OFFICIAL 2009 NC[AA]
MEN'S BASKETBALL
RECORDS BOOK

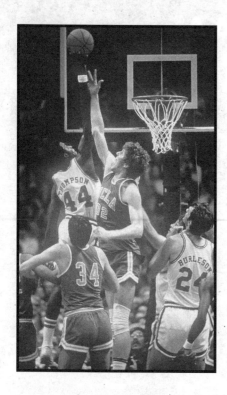

THE NATIONAL COLLEGIATE ATHLETIC ASSOCIATION
P.O. Box 6222, Indianapolis, Indiana 46206-6222
317/917-6222
NCAA.org
October 2008

Compiled By:
Gary K. Johnson, *Associate Director of Statistics*.
Sean W. Straziscar, *Associate Director of Statistics*.
Bonnie Senappe, *Assistant Director of Statistics*.
Jeff Williams, *Assistant Director of Statistics*.

ON THE COVER
Top row (left to right): Jim Boeheim, Syracuse; Freeman Williams, Portland State; Lionel Simmons, La Salle; Hersey Hawkins, Bradley. Middle Row: Troy Ruths, Washington-St. Louis; Pepe Sanchez, Temple; Bo Kimble, Loyola Marymount; Kevin Durant, Texas. Bottom Row: Dick Reynolds, Otterbein; Don Meyer and Kevin Ratzsch, Northern State.

Cover photos by Andres Alonso and Rich Clarkson of NCAA Photos; and the Sports Information offices at of Bradley, La Salle, Loyola Marymount, Northern State, Otterbein, Portland State, Syracuse, Temple and Texas.

Distributed to sports information directors and conference publicity directors.

ISSN 1089-5280
NCAA 65980-10/08

Contents

New To this Book

Division I Records

Individual Collegiate Records

Award Winners

Coaches

Playing-Rules History

School Name-Change/Abbreviation Key

The following players changed their names after their collegiate careers ended. They are listed throughout the book by the names under which they played in college (those listed at the left). Their current names are listed below. In addition, various schools have changed their name. The current school name is listed along with other names by which the schools have been referred.

PLAYER name changes

Name as a collegian:	Changed to:
Lew Alcindor (UCLA)	Kareem Abdul-Jabbar
Walt Hazzard (UCLA)	Mahdi Abdul-Rahmad
Chris Jackson (LSU)	Mahmoud Abdul-Rauf
Akeem Olajuwon (Houston)	Hakeem Olajuwon
Don Smith (Iowa St.)	Zaid Abdul-Aziz
Keith Wilkes (UCLA)	Jamaal Wilkes
Jason Williams (Duke)	Jay Williams

SCHOOL name changes

Current school name:	Changed from:
Akron	Buchtel
Alcorn St.	Alcorn A&M
Alliant Int'l	U.S. Int'l; Cal Western
Arcadia	Beaver
Arizona St.	Tempe St.
Ark.-Pine Bluff	Arkansas AM&N
Armstrong Atlantic	Armstrong St.
Auburn	Alabama Poly
Augusta St.	Augusta
Benedictine (Ill.)	Ill. Benedictine
Bradley	Bradley Tech
UC Davis	California Aggies
Cal St. East Bay	Cal St. Hayward
Cal St. Fullerton	Orange County State College; Orange St.
Cal St. L.A.	Los Angeles St.
Cal St. Northridge	San Fernando Valley St.
Carnegie Mellon	Carnegie Tech
Case Reserve	Case Institute of Technology
Central Ark.	Conway St.
Central Conn. St.	New Haven St.
Central Mich.	Mt. Pleasant
Central Mo.	Central Mo. St.
Central Okla.	Central St. (Okla.)
Charleston So.	Baptist (S.C.)
Charleston (W.V.)	Morris Harvey
Cleveland St.	Fenn
Colorado St.	Colorado A&M
Colorado St.-Pueblo	Southern Colo.
Columbus St.	Columbus
Concordia (Cal.)	Christ College-Irvine
Concordia Chicago	Concordia (Ill.)
Concordia (Tex.)	Concordia-Austin
Connecticut	Connecticut Aggies
Crown (Minn.)	St. Paul Bible
Dayton	St. Mary's Institute
Delaware Valley	National Aggies
DeSales	Allentown
Detroit	Detroit Mercy; Detroit Tech
Dist. Columbia	Federal City
Dominican (Ill.)	Rosary
Drexel	Drexel Tech
Dubuque	Columbia Col.
Duke	Trinity (N.C.)
Eastern Conn. St.	Willimantic St.
Eastern Mich.	Michigan Normal
Eckerd	Fla. Presbyterian
Emporia St.	Kansas St. Normal
FDU-Florham	FDU-Madison
Fort Hays St.	Kansas St. Normal-Western
Fresno St.	Fresno Pacific
Col. of Idaho	Albertson
Idaho St.	Academy of Idaho; Idaho Tech. Inst.; Idaho-Southern
Ill.-Chicago	Ill.-Chicago Circle
Illinois St.	Illinois St. Normal; Illinois Normal
Indiana (Pa.)	Indiana St. (Pa.)
Indianapolis	Indiana Central
Iowa	State University of Iowa
Iowa St.	Ames
James Madison	Madison

Current school name:	Also known as:
Johnson C. Smith	Johnson Smith
Kansas St.	Kansas Aggies
Kean	Newark St.
Kent St.	Kent
La Sierra	Loma Linda
Lamar	Lamar Tech
Liberty	Lynchburg Baptist; Liberty Baptist
La.-Lafayette	Southwestern La.
La.-Monroe	Northeast La.
Loyola Marymount	St. Vincent; Loyola U. of L.A.
Lycoming	Williamsport Dickinson Seminary
Lynn	College of Boca Raton
Lyon	Arkansas Col.
Me.-Farmington	Western State Normal School
Maritime (N.Y.)	N.Y. Maritime
Marycrest Int'l	Teikyo Marycrest
Md.-East. Shore	Maryland St.
Massachusetts	Massachusetts St.; Massachusetts Agriculture Col.
Mass.-Dartmouth	Southeastern Mass.
Mass.-Lowell	Lowell; Lowell St.; Lowell Tech
McDaniel	Western Md.
Memphis	Memphis St.; West Tenn. St. Normal
Michigan Tech	Michigan Mines and Tech
Millersville	Millersville St.
Millikin	James Millikin
Minn. St. Mankato	Mankato St.
Minn. St. Moorhead	Moorhead St.
Mississippi Col.	Mississippi A&M
Mississippi Val.	Mississippi Vocational
Missouri S&T	Missouri School of Mines; Mo.-Rolla
Missouri St.	Southwest Mo. St.
Mont. St.-Billings	Eastern Montana
Montana St.-Northern	Northern Montana
Neb.-Kearney	Kearney St.
Neb.-Omaha	Omaha
New England U.	St. Francis (Me.)
New Jersey City	Jersey City St.
New Mexico St.	New Mexico A&M
New Orleans	Louisiana St. (N.O.)
North Ala.	Florence St.
N.C. Central	North Caro. College
UNC Pembroke	Pembroke St.
North Central Texas	Cooke County
North Texas	North Tex. St.
Northeastern St.	Northeastern Okla. St.
Northern Ariz.	Arizona St.-Flagstaff
Northern Colo.	Colorado St. Col.; State Teachers
Okla. Panhandle	Panhandle A&M; Panhandle St.
Oklahoma St.	Oklahoma A&M
Old Dominion	William & Mary (Norfolk)
Penn St.-Berks	Penn St. Berks-Lehigh Val.; Berks & Lehigh
Penn St.-Harrisburg	Penn St.-Capitol
Pepperdine	George Pepperdine
Phila. Sciences	Phila. Pharmacy
Philadelphia U.	Phila. Textile
Pittsburgh	Western Pennsylvania
Plymouth St.	Plymouth Normal; Plymouth Teachers
Polytechnic (N.Y.)	New York Poly; Brooklyn Poly
Portland St.	Vanport
Post	Teikyo Post
Randolph	Randolph-Macon Woman's
Rhodes	Southwestern (Tenn.)
Rice	Rice Institute
Richard Stockton	Stockton St.
Rochester Inst.	Mechanics Institute
Rose-Hulman	Rose Polytechnic Institute
Rowan	Glassboro St.
Sage Colleges	Russell Sage
Salem Int'l	Salem-Teikyo; Salem
Samford	Howard Col.
S.C. Upstate	S.C.-Spartanburg
Southern Ark.	Magnolia A&M
Southern Conn. St.	New Britain St.
Southern Ind.	Indiana St.-Evansville
Southern Me.	Maine Portland-Gorham; Gorham St. (Me.)
Southern Miss.	Mississippi Southern Col.; Mississippi Normal
Southern N.H.	New Hamp. Col.

Current school name:	Changed from:
Southern U.	Southern B.R.
Southwest Minn. St.	Southwest St.
Stevens Institute	Stevens Tech
Stevenson	Villa Julie
Taylor-Ft. Wayne	Summit Christian
Tex. A&M-Commerce	East Texas St.
Tex. A&M-Kingsville	Texas A&I
Tex.-Pan American	Pan American
Texas St.	Southwest Tex. St.
Towson	Towson St.
Trine	Tri-State
Troy	Troy St.
Truman	Northeast Mo. St.; Truman St.
Tulsa	Henry Kendall
Washburn	Lincoln Col.
Washington-St. Louis	Washington (Mo.)
Washington St.	Washington Agricultural Col.
West Ala.	Livingston
West Tex. A&M	West Texas St.
Western N.M.	New Mexico Western
Western Ore.	Monmouth Normal; Oregon Tech; Oregon College of Education
Western St.	Colo. Western; Colorado Normal
Westmar	Western Union Col.; Teikyo Westmar
Wichita St.	Fairmount
Widener	Pennsylvania Military Col.
Wm. Paterson	Paterson St.
Wis.-Superior	Superior Normal
Xavier	St. Xavier

In the early days of colleges and universities, many schools used the designation of Teachers College. Due to the high numbers of such schools, they are not listed here.

SCHOOLS also known as

Current school name:	Also known as:
A&M-Corpus Christi	Tex. A&M-Corp. Chris.
Air Force	U.S. Air Force Academy
Apprentice School	Newport News
Army	U.S. Military Academy; West Point
Baruch	Bernard M. Baruch
BYU	Brigham Young
Case Reserve	Case Western Reserve
Charlotte	UNC Charlotte
Chattanooga	Tenn.-Chatt.
CCNY	City College of New York
City Tech	New York City Tech (was NYCCT)
Coast Guard	U.S. Coast Guard Academy
Georgia College	Georgia College & State, GCSU
Green Bay	Wis.-Green Bay
Hawthorne	Nathaniel Hawthorne
IPFW	Indiana/Purdue-Ft. Wayne
IUPUI	Indiana/Purdue-Indianapolis
Lehman	Herbert H. Lehman
Lipscomb	David Lipscomb
Long Island	LIU-Brooklyn
LSU	Louisiana St.
Mass. Liberal Arts	Massachusetts College (was North Adams St.)
Merchant Marine	King's Point; U.S. Merchant Marine Academy
Milwaukee	Wis.-Milwaukee
MIT	Massachusetts Institute of Technology
Navy	U.S. Naval Academy
NJIT	Newark Engineering (was N.J. Inst. of Tech.)
NYIT	New York Institute of Technology; New York Tech
Rensselaer	RPI, Rensselaer Poly Inst.
Rochester Inst.	RIT
Sewanee	University of the South
SMU	Southern Methodist
Southampton	LIU-Southampton
SUNYIT	Utica/Rome
TCNJ	The College of New Jersey (was Trenton St.)
TCU	Texas Christian (was AddRan Christian)
UAB	Alabama at Birmingham
UALR	Ark.-Little Rock
UCF	Central Fla. (was Florida Tech)
UCLA	University of California, Los Angeles
UMBC	Md.-Balt. County
UMKC	Mo.-Kansas City
UNI	Northern Iowa (was Iowa Normal; State Col. of Iowa)

Current school name:	Also known as:
UNLV	Nevada-Las Vegas (was Nevada Southern)
UTEP	Texas-El Paso (was Texas Western)
UTSA	Texas-San Antonio
VCU	Va. Commonwealth
VMI	Va. Military
WPI	Worcester Poly Inst.; Worcester Tech

SCHOOL MERGERS

Current school name:	Two Schools Merged & Year:
Case Reserve	Case Tech & Western Reserve; 1971-72
Martin Luther	Northwestern (Wis.) & Dr. Martin Luther, 1995-96
Mass.-Lowell	Lowell St. & Lowell Tech; 1975-76

Division I Records

Individual Records

Basketball records are confined to the "modern era," which began with the 1937-38 season, the first without the center jump after each goal scored. Except for the school's all-time won-lost record or coaches' records, only statistics achieved while an institution was an active member of the NCAA are included in team or individual categories. Official weekly statistics rankings in scoring and shooting began with the 1947-48 season; individual rebounds were added for the 1950-51 season, although team rebounds were not added until 1954-55. Individual assists were kept in 1950-51 and 1951-52, and permanently added in 1983-84. Blocked shots and steals were added in 1985-86 and three-point field goals were added in 1986-87. Assists to turnover ratio was added in 2007-08. For Triple-Doubles and Double-Doubles, the individual had to reach double figures in two or more of the following categories: points, rebounds, assists, blocked shots or steals. Triple-Doubles and Double-Doubles include only the years in which each category was officially kept by the NCAA. Scoring, rebounding, assists, blocked shots and steals are ranked on total number and on per-game average; shooting, on percentage. In statistical rankings, the rounding of percentages and/or averages may indicate ties where none exist. In these cases, the numerical order of the rankings is accurate. In 1973, freshmen became eligible to compete on the varsity level.

Scoring

POINTS
Game
100—Frank Selvy, Furman vs. Newberry, Feb. 13, 1954 (41 FGs, 18 FTs)
Season
1,381—Pete Maravich, LSU, 1970 (522 FGs, 337 FTs, 31 games)
Career
3,667—Pete Maravich, LSU, 1968-70 (1,387 FGs, 893 FTs, 83 games)

POINTS VS. DIVISION I OPPONENT
Game
72—Kevin Bradshaw, U.S. Int'l vs. Loyola Marymount, Jan. 5, 1991

AVERAGE PER GAME
Season
44.5—Pete Maravich, LSU, 1970 (1,381 in 31)
Career
44.2—Pete Maravich, LSU, 1968-70 (3,667 in 83)

POINTS IN FIRST CAREER GAME
Game
56—Lew Alcindor, UCLA vs. Southern California, Dec. 3, 1966

COMBINED POINTS, TWO TEAMMATES
Game
125—Frank Selvy (100) and Darrell Floyd (25), Furman vs. Newberry, Feb. 13, 1954

COMBINED POINTS, TWO TEAMMATES VS. DIVISION I OPPONENT
Game
92—Kevin Bradshaw (72) and Isaac Brown (20), U.S. Int'l vs. Loyola Marymount, Jan. 5, 1991

COMBINED POINTS, TWO OPPOSING PLAYERS ON DIVISION I TEAMS
Game
115—Pete Maravich (64), LSU and Dan Issel (51), Kentucky, Feb. 21, 1970

GAMES SCORING AT LEAST 50 POINTS
Season
10—Pete Maravich, LSU, 1970
Season—Consecutive Games
3—Pete Maravich, LSU, Feb. 10 to Feb. 15, 1969
Career
28—Pete Maravich, LSU, 1968-70

GAMES SCORING AT LEAST 40 POINTS
Career
56—Pete Maravich, LSU, 1968-70

GAMES SCORING IN DOUBLE FIGURES
Career
132—Danny Manning, Kansas, 1985-88

CONSECUTIVE GAMES SCORING IN DOUBLE FIGURES
Career
115—Lionel Simmons, La Salle, 1987-90

Field Goals

FIELD GOALS
Game
41—Frank Selvy, Furman vs. Newberry, Feb. 13, 1954 (66 attempts)
Season
522—Pete Maravich, LSU, 1970 (1,168 attempts)
Career
1,387—Pete Maravich, LSU, 1968-70 (3,166 attempts)

CONSECUTIVE FIELD GOALS
Game
16—Doug Grayson, Kent St. vs. North Carolina, Dec. 6, 1967 (18 of 19)
Season
25—Ray Voelkel, American, 1978 (during nine games, Nov. 24-Dec. 16)

FIELD-GOAL ATTEMPTS
Game
71—Jay Handlan, Wash. & Lee vs. Furman, Feb. 17, 1951 (30 made)
Season
1,168—Pete Maravich, LSU, 1970 (522 made)
Career
3,166—Pete Maravich, LSU, 1968-70 (1,387 made)

FIELD-GOAL PERCENTAGE
Game
(Min. 15 made) 100%—Clifford Rozier, Louisville vs. Eastern Ky., Dec. 11, 1993 (15 of 15)
(Min. 20 made) 95.5%—Bill Walton, UCLA vs. Memphis, March 26, 1973 (21 of 22)
*Season
74.6%—Steve Johnson, Oregon St., 1981 (235 of 315)

*Based on qualifiers for national championship.

Career
(Min. 400 made and 4 made per game) 67.8%—Steve Johnson, Oregon St., 1976-81 (828 of 1,222)

Three-Point Field Goals

THREE-POINT FIELD GOALS
Game
15—Keith Veney, Marshall vs. Morehead St., Dec. 14, 1996 (25 attempts)
Season
162—Stephen Curry, Davidson, 2008 (369 attempts)
Career
457—J.J. Redick, Duke, 2003-06 (1,126 attempts)

THREE-POINT FIELD GOALS MADE PER GAME
Season
5.6—Darrin Fitzgerald, Butler, 1987 (158 in 28)
Career
(Min. 200 made) 4.6—Timothy Pollard, Mississippi Val., 1988-89 (256 in 56)

CONSECUTIVE THREE-POINT FIELD GOALS
Game
11—Gary Bossert, Niagara vs. Siena, Jan. 7, 1987
Season
15—Todd Leslie, Northwestern, 1990 (during four games, Dec. 15-28)

CONSECUTIVE GAMES MAKING A THREE-POINT FIELD GOAL
Season
38—Steve Kerr, Arizona, Nov. 27, 1987, to April 2, 1988
Career
88—Cory Bradford, Illinois, Nov. 10, 1998 to Feb. 10, 2001

THREE-POINT FIELD-GOAL ATTEMPTS
Game
27—Bruce Seals, Manhattan vs. Canisius, Jan. 31, 2000 (9 made)
Season
376—Robert McKiver, Houston, 2008 (145 made)
Career
1,192—Keydren Clark, St. Peter's, 2003-06 (435 made)

THREE-POINT FIELD-GOAL ATTEMPTS PER GAME
Season
12.9—Darrin Fitzgerald, Butler, 1987 (362 in 28)
Career
10.1—Keydren Clark, St. Peter's, 2003-06 (1,192 in 118)

THREE-POINT FIELD-GOAL PERCENTAGE
Game
(Min. 10 made) 100%—Andre Smith, George Mason vs. James Madison, Jan. 19, 2008 (10 of 10)
(Min. 12 made) 85.7%—Gary Bossert, Niagara vs. Siena, Jan. 7, 1987 (12 of 14)
Season
(Min. 50 made) 63.4%—Glenn Tropf, Holy Cross, 1988 (52 of 82)
(Min. 100 made) 57.3%—Steve Kerr, Arizona, 1988 (114 of 199)
Career
(Min. 200 made and 2.0 made per game) 49.7%—Tony Bennett, Green Bay, 1989-92 (290 of 584)
(Min. 300 made) 46.9%—Stephen Sir, San Diego St. & Northern Ariz., 2003-07 (323 of 689)

Free Throws

FREE THROWS
Game
30—Pete Maravich, LSU vs. Oregon St., Dec. 22, 1969 (31 attempts)
Season
355—Frank Selvy, Furman, 1954 (444 attempts)
Career
(4 yrs.) 905—Dickie Hemric, Wake Forest, 1952-55 (1,359 attempts)
(3 yrs.) 893—Pete Maravich, LSU, 1968-70 (1,152 attempts)

CONSECUTIVE FREE THROWS MADE
Game
24—Arlen Clark, Oklahoma St. vs. Colorado, March 7, 1959 (24 of 24)
Season
73—Gary Buchanan, Villanova, 2000-01 (during 21 games, Nov. 17-Feb. 12)
Career
85—Darnell Archey, Butler, 2001-03 (during 57 games, Feb. 15, 2001-Jan. 18, 2003)

FREE THROWS ATTEMPTED
Game
36—Ed Tooley, Brown vs. Amherst, Dec. 4, 1954 (23 made)
Season
444—Frank Selvy, Furman, 1954 (355 made)
Career
(4 yrs.) 1,359—Dickie Hemric, Wake Forest, 1952-55 (905 made)
(3 yrs.) 1,152—Pete Maravich, LSU, 1968-70 (893 made)

FREE-THROW PERCENTAGE
Game
> *(Min. 24 made)* 100% —Arlen Clark, Oklahoma St. vs. Colorado, March 7, 1959 (24 of 24)

*Season
> 97.5%—Blake Ahearn, Missouri St., 2004 (117 of 120)

*Based on qualifiers for national championship.

Career
> *(Min. 300 made and 2.5 made per game)* 94.6%—Blake Ahearn, Missouri St., 2004-07 (435 of 460)
> *(Min. 600 made)* 91.2%—J.J. Redick, Duke, 2003-06 (662 of 726)

Rebounds

REBOUNDS
Game
> 51—Bill Chambers, William & Mary vs. Virginia, Feb. 14, 1953
> *(Since 1973)* 35—Larry Abney, Fresno St. vs. SMU, Feb. 17, 2000

Season
> 734—Walt Dukes, Seton Hall, 1953 (33 games)
> *(Since 1973)* 597—Marvin Barnes, Providence, 1974 (32 games)

Career
> *(4 yrs.)* 2,201—Tom Gola, La Salle, 1952-55 (118 games)
> *(3 yrs.)* 1,751—Paul Silas, Creighton, 1962-64 (81 games)
> *(Since 1973)* 1,570—Tim Duncan, Wake Forest, 1994-97 (128 games)

AVERAGE PER GAME
Season
> 25.6—Charlie Slack, Marshall, 1955 (538 in 21)
> *(Since 1973)* 20.4—Kermit Washington, American, 1973 (511 in 25)

Career
> *(Min. 800)* 22.7—Artis Gilmore, Jacksonville, 1970-71 (1,224 in 54)
> *(4 yrs.)* 21.8—Charlie Slack, Marshall, 1953-56 (1,916 in 88)
> *(Since 1973)* 15.2—Glenn Mosley, Seton Hall, 1974-77 (1,263 in 83)

Assists

ASSISTS
Game
> 22—Tony Fairley, Charleston So. vs. Armstrong Atlantic, Feb. 9, 1987; Avery Johnson, Southern U. vs. Texas Southern, Jan. 25, 1988; Sherman Douglas, Syracuse vs. Providence, Jan. 28, 1989

Season
> 406—Mark Wade, UNLV, 1987 (38 games)

Career
> 1,076—Bobby Hurley, Duke, 1990-93 (140 games)

AVERAGE PER GAME
Season
> 13.3—Avery Johnson, Southern U., 1988 (399 in 30)

Career
> *(Min. 600)* 12.0—Avery Johnson, Southern U., 1987-88 (732 in 61)
> *(4 yrs.)* 8.4—Chris Corchiani, North Carolina St., 1988-91 (1,038 in 124)

Assist-to-Turnover Ratio

ASSIST-TO-TURNOVER RATIO
(Since 2008)
Season
> *(Min. 3 assists per game)* 3.62—Cliff Clinkscales, DePaul, 2008 (123 assists to 34 turnovers)

Blocked Shots

BLOCKED SHOTS
Game
> 16—Mickell Gladness, Alabama A&M vs. Texas Southern, Feb. 24, 2007

Season
> 207—David Robinson, Navy, 1986 (35 games)

Career
> 535—Wojciech Myrda, La.-Monroe, 1999-2002 (115 games)

AVERAGE PER GAME
Season
> 6.5—Shawn James, Northeastern, 2006 (196 in 30)

Career
> *(Min. 225)* 5.9—Keith Closs, Central Conn. St., 1995-96 (317 in 54)
> *(4 yrs.)* 4.7—Wojciech Myrda, La.-Monroe, 1999-2002 (535 in 115)

Steals

STEALS
Game
> 13—Mookie Blaylock, Oklahoma vs. Centenary (La.), Dec. 12, 1987; and vs. Loyola Marymount, Dec. 17, 1988

Season
> 160—Desmond Cambridge, Alabama A&M, 2002 (29 games)

Career
> 385—John Linehan, Providence, 1998-2002 (122 games)

AVERAGE PER GAME
Season
> 5.5—Desmond Cambridge, Alabama A&M, 2002 (160 in 29)

Career
> *(Min. 225)* 3.9—Desmond Cambridge, Alabama A&M, 1999-2002 (330 in 84)
> *(4 yrs.)* 3.2—Eric Murdock, Providence, 1988-91 (376 in 117)

Double-Doubles

QUADRUPLE-DOUBLES
Season
> 1—Lester Hudson, Tenn.-Martin, 2008

TRIPLE-DOUBLES
Season
> 4—Michael Anderson, Drexel, 1986; Brian Shaw, UC Santa Barbara, 1988; Jason Kidd, California, 1994; Stephane Lasme, Massachusetts, 2007

Career
> 6—Michael Anderson, Drexel, 1985-88; Shaquille O'Neal, LSU, 1990-92

CONSECUTIVE GAMES MAKING A TRIPLE-DOUBLE
Season
> 2—Kevin Robertson, Vermont, Jan. 7-9, 1992; Shaquille O'Neal, LSU, Feb. 19-22, 1992; Anfernee Hardaway, Memphis, Jan. 4-6, 1993; Gerald Lewis, SMU, Mar. 3-6, 1993; David Edwards, Texas A&M, Mar. 5-10, 1994; Tony Lee, Robert Morris, Feb. 9-14, 2008

DOUBLE-DOUBLES
Season
> 31—David Robinson, Navy, 1986

Career
> 87—Tim Duncan, Wake Forest, 1994-97

DOUBLE-DOUBLES BY A FRESHMAN
Season
> 28—Michael Beasley, Kansas St., 2008

CONSECUTIVE GAMES MAKING A DOUBLE-DOUBLE
Season
> 29—Mel Counts, Oregon St., Nov. 30, 1963-Mar. 10, 1964

Career
> 40—Billy Cunningham, North Carolina, Dec, 5, 1962-Feb. 22, 1964

Fouls

SHORTEST PLAYING TIME BEFORE BEING DISQUALIFIED
Game
> 1:11—Ben Wardrop, San Diego St. vs. Colorado St., Jan. 24, 2004

MOST GAMES NEVER FOULING OUT
Full Career
> 138—Ed Cota, North Carolina, 1997-2000

Games

GAMES PLAYED (SINCE 1947-48)
Season
> 40—Mark Alarie, Tommy Amaker, Johnny Dawkins, Danny Ferry and Billy King, Duke, 1986; Larry Johnson, UNLV, 1990; Anthony Epps, Jamaal Magloire, Ron Mercer and Wayne Turner, Kentucky, 1997; Cole Aldrich, Darrell Arthur, Darnell Jackson, Sasha Kaun and Russell Robinson, Kansas, 2008; Antonio Anderson, Chris Douglas-Roberts, Willie Kemp and Derrick Rose, Memphis, 2008

Career
> 151—Wayne Turner, Kentucky, 1996-99

General

ACHIEVED 2,000 POINTS AND 2,000 REBOUNDS
Career
> Tom Gola, La Salle, 1952-55 (2,462 points and 2,201 rebounds)
> Joe Holup, George Washington, 1953-56 (2,226 points and 2,030 rebounds)

AVERAGED 20 POINTS AND 20 REBOUNDS
Career
> Bill Russell, San Francisco, 1954-56 (20.7 points and 20.3 rebounds)
> Paul Silas, Creighton, 1962-64 (20.5 points and 21.6 rebounds)
> Julius Erving, Massachusetts, 1970-71 (26.3 points and 20.2 rebounds)
> Artis Gilmore, Jacksonville, 1970-71 (24.3 points and 22.7 rebounds)
> Kermit Washington, American, 1971-73 (20.1 points and 20.2 rebounds)

Team Records

Note: Where records involve both teams, each team must be an NCAA Division I member institution.

SINGLE-GAME RECORDS

Scoring

POINTS
186—Loyola Marymount vs. U.S. Int'l (140), Jan. 5, 1991

POINTS BY LOSING TEAM
150—U.S. Int'l vs. Loyola Marymount (181), Jan. 31, 1989

POINTS, BOTH TEAMS
331—Loyola Marymount (181) vs. U.S. Int'l (150), Jan. 31, 1989

MARGIN OF VICTORY
117—Long Island (179) vs. Medgar Evers (62), Nov. 26, 1997

MARGIN OF VICTORY VS. DIVISION I OPPONENT
91—Tulsa (141) vs. Prairie View (50), Dec. 7, 1995

POINTS IN A HALF
98—Long Island vs. Medgar Evers, Nov. 26, 1997 (2nd)

POINTS IN A HALF VS. DIVISION I OPPONENT
97—Oklahoma vs. U.S. Int'l, Nov. 29, 1989 (1st)

POINTS IN A HALF, BOTH TEAMS
172—Loyola Marymount (86) vs. Gonzaga (86), Feb. 18, 1989 (2nd)

LEAD BEFORE OPPONENT SCORES AT START OF A GAME
34-0—Seton Hall vs. Kean, Nov. 29, 1998

LEAD BEFORE DIVISION I OPPONENT SCORES AT START OF A GAME
32-0—Connecticut vs. New Hampshire, Dec. 12, 1990

LARGEST SCORING RUN VS. A DIVISION I OPPONENT
37-0—Utah St. vs. Idaho, Feb. 15, 2006

DEFICIT OVERCOME TO WIN GAME
32—Duke (74) vs. Tulane (72), Dec. 30, 1950 (trailed 22-54 with 2:00 left in the first half)

SECOND-HALF DEFICIT OVERCOME TO WIN GAME
31—Duke (74) vs. Tulane (72), Dec. 30, 1950 (trailed 27-58 with 19:00 left in the second half); Kentucky (99) vs. LSU (95), Feb. 15, 1994 (trailed 37-68 with 15:34 left in the second half)

HALFTIME DEFICIT OVERCOME TO WIN GAME
29—Duke (74) vs. Tulane (72), Dec. 30, 1950 (trailed 27-56 at halftime)

DEFICIT OVERCOME BEFORE SCORING TO WIN GAME
28—New Mexico St. (117) vs. Bradley (109), Jan. 27, 1977 (trailed 0-28 with 13:49 left in first half)

Field Goals

FIELD GOALS
76—Long Island vs. Medgar Evers, Nov. 26, 1997 (124 attempts)

FIELD GOALS VS. DIVISION I OPPONENT
74—Houston vs. Valparaiso, Feb. 24, 1968 (112 attempts)

FIELD GOALS, BOTH TEAMS
130—Loyola Marymount (67) vs. U.S. Int'l (63), Jan. 31, 1989

FIELD GOALS IN A HALF
42—Oklahoma vs. U.S. Int'l, Nov. 29, 1989 (90 attempts) (1st half)

FIELD-GOAL ATTEMPTS
147—Oklahoma vs. U.S. Int'l, Nov. 29, 1989 (70 made)

FIELD-GOAL ATTEMPTS, BOTH TEAMS
245—Loyola Marymount (124) vs. U.S. Int'l (121), Jan. 7, 1989

FIELD-GOAL ATTEMPTS IN A HALF
90—Oklahoma vs. U.S. Int'l, Nov. 29, 1989 (42 made) (1st half)

FIELD-GOAL PERCENTAGE
(Min. 15 made) 83.3%—Maryland vs. South Carolina, Jan. 9, 1971 (15 of 18)
(Min. 30 made) 81.4%—New Mexico vs. Oregon St., Nov. 30, 1985 (35 of 43)

FIELD-GOAL PERCENTAGE, HALF
94.1%—North Carolina vs. Virginia, Jan. 7, 1978 (16 of 17) (2nd half)

Three-Point Field Goals

THREE-POINT FIELD GOALS
28—Troy vs. George Mason, Dec. 10, 1994 (74 attempts)

THREE-POINT FIELD GOALS, BOTH TEAMS
44—Troy (28) vs. George Mason (16), Dec. 10, 1994

CONSECUTIVE THREE-POINT FIELD GOALS MADE WITHOUT A MISS
11—Niagara vs. Siena, Jan. 7, 1987; Eastern Ky. vs. UNC Asheville, Jan. 14, 1987

THREE-POINT FIELD-GOAL ATTEMPTS WITHOUT MAKING ONE
22—Canisius vs. St. Bonaventure, Jan. 21, 1995

NUMBER OF DIFFERENT PLAYERS TO SCORE A THREE-POINT FIELD GOAL, ONE TEAM
9—Dartmouth vs. Boston College, Nov. 30, 1993

THREE-POINT FIELD-GOAL ATTEMPTS
74—Troy vs. George Mason, Dec. 10, 1994 (28 made)

THREE-POINT FIELD-GOAL ATTEMPTS, BOTH TEAMS
108—Troy (74) vs. George Mason (34), Dec. 10, 1994

THREE-POINT FIELD-GOAL PERCENTAGE
(Min. 10 made) 91.7%—Drexel vs. Delaware, Dec. 3, 2000 (11 of 12); Northern Ariz. vs. Willamette, Dec. 11, 2004 (11 of 12)
(Min. 15 made) 83.3%—Eastern Ky. vs. UNC Asheville, Jan. 14, 1987 (15 of 18)

THREE-POINT FIELD-GOAL PERCENTAGE, BOTH TEAMS
(Min. 10 made) 83.3%—Lafayette (7 of 8) vs. Marist (3 of 4), Dec. 6, 1986 (10 of 12)
(Min. 15 made) 76.2%—Florida (10 of 14) vs. California (6 of 7), Dec. 27, 1986 (16 of 21)
(Min. 20 made) 72.4%—Princeton (12 of 15) vs. Brown (9 of 14), Feb. 20, 1988 (21 of 29)

Free Throws

FREE THROWS MADE
56—TCU vs. Eastern Mich., Dec. 21, 1999 (70 attempts)

FREE THROWS MADE, BOTH TEAMS
88—Morehead St. (53) vs. Cincinnati (35), Feb. 11, 1956 (111 attempts)

FREE-THROW ATTEMPTS
79—Northern Ariz. vs. Arizona, Jan. 26, 1953 (46 made)

FREE THROWS, BOTH TEAMS
130—Northern Ariz. (79) vs. Arizona (51), Jan. 26, 1953 (78 made)

FREE-THROW PERCENTAGE
(Min. 32 made) 100.0%—UC Irvine vs. Pacific, Feb. 21, 1981 (34 of 34); Samford vs. UCF, Dec. 20, 1990 (34 of 34)
(Min. 35 made) 97.2%—Vanderbilt vs. Mississippi St., Feb. 26, 1986 (35 of 36); Butler vs. Dayton, Feb. 21, 1991 (35 of 36); Marquette vs. Memphis, Jan. 23, 1993 (35 of 36)
(Min. 40 made) 95.5%—UNLV vs. San Diego St., Dec. 11, 1976 (42 of 44)

FREE-THROW PERCENTAGE, BOTH TEAMS
100%—Purdue (25 of 25) vs. Wisconsin (22 of 22), Feb. 7, 1976 (47 of 47)

Rebounds

REBOUNDS
108—Kentucky vs. Mississippi, Feb. 8, 1964

REBOUNDS, BOTH TEAMS
152—Indiana (95) vs. Michigan (57), March 11, 1961

REBOUND MARGIN
84—Arizona (102) vs. Northern Ariz. (18), Jan. 6, 1951

Assists

ASSISTS (INCLUDING OVERTIMES)
44—Colorado vs. George Mason, Dec. 2, 1995 (ot)

ASSISTS (REGULATION)
43—TCU vs. Central Okla., Dec. 12, 1998.

ASSISTS, BOTH TEAMS (INCLUDING OVERTIMES)
67—Colorado (44) vs. George Mason (23), Dec. 2, 1995 (ot)

ASSISTS, BOTH TEAMS (REGULATION)
65—Dayton (34) vs. UCF (31), Dec. 3, 1988

Blocked Shots

BLOCKED SHOTS
21—Georgetown vs. Southern (N.O.), Dec. 1, 1993; Alabama A&M vs. Texas Southern, Feb. 24, 2007

BLOCKED SHOTS, BOTH TEAMS
29—Rider (17) vs. Fairleigh Dickinson (12), Jan. 9, 1989

Steals

STEALS
39—Long Island vs. Medgar Evers, Nov. 26, 1997

STEALS VS. DIVISION I OPPONENT
34—Oklahoma vs. Centenary (La.), Dec. 12, 1987

STEALS, BOTH TEAMS
44—Oklahoma (34) vs. Centenary (La.) (10), Dec. 12, 1987

Fouls

FOULS
50—Arizona vs. Northern Ariz., Jan. 26, 1953

FOULS, BOTH TEAMS
84—Arizona (50) vs. Northern Ariz. (34), Jan. 26, 1953

PLAYERS DISQUALIFIED
8—St. Joseph's vs. Xavier, Jan. 10, 1976

PLAYERS DISQUALIFIED, BOTH TEAMS
12—UNLV (6) vs. Hawaii (6), Jan. 19, 1979 (ot); Arizona (7) vs. West Tex. A&M (5), Feb. 14, 1952

Defense

FEWEST POINTS ALLOWED (Since 1938)
6—Tennessee (11) vs. Temple, Dec. 15, 1973; Kentucky (75) vs. Arkansas St., Jan. 8, 1945

FEWEST POINTS ALLOWED (Since 1986)
20—George Washington (49) vs. St. Louis, Jan. 10, 2008

FEWEST POINTS, BOTH TEAMS
(Since 1938)
  17—Tennessee (11) vs. Temple (6), Dec. 15, 1973

FEWEST POINTS, BOTH TEAMS
(Since 1986)
  62—Monmouth (41) vs. Princton (21), Dec. 14, 2005

FEWEST POINTS ALLOWED IN A HALF
(Since 1938)
  0—Duke (7) vs. North Carolina, Feb. 24, 1979 (1st)

FEWEST POINTS ALLOWED IN A HALF
(Since 1986)
  4—Kansas St. (48) vs. Savannah St., Jan. 7, 2008 (2nd)

FEWEST POINTS, BOTH TEAMS IN A HALF
(Since 1938)
  7—Duke (7) vs. North Carolina, Feb. 24, 1979 (1st)

FEWEST POINTS, BOTH TEAMS IN A HALF
(Since 1986)
  28—Mississippi (15) vs. South Carolina (13), Jan. 8, 2003 (1st)

LONGEST TIME HOLDING THE OPPONENT SCORELESS
  20:48—Duke vs. North Carolina, Feb. 25, 1979 (UNC scored its first points of the game at 19:12 in the 2nd half)

LONGEST TIME HOLDING THE OPPONENT SCORELESS
(Since 1986)
  16:08—Oklahoma vs. Texas A&M, Mar. 1, 2008 (last 12:50 of the 1st half and first 3:18 of the 2nd half)

FEWEST FIELD GOALS
(Since 1938)
  2—Duke vs. North Carolina St., Mar. 8, 1968 (11 attempts); Arkansas St. vs. Kentucky, Jan. 8, 1945

FEWEST FIELD GOALS IN A HALF
(Since 1986)
  1—Kansas St. vs. Savannah St., Jan. 7, 2008 (2nd)

FEWEST FIELD-GOAL ATTEMPTS
(Since 1938)
  9—Pittsburgh vs. Penn St., March 1, 1952 (3 made)

LOWEST FIELD-GOAL PERCENTAGE
(Since 1986)
  13.3%—Dayton vs. Miami (Ohio) (8 of 60), Dec. 29, 2001

LOWEST FIELD-GOAL PERCENTAGE IN A HALF
  4.3%—Kansas St. vs. Savannah St., Jan. 7, 2008 (1 of 23) (2nd)

FEWEST THREE-POINT FIELD GOALS MADE
  0—Many teams

FEWEST THREE-POINT FIELD-GOAL ATTEMPTS
  0—Many teams

FEWEST FREE THROWS MADE
  0—Many teams

FEWEST FREE-THROW ATTEMPTS
  0—Many teams

Overtimes

OVERTIME PERIODS
  7—Cincinnati (75) vs. Bradley (73), Dec. 21, 1981

POINTS IN ONE OVERTIME PERIOD
  26—Vermont vs. Hartford, Jan. 24, 1998

POINTS IN ONE OVERTIME PERIOD, BOTH TEAMS
  15   VCU (23) vs. Texas A&M (22), Dec. 2, 2000

POINTS IN OVERTIME PERIODS
  52—Baylor vs. Texas A&M, Jan. 23, 2008 (5 ot)

POINTS IN OVERTIME PERIODS, BOTH TEAMS
  98—Baylor (52) vs. Texas A&M (46), Jan. 23, 2008 (5 ot)

WINNING MARGIN IN OVERTIME GAME
  21—Nicholls St. (86) vs. Sam Houston St. (65), Feb. 4, 1999 (23-2 in the ot)

SEASON RECORDS

Scoring

POINTS
  4,012—Oklahoma, 1988 (39 games)

POINTS PER GAME
  122.4—Loyola Marymount, 1990 (3,918 in 32)

SCORING MARGIN AVERAGE
  30.3—UCLA, 1972 (94.6 offense, 64.3 defense)

GAMES AT LEAST 100 POINTS
  28—Loyola Marymount, 1990

CONSECUTIVE GAMES AT LEAST 100 POINTS
  12—UNLV, 1977; Loyola Marymount, 1990

Field Goals

FIELD GOALS
  1,533—Oklahoma, 1988 (3,094 attempts)

FIELD GOALS PER GAME
  46.3—UNLV, 1976 (1,436 in 31)

FIELD-GOAL ATTEMPTS
  3,094—Oklahoma, 1988 (1,533 made)

FIELD-GOAL ATTEMPTS PER GAME
  98.5—Oral Roberts, 1973 (2,659 in 27)

FIELD-GOAL PERCENTAGE
  57.2%—Missouri, 1980 (936 of 1,635)

Three-Point Field Goals

THREE-POINT FIELD GOALS
  442—VMI, 2007 (1,383 attempts)

THREE-POINT FIELD GOALS PER GAME
  13.4—VMI, 2007 (442 in 33)

THREE-POINT FIELD-GOAL ATTEMPTS
  1,383—VMI, 2007 (442 made)

THREE-POINT FIELD-GOAL ATTEMPTS PER GAME
  41.9—VMI, 2007 (1,383 in 33)

THREE-POINT FIELD-GOAL PERCENTAGE
  (Min. 100 made) 50.8%—Indiana, 1987 (130 of 256)
  (Min. 150 made) 50.0%—Mississippi Val., 1987 (161 of 322)
  (Min. 200 made) 49.2%—Princeton, 1988 (211 of 429)

CONSECUTIVE GAMES SCORING A THREE-POINT FIELD GOAL
(Multiple Seasons)
  668—UNLV, Nov. 26, 1986, to present

Free Throws

FREE THROWS MADE
  888—Duke, 1990 (1,165 attempts)

FREE THROWS MADE PER GAME
  28.9—Morehead St., 1956 (838 in 29)

CONSECUTIVE FREE THROWS MADE
  50—Wake Forest, 2005 (during two games, Jan. 15-18)

FREE THROW ATTEMPTS
  1,263—Bradley, 1954 (865 made)

FREE-THROW ATTEMPTS PER GAME
  41.0—Bradley, 1953 (1,107 in 27)

FREE-THROW PERCENTAGE
  82.2%—Harvard, 1984 (535 of 651)

Rebounds

REBOUNDS
  2,109—Kentucky, 1951 (34 games)

REBOUNDS PER GAME
  70.0—Connecticut, 1955 (1,751 in 25)

REBOUND MARGIN AVERAGE
  25.0—Morehead St., 1957 (64.3 offense, 39.3 defense)
  (Since 1973) 18.5—Manhattan, 1973 (56.5, 38.0)

Assists

ASSISTS
  926—UNLV, 1990 (40 games)

ASSISTS PER GAME
  24.7—UNLV, 1991 (863 in 35)

Assist-to-Turnover Ratio

ASSIST-TO-TURNOVER RATIO
(Since 2008)
  1.57—UMBC, 2008 (500 assists to 318 turnovers)

Blocked Shots

BLOCKED SHOTS
  315—Connecticut, 2004 (39 games)

BLOCKED SHOTS PER GAME
  9.1—Georgetown, 1989 (309 in 34)

Steals

STEALS
  490—VMI, 2007 (33 games)

STEALS PER GAME
  14.9—Long Island, 1998 (478 in 32)

Turnovers

FEWEST TURNOVERS PER GAME
(Since 2002)
  7.72—Temple, 2006 (247 in 32 games))

Fouls

FOULS
  966—Providence, 1987 (34 games)

FOULS PER GAME
  29.3—Indiana, 1952 (644 in 22)

FEWEST FOULS
  253—Air Force, 1962 (23 games)

FEWEST FOULS PER GAME
  11.0—Air Force, 1962 (253 in 23)

Defense

LOWEST SCORING AVERAGE PER GAME ALLOWED
  (Since 1938) 25.7—Oklahoma St., 1939 (693 in 27)
  (Since 1948) 32.5—Oklahoma St., 1948 (1,006 in 31)
  (Since 1965) 47.1—Fresno St., 1982 (1,412 in 30)

LOWEST FIELD-GOAL PERCENTAGE ALLOWED
  (Since 1978) 35.2—Stanford, 2000 (667 of 1,893)

Overtimes

OVERTIME GAMES
8—Western Ky., 1978 (won 5, lost 3); Portland, 1984 (won 4, lost 4); Valparaiso, 1993 (won 4, lost 4)

CONSECUTIVE OVERTIME GAMES
4—Jacksonville, 1982 (won 3, lost 1); Illinois St., 1985 (won 3, lost 1); Dayton, 1988 (won 1, lost 3)

OVERTIME WINS
6—Chattanooga, 1989 (6-0); Wake Forest, 1984 (6-1); Lafayette, 2008 (6-1)

OVERTIME HOME WINS
5—Cincinnati, 1967 (5-0)

OVERTIME ROAD WINS
5—Lafayette, 2008 (5-1)

OVERTIME PERIODS
14—Bradley, 1982 (3-3)

CONSECUTIVE OVERTIME WINS—ALL-TIME
11—Louisville, Feb. 10, 1968-March 29, 1975; Massachusetts, March 21, 1991-Feb. 28, 1996; Virginia, Dec. 5, 1991-Feb. 8, 1996

General Records

GAMES IN A SEASON
45—Oregon, 1945 (30-15)

**GAMES IN A SEASON
(Since 1948)**
40—Duke, 1986 (37-3); UNLV, 1990 (35-5); Kentucky, 1997 (35-5); Florida, 2007 (35-5); Kansas, 2008 (37-3); Memphis, 2008 (38-2)

VICTORIES IN A SEASON
38—Memphis, 2008 (38-2)

VICTORIES IN A PERFECT SEASON
32—North Carolina, 1957; Indiana, 1976

VICTORIES IN FIRST SEASON IN DIVISION I
29—Seattle, 1953 (29-4)

WON-LOST PERCENTAGE IN FIRST SEASON IN DIVISION I
.931—Md.-East. Shore, 1974 (27-2)

MOST-IMPROVED TEAM FROM ONE SEASON TO THE NEXT
17 games—Mercer, 2003 (from 6-23 to 23-6); UTEP, 2004 (from 6-24 to 24-8)

CONSECUTIVE VICTORIES IN A SEASON
34—UNLV, 1991 (34-1)

CONSECUTIVE VICTORIES
88—UCLA, from Jan. 30, 1971, through Jan. 17, 1974 (ended Jan. 19, 1974, at Notre Dame, 71-70; last UCLA defeat before streak also came at Notre Dame, 89-82)

CONSECUTIVE REGULAR-SEASON VICTORIES (NATIONAL POSTSEASON TOURNAMENTS NOT INCLUDED)
76—UCLA, 1971-74

CONSECUTIVE HOME-COURT VICTORIES
129—Kentucky, from Jan. 4, 1943, to Jan. 8, 1955 (ended by Georgia Tech, 59-58)

CONSECUTIVE ROAD VICTORIES (OPPONENTS' HOME SITE ONLY)
35—Kansas, Feb. 20, 1924-Jan. 13, 1928 (ended by Oklahoma, 45-19)

CONSECUTIVE NON-HOME VICTORIES (ROAD AND NEUTRAL SITE GAMES ONLY)
39—UCLA, Feb. 6, 1971-Jan. 7, 1974 (ended by Notre Dame, 71-70)

DEFEATS IN A SEASON
30—Grambling, 2000 (1-30)

DEFEATS IN A WINLESS SEASON
28—Prairie View, 1992 (0-28); Savannah St., 2005 (0-28)
Note: 29—NJIT, 2008 (0-29 while reclassifying)

CONSECUTIVE DEFEATS IN A SEASON
28—Prairie View, 1992 (0-28); Savannah St., 2005 (0-28)
Note: 29—NJIT, 2008 (0-29 while reclassifying)

CONSECUTIVE DEFEATS
34—Sacramento St., from Dec. 22, 1997, to Jan. 27, 1999

CONSECUTIVE HOME-COURT DEFEATS
32—New Hampshire, from Feb. 9, 1988, to Feb. 2, 1991 (ended vs. Holy Cross, 72-56)

CONSECUTIVE ROAD DEFEATS (INCLUDING ONLY GAMES AT THE OPPONENTS' HOME SITES)
64—Tex.-Pan American, from Nov. 25, 1995, to Jan. 8, 2000 (ended vs. Oral Roberts, 79-62)

CONSECUTIVE NON-HOME DEFEATS (INCLUDING GAMES AT THE OPPONENTS' HOME SITES AND AT NEUTRAL SITES)
56—Sacramento St., from Nov. 22, 1991, to Jan. 5, 1995 [ended at Loyola (Ill.), 68-56]

CONSECUTIVE 30-WIN SEASONS
3—Kentucky, 1947-49 and 1996-98; Memphis, 2006-08; UCLA, 2006-08

CURRENT CONSECUTIVE 30-WIN SEASONS
3—Memphis & UCLA, 2006-08

CONSECUTIVE 25-WIN SEASONS
10—UCLA, 1967-76; UNLV, 1983-92

CURRENT CONSECUTIVE 25-WIN SEASONS
3—Kansas, Memphis, Pittsburgh, Texas & UCLA, 2006-08

CONSECUTIVE 20-WIN SEASONS
31—North Carolina, 1971-2001

CURRENT CONSECUTIVE 20-WIN SEASONS
19—Kansas, 1990-2008

CONSECUTIVE WINNING SEASONS
54—UCLA, 1949-2002

CURRENT CONSECUTIVE WINNING SEASONS
38—Syracuse, 1971-2008

CONSECUTIVE NON-LOSING SEASONS (INCLUDES .500 RECORD)
60—Kentucky, 1928-52, 54-88# (two .500 seasons)
#Kentucky did not play basketball during the 1953 season.

CONSECUTIVE NON-LOSING SEASONS (INCLUDES .500 RECORD)-CURRENT
39—Syracuse, 1970-2008 (one .500 season)

UNBEATEN TEAMS (SINCE 1938; NUMBER OF VICTORIES IN PARENTHESES)
1939 Long Island (24)†
1940 Seton Hall (19)††
1944 Army (15)††
1954 Kentucky (25)††
1956 San Francisco (29)*
1957 North Carolina (32)*
1964 UCLA (30)*
1967 UCLA (30)*
1972 UCLA (30)*
1973 UCLA (30)*
1973 North Carolina St. (27)††
1976 Indiana (32)*

*NCAA champion; †NIT champion; ††not in either tournament

UNBEATEN IN REGULAR SEASON BUT LOST IN NCAA (*) OR NIT (†)
1939 Loyola (Ill.) (20; 21-1)†
1941 Seton Hall (19; 20-2)†
1951 Columbia (21; 21-1)*
1961 Ohio St. (24; 27-1)*
1968 Houston (28; 31-2)*
1968 St. Bonaventure (22; 23-2)*
1971 Marquette (26; 28-1)*
1971 Penn (26; 28-1)*
1975 Indiana (29; 31-1)*
1976 Rutgers (28; 31-2)*
1979 Indiana St. (27; 33-1)*
1979 Alcorn St. (25; 28-1)†
1991 UNLV (30; 34-1)*

**30-GAME WINNERS
(Since 1938)**
38—Memphis, 2008.
37—Duke, 1986 & 1999; Illinois, 2005; Kansas, 2008; UNLV, 1987.
36—Kentucky, 1948; North Carolina, 2008.
35—Arizona, 1988; Duke, 2001; Florida, 2007; Georgetown, 1985; Kansas, 1986 & 1998; Kentucky, 1997 & 1998; Massachusetts, 1996; UNLV, 1990; Ohio St., 2007; Oklahoma, 1988; UCLA, 2008.
34—Arkansas, 1991; Connecticut, 1999; Duke, 1992; Georgetown, 1984; Kansas, 1997; Kentucky, 1947 & 1996; UNLV, 1991; North Carolina, 1993 & 1998.
33—Connecticut, 2004; Florida, 2006; Indiana St., 1979; Kansas, 2007; Louisville, 1980 & 2005; Memphis, 2006 & 2007; Michigan St., 1999; UNLV, 1986; North Carolina, 2005.
32—Arkansas, 1978 & 1995; Bradley, 1950, 1951 & 1986; Connecticut, 1996 & 1998; Duke, 1991, 1998 & 2006; Houston, 1984; Indiana, 1976; Iowa St., 2000; Kentucky, 1949, 1951, 1986 & 2003; Louisville, 1983 & 1986; Marshall, 1947; Maryland, 2002; Michigan St., 2000; North Carolina, 1957, 1982 & 1987; Temple, 1987 & 1988; Tulsa, 2000; UCLA, 2006.
31—Arkansas, 1994; Cincinnati, 2002; Connecticut, 1990; Duke, 2002 & 2004; Houston, 1968 & 1983; Illinois, 1989; Indiana, 1975 & 1993; LSU, 1981; Memphis, 1985; Michigan, 1993; Minnesota, 1997; North Carolina, 2007; Oklahoma, 1985 & 2002; Oklahoma St., 1946 & 2004; Pittsburgh, 2004; Rutgers, 1976; St. John's (N.Y.), 1985 & 1986; Seton Hall, 1953 & 1989; Stanford, 2001; Syracuse, 1987; Tennessee, 2008; Texas, 2008; UCLA, 1995; Wisconsin, 2008; Wyoming, 1943.
30—Arizona, 1998 & 2005; Arkansas, 1990; Butler, 2008; California, 1946; Connecticut, 2006; Georgetown, 1982 & 2007; Indiana, 1987; Iowa, 1987; Kansas, 1990 & 2003; Kentucky, 1978 & 1993; La Salle, 1990; Massachusetts, 1992; Michigan, 1989; Navy, 1986; UNLV, 2007; North Carolina, 1946; North Carolina St., 1951 & 1974; Oklahoma, 1989; Oregon, 1945; St. Joseph's, 2004; Stanford 1998 & 2004; Syracuse, 1989 & 2003; Texas, 2006; Texas Tech, 1996; UCLA, 1964, 1967, 1972, 1973 & 2007; Utah, 1991 & 1998; Virginia, 1982; Western Ky., 1938, Wisconsin, 2007; Xavier, 2008.

All-Time Individual Leaders

Single-Game Records

SCORING HIGHS VS. DIVISION I OPPONENT

Pts.	Player, Team vs. Opponent	Date
72	Kevin Bradshaw, U.S. Int'l vs. Loyola Marymount	Jan. 5, 1991
69	Pete Maravich, LSU vs. Alabama	Feb. 7, 1970
68	Calvin Murphy, Niagara vs. Syracuse	Dec. 7, 1968
66	Jay Handlan, Wash. & Lee vs. Furman	Feb. 17, 1951
66	Pete Maravich, LSU vs. Tulane	Feb. 10, 1969
66	Anthony Roberts, Oral Roberts vs. N.C. A&T	Feb. 19, 1977
65	Anthony Roberts, Oral Roberts vs. Oregon	Mar. 9, 1977
65	Scott Haffner, Evansville vs. Dayton	Feb. 18, 1989
64	Pete Maravich, LSU vs. Kentucky	Feb. 21, 1970
63	Johnny Neumann, Mississippi vs. LSU	Jan. 30, 1971
63	Hersey Hawkins, Bradley vs. Detroit	Feb. 22, 1988
62	Darrell Floyd, Furman vs. Citadel	Jan. 14, 1956
62	Oscar Robertson, Cincinnati vs. North Texas	Feb. 6, 1960
62	Askia Jones, Kansas St. vs. Fresno St.	Mar. 24, 1994
61	Lew Alcindor, UCLA vs. Washington St.	Feb. 25, 1967
61	Pete Maravich, LSU vs. Vanderbilt	Dec. 11, 1969
61	Rick Mount, Purdue vs. Iowa	Feb. 28, 1970
61	Austin Carr, Notre Dame vs. Ohio	Mar. 7, 1970
61	Wayman Tisdale, Oklahoma vs. UTSA	Dec. 28, 1983
61	Eddie House, Arizona St. vs. California (2 ot)	Jan. 8, 2000
60	Elgin Baylor, Seattle vs. Portland	Jan. 30, 1958
60	Billy McGill, Utah vs. BYU	Feb. 24, 1962
60	John Mengelt, Auburn vs. Alabama	Feb. 14, 1970
60	Johnny Neumann, Mississippi vs. Baylor	Dec. 29, 1970
59	Pete Maravich, LSU vs. Alabama	Feb. 17, 1968
59	Ernie Fleming, Jacksonville vs. St. Peter's	Jan. 29, 1972
59	Kevin Bradshaw, U.S. Int'l vs. Florida Int'l	Jan. 14, 1991

SCORING HIGHS VS. NON-DIVISION I OPPONENT

Pts.	Player, Team vs. Opponent	Date
100	Frank Selvy, Furman vs. Newberry	Feb. 13, 1954
85	Paul Arizin, Villanova vs. Philadelphia NAMC	Feb. 12, 1949
81	Freeman Williams, Portland St. vs. Rocky Mountain	Feb. 3, 1978
73	Bill Mlkvy, Temple vs. Wilkes	Mar. 3, 1951
71	Freeman Williams, Portland St. vs. Southern Ore.	Feb. 9, 1977
67	Darrell Floyd, Furman vs. Morehead St.	Jan. 22, 1955
66	Freeman Williams, Portland St. vs. George Fox	Jan. 13, 1978
65	Bob Zawoluk, St. John's (N.Y.) vs. St. Peter's	Mar. 30, 1950
63	Sherman White, Long Island vs. John Marshall	Feb. 1950
63	Frank Selvy, Furman vs. Mercer	Feb. 11, 1953
62	Elvin Hayes, Houston vs. Valparaiso	Feb. 24, 1968
61	Matt Teahan, Denver vs. Neb. Wesleyan	Feb. 26, 1979
60	Bob Pettit, LSU vs. Louisiana College	Dec. 7, 1953
60	Harry Kelly, Texas Southern vs. Jarvis Christian	Feb. 23, 1983
60	Dave Jamerson, Ohio vs. Charleston (W.V.)	Dec. 21, 1989
59	Rick Barry, Miami (Fla.) vs. Rollins	Jan. 23, 1965
58	Frank Selvy, Furman vs. Wofford	Feb. 23, 1954
57	David Thompson, North Carolina St. vs. Buffalo St.	Dec. 5, 1974
57	Calvin Murphy, Niagara vs. Villa Madonna	Dec. 6, 1967
56	Stan Davis, Appalachian St. vs. Carson-Newman	Jan. 24, 1974
56	Tim Roberts, Southern U. vs. Faith Baptist	Dec. 12, 1994
55	Rick Barry, Miami (Fla.) vs. Tampa	Dec. 1, 1964
55	Elvin Hayes, Houston vs. Texas St.	Feb. 12, 1966
55	Wayman Tisdale, Oklahoma vs. Texas St.	Dec. 10, 1984
54	Rick Barry, Miami (Fla.) vs. Florida Southern	Jan. 13, 1965

FIELD-GOAL PERCENTAGE
(Minimum 12 field goals made)

Pct.	Player, Team vs. Opponent (FG-FGA)	Date
100	Clifford Rozier, Louisville vs. Eastern Ky. (15 of 15)	Dec. 11, 1993
100	Dan Henderson, Arkansas St. vs. Ga. Southern (14 of 14)	Feb. 26, 1976
100	Cornelius Holden, Louisville vs. Southern Miss. (14 of 14)	Mar. 3, 1990
100	Dana Jones, Pepperdine vs. Boise St. (14 of 14)	Nov. 30, 1991
100	Ted Guzek, Butler vs. Michigan (13 of 13)	Dec. 15, 1956
100	Rick Dean, Syracuse vs. Colgate (13 of 13)	Feb. 14, 1966
100	Gary Lechman, Gonzaga vs. Portland St. (13 of 13)	Jan. 21, 1967
100	Kevin King, Charlotte vs. South Ala. (13 of 13)	Feb. 20, 1978
100	Vernon Smith, Texas A&M vs. Alas. Anchorage (13 of 13)	Nov. 26, 1978
100	Steve Johnson, Oregon St. vs. Hawaii-Hilo (13 of 13)	Dec. 5, 1979
100	Antoine Carr, Wichita St. vs. Abilene Christian (13 of 13)	Nov. 28, 1980
100	Doug Hashley, Montana St. vs. Idaho St. (13 of 13)	Feb. 5, 1982
100	Brad Daugherty, North Carolina vs. UCLA (13 of 13)	Nov. 24, 1985
100	Ricky Butler, UC Irvine vs. Cal St. Fullerton (13 of 13)	Feb. 21, 1991
100	Rafael Solis, Brooklyn vs. Wagner (13 of 13)	Dec. 11, 1991

Pct.	Player, Team vs. Opponent (FG-FGA)	Date
100	Ben Handlogten, Western Mich. vs. Toledo (13 of 13)	Jan. 27, 1996
100	Mate Milisa, Long Beach St. vs. Cal St. Monterey (13 of 13)	Dec. 22, 1999
100	Leon Roberts, Northern Ill. vs. Rockford (13 of 13)	Dec. 6, 2000
100	Calvin Ento, Montana St. vs. Dickinson St. (13 of 13)	Dec. 10, 2002
100	23 tied (12 of 12)	

THREE-POINT FIELD GOALS MADE

3FG	Player, Team vs. Opponent	Date
15	Keith Veney, Marshall vs. Morehead St.	Dec. 14, 1996
14	Dave Jamerson, Ohio vs. Col. of Charleston	Dec. 21, 1989
14	Askia Jones, Kansas St. vs. Fresno St.	Mar. 24, 1994
14	Ronald Blackshear, Marshall vs. Akron	Mar. 1, 2002
12	Gary Bossert, Niagara vs. Siena	Jan. 7, 1987
12	Darrin Fitzgerald, Butler vs. Detroit	Feb. 9, 1987
12	Alex Dillard, Arkansas vs. Delaware St.	Dec. 11, 1993
12	Mitch Taylor, Southern U. vs. La. Christian	Dec. 1, 1994
12	David McMahan, Winthrop vs. Coastal Caro.	Jan. 15, 1996
12	Clarence Gilbert, Missouri vs. Colorado	Feb. 23, 2002
12	Terrence Woods, Florida A&M vs. Coppin St.	Mar. 1, 2003
12	Michael Jenkins, Winthrop vs. North Greenville	Nov. 11, 2006
11	Jeff Hodson, Augusta St. vs. Armstrong Atlantic	Jan. 28, 1986
11	Dennis Scott, Georgia Tech vs. Houston	Dec. 28, 1988
11	Scott Haffner, Evansville vs. Dayton	Feb. 18, 1989
11	Bobby Phills, Southern U. vs. Alcorn St.	Feb. 3, 1990
11	Dave Jamerson, Ohio vs. Kent St.	Feb. 24, 1990
11	Jeff Fryer, Loyola Marymount vs. Michigan	Mar. 18, 1990
11	Doug Day, Radford vs. Central Conn. St.	Dec. 12, 1990
11	Brent Price, Oklahoma vs. Loyola Marymount	Dec. 15, 1990
11	Bobby Phills, Southern U. vs. Manhattan	Dec. 28, 1990
11	Terry Brown, Kansas vs. North Carolina	Jan. 5, 1991
11	Marc Rybczyk, Central Conn. St. vs. Long Island	Nov. 26, 1991
11	Mark Alberts, Akron vs. Wright St.	Feb. 8, 1992
11	Mike Alcorn, Youngstown St. vs. Pitt.-Bradford	Feb. 24, 1992
11	Doug Day, Radford vs. Morgan St.	Dec. 9, 1992
11	Lindsey Hunter, Jackson St. vs. Kansas	Dec. 27, 1992
11	Keith Veney, Lamar vs. Prairie View	Feb. 2, 1993
11	Keith Veney, Lamar vs. UALR	Feb. 11, 1993
11	Scott Neely, Campbell vs. Coastal Caro.	Jan. 29, 1994
11	Chris Brown, UC Irvine vs. New Mexico St.	Mar. 13, 1994
11	Randy Rutherford, Oklahoma St. vs. Kansas	Mar. 5, 1995
11	Troy Hudson, Southern Ill. vs. Hawaii-Hilo	Dec. 29, 1995
11	Seth Chadwick, Wofford vs. Mercer	Feb. 15, 1997
11	Cory Schwab, Northern Ariz. vs. Cal Poly	Feb. 2, 2000
11	Ron Williamson, Howard vs. Georgetown	Dec. 16, 2000
11	T.J. Sorrentine, Vermont vs. Northeastern	Jan. 17, 2002
11	Ron Williamson, Howard vs. N.C. A&T	Jan. 21, 2003
11	Terrence Woods, Florida A&M vs. N.C. A&T	Feb. 1, 2003
11	Kevin Bettencourt, Bucknell vs. St. Francis (Pa.)	Dec. 6, 2003
11	Earnest Crumbley, Fla. Atlantic vs. Campbell	Feb. 26, 2004
11	Elton Nesbitt, Ga. Southern vs. Chattanooga	Jan. 17, 2005
11	Bobby Brown, Cal St. Fullerton vs. Bethune-Cookman	Dec. 16, 2006
11	Eric Moore, Buffalo vs. Bowling Green	Jan. 7, 2007
11	Gary Patterson, IUPUI vs. Southern Utah	Jan. 31, 2008

THREE-POINT FIELD-GOAL PERCENTAGE
(Minimum 7 three-point field goals made)

Pct.	Player, Team vs. Opponent (3FG-FGA)	Date
100	Andre Smith, George Mason vs. James Madison (10 of 10)	Jan. 19, 2008
100	Mark Poag, Old Dominion vs. VMI (9 of 9)	Nov. 25, 1997
100	Marcus Wilson, Evansville vs. Tenn.-Martin (9 of 9)	Nov. 18, 1998
100	Donnie McGrath, Providence vs. Virginia (9 of 9)	Feb. 2, 2005
100	Tomas Thompson, San Francisco vs. Loyola Marymount (8 of 8)	Mar. 7, 1992
100	Shawn Haughn, Dayton vs. St. Louis (8 of 8)	Feb. 13, 1994
100	James Singleton, Murray St. vs. Eastern Ill. (8 of 8)	Feb. 13, 2003
100	John Goldsberry, UNC Wilmington vs. Maryland (8 of 8)	Mar. 21, 2003
100	Doug D'Amore, Idaho St. vs. Montana (8 of 8)	Jan. 17, 2004
100	Draelon Burns, DePaul vs. A&M Corpus Christi (8 of 8)	Nov. 28, 2007
100	Kelvin Collins, La.-Monroe vs. Nevada (7 of 7)	Dec. 30, 1986
100	Wally Lancaster, Virginia Tech vs. San Fran. St. (7 of 7)	Jan. 3, 1987
100	Ramon Trice, St. Louis vs. Butler (7 of 7)	Feb. 16, 1987
100	Juan Sanchez, Temple vs. Rhode Island (7 of 7)	Feb. 16, 1997
100	DeMar Moore, Bowling Green vs. Western Mich. (7 of 7)	Jan. 3, 1998
100	Senque Carey, Washington vs. Old Dominion (7 of 7)	Dec. 4, 1999
100	Okechi Egbe, Tenn.-Martin vs. Bethel (7 of 7)	Nov. 20, 2000
100	Justin Brown, Montana St. vs. Western Ill. (7 of 7)	Dec. 6, 2000
100	Lionel Armstead, West Virginia vs. Ark.-Monticello (7 of 7)	Dec. 1, 2001
100	Bronski Dockery, St. Francis (N.Y.) vs. Central Conn. St. (7 of 7)	Dec. 3, 2001
100	Nick Moore, Toledo vs. Akron (7 of 7)	Feb. 13, 2002
100	Felton Freeman, Sam Houston St. vs. TCU (7 of 7)	Nov. 22, 2002
100	Matt Walsh, Florida vs. Miami (Fla.) (7 of 7)	Dec. 21, 2002

Pct.	Player, Team vs. Opponent (3FG-FGA)	Date
100	Ezra Williams, Georgia vs. LSU (7 of 7)	Jan. 5, 2003
100	Tyrone Green, N.C. A&T vs. N.C. Central (7 of 7)	Jan. 19, 2003
100	Avery Sheets, Butler vs. Loyola (Ill.) (7 of 7)	Feb. 3, 2005
100	Rashad Anderson, Connecticut vs. Morehead St. (7 of 7)	Dec. 23, 2005
100	Ricky Porter, UC Riverside vs. Pacific (7 of 7)	Jan. 7, 2006
100	Jawann McClellan, Arizona vs. New Mexico St. (7 of 7)	Nov. 19, 2006
100	Matt Lojeski, Hawaii vs. Boise St. (7 of 7)	Mar. 3, 2007
100	Bryce Taylor, Oregon vs. Southern California (7 of 7)	Mar. 10, 2007
100	Mike Schachtner, Green Bay vs. Valparaiso (7 of 7)	Jan. 12, 2008
100	Darnell Harris, La Salle vs. St. Bonaventure (7 of 7)	Jan. 30, 2008

FREE-THROW PERCENTAGE
(Minimum 18 free throws made)

Pct.	Player, Team vs. Opponent (FT-FTA)	Date
100	Arlen Clark, Oklahoma St. vs. Colorado (24 of 24)	Mar. 7, 1959
100	York Larese, North Carolina vs. Duke (21 of 21)	Dec. 29, 1959
100	Steve Nash, Santa Clara vs. St. Mary's (Cal.) (21 of 21)	Jan. 7, 1995
100	Paul Renfro, Texas-Arlington vs. Lafayette (20 of 20)	Feb. 11, 1979
100	Anthony Peeler, Missouri vs. Iowa St. (20 of 20)	Jan. 31, 1990
100	Donyell Marshall, Connecticut vs. St. John's (N.Y.)	Jan 15, 1994
100	Jeron Roberts, Wyoming vs. UTEP (20 of 20)	Feb. 7, 1998
100	Dick Ricketts, Duquesne vs. Dayton (19 of 19)	Dec. 29, 1955
100	Skip Chappelle, Maine vs. Massachusetts (19 of 19)	1961
100	Gene Phillips, SMU vs. Texas A&M (19 of 19)	Feb. 2, 1971
100	Jim Kennedy, Missouri vs. Hawaii (19 of 19)	Dec. 22, 1975
100	Kevin Smith, Michigan St. vs. Indiana (19 of 19)	Jan. 7, 1982
100	Sidney Goodman, Coppin St. vs. N.C. A&T (19 of 19)	Feb. 18, 1995
100	Geno Ford, Ohio vs. Eastern Mich. (19 of 19)	Feb. 12, 1997
100	Eddie Benton, Vermont vs. New Hampshire (19 of 19)	Feb. 18, 1993
100	Tommy Boyer, Arkansas vs. Texas Tech (18 of 18)	Feb. 19, 1963
100	Ted Kitchel, Indiana vs. Illinois (18 of 18)	Jan. 10, 1981
100	Eric Rhodes, Stephen F. Austin vs. Texas St. (18 of 18)	Feb. 21, 1987
100	Todd Lichti, Stanford vs. UC Santa Barbara (18 of 18)	Dec. 28, 1987
100	Lionel Simmons, La Salle vs. American (18 of 18)	Feb. 2, 1988
100	Jeff Webster, Oklahoma vs. SMU (18 of 18)	Jan. 2, 1994
100	Anquell McCollum, Western Caro. vs. Marshall (18 of 18)	Feb. 5, 1996
100	Keith Van Horn, Utah vs. TCU (18 of 18)	Feb. 13, 1997
100	Edwin Young, Dayton vs. La.-Monroe (18 of 18)	Dec. 18, 1997
100	Rayford Young, Texas Tech vs. Kansas (18 of 18)	Feb 13, 1993
100	Lynn Greer, Temple vs. St. Joseph's (18 of 18)	Feb. 2, 2002
100	Gabe Martin, Liberty vs. Fla. Atlantic (18 of 18)	Dec. 20, 2002
100	Matt Freije, Vanderbilt vs. Indiana (18 of 18)	Nov. 24, 2003
100	Ron Lewis, Bowling Green vs. Eastern Mich. (18 of 18)	Mar. 6, 2004
100	James Shuler, Winthrop vs. High Point (18 of 18)	Feb. 23, 2006
100	Shy Ely, Evansville vs. Creighton (18 of 18)	Feb. 13, 2008

REBOUNDS

Reb.	Player, Team vs. Opponent	Date
51	Bill Chambers, William & Mary vs. Virginia	Feb. 14, 1953
43	Charlie Slack, Marshall vs. Morris Harvey	Jan. 12, 1954
42	Tom Heinsohn, Holy Cross vs. Boston College	Mar. 1, 1955
40	Art Quimby, Connecticut vs. Boston U.	Jan. 11, 1955
40	John Tresvant, Seattle vs. Montana	Feb. 8, 1963
39	Maurice Stokes, St. Francis (Pa.) vs. John Carroll	Jan. 28, 1955
39	Dave DeBusschere, Detroit vs. Central Mich.	Jan. 30, 1960
39	Keith Swagerty, Pacific vs. UC Santa Barbara	Mar. 5, 1965
38	Jerry Koch, St. Louis vs. Bradley	Mar. 5, 1954
38	Charlie Tyra, Louisville vs. Canisius	Dec. 10, 1955
38	Steve Hamilton, Morehead St. vs. Florida St.	Jan. 2, 1957
38	Paul Silas, Creighton vs. Centenary (La.)	Feb. 19, 1962
38	Tommy Woods, East Tenn. St. vs. Middle Tenn.	Mar. 1, 1965
37	Elgin Baylor, Seattle vs. Pacific Lutheran	Feb. 28, 1958
36	Herb Neff, Tennessee vs. Georgia Tech	Jan. 26, 1952
36	Dickie Hemric, Wake Forest vs. Clemson	Feb. 4, 1955
36	Swede Halbrook, Oregon St. vs. Idaho	Feb. 15, 1955
36	Wilt Chamberlain, Kansas vs. Iowa St.	Feb. 15, 1958
36	Jim Barnes, UTEP vs. Western N.M.	Jan. 4, 1964
36	Paul Silas, Creighton vs. Marquette	Jan. 23, 1964
35	Don Lange, Navy vs. Loyola (Md.)	Feb. 18, 1953
35	Ronnie Shavlik, North Carolina St. vs. Villanova	Jan. 29, 1955
35	Bill Ebben, Detroit vs. BYU	Dec. 28, 1955
35	Larry Abney, Fresno St. vs. SMU	Feb. 17, 2000
34	Bob Burrow, Kentucky vs. Temple	Dec. 10, 1955
34	Ronnie Shavlik, North Carolina St. vs. South Carolina	Feb. 11, 1955
34	Fred Cohen, Temple vs. Connecticut	Mar. 16, 1956
34	Bailey Howell, Mississippi St. vs. LSU	Feb. 1, 1957
34	Cal Ramsey, New York U. vs. Boston College	Feb. 16, 1957
34	Artis Gilmore, Jacksonville vs. St. Peter's	Dec. 3, 1970
34	David Vaughn, Oral Roberts vs. Brandeis	Jan. 8, 1973

(Since 1973)

Reb.	Player, Team vs. Opponent	Date
35	Larry Abney, Fresno St. vs. SMU	Feb. 17, 2000
34	David Vaughn, Oral Roberts vs. Brandeis	Jan. 8, 1973
32	Durand Macklin, LSU vs. Tulane	Nov. 26, 1976
32	Jervaughn Scales, Southern U. vs. Grambling	Feb. 7, 1994
31	Jim Bradley, Northern Ill. vs. Milwaukee	Feb. 19, 1973
31	Calvin Natt, La.-Monroe vs. Ga. Southern	Dec. 29, 1976
30	Marvin Barnes, Providence vs. Assumption	Feb. 3, 1973
30	Brad Robinson, Kent St. vs. Central Mich.	Feb. 9, 1974
30	Monti Davis, Tennessee St. vs. Alabama St.	Feb. 8, 1979
30	Rashad Jones-Jennings, UALR vs. Ark.-Pine Bluff	Dec. 13, 2005
29	Lionel Garrett, Southern U. vs. Bishop	Feb. 16, 1979
29	Donald Newman, UALR vs. Centenary (La.)	Jan. 24, 1984
29	Hank Gathers, Loyola Marymount vs. U.S. Int'l	Jan. 31, 1989
28	Alvan Adams, Oklahoma vs. Indiana St.	Nov. 27, 1972
28	Cliff Robinson, Southern California vs. Portland St.	Jan. 20, 1978
28	Eric McArthur, UC Santa Barbara vs. New Mexico St.	Jan. 11, 1990
28	Marcus Mann, Mississippi Val. vs. Jackson St.	Mar. 9, 1996
28	David Bluthenthal, Southern California vs. Arizona St.	Jan. 20, 2000
28	Paul Millsap, Louisiana Tech vs. San Jose St.	Feb. 15, 2006
27	Andy Hopson, Oklahoma St. vs. Missouri	Jan. 30, 1973
27	Henry Ray, McNeese St. vs. Texas-Arlington	1974
27	Bill Walton, UCLA vs. Loyola (Ill.)	Jan. 25, 1973
27	Bill Walton, UCLA vs. Maryland	Dec. 1, 1973
27	Rick Kelley, Stanford vs. Kentucky	Dec. 22, 1974
27	Kerry Davis, Cal St. Fullerton vs. Central Mich.	Dec. 15, 1975
27	Hank Gathers, Loyola Marymount vs. U.S. Int'l	Dec. 7, 1989
27	Dikembe Mutombo, Georgetown vs. Connecticut	Mar. 8, 1991
27	Reginald Slater, Wyoming vs. Troy	Dec. 14, 1991
27	Ervin Johnson, New Orleans vs. Lamar	Feb. 18, 1993
27	Willie Fisher, Jacksonville vs. Louisiana Tech	Dec. 4, 1993
27	Kareem Carpenter, Eastern Mich. vs. Western Mich.	Feb. 8, 1995
27	Amien Hicks, Morris Brown vs. Clark Atlanta	Jan. 14, 2002
27	Andre Brown, DePaul vs. TCU	Feb. 6, 2002

ASSISTS

Ast.	Player, Team vs. Opponent	Date
22	Tony Fairley, Charleston So. vs. Armstrong Atlantic	Feb. 9, 1987
22	Avery Johnson, Southern U. vs. Texas Southern	Jan. 25, 1988
22	Sherman Douglas, Syracuse vs. Providence	Jan. 28, 1989
21	Mark Wade, UNLV vs. Navy	Dec. 29, 1986
21	Kelvin Scarborough, New Mexico vs. Hawaii	Feb. 13, 1987
21	Anthony Manuel, Bradley vs. UC Irvine	Dec. 19, 1987
21	Avery Johnson, Southern U. vs. Alabama St.	Jan. 16, 1988
20	Grayson Marshall, Clemson vs. Md.-East. Shore	Nov. 25, 1985
20	James Johnson, Middle Tenn. vs. Freed-Hardeman	Jan. 2, 1986
20	Avery Johnson, Southern U. vs. Texas Southern	Mar. 6, 1987
20	Avery Johnson, Southern U. vs. Mississippi Val.	Feb. 8, 1988
20	Howard Evans, Temple vs. Villanova	Feb. 10, 1988
20	Jasper Walker, St. Peter's vs. Holy Cross	Feb. 11, 1989
20	Chris Corchiani, North Carolina St. vs. Maryland	Feb. 27, 1991
20	Drew Henderson, Fairfield vs. Loyola (Md.)	Jan. 25, 1992
20	Dana Harris, UMBC vs. St. Mary's	Dec. 12, 1992
20	Sam Crawford, New Mexico St. vs. Sam Houston St.	Dec. 21, 1992
20	Ray Washington, Nicholls St. vs. McNeese St.	Jan. 28, 1995
20	Mateen Cleaves, Michigan St. vs. Michigan	Mar. 4, 2000
20	Brandon Brooks, Alabama St. vs. Jackson St.	Mar. 8, 2008
19	Frank Nardi, Green Bay vs. UNI	Feb. 24, 1986
19	Avery Johnson, Southern U. vs. Tex. A&M-Kingsville	Dec. 6, 1986
19	Avery Johnson, Southern U. vs. Jackson St.	Jan. 16, 1987
19	Andre Van Drost, Wagner vs. Long Island	Feb. 25, 1987
19	Todd Lehmann, Drexel vs. Liberty	Feb. 5, 1990
19	Greg Anthony, UNLV vs. Pacific	Dec. 29, 1990
19	Keith Jennings, East Tenn. St. vs. Appalachian St.	Feb. 2, 1991
19	Nelson Haggerty, Baylor vs. Oral Roberts	Feb. 27, 1993
19	Andres Rodriguez, American vs. Navy	Jan. 14, 2004
19	Jason Richards, Davidson vs. Mt. St. Mary (N.Y.)	Dec. 15, 2006

BLOCKED SHOTS

Blk.	Player, Team vs. Opponent	Date
16	Mickell Gladness, Alabama A&M vs. Texas Southern	Feb. 24, 2007
14	David Robinson, Navy vs. UNC Wilmington	Jan. 4, 1986
14	Shawn Bradley, BYU vs. Eastern Ky.	Dec. 7, 1990
14	Roy Rogers, Alabama vs. Georgia	Feb. 10, 1996
14	Loren Woods, Arizona vs. Oregon	Feb. 3, 2000
13	Kevin Roberson, Vermont vs. New Hampshire	Jan. 9, 1992
13	Jim McIlvaine, Marquette vs. Northeastern Ill.	Dec. 9, 1992
13	Keith Closs, Central Conn. St. vs. St. Francis (Pa.)	Dec. 21, 1994
13	D'or Fischer, Northwestern St. vs. Texas St.	Jan. 22, 2001
13	Kyle Davis, Auburn vs. Miami (Fla.)	Mar. 14, 2001
13	Wojciech Myrda, La.-Monroe vs. UTSA	Jan. 17, 2002
13	Anthony King, Miami (Fla.) vs. Fla. Atlantic	Nov. 29, 2004
13	Deng Gai, Fairfield vs. Siena	Jan. 22, 2005

DIVISION I

Blk.	Player, Team vs. Opponent	Date
13	Sean Williams, Boston College vs. Duquesne	Dec. 28, 2006
13	Joel Anthony, UNLV vs. TCU	Feb. 7, 2007
12	David Robinson, Navy vs. James Madison	Jan. 9, 1986
12	Derrick Lewis, Maryland vs. James Madison	Jan. 28, 1987
12	Rodney Blake, St. Joseph's vs. Cleveland St.	Dec. 2, 1987
12	Walter Palmer, Dartmouth vs. Harvard	Jan. 9, 1988
12	Alan Ogg, UAB vs. Florida A&M	Dec. 16, 1988
12	Dikembe Mutombo, Georgetown vs. St. John's (N.Y.)	Jan. 23, 1989
12	Shaquille O'Neal, LSU vs. Loyola Marymount	Feb. 3, 1990
12	Cedric Lewis, Maryland vs. South Fla.	Jan. 19, 1991
12	Ervin Johnson, New Orleans vs. Texas A&M	Dec. 29, 1992
12	Kurt Thomas, TCU vs. Texas A&M	Feb. 25, 1995
12	Keith Closs, Central Conn. St. vs. Troy	Jan. 20, 1996
12	Adonal Foyle, Colgate vs. Fairfield	Nov. 26, 1996
12	Adonal Foyle, Colgate vs. Navy	Feb. 5, 1997
12	Tarvis Williams, Hampton vs. N.C. A&T	Jan. 9, 1999
12	Darrick Davenport, TCU vs. Alas. Fairbanks	Nov. 20, 1999
12	Tarvis Williams, Hampton vs. Delaware St.	Jan. 13, 2001
12	D'or Fischer, Northwestern St. vs. Siena	Nov. 21, 2001
12	Justin Williams, Wyoming vs. Utah	Mar. 10, 2006
12	Sean Williams, Boston College vs. Providence	Nov. 22, 2006
12	Brook Lopez, Stanford vs. Southern California	Jan. 25, 2007
12	Shawn James, Duquesne vs. Oakland	Nov. 20, 2007

STEALS

Stl.	Player, Team vs. Opponent	Date
13	Mookie Blaylock, Oklahoma vs. Centenary (La.)	Dec. 12, 1987
13	Mookie Blaylock, Oklahoma vs. Loyola Marymount	Dec. 17, 1988
12	Kenny Robertson, Cleveland St. vs. Wagner	Dec. 3, 1988
12	Terry Evans, Oklahoma vs. Florida A&M	Jan. 27, 1993
12	Richard Duncan, Middle Tenn. vs. Eastern Ky.	Feb. 20, 1999
12	Greedy Daniels, TCU vs. Ark.-Pine Bluff	Dec. 30, 2000
12	Jehiel Lewis, Navy vs. Bucknell	Jan. 12, 2002
12	Carldwell Johnson, UAB vs. South Carolina St.	Nov. 27, 2005
11	Darron Brittman, Chicago St. vs. McKendree	Jan. 24, 1986
11	Darron Brittman, Chicago St. vs. St. Xavier	Feb. 8, 1986
11	Marty Johnson, Towson vs. Bucknell	Feb. 17, 1988
11	Aldwin Ware, Florida A&M vs. Tuskegee	Feb. 24, 1988
11	Mark Macon, Temple vs. Notre Dame	Jan. 29, 1989
11	Carl Thomas, Eastern Mich. vs. Chicago St.	Feb. 20, 1991
11	Ron Arnold, St. Francis (N.Y.) vs. Mt. St. Mary's	Feb. 4, 1993
11	Tyus Edney, UCLA vs. George Mason	Dec. 22, 1995
11	Philip Huler, Fla. Atlantic vs. Campbell	Jan. 18, 1997
11	Ali Ton, Davidson vs. Tufts	Nov. 29, 1997
11	Chris Thomas, Notre Dame vs. New Hampshire	Nov. 16, 2001
11	Drew Schifino, West Virginia vs. Ark.-Monticello	Dec. 1, 2001
11	John Linehan, Providence vs. Rutgers	Jan. 22, 2002
11	Travis Demanby, Fresno St. vs. Oklahoma St.	Feb. 10, 2002
11	Travis Holmes, VMI vs. Bridgewater (Va.)	Jan. 18, 2007
10	38 tied	

QUADRUPLE-DOUBLES

Player, Team	Date
Lester Hudson, Tenn.-Martin vs. Central Baptist	Nov. 11, 2007
(25 points, 12 rebounds, 10 assists, 10 steals)	

Season Records

POINTS

Player, Team	Season	G	FG	3FG	FT	Pts.
Pete Maravich, LSU	†1970	31	522	—	337	1,381
Elvin Hayes, Houston	†1968	33	519	—	176	1,214
Frank Selvy, Furman	†1954	29	427	—	355	1,209
Pete Maravich, LSU	†1969	26	433	—	282	1,148
Pete Maravich, LSU	1968	26	432	—	274	1,138
Bo Kimble, Loyola Marymount	†1990	32	404	92	231	1,131
Hersey Hawkins, Bradley	†1988	31	377	87	284	1,125
Austin Carr, Notre Dame	1970	29	444	—	218	1,106
Austin Carr, Notre Dame	†1971	29	430	—	241	1,101
Otis Birdsong, Houston	†1977	36	452	—	186	1,090
Dwight Lamar, La.-Lafayette	†1972	29	429	—	196	1,054
Kevin Bradshaw, U.S. Int'l	†1991	28	358	60	278	1,054
Glenn Robinson, Purdue	†1994	34	368	79	215	1,030
Hank Gathers, Loyola Marymount	†1989	31	419	0	177	1,015
Oscar Robertson, Cincinnati	†1960	30	369	—	273	1,011
Freeman Williams, Portland St.	1977	26	417	—	176	1,010
Billy McGill, Utah	†1962	26	394	—	221	1,009
Rich Fuqua, Oral Roberts	1972	28	423	—	160	1,006
Oscar Robertson, Cincinnati	†1958	28	352	—	280	984
Oscar Robertson, Cincinnati	†1959	30	331	—	316	978

Player, Team	Season	G	FG	3FG	FT	Pts.
Rick Barry, Miami (Fla.)	†1965	26	340	—	293	973
Larry Bird, Indiana St.	†1979	34	376	—	221	973
Dennis Scott, Georgia Tech	1990	35	336	137	161	970
Freeman Williams, Portland St.	†1978	27	410	—	149	969
Chris Jackson, LSU	1989	32	359	84	163	965

†national leader

SCORING AVERAGE

Player, Team	Season	G	FG	3FG	FT	Pts.	Avg.
Pete Maravich, LSU	†1970	31	522	—	337	1,381	44.5
Pete Maravich, LSU	†1969	26	433	—	282	1,148	44.2
Pete Maravich, LSU	†1968	26	432	—	274	1,138	43.8
Frank Selvy, Furman	†1954	29	427	—	355	1,209	41.7
Johnny Neumann, Mississippi	†1971	23	366	—	191	923	40.1
Freeman Williams, Portland St.	†1977	26	417	—	176	1,010	38.8
Billy McGill, Utah	†1962	26	394	—	221	1,009	38.8
Calvin Murphy, Niagara	1968	24	337	—	242	916	38.2
Austin Carr, Notre Dame	1970	29	444	—	218	1,106	38.1
Austin Carr, Notre Dame	1971	29	430	—	241	1,101	38.0
Kevin Bradshaw, U.S. Int'l	†1991	28	358	60	278	1,054	37.6
Rick Barry, Miami (Fla.)	†1965	26	340	—	293	973	37.4
Elvin Hayes, Houston	1968	33	519	—	176	1,214	36.8
Marshall Rogers, Tex.-Pan American	†1976	25	361	—	197	919	36.8
Howard Komives, Bowling Green	†1964	23	292	—	260	844	36.7
Dwight Lamar, La.-Lafayette	†1972	29	429	—	196	1,054	36.3
Hersey Hawkins, Bradley	†1988	31	377	87	284	1,125	36.3
Darrell Floyd, Furman	†1955	25	344	—	209	897	35.9
Rich Fuqua, Oral Roberts	1972	28	423	—	160	1,006	35.9
Freeman Williams, Portland St.	†1978	27	410	—	149	969	35.9
Rick Mount, Purdue	1970	20	285	—	138	708	35.4
Bo Kimble, Loyola Marymount	†1990	32	404	92	231	1,131	35.3
Oscar Robertson, Cincinnati	†1958	28	352	—	280	984	35.1
Anthony Roberts, Oral Roberts	1977	28	402	—	147	951	34.0
Dan Issel, Kentucky	1970	28	369	—	210	948	33.9
William Averitt, Pepperdine	†1973	25	352	—	144	848	33.9

†national leader

FIELD-GOAL PERCENTAGE
(Based on qualifiers for annual championship)

Player, Team	Season	G	FG	FGA	Pct.
Steve Johnson, Oregon St.	†1981	28	235	315	74.6
Dwayne Davis, Florida	†1989	33	179	248	72.2
Keith Walker, Utica	†1985	27	154	216	71.3
Steve Johnson, Oregon St.	†1980	30	211	297	71.0
Adam Mark, Belmont	†2002	26	150	212	70.8
Oliver Miller, Arkansas	†1991	38	254	361	70.4
Alan Williams, Princeton	†1987	25	163	232	70.3
Mark McNamara, California	†1982	27	231	329	70.2
Warren Kidd, Middle Tenn.	1991	30	173	247	70.0
Pete Freeman, Akron	1991	28	175	250	70.0
Joe Senser, West Chester	†1977	25	130	186	69.9
Lee Campbell, Missouri St.	†1990	29	192	275	69.8
Stephen Scheffler, Purdue	1990	30	173	248	69.8
Brendan Haywood, North Carolina	†2000	36	191	274	69.7
Kenny George, UNC Asheville	†2008	28	151	217	69.6
Mike Atkinson, Long Beach St.	†1994	26	141	203	69.5
Lester James, St. Francis (N.Y.)	1991	29	149	215	69.3
Micheal Bradley, Villanova	†2001	31	254	367	69.2
Murray Brown, Florida St.	†1979	29	237	343	69.1
Joe Senser, West Chester	†1978	25	135	197	68.5
Charles Outlaw, Houston	†1992	31	156	228	68.4
Shane Kline-Ruminski, Bowling Green	†1995	26	181	265	68.3
Marcus Kennedy, Eastern Mich.	1991	33	240	352	68.2
Felton Spencer, Louisville	1990	35	188	276	68.1
Tyrone Howard, Eastern Ky.	1987	30	156	230	67.8
Nigel Dixon, Western Ky.	†2004	28	179	264	67.8
Mike Freeman, Hampton	†2007	30	162	239	67.8

†national leader

THREE-POINT FIELD GOALS MADE

Player, Team	Season	G	3FG
Stephen Curry, Davidson	†2008	36	162
Darrin Fitzgerald, Butler	†1987	28	158
Freddie Banks, UNLV	1987	39	152
Randy Rutherford, Oklahoma St.	†1995	37	146
Robert McKiver, Houston	2008	34	145
Robert Vaden, UAB	2008	33	142
Terrence Woods, Florida A&M	†2004	31	140
Terrence Woods, Florida A&M	†2003	28	139
J.J. Redick, Duke	†2006	36	139
Dennis Scott, Georgia Tech	†1990	35	137

Player, Team	Season	G	3FG
Demon Brown, Charlotte	2003	29	137
Will Whittington, Marist	†2007	30	137
Rashad Phillips, Detroit	†2001	35	136
Pat Carroll, St. Joseph's	†2005	35	135
Garrison Carr, American	2008	33	135
Troy Hudson, Southern Ill.	†1997	30	134
Shan Foster, Vanderbilt	2008	34	134
Timothy Pollard, Mississippi Val.	†1988	28	132
Jason Williams, Duke	2001	39	132
Dave Jamerson, Ohio	1990	28	131
Sydney Grider, La.-Lafayette	1990	29	131
Keith Veney, Marshall	1997	29	130
Curtis Staples, Virginia	†1998	30	130
David Holston, Chicago St.	2008	28	130
Kyle Korver, Creighton	2003	34	129

†national leader

THREE-POINT FIELD GOALS MADE PER GAME
(Based on qualifiers for annual championship)

Player, Team	Season	G	3FG	Avg.
Darrin Fitzgerald, Butler	†1987	28	158	5.64
Terrence Woods, Florida A&M	†2003	28	139	4.96
Demon Brown, Charlotte	2003	29	137	4.72
Timothy Pollard, Mississippi Val.	†1988	28	132	4.71
Chris Brown, UC Irvine	†1994	26	122	4.69
Dave Jamerson, Ohio	†1990	28	131	4.68
David Holston, Chicago St.	†2008	28	130	4.64
William Fourche, Southern U.	†1997	27	122	4.52
Sydney Grider, La.-Lafayette	1990	29	131	4.52
Terrence Woods, Florida A&M	†2004	31	140	4.52
Stephen Curry, Davidson	2008	36	162	4.50
Keith Veney, Marshall	1997	29	130	4.48
Troy Hudson, Southern Ill.	1997	30	134	4.47
Timothy Pollard, Mississippi Val.	†1989	28	124	4.43
Keke Hicks, Coastal Caro.	1994	26	115	4.42
Bobby Phills, Southern U.	†1991	28	123	4.39
Mitch Taylor, Southern U.	†1995	25	109	4.36
Mark Alberts, Akron	1990	28	122	4.36
Curtis Staples, Virginia	†1998	30	130	4.33
Jeff Fryer, Loyola Marymount	1990	28	121	4.32
Robert Vaden, UAB	2008	33	142	4.30
Robert McKiver, Houston	2008	34	145	4.26
Shawn Respert, Michigan St.	1995	28	119	4.25
Andre Collins, Loyola (Md.)	†2006	28	118	4.21
Sydney Grider, La.-Lafayette	1989	29	122	4.21

†national leader

THREE-POINT FIELD-GOAL PERCENTAGE
(Based on qualifiers for annual championship)

Player, Team	Season	G	3FG	3FGA	Pct.
Glenn Tropf, Holy Cross	†1988	29	52	82	63.4
Sean Wightman, Western Mich.	†1992	30	48	76	63.2
Keith Jennings, East Tenn. St.	†1991	33	84	142	59.2
Dave Calloway, Monmouth	†1989	28	48	82	58.5
Steve Kerr, Arizona	1988	38	114	199	57.3
Reginald Jones, Prairie View	†1987	28	64	112	57.1
Jim Cantamessa, Siena	†1998	29	66	117	56.4
Joel Tribelhorn, Colorado St.	1989	33	76	135	56.3
Mike Joseph, Bucknell	1988	28	65	116	56.0
Brian Jackson, Evansville	†1995	27	53	95	55.8
Amory Sanders, Southeast Mo. St.	†2001	24	53	95	55.8
Christian Laettner, Duke	1992	35	54	97	55.7
Reginald Jones, Prairie View	1988	27	85	155	54.8
Eric Rhodes, Stephen F. Austin	1987	30	58	106	54.7
Dave Orlandini, Princeton	1988	26	60	110	54.5
David Falknor, Akron	2001	22	47	87	54.0
Mike Joseph, Bucknell	1989	31	62	115	53.9
John Bays, Towson	1989	29	71	132	53.8
Jeff Anderson, Kent St.	†1993	26	44	82	53.7
Jay Edwards, Indiana	1988	23	59	110	53.6
Anthony Davis, George Mason	1987	27	45	84	53.6
Mark Anglavar, Marquette	1989	28	53	99	53.5
Scot Dimak, Stephen F. Austin	1987	30	46	86	53.5
Matt Lapin, Princeton	†1990	27	71	133	53.4
Michael Charles, UAB	1988	28	63	118	53.4

†national leader

FREE THROWS MADE

Player, Team	Season	G	FT	FTA	Pct.
Frank Selvy, Furman	+1954	29	355	444	80.0
Pete Maravich, LSU	+1970	31	337	436	77.3
Johnny O'Brien, Seattle	+1953	32	348	430	80.9
Walter Dukes, Seton Hall	1953	33	317	425	74.6
Oscar Robertson, Cincinnati	+1959	30	316	398	79.4
Tyler Hansbrough, North Carolina	+2008	39	304	377	80.6
Dickie Hemric, Wake Forest	+1955	27	302	403	74.9
Rick Barry, Miami (Fla.)	+1965	26	293	341	85.9
Terry Dischinger, Purdue	+1962	24	292	350	83.4
Lennie Rosenbluth, North Carolina	+1957	32	285	376	75.8
Hersey Hawkins, Bradley	+1988	31	284	335	84.8
Pete Maravich, LSU	+1969	26	282	378	74.6
Oscar Robertson, Cincinnati	+1958	28	280	355	78.9
Len Chappell, Wake Forest	1962	31	278	383	72.6
Kevin Bradshaw, U.S. Int'l	+1991	28	278	338	82.2
Caleb Green, Oral Roberts	+2007	34	278	366	76.0
Pete Maravich, LSU	+1968	26	274	338	81.1
Oscar Robertson, Cincinnati	+1960	30	273	361	75.6
Bill Bradley, Princeton	1965	29	273	308	88.6
Alonzo Mourning, Georgetown	+1992	32	272	359	75.8
Darrel Floyd, Furman	+1956	28	268	350	76.6
Joe Dumars, McNeese St.	+1984	31	267	324	82.4
Dick Groat, Duke	+1951	33	261	331	78.9
Troy Murphy, Notre Dame	+2000	37	261	323	80.8
Howard Komives, Bowling Green	+1964	23	260	303	85.8
Bill Bradley, Princeton	1964	29	260	306	85.0

FREE THROWS ATTEMPTED

Player, Team	Season	G	FT	FTA	Pct.
Frank Selvy, Furman	+1954	29	355	444	80.0
Pete Maravich, LSU	+1970	31	337	436	77.3
Johnny O'Brien, Seattle	+1953	32	348	430	80.9
Walter Dukes, Seton Hall	1953	33	317	425	74.6
Dickie Hemric, Wake Forest	+1955	27	302	403	74.9
Wilt Chamberlain, Kansas	+1957	27	250	399	62.7
Oscar Robertson, Cincinnati	+1959	30	316	398	79.4
Len Chappell, Wake Forest	+1962	31	278	383	72.6
Pete Maravich, LSU	+1969	26	282	378	74.6
Tyler Hansbrough, North Carolina	+2008	39	304	377	80.6
Lennie Rosenbluth, North Carolina	1957	32	285	376	75.8
Caleb Green, Oral Roberts	+2007	34	278	366	76.0
Oscar Robertson, Cincinnati	+1960	30	273	361	75.6
Alonzo Mourning, Georgetown	+1992	32	272	359	75.8
Oscar Robertson, Cincinnati	+1958	28	280	355	78.9
Darrel Floyd, Furman	+1956	28	268	350	76.6
Terry Dischinger, Purdue	1962	24	292	350	83.4
Howard Crittenden, Murray St.	1954	31	222	348	63.8
Nick Werkman, Seton Hall	1962	24	251	347	72.3
Rick Barry, Miami (Fla.)	+1965	26	293	341	85.9
Pete Maravich, LSU	+1968	26	274	338	81.1
Kevin Bradshaw, U.S. Int'l	+1991	28	278	338	82.2
Jerry West, West Virginia	1960	31	258	337	76.6
Dickie Hemric, Wake Forest	1953	25	199	336	59.2
McEverett Powers, UTSA	+2002	29	218	336	64.9
Mike Sweetney, Georgetown	+2003	34	248	336	73.8

FREE-THROW PERCENTAGE
(Based on qualifiers for annual championship)

Player, Team	Season	G	FT	FTA	Pct.
Blake Ahearn, Missouri St.	†2004	33	117	120	97.5
Derek Raivio, Gonzaga	†2007	34	148	154	96.1
Craig Collins, Penn St.	†1985	27	94	98	95.9
J.J. Redick, Duke	2004	37	143	150	95.3
Steve Drabyn, Belmont	†2003	29	78	82	95.1
Rod Foster, UCLA	†1982	27	95	100	95.0
Clay McKnight, Pacific	†2000	24	74	78	94.9
Matt Logie, Lehigh	2003	28	91	96	94.8
A.J. Green, Butler	2007	35	145	153	94.8
Blake Ahearn, Missouri St.	†2005	32	90	95	94.7
Carlos Gibson, Marshall	†1978	28	84	89	94.4
Danny Basile, Marist	†1994	27	84	89	94.4
Jim Barton, Dartmouth	†1986	26	65	69	94.2
Gary Buchanon, Villanova	†2001	31	97	103	94.2
Jack Moore, Nebraska	1982	27	123	131	93.9
J.J. Redick, Duke	2005	33	196	209	93.8
Tyler Relph, St. Bonaventure	†2008	29	75	80	93.8
Blake Ahearn, Missouri St.	†2006	31	117	125	93.6
Rob Robbins, New Mexico	†1990	34	101	108	93.5
Dandrea Evans, Troy	1994	27	72	77	93.5
Tommy Boyer, Arkansas	†1962	23	125	134	93.3
Jake Sullivan, Iowa St.	2003	33	83	89	93.3

Player, Team	Season	G	FT	FTA	Pct.
Damon Goodwin, Dayton	1986	30	95	102	93.1
Brent Jolly, Tennessee Tech	2001	29	95	102	93.1
Ryan Mendez, Stanford	2001	34	94	101	93.1

†national leader

REBOUNDS

Player, Team	Ht.	Season	G	Reb.
Walt Dukes, Seton Hall	6-10	†1953	33	734
Leroy Wright, Pacific	6-8	†1959	26	652
Tom Gola, La Salle	6-6	†1954	30	652
Charlie Tyra, Louisville	6-8	†1956	29	645
Paul Silas, Creighton	6-7	†1964	29	631
Elvin Hayes, Houston	6-8	†1968	33	624
Artis Gilmore, Jacksonville	7-2	†1970	28	621
Tom Gola, La Salle	6-6	†1955	31	618
Ed Conlin, Fordham	6-5	1953	26	612
Art Quimby, Connecticut	6-5	1955	25	611
Bill Russell, San Francisco	6-9	1956	29	609
Jim Ware, Oklahoma City	6-8	†1966	29	607
Joe Holup, George Washington	6-6	1956	26	604
Artis Gilmore, Jacksonville	7-2	†1971	26	603
Elton Tuttle, Creighton	6-5	1954	30	601
Marvin Barnes, Providence	6-9	†1974	32	597
Bill Russell, San Francisco	6-9	1955	29	594
Art Quimby, Connecticut	6-5	1954	26	588
Ed Conlin, Fordham	6-5	1955	27	578
Marvin Barnes, Providence	6-9	†1973	30	571
Bill Spivey, Kentucky	7-0	†1951	33	567
Bob Pelkington, Xavier	6-7	1964	26	567
Paul Silas, Creighton	6-7	†1962	25	563
Elgin Baylor, Seattle	6-6	†1959	29	559
Paul Silas, Creighton	6-7	†1963	27	557

†national leader

(Since 1973)

Player, Team	Ht.	Season	G	Reb.
Marvin Barnes, Providence	6-9	†1974	32	597
Marvin Barnes, Providence	6-9	†1973	30	571
Kermit Washington, American	6-8	1973	25	511
Bill Walton, UCLA	6-11	1973	30	506
Larry Bird, Indiana St.	6-9	†1979	34	505
Larry Kenon, Memphis	6-9	1973	30	501
Akeem Olajuwon, Houston	7-0	†1984	37	500
Glenn Mosley, Seton Hall	6-8	†1977	29	473
Popeye Jones, Murray St.	6-8	†1991	33	469
Pete Padgett, Nevada	6-8	†1973	26	462
Xavier McDaniel, Wichita St.	6-8	†1985	31	460
Larry Johnson, UNLV	6-7	†1990	40	457
Tim Duncan, Wake Forest	6-11	†1997	31	457
Anthony Bonner, St. Louis	6-8	1990	33	456
Bill Cartwright, San Francisco	7-1	1979	29	455
David Robinson, Navy	6-11	†1986	35	455
Benoit Benjamin, Creighton	7-0	1985	32	451
Jerome Lane, Pittsburgh	6-6	†1987	33	444
Robert Elmore, Wichita St.	6-10	1977	28	441
John Irving, Hofstra	6-9	1977	27	440
Paul Millsap, Louisiana Tech	6-8	†2006	33	438
Lionel Garrett, Southern U.	6-9	1979	28	433
Popeye Jones, Murray St.	6-8	†1992	30	431
Andrew Bogut, Utah	7-0	†2005	35	427
Jim Bradley, Northern Ill.	6-10	1973	24	426
Hank Gathers, Loyola Marymount	6-7	†1989	31	426

†national leader

REBOUND AVERAGE

Player, Team	Ht.	Season	G	Reb.	Avg.
Charlie Slack, Marshall	6-5	†1955	21	538	25.6
Leroy Wright, Pacific	6-8	†1959	26	652	25.1
Art Quimby, Connecticut	6-5	1955	25	611	24.4
Charlie Slack, Marshall	6-5	1956	22	520	23.6
Ed Conlin, Fordham	6-5	†1953	26	612	23.5
Joe Holup, George Washington	6-6	††1956	26	604	23.2
Artis Gilmore, Jacksonville	7-2	†1971	26	603	23.2
Art Quimby, Connecticut	6-5	1954	26	588	22.6
Paul Silas, Creighton	6-7	1962	25	563	22.5
Leroy Wright, Pacific	6-8	†1960	17	380	22.4
Walt Dukes, Seton Hall	6-10	1953	33	734	22.2
Charlie Tyra, Louisville	6-8	1956	29	645	22.2
Charlie Slack, Marshall	6-5	1954	21	466	22.2
Artis Gilmore, Jacksonville	7-2	†1970	28	621	22.2
Bill Chambers, William & Mary	6-4	1953	22	480	21.8
Bob Pelkington, Xavier	6-7	†1964	26	567	21.8
Dick Cunningham, Murray St.	6-10	†1967	22	479	21.8

Player, Team	Ht.	Season	G	Reb.	Avg.
Paul Silas, Creighton	6-7	1964	29	631	21.8
Tom Gola, La Salle	6-6	1954	30	652	21.7
Jerry Harper, Alabama	6-8	1956	24	517	21.5
Spencer Haywood, Detroit	6-8	†1969	22	472	21.5
Ed Conlin, Fordham	6-5	1955	27	578	21.4
Tom Heinsohn, Holy Cross	6-7	1956	26	549	21.1
Bill Russell, San Francisco	6-9	1956	29	609	21.0
Toby Kimball, Connecticut	6-8	†1965	23	483	21.0

†national leader; ††From 1956 through 1962, individual champions were determined by percentage of all recoveries; Holup led in percentage of recoveries and Slack led in average in 1956.

(Since 1973)

Player, Team	Ht.	Season	G	Reb.	Avg.
Kermit Washington, American	6-8	†1973	25	511	20.4
Marvin Barnes, Providence	6-9	1973	30	571	19.0
Marvin Barnes, Providence	6-9	1974	32	597	18.7
Pete Padgett, Nevada	6-8	1973	26	462	17.8
Jim Bradley, Northern Ill.	6-10	1973	24	426	17.8
Bill Walton, UCLA	6-11	1973	30	506	16.9
Larry Kenon, Memphis	6-9	1973	30	501	16.7
Glenn Mosley, Seton Hall	6-8	†1977	29	473	16.3
John Irving, Hofstra	6-9	1977	27	440	16.3
Carlos McCullough, Tex.-Pan American	6-7	1974	22	358	16.3
Brad Robinson, Kent St.	6-7	1974	26	423	16.3
Monti Davis, Tennessee St.	6-7	†1979	26	421	16.2
Sam Pellom, Buffalo	6-8	†1976	26	420	16.2
Robert Elmore, Wichita St.	6-10	1977	28	441	15.8
Bill Cartwright, San Francisco	7-1	1979	29	455	15.7
Bill Champion, Manhattan	6-10	1973	26	402	15.5
Bill Champion, Manhattan	6-10	1974	27	419	15.5
Lionel Garrett, Southern U.	6-9	1979	28	433	15.5
Dwayne Barnett, Samford	6-6	1976	23	354	15.4
John Irving, Hofstra	6-9	†1975	21	323	15.4
Cornelius Cash, Bowling Green	6-8	1973	26	396	15.2
Pete Padgett, Nevada	6-8	1974	26	395	15.2
Jimmie Baker, UNLV	6-9	1973	28	424	15.1
Larry Smith, Alcorn St.	6-8	†1980	26	392	15.1
Charles McKinney, Baylor	6-6	1974	25	375	15.0
Lewis Lloyd, Drake	6-6	1980	27	406	15.0

†national leader

ASSISTS

Player, Team	Season	G	Ast.
Mark Wade, UNLV	†1987	38	406
Avery Johnson, Southern U.	†1988	30	399
Anthony Manuel, Bradley	1988	31	373
Avery Johnson, Southern U.	1987	31	333
Mark Jackson, St. John's (N.Y.)	†1986	32	328
Sherman Douglas, Syracuse	†1989	38	326
Greg Anthony, UNLV	†1991	35	310
Sam Crawford, New Mexico St.	†1993	34	310
Reid Gettys, Houston	†1984	37	309
Carl Golston, Loyola (Ill.)	†1985	33	305
Craig Neal, Georgia Tech	1988	32	303
Keith Jennings, East Tenn. St.	1991	33	301
Doug Gottlieb, Oklahoma St.	†1999	34	299
Chris Corchiani, North Carolina St.	1991	31	299
Keith Jennings, East Tenn. St.	†1990	34	297
Howard Evans, Temple	1988	34	294
Ahlon Lewis, Arizona St.	†1998	32	294
Doug Gottlieb, Oklahoma St.	†2000	34	293
Jason Richards, Davidson	†2008	36	293
Danny Tarkanian, UNLV	1984	34	289
Sherman Douglas, Syracuse	1987	38	289
Bobby Hurley, Duke	1991	39	289
Greg Anthony, UNLV	1990	39	289
Sherman Douglas, Syracuse	1988	35	288
Bobby Hurley, Duke	1990	38	288

†national leader

ASSIST AVERAGE

Player, Team	Season	G	Ast.	Avg.
Avery Johnson, Southern U.	†1988	30	399	13.30
Anthony Manuel, Bradley	1988	31	373	12.03
Avery Johnson, Southern U.	†1987	31	333	10.74
Mark Wade, UNLV	1987	38	406	10.68
Nelson Haggerty, Baylor	†1995	28	284	10.14
Glenn Williams, Holy Cross	†1989	28	278	9.92
Chris Corchiani, North Carolina St.	†1991	31	299	9.65
Tony Fairley, Charleston So.	1987	28	270	9.64
Tyrone Bogues, Wake Forest	1987	29	276	9.52
Ron Weingard, Hofstra	†1985	24	228	9.50

Player, Team	Season	G	Ast.	Avg.
Craig Neal, Georgia Tech	1988	32	303	9.47
Craig Lathan, Ill.-Chicago	†1984	29	274	9.45
Curtis McCants, George Mason	1995	27	251	9.30
Andre Van Drost, Wagner	1987	28	260	9.29
Todd Lehmann, Drexel	†1990	28	260	9.29
Danny Tirado, Jacksonville	1991	28	259	9.25
Carl Golston, Loyola (Ill.)	1985	33	305	9.24
Ahlon Lewis, Arizona St.	†1998	32	294	9.19
Terrell Lowery, Loyola Marymount	1991	31	283	9.13
Keith Jennings, East Tenn. St.	1991	33	301	9.12
Sam Crawford, New Mexico St.	†1993	34	310	9.12
Mark Jackson, St. John's (N.Y.)	†1986	36	328	9.11
Aaron Mitchell, La.-Lafayette	1990	29	264	9.10
Jason Kidd, California	†1994	30	272	9.07
Mark Dickel, UNLV	†2000	31	280	9.03

†national leader

BLOCKED SHOTS

Player, Team	Season	G	Blk.
David Robinson, Navy	†1986	35	207
Shawn James, Northeastern	†2006	30	196
Mickell Gladness, Alabama A&M	†2007	30	188
Adonal Foyle, Colgate	†1997	28	180
Keith Closs, Central Conn. St.	†1996	28	178
Shawn Bradley, BYU	1991	34	177
Wojciech Myrda, La.-Monroe	†2002	32	172
Alonzo Mourning, Georgetown	†1989	34	169
Stephane Lasme, Massachusetts	2007	33	168
Adonal Foyle, Colgate	1996	29	165
Deng Gai, Fairfield	†2005	30	165
Justin Williams, Wyoming	2006	30	163
Ken Johnson, Ohio St.	†2000	30	161
Alonzo Mourning, Georgetown	†1992	32	160
Shaquille O'Neal, LSU	1992	30	157
Jarvis Varnado, Mississippi St.	†2008	34	157
Roy Rogers, Alabama	1996	32	156
Emeka Okafor, Connecticut	†2003	33	156
Dikembe Mutombo, Georgetown	1991	32	151
Adonal Foyle, Colgate	†1995	30	147
Tarvis Williams, Hampton	†2001	32	147
Emeka Okafor, Connecticut	†2004	36	147
Hasheem Thabeet, Connecticut	2008	33	147
Theo Ratliff, Wyoming	1995	28	144
David Robinson, Navy	†1987	32	144
Wojciech Myrda, La.-Monroe	2000	28	144

†national leader

BLOCKED-SHOT AVERAGE

Player, Team	Season	G	Blk.	Avg.
Shawn James, Northeastern	†2006	30	196	6.53
Adonal Foyle, Colgate	†1997	28	180	6.43
Keith Closs, Central Conn. St.	†1996	28	178	6.36
Mickell Gladness, Alabama A&M	†2007	30	188	6.27
David Robinson, Navy	†1986	35	207	5.91
Adonal Foyle, Colgate	1996	29	165	5.69
Deng Gai, Fairfield	†2005	30	165	5.50
Shawn James, Northeastern	2005	25	136	5.44
Justin Williams, Wyoming	2006	30	163	5.43
Wojciech Myrda, La.-Monroe	†2002	32	172	5.38
Ken Johnson, Ohio St.	†2000	30	161	5.37
Keith Closs, Central Conn. St.	†1995	26	139	5.35
Shaquille O'Neal, LSU	†1992	30	157	5.23
Shawn Bradley, BYU	†1991	34	177	5.21
Theo Ratliff, Wyoming	1995	28	144	5.14
Wojciech Myrda, La.-Monroe	2000	28	144	5.14
Cedric Lewis, Maryland	1991	28	143	5.11
Stephane Lasme, Massachusetts	2007	33	168	5.09
Shaquille O'Neal, LSU	1991	28	140	5.00
Alonzo Mourning, Georgetown	1992	32	160	5.00
Tarvis Williams, Hampton	†1999	27	135	5.00
Alonzo Mourning, Georgetown	†1989	34	169	4.97
Kevin Roberson, Vermont	1992	28	139	4.96
Adonal Foyle, Colgate	1995	30	147	4.90
Roy Rogers, Alabama	1996	32	156	4.88

†national leader

STEALS

Player, Team	Season	G	Stl.
Desmond Cambridge, Alabama A&M	†2002	29	160
Mookie Blaylock, Oklahoma	†1988	39	150
Aldwin Ware, Florida A&M	1988	29	142
Darron Brittman, Chicago St.	†1986	28	139
John Linehan, Providence	2002	31	139
Nadav Henefeld, Connecticut	†1990	37	138
Mookie Blaylock, Oklahoma	†1989	35	131
Ronn McMahon, Eastern Wash.	1990	29	130
Obie Trotter, Alabama A&M	†2005	32	125
Marty Johnson, Towson	1988	30	124
Allen Iverson, Georgetown	†1996	37	124
Eric Coley, Tulsa	†2000	37	123
Jim Paguaga, St. Francis (N.Y.)	1986	28	120
Shawn Griggs, La.-Lafayette	†1994	30	120
Pointer Williams, McNeese St.	1996	27	118
Tony Fairley, Charleston So.	†1987	28	114
Scott Burrell, Connecticut	†1991	31	112
Kenny Robertson, Cleveland St.	1989	28	111
Lance Blanks, Texas	1989	34	111
Eric Murdock, Providence	1991	32	111
Travis Holmes, VMI	†2007	33	111
Jason Kidd, California	†1993	29	110
Johnny Rhodes, Maryland	1996	30	110
Robert Dowdell, Coastal Caro.	1990	29	109
Keith Jennings, East Tenn. St.	1991	33	109
Mark Woods, Wright St.	1993	30	109
Gerald Walker, San Francisco	1994	28	109

†national leader

STEAL AVERAGE

Player, Team	Season	G	Stl.	Avg.
Desmond Cambridge, Alabama A&M	†2002	29	160	5.52
Darron Brittman, Chicago St.	†1986	28	139	4.96
Aldwin Ware, Florida A&M	†1988	29	142	4.90
John Linehan, Providence	2002	31	139	4.48
Ronn McMahon, Eastern Wash.	1990	29	130	4.48
Pointer Williams, McNeese St.	†1996	27	118	4.37
Greedy Daniels, TCU	†2001	25	108	4.32
Jim Paguaga, St. Francis (N.Y.)	1986	28	120	4.29
Marty Johnson, Towson	1988	30	124	4.13
Tony Fairley, Charleston So.	†1987	28	114	4.07
Shawn Griggs, La.-Lafayette	†1994	30	120	4.00
Kenny Robertson, Cleveland St.	†1989	28	111	3.96
Marques Green, St. Bonaventure	†2004	27	107	3.96
Alexis McMillan, Stetson	†2003	22	87	3.95
Obie Trotter, Alabama A&M	†2005	32	125	3.91
Gerald Walker, San Francisco	1994	28	109	3.89
Mookie Blaylock, Oklahoma	1988	39	150	3.85
Carl Williams, Liberty	†2000	28	107	3.82
Desmond Cambridge, Alabama A&M	2001	28	107	3.82
Jason Kidd, California	†1993	29	110	3.79
Jay Goodman, Utah St.	1993	27	102	3.78
Andre Cradle, Long Island	1994	21	79	3.76
Robert Dowdell, Coastal Caro.	1990	29	109	3.76
Mookie Blaylock, Oklahoma	1989	35	131	3.74
Johnny Rhodes, Maryland	1996	30	110	3.67

†national leader

QUADRUPLE-DOUBLES

Player, Team	Class	Season	QD-2Bs
Lester Hudson, Tenn.-Martin	Sr.	2008	1

TRIPLE-DOUBLES

Player, Team	Class	Season	3B-2Bs
Michael Anderson, Drexel	So.	1986	4
Brian Shaw, UC Santa Barbara	Sr.	1988	4
Jason Kidd, California	So.	1994	4
Stephane Lasme, Massachusetts	Sr.	2007	4
David Robinson, Navy	Jr.	1986	3
Shaquille O'Neal, LSU	Jr.	1992	3
Gerald Lewis, SMU	Sr.	1993	3
David Edwards, Texas A&M	Sr.	1994	3
Andre Iguodala, Arizona	So.	2004	3
Derrick Lewis, Maryland	Jr.	1987	2
Luc Longley, New Mexico	Jr.	1990	2
Shaquille O'Neal, LSU	Fr.	1990	2
Kevin Roberson, Vermont	So.	1990	2
Dave Barnett, Fresno St.	Sr.	1991	2
Kevin Roberson, Vermont	Sr.	1992	2
Anfernee Hardaway, Memphis	Jr.	1993	2
Sharone Wright, Clemson	So.	1993	2
Roy Rogers, Alabama	Sr.	1996	2
Keith Closs, Central Conn. St.	So.	1996	2
Adonal Foyle, Colgate	Jr.	1997	2
Jerome James, Florida A&M	Jr.	1997	2

Player, Team	Class	Season	3B-2Bs
Sean Kennedy, Marist	Sr.	2002	2
Wojciech Murda, La.-Monroe	Sr.	2002	2
David Harrison, Colorado	So.	2003	2
Damitrius Coleman, Mercer	Jr.	2005	2
Shawn James, Northeastern	Fr.	2005	2
Shawn James, Northeastern	So.	2006	2
Dominic McGuire, Fresno St.	Jr.	2007	2
Jared Jordan, Marist	Sr.	2007	2
Tony Lee, Robert Morris	Sr.	2008	2
Terrence Williams, Louisville	Jr.	2008	2

CONSECUTIVE TRIPLE-DOUBLES

Player, Team	Class	Dates	3B-2Bs
Kevin Roberson, Vermont	Sr.	Jan. 7-9, 1992	2
Shaquille O'Neal, LSU	Jr.	Feb. 19-22, 1992	2
Anfernee Hardaway, Memphis	Jr.	Jan. 4-6, 1993	2
Gerald Lewis, SMU	Sr.	Mar. 3-6, 1993	2
David Edwards, Texas A&M	Sr.	Mar. 5-10, 1994	2
Tony Lee, Robert Morris	Sr.	Feb. 9-14, 2008	2

DOUBLE-DOUBLES

Player, Team	Class	Season	2B-2Bs
David Robinson, Navy	Jr.	1986	31
Jerry West, West Virginia	Sr.	1960	30
Xavier McDaniel, Wichita St.	Sr.	1985	30
Mel Counts, Oregon St.	Sr.	1964	29
Rudy Hackett, Syracuse	Sr.	1975	29
Benoit Benjamin, Creighton	Jr.	1985	29
Derrick Coleman, Syracuse	Jr.	1989	29
Tim Duncan, Wake Forest	Sr.	1997	29
Oscar Robertson, Cincinnati	Jr.	1959	28
Lew Alcindor, UCLA	So.	1967	28
Larry Bird, Indiana St.	Sr.	1979	28
Michael Beasley, Kansas St.	Fr.	2008	28
Oscar Robertson, Cincinnati	Jr.	1960	27
Mel Counts, Oregon St.	Jr.	1963	27
Paul Silas, Creighton	Sr.	1964	27
Lew Alcindor, UCLA	Jr.	1968	27
Artis Gilmore, Jacksonville	Jr.	1970	27
Bill Walton, UCLA	Jr.	1973	27
Willie Naulls, UCLA	Sr.	1956	26
Jerry Lucas, Ohio St.	So.	1960	26
Jerry Lucas, Ohio St.	Jr.	1961	26
Jerry Lucas, Ohio St.	Sr.	1962	26
Len Chappell, Wake Forest	Sr.	1962	26
Dan Issel, Kentucky	Sr.	1970	26
Xavier McDaniel, Wichita St.	So.	1983	26
Jerome Lane, Pittsburgh	Jr.	1987	26
Brad Sellers, Ohio St.	Sr.	1986	26
Hank Gathers, Loyola Marymount	Jr.	1989	26
Andrew Bogut, Utah	So.	2005	26

DOUBLE-DOUBLES FOR A FRESHMAN

Player, Team	Season	2B-2Bs
Michael Beasley, Kansas St.	2008	28
Kevin Love, UCLA	2008	23
Carmelo Anthony, Syracuse	2003	22
Ralph Sampson, Virginia	1980	21
Kenny Miller, Loyola (Ill.)	1988	21
Eddie Griffin, Seton Hall	2001	21
Gary Winton, Army	1975	20
Kevin Durant, Texas	2007	20
Wayman Tisdale, Oklahoma	1983	19
Rickey Brown, Mississippi St.	1977	18
Steve Stielper, James Madison	1977	18
Herb Williams, Ohio St.	1978	18
Alvan Adams, Oklahoma	1973	17
Malik Rose, Drexel	1993	15
Caleb Green, Oral Roberts	2004	15
Gene Banks, Duke	1978	14
Andrew Bogut, Utah	2004	14
Leon Powe, California	2004	14
Tyrus Thomas, LSU	2006	14
Greg Oden, Ohio St.	2007	14
DeJuan Blair, Pittsburgh	2008	14
Ron Baxter, Texas	1977	13
Vernon Butler, Navy	1983	13
Derrick Coleman, Syracuse	1987	13
Tim Duncan, Wake Forest	1994	13

CONSECUTIVE DOUBLE-DOUBLES

Player, Team	Class	Dates	2B-2Bs
Mel Counts, Oregon St.	Sr.	Nov. 30, 1963-Mar. 10, 1964	29
Benoit Benjamin, Creighton	Jr.	Nov. 24, 1984-Feb. 16, 1985	27
Lew Alcindor, UCLA	Jr.	Dec. 27, 1967-Mar. 23, 1968	26
Willie Naulls, UCLA	Sr.	Dec. 2, 1955-Mar. 9, 1956	25
Oscar Robertson, Cincinnati	Jr.	Dec. 31, 1958-Mar. 21, 1959	23
#Jerry Lucas, Ohio St.	Jr.	Dec. 1, 1960-Mar. 11, 1961	23
Xavier McDaniel, Wichita St.	Sr.	Dec. 21, 1984-Mar. 15, 1985	23
Jerry Lucas, Ohio St.	Sr.	Dec. 2, 1961-Feb. 24, 1962	21
Mike Lewis, Duke	Sr.	Dec. 1, 1967-Feb. 20, 1968	20
Jerry West, West Virginia	Sr.	Jan. 5-Mar. 12, 1960	20
Billy Cunningham, North Carolina	So.	Dec. 5, 1962-Mar. 1, 1963	20
Billy Cunningham, North Carolina	Jr.	Dec. 2, 1963-Feb. 22, 1964	20
Dave Gunther, Iowa	Sr.	Dec. 8, 1958-Feb. 21, 1959	19
Artis Gilmore, Jacksonville	Sr.	Dec. 1, 1970-Feb. 8 1971	18
Steve Smith, Loyola Marymount	Jr.	Jan. 4-Mar. 4, 1972	18
Jack Twyman, Cincinnati	Jr.	Dec. 17, 1953-Mar. 4, 1954	17
Artis Gilmore, Jacksonville	Jr.	Dec. 9, 1969-Feb. 13, 1970	17
Tim Duncan, Wake Forest	Sr.	Nov. 24, 1996-Jan. 28, 1997	17
Len Chappell, Wake Forest	Sr.	Feb. 3-Mar. 24, 1962	16
Larry Bird, Indiana St.	Sr.	Dec. 9, 1978-Feb. 6, 1979	16
Jerry Lucas, Ohio St.	So.	Jan. 23-Mar. 19, 1960	15
Bill Walton, UCLA	So.	Dec. 10, 1971-Jan. 28, 1972	15
Rickey Brown, Mississippi St.	Sr.	Nov. 30, 1979-Jan. 17, 1980	15
David Robinson, Navy	Jr.	Feb. 12-Nov. 29, 1986	15
Andre Moore, Loyola (Ill.)	Sr.	Jan. 12-Feb. 23, 1987	15
Spencer Dunkley, Delaware	Sr.	Dec. 10, 1992-Feb. 6, 1993	15

#Missed the Jan. 9, 1961, game because of injury.

Top Season Performances by Class

SCORING AVERAGE

Class	Player, Team	Season	G	FG	3FG	FT	Pts.	Avg.
Senior	Pete Maravich, LSU	1970	31	522	—	337	1,381	44.5
Junior	Pete Maravich, LSU	1969	26	433	—	282	1,148	44.2
Sophomore	Pete Maravich, LSU	1968	26	432	—	274	1,138	43.8
Freshman	Chris Jackson, LSU	1989	32	359	84	163	965	30.2

FIELD-GOAL PERCENTAGE

Class	Player, Team	Season	G	FG	FGA	Pct.
Senior	Steve Johnson, Oregon St.	1981	28	235	315	74.6
Junior	Steve Johnson, Oregon St.	1980	30	211	297	71.0
Sophomore	Dwayne Davis, Florida	1989	33	179	248	72.2
Freshman	Mike Freeman, Hampton	2007	30	162	239	67.8

THREE-POINT FIELD GOALS MADE PER GAME

Class	Player, Team	Season	G	3FG	Avg.
Senior	Darrin Fitzgerald, Butler	1987	28	158	5.64
Junior	Terrence Woods, Florida A&M	2003	28	139	4.96
Sophomore	Stephen Curry, Davidson	2008	36	162	4.50
Freshman	Keith Veney, Lamar	1993	27	106	3.93

THREE-POINT FIELD-GOAL PERCENTAGE

Class	Player, Team	Season	G	3FG	3FGA	Pct.
Senior	Keith Jennings, East Tenn. St.	1991	33	84	142	59.2
Junior	Glenn Tropf, Holy Cross	1988	29	52	82	63.4
Sophomore	Dave Calloway, Monmouth	1989	28	48	82	58.5
Freshman	Jay Edwards, Indiana	1988	23	59	110	53.6

FREE-THROW PERCENTAGE

Class	Player, Team	Season	G	FT	FTA	Pct.
Senior	Derek Raivio, Gonzaga	2007	34	148	154	96.1
Junior	Steve Drabyn, Belmont	2003	29	78	82	95.1
Sophomore	J.J. Redick, Duke	2004	37	143	150	95.3
Freshman	Blake Ahearn, Missouri St.	2004	33	117	120	97.5

REBOUND AVERAGE

Class	Player, Team	Season	G	Reb.	Avg.
Senior	Art Quimby, Connecticut	1955	25	611	24.4
Junior	Charlie Slack, Marshall	1955	21	538	25.6
Sophomore	Ed Conlin, Fordham	1953	26	612	23.5
Freshman	Pete Padgett, Nevada	1973	26	462	17.8

REBOUND AVERAGE
(Since 1973)

Class	Player, Team	Season	G	Reb.	Avg.
Senior	Kermit Washington, American	1973	22	439	20.0
Junior	Marvin Barnes, Providence	1973	30	571	19.0
Sophomore	Brad Robinson, Kent St.	1974	26	423	16.3
Freshman	Pete Padgett, Nevada	1973	26	462	17.8

ASSIST AVERAGE

Class	Player, Team	Season	G	Ast.	Avg.
Senior	Avery Johnson, Southern U.	1988	30	399	13.30
Junior	Anthony Manuel, Bradley	1988	31	373	12.03
Sophomore	Curtis McCants, George Mason	1995	27	251	9.30
Freshman	Omar Cook, St. John's (N.Y.)	2001	29	252	8.69

ASSIST-TO-TURNOVER RATIO

Class	Player, Team	Season	G	Ast.	TO	Ratio
Senior	Cliff Clinkscales, DePaul	2008	30	123	34	3.62
Junior	Jay Greene, UMBC	2008	33	236	68	3.47
Sophomore	Jermaine Beal, Vanderbilt	2008	34	158	51	3.10
Freshman	Julyan Stone, UTEP	2008	33	114	50	2.28

BLOCKED-SHOT AVERAGE

Class	Player, Team	Season	G	Blk.	Avg.
Senior	Deng Gai, Fairfield	2005	30	165	5.50
Junior	Adonal Foyle, Colgate	1997	28	180	6.43
Sophomore	Shawn James, Northeastern	2006	30	196	6.53
Freshman	Shawn James, Northeastern	2005	26	136	5.44

STEAL AVERAGE

Class	Player, Team	Season	G	Stl.	Avg.
Senior	Desmond Cambridge, Alabama A&M	2002	29	160	5.52
Junior	Kenny Robertson, Cleveland St.	1989	28	111	3.96
Sophomore	Gerald Walker, San Francisco	1994	28	109	3.89
Freshman	Jason Kidd, California	1993	29	110	3.79

Top Season Performances by a Freshman

POINTS

Player, Team	Season	G	FG	3FG	FT	Pts.
Chris Jackson, LSU	1989	32	359	84	163	965
Kevin Durant, Texas	2007	35	306	82	209	903
Michael Beasley, Kansas St.	2008	33	307	36	216	866
James Williams, Austin Peay	1973	29	360	—	134	854
Jason Conley, VMI	2002	28	285	79	171	820

SCORING AVERAGE

Player, Team	Season	G	FG	3FG	FT	Pts.	Avg.
Chris Jackson, LSU	1989	32	359	84	163	965	30.2
Alphonso Ford, Mississippi Val.	1990	27	289	104	126	808	29.9
James Williams, Austin Peay	1973	29	360	—	134	854	29.4
Jason Conley, VMI	2002	28	285	79	171	820	29.3
Harry Kelly, Texas Southern	1980	26	313	—	127	753	29.0

FIELD-GOAL PERCENTAGE

Player, Team	Season	G	FG	FGA	Pct.
Mike Freeman, Hampton	2007	30	162	239	67.8
Sidney Moncrief, Arkansas	1976	28	149	224	66.5
Gary Trent, Ohio	1993	27	194	298	65.1
Brandan Wright, North Carolina	2007	37	228	353	64.6
Ed Pinckney, Villanova	1982	32	169	264	64.0

THREE-POINT FIELD GOALS MADE

Player, Team	Season	G	3FG
Stephen Curry, Davidson	2007	34	122
Tajuan Porter, Oregon	2007	35	110
Keydren Clark, St. Peter's	2003	29	109
Keith Veney, Lamar	1993	27	106
Alphonso Ford, Mississippi Val.	1990	27	104
Tony Ross, San Diego St.	1987	28	104
Adam Leonard, Eastern Ky.	2007	33	104

THREE-POINT FIELD GOALS MADE PER GAME

Player, Team	Season	G	3FG	Avg.
Keith Veney, Lamar	1993	27	106	3.93
Alphonso Ford, Mississippi Val.	1990	27	104	3.85
Keydren Clark, St. Peter's	2003	29	109	3.76
Tony Ross, San Diego St.	1987	28	104	3.71
Donnie Carr, La Salle	1997	27	99	3.67

THREE-POINT FIELD-GOAL PERCENTAGE

Player, Team	Season	G	3FG	3FGA	Pct.
Jay Edwards, Indiana	1988	23	59	110	53.6
Ross Richardson, Loyola Marymount	1991	25	61	116	52.6
Lance Barker, Valparaiso	1992	26	61	117	52.1
Ed Peterson, Yale	1989	28	53	104	51.0
Ross Land, Northern Ariz.	1997	28	64	126	50.8
Willie Brand, Texas-Arlington	1988	29	65	128	50.8

FREE-THROW PERCENTAGE

Player, Team	Season	G	FT	FTA	Pct.
Blake Ahearn, Missouri St.	2004	33	117	120	97.5
Jim Barton, Dartmouth	1986	26	65	69	94.2
J.J. Redick, Duke	2003	33	102	111	91.9
David Kool, Western Mich.	2007	29	99	108	91.7
Steve Alford, Indiana	1984	31	137	150	91.3

REBOUNDS

Player, Team	Season	G	Reb.
Pete Padgett, Nevada	1973	26	462
Kevin Love, UCLA	2008	39	415
Michael Beasley, Kansas St.	2008	33	408
Kenny Miller, Loyola (Ill.)	1988	29	395
Kevin Durant, Texas	2007	35	390

REBOUND AVERAGE

Player, Team	Season	G	Reb.	Avg.
Pete Padgett, Nevada	1973	26	462	17.8
Glenn Mosley, Seton Hall	1974	21	299	14.2
Ira Terrell, SMU	1973	25	352	14.1
Kenny Miller, Loyola (Ill.)	1988	29	395	13.6
Bob Stephens, Drexel	1976	23	307	13.3

ASSISTS

Player, Team	Season	G	Ast.
Bobby Hurley, Duke	1990	38	288
Kenny Anderson, Georgia Tech	1990	35	285
T.J. Ford, Texas	2002	33	273
Andre LaFleur, Northeastern	1984	32	252
Omar Cook, St. John's (N.Y.)	2001	29	252
Chris Thomas, Notre Dame	2002	33	252

ASSIST AVERAGE

Player, Team	Season	G	Ast.	Avg.
Omar Cook, St. John's (N.Y.)	2001	29	252	8.69
T.J. Ford, Texas	2002	33	273	8.27
Orlando Smart, San Francisco	1991	29	237	8.17
Kenny Anderson, Georgia Tech	1990	35	285	8.14
Taurence Chisholm, Delaware	1985	28	224	8.00

ASSIST-TO-TURNOVER RATIO

Player, Team	Season	G	Ast.	TO	Ratio
Julyan Stone, UTEP	2008	33	114	50	2.28
Nick Calathes, Florida	2008	36	221	104	2.13
Sam Maniscalco, Bradley	2008	38	114	54	2.11

BLOCKED SHOTS

Player, Team	Season	G	Blk.
Shawn Bradley, BYU	1991	34	177
Alonzo Mourning, Georgetown	1989	34	169
Adonal Foyle, Colgate	1995	30	147
Alvin Jones, Georgia Tech	1998	33	141
Keith Closs, Central Conn. St.	1995	26	139

BLOCKED-SHOT AVERAGE

Player, Team	Season	G	Blk.	Avg.
Shawn James, Northeastern	2005	25	136	5.44
Keith Closs, Central Conn. St.	1995	26	139	5.35
Shawn Bradley, BYU	1991	34	177	5.21
Alonzo Mourning, Georgetown	1989	34	169	4.97
Adonal Foyle, Colgate	1995	30	147	4.90

STEALS

Player, Team	Season	G	Stl.
Nadav Henefeld, Connecticut	1990	37	138
Jason Kidd, California	1993	29	110
Kellii Taylor, Pittsburgh	1997	32	101
Ben Larson, Cal Poly	1996	29	100
Devin Gibson, UTSA	2008	28	93

STEAL AVERAGE

Player, Team	Season	G	Stl.	Avg.
Jason Kidd, California	1993	29	110	3.79
Nadav Henefeld, Connecticut	1990	37	138	3.73
Ben Larson, Cal Poly	1996	29	100	3.45
Devin Gibson, UTSA	2008	28	93	3.32
Eric Murdock, Providence	1988	28	90	3.21
Pat Baldwin, Northwestern	1991	28	90	3.21
Joel Hoover, Md.-East. Shore	1997	28	90	3.21

Career Records

POINTS

Player, Team	Ht.	Last Season	Yrs.	G	FG	3FG#	FT	Pts.
Pete Maravich, LSU	6-5	1970	3	83	1,387	—	893	3,667
Freeman Williams, Portland St.	6-4	1978	4	106	1,369	—	511	3,249
Lionel Simmons, La Salle	6-7	1990	4	131	1,244	56	673	3,217
Alphonso Ford, Mississippi Valley	6-2	1993	4	109	1,121	333	590	3,165
Harry Kelly, Texas Southern	6-7	1983	4	110	1,234	—	598	3,066
Keydren Clark, St. Peter's	5-9	2006	4	118	967	435	689	3,058
Hersey Hawkins, Bradley	6-3	1988	4	125	1,100	118	690	3,008
Oscar Robertson, Cincinnati	6-5	1960	3	88	1,052	—	869	2,973
Danny Manning, Kansas	6-10	1988	4	147	1,216	10	509	2,951
Alfredrick Hughes, Loyola (Ill.)	6-5	1985	4	120	1,226	—	462	2,914
Elvin Hayes, Houston	6-8	1968	3	93	1,215	—	454	2,884
Larry Bird, Indiana St.	6-9	1979	3	94	1,154	—	542	2,850
Otis Birdsong, Houston	6-4	1977	4	116	1,176	—	480	2,832
Kevin Bradshaw, Bethune-Cookman & U.S. Int'l	6-6	1991	4	111	1,027	132	618	2,804
Allan Houston, Tennessee	6-5	1993	4	128	902	346	651	2,801
J.J. Redick, Duke	6-4	2006	4	139	825	457	662	2,769
Hank Gathers, Southern Cal & Loyola Marymount	6-7	1990	4	117	1,127	0	469	2,723
Reggie Lewis, Northeastern	6-7	1987	4	122	1,043	30(1)	592	2,708
Daren Queenan, Lehigh	6-5	1988	4	118	1,024	29	626	2,703
Byron Larkin, Xavier	6-3	1988	4	121	1,022	51	601	2,696
Bo McCalebb, New Orleans	6-0	2008	5	128	977	115	610	2,679
David Robinson, Navy	7-1	1987	4	127	1,032	1	604	2,669
Wayman Tisdale, Oklahoma	6-9	1985	3	104	1,077	—	507	2,661
Troy Bell, Boston College	6-1	2003	4	122	761	300	810	2,632
Michael Brooks, La Salle	6-7	1980	4	114	1,064	—	500	2,628
Calbert Cheaney, Indiana	6-6	1993	4	132	1,018	148	429	2,613
Mark Macon, Temple	6-5	1991	4	126	980	246	403	2,609
Don MacLean, UCLA	6-10	1992	4	127	943	11	711	2,608
Joe Dumars, McNeese St.	6-3	1985	4	116	941	(5)	723	2,605
Henry Domercant, Eastern Ill.	6-4	2003	4	120	861	285	595	2,602
Terrance Bailey, Wagner	6-2	1987	4	110	985	42	579	2,591
Dickie Hemric, Wake Forest	6-6	1955	4	104	841	—	905	2,587
Calvin Natt, La.-Monroe	6-5	1979	4	108	1,017	—	547	2,581
Derrick Chievous, Missouri	6-7	1988	4	130	893	30	764	2,580
Skip Henderson, Marshall	6-2	1988	4	125	1,000	133	441	2,574
Austin Carr, Notre Dame	6-3	1971	3	74	1,017	—	526	2,560
Reggie Williams, VMI	6-6	2008	4	112	933	196	494	2,556
Sean Elliott, Arizona	6-8	1989	4	133	896	140	623	2,555
Rodney Monroe, North Carolina St.	6-3	1991	4	124	885	322	459	2,551
Calvin Murphy, Niagara	5-10	1970	3	77	947	—	654	2,548
Keith Van Horn, Utah	6-9	1997	4	122	891	206	554	2,542
Frank Selvy, Furman	6-3	1954	3	78	922	—	694	2,538
Johnny Dawkins, Duke	6-2	1986	4	133	1,026	(19)	485	2,537
Willie Jackson, Centenary (La.)	6-6	1984	4	114	995	(18)	545	2,535
Steve Rogers, Alabama St.	6-5	1992	4	113	817	107	713	2,534
Steve Burtt, Iona	6-2	1984	4	121	1,003	—	528	2,534
Shawn Respert, Michigan St.	6-3	1995	4	118	866	331	468	2,531
Joe Jakubick, Akron	6-5	1984	4	108	973	(53)	584	2,530
Andrew Toney, La.-Lafayette	6-3	1980	4	107	996	—	534	2,526
Ron Perry, Holy Cross	6-2	1980	4	109	922	—	680	2,524

Player, Team	Ht.	Last Season	Yrs.	G	FG	3FG#	FT	Pts.
Ronnie McCollum, Centenary (La.)	6-4	2001	4	113	822	345	535	2,524
Jaycee Carroll, Utah St.	6-2	2008	4	134	880	369	393	2,522
Mike Olliver, Lamar	6-1	1981	4	122	1,130	—	258	2,518
Bryant Stith, Virginia	6-5	1992	4	131	856	114	690	2,516
Bill Bradley, Princeton	6-5	1965	3	83	856	—	791	2,503
Caleb Green, Oral Roberts	6-8	2007	4	128	821	9	852	2,503
Jeff Grayer, Iowa St.	6-5	1988	4	125	974	27	527	2,502
Elgin Baylor, Albertson & Seattle	6-6	1958	3	80	956	—	588	2,500

#Listed is the number of three-pointers scored since it became the national rule in 1987; the number in the parenthesis is number scored before 1987—these counted as three points in the game but counted as two-pointers in the national rankings. The three-pointers in the parenthesis are not included in total points.

2,000-POINT SCORERS

A total of 448 players in Division I history have scored at least 2,000 points over their careers. The first was Jim Lacy, Loyola (Md.), with 2,154 over four seasons ending with 1949. The first to reach 2,000 in a three-season career was Furman's Frank Selvy, 2,538 through 1954. The 448 come from 218 different colleges. Duke leads with nine 2,000-pointers: Jim Spanarkel (last season was 1979), Mike Gminski (1980), Gene Banks (1981), Mark Alarie (1986), Johnny Dawkins (1986), Danny Ferry (1989), Christian Laettner (1992), Jason Williams (2002) and J.J. Redick (2006). Next are Boston College, Georgia Tech, La Salle, North Carolina, Notre Dame, Syracuse, Tennessee and Villanova with six, followed by Indiana, Michigan, Murray State, Oklahoma, Virginia, Wake Forest and Xavier with five apiece.

SCORING AVERAGE
(Minimum 1,400 points)

Player, Team	Last Season	Yrs.	G	FG	3FG	FT	Pts.	Avg.
Pete Maravich, LSU	1970	3	83	1,387	—	893	3,667	44.2
Austin Carr, Notre Dame	1971	3	74	1,017	—	526	2,560	34.6
Oscar Robertson, Cincinnati	1960	3	88	1,052	—	869	2,973	33.8
Calvin Murphy, Niagara	1970	3	77	947	—	654	2,548	33.1
Dwight Lamar, La.-Lafayette	†1973	2	57	768	—	326	1,862	32.7
Frank Selvy, Furman	1954	3	78	922	—	694	2,538	32.5
Rick Mount, Purdue	1970	3	72	910	—	503	2,323	32.3
Darrell Floyd, Furman	1956	3	71	868	—	545	2,281	32.1
Nick Werkman, Seton Hall	1964	3	71	812	—	649	2,273	32.0
Willie Humes, Idaho St.	1971	2	48	565	—	380	1,510	31.5
William Averitt, Pepperdine	1973	2	49	615	—	311	1,541	31.4
Elgin Baylor, Albertson & Seattle	1958	3	80	956	—	588	2,500	31.3
Elvin Hayes, Houston	1968	3	93	1,215	—	454	2,884	31.0
Freeman Williams, Portland St.	1978	4	106	1,369	—	511	3,249	30.7
Larry Bird, Indiana St.	1979	3	94	1,154	—	542	2,850	30.3
Bill Bradley, Princeton	1965	3	83	856	—	791	2,503	30.2
Rich Fuqua, Oral Roberts	†1973	2	54	692	—	233	1,617	29.9
Wilt Chamberlain, Kansas	1958	2	48	503	—	427	1,433	29.9
Rick Barry, Miami (Fla.)	1965	3	77	816	—	666	2,298	29.8
Doug Collins, Illinois St.	1973	3	77	894	—	452	2,240	29.1
Alphonso Ford, Mississippi Val.	1993	4	109	1,121	333	590	3,165	29.0
Chris Jackson, LSU	1990	2	64	664	172	354	1,854	29.0
Dave Schellhase, Purdue	1966	3	74	746	—	582	2,074	28.8
Dick Wilkinson, Virginia	1955	3	78	783	—	665	2,233	28.6
James Williams, Austin Peay	1974	2	54	632	—	277	1,541	28.5

†Each played two years of non-Division I competition (Lamar—four years, 3,493 points and 31.2 average; Fuqua—four years, 3,004 points and 27.1 average).

FIELD-GOAL PERCENTAGE
(Minimum 400 field goals made and 4 field goals made per game)

Player, Team	Ht.	Last Season	Yrs.	G	FG	FGA	Pct.
Steve Johnson, Oregon St.	6-10	1981	4	116	828	1,222	67.8
Michael Bradley, Kentucky & Villanova	6-10	2001	3	100	441	651	67.7
Murray Brown, Florida St.	6-8	1980	4	106	566	847	66.8
Lee Campbell, Middle Tenn. & Missouri St.	6-7	1990	3	88	411	618	66.5
Warren Kidd, Middle Tenn.	6-9	1993	3	83	496	747	66.4
Todd MacCulloch, Washington	7-0	1999	4	115	702	1,058	66.4
Joe Senser, West Chester	6-5	1979	4	96	476	719	66.2
Kevin Magee, UC Irvine	6-8	1982	2	56	552	841	65.6
Orlando Phillips, Pepperdine	6-7	1983	2	58	404	618	65.4
Bill Walton, UCLA	6-11	1974	3	87	747	1,147	65.1
William Herndon, Massachusetts	6-3	1992	4	100	472	728	64.8
Larry Stewart, Coppin St.	6-8	1991	3	91	676	1,046	64.6
Adam Mark, Belmont	6-8	2004	4	112	656	1,018	64.4
Larry Johnson, UNLV	6-7	1991	2	75	612	952	64.3
Dwayne Davis, Florida	6-7	1991	4	124	572	892	64.1
Nate Harris, Utah St.	6-7	2006	5	126	588	918	64.1
Lew Alcindor, UCLA	7-2	1969	3	88	943	1,476	63.9
Akeem Olajuwon, Houston	7-0	1984	3	100	532	833	63.9
Oliver Miller, Arkansas	6-9	1992	4	137	680	1,069	63.6

Player, Team	Ht.	Last Season	Yrs.	G	FG	FGA	Pct.
Mike Coleman, Liberty	6-7	1992	4	105	421	663	63.5
Jeff Ruland, Iona	6-10	1980	3	89	717	1,130	63.5
Mark McNamara, California	6-10	1982	4	107	709	1,119	63.4
Vladimir Kulijanin, UNC Wilmington	6-10	2008	4	121	465	736	63.2
Dan McClintock, Northern Ariz.	7-0	2000	4	115	542	858	63.2
Cherokee Rhone, Centenary (La.)	6-8	1982	4	63	421	667	63.1
Carlos Boozer, Duke	6-9	2002	3	101	554	878	63.1
Bobby Lee Hunt, Alabama	6-9	1985	4	126	646	1,024	63.1

THREE-POINT FIELD GOALS

Player, Team	Ht.	Last Season	Yrs.	G	3FG
J.J. Redick, Duke	6-4	2006	4	139	457
Keydren Clark, St. Peter's	5-9	2006	4	118	435
Chris Lofton, Tennessee	6-2	2008	4	128	431
Curtis Staples, Virginia	6-3	1998	4	122	413
Jack Leasure, Coastal Caro.	6-3	2008	4	117	411
Keith Veney, Lamar & Marshall	6-3	1997	4	111	409
Doug Day, Radford	6-1	1993	4	117	401
Gerry McNamara, Syracuse	6-2	2006	4	135	400
Michael Watson, UMKC	6-0	2004	4	117	391
Ronnie Schmitz, UMKC	6-3	1993	4	112	378
Mark Alberts, Akron	6-1	1993	4	107	375
Brett Blizzard, UNC Wilmington	6-4	2003	4	125	371
Kyle Korver, Creighton	6-7	2003	4	128	371
Jaycee Carroll, Utah St.	6-2	2008	4	134	369
Shan Foster, Vanderbilt	6-6	2008	4	132	367
Pat Bradley, Arkansas	6-2	1999	4	132	366
Bryce Drew, Valparaiso	6-3	1998	4	121	364
Jeff Fryer, Loyola Marymount	6-2	1990	4	112	363
Will Whittington, Marist	6-3	2007	4	114	362
Taquan Dean, Louisville	6-3	2006	4	128	359
Antoine Agudio, Hofstra	6-3	2008	4	122	357
T.J. Sorrentine, Vermont	6-3	2005	4	120	354
Steve Novak, Marquette	6-10	2006	4	126	354
Terrence Woods, Florida A&M	6-3	2004	4	123	353
Dennis Scott, Georgia Tech	6-8	1990	3	99	351

THREE-POINT FIELD GOALS PER GAME
(Minimum 200 three-point field goals made)

Player, Team	Ht.	Last Season	Yrs.	G	3FG	Avg.
Timothy Pollard, Mississippi Val.	6-3	1989	2	56	256	4.57
Sydney Grider, La.-Lafayette	6-3	1990	2	58	253	4.36
Brian Merriweather, Tex.-Pan American	6-3	2001	3	84	332	3.95
Josh Heard, Tennessee Tech	6-2	2000	2	55	210	3.82
Kareem Townes, La Salle	6-3	1995	3	81	300	3.70
Keydren Clark, St. Peter's	5-9	2006	4	118	435	3.69
Keith Veney, Lamar & Marshall	6-3	1997	4	111	409	3.68
Dave Mooney, Coastal Caro.	6-4	1988	2	56	202	3.61
Dennis Scott, Georgia Tech	6-8	1990	3	99	351	3.55
Jack Leasure, Coastal Caro.	6-3	2008	4	117	411	3.51
Mark Alberts, Akron	6-1	1993	4	107	375	3.50
Doug Day, Radford	6-1	1993	4	117	401	3.43
Curtis Staples, Virginia	6-3	1998	4	122	413	3.39
Ronnie Schmitz, UMKC	6-3	1993	4	112	378	3.38
Chris Lofton, Tennessee	6-2	2008	4	128	431	3.37
Michael Watson, UMKC	6-0	2004	4	117	391	3.34
J.J. Redick, Duke	6-4	2006	4	139	457	3.29
Jeff Fryer, Loyola Marymount	6-2	1990	4	112	363	3.24
Keddric Mays, Chattanooga	6-0	2007	2	65	209	3.22
Dana Barros, Boston College	5-11	1989	3	91	291	3.20
Tony Ross, San Diego St.	6-3	1989	3	85	270	3.18
Will Whittington, Marist	6-3	2007	4	114	362	3.18
Randy Woods, La Salle	6-0	1992	3	88	278	3.16
Dominick Young, Fresno St.	5-10	1997	3	89	279	3.13
Wally Lancaster, Virginia Tech	6-5	1989	3	82	257	3.13
David Sivulich, St. Mary's (Cal.)	5-10	1998	3	76	238	3.13

THREE-POINT FIELD-GOAL PERCENTAGE
(Minimum 200 three-point field goals made and 2.0 three-point field goals made per game)

Player, Team	Ht.	Last Season	Yrs.	G	3FG	3FGA	Pct.
Tony Bennett, Green Bay	6-0	1992	4	118	290	584	49.7
Stephen Sir, San Diego St. & Northern Ariz.	6-5	2007	5	111	323	689	46.9
David Olson, Eastern Ill.	6-4	1992	4	111	262	562	46.6
Jaycee Carroll, Utah St.	6-2	2008	4	134	369	793	46.5
Ross Land, Northern Ariz.	6-5	2000	4	117	308	664	46.4

Player, Team	Ht.	Last Season	Yrs.	G	3FG	3FGA	Pct.
Dan Dickau, Washington & Gonzaga	6-0	2002	4	97	215	465	46.2
Steve Novak, Marquette	6-10	2006	4	126	354	768	46.1
Sean Jackson, Ohio & Princeton	5-11	1992	4	104	243	528	46.0
Barry Booker, Vanderbilt	6-3	1989	3	98	246	535	46.0
Kevin Booth, Mt. St. Mary's	6-0	1993	5	110	265	577	45.9
Dave Calloway, Monmouth	6-3	1991	4	115	260	567	45.9
Tony Ross, San Diego St.	6-3	1992	3	85	270	589	45.8
Salim Stoudamire, Arizona	6-1	2005	4	129	342	747	45.8
Jason Matthews, Pittsburgh	6-3	1991	4	123	259	567	45.7
Corey Reed, Radford	6-6	1998	4	104	232	510	45.5
Jim Barton, Dartmouth	6-4	1989	3	78	242	532	45.5
Shawn Respert, Michigan St.	6-3	1995	4	118	331	728	45.5
Kyle Korver, Creighton	6-7	2003	4	128	371	819	45.3
Carlton Becton, N.C. A&T	6-6	1989	3	84	209	462	45.2
Eric Channing, New Mexico St.	6-4	2002	4	124	283	627	45.1
Pete Campbell, IPFW & Butler	6-7	2008	3	94	248	550	45.1
Ray Allen, Connecticut	6-5	1996	3	101	233	520	44.8
Curtis Shelton, Southeast Mo. St.	5-9	1994	4	107	215	480	44.8
Jeff McCool, New Mexico St.	6-5	1989	3	92	201	450	44.7
Jason Kapono, UCLA	6-8	2003	4	127	317	710	44.6

FREE THROWS MADE

Player, Team	Ht.	Last Season	Yrs.	G	FT	FTA	Pct.
Dickie Hemric, Wake Forest	6-6	1955	4	104	905	1,359	66.6
Pete Maravich, LSU	6-5	1970	3	83	893	1,152	77.5
Oscar Robertson, Cincinnati	6-5	1960	3	88	869	1,114	78.0
Caleb Green, Oral Roberts	6-8	2007	4	128	852	1,134	75.1
Don Schlundt, Indiana	6-10	1955	4	94	826	1,076	76.8
Troy Bell, Boston College	6-1	2003	4	122	810	933	86.8
Bill Bradley, Princeton	6-5	1965	3	83	791	903	87.6
Alonzo Mourning, Georgetown	6-10	1992	4	120	771	1,023	75.4
Derrick Chievous, Missouri	6-7	1988	4	130	764	963	79.3
Eddie Benton, Vermont	5-11	2008	4	104	739	891	82.9
+Tyler Hansbrough, North Carolina	6-9	2008	3	108	733	945	77.6
Howard Crittenden, Murray St.	6-0	1956	4	104	731	1,041	70.2
Joe Dumars, McNeese St.	6-3	1985	4	116	723	917	78.8
Chris Monroe, George Washington	6-3	2003	4	118	719	955	75.3
Joe Holup, George Washington	6-6	1956	4	104	714	961	74.3
Terry Dischinger, Purdue	6-7	1962	3	70	713	871	81.9
Christian Laettner, Duke	6-11	1992	4	148	713	885	80.6
Steve Rogers, Middle Tenn. & Alabama St.	6-5	1992	4	113	713	955	74.7
Don MacLean, UCLA	6-10	1992	4	127	711	827	86.0
Michael Anderson, Drexel	5-11	1988	4	115	705	958	73.6
Danya Abrams, Boston College	6-7	1997	4	122	698	1,003	69.6
Byron Houston, Oklahoma St.	6-7	1992	4	127	698	957	72.9
Dom Flora, Washington & Lee	62	1958	4	109	696	954	73.0
Larry Chanay, Montana St.	6-4	1960	4	101	696	947	73.5
Frank Selvy, Furman	6-3	1954	3	78	694	906	76.6

+active player

FREE THROWS ATTEMPTED

Player, Team	Ht.	Last Season	Yrs.	G	FT	FTA	Pct.
Dickie Hemric, Wake Forest	6-6	1955	4	104	905	1,359	66.6
Pete Maravich, LSU	6-5	1970	3	83	893	1,152	77.5
Caleb Green, Oral Roberts	6-8	2007	4	128	852	1,134	75.1
Oscar Robertson, Cincinnati	6-5	1960	3	88	869	1,114	78.0
Don Schlundt, Indiana	6-10	1955	4	94	826	1,076	76.8
Howard Crittenden, Murray St.	6-0	1956	4	104	731	1,041	70.2
Alonzo Mourning, Georgetown	6-10	1992	4	120	771	1,023	75.4
Danya Abrams, Boston College	6-7	1997	4	122	698	1,003	69.6
Jesse Arnelle, Penn St.	6-5	1955	4	102	662	992	66.7
Nick Werkman, Seton Hall	6-3	1964	3	71	649	980	66.2
David Robinson, Navy	7-0	1987	4	127	604	964	62.7
Derrick Chievous, Missouri	6-7	1988	4	130	764	963	79.3
Joe Holup, George Washington	6-6	1956	4	104	714	961	74.3
Michael Anderson, Drexel	5-11	1988	4	115	705	958	73.6
Byron Houston, Oklahoma St.	6-7	1992	4	127	698	957	72.9
Chris Monroe, George Washington	6-3	2003	4	118	719	955	75.3
Steve Rogers, Middle Tenn. & Alabama St.	6-5	1992	4	113	713	955	74.7
Dom Flora, Washington & Lee	62	1958	4	109	696	954	73.0
Bryant Reeves, Oklahoma St.	7-0	1995	4	136	618	953	64.8
Larry Chanay, Montana St.	6-4	1960	4	101	696	947	73.5
+Tyler Hansbrough, North Carolina	6-9	2008	3	108	733	945	77.6
Walter Dukes, Seton Hall	6-10	1953	3	90	615	933	65.9
Troy Bell, Boston College	6-1	2003	4	122	810	933	86.8
Lionel Simmons, La Salle	6-7	1990	4	131	673	932	72.2
Ralph Crosthwaite, Western Ky.	6-9	1959	4	103	608	930	65.4

+active player

FREE-THROW PERCENTAGE
(Minimum 300 free throws made and 2.5 free throws made per game)

Player, Team	Ht.	Last Season	Yrs.	G	FT	FTA	Pct.
Blake Ahearn, Missouri St.	6-2	2007	4	129	435	460	94.6
Derek Raivio, Gonzaga	6-1	2007	4	127	343	370	92.7
Gary Buchanan, Villanova	6-3	2003	4	122	324	355	91.3
J.J. Redick, Duke	6-4	2006	4	139	662	726	91.2
Greg Starrick, Kentucky & Southern Ill.	6-2	1972	4	72	341	375	90.9
Jack Moore, Nebraska	5-9	1982	4	105	446	495	90.1
A.J. Graves, Butler	6-1	2008	4	130	362	402	90.0
Steve Henson, Kansas St.	6-1	1990	4	127	361	401	90.0
Steve Alford, Indiana	6-2	1987	4	125	535	596	89.8
Bob Lloyd, Rutgers	6-1	1967	3	77	543	605	89.8
Jake Sullivan, Iowa St.	6-1	2004	4	123	354	395	89.6
Jim Barton, Dartmouth	6-4	1989	4	104	394	440	89.5
Tommy Boyer, Arkansas	6-6	1963	3	70	315	353	89.2
Gerry McNamara, Syracuse	6-2	2006	4	135	435	490	88.8
Brent Jolly, Tennessee Tech	6-6	2003	4	123	347	391	88.7
Marcus Wilson, Evansville	6-3	1999	4	119	455	513	88.7
Joe Crispin, Penn St.	6-1	2001	4	127	448	506	88.5
Ron Perry, Holy Cross	6-2	1980	4	109	680	768	88.5
Joe Dykstra, Western Ill.	6-6	1983	4	117	587	663	88.5
Mike Joseph, Bucknell	6-0	1990	4	115	397	449	88.4
Kyle Macy, Purdue & Kentucky	6-3	1980	5	125	416	471	88.3
Matt Hildebrand, Liberty	6-3	1994	4	117	398	451	88.2
Jimmy England, Tennessee	6-1	1971	3	81	319	362	88.1
Rod Foster, UCLA	6-1	1983	4	113	309	351	88.0
Michael Smith, BYU	6-10	1989	4	122	431	491	87.8
Jason Matthews, Pittsburgh	6-3	1991	4	123	481	548	87.8
Mike Iuzzolino, Penn St. & St. Francis (Pa.)	5-10	1991	4	112	402	458	87.8

REBOUNDS

Player, Team	Ht.	Last Season	Yrs.	G	Reb.
Tom Gola, La Salle	6-6	1955	4	118	2,201
Joe Holup, George Washington	6-6	1956	4	104	2,030
Charlie Slack, Marshall	6-5	1956	4	88	1,916
Ed Conlin, Fordham	6-5	1955	4	102	1,884
Dickie Hemric, Wake Forest	6-6	1955	4	104	1,802
Paul Silas, Creighton	6-7	1964	3	81	1,751
Art Quimby, Connecticut	6-5	1955	4	80	1,716
Jerry Harper, Alabama	6-8	1956	4	93	1,688
Jeff Cohen, William & Mary	6-7	1961	4	103	1,679
Steve Hamilton, Morehead St.	6-7	1958	4	102	1,675
Charlie Tyra, Louisville	6-8	1957	4	95	1,617
Bill Russell, San Francisco	6-9	1956	3	79	1,606
Elvin Hayes, Houston	6-8	1968	3	93	1,602
Marvin Barnes, Providence	6-9	1974	3	89	1,592
Tim Duncan, Wake Forest	6-11	1997	4	128	1,570
Ron Shavlik, North Carolina St.	6-8	1956	3	93	1,567
Elgin Baylor, Albertson & Seattle	6-6	1958	3	80	1,559
Ernie Beck, Penn	6-4	1953	3	82	1,557
Dave DeBusschere, Detroit	6-5	1962	3	80	1,552
Wes Unseld, Louisville	6-8	1968	3	82	1,551
Derrick Coleman, Syracuse	6-9	1990	4	143	1,537
Malik Rose, Drexel	6-7	1996	4	120	1,514
Ralph Sampson, Virginia	7-4	1983	4	132	1,511
Chris Smith, Virginia Tech	6-6	1961	4	88	1,508
Keith Swagerty, Pacific	6-7	1967	3	82	1,505

(For careers beginning in 1973 or after)

Player, Team	Ht.	Last Season	Yrs.	G	Reb.
Tim Duncan, Wake Forest	6-11	1997	4	128	1,570
Derrick Coleman, Syracuse	6-9	1990	4	143	1,537
Malik Rose, Drexel	6-7	1996	4	120	1,514
Ralph Sampson, Virginia	7-4	1983	4	132	1,511
Pete Padgett, Nevada	6-8	1976	4	104	1,464
Lionel Simmons, La Salle	6-7	1990	4	131	1,429
Anthony Bonner, St. Louis	6-7	1990	4	133	1,424
Tyrone Hill, Xavier	6-9	1990	4	126	1,380
Popeye Jones, Murray St.	6-8	1992	4	123	1,374
Michael Brooks, La Salle	6-7	1980	4	114	1,372
Xavier McDaniel, Wichita St.	6-7	1985	4	117	1,359
John Irving, Arizona & Hofstra	6-9	1977	4	103	1,348
Sam Clancy, Pittsburgh	6-6	1981	4	116	1,342
Keith Lee, Memphis	6-10	1985	4	128	1,336
Larry Smith, Alcorn St.	6-8	1980	4	111	1,334
Clarence Weatherspoon, Southern Miss.	6-7	1992	4	117	1,320
Michael Cage, San Diego St.	6-9	1984	4	112	1,317

Player, Team	Ht.	Last Season	Yrs.	G	Reb.
Bob Stephens, Drexel	6-7	1979	4	99	1,316
Patrick Ewing, Georgetown	7-0	1985	4	143	1,316
David Robinson, Navy	7-1	1987	4	127	1,314
Wayne Rollins, Clemson	7-1	1977	4	110	1,311
David West, Xavier	6-9	2003	4	126	1,309
Bob Warner, Maine	6-6	1976	4	96	1,304
Ervin Johnson, New Orleans	6-11	1993	4	123	1,287
Calvin Natt, La.-Monroe	6-5	1979	4	108	1,285

REBOUND AVERAGE
(Minimum 800 rebounds)

Player, Team	Ht.	Last Season	Yrs.	G	Reb.	Avg.
Artis Gilmore, Jacksonville	7-2	1971	2	54	1,224	22.7
Charlie Slack, Marshall	6-5	1956	4	88	1,916	21.8
Paul Silas, Creighton	6-7	1964	3	81	1,751	21.6
Leroy Wright, Pacific	6-8	1960	3	67	1,442	21.5
Art Quimby, Connecticut	6-5	1955	4	80	1,716	21.5
Walt Dukes, Seton Hall	6-10	1953	2	59	1,247	21.1
Bill Russell, San Francisco	6-9	1956	3	79	1,606	20.3
Kermit Washington, American	6-8	1973	3	73	1,478	20.2
Julius Erving, Massachusetts	6-6	1971	2	52	1,049	20.2
Joe Holup, George Washington	6-6	1956	4	104	2,030	19.5
Elgin Baylor, Albertson & Seattle	6-6	1958	3	80	1,559	19.5
Dave DeBusschere, Detroit	6-5	1962	3	80	1,552	19.4
Ernie Beck, Penn	6-4	1953	3	82	1,557	19.0
Wes Unseld, Louisville	6-8	1968	3	82	1,551	18.9
Tom Gola, La Salle	6-6	1955	4	118	2,201	18.7
Ed Conlin, Fordham	6-5	1955	4	102	1,884	18.5
Keith Swagerty, Pacific	6-7	1967	3	82	1,505	18.4
Wilt Chamberlain, Kansas	7-0	1958	2	48	877	18.3
Jerry Harper, Alabama	6-8	1956	4	93	1,688	18.2
Dick Cunningham, Murray St.	6-10	1968	3	71	1,292	18.2
Marvin Barnes, Providence	6-9	1974	3	89	1,592	17.9
Jim Barnes, UTEP	6-8	1964	2	54	965	17.9
Alex Ellis, Niagara	6-5	1958	3	77	1,376	17.9
Dickie Hemric, Wake Forest	6-6	1955	4	104	1,802	17.3
Elvin Hayes, Houston	6-8	1968	3	93	1,602	17.2

(For careers beginning in 1973 or after; minimum 800 rebounds)

Player, Team	Ht.	Last Season	Yrs.	G	Reb.	Avg.
Glenn Mosley, Seton Hall	6-8	1977	4	83	1,263	15.2
Bill Campion, Manhattan	6-10	1975	3	74	1,070	14.6
Pete Padgett, Nevada	6-8	1976	4	104	1,464	14.1
Bob Warner, Maine	6-6	1976	4	96	1,304	13.6
Shaquille O'Neal, LSU	7-1	1992	3	90	1,217	13.5
Cornelius Cash, Bowling Green	6-8	1975	3	79	1,068	13.5
Ira Terrell, SMU	6-8	1976	3	80	1,077	13.5
Bob Stephens, Drexel	6-7	1979	4	99	1,316	13.3
Larry Bird, Indiana St.	6-9	1979	3	94	1,247	13.3
Bernard King, Tennessee	6-7	1977	3	76	1,004	13.2
John Irving, Arizona & Hofstra	6-9	1977	4	103	1,348	13.1
Andy Hopson, Oklahoma St.	6-8	1975	3	78	1,020	13.1
Alvan Adams, Oklahoma	6-9	1975	3	73	938	12.8
Carey Scurry, Long Island	6-9	1985	3	79	1,013	12.8
Paul Millsap, Louisiana Tech	6-8	2006	3	92	1,172	12.7
Adonal Foyle, Colgate	6-10	1997	3	87	1,103	12.7
Warren Kidd, Middle Tenn.	6-6	1993	3	83	1,048	12.6
Malik Rose, Drexel	6-7	1996	4	120	1,514	12.6
Jervaughn Scales, Southern U.	6-6	1994	3	88	1,099	12.5
Tim Duncan, Wake Forest	6-11	1997	4	128	1,570	12.3
Michael Brooks, La Salle	6-7	1980	4	114	1,372	12.0
Larry Smith, Alcorn St.	6-8	1980	4	111	1,334	12.0
Wayne Rollins, Clemson	7-1	1977	4	110	1,311	11.9
Calvin Natt, La.-Monroe	6-5	1979	4	108	1,285	11.9
Ed Lawrence, McNeese St.	7-0	1976	4	102	1,212	11.9

ASSISTS

Player, Team	Ht.	Last Season	Yrs.	G	Ast.
Bobby Hurley, Duke	6-0	1993	4	140	1,076
Chris Corchiani, North Carolina St.	6-1	1991	4	124	1,038
Ed Cota, North Carolina	6-2	2000	4	138	1,030
Keith Jennings, East Tenn. St.	5-7	1991	4	127	983
Steve Blake, Maryland	6-3	2003	4	138	972
Sherman Douglas, Syracuse	6-0	1989	4	138	960
Tony Miller, Marquette	6-0	1995	4	123	956
Aaron Miles, Kansas	6-1	2005	4	138	954
Greg Anthony, Portland & UNLV	6-1	1991	4	138	950
Doug Gottlieb, Notre Dame & Oklahoma St.	6-1	2000	4	124	947
Gary Payton, Oregon St.	6-2	1990	4	120	939
Orlando Smart, San Francisco	6-0	1994	4	116	902

Player, Team	Ht.	Last Season	Yrs.	G	Ast.
Andre LaFleur, Northeastern	6-3	1987	4	128	894
Chico Fletcher, Arkansas St.	5-6	2000	4	114	893
Jim Les, Bradley	5-11	1986	4	118	884
Frank Smith, Old Dominion	6-0	1988	4	120	883
Taurence Chisholm, Delaware	5-7	1988	4	110	877
Grayson Marshall, Clemson	6-2	1988	4	122	857
Anthony Manuel, Bradley	5-11	1989	4	108	855
Pooh Richardson, UCLA	6-1	1989	4	122	833
Chris Thomas, Notre Dame	6-1	2005	4	128	833
Butch Moore, SMU	5-10	1986	4	125	828
Chris Duhon, Duke	6-1	2004	4	144	819
Mateen Cleaves, Michigan St.	6-3	2000	4	123	816
Jared Jordan, Marist	6-2	2007	4	117	813

ASSIST AVERAGE
(Minimum 550 assists)

Player, Team	Ht.	Last Season	Yrs.	G	Ast.	Avg.
Avery Johnson, Southern U.	5-11	1988	2	61	732	12.00
Sam Crawford, New Mexico St.	5-8	1993	2	67	592	8.84
Mark Wade, Oklahoma & UNLV	6-0	1987	3	79	693	8.77
Chris Corchiani, North Carolina St.	6-1	1991	4	124	1,038	8.37
Taurence Chisholm, Delaware	5-7	1988	4	110	877	7.97
Van Usher, Tennessee Tech	6-0	1992	3	85	676	7.95
Anthony Manuel, Bradley	5-11	1989	4	108	855	7.92
Chico Fletcher, Arkansas St.	5-6	2000	4	114	893	7.83
Gary Payton, Oregon St.	6-2	1990	4	120	938	7.82
Orlando Smart, San Francisco	6-0	1994	4	116	902	7.78
Tony Miller, Marquette	6-0	1995	4	123	956	7.77
Keith Jennings, East Tenn. St.	5-7	1991	4	127	983	7.74
Bobby Hurley, Duke	6-0	1993	4	140	1,076	7.69
Doug Gottlieb, Notre Dame & Oklahoma St.	6-1	2000	4	124	947	7.63
Chuck Evans, Old Dominion & Mississippi St.	5-11	1993	3	85	648	7.62
Jim Les, Bradley	5-11	1986	4	118	884	7.49
Ed Cota, North Carolina	6-2	2000	4	138	1,030	7.46
Curtis McCants, George Mason	6-0	1998	3	81	598	7.38
Frank Smith, Old Dominion	6-0	1988	4	120	883	7.36
Doug Wojcik, Navy	6-1	1987	3	99	714	7.21
Mark Woods, Wright St.	6-1	1993	4	113	811	7.18
Nelson Haggerty, Baylor	6-0	1995	4	98	699	7.13
Steve Blake, Maryland	6-3	2003	4	138	972	7.04
Grayson Marshall, Clemson	6-2	1988	4	122	857	7.02
Drafton Davis, Marist	6-0	1988	4	115	804	6.99

BLOCKED SHOTS

Player, Team	Ht.	Last Season	Yrs.	G	Blk.
Wojciech Mydra, La.-Monroe	7-2	2002	4	115	535
Adonal Foyle, Colgate	6-10	1997	3	87	492
Tim Duncan, Wake Forest	6-11	1997	4	128	481
Alonzo Mourning, Georgetown	6-10	1992	4	120	453
Tarvis Williams, Hampton	6-9	2001	4	114	452
Ken Johnson, Ohio St.	6-11	2001	4	127	444
Deng Gai, Fairfield	6-9	2005	4	100	442
Emeka Okafor, Connecticut	6-9	2004	3	103	441
Lorenzo Coleman, Tennessee Tech	7-1	1997	4	113	437
Calvin Booth, Penn St.	6-11	1999	4	114	428
Theo Ratliff, Wyoming	6-10	1995	4	111	425
Troy Murphy, Notre Dame	6-9	2001	3	94	425
Etan Thomas, Syracuse	6-9	2000	4	122	424
Shelden Williams, Duke	6-9	2006	4	139	422
Rodney Blake, St. Joseph's	6-8	1988	4	116	419
Shaquille O'Neal, LSU	7-1	1992	3	90	412
Kevin Roberson, Vermont	6-7	1992	4	112	409
Jim McIlvaine, Marquette	7-1	1994	4	118	399
Stephane Lasme, Massachusetts	6-8	2007	4	118	399
Mickell Gladness, Alabama A&M	6-11	2008	3	85	396
Tim Perry, Temple	6-9	1988	4	130	392
D'or Fischer, Northwestern St. & West Virginia	6-11	2005	4	127	392
Jason Lawson, Villanova	6-11	1997	4	131	375
Pervis Ellison, Louisville	6-9	1989	4	136	374
Peter Aluma, Liberty	6-10	1997	4	119	366

BLOCKED-SHOT AVERAGE
(Minimum 225 blocked shots)

Player, Team	Ht.	Last Season	Yrs.	G	Blk.	Avg.
Keith Closs, Central Conn. St.	7-2	1996	2	54	317	5.87
Adonal Foyle, Colgate	6-10	1997	3	87	492	5.66
David Robinson, Navy	6-11	1987	2	67	351	5.24
Mickell Gladness, Alabama A&M	6-11	2008	3	85	396	4.66
Wojciech Mydra, La.-Monroe	7-2	2002	4	115	535	4.65
Shaquille O'Neal, LSU	7-1	1992	3	90	412	4.58
Troy Murphy, Notre Dame	6-9	2001	3	94	425	4.52
Jerome James, Florida A&M	7-1	1998	3	81	363	4.48
Deng Gai, Fairfield	6-9	2005	4	100	442	4.42
Emeka Okafor, Connecticut	6-9	2004	3	103	441	4.28
Justin Williams, Wyoming	6-10	2006	2	58	244	4.21
Justin Rowe, Maine	7-0	2003	2	55	226	4.11
Tarvis Williams, Hampton	6-9	2001	4	114	452	3.96
Lorenzo Coleman, Tennessee Tech	7-1	1997	4	113	437	3.87
Theo Ratliff, Wyoming	6-10	1995	4	111	425	3.83
Alonzo Mourning, Georgetown	6-10	1992	4	120	453	3.78
Tim Duncan, Wake Forest	6-11	1997	4	128	481	3.76
Calvin Booth, Penn St.	6-11	1999	4	114	428	3.75
Lorenzo Williams, Stetson	6-9	1991	2	63	234	3.71
Dikembe Mutombo, Georgetown	7-2	1991	3	96	354	3.69
Marcus Camby, Massachusetts	6-11	1996	3	92	336	3.65
Kevin Roberson, Vermont	6-7	1992	4	112	409	3.65
Rodney Blake, St. Joseph's	6-8	1988	4	116	419	3.61
Ken Johnson, Ohio St.	6-11	2001	4	127	444	3.50
Etan Thomas, Syracuse	6-9	2000	4	122	424	3.48

STEALS

Player, Team	Ht.	Last Season	Yrs.	G	Stl.
John Linehan, Providence	5-9	2002	5	122	385
Eric Murdock, Providence	6-2	1991	4	117	376
Pepe Sanchez, Temple	6-0	2000	4	116	365
Cookie Belcher, Nebraska	6-4	2001	5	131	353
Kevin Braswell, Georgetown	6-2	2002	4	128	349
Bonzi Wells, Ball St.	6-5	1998	4	116	347
Obie Trotter, Alabama A&M	6-1	2006	4	114	346
Gerald Walker, San Francisco	6-1	1996	4	111	344
Johnny Rhodes, Maryland	6-6	1996	4	122	344
Michael Anderson, Drexel	5-11	1988	4	115	341
Kenny Robertson, Cleveland St.	6-0	1990	4	119	341
Keith Jennings, East Tenn. St.	5-7	1991	4	127	334
Juan Dixon, Maryland	6-3	2002	4	141	333
Desmond Cambridge, Alabama A&M	6-1	2002	3	84	330
Greg Anthony, Portland & UNLV	6-1	1991	4	138	329
Jason Hart, Syracuse	6-3	2000	4	132	329
Chris Corchiani, North Carolina St.	6-1	1991	4	124	328
Marques Green, St. Bonaventure	5-7	2004	4	112	325
Gary Payton, Oregon St.	6-2	1990	4	120	321
Chris Garner, Memphis	5-10	1997	4	123	321
Tim Winn, St. Bonaventure	5-10	2000	4	108	319
Mark Woods, Wright St.	6-1	1993	4	113	314
Pointer Williams, Tulane & McNeese St.	6-0	1996	4	115	314
Tim Smith, East Tenn. St.	5-9	2006	4	114	313
Scott Burrell, Connecticut	6-7	1993	4	119	310
Clarence Ceasar, LSU	6-7	1995	4	112	310
Shawnta Rogers, George Washington	5-4	1999	4	114	310

STEAL AVERAGE
(Minimum 225 steals)

Player, Team	Ht.	Last Season	Yrs.	G	Stl.	Avg.
Desmond Cambridge, Alabama A&M	6-1	2002	3	84	330	3.93
Mookie Blaylock, Oklahoma	6-0	1989	2	74	281	3.80
Ronn McMahon, Eastern Wash.	5-9	1990	3	64	225	3.52
Eric Murdock, Providence	6-2	1991	4	117	376	3.21
Van Usher, Tennessee Tech	6-0	1992	3	85	270	3.18
John Linehan, Providence	5-9	2002	5	122	385	3.16
Pepe Sanchez, Temple	6-0	2000	4	116	365	3.15
Gerald Walker, San Francisco	6-1	1996	4	111	344	3.10
Obie Trotter, Alabama A&M	6-1	2006	4	114	346	3.04
Bonzi Wells, Ball St.	6-5	1998	4	116	347	2.99
Michael Anderson, Drexel	5-11	1988	4	115	341	2.97
Tim Winn, St. Bonaventure	5-10	2000	4	108	319	2.95
Haywoode Workman, Oral Roberts	6-3	1989	3	85	250	2.94
Shawn Griggs, LSU & La.-Lafayette	6-6	1994	3	89	260	2.92
Marques Green, St. Bonaventure	5-7	2004	4	112	325	2.90
Morris Scott, Florida A&M	6-0	2001	4	87	252	2.90
Kenny Robertson, Cleveland St.	6-0	1990	4	119	341	2.87
Jason Rowe, Loyola (Md.)	5-10	2000	4	95	272	2.86
Darnell Mee, Western Ky.	6-3	1993	3	91	259	2.85
Pat Baldwin, Northwestern	6-1	1994	4	96	272	2.83
Johnny Rhodes, Maryland	6-6	1996	4	122	344	2.82
Mark Woods, Wright St.	6-1	1993	4	113	314	2.78
Clarence Ceasar, LSU	6-7	1995	4	112	310	2.77
Louis Ford, Howard	5-6	2006	4	86	238	2.77
Aldwin Ware, Florida A&M	6-2	1988	4	110	301	2.74

2,000 POINTS & 1,000 REBOUNDS

Player, Team	Ht.	Last Season	Yrs.	G	Pts.	Reb.
Lionel Simmons, La Salle	6-7	1990	4	131	3,217	1,429
Harry Kelly, Texas Southern	6-7	1983	4	110	3,066	1,085
Oscar Robertson, Cincinnati	6-5	1960	3	88	2,973	1,338
Danny Manning, Kansas	6-10	1988	4	147	2,951	1,187
Elvin Hayes, Houston	6-8	1968	3	93	2,884	1,602
Larry Bird, Indiana St.	6-9	1979	3	94	2,850	1,247
Hank Gathers, Southern California & Loyola Marymount	6-7	1990	4	117	2,723	1,128
Daren Queenan, Lehigh	6-5	1988	4	118	2,703	1,013
David Robinson, Navy	7-1	1987	4	127	2,669	1,314
Wayman Tisdale, Oklahoma	6-9	1985	3	104	2,661	1,048
Michael Brooks, La Salle	6-7	1980	4	114	2,628	1,372
Dickie Hemric, Wake Forest	6-6	1955	4	104	2,587	1,802
Calvin Natt, La.-Monroe	6-5	1979	4	108	2,581	1,285
Keith Van Horn, Utah	6-9	1997	4	122	2,542	1,074
Willie Jackson, Centenary (La.)	6-6	1984	4	114	2,535	1,013
Caleb Green, Oral Roberts	6-8	2007	4	128	2,503	1,189
Bill Bradley, Princeton	6-5	1965	3	83	2,503	1,008
Elgin Baylor, Albertson & Seattle	6-6	1958	3	80	2,500	1,559
Nick Fazekas, Nevada	6-11	2007	4	131	2,464	1,254
Tom Gola, La Salle	6-6	1955	4	118	2,462	2,201
Christian Laettner, Duke	6-11	1992	4	148	2,460	1,149
Keith Lee, Memphis	6-11	1985	4	128	2,408	1,336
Phil Sellers, Rutgers	6-5	1976	4	114	2,399	1,115
Byron Houston, Oklahoma St.	6-7	1992	4	127	2,379	1,190
Ron Harper, Miami (Ohio)	6-6	1986	4	120	2,377	1,119
Bryant Reeves, Oklahoma St.	7-0	1995	4	136	2,367	1,152
Craig Smith, Boston College	6-7	2006	4	130	2,349	1,114
Lew Alcindor, UCLA	7-2	1969	3	88	2,325	1,367
Mike Gminski, Duke	6-11	1980	4	122	2,323	1,242
Billy McGill, Utah	6-9	1962	3	86	2,321	1,106
Adam Keefe, Stanford	6-9	1992	4	125	2,319	1,119
Jerry West, West Virginia	6-3	1960	3	93	2,309	1,240
Tunji Awojobi, Boston U.	6-5	1997	4	114	2,308	1,237
Jonathan Moore, Furman	6-8	1980	4	117	2,299	1,242
Rick Barry, Miami (Fla.)	6-7	1965	3	77	2,298	1,274
Gary Winton, Army	6-5	1978	4	105	2,296	1,168
Kenneth Lyons, North Texas	6-7	1983	4	111	2,291	1,020
Tom Davis, Delaware St.	6-6	1991	4	95	2,274	1,013
Nick Werkman, Seton Hall	6-3	1964	3	71	2,273	1,036
Jim McDaniels, Western Ky.	7-0	1971	3	81	2,238	1,118
Joe Holup, George Washington	6-6	1956	4	104	2,226	2,030
Ralph Sampson, Virginia	7-4	1983	4	132	2,225	1,511
Juan Mendez, Niagara	6-7	2005	4	123	2,210	1,053
Kyle Hines, UNC Greensboro	6-6	2008	4	120	2,187	1,047
Patrick Ewing, Georgetown	7-0	1985	4	143	2,184	1,316
Doug Smith, Missouri	6-10	1991	4	128	2,184	1,054
Jenny Sanders, George Mason	6-5	1989	4	107	2,177	1,026
Joe Barry Carroll, Purdue	7-1	1980	4	123	2,175	1,148
Reggie King, Alabama	6-6	1979	4	118	2,168	1,279
Len Chappell, Wake Forest	6-8	1962	3	87	2,165	1,213
Danny Ferry, Duke	6-10	1989	4	143	2,155	1,003
Xavier McDaniel, Wichita St.	6-7	1985	4	117	2,152	1,359
Derrick Coleman, Syracuse	6-9	1990	4	143	2,143	1,537
Joe Binion, N.C. A&T	6-8	1984	4	116	2,143	1,194
Pervis Ellison, Louisville	6-9	1989	4	136	2,143	1,149
Dan Issel, Kentucky	6-9	1970	3	83	2,138	1,078
Jesse Arnelle, Penn St.	6-5	1955	4	102	2,138	1,238
Ryan Gomes, Providence	6-7	2005	4	116	2,138	1,028
Sam Perkins, North Carolina	6-10	1984	4	135	2,133	1,167
David West, Xavier	6-9	2003	4	126	2,132	1,309
Bob Elliott, Arizona	6-10	1977	4	114	2,131	1,083
Clarence Weatherspoon, Southern Miss.	6-7	1992	4	117	2,130	1,320
Reggie Jackson, Nicholls St.	6-6	1995	4	110	2,124	1,271
Greg Grant, Utah St.	6-7	1986	4	115	2,124	1,003
John Wallace, Syracuse	6-8	1996	4	127	2,119	1,065
Tim Duncan, Wake Forest	6-11	1997	4	128	2,117	1,570
Odell Hodge, Old Dominion	6-9	1997	5	128	2,117	1,086
Bill Cartwright, San Francisco	6-11	1979	4	111	2,116	1,137
Bob Harstad, Creighton	6-6	1991	4	128	2,110	1,126
Gary Trent, Ohio	6-8	1995	3	93	2,108	1,050
Nick Collison, Kansas	6-9	2003	4	142	2,097	1,143
B.B. Davis, Lamar	6-8	1981	4	119	2,084	1,122
Durand Macklin, LSU	6-7	1981	5	123	2,080	1,276
Ralph Crosthwaite, Western Ky.	6-9	1959	4	103	2,076	1,309
Hakim Warrick, Syracuse	6-8	2005	4	135	2,073	1,025
Sidney Green, UNLV	6-9	1983	4	119	2,069	1,276
Arizona Reid, High Point	6-5	2008	4	120	2,069	1,013
Bob Lanier, St. Bonaventure	6-11	1970	3	75	2,067	1,180
Raef LaFrentz, Kansas	6-11	1998	4	131	2,066	1,186
Fred West, Texas Southern	6-9	1990	4	118	2,066	1,136
Sidney Moncrief, Arkansas	6-4	1979	4	122	2,066	1,015
Popeye Jones, Murray St.	6-8	1992	4	123	2,057	1,374
Danya Abrams, Boston College	6-7	1997	4	122	2,053	1,029
Jason Thompson, Rider	6-11	2008	4	122	2,040	1,171
Mark Acres, Oral Roberts	6-11	1985	4	110	2,038	1,051
Fred Hetzel, Davidson	6-8	1965	3	79	2,032	1,094
Bailey Howell, Mississippi St.	6-7	1959	3	75	2,030	1,277
Malik Rose, Drexel	6-7	1996	4	120	2,024	1,514
Larry Krystkowiak, Montana	6-9	1986	4	120	2,017	1,105
Greg Kelser, Michigan St.	6-7	1979	4	115	2,014	1,092
Michael Harris, Rice	6-6	2005	4	121	2,014	1,111
Brandon Hunter, Ohio	6-7	2003	4	119	2,012	1,103
Herb Williams, Ohio St.	6-10	1981	4	114	2,011	1,111
Stacey Augmon, UNLV	6-8	1991	4	145	2,011	1,005
Jeff Cohen, William & Mary	6-7	1961	4	103	2,003	1,679
Tyrone Hill, Xavier	6-9	1990	4	126	2,003	1,380
Alonzo Mourning, Georgetown	6-10	1992	4	120	2,001	1,032
Josh Grant, Utah	6-9	1993	5	131	2,000	1,066

QUADRUPLE-DOUBLES

Player, Team	Last Season	Yrs.	QD-2Bs
Lester Hudson, Tenn.-Martin	2008	4	1

TRIPLE-DOUBLES

Player, Team	Last Season	Yrs.	3B-2Bs
Michael Anderson, Drexel	1988	4	6
Shaquille O'Neal, LSU	1992	3	6
Kevin Roberson, Vermont	1992	4	5
David Robinson, Navy	1987	4	4
Brian Shaw, UC Santa Barbara	1988	2	4
Jason Kidd, California	1994	3	4
David Edwards, Texas A&M	1994	4	4
Adonal Foyle, Colgate	1997	3	4
Shawn James, Northeastern	2006	2	4
Stephane Lasme, Massachusetts	2007	4	4
Gerald Lewis, SMU	1993	4	3
Trenton Hassell, Austin Peay	2001	3	3
Wojciech Murda, La.-Monroe	2002	3	3
Andre Iguodala, Arizona	2004	3	3
Derrick Lewis, Maryland	1988	4	2
Luc Longley, New Mexico	1991	4	2
Dave Barnett, Fresno St.	1991	2	2
Alonzo Mourning, Georgetown	1991	4	2
Stacey Augmon, UNLV	1991	4	2
Chris Mills, Kentucky & Arizona	1993	4	2
Anfernee Hardaway, Memphis	1993	3	2
Sharone Wright, Clemson	1994	3	2
Mark Davis, Texas Tech	1995	3	2
Keith Closs, Central Conn. St.	1996	2	2
Roy Rogers, Alabama	1996	4	2
Brian Skinner, Baylor	1998	4	2
Jerome James, Florida A&M	1998	4	2
Bonzi Wells, Ball St.	1998	4	2
Kenyon Martin, Cincinnati	2000	4	2
Loren Woods, Arizona	2001	2	2
D'or Fischer, Northwestern St. & West Virginia	2005	4	2
Sean Kennedy, Marist	2002	4	2
Luke Jackson, Oregon	2004	4	2
David Harrison, Colorado	2004	3	2
Damitrius Coleman, Mercer & Bethune-Cookman	2007	2	2
Dominic McGuire, California & Fresno St.	2007	3	2
Jared Jordan, Marist	2007	4	2
Tony Lee, Robert Morris	2008	4	2
Terrence Williams, Louisville	2008	3	2

DOUBLE-DOUBLES

Player, Team	Last Season	Yrs.	2B-2Bs
Tim Duncan, Wake Forest	1997	4	87
Ralph Sampson, Virginia	1983	4	84
Derrick Coleman, Syracuse	1990	4	83
Malik Rose, Drexel	1996	4	80
Oscar Robertson, Cincinnati	1960	3	79
Jerry Lucas, Ohio St.	1962	3	78
Mel Counts, Oregon St.	1964	3	78
Lew Alcindor, UCLA	1969	3	78
Keith Lee, Memphis	1985	4	74
David Robinson, Navy	1987	4	74
Don May, Dayton	1968	3	72
Bill Walton, UCLA	1974	3	72

Player, Team	Last Season	Yrs.	2B-2Bs
Paul Silas, Creighton	1964	3	71
Gary Winton, Army	1978	4	71
Hank Finkel, Dayton	1966	3	69
Larry Bird, Indiana St.	1979	3	68
David West, Xavier	2003	4	68
Bob Stephens, Drexel	1979	4	67
Tyrone Hill, Xavier	1990	4	67
Len Chappell, Wake Forest	1962	3	66
Jim Haderlein, Loyola Marymount	1971	3	66
Sam Clancy, Pittsburgh	1981	4	66
Dan Issel, Kentucky	1970	3	64
Mike Gminski, Duke	1980	3	63
Jack Twyman, Cincinnati	1955	4	62
Dave Cowens, Florida St.	1970	3	62

CONSECUTIVE DOUBLE-DOUBLES

Player, Team	Dates	2B-2Bs
Billy Cunningham, North Carolina	Dec. 5, 1962-Feb. 22, 1964	40
#Jerry Lucas, Ohio St.	Jan. 23, 1960-Mar. 11, 1961	38
Oscar Robertson, Cincinnati	Dec. 31, 1958-Jan. 2, 1960	33
Mel Counts, Oregon St.	Mar. 23, 1963-Mar. 10, 1964	30
Lew Alcindor, UCLA	Dec. 27, 1967-Dec. 6, 1968	28
Benoit Benjamin, Creighton	Mar. 15, 1984-Feb. 16, 1985	28
Artis Gilmore, Jacksonville	Feb. 18, 1970-Feb. 8 1971	27
Willie Naulls, UCLA	Dec. 2, 1955-Mar. 9, 1956	25
Jerry Lucas, Ohio St.	Mar. 18, 1961-Feb. 24, 1962	24
Mike Lewis, Duke	Mar. 13, 1967-Feb. 20, 1968	21
Jack Twyman, Cincinnati	Dec. 17, 1953-Jan. 6, 1955	20
Jerry West, West Virginia	Jan. 5-Mar. 12, 1960	20
Jim Haderlein, Loyola Marymount	Feb. 21, 1969-Jan. 29, 1970	20
Steve Smith, Loyola Marymount	Jan. 4-Dec. 4, 1972	20
Dave Gunther, Iowa	Dec. 8, 1958-Feb. 21, 1959	19
Jerry West, West Virginia	Feb. 18-Dec. 29, 1959	17
Marvin Roberts, Utah St.	Feb. 26, 1970-Jan. 14, 1971	17
Artis Gilmore, Jacksonville	Dec. 9, 1969-Feb. 13, 1970	17
Tim Duncan, Wake Forest	Nov. 24, 1996-Jan. 28, 1997	17
Len Chappell, Wake Forest	1962	16
Larry Bird, Indiana St.	Dec. 9-Feb. 6, 1979	16
Rickey Brown, Mississippi St.	Mar. 8, 1979-Jan. 17, 1980	16
Shaun Vandiver, Colorado	Feb. 13-Dec. 12, 1990	16
Bill Walton, UCLA	Dec. 10, 1971-Jan. 28, 1972	15
David Robinson, Navy	Feb. 12-Nov. 29, 1986	15
Andre Moore, Loyola (Ill.)	Jan. 12-Feb. 23, 1987	15

Player, Team	Dates	2B-2Bs
Spencer Dunkley, Delaware	Dec. 10, 1992-Feb. 6, 1993	15

#Missed the Jan. 9, 1961, game because of injury.

Note: Triple-Doubles and Double-Doubles include only statistics from points, rebounds (since 1951), assists (since 1984), blocked shots (since 1986) or steals (since 1986).

GAMES PLAYED

Player, Team	Last Season	Yrs.	G
Wayne Turner, Kentucky	1999	4	151
Joey Dorsey, Memphis	2008	4	149
Christian Laettner, Duke	1992	4	148
Danny Manning, Kansas	1988	4	147
Greg Koubek, Duke	1991	4	147
Shane Battier, Duke	2001	4	146
Stacey Augmon, UNLV	1991	4	145
Jamaal Magloire, Kentucky	2000	4	145
Chris Duhon, Duke	2004	4	144
Patrick Ewing, Georgetown	1985	4	143
Danny Ferry, Duke	1989	4	143
Derrick Coleman, Syracuse	1990	4	143
Jared Prickett, Kentucky	1997	4	143
Ryan Robertson, Kansas	1999	4	142
Nick Collison, Kansas	2003	4	142
Brian Davis, Duke	1992	4	141
Thomas Hill, Duke	1993	4	141
Anthony Epps, Kentucky	1997	4	141
Brendan Haywood, North Carolina	2001	4	141
Juan Dixon, Maryland	2002	4	141
Kirk Hinrich, Kansas	2003	4	141
Chris Richard, Duke	2007	4	141
Daris Nichols, West Virginia	2008	4	141
Bobby Hurley, Duke	1993	4	140
Kevin Freeman, Connecticut	2000	4	140
Charlie Bell, Michigan St.	2001	4	140

Top 10 Individual Scoring Leaders

Year-by-Year Top 10

1948

Rk. Player, School	G	Pts.	Avg.
1. Murray Wier, Iowa	19	399	21.0
2. Tony Lavelli, Yale	27	554	20.5
3. Frank Kudelka, St. Mary's	24	489	20.4
4. Ernie Vandeweghe, Colgate	19	385	20.3
5. Hal Haskins, Hamline	31	605	19.5
6. George Kok, Arkansas	24	469	19.5
7. Jim McIntyre, Minnesota	19	360	18.9
8. William Hatchett, Rutgers	11	201	18.3
9. Gene Berce, Marquette	22	390	17.7
10. Duane Klueh, Indiana St.	34	597	17.6

1949

Rk. Player, School	G	Pts.	Avg.
1. Tony Lavelli, Yale	30	671	22.4
2. Paul Arizin, Villanova	27	594	22.0
3. Chet Giermak, William & Mary	34	740	21.8
4. George Senesky, St. Joseph's	23	483	21.0
5. Ernie Vandeweghe, Colgate	19	397	20.9
6. Alex Groza, Kentucky	34	698	20.5
7. Billy Goodwin, Rhode Island	22	433	19.7
8. Joe Noertker, Virginia	23	442	19.2
9. Vince Boryla, Denver	33	624	18.9
10. Fred Schaus, West Virginia	24	442	18.4

1950

Rk. Player, School	G	Pts.	Avg.
1. Paul Arizin, Villanova	29	735	25.3
2. George Senesky, St. Joseph's	24	537	22.4
3. Sherm White, Long Island	25	551	22.0
4. Clyde Lovellette, Kansas	25	545	21.8
5. Bobby Lavoy, Western Ky.	31	671	21.6
6. Dick Schnittker, Ohio St.	22	469	21.3
7. Chet Giermak, William & Mary	31	646	20.8
8. Jay Handlan, Wash. & Lee	20	406	20.3
9. Bob Zawoluk, St. John's (N.Y.)	29	588	20.3
10. Joe Noertker, Virginia	25	503	20.1

1951

Rk. Player, School	G	Pts.	Avg.
1. Bill Milkvy, Temple	25	731	29.2
2. Jay Handlan, Wash. & Lee	25	656	26.2
3. Mark Workman, West Virginia	27	705	26.1
4. Dick Groat, Duke	33	831	25.2
5. Clyde Lovellette, Kansas	24	548	22.8
6. Fred Slaughter, South Carolina	25	569	22.8
7. Larry Hennessey, Villanova	32	703	22.0
8. Jim Ove, Valparaiso	22	469	21.3
9. Bob Zawoluk, St. John's (N.Y.)	31	654	21.1
10. Sam Ranzino, North Carolina St.	34	706	20.8

1952

Rk. Player, School	G	Pts.	Avg.
1. Clyde Lovellette, Kansas	28	795	28.4
2. Dick Groat, Duke	30	780	26.0
3. Bob Pettit, LSU	24	612	25.5
4. Chuck Darling, Iowa	22	561	25.5
5. Frank Selvy, Furman	24	591	24.6
6. Mark Workman, West Virginia	25	577	23.1
7. Dick Retherford, Baldwin-Wallace	21	457	21.8
8. Dickie Hemric, Wake Forest	29	629	21.7
9. Cliff Hagan, Kentucky	32	692	21.6
10. John Clune, Navy	23	487	21.2

1953

Rk. Player, School	G	Pts.	Avg.
1. Frank Selvy, Furman	25	738	29.5
2. Larry Hennessey, Villanova	15	438	29.2
3. Johnny O'Brien, Seattle	31	884	28.5
4. Walter Dukes, Seton Hall	33	861	26.1
5. Ernie Beck, Penn	26	673	25.9
6. Bob Houbregs, Washington	31	800	25.8
7. Don Schlundt, Indiana	26	661	25.4
8. Dickie Hemric, Wake Forest	25	623	24.9
9. George Dalton, John Carroll	27	669	24.8
10. Bob Pettit, LSU	21	519	24.7

1954

Rk. Player, School	G	Pts.	Avg.
1. Frank Selvy, Furman	29	1,209	41.7
2. Bob Pettit, LSU	25	785	31.4
3. Buzz Wilkinson, Virginia	25	814	30.1
4. Arney Short, Oklahoma City	25	696	27.8
5. Bob Schafer, Villanova	31	836	27.0
6. Walt Walowac, Marshall	21	548	26.1
7. Tom Marshall, Western Ky.	32	829	25.9
8. John Kerr, Illinois	22	556	25.3
9. Al Bianchi, Bowling Green	24	600	25.0
10. Togo Palazzi, Holy Cross	27	670	24.8

1955

Rk. Player, School	G	Pts.	Avg.
1. Darrel Floyd, Furman	25	897	35.9
2. Buzz Wilkinson, Virginia	28	898	32.1
3. Robin Freeman, Ohio St.	13	409	31.5
4. Bill Yarborough, Clemson	23	651	28.3
5. Dick O'Neal, TCU	24	676	28.2
6. Dickie Hemric, Wake Forest	27	746	27.6
7. Bob Patterson, Tulsa	28	773	27.6
8. Johnny Mahoney, William & Mary	24	656	27.3
9. Denver Brackeen, Mississippi	22	599	27.2
10. Jesse Arnelle, Penn St.	28	731	26.1

1956

Rk. Player, School	G	Pts.	Avg.
1. Darrel Floyd, Furman	28	946	33.8
2. Robin Freeman, Ohio St.	22	723	32.9
3. Dan Swartz, Morehead St.	29	828	28.6
4. Tom Heinsohn, Holy Cross	27	740	27.4
5. Julius McCoy, Michigan St.	22	600	27.3
6. Len Rosenbluth, No. Carolina	23	614	26.7
7. Rod Hundley, West Virginia	30	798	26.6
8. Raymond Downs, Texas	22	580	26.4
9. Jim Ray, Toledo	22	563	25.6
10. Roger Sigler, LSU	20	501	25.1

1957

Rk. Player, School	G	Pts.	Avg.
1. Grady Wallace, South Carolina	29	906	31.2
2. Joe Gibbon, Mississippi	21	631	30.0
3. Elgin Baylor, Seattle	25	743	29.7
4. Wilt Chamberlain, Kansas	27	800	29.6
5. Chet Forte, Columbia	24	694	28.9
6. Jim Ashmore, Mississippi St.	25	708	28.3
7. Lennie Rosenbluth, North Carolina	32	895	28.0
8. Bill Ebben, Detroit	26	724	27.8
9. Bailey Howell, Mississippi St.	25	647	25.9
10. Archie Dees, Indiana	22	550	25.0

1958

Rk. Player, School	G	Pts.	Avg.
1. Oscar Robertson, Cincinnati	28	984	35.1
2. Elgin Baylor, Seattle	29	943	32.5
3. Wilt Chamberlain, Kansas	21	633	30.1
4. Bailey Howell, Mississippi St.	25	695	27.8
5. Phil Murrell, Drake	25	668	26.7
6. King Coleman, Ky. Wesleyan	24	639	26.6
7. Don Hennon, Pittsburgh	25	651	26.0
8. Hub Reed, Oklahoma City	26	666	25.6
9. Archie Dees, Indiana	24	613	25.5
10. Dom Flora, Wash. & Lee	25	634	25.4

1959

Rk. Player, School	G	Pts.	Avg.
1. Ocsar Robertson, Cincinnati	30	978	32.6
2. Leo Byrd, Marshall	24	704	29.3
3. Jim Hagan, Tennessee Tech	25	720	28.8
4. Bailey Howell, Miss. St.	25	688	27.5
5. Jerry West, West Virginia	34	903	26.6
6. Bob Ayersman, Virginia Tech	21	556	26.5
7. Don Hennon, Pittsburgh	24	617	25.7
8. Bob Boozer, Kansas St.	27	691	25.6
9. Tony Windis, Wyoming	19	463	24.4
10. Tom Hawkins, Notre Dame	22	514	23.4

1960

Rk. Player, School	G	Pts.	Avg.
1. Oscar Robertson, Cincinnati	30	1,011	33.7
2. Tom Stith, St. Bonaventure	26	819	31.5
3. Jim Darrow, Bowling Green	24	705	29.4
4. Jerry West, West Virginia	31	908	29.3
5. Frank Burgess, Gonzaga	26	751	28.9
6. Al Butler, Niagara	25	714	28.6
7. Terry Dischinger, Purdue	23	605	26.3
8. Jerry Lucas, Ohio St.	27	710	26.3
9. Dave DeBusschere, Detroit	27	691	25.6
10. Jim Mudd, North Texas	24	605	25.2

1961

Rk. Player, School	G	Pts.	Avg.
1. Frank Burgess, Gonzaga	26	842	32.4
2. Tom Chilton, East Tennessee	24	771	32.1
3. Tom Stith, St. Bonaventure	28	830	29.6
4. Terry Dischinger, Purdue	23	648	28.2
5. Billy McGill, Utah	31	862	27.8
6. Len Chappell, Wake Forest	28	745	26.6
7. Jack Foley, Holy Cross	26	688	26.5
8. Chet Walker, Bradley	26	656	25.2
9. Art Heyman, Duke	25	629	25.2
10. Ronald Warner, Gettysburg	25	623	24.9

1962

Rk. Player, School	G	Pts.	Avg.
1. Bill McGill, Utah	26	1,009	38.8
2. Jack Foley, Holy Cross	26	866	33.3
3. Nick Werkman, Seton Hall	24	793	33.0
4. Terry Dischinger, Purdue	24	726	30.3
5. Len Chappell, Wake Forest	31	932	30.1
6. Jimmy Rayl, Indiana	24	714	29.8
7. Jerry Smith, Furman	27	728	27.0
8. Dave DeBusschere, Detroit	26	696	26.8
9. Bob Duffy, Colgate	23	611	26.6
10. Chet Walker, Bradley	26	687	26.4

1963

Rk.	Player, School	G	Pts.	Avg.
1.	Nick Werkman, Seton Hall	22	650	29.5
2.	Berry Kramer, New York U.	23	675	29.3
3.	Bill Green, Colorado St.	23	649	28.2
4.	Gary Bradds, Ohio St.	24	672	28.0
5.	Bill Bradley, Princeton	25	682	27.3
6.	Flynn Robinson, Wyoming	26	682	26.2
7.	Eddie Miles, Seattle	27	697	25.8
8.	Jimmy Rayl, Indiana	24	608	25.3
9.	Art Heyman, Duke	30	747	24.9
10.	Art Crump, Idaho St.	24	595	24.8

1964

Rk.	Player, School	G	Pts.	Avg.
1.	Butch Komives, Bowling Green	23	844	36.7
2.	Nick Werkman, Seton Hall	25	830	33.2
3.	Manny Newsome, Western Mich.	20	653	32.7
4.	Bill Bradley, Princeton	29	936	32.3
5.	Rick Barry, Miami (Fla.)	27	870	32.2
6.	Gary Bradds, Ohio St.	24	735	30.6
7.	Steve Thomas, Xavier	26	779	30.0
8.	John Austin, Boston College	21	614	29.2
9.	Jim Barnes, Texas Western	28	816	29.1
10.	Wayne Estes, Utah St.	29	821	28.3

1965

Rk.	Player, School	G	Pts.	Avg.
1.	Rick Barry, Miami (Fla.)	26	973	37.4
2.	Wayne Estes, Utah St.	19	641	33.7
3.	Bill Bradley, Princeton	29	885	30.5
4.	Dave Schellhase, Purdue	24	704	29.3
5.	Steve Thomas, Xavier	14	405	28.9
6.	Flynn Robinson, Wyoming	26	701	27.0
7.	John Austin, Boston College	25	673	26.9
8.	Fred Hetzel, Davidson	26	689	26.5
9.	John Beasley, Texas A&M	24	619	25.8
10.	Cazzie Russell, Michigan	27	694	25.7

1966

Rk.	Player, School	G	Pts.	Avg.
1.	Dave Schellhase, Purdue	24	781	32.5
2.	Dave Wagnon, Idaho St.	26	845	32.5
3.	Cazzie Russell, Michigan	26	800	30.8
4.	Jerry Chambers, Utah	31	892	28.8
5.	Dave Bing, Syracuse	28	794	28.4
6.	Tom Kerwin, Centenary (La.)	26	726	27.9
7.	Don Freeman, Illinois	24	668	27.8
8.	John Beasley, Texas A&M	24	668	27.8
9.	Bill Melchionni, Villanova	29	801	27.6
10.	Bob Lewis, North Carolina	27	740	27.4

1967

Rk.	Player, School	G	Pts.	Avg.
1.	Jimmy Walker, Providence	28	851	30.4
2.	Lew Alcindor, UCLA	30	870	29.0
3.	Mal Graham, New York U.	24	688	28.7
4.	Elvin Hayes, Houston	31	881	28.4
5.	Wes Bialosuknia, Connecticut	24	673	28.0
6.	Bob Lloyd, Rutgers	29	809	27.9
7.	Gary Gray, Oklahoma City	26	715	27.5
8.	Cliff Anderson, St. Joseph's	26	690	26.5
9.	Bob Verga, Duke	27	705	26.1
10.	Jim Tillman, Loyola (Ill.)	22	553	25.1

1968

Rk.	Player, School	G	Pts.	Avg.
1.	Pete Maravich, LSU	26	1,138	43.8
2.	Calvin Murphy, Niagara	24	916	38.2
3.	Elvin Hayes, Houston	33	1,214	36.8
4.	Rich Travis, Oklahoma City	27	808	29.9
5.	Bob Portman, Creighton	25	738	29.5
6.	Rick Mount, Purdue	24	683	28.5
7.	Bobby Joe Hill, West Texas St.	21	573	27.3
8.	Shaler Halimon, Utah St.	25	671	26.8
9.	Fred Foster, Miami (Ohio)	23	617	26.8
10.	Neal Walk, Florida	25	663	26.5

1969

Rk.	Player, School	G	Pts.	Avg.
1.	Pete Maravich, LSU	26	1,148	44.2
2.	Rick Mount, Purdue	28	932	33.3
3.	Calvin Murphy, Niagara	24	778	32.4
4.	Spencer Haywood, Detroit	22	699	31.8
5.	Bob Tallent, George Washington	25	723	28.9
6.	Marv Roberts, Utah St.	26	718	27.6
7.	Don Curnutt, Miami (Fla.)	24	661	27.5
8.	Bob Lanier, St. Bonaventure	24	654	27.3
9.	Rich Travis, Oklahoma City	27	729	27.0
10.	Rex Morgan, Jacksonville	23	613	26.7

1970

Rk.	Player, School	G	Pts.	Avg.
1.	Pete Maravich, LSU	31	1,381	44.5
2.	Austin Carr, Notre Dame	29	1,106	38.1
3.	Rick Mount, Purdue	20	708	35.4
4.	Dan Issel, Kentucky	28	948	33.9
5.	Willie Humes, Idaho St.	24	733	30.5
6.	Rich Yunkus, Georgia Tech	27	814	30.1
7.	Rudy Tomjanovich, Michigan	24	722	30.1
8.	Calvin Murphy, Niagara	29	854	29.4
9.	Bob Lanier, St. Bonaventure	26	757	29.1
10.	Ralph Simpson, Michigan St.	23	667	29.0

1971

Rk.	Player, School	G	Pts.	Avg.
1.	Johnny Neumann, Mississippi	23	923	40.1
2.	Austin Carr, Notre Dame	29	1,101	38.0
3.	Willie Humes, Idaho St.	24	777	32.4
4.	George McGinnis, Indiana	24	719	30.0
5.	Jim McDaniels, Western Ky.	30	878	29.3
6.	Rich Rinaldi, St. Peter's	24	687	28.6
7.	John Mengelt, Auburn	26	738	28.4
8.	Gene Phillips, SMU	26	737	28.3
9.	Cliff Meely, Colorado	26	729	28.0
10.	Wiley Brown, Iowa	24	662	27.6

1972

Rk.	Player, School	G	Pts.	Avg.
1.	Bo Lamar, La.-Lafayette	29	1,054	36.3
2.	Richie Fuqua, Oral Roberts	28	1,006	35.9
3.	Doug Collins, Illinois St.	26	847	32.6
4.	Wil Robertson, West Virginia	24	706	29.4
5.	Bird Averitt, Pepperdine	24	693	28.9
6.	John Williamson, New Mexico St.	25	678	27.1
7.	Greg Kohls, Syracuse	28	748	26.7
8.	Tony Miller, Florida	19	507	26.7
9.	Les Taylor, Murray St.	21	538	25.6
10.	Ted Martiniuk, St. Peter's	24	611	25.5

1973

Rk.	Player, School	G	Pts.	Avg.
1.	Bird Averitt, Pepperdine	25	848	33.9
2.	Ray Lewis, LSU	24	789	32.9
3.	Willie Biles, Tulsa	26	788	30.3
4.	Aron Stewart, Richmond	19	574	30.2
5.	Fly Williams, Austin Peay	29	854	29.4
6.	Bo Lamar, La.-Lafayette	28	808	28.9
7.	Ozie Edwards, Oklahoma City	27	767	28.4
8.	Martin Terry, Arkansas	26	735	28.3
9.	John Williamson, New Mexico St.	18	490	27.2
10.	Doug Collins, Illinois St.	25	650	26.0

1974

Rk.	Player, School	G	Pts.	Avg.
1.	Larry Fogle, Canisius	25	835	33.4
2.	Bruce King, Tex.-Pan Americn	22	681	31.0
3.	Fly Williams, Austin Peay	25	687	27.5
4.	Aaron Stewart, Richmond	25	663	26.5
5.	David Thompson, North Caro. St.	31	805	26.0
6.	Larry Bullington, Ball St.	26	664	25.5
7.	Frank Oleynick, Seattle	26	653	25.1
8.	James Outlaw, N.C. A&T	26	647	24.9
9.	Willie Biles, Tulsa	26	641	24.7
10.	John Shumate, Notre Dame	29	703	24.2

1975

Rk.	Player, School	G	Pts.	Avg.
1.	Bob McCurdy, Richmond	26	855	32.9
2.	Adrien Dantley, Notre Dame	29	883	30.4
3.	David Thompson, North Caro. St.	28	838	29.9
4.	Luther Burden, Utah	26	747	28.7
5.	Hercle Ivy, Iowa St.	26	737	28.3
6.	Mike Coleman, Southern Miss.	20	564	28.2
7.	Frank Oleynick, Seattle	26	709	27.3
8.	Don Scaife, Arkansas St.	25	678	27.1
9.	Marshall Rogers, Tex.-Pan Am.	22	588	26.7
10.	Alvan Adams, Oklahoma	26	691	26.6

1976

Rk.	Player, School	G	Pts.	Avg.
1.	Marshall Rogers, Tex.-Pan Am.	25	919	36.8
2.	Freeman Williams, Portland St.	27	834	30.9
3.	Terry Furlow, Michigan St.	27	793	29.4
4.	Adrian Dantley, Notre Dame	29	829	28.6
5.	Kenny Carr, North Carolina St.	30	798	26.6
6.	Lee Dixon, Hard-Simmons	27	707	26.2
7.	Tracy Tripucka, Lafayette	26	679	26.1
8.	Otis Birdsong, Houston	28	730	26.1
9.	Ernie Grunfeld, Tennessee	27	683	25.3
10.	Willie Smith, Missouri	31	783	25.3

1977

Rk.	Player, School	G	Pts.	Avg.
1.	Freeman Williams, Portland St.	26	1,010	38.8
2.	Anthony Roberts, Oral Roberts	28	951	34.0
3.	Larry Bird, Indiana St.	28	918	32.8
4.	Otis Birdsong, Houston	36	1,090	30.3
5.	Rich Laurel, Hofstra	30	908	30.3
6.	Calvin Natt, La.-Monroe	27	782	29.0
7.	Mike McConathy, Louisiana Tech	26	716	27.5
8.	Roger Phegley, Bradley	27	739	27.4
9.	Billy Reynolds, Northwestern St.	26	686	26.4
10.	Tony Hanson, Connecticut	27	702	26.0

1978

Rk.	Player, School	G	Pts.	Avg.
1.	Freeman Williams, Portland St.	27	969	35.9
2.	Larry Bird, Indiana St.	32	959	30.0
3.	Purvis Short, Jackson St.	22	650	29.5
4.	Oliver Mack, East Carolina	25	699	28.0
5.	Roger Phegley, Bradley	24	663	27.6
6.	Frankie Sanders, Southern U.	27	740	27.4
7.	Ron Carter, VMI	28	736	26.3
8.	John Gerdy, Davidson	26	670	25.8
9.	Michael Brooks, La Salle	28	696	24.9
10.	Mike Mitchell, Auburn	27	671	24.9

1979

Rk.	Player, School	G	Pts.	Avg.
1.	Lawrence Butler, Idaho St.	27	812	30.1
2.	Larry Bird, Indiana St.	34	973	28.6
3.	Nick Galis, Seton Hall	27	743	27.5
4.	James Tillman, Eastern Ky.	29	780	26.9
5.	Paul Dawkins, Northern Ill.	26	695	26.7
6.	John Gerdy, Davidson	27	721	26.7
7.	Ernie Hill, Oklahoma City	29	771	26.6
8.	John Stroud, Mississippi	27	709	26.3
9.	John Manning, North Texas	27	699	25.9
10.	Steve Stielper, James Madison	26	668	25.7

1980

Rk.	Player, School	G	Pts.	Avg.
1.	Tony Murphy, Southern	29	932	32.1
2.	Lewis Lloyd, Drake	27	815	30.2
3.	Harry Kelly, Texas Southern	26	753	29.0
4.	Kenny Page, New Mexico	28	784	28.0
5.	James Tillman, Eastern Ky.	27	734	27.2
6.	Earl Belcher, St. Bonaventure	24	646	26.9
7.	Russel Bowers, American	27	726	26.9
8.	Carl Nicks, Indiana St.	27	723	26.8
9.	Mark Aguirre, DePaul	28	749	26.8
10.	Andrew Toney, La.-Lafayette	24	627	26.1

1981

Rk. Player, School	G	Pts.	Avg.
1. Zam Fredrick, South Carolina	27	781	28.9
2. Mike Ferrara, Colgate	27	772	28.6
3. Kevin Magee, UC Irvine	27	743	27.5
4. Lewis Lloyd, Drake	29	762	26.3
5. Rob Williams, Houston	30	749	25.0
6. Rubin Jackson, Oklahoma City	29	719	24.8
7. Frank Edwards, Cleveland St.	27	664	24.6
8. Earl Belcher, St. Bonaventure	26	637	24.5
9. Danny Ainge, BYU	32	787	24.4
10. Mike McGee, Michigan	30	732	24.4

1982

Rk. Player, School	G	Pts.	Avg.
1. Harry Kelly, Texas Southern	29	862	29.7
2. Ricky Pierce, Rice	30	805	26.8
3. Dan Callandrillo, Seton Hall	27	698	25.9
4. Kevin Magee, UC Irvine	29	732	25.2
5. Quintin Dailey, San Francisco	30	755	25.2
6. Willie Jackson, Centenary (La.)	29	693	23.9
7. Mitchell Wiggins, Florida St.	22	523	23.8
8. Perry Moss, Northeastern	30	710	23.7
9. Melvin McLaughlin, Central Mich.	25	581	23.2
10. Joe Jakubick, Akron	26	594	22.8

1983

Rk. Player, School	G	Pts.	Avg.
1. Harry Kelly, Texas Southern	29	835	28.8
2. Jeff Malone, Mississippi St.	29	777	26.8
3. Carlos Yates, George Mason	27	723	26.8
4. Charlie Bradley, South Florida	32	855	26.7
5. Joe Jakubick, Akron	29	774	26.7
6. Greg Goorjian, Loyola Marymount	23	601	26.1
7. Alfredrick Hughes, Loyola (Ill.)	29	744	25.7
8. Wayman Tisdale, Oklahoma	33	810	24.5
9. Kenneth Lyons, North Texas St.	30	728	24.3
10. Willie Jackson, Centenary (La.)	29	697	24.0

1984

Rk. Player, School	G	Pts.	Avg.
1. Joe Jakublick, Akron	27	814	30.1
2. Lewis Jackson, Alabama St.	28	812	29.0
3. Devin Durrant, BYU	31	866	27.9
4. Alfredrick Hughes, Loyola (Ill.)	29	800	27.6
5. Wayman Tisdale, Oklahoma	34	919	27.0
6. Joe Dumars, McNeese St.	31	817	26.4
7. Brett Crawford, U.S. Int'l	25	614	24.6
8. Michael Cage, San Diego St.	28	686	24.5
9. Steve Burtt, Iona	31	749	24.2
10. Leon Wood, Cal. St.-Fullerton	30	719	24.0

1985

Rk. Player, School	G	Pts.	Avg.
1. Xavier McDaniel, Wichita St.	31	844	27.2
2. Alfredrick Hughes, Loyola (Ill.)	33	868	26.3
3. Dan Palombizio, Ball St.	29	762	26.3
4. Joe Dumars, McNeese St.	27	697	25.8
5. Terry Catledge, South Ala.	28	718	25.6
6. Derrick Gervin, Tex.-San Antonio	28	718	25.6
7. Wayman Tisdale, Oklahoma	37	932	25.2
8. Keith Smith, Loyola Marymount	27	678	25.1
9. Sam Mitchell, Mercer	31	774	25.0
10. Ron Harper, Miami (Ohio)	31	772	24.9

1986

Rk. Player, School	G	Pts.	Avg.
1. Terrance Bailey, Wagner	29	854	29.4
2. Scott Skiles, Michigan St.	31	850	27.4
3. Joe Yezback, U.S. Int'l	28	755	27.0
4. Reggie Miller, UCLA	29	750	25.9
5. Ron Harper, Miami (Ohio)	31	757	24.4
6. Dell Curry, Virginia Tech	30	722	24.1
7. Reggie Lewis, Northeastern	30	714	23.8
8. Len Bias, Maryland	32	743	23.2
9. Frank Ross, American	28	645	23.0
10. Walter Berry, St. John's (N.Y.)	36	828	23.0

1987

Rk. Player, School	G	Pts.	Avg.
1. Kevin Houston, Army	29	953	32.9
2. Dennis Hopson, Ohio St.	33	958	29.0
3. Dave Robinson, Navy	32	903	28.2
4. Terrance Bailey, Wagner	28	788	28.1
5. Hersey Hawkins, Bradley	29	788	28.1
6. Darrin Fitzgerald, Butler	28	734	26.2
7. Gay Elmore, VMI	28	713	25.5
8. Frank Ross, American	27	683	25.3
9. Daren Queenan, Lehigh	29	720	24.8
10. Byron Larkin, Xavier	32	792	24.7

1988

Rk. Player, School	G	Pts.	Avg.
1. Hershey Hawkins, Bradley	31	1,125	36.3
2. Daren Queenan, Lehigh	31	882	28.5
3. Anthony Mason, Tennessee St.	28	783	28.0
4. Gerald Hayward, Loyola (Ill.)	29	756	26.1
5. Jeff Martin, Murray St.	31	806	26.0
6. Marty Simmons, Evansville	29	750	25.9
7. Steve Middleton, Southern Ill.	28	711	25.4
8. Jeff Grayer, Iowa St.	32	811	25.3
9. Byron Larkin, Xavier	30	758	25.3
10. Skip Henderson, Marshall	32	804	25.1

1989

Rk. Player, School	G	Pts.	Avg.
1. Hank Gathers, Loyola Marymount	31	1,015	32.7
2. Chris Jackson, Louisiana St.	32	965	30.2
3. Lionel Simmons, La Salle	32	908	28.4
4. Gerald Glass, Mississippi	30	841	28.0
5. Blue Edwards, East Carolina	29	773	26.7
6. Raymond Dudley, Air Force	28	746	26.6
7. Bimbo Coles, Virginia Tech	27	717	26.6
8. Michael Smith, BYU	29	765	26.4
9. Stacey King, Oklahoma	33	859	26.0
10. John Taft, Marshall	27	701	26.0

1990

Rk. Player, School	G	Pts.	Avg.
1. Bo Kimble, Loyola Marymount	32	1,131	35.3
2. Kevin Bradshaw, U.S. Int'l	28	875	31.3
3. Dave Jamerson, Ohio	28	874	31.2
4. Alphonzo Ford, Miss. Val.	27	808	29.9
5. Steve Rogers, Alabama St.	28	831	29.7
6. Hank Gathers, Loyola Marymount	26	754	29.0
7. Darryl Brooks, Tennessee St.	24	690	28.8
8. Chris Jackson, LSU	32	889	27.8
9. Dennis Scott, Georgia Tech	35	970	27.7
10. Mark Stevenson, Duquesne	29	788	27.2

1991

Rk. Player, School	G	Pts.	Avg.
1. Kevin Bradshaw, U.S. Int'l	28	1,054	37.6
2. Alphonso Ford, Miss. Valley	28	915	32.7
3. Von McDade, Milwaukee	28	830	29.6
4. Steve Rogers, Alabama St.	29	852	29.4
5. Terrell Lowery, Loyola Marymount	31	884	28.5
6. Bibby Phills, Southern U.	28	795	28.4
7. Shaquille O'Neal, LSU	28	774	27.6
8. John Taft, Marshall	28	764	27.3
9. Rodney Monroe, North Caro. St.	31	836	27.0
10. Terrell Brandon, Oregon	28	745	26.6

1992

Rk. Player, School	G	Pts.	Avg.
1. Brett Roberts, Morehead St.	29	815	28.1
2. Vin Baker, Hartford	27	745	27.6
3. Alphonso Ford, Mississippi Val.	26	714	27.5
4. Randy Woods, La Salle	31	847	27.3
5. Steve Rogers, Alabama St.	28	764	27.3
6. Walt Williams, Maryland	29	776	26.8
7. Harold Miner, Southern California	30	709	26.3
8. Terrell Lowery, Loyola Marymount	26	675	26.0
9. Reggie Cunningham, Beth.-Cook.	29	744	25.7
10. Parrish Casebier, Evansville	25	634	25.4

1993

Rk. Player, School	G	Pts.	Avg.
1. Greg Guy, Tex.-Pan American	19	556	29.3
2. J.R.Rider, UNLV	28	814	29.1
3. John Best, Tennessee Tech	28	799	28.5
4. Vin Baker, Hartford	28	792	28.3
5. Lindsey Hunter, Jackson St.	34	907	26.7
6. Alphonzo Ford, Mississippi Val.	28	728	26.0
7. Bill Edwards, Wright St.	30	757	25.2
8. Billy Ross, Appalachian St.	28	683	24.4
9. Glenn Robinson, Purdue	28	676	24.1
10. Kenneth Sykes, Grambling	27	644	23.9

1994

Rk. Player, School	G	Pts.	Avg.
1. Glenn Robinson, Purdue	34	1,030	30.3
2. Rob Feaster, Holy Cross	28	785	28.0
3. Jervaughn Scales, Southern U.	27	733	27.1
4. Frankie King, Western Caro.	28	752	26.9
5. Tucker Neale, Colgate	29	771	26.6
6. Eddie Benton, Vermont	26	687	26.4
7. Doremus Bennerman, Siena	33	858	26.0
8. Tony Dumas, UMKC	29	753	26.0
9. Otis Jones, Air Force	26	663	25.5
10. Izett Buchanan, Marist	27	685	25.4

1995

Rk. Player, School	G	Pts.	Avg.
1. Kurt Thomas, TCU	27	781	28.9
2. Frankie King, Western Caro.	28	743	26.5
3. Kenny Sykes, Grambling	26	684	26.3
4. Sherell Ford, Ill.-Chicago	27	707	26.2
5. Tim Roberts, Southern U.	26	680	26.2
6. Kareem Townes, La Salle	27	699	25.9
7. Joe Griffin, Long Island	28	723	25.8
8. Shawn Respert, Michigan St.	28	716	25.6
9. Rob Feaster, Holy Cross	27	672	24.9
10. Shannon Smith, Milwaukee	27	661	24.5

1996

Rk. Player, School	G	Pts.	Avg.
1. Kevin Granger, Texas Southern	24	648	27.0
2. Marcus Brown, Murray St.	29	767	26.4
3. Bubba Wells, Austin Peay	30	789	26.3
4. JaFonde Williams, Hampton	26	669	25.7
5. Bonzi Wells, Ball St.	28	712	25.4
6. Anquell McCollum, Western Caro.	30	751	25.0
7. Allen Iverson, Georgetown	37	926	25.0
8. Eddie Benton, Vermont	26	636	24.5
9. Matt Alosa, New Hampshire	26	624	24.0
10. Ray Allen, Connecticut	35	818	23.4

1997

Rk. Player, School	G	Pts.	Avg.
1. Charles Jones, Long Island	30	903	30.1
2. Ed Gray, California	26	644	24.8
3. Adonal Foyle, Colgate	28	682	24.4
4. Raymond Tutt, UC Santa Barbara	27	649	24.0
5. Antonio Daniels, Bowling Green	32	767	24.0
6. Donnie Carr, La Salle	27	646	23.9
7. Oliver Saint-Jean, San Jose St.	26	619	23.8
8. James Cotton, Long Beach St.	27	634	23.5
9. Roderick Blakney, South Caro. St.	28	655	23.4
10. Cory Carr, Texas Tech	28	646	23.1

1998

Rk. Player, School	G	Pts.	Avg.
1. Charles Jones, Long Island	30	869	29.0
2. Earl Boykins, Eastern Mich.	29	746	25.7
3. Lee Nailon, TCU	32	796	24.9
4. Brett Eppehimer, Lehigh	27	667	24.7
5. Cory Carr, Texas Tech	27	628	23.3
6. Pat Garrity, Notre Dame	27	627	23.2
7. Mike Powell, Loyola (Md.)	28	647	23.1
8. Bonzi Wells, Ball St.	29	662	22.8
9. Xavier Singletary, Howard	23	514	22.3
10. Michael Olowokandi, Pacific	33	734	22.2

1999

Rk.	Player, School	G	Pts.	Avg.
1.	Alvin Young, Niagara	29	728	25.1
2.	Ray Minlend, St. Francis (N.Y.)	28	680	24.3
3.	Wally Szczerbiak, Miami (Ohio)	32	775	24.2
4.	Brian Merriweather, Tex.-Pan American	27	641	23.7
5.	Damian Woolfolk, Norfolk St.	27	635	23.5
6.	Quincy Lewis, Minnesota	27	625	23.1
7.	Jason Hartman, Portland St.	28	639	22.8
8.	Lee Nailon, TCU	31	707	22.8
9.	Maurice Evans, Wichita St.	28	632	22.6
10.	Harold Arceneaux, Weber St.	32	713	22.3

2000

Rk.	Player, School	G	Pts.	Avg.
1.	Courtney Alexander, Fresno St.	27	669	24.8
2.	SirValiant Brown, George Washington	30	738	24.6
3.	Ronnie McCollum, Centenary (La.)	28	667	23.8
4.	Eddie House, Arizona St.	32	736	23.0
5.	Harold Arceneaux, Weber St.	28	644	23.0
6.	Rashad Phillips, Detroit	32	735	23.0
7.	Demond Stewart, Niagara	29	665	22.9
8.	Marcus Fizer, Iowa St.	37	844	22.8
9.	Craig Claxton, Hofstra	31	706	22.8
10.	Troy Murphy, Notre Dame	37	839	22.7

2001

Rk.	Player, School	G	Pts.	Avg.
1.	Ronnie McCollum, Centenary (La.)	27	787	29.1
2.	Kyle Hill, Eastern Ill.	31	737	23.8
3.	DeWayne Jefferson, Miss. Val.	27	637	23.6
4.	Tarise Bryson, Illinois St.	30	685	22.8
5.	Henry Domercant, Eastern Ill.	31	706	22.8
6.	Rahsad Phillips, Detroit	35	785	22.4
7.	Brandon Wolfram, UTEP	32	714	22.3
8.	Rasual Butler, La Salle	29	641	22.1
9.	Brandon Armstrong, Pepperdine	31	684	22.1
10.	Marvin O'Connor, St. Joseph's	32	706	22.1

2002

Rk.	Player, School	G	Pts.	Avg.
1.	Jason Conley, VMI	28	820	29.3
2.	Henry Domercant, Eastern Ill.	31	817	26.4
3.	Mire Chatman, Tex.-Pan American	29	760	26.2
4.	Ernest Bremer, St. Bonaventure	30	738	24.6
5.	Melvin Ely, Fresno St.	28	653	23.3
6.	Lynn Greer, Temple	31	719	23.2
7.	Nick Stapleton, Austin Peay	32	742	23.2
8.	Keith McLeod, Bowling Green	33	755	22.9
9.	Chris Davis, North Texas	29	653	22.5
10.	Ricky Minard, Morehead St.	29	646	22.3

2003

Rk.	Player, School	G	Pts.	Avg.
1.	Ruben Douglas, New Mexico	28	783	28.0
2.	Henry Domercant, Eastern Ill.	29	810	27.9
3.	Mike Helms, Oakland	28	752	26.9
4.	Michael Watson, UMKC	29	740	25.5
5.	Troy Bell, Boston College	31	781	25.2
6.	Keydren Clark, St. Peter's	29	722	24.9
7.	Luis Flores, Manhattan	30	739	24.6
8.	Chris Williams, Ball St.	30	736	24.5
9.	Mike Sweetney, Georgetown	34	776	22.8
10.	Kevin Martin, Western Caro.	24	546	22.8

2004

Rk.	Player, School	G	Pts.	Avg.
1.	Keydren Clark, St. Peter's	29	775	26.7
2.	Kevin Martin, Western Caro.	27	673	24.9
3.	David Hawkins, Temple	29	709	24.4
4.	Taylor Coppenrath, Vermont	24	579	24.1
5.	Luis Flores, Manhattan	31	744	24.0
6.	Michael Watson, UMKC	29	680	23.4
7.	Mike Helms, Oakland	30	695	23.2
8.	Odell Bradley, IUPUI	29	671	23.1
9.	Ike Diogu, Arizona St.	27	615	22.8
10.	Derrick Tarver, Akron	27	612	22.7

2005

Rk.	Player, School	G	Pts.	Avg.
1.	Keydren Clark, St. Peter's	28	721	25.8
2.	Taylor Coppenrath, Vermont	31	777	25.1
3.	Juan Mendez, Niagara	30	705	23.5
4.	Rob Monroe, Quinnipiac	26	589	22.7
5.	Bo McCalebb, New Orleans	30	679	22.6
6.	Ike Diogu, Arizona St.	32	724	22.6
7.	Tim Smith, East Tenn. St.	29	645	22.2
8.	Jose Juan Barea, Northeastern	30	665	22.2
9.	J.J. Redick, Duke	33	721	21.8
10.	Ryan Gomes, Providence	31	670	21.6

2006

Rk.	Player, School	G	Pts.	Avg.
1.	Adam Morrison, Gonzaga	33	926	28.1
2.	J.J. Redick, Duke	36	964	26.8
3.	Keydren Clark, St. Peter's	32	840	26.3
4.	Andre Collins, Loyola (Md.)	28	731	26.1
5.	Brion Rush, Grambling	21	541	25.8
6.	Quincy Douby, Rutgers	33	839	25.4
7.	Steve Burtt, Iona	31	780	25.2
8.	Rodney Stuckey, Eastern Wash.	30	726	24.2
9.	Alan Daniels, Lamar	31	730	23.5
10.	Trey Johnson, Jackson St.	32	751	23.5

2007

Rk.	Player, School	G	Pts.	Avg.
1.	Reggie Williams, VMI	33	928	28.1
2.	Trey Johnson, Jackson St.	35	947	27.1
3.	Morris Almond, Rice	32	844	26.4
4.	Kevin Durant, Texas	35	903	25.8
5.	Gary Neal, Towson	32	810	25.3
6.	Bo McCalebb, New Orleans	31	776	25.0
7.	Rodney Stuckey, Eastern Wash.	29	712	24.6
8.	Gerald Brown, Loyola (Md.)	29	643	22.2
9.	Stephen Curry, Davidson	34	730	21.5
10.	Jaycee Carroll, Utah St.	35	746	21.3

2008

Rk.	Player, School	G	Pts.	Avg.
1.	Reggie Williams, VMI	25	695	27.8
2.	Charron Fisher, Niagara	29	800	27.6
3.	Michael Beasley, Kansas St.	33	866	26.2
4.	Stephen Curry, Davidson	36	931	25.9
5.	Lester Hudson, Tenn.-Martin	33	847	25.7
6.	Arizona Reid, High Point	31	742	23.9
7.	Stefon Jackson, UTEP	33	778	23.6
8.	Robert McKiver, Houston	34	801	23.6
9.	Bo McCalebb, New Orleans	32	742	23.2
10.	David Holston, Chicago St.	28	646	23.1

Annual Individual Champions

DIVISION I

Scoring Average

Season	Player, Team	Ht.	Cl.	G	FG	FT	Pts.	Avg.
1948	Murray Wier, Iowa	5-9	Sr.	19	152	95	399	21.0
1949	Tony Lavelli, Yale	6-3	Sr.	30	228	215	671	22.4
1950	Paul Arizin, Villanova	6-3	Sr.	29	260	215	735	25.3
1951	Bill Mlkvy, Temple	6-4	Sr.	25	303	125	731	29.2
1952	Clyde Lovellette, Kansas	6-9	Sr.	28	315	165	795	28.4
1953	Frank Selvy, Furman	6-3	Jr.	25	272	194	738	29.5
1954	Frank Selvy, Furman	6-3	Sr.	29	427	*355	1,209	41.7
1955	Darrell Floyd, Furman	6-1	Jr.	25	344	209	897	35.9
1956	Darrell Floyd, Furman	6-1	Sr.	28	339	268	946	33.8
1957	Grady Wallace, South Carolina	6-4	Sr.	29	336	234	906	31.2
1958	Oscar Robertson, Cincinnati	6-5	So.	28	352	280	984	35.1
1959	Oscar Robertson, Cincinnati	6-5	Jr.	30	331	316	978	32.6
1960	Oscar Robertson, Cincinnati	6-5	Sr.	30	369	273	1,011	33.7
1961	Frank Burgess, Gonzaga	6-1	Sr.	26	304	234	842	32.4
1962	Billy McGill, Utah	6-9	Sr.	26	394	221	1,009	38.8
1963	Nick Werkman, Seton Hall	6-3	Jr.	22	221	208	650	29.5
1964	Howard Komives, Bowling Green	6-1	Sr.	23	292	260	844	36.7
1965	Rick Barry, Miami (Fla.)	6-7	Sr.	26	340	293	973	37.4
1966	Dave Schellhase, Purdue	6-4	Sr.	24	284	213	781	32.5
1967	Jim Walker, Providence	6-3	Sr.	28	323	205	851	30.4
1968	Pete Maravich, LSU	6-5	So.	26	432	274	1,138	43.8
1969	Pete Maravich, LSU	6-5	Jr.	26	433	282	1,148	44.2
1970	Pete Maravich, LSU	6-5	Sr.	31	*522	337	*1,381	*44.5
1971	Johnny Neumann, Mississippi	6-6	So.	23	366	191	923	40.1
1972	Dwight Lamar, La.-Lafayette	6-1	Jr.	29	429	196	1,054	36.3
1973	William Averitt, Pepperdine	6-1	Sr.	25	352	144	848	33.9
1974	Larry Fogle, Canisius	6-5	So.	25	326	183	835	33.4
1975	Bob McCurdy, Richmond	6-7	Sr.	26	321	213	855	32.9
1976	Marshall Rodgers, Tex.-Pan American	6-2	Sr.	25	361	197	919	36.8
1977	Freeman Williams, Portland St.	6-4	Jr.	26	417	176	1,010	38.8
1978	Freeman Williams, Portland St.	6-4	Sr.	27	410	149	969	35.9
1979	Lawrence Butler, Idaho St.	6-3	Sr.	27	310	192	812	30.1
1980	Tony Murphy, Southern U.	6-3	Sr.	29	377	178	932	32.1
1981	Zam Fredrick, South Carolina	6-2	Sr.	27	300	181	781	28.9
1982	Harry Kelly, Texas Southern	6-7	Jr.	29	336	190	862	29.7
1983	Harry Kelly, Texas Southern	6-7	Sr.	29	333	169	835	28.8
1984	Joe Jakubick, Akron	6-5	Sr.	27	304	206	814	30.1
1985	Xavier McDaniel, Wichita St.	6-8	Sr.	31	351	142	844	27.2
1986	Terrance Bailey, Wagner	6-2	Jr.	29	321	212	854	29.4
1987	Kevin Houston, Army	5-11	Sr.	29	311	268	953	32.9
1988	Hersey Hawkins, Bradley	6-3	Sr.	31	377	87	284	1,125	36.3
1989	Hank Gathers, Loyola Marymount	6-7	Jr.	31	419	0	177	1,015	32.7
1990	Bo Kimble, Loyola Marymount	6-5	Sr.	32	404	92	231	1,131	35.3
1991	Kevin Bradshaw, U.S. Int'l	6-6	Sr.	28	358	60	278	1,054	37.6
1992	Brett Roberts, Morehead St.	6-8	Sr.	29	278	66	193	815	28.1
1993	Greg Guy, Tex.-Pan American	6-1	Jr.	19	189	67	111	556	29.3
1994	Glenn Robinson, Purdue	6-8	Jr.	34	368	79	215	1,030	30.3
1995	Kurt Thomas, TCU	6-9	Sr.	27	288	3	202	781	28.9
1996	Kevin Granger, Texas Southern	6-3	Sr.	24	194	30	230	648	27.0
1997	Charles Jones, Long Island	6-3	Jr.	30	338	109	118	903	30.1
1998	Charles Jones, Long Island	6-3	Sr.	30	326	116	101	869	29.0
1999	Alvin Young, Niagara	6-3	Sr.	29	253	65	157	728	25.1
2000	Courtney Alexander, Fresno St.	6-6	Sr.	27	252	58	107	669	24.8
2001	Ronnie McCollum, Centenary (La.)	6-4	Sr.	27	244	85	214	787	29.1
2002	Jason Conley, VMI	6-5	Fr.	28	285	79	171	820	29.3
2003	Ruben Douglas, New Mexico	6-5	Sr.	28	218	94	253	783	28.0
2004	Keydren Clark, St. Peter's	5-8	So.	29	233	112	197	775	26.7
2005	Keydren Clark, St. Peter's	5-9	Jr.	28	230	109	152	721	25.8
2006	Adam Morrison, Gonzaga	6-8	Jr.	33	306	74	240	926	28.1
2007	Reggie Williams, VMI	6-6	Jr.	33	338	76	176	928	28.1
2008	Reggie Williams, VMI	6-6	Sr.	25	269	43	114	695	27.8

*record

Field-Goal Percentage

Season	Player, Team	Cl.	G	FG	FGA	Pct.
1948	Alex Peterson, Oregon St.	Jr.	27	89	187	47.6
1949	Ed Macauley, St. Louis	Sr.	26	144	275	52.4
1950	Jim Moran, Niagara	Jr.	27	98	185	53.0
1951	Don Meineke, Dayton	Jr.	32	240	469	51.2
1952	Art Spoelstra, Western Ky.	So.	31	178	345	51.6
1953	Vernon Stokes, St. Francis (N.Y)	Jr.	24	147	247	59.5
1954	Joe Holup, George Washington	So.	26	179	313	57.2
1955	Ed O'Connor, Manhattan	Sr.	23	147	243	60.5
1956	Joe Holup, George Washington	Sr.	26	200	309	64.7
1957	Bailey Howell, Mississippi St.	So.	25	217	382	56.8
1958	Ralph Crosthwaite, Western Ky.	Jr.	25	202	331	61.0
1959	Ralph Crosthwaite, Western Ky.	Sr.	26	191	296	64.5
1960	Jerry Lucas, Ohio St.	So.	27	283	444	63.7
1961	Jerry Lucas, Ohio St.	Jr.	27	256	411	62.3
1962	Jerry Lucas, Ohio St.	Sr.	28	237	388	61.1
1963	Lyle Harger, Houston	Sr.	26	193	294	65.6
1964	Terry Holland, Davidson	Sr.	26	135	214	63.1
1965	Tim Kehoe, St. Peter's	Sr.	19	138	209	66.0
1966	Julian Hammond, Tulsa	Sr.	29	172	261	65.9
1967	Lew Alcindor, UCLA	So.	30	346	519	66.7
1968	Joe Allen, Bradley	Sr.	28	258	394	65.5
1969	Lew Alcindor, UCLA	Sr.	30	303	477	63.5
1970	Willie Williams, Florida St.	Sr.	26	185	291	63.6
1971	John Belcher, Arkansas St.	Jr.	24	174	275	63.3
1972	Kent Martens, Abilene Christian	Sr.	21	136	204	66.7
1973	Elton Hayes, Lamar	Sr.	24	146	222	65.8
1974	Al Fleming, Arizona	So.	26	136	204	66.7
1975	Bernard King, Tennessee	Fr.	25	273	439	62.2
1976	Sidney Moncrief, Arkansas	Fr.	28	149	224	66.5
1977	Joe Senser, West Chester	So.	25	130	186	69.9
1978	Joe Senser, West Chester	Jr.	25	135	197	68.5
1979	Murray Brown, Florida St.	Sr.	29	237	343	69.1
1980	Steve Johnson, Oregon St.	Jr.	30	211	297	71.0
1981	Steve Johnson, Oregon St.	Sr.	28	235	315	*74.6
1982	Mark McNamara, California	Sr.	27	231	329	70.2
1983	Troy Lee Mikel, East Tenn. St.	Sr.	29	197	292	67.5
1984	Akeem Olajuwon, Houston	Jr.	37	249	369	67.5
1985	Keith Walker, Utica	Sr.	27	154	216	71.3
1986	Brad Daugherty, North Carolina	Sr.	34	284	438	64.8
1987	Alan Williams, Princeton	Sr.	25	163	232	70.3
1988	Arnell Jones, Boise St.	Sr.	30	187	283	66.1
1989	Dwayne Davis, Florida	So.	33	179	248	72.2
1990	Lee Campbell, Missouri St.	Sr.	29	192	275	69.8
1991	Oliver Miller, Arkansas	Jr.	38	254	361	70.4
1992	Charles Outlaw, Houston	Jr.	31	156	228	68.4
1993	Charles Outlaw, Houston	Sr.	30	196	298	65.8
1994	Mike Atkinson, Long Beach St.	Jr.	26	141	203	69.5
1995	Shane Kline-Ruminski, Bowling Green	Sr.	26	181	265	68.3
1996	Quadre Lollis, Montana St.	Sr.	30	212	314	67.5
1997	Todd MacCulloch, Washington	So.	28	163	241	67.6
1998	Todd MacCulloch, Washington	Jr.	30	225	346	65.0
1999	Todd MacCulloch, Washington	Sr.	29	210	317	66.2
2000	Brendan Haywood, North Carolina	Jr.	36	191	274	69.7
2001	Michael Bradley, Villanova	Jr.	31	254	367	69.2
2002	Adam Mark, Belmont	So.	26	150	212	70.8
2003	Adam Mark, Belmont	Jr.	28	199	297	67.0
2004	Nigel Dixon, Western Ky.	Sr.	28	179	264	67.8
2005	Bruce Brown, Hampton	Jr.	30	178	269	66.2
2006	Randall Hanke, Providence	So.	27	149	220	67.7
2007	Mike Freeman, Hampton	Fr.	30	162	239	67.8
2008	Kenny George, UNC Asheville	Jr.	28	151	217	69.6

*record

Three-Point Field Goals Made Per Game

Season	Player, Team	Cl.	G	3FG	Avg.
1987	Darrin Fitzgerald, Butler	Sr.	28	158	*5.64
1988	Timothy Pollard, Mississippi Val.	Jr.	28	132	4.71
1989	Timothy Pollard, Mississippi Val.	Sr.	28	124	4.43
1990	Dave Jamerson, Ohio	Sr.	28	131	4.68
1991	Bobby Phills, Southern U.	Sr.	28	123	4.39
1992	Doug Day, Radford	Jr.	29	117	4.03
1993	Bernard Haslett, Southern Miss.	Jr.	26	109	4.19
1994	Chris Brown, UC Irvine	Jr.	26	122	4.69
1995	Mitch Taylor, Southern U.	Jr.	25	109	4.36

Season	Player, Team	Cl.	G	3FG	Avg.
1996	Dominick Young, Fresno St.	Jr.	29	120	4.14
1997	William Fourche, Southern U.	Sr.	27	122	4.52
1998	Curtis Staples, Virginia	Sr.	30	130	4.33
1999	Brian Merriweather, Tex.-Pan American	So.	27	110	4.07
2000	Brian Merriweather, Tex.-Pan American	Jr.	28	114	4.07
2001	DeWayne Jefferson, Mississippi Val.	Sr.	27	107	3.96
2002	Cain Doliboa, Wright St.	Sr.	28	104	3.71
2003	Terrence Woods, Florida A&M	Jr.	28	139	4.96
2004	Terrence Woods, Florida A&M	Sr.	31	140	4.52
2005	Brendan Plavich, Charlotte	Sr.	29	114	3.93
2006	Andre Collins, Loyola (Md.)	Sr.	28	118	4.21
2007	Stephen Sir, Northern Ariz.	Sr.	30	124	4.13
2008	David Holston, Chicago St.	Jr.	28	130	4.64

*record

Three-Point Field-Goal Percentage

Season	Player, Team	Cl.	G	3FG	3FGA	Pct.
1987	Reginald Jones, Prairie View	Jr.	28	64	112	57.1
1988	Glenn Tropf, Holy Cross	Jr.	29	52	82	*63.4
1989	Dave Calloway, Monmouth	So.	28	48	82	58.5
1990	Matt Lapin, Princeton	Sr.	27	71	133	53.4
1991	Keith Jennings, East Tenn. St.	Sr.	33	84	142	59.2
1992	Sean Wightman, Western Mich.	Jr.	30	48	76	63.2
1993	Jeff Anderson, Kent St.	Jr.	26	44	82	53.7
1994	Brent Kell, Evansville	So.	29	62	123	50.4
1995	Brian Jackson, Evansville	Jr.	27	53	95	55.8
1996	Joe Stafford, Western Caro.	Jr.	30	58	110	52.7
1997	Kent McCausland, Iowa	So.	29	70	134	52.2
1998	Jim Cantamessa, Siena	So.	29	66	117	56.4
1999	Rodney Thomas, IUPUI	Jr.	26	59	113	52.2
2000	Jonathan Whitworth, Middle Tenn.	Jr.	28	50	99	50.5
2001	Amory Sanders, Southeast Mo. St.	Sr.	24	53	95	55.8
2002	Dante Swanson, Tulsa	Jr.	33	73	149	49.0
2003	Jeff Schiffner, Penn	Jr.	28	74	150	49.3
2004	Brad Lechtenberg, San Diego	Jr.	23	71	139	51.1
2005	Salim Stoudamire, Arizona	Sr.	36	120	238	50.4
2006	Stephen Sir, Northern Ariz.	Sr.	32	93	190	48.9
2007	Josh Carter, Texas A&M	So.	34	86	172	50.0
	Jeremy Crouch, Bradley	Jr.	27	83	166	50.0
2008	Jaycee Carroll, Utah St.	Sr.	35	114	229	49.8

*record

Free-Throw Percentage

Season	Player, Team	Cl.	G	FT	FTA	Pct.
1948	Sam Urzetta, St. Bonaventure	So.	22	59	64	92.2
1949	Bill Schroer, Valparaiso	So.	24	59	68	86.8
1950	Sam Urzetta, St. Bonaventure	Sr.	22	54	61	88.5
1951	Jay Handlan, Wash. & Lee	Jr.	22	148	172	86.0
1952	Sy Chadroff, Miami (Fla.)	Sr.	22	99	123	80.5
1953	John Weber, Yale	Sr.	24	117	141	83.0
1954	Dick Daugherty, Arizona St.	Sr.	23	75	86	87.2
1955	Jim Scott, West Tex. A&M	Sr.	23	153	171	89.5
1956	Bill Von Weyhe, Rhode Island	Jr.	25	180	208	86.5
1957	Ernie Wiggins, Wake Forest	Sr.	28	93	106	87.7
1958	Semi Mintz, Davidson	Sr.	24	105	119	88.2
1959	Arlen Clark, Oklahoma St.	Sr.	25	201	236	85.2
1960	Jack Waters, Mississippi	Jr.	24	103	118	87.3
1961	Stew Sherard, Army	Jr.	24	135	154	87.7
1962	Tommy Boyer, Arkansas	Jr.	23	125	134	93.3
1963	Tommy Boyer, Arkansas	Sr.	24	147	161	91.3
1964	Rick Park, Tulsa	Jr.	25	121	134	90.3
1965	Bill Bradley, Princeton	Sr.	29	273	308	88.6
1966	Bill Blair, Providence	Sr.	27	101	112	90.2
1967	Bob Lloyd, Rutgers	Sr.	29	255	277	92.1
1968	Joe Heiser, Princeton	Sr.	26	117	130	90.0
1969	Bill Justus, Tennessee	Sr.	28	133	147	90.5
1970	Steve Kaplan, Rutgers	So.	23	102	110	92.7
1971	Greg Starrick, Southern Ill.	Jr.	23	119	132	90.2
1972	Greg Starrick, Southern Ill.	Sr.	26	148	160	92.5
1973	Don Smith, Dayton	Jr.	26	111	122	91.0
1974	Rickey Medlock, Arkansas	Jr.	26	87	95	91.6
1975	Frank Oleynick, Seattle	Jr.	26	135	152	88.8
1976	Tad Dufelmeier, Loyola (Ill.)	Jr.	25	71	80	88.8
1977	Robert Smith, UNLV	Sr.	32	98	106	92.5
1978	Carlos Gibson, Marshall	Jr.	28	84	89	94.4
1979	Darrell Mauldin, Campbell	Jr.	26	70	76	92.1
1980	Brian Magid, George Washington	Sr.	26	79	85	92.9

Season	Player, Team	Cl.	G	FT	FTA	Pct.
1981	Dave Hildahl, Portland St.	Sr.	21	76	82	92.7
1982	Rod Foster, UCLA	Jr.	27	95	100	95.0
1983	Rob Gonzalez, Colorado	Sr.	28	75	82	91.5
1984	Steve Alford, Indiana	Fr.	31	137	150	91.3
1985	Craig Collins, Penn St.	Sr.	27	94	98	95.9
1986	Jim Barton, Dartmouth	Fr.	26	65	69	94.2
1987	Kevin Houston, Army	Sr.	29	268	294	91.2
1988	Steve Henson, Kansas St.	So.	34	111	120	92.5
1989	Michael Smith, BYU	Sr.	29	160	173	92.5
1990	Rob Robbins, New Mexico	Jr.	34	101	108	93.5
1991	Darin Archbold, Butler	Jr.	29	187	205	91.2
1992	Don MacLean, UCLA	Sr.	32	197	214	92.1
1993	Josh Grant, Utah	Sr.	31	104	113	92.0
1994	Danny Basile, Marist	So.	27	84	89	94.4
1995	Greg Bibb, Tennessee Tech	Jr.	27	106	117	90.6
1996	Mike Dillard, Sam Houston St.	Jr.	25	63	68	92.6
1997	Aaron Zobrist, Bradley	Sr.	30	77	85	90.6
1998	Matt Sundblad, Lamar	Jr.	27	96	104	92.3
1999	Lonnie Cooper, Louisiana Tech	Sr.	25	70	76	92.1
2000	Clay McKnight, Pacific	Sr.	24	74	78	94.9
2001	Gary Buchanan, Villanova	So.	31	97	103	94.2
2002	Cary Cochran, Nebraska	Sr.	28	71	77	92.2
2003	Steve Drabyn, Belmont	Jr.	29	78	82	95.1
2004	Blake Ahearn, Missouri St.	Fr.	33	117	120	*97.5
2005	Blake Ahearn, Missouri St.	So.	32	90	95	94.7
2006	Blake Ahearn, Missouri St.	Jr.	31	117	125	93.6
2007	Derek Raivio, Gonzaga	Sr.	34	148	154	96.1
2008	Tyler Relph, St. Bonaventure	Sr.	29	75	80	93.8

*record

Rebound Average

Season	Player, Team	Ht.	Cl.	G	Reb.	Avg.
1951	Ernie Beck, Penn	6-4	So.	27	556	20.6
1952	Bill Hannon, Army	6-3	So.	17	355	20.9
1953	Ed Conlin, Fordham	6-5	So.	26	612	23.5
1954	Art Quimby, Connecticut	6-5	Jr.	26	588	22.6
1955	Charlie Slack, Marshall	6-5	Jr.	21	538	*25.6
1956	Joe Holup, George Washington	6-6	Sr.	26	604	†.256
1957	Elgin Baylor, Seattle	6-6	Jr.	25	508	†.235
1958	Alex Ellis, Niagara	6-5	Sr.	25	536	†.262
1959	Leroy Wright, Pacific	6-8	Jr.	26	652	†.238
1960	Leroy Wright, Pacific	6-8	Sr.	17	380	†.234
1961	Jerry Lucas, Ohio St.	6-8	Jr.	27	470	†.198
1962	Jerry Lucas, Ohio St.	6-8	Sr.	28	499	†.211
1963	Paul Silas, Creighton	6-7	Sr.	27	557	20.6
1964	Bob Pelkington, Xavier	6-7	Sr.	26	567	21.8
1965	Toby Kimball, Connecticut	6-8	Sr.	23	483	21.0
1966	Jim Ware, Oklahoma City	6-8	Sr.	29	607	20.9
1967	Dick Cunningham, Murray St.	6-10	Jr.	22	479	21.8
1968	Neal Walk, Florida	6-10	Jr.	25	494	19.8
1969	Spencer Haywood, Detroit	6-8	So.	22	472	21.5
1970	Artis Gilmore, Jacksonville	7-2	Jr.	28	621	22.2
1971	Artis Gilmore, Jacksonville	7-2	Sr.	26	603	23.2
1972	Kermit Washington, American	6-8	Jr.	23	455	19.8
1973	Kermit Washington, American	6-8	Sr.	22	439	20.0
1974	Marvin Barnes, Providence	6-9	Sr.	32	597	18.7
1975	John Irving, Hofstra	6-9	So.	21	323	15.4
1976	Sam Pellom, Buffalo	6-8	So.	26	420	16.2
1977	Glenn Mosley, Seton Hall	6-8	Sr.	29	473	16.3
1978	Ken Williams, North Texas	6-7	Sr.	28	411	14.7
1979	Monti Davis, Tennessee St.	6-7	Jr.	26	421	16.2
1980	Larry Smith, Alcorn St.	6-8	Sr.	26	392	15.1
1981	Darryl Watson, Mississippi Val.	6-7	Sr.	27	379	14.0
1982	LaSalle Thompson, Texas	6-10	Jr.	27	365	13.5
1983	Xavier McDaniel, Wichita St.	6-7	So.	28	403	14.4
1984	Akeem Olajuwon, Houston	7-0	Jr.	37	500	13.5
1985	Xavier McDaniel, Wichita St.	6-8	Sr.	31	460	14.8
1986	David Robinson, Navy	6-11	Jr.	35	455	13.0
1987	Jerome Lane, Pittsburgh	6-6	So.	33	444	13.5
1988	Kenny Miller, Loyola (Ill.)	6-9	Fr.	29	395	13.6
1989	Hank Gathers, Loyola Marymount	6-7	Jr.	31	426	13.7
1990	Anthony Bonner, St. Louis	6-8	Sr.	33	456	13.8
1991	Shaquille O'Neal, LSU	7-1	So.	28	411	14.7
1992	Popeye Jones, Murray St.	6-8	Sr.	30	431	14.4
1993	Warren Kidd, Middle Tenn.	6-9	Sr.	26	386	14.8
1994	Jerome Lambert, Baylor	6-8	Jr.	24	355	14.8
1995	Kurt Thomas, TCU	6-9	Sr.	27	393	14.6
1996	Marcus Mann, Mississippi Val.	6-8	Sr.	29	394	13.6
1997	Tim Duncan, Wake Forest	6-11	Sr.	31	457	14.7
1998	Ryan Perryman, Dayton	6-7	Sr.	33	412	12.5

Season	Player, Team	Ht.	Cl.	G	Reb.	Avg.
1999	Ian McGinnis, Dartmouth	6-8	So.	26	317	12.2
2000	Darren Phillip, Fairfield	6-7	Sr.	29	405	14.0
2001	Chris Marcus, Western Ky.	7-1	Jr.	31	374	12.1
2002	Jeremy Bishop, Quinnipiac	6-6	Jr.	29	347	12.0
2003	Brandon Hunter, Ohio	6-7	Sr.	30	378	12.6
2004	Paul Millsap, Louisiana Tech	6-7	Fr.	30	374	12.5
2005	Paul Millsap, Louisiana Tech	6-8	So.	29	360	12.4
2006	Paul Millsap, Louisiana Tech	6-8	Jr.	33	438	13.3
2007	Rashad Jones-Jennings, UALR	6-8	Sr.	30	392	13.1
2008	Michael Beasley, Kansas St.	6-10	Fr.	33	408	12.4

*record; †From 1956 through 1962, championship was determined on highest individual recoveries out of total by both teams in all games.

Assist Average

Season	Player, Team	Cl.	G	Ast.	Avg.
1951	Bill Walker, Toledo	Sr.	29	210	7.24
1952	Tom O'Toole, Boston College	Sr.	27	213	7.89
1984	Craig Lathen, Ill.-Chicago	Jr.	29	274	9.45
1985	Rob Weingard, Hofstra	Sr.	24	228	9.50
1986	Mark Jackson, St. John's (N.Y.)	Jr.	36	328	9.11
1987	Avery Johnson, Southern U.	Jr.	31	333	10.74
1988	Avery Johnson, Southern U.	Sr.	30	399	*13.30
1989	Glenn Williams, Holy Cross	Sr.	28	278	9.93
1990	Todd Lehmann, Drexel	Sr.	28	260	9.29
1991	Chris Corchiani, North Carolina St.	Sr.	31	299	9.65
1992	Van Usher, Tennessee Tech	Sr.	29	254	8.76
1993	Sam Crawford, New Mexico St.	Sr.	34	310	9.12
1994	Jason Kidd, California	So.	30	272	9.07
1995	Nelson Haggerty, Baylor	Sr.	28	284	10.14
1996	Raimonds Miglinieks, UC Irvine	Sr.	27	230	8.52
1997	Kenny Mitchell, Dartmouth	Sr.	26	203	7.81
1998	Ahlon Lewis, Arizona St.	Sr.	32	294	9.19
1999	Doug Gottlieb, Oklahoma St.	Jr.	34	299	8.79
2000	Mark Dickel, UNLV	Sr.	31	280	9.03
2001	Markus Carr, Cal St. Northridge	Jr.	32	286	8.94
2002	T.J. Ford, Texas	Fr.	33	273	8.27
2003	Martell Bailey, Ill.-Chicago	Jr.	30	244	8.13
2004	Greg Davis, Troy	Sr.	31	256	8.26
2005	Damitrius Coleman, Mercer	Jr.	28	224	8.00
	Will Funn, Portland St.	Sr.	28	224	8.00
2006	Jared Jordan, Marist	Jr.	29	247	8.52
2007	Jared Jordan, Marist	Sr.	33	286	8.67
2008	Jason Richards, Davidson	Sr.	36	293	8.14

*record

Assist-to-Turnover Ratio

Season	Player, Team	Cl.	G	Ast.	TO	Ratio
2008	Cliff Clinkscales, DePaul	Sr.	30	123	34	3.62

Blocked-Shot Average

Season	Player, Team	Cl.	G	Blk.	Avg.
1986	David Robinson, Navy	Jr.	35	207	5.91
1987	David Robinson, Navy	Sr.	32	144	4.50
1988	Rodney Blake, St. Joseph's	Sr.	29	116	4.00
1989	Alonzo Mourning, Georgetown	Fr.	34	169	4.97
1990	Kenny Green, Rhode Island	Sr.	26	124	4.77
1991	Shawn Bradley, BYU	Fr.	34	177	5.21
1992	Shaquille O'Neal, LSU	Jr.	30	157	5.23
1993	Theo Ratliff, Wyoming	Jr.	28	124	4.43
1994	Grady Livingston, Howard	Jr.	26	115	4.42
1995	Keith Closs, Central Conn. St.	Fr.	26	139	5.35
1996	Keith Closs, Central Conn. St.	So.	28	178	6.36
1997	Adonal Foyle, Colgate	Jr.	28	180	*6.43
1998	Jerome James, Florida A&M	Sr.	27	125	4.63
1999	Tarvis Williams, Hampton	So.	27	135	5.00
2000	Ken Johnson, Ohio St.	Sr.	30	161	5.37
2001	Tarvis Williams, Hampton	Sr.	32	147	4.59
2002	Wojciech Myrda, La.-Monroe	Sr.	32	172	5.38
2003	Emeka Okafor, Connecticut	So.	33	156	4.73
2004	Anwar Ferguson, Houston	Sr.	27	111	4.11
2005	Deng Gai, Fairfield	Sr.	30	165	5.50
2006	Shawn James, Northeastern	So.	30	196	6.53
2007	Mickell Gladness, Alabama A&M	Jr.	30	188	6.27
2008	Jarvis Varnado, Mississippi St.	So.	34	157	4.62

*record

Steal Average

Season	Player, Team	Cl.	G	Stl.	Avg.
1986	Darron Brittman, Chicago St.	Sr.	28	139	4.96
1987	Tony Fairley, Charleston So.	Sr.	28	114	4.07
1988	Aldwin Ware, Florida A&M	Sr.	29	142	4.90
1989	Kenny Robertson, Cleveland St.	Jr.	28	111	3.96
1990	Ronn McMahon, Eastern Wash.	Sr.	29	130	4.48
1991	Van Usher, Tennessee Tech	Jr.	28	104	3.71
1992	Victor Snipes, Northeastern Ill.	So.	25	86	3.44
1993	Jason Kidd, California	Fr.	29	110	3.79
1994	Shawn Griggs, La.-Lafayette	Sr.	30	120	4.00
1995	Roderick Anderson, Texas	Sr.	30	101	3.37
1996	Pointer Williams, McNeese St.	Sr.	27	118	4.37
1997	Joel Hoover, Md.-East. Shore	Fr.	28	90	3.21
1998	Bonzi Wells, Ball St.	Sr.	29	103	3.55
1999	Shawnta Rogers, George Washington	Sr.	29	103	3.55
2000	Carl Williams, Liberty	Sr.	28	107	3.82
2001	Greedy Daniels, TCU	Jr.	25	108	4.32
2002	Desmond Cambridge, Alabama A&M	Sr.	29	160	*5.52
2003	Alexis McMillan, Stetson	Sr.	22	87	3.95
2004	Marques Green, St. Bonaventure	Sr.	27	107	3.96
2005	Obie Trotter, Alabama A&M	Jr.	32	125	3.91
2006	Tim Smith, East Tenn. St.	Sr.	28	95	3.39
2007	Travis Holmes, VMI	So.	33	111	3.36
2008	Devin Gibson, UTSA	Fr.	28	93	3.32

*record

Miscellaneous Player Information

Declared Early for the NBA Draft

Year	4-Year College Underclassmen	Jr. Col.	High School	U.S.	Foreign Country	Declared	Drafted	Total W/drew#
1971	6	0	0	6	0	6	5	0
1972	6	2	0	8	0	8	3	2
1973	10	1	0	11	0	11	7	2
1974	18	2	1	21	0	21	11	7
1975	13	1	2	16	0	16	14	0
1976	12	1	0	13	0	13	7	0
1977	6	0	0	6	0	6	4	0
1978	4	1	0	5	0	5	4	0
1979	4	0	0	4	0	4	4	0
1980	6	1	0	7	0	7	4	0
1981	5	0	0	5	0	5	5	0
1982	13	0	0	13	0	13	9	1
1983	6	0	0	6	0	6	4	0
1984	9	0	0	9	0	9	8	0
1985	12	0	0	12	0	12	11	0
1986	9	0	0	9	0	9	7	0
1987	9	0	0	9	0	9	5	0
1988	12	0	0	12	0	12	8	0

Year	4-Year College Underclassmen	Jr. Col.	High School	U.S.	Foreign Country	Declared	Drafted	Total W/drew#
1989	10	3	0	13	1	14	6	0
1990	22	1	0	23	0	23	7	0
1991	11	0	0	11	1	12	6	0
1992	14	2	0	16	0	16	4	0
1993	13	5	0	18	1	19	7	0
1994	20	0	0	20	0	20	12	2
1995	14	2	1	17	0	17	13	3
1996	25	4	4	33	4	37	21	6
1997	19	0	1	20	0	20	12	6
1998	26	2	4	32	3	35	20	3
1999	18	3	2	23	4	27	15	12
2000	25	2	2	29	8	37	25	19
2001	34	7	6	47	8	55	37	23
2002	33	8	4	45	9	54	29	24
2003	22	3	5	30	21	51	35	29
2004	19	3	10	32	10	42	27	54
2005	35	4	11	50	10	60	37	65
2006	33	4	0	37	10	47	33	41
2007	43	2	0	45	12	57	32	15
2008	43	3	0	46	39	85	41	22

#Those athletes who withdrew before the draft are not included in any of the other columns.

Foreign Players at NCAA Division I Schools

Players whose home towns on their schools' rosters were listed as being from a country other than the U.S.

Year	Div. I Schools	Foreign Players
1993	298	135
1994	301	—
1995	302	178
1996	305	212
1997	305	238
1998	306	268

Year	Div. I Schools	Foreign Players
1999	310	291
2000	318	285
2001	318	340
2002	321	366
2003	325	392
2004	326	392
2005	326	396
2006	326	402
2007	325	424
2008	328	406

All-Time Team Leaders

Single-Game Records

SCORING HIGHS

Pts.	Team vs. Opponent (Opp. Pts.)	Date
186	Loyola Marymount vs. U.S. Int'l (140)	Jan. 5, 1991
181	Loyola Marymount vs. U.S. Int'l (150)	Jan. 31, 1989
179	Long Island vs. Medgar Evers (62)	Nov. 26, 1997
173	Oklahoma vs. U.S. Int'l (101)	Nov. 29, 1989
172	Oklahoma vs. Loyola Marymount (112)	Dec. 15, 1990
166	Arkansas vs. U.S. Int'l (101)	Dec. 9, 1989
164	UNLV vs. Hawaii-Hilo (111)	Feb. 19, 1976
164	Loyola Marymount vs. Azusa-Pacific (138)	Nov. 28, 1988
162	Loyola Marymount vs. U.S. Int'l (144)	Jan. 7, 1989
162	Loyola Marymount vs. Chaminade (129)	Nov. 25, 1990
162	Oklahoma vs. Angelo St. (99)	Dec. 1, 1990
162	Drake vs. Grinnell (110)	Dec. 11, 2002
159	Southern U. vs. Texas College (65)	Dec. 6, 1990
159	LSU vs. Northern Ariz. (86)	Dec. 28, 1991
159	Cal St. Northridge vs. Redlands (97)	Nov. 15, 2006
157	Loyola Marymount vs. San Francisco (115)	Feb. 5, 1990
156	Southern U. vs. Baptist Christian (91)	Dec. 14, 1992
156	South Ala. vs. Prairie View (114)	Dec. 2, 1994
156	VMI vs. Va. Intermont (95)	Nov. 15, 2006
156	VMI vs. Columbia Union (91)	Nov. 28, 2007
155	Oral Roberts vs. Union (Tenn.) (113)	Feb. 24, 1972
155	Southern U. vs. Prairie View (91)	Feb. 22, 1993
154	Texas-Arlington vs. Huston-Tillotson (85)	Nov. 29, 1990
154	Southern U. vs. Patten (57)	Nov. 26, 1993
153	TCU vs. Tex.-Pan American (87)	Nov. 29, 1997

SCORING HIGHS BY LOSING TEAM

Pts.	Team vs. Opponent (Opp. Pts.)	Date
150	U.S. Int'l vs. Loyola Marymount (181)	Jan. 31, 1989
144	U.S. Int'l vs. Loyola Marymount (162)	Jan. 7, 1989
141	Loyola Marymount vs. LSU (148) (ot)	Feb. 3, 1990
140	Utah St. vs. UNLV (142) (3 ot)	Jan. 2, 1985
140	U.S. Int'l vs. Loyola Marymount (186)	Jan. 5, 1991
140	Long Island vs. St. Francis (N.Y.) (142) (2 ot)	Feb. 22, 2003
137	U.S. Int'l vs. Loyola Marymount (152)	Dec. 7, 1989
136	Gonzaga vs. Loyola Marymount (147)	Feb. 18, 1989
132	Troy vs. George Mason (148)	Dec. 10, 1994
130	Fairleigh Dickinson vs. Sacred Heart (133) (4 ot)	Dec. 1, 2001
127	Pepperdine vs. Loyola Marymount (142)	Feb. 20, 1988
127	Troy vs. George Mason (142)	Nov. 28, 1995
126	Western Mich. vs. Marshall (127)	Dec. 20, 1999
125	Nevada vs. Loyola Marymount (130)	Dec. 30, 1988
123	San Francisco vs. Loyola Marymount (137)	Feb. 9, 1990
123	Loyola Marymount vs. Pepperdine (148)	Feb. 17, 1990
123	Loyola Marymount vs. Northeastern (152)	Nov. 24, 1990
123	Sam Houston St. vs. Texas-Arlington (125)	Dec. 28, 1998
122	Oral Roberts vs. Oklahoma (152)	Dec. 10, 1988
121	Loyola Marymount vs. LSU (148) (ot)	Feb. 3, 1990
121	Loyola Marymount vs. Oklahoma (136)	Dec. 23, 1989
121	Central Mich. vs. Ohio (122) (2 ot)	Feb. 5, 1998

SCORING HIGHS BOTH TEAMS COMBINED

Pts.	Team (Pts.) vs. Team (Pts.)	Date
331	Loyola Marymount (181) vs. U.S. Int'l (150)	Jan. 31, 1989
326	Loyola Marymount (186) vs. U.S. Int'l (140)	Jan. 5, 1991
306	Loyola Marymount (162) vs. U.S. Int'l (144)	Jan. 7, 1989

Pts.	Team (Pts.) vs. Team (Pts.)	Date
289	Loyola Marymount (152) vs. U.S. Int'l (137)	Dec. 7, 1989
289	LSU (148) vs. Loyola Marymount (141) (ot)	Feb. 3, 1990
284	Oklahoma (172) vs. Loyola Marymount (112)	Dec. 15, 1990
283	Loyola Marymount (147) vs. Gonzaga (136)	Feb. 18, 1989
282	UNLV (142) vs. Utah St. (140) (3 ot)	Jan. 2, 1985
282	St. Francis (N.Y.) (142) vs. Long Island (140) (2 ot)	Feb. 22, 2003
280	George Mason (148) vs. Troy (132)	Dec. 10, 1994
275	Northeastern (152) vs. Loyola Marymount (123)	Nov. 24, 1990
274	Oklahoma (152) vs. Oral Roberts (122)	Dec. 10, 1988
274	Oklahoma (173) vs. U.S. Int'l (101)	Nov. 29, 1989
272	Loyola Marymount (157) vs. San Francisco (115)	Feb. 4, 1990
269	Loyola Marymount (142) vs. Pepperdine (127)	Feb. 20, 1988
269	Loyola Marymount (150) vs. St. Mary's (Cal.) (119)	Feb. 1, 1990
269	George Mason (142) vs. Troy (127)	Nov. 28, 1995

MARGIN OF VICTORY

Pts.	Team (Pts.) vs. Opponent (Opp. Pts.)	Date
117	Long Island (179) vs. Medgar Evers (62)	Nov. 26, 1997
106	Purdue (112) vs. Indiana St. (6)	Jan. 10, 1911
101	Texas (102) vs. San Marcos Baptist (1)	Jan. 10, 1916
97	Southern U. (154) vs. Patten (57)	Nov. 26, 1993
97	Winthrop (130) vs. Johnson & Wales (33)	Dec. 7, 1996
96	Western Ky. (103) vs. Adairville Independents (7)	Jan. 10, 1923
95	Oklahoma (146) vs. Northeastern Ill. (51)	Dec. 2, 1989
94	Southern U. (159) vs. Texas College (65)	Dec. 6, 1990
93	Washington (100) vs. Puget Sound (7)	Jan. 14, 1921
93	Furman (126) vs. Va. Intermont (33)	Dec. 29, 2004
92	Villanova (117) vs. Philadelphia NAMC (25)	Feb. 12, 1949
91	LSU (124) vs. Rhodes (33)	Dec. 8, 1952
91	Tennessee St. (148) vs. Fisk (57)	Dec. 6, 1993
91	Tulsa (141) vs. Prairie View (50)	Dec. 7, 1995
89	Northwestern La. vs. LeTourneau (51)	Jan. 20, 1992
89	Nicholls St. (140) vs. Faith Baptist (51)	Dec. 17, 1994
88	Southern U. (132) vs. Faith Baptist (44)	Dec. 12, 1994
88	Prairie View (129) vs. Okla. Baptist (41)	Jan. 21, 1997
87	Canisius (107) vs. St. Ann's (20)	Dec. 8, 1907
86	Ohio St. (88) vs. Ohio (2)	Feb. 6, 1903
86	Southeastern La. (126) vs. Dallas Christian (40)	Nov. 16, 2007
84	Rhode Island (118) vs. Fort Varnum (34)	Nov. 20, 1943
83	Texas (89) vs. Texas St. (6)	Feb. 11, 1919
82	Navy (126) vs. McDaniel (44)	Dec. 3, 1952
82	Morehead St. (130) vs. Asbury (48)	Nov. 30, 1996

MARGIN OF VICTORY VS. DIVISION I OPPONENT (SINCE 1938)

Pts.	Team (Pts.) vs. Opponent (Opp. Pts.)	Date
91	Tulsa (141) vs. Prairie View (50)	Dec. 7, 1995
81	Oklahoma (146) vs. Florida A&M (65)	Jan. 27, 1993
80	Minnesota (114) vs. Alabama St. (34)	Dec. 23, 1996
77	Kentucky (143) vs. Georgia (66)	Feb. 27, 1956
76	Duke (130) vs. Harvard (54)	Nov. 25, 1989
75	Maryland (132) vs. North Texas (57)	Dec. 23, 1998
75	LSU (112) vs. Grambling (37)	Nov. 20, 1999
75	Florida (125) vs. Florida A&M (50)	Dec. 10, 2000
74	Kentucky (124) vs. Tenn.-Martin (50)	Nov. 26, 1994
74	Texas A&M (101) vs. Grambling (27)	Dec. 28, 2006
73	LSU (159) vs. Northern Ariz. (86)	Dec. 28, 1991
72	Iowa (103) vs. Chicago (31)	Feb. 5, 1944
72	Oklahoma (173) vs. U.S. Int'l (101)	Nov. 29, 1989
72	Ohio St. (116) vs. Chicago St. (44)	Nov. 30, 1991
72	Missouri (117) vs. Chicago St. (45)	Dec. 2, 1995
72	Texas Tech (107) vs. Nicholls (35)	Dec. 7, 2002
71	Ohio St. (109) vs. Delaware (38)	Jan. 11, 1960
71	New Mexico (71) vs. Dartmouth (36)	Dec. 29, 1972
71	Dayton (109) vs. Bowling Green (38)	Dec. 11, 1954
70	Massachusetts (108) vs. Maine (38)	Feb. 23, 1974
70	Kansas (115) vs. Brown (45)	Jan. 3, 1989
70	Connecticut (116) vs. Central Conn. St. (46)	Jan. 23, 1996
70	Memphis (112) vs. Howard (42)	Jan. 3, 2001
70	Duquesne (129) vs. Howard (59)	Nov. 9, 2007
69	Kentucky (98) vs. Vanderbilt (29)	Feb. 27, 1947
69	Lamar (126) vs. Sam Houston St. (57)	Dec. 30, 1991
69	Tennessee (109) vs. Middle Tenn. (40)	Nov. 20, 2007

SCORING HIGHS IN A HALF

Pts.	Team vs. Opponent (Half)	Date
98	Long Island vs. Medgar Evers (2nd)	Nov. 26, 1997
97	Oklahoma vs. U.S. Int'l (1st)	Nov. 29, 1989
96	Southern U. vs. Texas College (2nd)	Dec. 6, 1990
94	Loyola Marymount vs. U.S. Int'l (1st)	Jan. 31, 1989
94	Oklahoma vs. Northeastern Ill. (2nd)	Dec. 2, 1989
94	Loyola Marymount vs. U.S. Int'l (1st)	Jan. 5, 1991

Pts.	Team vs. Opponent (Half)	Date
93	Loyola Marymount vs. U.S. Int'l (1st)	Jan. 7, 1989
93	Oklahoma vs. Loyola Marymount (2nd)	Dec. 15, 1990
92	Loyola Marymount vs. U.S. Int'l (2nd)	Jan. 5, 1991
92	Alabama St. vs. Grambling (2nd)	Jan. 21, 1991
91	Oklahoma vs. Angelo St. (2nd)	Dec. 1, 1990
87	Oklahoma vs. Oral Roberts (2nd)	Dec. 10, 1988
87	Loyola Marymount vs. U.S. Int'l (2nd)	Jan. 31, 1989
86	Jacksonville vs. St. Peter's (2nd)	Dec. 3, 1970
86	Lamar vs. Portland St. (2nd)	Jan. 12, 1980
86	Loyola Marymount vs. Gonzaga (2nd)	Feb. 18, 1989
86	Gonzaga vs. Loyola Marymount (2nd)	Feb. 18, 1989
86	Kentucky vs. LSU (1st)	Jan. 16, 1996
86	Cal St. Northridge vs. Redlands (2nd)	Nov. 15, 2006

SCORING HIGHS IN A HALF BOTH TEAMS COMBINED

Pts.	Team (Pts.) vs. Team (Pts.) (Half)	Date
172	Loyola Marymount (86) vs. Gonzaga (86) (2nd)	Feb. 18, 1989
170	Loyola Marymount (94) vs. U.S. Int'l (76) (1st)	Jan. 31, 1989
164	Loyola Marymount (94) vs. U.S. Int'l (70) (1st)	Jan. 5, 1991
162	Loyola Marymount (92) vs. U.S. Int'l (70) (2nd)	Jan. 5, 1991
161	Loyola Marymount (93) vs. U.S. Int'l (68) (1st)	Jan. 7, 1989
161	Loyola Marymount (87) vs. U.S. Int'l (74) (2nd)	Jan. 31, 1989
160	Oklahoma (87) vs. Oral Roberts (73) (2nd)	Dec. 10, 1988

FEWEST POINTS SCORED IN A GAME SINCE 1938

Pts.	Team vs. Opponent (Opp. Pts.)	Date
6	Temple vs. Tennessee (11)	Dec. 15, 1974
9	Pittsburgh vs. Penn St. (24)	Mar. 1, 1952
10	Duke vs. North Carolina St. (12)	Mar. 8, 1968
11	Oklahoma vs. Oklahoma St. (14)	Feb. 19, 1944
11	Tennessee vs. Temple (6)	Dec. 15, 1974
11	Cincinnati vs. Kentucky (24)	Dec. 20, 1983
12	Marquette vs. Creighton (57)	Dec. 16, 1940
12	Pittsburgh vs. Penn St. (15)	Jan. 15, 1944
12	North Carolina St. vs. Duke (10)	Mar. 8, 1968
13	Pittsburgh vs. Penn St. (32)	Feb. 20, 1943
13	Illinois vs. Purdue (23)	Feb. 7, 1938
14	Virginia vs. Navy (36)	Jan. 12, 1938
14	Michigan St. vs. Michigan (42)	Dec. 7, 1940
14	Kansas St. vs. Missouri (38)	Mar. 4, 1944
14	Oklahoma St. vs. Oklahoma (11)	Feb. 19, 1944
14	Alabama vs. Tennessee (23)	Jan. 11, 1945
15	Alabama vs. Tennessee (37)	Jan. 9, 1942
15	Arkansas vs. Oklahoma St. (17)	Jan. 28, 1944
15	Penn St. vs. Pittsburgh (12)	Jan. 15, 1944
15	Creighton vs. Oklahoma St. (35)	Feb. 9, 1948
15	Charleston So. vs. Col. of Charleston (18)	Feb. 6, 1980
16	Vanderbilt vs. Tennessee Tech (21)	1938
16	Miami (Ohio) vs. Marshall (22)	Feb. 19, 1938
16	South Carolina vs. Clemson (38)	Feb. 10, 1939
16	South Carolina vs. Clemson (43)	Feb. 18, 1939
16	Stanford vs. Oregon St. (18)	Jan. 28, 1980

FEWEST POINTS SCORED IN A GAME SINCE 1986

Pts.	Team vs. Opponent (Opp. Pts.)	Date
20	St. Louis vs. George Washington (49)	Jan. 10, 2008
21	Ga. Southern vs. Coastal Caro. (61)	Jan. 2, 1997
21	Princeton vs. Monmouth (41)	Dec. 14, 2005
22	Hartford vs. Boston U. (73)	Jan. 6, 2005
23	Miami (Ohio) vs. Dayton (60)	Dec. 29, 2001
23	Army vs. Bucknell (56)	Jan. 23, 2004
24	Nicholls St. vs. LSU (68)	Nov. 22, 2002
24	Ark.-Pine Bluff vs. Oklahoma (94)	Dec. 2, 2003
25	Tex.-Pan American vs. North Carolina St. (75)	Jan. 7, 1997
25	Valparaiso vs. Green Bay (69)	Mar. 2, 1992
25	Army vs. Bucknell (75)	Feb. 22, 2004
25	Savannah St. vs. Kansas St. (85)	Jan. 7, 2008
26	Northwestern vs. Evansville (48)	Nov. 26, 1999
26	Bethune-Cookman vs. Nebraska (70)	Dec. 20, 2003
27	New Hampshire vs. Providence (56)	Dec. 5, 1992
27	Yale vs. Princeton (55)	Jan. 11, 1991
27	Bucknell vs. Princeton (68)	Dec. 9, 1998
27	Eastern Wash. vs. California (56)	Nov. 16, 2001
27	Southern U. vs. Florida (83)	Nov. 28, 2006
27	Grambling vs. Texas A&M (101)	Dec. 28, 2006
28	Dartmouth vs. Princeton (66)	Feb. 10, 1990
28	Wofford vs. North Carolina St. (57)	Dec. 3, 1996
28	Winthrop vs. North Carolina St. (57)	Dec. 3, 1996
28	Rice vs. Princeton (51)	Jan. 6, 2007
28	Mississippi Val. vs. Washington St. (71)	Nov. 24, 2007

FEWEST POINTS SCORED BY BOTH TEAMS IN A GAME SINCE 1938

Pts.	Team vs. Opponent (Opp. Pts.)	Date
17	Tennessee (11) vs. Temple (6)	Dec. 15, 1974
22	North Carolina St. (12) vs. Duke (10)	Mar. 8, 1968
25	Oklahoma St. (14) vs. Oklahoma (11)	Feb. 19, 1944
27	Penn St. (15) vs. Pittsburgh (12)	Jan. 15, 1944
32	Oklahoma St. (17) vs. Arkansas (15)	Jan. 28, 1944
33	Penn St. (24) vs. Pittsburgh (9)	Mar. 1, 1952
33	Col. of Charleston (18) vs. Charleston So. (15)	Feb. 6, 1980
34	Oregon St. (18) vs. Stanford (16)	Jan. 28, 1980
35	Kentucky (24) vs. Cincinnati (11)	Dec. 20, 1983
36	Purdue (23) vs. Illinois (13)	Feb. 7, 1958
37	Tennessee (23) vs. Alabama (14)	Jan. 11, 1945
37	Tennessee Tech (21) vs. Vanderbilt (16)	1938
38	Marshall (22) vs. Miami (Ohio) (16)	Feb. 19, 1938

FEWEST POINTS SCORED BY BOTH TEAMS IN A GAME SINCE 1986

Pts.	Team vs. Opponent (Opp. Pts.)	Date
62	Monmouth (41) vs. Princeton (21)	Dec. 14, 2005
67	SMU (36) vs. Tex.-Arlington (31)	Dec. 16, 1989
67	Green Bay (46) vs. Northern Mich. (21)	Nov. 22, 1996
68	George Mason (35) vs. UNC Wilmington (33)	Mar. 4, 2001
69	George Washington (49) vs. St. Louis (20)	Jan. 10, 2008
72	Princeton (37) vs. Monmouth (35)	Nov. 20, 1999
72	Binghamton (38) vs. Charleston So. (34)	Nov. 30, 2003
72	Tex.-Pan American (37) vs. Air Force (35)	Feb. 16, 2004
74	Princeton (38) vs. North Carolina St. (36)	Nov. 12, 1997
74	Evansville (48) vs. Northwestern (26)	Nov. 26, 1999
75	Fresno St. (46) vs. Washington St. (29)	Dec. 22, 2003
75	Missouri St. (43) vs. Wisconsin (32)	Mar. 12, 1999
75	Samford (41) vs. Jacksonville St. (34)	Dec. 6, 2007
76	Princeton (43) vs. Colgate (33)	Nov. 30, 1988
76	Yale (39) vs. Princeton (37)	Jan. 12, 1990
76	Cornell (41) vs. Columbia (35)	Jan. 27, 2001
76	Utah (41) vs. St. Mary's (Cal.) (35)	Jan. 7, 2002
76	Alabama St. (43) vs. Ark.-Pine Bluff (33)	Jan. 11, 2003
77	Idaho (40) vs. UC Santa Barbara (37)	Feb. 2, 2002
78	UNLV (49) vs. Long Beach St. (29)	Mar. 9, 1991
78	Northern Ill. (48) vs. Akron (30)	Jan. 26, 1991
78	Auburn (43) vs. Tennessee (35)	Jan. 15, 1997
78	Richmond (41) vs. UNC Wilmington (37)	Jan. 17, 2001
78	Yale (43) vs. Princeton (35)	Feb. 2, 2007
79	Princeton (48) vs. Cornell (31)	Feb. 8, 1992
79	Butler (43) vs. La Salle (36)	Dec. 29, 1999
79	Bucknell (56) vs. Army (23)	Jan. 23, 2004
79	Northwestern (40) vs. Purdue (39)	Feb. 11, 2004
79	Princeton (51) vs. Rice (28)	Jan. 6, 2007
79	Iowa (43) vs. Michigan St. (36)	Jan. 12, 2008

FIELD-GOAL PERCENTAGE

Pct.	Team (FG-FGA) vs. Opponent	Date
83.3	Maryland (15-18) vs. South Carolina	Jan. 9, 1971
81.4	New Mexico (35-43) vs. Oregon St.	Nov. 30, 1985
81.0	Fresno St. (34-42) vs. Portland St.	Dec. 3, 1977
81.0	St. Peter's (34-42) vs. Utica	Dec. 4, 1984
80.5	Fordham (33-41) vs. Fairfield	Feb. 27, 1984
80.0	Holy Cross (32-40) vs. Vermont	Nov. 30, 1981
80.0	Oklahoma St. (28-35) vs. Tulane	Mar. 22, 1992
80.0	Long Beach St. (56-70) vs. Cal St. Monterey Bay	Dec. 22, 1999
80.0	Utah (24-30) vs. Air Force	Jan. 24, 2005
79.4	Arkansas (27-34) vs. Texas Tech	Feb. 20, 1979
79.4	Columbia (27-34) vs. Dartmouth	Mar. 2, 1984
79.0	North Carolina (49-62) vs. Loyola Marymount	Mar. 19, 1988
78.6	Villanova (22-28) vs. Georgetown	Apr. 1, 1985
78.6	St. Peter's (22-28) vs. Army	Jan. 9, 1982
78.4	Western Ky. (29-37) vs. Dayton	Jan. 24, 1979
78.1	Army (25-32) vs. Manhattan	Jan. 20, 1979
78.0	Southern Utah (32-41) vs. Montana Tech	Dec. 19, 2002
77.8	Samford (35-45) vs. Loyola (La.)	Dec. 12, 1992
77.8	Utah St. (28-36) vs. UC Davis	Nov. 27, 2004
77.5	Nicholls St. (31-40) vs. Samford	Dec. 30, 1983
77.4	Richmond (24-31) vs. Citadel	Feb. 8, 1976
77.2	Stephen F. Austin (44-57) vs. LeTourneau	Nov. 26, 2002
77.0	Purdue (47-61) vs. Long Island	Nov. 14, 1997

THREE-POINT FIELD GOALS

3FG	Team vs. Opponent	Date
28	Troy vs. George Mason	Dec. 10, 1994
26	Troy vs. Oakwood	Nov. 24, 2003
24	Cincinnati vs. Oakland	Dec. 5, 1998
23	Lamar vs. Louisiana Tech	Feb. 28, 1993
23	Kansas St. vs. Fresno St.	Mar. 24, 1994
23	Troy vs. George Mason	Nov. 28, 1995
23	Samford vs. Troy	Jan. 13, 2001
22	Gonzaga vs. San Francisco	Feb. 23, 1995
22	Troy vs. Mercer	Jan. 31, 2005
22	Ga. Southern vs. Chattanooga	Jan. 17, 2005
22	VMI vs. Lees-McRae	Dec. 6, 2006
22	Louisville vs. Hartford	Nov. 17, 2007
21	Kentucky vs. North Carolina	Dec. 27, 1989
21	Loyola Marymount vs. Michigan	Mar. 18, 1990
21	UNLV vs. Nevada	Dec. 8, 1990
21	Troy vs. Loyola (La.)	Dec. 22, 1993
21	Cal Poly vs. Cal Baptist	Dec. 3, 1996
21	Mississippi Val. vs. Troy	Dec. 6, 1996
21	Arkansas vs. Troy	Dec. 10, 1996
21	Long Island vs. Robert Morris	Feb. 3, 1997
21	Troy vs. Lipscomb	Jan. 10, 2004
21	Furman vs. Va. Intermont	Dec. 29, 2004
21	Pepperdine vs. Nicholls St.	Nov. 14, 2006
21	VMI vs. Va. Intermont	Nov. 15, 2006
21	Morgan St. vs. East Carolina	Dec. 18, 2006
21	N.C. A&T vs. Arizona St.	Dec. 21, 2006
21	VMI vs. Charleston So.	Jan. 13, 2007
21	Nicholls St. vs. A&M-Corpus Christi	Feb. 8, 2007
21	Citadel vs. Daniel Webster	Nov. 9, 2007

THREE-POINT FIELD GOALS ATTEMPTED

3FGA	Team vs. Opponent	Date
74	Troy vs. George Mason	Dec 10, 1994
67	Mississippi Val. vs. Troy	Dec. 6, 1996
61	VMI vs. Va. Intermont	Nov. 15, 2006
59	VMI vs. Southern Va.	Nov. 20, 2006
58	Cal Poly vs. Cal Baptist	Dec. 3, 1996
56	VMI vs. Charleston So.	Jan. 13, 2007
55	VMI vs. Bridgewater (Va.)	Jan. 18, 2007
54	VMI vs. Cornell	Dec. 1, 2006
54	VMI vs. Penn St.	Dec. 30, 2006
53	Kentucky vs. La.-Lafayette	Dec. 23, 1989
52	Troy vs. Oakwood	Nov. 24, 2003
51	Texas-Arlington vs. New Mexico	Nov. 23, 1990
51	Arizona St. vs. BYU	Dec. 1, 1992
50	Morehead St. vs. George Mason	Dec. 3, 1996
50	Cal Poly vs. Air Force	Dec. 5, 1997
50	VMI vs. Coastal Caro.	Jan. 15, 2007
49	VMI vs. Lees-McRae	Dec. 6, 2006
48	Kentucky vs. North Carolina	Dec. 27, 1989
48	Cincinnati vs. Oakland	Dec. 5, 1998
48	VMI vs. Mercer	Dec. 9, 2006
47	Kentucky vs. Furman	Dec. 19, 1989
47	Charleston So. vs. Clemson	Dec. 1, 1993
47	Centenary (La.) vs. UCF	Jan. 11, 1993
47	VMI vs. Ohio St.	Nov. 10, 2006
47	VMI vs. South Dakato St.	Nov. 12, 2006

THREE-POINT FIELD-GOAL PERCENTAGE
(Minimum 10 three-point field goals made)

Pct.	Team (3FG-3FGA) vs. Opponent	Date
91.7	Drexel (11-12) vs. Delaware	Dec. 3, 2000
91.7	Northern Ariz. (11-12) vs. Willamette	Dec. 11, 2004
90.9	Duke (10-11) vs. Clemson	Feb. 1, 1988
90.9	Hofstra (10-11) vs. Rhode Island	Jan. 16, 1993
87.5	Stetson (14-16) vs. Centenary (La.)	Jan. 13, 1996
85.7	Western Ill. (12-14) vs. Valparaiso	Jan. 13, 1992
84.6	Murray St. (11-13) vs. Southeast Mo. St.	Jan. 16, 1993
84.6	Clemson (11-13) vs. North Carolina	Jan. 31, 2004
83.3	Eastern Ky. (15-18) vs. UNC Asheville	Jan. 14, 1987
83.3	Princeton (10-12) vs. Penn	Jan. 6, 1990
83.3	Evansville (10-12) vs. Butler	Feb. 9, 1991
83.3	Southern Utah (10-12) vs. Cal St. Northridge	Mar. 1, 1991
83.3	Milwaukee (10-12) vs. Eastern Mich.	Feb. 19, 1992
83.3	Purdue (10-12) vs. Michigan	Feb. 7, 1993
83.3	UNLV (10-12) vs. William & Mary	Feb. 11, 1995
83.3	Evansville (10-12) vs. Southern Ill.	Feb. 24, 1996
83.3	Green Bay (10-12) vs. Miami (Ohio)	Dec. 5, 1998
81.3	Niagara (13-16) vs. Siena	Jan. 7, 1987
81.3	BYU (13-16) vs. New Mexico	Jan. 26, 2008
80.0	Marshall (12-15) vs. Wyoming	Dec. 7, 1991
80.0	Washington St. (12-15) vs. Princeton	Dec. 29, 1992
80.0	Princeton (12-15) vs. Columbia	Feb. 13, 1993
80.0	Niagara (12-15) vs. Iona	Feb. 17, 1995
80.0	Marquette (12-15) vs. Tulane	Jan. 27, 2001
80.0	Iona (12-15) vs. St. Peter's	Feb. 27, 2004

DIVISION I

FREE-THROW PERCENTAGE
(Minimum 30 free throws made)

Pct.	Team (FT-FTA) vs. Opponent	Date
100	UC Irvine (34-34) vs. Pacific	Feb. 21, 1981
100	Samford (34-34) vs. UCF	Dec. 20, 1990
100	Wake Forest (32-32) vs. North Carolina	Jan. 15, 2005
100	Marshall (31-31) vs. Davidson	Dec. 17, 1979
100	Indiana St. (31-31) vs. Wichita St.	Feb. 18, 1991
97.2	Vanderbilt (35-36) vs. Mississippi St.	Feb. 26, 1986
97.2	Butler (35-36) vs. Dayton	Feb. 21, 1991
97.2	Marquette (35-36) vs. Memphis	Jan. 23, 1993
97.1	Bowling Green (34-35) vs. Kent St.	Jan. 26, 2006
97.0	Miami (Fla.) (32-33) vs. Creighton	Feb. 10, 1964
97.0	Toledo (32-33) vs. Old Dominion	Dec. 9, 1995
97.0	Hawaii (32-33) vs. New Mexico	Feb. 24, 1996
96.8	Oregon St. (30-31) vs. Memphis	Dec. 19, 1990
96.8	Niagara (30-31) vs. Fairfield	Jan. 31, 1998
95.5	UNLV (42-44) vs. San Diego St.	Dec. 11, 1976
94.7	Missouri St. (36-38) vs. Evansville	Dec. 30, 2001
94.6	TCU (35-37) vs. Tex.-Arlington	Dec. 23, 1996
94.4	Eastern Mich. (34-36) vs. Jackson St.	Dec. 20, 1994
93.8	North Carolina St. (30-32) vs. North Carolina	Feb. 21, 1998
93.8	BYU (30-32) vs. Weber St.	Dec. 28, 2000
93.7	Mount St. Mary's (30-32) vs. Robert Morris	Feb. 6, 1990

REBOUNDS

Reb.	Team vs. Opponent	Date
108	Kentucky vs. Mississippi	Feb. 8, 1964
103	Holy Cross vs. Boston College	Mar. 1, 1956
102	Arizona vs. Northern Ariz.	Jan. 6, 1951
101	Weber St. vs. Idaho St.	Jan. 22, 1966
100	William & Mary vs. Virginia	Feb. 14, 1954
95	Indiana vs. Michigan	Mar. 11, 1961
95	Murray St. vs. MacMurray	Jan. 2, 1967
92	Santa Clara vs. St. Mary's (Cal.)	Feb. 15, 1971
92	Oral Roberts vs. Brandeis	Jan. 8, 1973
91	Notre Dame vs. St. Norbert	Dec. 7, 1965
91	Southern Miss. vs. Tex.-Pan American	Feb. 9, 1970
91	Houston vs. Rice	Mar. 7, 1974
90	Vanderbilt vs. Sewanee	Dec. 4, 1954

ASSISTS

Ast.	Team vs. Opponent	Date
44	Colorado vs. George Mason (ot)	Dec. 2, 1995
43	TCU vs. Central Okla.	Dec. 12, 1998
41	North Carolina vs. Manhattan	Dec. 27, 1985
41	Weber St. vs. Northern Ariz.	Mar. 2, 1991
40	New Mexico vs. Texas-Arlington	Nov. 23, 1990
40	Loyola Marymount vs. U.S. Int'l	Jan. 5, 1991
40	Southern Utah vs. Texas Wesleyan	Jan. 25, 1992
40	Lamar vs. Prairie View	Feb. 2, 1993
40	TCU vs. North Texas	Dec. 1, 1998
39	Southern Miss. vs. Virginia Tech	Jan. 16, 1988
39	UNLV vs. Pacific	Feb. 8, 1990
39	UNLV vs. Rutgers	Feb. 3, 1991
39	Davidson vs. Warren Wilson	Dec. 9, 1991
39	TCU vs. Midwestern St.	Nov. 30, 1994
39	Arizona St. vs. Delaware St.	Dec. 1, 1997
39	TCU vs. Central Okla.	Dec. 9, 2000
38	New Mexico vs. U.S. Int'l	Dec. 3, 1985
38	Pepperdine vs. U.S. Int'l	Jan. 7, 1986
38	UCLA vs. Loyola Marymount	Dec. 2, 1990
38	Arizona vs. Northern Ariz.	Dec. 18, 1991
38	Tex.-Pan American vs. Concordia Lutheran	Dec. 4, 1993
38	LSU vs. George Mason	Dec. 3, 1994
38	Arizona vs. Morgan St.	Nov. 20, 1997
38	TCU vs. Ark.-Pine Bluff	Dec. 30, 2000
37	15 tied	

BLOCKED SHOTS

Blk.	Team vs. Opponent	Date
21	Georgetown vs. Southern (N.O.)	Dec. 1, 1993
21	Alabama A&M vs. Texas Southern	Feb. 24, 2007
20	Iona vs. Northern Ill.	Jan. 7, 1989
20	Georgia vs. Bethune-Cookman	Dec. 7, 1993
20	Massachusetts vs. West Virginia	Jan. 3, 1995
19	Seton Hall vs. Norfolk St.	Dec. 4, 2000
19	Connecticut vs. Florida Int'l	Nov. 30, 2004
19	UNLV vs. TCU	Feb. 7, 2007
19	Stanford vs. Southern California	Jan. 25, 2007
18	North Carolina vs. Stanford	Dec. 20, 1985
18	Cincinnati vs. Marquette	Jan. 7, 2006
18	Boston College vs. Duquesne	Dec. 28, 2006

Blk.	Team vs. Opponent	Date
17	Maryland vs. Md.-East. Shore	Feb. 27, 1987
17	Rider vs. Fairleigh Dickinson	Jan. 9, 1989
17	Georgetown vs. Providence	Feb. 22, 1989
17	Georgetown vs. Hawaii-Loa	Nov. 23, 1990
17	BYU vs. Eastern Ky.	Dec. 7, 1990
17	Northwestern St. vs. Ouachita Baptist	Nov. 30, 1991
17	New Orleans vs. Texas A&M	Dec. 29, 1992
17	Massachusetts vs. Hartford	Dec. 28, 1993
17	Louisville vs. Kentucky	Jan. 1, 1995
17	William & Mary vs. George Mason	Feb. 26, 1996
17	Miami (Fla.) vs. Hartford	Dec. 13, 1996
17	Fairleigh Dickinson vs. Hartford	Nov. 11, 1997
17	Kentucky vs. Morehead St.	Nov. 20, 1997
17	Duke vs. Virginia	Jan. 10, 1999
17	La.-Monroe vs. Lamar	Feb. 3, 2000
17	Georgetown vs. Southern-N.O.	Feb. 10, 2000
17	Connecticut vs. Quinnipiac	Dec. 30, 2004

STEALS

Stl.	Team vs. Opponent	Date
39	Long Island vs. Medgar Evers	Nov. 26, 1997
35	VMI vs. Va. Intermont	Nov. 15, 2006
34	Oklahoma vs. Centenary (La.)	Dec. 12, 1987
34	Northwestern St. vs. LeTourneau	Jan. 20, 1992
33	Connecticut vs. Pittsburgh	Jan. 6, 1990
32	Manhattan vs. Lehman	Dec. 14, 1987
32	Oklahoma vs. Angelo St.	Dec. 1, 1990
32	Long Island vs. Medgar Evers	Nov. 29, 1994
32	La.-Lafayette vs. Baptist Christian	Nov. 25, 1995
30	Southern U. vs. Baptist Christian	Dec. 14, 1992
30	Cal Poly vs. Notre Dame (Cal.)	Nov. 25, 1995
30	TCU vs. Ark.-Pine Bluff	Dec. 30, 2000
29	Cleveland St. vs. Canisius	Dec. 28, 1986
29	Oklahoma vs. U.S. Int'l	Nov. 19, 1989
29	Centenary (La.) vs. East Texas Baptist	Dec. 12, 1992
29	TCU vs. Delaware St.	Dec. 3, 1997
28	Oklahoma vs. Morgan St.	Dec. 21, 1991
28	Memphis vs. Southeastern La.	Jan. 11, 1993
28	Oklahoma vs. Florida A&M	Jan. 27, 1993
28	VMI vs. Southern Va.	Nov. 20, 2006
27	Oregon St. vs. Hawaii-Loa	Dec. 22, 1985
27	Cal St. Fullerton vs. Lamar	Nov. 24, 1989
27	UTSA vs. Samford	Jan. 19, 1991
27	Iowa St. vs. Bethune-Cookman	Dec. 31, 1992
27	San Francisco vs. Delaware St.	Nov. 27, 1993
27	Charleston So. vs. Warner Southern	Dec. 11, 1993
27	Georgetown vs. Southern (N.O.)	Feb. 13, 1999
27	TCU vs. Alabama St.	Nov. 20, 2000

Season Records

VICTORIES

Team	Season	Won	Lost	Pct.
Memphis	†2008	38	2	.950
UNLV	†1987	37	2	.949
Duke	†1999	37	2	.949
Illinois	†2005	37	2	.949
Duke	†1986	37	3	.925
Kansas	2008	37	3	.925
Kentucky	†1948	36	3	.923
North Carolina	2008	36	3	.923
Massachusetts	†1996	35	2	.946
Georgetown	†1985	35	3	.921
Arizona	†1988	35	3	.921
Kansas	1986	35	4	.897
Oklahoma	†1988	35	4	.897
Kansas	†1998	35	4	.897
Kentucky	†1998	35	4	.897
Duke	†2001	35	4	.897
Ohio St.	†2007	35	4	.897
UCLA	2008	35	4	.897
UNLV	†1990	35	5	.875
Kentucky	†1997	35	5	.875
Florida	2007	35	5	.875
UNLV	†1991	34	1	.971
Duke	†1992	34	2	.944
Kentucky	1996	34	2	.944
Kansas	1997	34	2	.944
Connecticut	1999	34	2	.944
Kentucky	†1947	34	3	.919

Team	Season	Won	Lost	Pct.
Georgetown	†1984	34	3	.919
Arkansas	†1991	34	4	.895
North Carolina	†1993	34	4	.895
North Carolina	1998	34	4	.895

†national leader

VICTORIES IN FIRST SEASON IN DIVISION I

Team	Season	Won	Lost	Pct.
Seattle#	1953	29	4	.879
Md.-East. Shore	1974	27	2	.931
Oral Roberts	1972	26	2	.929
Old Dominion	1977	25	4	.862
Long Beach St.#	1970	24	5	.828
La.-Lafayette#	1972	23	3	.885
Southern U.	1978	23	5	.821
Hawaii	1971	23	5	.821
Alabama St.	1983	22	6	.786
Alcorn St.	1978	22	7	.759
Stephen F. Austin	1987	22	8	.733
Idaho St.#	1959	21	7	.750
McNeese St.	1974	20	5	.800
Memphis#	1956	20	7	.741
Birmingham So.	2004	20	7	.741
Loyola (La.)	1952	20	14	.588
Jackson St.	1978	19	5	.792
Northeastern	1973	19	7	.731
Ga. Southern	1974	19	7	.731
Miami (Fla.)	1949	19	8	.704
Col. of Charleston	1992	19	8	.704
Morehead St.#	1956	19	10	.655
New Mexico St.	1951	19	14	.576
New Orleans	1976	18	8	.692
Florida A&M	1979	18	9	.667
Alabama A&M	2000	18	10	.643

#appeared in NCAA tournament

WON-LOST PERCENTAGE

Team	Season	Won	Lost	Pct.
North Carolina	†1957	32	0	1.000
Indiana	†1976	32	0	1.000
UCLA	†1964	30	0	1.000
UCLA	†1967	30	0	1.000
UCLA	†1972	30	0	1.000
UCLA	†1973	30	0	1.000
San Francisco	†1956	29	0	1.000
North Carolina St.	1973	27	0	1.000
Kentucky	†1954	25	0	1.000
Long Island	†1939	24	0	1.000
Seton Hall	†1940	19	0	1.000
Army	†1944	15	0	1.000
UNLV	†1991	34	1	.971
Indiana St.	†1979	33	1	.971
Indiana	†1975	31	1	.969
North Carolina St.	†1974	30	1	.968
UCLA	†1968	29	1	.967
UCLA	†1969	29	1	.967
UCLA	†1971	29	1	.967
San Francisco	†1955	28	1	.966
UTEP	†1966	28	1	.966
Marquette	1971	28	1	.966
Penn	1971	28	1	.966
Alcorn St.	1979	28	1	.966
Ohio St.	†1961	27	1	.964

†national leader

WON-LOST PERCENTAGE IN FIRST SEASON IN DIVISION I

Team	Season	Won	Lost	Pct.
Md.-East. Shore	1974	27	2	.931
Oral Roberts	1972	26	2	.929
Seattle#	1953	29	4	.879
La.-Lafayette#	1972	25	4	.862
Old Dominion	1977	25	4	.862
Long Beach St.#	1970	24	5	.828
Southern U.	1978	23	5	.821
Hawaii	1971	23	5	.821
McNeese St.	1974	20	5	.800
Jackson St.	1978	19	5	.792
Alabama St.	1983	22	6	.786
Alcorn St.	1978	22	7	.759
Idaho St.#	1959	21	7	.750
Memphis#	1956	20	7	.741

Team	Season	Won	Lost	Pct.
Birmingham So.	2004	20	7	.741
Air Force	1958	17	6	.739
Stephen F. Austin	1987	22	8	.733
Northeastern	1973	19	7	.731
Ga. Southern	1974	19	7	.731
VCU	1974	17	7	.708
Miami (Fla.)	1949	19	8	.704
Col. of Charleston	1992	19	8	.704
New Orleans	1976	18	8	.692
Weber St.	1964	17	8	.680
George Mason	1979	17	8	.680
Florida A&M	1979	18	9	.667
Mercer	1974	16	8	.667
Tennessee Tech	1956	14	7	.667
American	1967	16	8	.667
Fairfield	1965	14	7	.667

#appeared in NCAA tournament

MOST-IMPROVED TEAMS (Since 1974)

Team	Season	W-L Record	Previous Yr. W-L	Games Imp.
Mercer	†2003	23-6	6-23	17
UTEP	†2004	24-8	6-24	17
N.C. A&T	†1978	20-8	3-24	16½
Murray St.	†1980	23-8	4-22	16½
Liberty	†1992	22-7	5-23	16½
North Texas	†1976	22-4	6-20	16
Ohio State	†1999	27-9	8-22	16
Tulsa	†1981	26-7	8-19	15
Utah St.	†1983	20-9	4-23	15
Radford	†1991	22-7	7-22	15
Boston College	†2001	27-5	11-19	15
Western Mich.	1992	21-9	5-22	14½
Tennessee St.	†1993	19-10	4-24	14½
Central Mich.	2001	20-8	6-23	14½
Fresno St.	1978	21-6	7-20	14
James Madison	†1987	20-10	5-23	14
Loyola Marymount	†1988	28-4	12-16	14
Cal Poly	†1996	16-13	1-26	14
Northern Ariz.	†1997	21-7	6-20	14
McNeese St.	2001	22-9	6-21	14
Central Mich.	2003	25-7	9-19	14
Michigan St.	1978	25-5	10-17	13½
Loyola (Md.)	†1994	17-13	2-25	13½
UTSA	†1998	16-11	3-25	13½
Iowa St.	†2000	32-5	15-15	13½
UALR	2001	18-11	4-24	13½

†national leader

POINTS

Team	Season	G	Pts.
Oklahoma	†1988	39	4,012
Loyola Marymount	†1990	32	3,918
Arkansas	†1991	38	3,783
UNLV	1990	40	3,739
Oklahoma	†1989	36	3,680
UNLV	†1987	39	3,612
Duke	†1999	39	3,581
Duke	†2001	39	3,538
Loyola Marymount	1988	32	3,528
Loyola Marymount	1989	31	3,486
Houston	†1977	37	3,482
North Carolina	†2008	39	3,454
UNLV	†1976	31	3,426
UNLV	1977	32	3,426
Duke	1991	39	3,421
UNLV	1991	35	3,420
Arkansas	†1995	39	3,416
Syracuse	1989	38	3,410
Michigan	1989	37	3,393
Duke	1990	38	3,386
Kansas	†2002	37	3,365
Oklahoma	1991	35	3,363
Arkansas	1990	35	3,345
North Carolina	1989	37	3,331
VMI	†2007	33	3,331

†national leader

DIVISION I

SCORING OFFENSE

Team	Season	G	Pts.	Avg.
Loyola Marymount	†1990	32	3,918	122.4
Loyola Marymount	†1989	31	3,486	112.5
UNLV	†1976	31	3,426	110.5
Loyola Marymount	†1988	32	3,528	110.3
UNLV	†1977	32	3,426	107.1
Oral Roberts	†1972	28	2,943	105.1
Southern U.	†1991	28	2,924	104.4
Loyola Marymount	1991	31	3,211	103.6
Oklahoma	1988	39	4,012	102.9
Oklahoma	1989	36	3,680	102.2
Oklahoma	1990	32	3,243	101.3
Southern U.	†1994	27	2,727	101.0
VMI	†2007	33	3,331	100.9
Jacksonville	†1970	28	2,809	100.3
Jacksonville	†1971	26	2,598	99.9
Arkansas	1991	38	3,783	99.6
Southern U.	1990	31	3,078	99.3
Syracuse	†1966	28	2,773	99.0
Iowa	1970	25	2,467	98.7
Miami (Fla.)	†1965	26	2,558	98.4
Houston	1966	29	2,845	98.1
La.-Lafayette	1972	29	2,840	97.9
U.S. Int'l	1990	28	2,738	97.8
Houston	†1968	33	3,226	97.8
UNLV	1991	35	3,420	97.7

†national leader

SCORING DEFENSE

Team	Season	G	Pts.	Avg.
Oklahoma St.	†1948	31	1,006	32.5
Oklahoma St.	†1949	28	985	35.2
Oklahoma St.	†1950	27	1,059	39.2
Alabama	1948	27	1,070	39.6
Creighton	1948	23	925	40.2
Wyoming	1948	27	1,101	40.8
Wyoming	1950	36	1,491	41.4
Siena	1948	28	1,161	41.5
St. Bonaventure	1948	22	921	41.9
Siena	1949	29	1,215	41.9
Tulane	1948	26	1,102	42.4
Wyoming	1949	35	1,509	43.1
Texas	1948	25	1,079	43.2
Utah	1948	20	868	43.4
Minnesota	1949	21	912	43.4
Washington-St. Louis	1948	21	915	43.6
St. Bonaventure	1949	26	1,137	43.7
St. Louis	1948	27	1,183	43.8
Kentucky	1949	34	1,492	43.9
Washington St.	1949	30	1,317	43.9
Texas A&M	†1951	29	1,275	44.0
Kentucky	1948	39	1,730	44.4
Baylor	1949	24	1,068	44.5
Tulsa	1950	23	1,027	44.7
Hamline	1948	31	1,389	44.8

†national leader

(Since 1965)

Team	Season	G	Pts.	Avg.
Fresno St.	†1982	30	1,412	47.1
Princeton	†1992	28	1,349	48.2
Princeton	†1991	27	1,320	48.9
North Carolina St.	1982	32	1,570	49.1
Princeton	1982	26	1,277	49.1
Princeton	†1984	28	1,403	50.1
St. Peter's	†1980	31	1,563	50.4
Fresno St.	†1981	29	1,470	50.7
Air Force	†2004	29	1,475	50.9
Princeton	†1990	27	1,378	51.0
Princeton	1981	28	1,438	51.4
Princeton	†1998	29	1,491	51.4
St. Peter's	1981	26	1,338	51.5
Wyoming	1982	30	1,545	51.5
Princeton	†1977	26	1,343	51.7
Princeton	†1996	29	1,498	51.7
Princeton	†1983	29	1,507	52.0
James Madison	1982	30	1,559	52.0
Fresno St.	†1978	27	1,417	52.5
Princeton	†1999	30	1,581	52.7
Princeton	†1976	27	1,427	52.9
Columbia	1982	26	1,375	52.9
Princeton	†1989	27	1,430	53.0
Fresno St.	†1985	32	1,696	53.0
Princeton	†2007	28	1,493	53.3

†national leader

SCORING MARGIN

Team	Season	Off.	Def.	Mar.
UCLA	†1972	94.6	64.3	30.3
North Carolina St.	†1948	75.3	47.2	28.1
Kentucky	1954	87.5	60.3	27.2
Kentucky	†1952	82.3	55.4	26.9
UNLV	†1991	97.7	71.0	26.7
UCLA	†1968	93.4	67.2	26.2
UCLA	†1967	89.6	63.7	25.9
Houston	1968	97.8	72.5	25.3
Duke	†1999	91.8	67.2	24.7
Kentucky	1948	69.0	44.3	24.6
Kentucky	†1949	68.2	43.9	24.3
Bowling Green	1948	70.5	46.7	23.8
Loyola (Ill.)	†1963	91.8	68.1	23.7
Charlotte	1975	88.9	65.2	23.7
Arizona St.	†1962	90.1	67.6	22.5
St. Bonaventure	†1970	88.4	65.9	22.5
Kentucky	†1951	74.7	52.5	22.2
Indiana	1975	88.0	65.9	22.1
Kentucky	†1996	91.4	69.4	22.1
Cincinnati	†1960	86.7	64.7	22.0
Oklahoma	†1988	102.9	81.0	21.9
North Carolina St.	†1973	92.9	71.1	21.8
Jacksonville	1970	100.3	78.5	21.8
UNLV	†1976	110.5	89.0	21.5
Duke	†1998	85.6	64.1	21.5

†national leader

FIELD-GOAL PERCENTAGE

Team	Season	FG	FGA	Pct.
Missouri	†1980	936	1,635	57.2
Michigan	†1989	1,325	2,341	56.6
Oregon St.	†1981	862	1,528	56.4
UC Irvine	†1982	920	1,639	56.1
Michigan St.	†1986	1,043	1,860	56.1
North Carolina	1986	1,197	2,140	55.9
Kansas	1986	1,260	2,266	55.6
Kentucky	†1983	869	1,564	55.6
Notre Dame	1981	824	1,492	55.2
Houston Baptist	†1984	797	1,445	55.2
Maryland	1980	985	1,789	55.1
Idaho	1981	816	1,484	55.0
UC Irvine	1981	934	1,703	54.8
Navy	†1985	946	1,726	54.8
Stanford	1983	752	1,373	54.8
Maryland	†1975	1,049	1,918	54.7
New Orleans	1983	937	1,714	54.7
Georgia Tech	1986	1,008	1,846	54.6
Arkansas	†1978	1,060	1,943	54.6
Michigan	†1988	1,198	2,196	54.6
New Mexico	1989	992	1,819	54.5
Southern U.	1978	1,107	2,031	54.5
Arkansas	†1977	849	1,558	54.5
Arizona	1988	1,147	2,106	54.5
Pepperdine	1983	900	1,653	54.4
Oregon St.	1980	943	1,732	54.4
Ohio St.	†1970	831	1,527	54.4
UNC Wilmington	1977	816	1,500	54.4
Davidson	†1964	894	1,644	54.4

†national leader

FIELD-GOAL PERCENTAGE DEFENSE (Since 1978)

Team	Season	FG	FGA	Pct.
Stanford	†2000	667	1,893	35.2
Marquette	†1994	750	2,097	35.8
Marquette	†1997	628	1,735	36.2
Temple	2000	633	1,747	36.2
Wake Forest	1997	667	1,832	36.4
UNLV	†1992	628	1,723	36.5
Green Bay	1997	499	1,368	36.5
Georgetown	†2008	669	1,827	36.6
Georgetown	†1991	680	1,847	36.8
Temple	†1994	621	1,686	36.8
Connecticut	†2004	924	2,502	36.9
Mississippi St.	2008	790	2,137	37.0
Kansas	†2006	702	1,896	37.0
Princeton	2000	577	1,558	37.0

Team	Season	FG	FGA	Pct.
Connecticut	†2007	677	1,824	37.1
Boston U.	†2005	588	1,584	37.1
Kansas St.	†1999	729	1,963	37.1
St. Joseph's	†2003	609	1,639	37.2
Detroit	1999	590	1,583	37.3
Northwestern	1999	577	1,548	37.3
Texas St.	1999	597	1,601	37.3
Cincinnati	2005	749	2,008	37.3
Green Bay	1994	664	1,777	37.4
VCU	†2002	767	2,052	37.4
Cincinnati	2002	761	2,035	37.4

†national leader

THREE-POINT FIELD GOALS MADE

Team	Season	G	3FG
VMI	†2007	33	442
Duke	†2001	39	407
Houston	†2008	34	375
West Virginia	2007	36	371
Troy	†2004	31	364
Arkansas	†1995	39	361
Louisville	†2005	38	361
Belmont	2008	34	357
Oregon	2007	37	350
Bradley	2007	35	349
Bradley	2008	38	346
Illinois	2005	39	344
Troy	†2006	29	344
Kentucky	†1993	34	340
West Virginia	2006	33	337
VMI	2008	29	336
Troy	2008	31	335
Massachusetts	2008	36	331
Houston	2007	33	330
Valparaiso	2008	36	330
Davidson	2007	34	328
Davidson	2008	36	328
Tennessee	2007	35	327
Missouri	†2002	36	326
Butler	2007	36	321

†national leader

THREE-POINT FIELD GOALS MADE PER GAME

Team	Season	G	3FG	Avg.
VMI	†2007	33	442	13.39
Troy	†2006	29	344	11.86
Troy	†2004	31	364	11.74
VMI	†2008	29	336	11.59
Troy	†2005	30	338	11.27
Troy	†1996	27	300	11.11
Houston	2008	34	375	11.03
Troy	2008	31	335	10.81
Mississippi Val.	†1997	29	309	10.66
Troy	†1995	27	287	10.63
Belmont	2008	34	357	10.50
St. Bonaventure	†2002	30	314	10.47
Duke	†2001	39	407	10.44
Samford	1995	27	279	10.33
Mississippi Val.	†2003	29	299	10.31
West Virginia	2007	36	371	10.31
Belmont	2001	28	288	10.29
West Virginia	2006	33	337	10.21
Marshall	1996	28	284	10.14
Lamar	†1993	27	271	10.04
St. Bonaventure	2003	27	271	10.04
Kentucky	†1990	28	281	10.04
Long Island	1997	30	301	10.03
Kentucky	1993	34	340	10.00
Houston	2007	35	330	10.00

†national leader

THREE-POINT FIELD-GOAL PERCENTAGE
(Minimum 100 three-point field goals made)

Team	Season	G	3FG	3FGA	Pct.
Indiana	†1987	34	130	256	50.8
Mississippi Val.	1987	28	161	322	50.0
Stephen F. Austin	1987	30	120	241	49.8
Princeton	†1988	26	211	429	49.2
Prairie View	1988	27	129	266	48.5
Kansas St.	1988	34	179	370	48.4
Arizona	1988	38	254	526	48.3
Indiana	†1989	35	121	256	47.3

Team	Season	G	3FG	3FGA	Pct.
Bucknell	1988	28	154	328	47.0
Holy Cross	1988	29	158	337	46.9
Michigan	1989	37	196	419	46.8
Green Bay	†1992	30	204	437	46.7
Citadel	1989	28	153	328	46.6
Niagara	1987	31	128	275	46.5
Eastern Mich.	1987	29	144	310	46.5
Green Bay	†1991	31	189	407	46.4
Colorado St.	1989	33	141	305	46.2
Bucknell	1989	31	160	347	46.1
Illinois	1987	31	112	243	46.1
Illinois St.	1987	32	110	240	45.8
Jacksonville	1987	30	188	412	45.6
Rider	1987	28	151	331	45.6
Davidson	1987	30	138	303	45.5
New Mexico St.	1988	32	143	314	45.5
Gonzaga	1989	28	119	262	45.4
Indiana	†1994	30	182	401	45.4

†national leader

FREE-THROW PERCENTAGE

Team	Season	FT	FTA	Pct.
Harvard	†1984	535	651	82.2
BYU	†1989	527	647	81.5
Harvard	†1985	450	555	81.1
Ohio St.	†1970	452	559	80.9
Siena	†1998	574	715	80.3
Vanderbilt	†1974	477	595	80.2
Michigan St.	†1986	490	613	79.9
St. Joseph's	†2006	525	657	79.9
North Carolina St.	†2004	481	602	79.9
Butler	†1988	413	517	79.9
Miami (Fla.)	†1965	642	807	79.6
Tulane	†1963	390	492	79.3
Tennessee	†1971	538	679	79.2
UTEP	†2005	606	765	79.2
Auburn	†1966	476	601	79.2
Utah St.	†2008	532	672	79.2
Oklahoma St.	†1958	488	617	79.1
Duke	†1978	665	841	79.1
Utah	†1993	476	602	79.1
Gonzaga	1989	485	614	79.0
Western Ky.	†1997	342	433	79.0
Montana St.	†2000	481	609	79.0
Oral Roberts	†1980	481	610	78.9
Marshall	1958	479	608	78.8
Bucknell	1989	590	749	78.8
Manhattan	†2003	560	711	78.8

†national leader

REBOUNDS

Team	Season	G	Reb.
Kentucky	†1951	34	2,109
North Carolina St.	1951	37	2,091
Houston	†1968	33	2,074
Columbia	†1957	24	2,016
Fordham	†1953	27	1,879
North Carolina St.	†1955	32	1,864
Houston	†1967	31	1,862
Fordham	†1952	29	1,859
Kentucky	1952	32	1,817
West Virginia	†1959	34	1,810
Western Ky.	†1954	32	1,810
Creighton	†1964	29	1,803
North Carolina St.	1952	34	1,782
Connecticut	†2004	39	1,742
Dayton	1955	29	1,738
North Carolina St.	1954	35	1,735
Notre Dame	†1965	27	1,722
Dayton	†1956	29	1,713
New Mexico St.	1970	31	1,713
Seton Hall	1953	33	1,706
La Salle	1955	31	1,697
North Carolina	2008	39	1,695
LSU	†1970	32	1,691
Middle Tenn.	†1969	26	1,685
Kansas	†1998	39	1,682

†national leader

DIVISION I

REBOUND MARGIN
(Since 1973)

Team	Season	Off.	Def.	Mar.
Manhattan	†1973	56.5	38.0	18.5
American	1973	56.7	40.3	16.4
Alcorn St.	†1978	52.3	36.0	16.3
Oral Roberts	1973	66.9	50.3	15.6
Alcorn St.	†1980	49.2	33.8	15.4
Michigan St.	†2001	42.5	27.1	15.4
UCLA	1973	49.0	33.9	15.1
Houston	1973	54.7	40.8	13.9
Massachusetts	†1974	44.5	30.7	13.8
Alcorn St.	†1979	50.1	36.3	13.8
Minnesota	1973	49.0	36.0	13.0
VCU	1974	55.1	42.1	13.0
Northeastern	†1981	44.9	32.0	12.9
Stetson	†1975	47.1	34.7	12.4
Notre Dame	†1976	46.3	34.1	12.2
Harvard	1973	53.5	41.3	12.2
Tennessee St.	1980	46.5	34.3	12.2
Tennessee St.	1979	49.7	37.9	11.8
Buffalo	1976	51.5	39.7	11.8
Southern U.	1978	43.1	31.4	11.7
Wyoming	1981	42.0	30.3	11.7
Michigan St.	†2000	39.0	27.3	11.7
Alabama	1973	50.9	39.3	11.6
Mississippi Val.	†1996	48.3	36.8	11.6
Iowa	†1987	43.1	31.5	11.5

†national leader

ASSISTS

Team	Season	G	Ast.
UNLV	†1990	40	926
UNLV	†1991	35	863
Oklahoma	†1988	39	862
UNLV	†1987	39	853
Oklahoma	†1985	37	828
Arkansas	1991	38	819
Kansas	†1986	39	814
North Carolina	1986	34	800
North Carolina	†1989	37	788
SMU	1988	35	786
Kentucky	†1996	36	783
North Carolina	1987	36	782
Kentucky	†1997	40	776
Kansas	†2002	37	767
Loyola Marymount	1990	32	763
Kansas	1990	35	762
Kansas	†1998	39	746
Oklahoma	1989	36	743
Illinois	†2005	39	727
Arkansas	†1995	39	721
Kansas	†2008	40	721
Maryland	2002	36	714
North Carolina	2005	37	706
Duke	†2001	39	701
North Carolina	1991	35	699
North Carolina	1998	38	699

†national leader

ASSISTS PER GAME

Team	Season	G	Ast.	Avg.
UNLV	†1991	35	863	24.7
Loyola Marymount	†1990	32	762	23.8
North Carolina	1986	34	800	23.5
UNLV	1990	40	926	23.2
SMU	†1987	29	655	22.6
SMU	†1988	35	786	22.5
Oklahoma	†1985	37	828	22.4
Oklahoma	1988	39	862	22.1
Northwestern St.	†1993	26	570	21.9
UNLV	1987	39	853	21.9
Kansas	1990	35	763	21.8
Kentucky	†1996	36	783	21.8
North Carolina	1987	36	782	21.7
Iowa St.	1988	32	694	21.7
Arkansas	1991	38	819	21.6
North Carolina	†1989	37	788	21.3
Georgia Tech	1988	32	680	21.3
Montana St.	1996	30	627	20.9
Montana St.	†1995	29	606	20.9
Montana St.	†1998	30	624	20.8

Team	Season	G	Ast.	Avg.
Kansas	†2002	37	767	20.7
VMI	†2007	33	681	20.6
TCU	†1999	32	650	20.3
Arkansas	†1994	34	687	20.2
Fresno St.	1998	34	685	20.2

†national leader

BLOCKED SHOTS

Team	Season	G	Blk.
Connecticut	†2004	39	315
Georgetown	†1989	34	309
Connecticut	†2006	34	298
Connecticut	†2008	33	285
Connecticut	†2005	31	275
Massachusetts	†1995	34	273
Mississippi St.	2008	34	267
UNLV	†1991	35	266
Connecticut	†2007	31	264
Massachusetts	2008	36	264
Connecticut	†2003	33	253
Syracuse	2007	35	250
Old Dominion	†1999	34	248
Syracuse	2003	35	247
BYU	1991	34	246
Massachusetts	2007	33	246
Kansas	2007	38	246
Duke	1999	39	245
Memphis	2008	40	244
Kentucky	†1998	39	240
Duke	2004	37	240
Northeastern	2006	30	240
Seton Hall	†2001	31	236
Connecticut	†2002	34	236
LSU	2006	36	236
Alabama A&M	2007	30	236

†national leader

BLOCKED SHOTS PER GAME

Team	Season	G	Blk.	Avg.
Georgetown	†1989	34	309	9.09
Connecticut	†2005	31	275	8.87
Connecticut	†2006	34	298	8.76
Connecticut	†2008	33	285	8.64
Connecticut	†2007	31	264	8.52
Central Conn. St.	†1996	28	235	8.39
Connecticut	†2004	39	315	8.08
Massachusetts	†1995	34	273	8.03
Northeastern	2006	30	240	8.00
Alabama A&M	2007	30	236	7.87
Mississippi St.	2008	34	267	7.85
Colgate	†1997	28	217	7.75
Connecticut	†2003	33	253	7.67
Seton Hall	†2001	31	236	7.61
UNLV	†1991	35	266	7.60
Georgetown	†1990	31	233	7.52
Central Conn. St.	1995	26	194	7.46
Massachusetts	2007	33	246	7.45
La.-Monroe	†2000	28	207	7.39
Georgetown	1991	32	235	7.34
Florida A&M	1996	27	198	7.33
Iona	†1999	30	220	7.33
Massachusetts	2008	36	264	7.33
Duquesne	2008	30	220	7.33
Old Dominion	1999	34	248	7.29

†national leader

STEALS

Team	Season	G	Stl.
VMI	†2007	33	490
Oklahoma	†1988	39	486
Connecticut	†1990	37	484
Kentucky	†1997	40	480
Long Island	†1998	32	478
Cleveland St.	†1987	33	473
Arkansas	†1991	38	467
Texas	†1994	34	453
Loyola Marymount	1990	32	450
Arkansas	†1995	39	445
Cleveland St.	†1986	33	436
Kentucky	†1996	36	435
Tulsa	†2000	37	433
Georgetown	1996	37	431

Team	Season	G	Stl.
Maryland	†1999	34	431
UTSA	1991	29	430
Duke	†2001	39	411
West Virginia	1998	33	407
Oklahoma	†1993	32	405
UNLV	1991	35	399
Long Island	1997	30	396
Florida A&M	1988	30	395
Alabama A&M	†2002	27	395
Kentucky	1994	34	394
Syracuse	2002	36	394
UAB	†2003	34	394

†national leader

STEALS PER GAME

Team	Season	G	Stl.	Avg.
Long Island	†1998	32	478	14.94
VMI	†2007	33	490	14.85
UTSA	†1991	29	430	14.83
Cleveland St.	†1987	33	473	14.33
Centenary (La.)	†1993	27	380	14.07
Loyola Marymount	†1990	32	450	14.06
Alabama A&M	†2002	27	395	13.62
Liberty	†2000	28	376	13.43
Texas	†1994	34	453	13.32
Cleveland St.	†1986	33	436	13.21
Long Island	1997	30	396	13.20
Florida A&M	†1988	30	395	13.17
Connecticut	1990	37	484	13.08
Alabama A&M	2000	28	366	13.07
Charlotte	1991	28	363	12.96
Northeastern Ill.	†1992	28	358	12.79
VMI	†2008	29	369	12.72
Maryland	†1999	34	431	12.68
Oklahoma	1993	32	405	12.66
Southern U.	1991	28	352	12.57
Cleveland St.	1988	30	376	12.53
Nicholls St.	†1995	30	376	12.53
Tulane	1992	31	388	12.52
Southern U.	1993	31	387	12.48
Drake	1994	27	337	12.48

†national leader

FEWEST TURNOVERS PER GAME
(Since 2002)

Team	Season	G	TO	Avg.
Temple	+2006	32	247	7.72
West Virginia	2006	33	287	8.70
Butler	2006	33	292	8.85
Temple	+2004	29	260	8.97
Temple	+2005	30	275	9.17
Texas	+2008	38	359	9.45
Butler	+2007	36	341	9.47
UMBC	2008	33	318	9.64
Air Force	2005	30	295	9.83
Temple	+2003	34	336	9.88
Wisconsin	2004	32	320	10.00
Butler	+2002	32	322	10.06
Butler	2005	28	282	10.07
Washington St.	2008	35	358	10.23
Air Force	2007	35	359	10.26
Butler	2004	30	308	10.27
Richmond	2002	36	370	10.28
Notre Dame	2004	32	329	10.28
Butler	2008	34	352	10.35
Samford	2007	32	334	10.44

Team	Season	G	TO	Avg.
Wisconsin	2003	32	334	10.44
Washington St.	2007	34	355	10.44
Temple	2002	34	356	10.47
South Carolina	2008	32	337	10.53
Cincinnati	2003	29	307	10.59

FEWEST PERSONAL FOULS PER GAME
(Since 2003)

Team	Season	G	PF	Avg.
West Virginia	+2006	33	419	12.70
Eastern Ky.	+2007	33	449	13.61
Ohio St.	2007	39	534	13.69
Arizona	2007	31	425	13.71
Utah St.	+2005	32	441	13.78
Eastern Ky.	2006	30	414	13.80
Alabama	2006	31	433	13.97
Penn St.	2006	30	422	14.07
UNC Asheville	+2008	33	465	14.09
Central Conn. St.	2008	30	425	14.17
Samford	2008	30	430	14.33
Utah St.	+2004	29	416	14.34
Wisconsin	2008	36	517	14.36
Alabama	2007	32	460	14.38
Troy	2004	31	446	14.39
Samford	2006	31	447	14.42
South Carolina	2006	38	548	14.42
Utah	2005	35	506	14.46
Ohio St.	2008	37	537	14.51
UNI	2006	33	480	14.55
UCLA	2008	39	569	14.59
Samford	2007	32	467	14.59
Pacific	2005	31	455	14.68
Samford	2005	28	412	14.71
Alabama	2005	32	471	14.72

MOST GAMES PLAYED
(Since 1947-48)

Team	Season	W	L	G
Duke	†1986	37	3	40
UNLV	†1990	35	5	40
Kentucky	†1997	35	5	40
Florida	†2007	35	5	40
Memphis	†2008	38	2	40
Kansas	†2008	37	3	40
Kentucky	†1948	36	3	39
Kansas	†1986	35	4	39
Louisville	†1986	32	7	39
UNLV	†1987	37	2	39
LSU	†1987	24	15	39
Oklahoma	†1988	35	4	39
Duke	†1991	32	7	39
Arkansas	†1995	32	7	39
Kansas	†1998	35	4	39
Kentucky	†1998	35	4	39
Duke	†1999	37	2	39
Michigan St.	†2000	32	7	39
Duke	†2001	35	4	39
Duke	†2004	33	6	39
Illinois	†2005	37	2	39
Florida	†2006	33	6	39
UCLA	†2006	32	7	39
Ohio St.	2007	35	4	39
North Carolina	2008	36	3	39
UCLA	2008	35	4	39

†national leader

Annual Team Champions

Won-Lost Percentage

Season	Team	Won	Lost	Pct.
1948	Western Ky.	28	2	.933
1949	Kentucky	32	2	.941
1950	Holy Cross	27	4	.871
1951	Columbia	21	1	.956
1952	Kansas	26	2	.929
1953	Seton Hall	31	2	.939
1954	Kentucky	25	0	1.000
1955	San Francisco	28	1	.966
1956	San Francisco	29	0	1.000
1957	North Carolina	32	0	1.000
1958	West Virginia	26	2	.929
1959	Mississippi St.	24	1	.960
1960	California	28	2	.933
	Cincinnati	28	2	.933
1961	Ohio St.	27	1	.964
1962	Mississippi St.	24	1	.960
1963	Loyola (Ill.)	29	2	.935
1964	UCLA	30	0	1.000
1965	UCLA	28	2	.933
1966	UTEP	28	1	.966
1967	UCLA	30	0	1.000
1968	UCLA	29	1	.967
1969	UCLA	29	1	.967
1970	UCLA	28	2	.933
1971	UCLA	29	1	.967
1972	UCLA	30	0	1.000
1973	UCLA	30	0	1.000
	North Carolina St.	27	0	1.000
1974	North Carolina St.	30	1	.968
1975	Indiana	31	1	.969
1976	Indiana	32	0	1.000
1977	San Francisco	29	2	.935
1978	Kentucky	30	2	.938
1979	Indiana St.	33	1	.971
1980	Alcorn St.	28	2	.933
1981	DePaul	27	2	.931
1982	North Carolina	32	2	.941
1983	Houston	31	3	.912
1984	Georgetown	34	3	.919
1985	Georgetown	35	3	.921
1986	Duke	37	3	.925
1987	UNLV	37	2	.949
1988	Temple	32	2	.941
1989	Ball St.	29	3	.906
1990	La Salle	30	2	.938
1991	UNLV	34	1	.971
1992	Duke	34	2	.944
1993	North Carolina	34	4	.895
1994	Arkansas	31	3	.912
1995	UCLA	31	2	.939
1996	Massachusetts	35	2	.946
1997	Kansas	34	2	.944
1998	Princeton	27	2	.931
1999	Duke	37	2	.949
2000	Cincinnnati	29	4	.879
2001	Stanford	31	3	.912
2002	Kansas	33	4	.892
2003	Kentucky	32	4	.889
2004	St. Joseph's	30	2	.938
	Stanford	30	2	.938
2005	Illinois	37	2	.949
2006	George Washington	27	3	.900
2007	Ohio St.	35	4	.897
2008	Memphis	38	2	.950

Most-Improved Teams

Season	Team	W-L Record	Previous Yr. W-L	Games Imp.
1974	Kansas	23-7	8-18	13
1975	Holy Cross	20-8	8-18	11
1976	North Texas	22-4	6-20	16
1977	La.-Lafayette	21-8	7-19	12½
1978	N.C. A&T	20-8	3-24	16½
1979	Wagner	21-7	7-19	13

Season	Team	W-L Record	Previous Yr. W-L	Games Imp.
1980	Murray St.	23-8	4-22	16½
1981	Tulsa	26-7	8-19	15
1982	Cal St. Fullerton	18-14	4-23	11½
1983	Utah St.	20-9	4-23	15
1984	Northeastern	27-5	13-15	12
	Loyola (Md.)	16-12	4-24	12
1985	Cincinnati	17-14	3-25	12½
1986	Bradley	32-3	17-13	12½
1987	James Madison	20-10	5-23	14
1988	Loyola Marymount	28-4	12-16	14
1989	Ball St.	29-3	14-14	13
1990	South Fla.	20-11	7-21	11½
	George Washington	14-17	1-27	11½
1991	Radford	22-7	7-22	15
1992	Liberty	22-7	5-23	16½
1993	Tennessee St.	19-10	4-24	14½
1994	Loyola (Md.)	17-13	2-25	13½
1995	Western Ill.	20-8	7-20	12½
1996	Cal Poly	16-13	1-26	14
1997	Northern Ariz.	21-7	6-20	14
1998	UTSA	16-11	3-25	13½
1999	Ohio St.	27-9	8-22	16
2000	Iowa St.	32-5	15-15	13½
2001	Boston College	27-5	11-19	15
2002	Fla. Atlantic	19-12	7-24	12
	Texas Tech	23-9	9-19	12
2003	Mercer	23-6	6-23	*17
2004	UTEP	24-8	6-24	*17
2005	Texas A&M	21-10	7-21	12½
	San Diego	16-13	4-26	12½
2006	South Ala.	24-7	10-18	12½
2007	Jacksonville	15-14	1-26	13
2008	Wagner	23-8	11-19	11½

*record

Scoring Offense

Season	Team	G	W-L	Pts.	Avg.
1948	Rhode Island	23	17-6	1,755	76.3
1949	Rhode Island	22	16-6	1,575	71.6
1950	Villanova	29	25-4	2,111	72.8
1951	Cincinnati	22	18-4	1,694	77.0
1952	Kentucky	32	29-3	2,635	82.3
1953	Furman	27	21-6	2,435	90.2
1954	Furman	29	20-9	2,658	91.7
1955	Furman	27	17-10	2,572	95.3
1956	Morehead St.	29	19-10	2,782	95.9
1957	Connecticut	25	17-8	2,183	87.3
1958	Marshall	24	17-7	2,113	88.0
1959	Miami (Fla.)	25	18-7	2,190	87.6
1960	Ohio St.	28	25-3	2,532	90.4
1961	St. Bonaventure	28	24-4	2,479	88.5
1962	Loyola (Ill.)	27	23-4	2,436	90.2
1963	Loyola (Ill.)	31	29-2	2,847	91.8
1964	Detroit	25	14-11	2,402	96.1
1965	Miami (Fla.)	26	22-4	2,558	98.4
1966	Syracuse	28	22-6	2,773	99.0
1967	Oklahoma City	26	16-10	2,496	96.0
1968	Houston	33	31-2	3,226	97.8
1969	Purdue	28	23-5	2,605	93.0
1970	Jacksonville	28	26-2	2,809	100.3
1971	Jacksonville	26	22-4	2,598	99.9
1972	Oral Roberts	28	26-2	2,943	105.1
1973	Oral Roberts	27	21-6	2,626	97.3
1974	Md.-East. Shore	29	27-2	2,831	97.6
1975	South Ala.	26	19-7	2,412	92.8
1976	UNLV	31	29-2	3,426	110.5
1977	UNLV	32	29-3	3,426	107.1
1978	New Mexico	28	24-4	2,731	97.5
1979	UNLV	29	21-9	2,700	93.1
1980	Alcorn St.	30	28-2	2,729	92.0
1981	UC Irvine	27	17-10	2,332	86.4
1982	Long Island	30	20-10	2,605	86.8
1983	Boston College	32	25-7	2,697	84.3
1984	Tulsa	31	27-4	2,816	90.8
1985	Oklahoma	37	31-6	3,328	89.9
1986	U.S. Int'l	28	8-20	2,542	90.8

Season	Team	G	W-L	Pts.	Avg.
1987	UNLV	39	37-2	3,612	92.6
1988	Loyola Marymount	32	28-4	3,528	110.3
1989	Loyola Marymount	31	20-11	3,486	112.5
1990	Loyola Marymount	32	26-6	3,918	*122.4
1991	Southern U.	28	19-9	2,924	104.4
1992	Northwestern St.	28	15-13	2,660	95.0
1993	Southern U.	31	21-10	3,011	97.1
1994	Southern U.	27	16-11	2,727	101.0
1995	TCU	27	16-11	2,529	93.7
1996	Troy	27	11-16	2,551	94.5
1997	Long Island	30	21-9	2,746	91.5
1998	TCU	33	27-6	3,209	97.2
1999	Duke	39	37-2	3,581	91.8
2000	Duke	34	29-5	2,992	88.0
2001	TCU	31	20-11	2,902	93.6
2002	Kansas	37	33-4	3,365	90.9
2003	Arizona	32	28-4	2,725	85.2
2004	Arizona	30	20-10	2,614	87.1
2005	North Carolina	37	33-4	3,257	88.0
2006	Long Beach St.	30	18-12	2,498	83.3
2007	VMI	33	14-19	3,331	100.9
2008	VMI	29	14-15	2,649	91.3

*record

Scoring Defense

Season	Team	G	W-L	Pts.	Avg.
1948	Oklahoma St.	31	27-4	1,006	*32.5
1949	Oklahoma St.	28	23-5	985	35.2
1950	Oklahoma St.	27	18-9	1,059	39.2
1951	Texas A&M	29	17-12	1,275	44.0
1952	Oklahoma St.	27	19-8	1,228	45.5
1953	Oklahoma St.	30	23-7	1,614	53.8
1954	Oklahoma St.	29	24-5	1,539	53.1
1955	San Francisco	29	28-1	1,511	52.1
1956	San Francisco	29	29-0	1,514	52.2
1957	Oklahoma St.	26	17-9	1,420	54.6
1958	San Francisco	27	25-2	1,363	50.5
1959	California	29	25-4	1,480	51.0
1960	California	30	28-2	1,486	49.5
1961	Santa Clara	27	18-9	1,314	48.7
1962	Santa Clara	25	19-6	1,302	52.1
1963	Cincinnati	28	26-2	1,480	52.9
1964	San Jose St.	24	14-10	1,307	54.5
1965	Tennessee	25	20-5	1,391	55.6
1966	Oregon St.	28	21-7	1,527	54.5
1967	Tennessee	28	21-7	1,511	54.0
1968	Army	25	20-5	1,448	57.9
1969	Army	28	18-10	1,498	53.5
1970	Army	28	22-6	1,515	54.1
1971	Fairleigh Dickinson	23	16-7	1,236	53.7
1972	Minnesota	25	18-7	1,451	58.0
1973	UTEP	26	16-10	1,460	56.2
1974	UTEP	25	18-7	1,413	56.5
1975	UTEP	26	20-6	1,491	57.3
1976	Princeton	27	22-5	1,427	52.9
1977	Princeton	26	21-5	1,343	51.7
1978	Fresno St.	27	21-6	1,417	52.5
1979	Princeton	26	14-12	1,452	55.8
1980	St. Peter's	31	22-9	1,563	50.4
1981	Fresno St.	29	25-4	1,470	50.7
1982	Fresno St.	30	27-3	1,412	47.1
1983	Princeton	29	20-9	1,507	52.0
1984	Princeton	28	18-10	1,403	50.1
1985	Fresno St.	32	23-9	1,696	53.0
1986	Princeton	26	13-13	1,429	55.0
1987	Missouri St.	34	28-6	1,958	57.6
1988	Ga. Southern	31	24-7	1,725	55.6
1989	Princeton	27	19-8	1,430	53.0
1990	Princeton	27	20-7	1,378	51.0
1991	Princeton	27	24-3	1,320	48.9
1992	Princeton	28	22-6	1,349	48.2
1993	Princeton	26	15-11	1,421	54.7
1994	Princeton	26	18-8	1,361	52.3
1995	Princeton	26	16-10	1,501	57.7
1996	Princeton	29	22-7	1,498	51.7
1997	Princeton	28	24-4	1,496	53.4
1998	Princeton	29	27-2	1,491	51.4
1999	Princeton	30	22-8	1,581	52.7
2000	Princeton	30	19-11	1,637	54.6
2001	Wisconsin	29	18-11	1,641	56.6

Season	Team	G	W-L	Pts.	Avg.
2002	Columbia	28	11-17	1,596	57.0
2003	Air Force	28	12-16	1,596	57.0
2004	Air Force	29	22-7	1,475	50.9
2005	Air Force	30	18-12	1,629	54.3
2006	Air Force	31	24-7	1,695	54.7
2007	Princeton	28	11-17	1,493	53.3
2008	Wisconsin	36	31-5	1,958	54.4

*record

Scoring Margin

Season	Team	G	Off.	Def.	Mar.
1949	Kentucky	34	68.2	43.9	24.3
1950	Holy Cross	31	72.6	55.4	17.2
1951	Kentucky	34	74.7	52.5	22.2
1952	Kentucky	32	82.3	55.4	26.9
1953	La Salle	28	80.1	61.8	18.3
1954	Kentucky	25	87.5	60.3	27.2
1955	Utah	28	79.0	59.9	19.1
1956	San Francisco	29	72.2	52.2	20.0
1957	Kentucky	28	84.2	69.4	14.8
1958	Cincinnati	28	86.5	65.9	20.6
1959	Idaho St.	28	74.2	53.7	20.5
1960	Cincinnati	30	86.7	64.7	22.0
1961	Memphis	23	85.0	64.2	20.8
1962	Arizona St.	27	90.1	67.6	22.5
1963	Loyola (Ill.)	31	91.8	68.1	23.7
1964	Davidson	26	89.3	70.5	18.8
1965	Connecticut	26	85.1	66.5	18.6
1966	Loyola (Ill.)	25	97.5	76.6	20.9
1967	UCLA	30	89.6	63.7	25.9
1968	UCLA	30	93.4	67.2	26.2
1969	UCLA	30	84.7	63.8	20.9
1970	St. Bonaventure	28	88.4	65.9	22.5
1971	Jacksonville	26	99.9	79.0	20.9
1972	UCLA	30	94.6	64.3	*30.3
1973	North Carolina St.	27	92.9	71.1	21.8
1974	Charlotte	26	90.2	69.4	20.8
1975	Charlotte	26	88.9	65.2	23.7
1976	UNLV	31	110.5	89.0	21.5
1977	UNLV	32	107.1	87.7	19.4
1978	UCLA	28	85.3	67.4	17.9
1979	Syracuse	30	88.7	71.5	17.2
1980	Alcorn St.	30	91.0	73.6	17.4
1981	Wyoming	30	73.6	57.5	16.1
1982	Oregon St.	27	69.6	55.0	14.6
1983	Houston	34	82.4	64.9	17.4
1984	Georgetown	37	74.3	57.9	16.4
1985	Georgetown	38	74.3	57.3	17.1
1986	Cleveland St.	33	88.9	69.6	19.3
1987	UNLV	39	92.6	75.5	17.1
1988	Oklahoma	39	102.9	81.0	21.9
1989	St. Mary's (Cal.)	30	76.1	57.6	18.5
1990	Oklahoma	32	101.3	80.4	21.0
1991	UNLV	35	97.7	71.0	26.7
1992	Indiana	34	83.4	65.8	17.6
1993	North Carolina	38	86.1	68.3	17.8
1994	Arkansas	34	93.4	75.6	17.9
1995	Kentucky	33	87.4	69.0	18.4
1996	Kentucky	36	91.4	69.4	22.1
1997	Kentucky	40	83.1	62.8	20.3
1998	Duke	36	85.6	64.1	21.5
1999	Duke	39	91.8	67.2	24.7
2000	Stanford	31	78.9	59.7	19.3
2001	Duke	39	90.7	70.5	20.2
2002	Duke	35	88.9	69.2	19.7
2003	Kansas	38	82.7	66.9	15.8
2004	Gonzaga	31	81.8	66.2	15.6
2005	North Carolina	37	88.0	70.3	17.8
2006	A&M-Corpus Christi	28	82.4	67.4	15.0
2007	Florida	40	79.8	62.6	17.2
2008	Kansas	40	80.5	61.5	19.0

*record

Field-Goal Percentage

Season	Team	FG	FGA	Pct.
1948	Oregon St.	668	1,818	36.7
1949	Muhlenberg	593	1,512	39.2

Season	Team	FG	FGA	Pct.
1950	TCU	476	1,191	40.0
1951	Maryland	481	1,210	39.8
1952	Boston College	787	1,893	41.6
1953	Furman	936	2,106	44.4
1954	George Washington	744	1,632	45.6
1955	George Washington	867	1,822	47.6
1956	George Washington	725	1,451	50.0
1957	Manhattan	679	1,489	45.6
1958	Fordham	693	1,440	48.1
1959	Auburn	593	1,216	48.8
1960	Auburn	532	1,022	52.1
1961	Ohio St.	939	1,886	49.8
1962	Florida St.	709	1,386	51.2
1963	Duke	984	1,926	51.1
1964	Davidson	894	1,644	54.4
1965	St. Peter's	579	1,089	53.2
1966	North Carolina	838	1,620	51.7
1967	UCLA	1,082	2,081	52.0
1968	Bradley	927	1,768	52.4
1969	UCLA	1,027	1,999	51.4
1970	Ohio St.	831	1,527	54.4
1971	Jacksonville	1,077	2,008	53.6
1972	North Carolina	1,031	1,954	52.8
1973	North Carolina	1,150	2,181	52.7
1974	Notre Dame	1,056	1,992	53.0
1975	Maryland	1,049	1,918	54.7
1976	Maryland	996	1,854	53.7
1977	Arkansas	849	1,558	54.5
1978	Arkansas	1,060	1,943	54.6
1979	UCLA	1,053	1,897	55.5
1980	Missouri	936	1,635	*57.2
1981	Oregon St.	862	1,528	56.4
1982	UC Irvine	920	1,639	56.1
1983	Kentucky	869	1,564	55.6
1984	Houston Baptist	797	1,445	55.2
1985	Navy	946	1,726	54.8
1986	Michigan St.	1,043	1,860	56.1
1987	Princeton	601	1,111	54.1
1988	Michigan	1,198	2,196	54.6
1989	Michigan	1,325	2,341	56.6
1990	Kansas	1,204	2,258	53.3
1991	UNLV	1,305	2,441	53.5
1992	Duke	1,108	2,069	53.6
1993	Indiana	1,076	2,062	52.2
1994	Auburn	854	1,689	50.6
1995	Washington St.	902	1,743	51.7
1996	UCLA	897	1,698	52.8
1997	UCLA	932	1,791	52.0
1998	North Carolina	1,131	2,184	51.8
1999	Northern Ariz.	783	1,497	52.3
2000	Samford	825	1,649	50.0
2001	Stanford	953	1,865	51.1
2002	Kansas	1,259	2,487	50.6
2003	Morehead St.	854	1,674	51.0
2004	Oklahoma St.	1,002	1,953	51.3
2005	Utah St.	851	1,621	52.5
2006	A&M-Corpus Christi	837	1,671	50.1
2007	Florida	1,125	2,138	52.6
2008	Utah St.	923	1,797	51.4

*record

Field-Goal Percentage Defense

Season	Team	FG	FGA	Pct.
1977	Minnesota	766	1,886	40.6
1978	Delaware St.	733	1,802	40.7
1979	Illinois	738	1,828	40.4
1980	Penn St.	543	1,309	41.5
1981	Wyoming	637	1,589	40.1
1982	Wyoming	584	1,470	39.7
1983	Wyoming	599	1,441	41.6
1984	Georgetown	799	2,025	39.5
1985	Georgetown	833	2,064	40.4
1986	St. Peter's	574	1,395	41.1
1987	San Diego	660	1,645	40.1
1988	Temple	777	1,981	39.2
1989	Georgetown	795	1,993	39.9
1990	Georgetown	713	1,929	37.0
1991	Georgetown	680	1,847	36.8
1992	UNLV	628	1,723	36.4
1993	Marquette	634	1,613	39.3

Season	Team	FG	FGA	Pct.
1994	Marquette	750	2,097	35.8
1995	Alabama	771	2,048	37.6
1996	Temple	670	1,741	38.5
1997	Marquette	628	1,735	36.2
1998	Miami (Fla.)	634	1,672	37.9
1999	Kansas St.	729	1,963	37.1
2000	Stanford	667	1,893	*35.2
2001	Kansas	782	2,069	37.8
2002	VCU	767	2,052	37.4
2003	St. Joseph's	609	1,639	37.2
2004	Connecticut	924	2,502	36.9
2005	Boston U.	588	1,584	37.1
2006	Kansas	702	1,896	37.0
2007	Connecticut	677	1,824	37.1
2008	Georgetown	669	1,827	36.6

*record

Three-Point Field Goals Made Per Game

Season	Team	G	3FG	Avg.
1987	Providence	34	280	8.24
1988	Princeton	26	211	8.12
1989	Loyola Marymount	31	287	9.26
1990	Kentucky	28	281	10.04
1991	Texas-Arlington	29	265	9.14
1992	La Salle	31	294	9.48
1993	Lamar	27	271	10.04
1994	Troy	27	262	9.70
1995	Troy	27	287	10.63
1996	Troy	27	300	11.11
1997	Mississippi Val.	29	309	10.66
1998	Florida	29	285	9.83
1999	Cal Poly	27	255	9.44
2000	Tennessee Tech	28	279	9.96
2001	Duke	39	407	10.44
2002	St. Bonaventure	30	314	10.47
2003	Mississippi Val.	29	299	10.31
2004	Troy	31	364	11.74
2005	Troy	30	338	11.27
2006	Troy	29	344	11.86
2007	VMI	33	442	*13.39
2008	VMI	29	336	11.59

*record

Three-Point Field-Goal Percentage

Season	Team	G	3FG	3FGA	Pct.
1987	Indiana	34	130	256	*50.8
1988	Princeton	26	211	429	49.2
1989	Indiana	35	121	256	47.3
1990	Princeton	27	208	460	45.2
1991	Green Bay	31	189	407	46.4
1992	Green Bay	30	204	437	46.7
1993	Valparaiso	28	214	500	42.8
1994	Indiana	30	182	401	45.4
1995	Southern Utah	28	244	571	42.7
1996	Weber St.	30	245	577	42.5
1997	Northern Ariz.	28	221	527	41.9
1998	Northern Ariz.	29	254	591	43.0
1999	Northern Ariz.	29	243	546	44.5
2000	Colorado St.	30	255	579	44.0
2001	Akron	28	189	436	43.3
2002	Marshall	30	252	595	42.4
2003	Illinois St.	29	188	427	44.0
2004	Birmingham-So.	27	243	565	43.0
2005	Oklahoma St.	33	240	564	42.6
2006	Southern Utah	30	226	527	42.9
2007	Northern Ariz.	30	229	537	42.7
2008	IUPUI	33	246	582	42.3

*record

Free-Throw Percentage

Season	Team	FT	FTA	Pct.
1948	Texas	351	481	73.0
1949	Davidson	347	489	71.0

Season	Team	FT	FTA	Pct.
1950	Temple	342	483	70.8
1951	Minnesota	287	401	71.6
1952	Kansas	491	707	69.4
1953	George Washington	502	696	72.1
1954	Wake Forest	734	1,010	72.7
1955	Wake Forest	709	938	75.6
1956	SMU	701	917	76.4
1957	Oklahoma St.	569	752	75.7
1958	Oklahoma St.	488	617	79.1
1959	Tulsa	446	586	76.1
1960	Auburn	424	549	77.2
1961	Tulane	459	604	76.0
1962	Arkansas	647	502	77.6
1963	Tulane	390	492	79.3
1964	Miami (Fla.)	593	780	76.0
1965	Miami (Fla.)	642	807	79.6
1966	Auburn	476	601	79.2
1967	West Tex. A&M	400	518	77.2
1968	Vanderbilt	527	684	77.0
1969	Jacksonville	574	733	78.3
1970	Ohio St.	452	559	80.9
1971	Tennessee	538	679	79.2
1972	Lafayette	656	844	77.7
1973	Duke	496	632	78.5
1974	Vanderbilt	477	595	80.2
1975	Vanderbilt	530	692	76.6
1976	Morehead St.	452	577	78.3
1977	Utah	499	638	78.2
1978	Duke	665	841	79.1
1979	St. Francis (Pa.)	350	446	78.5
1980	Oral Roberts	481	610	78.9
1981	Connecticut	487	623	78.2
1982	Western Ill.	447	569	78.6
1983	Western Ill.	526	679	77.5
1984	Harvard	535	651	*82.2
1985	Harvard	450	555	81.1
1986	Michigan St.	490	613	79.9
1987	Alabama	521	662	78.7
1988	Butler	413	517	79.9
1989	BYU	527	647	81.5
1990	Lafayette	461	588	78.4
1991	Butler	725	922	78.6
1992	Northwestern	497	651	76.3
1993	Utah	476	602	79.1
1994	Colgate	511	665	76.8
1995	BYU	617	798	77.3
1996	Utah	649	828	78.4
1997	Western Ky.	342	433	79.0
1998	Siena	574	715	80.3
1999	Siena	672	854	78.7
2000	Montana St.	481	609	79.0
2001	BYU	651	835	78.0
2002	Morehead St.	485	619	78.4
2003	Manhattan	560	711	78.8
2004	North Carolina St.	481	602	79.9
2005	UTEP	606	765	79.2
2006	St. Joseph's	525	657	79.9
2007	Villanova	594	761	78.1
2008	Utah St.	532	672	79.2

*record

Rebounding

Season	Team	G	Reb.	Pct.
1955	Niagara	26	1,507	.624
1956	George Washington	26	1,451	.616
1957	Morehead St.	27	1,735	.621
1958	Manhattan	26	1,437	.591
1959	Mississippi St.	25	1,012	.589
1960	Iona	18	1,054	.607
1961	Bradley	26	1,330	.592
1962	Cornell	25	1,463	.590
1963	UTEP	26	1,167	.591
1964	Iona	20	1,071	.640
1965	Iona	23	1,191	.628
1966	UTEP	29	1,430	.577
1967	Florida	25	1,275	.600

Season	Team	G	Reb.	Avg.
1968	Houston	33	2,074	62.8
1969	Middle Tenn.	26	1,685	64.8
1970	Florida St.	26	1,451	55.8

Season	Team	G	Reb.	Avg.
1971	Pacific	28	1,643	58.7
1972	Oral Roberts	28	1,686	60.2

Season	Team	G	Off.	Def.	Pct.
1973	Manhattan	26	56.5	38.0	*18.5
1974	Massachusetts	26	44.5	30.7	13.8
1975	Stetson	26	47.1	34.7	12.4
1976	Notre Dame	29	46.3	34.1	12.2
1977	Notre Dame	29	42.4	31.6	10.8
1978	Alcorn St.	29	52.3	36.0	16.3
1979	Alcorn St.	29	50.1	36.3	13.8
1980	Alcorn St.	30	49.2	33.8	15.4
1981	Northeastern	30	44.9	32.0	12.9
1982	Northeastern	30	41.2	30.8	10.4
1983	Wichita St.	28	42.4	33.6	8.8
1984	Northeastern	32	40.1	30.3	9.8
1985	Georgetown	38	39.6	30.5	9.1
1986	Notre Dame	29	36.4	27.8	8.6
1987	Iowa	35	43.1	31.5	11.5
1988	Notre Dame	29	36.0	26.2	9.9
1989	Iowa	33	41.4	31.8	9.6
1990	Georgetown	31	44.8	34.0	10.8
1991	New Orleans	31	41.7	32.4	9.3
1992	Delaware	31	42.1	33.8	8.3
1993	Massachusetts	31	43.9	32.8	11.2
1994	Utah St.	27	38.4	29.8	8.6
1995	Navy	29	40.6	29.6	11.0
1996	Mississippi Val.	29	48.3	36.8	11.6
1997	Utah St.	29	37.4	26.6	10.9
1998	Utah	34	37.0	27.1	10.0
1999	Navy	27	43.6	33.7	10.0
2000	Michigan St.	39	39.0	27.3	11.7
2001	Michigan St.	33	42.5	27.1	15.4
2002	Gonzaga	33	41.5	32.6	8.9
2003	Wake Forest	31	41.7	32.0	9.6
2004	Connecticut	39	44.7	34.9	9.7
2005	Connecticut	31	45.5	34.3	11.3
2006	Texas	37	40.5	29.9	10.6
2007	Vermont	33	40.7	31.1	9.6
2008	North Carolina	39	43.5	32.5	11.0

Note: From 1955 through 1967, the rebounding champion was determined by highest team recoveries out of the total by both teams in all games. From 1968 through 1972, the champion was determined by rebound average per game. Beginning with the 1973 season, the champion is determined by rebounding margin.

*record

Assists

Season	Team	G	Ast.	Avg.
1984	Clemson	28	571	20.4
1985	Oklahoma	37	828	22.4
1986	North Carolina	34	800	23.5
1987	SMU	29	655	22.6
1988	SMU	35	786	22.5
1989	North Carolina	37	788	21.3
1990	Loyola Marymount	32	762	23.8
1991	UNLV	35	863	*24.7
1992	Arkansas	34	674	19.8
1993	Northwestern St.	26	570	21.9
1994	Arkansas	34	687	20.2
1995	Montana St.	29	606	20.9
1996	Kentucky	36	783	21.8
1997	Kentucky	40	776	19.4
1998	Montana St.	30	624	20.8
1999	TCU	32	650	20.3
2000	UNLV	31	623	20.1
2001	Kansas	33	641	19.4
2002	Kansas	37	767	20.7
2003	Maryland	31	573	18.5
2004	Sam Houston St.	28	530	18.9
2005	North Carolina	37	706	19.1
2006	A&M-Corpus Christi	28	550	19.6
2007	VMI	33	681	20.6
2008	Notre Dame	33	608	18.4

*record

Assist-to-Turnover Ratio

Season	Team	G	Ast.	TO	Ratio
2008	UMBC	33	500	318	1.57

Blocked Shots

Season	Team	G	Blk.	Avg.
1986	Navy	35	233	6.66
1987	Siena	29	188	6.48
1988	Siena	29	193	6.66
1989	Georgetown	34	309	*9.09
1990	Georgetown	31	233	7.52
1991	UNLV	35	266	7.60
1992	Vermont	29	198	6.83
1993	Wyoming	28	184	6.57
1994	Howard	27	179	6.63
1995	Massachusetts	34	273	8.03
1996	Central Conn. St.	28	235	8.39
1997	Colgate	28	217	7.75
1998	Texas	31	203	6.55
1999	Iona	30	220	7.33
2000	La.-Monroe	28	207	7.39
2001	Seton Hall	31	236	7.61
2002	Connecticut	34	236	6.94
2003	Connecticut	33	253	7.67
2004	Connecticut	39	315	8.08
2005	Connecticut	31	275	8.87
2006	Connecticut	34	298	8.76
2007	Connecticut	31	264	8.52
2008	Connecticut	33	285	8.64

*record

Steals

Season	Team	G	Stl.	Avg.
1986	Cleveland St.	33	436	13.2
1987	Cleveland St.	33	473	14.3
1988	Florida A&M	30	395	13.2
1989	Arkansas	32	372	11.6
1990	Loyola Marymount	32	450	14.1

1991	UTSA	29	430	14.8
1992	Northeastern Ill.	28	358	12.8
1993	Centenary (La.)	27	380	14.1
1994	Texas	34	453	13.3
1995	Nicholls St.	30	376	12.5
1996	McNeese St.	27	330	12.2
1997	Long Island	30	396	13.2
1998	Long Island	32	478	*14.9
1999	Maryland	34	431	12.7
2000	Liberty	28	376	13.4
2001	Alabama A&M	28	339	12.1
2002	Alabama A&M	29	395	13.6
2003	UAB	34	394	11.6
2004	UAB	32	371	11.6
2005	UAB	33	382	11.6
2006	Houston	31	385	12.4
2007	VMI	33	490	14.8
2008	VMI	29	369	12.7

*record

Fewest Turnovers

Season	Team	G	TO	Avg.
2002	Butler	32	322	10.06
2003	Temple	34	336	9.88
2004	Temple	29	260	8.97
2005	Temple	30	275	9.17
2006	Temple	32	247	7.72
2007	Butler	36	341	9.47
2008	Texas	38	359	9.45

Fewest Personal Fouls

Season	Team	G	PF	Avg.
2003	Wisconsin	32	478	14.9
2004	Utah St.	29	416	14.3
2005	Utah St.	32	441	13.8
2006	West Virginia	33	419	12.7
2007	Eastern Ky.	33	449	13.6
2008	UNC Asheville	33	465	14.1

Statistical Trends

Year	Teams	Games	FG Made	FG Att.	Pct.	FT Made	FT Att.	Pct.	PF	Pts.
1948	160	24.7	20.3	69.4	29.3	12.7	21.1	59.8	18.5	53.3
1949	148	25.3	20.7	67.4	30.8	13.4	21.7	61.6	19.4	54.8
1950	145	25.2	21.6	68.4	31.6	14.4	23.3	61.8	19.5	57.6
1951	153	26.0	22.8	68.9	33.1	15.1	24.1	62.8	21.4	60.7
1952	156	25.7	23.8	*70.3	33.7	15.8	25.3	62.6	*22.5	63.3
1953	158	23.8	24.0	69.1	34.7	21.1	*32.9	64.0	21.3	69.1
1954	160	24.6	24.4	67.8	35.4	21.0	32.2	65.2	21.0	69.0
1955	162	23.6	25.6	69.3	36.9	*21.6	32.4	66.5	19.0	72.7
1956	166	24.7	26.1	69.5	37.5	21.2	31.7	66.8	18.9	73.3
1957	167	24.6	25.8	67.6	38.2	20.4	30.3	67.3	18.3	72.0
1958	173	24.0	25.8	67.1	38.4	16.8	25.3	66.4	18.2	68.4
1959	174	24.3	25.9	66.2	39.1	17.0	25.4	67.1	18.2	68.7
1960	175	24.5	26.3	66.2	39.8	17.4	25.8	67.4	18.4	70.0
1961	173	24.5	26.7	65.6	40.7	17.4	25.5	68.2	18.2	70.7
1962	178	24.4	27.0	67.3	40.2	16.5	24.3	67.9	18.1	70.5
1963	178	23.5	26.6	63.8	41.7	16.3	23.9	68.2	18.2	69.5
1964	179	24.3	28.7	67.4	42.5	17.1	25.1	68.3	19.1	74.4
1965	182	24.8	29.2	67.7	43.1	17.4	25.2	69.0	19.3	75.7
1966	182	21.9	30.0	68.8	43.6	17.5	25.3	69.2	19.2	77.5
1967	185	24.9	28.9	66.0	43.8	17.2	24.9	69.0	19.2	74.9
1968	189	25.1	29.1	66.6	43.7	17.4	25.1	69.1	19.0	75.5
1969	193	25.3	29.1	66.4	43.8	17.4	25.4	68.4	19.0	75.6
1970	196	25.4	30.0	67.8	44.2	17.7	25.7	68.7	19.3	77.6
1971	203	25.8	30.1	67.8	44.4	17.5	25.7	68.1	19.3	*77.7
1972	210	25.7	30.1	67.2	44.8	17.5	25.6	68.6	19.2	*77.7
1973	216	25.8	31.2	69.6	44.8	13.1	19.2	68.4	19.2	75.5
1974	233	26.0	31.0	68.3	45.4	12.8	18.7	68.4	19.2	74.8
1975	235	26.2	*31.5	68.4	46.0	13.7	19.9	69.0	20.2	76.6
1976	235	26.6	31.0	66.3	46.7	13.8	19.9	69.2	20.2	75.7
1977	245	27.2	30.4	64.9	46.7	14.2	20.5	69.4	20.1	74.9
1978	254	27.2	30.1	63.6	47.3	14.3	20.7	69.2	20.2	74.5
1979	257	27.7	29.6	62.1	47.7	14.8	21.1	*69.7	20.6	74.0
1980	261	28.0	28.6	59.7	47.9	14.9	21.3	69.6	20.2	72.0
1981	264	28.1	27.8	58.0	48.0	14.5	21.0	68.9	20.1	70.1
1982	273	28.0	26.7	55.6	47.9	14.3	20.8	68.6	19.4	67.6
1983	274	29.0	27.2	57.0	47.7	14.5	21.2	68.5	19.9	69.3
1984	276	29.1	26.7	55.6	*48.1	14.8	21.4	68.9	20.0	68.2
1985	282	29.3	27.3	57.0	47.9	14.7	21.3	68.9	19.7	69.2
1986	283	29.5	27.4	57.3	47.7	14.7	21.3	69.1	19.6	69.4

Year	Teams	Games	FG Made	FG Att.	Pct.	3FG Made	3FG Att.	Pct.	FT Made	FT Att.	Pct.	PF	Pts.
1987	290	29.6	27.2	58.7	46.4	3.5	9.2	*38.4	14.9	21.5	69.1	19.7	72.8
1988	290	29.6	27.6	58.4	47.3	4.0	10.4	38.3	15.2	22.0	68.9	19.7	74.4
1989	293	29.6	28.1	59.4	47.3	4.4	11.8	37.8	15.6	22.6	69.1	20.1	76.2
1990	292	29.6	27.5	59.5	46.2	4.7	12.8	36.8	15.6	22.6	68.9	19.8	75.3
1991	295	29.6	27.9	60.6	46.1	5.0	13.8	36.2	15.9	23.2	68.6	19.6	76.7
1992	298	29.5	26.7	58.4	45.7	5.0	14.0	35.6	15.9	23.3	68.1	20.0	74.2
1993	298	28.6	26.5	58.6	45.2	5.3	14.9	35.4	15.4	22.8	67.7	19.6	73.6
1994	301	28.7	26.8	60.6	44.3	5.7	16.5	34.5	15.6	23.2	67.1	19.9	75.0
1995	302	28.7	26.5	59.7	44.4	5.9	17.2	34.4	15.3	22.6	67.6	19.7	74.2
1996	305	28.7	25.8	58.5	44.1	5.8	17.1	34.2	15.1	22.4	67.4	19.4	72.5
1997	305	28.92	24.85	57.18	43.46	5.81	17.10	33.97	14.69	21.79	67.43	19.30	70.19
1998	306	30.26	25.31	57.67	43.88	5.98	17.37	34.44	14.85	22.00	67.52	19.35	71.44
1999	310	29.05	24.84	57.02	43.57	5.94	17.37	34.21	14.65	21.60	67.83	19.04	70.28
2000	318	29.96	24.99	57.44	43.50	6.10	17.70	34.44	14.45	21.21	68.14	18.94	70.53
2001	318	29.84	24.98	56.79	43.99	6.13	17.70	34.63	15.35	22.40	68.54	19.92	71.45
2002	321	30.17	25.06	57.23	43.79	6.33	18.29	34.58	14.81	21.48	68.96	19.19	71.26
2003	325	29.68	24.81	56.35	44.03	6.28	18.05	34.79	14.38	20.66	69.43	19.08	70.24
2004	326	29.65	24.49	55.93	43.78	6.32	18.27	34.59	14.25	20.71	68.82	19.01	69.55
2005	326	29.94	24.42	55.69	43.85	6.37	18.33	34.73	14.01	20.39	68.68	18.59	69.21
2006	326	30.06	24.43	55.59	43.94	6.44	18.43	34.94	13.88	20.09	69.12	18.40	69.17
2007	325	31.68	24.43	55.21	44.25	6.62	18.89	35.04	13.98	20.25	69.03	18.65	69.46
2008	*328	*31.94	24.45	55.43	44.10	*6.72	*19.07	35.23	13.94	20.17	69.11	18.58	69.55

Year	Teams	Games	Reb.	Ast.	Blk.	St.	TO
1993	298	28.6	36.1	*14.5	3.2	7.6	15.8
1994	301	28.7	*37.8	*14.5	3.3	*7.8	15.9
1995	302	28.7	37.2	*14.5	3.3	7.5	15.8
1996	305	28.7	36.7	14.1	3.2	7.4	15.6
1997	305	28.92	36.12	13.85	3.17	7.48	15.73
1998	306	30.26	36.41	14.02	3.22	7.64	15.91
1999	310	29.05	36.13	13.90	3.32	*7.84	*15.99
2000	318	29.96	36.28	14.01	*3.37	7.62	15.78
2001	318	29.84	35.86	13.89	3.33	7.14	15.24
2002	321	30.17	35.93	13.89	3.35	7.29	15.09
2003	325	29.68	35.07	13.75	3.30	7.17	14.89
2004	326	29.65	35.10	13.69	3.23	7.22	14.85
2005	326	29.94	34.88	13.65	3.31	7.21	14.67
2006	326	30.06	34.71	13.66	3.34	7.11	14.66
2007	325	31.68	34.35	13.55	3.29	6.81	14.52
2008	*328	*31.94	34.60	13.47	3.36	6.81	14.37

*all-time high

All-Time Winningest Teams

DIVISION I

By Victories

(Minimum 25 years in Division I)

No.	Team	First Season	Yrs.	Won	Lost	Tied	Pct.
1.	Kentucky	1903	105	1,966	621	1	.760
2.	North Carolina	1911	98	1,950	699	0	.736
3.	Kansas	1899	110	1,943	785	0	.712
4.	Duke	1906	103	1,846	808	0	.696
5.	Syracuse	1901	107	1,725	796	0	.684
6.	Temple	1895	112	1,689	948	0	.641
7.	St. John's (N.Y.)	1908	101	1,670	850	0	.663
8.	Penn	1897	108	1,647	931	2	.639
9.	UCLA	1920	89	1,646	717	0	.697
10.	Indiana	1901	108	1,635	884	0	.649
11.	Notre Dame	1898	103	1,630	893	1	.646
12.	Utah	1909	100	1,613	848	0	.655
13.	Illinois	1906	103	1,585	843	0	.653
14.	Western Ky.	1915	89	1,577	771	0	.672
15.	Oregon St.	1902	107	1,576	1,162	0	.576
16.	Washington	1896	106	1,564	1,038	0	.601
17.	Texas	1906	102	1,563	933	0	.626
18.	Louisville	1912	94	1,556	825	0	.654
19.	BYU	1903	106	1,553	986	0	.612
20.	Arizona	1905	103	1,547	844	1	.647
21.	Princeton	1901	108	1,539	972	0	.613
22.	Purdue	1897	110	1,538	917	0	.626
23.	Cincinnati	1902	107	1,535	901	0	.630
24.	West Virginia	1904	99	1,527	960	0	.614
25.	North Carolina St.	1913	96	1,518	910	0	.625
26.	Bradley	1903	104	1,516	991	0	.605
27.	Missouri St.	1909	96	1,487	813	0	.647
28.	Villanova	1921	88	1,475	842	0	.637
29.	Arkansas	1924	85	1,473	806	0	.646
30.	Oklahoma	1908	101	1,469	934	0	.611
31.	Connecticut	1901	105	1,468	834	0	.638
32.	Alabama	1913	95	1,464	884	1	.623
33.	Georgetown	1907	100	1,460	909	0	.616
33.	St. Joseph's	1910	99	1,460	951	0	.606
35.	Oklahoma St.	1908	99	1,452	1,018	0	.588
36.	Iowa	1902	107	1,451	989	0	.595
37.	Washington St.	1902	107	1,440	1,325	0	.521
38.	Southern California	1907	102	1,437	1,029	0	.583
39.	Fordham	1903	105	1,432	1,165	0	.551
40.	Montana St.	1902	106	1,427	1,131	0	.558
41.	Missouri	1907	102	1,422	1,010	0	.585
42.	Tennessee	1909	99	1,421	906	2	.611
43.	Michigan St.	1899	109	1,418	988	0	.589
44.	Illinois St.	1899	110	1,416	1,026	0	.580
45.	Ohio St.	1899	107	1,414	970	0	.593
46.	Oregon	1903	103	1,410	1,227	0	.535
47.	Kansas St.	1903	104	1,407	1,024	0	.579
48.	Vanderbilt	1901	106	1,404	1,003	0	.583
49.	Southern Ill.	1914	94	1,402	935	0	.600
50.	Marquette	1917	91	1,399	867	0	.617

By Percentage

(Minimum 25 years in Division I)

No.	Team	First Season	Yrs.	Won	Lost	Tied	Pct.
1.	Kentucky	1903	105	1,966	621	1	.760
2.	North Carolina	1911	98	1,950	699	0	.736
3.	UNLV	1959	50	1,037	418	0	.713
4.	Kansas	1899	110	1,943	785	0	.712
5.	UCLA	1920	89	1,646	717	0	.697
6.	Duke	1906	103	1,846	808	0	.696
7.	Syracuse	1901	107	1,725	796	0	.684
8.	Western Ky.	1915	89	1,577	771	0	.672
9.	St. John's (N.Y.)	1908	101	1,670	850	0	.663
10.	Utah	1909	100	1,613	848	0	.655
11.	Louisville	1912	94	1,556	825	0	.654
12.	Illinois	1906	103	1,585	843	0	.653
13.	Indiana	1901	108	1,635	884	0	.649
14.	Arizona	1905	103	1,547	844	1	.647
15.	Missouri St.	1909	96	1,487	813	0	.647
16.	Notre Dame	1898	103	1,630	893	1	.646
17.	Arkansas	1924	85	1,473	806	0	.646
18.	Temple	1895	112	1,689	948	0	.641

Team	First Season	Yrs.	Won	Lost	Tied	Pct.
19. Penn	1897	108	1,647	931	2	.639
20. Connecticut	1901	105	1,468	834	0	.638
21. Villanova	1921	88	1,475	842	0	.637
22. Murray St.	1926	83	1,378	794	0	.634
23. DePaul	1924	85	1,343	785	0	.631
24. Weber St.	1963	46	831	486	0	.631
25. Cincinnati	1902	107	1,535	901	0	.630
26. Texas	1906	102	1,563	933	0	.626
27. Purdue	1897	110	1,538	917	0	.626
28. VCU	1971	38	683	408	0	.626
29. UAB	1979	30	595	355	0	.626
30. North Carolina St.	1913	96	1,518	910	0	.625
31. Memphis	1921	87	1,336	801	0	.625
32. Alabama	1913	95	1,464	884	1	.623
33. Marquette	1917	91	1,399	867	0	.617
34. Georgetown	1907	100	1,460	909	0	.616
35. Jackson St.	1951	57	984	616	0	.615
36. West Virginia	1904	99	1,527	960	0	.614
37. Old Dominion	1951	58	929	584	0	.614
38. Princeton	1901	108	1,539	972	0	.613
39. BYU	1903	106	1,553	986	0	.612
40. Oklahoma	1908	101	1,469	934	0	.611
41. Tennessee	1909	99	1,421	906	2	.611
42. Holy Cross	1901	89	1,262	813	0	.608
43. St. Joseph's	1910	99	1,460	951	0	.606
44. Bradley	1903	104	1,516	991	0	.605
45. Akron	1902	107	1,364	897	0	.603
46. Washington	1896	106	1,564	1,038	0	.601
47. Providence	1921	83	1,255	833	0	.601
48. Tennessee St.	1945	64	1,049	697	0	.601
49. Southern Ill.	1914	94	1,402	935	0	.600
50. New Orleans	1970	39	674	449	0	.600

(Alphabetical Listing; No Minimum Seasons of Competition)

Team	First Season	Yrs.	Won	Lost	Tied	Pct.
Air Force	1957	52	609	762	0	.444
Akron	1902	107	1,364	897	0	.603
Alabama	1913	95	1,464	884	1	.623
Alabama A&M	1951	51	747	597	0	.556
Alabama St.	1935	69	1,061	719	0	.596
UAB	1979	30	595	355	0	.626
Albany (N.Y.)	1910	95	1,072	783	0	.578
Alcorn St.	1945	63	1,072	771	0	.582
American	1935	74	958	907	0	.514
Appalachian St.	1920	83	1,082	935	0	.536
Arizona	1905	103	1,547	844	1	.647
Arizona St.	1912	96	1,182	1,070	0	.525
Arkansas	1924	85	1,473	806	0	.646
Arkansas St.	1927	80	1,021	974	0	.512
UALR	1968	41	620	529	0	.540
Ark.-Pine Bluff	1957	40	498	556	0	.472
Army	1903	106	1,083	1,065	0	.504
Auburn	1906	102	1,176	1,027	1	.534
Austin Peay	1930	77	1,039	899	0	.536
Ball St.	1921	87	1,065	963	1	.525
Baylor	1907	102	1,089	1,245	0	.467
Belmont	1953	56	877	727	0	.547
Bethune-Cookman	1962	47	573	712	0	.446
Binghamton	1947	62	581	792	0	.423
Boise St.	1969	40	620	516	0	.546
Boston College	1905	75	1,045	800	0	.566
Boston U.	1902	99	986	973	0	.503
Bowling Green	1916	93	1,212	1,003	0	.547
Bradley	1903	104	1,516	991	0	.605
BYU	1903	106	1,553	986	0	.612
Brown	1901	102	912	1,338	0	.405
Bucknell	1896	113	1,224	1,090	0	.529
Buffalo	1916	91	977	983	0	.498
Butler	1897	110	1,336	1,020	0	.567
Cal Poly	1922	77	941	892	0	.513
California	1908	99	1,379	1,050	0	.568
UC Davis	1911	96	942	1,130	0	.455
UC Irvine	1966	43	599	613	0	.494
UC Riverside	1955	54	780	621	0	.557
UC Santa Barbara	1922	83	1,033	971	0	.515
Cal St. Fullerton	1961	48	617	701	0	.468
Cal St. Northridge	1959	50	660	701	0	.485

Team	First Season	Yrs.	Won	Lost	Tied	Pct.
Campbell	1962	47	603	696	0	.464
Canisius	1904	104	1,134	1,084	0	.511
Centenary (La.)	1922	82	1,040	1,072	0	.492
Central Conn. St.	1935	72	986	740	0	.571
UCF	1970	39	611	466	0	.567
Central Mich.	1905	104	1,145	1,067	1	.518
Col. of Charleston	1899	98	1,038	861	0	.547
Charleston So.	1966	43	488	679	0	.418
Charlotte	1966	43	694	539	0	.563
Chattanooga	1916	87	1,123	884	0	.560
Chicago St.	1967	42	479	693	0	.409
Cincinnati	1902	107	1,535	901	0	.630
Citadel	1913	96	874	1,141	0	.434
Clemson	1912	97	1,116	1,155	2	.491
Cleveland St.	1930	77	713	1,015	0	.413
Coastal Caro.	1975	34	460	506	0	.476
Colgate	1901	108	1,140	1,198	0	.488
Colorado	1902	105	1,104	1,051	0	.512
Colorado St.	1902	104	1,068	1,108	0	.491
Columbia	1901	108	1,139	1,142	0	.499
Connecticut	1901	105	1,468	834	0	.638
Coppin St.	1965	44	672	523	0	.562
Cornell	1899	110	1,118	1,259	0	.470
Creighton	1912	91	1,341	914	0	.595
Dartmouth	1901	107	1,191	1,302	0	.478
Davidson	1909	99	1,224	1,092	0	.528
Dayton	1904	103	1,397	992	0	.585
Delaware	1906	103	1,030	1,119	2	.479
Delaware St.	1957	51	584	750	0	.438
Denver	1904	104	1,122	1,160	0	.492
DePaul	1924	85	1,343	785	0	.631
Detroit	1906	101	1,263	1,037	0	.549
Drake	1907	102	1,087	1,281	0	.459
Drexel	1921	87	1,040	861	0	.547
Duke	1906	103	1,846	808	0	.696
Duquesne	1914	92	1,235	941	0	.568
East Carolina	1932	76	925	954	0	.492
East Tenn. St.	1922	79	1,067	861	0	.553
Eastern Ill.	1909	97	1,164	1,070	0	.521
Eastern Ky.	1910	96	1,076	1,015	1	.515
Eastern Mich.	1904	101	1,069	1,085	0	.496
Eastern Wash.	1904	100	1,257	1,049	0	.545
Elon	1911	96	1,255	1,121	0	.528
Evansville	1920	89	1,204	921	0	.567
Fairfield	1949	60	772	791	0	.494
Fairleigh Dickinson	1950	59	829	718	0	.536
Florida	1916	89	1,165	996	0	.539
Florida A&M	1951	58	879	701	0	.556
Fla. Atlantic	1989	20	207	361	0	.364
Florida Int'l	1982	27	287	442	0	.394
Florida St.	1948	61	969	724	0	.572
Fordham	1903	105	1,432	1,165	0	.551
Fresno St.	1922	86	1,154	958	1	.546
Furman	1909	95	1,084	1,094	0	.498
Gardner-Webb	1970	27	487	292	0	.625
George Mason	1967	42	592	596	0	.498
George Washington	1907	94	1,177	995	0	.542
Georgetown	1907	100	1,460	909	0	.616
Georgia	1906	103	1,235	1,137	0	.521
Ga. Southern	1927	76	1,121	798	0	.584
Georgia St.	1964	45	426	781	0	.353
Georgia Tech	1906	93	1,205	1,055	0	.533
Gonzaga	1908	100	1,336	1,036	0	.563
Grambling	1957	52	799	673	0	.543
Green Bay	1970	39	682	456	0	.599
Hampton	1953	56	817	674	0	.548
Hartford	1963	46	588	631	0	.482
Harvard	1901	97	931	1,219	0	.433
Hawaii	1938	65	645	783	0	.452
High Point	1928	81	1,241	897	0	.580
Hofstra	1937	70	1,062	789	0	.574
Holy Cross	1901	89	1,262	813	0	.608
Houston	1946	63	1,065	712	0	.599
Howard	1902	94	993	1,089	0	.477
Idaho	1906	103	1,171	1,321	0	.470
Idaho St.	1927	81	1,058	997	0	.515
Illinois	1906	103	1,585	843	0	.653
Illinois St.	1899	110	1,416	1,026	0	.580
Ill.-Chicago	1948	61	735	755	0	.493
Indiana	1901	108	1,635	884	0	.649
Indiana St.	1900	109	1,320	1,109	0	.543
IPFW	1974	35	387	572	0	.404
IUPUI	1972	37	534	533	0	.500

Team	First Season	Yrs.	Won	Lost	Tied	Pct.
Iona	1941	65	958	729	0	.568
Iowa	1902	107	1,451	989	0	.595
Iowa St.	1908	101	1,148	1,178	0	.494
Jackson St.	1951	57	984	616	0	.615
Jacksonville	1949	60	835	747	0	.528
Jacksonville St.	1926	65	1,017	637	0	.615
James Madison	1970	39	592	495	0	.545
Kansas	1899	110	1,943	785	0	.712
Kansas St.	1903	104	1,407	1,024	0	.579
Kent St.	1914	92	1,006	1,098	0	.478
Kentucky	1903	105	1,966	621	1	.760
La Salle	1932	77	1,204	811	0	.598
Lafayette	1901	98	1,195	1,064	0	.529
Lamar	1952	57	850	703	0	.547
Lehigh	1902	107	903	1,272	0	.415
Liberty	1973	36	501	543	0	.480
Lipscomb	1937	58	1,044	530	0	.663
Long Beach St.	1951	58	801	744	0	.518
Long Island	1929	74	1,080	806	2	.573
Longwood	1977	32	427	450	0	.487
LSU	1909	100	1,359	1,028	0	.569
Louisiana Tech	1926	81	1,133	897	0	.558
La.-Lafayette	1912	92	1,221	935	0	.566
La.-Monroe	1952	57	864	685	0	.558
Louisville	1912	94	1,556	825	0	.654
Loyola (Ill.)	1914	92	1,157	1,001	0	.536
Loyola (Md.)	1908	98	1,124	1,133	0	.498
Loyola Marymount	1924	80	900	1,079	0	.455
Maine	1902	93	899	988	0	.476
Manhattan	1905	102	1,205	1,058	0	.532
Marist	1967	42	591	570	0	.509
Marquette	1917	91	1,399	867	0	.617
Marshall	1907	96	1,304	947	2	.579
Maryland	1905	89	1,322	936	0	.585
UMBC	1971	38	444	598	0	.426
Md.-East. Shore	1949	59	692	825	0	.456
Massachusetts	1900	99	1,113	988	0	.530
McNeese St.	1941	66	937	770	0	.549
Memphis	1921	87	1,336	801	0	.625
Mercer	1909	91	1,045	1,030	0	.504
Miami (Fla.)	1928	56	788	627	0	.557
Miami (Ohio)	1906	103	1,235	999	0	.553
Michigan	1909	92	1,233	915	0	.574
Michigan St.	1899	109	1,418	988	0	.589
Middle Tenn.	1914	85	1,001	940	0	.516
Milwaukee	1897	112	1,189	1,095	1	.521
Minnesota	1896	113	1,397	1,066	2	.567
Mississippi	1909	98	1,091	1,165	0	.484
Mississippi St.	1909	96	1,225	1,031	0	.543
Mississippi Val.	1962	40	524	597	0	.467
Missouri	1907	102	1,422	1,010	0	.585
Missouri St.	1909	96	1,487	813	0	.647
UMKC	1970	39	547	556	0	.496
Monmouth	1957	52	821	595	0	.580
Montana	1906	100	1,267	1,123	0	.530
Montana St.	1902	106	1,427	1,131	0	.558
Morehead St.	1930	79	971	946	0	.507
Morgan St.	1948	61	662	905	0	.422
Mt. St. Mary's	1955	54	890	615	0	.591
Murray St.	1926	83	1,378	794	0	.634
Navy	1907	102	1,252	868	0	.591
Nebraska	1897	112	1,334	1,188	0	.529
Nevada	1913	95	1,127	1,044	0	.519
UNLV	1959	50	1,037	418	0	.713
New Hampshire	1903	104	790	1,288	0	.380
New Mexico	1900	105	1,286	1,005	0	.561
New Mexico St.	1905	99	1,274	975	2	.566
New Orleans	1970	39	674	449	0	.600
Niagara	1906	102	1,321	1,040	1	.559
Nicholls St.	1964	43	499	653	0	.433
Norfolk St.	1963	45	879	408	0	.683
North Carolina	1911	98	1,950	699	0	.736
N.C. A&T	1953	56	888	641	0	.581
UNC Asheville	1965	44	626	641	0	.494
UNC Greensboro	1968	41	484	574	0	.457
North Carolina St.	1913	96	1,518	910	0	.625
UNC Wilmington	1964	45	636	607	0	.512
North Dakota St.	1898	109	1,403	1,000	0	.584
North Texas	1915	91	982	1,147	0	.461
Northeastern	1921	88	1,032	965	0	.517
Northern Ariz.	1910	96	1,032	1,043	0	.497
Northern Colo.	1902	104	984	1,093	0	.474
Northern Ill.	1955	51	612	718	0	.460

Team	First Season	Yrs.	Won	Lost	Tied	Pct.
UNI	1901	103	1,086	1,012	0	.518
Northwestern	1905	103	900	1,346	1	.401
Northwestern St.	1966	43	545	648	0	.457
Notre Dame	1898	103	1,630	893	1	.646
Oakland	1968	41	575	560	0	.507
Ohio	1908	101	1,316	999	0	.568
Ohio St.	1899	107	1,414	970	0	.593
Oklahoma	1908	101	1,469	934	0	.611
Oklahoma St.	1908	99	1,452	1,018	0	.588
Old Dominion	1951	58	929	584	0	.614
Oral Roberts	1970	35	602	409	0	.595
Oregon	1903	103	1,410	1,227	0	.535
Oregon St.	1902	107	1,576	1,162	0	.576
Pacific	1911	98	1,119	1,085	0	.508
Penn	1897	108	1,647	931	2	.639
Penn St.	1897	112	1,292	1,001	1	.563
Pepperdine	1939	70	1,102	879	0	.556
Pittsburgh	1906	101	1,380	1,028	0	.573
Portland	1923	83	1,030	1,118	0	.480
Portland St.	1947	47	621	602	0	.508
Prairie View	1957	48	466	822	0	.362
Princeton	1901	108	1,539	972	0	.613
Providence	1921	83	1,255	833	0	.601
Purdue	1897	110	1,538	917	0	.626
Quinnipiac	1952	57	784	721	0	.521
Radford	1975	34	522	432	0	.547
Rhode Island	1904	102	1,307	980	0	.571
Rice	1915	94	960	1,201	0	.444
Richmond	1913	96	1,160	1,050	0	.525
Rider	1928	78	1,009	892	0	.531
Robert Morris	1977	32	414	492	0	.457
Rutgers	1907	96	1,100	1,016	0	.520
Sacramento St.	1949	60	658	935	0	.413
Sacred Heart	1966	43	703	526	0	.572
St. Bonaventure	1920	88	1,148	892	0	.563
St. Francis (N.Y.)	1902	89	1,074	1,092	0	.496
St. Francis (Pa.)	1919	82	984	958	2	.507
St. John's (N.Y.)	1908	101	1,670	850	0	.663
St. Joseph's	1910	99	1,460	951	0	.606
St. Louis	1916	92	1,223	1,057	0	.536
St. Mary's (Cal.)	1910	85	1,054	1,102	0	.489
St. Peter's	1931	75	936	892	0	.512
Sam Houston St.	1918	86	1,097	985	0	.527
Samford	1902	92	977	1,154	0	.458
San Diego	1956	53	751	702	0	.517
San Diego St.	1922	87	1,180	1,012	0	.538
San Francisco	1924	81	1,198	842	0	.587
San Jose St.	1910	95	1,058	1,192	0	.470
Santa Clara	1905	101	1,322	920	0	.590
Savannah St.	1965	44	504	677	0	.427
Seton Hall	1904	96	1,311	930	2	.585
Siena	1939	67	941	781	0	.546
South Ala.	1969	40	655	478	0	.578
South Carolina	1909	100	1,237	1,086	1	.532
South Carolina St.	1956	53	843	625	0	.574
South Dakota St.	1906	100	1,285	900	1	.588
South Fla.	1972	37	502	550	0	.477
Southeast Mo. St.	1953	50	749	552	0	.576
Southeastern La.	1948	60	690	866	0	.443
Southern California	1907	102	1,437	1,029	0	.583
Southern Ill.	1914	94	1,402	935	0	.600
SMU	1917	92	1,124	1,073	0	.512
Southern Miss.	1913	89	1,062	912	1	.538
Southern U.	1950	46	755	547	0	.580
Southern Utah	1969	40	587	499	0	.541
Stanford	1914	93	1,328	996	0	.571
Stephen F. Austin	1925	82	1,235	833	0	.597
Stetson	1901	92	1,117	943	0	.542
Stony Brook	1961	48	589	592	0	.499
Syracuse	1901	107	1,725	796	0	.684
Temple	1895	112	1,689	948	0	.641
Tennessee	1909	99	1,421	906	2	.611
Tennessee St.	1945	64	1,049	697	0	.601
Tennessee Tech	1925	84	971	936	1	.509
Tenn.-Martin	1952	57	639	786	0	.448
Texas	1906	102	1,563	933	0	.626
Texas A&M	1913	96	1,201	1,130	0	.515
A&M-Corpus Chris	2000	9	143	111	0	.563
TCU	1909	97	1,050	1,201	0	.466
Texas Southern	1950	58	940	728	0	.564
Texas St.	1921	87	1,144	980	0	.539
Texas Tech	1926	83	1,237	930	0	.571
Texas-Arlington	1960	49	540	788	0	.407
UTEP	1915	87	1,180	911	0	.564
Tex.-Pan American	1953	56	724	774	0	.483
UTSA	1982	27	399	371	0	.518
Toledo	1916	93	1,278	898	0	.587
Towson	1959	50	563	729	0	.436
Troy	1951	58	917	697	0	.568
Tulane	1906	98	1,081	1,088	0	.498
Tulsa	1908	97	1,237	1,015	0	.549
UCLA	1920	89	1,646	717	0	.697
Utah	1909	100	1,613	848	0	.655
Utah St.	1904	102	1,356	981	0	.580
Valparaiso	1918	91	1,148	1,078	0	.516
Vanderbilt	1901	106	1,404	1,003	0	.583
Vermont	1901	94	1,001	1,015	0	.497
Villanova	1921	88	1,475	842	0	.637
Virginia	1906	103	1,368	1,061	1	.563
VCU	1971	38	683	408	0	.626
VMI	1909	100	746	1,341	0	.357
Virginia Tech	1909	100	1,260	1,057	0	.544
Wagner	1923	71	889	905	0	.496
Wake Forest	1906	102	1,366	1,042	0	.567
Washington	1896	106	1,564	1,038	0	.601
Washington St.	1902	107	1,440	1,325	0	.521
Weber St.	1963	46	831	486	0	.631
West Virginia	1904	99	1,527	960	0	.614
Western Caro.	1929	80	1,061	1,022	0	.509
Western Ill.	1948	61	852	808	0	.513
Western Ky.	1915	89	1,577	771	0	.672
Western Mich.	1914	95	1,154	1,031	0	.528
Wichita St.	1906	101	1,289	1,110	0	.537
William & Mary	1906	103	1,060	1,228	0	.463
Winthrop	1979	30	501	406	0	.552
Wisconsin	1899	110	1,345	1,094	0	.551
Wofford	1916	84	1,053	1,049	0	.501
Wright St.	1971	38	634	430	0	.596
Wyoming	1905	103	1,349	1,007	0	.573
Xavier	1920	87	1,229	884	0	.582
Yale	1896	113	1,283	1,339	1	.489
Youngstown St.	1928	78	965	955	0	.503

YNote: Records are adjusted with vacated and forfeited games.

Schools in the process of becoming Division I

Team	First Season	Yrs.	Won	Lost	Tied	Pct.
Bryant	1964	45	622	600	0	.509
Cal St. Bakersfield	1972	37	738	328	0	.692
Central Ark.	1921	86	1,371	858	1	.615
Fla. Gulf Coast	2003	6	124	60	0	.674
Kennesaw St.	1986	23	375	301	0	.555
Houston Baptist	1968	22	270	322	0	.456
New Haven	1951	56	809	641	0	.558
NJIT	1924	77	799	683	0	.539
N.C. Central	1928	75	1,030	830	0	.554
North Dakota	1905	103	1,422	887	0	.616
North Fla.	1993	16	164	281	0	.369
Presbyterian	1914	95	1,038	1,019	2	.505
Seattle	1946	63	929	832	0	.528
S.C. Upstate	1975	34	574	405	0	.586
South Dakota	1909	98	1,139	938	0	.548
SIU-Edwardsville	1968	40	548	516	0	.515
Utah Valley	2004	5	92	51	0	.643
Winston-Salem	1947	62	1,068	640	0	.625

Vacated and Forfeited Games

Teams	Coach	Year	Actual W-L	Adjusted W-L	Games Affected*
Alabama	Wimp Sanderson	1987	28-5	26-4	V: Tr 2-1
Arizona	Lute Olson	1999	22-7	22-6	V: Tr 0-1
Arizona St.	Bill Freider	1995	24-9	22-8	V: Tr 2-1
Austin Peay	Lake Kelly	1973	22-7	21-5	V: Tr 1-2
California	Todd Bozeman	1995	13-14	0-27	F: RS 13 wins
California	Todd Bozeman	1996	17-11	2-25	F: RS 15 wins; V: 0-1
Clemson	Cliff Ellis	1990	26-9	24-8	V: Tr 2-1
Connecticut	Jim Calhoun	1996	32-3	30-2	V: Tr 2-1
DePaul	Joey Meyer	1986	18-13	16-12	V: Tr 2-1
DePaul	Joey Meyer	1987	28-3	26-2	V: Tr 2-1
DePaul	Joey Meyer	1988	22-8	21-7	V: Tr 1-1
DePaul	Joey Meyer	1989	21-12	20-11	V: Tr 1-1
Florida	Norm Sloan	1987	23-11	21-10	V: Tr 2-1
Florida	Norm Sloan	1988	23-12	22-11	V: Tr 1-1
Florida Int'l	Donnie Marsh	2003	8-21	1-21	V: RS 7 wins
Florida Int'l	Donnie Marsh	2004	5-22	0-22	V: RS 5 wins
Florida Int'l	Sergio Rouco	2005	13-17	0-17	V: RS 13 wins
Florida Int'l	Sergio Rouco	2006	8-20	1-20	V: RS 7 wins
Fresno St.	Jerry Tarkanian	1999	21-12	1-12	V: RS 20 wins
Fresno St.	Jerry Tarkanian	2000	24-10	12-9	V: RS 12 wins, Tr 0-1
Fresno St.	Jerry Tarkanian	2001	26-7	9-7	V: RS 17 wins
Georgia	Hugh Durham	1985	22-9	21-8	V: Tr 1-1
Georgia	Jim Harrick	2002	22-10	21-9	V: Tr 1-1
Iona	Jim Valvano	1980	29-5	28-4	V: Tr 1-1
Kentucky	Eddie Sutton	1988	27-6	25-5	V: Tr 2-1
Long Beach St.	Jerry Tarkanian	1971	24-5	22-4	V: Tr 2-1
Long Beach St.	Jerry Tarkanian	1972	25-4	23-3	V: Tr 2-1
Long Beach St.	Jerry Tarkanian	1973	26-3	24-2	V: Tr 2-1
Long Beach St.	Larry Reynolds	2006	18-12	0-12	V: RS 18 wins
La.-Lafayette	Berly Shipley	1972	25-4	23-3	V: Tr 2-1
La.-Lafayette	Berly Shipley	1973	24-5	23-3	V: Tr 1-2
La.-Lafayette	Jessie Evans	2004	20-9	6-8	V: RS 14 wins, Tr 0-1
La.-Lafayette	Robert Lee	2005	20-11	3-10	V: RS 17 wins, Tr 0-1
Loyola Marymount	Ron Jacobs	1980	14-14	14-13	V: Tr 0-1
Marshall	Ricky Huckabay	1987	25-6	25-5	V: Tr 0-1
Maryland	Bob Wade	1988	18-13	17-12	V: Tr 1-1
Massachusetts	John Calipari	996	35-2	31-1	V: Tr 4-1
Memphis	Dana Kirk	1982	24-5	23-4	V: Tr 1-1
Memphis	Dana Kirk	1983	23-8	22-7	V: Tr 1-1
Memphis	Dana Kirk	1984	26-7	24-6	V: Tr 2-1
Memphis	Dana Kirk	1985	31-4	27-3	V: Tr 4-1
Memphis	Dana Kirk	1986	28-6	27-5	V: Tr 1-1
Miami (Ohio)	Jerry Pierson	1989	13-15	5-23	F: RS 8 wins
Michigan	Steve Fisher	1992	25-9	20-8	V: Tr 5-1
Michigan	Steve Fisher	1993	31-5	0-5	V: RS 26 wins, Tr 5-1
Michigan	Steve Fisher	1996	21-11	0-11	V: RS 21 wins, Tr 0-1
Michigan	Steve Fisher	1997	24-11	0-11	V: RS 24 wins
Michigan	Brian Ellerbe	1998	25-9	0-9	V: RS 24 wins, Tr 1-1
Michigan	Brian Ellerbe	1999	12-19	0-19	V: RS 12 wins
Minnesota	Bill Musselman	1972	18-7	17-6	V: Tr 1-1
Minnesota	Jim Dutcher	1977	24-3	0-27	F: RS 24 wins
Minnesota	Clem Haskins	1994	22-13	21-12	V: Tr 1-1
Minnesota	Clem Haskins	1995	19-13	19-12	V: Tr 0-1
Minnesota	Clem Haskins	1996	19-13	18-12	V: NIT 1-1
Minnesota	Clem Haskins	1997	35-5	31-4	V: Tr 4-1
Minnesota	Clem Haskins	1998	20-15	15-15	V: NIT 5-0
Missouri	Norm Stewart	1994	28-4	25-3	V: Tr 3-1
New Mexico St.	Neil McCarthy	1992	25-8	23-7	V: Tr 2-1
New Mexico St.	Neil McCarthy	1993	26-8	25-7	V: Tr 1-1
New Mexico St.	Neil McCarthy	1994	23-8	23-7	V: Tr 0-1
New Mexico St.	Neil McCarthy	1997	19-9	0-0	V: RS 19 wins
New Mexico St.	Lou Henson	1998	18-12	0-0	V: RS 18 wins
North Carolina St.	Jim Valvano	1987	20-14	20-13	V: Tr 0-1
North Carolina St.	Jim Valvano	1988	24-7	24-6	V: Tr 0-1
Ohio St.	Jim O'Brien	1999	27-9	1-1	V: RS 22-7, Tr 4-1
Ohio St.	Jim O'Brien	2000	23-7	11-3	V: RS 11-3, Tr 1-1
Ohio St.	Jim O'Brien	2001	20-11	0-0	V: RS 20-10, Tr 0-1
Ohio St.	Jim O'Brien	2002	24-8	0-0	V: RS 23-7, Tr 1-1
Oregon St.	Ralph Miller	1976	18-9	3-24	F: RS 15 wins
Oregon St.	Ralph Miller	1980	26-4	26-3	V: Tr 0-1
Oregon St.	Ralph Miller	1981	26-2	26-1	V: Tr 0-1
Oregon St.	Ralph Miller	1982	25-5	23-4	V: Tr 2-1
Purdue	Gene Keady	1996	26-6	7-23	F: RS 18 wins; V: Tr 1-1
St. Bonaventure	Jan van Breda Kolff	2002	13-14	1-14	V: RS 12 wins
St. John's (N.Y.)	Mike Jarvis	2001	14-15	5-15	V: RS 9 wins
St. John's (N.Y.)	Mike Jarvis	2002	20-12	7-11	V: RS 13 wins, Tr 0-1
St. John's (N.Y.)	Mike Jarvis	2003	21-13	1-13	V: RS 20 wins
St. John's (N.Y.)	Mike Jarvis	2004	6-21	2-21	V: RS 4 wins
St. Joseph's	Jack Ramsay	1961	25-5	22-4	V: Tr 3-1
Texas Tech	James Dickey	1996	30-2	28-1	V: Tr 2-1
UCLA	Larry Brown	1980	22-10	17-9	V: Tr 5-1
UCLA	Steve Lavin	1999	22-9	22-8	V: Tr 0-1
Villanova	Jack Kraft	1971	27-7	23-6	V: Tr 4-1
Western Ky.	Johnny Oldham	1971	24-6	20-5	V: Tr 4-1

*F=Forfeited, V=Vacated; NIT=National Invitational Tournament; RS=Regular Season; Tr=NCAA Tournament.

Winningest Teams by Decade

DIVISION I

1930-39

Rk.	Team	Won	Lost	Pct.
1.	Long Island	198	38	.839
2.	Kentucky	162	34	.827
3.	St. John's (N.Y.)	181	40	.819
4.	Kansas	153	37	.805
5.	Syracuse	143	37	.794
6.	Purdue	148	39	.791
7.	Western Ky.	197	52	.791
8.	Rhode Island	142	39	.785
9.	Notre Dame	170	49	.776
10.	CCNY	120	35	.774
11.	Washington	206	63	.766
12.	DePaul	142	44	.763
13.	Arkansas	167	57	.746
14.	Duquesne	143	50	.741
15.	Wyoming	147	52	.739
16.	Navy	108	40	.730
17.	North Carolina	163	61	.728
18.	George Washington	129	50	.721
19.	New York U.	124	49	.717
20.	Western Mich.	123	50	.711

1940-49

Rk.	Team	Won	Lost	Pct.
1.	Kentucky	239	42	.851
2.	Oklahoma St.	237	55	.812
3.	Rhode Island	178	44	.802
4.	Eastern Ky.	145	40	.784
5.	Western Ky.	222	66	.771
6.	Tennessee	152	46	.768
7.	Bowling Green	204	66	.756
8.	Notre Dame	162	55	.747
9.	Toledo	176	65	.730
10.	St. John's (N.Y.)	162	60	.730
11.	North Carolina	196	75	.723
12.	West Virginia	157	59	.727
13.	Illinois	150	57	.725
14.	DePaul	180	69	.723
15.	Bradley	144	56	.720
16.	New York U.	150	60	.714
17.	Utah	159	68	.700
18.	Wyoming	163	70	.700
19.	Texas	168	73	.697
20.	CCNY	133	62	.682
Played only seven seasons:				
	Seton Hall	128	22	.853
	Duquesne	118	32	.787
	George Washington	117	47	.713

1950-59

Rk.	Team	Won	Lost	Pct.
1.	Kentucky	224	33	.872
2.	North Carolina St.	240	65	.787
3.	Seattle	233	69	.772
4.	La Salle	209	65	.763
5.	Dayton	228	71	.763
6.	Holy Cross	199	65	.754
7.	Kansas St.	179	63	.740
8.	Connecticut	187	67	.736
9.	West Virginia	205	74	.735
10.	Louisville	202	77	.724
11.	Illinois	165	64	.721
12.	Western Ky.	205	82	.714
13.	UCLA	193	78	.712
14.	Duquesne	187	76	.711
15.	Kansas	171	74	.698
16.	St. John's (N.Y.)	176	77	.696
17.	Cincinnati	175	80	.686
18.	Oklahoma St.	192	88	.686
19.	Lafayette	171	81	.679
20.	St. Louis	185	88	.678

1960-69

Rk.	Team	Won	Lost	Pct.
1.	UCLA	234	52	.818
2.	Cincinnati	214	63	.773
3.	Providence	204	64	.761
4.	Duke	213	67	.761
5.	Kentucky	197	69	.741
6.	Ohio St.	188	69	.732
7.	St. Joseph's	201	74	.731
8.	Dayton	207	77	.729
9.	Bradley	197	74	.727
10.	Princeton	188	71	.726
11.	Vanderbilt	182	69	.725
12.	North Carolina	184	72	.719
13.	St. Bonaventure	172	69	.714
14.	Villanova	193	79	.710
15.	Houston	198	82	.707
16.	St. John's (N.Y.)	185	79	.701
17.	Miami (Fla.)	183	82	.691
18.	West Virginia	197	89	.689
19.	Temple	183	83	.688
20.	UTEP	177	81	.686
Played only seven seasons:				
	Weber St.	147	36	.803

1970-79

Rk.	Team	Won	Lost	Pct.
1.	UCLA	273	27	.910
2.	Marquette	251	41	.860
3.	Penn	223	56	.799
4.	North Carolina	239	65	.786
5.	Kentucky	223	69	.764
6.	Louisville	224	70	.762
7.	Syracuse	213	69	.755
8.	Long Beach St.	209	71	.746
9.	Indiana	208	75	.735
10.	Florida St.	201	74	.731
11.	UNLV	203	78	.722
12.	North Carolina St.	208	80	.722
13.	San Francisco	202	79	.719
14.	Houston	210	84	.714
15.	Providence	209	84	.713
16.	South Carolina	198	80	.712
17.	St. John's (N.Y.)	205	85	.707
18.	Maryland	199	85	.701
19.	Rutgers	193	84	.697
20.	Notre Dame	202	89	.694
Played only eight seasons:				
	Oral Roberts	161	59	.732

1980-89

Rk.	Team	Won	Lost	Pct.
1.	North Carolina	281	63	.817
2.	UNLV	271	65	.807
3.	Georgetown	269	69	.796
4.	DePaul	235	67	.778
5.	Temple	225	78	.743
6.	Syracuse	243	87	.736
7.	UTEP	227	82	.735
8.	Oklahoma	245	90	.731
9.	Kentucky	233	86	.730
10.	St. John's (N.Y.)	228	85	.728
11.	Indiana	228	86	.726
12.	Oregon St.	212	80	.726
13.	Louisville	250	96	.723
14.	Illinois	233	90	.721
15.	Memphis	225	89	.717
16.	Northeastern	213	86	.712
17.	Chattanooga	215	89	.707
18.	Arkansas	218	92	.703
19.	Missouri	227	99	.696
20.	West Virginia	217	95	.696

1990-99

Rk.	Team	Won	Lost	Pct.
1.	Kansas	286	60	.827
2.	Kentucky	282	63	.817
3.	Arizona	256	67	.793
4.	Duke	271	78	.777
5.	North Carolina	270	78	.776
6.	Connecticut	259	75	.775
7.	Utah	250	76	.767
8.	Princeton	210	66	.761
9.	Arkansas	260	83	.758
10.	UCLA	240	79	.752
11.	Cincinnati	246	83	.748
12.	Xavier	217	86	.716
13.	Syracuse	232	92	.716
14.	Massachusetts	237	94	.716
15.	Murray St.	219	88	.713
16.	Indiana	229	94	.709
17.	New Mexico St.	219	91	.706
18.	Green Bay	211	90	.701
19.	Purdue	222	96	.698
20.	New Mexico	224	97	.698

Played only eight seasons:

	Col. of Charleston	191	42	.820

2000-08

Rk.	Team	Won	Lost	Pct.
1.	Duke	261	53	.831
2.	Kansas	255	61	.807
3.	Gonzaga	236	60	.797
4.	Florida	236	74	.761
5.	Utah St.	222	73	.753
6.	Memphis	234	81	.743
7.	Texas	228	80	.740
8.	Illinois	228	81	.738
9.	Stanford	212	76	.736
10.	Connecticut	222	80	.735
11.	Pittsburgh	221	80	.734
12.	Oklahoma	215	81	.726
13.	Kentucky	218	83	.724
14.	Syracuse	222	85	.723
15.	Xavier	213	82	.722
16.	Kent St.	214	83	.721
17.	Butler	208	81	.720
18.	Arizona	216	85	.718
19.	Wisconsin	213	85	.715
20.	Creighton	206	84	.710

Winningest Teams Over Periods of Time

Victories Over a Two-Year Period

Team	First Year	Last Year	Won	Lost
Montana St.	1928	1929	72	4
Memphis	2007	2008	71	6
Kentucky	1947	1948	70	6
UNLV	1986	1987	70	7
Kansas	2007	2008	70	8
Kentucky	1997	1998	70	9
Georgetown	1984	1985	69	6
UNLV	1990	1991	69	6
Kansas	1997	1998	69	6
Duke	1998	1999	69	6
Kentucky	1996	1997	69	7
Kentucky	1948	1949	68	5
Florida	2006	2007	68	11
North Carolina	2007	2008	67	10
Connecticut	1998	1999	66	7
Duke	1999	2000	66	7
Duke	2001	2002	66	8
Memphis	2006	2007	66	8
Montana St.	1927	1928	66	9
Duke	1991	1992	66	9
Oklahoma	1988	1989	65	10
UCLA	2007	2008	65	10
Michigan St.	1999	2000	65	12
UNLV	1987	1988	65	8
Temple	1987	1988	64	6
Arizona	1988	1989	64	7
Massachusetts	1995	1996	64	7
Arkansas	1990	1991	64	9
Duke	2000	2001	64	9
Bradley	1950	1951	64	11
UNLV	1989	1990	64	13

Victories Over a Three-Year Period

Team	First Year	Last Year	Won	Lost
Memphis	2006	2008	104	10
Kentucky	1996	1998	104	11
Kentucky	1947	1949	102	8
Montana St.	1927	1929	102	11
Duke	1999	2001	101	11
Kentucky	1946	1948	98	8
Kansas	1996	1998	98	11
Duke	1998	2000	98	11
UNLV	1985	1987	98	11
UNLV	1986	1988	98	13
UNLV	1989	1991	98	14
Kentucky	1997	1999	98	18
Kentucky	1995	1997	97	12
UCLA	2006	2008	97	17
UNLV	1990	1992	95	8
Duke	2000	2002	95	13
Kansas	2006	2008	95	16
Duke	1990	1992	95	18
UNLV	1987	1989	94	16
Kentucky	1948	1950	93	10
Montana St.	1928	1930	93	14
Georgetown	1984	1986	93	14
Duke	1997	1999	93	15
Michigan St.	1999	2001	93	17
Massachusetts	1994	1996	92	14
Oklahoma	1988	1990	92	15
Duke	2001	2003	92	15
Kansas	1997	1999	92	16
UNLV	1988	1990	92	19
Florida	2005	2007	92	19
Florida	2006	2008	92	23

Victories Over a Four-Year Period

Team	First Year	Last Year	Won	Lost
Duke	1998	2001	133	15
Duke	1999	2002	132	15
Kentucky	1995	1998	132	16
Kentucky	1996	1999	132	20
Kentucky	1946	1949	130	10
UNLV	1987	1990	129	21
Kentucky	1947	1950	127	13
UNLV	1984	1987	127	17
UNLV	1986	1989	127	21
UNLV	1985	1988	126	17
UNLV	1988	1991	126	20
Memphis	2005	2008	126	26
Kentucky	1948	1951	125	12
UNLV	1989	1992	124	16
Kentucky	1994	1997	124	19
Kansas	1995	1998	123	17
Montana St.	1927	1930	123	21
Duke	2001	2004	123	21
North Carolina	2005	2008	123	22
Duke	1989	1992	123	26
Georgetown	1984	1987	122	19

Team	First Year	Last Year	Won	Lost
Duke	1997	2000	122	20
Montana St.	1926	1929	122	23
Duke	2000	2003	121	20
Kansas	1996	1999	121	21
Georgetown	1982	1985	121	23
Kentucky	1997	2000	121	28

Winning Percentage Over a Two-Year Period

(Minimum 40 games)

Team	First Year	Last Year	Won	Lost	Pct.
UCLA	1972	1973	60	0	1.000
Indiana	1975	1976	63	1	.984
UCLA	1967	1968	59	1	.983
UCLA	1971	1972	59	1	.983
North Carolina St.	1973	1974	57	1	.983
North Carolina	1923	1924	41	1	.976
UCLA	1964	1965	58	2	.967
UCLA	1968	1969	58	2	.967
Long Island	1935	1936	49	2	.961
St. John's (N.Y.)	1930	1931	46	2	.958
UNLV	1991	1992	60	3	.952
Seton Hall	1940	1941	39	2	.951
Arkansas	1928	1929	38	2	.950
Notre Dame	1926	1927	38	2	.950
UCLA	1969	1970	57	3	.950
UCLA	1970	1971	57	3	.950
Alcorn St.	1978	1979	56	3	.949
Montana St.	1928	1929	72	4	.947
Long Island	1936	1937	53	3	.946
Penn	1970	1971	53	3	.946
Ohio St.	1961	1962	53	3	.946
Long Island	1934	1935	50	3	.943
Kentucky	1954	1955	48	3	.941
St. John's (N.Y.)	1929	1930	46	3	.939
Penn	1920	1921	43	3	.935

Winning Percentage Over a Three-Year Period

(Minimum 60 games)

Team	First Year	Last Year	Won	Lost	Pct.
UCLA	1971	1973	89	1	.989
UCLA	1967	1969	88	2	.978
UCLA	1970	1972	87	3	.967
Long Island	1934	1936	75	3	.962
UCLA	1968	1970	86	4	.956
UCLA	1969	1971	86	4	.956
UCLA	1972	1974	86	4	.956
St. John's (N.Y.)	1929	1931	67	4	.944
Long Island	1935	1937	77	5	.939
Penn	1919	1921	58	4	.935
Indiana	1974	1976	86	6	.935
Ohio St.	1960	1962	78	6	.929
Penn	1970	1972	78	6	.929
Kentucky	1947	1949	102	8	.927
Kentucky	1946	1948	98	8	.925
Kentucky	1951	1953	61	5	.924
Cincinnati	1960	1962	84	7	.923
UCLA	1973	1975	84	7	.923
UNLV	1990	1992	95	8	.922
Cincinnati	1961	1963	82	7	.921
North Carolina St.	1973	1975	79	7	.919
DePaul	1980	1982	79	7	.917
Arkansas	1926	1928	56	5	.918
Penn	1920	1922	67	6	.918
St. John's (N.Y.)	1930	1932	66	6	.917
Seton Hall	1940	1942	55	5	.917

Winning Percentage Over a Four-Year Period

(Minimum 80 games)

Team	First Year	Last Year	Won	Lost	Pct.
UCLA	1970	1973	117	3	.975
UCLA	1967	1970	116	4	.967
UCLA	1969	1972	116	4	.967
UCLA	1968	1971	115	5	.958
UCLA	1971	1974	115	5	.958
Kentucky	1951	1954	86	5	.945
Long Island	1934	1937	103	6	.945
UCLA	1972	1975	114	7	.942
Kentucky	1946	1949	130	10	.929
Kentucky	1952	1955	77	6	.928
Penn	1918	1921	76	6	.927
Arkansas	1926	1929	75	6	.929
Long Island	1936	1939	99	8	.925
Cincinnati	1960	1963	110	9	.924
Penn	1919	1922	82	7	.921
St. John's (N.Y.)	1929	1932	89	8	.918
St. John's (N.Y.)	1928	1931	85	8	.914
UCLA	1964	1967	106	10	.914
UCLA	1966	1969	106	10	.914
Kentucky	1948	1951	125	12	.912
Long Island	1939	1942	92	9	.911
UCLA	1973	1976	112	11	.911
Long Island	1935	1938	100	10	.909
Kentucky	1945	1948	120	12	.909
Cincinnati	1959	1962	110	11	.909

Winning Streaks

Full Season

Wins	Team	Seasons	Ended By	Score
88	UCLA	1971-74	Notre Dame	71-70
60	San Francisco	1955-57	Illinois	62-33
47	UCLA	1966-68	Houston	71-69
45	UNLV	1990-91	Duke	79-77
44	Texas	1913-17	Rice	24-18
43	Seton Hall	1939-41	Long Island	49-26
43	Long Island	1935-37	Stanford	45-31
41	UCLA	1968-69	Southern California	46-44
39	Marquette	1970-71	Ohio St.	60-59
37	Cincinnati	1962-63	Wichita St.	65-64
37	North Carolina	1957-58	West Virginia	75-64
36	North Carolina St.	1974-75	Wake Forest	83-78
35	Arkansas	1927-29	Texas	26-25

Regular Season

(Does not include national postseason tournaments)

Wins	Team	Seasons	Ended By	Score
76	UCLA	1971-74	Notre Dame	71-70
57	Indiana	1975-77	Toledo	59-57
56	Marquette	1970-72	Detroit	70-49
54	Kentucky	1952-55	Georgia Tech	59-58
51	San Francisco	1955-57	Illinois	62-33
48	Penn	1970-72	Temple	57-52
47	Ohio St.	1960-62	Wisconsin	86-67
44	Texas	1913-17	Rice	24-18
43	UCLA	1966-68	Houston	71-69
43	Long Island	1935-37	Stanford	45-31
42	Seton Hall	1939-41	Long Island	49-26

Home Court

Wins	Team	Seasons	Ended By	Score
129	Kentucky	1943-55	Georgia Tech	59-58
99	St. Bonaventure	1948-61	Niagara	87-77
98	UCLA	1970-76	Oregon	65-45
86	Cincinnati	1957-64	Bradley	87-77
81	Arizona	1945-51	Kansas St.	76-57
81	Marquette	1967-73	Notre Dame	71-69
80	Lamar	1978-84	Louisiana Tech	68-65
75	Long Beach St.	1968-74	San Francisco	94-84
72	UNLV	1974-78	New Mexico	102-98
71	Arizona	1987-92	UCLA	89-87
68	Cincinnati	1972-78	Georgia Tech	59-56
67	Western Ky.	1949-55	Xavier	(ot) 82-80

Current Home Court

Wins	Team	Wins	Team
47	BYU	15	UNLV
37	Notre Dame	14	Morgan St.
32	Tennessee	13	Lamar
24	Kansas	12	Tulsa
22	Georgetown	11	Austin Peay
21	Michigan St.	10	Davidson
19	Vanderbilt	10	Gonzaga
17	Utah St.	10	Portland St.
16	IUPUI	10	Purdue
16	Kent St.	10	Texas
		10	Western Mich.
		10	Xavier

Rivalries

Consecutive Years

Years	Opponents	First Year	Last Year
107	Columbia vs. Yale	1902	2008
107	Princeton vs. Yale	1902	2008
107	Penn vs. Princeton	1903	2008
105	Columbia vs. Penn	1904	2008
105	Cornell vs. Penn	1904	2008
104	Maine vs. New Hampshire	1905	2008
103	Idaho vs. Washington St.	1906	2008
102	Kansas vs. Kansas St.	1907	2008
102	Kansas vs. Missouri	1907	2008
101	Kansas St. vs. Nebraska	1908	2008

Games Played

Games	Opponents	First Year	Last Year
329	Oregon vs. Oregon St.	1903	2008
282	Oregon vs. Washington	1904	2008
281	Oregon St. vs. Washington	1904	2008
276	Oregon St. vs. Washington St.	1907	2008
273	Oregon vs. Washington St.	1908	2008
265	Washington vs. Washington St.	1910	2008
264	Kansas vs. Kansas St.	1907	2008
258	Kansas vs. Missouri	1907	2008
251	California vs. Stanford	1912	2008
244	BYU vs. Utah	1909	2008

Victories for One Opponent

W-L	Opponents	First Year	Last Year
180-102	Washington vs. Oregon	1904	2008
180-149	Oregon St. vs. Oregon	1903	2008
174-90	Kansas vs. Kansas St.	1907	2008
167-98	Washington vs. Washington St.	1910	2008
166-93	Kansas vs. Missouri	1907	2008
164-58	Kansas vs. Iowa St.	1908	2008
164-71	Kansas vs. Nebraska	1900	2008
161-115	Oregon St. vs. Washington St.	1909	2008
155-107	Washington St. vs. Idaho	1906	2008
154-119	Oregon vs. Washington St.	1908	2008

Consecutive Victories

Won	Opponents	First Year	Last Year
52	UCLA vs. California	1961	1985
42	Syracuse vs. Colgate	1963	†2008
41	Southern California vs. UCLA	1932	1943
39	Kentucky vs. Mississippi	1929	1972
39	Rhode Island vs. Maine	1924	1952
38	Arizona vs. Washington St.	1986	2004
38	Providence vs. Brown	1959	1978
35	Connecticut vs. New Hampshire	1939	1961
35	Marquette vs. Milwaukee	1917	†2008
35	South Carolina vs. Citadel	1945	1988

†active streak

Current Consecutive Victories

Won	Opponents	First Year	Last Year
42	Syracuse vs. Colgate	1963	2008
35	Marquette vs. Milwaukee	1917	2008
33	North Carolina vs. VMI	1922	1997
30	Syracuse vs. Cornell	1969	2008
29	Pittsburgh vs. St. Francis (Pa.)	1973	2005
25	Kentucky vs. Xavier	1942	1968
21	Duke vs. Davidson	1982	2008
20	Duke vs. East Carolina	1969	1991

Consecutive Home Victories

Won	Opponents	First Year	Last Year
52	Princeton vs. Brown	1929	2002
53	North Carolina vs. Clemson	1926	†2008
47	UCLA vs. Washington St.	1950	2003
41	Kentucky vs. Mississippi	1929	1996
37	Southern California vs. UCLA	1932	1944
34	Indiana vs. Northwestern	1969	†2008
34	Kentucky vs. Georgia	1930	1984
33	Rhode Island vs. Northeastern	1917	1988
32	Marquette vs. Milwaukee	1920	†2008
32	Rhode Island vs. New Hampshire	1937	1973
32	UCLA vs. California	1961	1989

†active streak

Current Consecutive Home Victories

Won	Opponents	First Year	Last Year
53	North Carolina vs. Clemson	1926	2008
34	Indiana vs. Northwestern	1969	2008
32	Marquette vs. Milwaukee	1920	2008
30	Syracuse vs. Colgate	1963	2008
26	Syracuse vs. Cornell	1966	2008
20	Oklahoma St. vs. Drake	1931	1958
19	Pittsburgh vs. St. Francis (Pa.)	1973	2005
19	Duke vs. East Carolina	1969	1991
16	Duke vs. William & Mary	1925	2000
14	Syracuse vs. Canisius	1970	2004

Consecutive Victories on an Opponent's Home Court

Won	Opponents	First Year	Last Year
29	Southern California at UCLA	1933	1942
26	UCLA at California	1962	1985
24	Connecticut vs. New Hampshire	1939	1968
24	Kansas at Kansas St.	1984	2007
23	Rhode Island vs. Maine	1927	1957
20	Arizona vs. Washington St.	1987	2006
20	South Carolina at Citadel	1945	†2007
13	Syracuse vs. Colgate	1963	†1997
12	Providence vs. Brown	1959	†1972

†active streak

Victories for One Opponent in One Year

W-L	Opponents	Year
5-0	Kansas vs. Nebraska	1909
5-0	Kansas vs. Kansas St.	1935
4-0	by many	

Associated Press (A.P.) Poll Records

Full Season at No. 1

1956, San Francisco, 14 weeks
1960, Cincinnati, 12 weeks
1961, Ohio St., 13 weeks
1962, Ohio St., 14 weeks
1963, Cincinnati, 16 weeks

1967, UCLA, 15 weeks
1969, UCLA, 15 weeks
1972, UCLA, 16 weeks
1973, UCLA, 16 weeks
1976, Indiana, 17 weeks

1991, UNLV, 17 weeks
1992, Duke, 18 weeks

Most Consecutive Weeks at No. 1

46, UCLA, Feb. 9, 1971 to Jan. 15, 1974
27, Ohio St., Dec. 13, 1960 to March 13, 1962
23, UCLA, Preseason Nov. 1966 to Jan. 16, 1968
19, San Francisco, Feb. 8, 1955 to March 6, 1956
18, Duke, Preseason Nov. 1991 to March 16, 1992

17, Indiana, Preseason Nov. 1975 to March 16, 1976
17, UNLV, Preseason Nov. 1990 to March 12, 1991
16, Cincinnati, Preseason Nov. 1962 to March 12, 1963
15, UCLA, Preseason Nov. 1968 to March 4, 1969
15, North Carolina, Dec. 6, 1983 to March 13, 1984

15, Kansas, Dec. 3, 1996 to March 11, 1997
15, Illinois, Dec. 7, 2004 to March 15, 2005

Preseason No. 1 to not Ranked No. 1 the Rest of the Season

1970, South Carolina
1978, North Carolina
1981, Kentucky
1986, Georgia Tech
1988, Syracuse

1990, UNLV
2000, Connecticut

Biggest Jump to No. 1 from Previous Week

8th, West Virginia, Dec. 17 to Dec. 24, 1957
6th, Duke, Dec. 7 to Dec. 14, 1965
6th, Kansas, Nov. 25 to Dec. 2, 2003

5th, Holy Cross, Jan. 10 to Jan. 17, 1950
5th, Kansas St., Dec. 23 to Dec. 30, 1952

5th, Indiana, Dec. 21 to Dec. 28, 1982
5th, UCLA, Jan. 11 to Jan. 18, 1983
5th, Temple, Feb. 2 to Feb. 9, 1988
5th, Oklahoma, Feb. 7 to Feb. 14, 1989
5th, Oklahoma, Feb. 27 to March 6, 1990

5th, Illinois, Nov. 30 to Dec. 7, 2004
5th, UCLA, Nov. 21 to Nov. 28, 2006

Biggest Jump from Not Ranked the Previous Week

(at least 20 ranked)
4th, Kansas, Preseason to Nov. 27, 1989
5th, St. Louis, Dec. 26, 1950 to Jan. 3, 1951
5th, Cincinnati, Jan. 31 to Feb. 7, 1961
6th, Notre Dame, Jan. 12 to Jan. 19, 1954
6th, Missouri, Dec. 7 to Dec. 14, 1954

6th, Maryland, Dec. 10 to Dec. 17, 1957
6th, Oklahoma St., Jan. 21 to Jan. 28, 1958
7th, Bradley, March 9 to March 23, 1954
7th, Oklahoma City, Jan. 14 to Jan. 21, 1958
7th, Iowa, Dec. 27, 1960, to Jan. 3, 1961

7th, Wake Forest, Jan. 30 to Feb. 6, 1976
7th, North Carolina St., Preseason to Nov. 29, 1983

Biggest Jump from Not Ranked the Previous Week

(at least 25 ranked)
4th, Kansas, Preseason to Nov. 27, 1989
8th, Arizona, Preseason to Nov. 20, 2001
10th, Notre Dame, Dec. 3 to Dec. 10, 2002
12th, Arizona St., Nov. 21 to Nov. 28, 1994
12th, Duke, Nov. 20 to Nov. 27, 1995

12th, North Carolina, Nov. 26 to Dec. 3, 2002
13th, Wake Forest, Jan. 25 to Feb. 1, 1993
13th, Oregon, Jan. 29 to Feb. 5, 2002
13th, Georgia Tech, Nov. 25 to Dec. 2, 2003
14th, Iowa, Jan. 9 to Jan. 16, 2001

14th, Pittsburgh, Feb. 5 to Feb. 12, 2002
14th, Florida, Nov. 15 to Nov. 22, 2005

Biggest Drop from No. 1 from Previous Week

15th, Florida, Dec. 9 to Dec. 15, 2003
9th, UNLV, Feb. 22 to March 1, 1983
8th, UCLA, Dec. 7 to Dec. 14, 1965
8th, South Carolina, Preseason Nov. to Dec. 9, 1969
8th, Duke, Jan. 17 to Jan. 24, 1989

8th, Connecticut, Preseason Nov. to Nov. 16, 1999
7th, St. John (N.Y.), Dec. 18 to Dec. 26, 1951
7th, UCLA, Jan. 25 to Feb. 1, 1983
7th, Cincinnati, March 7 to March 14, 2000
6th, Michigan St., Jan. 9 to Jan. 16, 1979

6th, Memphis, Jan. 11 to Jan. 18, 1983
6th, UNLV, Preseason Nov. 1989 to Nov. 27, 1989
6th, Syracuse, Jan. 2 to Jan. 9, 1990
6th, Michigan, Nov. 30 to Dec. 7, 1992
6th, Kentucky, Nov. 29 to Dec. 6, 1993

6th, Wake Forest, Nov. 30 to Dec. 7, 2004

Biggest Drop to Not Ranked from the Previous Week

(at least 20 ranked)
2nd, Louisville, Preseason to Dec. 2, 1986
4th, Indiana, Dec. 27, 1960, to Jan. 3, 1961
5th, Kansas, Dec. 8 to Dec. 15, 1953
6th, Iowa, Dec. 27, 1955, to Jan. 3, 1956
6th, Louisville, Preseason to Nov. 29, 1983

7th, Indiana, Dec. 14 to Dec. 21, 1954
7th, Missouri, Dec. 21 to Dec. 28, 1954
7th, Utah, Dec. 27, 1955, to Jan. 3, 1956
7th, Kansas, Dec. 9 to Dec. 16, 1958
7th, Duquesne, Dec. 9 to Dec. 16, 1969

7th, Ohio St., Dec. 16 to Dec. 23, 1980

Biggest Drop to Not Ranked from the Previous Week

(at least 25 ranked)
11th, Indiana, Dec. 21 to Dec. 28, 1994
13th, Stanford, Nov. 13 to Nov. 22, 2005
13th, West Virginia, Nov. 22 to Nov. 29, 2005
14th, UCLA, Nov. 26 to Dec. 3, 2002
15th, St. John's (N.Y.), Nov. 15 to Nov. 23, 1999

15th, UCLA, Nov. 21 to Nov. 28, 2000
15th, St. Joseph's, Dec. 18 to Dec. 25, 2001
15th, Marquette, Jan. 2 to Jan. 9, 2007
16th, Oklahoma, Feb. 1 to Feb. 8, 1993
16th, Duke, Jan. 9 to Jan. 16, 1995

16th, Minnesota, Dec. 19 to Dec. 26, 1994
16th, Arkansas, Preseason to Nov. 20, 1995
16th, Temple, Dec. 8 to Dec. 15, 1998
16th, Wichita St., Dec. 26 to Jan. 2, 2007
16th, Virginia Tech, Jan. 30 to Feb. 6, 2007

16th, Duke, Feb. 6 to Feb. 13, 2007
16th, Dayton, Jan. 22 to Jan. 29, 2008

Lowest Ranking to Rise to No. 1 during the Season

(does not include 1962-69 when only 10 ranked)
NR, Indiana St., Dec. 5, 1978 to Feb. 13, 1979 (only 20 ranked)
21st, Stanford, Dec. 2, 2003 to Feb. 17, 2004
20th, UNLV, Preseason Nov. 1982 to Feb. 15, 1983
20th, Kentucky, Dec. 31, 2002 to March 18, 2003
19th, Indiana, Dec. 16, 1952 to March 3, 1953

19th, Houston, Jan. 4 to March 1, 1983
19th, Connecticut, Preseason Nov. 1994 to Feb. 13, 1995
18th, North Carolina, Jan. 4 to Feb. 1, 1983
18th, Duke, Nov. 16, 1999 to March 14, 2000
17th, San Francisco, Dec. 21, 1954 to Feb. 8, 1955

17th, Arizona, Preseason Nov. to Dec. 22, 1987
17th, Oklahoma, Nov. 27, 1989 to March 6, 1990
17th, UCLA, Jan. 24 to March 17, 1994
17th, St. Joseph's, Preseason Nov. 2003 to March 9, 2004

Lowest Ranking to Drop from No. 1 during the Season

(does not include 1962-69 when only 10 ranked)
NR, St. John's (N.Y.), Dec. 18, 1951 to Jan. 15, 1952 (only 20 ranked)
NR, Duke, Jan. 8 to Feb. 26, 1980 (only 20 ranked)
NR, Alabama, Dec. 31, 2002 to Feb. 11, 2003
NR, Florida, Dec. 9, 2003 to Feb. 17, 2004
24th, Connecticut, Preseason Nov. 1999 to Feb, 29, 2000

21st, Arizona, Nov. 21, 2000 to Jan. 9, 2001
21st, Kansas, Dec. 2, 2003 to Feb. 17, 2004
20th, Indiana, Dec. 11, 1979 to Feb. 5, 1980
17th, Memphis, Jan. 11 to March 1, 1983
17th, Syracuse, Preseason Nov. 1987 to Jan. 26, 1988

Most Teams at No. 1 in One Season

7, 1983 Houston, Indiana, Memphis, UNLV, North Carolina, UCLA and Virginia
6, 1993 Duke, Indiana, Kansas, Kentucky, Michigan and North Carolina
6, 1994 Arkansas, Duke, Kansas, Kentucky, North Carolina and UCLA
6, 1995 Arkansas, Connecticut, Kansas, Massachusetts, North Carolina and UCLA
6, 2004 Connecticut, Duke, Florida, Kansas, St. Joseph's and Stanford

5, 1979 Duke, Indiana, Michigan St., Notre Dame and UCLA
5, 1990 Kansas, Missouri, UNLV, Oklahoma and Syracuse
5, 2001 Arizona, Duke, Michigan St., North Carolina and Stanford
5, 2003 Alabama, Arizona, Duke, Florida and Kentucky
5, 2007 Florida, North Carolina, Ohio St., UCLA and Wisconsin

Most Consecutive Weeks with a Different No. 1

7, Jan. 3 to Feb. 14, 1994 (in order: Arkansas, North Carolina, Kansas, UCLA, Duke, North Carolina and Arkansas)
5, Jan. 17 to Feb. 14, 1989 (in order: Duke, Illinois, Oklahoma, Arizona and Oklahoma)
5, Feb. 6 to March 6, 1990 (in order: Missouri, Kansas, Missouri, Kansas and Oklahoma)
5, Jan. 30 to Feb. 27, 1995 (in order: Massachusetts, North Carolina, Connecticut, Kansas and UCLA)
4, Dec. 11, 1951 to Jan. 2, 1952 [in order: Kentucky, St. John's (N.Y.), Kentucky and Kansas]
4, Feb. 17 to March 10, 1970 (in order: UCLA, Kentucky, UCLA and Kentucky)
4, Feb. 7 to Feb. 28, 1978 (in order: Kentucky, Arkansas, Marquette and Kentucky)
4, Feb. 6 to Feb. 27, 1979 (in order: Notre Dame, Indiana St., UCLA and Indiana St.)
4, Jan. 13 to Feb. 3, 1987 (in order: UNLV, Iowa, North Carolina and UNLV)
4, Nov. 25 to Dec. 16, 2003 (in order: Connecticut, Kansas, Florida and Connecticut)

Most Times No. 1 Defeated in a Season

10, 1993-94
9, 2003-04
8, 1978-79
8, 1982-83
8, 1989-90

7, 1987-88
7, 1988-89
7, 1992-93
7, 1997-98
7, 1999-2000

7, 2002-03
7, 2006-07

Largest Point Margin in Defeating No. 1

41, No. 2 Kentucky (81) vs. No. 1 St. John's (N.Y.), Lexington, KY, Dec. 17, 1951
32, No. 2 UCLA (101) vs. No. 1 Houston (69), Los Angeles (NSF), March 22, 1968
24, No. 3 Massachusetts (104) vs. No. 1 Arkansas (80), Springfield, MA, Nov. 25, 1994
24, No. 2 North Carolina (97) vs. No. 1 Duke (73), Chapel Hill, NC, Feb. 5, 1998
23, No. 15 Villanova (96) vs. No. 1 Connecticut (73), Storrs, CT, Feb. 18, 1995

22, Tied No. 5 Oklahoma (100) vs. No. 1 Kansas (78), Norman, OK, Feb. 27, 1990
20, No. 5 Arizona St. (87) vs. No. 1 Oregon St. (67), Corvallis, OR, March 7, 1981
20, No. 13 North Carolina (91) vs. No. 1 Duke (71), Durham, NC, Jan. 18, 1989
20, No. 17 Georgia Tech (89) vs. No. 1 North Carolina (69), Atlanta, Jan. 12, 1994
20, NR Xavier (87) vs. No. 1 St. Joseph's (67), Dayton, OH, March 11, 2004

Largest Point Margin for an Unranked Opponent Defeating No. 1

20, Xavier (87) vs. St. Joseph's (67), Dayton, OH, March 11, 2004
19, Wisconsin (86) vs. Ohio St. (67), Madison, WI, March 3, 1962
19, Villanova (93) vs. Syracuse (74), Syracuse, NY, Jan. 6, 1990
18, Maryland (69) vs. North Carolina (51), College Park, MD, Feb. 21, 1959
16, Alabama (78) vs. Kentucky (62), Tuscaloosa, AL, Jan. 23, 1978

16, Nebraska (67) vs. Missouri (51), Columbia, MO, Feb. 6, 1982
16, Georgia Tech (77) vs. Connecticut (61), New York, Nov. 26, 2003
15, Vanderbilt (101) vs. Kentucky (86), Nashville, TN, Jan. 13, 1993
15, Long Beach St. (64) vs. Kansas (49), Lawrence, KS, Jan. 25, 1993
15, California (85) vs. UCLA (70), Oakland, CA, Jan. 30, 1994

Most Weeks at No. 1 - All-Time

(Complete List)

134	UCLA	1964-2007
110	Duke	1966-2006
99	North Carolina	1957-2008
80	Kentucky	1949-2003
45	Cincinnati	1959-2000
44	Indiana	1953-93
42	Kansas	1952-2005
32	UNLV	1983-91
30	Ohio St.	1961-2007
29	Arizona	1988-2003
28	San Francisco	1955-77
24	Connecticut	1995-2006
21	Michigan	1965-93
17	Illinois	1952-2005
16	Kansas St.	1952-59
16	Stanford	2000-04
15	DePaul	1980-81
15	Massachusetts	1995-96
13	North Carolina St.	1975
12	Arkansas	1978-95
12	Georgetown	1985
12	Virginia	1981-83
11	Houston	1968-83
10	Florida	2003-07
8	St. John's (N.Y.)	1950-85
8	West Virginia	1958
7	Syracuse	1988-90
6	Memphis	1983-2008
6	Missouri	1982-90
6	Seton Hall	1953
6	Temple	1988
5	Bradley	1950-51
5	Holy Cross	1950
5	Notre Dame	1974-79
5	Oklahoma	1989-90
5	Oregon St.	1981
4	Indiana St.	1979
4	La Salle	1953-55
4	Loyola (Ill.)	1964
4	Michigan St.	1979-2001
3	Marquette	1971-78
2	Alabama	2003
2	Duquesne	1954
2	St. Louis	1949
2	Wake Forest	2005
1	Georgia Tech	1986
1	Iowa	1987
1	Oklahoma St.	1951
1	St. Joseph's	2004
1	South Carolina	1970
1	Tennessee	2008
1	Wichita St.	1965
1	Wisconsin	2007

Most Times Defeating No. 1

(Complete List)

12	North Carolina	1959-2006
10	Maryland	1959-2008
10	UCLA	1965-2003
8	Duke	1958-97
8	Georgia Tech	1955-2004
8	Ohio St.	1965-2007
7	Kansas	1953-2008
7	Notre Dame	1971-87
7	Oklahoma	1951-2002
7	Vanderbilt	1951-2008
6	Kentucky	1951-2003

5	Cincinnati	1954-98
5	Indiana	1984-2002
5	North Carolina St.	1983-2004
5	St. John's (N.Y.)	1951-85
5	Villanova	1983-2006
4	Alabama	1978-2004
4	Arizona	1987-2001
4	Missouri	1989-97
4	Stanford	1988-2003
4	Wake Forest	1975-92
3	DePaul	1950-52
3	Georgetown	1963-2006
3	Louisville	1953-2004
3	Massachusetts	1993-95
3	Minnesota	1951-89
3	Nebraska	1958-82
3	Oregon	1970-2007
3	St. Louis	1951-2000
3	Syracuse	1985-2006
3	Tennessee	1965-2008
3	Utah	1954-2002
3	West Virginia	1957-83
3	Xavier	1996-2004
2	California	1960-94
2	CCNY	1950
2	Clemson	1980-2001
2	Dayton	1953-54
2	Florida	2000-07
2	Florida St.	2002-06
2	George Washington	1995-96
2	Houston	1968-78
2	Illinois	1979-2005
2	Iowa	1965-99
2	Kansas St.	1990-94
2	Loyola (Ill.)	1949-63
2	LSU	1978-2002
2	Michigan	1964-97
2	Michigan St.	1979-2007
2	Mississippi St.	1959-96
2	Oklahoma St.	1949-89
2	Oregon St.	1953-74
2	Purdue	1979-2000
2	Southern California	1969-70
2	Temple	1995-2000
2	Virginia Tech	1983-2007
2	Washington	1979-2004
1	Arizona St.	1981
1	Arkansas	1984
1	Auburn	1988
1	Boston College	1994
1	Bradley	1960
1	Cal St. Fullerton	1983
1	Chaminade	1982
1	Charlotte	1977
1	Connecticut	1999
1	Detroit	1951
1	Iowa St.	1957
1	Jacksonville	1970
1	Long Beach St.	1993
1	Manhattan	1958
1	Marquette	2003
1	New Mexico	1988
1	Old Dominion	1981
1	Providence	1976
1	St. Joseph's	1981
1	UNLV	1989
1	UTEP	1966
1	Virginia	1986
1	Wichita St.	1963
1	Wisconsin	1962

Notes About No. 1

No. 1 has been defeated 245 times.
No. 1 has been defeated 11 times in overtime.
No. 1 has been defeated 34 times by one point.
No. 1 has been defeated 122 times by a non-ranked opponent.
Chaminade is the only non-Division I team to upset the nation's top team. It happened in Honolulu December 24, 1982, when Chaminade defeated No. 1 Virginia, 77-72.
California, CCNY, Louisville, Maryland, UTEP and Villanova have never been ranked No. 1 despite winning the NCAA championship.
The following men's and women's programs from the same school have been ranked No. 1 at the same time:
Connecticut, Feb. 13, 1995
Connecticut, Nov. 30, 1998
Duke, Jan. 7-14, 2003
Connecticut, Preseason 2003 to Nov. 25, 2003
Duke, Feb. 21, 2006

No. 1 vs. No. 2

Date	No. 1, Score	W-L	No. 2, Score	Site
Mar. 26, 1949	Kentucky 46	W	Oklahoma St. 36	Seattle (CH)
Dec. 17, 1951	St. John's (N.Y.) 40	L	Kentucky 81	Lexington, KY
Dec. 21, 1954	Kentucky 70	W	Utah 65	Lexington, KY
Mar. 23, 1957	North Carolina 54	W	Kansas 53	Kansas City, MO (CH)
Mar. 18, 1960	Cincinnati 69	L	California 77	San Francisco (NSF)
Mar. 25, 1961	Ohio St. 65	L (ot)	Cincinnati 70	Kansas City, MO (CH)
Mar. 24, 1962	Ohio St. 59	L	Cincinnati 71	Louisville, KY (CH)
Dec. 14, 1964	Wichita St. 85	L	Michigan 87	Detroit
Mar. 20, 1965	Michigan 80	L	UCLA 91	Portland, OR (CH)
Mar. 18, 1966	Kentucky 83	W	Duke 79	College Park, MD (NSF)
Jan. 20, 1968	UCLA 69	L	Houston 71	Houston
Mar. 22, 1968	Houston 69	L	UCLA 101	Los Angeles (NSF)
Dec. 15, 1973	UCLA 84	W	North Carolina St. 66	St. Louis
Jan. 19, 1974	UCLA 70	L	Notre Dame 71	South Bend, IN
Jan. 26, 1974	Notre Dame 75	L	UCLA 94	Los Angeles
Mar. 25, 1974	North Carolina St. 80	W	UCLA 77	Greensboro, NC (NSF)
Mar. 31, 1975	UCLA 92	W	Kentucky 85	San Diego (CH)
Nov. 29, 1975	Indiana 84	W	UCLA 64	St. Louis
Mar. 22, 1976	Indiana 65	W	Marquette 56	Baton Rouge, LA
Dec. 26, 1981	North Carolina 82	W	Kentucky 69	East Rutherford, NJ
Jan. 9, 1982	North Carolina 65	W	Virginia 60	Chapel Hill, NC
April 2, 1983	Houston 94	W	Louisville 81	Albuquerque, NM (NSF)
Dec. 15, 1984	Georgetown 77	W	DePaul 57	Landover, MD
Jan. 26, 1985	Georgetown 65	L	St. John's (N.Y.) 66	Washington, DC
Feb. 27, 1985	St. John's (N.Y.) 69	L	Georgetown 85	New York
Mar. 9, 1985	Georgetown 92	W	St. John's (N.Y.) 80	New York
Feb. 4, 1986	North Carolina 78	W (ot)	Georgia Tech 77	Atlanta
Mar. 29, 1986	Duke 71	W	Kansas 67	Dallas (NSF)
Feb. 13, 1990	Kansas 71	L	Missouri 77	Lawrence, KS
Mar. 10, 1990	Oklahoma 95	W	Kansas 77	Kansas City, MO
Feb. 10, 1991	UNLV 112	W	Arkansas 105	Fayetteville, AR
Feb. 3, 1994	Duke 78	L	North Carolina 89	Chapel Hill, NC
Mar. 30, 1996	Massachusetts 74	L	Kentucky 81	East Rutherford, NJ (NSF)
Feb. 5, 1998	Duke 73	L	North Carolina 97	Chapel Hill, NC
April 4, 2005	Illinois 70	L	North Carolina 75	St. Louis (CH)
Dec. 10, 2005	Duke 97	W	Texas 66	East Rutherford, NJ
Feb. 25, 2007	Wisconsin 48	L	Ohio State 49	Columbus, OH
Feb. 23, 2008	Memphis 62	L	Tennessee 66	Memphis, TN

Schools Defeating No. 1

Date	Rank	School	No. 1 Team	Score	Site
Jan. 20, 1949	3	Oklahoma St.	St. Louis	29-27	Stillwater, OK
Mar. 14, 1949	16	Loyola (Ill.)	Kentucky	67-56	New York
Jan. 17, 1950	NR	DePaul	St. John's (N.Y.)	74-68	New York
Mar. 18, 1950	NR	CCNY	Bradley	69-61	New York
Mar. 28, 1950	NR	CCNY	Bradley	71-68	New York (CH)
Dec. 29, 1950	NR	St. Louis	Kentucky	43-42	New Orleans
Jan. 11, 1951	11	St. John's (N.Y.)	Bradley	68-59	New York
Jan. 15, 1951	NR	Detroit	Bradley	70-65	Peoria, IL
Jan. 20, 1951	NR	Oklahoma	Oklahoma St.	44-40	Norman, OK
Mar. 3, 1951	NR	Vanderbilt	Kentucky	61-57	Louisville, KY
Dec. 13, 1951	NR	Minnesota	Kentucky	61-57	Minneapolis
Dec. 17, 1951	2	Kentucky	St. John's (N.Y.)	81-40	Lexington, KY
Dec. 29, 1951	12	St. Louis	Kentucky	61-60	New Orleans
Jan. 28, 1952	NR	DePaul	Illinois	69-65	Chicago
Mar. 22, 1952	10	St. John's (N.Y.)	Kentucky	64-57	Raleigh, NC (RF)
Dec. 27, 1952	NR	DePaul	La Salle	63-61	Chicago
Jan. 17, 1953	15	Kansas	Kansas St.	80-66	Lawrence, KS
Mar. 1, 1953	NR	Dayton	Seton Hall	70-65	Dayton, OH
Mar. 2, 1953	18	Louisville	Seton Hall	73-67	Louisville, KY
Mar. 7, 1953	NR	Minnesota	Indiana	65-63	Minneapolis
Dec. 22, 1953	12	Oregon St.	Indiana	67-51	Eugene, OR
Feb. 25, 1954	NR	Cincinnati	Duquesne	66-52	Cincinnati
Feb. 27, 1954	16	Dayton	Duquesne	64-54	Dayton, OH
Dec. 18, 1954	15	Utah	La Salle	79-69	New York
Jan. 8, 1955	NR	Georgia Tech	Kentucky	59-58	Lexington, KY
Jan. 31, 1955	NR	Georgia Tech	Kentucky	65-59	Atlanta
Jan. 14, 1957	9	Iowa St.	Kansas	39-37	Ames, IA
Dec. 21, 1957	8	West Virginia	North Carolina	75-64	Lexington, KY
Jan. 27, 1958	NR	Duke	West Virginia	72-68	Durham, NC
Mar. 3, 1958	NR	Nebraska	Kansas St.	55-48	Lincoln, NE
Mar. 8, 1958	10	Kansas	Kansas St.	61-44	Manhattan, KS
Mar. 11, 1958	NR	Manhattan	West Virginia	89-84	New York
Jan. 6, 1959	NR	Vanderbilt	Kentucky	75-66	Nashville, TN
Jan. 14, 1959	3	North Carolina	North Carolina St.	72-68	Raleigh, NC
Feb. 9, 1959	10	Mississippi St.	Kentucky	66-58	Mississippi State, MS
Feb. 21, 1959	NR	Maryland	North Carolina	69-51	College Park, MD

Date	Rank	School	No. 1 Team	Score	Site
Mar. 14, 1959	5	Cincinnati	Kansas St.	85-75	Lawrence, KS (RF)
Jan. 16, 1960	4	Bradley	Cincinnati	91-90	Peoria, IL
Mar. 18, 1960	2	California	Cincinnati	77-69	San Francisco (NSF)
Mar. 25, 1961	2	Cincinnati	Ohio St.	70-65 (ot)	Kansas City, MO (CH)
Mar. 3, 1962	NR	Wisconsin	Ohio St.	86-67	Madison, WI
Mar. 24, 1962	2	Cincinnati	Ohio St.	71-59	Louisville, KY (CH)
Feb. 16, 1963	NR	Wichita St.	Cincinnati	65-64	Wichita, KS
Mar. 23, 1963	3	Loyola (Ill.)	Cincinnati	60-58	Louisville, KY
Dec. 28, 1963	NR	Georgetown	Loyola (Ill.)	69-58	Philadelphia
Jan. 4, 1964	NR	Georgia Tech	Kentucky	76-67	Atlanta
Jan. 6, 1964	6	Vanderbilt	Kentucky	85-83	Nashville, TN
Dec. 12, 1964	NR	Nebraska	Michigan	74-73	Lincoln, NE
Dec. 14, 1964	2	Michigan	Wichita St.	87-85	Detroit
Jan. 2, 1965	NR	St. John's (N.Y.)	Michigan	75-74	New York
Jan. 29, 1965	NR	Iowa	UCLA	87-82	Chicago
Mar. 8, 1965	NR	Ohio St.	Michigan	93-85	Columbus, OH
Mar. 20, 1965	2	UCLA	Michigan	91-80	Portland, OR (CH)
Dec. 10, 1965	6	Duke	UCLA	82-66	Durham, NC
Dec. 11, 1965	6	Duke	UCLA	94-75	Charlotte, NC
Feb. 7, 1966	NR	West Virginia	Duke	94-90	Morgantown, WV
Mar. 5, 1966	NR	Tennessee	Kentucky	69-62	Nashville, TN
Mar. 19, 1966	3	UTEP	Kentucky	72-65	College Park, MD (CH)
Jan. 20, 1968	2	Houston	UCLA	71-69	Houston
Mar. 22, 1968	2	UCLA	Houston	101-69	Los Angeles (NSF)
Mar. 23, 1968	NR	Ohio St.	Houston	89-85	Los Angeles (N3rd)
Mar. 8, 1969	NR	Southern California	UCLA	46-44	Los Angeles
Dec. 6, 1969	NR	Tennessee	South Carolina	55-54	Columbia, SC
Feb. 21, 1970	NR	Oregon	UCLA	78-65	Eugene, OR
Mar. 6, 1970	NR	Southern California	UCLA	87-86	Los Angeles
Mar. 14, 1970	4	Jacksonville	Kentucky	106-100	Columbus, OH (RF)
Jan. 23, 1971	9	Notre Dame	UCLA	89-82	South Bend, IN
Jan. 19, 1974	2	North Carolina	UCLA	71-70	South Bend, IN
Jan. 26, 1974	2	UCLA	Notre Dame	94-75	Los Angeles
Feb. 15, 1974	NR	Oregon St.	UCLA	61-57	Corvallis, OR
Feb. 16, 1974	NR	Oregon	UCLA	56-51	Eugene, OR
Jan. 3, 1975	NR	Wake Forest	North Carolina St.	83-78	Greensboro, NC
Mar. 22, 1975	5	Kentucky	Indiana	92-90	Dayton, OH (RF)
Dec. 29, 1976	NR	Providence	Michigan	82-81 (2ot)	Providence, RI
Mar. 1, 1977		Notre Dame	San Francisco	93-82	South Bend, IN
Mar. 19, 1977	17	Charlotte	Michigan	75-68	Lexington, KY (RF)
Jan. 23, 1978	NR	Alabama	Kentucky	78-62	Tuscaloosa, AL
Feb. 11, 1978	NR	LSU	Kentucky	95-94	Baton Rouge, LA
Feb. 18, 1978	NR	Houston	Arkansas	84-75	Houston
Feb. 26, 1978	9	Notre Dame	Marquette	65-59	South Bend, IN
Dec. 29, 1978	NR	Ohio St.	Duke	90-84	New York
Dec. 30, 1978	NR	St. John's (N.Y.)	Duke	69-66	New York
Jan. 11, 1979	4	Illinois	Michigan St.	57-55	Champaign, IL
Jan. 13, 1979		Purdue	Michigan St.	52-50	West Lafayette, IN
Jan. 27, 1979	NR	Maryland	Notre Dame	67-66	College Park, MD
Feb. 11, 1979	4	UCLA	Notre Dame	56-52	South Bend, IN
Feb. 22, 1979	NR	Washington	UCLA	69-68	Seattle
Mar. 26, 1979	3	Michigan St.	Indiana St.	75-64	Salt Lake City
Dec. 18, 1979	5	Kentucky	Indiana	69-58	Lexington, KY
Jan. 9, 1980	18	Clemson	Duke	87-82	Clemson, SC
Jan. 12, 1980	15	North Carolina	Duke	82-67	Durham, NC
Feb. 27, 1980	14	Notre Dame	DePaul	76-74 (2 ot)	South Bend, IN
Mar. 9, 1980	NR	UCLA	DePaul	77-71	Tempe, AZ (2nd)
Jan. 10, 1981	NR	Old Dominion	DePaul	63-62	Chicago
Feb. 22, 1981	11	Notre Dame	Virginia	57-56	Chicago
Mar. 7, 1981	5	Arizona St.	Oregon St.	87-67	Corvallis, OR
Mar. 14, 1981	NR	St. Joseph's	DePaul	49-48	Dayton, OH (1st)
Jan. 21, 1982	NR	Wake Forest	North Carolina	55-48	Chapel Hill, NC
Feb. 6, 1982	NR	Nebraska	Missouri	67-51	Columbia, MO
Feb. 27, 1982	NR	Maryland	Virginia	47-46 (ot)	College Park, MD
Dec. 24, 1982	NR	Chaminade	Virginia	77-72	Honolulu
Jan. 8, 1983	NR	Ohio St.	Indiana	70-67	Columbus, OH
Jan. 10, 1983	NR	Virginia Tech	Memphis	64-56	Blacksburg, VA
Jan. 28, 1983	NR	Alabama	UCLA	70-67	Los Angeles
Feb.13, 1983	12	Villanova	North Carolina	56-53	Chapel Hill, NC
Feb. 24, 1983	NR	Cal St. Fullerton	UNLV	86-78	Fullerton, CA
Feb. 27, 1983	NR	West Virginia	UNLV	87-78	Morgantown, WV
Apr. 4, 1983	16	North Carolina St.	Houston	54-52	Albuquerque, NM (CH)
Feb. 12, 1984	NR	Arkansas	North Carolina	65-64	Pine Bluff, NC
Mar. 10, 1984	16	Duke	North Carolina	77-75	Greensboro, NC
Mar. 22, 1984	NR	Indiana	North Carolina	72-68	Atlanta (RSF)
Jan. 26, 1985	2	St. John's (N.Y.)	Georgetown	66-65	Washington, DC
Jan. 28, 1985	11	Syracuse	Georgetown	65-63	Syracuse, NY
Feb. 27, 1985	2	Georgetown	St. John's (N.Y.)	85-69	New York
Apr. 1, 1985	NR	Villanova	Georgetown	66-64	Lexington, KY
Jan. 30, 1986	NR	Virginia	North Carolina	86-73	Charlottesville, VA
Feb. 20, 1986	NR	Maryland	North Carolina	77-72	Chapel Hill, NC
Feb. 23, 1986	20	North Carolina St.	North Carolina	76-65	Raleigh, NC
Mar. 31, 1986	7	Louisville	Duke	72-69	Dallas (CH)
Dec. 1, 1986	NR	UCLA	North Carolina	89-84	Los Angeles

Date	Rank	School	No. 1 Team	Score	Site
Jan. 17, 1987	16	Oklahoma	UNLV	89-88	Norman, OK
Jan. 24, 1987	NR	Ohio St.	Iowa	80-76	Iowa City, IA
Feb. 1, 1987	NR	Notre Dame	North Carolina	60-58	South Bend, IN
Mar. 28, 1987	3	Indiana	UNLV	97-93	New Orleans (NSF)
Nov. 21, 1987	3	North Carolina	Syracuse	96-93	Springfield, MA
Nov. 30, 1987	17	Arizona	Syracuse	80-69	Anchorage, AK
Dec. 5, 1987	NR	Vanderbilt	North Carolina	78-76	Nashville, TN
Jan. 2, 1988	NR	New Mexico	Arizona	61-59	Albuquerque, NM
Jan. 9, 1988	NR	Auburn	Kentucky	53-52	Lexington, KY
Feb. 4, 1988	NR	Stanford	Arizona	82-74	Palo Alto, CA
Mar. 26, 1988	5	Duke	Temple	63-53	East Rutherford, NJ (RF)
Jan. 18, 1989	13	North Carolina	Duke	91-71	Durham, NC
Jan. 21, 1989	NR	Wake Forest	Duke	75-71	Winston-Salem, NC
Jan. 26, 1989	NR	Minnesota	Illinois	69-62	Minneapolis
Feb. 4, 1989	NR	Oklahoma St.	Oklahoma	77-73	Stillwater, OK
Feb. 12, 1989	5	Oklahoma	Arizona	82-80	Norman, OK
Feb. 25, 1989	7	Missouri	Oklahoma	97-84	Columbia, MO
Mar. 23, 1989	15	UNLV	Arizona	68-67	Denver (RSF)
Nov. 22, 1989	NR	Kansas	UNLV	91-77	New York
Jan. 6, 1990	NR	Villanova	Syracuse	93-74	Greensboro, NC
Jan. 20, 1990	4	Missouri	Kansas	95-87	Columbia, MO
Feb. 8, 1990	NR	Kansas St.	Missouri	65-58	Manhattan, KS
Feb. 13, 1990	2	Missouri	Kansas	77-71	Lawrence, KS
Feb. 25, 1990	10	Oklahoma	Missouri	107-90	Norman, OK
Feb. 27, 1990	T5	Oklahoma	Kansas	100-78	Norman, OK
Mar. 17, 1990	NR	North Carolina	Oklahoma	79-77	Austin, TX (2nd)
Mar. 30, 1991	6	Duke	UNLV	79-77	Indianapolis (NSF)
Feb. 5, 1992	9	North Carolina	Duke	75-73	Chapel Hill, NC
Feb. 23, 1992	NR	Wake Forest	Duke	72-68	Winston-Salem, NC
Dec. 5, 1992	4	Duke	Michigan	79-68	Durham, NC
Jan. 10, 1993	10	Georgia Tech	Duke	80-79	Atlanta
Jan. 13, 1993	NR	Vanderbilt	Kentucky	101-86	Nashville, TN
Jan. 25, 1993	NR	Long Beach St.	Kansas	64-49	Lawrence, KS
Feb. 23, 1993	NR	Ohio St.	Indiana	81-77 (ot)	Columbus, OH
Mar. 14, 1993	NR	Georgia Tech	North Carolina	77-75	Charlotte, NC
Mar. 27, 1993	9	Kansas	Indiana	83-77	St. Louis (RF)
Nov. 24, 1993	18	Massachusetts	North Carolina	91-86 (ot)	New York
Dec. 4, 1993	21	Indiana	Kentucky	96-84	Indianapolis
Jan. 8, 1994	NR	Alabama	Arkansas	66-64	Tuscaloosa, AL
Jan. 12, 1994	17	Georgia Tech	North Carolina	89-69	Atlanta
Jan. 17, 1994	NR	Kansas St.	Kansas	68-64	Lawrence, KS
Jan. 30, 1994	NR	California	UCLA	85-70	Oakland, CA
Feb. 3, 1994	2	North Carolina	Duke	89-78	Chapel Hill, NC
Feb. 12, 1994	NR	Georgia Tech	North Carolina	96-89	Chapel Hill, NC
Mar. 12, 1994	10	Kentucky	Arkansas	90-78	Memphis, TN
Mar. 20, 1994	NR	Boston College	North Carolina	75-72	Landover, MD (2nd)
Nov. 25, 1994	3	Massachusetts	Arkansas	104-80	Springfield, MA
Dec. 3, 1994	7	Kansas	Massachusetts	81-75	New York
Jan. 4, 1995	NR	North Carolina St.	North Carolina	80-70	Raleigh, NC
Feb. 4, 1995	NR	George Washington	Massachusetts	78-75	Washington, DC
Feb. 7, 1995	8	Maryland	North Carolina	86-73	College Park, MD
Feb. 18, 1995	15	Villanova	Connecticut	96-73	Storrs, CT
Feb. 20, 1995	25	Oklahoma	Kansas	76-73	Norman, OK
Nov. 28, 1995	5	Massachusetts	Kentucky	92-82	Auburn Hills, MI
Dec. 22, 1995	NR	Temple	Kansas	75-66	East Rutherford, NJ
Feb. 24, 1996	NR	George Washington	Massachusetts	86-76	Amherst, MA
Mar. 10, 1996	NR	Mississippi St.	Kentucky	84-73	New Orleans
Mar. 30, 1996	2	Kentucky	Massachusetts	81-74	East Rutherford, NJ (NSF)
Nov. 26, 1996	NR	Xavier	Cincinnati	71-69	Cincinnati
Feb. 4, 1997	NR	Missouri	Kansas	96-94	Columbia, MO
Mar. 21, 1997	15	Arizona	Kansas	85-82	Birmingham, AL (RSF)
Nov. 26, 1997	3	Duke	Arizona	95-87	Lahaina, HI
Dec. 13, 1997	NR	Michigan	Duke	81-73	Ann Arbor, MI
Jan. 14, 1998	NR	Maryland	North Carolina	89-83 (ot)	College Park, MD
Feb. 5, 1998	2	North Carolina	Duke	97-73	Chapel Hill, NC
Feb. 21, 1998	NR	North Carolina St.	North Carolina	86-72	Chapel Hill, NC
Mar. 8, 1998	4	North Carolina	Duke	83-68	Greensboro, NC
Mar. 28, 1998	7	Utah	North Carolina	65-59	San Antonio, TX (NSF)
Nov. 28, 1998	15	Cincinnati	Duke	77-75	Anchorage, AK
Feb. 1, 1999	17	Syracuse	Connecticut	59-42	Hartford, CT
Mar. 29, 1999	3	Connecticut	Duke	77-74	St. Petersburg, FL (CH)
Nov. 11, 1999	NR	Iowa	Connecticut	70-68	New York
Nov. 18, 1999	NR	Xavier	Cincinnati	66-64	Cincinnati
Jan. 8, 2000	5	Arizona	Stanford	68-65	Palo Alto, CA
Feb. 12, 2000	15	Temple	Cincinnati	77-69	Cincinnati
Mar. 4, 2000	NR	UCLA	Stanford	94-93 (ot)	Palo Alto, CA
Mar. 9, 2000	NR	St. Louis	Cincinnati	68-58	Memphis, TN
Mar. 24, 2000	11	Florida	Duke	87-78	Syracuse, NY (RSF)
Nov. 25, 2000	NR	Purdue	Arizona	72-69	Indianapolis
Dec. 21, 2000	3	Stanford	Duke	84-83	Oakland, CA
Jan. 7, 2001	NR	Indiana	Michigan St.	59-58	Bloomington, IN
Feb. 3, 2001	NR	UCLA	Stanford	79-73	Palo Alto, CA
Feb. 18, 2001	NR	Clemson	North Carolina	75-65	Clemson, SC
Mar. 8, 2001	8	Arizona	Stanford	76-75	Palo Alto, CA

Date	Rank	School	No. 1 Team	Score	Site
Jan. 6, 2002	NR	Florida St.	Duke	77-76	Tallahassee, FL
Jan. 12, 2002	11	UCLA	Kansas	87-77	Los Angeles
Feb. 17, 2002	3	Maryland	Duke	87-73	College Park, MD
Mar. 10, 2002	4	Oklahoma	Kansas	64-55	Kansas City, MO
Mar. 21, 2002	NR	Indiana	Duke	74-73	Lexington, KY (RSF)
Dec. 21, 2002	NR	LSU	Arizona	66-65	Baton Rouge, LA
Dec. 30, 2002	NR	Utah	Alabama	51-49	Salt Lake City
Jan. 18, 2003	17	Maryland	Duke	87-72	College Park, MD
Jan. 30, 2003	24	Stanford	Arizona	82-77	Tucson, AZ
Feb. 4, 2003	6	Kentucky	Florida	70-55	Lexington, KY
Mar. 13, 2003	NR	UCLA	Arizona	96-89 (ot)	Los Angeles
Mar. 29, 2003	9	Marquette	Kentucky	83-69	Minneapolis (RF)
Nov. 26, 2003	NR	Georgia Tech	Connecticut	77-61	New York
Dec. 6, 2003	21	Stanford	Kansas	64-58	Los Angeles
Dec. 10, 2003	NR	Maryland	Florida	69-68 (ot)	Gainesville, FL
Dec. 13, 2003	NR	Louisville	Florida	73-65	Louisville, KY
Jan. 17, 2004	11	North Carolina	Connecticut	86-83	Chapel Hill, NC
Feb. 15, 2004	21	North Carolina St.	Duke	78-74	Raleigh, NC
Mar. 6, 2004	NR	Washington	Stanford	75-62	Seattle
Mar. 11, 2004	NR	Xavier	St. Joseph's	87-67	Dayton, OH
Mar. 20, 2004	NR	Alabama	Stanford	70-67	Seattle, (2nd)
Dec. 1, 2004	5	Illinois	Wake Forest	91-73	Champaign, IL
Mar. 6, 2005	NR	Ohio St.	Illinois	65-64	Columbus, OH
Apr. 4, 2005	2	North Carolina	Illinois	75-70	St. Louis (CH)
Jan. 21, 2006	NR	Georgetown	Duke	87-84	Washington
Feb. 13, 2006	4	Villanova	Connecticut	69-64	Philadelphia
Mar. 1, 2006	NR	Florida St.	Duke	79-74	Tallahassee, FL
Mar. 4, 2006	15	North Carolina	Duke	83-76	Durham, NC
Mar. 9, 2006	NR	Syracuse	Connecticut	86-84	New York
Nov. 26, 2006	10	Kansas	Florida	82-80 (ot)	Las Vegas
Jan. 6, 2007	17	Oregon	UCLA	68-66	Eugene, OR
Jan. 13, 2007	NR	Virginia Tech	North Carolina	94-88	Blacksburg, VA
Feb. 17, 2007	NR	Vanderbilt	Florida	83-70	Nashville, TN
Feb. 20, 2007	NR	Michigan St.	Wisconsin	64-55	East Lansing, MI
Feb. 25, 2007	2	Ohio St.	Wisconsin	49-48	Columbus, OH
Apr. 2, 2007	3	Florida	Ohio St.	84-75	Atlanta, GA (CH)
Jan. 19, 2008	NR	Maryland	North Carolina	82-80	Chapel Hill, NC
Feb. 23, 2008	2	Tennessee	Memphis	66-62	Memphis, TN
Feb. 26, 2008	18	Vanderbilt	Tennessee	72-69	Nashville, TN
Apr. 5, 2008	4	Kansas	North Carolina	84-66	San Antonio, TX (NSF)

NR=Not Rated
NCAA Tournament Abbreviations After Site:
CH=National Final or Championship Game
NSF=National Semifinal
N3rd= NCAA National Consolation Game
RF=Regional Final
RSF=Regional Semifinal
2nd=Second-Round Game
1st=First-Round Game

Week-by-Week A.P. Polls

REGULAR-SEASON POLLS

The Associated Press began its basketball poll on January 20, 1949. The following are those polls, year by year and week by week. Starting in the 1961-62 season, A.P. provided a preseason (PS) poll. A.P. did a post-tournament poll in 1953, 1954, 1974 and 1975. If two teams are ranked the same in the same column, then it was a tie for that week.

1948-49

| | January | | February | | | | March | |
	18	25	1	8	15	22	1	8
Arkansas	-	-	-	-	-	-	20	-
Baylor	-	18	-	-	-	-	-	-
Bowling Green	15	-	14	14	10	9	9	10
Bradley	16	19	18	-	12	10	10	7
Butler	19	17	16	16	11	11	11	18
Cincinnati	13	-	-	-	-	-	-	-
DePaul	-	16	-	-	17	-	-	-
Duquesne	-	-	-	20	20	17	-	-
Eastern Ky.	-	-	20	-	-	-	-	-
Hamline	8	7	8	5	9	15	16	19
Holy Cross	14	20	19	15	-	-	-	-
Illinois	7	6	4	4	4	4	4	4
Kentucky	2	2	1	1	1	1	1	1
Loyola (Ill.)	12	13	13	11	13	12	14	16
Minnesota	4	5	5	7	6	5	5	6
North Carolina St.	-	15	17	-	18	-	15	13
New York U.	20	-	15	-	-	-	-	-
Ohio St.	-	-	-	18	-	18	19	20
Oklahoma	-	-	-	-	16	-	-	-
Oklahoma St.	5	3	3	3	3	3	2	2
St. Louis	1	1	2	2	2	2	3	3
San Francisco	6	9	10	9	8	8	8	8
Southern California	-	-	-	-	-	19	-	-
Stanford	17	11	9	10	20	-	-	-
Texas	-	-	-	-	-	20	-	-
Tulane	11	12	11	8	5	6	7	9
UCLA	-	-	-	-	-	-	-	15
Utah	10	10	12	12	14	16	13	12
Villanova	9	8	7	13	15	-	17	14
Western Ky.	3	4	6	6	7	7	6	5
Washington St.	18	14	-	17	-	-	-	-
Wyoming	-	-	-	19	19	14	12	17
Yale	-	-	-	-	20	13	18	11

1949-50

| | January | | | | | February | | | | March |
	5	10	17	24	31	7	14	21	28	7
Arizona	-	-	-	-	-	18	17	19	15	15
Bowling Green	19	-	-	-	-	-	-	-	-	-
Bradley	3	6	4	6	3	2	2	1	1	1
CCNY	14	7	7	8	10	14	13	20	-	-
Cincinnati	-	12	20	-	-	-	-	-	-	-
Duquesne	8	8	6	2	2	3	7	4	5	6
Hamline	-	-	-	-	-	20	-	-	-	-
Holy Cross	6	5	1	1	1	1	1	2	3	4
Illinois	16	-	-	20	-	-	-	-	-	-
Indiana	5	4	8	9	12	16	-	17	-	20
Kansas	-	-	-	-	-	-	-	-	-	19
Kansas St.	20	-	13	12	11	10	14	13	12	14
Kentucky	2	5	4	4	6	7	5	5	4	3
La Salle	18	13	10	7	8	9	11	12	9	10
Long Island	4	3	3	3	4	6	6	10	14	13
Louisville	-	-	19	-	15	13	-	-	-	-
Minnesota	10	11	16	18	-	-	-	-	-	-
Missouri	12	16	-	-	-	-	-	-	-	-
Nebraska	-	-	-	-	-	-	-	-	16	-
North Carolina St.	7	9	12	10	9	8	8	9	8	5
Notre Dame	-	-	-	-	16	-	-	-	-	-
Ohio St.	-	15	11	13	7	4	3	3	2	2
Oklahoma	17	19	-	-	-	-	-	-	-	-
Oklahoma St.	-	-	-	-	19	-	-	-	-	-
St. John's (N.Y.)	1	1	2	5	5	4	4	6	10	9
St. Louis	11	-	-	-	-	19	18	15	-	-
San Francisco	-	-	-	-	-	15	12	11	13	12
San Jose St.	-	-	-	-	-	-	-	18	19	17
Siena	-	18	-	-	-	-	-	-	-	-
Southern California	-	-	-	-	-	-	19	16	-	-
Tennessee	-	-	17	-	-	-	-	-	-	-
Toledo	-	-	-	-	-	-	-	-	14	17
Tulane	-	-	15	-	-	-	-	-	-	-
UCLA	9	10	9	11	13	12	10	7	6	7
Vanderbilt	-	-	-	-	18	-	20	-	20	-
Villanova	13	17	18	19	-	-	15	-	11	11
Washington	-	20	-	16	-	-	-	-	-	-
Washington St.	-	-	-	-	-	17	16	-	-	18
Western Ky.	-	14	14	17	14	11	9	8	7	8
Wisconsin	15	-	-	15	17	-	-	-	-	16
Wyoming	-	-	14	-	20	-	-	-	18	-

1950-51

| | December | | January | | | | | February | | | | Mar. |
	19	26	3	9	16	23	30	6	13	20	27	7
Arizona	-	-	16	-	-	14	15	13	16	11	12	12
Beloit	-	-	-	-	-	-	-	-	18	20	16	-
Bradley	2	2	1	1	3	4	5	5	8	7	5	6
BYU	15	-	-	-	19	12	14	12	12	11	-	11
CCNY	6	11	-	-	-	-	-	-	-	-	-	-
Cincinnati	17	17	17	-	16	15	16	11	15	18	-	17
Columbia	-	8	14	8	7	7	6	6	4	3	3	3
Cornell	19	18	14	-	-	-	-	-	-	-	-	-
Dayton	-	-	-	-	-	-	-	18	17	14	14	13
Duquesne	-	-	13	15	20	-	-	-	-	-	-	-
Illinois	-	20	-	14	14	16	14	16	11	10	6	5
Indiana	4	5	6	6	6	5	3	3	6	4	7	7
Kansas	11	10	20	17	-	-	17	20	-	-	-	-
Kansas St.	20	-	9	9	10	9	7	4	3	5	4	4
Kentucky	1	1	3	3	2	1	1	1	1	1	1	1
La Salle	-	16	-	19	-	17	-	-	-	-	-	-
Long Island	7	4	4	4	2	4	12	19	16	-	-	-
Louisville	-	-	-	-	-	17	14	-	-	-	-	-
Missouri	8	9	-	-	-	-	-	-	-	-	-	-
Murray St.	-	-	-	-	-	-	-	-	-	-	20	16
North Carolina St.	3	6	7	7	9	8	8	10	9	9	8	8
Notre Dame	14	-	-	-	-	-	-	-	-	-	-	-
Oklahoma	16	-	-	-	-	18	18	-	-	17	-	-
Oklahoma St.	5	3	2	1	3	2	2	2	2	2	2	2
Princeton	-	-	18	20	-	-	-	-	-	-	-	-
St. Bonaventure	-	-	-	-	17	-	-	-	-	-	-	-
St. John's (N.Y.)	13	12	11	11	5	6	9	7	7	8	9	9
St. Louis	-	-	5	5	8	10	8	5	6	10	-	10
Seattle	-	-	-	-	-	-	-	20	-	-	-	-
Siena	-	-	-	-	18	13	-	19	-	-	-	18
Southern California	-	-	13	19	12	13	15	13	13	18	-	19
Toledo	10	13	19	18	12	-	20	-	-	-	13	14
UCLA	9	-	-	-	-	-	19	-	-	17	-	-
Villanova	18	7	8	16	11	11	11	9	10	15	15	20
Washington	12	15	12	12	15	-	-	-	-	19	19	15
West Virginia	-	19	-	-	-	-	-	-	-	-	-	-
Wyoming	-	14	10	10	13	20	-	-	-	-	-	-

1951-52

| | December | | | January | | | | | February | | | | March |
	10	17	25	1	8	15	22	29	5	12	19	26	4
Dayton	-	-	-	20	19	16	14	11	11	11	11	11	11
DePaul	-	-	-	-	-	-	-	19	-	18	-	-	-
Duke	12	19	-	-	-	-	-	-	-	-	-	15	12
Duquesne	-	-	-	16	7	10	7	5	3	3	4	4	-
Eastern Ky.	19	-	-	-	-	-	-	-	-	-	-	-	-
Fordham	-	-	-	-	-	-	20	-	-	-	-	-	-
Holy Cross	-	17	-	-	-	20	11	17	-	19	17	17	13
Illinois	3	3	2	2	2	2	1	3	3	6	5	2	2
Indiana	11	6	5	5	4	14	20	13	18	20	-	-	-
Iowa	-	-	-	12	10	4	4	8	9	5	4	7	7
Kansas	8	7	4	1	1	1	2	4	6	9	7	8	8
Kansas St.	5	5	8	9	7	9	7	2	2	2	2	3	3
Kentucky	1	2	1	4	3	3	3	1	1	1	1	1	1
La Salle	9	12	17	13	-	15	18	-	19	-	20	-	-
Louisville	17	-	-	-	15	13	14	12	13	15	15	13	17
Michigan St.	-	-	-	20	19	-	-	-	-	-	-	-	-
Minnesota	-	15	-	-	-	-	-	-	-	-	-	-	-
Murray St.	-	-	18	16	-	-	-	-	-	-	-	-	-
North Carolina St.	10	9	19	17	-	17	-	-	-	-	-	-	-
Notre Dame	14	20	9	14	-	-	-	-	-	-	-	-	-
New York U.	20	11	6	6	13	-	-	-	-	-	-	-	-
Oklahoma City	-	-	15	18	18	-	16	15	13	-	-	-	-
Oklahoma St.	13	13	-	-	-	-	-	-	16	-	-	-	-
Penn St.	-	-	-	-	-	-	-	14	17	13	-	-	-
St. Bonaventure	-	-	-	10	8	6	5	4	4	10	12	-	15
St. John's (N.Y.)	2	1	7	8	12	-	15	15	10	10	8	9	10
St. Louis	4	4	12	7	5	5	8	6	7	9	5	-	5
Seattle	-	-	-	-	-	-	-	-	-	-	-	16	18
Seton Hall	7	10	10	11	9	12	13	11	17	12	14	14	14

	December			January					February				March
	10	17	25	1	8	15	22	29	5	12	19	26	4
Siena	-	-	-	-	17	11	19	18	-	16	18	20	-
Stanford	16	-	13	-	-	-	-	-	-	-	-	-	-
Texas St.	-	-	-	-	-	-	-	-	-	-	-	-	20
Syracuse	-	-	20	19	14	-	-	-	-	-	-	-	-
TCU	-	-	-	-	-	15	12	-	-	-	-	-	-
UCLA	-	-	16	-	-	-	-	-	-	-	-	-	19
Utah	-	-	15	18	-	-	17	-	-	-	-	-	-
Vanderbilt	18	-	-	-	-	-	-	-	-	-	-	-	-
Villanova	15	18	14	-	-	-	-	-	-	-	-	19	-
Washington	6	8	3	3	6	8	6	9	8	8	6	6	6
West Virginia	-	-	-	-	11	10	9	10	12	14	12	10	9
Western Ky.	-	16	11	-	-	-	-	-	20	-	-	18	-
Wyoming	-	14	-	-	-	-	-	-	-	-	19	16	16

1952-53

	December			January				February				March		
	16	23	30	6	13	20	27	3	10	17	24	3	10	24
California	18	-	-	20	-	14	-	14	19	19	-	-	-	-
Colorado	-	18	-	-	-	-	-	-	-	-	-	-	-	-
DePaul	-	-	14	-	-	-	10	7	7	14	15	-	-	19
Duke	-	-	-	-	-	-	-	-	-	18	-	-	-	-
Duquesne	-	-	-	-	-	-	-	-	-	-	19	18	11	9
Eastern Ky.	-	-	-	-	-	18	15	-	-	20	-	17	-	-
Fordham	-	-	-	8	7	10	7	13	16	-	-	-	-	-
Georgetown	-	-	-	-	20	-	-	-	-	-	-	-	-	-
Holy Cross	8	4	6	14	17	-	-	17	-	-	-	20	-	13
Idaho	-	20	-	18	-	-	-	-	-	-	-	-	-	-
Illinois	3	2	4	4	4	6	6	6	5	5	10	10	13	11
Indiana	19	15	12	7	6	2	2	2	2	2	2	1	1	1
Kansas	20	-	-	-	15	9	14	18	14	10	5	6	5	3
Kansas St.	2	5	1	1	1	4	5	5	10	8	9	8	8	12
La Salle	1	1	3	3	3	5	4	4	4	4	4	2	3	6
LSU	10	8	17	11	14	14	11	10	8	6	6	5	7	5
Louisville	-	-	-	-	-	-	-	-	17	16	18	14	14	-
Manhattan	-	-	-	-	-	20	19	19	15	13	16	-	20	-
Miami (Ohio)	-	-	-	-	-	-	-	-	-	12	-	16	-	-
Minnesota	16	17	9	19	-	19	-	-	-	-	-	-	-	-
Missouri St.	-	-	-	-	-	-	-	-	-	-	-	-	-	20
Murray St.	-	-	-	-	-	-	-	-	17	-	-	-	-	-
Navy	20	13	-	15	-	-	16	-	-	-	-	18	19	-
Niagara	-	-	-	-	-	-	-	20	17	-	-	-	-	-
North Carolina	-	-	-	-	-	-	18	12	-	-	-	-	-	-
North Carolina St.	6	6	11	9	8	8	12	15	12	15	13	12	18	18
Notre Dame	7	11	19	13	11	16	17	-	-	-	17	13	17	10
Oklahoma City	13	19	16	-	18	17	-	16	13	12	11	11	10	-
Oklahoma St.	5	9	7	5	9	7	8	9	6	7	7	7	6	8
St. Bonaventure	14	12	15	-	-	-	-	-	-	-	-	-	-	-
St. John's (N.Y.)	-	-	-	-	-	-	-	-	-	-	-	-	20	7
St. Louis	17	-	-	-	-	-	-	-	-	-	-	-	-	-
Santa Clara	-	-	-	-	-	-	-	-	-	-	-	-	-	16
Seattle	-	15	13	16	16	13	13	11	11	11	14	15	14	14
Seton Hall	4	3	2	2	2	1	1	1	1	1	1	3	4	2
Southern California	-	-	-	12	12	-	-	-	-	-	-	-	-	-
Toledo	-	-	18	-	-	-	-	-	-	-	-	-	-	-
Tulsa	15	14	8	17	13	11	20	-	-	19	-	-	-	-
UCLA	12	20	-	-	-	19	-	-	-	-	-	-	-	-
Villanova	-	-	-	-	-	-	-	-	-	-	19	-	-	-
Wake Forest	-	-	-	-	-	-	-	-	-	-	-	-	12	15
Washington	9	7	5	6	5	3	3	3	3	3	3	4	2	4
Wayne St. (Mich.)	-	-	20	-	-	-	-	-	-	-	-	-	-	-
Western Ky.	15	14	10	10	10	12	9	8	9	9	8	9	9	17
Wyoming	-	-	-	-	-	-	-	-	-	-	-	-	16	-

1953-54

	December				January				February				March		
	8	15	22	29	5	12	19	26	2	9	16	23	2	9	23
Bradley	-	-	-	-	-	-	-	-	18	-	-	-	-	-	7
BYU	-	-	-	19	-	-	-	-	-	-	-	-	-	-	-
California	17	15	-	-	-	-	15	14	15	14	-	-	-	-	-
Colorado A&M	-	-	-	-	-	18	-	-	-	-	19	18	-	19	-
Connecticut	-	-	-	-	-	-	-	18	-	-	-	-	19	-	-
Dayton	15	-	16	-	14	17	-	18	-	-	17	16	14	15	-
Duke	-	13	-	-	8	9	13	20	8	15	14	10	11	18	15
Duquesne	3	3	3	2	2	2	2	2	2	2	1	1	4	3	5
Fordham	-	9	7	10	-	-	-	-	-	-	-	-	-	-	-
George Washington	-	-	-	-	-	7	10	10	11	10	8	8	9	7	12
Holy Cross	19	14	10	12	7	6	8	7	10	9	9	7	13	9	3
Idaho	-	-	20	17	-	20	-	-	-	-	-	-	-	-	-
Illinois	9	4	4	8	15	19	20	-	-	-	-	20	-	-	19
Indiana	1	1	1	3	3	3	3	3	3	3	3	3	2	2	4
Iowa	-	-	-	-	-	-	-	-	-	-	10	20	16	16	13
Kansas	5	-	-	-	16	11	17	17	19	20	-	17	15	13	18
Kansas St.	8	-	-	-	-	-	-	-	-	-	-	-	-	-	-
Kentucky	2	2	2	1	1	1	1	1	1	1	2	2	1	1	1
La Salle	6	20	16	13	-	-	19	12	9	7	12	13	8	12	2
LSU	10	5	14	18	-	16	12	14	17	13	12	-	7	8	14
Louisville	-	-	-	-	-	-	-	-	20	-	-	-	20	-	-
Maryland	-	-	-	-	-	-	14	13	13	11	11	11	17	14	20
Minnesota	12	6	8	6	6	10	9	8	12	12	18	-	-	-	-
Navy	-	-	-	-	18	-	-	-	-	16	20	-	-	-	-
Niagara	-	18	-	-	-	12	13	18	-	-	-	-	-	-	16
North Carolina St.	7	8	9	9	20	-	-	-	-	19	-	-	18	10	-
Notre Dame	-	16	19	-	-	-	6	6	7	6	6	6	5	6	6
Oklahoma City	19	12	15	11	9	8	7	9	16	13	16	15	6	5	10
Oklahoma St.	4	7	5	5	4	4	5	4	5	4	5	5	-	-	-
Oregon St.	13	11	12	4	10	-	-	-	-	-	-	-	-	16	-
Penn St.	-	-	-	-	-	-	-	-	-	-	-	-	-	-	9
Rice	-	-	11	16	11	15	-	-	-	-	-	-	-	-	-
St. Louis	18	-	-	-	-	-	-	-	-	-	-	-	-	-	-
Santa Clara	16	-	-	-	-	-	-	-	-	-	-	-	-	-	-
Seattle	-	-	-	15	16	14	16	11	6	8	7	9	10	11	17
Siena	-	19	-	-	-	-	-	-	-	-	-	-	-	-	-
Southern California	-	-	-	-	-	-	-	-	-	-	-	-	-	-	11
UCLA	-	17	13	14	-	-	-	-	-	19	-	-	-	-	-
Vanderbilt	-	-	20	20	19	-	-	-	-	-	-	-	-	-	-
Western Ky.	11	10	6	7	5	5	4	4	5	4	4	4	3	4	8
Wichita St.	-	-	-	-	-	11	11	16	14	18	15	14	12	20	-
Wisconsin	-	-	18	-	-	-	-	-	-	-	-	-	-	-	-
Wyoming	14	-	-	20	-	-	-	-	-	-	-	-	-	-	-

1954-55

	December				January				February				March	
	7	14	21	28	4	11	18	25	1	8	15	22	1	8
Alabama	-	-	19	12	20	16	12	14	13	13	17	12	11	12
Auburn	-	-	-	-	-	20	-	-	-	-	-	-	-	-
Cincinnati	-	-	-	-	-	-	-	-	-	17	12	17	-	-
Colorado	-	-	-	-	-	-	-	-	-	-	-	-	-	15
Dayton	7	5	6	4	10	12	18	15	15	16	13	11	10	9
Duke	17	-	-	18	17	-	-	-	-	-	-	-	-	-
Duquesne	3	9	9	8	2	3	5	4	4	4	4	4	8	6
George Washington	-	11	8	9	6	8	9	6	7	6	5	10	13	14
Holy Cross	5	19	-	-	-	-	16	13	14	-	-	-	17	-
Illinois	14	3	3	6	12	7	7	10	10	10	14	13	17	18
Indiana	6	7	-	-	-	-	-	-	-	-	-	-	-	-
Iowa	4	13	20	19	14	19	19	19	-	15	15	16	12	5
Kansas	-	-	20	16	-	-	-	-	-	-	-	-	-	-
Kentucky	2	2	1	1	1	1	1	1	1	2	2	2	2	2
La Salle	1	1	4	3	4	4	4	5	3	3	3	3	3	3
Louisville	-	12	14	13	16	20	-	-	-	-	-	-	-	-
Marquette	-	-	-	-	-	-	15	11	9	9	6	5	4	8
Maryland	-	-	-	-	11	11	6	8	12	11	11	17	18	-
Memphis	-	-	-	-	-	-	-	-	-	-	-	15	19	-
Minnesota	-	-	-	11	13	14	14	-	11	12	8	7	6	11
Missouri	-	6	7	-	9	6	8	12	17	14	-	20	20	-
Niagara	8	10	10	10	15	15	20	20	16	-	-	-	-	-
North Carolina St.	10	4	5	2	3	2	2	3	6	7	7	6	5	4
Northwestern	-	-	-	-	-	-	-	16	-	-	-	-	-	-
Notre Dame	9	20	-	-	20	-	-	-	-	-	-	-	-	-
Ohio St.	-	14	11	20	-	-	-	-	-	-	-	-	-	-
Oklahoma St.	11	-	-	-	-	-	-	-	-	-	-	-	-	-
Oregon St.	-	-	-	-	-	-	-	-	-	19	18	16	14	10
Penn	-	-	16	17	19	-	-	-	-	-	-	-	-	-
Penn St.	19	-	-	-	-	-	-	-	-	-	-	-	-	-
Purdue	-	-	-	-	-	17	-	-	-	-	-	-	-	-
Richmond	-	-	-	-	-	13	13	17	-	-	-	-	-	-
St. John's (N.Y.)	-	16	-	-	-	-	-	-	-	-	-	-	-	-
St. Louis	12	-	-	-	-	-	-	-	-	-	-	-	-	20
San Francisco	-	-	17	5	5	5	3	2	2	1	1	1	1	1
Seton Hall	-	-	-	-	-	-	20	-	-	-	-	-	-	-
Southern California	-	13	14	-	-	18	-	-	-	-	-	-	-	-
Tennessee	-	-	-	-	-	-	-	-	-	-	-	18	-	-
TCU	-	-	-	-	-	20	-	-	-	-	-	-	-	-
Tulsa	-	-	-	-	-	-	-	-	-	19	19	-	15	16
UCLA	13	8	17	15	7	10	10	9	8	8	9	9	9	13
Utah	16	15	2	7	8	9	10	7	5	5	10	8	7	7
Vanderbilt	-	-	17	18	-	-	-	-	20	20	20	14	16	17
Villanova	-	-	-	-	17	-	-	-	17	19	-	-	-	-
Wake Forest	17	17	-	-	-	-	-	-	-	-	-	-	-	-
West Virginia	-	-	12	-	-	-	-	-	-	-	-	-	-	19
Western Ky.	20	-	-	-	-	-	-	-	-	-	-	-	-	-
Wichita St.	15	17	14	-	-	-	-	-	-	-	-	-	-	-

1955-56

Team	Dec 6	13	20	27	Jan 3	10	17	24	31	Feb 7	14	21	28	Mar 6
Alabama	6	5	16	19	17	19	13	12	12	10	8	7	4	4
BYU	10	8	5	20	-	-	-	-	-	-	-	-	-	-
Cincinnati	-	14	-	-	20	-	-	14	-	20	-	-	-	-
Dayton	7	7	4	2	3	2	2	2	2	2	2	4	3	3
Duke	-	-	14	8	11	6	7	10	10	8	11	11	11	19
Duquesne	9	6	20	-	-	-	-	-	-	-	-	-	-	-
George Washington	13	13	11	12	7	14	-	-	-	19	-	19	-	-
Holy Cross	11	10	7	14	14	11	12	11	14	13	16	17	15	12
Houston	-	-	-	-	-	-	-	-	-	-	18	14	18	17
Illinois	8	-	17	9	9	8	6	5	6	6	3	2	2	7
Indiana	-	19	18	-	13	12	-	-	-	-	-	-	-	-
Iowa	4	4	10	6	-	-	20	13	19	17	15	13	10	5
Iowa St.	-	-	-	-	8	15	-	-	-	-	-	20	-	-
Kansas	-	18	-	-	-	-	-	-	-	-	-	-	-	-
Kansas St.	-	-	-	-	-	-	-	-	-	-	-	-	17	-
Kentucky	2	12	9	13	6	5	4	3	8	7	7	8	12	9
La Salle	18	-	-	-	-	-	-	-	-	-	-	-	-	-
Louisville	-	-	-	11	-	13	10	9	5	5	4	3	6	6
Marquette	14	-	13	-	-	-	-	-	-	-	-	-	-	-
Marshall	-	-	-	-	-	-	-	-	18	-	-	-	-	-
Memphis	-	-	18	-	12	17	15	19	16	-	19	-	-	-
Michigan St.	-	-	-	16	20	-	-	-	-	-	-	-	-	-
Minnesota	20	-	-	-	-	-	-	-	-	-	-	-	-	-
North Carolina	-	16	6	4	5	9	9	8	9	12	10	9	8	15
North Carolina St.	3	2	2	3	2	3	3	4	4	4	5	6	5	2
Ohio St.	16	-	-	15	10	7	11	-	-	-	-	-	-	-
Oklahoma City	12	20	15	10	-	16	14	16	15	14	14	18	16	16
Oklahoma St.	-	-	-	-	-	20	-	20	-	-	-	-	-	-
Rice	-	-	-	17	18	-	-	-	-	-	-	-	-	-
St. Francis (N.Y.)	-	-	-	-	-	-	-	15	13	16	13	16	-	-
St. Louis	-	17	-	-	-	-	17	17	11	11	17	-	19	-
San Francisco	1	1	1	1	1	1	1	1	1	1	1	1	1	1
SMU	-	-	-	-	-	-	19	18	17	15	12	12	9	8
Stanford	19	-	-	-	-	-	-	-	-	-	-	-	-	-
Temple	-	11	12	17	16	10	8	6	7	9	9	10	14	13
Tulsa	-	-	-	-	15	-	-	-	-	-	-	-	-	-
UCLA	16	-	-	-	-	-	18	-	20	18	20	15	13	10
Utah	5	3	3	7	-	20	16	-	-	-	-	-	-	20
Vanderbilt	-	9	8	5	4	4	5	7	3	3	6	5	7	11
Wake Forest	-	-	-	-	-	18	-	-	-	-	-	-	20	18
West Virginia	14	15	-	-	19	-	-	-	-	-	-	-	-	14

1956-57

Team	Dec 11	18	26	Jan 2	8	15	22	29	Feb 5	12	19	26	Mar 5	12
Alabama	9	17	-	-	-	-	-	-	-	-	-	-	-	-
Bradley	-	-	-	-	12	10	10	-	8	5	5	7	13	19
California	-	-	-	-	19	19	15	-	19	12	15	-	14	13
Canisius	10	18	17	15	14	14	14	12	14	14	-	-	-	20
Dayton	15	-	-	-	-	-	-	-	-	-	-	-	-	-
Duke	-	13	9	-	15	16	15	19	-	17	16	-	-	-
Idaho St.	-	-	20	-	-	-	-	17	20	-	-	15	15	16
Illinois	7	5	6	5	10	8	9	7	15	16	-	-	-	-
Indiana	-	-	-	-	-	-	-	-	-	18	11	10	-	-
Iowa St.	17	14	14	7	7	9	3	8	9	9	9	16	17	-
Kansas	1	1	1	1	1	1	2	2	2	2	2	2	2	2
Kansas St.	14	10	-	-	-	-	-	-	-	17	12	-	-	-
Kentucky	3	7	3	3	3	4	5	4	3	3	3	3	3	3
Louisville	4	6	8	6	5	5	4	3	6	8	7	8	6	6
Manhattan	-	-	-	13	-	-	-	-	-	-	-	-	-	-
Memphis	-	-	-	20	-	-	-	-	16	-	20	19	19	12
Michigan St.	-	-	-	-	-	-	-	-	-	-	-	-	8	11
Minnesota	-	-	-	-	-	19	-	-	-	-	-	-	-	-
Mississippi St.	-	-	-	-	-	-	-	-	-	-	19	20	18	15
Niagara	16	-	-	-	-	-	-	-	-	-	-	-	-	-
North Carolina	6	3	2	2	2	2	1	1	1	1	1	1	1	1
North Carolina St.	8	19	-	-	-	-	-	-	-	-	-	-	-	-
Notre Dame	-	-	-	-	-	-	-	-	-	-	-	-	-	17
Ohio St.	11	11	-	-	17	12	11	-	12	-	-	-	-	-
Oklahoma City	18	15	11	17	11	13	16	16	13	13	13	18	10	9
Oklahoma St.	19	12	10	11	12	19	-	20	-	-	-	17	16	20
Purdue	-	-	-	-	-	-	-	-	17	-	-	-	-	-
St. John's (N.Y.)	-	15	-	-	-	-	-	-	-	-	-	-	-	-
St. Louis	-	9	5	16	17	-	-	-	-	20	-	14	12	10
San Francisco	2	2	19	-	-	-	-	-	-	-	-	-	-	-
Seattle	20	-	18	10	9	7	8	9	7	4	9	5	5	5
SMU	5	4	7	4	4	3	6	4	4	6	4	4	4	4
Tennessee	-	-	12	12	16	-	-	-	-	-	-	-	-	-
Tulane	-	-	16	-	-	-	18	14	-	-	-	-	-	-
UCLA	-	-	-	-	8	6	7	5	5	7	8	6	7	14
Vanderbilt	-	-	12	9	6	10	13	-	18	18	10	9	9	8
Wake Forest	-	-	-	18	13	11	11	13	10	11	12	13	20	18
West Virginia	13	8	4	19	18	15	17	18	11	10	14	11	11	7
West Va. Tech	-	-	-	-	-	-	-	-	-	15	18	-	-	-
Western Ky.	12	20	15	14	20	18	20	-	-	-	-	-	-	-

1957-58

Team	Dec 10	17	24	31	Jan 7	14	21	28	Feb 4	11	18	25	Mar 4	11
Arkansas	-	-	-	-	-	-	20	17	18	-	-	-	-	-
Auburn	-	-	-	-	-	-	-	-	-	-	-	20	16	16
Bradley	4	11	11	12	10	10	10	12	11	13	15	14	11	14
California	-	-	-	19	-	-	-	-	-	-	-	19	-	-
Cincinnati	19	4	5	5	7	5	4	3	3	3	2	3	3	2
Dartmouth	-	-	-	-	19	18	19	-	20	-	19	-	-	-
Dayton	-	-	-	-	-	17	16	-	14	14	11	10	8	11
Duke	-	-	-	-	-	-	-	-	13	8	7	6	6	10
Georgia Tech	-	-	-	-	-	-	-	-	19	-	-	-	-	-
Illinois	-	-	-	-	17	-	-	-	-	-	-	-	-	-
Indiana	-	-	-	-	-	-	-	-	-	-	-	-	-	12
Iowa St.	-	-	20	-	-	-	-	-	-	-	-	-	-	-
Kansas	2	2	2	-	3	2	2	-	2	4	4	7	10	7
Kansas St.	5	3	3	-	4	2	3	4	4	1	1	1	1	3
Kentucky	3	5	9	10	9	9	9	8	12	12	13	12	9	9
La Salle	-	-	-	20	-	-	-	-	-	-	-	-	-	-
Maryland	-	6	6	7	11	8	6	9	8	9	14	17	17	6
Memphis	20	-	-	-	18	-	-	-	-	-	-	-	-	-
Michigan St.	7	9	8	8	14	18	15	16	15	19	12	15	12	17
Minnesota	11	10	-	-	-	-	-	-	-	-	-	-	-	-
Mississippi St.	-	18	10	9	5	11	14	14	17	18	18	16	15	15
North Carolina	1	1	4	4	3	6	8	7	7	11	16	9	13	13
North Carolina St.	12	20	13	11	13	20	12	10	9	10	9	11	14	20
Notre Dame	15	-	-	-	-	-	-	-	-	17	10	8	7	8
Oklahoma	-	-	-	-	-	14	-	-	-	20	-	-	-	-
Oklahoma St.	18	16	14	14	8	7	7	6	6	6	8	13	18	19
Oregon St.	-	17	-	18	15	16	-	20	-	-	-	-	-	-
Rice	16	14	-	-	-	-	-	-	-	-	-	-	-	-
Richmond	-	19	17	-	-	-	-	-	-	-	-	-	-	-
St. Bonaventure	-	-	-	-	-	-	-	-	-	-	-	-	20	-
St. John's (N.Y.)	-	-	19	17	16	15	13	13	-	-	-	-	-	-
St. Louis	9	-	18	-	-	-	-	-	-	-	-	-	-	-
San Francisco	6	7	7	6	6	4	5	5	5	5	4	4	4	4
Seattle	14	12	15	-	20	-	-	-	16	16	17	18	19	18
Syracuse	17	-	-	-	-	-	-	-	-	-	-	-	-	-
Temple	10	-	13	-	12	12	11	11	10	7	6	5	5	5
Tennessee	-	-	-	-	-	13	16	-	-	15	20	-	-	-
TCU	-	-	16	-	-	-	-	-	-	-	-	-	-	-
UCLA	13	13	-	-	-	-	-	-	-	-	-	-	-	-
Utah	-	15	12	15	19	-	-	-	-	-	-	-	-	-
West Virginia	8	8	1	1	1	1	1	1	1	2	3	2	2	1
Western Ky.	-	-	16	-	-	-	-	-	-	-	-	-	-	-
Wichita St.	-	-	-	-	20	17	19	18	-	-	-	-	-	-

1958-59

Team	Dec 9	16	23	30	Jan 6	13	20	27	Feb 3	10	17	24	Mar 2	9
Auburn	12	13	8	9	6	5	5	4	4	4	2	6	7	8
Bradley	-	11	13	10	9	7	9	9	8	7	10	9	9	4
California	-	15	14	20	-	20	-	20	19	18	15	12	11	11
Cincinnati	1	1	2	2	7	6	6	5	5	5	6	4	3	5
Dayton	-	-	20	-	-	-	-	-	-	-	-	-	-	-
Illinois	-	-	-	-	20	-	-	18	-	-	-	-	-	-
Indiana	19	-	-	-	-	19	-	-	-	15	19	-	-	-
Kansas	7	-	-	-	-	-	-	-	-	-	-	-	-	-
Kansas St.	3	3	4	3	4	4	3	3	3	3	4	2	2	1
Kentucky	2	2	1	1	1	2	1	1	1	1	3	1	1	2
Louisville	-	-	-	-	-	-	17	-	-	-	-	-	-	-
Marquette	17	-	17	15	15	13	12	12	12	11	13	13	13	20
Memphis	-	-	18	-	-	-	-	-	-	-	-	-	-	-
Michigan St.	15	11	9	7	5	8	8	8	7	12	9	8	6	7
Mississippi St.	8	8	7	8	12	12	11	11	11	10	5	5	4	3
North Carolina	13	10	3	4	3	3	2	2	2	2	1	3	5	9
North Carolina St.	5	4	6	5	2	1	4	6	6	6	6	7	10	6
Northwestern	10	6	12	6	8	11	18	-	-	-	-	-	-	-
Notre Dame	11	-	-	-	-	-	-	-	-	-	-	-	-	-
Oklahoma City	-	-	-	17	13	17	15	14	13	14	18	15	14	17
Oklahoma St.	20	-	-	-	-	-	-	-	-	-	-	-	-	-
Pittsburgh	-	18	-	-	-	-	-	-	-	-	-	-	-	-
Portland	-	-	-	-	-	18	17	-	-	-	-	19	-	-
Purdue	-	-	18	-	-	-	-	-	20	20	-	-	-	-
St. Bonaventure	-	-	-	-	-	14	13	16	18	-	14	18	19	19
St. John's (N.Y.)	20	-	-	13	10	9	7	7	15	15	-	17	18	-
St. Joseph's	-	14	-	12	-	-	-	-	-	20	-	-	20	14
St. Louis	9	17	16	16	14	15	14	15	9	8	8	11	12	12

	December				January				February				March	
	9	16	23	30	6	13	20	27	3	10	17	24	2	9
St. Mary's (Cal.)	14	-	-	-	-	-	-	20	-	-	-	-	17	15
Seattle	-	16	-	-	16	16	16	13	14	13	12	16	-	13
SMU	18	20	-	-	-	-	-	-	-	-	-	-	-	-
Tennessee	6	5	11	14	17	-	-	-	-	-	-	-	-	-
Texas A&M	-	-	-	-	19	-	-	-	-	-	-	-	-	-
TCU	-	-	-	19	-	-	-	19	17	16	16	14	15	16
UCLA	-	19	-	-	-	-	-	-	-	-	-	-	-	-
Utah	-	-	-	-	-	-	20	-	16	17	17	-	16	18
Villanova	-	-	15	-	18	-	19	-	-	-	-	-	-	-
Washington	-	-	19	-	-	-	-	-	-	-	-	-	-	-
West Virginia	4	7	5	11	11	10	10	10	10	9	11	10	8	10
Xavier	16	9	10	-	-	-	-	-	-	-	-	-	-	-

1959-60

	December		January				February				March	
	22	29	5	12	19	26	2	9	16	23	1	8
Auburn	-	-	-	-	-	-	-	17	17	13	11	11
Bradley	5	9	4	4	2	2	2	2	2	3	4	4
California	4	3	2	2	3	3	3	3	3	4	3	2
Cincinnati	1	1	1	1	1	1	1	1	1	1	1	1
Dayton	-	-	-	-	19	19	13	15	-	-	-	-
DePaul	-	20	-	-	-	-	-	-	-	-	-	-
Detroit	17	11	15	20	20	14	14	19	-	-	-	-
Duke	16	18	-	-	-	-	-	-	-	-	-	18
Georgia Tech	8	10	6	6	6	6	6	6	6	6	7	13
Holy Cross	-	-	-	-	-	-	16	13	17	-	20	16
Illinois	10	8	9	14	13	-	19	20	20	-	-	-
Indiana	9	7	11	-	-	-	-	-	-	20	12	7
Iowa	19	14	-	-	15	-	-	-	-	-	-	-
Kansas St.	-	-	-	-	-	-	15	-	-	-	-	-
Kentucky	13	13	-	17	16	15	-	-	-	-	-	-
La Salle	14	-	-	19	-	-	-	-	-	-	-	-
Miami (Fla.)	-	15	14	15	11	11	11	10	10	9	8	10
Michigan St.	11	-	-	-	-	-	-	-	-	-	-	-
New York U.	12	12	-	-	-	-	-	-	-	14	14	12
North Carolina	-	-	19	16	12	12	17	13	19	-	16	-
Ohio	-	-	-	-	-	-	-	-	18	-	-	-
Ohio St.	3	5	7	5	5	5	4	4	4	2	2	3
Providence	-	-	-	-	-	20	16	14	16	15	15	14
St. Bonaventure	-	-	-	-	-	-	19	-	14	10	9	9
St. John's (N.Y.)	-	-	-	-	-	-	-	-	15	11	19	20
St. Louis	7	6	12	11	18	16	18	18	-	16	13	15
Southern California	20	-	10	10	14	18	-	-	-	-	-	-
Texas A&M	18	-	13	8	10	10	10	12	11	18	-	-
Toledo	-	16	20	18	17	13	12	11	12	19	-	-
Utah	6	4	5	7	7	7	9	8	5	-	6	6
Utah St.	-	-	17	12	9	9	9	7	7	8	10	8
Villanova	15	17	16	9	8	8	8	9	9	12	17	17
Virginia Tech	-	-	-	-	-	17	-	-	-	-	-	-
Wake Forest	-	19	8	13	-	20	-	-	-	-	18	19
West Virginia	2	2	3	3	4	4	5	5	5	7	5	5
Western Ky.	-	-	18	-	-	-	-	-	-	-	-	-

1960-61

	December			January					February				March
	13	20	27	3	10	17	24	31	7	14	21	28	7
Auburn	11	9	9	10	-	-	-	-	-	-	-	-	-
Bradley	2	2	2	2	2	3	3	3	4	5	4	4	6
Cincinnati	-	-	-	-	-	-	-	-	5	4	3	3	2
Colorado	-	15	-	-	-	-	-	-	-	-	-	-	-
Dayton	20	-	-	-	-	-	-	-	-	-	-	-	-
DePaul	-	-	-	-	-	7	-	-	-	-	-	-	-
Detroit	3	8	13	-	-	-	-	-	-	-	-	-	-
Drake	-	20	14	-	-	-	-	-	-	-	-	-	-
Duke	8	7	6	8	8	8	5	4	3	3	6	9	10
Georgia Tech	15	-	-	-	-	-	-	-	-	-	-	-	-
Illinois	19	-	-	-	-	-	-	-	-	-	-	-	-
Indiana	4	4	4	-	-	-	-	-	-	-	-	-	-
Iowa	-	-	-	7	6	4	6	6	9	9	5	6	8
Kansas	16	20	-	-	-	-	-	-	-	-	-	-	-
Kansas St.	20	12	12	-	9	10	-	10	7	6	8	7	4
Kentucky	20	-	19	-	-	-	-	-	-	-	-	-	-
Louisville	9	5	5	4	4	5	8	8	10	-	-	-	-
Maryland	12	-	-	-	-	-	-	-	-	-	-	-	-
Memphis	-	-	19	-	-	-	-	-	-	-	-	-	-
North Carolina	5	10	11	6	7	6	4	6	5	7	7	5	5
North Carolina St.	10	10	10	-	-	-	-	-	-	-	-	-	-
Ohio St.	1	1	1	1	1	1	1	1	1	1	1	1	1
Providence	-	13	15	-	-	-	-	-	-	-	-	-	-
Purdue	-	-	-	-	-	-	-	10	-	-	-	-	-
St. Bonaventure	6	3	3	3	3	2	2	2	2	2	2	2	3
St. John's (N.Y.)	7	6	7	5	5	9	7	7	-	-	-	-	-

	December			January					February				March
	13	20	27	3	10	17	24	31	7	14	21	28	7
St. Louis	-	16	8	-	-	-	-	-	-	-	-	-	-
Southern California	-	-	-	-	-	-	9	9	8	8	10	10	7
UCLA	13	14	16	9	10	-	-	-	-	-	-	-	-
Utah	18	18	-	-	-	-	-	-	-	-	-	-	-
Utah St.	14	-	-	-	-	-	-	-	-	-	-	-	-
Vanderbilt	-	17	16	-	-	-	-	-	-	-	-	-	-
Wake Forest	-	19	-	-	-	-	-	-	-	-	-	-	-
West Virginia	-	-	-	-	-	-	-	-	-	10	9	8	9
Wichita St.	16	-	18	-	-	-	-	-	-	-	-	-	-

1961-62

	December			January					February				March	
	PS	19	26	2	9	16	23	30	6	13	20	27	6	13
Arizona St.	-	10	-	-	-	-	-	-	-	-	-	-	-	-
Bowling Green	-	-	-	10	9	8	8	8	8	10	7	7	8	8
Bradley	-	-	-	-	-	9	9	9	7	5	6	6	6	5
Cincinnati	2	2	2	2	3	3	3	3	3	2	2	2	2	2
Colorado	-	-	-	-	-	-	-	-	-	-	-	-	9	9
Duke	7	-	10	8	10	7	7	6	5	7	8	8	9	10
Duquesne	-	7	3	7	8	5	6	7	6	9	-	-	-	-
Kansas St.	8	4	5	4	5	4	4	4	4	4	3	3	3	6
Kentucky	-	-	6	3	3	2	2	2	2	2	3	4	4	3
Loyola (Ill.)	-	-	-	-	-	-	-	-	-	-	-	-	10	-
Mississippi St.	-	-	-	9	7	10	10	10	9	8	5	5	5	4
Ohio St.	1	1	1	1	1	1	1	1	1	1	1	1	1	1
Oregon St.	-	-	-	-	-	-	-	-	10	6	10	-	-	-
Providence	5	3	-	-	-	-	-	-	-	-	-	-	-	-
Purdue	6	8	9	-	-	-	-	-	-	-	-	-	-	-
St. Bonaventure	-	9	-	-	-	-	-	-	-	-	-	-	-	-
St. John's (N.Y.)	9	-	-	-	-	-	-	-	-	-	-	-	-	-
Seattle	10	10	-	-	-	-	-	-	-	-	-	-	-	-
Southern California	4	6	4	6	4	6	5	5	-	-	-	-	-	-
Utah	-	-	-	-	-	-	-	-	-	-	-	10	7	7
Villanova	-	-	-	5	6	-	-	-	-	-	-	-	-	-
Wake Forest	3	-	-	-	-	-	-	-	-	-	-	-	-	-
West Virginia	-	5	7	-	-	-	-	-	-	-	-	-	-	-
Wichita St.	-	8	-	-	-	-	-	-	-	-	-	-	-	-

1962-63

	December					January					February				March	
	PS	4	11	18	25	1	8	15	22	29	5	12	19	26	5	12
Arizona St.	-	-	-	-	-	6	4	3	4	5	5	5	5	4	4	4
Auburn	-	-	-	-	-	-	-	-	-	-	-	9	-	-	-	-
Cincinnati	1	1	1	1	1	1	1	1	1	1	1	1	1	1	1	1
Colorado	-	-	8	6	-	-	-	-	8	-	7	7	-	-	-	10
Duke	2	2	2	2	8	7	6	5	4	3	3	3	2	2	2	2
Georgia Tech	-	-	-	-	-	-	7	6	7	6	6	10	-	10	-	-
Illinois	8	-	10	8	4	3	5	3	3	4	4	4	6	6	8	4
Indiana	-	8	-	-	-	-	-	-	-	-	-	-	-	-	-	-
Kentucky	3	9	-	9	5	6	-	-	-	-	-	-	-	-	-	-
Loyola (Ill.)	4	4	4	3	2	2	2	2	2	2	2	3	3	5	5	3
Mississippi St.	6	5	5	5	10	-	-	9	9	-	8	6	8	7	7	6
New York U.	-	-	-	-	-	-	-	-	-	-	-	-	10	9	-	9
North Carolina	-	-	-	-	-	-	-	10	-	-	-	-	-	-	-	-
Ohio St.	-	3	3	3	5	4	8	-	-	-	-	9	5	5	3	7
Oregon St.	7	7	9	-	-	-	10	-	9	-	-	-	-	-	-	-
Providence	-	-	-	-	-	-	-	-	-	-	-	-	-	-	10	-
St. Bonaventure	9	-	-	-	-	-	-	-	-	-	-	-	-	-	-	-
Seattle	-	-	10	-	-	-	-	-	-	-	-	-	-	-	-	-
Southern California	-	-	7	-	-	-	-	-	-	-	-	-	-	-	-	-
Stanford	-	-	-	-	9	-	-	10	7	10	8	-	-	-	9	-
UCLA	-	-	-	-	-	9	-	-	-	-	-	-	-	-	-	-
West Virginia	5	3	6	7	-	9	-	6	-	-	-	-	-	-	-	-
Wichita St.	-	10	-	-	-	8	8	7	8	10	9	-	7	8	6	5
Wisconsin	10	6	7	-	-	-	-	-	-	-	-	-	-	-	-	-

1963-64

	December					January				February				March	
	PS	10	17	24	31	7	14	21	28	4	11	18	25	3	10
Arizona St.	6	4	-	-	-	-	-	-	-	-	-	-	-	-	-
Cincinnati	3	6	4	5	4	8	8	-	-	-	-	-	-	-	-
Davidson	-	-	10	7	7	5	5	4	3	5	4	8	7	10	10
DePaul	-	-	-	-	-	-	9	9	-	10	10	9	9	8	9
Drake	-	-	-	-	-	-	-	-	-	-	10	-	-	-	-
Duke	4	3	5	8	9	9	10	8	8	7	5	4	4	4	3
Kansas	-	10	-	-	-	-	-	-	-	-	-	-	-	-	-
Kentucky	9	5	2	1	2	4	5	4	3	3	2	3	3	3	4
Loyola (Ill.)	1	1	1	2	1	2	2	3	10	9	-	-	10	9	8
Michigan	8	7	3	3	5	4	3	2	2	-	-	-	-	-	-
New York U.	2	2	7	10	-	-	-	-	-	-	-	-	-	-	-
Ohio St.	7	8	-	-	-	-	-	-	-	-	-	-	-	-	-
Oregon St.	10	9	-	9	8	6	7	10	-	-	9	7	6	6	6
Toledo	-	-	9	-	-	-	-	-	-	-	-	-	-	-	-

	PS	December				January				February				March	
		10	17	24	31	7	14	21	28	4	11	18	25	3	10
UCLA	-	-	6	4	2	1	1	1	1	1	1	1	1	1	1
Vanderbilt	-	-	8	6	6	7	6	6	5	8	7	-	-	-	-
Villanova	-	-	-	-	10	10	9	7	6	6	8	5	8	7	7
Wichita St.	5	-	-	-	-	-	-	10	7	4	6	6	5	5	5

1964-65

	PS	December				January				February				March	
		8	15	22	29	5	12	19	26	2	9	16	23	2	9
Bradley	14	-	-	-	-	-	-	-	-	-	-	-	-	-	-
BYU	19	-	-	-	-	-	-	-	-	-	-	-	-	10	9
Davidson	4	-	-	10	-	10	8	7	6	5	5	5	6	7	6
DePaul	20	-	-	-	-	-	-	-	-	-	-	-	-	-	-
Duke	5	8	6	6	8	6	10	10	10	6	6	6	5	8	10
Illinois	-	-	-	7	6	-	-	-	-	-	10	-	-	-	-
Indiana	-	-	-	8	7	2	5	5	9	7	8	7	7	-	-
Kansas	18	-	-	-	-	-	-	-	-	-	-	-	-	-	-
Kansas St.	8	-	-	-	-	-	-	-	-	-	-	-	-	-	-
Kentucky	11	9	8	-	-	-	-	-	-	-	-	-	-	-	-
Michigan	1	1	2	1	1	3	2	2	2	1	1	1	1	1	1
Minnesota	11	6	4	3	3	-	-	-	-	-	-	9	8	6	7
New Mexico	-	-	-	-	-	-	-	-	-	-	-	-	10	-	-
North Carolina	13	-	-	-	-	-	-	-	-	-	-	-	-	-	-
Notre Dame	17	-	-	-	-	-	-	-	-	-	-	-	-	-	-
Providence	-	-	-	-	-	9	6	6	4	4	4	4	4	4	4
St. John's (N.Y.)	10	10	7	-	-	7	7	8	7	-	-	-	-	-	-
St. Joseph's	-	-	-	-	10	4	4	3	3	3	3	3	3	3	3
St. Louis	-	4	10	9	9	-	-	-	-	-	-	-	-	-	-
San Francisco	9	5	3	5	5	8	9	9	8	10	-	-	-	-	-
Seattle	15	-	-	-	-	-	-	-	-	-	-	-	-	-	-
Syracuse	7	-	-	-	-	-	-	-	-	-	-	-	-	-	-
Tennessee	-	-	-	-	-	-	-	-	-	-	-	8	-	-	-
UCLA	2	7	5	4	4	1	1	1	1	2	2	2	2	2	2
Vanderbilt	6	3	9	-	-	-	-	-	-	9	7	-	9	5	5
Villanova	16	-	-	-	-	-	-	-	-	-	-	-	-	9	8
Wichita St.	3	2	1	2	2	5	3	4	5	8	9	10	-	-	-

1965-66

	PS	December				January				February				March	
		7	14	21	28	4	11	18	25	1	8	15	22	1	8
Bradley	9	9	9	5	3	5	5	7	-	-	-	-	-	-	-
BYU	-	-	-	-	6	8	7	-	-	-	-	-	-	-	-
Cincinnati	-	-	-	-	-	-	-	-	8	10	-	-	-	10	7
Duke	3	6	1	1	1	1	1	1	1	1	2	2	2	3	2
Iowa	-	-	-	9	4	7	-	-	-	-	-	-	-	-	-
Kansas	8	7	4	-	-	-	10	6	9	7	7	7	6	6	4
Kansas St.	10	-	-	-	-	-	-	-	-	-	-	-	-	-	-
Kentucky	-	-	-	10	5	2	2	2	2	2	1	1	1	1	1
Loyola (Ill.)	-	-	-	-	-	-	-	9	7	5	3	4	4	4	6
Michigan	2	2	3	3	7	-	-	-	-	9	10	10	10	-	9
Minnesota	7	5	6	6	9	-	-	-	-	-	-	-	-	-	-
Nebraska	-	-	-	-	-	-	-	-	-	-	9	9	8	9	-
Providence	6	8	7	7	10	6	6	4	3	4	6	6	9	8	-
St. Joseph's	4	3	2	2	8	4	4	3	5	8	8	8	7	7	5
South Carolina	-	10	-	-	-	-	-	-	-	-	-	-	-	-	-
UTEP	-	-	-	-	-	9	8	8	6	6	4	3	3	2	3
UCLA	1	1	8	-	-	10	9	10	10	-	-	-	-	-	-
Vanderbilt	5	4	5	4	2	3	3	5	4	3	5	5	5	5	8
Western Ky.	-	-	-	-	-	-	-	-	-	-	-	-	-	-	10
Wichita St.	-	-	10	8	-	-	-	-	-	-	-	-	-	-	-

1966-67

	PS	December				January					February				March
		6	13	20	27	3	10	17	24	31	7	14	21	28	7
Boston College	-	-	-	-	-	-	-	-	-	-	10	-	-	10	9
Bradley	-	-	-	-	-	10	-	-	-	-	-	-	-	-	-
BYU	-	9	7	-	-	-	-	-	-	-	-	-	-	-	-
Cincinnati	10	10	10	7	7	8	-	-	-	-	-	-	-	-	-
Duke	4	7	-	-	-	-	-	-	-	-	-	-	-	-	-
Florida	-	-	-	-	-	-	10	8	-	-	-	-	-	-	-
Houston	7	5	9	8	6	5	4	3	3	6	5	7	7	7	7
Kansas	-	-	-	9	-	9	8	7	7	7	7	6	4	4	3
Kentucky	3	3	4	-	-	-	-	-	-	-	-	-	-	-	-
Louisville	5	4	3	2	2	2	2	2	4	3	3	2	2	2	2
Michigan St.	-	-	8	5	10	-	-	-	-	-	-	-	-	-	-
Mississippi St.	-	-	-	-	-	10	-	-	-	-	-	-	-	-	-
New Mexico	6	6	5	6	5	4	3	9	-	-	-	-	-	-	-
North Carolina	9	8	6	3	3	3	5	4	2	2	2	4	5	3	4
Princeton	-	-	-	-	-	-	7	5	5	5	4	3	6	5	5
Providence	-	-	-	-	-	7	9	10	10	10	9	-	-	-	-
St. John's (N.Y.)	-	-	-	-	8	-	-	-	-	-	-	-	-	-	-
Syracuse	-	-	-	-	-	-	-	-	-	-	-	10	8	-	-
Tennessee	-	-	-	-	-	-	-	-	-	-	-	-	9	8	8
UTEP	2	2	2	4	4	6	6	6	6	4	8	8	10	9	10
UCLA	1	1	1	1	1	1	1	1	1	1	1	1	1	1	1
Vanderbilt	-	-	-	10	9	-	-	-	9	9	-	9	-	-	-
Western Ky.	8	-	-	-	-	-	-	-	8	8	6	5	3	6	6

1967-68

	PS	December				January					February				March	
		5	12	19	26	2	9	16	23	30	6	13	20	27	5	12
Boston College	7	10	6	8	10	-	-	-	-	-	-	-	-	-	-	-
Bradley	-	-	-	10	-	-	-	-	-	-	-	-	-	-	-	-
Columbia	-	-	-	-	-	-	10	10	8	8	7	6	6	6	8	7
Davidson	10	-	8	6	8	-	-	-	-	-	-	-	-	-	10	8
Dayton	6	6	-	-	-	-	-	-	-	-	-	-	-	-	-	-
Duke	-	-	-	-	-	-	-	-	-	9	-	10	8	10	6	10
Houston	2	2	2	2	2	2	2	2	1	1	1	1	1	1	1	1
Indiana	-	-	9	5	3	-	-	-	-	-	-	-	-	-	-	-
BKansas	5	4	-	-	-	-	-	-	-	-	-	-	-	-	-	-
Kentucky	-	9	4	7	6	5	4	8	9	10	8	8	5	5	4	5
Louisville	3	3	5	-	-	-	-	-	-	-	-	-	-	9	9	9
Marquette	-	-	-	-	-	-	-	-	-	-	-	-	10	8	-	-
New Mexico	-	-	-	-	-	10	9	6	4	4	6	5	7	7	7	6
New Mexico St.	-	-	-	-	-	-	-	-	-	-	10	-	-	-	-	-
North Carolina	4	5	7	4	5	3	3	3	3	3	3	3	3	3	5	4
Oklahoma City	-	-	-	-	-	8	-	-	-	-	-	-	-	-	-	-
Princeton	8	-	10	-	-	-	-	-	-	-	-	-	-	-	-	-
Purdue	-	7	-	-	-	-	-	-	-	-	-	-	-	-	-	-
St. Bonaventure	-	-	-	-	-	9	7	7	5	5	4	4	4	4	3	3
Tennessee	-	-	-	9	4	6	5	4	6	6	5	7	-	-	-	-
UCLA	1	1	1	1	1	1	1	1	2	2	2	2	2	2	2	2
Utah	-	-	-	-	7	7	6	5	10	-	-	-	-	-	-	-
Vanderbilt	9	8	3	3	9	4	8	9	7	7	9	9	9	-	-	-

1968-69

	PS	December					January				February				March
		3	10	17	24	31	7	14	21	28	4	11	18	25	4
Baylor	-	-	-	-	-	-	-	18	-	-	-	19	-	-	-
Boston College	-	-	-	-	-	-	-	-	-	-	-	-	-	20	16
California	-	19	18	15	-	-	-	-	-	-	-	-	-	-	-
Cincinnati	14	9	6	6	10	10	19	19	-	-	-	-	-	-	-
Colorado	-	-	-	-	-	-	-	20	17	17	20	14	18	-	18
Columbia	-	-	-	-	-	-	-	-	19	18	14	-	-	-	-
Davidson	6	6	3	3	3	2	6	4	4	4	6	6	5	5	5
Dayton	-	-	-	-	-	-	-	-	20	20	19	17	-	-	-
Detroit	18	15	14	13	11	7	13	-	-	-	-	-	-	-	-
Drake	-	-	-	-	-	-	18	-	-	-	-	-	-	-	11
Duke	17	16	9	-	-	-	-	-	-	-	-	-	-	-	-
Duquesne	-	-	-	-	-	15	15	12	10	11	15	13	8	10	9
Florida	19	-	-	-	-	-	-	-	-	-	-	-	-	-	-
Houston	8	6	12	20	-	-	-	-	-	-	-	-	-	-	-
Illinois	-	-	-	-	12	8	4	8	8	7	10	10	19	15	20
Iowa	-	20	19	-	-	-	-	-	-	-	-	-	-	-	-
Kansas	5	4	11	11	8	5	5	10	13	15	13	12	16	13	19
Kentucky	3	3	4	4	4	3	7	5	5	5	4	4	6	6	7
La Salle	-	-	20	16	17	11	11	11	9	9	7	5	4	3	2
Louisville	-	-	-	19	14	14	14	-	-	-	-	20	13	11	15
Marquette	15	20	-	-	-	-	20	15	16	16	17	18	20	18	14
New Mexico	9	8	5	5	6	18	-	-	-	-	18	-	-	-	-
New Mexico St.	-	-	-	14	15	12	10	7	7	8	16	15	15	16	12
North Carolina	2	2	2	2	2	4	2	2	2	2	2	2	3	2	4
Northwestern	-	-	-	-	-	19	12	17	-	-	-	-	-	-	-
Notre Dame	4	5	7	7	7	16	17	16	15	-	-	-	-	-	17
Ohio St.	12	13	17	17	16	13	16	13	12	12	12	16	10	14	-
Purdue	10	14	13	12	18	-	-	-	18	14	9	8	9	9	6
St. Bonaventure	7	11	10	9	13	20	-	-	-	-	-	-	-	-	-
St. John's (N.Y.)	-	-	-	-	-	17	8	6	6	6	5	9	7	7	8
Santa Clara	-	18	16	10	9	6	3	3	3	3	3	3	2	4	3
South Carolina	-	-	-	-	-	-	-	-	-	19	-	-	12	8	13
Tennessee	20	20	-	-	20	-	-	-	-	-	-	-	17	17	-
Tulsa	-	-	-	-	-	-	-	14	14	13	11	7	14	19	-
UCLA	1	1	1	1	1	1	1	1	1	1	1	1	1	1	1
Vanderbilt	13	12	-	-	-	-	-	-	-	-	-	-	-	-	-
Villanova	11	10	8	8	5	9	9	9	11	10	8	11	11	12	10
Western Ky.	16	17	15	18	-	-	-	-	-	-	-	-	-	-	-
Wyoming	-	-	-	-	19	-	-	-	-	-	-	-	-	-	-

1969-70

	PS	December				January				February				March	
		9	16	23	30	6	13	20	27	3	10	17	24	3	10
Cincinnati	-	-	-	-	-	-	-	-	-	-	-	-	-	19	-
Colorado	10	17	16	-	20	-	-	-	-	-	-	-	-	-	-
Columbia	-	-	-	-	15	17	13	-	17	17	19	-	18	-	-
Davidson	5	4	4	9	11	8	8	11	11	15	13	9	11	10	15
Drake	19	-	-	-	-	-	-	-	16	13	11	17	16	14	14

	December					January				February				March	
	PS	9	16	23	30	6	13	20	27	3	10	17	24	3	10
Duke	-	-	-	-	-	19	19	16	-	-	-	-	-	-	-
Duquesne	11	7	-	-	-	-	-	-	-	-	-	-	-	-	-
Florida St.	-	-	-	-	-	-	-	-	18	12	9	8	10	11	11
Georgia	-	-	-	-	-	-	-	-	-	-	20	-	-	-	-
Houston	20	-	19	8	8	11	9	7	12	16	15	15	15	13	12
Illinois	-	-	-	15	-	-	17	12	10	14	-	-	-	-	-
Iowa	-	-	-	-	-	-	-	18	20	20	14	11	9	8	7
Jacksonville	-	18	18	13	10	7	6	6	6	8	7	6	6	6	4
Kansas	-	-	-	16	-	-	-	-	-	-	-	-	-	-	-
Kansas St.	-	-	-	-	-	-	-	17	19	18	-	18	17	16	-
Kentucky	2	1	1	1	1	2	2	2	2	3	3	2	1	2	1
Long Beach St.	-	-	-	-	-	-	-	-	-	-	-	-	-	-	19
LSU	-	-	15	-	-	-	-	-	-	-	-	-	-	-	-
Louisville	15	11	14	14	-	20	18	18	-	-	-	19	-	-	-
Marquette	8	12	17	-	18	13	10	8	7	9	12	10	8	9	8
New Mexico St.	6	3	3	7	7	6	5	5	5	6	6	5	5	5	5
Niagara	-	-	-	-	-	15	12	-	-	-	-	-	-	-	17
North Carolina	7	5	7	4	4	4	7	9	9	7	10	13	19	-	-
North Carolina St.	-	-	-	-	15	10	11	10	8	5	5	12	14	19	10
Notre Dame	13	10	6	11	13	-	-	20	-	-	16	14	13	15	9
Ohio	-	19	10	5	5	9	14	13	13	-	-	-	-	17	-
Ohio St.	18	16	-	-	-	-	-	-	-	-	-	-	-	-	-
Oklahoma	-	-	-	-	-	16	-	-	-	-	-	-	-	-	-
Penn	-	-	-	17	14	18	15	14	14	10	8	7	7	7	13
Purdue	3	14	12	18	17	-	-	-	-	-	-	-	-	-	-
St. Bonaventure	17	20	-	19	12	5	4	4	3	4	4	3	3	4	3
St. John's (N.Y.)	14	-	-	-	-	-	-	-	-	-	-	-	-	-	-
Santa Clara	12	15	11	-	-	-	-	-	-	-	-	20	-	-	-
South Carolina	1	8	5	3	3	3	3	3	4	2	2	4	4	3	6
Southern California	16	6	13	12	19	-	20	15	15	11	18	-	-	-	20
Tennessee	-	9	8	6	6	12	-	-	-	-	-	-	-	-	-
UCLA	4	2	2	2	2	1	1	1	1	1	1	1	2	1	2
Utah St.	-	-	-	-	-	-	-	-	-	-	-	-	20	18	16
Villanova	9	12	9	20	-	-	-	-	-	19	-	-	-	-	-
Washington	-	-	20	10	9	14	15	-	-	-	-	-	-	-	-
Western Ky.	-	-	-	-	-	-	-	-	-	-	17	16	12	12	18

1970-71

	December					January				February				March		
	PS	8	15	22	29	5	12	19	26	2	9	16	23	2	9	16
Army	-	14	-	-	-	-	-	-	-	-	-	-	-	-	-	-
BYU	-	-	-	-	-	-	-	-	-	-	-	-	-	-	-	20
Drake	10	7	9	9	7	16	-	-	-	-	-	-	-	-	-	18
Duke	13	-	-	-	-	-	-	-	-	-	-	-	-	-	19	-
Duquesne	-	-	-	-	-	-	-	-	17	14	12	10	8	11	11	15
Florida St.	-	-	17	-	-	-	-	-	-	-	-	-	-	-	-	-
Fordham	-	-	-	-	-	18	14	17	-	-	20	18	11	10	10	9
Houston	17	-	-	-	-	-	-	-	-	18	15	-	-	15	18	14
Illinois	-	-	-	-	-	-	-	-	18	15	-	-	-	-	-	-
Indiana	16	11	13	11	14	12	11	18	-	-	-	-	-	18	-	-
Jacksonville	4	3	5	4	9	7	7	6	6	6	6	6	6	9	9	11
Kansas	14	11	12	8	12	8	8	5	5	5	5	5	5	4	5	4
Kentucky	3	5	3	7	8	11	10	12	11	8	8	12	10	8	8	8
La Salle	-	-	-	-	-	-	-	15	14	10	13	11	14	19	-	-
Long Beach St.	18	-	-	-	-	-	-	-	-	-	-	-	20	17	17	16
LSU	-	-	-	-	18	-	-	-	-	-	-	-	-	-	-	-
Louisville	-	20	-	-	17	13	16	-	-	-	-	19	15	-	-	-
Marquette	6	4	4	3	3	3	2	2	1	1	2	2	2	2	2	2
Memphis	-	-	-	-	-	-	19	-	-	-	-	-	-	-	-	-
Miami (Ohio)	-	-	-	-	-	-	-	-	-	-	-	-	-	-	20	-
Michigan	-	-	-	-	-	-	-	-	-	20	16	16	12	-	-	-
Murray St.	-	-	-	-	-	-	-	-	19	19	17	17	-	-	-	-
New Mexico St.	15	15	17	20	-	-	-	-	-	-	-	-	-	-	-	-
North Carolina	-	-	20	17	-	20	15	20	20	16	11	8	13	12	13	13
North Caro. St.	19	-	-	-	-	-	-	-	-	-	-	-	-	-	-	-
Notre Dame	5	6	7	14	15	9	9	9	7	12	9	14	19	16	14	12
Ohio St.	-	-	-	-	-	-	-	-	-	-	-	20	18	13	12	10
Oregon	-	18	16	17	16	-	-	16	13	-	-	-	-	-	-	-
Oregon St.	-	-	-	-	-	-	20	-	-	-	-	-	-	-	-	-
Penn	11	8	6	5	6	5	4	4	4	4	4	4	4	5	4	3
Purdue	-	-	-	16	20	19	-	-	-	-	-	-	-	-	-	-
St. Bonaventure	20	19	19	15	13	10	12	10	-	-	-	-	-	-	-	-
St. John's (N.Y.)	-	-	-	19	-	-	-	-	-	-	-	-	-	-	-	-
South Carolina	2	2	2	2	2	2	6	11	10	7	10	7	7	6	6	6
Southern California	7	9	8	6	4	4	3	3	3	2	3	3	3	3	3	5
Tennessee	-	17	14	12	10	17	18	8	8	11	14	13	17	14	15	17
UCLA	1	1	1	1	1	1	1	1	2	3	1	1	1	1	1	1
Utah St.	12	16	15	-	19	15	17	12	9	13	19	15	16	20	16	-
Villanova	8	10	10	13	11	14	13	14	16	17	18	-	-	-	-	19
Virginia	-	-	-	-	-	-	-	19	15	-	-	-	-	-	-	-
Western Ky.	9	13	11	10	5	6	5	7	12	9	7	9	9	7	7	7

1971-72

	December					January					February				March	
	PS	7	14	21	28	4	11	18	25	1	8	15	22	29	7	14
Arizona St.	-	17	-	-	-	-	-	-	-	-	-	-	-	-	-	-
BYU	19	15	6	7	8	18	14	13	13	10	10	11	7	7	8	9
Duquesne	-	-	-	-	-	-	-	-	-	-	20	-	-	-	-	-
Florida St.	-	18	9	14	-	20	12	11	10	12	14	14	11	10	14	10
Hawaii	-	-	-	-	18	16	19	18	15	14	18	16	17	15	12	-
Houston	7	12	20	-	-	-	-	-	-	-	-	-	16	13	19	-
Illinois	-	-	-	-	-	-	16	-	-	-	-	-	-	-	-	-
Indiana	-	-	12	8	7	5	17	-	-	-	-	-	-	-	20	17
Jacksonville	11	8	14	16	-	-	-	-	-	17	16	-	-	-	-	-
Kansas	14	-	-	-	-	-	-	-	-	-	-	-	-	-	-	-
Kentucky	10	7	7	11	12	19	15	-	-	-	-	17	18	-	-	18
Long Beach St.	8	6	13	9	10	8	7	4	5	5	8	9	6	6	5	5
La.-Lafayette	-	-	16	12	13	15	13	12	12	13	13	12	10	11	9	8
Louisville	9	16	17	19	15	7	5	6	4	3	4	4	3	2	4	4
Marquette	4	2	2	2	2	2	2	2	2	2	2	2	2	5	7	7
Marshall	-	-	-	20	17	13	20	16	14	11	11	10	8	9	10	12
Maryland	6	5	15	15	16	12	-	-	18	-	-	19	12	18	13	14
Memphis	-	-	-	-	-	-	-	-	-	-	15	18	19	20	11	13
Michigan	13	9	-	-	-	-	-	-	-	20	-	-	-	16	-	-
Minnesota	-	-	-	-	-	-	-	17	16	19	19	-	-	-	16	11
Missouri	-	-	-	-	-	-	18	-	20	15	17	15	14	19	18	-
New Mexico	16	-	-	-	-	-	-	-	-	-	-	-	-	-	-	-
North Carolina	2	3	4	4	4	3	3	3	3	4	3	3	5	3	3	2
North Caro. St.	-	20	-	-	-	-	-	-	-	-	-	-	-	-	-	-
Northern Ill.	-	-	-	-	-	-	-	20	19	-	-	-	-	-	-	-
Ohio	-	-	-	17	-	-	-	-	-	-	-	-	-	-	-	-
Ohio St.	5	4	10	6	6	10	9	7	6	9	7	8	15	14	-	19
Oklahoma	20	-	-	-	-	-	-	-	-	-	-	-	-	-	-	-
Oral Roberts	-	-	-	-	-	-	-	-	-	-	-	-	20	17	17	16
Penn	15	10	5	13	14	6	6	10	9	6	5	5	4	4	2	3
Princeton	-	-	18	-	-	-	-	14	17	-	-	-	-	-	-	-
Providence	-	-	-	-	-	-	-	-	-	16	12	13	-	-	-	-
St. John's (N.Y.)	17	14	8	10	9	17	-	-	-	-	-	-	-	-	-	-
South Carolina	12	11	3	3	3	4	4	5	11	8	9	7	9	8	6	6
Southern California	3	13	10	5	5	11	10	8	7	18	-	-	-	-	-	-
Tennessee	-	-	-	-	20	-	-	19	-	-	-	20	-	-	-	-
UCLA	1	1	1	1	1	1	1	1	1	1	1	1	1	1	1	1
Villanova	18	18	-	-	-	14	11	15	-	-	-	-	-	-	-	15
Virginia	-	-	19	18	11	9	8	9	8	7	6	6	13	12	15	20
West Virginia	-	-	-	-	19	-	-	-	-	-	-	-	-	-	-	-

1972-73

	December					January					February				March	
	PS	5	12	19	26	2	9	16	23	30	6	13	20	27	6	13
Alabama	-	-	-	-	18	14	14	11	9	6	10	17	18	-	-	-
Arizona St.	-	-	-	-	-	-	-	-	-	-	-	-	-	-	-	16
Austin Peay	-	-	-	-	-	-	-	-	-	-	-	-	-	-	-	19
BYU	12	-	17	15	14	15	-	-	-	-	-	20	-	-	-	-
Florida St.	2	2	2	7	12	19	18	19	-	-	-	-	-	-	-	-
Houston	15	20	16	14	13	10	10	12	11	11	11	7	9	8	7	13
Indiana	-	-	15	9	15	20	16	16	6	5	4	11	10	12	9	6
Jacksonville	-	-	-	-	-	-	15	15	13	15	16	13	20	18	16	-
Kansas St.	17	16	20	17	16	18	17	14	18	18	18	15	13	16	11	9
Kentucky	13	8	-	-	-	-	-	-	-	-	-	-	-	-	19	17
Long Beach St.	6	7	7	6	6	5	6	5	5	4	3	3	3	4	4	3
La.-Lafayette	7	10	8	8	9	8	13	13	12	13	13	14	12	11	14	7
Louisville	20	-	-	-	-	-	20	20	-	-	-	-	-	-	-	-
Marquette	5	5	4	3	3	3	4	7	10	10	7	5	5	5	6	5
Maryland	3	3	3	2	2	2	2	3	4	3	9	10	8	9	10	8
Memphis	11	11	19	-	-	-	-	-	17	17	15	16	14	10	15	12
Michigan	19	18	18	-	-	-	-	-	-	-	-	-	-	-	-	-
Minnesota	4	4	5	5	5	6	8	6	8	9	5	4	4	3	3	10
Missouri	-	-	12	10	7	7	5	8	7	7	8	12	16	13	12	15
New Mexico	-	-	-	-	-	16	-	-	19	-	20	18	15	15	-	-
North Carolina	-	13	11	13	11	9	7	4	3	8	6	6	6	7	8	11
North Carolina St.	8	6	6	4	4	4	3	2	2	2	2	2	2	2	2	2
Ohio St.	10	15	-	-	-	-	-	-	-	-	-	-	-	-	-	-
Oklahoma	-	-	-	19	19	-	-	-	-	-	-	-	-	-	-	-
Oral Roberts	18	12	10	16	-	-	-	-	-	19	19	-	-	-	-	-
Penn	9	9	9	11	8	17	-	-	-	-	-	-	-	-	-	18
Providence	-	19	14	18	17	13	11	9	14	12	12	8	7	6	5	4
Purdue	-	-	-	-	-	-	-	-	20	-	-	-	17	20	-	-
St. John's (N.Y.)	-	-	-	-	-	-	18	17	15	14	14	9	11	17	17	-
St. Joseph's	-	-	-	-	-	-	-	-	-	-	-	-	-	-	18	-
San Francisco	-	-	-	-	20	12	12	10	16	16	17	-	-	-	19	20
Santa Clara	-	-	-	20	-	-	-	-	-	-	-	-	-	-	-	-
South Carolina	16	-	-	-	-	-	-	-	-	-	-	-	-	19	-	-
Southern California	20	17	-	-	-	-	-	-	-	20	-	-	-	-	-	-
Syracuse	-	-	-	-	-	-	-	-	-	-	-	-	-	14	13	14
Tennessee	14	14	-	-	-	-	-	-	-	-	-	-	-	-	-	-
UCLA	1	1	1	1	1	1	1	1	1	1	1	1	1	1	1	1

		December				January					February				March	
	PS	5	12	19	26	2	9	16	23	30	6	13	20	27	6	13
Vanderbilt	-	-	13	12	10	11	9	18	-	-	-	-	-	-	-	-
Virginia Tech	-	-	-	-	-	-	-	-	-	-	-	19	19	-	-	-

1973-74

		December				January					February				March			
	PS	4	11	18	25	2	8	15	22	29	5	12	19	26	5	12	19	27
Alabama	18	18	13	10	13	7	12	10	9	8	8	8	8	7	12	11	13	14
Arizona	15	15	14	14	12	15	-	-	-	-	-	20	-	18	-	-	-	-
Arizona St.	-	-	-	-	-	-	-	-	20	-	-	-	-	-	-	-	-	-
Austin Peay	-	-	-	-	20	20	-	-	-	-	-	-	-	-	-	-	-	-
Centenary (La.)	-	-	-	-	-	-	-	-	18	-	-	-	-	-	-	-	-	-
Cincinnati	-	-	-	20	-	-	-	20	-	-	-	-	-	-	-	-	-	-
Creighton	-	-	-	-	-	-	-	-	-	-	-	17	15	16	19	19	-	-
Dayton	-	-	-	-	-	-	-	-	-	-	-	-	-	-	-	20	16	20
Hawaii	-	-	-	-	-	-	20	-	-	-	-	-	-	-	-	-	-	-
Houston	14	14	-	-	-	-	-	-	-	-	-	-	-	-	-	-	-	-
Indiana	3	3	3	7	7	8	13	12	11	12	12	12	10	9	13	10	11	9
Jacksonville	17	17	19	19	-	-	-	-	-	-	-	-	-	-	-	-	-	-
Kansas	13	-	-	-	-	-	-	-	-	18	17	16	16	15	15	14	6	7
Kansas St.	-	13	15	13	18	-	-	-	-	-	-	-	18	-	-	-	-	-
Kentucky	10	10	-	-	-	-	-	-	-	-	-	-	-	-	-	-	-	-
Long Beach St.	12	12	12	11	10	9	9	9	10	10	9	10	13	13	9	9	9	10
Louisville	9	9	9	8	8	13	11	16	14	15	15	18	20	20	18	16	-	-
Marquette	7	7	7	6	6	6	7	6	6	5	6	9	9	8	11	7	3	3
Maryland	4	4	4	2	2	3	3	4	5	6	7	6	5	5	4	4	4	4
Md.-East. Shore	-	-	-	-	-	-	-	-	-	-	20	-	-	-	-	-	-	-
Memphis	20	20	10	12	16	18	19	-	-	-	-	-	-	-	-	-	-	-
Michigan	-	-	-	-	-	-	18	14	15	20	16	15	19	17	16	12	7	6
Missouri	-	-	-	-	-	-	-	18	-	-	-	-	-	-	-	-	-	-
UNLV	19	19	-	-	19	15	16	-	-	-	-	-	-	-	-	-	-	-
New Mexico	-	-	-	-	17	12	8	15	19	17	-	-	-	19	17	17	20	-
North Carolina	5	5	5	4	4	4	5	5	4	4	4	4	6	4	6	8	10	12
North Carolina St.	2	2	2	5	5	5	4	3	3	2	2	2	1	1	1	1	1	1
Notre Dame	8	8	6	3	3	2	2	2	1	3	3	3	2	2	2	3	5	5
Oral Roberts	-	-	-	-	-	-	-	-	-	19	19	-	-	-	20	-	18	18
Penn	16	16	11	-	-	-	-	-	-	-	-	-	-	-	-	-	-	-
Pittsburgh	-	-	-	-	-	-	-	17	16	13	10	7	7	11	14	13	15	16
Providence	6	6	8	9	9	14	10	7	8	9	11	11	11	12	8	5	8	8
Purdue	-	-	-	-	-	-	-	-	-	-	-	-	-	-	-	-	18	11
San Francisco	11	11	17	-	-	-	-	-	-	-	-	-	-	-	-	-	-	-
South Carolina	-	-	16	15	-	-	15	11	13	14	13	14	14	14	10	18	17	19
Southern California	-	-	20	16	14	11	17	13	12	11	14	13	12	10	7	15	14	17
Syracuse	-	-	18	18	15	19	-	-	-	-	-	-	-	-	-	-	-	-
UTEP	-	-	-	-	-	-	-	-	-	-	18	-	-	-	-	-	-	-
UCLA	1	1	1	1	1	1	1	1	2	1	1	1	3	3	3	2	2	2
Utah	-	-	-	-	-	-	-	-	-	-	-	19	17	-	-	-	-	15
Vanderbilt	-	-	-	17	11	10	6	8	7	7	5	5	4	6	5	6	11	13
Wisconsin	-	-	-	-	-	17	13	19	17	16	-	-	-	-	-	-	-	-

1974-75

		December					January				February				March				Apr.
	PS	3	10	17	24	31	7	14	21	28	4	11	18	25	4	11	18	25	2
Alabama	9	11	10	8	7	6	8	7	6	9	7	7	5	8	7	10	11	11	10
Arizona	19	18	17	13	10	14	10	13	13	15	17	19	15	19	19	-	-	-	-
Arizona St.	-	-	-	-	-	16	12	9	10	12	10	8	8	9	9	8	7	7	8
Auburn	-	-	-	-	-	-	-	-	20	14	-	-	-	-	-	-	-	-	-
Centenary (La.)	-	-	-	-	-	-	-	-	-	-	-	-	18	-	-	17	19	18	-
Cincinnati	-	-	-	-	-	-	-	-	-	-	-	-	-	-	-	17	12	12	13
Clemson	-	-	-	-	-	-	-	-	-	-	16	18	16	11	14	14	-	-	-
Creighton	-	-	-	-	-	-	-	-	-	-	18	20	14	13	13	-	-	-	-
Drake	-	-	-	-	-	-	-	-	-	-	-	-	-	-	-	-	14	16	16
Houston	-	20	-	-	-	-	-	-	-	-	-	-	-	-	-	-	-	-	-
Indiana	3	3	3	2	2	2	1	1	1	1	1	1	1	1	1	1	1	3	3
Kansas	6	7	9	18	-	-	-	-	18	20	-	-	-	-	-	-	-	-	-
Kansas St.	-	-	-	-	-	-	-	-	-	-	-	-	-	-	-	-	17	15	15
Kentucky	16	15	-	20	17	9	7	10	11	5	5	4	7	4	6	6	5	2	2
La Salle	-	-	-	-	-	-	14	11	9	7	13	12	17	-	-	-	-	-	-
Louisville	8	6	4	4	4	4	3	3	2	3	3	6	6	3	3	3	3	4	4
Marquette	5	8	7	6	14	13	13	12	12	13	11	9	9	6	5	5	10	10	11
Maryland	4	4	5	5	5	7	5	5	3	8	4	3	3	2	2	4	4	5	5
Memphis	15	16	14	11	16	19	-	-	-	-	-	-	-	-	-	-	-	-	-
Michigan	17	19	16	-	-	17	11	19	-	-	-	-	-	-	-	-	-	19	19
Minnesota	18	-	-	-	-	-	17	16	17	-	-	-	-	-	-	-	-	-	-
UNLV	-	-	-	-	-	-	-	-	-	-	-	-	-	-	-	-	16	20	17
North Carolina	11	9	8	10	8	8	15	14	14	10	12	11	13	14	12	7	6	9	9
North Caro. St.	1	1	1	1	1	1	4	4	5	2	6	5	4	7	8	9	8	8	7
Notre Dame	12	13	11	12	13	19	-	-	-	16	14	16	11	16	16	12	9	14	14
Oklahoma	-	-	19	17	18	-	-	-	-	-	-	-	-	-	-	-	-	-	-
Oregon	-	-	18	19	19	11	9	8	8	11	9	13	-	-	-	-	-	-	-
Oregon St.	-	-	-	-	-	-	-	-	-	-	-	17	20	17	15	15	13	-	18
Penn	20	14	12	9	9	12	-	-	-	-	20	14	12	10	10	11	15	17	-
Princeton	-	-	-	-	-	-	-	-	-	-	-	-	-	-	-	-	-	13	12
Providence	14	17	20	16	12	10	19	15	16	-	-	-	-	-	-	-	-	-	20
Purdue	13	12	15	15	15	18	-	-	20	-	-	-	-	-	-	-	-	-	-
Rutgers	-	-	-	-	20	-	-	17	19	-	19	-	-	-	20	16	-	-	-
South Carolina	7	5	13	14	11	15	16	20	-	19	-	-	-	-	-	-	-	-	-
Southern California	10	10	6	7	6	5	6	6	7	6	8	10	10	12	11	13	18	-	-
Stanford	-	-	-	-	-	-	-	-	15	17	-	-	-	-	-	-	-	-	-
Syracuse	-	-	-	-	-	-	-	-	-	-	-	-	-	-	-	-	20	6	6
Tennessee	-	-	-	-	-	-	18	18	-	18	15	-	-	-	-	-	-	-	-
UTEP	-	-	-	-	-	-	-	-	-	-	-	-	-	15	18	17	-	-	-
Tex.-Pan American	-	-	-	-	-	-	-	-	-	-	-	15	19	18	17	20	-	-	-
UCLA	2	2	2	3	3	3	2	2	4	4	2	2	2	5	4	2	2	1	1
Wake Forest	-	-	-	-	-	-	19	-	-	-	-	-	-	-	-	-	-	-	-
Washington	-	-	-	-	-	-	-	-	-	-	-	-	-	20	-	-	-	-	-

1975-76

		December					January				February				March		
	PS	2	9	16	23	30	6	13	20	27	3	10	17	24	2	9	16
Alabama	12	14	11	8	8	8	10	11	12	11	14	11	10	7	6	8	6
Arizona	11	11	10	-	-	-	-	-	-	-	-	-	-	-	-	18	15
Arizona St.	18	19	19	19	-	-	-	-	-	-	-	-	-	-	-	-	-
Auburn	-	17	17	17	-	-	-	-	-	-	-	-	-	-	-	-	-
Centenary (La.)	-	-	-	-	19	18	-	18	-	19	18	19	20	19	20	20	19
Cincinnati	10	10	9	7	6	7	15	14	16	18	16	13	13	18	13	15	12
DePaul	-	-	-	-	-	-	-	-	-	-	-	-	-	-	-	-	17
Florida St.	-	-	-	-	-	-	-	-	-	-	-	-	-	-	18	-	-
Indiana	1	1	1	1	1	1	1	1	1	1	1	1	1	1	1	1	1
Kansas St.	14	18	-	-	-	-	-	-	-	-	-	-	-	-	-	-	-
Kentucky	6	7	14	20	18	-	-	-	-	-	-	-	-	-	-	-	-
La Salle	-	-	-	-	-	20	-	-	-	-	-	-	-	-	-	-	-
Louisville	8	6	6	10	11	11	16	-	-	-	-	-	19	-	-	-	-
Marquette	4	3	3	3	7	6	4	3	3	2	2	2	2	2	2	2	2
Maryland	3	2	2	2	2	2	2	2	2	7	5	4	7	10	9	12	11
Memphis	19	-	-	-	-	-	-	-	-	-	-	-	-	-	-	-	-
Michigan	16	16	18	16	16	17	19	16	17	15	-	16	15	13	11	14	9
Minnesota	-	-	-	-	20	16	17	-	-	-	-	-	-	-	-	-	-
Missouri	-	-	20	-	-	-	-	20	-	13	13	14	14	12	15	10	14
UNLV	-	-	16	13	12	10	5	4	4	3	3	7	6	5	5	4	3
North Carolina	5	4	4	4	3	3	6	7	5	4	4	3	3	4	4	5	8
North Carolina St.	13	13	13	9	9	9	11	13	11	8	10	12	12	15	17	-	-
North Texas	-	-	-	-	-	-	-	-	-	-	20	20	-	-	-	-	-
Notre Dame	7	9	8	5	5	5	13	15	15	10	11	10	8	6	8	7	7
Oregon	-	-	-	-	-	-	-	-	-	-	-	-	-	17	-	-	-
Oregon St.	-	-	-	-	-	-	-	17	13	16	-	-	-	-	-	-	-
Pepperdine	-	-	-	-	-	-	-	-	-	-	-	-	-	-	-	-	20
Princeton	-	-	-	-	-	-	-	-	-	17	15	-	-	-	-	-	-
Providence	17	15	-	-	-	-	-	-	-	-	-	-	-	-	-	-	-
Rutgers	-	-	-	15	15	14	12	10	7	5	7	5	4	3	3	3	4
St. John's (N.Y.)	-	-	-	18	17	15	14	12	9	14	12	17	16	14	16	17	-
San Francisco	15	12	12	14	14	19	20	-	-	-	-	-	-	-	-	-	-
Southern California	-	-	-	-	-	-	18	-	-	-	-	-	-	-	-	-	-
Syracuse	20	-	-	-	-	-	-	-	-	-	-	-	-	-	-	-	-
Tennessee	9	8	7	11	10	12	9	9	10	9	8	8	9	11	12	9	13
Texas A&M	-	-	-	-	-	-	-	-	-	-	-	-	-	20	19	-	-
Texas Tech	-	-	-	-	-	-	-	-	-	-	-	-	-	-	-	19	16
UCLA	2	5	5	6	4	4	3	8	6	12	9	6	5	9	7	6	5
Virginia	-	-	-	-	-	-	-	-	-	-	-	-	-	-	-	13	18
Virginia Tech	-	-	-	-	-	-	-	-	-	-	19	18	18	-	-	-	-
VMI	-	-	-	-	-	-	-	-	20	-	-	-	-	-	-	-	-
Wake Forest	-	-	-	-	-	-	7	5	14	-	-	-	-	-	-	-	-
Washington	-	20	15	12	13	13	8	6	8	6	6	9	11	8	10	11	-
West Tex. A&M	-	-	-	-	-	-	-	19	19	20	-	-	-	-	-	-	-
Western Mich.	-	-	-	-	-	-	-	-	-	-	17	15	17	16	14	16	10
Wisconsin	-	-	-	-	-	-	-	-	18	-	-	-	-	-	-	-	-

1976-77

		Nov.	December				January				February				March		
	PS	30	7	14	21	28	4	11	18	25	1	8	15	22	1	8	15
Alabama	13	13	10	7	5	4	4	4	3	3	8	7	4	8	12	12	11
Arizona	10	11	9	8	14	13	11	10	16	16	19	18	17	20	17	20	-
Arkansas	-	-	-	19	18	17	18	16	17	15	14	13	11	6	7	8	18
Auburn	-	-	-	-	-	20	-	-	-	-	-	-	-	-	-	-	-
Charlotte	19	20	-	-	-	-	-	-	-	-	-	-	-	-	-	18	17
Cincinnati	12	12	8	6	4	5	2	3	2	12	12	12	10	14	14	11	-
Clemson	-	-	16	13	11	10	16	17	-	19	16	15	18	19	18	-	-
DePaul	18	18	19	-	-	-	-	-	-	-	-	-	-	-	-	-	-
Detroit	-	-	-	-	-	-	-	-	-	-	20	19	15	16	15	17	12
Indiana	5	4	13	16	-	-	-	-	-	-	-	-	-	-	-	-	-
Kansas St.	-	-	-	-	-	-	-	-	-	-	-	-	-	-	-	-	16
Kentucky	6	5	4	3	7	6	3	2	6	6	3	3	2	2	2	6	3
Louisville	9	7	14	17	13	14	14	13	12	11	9	6	8	10	10	14	19
Marquette	2	2	2	2	6	12	12	11	8	9	6	9	9	18	19	16	7
Maryland	8	16	17	14	15	16	15	14	13	-	-	-	-	-	-	-	-

		Nov.	December				January				February				March		
	PS	30	7	14	21	28	4	11	18	25	1	8	15	22	1	8	15
Memphis	-	-	-	-	-	-	20	18	18	20	-	-	-	-	-	-	-
Michigan	1	1	1	1	1	1	5	6	5	2	7	5	5	3	3	1	1
Minnesota	-	-	-	-	20	15	13	9	11	13	10	8	12	13	9	9	13
Missouri	20	-	-	-	-	-	-	-	-	-	-	-	-	-	-	-	-
UNLV	7	6	5	12	12	11	9	8	7	5	4	10	6	4	5	5	4
North Carolina	3	9	12	11	10	9	6	5	4	4	13	14	13	9	6	4	5
North Carolina St.	15	-	-	-	-	-	-	-	-	-	-	-	-	-	-	-	-
Notre Dame	14	8	7	4	2	2	8	19	-	-	-	-	-	-	-	15	10
Oregon	-	-	-	-	-	-	-	20	-	-	-	-	-	17	-	-	-
Providence	-	-	-	-	-	-	17	15	15	14	15	16	16	12	8	13	-
Purdue	-	-	-	-	-	-	-	-	19	18	18	-	-	-	-	-	-
Rutgers	17	19	-	-	-	-	-	-	-	-	-	-	-	-	-	-	-
St. John's (N.Y.)	-	-	-	20	-	-	-	-	-	-	-	-	-	-	-	-	-
San Francisco	11	10	6	5	3	3	1	1	1	1	1	1	1	1	1	3	8
Southern Ill.	-	17	18	18	-	-	-	-	-	-	-	-	-	-	-	-	-
Syracuse	-	-	20	15	17	18	19	-	20	17	17	17	20	15	13	10	6
Tennessee	16	15	15	-	19	-	-	-	14	7	11	11	14	7	11	7	15
UCLA	4	3	3	9	8	8	7	12	10	8	2	2	3	5	4	2	2
Utah	-	-	-	-	16	19	-	-	-	-	-	-	-	-	20	19	14
VMI	-	-	-	-	-	-	-	-	-	-	-	20	19	-	-	-	20
Wake Forest	-	14	11	10	9	7	10	7	9	10	5	4	7	11	16	-	9

1977-78

		Nov.	December				January					February				March	
	PS	29	6	13	20	27	3	10	17	24	31	7	14	21	28	6	13
Alabama	15	15	-	-	18	-	-	-	-	-	-	-	-	-	-	-	-
Arkansas	7	7	6	4	4	3	3	3	6	4	2	2	1	4	4	7	5
Cincinnati	9	8	7	6	12	11	12	19	-	-	-	-	-	-	-	-	-
DePaul	-	-	-	-	-	-	-	20	18	19	13	11	8	7	6	4	3
Detroit	19	19	17	16	15	20	-	-	-	-	-	17	19	16	16	19	18
Duke	-	-	-	-	-	-	-	-	17	11	17	-	20	13	15	8	7
Florida St.	-	-	-	-	-	18	-	-	-	17	15	16	14	12	11	13	15
Georgetown	-	-	-	-	-	-	20	17	19	16	14	-	18	18	17	-	-
Holy Cross	18	17	15	13	12	12	16	13	14	-	-	-	-	-	-	-	-
Houston	-	-	-	-	-	-	-	-	-	-	-	-	-	-	-	14	-
Illinois St.	-	-	-	-	-	-	-	-	-	20	19	15	15	15	13	17	-
Indiana	-	-	-	-	-	15	11	18	-	-	-	-	-	-	-	-	13
Indiana St.	-	-	11	7	6	6	6	6	4	13	-	-	-	-	-	-	-
Kansas	-	-	19	20	16	17	14	10	8	8	8	8	6	6	5	9	10
Kansas St.	-	-	-	19	-	-	-	-	-	-	-	-	-	-	-	-	-
Kentucky	2	1	1	1	1	1	1	1	1	1	1	1	3	2	1	1	1
Louisville	10	9	16	10	8	7	10	9	9	12	9	9	9	20	20	12	9
Marquette	3	4	4	3	2	5	4	4	2	2	3	3	2	1	3	3	8
Maryland	14	14	12	18	20	14	15	-	-	-	-	-	-	-	-	-	-
Miami (Ohio)	-	-	-	-	-	-	-	-	-	-	-	-	-	-	-	-	19
Michigan	13	13	9	15	-	-	-	-	-	-	-	-	-	-	-	-	-
Michigan St.	-	-	-	-	-	-	18	12	10	7	7	10	10	10	9	6	4
Minnesota	16	-	-	-	-	-	-	-	-	-	-	-	-	19	-	-	-
Nebraska	-	-	-	-	-	-	-	-	-	-	-	19	-	-	-	-	-
UNLV	8	10	10	9	9	9	9	11	16	-	-	-	-	-	-	-	-
New Mexico	-	-	-	-	-	-	-	-	20	14	10	6	5	5	8	5	12
North Carolina	1	2	2	5	3	2	2	2	5	3	6	7	11	8	10	11	16
North Caro. St.	-	-	-	-	-	-	-	16	-	-	-	-	-	-	-	-	-
Notre Dame	4	3	3	2	5	4	5	5	7	5	4	4	7	9	7	10	6
Penn	-	-	-	-	-	-	-	-	-	-	-	-	-	-	-	-	20
Providence	-	-	20	14	14	13	17	14	12	9	16	20	13	11	18	-	-
Purdue	12	11	-	17	-	-	-	-	-	-	-	-	-	-	-	-	-
St. John's (N.Y.)	20	16	13	-	-	-	-	-	-	-	-	-	-	-	-	-	-
San Francisco	5	5	8	11	11	19	19	-	-	-	20	-	-	-	-	20	11
Syracuse	11	12	18	12	10	10	8	8	11	10	18	18	16	17	14	18	-
Texas	-	-	-	-	-	-	-	-	15	15	12	12	12	14	12	16	17
UCLA	6	6	5	8	7	8	7	7	3	6	5	5	4	3	2	2	2
Utah	-	20	14	-	17	-	-	-	-	-	-	-	-	-	19	15	14
Virginia	-	-	-	-	19	16	13	15	13	18	11	13	17	-	-	-	-
Wake Forest	17	18	-	-	-	-	-	-	-	-	-	14	-	-	-	-	-

1978-79

		Nov.	December				January					February				March	
	PS	28	5	12	19	26	3	9	16	23	30	6	13	20	27	6	13
Alabama	19	-	-	-	-	-	-	-	18	18	15	16	20	-	-	-	-
Arkansas	-	-	-	-	-	20	14	10	11	15	14	14	11	10	9	7	5
DePaul	-	-	-	-	-	-	-	-	-	-	-	-	-	20	15	8	6
Detroit	-	-	-	-	-	-	-	-	-	-	-	-	18	16	18	17	-
Duke	1	1	1	1	1	1	5	7	8	7	3	3	5	6	5	6	11
Georgetown	-	-	20	16	14	15	12	14	10	11	17	18	16	17	16	11	-
Illinois	-	-	-	18	15	6	4	4	4	8	19	20	-	-	-	-	-
Indiana	10	20	-	-	-	-	-	-	-	-	-	-	-	-	-	-	-
Indiana St.	-	-	-	20	16	11	11	9	5	3	2	2	1	2	1	1	1
Iowa	-	-	-	-	-	-	-	-	-	-	18	15	14	12	11	14	20
Kansas	5	4	5	8	7	18	19	15	20	-	-	-	-	-	-	-	-
Kentucky	11	10	10	6	11	13	9	17	-	-	-	-	-	-	-	-	-
Long Beach St.	-	-	-	-	-	17	15	19	-	-	-	-	-	-	-	-	-
LSU	14	11	12	11	10	7	7	5	9	9	9	8	6	5	8	9	7
Louisville	4	5	7	4	12	10	16	12	7	5	5	5	9	13	13	18	13
Marquette	18	17	16	14	13	16	17	13	13	13	10	9	10	9	10	12	10
Maryland	-	19	19	-	-	-	20	-	19	-	-	-	-	-	-	-	-
Michigan	8	8	6	9	9	8	13	16	-	-	-	-	-	-	-	-	-
Michigan St.	7	7	4	3	5	4	1	1	6	4	4	10	8	7	4	4	3
Mississippi St.	-	-	-	-	-	-	18	-	-	-	-	-	-	-	-	-	-
UNLV	20	18	15	15	18	14	-	-	-	-	-	-	-	-	-	-	-
North Carolina	16	14	14	13	6	5	3	3	2	2	7	6	4	4	7	3	9
North Caro. St.	12	6	8	7	4	9	8	8	14	20	-	-	-	-	-	-	-
Notre Dame	3	3	3	2	2	2	2	2	1	1	1	1	3	3	2	5	4
Ohio St.	-	-	-	-	-	-	-	-	16	10	13	13	17	14	17	-	-
Oklahoma	-	-	-	-	-	-	-	-	-	-	-	-	-	-	-	-	16
Penn	-	-	-	-	-	-	-	-	-	-	-	-	-	-	-	-	14
Purdue	-	-	-	-	-	-	-	-	-	-	-	-	13	18	19	16	15
Rutgers	15	16	18	-	-	-	-	-	-	-	-	-	-	-	-	-	18
St. John's (N.Y.)	-	-	-	-	-	-	-	-	-	-	-	-	-	-	-	-	17
San Francisco	17	15	17	19	-	-	-	-	-	-	-	-	-	-	20	19	12
Southern Cal	13	12	11	12	20	-	-	-	-	-	-	-	-	-	-	-	-
Syracuse	9	9	9	10	8	19	-	20	12	12	8	7	7	8	6	10	8
Temple	-	-	-	-	-	-	-	18	17	16	20	19	15	15	12	13	-
Tennessee	-	-	-	-	-	-	-	-	-	-	-	-	-	-	-	20	-
Texas	6	13	13	17	19	-	-	-	-	17	11	12	12	11	14	15	-
Texas A&M	-	-	-	-	17	12	10	11	15	14	12	11	-	-	-	-	-
Toledo	-	-	-	-	-	-	-	-	-	-	-	-	-	-	-	-	19
UCLA	2	2	2	5	3	3	6	6	3	6	6	4	2	1	3	2	2
Vanderbilt	-	-	-	-	-	-	-	-	-	19	16	17	19	19	-	-	-

1979-80

		December				January					February				March
	PS	4	11	18	26	2	8	15	22	29	5	12	19	26	4
Arizona St.	-	-	-	-	-	-	-	-	-	-	19	18	18	15	18
Arkansas	-	-	20	20	19	-	-	-	-	-	-	-	-	-	-
BYU	15	18	18	18	20	19	17	18	20	19	14	13	14	12	12
Clemson	-	-	-	-	-	-	18	17	12	16	16	10	12	17	-
DePaul	9	10	11	6	4	3	2	1	1	1	1	1	1	1	1
Duke	3	2	2	1	1	1	1	5	3	5	10	16	17	-	14
Georgetown	19	17	16	17	17	18	20	-	-	-	-	-	-	20	11
Illinois	-	-	-	-	-	20	-	-	-	-	-	-	-	-	-
Indiana	1	1	1	5	10	11	19	19	16	18	20	-	19	13	7
Iona	-	-	-	-	-	-	-	-	-	-	-	-	-	-	19
Iowa	-	20	17	13	11	10	12	13	-	-	-	20	-	-	-
Kansas	20	19	-	-	-	-	-	-	-	-	-	-	-	-	-
Kansas St.	-	-	-	-	-	-	-	-	-	20	-	19	-	-	-
Kentucky	2	5	5	3	2	2	4	6	5	3	6	5	3	2	4
LSU	7	6	6	7	5	4	6	14	11	10	7	6	5	5	3
Louisville	10	14	12	11	12	15	11	7	7	7	3	3	2	4	2
Marquette	18	16	-	-	-	-	-	-	-	-	-	-	-	-	-
Maryland	-	-	-	-	-	-	-	-	15	12	5	8	9	7	8
Missouri	-	-	19	16	13	12	13	15	10	14	15	14	13	11	16
North Carolina	6	8	8	8	6	6	15	9	13	11	11	11	8	10	15
North Caro. St.	-	-	-	-	-	-	-	16	-	-	-	-	-	19	-
Notre Dame	5	4	4	4	3	7	7	8	8	8	9	12	10	14	9
Ohio St.	4	3	3	2	7	5	3	2	4	6	13	9	11	9	10
Oregon St.	17	15	14	19	18	14	9	4	2	2	4	4	6	6	5
Purdue	11	12	9	9	8	8	10	11	14	17	12	15	15	18	20
St. John's (N.Y.)	16	9	15	15	15	17	14	10	9	9	8	7	7	8	13
Syracuse	12	11	10	10	9	9	5	3	6	4	2	2	4	3	6
Tennessee	-	-	-	-	-	-	-	20	19	-	-	-	-	-	-
Texas A&M	14	-	-	-	-	-	-	-	-	-	-	-	-	-	-
UCLA	8	7	7	14	16	16	16	-	-	-	-	-	-	-	-
Virginia	13	13	13	12	14	13	8	12	17	13	18	-	-	-	-
Washington St.	-	-	-	-	-	-	-	-	-	-	-	-	20	-	-
Weber St.	-	-	-	-	-	-	-	-	18	15	17	17	16	16	17

1980-81

		December					January				February				March	
	PS	2	9	16	23	30	6	13	20	27	3	10	17	24	3	10
Arizona St.	-	-	15	14	11	13	14	12	7	5	5	5	7	5	5	3
Arkansas	20	11	17	19	17	-	-	-	-	-	-	-	-	18	15	20
BYU	18	19	19	18	20	19	17	15	18	15	16	15	17	15	18	16
Clemson	-	-	-	-	-	-	20	19	19	-	-	-	-	-	-	-
Connecticut	-	-	-	-	-	-	-	-	20	20	-	-	-	-	-	-
DePaul	2	1	1	1	1	1	1	4	T3	3	3	3	3	4	2	1
Georgetown	16	19	-	-	-	-	-	-	-	-	-	-	-	-	-	-
Illinois	-	-	-	17	18	16	12	18	15	-	18	17	15	14	16	19
Indiana	5	5	7	11	15	15	-	-	-	-	17	20	16	16	14	9
Iowa	14	12	16	16	14	14	11	14	9	13	15	14	12	8	8	13
Kansas	-	-	-	-	-	-	-	-	-	18	-	-	-	-	-	-
Kentucky	1	2	2	2	2	5	4	3	6	7	6	11	10	9	7	8
Lamar	-	-	-	-	-	-	-	-	-	-	-	-	19	-	-	-
LSU	12	15	11	10	10	10	9	6	5	4	4	4	4	2	3	4
Louisville	3	8	-	20	-	-	-	-	-	-	-	-	-	20	17	12

		December					January				February				March	
	PS	2	9	16	23	30	6	13	20	27	3	10	17	24	3	10
Maryland	4	4	4	9	9	9	8	10	10	14	13	19	20	17	20	18
Michigan	-	-	18	15	13	12	10	9	16	17	14	13	18	-	-	-
Minnesota	-	-	-	-	-	-	19	20	-	19	-	-	-	-	-	-
Missouri	11	17	14	-	-	-	-	-	-	-	-	-	-	-	-	-
North Carolina	13	10	10	8	6	6	16	17	17	12	11	10	13	11	12	6
Notre Dame	10	13	9	6	8	4	5	7	13	8	9	12	11	6	6	7
Ohio St.	9	9	8	7	-	-	-	-	-	-	-	-	-	-	-	-
Oregon St.	7	6	5	4	4	2	2	1	1	T1	2	2	2	1	1	2
St. John's (N.Y.)	17	16	-	-	-	-	-	-	-	-	-	-	-	-	-	-
South Ala.	-	-	-	-	16	17	15	13	11	16	20	18	-	-	-	-
Syracuse	19	18	20	-	-	-	-	-	-	-	-	-	-	-	-	-
Tennessee	-	-	-	-	-	18	13	11	8	11	10	9	8	10	10	15
Texas A&M	15	14	12	13	12	11	-	-	-	-	-	-	-	-	-	-
UCLA	6	3	3	3	3	7	7	8	12	10	12	8	6	13	13	10
Utah	-	-	-	-	19	20	18	16	14	9	7	6	9	7	9	14
Virginia	8	7	6	5	5	3	3	2	2	T1	1	1	1	3	4	5
Wake Forest	-	-	13	12	7	8	6	5	T3	6	8	7	5	12	11	11
Wichita St.	-	-	-	-	-	-	-	-	-	-	19	16	14	19	-	-
Wyoming	-	-	-	-	-	-	-	-	-	-	-	-	-	-	19	17

1981-82

		December					January				February				March	
	PS	1	8	15	22	29	5	12	19	26	2	9	16	23	2	9
Alabama	20	17	16	14	12	12	16	13	16	13	8	10	19	17	18	13
UAB	14	11	9	16	19	-	-	-	-	-	-	-	-	-	20	17
Arkansas	18	13	11	9	6	5	11	9	15	12	14	8	17	15	14	12
BYU	-	15	-	-	-	-	-	-	-	-	-	-	-	-	-	-
DePaul	8	7	7	7	13	8	5	4	4	4	4	3	3	3	2	2
Fresno St.	-	-	-	-	-	-	-	-	-	19	17	18	15	14	12	11
Georgetown	5	20	20	19	17	17	13	8	13	-	-	20	13	12	8	6
Georgia	16	-	-	-	-	-	-	-	-	-	-	-	-	-	-	-
Houston	-	-	-	-	18	18	14	10	19	-	-	-	-	-	-	-
Idaho	-	-	-	-	-	-	18	14	8	11	15	13	11	9	6	8
Indiana	12	12	10	13	11	11	-	-	-	-	-	-	20	-	-	-
Iowa	9	6	6	6	10	10	7	5	6	6	5	5	7	11	11	16
Kansas St.	-	-	-	-	-	-	-	-	18	14	T19	15	18	-	17	-
Kentucky	3	2	2	2	2	4	3	6	9	7	9	12	10	7	15	15
La.-Lafayette	-	-	18	15	-	-	-	-	-	-	-	-	-	-	-	-
LSU	17	-	-	-	-	-	-	-	-	-	-	-	-	-	-	-
Louisville	4	3	3	3	8	14	12	17	17	-	-	-	-	-	-	20
Memphis	-	-	-	-	-	-	-	-	-	-	T19	14	12	10	13	9
Minnesota	10	10	8	8	5	9	6	11	5	10	6	9	8	13	7	7
Missouri	15	16	13	11	9	7	4	2	2	1	1	4	4	5	5	5
UNLV	-	18	15	-	-	-	-	-	-	-	-	-	-	-	-	-
North Carolina	1	1	1	1	1	1	1	1	1	2	2	2	2	2	1	1
North Caro. St.	-	-	-	-	-	20	15	12	14	17	-	-	-	-	-	-
Notre Dame	19	19	-	-	-	-	-	-	-	-	-	-	-	-	-	-
Oregon St.	-	-	19	20	16	15	17	15	12	8	10	6	5	4	4	4
St. John's (N.Y.)	-	-	-	-	-	-	20	-	-	-	-	-	-	-	-	-
San Francisco	-	14	12	10	7	6	8	7	11	9	7	17	16	16	-	-
Tennessee	-	-	-	-	-	-	-	-	20	15	16	-	-	19	-	-
Texas	-	-	-	-	-	-	-	19	7	5	12	-	-	-	-	-
Tulsa	11	9	14	12	14	13	10	18	10	16	11	7	6	8	10	10
UCLA	2	8	17	17	15	16	19	-	-	-	-	-	-	20	19	19
Villanova	-	-	-	18	20	19	-	-	-	20	-	-	-	-	-	-
Virginia	7	5	5	5	4	3	2	3	3	3	3	1	1	1	3	3
Virginia Tech	-	-	-	-	-	-	-	20	-	-	-	-	-	-	-	-
Wake Forest	13	-	-	-	-	-	-	-	-	18	13	16	14	18	16	18
Washington	-	-	-	-	-	-	-	-	-	-	-	19	-	-	-	-
West Virginia	-	-	-	-	-	-	-	-	-	-	18	11	9	6	9	14
Wichita St.	6	4	4	4	3	2	9	16	-	-	-	-	-	-	-	-

1982-83

		Nov.	December				January				February				March		
	PS	30	7	14	21	28	4	11	18	25	1	8	15	22	1	8	15
Alabama	12	13	11	10	8	6	5	10	-	-	-	-	-	-	-	-	-
Arkansas	17	16	15	13	12	11	10	7	4	12	9	8	7	6	5	6	9
Auburn	-	-	-	-	-	-	-	-	20	-	-	-	-	-	-	-	-
Boston College	-	-	-	-	-	-	-	-	-	-	-	-	18	19	15	14	11
Chattanooga	-	-	-	-	-	-	-	-	-	-	-	-	-	-	19	18	15
Georgetown	2	2	3	T5	11	10	17	-	19	15	14	14	14	18	16	15	20
Georgia	-	-	-	-	-	-	-	-	-	-	19	-	-	-	-	-	18
Houston	14	11	9	14	19	18	19	16	14	9	8	6	4	2	1	1	1
Illinois St.	-	-	-	-	-	-	-	-	-	17	16	17	-	-	-	-	-
Indiana	9	8	6	T5	5	1	1	4	2	2	6	4	2	4	11	7	5
Iowa	11	10	7	7	10	9	8	12	10	14	13	20	16	17	-	-	-
Kentucky	4	3	2	2	2	3	3	6	11	10	15	13	11	10	7	10	12
Louisville	8	7	13	12	14	13	13	9	9	8	12	11	9	5	3	3	2
Marquette	18	17	16	-	-	-	-	-	-	-	-	-	-	-	-	-	-
Memphis	6	5	4	3	4	2	2	1	6	5	4	9	13	14	17	17	17
Minnesota	-	-	-	-	-	-	-	17	16	16	17	19	-	-	-	-	-
Missouri	15	9	8	8	6	12	15	14	12	13	10	10	12	T15	13	12	10
UNLV	T20	19	18	18	17	15	11	8	5	4	2	2	1	1	9	9	6
North Carolina	3	15	17	17	-	-	18	11	3	3	1	1	3	11	8	5	8
North Caro. St.	16	18	18	15	15	17	16	19	-	-	-	-	-	-	-	-	16
Ohio St.	-	-	-	-	-	-	-	20	-	-	-	-	20	T15	14	16	-
Oklahoma	T20	-	-	-	-	-	-	-	-	-	-	-	19	-	-	19	-
Oklahoma St.	-	-	-	-	-	-	-	-	18	20	-	-	-	-	-	-	19
Oregon St.	10	19	-	-	-	-	-	-	-	-	-	-	-	-	-	-	-
Purdue	-	-	20	-	-	-	20	-	-	-	-	18	-	-	20	-	-
St. John's (N.Y.)	19	12	12	9	7	7	7	3	8	7	5	7	6	9	10	8	3
Syracuse	-	-	-	16	13	14	9	13	15	18	20	15	17	13	18	20	-
Tennessee	13	14	14	11	9	8	12	18	-	-	-	-	-	20	-	-	-
Tulsa	-	-	-	-	20	19	-	-	-	-	-	-	-	-	-	-	-
UCLA	7	6	5	4	3	5	6	5	1	1	7	5	10	8	6	4	7
Villanova	5	4	10	19	18	16	14	15	13	11	11	12	8	7	4	13	13
Virginia	1	1	1	1	1	4	4	2	7	6	3	3	5	3	2	2	4
Virginia Tech	-	-	-	-	-	-	-	-	17	-	-	-	-	-	-	-	-
Wake Forest	-	-	-	-	-	-	-	-	-	19	-	-	-	-	-	-	-
Washington St.	-	-	-	-	-	-	-	-	-	-	18	-	-	-	-	-	-
West Virginia	-	-	-	20	16	20	-	-	-	-	-	-	-	-	-	-	-
Wichita St.	-	-	-	-	-	-	-	-	-	-	-	16	15	12	12	11	14

1983-84

		Nov.	December				January					February				March	
	PS	29	6	13	20	27	3	10	17	24	31	7	14	21	28	6	13
Arkansas	14	14	15	-	-	-	-	-	-	16	-	-	14	11	12	8	8
Auburn	-	-	-	-	-	-	-	-	-	-	19	16	-	19	-	-	-
Boston College	15	15	12	8	6	12	17	18	16	-	-	-	-	-	-	-	-
DePaul	18	16	13	4	4	4	3	3	2	2	2	2	3	5	5	4	4
Duke	-	-	-	-	-	-	-	-	-	-	-	-	19	14	15	16	14
Fresno St.	13	17	20	-	-	-	16	13	17	-	-	-	-	-	-	-	-
Georgetown	4	3	3	5	5	5	4	4	6	4	4	3	2	2	4	2	2
Georgia	16	13	10	12	14	11	11	15	-	18	-	-	-	-	-	-	-
Georgia Tech	-	-	-	-	-	-	-	-	-	-	18	18	-	-	-	-	-
Houston	3	8	6	3	3	3	7	7	4	7	6	5	4	3	2	5	5
Illinois	-	-	-	-	-	20	14	9	10	9	8	8	7	6	10	7	6
Indiana	19	-	-	-	-	-	-	-	-	-	-	-	T17	-	-	-	-
Iowa	7	5	5	18	19	-	-	-	-	-	-	-	-	-	-	-	-
Kansas	17	-	-	-	-	-	-	-	-	-	-	-	-	-	-	-	-
Kentucky	2	1	2	2	2	2	2	2	3	3	3	6	6	4	3	3	3
LSU	11	12	9	10	11	9	9	11	15	10	14	20	T17	-	-	-	-
Louisville	6	-	-	16	10	14	-	-	-	14	17	15	-	-	-	18	-
Maryland	8	6	11	9	8	6	5	5	7	5	10	13	-	-	19	14	11
Memphis	5	4	4	T6	16	17	19	19	18	13	9	9	8	12	14	17	16
Michigan	-	-	-	-	20	15	-	-	-	-	-	-	-	-	-	-	-
Michigan St.	12	11	17	17	-	-	-	-	-	-	-	-	-	-	-	-	-
UNLV	-	-	-	-	-	-	18	14	8	6	5	4	5	7	7	10	13
North Carolina	1	2	1	1	1	1	1	1	1	1	1	1	1	1	1	1	1
North Caro. St.	-	7	8	T6	13	13	12	-	-	-	-	-	-	-	-	-	-
Oklahoma	20	-	-	-	-	-	-	17	20	11	12	10	9	8	6	6	7
Oregon St.	10	10	18	14	15	19	15	16	11	-	-	-	-	20	20	20	17
Purdue	-	-	19	11	7	18	-	-	19	-	16	11	11	13	11	11	10
St. John's (N.Y.)	-	19	16	13	12	8	13	10	14	-	-	-	-	-	-	-	-
Syracuse	-	-	-	-	-	-	-	-	-	20	13	19	16	16	16	-	18
Temple	-	-	-	-	-	-	-	-	-	-	-	-	20	17	18	15	20
UTEP	-	-	-	20	18	16	10	8	5	8	7	7	10	9	8	9	9
Tulsa	-	-	-	-	-	-	-	20	13	12	11	12	12	10	9	12	12
UCLA	9	9	7	15	9	7	6	6	9	15	20	-	-	-	-	-	-
Virginia	-	-	-	-	-	-	20	-	-	19	-	-	-	-	-	-	-
Va. C'wealth	-	20	-	-	-	-	-	-	-	-	-	-	-	-	-	-	-
Wake Forest	-	-	-	19	17	10	8	12	12	17	15	14	13	15	17	19	19
Washington	-	-	-	-	-	-	-	-	-	-	-	17	15	18	13	13	15
Wichita St.	-	18	14	-	-	-	-	-	-	-	-	-	-	-	-	-	-

1984-85

		Nov.	December				January					February				March	
	PS	27	4	11	18	25	1	8	15	22	29	5	12	19	26	5	12
UAB	-	13	18	17	-	-	-	-	-	-	20	-	19	-	-	-	-
Arizona	-	-	-	-	-	-	-	-	-	-	-	-	-	-	19	-	-
Arkansas	16	17	-	-	-	-	-	-	-	-	-	-	-	-	-	-	-
Boston College	-	-	-	-	-	-	-	12	15	-	-	-	20	-	-	-	-
DePaul	3	2	2	2	5	9	10	13	10	7	13	18	-	-	-	-	-
Duke	6	4	4	3	2	2	2	2	2	5	6	5	7	6	5	7	10
Georgetown	1	1	1	1	1	1	1	1	1	1	2	2	2	2	2	1	1
Georgia	-	-	-	-	-	-	-	-	-	-	-	-	-	18	14	17	19
Georgia Tech	20	18	15	12	13	10	8	9	17	16	8	10	6	8	10	9	6
Illinois	2	7	7	6	4	8	6	15	11	6	5	9	17	16	18	14	12
Indiana	4	12	11	16	16	15	12	11	8	13	-	-	-	-	-	-	-
Iowa	-	-	-	-	-	-	-	19	-	-	-	12	11	14	-	-	-
Kansas	19	20	19	18	15	12	11	10	9	15	19	13	10	15	11	10	13
Kentucky	18	-	-	-	-	-	-	-	-	-	-	-	-	-	-	-	-
LSU	14	16	13	19	19	18	14	-	-	-	-	-	-	-	-	19	20
Louisiana Tech	-	-	-	-	20	19	18	14	12	12	15	14	12	10	7	8	8
Louisville	17	6	6	14	12	20	-	-	-	-	-	-	-	-	-	-	-

		Nov.	December					January				February				March	
	PS	27	4	11	18	25	1	8	15	22	29	5	12	19	26	5	12
Loyola (Ill.)	-	-	-	-	-	-	-	-	-	-	-	-	-	-	20	16	14
Maryland	-	-	-	-	-	-	19	-	-	-	17	20	20	-	-	-	-
Memphis	8	5	5	5	3	3	3	6	5	4	3	3	5	4	4	5	5
Michigan	-	-	-	20	18	13	16	-	-	18	10	8	3	3	3	3	2
Michigan St.	-	-	-	-	-	-	-	17	19	-	-	-	-	-	-	-	-
UNLV	11	20	20	-	-	-	-	-	-	20	16	11	14	11	9	11	9
North Carolina	-	19	16	13	10	7	9	5	6	8	11	15	13	13	8	6	7
North Caro. St.	13	11	10	9	14	14	17	-	-	-	-	-	-	-	16	18	16
Oklahoma	5	10	17	15	11	17	13	8	13	9	7	7	4	5	6	4	4
Oregon St.	-	-	-	-	-	-	-	20	14	10	14	16	18	19	-	-	-
St. John's (N.Y.)	7	3	3	4	8	5	4	3	4	2	1	1	1	1	1	2	3
SMU	10	9	8	7	6	4	7	4	3	2	4	4	9	9	13	20	-
Syracuse	12	14	12	10	9	6	5	7	7	11	9	6	8	7	12	13	15
Texas Tech	-	-	-	-	-	-	-	-	-	-	-	-	-	-	-	-	17
Tulsa	-	-	-	-	-	-	-	-	20	17	12	17	15	12	15	15	18
VCU	-	-	-	-	-	-	20	18	16	19	-	-	-	17	17	12	11
Virginia Tech	15	15	14	11	17	16	-	-	-	-	-	-	-	-	-	-	-
Villanova	-	-	-	-	-	-	-	16	18	14	18	19	16	-	-	-	-
Washington	9	8	9	8	7	11	15	-	-	-	-	-	-	-		-	-

1985-86

		Nov.	December					January				February				March	
	PS	26	3	10	17	24	31	7	14	21	28	4	11	18	25	4	11
Alabama	-	-	-	-	-	-	-	-	-	-	-	20	18	-	-	-	-
UAB	16	20	17	16	14	14	16	14	12	18	-	-	-	-	-	-	-
Auburn	10	19	19	-	-	-	-	-	-	-	-	-	-	-	-	-	-
Bradley	-	-	-	-	-	-	-	-	20	17	13	13	13	12	11	9	14
DePaul	-	-	19	18	18	20	-	-		-	-	-	-	-	-	-	-
Duke	6	6	3	3	3	3	3	3	3	2	5	4	2	2	1	1	1
Georgetown	8	8	6	5	5	5	11	13	15	12	12	11	9	13	15	14	13
Georgia Tech	1	2	5	5	7	7	6	5	5	4	3	2	5	5	4	6	6
Illinois	7	7	12	10	15	16	14	18	-	-	-	-	-	-	-	19	19
Indiana	-	-	19	18	17	17	15	-	-	-	15	18	16	15	16	16	16
Iowa	-	-	18	-	-	-	-	-	-	-	-	-	-	-	-	-	-
Kansas	5	5	7	7	6	6	5	9	8	7	4	6	3	3	2	2	2
Kentucky	11	10	9	9	13	13	12	11	11	11	8	12	11	8	5	3	3
LSU	14	12	11	11	9	9	8	8	14	14	17	-	-	-	-	-	-
Louisville	9	9	16	15	16	15	18	17	18	13	18	16	19	16	13	11	7
Maryland	19	17	-	-	-	-	-	-	-	-	-	-	-	-	-	-	-
Memphis	15	14	13	12	10	10	9	6	6	3	2	3	4	4	7	10	12
Michigan	3	3	2	2	2	2	2	2	2	6	9	7	10	7	10	7	5
Michigan St.	-	-	-	-	-	-	-	-	-	-	-	-	-	19	17	17	18
Navy	19	-	-	-	-	-	-	-	-	-	-	-	-	17	19	18	17
UNLV	18	16	14	13	12	12	13	12	10	10	10	9	6	11	9	13	11
North Carolina	2	1	1	1	1	1	1	1	1	1	1	1	1	1	3	4	8
North Caro. St.	17	15	-	-	-	-	-	-	-	-	-	-	17	20	18	20	-
Notre Dame	12	11	10	17	19	18	17	16	13	16	14	14	14	14	12	12	10
Ohio St.	-	-	-	20	-	-	-	-	-	-	-	-	-	-	-	-	-
Oklahoma	13	13	8	8	8	8	7	7	7	5	6	5	8	10	14	15	15
Purdue	-	-	-	-	-	-	-	20	19	15	-	-	-	-	20	-	-
Richmond	-	-	-	-	-	-	-	-	-	-	20	-	-	-	-	-	-
St. John's (N.Y.)	-	18	15	14	11	11	10	10	9	8	7	10	7	6	8	5	4
Syracuse	4	4	4	4	4	4	4	4	4	9	11	8	12	9	6	8	9
UTEP	-	-	-	-	-	-	19	15	17	19	19	17	15	-	-	-	20
Virginia Tech	-	-	-	-	20	19	20	19	16	20	16	15	20	18	-	-	-
Western Ky.	-	-	-	-	-	-	-	-	-	-	-	19	-	-	-	-	-

1986-87

		December					January				February				March	
	PS	2	9	16	23	30	6	13	20	27	3	10	17	24	3	10
Alabama	13	8	18	-	-	-	-	15	13	9	9	14	12	10	9	9
Arizona	19	20	-	-	-	-	-	-	-	-	-	-	-	-	-	-
Arkansas	-	-	20	-	-	-	-	-	-	-	-	-	-	-	-	-
Auburn	12	7	7	6	5	5	13	10	17	18	20	-	-	-	-	-
Clemson	-	-	-	-	-	-	20	12	10	14	12	12	10	13	13	13
Cleveland St.	20	-	-	-	-	-	-	-	-	-	-	-	-	-	-	-
DePaul	-	-	-	19	17	15	7	7	6	8	5	5	4	4	5	5
Duke	-	-	-	-	-	20	17	14	12	13	16	15	17	17	14	17
Florida	-	-	-	-	20	-	-	-	-	19	-	19	18	18	-	-
Georgetown	18	16	13	10	10	8	16	9	15	11	10	13	11	8	7	4
Georgia Tech	6	15	16	16	19	18	-	-	-	-	-	-	-	-	-	-
Illinois	14	9	6	5	9	16	12	8	9	12	14	11	14	14	12	11
Indiana	3	3	2	8	8	6	4	4	3	4	2	2	2	3	4	3
Iowa	10	5	4	3	3	3	2	2	1	2	4	4	7	7	6	6
Kansas	8	6	14	13	13	12	19	20	-	20	18	17	15	16	-	20
Kentucky	11	13	19	18	18	11	9	-	-	-	-	-	-	-	-	-
Louisville	2	-	-	-	-	-	-	-	-	-	-	-	-	-	-	-
Missouri	-	-	-	-	-	-	-	-	-	-	-	-	-	-	19	14
Navy	9	10	10	11	12	9	15	19	18	-	-	-	-	-	-	-
UNLV	5	2	1	1	1	1	1	1	4	3	1	1	1	1	1	1
New Orleans	-	-	-	-	-	-	-	-	-	-	-	-	-	19	16	16
North Carolina	1	1	5	4	4	4	3	3	2	1	3	3	3	2	2	2
North Caro. St.	17	18	15	12	11	19	18	17	20	-	-	-	-	-	-	-
Northeastern	-	19	-	-	-	-	-	-	-	-	-	-	-	-	-	-
Notre Dame	-	-	-	-	-	-	-	-	-	-	-	-	-	-	20	18
Oklahoma	7	11	9	7	6	13	11	16	11	10	8	8	13	12	17	-
Pittsburgh	16	12	17	14	14	17	14	18	16	17	13	10	8	9	11	12
Providence	-	-	-	-	-	-	-	-	-	-	17	20	19	20	-	-
Purdue	4	4	3	2	2	2	6	6	5	4	7	7	6	6	3	7
St. John's (N.Y.)	-	-	-	15	15	10	10	13	14	15	19	16	20	-	-	-
Syracuse	15	17	12	9	7	7	5	5	7	6	11	9	9	11	10	10
Temple	-	-	-	20	16	14	8	11	8	7	6	6	5	5	8	8
TCU	-	-	-	-	-	-	-	-	19	16	15	18	16	15	15	19
UCLA	-	-	11	17	-	-	-	-	-	-	-	-	-	-	18	15
Western Ky.	-	14	8	-	-	-	-	-	-	-	-	-	-	-	-	-

1987-88

		December					January				February				March		
	PS	1	8	15	22	29	5	12	19	26	2	9	16	23	1	8	15
Arizona	17	9	4	2	1	1	3	1	1	1	1	3	3	3	3	3	2
Auburn	-	-	-	-	-	-	-	19	-	-	-	-	-	-	-	-	-
Bradley	-	-	-	-	-	-	-	-	-	-	18	15	17	14	14	12	11
BYU	-	-	-	-	-	-	-	-	12	7	4	8	7	11	15	17	19
DePaul	20	-	-	-	-	-	-	-	-	-	-	-	-	-	-	-	-
Duke	15	13	10	10	9	9	9	7	9	5	3	8	6	5	9	8	5
Florida	14	7	12	11	8	8	15	-	-	14	19	-	-	-	-	-	-
Georgia Tech	18	-	-	-	-	-	-	-	-	-	-	-	-	20	13	18	-
Georgetown	16	17	14	18	19	18	14	11	15	15	14	-	18	-	-	-	-
Illinois	-	-	-	-	-	-	19	20	13	13	17	-	-	-	-	19	16
Indiana	6	5	6	5	13	13	12	15	-	-	-	19	-	-	-	-	-
Iowa	11	6	3	7	14	14	16	17	19	16	13	13	13	13	11	15	17
Iowa St.	-	-	-	20	16	16	17	14	10	12	16	-	-	-	-	-	-
Kansas	7	16	18	17	18	17	18	16	16	-	-	-	-	-	-	-	-
Kansas St.	-	-	-	-	-	-	-	-	-	-	-	14	-	-	-	-	20
Kentucky	5	2	1	1	2	2	1	5	4	9	10	10	9	12	8	6	6
Louisville	13	14	-	-	-	20	-	-	-	-	-	-	-	-	-	-	-
Loyola Marymnt.	-	-	-	-	-	-	-	-	-	-	-	-	20	19	18	16	15
Memphis	-	20	20	19	20	19	-	-	-	-	-	-	-	-	-	-	-
Michigan	9	15	15	13	11	12	11	10	7	8	11	12	10	7	10	10	10
Missouri	8	8	9	16	17	-	-	-	-	-	-	-	15	15	-	-	-
UNLV	-	19	17	15	15	15	13	13	8	4	2	7	11	8	5	7	12
New Mexico	-	-	-	-	-	-	-	18	-	-	-	-	-	-	-	-	-
North Carolina	3	1	5	4	4	4	4	2	2	3	8	6	5	9	6	9	7
North Caro. St. -	-	-	-	-	-	-	-	20	-	-	-	-	14	16	11	14	
Notre Dame	-	-	19	-	-	-	-	-	-	-	-	-	-	-	-	-	-
Oklahoma	19	18	16	14	12	10	8	3	11	10	7	4	4	4	4	4	4
Pittsburgh	4	4	2	3	3	3	2	6	6	11	9	5	8	6	7	5	8
Purdue	2	11	13	12	10	11	10	8	5	2	6	2	2	2	2	2	3
St. John's (N.Y.)	-	-	-	-	-	-	20	-	-	-	20	-	-	-	-	-	-
Southern Miss.	-	-	-	-	-	-	-	-	-	20	-	16	-	18	-	-	-
Syracuse	1	3	8	9	7	7	7	9	14	17	12	11	12	10	12	13	9
Temple	12	12	11	8	6	6	6	4	3	6	5	1	1	1	1	1	1
UTEP	-	-	-	-	-	-	-	-	18	18	-	-	-	-	-	-	-
Vanderbilt	-	-	-	-	-	-	-	-	-	-	15	17	16	17	19	-	-
Villanova	-	-	-	-	-	-	-	-	-	19	-	20	-	-	-	-	-
Wyoming	10	10	7	6	5	5	5	12	17	-	-	18	19	16	17	14	13
Xavier	-	-	-	-	-	-	-	-	-	-	-	-	-	-	20	20	18

1988-89

		Nov.		December				January					February				March	
	PS	22	29	6	13	20	27	3	10	17	24	31	7	14	21	28	7	14
Alabama	-	-	-	-	-	-	-	-	-	-	-	-	-	-	-	-	-	20
Arizona	11	10	11	10	9	9	8	8	12	9	6	4	1	2	2	1	1	1
Ball St.	-	-	-	-	-	-	-	-	-	-	-	-	-	-	20	19	19	18
Connecticut	-	-	-	18	-	-	-	-	-	-	-	-	-	-	-	-	-	-
Duke	1	1	1	1	1	1	1	1	1	1	8	12	14	11	9	9	7	9
Florida	15	15	19	-	-	-	-	-	-	-	-	-	-	-	-	-	-	-
Florida St.	16	17	14	13	12	11	10	15	14	14	11	8	12	7	12	16	14	16
Georgetown	2	2	3	4	5	6	5	5	7	3	2	6	2	4	3	2	3	2
Georgia	-	-	-	-	-	-	-	20	-	-	-	-	-	-	-	-	-	-
Georgia Tech	13	14	12	12	11	16	17	19	19	-	-	-	20	-	-	-	-	-
Illinois	9	9	7	7	6	5	4	3	2	2	1	2	7	5	10	8	4	3
Indiana	-	20	-	-	-	-	-	-	-	19	16	17	13	9	4	3	6	8
Iowa	7	7	6	5	4	4	9	9	5	7	12	9	8	15	14	11	15	14
Kansas	-	-	-	-	-	20	20	18	16	17	18	-	-	-	-	-	-	-
LSU	-	-	-	-	-	-	-	-	-	-	-	19	-	20	-	-	-	-
Louisville	4	12	13	15	15	14	14	13	9	4	3	7	4	10	8	14	16	12
Michigan	3	3	2	2	2	2	2	7	6	6	10	11	10	13	13	10	8	10
Missouri	14	13	8	11	10	10	11	11	10	8	5	5	3	3	7	7	10	6
UNLV	10	8	9	9	13	13	12	12	11	10	13	16	19	18	18	18	18	15
North Carolina	6	5	10	8	8	8	7	6	8	13	7	3	6	8	5	5	9	5
North Caro. St.	18	18	16	19	18	17	18	16	15	15	15	13	17	19	17	20	17	19
Notre Dame	-	-	-	-	19	-	-	-	-	-	-	-	-	-	-	-	-	-
Ohio St.	17	16	15	14	14	12	15	14	18	16	17	15	16	16	-	-	-	-
Oklahoma	5	4	5	6	7	7	6	4	3	5	4	1	5	1	1	4	2	4

Team	PS	Nov.		December				January					February				March	
		22	29	6	13	20	27	3	10	17	24	31	7	14	21	28	7	14
Providence	-	-	-	-	-	-	-	-	20	-	20	-	-	-	-	-	-	-
St. Mary's (Cal.)	-	-	-	-	-	-	-	-	-	-	-	-	-	-	19	17	20	-
Seton Hall	-	-	20	17	15	13	10	13	12	9	10	11	12	15	12	11	11	-
South Carolina	-	-	-	-	18	16	-	-	-	-	-	-	-	-	-	-	-	-
Stanford	20	-	-	-	-	-	-	-	20	19	20	18	17	16	13	12	13	-
Syracuse	8	6	4	3	3	3	3	2	4	11	14	14	9	6	6	6	5	7
Temple	19	19	17	-	-	-	-	-	-	-	-	-	-	-	-	-	-	-
Tennessee	-	-	20	16	16	19	19	17	17	18	-	-	-	-	-	-	-	-
UCLA	-	-	-	-	20	-	-	-	-	-	-	-	-	-	-	-	-	-
Villanova	12	11	18	17	-	-	-	-	-	-	-	-	-	-	-	-	-	-
West Virginia	-	-	-	-	-	-	-	-	-	-	18	15	14	11	15	13	17	-

1989-90

Team	PS	Nov.	December				January					February				March	
		27	5	12	19	26	2	9	16	23	30	6	13	20	27	6	13
Alabama	-	-	21	19	20	22	22	24	25	24	-	-	-	-	-	-	23
Arizona	6	2	20	20	22	21	19	18	23	19	24	22	20	21	23	15	14
Arkansas	9	11	10	7	10	11	14	12	12	6	3	3	8	13	12	9	7
Clemson	-	-	-	-	-	-	-	-	-	-	-	-	23	20	17	17	-
Connecticut	-	-	-	-	-	-	-	-	20	13	8	10	6	4	8	4	-
Duke	10	7	6	12	12	13	13	10	8	8	5	4	6	3	5	12	15
Florida	23	24	25	24	-	-	-	-	-	-	-	-	-	-	-	-	-
Georgetown	5	3	3	3	3	2	2	6	5	3	6	5	3	5	7	5	8
Georgia	-	-	-	-	-	-	-	-	-	-	-	-	-	25	25	-	-
Georgia Tech	22	21	18	15	14	14	12	9	11	13	17	16	13	8	11	14	9
Illinois	8	8	7	5	5	4	4	8	7	10	11	12	15	19	18	20	18
Indiana	14	14	14	11	11	9	13	14	12	22	25	-	25	-	-	-	-
Iowa	-	-	-	21	16	18	20	-	-	-	-	-	-	-	-	-	-
Kansas	-	4	2	2	2	2	2	1	1	2	2	2	1	2	1	2	5
La Salle	-	-	-	23	20	17	21	17	18	15	14	14	14	13	11	12	-
LSU	2	9	9	9	8	9	11	14	13	16	14	11	9	12	15	16	19
Louisville	12	13	11	10	9	8	8	11	10	4	10	15	18	16	21	18	16
Loyola Marymount	-	-	-	-	-	-	25	23	21	22	20	20	19	22	22	21	21
Memphis	24	22	16	17	17	15	21	20	-	-	-	-	-	-	-	-	-
Michigan	4	10	8	6	6	5	5	3	6	7	4	7	5	7	8	13	13
Michigan St.	-	-	-	25	25	-	-	-	-	-	-	23	21	15	14	7	3
Minnesota	20	-	-	-	-	25	24	16	22	21	19	17	17	18	17	19	20
Missouri	11	5	4	4	4	7	7	5	4	1	1	1	2	1	3	6	11
UNLV	1	6	5	14	13	12	10	7	9	5	12	9	7	4	2	3	2
New Mexico St.	-	-	-	-	-	-	-	-	-	-	-	25	24	24	23	24	-
North Carolina	7	12	17	-	-	24	-	-	-	-	25	-	-	-	-	-	-
North Caro. St.	19	25	19	16	15	19	18	17	19	-	-	-	-	-	-	-	-
Notre Dame	17	19	-	-	-	-	-	-	-	-	-	-	-	-	-	-	-
Oklahoma	16	17	12	8	7	6	4	3	9	9	13	11	10	5	1	1	-
Oklahoma St.	21	23	-	22	24	-	-	-	-	-	-	-	-	-	-	-	-
Oregon St.	-	-	24	21	23	23	22	18	17	14	16	17	16	22	-	-	-
Pittsburgh	18	18	22	-	-	-	-	-	-	-	-	-	-	-	-	-	-
Purdue	-	-	-	-	-	-	24	13	8	10	12	9	9	10	10	-	-
St. John's (N.Y.)	25	20	15	18	19	17	16	15	15	15	18	24	24	-	-	-	-
Syracuse	3	1	1	1	1	1	1	6	5	11	7	6	4	11	10	4	6
Temple	15	16	23	-	-	-	-	-	-	-	-	-	-	-	-	-	-
UCLA	13	15	13	13	18	16	15	19	16	23	16	19	23	-	-	-	-
Xavier	-	-	-	-	-	25	20	25	23	21	22	19	19	24	25	-	-

1990-91

Team	PS	Nov.	December				January					February				March	
		27	4	11	18	25	1	8	15	22	29	5	12	19	26	5	12
Alabama	7	6	12	20	-	-	-	-	-	-	-	-	-	-	24	24	19
Arizona	3	2	2	4	4	4	6	6	5	5	6	5	6	9	7	9	8
Arkansas	2	3	3	2	2	2	2	2	2	2	2	2	2	3	3	5	2
Connecticut	17	15	14	16	15	13	12	9	13	19	-	-	-	-	-	-	-
DePaul	-	-	-	-	-	-	-	-	-	-	-	-	-	-	-	25	24
Duke	6	8	5	10	9	8	8	14	12	9	7	6	5	7	8	6	6
East Tenn. St.	-	-	-	24	21	20	17	16	15	12	16	10	13	13	19	15	17
Georgetown	9	9	6	5	12	16	15	15	19	21	18	20	18	25	-	-	-
Georgia	21	17	13	11	17	17	-	-	-	-	-	-	-	-	-	-	-
Georgia Tech	16	14	20	23	-	24	24	-	23	-	-	-	-	-	-	-	-
Indiana	8	10	7	7	6	5	5	3	3	4	4	4	4	4	5	3	3
Iowa	-	-	-	-	23	22	22	24	-	-	-	-	-	-	-	-	-
Kansas	-	-	-	-	-	-	24	18	11	8	10	12	12	-	-	-	-
Kentucky	-	-	25	18	18	18	16	11	9	8	10	16	12	13	10	9	-
LSU	14	20	18	12	10	15	14	20	20	16	14	19	20	19	18	16	22
Louisville	23	25	-	-	-	-	-	-	-	-	-	-	-	-	-	-	-
Michigan St.	4	5	19	21	24	25	25	-	22	-	-	-	-	-	-	-	-
Mississippi St.	-	-	-	-	-	-	-	-	-	-	-	23	21	23	18	21	-
Missouri	20	23	-	-	-	-	-	-	-	-	-	-	-	-	-	-	-
Nebraska	-	-	-	-	22	22	19	18	17	14	11	15	15	-	-	-	-
UNLV	1	1	1	1	1	1	1	1	1	1	1	1	1	1	1	1	1
New Mexico St.	-	-	-	24	23	23	21	23	20	16	12	15	11	11	15	-	-
New Orleans	-	-	-	-	-	-	-	24	22	21	-	-	-	-	-	-	-
North Carolina	5	4	10	9	8	7	7	5	5	7	9	9	8	6	4	7	4
Ohio St.	10	11	9	8	7	6	4	4	4	3	2	2	5				

Team	PS	Nov.	December				January					February				March	
		27	4	11	18	25	1	8	15	22	29	5	12	19	26	5	12
Oklahoma	15	18	16	13	11	14	13	12	11	13	21	23	-	-	-	-	-
Oklahoma St.	-	-	-	-	-	-	-	-	-	-	22	21	16	12	14	14	-
Pittsburgh	12	13	-	11	15	14	11	11	17	16	17	19	24	22	22	22	-
Princeton	-	-	-	-	25	-	-	-	-	-	-	25	23	21	19	18	-
St. John's (N.Y.)	25	21	17	14	13	9	9	10	10	10	5	8	13	18	17	20	20
Seton Hall	-	-	-	-	-	-	-	25	-	25	-	-	24	20	21	13	-
South Carolina	-	-	21	17	16	12	20	21	22	25	-	-	-	-	-	-	-
Southern Miss.	24	19	15	22	20	21	21	19	18	15	17	12	9	11	14	22	25
Syracuse	13	7	4	3	3	3	8	8	6	8	6	7	7	5	6	4	7
Temple	19	-	24	-	-	-	-	-	-	-	-	-	-	-	-	-	-
Texas	22	22	23	25	23	-	-	-	-	-	-	-	-	24	-	23	23
UTEP	-	-	-	-	-	-	-	25	-	-	-	-	-	-	-	-	-
UCLA	11	12	8	6	5	10	10	7	7	11	12	14	15	17	16	17	16
Utah	-	-	-	-	-	-	-	-	23	20	13	17	14	10	9	8	10
Villanova	-	24	-	-	-	-	-	-	-	-	-	-	-	-	-	-	-
Virginia	18	16	21	19	19	19	18	13	14	18	15	11	19	20	25	-	-

1991-92

Team	PS	Nov.	December					January				February				March		
		25	2	9	16	23	30	6	13	20	27	3	10	17	24	2	9	16
Alabama	17	16	15	20	20	20	19	16	9	15	22	18	16	14	16	20	17	13
Arizona	5	3	3	2	2	6	6	6	7	11	9	7	7	5	5	4	2	10
Arizona St.	24	25	-	-	-	-	-	-	-	-	-	-	-	-	-	-	-	-
Arkansas	3	2	11	19	19	15	16	13	12	9	7	5	11	10	9	7	6	9
Charlotte	-	-	-	24	24	25	21	22	18	19	17	20	22	-	-	-	-	-
Cincinnati	-	-	-	-	-	-	-	-	-	-	-	-	24	19	19	14	12	12
Connecticut	15	15	12	8	7	5	5	8	7	6	10	18	21	24	-	-	-	-
DePaul	18	20	20	-	-	-	-	-	-	-	-	-	-	-	21	15	19	24
Duke	1	1	1	1	1	1	1	1	1	1	1	1	1	1	1	1	1	1
Florida St.	-	-	-	-	-	-	-	-	-	-	23	23	16	22	19	18	20	-
Georgetown	16	17	18	23	23	24	22	-	22	-	-	-	-	25	18	17	21	22
Georgia Tech	23	18	17	13	13	13	15	14	16	18	20	24	-	-	-	-	-	-
Indiana	2	10	9	13	14	10	10	10	5	4	4	6	4	7	2	2	4	5
Iowa	21	21	21	16	22	23	-	-	-	-	-	-	-	-	-	-	-	-
Iowa St.	-	-	-	-	-	-	-	-	-	24	-	-	-	-	23	-	-	-
Kansas	12	12	10	7	6	4	4	4	6	5	5	3	4	3	3	3	3	2
Kentucky	4	13	14	9	8	17	17	15	10	8	14	19	19	13	11	10	9	6
LSU	6	9	16	25	-	-	-	-	-	-	-	22	20	-	-	23	23	25
Louisville	25	-	-	-	25	21	24	-	25	20	24	-	-	-	-	-	-	-
Massachusetts	-	-	-	-	-	-	-	-	25	-	-	-	-	-	-	25	22	17
Michigan	20	23	25	18	15	11	11	11	15	16	15	15	17	20	17	18	14	15
Michigan St.	-	-	22	13	12	9	9	9	11	14	13	11	12	11	12	13	16	14
Missouri	-	-	-	21	17	16	13	12	13	12	8	12	9	9	6	11	13	16
Nebraska	-	-	-	-	-	-	-	-	-	-	-	-	-	-	25	-	-	-
UNLV	-	24	-	-	-	-	-	-	-	-	25	21	17	15	12	7	6	7
North Carolina	8	6	5	5	9	8	8	8	14	10	11	9	6	4	10	16	20	18
Ohio St.	7	5	4	4	4	7	7	7	4	6	10	8	8	6	8	5	5	3
Oklahoma	19	19	19	17	16	14	14	14	21	23	17	18	21	-	-	-	24	23
Oklahoma St.	13	11	8	6	5	3	3	3	3	3	2	2	4	4	12	11	11	6
Pittsburgh	-	24	-	-	-	-	-	-	-	-	-	-	-	-	-	-	-	-
St. John's (N.Y.)	10	8	7	11	10	18	18	17	17	22	-	-	-	-	24	20	-	25
Seton Hall	9	7	6	12	11	12	12	18	21	-	-	-	25	22	-	22	15	19
Southern Cal.	-	-	-	-	-	-	25	-	23	-	-	16	13	15	13	8	10	8
Stanford	-	-	-	-	-	-	-	-	-	24	-	-	-	-	-	-	-	-
Syracuse	-	-	-	-	-	23	20	20	13	13	10	17	22	24	-	21	-	-
UTEP	-	-	-	-	-	-	-	-	-	-	-	23	19	25	21	-	-	-
Tulane	-	-	-	-	-	-	-	-	24	19	21	16	14	14	18	15	21	-
UCLA	11	4	2	3	3	2	2	2	2	2	2	4	3	2	4	9	8	4
Utah	14	14	13	10	18	19	-	-	-	-	-	-	-	-	-	-	-	-
Wake Forest	22	22	23	22	21	22	20	19	-	-	-	-	-	-	-	-	-	-

1992-93

Team	PS	Nov.		December				January				February				March		
		23	30	7	14	21	28	4	11	18	25	1	8	15	22	1	8	15
Arizona	10	10	9	14	15	14	22	20	12	11	8	8	5	4	4	3	6	5
Arkansas	-	-	-	16	12	10	9	13	9	8	16	17	14	13	15	13	14	12
Boston College	-	-	-	-	-	-	-	22	-	-	-	21	-	-	-	-	-	-
BYU	-	-	-	-	-	25	-	-	-	-	-	-	-	-	23	21	25	-
California	-	-	-	-	25	21	19	-	-	-	-	-	-	-	-	-	-	-
Cincinnati	21	23	22	19	19	23	21	16	11	9	6	4	8	8	10	12	11	7
Connecticut	16	16	25	-	24	22	23	19	15	17	22	-	-	-	-	-	-	-
Duke	3	3	4	1	1	1	1	1	3	6	7	5	3	7	9	6	8	10
Florida St.	9	7	11	10	10	18	23	18	-	19	12	10	9	6	9	11	10	11
Georgetown	12	13	14	11	11	11	10	17	20	18	22	23	-	-	-	-	-	-
Georgia Tech	14	14	13	17	17	16	14	10	8	16	18	22	-	-	-	-	-	18
Houston	-	-	-	-	-	-	-	-	-	-	-	25	-	-	-	-	-	-
Indiana	4	4	2	4	4	4	4	5	6	2	2	1	1	1	1	1	2	1
Iowa	11	11	10	8	9	7	8	13	14	11	9	13	20	18	15	17	13	-
Iowa St.	19	24	-	-	-	-	-	-	-	-	-	-	-	-	-	-	-	-
Kansas	2	2	3	2	2	2	2	4	4	1	1	3	7	6	7	8	7	9
Kansas St.	-	-	-	-	-	-	-	-	-	-	23	-	-	-	-	-	-	-
Kentucky	5	5	5	3	3	3	3	2	1	4	4	2	2	2	2	5	4	2
Long Beach St.	-	-	-	-	-	-	-	-	-	-	-	25	-	-	-	-	-	-

		Nov.		December				January				February				March		
	PS	23	30	7	14	21	28	4	11	18	25	1	8	15	22	1	8	15
Louisville	13	12	12	9	21	-	-	-	-	-	-	-	-	22	-	22	16	15
Marquette	-	-	-	-	-	-	-	-	-	-	24	20	15	24	20	-	-	-
Massachusetts	23	20	19	23	-	-	-	22	-	-	-	-	22	19	21	23	20	14
Memphis	8	9	8	21	-	-	-	-	-	-	-	-	-	-	-	-	-	-
Michigan	1	1	1	6	6	6	6	3	2	5	5	7	4	5	5	4	3	3
Michigan St.	20	18	18	24	23	20	17	14	23	21	-	25	-	-	-	-	-	-
Minnesota	-	-	-	-	-	-	-	-	19	-	-	-	-	-	-	-	-	-
Nebraska	25	25	-	25	20	17	20	-	-	-	-	-	-	-	-	-	-	-
UNLV	22	22	23	22	22	19	16	12	18	15	10	10	12	15	13	16	19	25
New Mexico	-	-	-	-	-	-	-	-	-	-	-	-	-	-	-	-	-	21
New Mexico St.	-	-	21	-	-	-	-	-	-	-	-	-	-	-	-	-	24	24
New Orleans	-	-	-	-	-	-	-	-	-	-	-	-	25	21	19	17	13	17
North Carolina	7	8	7	5	5	5	5	6	5	3	3	6	6	3	3	1	1	4
Ohio St.	-	-	-	-	-	-	-	-	21	24	-	-	-	-	-	-	-	-
Oklahoma	15	15	15	11	9	9	15	11	10	12	20	16	-	-	-	-	-	-
Oklahoma St.	-	-	-	-	-	-	-	-	-	-	-	-	-	-	-	19	21	23
Pittsburgh	-	-	-	-	-	-	-	24	-	20	13	15	17	17	25	-	-	-
Purdue	-	-	24	18	16	15	13	9	17	13	14	19	18	14	17	24	18	22
St. John's (N.Y.)	-	-	-	-	-	-	-	-	-	-	-	-	-	25	-	25	-	-
Seton Hall	6	6	6	7	7	7	7	7	7	10	9	14	19	16	14	10	9	6
Syracuse	18	17	17	15	14	13	12	21	24	-	-	-	-	-	-	-	-	-
Tulane	17	19	20	20	18	24	-	-	-	-	23	18	20	18	16	20	23	-
UCLA	24	21	16	13	13	12	11	15	16	23	-	-	-	-	-	-	-	-
Utah	-	-	-	-	-	-	-	-	25	22	17	21	16	12	11	9	15	19
Vanderbilt	-	-	-	-	-	25	24	18	-	19	11	11	11	11	8	7	5	8
Virginia	-	-	-	-	-	-	-	25	14	7	15	24	24	23	22	-	-	-
Wake Forest	-	-	-	-	-	-	-	-	-	-	-	13	9	10	12	14	12	16
Western Ky.	-	-	-	-	-	-	-	-	-	-	-	-	-	-	-	-	-	20
Xavier	-	-	-	-	-	-	-	-	-	-	-	-	-	-	24	18	22	-

1993-94

		Nov.		December				January					February				March	
	PS	22	29	6	13	20	27	3	10	17	24	31	7	14	21	28	7	14
UAB	-	-	-	-	-	-	-	-	22	18	20	17	19	21	-	24	22	-
Arizona	18	19	19	14	13	13	12	9	6	9	13	12	16	15	9	8	7	9
Arkansas	3	3	2	1	1	1	1	1	4	3	5	6	3	1	1	1	1	2
Boston College	-	-	-	-	20	18	23	20	20	-	-	-	-	-	21	23	-	-
California	6	12	13	25	-	-	-	24	19	21	-	19	18	19	17	20	16	16
Cincinnati	19	22	23	20	17	20	18	17	21	19	-	25	-	23	-	-	-	25
Connecticut	-	-	-	21	16	15	14	16	14	10	6	5	6	3	5	4	2	4
Duke	4	4	6	4	3	3	3	3	2	5	2	1	2	6	2	2	5	6
Florida	-	-	-	-	-	-	-	-	-	-	-	24	20	17	16	19	17	14
Florida St.	25	-	-	-	-	-	-	-	-	-	-	-	-	-	-	-	-	-
Geo. Washington	24	23	22	24	23	23	21	23	-	-	-	-	-	-	-	-	-	-
Georgetown	15	15	25	-	-	-	-	-	-	-	-	-	-	-	-	-	-	-
Georgia Tech	14	13	17	18	14	14	15	12	17	17	21	-	-	25	23	-	-	-
Illinois	17	17	16	16	19	19	22	21	-	-	-	-	24	-	-	-	-	-
Indiana	12	11	21	12	12	12	13	14	11	8	11	14	12	16	12	17	18	18
Kansas	9	6	3	7	6	6	6	5	3	1	3	3	5	4	10	13	11	13
Kentucky	2	2	1	6	5	5	5	4	8	7	9	7	4	11	7	7	10	7
LSU	-	-	-	-	25	-	-	-	-	-	-	-	-	-	-	-	-	-
Louisville	7	7	11	10	10	11	11	11	15	13	12	9	7	5	13	10	14	10
Marquette	-	-	-	-	-	24	24	25	-	-	22	-	22	22	22	22	19	21
Maryland	-	-	-	-	-	-	-	-	-	25	18	21	-	-	-	-	-	-
Massachusetts	22	18	9	8	8	8	9	8	7	6	8	11	13	10	11	11	9	8
Michigan	5	5	5	3	7	7	7	13	10	15	15	13	11	7	3	3	8	11
Minnesota	10	9	15	17	15	16	16	19	18	20	17	22	23	20	20	18	20	23
Missouri	-	-	-	-	-	-	-	-	25	-	24	20	15	12	6	6	3	5
Nebraska	-	-	-	-	-	-	-	-	-	-	-	-	-	-	-	-	-	22
New Mexico St.	-	-	-	-	-	-	-	-	-	-	25	23	-	-	25	-	-	-
North Carolina	1	1	4	2	2	2	2	2	1	4	4	2	1	2	4	5	4	1
Oklahoma St.	11	10	8	15	22	22	20	-	-	-	-	-	-	-	24	21	23	19
Penn	-	-	-	-	-	-	-	-	-	-	-	-	-	-	-	25	24	-
Purdue	21	21	14	11	11	10	10	10	9	12	7	8	10	9	14	9	6	3
St. Louis	-	-	-	-	-	-	-	-	-	23	23	18	17	18	19	16	21	24
Syracuse	20	20	18	13	21	21	19	18	16	16	14	15	14	14	18	14	13	15
Temple	8	8	7	5	4	4	4	7	13	11	10	10	8	13	8	12	12	12
Texas	-	-	-	-	-	-	-	-	-	-	-	-	-	-	-	-	25	20
UCLA	13	14	10	9	9	9	8	6	5	2	1	4	9	8	15	15	15	17
Vanderbilt	23	24	20	23	24	-	-	22	24	-	-	-	-	-				
Virginia	16	16	12	22	-	-	-	-	-	-	-	-	-	-	-	-	-	-
West Virginia	-	-	-	-	-	-	-	-	23	24	19	-	-	-	-	-	-	-
Western Ky.	-	-	-	-	-	25	25	-	-	-	-	-	-	-	-	-	-	-
Wisconsin	-	25	24	19	18	17	17	15	12	14	16	16	21	24	-	-	-	-
Xavier	-	-	-	-	-	-	-	-	25	22	-	-	25	-	-	-	-	-

1994-95

		Nov.		December				January					February				March	
	PS	21	28	5	12	19	26	2	9	16	23	30	6	13	20	27	6	13
Alabama	18	25	-	-	-	-	-	-	-	-	-	20	23	18	20	21	20	20
Arizona	5	5	9	8	7	6	10	9	13	11	12	12	9	12	13	12	12	15
Arizona St.	-	-	12	16	13	15	16	15	12	13	13	16	14	13	15	15	18	16
Arkansas	1	1	4	3	4	3	3	3	5	9	9	8	12	10	8	7	5	6
California	-	-	-	-	-	24	14	17	20	-	-	-	-	-	-	-	-	-
Cincinnati	13	12	10	13	17	13	20	-	-	23	19	23	-	-	-	-	-	-
Clemson	-	-	-	-	-	-	-	-	18	-	-	-	-	-	-	-	-	-
Connecticut	19	16	16	10	10	10	8	6	2	2	2	4	3	1	4	4	6	8
Duke	8	8	6	9	9	9	7	11	16	-	-	-	-	-	-	-	-	-
Florida	10	10	8	6	8	8	13	13	15	24	23	25	-	-	-	-	-	-
Georgetown	15	14	19	18	15	12	12	12	10	10	14	13	20	-	-	23	24	22
Georgia Tech	23	22	20	17	14	18	17	24	22	22	21	21	18	20	24	-	-	-
Illinois	25	-	-	-	-	23	-	-	-	20	-	-	-	-	-	-	-	-
Indiana	9	11	-	-	-	-	24	21	-	-	-	-	-	-	-	-	-	-
Iowa	-	-	-	-	-	-	-	22	19	-	-	-	-	-	-	-	-	-
Iowa St.	-	-	-	-	-	25	21	16	23	14	11	11	19	21	23	24	-	24
Kansas	11	9	7	4	3	7	6	5	3	7	7	3	2	3	1	3	2	5
Kentucky	4	4	3	7	6	5	5	8	7	5	5	6	5	4	6	5	3	2
Maryland	7	7	11	11	12	11	9	7	9	8	8	5	8	7	7	6	10	10
Massachusetts	3	3	1	5	5	4	4	4	1	1	1	1	4	5	5	8	8	7
Michigan	16	13	17	23	25	-	-	-	-	-	-	-	-	-	-	-	-	-
Michigan St.	20	17	18	15	18	17	15	14	11	12	10	9	7	8	12	10	9	11
Minnesota	-	-	15	12	11	16	-	-	-	-	-	-	-	24	22	-	-	-
Mississippi St.	-	-	-	-	-	-	-	-	-	-	-	-	21	23	16	14	15	18
Missouri	-	-	-	-	-	-	-	-	17	16	20	18	13	9	14	19	17	23
Nebraska	-	-	-	-	-	-	23	19	-	-	-	-	-	-	-	-	-	-
New Mexico St.	-	-	25	22	24	21	22	20	24	19	24	-	-	-	-	-	-	-
North Carolina	2	2	2	1	1	1	1	1	4	3	3	2	1	2	3	2	4	4
Ohio	-	23	14	21	19	-	-	-	-	-	-	-	-	-	-	-	-	-
Oklahoma	-	-	-	-	-	-	-	-	-	-	25	24	-	-	25	16	16	17
Oklahoma St.	21	19	-	-	-	-	-	-	-	-	-	-	24	22	18	18	19	14
Oregon	-	-	-	-	-	-	-	-	25	17	18	22	22	19	-	-	25	-
Penn	-	-	-	-	-	-	-	25	21	25	-	-	-	-	-	-	-	-
Purdue	-	-	-	-	-	-	-	-	-	-	-	-	25	25	21	17	14	12
St. John's (N.Y.)	-	-	-	-	-	-	25	-	-	-	-	-	-	-	-	-	-	-
Stanford	-	-	-	-	-	-	-	23	-	21	17	17	15	17	19	20	-	-
Syracuse	12	18	22	19	16	14	11	10	8	6	6	10	10	11	17	22	21	25
UCLA	6	6	5	2	2	2	2	2	6	4	4	7	6	6	2	1	1	1
Utah	-	-	-	-	-	-	-	-	-	-	-	-	-	-	-	-	22	19
Villanova	22	21	24	24	22	-	-	-	-	-	22	19	16	15	9	11	13	9
Virginia	14	20	23	20	23	22	-	-	-	18	15	15	17	16	11	13	11	13
Wake Forest	24	24	21	25	21	19	18	18	14	15	16	14	11	14	10	9	7	3
Western Ky.	-	-	-	-	-	-	-	-	-	-	-	-	-	-	-	-	23	21
Wisconsin	17	15	13	14	20	20	19	-	-	-	-	-	-	-	-	-	-	-
Xavier	-	-	-	-	-	-	-	-	-	-	-	-	-	-	-	25	-	-

1995-96

		Nov.		December				January					February				March	
	PS	20	27	4	11	18	26	2	8	15	22	29	5	12	19	26	5	12
Arizona	-	19	4	4	4	3	9	9	18	18	13	14	16	13	13	11	11	11
Arkansas	16	-	25	-	-	-	-	-	-	-	-	-	-	-	-	-	-	-
Auburn	-	-	-	-	-	-	-	-	-	23	21	22	-	-	-	-	-	-
Boston College	-	-	-	-	-	-	-	24	-	24	20	21	22	21	20	-	-	-
California	25	-	-	-	-	24	-	-	-	-	25	-	-	-	-	-	-	-
Cincinnati	21	21	21	17	12	9	5	5	4	3	5	5	5	6	6	7	8	7
Clemson	-	-	-	-	-	-	24	22	16	19	18	24	-	-	-	-	-	-
Connecticut	6	6	9	9	8	8	7	7	6	5	4	4	4	3	3	4	3	3
Duke	-	-	12	18	21	20	20	19	-	-	-	-	-	-	-	-	-	-
Eastern Mich.	-	-	-	-	-	-	-	-	-	-	-	23	24	23	-	-	-	-
Geo. Washington	-	-	-	-	-	-	-	-	-	-	-	-	-	-	-	24	-	-
Georgetown	5	5	6	6	7	6	6	6	5	8	6	9	8	14	11	8	6	4
Georgia	-	-	-	-	-	18	16	14	19	22	-	-	-	-	-	-	-	-
Georgia Tech	-	25	20	16	19	21	-	-	-	-	-	25	-	-	23	18	18	13
Green Bay	-	-	-	-	-	-	-	-	-	-	-	-	-	-	25	22	24	-
Illinois	-	-	-	21	16	14	12	13	21	-	-	-	-	-	-	-	-	-
Indiana	23	23	-	-	-	-	-	-	-	-	-	-	-	-	-	-	-	-
Iowa	8	10	11	12	9	10	10	10	11	16T	22	16	19	19	18	20	19	21
Iowa St.	-	-	-	-	-	-	-	-	-	-	-	-	21	22	22	23	23	17
Kansas	2	2	2	1	1	1	4	4	3	4	3	3	3	5	5	3	5	4
Kentucky	1	1	1	5	5	4	2	2	2	2	2	2	2	2	2	1	1	2
Louisville	12	13	18	23	20	25	-	-	-	-	-	-	20	24	21	21	22	24
Marquette	-	-	-	-	-	-	-	-	-	-	24	-	-	-	-	-	21	20
Maryland	15	14	19	20	-	-	-	-	-	-	-	-	-	-	-	-	-	-
Massachusetts	7	7	5	3	3	2	1	1	1	1	1	1	1	1	1	2	2	1
Memphis	13	12	7	7	6	5	3	3	9	9	12	11	15	15	19	14	14	16
Michigan	17	16	24	22	18	17	19	21	23	20	16	20	23	-	-	-	-	-
Mississippi St.	9	9	8	8	15	16	17	17	12	21	-	-	-	25	-	-	25	19
Missouri	14	15	13	11	14	15	18	-	-	-	-	-	-	-	-	-	-	-
New Mexico	-	-	-	-	-	-	-	25	25	-	-	-	-	-	-	-	-	23
North Carolina	20	20	17	13	10	11	11	16	10	10	11	8	12	17	17	19	20	25
Penn St.	-	-	-	-	-	-	-	-	20	14	14	10	10	9	14	12	16	18
Purdue	24	24	-	-	-	-	-	-	22	17	19	17	14	11	7	5	4	4
Santa Clara	-	-	-	25	22	-	-	-	-	-	-	-	-	-	-	-	-	-
Stanford	18	18	16	24	-	-	-	-	24	-	-	-	25	20	24	25	-	-
Syracuse	-	-	-	-	25	19	13	11	14	12	17	18	18	16	15	15	13	15

		Nov.		December				January					February				March	
	PS	20	27	4	11	18	26	2	8	15	22	29	5	12	19	26	5	12
Texas	-	-	-	-	-	-	-	23	-	-	-	-	-	-	-	-	-	-
Texas Tech	-	-	-	-	-	-	-	-	-	25	T22	15	13	12	9	9	7	8
Tulsa	-	-	-	-	-	-	25	-	-	-	-	-	-	-	-	-	-	-
UCLA	4	4	23	-	24	-	23	20	17	13	15	19	17	18	16	17	17	14
Utah	10	8	14	14	13	13	15	15	13	15	10	7	7	7	8	10	10	12
Villanova	3	3	3	2	2	7	8	8	7	7	7	6	6	4	4	6	9	10
Virginia	19	17	15	15	23	23	22	-	-	-	-	-	-	-	-	-	-	-
Virginia Tech	22	22	22	19	17	22	21	18	15	11	8	13	11	10	12	16	15	22
Wake Forest	11	11	10	10	11	12	14	12	8	6	9	12	9	8	10	13	12	9

1996-97

		Nov.		December					January				February				March	
	PS	19	26	3	10	17	24	31	7	14	21	28	4	11	18	25	4	11
Alabama	-	-	-	-	24	20	19	-	-	-	-	-	-	-	-	-	-	-
Arizona	19	19	11	15	8	6	9	9	7	6	11	10	14	11	13	15	12	15
Arkansas	13	16	16	22	20	19	22	22	-	-	-	-	-	-	-	-	-	-
Boston College	21	21	23	20	25	-	25	25	23	19	22	-	-	-	-	-	-	23
California	-	-	-	-	-	-	-	-	-	-	-	-	-	-	25	-	-	-
Col. of Charleston	-	-	-	-	-	-	-	-	-	-	-	-	-	25	22	20	17	16
Cincinnati	1	1	1	4	7	7	7	6	6	4	9	8	12	8	11	9	10	10
Clemson	20	12	10	12	10	8	6	5	5	3	2	7	10	7	8	12	13	14
Colorado	-	-	-	-	-	-	-	-	-	-	18	18	15	15	21	19	18	24
Duke	10	10	6	10	14	11	12	13	10	13	10	12	8	6	6	7	7	8
Fresno St.	14	14	15	13	16	21	-	-	-	-	-	-	-	-	-	-	-	-
Geo. Washington	24	24	25	-	-	-	-	-	-	-	-	-	-	-	-	-	-	-
Georgia	-	-	-	-	-	-	-	-	24	21	-	-	-	-	-	-	24	17
Illinois	-	-	-	-	-	-	-	24	25	-	-	-	-	20	23	21	15	19
Indiana	-	22	20	8	12	13	13	12	15	17	21	17	24	-	24	22	25	-
Iowa	23	25	-	-	-	-	-	-	-	-	-	-	25	-	-	-	-	-
Iowa St.	11	11	9	9	6	5	5	4	4	8	14	11	6	9	7	13	16	18
Kansas	2	2	2	1	1	1	1	1	1	1	1	1	1	1	1	1	1	1
Kentucky	3	8	8	6	3	3	3	3	3	5	3	3	3	4	3	3	6	5
Louisville	-	-	-	-	22	18	16	14	14	10	6	9	11	17	15	17	20	25
Marquette	25	-	-	-	-	-	-	-	-	-	25	24	-	-	-	-	-	-
Maryland	-	-	-	-	-	25	21	19	19	11	7	5	7	10	14	16	22	22
Massachusetts	15	15	17	-	-	-	-	-	-	-	-	-	-	-	-	-	-	-
Michigan	9	9	7	7	5	4	4	8	16	18	13	16	13	14	18	24	-	-
Minnesota	22	23	24	16	17	16	15	15	11	7	8	6	4	3	2	2	2	3
Mississippi	-	-	-	-	-	-	-	-	-	20	-	-	-	-	-	-	-	-
New Mexico	17	18	19	11	15	15	14	16	18	12	15	13	9	13	10	11	14	11
North Carolina	8	7	14	14	11	12	11	11	13	22	19	19	20	16	12	8	5	4
Oregon	-	-	-	-	-	-	24	20	17	24	-	-	-	-	-	-	-	-
St. Joseph's	-	-	-	-	-	-	-	-	-	-	-	-	-	-	-	23	19	12
South Carolina	-	-	-	-	-	-	-	-	-	-	-	25	19	12	9	6	4	6
Stanford	18	20	21	24	21	22	23	21	21	15	17	15	18	22	20	25	23	21
Syracuse	12	13	12	19	-	-	-	-	-	-	-	-	-	-	-	-	-	-
Texas	16	17	18	18	13	14	18	18	22	23	23	23	-	-	-	-	-	-
Texas Tech	-	-	-	-	18	23	20	23	20	25	20	22	23	21	-	-	-	-
Tulane	-	-	-	-	-	-	-	-	-	-	-	-	21	23	-	-	-	-
Tulsa	-	-	22	21	-	-	-	-	-	-	24	21	22	-	-	-	-	-
UCLA	5	5	13	17	23	24	-	-	-	-	-	-	-	24	17	10	9	7
Utah	6	4	4	3	9	9	8	7	9	9	5	4	5	5	5	4	3	2
Villanova	7	6	5	5	4	10	10	10	8	16	12	14	16	18	19	18	21	20
Virginia	-	-	-	25	-	-	-	-	-	-	-	-	-	-	-	-	-	-
Wake Forest	4	3	3	2	2	2	2	2	2	2	4	2	2	2	4	5	8	9
Xavier	-	-	-	23	19	17	17	17	12	14	16	20	17	19	16	14	11	13

1997-98

		Nov.		December					January				February				March	
	PS	18	25	2	9	16	23	30	6	13	20	27	3	10	17	24	3	10
Arizona	1	1	1	4	6	5	5	8	5	5	6	6	4	3	3	2	2	4
Arkansas	-	-	-	18	15	13	12	23	22	22	18	15	14	12	16	12	16	17
Charlotte	18	17	25	-	-	-	-	-	-	-	-	-	-	-	-	-	-	-
Cincinnati	-	-	-	-	-	-	-	-	-	-	21	18	20	19	17	17	14	9
Clemson	5	5	13	17	17	-	21	21	24	-	25	-	-	-	-	-	-	-
Connecticut	12	12	11	13	13	12	11	10	8	10	8	9	7	6	7	6	6	6
Duke	3	3	3	1	1	3	3	3	2	2	1	1	1	2	2	1	1	3
Florida St.	-	-	-	19	16	17	17	15	13	17	20	-	-	-	-	-	-	-
Fresno St.	13	13	12	16	18	-	-	-	-	-	-	-	-	-	-	-	-	-
Geo. Washington	-	-	-	-	-	-	-	-	-	-	-	-	22	17	24	-	-	-
Georgia	19	25	22	21	23	20	-	-	-	-	-	-	-	-	-	-	-	-
Georgia Tech	-	-	-	22	24	-	-	-	-	-	-	-	-	-	-	-	-	-
Hawaii	-	-	-	-	-	-	-	-	21	24	24	-	-	-	-	-	-	-
Illinois	-	-	-	-	-	-	-	-	-	-	-	-	-	-	23	22	18	22
Illinois St.	-	24	-	-	-	-	-	-	-	-	-	-	-	-	-	-	-	-
Indiana	17	23	21	-	-	-	-	-	-	-	-	25	-	-	-	-	-	-
Iowa	15	14	14	10	10	15	15	14	11	13	10	16	24	-	-	-	-	-
Kansas	2	2	2	2	3	2	2	2	4	3	3	5	3	4	4	4	3	2
Kentucky	8	9	8	7	4	4	4	6	6	6	7	7	8	7	8	7	7	5
Louisville	25	22	19	-	-	-	-	-	-	-	-	-	-	-	-	-	-	-
Marquette	-	-	-	-	-	-	-	25	20	23	-	-	-	-	-	-	-	-
Maryland	-	-	24	23	19	22	20	20	-	-	-	23	25	24	25	-	21	20
Massachusetts	-	-	-	-	-	-	-	-	-	-	-	-	23	20	18	20	-	-
Michigan	-	-	-	-	-	21	-	18	17	19	16	19	18	21	22	21	17	12
Michigan St.	-	-	-	-	-	-	-	-	-	-	-	22	16	13	14	10	12	16
Mississippi	23	21	17	14	21	18	16	16	14	11	13	12	17	18	15	13	10	13
Murray St.	-	-	-	-	-	-	-	-	-	-	-	-	-	-	-	-	-	25
New Mexico	11	11	10	8	14	14	14	12	12	T15	17	14	12	11	11	16	20	18
North Carolina	4	4	4	3	2	1	1	1	1	1	2	2	2	1	1	3	4	1
Oklahoma	20	19	18	-	-	-	-	-	-	-	-	-	-	-	-	-	-	-
Oklahoma St.	-	-	-	-	-	-	-	-	-	25	-	-	-	-	-	25	25	-
Princeton	-	-	-	25	22	19	18	17	15	12	11	11	11	10	9	9	8	8
Purdue	9	8	6	6	8	8	7	5	9	9	12	10	10	8	5	11	9	11
Rhode Island	21	20	23	-	-	-	22	24	23	20	22	21	-	25	-	-	-	-
South Carolina	7	6	5	5	5	6	10	11	16	14	14	13	13	15	13	14	15	14
Stanford	14	15	15	12	11	9	8	7	7	7	5	4	9	14	10	8	11	10
Syracuse	-	-	-	-	-	25	19	19	18	T15	15	20	19	23	21	23	22	21
Temple	24	18	20	20	20	16	24	-	-	-	-	-	-	-	-	24	24	24
Texas	22	-	-	-	-	-	-	-	-	-	-	-	-	-	-	-	-	-
TCU	-	-	-	-	-	24	25	-	-	-	-	-	-	22	19	15	13	15
UCLA	6	7	7	15	12	11	9	9	10	8	9	8	6	9	12	18	19	19
Utah	16	16	16	11	9	7	6	4	3	4	4	3	5	5	6	5	5	7
Wake Forest	-	-	-	24	25	23	-	-	-	-	-	-	-	-	-	-	-	-
West Virginia	-	-	-	-	-	-	23	22	25	21	23	17	15	16	20	19	23	-
Xavier	10	10	9	9	7	10	13	13	19	18	19	24	21	-	-	-	-	23

1998-99

		Nov.		December					January				February				March	
	PS	17	24	1	8	15	22	29	5	12	19	26	2	9	16	23	2	9
Arizona	18	12	11	13	8	8	8	6	11	7	9	13	10	10	8	7	13	12
Arkansas	19	19	21	19	23	20	19	20	18	24	22	21	23	-	-	-	22	17
Auburn	-	-	-	-	-	19	18	17	14	8	6	7	6	3	3	2	4	4
Charlotte	-	-	-	-	-	-	-	-	-	-	-	-	-	-	-	-	-	24
Col. of Charleston	-	-	-	-	-	-	-	-	-	-	-	-	22	20	18	17	16	16
Cincinnati	15	17	15	6	4	4	4	3	3	3	5	5	3	4	9	9	7	11
Clemson	-	24	22	24	17	16	16	14	20	25	-	-	-	-	-	-	-	-
Connecticut	2	2	2	1	1	1	1	1	1	1	1	1	1	2	2	4	3	3
Duke	1	1	1	4	3	2	2	2	2	2	2	2	2	1	1	1	1	1
Florida	-	-	-	-	-	-	-	-	-	-	-	25	-	23	23	19	21	23
Indiana	22	21	17	16	11	10	10	8	13	23	18	20	21	17	19	20	17	19
Iowa	-	-	-	-	-	25	21	21	19	12	14	16	14	19	20	18	20	21
Kansas	8	8	8	7	10	13	13	18	16	15	19	22	-	24	-	-	-	22
Kentucky	4	4	4	8	5	3	3	7	5	6	7	6	5	8	6	13	14	8
Louisville	-	-	-	-	-	-	-	-	-	-	24	-	-	-	-	-	-	-
Maryland	6	6	5	2	2	5	5	4	6	5	4	4	7	7	5	5	5	5
Massachusetts	24	23	-	-	-	-	-	-	-	-	-	-	-	-	-	-	-	-
Miami (Fla.)	-	-	-	-	-	-	-	-	-	-	25	23	25	16	15	11	9	10
Miami (Ohio)	-	-	24	22	-	-	-	-	-	-	-	-	-	-	25	-	-	-
Michigan St.	5	5	7	9	14	14	15	13	12	14	11	8	8	5	4	3	2	2
Minnesota	-	-	-	-	24	17	17	16	17	19	17	19	18	22	-	-	23	-
Missouri	-	-	-	-	-	-	-	-	-	-	-	-	24	-	22	-	24	-
New Mexico	20	20	20	17	12	11	11	15	15	16	12	18	17	25	24	21	25	25
North Carolina	11	10	9	3	7	7	7	9	10	9	10	10	12	12	14	14	15	13
Ohio St.	-	-	-	-	-	-	-	-	25	21	-	15	15	13	11	10	11	14
Oklahoma	-	-	-	-	-	24	23	-	-	-	-	-	-	-	-	-	-	-
Oklahoma St.	13	13	12	11	19	18	25	25	22	22	23	-	-	-	-	-	-	-
Pittsburgh	-	-	-	20	20	22	24	23	-	-	-	-	-	-	-	-	-	-
Purdue	16	15	14	14	9	8	9	11	7	13	16	14	18	21	17	23	-	-
Rhode Island	23	25	-	-	-	-	-	-	-	-	-	-	-	-	-	-	-	-
St. John's (N.Y.)	-	-	23	25	18	15	14	12	9	11	8	9	9	11	10	8	10	9
Stanford	3	3	3	5	6	6	6	5	4	4	3	3	4	6	7	6	6	7
Syracuse	20	22	19	12	13	21	22	22	21	18	20	17	16	18	21	24	-	-
Temple	7	7	6	10	16	-	-	-	-	-	-	-	-	-	-	24	-	-
Tennessee	9	18	25	-	21	-	-	-	-	-	-	-	-	-	-	-	18	20
Texas	-	-	-	-	-	-	-	-	-	-	-	-	-	-	-	22	-	-
TCU	25	-	-	-	-	-	-	24	24	20	21	24	-	-	-	-	-	-
UCLA	12	11	10	18	15	12	12	10	8	10	13	11	13	9	16	15	12	15
Utah	10	9	18	21	25	-	-	-	-	-	-	-	20	14	12	12	8	6
Washington	14	14	16	15	22	-	-	-	-	-	-	-	-	-	-	-	-	-
Wisconsin	-	-	-	-	-	23	20	19	23	17	15	12	11	15	13	16	19	18
Xavier	17	16	13	23	-	-	-	-	-	-	-	-	-	-	-	-	-	-

1999-2000

		Nov.			December				January				February					March	
	PS	16	23	30	7	14	21	28	4	11	18	25	1	8	15	22	29	7	14
Arizona	9	10	8	4	2	4	3	5	5	2	2	5	9	7	4	4	3	9	4
Auburn	4	3	2	7	8	6	7	4	4	4	4	7	10	9	12	11	19	-	24
Cincinnati	2	1	1	1	1	1	4	3	3	1	1	1	1	1	1	3	2	1	7
Connecticut	1	8	7	5	6	3	2	2	2	5	8	6	7	13	18	22	24	21	20
DePaul	20	20	18	22	20	19	24	24	23	21	23	-	-	-	-	-	-	-	-
Duke	10	18	16	17	14	11	10	9	8	6	5	3	3	3	3	2	4	3	1
Florida	8	7	6	11	9	9	8	6	6	10	9	10	12	12	11	9	8	11	13
Gonzaga	24	25	25	25	24	22	22	-	-	-	-	-	-	-	-	-	-	-	-
Illinois	16	17	15	16	22	20	15	20	19	22	-	-	-	-	-	-	25	25	21
Indiana	-	-	-	23	15	21	20	12	10	9	11	14	11	10	10	16	14	18	22

	PS	Nov. 16	23	30	December 7	14	21	28	January 4	11	18	25	February 1	8	15	22	29	March 7	14
Iowa	-	22	23	-	-	-	-	-	-	-	-	-	-	-	-	-	-	-	-
Iowa St.	-	-	-	-	-	-	-	-	-	-	-	-	20	17	14	17	10	7	6
Kansas	11	11	10	6	5	8	12	10	9	8	7	12	15	20	24	23	23	24	-
Kentucky	14	14	11	13	23	-	-	-	25	20	18	16	14	11	19	18	22	16	19
LSU	-	-	-	-	-	-	-	-	21	24	-	-	22	25	16	15	12	10	10
Louisville	-	-	-	-	-	-	-	-	-	25	-	-		-	-	-	-	-	-
Maryland	-	-	24	24	21	16	17	14	12	18	24	22	25	23	22	19	17	20	17
Miami (Fla.)	25	-	-	-	-	-	-	-	-	-	-	-	-	-	-	-	-	23	23
Michigan St.	3	2	3	8	4	5	5	8	11	11	10	9	8	6	6	5	7	5	2
North Carolina	6	5	4	2	7	7	6	13	14	13	21	-	-	-	-	-	-	-	-
North Caro. St.	-	-	-	-	-	25	-	-	-	-	21	-	-	-	-	-	-	-	
Ohio St.	5	4	12	15	13	12	16	15	13	17	13	8	5	5	7	6	6	4	8
Oklahoma	-	-	-	-	-	23	21	22	20	16	17	18	18	16	20	20	21	15	12
Oklahoma St.	22	23	21	21	17	14	13	11	16	14	12	15	13	14	8	10	13	17	14
Oregon	-	-	-	-	-	-	-	-	-	-	-	-	23	24	-	-	-	-	-
Purdue	23	24	22	19	25	24	-	-	-	-	-	-	-	-	25	21	20	22	25
St. John's (N.Y.)	18	15	-	-	-	-	-	-	-	-	19	25	-	-	-	-	18	19	9
Seton Hall	-	-	-	-	-	-	-	-	-	-	-	-	-	-	23	-	-	-	-
Southern Cal.	-	-	-	-	-	-	-	-	-	-	-	23	-	-	-	-	-	-	-
Stanford	13	9	9	3	3	2	1	1	1	3	3	2	2	2	2	1	1	2	3
Syracuse	17	13	14	14	12	10	9	7	7	7	6	4	4	4	9	13	9	12	16
Temple	7	6	5	10	19	17	19	17	-	23	-	23	21	19	15	8	5	6	5
Tennessee	19	19	17	18	16	13	11	16	15	12	16	11	6	8	5	7	11	8	11
Texas	21	21	20	9	10	15	14	18	17	15	14	17	16	18	17	14	16	13	15
Tulsa	-	-	-	-	-	-	-	25	22	19	15	13	17	15	13	12	15	14	18
UCLA	12	12	13	12	11	18	18	23	24	-	25	-	-	-	-	-	-	-	-
Utah	15	16	19	20	-	-	-	21	18	-	22	19	19	21	21	25	-	-	-
Vanderbilt	-	-	-	-	-	-	-	-	-	-	20	20	24	22	-	24	-	-	-
Wake Forest	-	-	-	-	18	25	23	19	-	-	-	-	-	-	-	-	-	-	-

2000-01

	PS	Nov. 14	21	28	December 5	12	19	26	January 2	9	16	23	30	February 6	13	20	27	March 6	13
Alabama	-	-	-	-	23	18	17	20	18	16	15	18	17	18	21	14	20	-	-
Arizona	1	1	1	5	5	7	10	12	16	21	17	12	7	11	8	8	9	8	5
Arkansas	15	15	24	25	21	25	25	-	-	-	-	-	-	-	-	-	-	-	-
Boston College	-	-	-	-	-	-	-	-	-	24	25	23	20	17	9	10	11	10	7
Cincinnati	18	17	16	22	18	17	22	19	25	-	-	-	-	-	-	-	-	-	-
Connecticut	14	13	12	16	15	11	11	10	10	13	15	24	-	-	-	-	-	-	-
Dayton	-	-	-	24	-	-	-	-	-	-	-	-	-	-	-	-	-	-	-
DePaul	21	22	21	-	-	-	-	-	-	-	-	-	-	-	-	-	-	-	-
Duke	2	2	2	1	1	1	1	3	3	2	2	2	2	3	3	4	2	3	1
Florida	11	11	11	10	8	8	7	5	5	8	7	14	13	8	11	7	6	5	8
Fresno St.	-	-	-	-	-	-	-	-	-	-	-	22	19	23	20	-	-	25	-
Georgetown	-	-	-	-	-	24	23	21	19	12	9	10	14	15	18	21	21	18	21
Georgia	-	-	-	-	-	-	-	-	-	-	-	-	25	-	-	-	-	-	-
Illinois	8	8	8	9	9	5	5	9	9	7	11	7	6	7	4	3	5	4	4
Indiana	-	-	-	-	-	-	-	-	-	-	-	-	-	-	-	-	-	-	20
Iowa	-	-	-	-	-	22	19	23	-	-	14	21	18	14	25	-	-	-	24
Iowa St.	25	-	-	-	25	-	-	25	23	18	23	17	15	12	7	6	8	7	10
Kansas	7	4	3	2	3	10	9	7	7	5	5	4	3	5	6	11	10	9	12
Kentucky	12	20	22	-	-	-	-	-	-	-	-	-	-	-	22	13	15	15	9
Maryland	5	6	6	13	19	20	20	18	17	14	12	8	9	13	17	20	16	11	11
Michigan St.	3	3	4	3	2	2	2	1	1	3	3	3	5	4	5	5	3	2	3
Mississippi	-	-	-	-	-	23	24	24	22	20	21	19	-	25	16	12	14	14	14
Missouri	-	-	-	-	-	-	-	-	-	-	20	-	-	-	-	-	-	-	-
No. Carolina	6	7	7	6	14	15	15	14	13	9	6	5	4	1	1	2	4	6	6
Notre Dame	15	16	14	11	10	21	21	22	21	25	-	-	23	20	14	18	13	19	19
Ohio St.	-	-	-	-	-	-	-	-	-	-	-	-	-	-	-	-	-	24	-
Oklahoma	22	21	19	14	20	19	18	17	15	22	22	-	24	21	13	16	17	16	13
Providence	-	-	-	-	-	-	-	-	-	-	-	-	-	-	-	25	-	-	-
St. John's (N.Y.)	24	23	19	24	-	-	-	-	-	-	-	-	-	-	-	-	-	-	
St. Joseph's	-	-	-	-	-	-	-	-	-	-	-	-	-	-	-	23	18	21	22
Seton Hall	10	10	10	8	7	9	8	11	11	15	18	16	22	-	-	-	-	-	-
Southern Cal	23	23	20	15	12	13	13	16	20	19	24	25	21	22	-	-	-	-	-
Stanford	4	5	5	4	4	3	3	2	2	1	1	1	1	2	2	1	1	1	2
Syracuse	-	-	-	20	13	12	12	15	14	11	8	11	12	9	10	17	19	17	17
Temple	-	-	-	17	-	-	-	-	-	-	-	-	-	-	-	-	-	-	-
Tennessee	9	9	9	7	6	4	4	6	6	4	4	6	8	10	15	22	-	-	-
Texas	-	-	-	-	-	-	-	-	24	23	-	20	-	-	-	-	24	20	18
UCLA	17	14	15	-	-	-	-	-	-	-	-	-	-	-	24	15	12	13	15
Utah	13	12	13	18	22	-	-	-	-	-	-	-	-	-	-	-	-	-	-
Virginia	24	25	25	21	16	14	14	8	8	10	13	13	11	6	12	9	7	12	16
Wake Forest	20	18	17	12	11	6	6	4	4	6	10	9	16	19	23	24	23	22	23
Wisconsin	19	19	18	23	17	16	16	13	12	17	19	15	10	16	19	19	22	23	25
Xavier	-	-	-	-	-	-	-	-	-	-	-	-	-	24	-	-	25	-	-

2001-02

	PS	Nov. 20	27	December 4	11	18	25	January 1	8	15	22	29	February 5	12	19	26	March 5	12
Alabama	24	22	21	16	22	23	21	18	14	16	14	7	5	7	5	6	8	8
Arizona	-	8	4	7	6	11	14	15	20	15	10	19	11	9	14	14	15	7
Ball St.	-	-	16	15	20	21	-	-	-	-	-	-	-	-	-	-	-	-
Boston College	17	17	15	13	11	10	11	11	16	22	-	-	-	-	-	-	-	-
Butler	-	-	-	-	-	-	23	20	24	-	-	-	-	-	-	-	-	-
California	-	-	-	-	-	-	-	-	-	-	-	-	-	-	-	21	25	-
Cincinnati	-	-	-	-	-	25	17	13	10	7	4	4	6	5	4	4	5	5
Connecticut	-	-	-	-	-	-	-	-	-	-	25	17	-	-	-	23	19	10
Duke	1	1	1	1	1	1	1	1	2	1	1	1	1	1	3	3	3	1
Florida	6	7	6	6	5	4	3	3	3	2	5	5	8	6	8	8	11	15
Fresno St.	-	23	24	21	-	-	-	-	-	-	-	-	-	-	-	-	-	-
Georgetown	14	16	18	19	18	16	20	24	-	-	-	-	-	-	-	-	-	-
Georgia	-	-	-	-	-	-	-	-	-	20	15	16	17	21	18	16	17	23
Gonzaga	-	-	-	-	25	24	22	22	18	13	16	11	9	8	7	7	6	6
Hawaii	-	-	-	-	-	-	-	-	-	-	-	-	-	-	-	-	-	25
Illinois	3	2	2	5	10	9	7	7	9	11	9	12	21	18	16	15	10	13
Indiana	22	20	-	-	21	-	-	-	-	25	-	-	-	22	23	25	23	-
Iowa	9	9	7	12	15	12	9	9	13	17	-	-	-	-	-	-	-	-
Kansas	7	4	8	4	4	3	2	2	1	4	2	2	2	2	1	1	1	2
Kentucky	4	10	13	11	9	7	6	6	8	12	8	10	7	10	12	11	12	16
Marquette	-	-	23	17	14	14	19	25	-	-	-	-	18	11	9	9	13	12
Maryland	2	6	5	3	3	2	8	8	4	3	3	3	3	3	2	2	2	4
Memphis	12	12	20	22	-	-	-	-	-	-	-	-	-	-	-	-	-	-
Miami (Fla.)	-	-	-	-	-	-	24	21	21	24	22	15	12	13	17	22	20	21
Michigan St.	15	13	22	24	23	17	13	19	25	-	-	-	-	-	-	-	-	-
Mississippi St.	-	-	-	-	-	-	-	-	22	-	-	-	-	-	-	-	-	17
Missouri	8	5	3	2	2	8	10	17	17	21	18	22	22	-	-	-	-	-
North Carolina	19	-	-	-	-	-	-	-	-	-	-	-	-	-	-	-	-	-
North Caro. St.	-	-	-	-	-	-	-	-	-	-	-	-	24	-	-	-	-	
Ohio St.	-	-	-	-	-	-	-	-	-	-	20	25	16	23	19	18	21	14
Oklahoma	25	-	-	-	24	22	12	10	5	5	6	6	4	4	6	5	4	3
Oklahoma St.	18	15	14	10	8	6	5	5	6	6	11	9	14	16	13	12	14	20
Oregon	-	-	-	-	-	-	-	-	-	23	19	-	13	17	15	13	9	11
Pittsburgh	-	-	-	-	-	-	-	-	23	-	-	21	-	14	11	10	7	9
St. Joseph's	10	19	19	18	16	15	-	-	-	-	-	-	-	-	-	-	-	-
Southern Cal	20	24	-	-	-	-	-	-	-	18	23	23	25	25	20	19	22	18
Stanford	13	14	11	14	12	13	16	12	14	19	17	18	20	12	10	17	16	24
Syracuse	21	18	12	9	13	18	18	16	12	8	12	14	23	-	-	-	-	-
Temple	16	25	-	-	-	-	-	-	-	-	-	-	-	-	-	-	-	-
Texas	23	-	-	-	-	-	-	-	-	-	24	-	-	-	-	-	-	-
Texas Tech	-	-	-	-	-	-	-	-	-	-	-	20	24	-	-	-	-	-
UCLA	5	3	10	20	17	19	15	14	11	9	13	13	15	20	25	-	-	-
Virginia	11	11	9	8	7	5	4	4	7	10	7	8	10	15	22	-	-	-
Wake Forest	-	-	25	23	19	20	25	23	19	14	21	24	19	19	20	24	-	-
Western Ky.	-	21	17	25	-	-	-	-	-	-	-	-	-	-	24	20	18	19
Xavier	-	-	-	-	-	-	-	-	-	-	-	-	-	-	-	-	24	22

2002-03

	PS	Nov. 19	26	December 3	10	17	24	31	January 7	14	21	28	February 4	11	18	25	March 4	11	18
Alabama	8	4	4	3	2	2	1	1	4	9	15	23	22	-	-	-	-	-	-
Arizona	1	1	1	1	1	1	4	4	2	2	1	1	2	1	1	1	1	1	2
Auburn	-	-	-	-	-	-	-	-	-	-	24	-	-	-	-	-	-	-	-
California	-	-	-	-	-	-	-	-	-	-	25	20	-	22	18	23	22	24	-
Col. of Charleston	-	-	-	-	25	-	-	-	-	-	-	-	-	-	-	-	-	-	-
Cincinnati	23	23	21	-	23	-	-	-	-	-	-	-	-	-	-	-	-	-	-
Connecticut	15	14	12	11	9	8	6	5	3	6	11	14	18	23	-	-	-	-	23
Creighton	-	-	-	-	-	20	18	15	16	13	10	16	13	12	17	17	19	19	15
Dayton	-	-	-	-	-	-	-	-	-	-	-	-	-	-	25	25	21	22	16
Duke	6	6	6	4	3	3	3	3	1	1	3	5	9	8	8	6	10	12	7
Florida	7	8	7	8	14	13	12	12	11	6	5	4	1	4	7	4	3	7	10
Georgia	16	18	17	-	-	-	-	-	20	20	19	15	17	20	22	21	25	21	25
Gonzaga	22	21	20	-	-	-	-	-	-	-	-	-	-	-	-	-	-	-	-
Illinois	-	-	-	25	15	12	7	11	10	8	18	13	16	14	20	18	14	13	11
Indiana	21	22	19	10	7	6	10	17	15	18	14	19	-	-	-	-	-	-	-
Kansas	2	2	2	14	20	19	19	18	14	12	6	12	12	9	6	7	6	4	6
Kentucky	17	17	15	18	12	18	14	20	18	16	8	7	6	3	2	2	2	2	1
LSU	-	-	-	-	-	-	24	21	-	23	-	-	-	-	-	-	-	-	-
Louisville	-	-	-	-	-	-	-	24	19	15	9	8	5	2	4	11	15	20	14
Marquette	18	16	13	13	16	14	13	13	24	21	20	18	15	11	11	10	8	8	9
Maryland	13	12	11	9	18	24	23	22	21	17	12	10	8	16	13	14	13	14	17
Memphis	-	-	-	-	-	-	-	-	-	-	-	-	-	-	-	24	18	16	19
Michigan St.	9	9	9	21	21	15	15	14	25	-	-	-	-	-	-	-	-	-	-
Minnesota	24	24	24	20	-	25	-	-	-	-	-	-	-	-	-	-	-	-	-
Mississippi St.	12	12	23	24	24	16	16	8	7	14	22	21	23	19	19	20	23	-	20
Missouri	19	20	18	15	11	11	17	16	13	11	21	25	21	21	-	-	-	-	24
North Carolina	-	-	-	12	22	23	22	-	-	-	-	-	-	-	-	-	-	-	-
Notre Dame	-	-	-	-	10	9	8	6	5	10	16	11	10	10	12	9	16	17	22
Oklahoma	3	7	8	6	6	7	5	10	9	5	7	6	7	5	5	3	5	6	3
Oklahoma St.	-	-	-	-	-	-	-	-	-	24	13	9	11	13	16	16	20	23	-

		Nov.		December					January				February				March		
	PS	19	26	3	10	17	24	31	7	14	21	28	4	11	18	25	4	11	18
Oregon	11	10	10	7	5	5	11	9	12	22	23	22	-	-	-	-	-	-	-
Pittsburgh	5	5	5	5	4	4	2	2	6	3	2	2	4	7	9	8	7	5	4
Purdue	-	-	-	-	-	-	-	-	-	-	-	-	24	-	24	-	-	-	-
St. Joseph's	-	-	-	-	-	-	-	-	-	-	-	-	-	25	-	-	-	25	-
Stanford	-	-	-	17	19	17	-	-	-	-	-	-	25	24	21	19	17	15	18
Syracuse	-	-	-	-	-	-	-	-	-	25	-	24	19	17	15	15	12	11	13
Texas	4	3	3	2	8	10	9	7	8	4	4	3	3	6	3	5	4	3	5
Texas Tech	-	-	-	-	-	-	-	25	23	-	-	-	-	-	-	-	-	-	-
Tulsa	25	25	22	19	17	22	20	-	-	-	-	-	-	-	-	-	-	-	-
UCLA	14	15	14	-	-	-	-	-	-	-	-	-	-	-	-	-	-	-	-
Utah	-	-	-	-	-	-	-	-	-	-	-	-	-	-	23	22	-	-	-
Virginia	-	-	-	22	-	-	-	-	-	-	-	-	-	-	-	-	-	-	-
Wake Forest	-	-	-	-	-	-	25	23	17	19	17	17	14	15	10	12	9	9	8
Western Ky.	20	19	-	-	-	-	-	-	-	-	-	-	-	-	-	-	-	-	-
Wisconsin	-	-	25	23	-	-	-	-	-	-	-	-	-	-	-	-	24	18	21
Xavier	10	11	16	16	13	21	21	19	21	-	-	-	20	18	14	13	11	10	12

2003-04

		Nov.	December					January				February				March		
	PS	25	2	9	16	23	31	6	13	20	27	3	10	17	24	2	9	16
Air Force	-	-	-	-	-	-	-	-	-	-	-	-	-	-	-	-	25	-
Arizona	4	4	7	9	7	5	4	3	7	14	9	12	16	14	17	22	21	22
Boston College	-	-	-	-	-	-	-	-	-	-	-	-	-	-	-	-	-	25
Cincinnati	18	19	19	18	16	14	12	11	10	6	8	10	13	17	15	13	13	11
Connecticut	1	1	3	2	1	1	1	1	1	4	6	5	5	8	8	7	9	7
Creighton	-	-	-	-	-	-	-	-	24	-	-	-	-	-	-	-	-	-
Dayton	-	-	-	25	24	23	-	-	-	-	-	-	-	-	-	-	-	-
Duke	2	2	6	4	3	3	2	2	2	1	1	1	1	3	5	3	5	6
Florida	8	8	2	1	15	13	14	14	15	17	22	21	22	-	-	-	-	-
Georgia Tech	-	-	13	10	5	4	3	8	12	11	14	15	15	18	18	19	14	14
Gonzaga	10	16	17	17	13	15	16	16	16	15	10	8	7	6	4	4	3	3
Illinois	13	12	11	14	21	21	20	19	25	-	-	-	-	-	23	18	12	13
Iowa	-	-	-	24	-	-	-	-	-	-	-	-	-	-	-	-	-	-
Kansas	6	6	1	5	6	12	13	13	14	12	15	20	12	21	20	21	18	16
Kentucky	11	10	9	8	2	2	8	7	5	9	5	9	8	9	9	9	8	2
LSU	-	-	-	-	-	-	-	-	-	-	-	-	-	24	-	-	-	-
Louisville	16	17	-	-	20	20	11	10	8	5	4	6	9	10	21	25	-	-
Marquette	23	23	24	22	23	-	25	23	21	-	-	-	-	-	-	-	-	-
Maryland	-	-	-	-	25	24	-	-	-	-	-	-	-	-	-	-	-	19
Memphis	-	-	-	-	-	-	-	-	-	-	-	-	-	23	19	20	23	24
Michigan St.	3	3	5	21	-	-	-	-	-	-	-	-	-	-	-	-	-	-
Mississippi St.	-	-	-	-	-	-	24	22	20	19	11	7	6	4	7	5	4	8
Missouri	5	5	4	3	10	11	23	-	-	-	-	-	-	-	-	-	-	-
North Carolina	9	9	10	7	4	9	9	12	9	7	12	17	14	16	12	14	16	18
North Caro. St.	24	25	-	-	-	-	-	-	-	-	-	-	21	13	14	16	17	15
Notre Dame	21	21	23	-	-	-	-	-	-	-	-	-	-	-	-	-	-	-
Oklahoma	14	14	14	11	8	7	7	6	11	20	25	22	-	-	-	-	-	-
Oklahoma St.	25	24	25	-	-	-	-	-	-	24	18	13	10	7	6	8	7	4
Pittsburgh	22	22	22	20	18	16	15	15	13	8	7	4	4	5	3	6	6	9
Providence	-	-	-	-	-	-	-	25	-	-	23	23	24	19	13	12	20	21
Purdue	-	-	20	16	17	22	21	24	-	23	21	-	-	-	-	-	-	-
St. Joseph's	17	13	12	12	11	10	10	9	6	3	3	3	3	2	2	2	1	5
South Carolina	-	-	-	-	-	-	-	-	-	25	24	25	25	25	-	-	-	23
Southern Ill.	-	-	-	-	-	-	-	-	-	-	-	-	23	20	16	15	24	-
Stanford	19	20	21	13	9	6	5	4	3	2	2	2	2	1	1	1	2	1
Syracuse	7	7	16	19	19	17	17	17	17	13	20	18	-	-	-	24	19	20
Texas	12	11	8	6	11	18	19	18	18	16	16	11	11	11	10	10	11	12
Texas Tech	-	-	-	-	-	-	-	-	22	18	13	19	18	22	25	-	-	-
Utah St.	-	-	-	-	-	-	-	-	-	-	-	24	19	-	24	23	22	25
Vanderbilt	-	-	-	-	-	25	22	20	23	22	-	-	-	-	-	-	-	-
Wake Forest	20	18	18	15	14	8	6	5	4	10	19	16	20	15	11	11	15	17
Wisconsin	15	15	15	23	22	19	18	21	19	21	17	14	17	12	22	17	10	10

2004-05

		Nov.			December				January				February				March		
	PS	16	23	30	7	14	21	28	4	11	18	25	1	8	15	22	1	8	15
Alabama	18	18	19	22	18	17	19	18	19	23	22	14	11	17	16	16	21	20	21
Arizona	10	10	18	21	15	15	14	14	13	17	13	11	14	12	10	9	11	8	9
Boston College	-	-	-	-	-	-	-	-	25	13	9	8	5	4	6	3	5	7	14
Charlotte	-	-	-	-	-	-	-	-	-	-	-	-	-	-	23	21	18	25	-
Cincinnati	-	-	-	-	-	25	22	22	23	18	20	21	18	21	24	24	22	21	23
Connecticut	8	8	7	7	7	11	11	11	10	12	16	19	23	19	18	17	15	12	13
Duke	11	11	9	10	9	7	6	6	5	5	4	2	4	7	7	7	6	5	3
Florida	23	23	23	19	-	-	-	-	-	-	-	-	-	-	-	-	-	-	16
Geo. Washington	-	-	-	-	21	19	20	20	24	21	-	-	-	-	-	-	-	-	-
Georgia Tech	3	3	3	4	3	3	9	9	9	8	12	22	25	-	-	-	-	-	25
Gonzaga	25	25	24	-	25	22	13	12	11	16	11	17	17	14	13	12	12	11	10
Illinois	5	6	5	5	1	1	1	1	1	1	1	1	1	1	1	1	1	1	1
Iowa	-	-	-	23	17	16	17	16	14	24	23	23	-	-	-	-	-	-	-
Kansas	1	1	2	2	2	2	2	2	2	2	2	6	3	3	2	8	7	9	12
Kentucky	9	9	8	8	10	9	8	8	8	9	8	7	6	5	3	5	3	4	7
Louisville	14	14	12	17	13	13	18	19	17	19	14	12	9	9	12	11	9	6	4
Marquette	-	-	-	-	-	-	-	-	-	22	25	-	-	-	-	-	-	-	-
Maryland	15	15	13	12	23	23	24	24	22	-	-	-	22	-	22	-	-	-	-
Memphis	24	24	25	-	-	-	-	-	-	-	-	-	-	-	-	-	-	-	-
Michigan St.	13	13	10	11	20	21	23	23	20	15	19	15	12	13	11	10	14	13	15
Mississippi St.	12	12	14	15	22	20	21	21	18	11	17	24	-	-	-	-	-	-	-
Nevada	-	-	-	-	-	-	-	-	-	-	-	-	-	-	-	25	25	24	-
North Carolina	4	4	11	9	8	5	4	4	3	3	6	3	2	2	4	2	2	2	2
North Caro. St.	19	19	17	16	12	12	16	17	-	-	-	-	-	-	-	-	-	-	-
Notre Dame	20	20	21	20	-	-	-	-	-	-	-	-	-	-	-	-	-	-	-
Oklahoma	-	-	-	-	-	-	-	-	-	25	18	13	15	16	21	22	20	17	17
Oklahoma St.	7	7	6	6	5	4	3	3	7	6	5	9	10	10	8	4	8	10	6
Pacific	-	-	-	-	-	-	-	-	-	-	-	-	-	24	19	19	17	18	22
Pittsburgh	17	17	16	13	11	10	10	10	16	20	21	20	16	18	17	18	24	22	-
Syracuse	6	5	4	3	4	8	7	7	6	7	7	4	8	8	9	15	13	16	11
Texas	16	16	15	18	14	14	15	15	15	10	15	16	20	23	-	-	-	-	-
Texas Tech	-	-	-	-	-	-	-	-	-	-	-	-	-	25	-	-	-	-	24
Utah	-	-	-	-	-	-	-	-	-	-	-	25	21	15	14	13	16	15	18
Villanova	-	-	-	-	-	-	-	-	-	-	-	-	24	22	25	23	19	19	19
Virginia	-	-	-	24	19	24	25	25	-	-	-	-	-	-	-	-	-	-	-
Wake Forest	2	2	1	1	6	6	5	5	4	4	3	5	7	6	5	6	4	3	5
Washington	22	22	22	14	16	18	12	13	12	14	10	10	13	11	15	14	10	14	8
West Virginia	-	-	-	-	-	-	-	-	21	-	-	-	-	-	-	-	-	-	-
Wisconsin	21	21	20	25	24	-	-	-	-	-	24	18	19	20	20	20	23	23	20

2005-06

	November				December				January					February				Mar.	
	PS	15	22	29	6	13	20	27	3	10	17	24	31	7	14	21	28	7	14
Alabama	15	15	19	21	22	-	-	-	-	-	-	-	-	-	-	-	-	-	-
UAB	-	-	-	-	-	-	-	-	-	-	-	-	-	-	-	-	-	24	25
Arizona	10	10	9	15	24	24	-	-	21	24	-	-	-	-	-	-	-	-	-
Boston College	11	11	10	8	6	13	14	13	11	15	21	20	15	17	13	11	12	11	7
Bucknell	-	-	-	-	-	-	-	-	-	-	-	-	-	-	24	-	-	-	-
Cincinnati	-	-	-	-	-	-	-	-	-	25	-	-	-	-	-	-	-	-	-
Connecticut	3	3	3	3	3	2	2	2	2	4	3	1	1	1	1	3	2	1	2
Duke	1	1	1	1	1	1	1	1	1	1	1	2	2	2	2	1	1	3	1
Florida	-	-	14	11	10	7	5	5	5	2	2	5	8	7	10	12	17	16	11
Geo. Washington	21	21	21	19	19	15	13	12	20	17	16	14	10	8	7	6	7	6	14
Georgetown	-	-	-	-	-	-	-	-	-	-	-	21	17	15	17	23	20	23	23
Gonzaga	8	9	8	6	9	10	8	8	8	6	6	7	5	5	5	5	5	4	5
Houston	-	-	-	-	-	25	-	-	-	-	-	-	-	-	-	-	-	-	-
Illinois	17	17	15	12	11	9	6	6	6	7	7	8	6	10	14	8	10	9	13
Indiana	24	23	20	17	18	18	18	17	16	9	13	13	22	24	-	-	-	-	-
Iowa	20	20	18	14	12	22	25	-	-	-	23	-	23	18	18	20	23	20	15
Iowa St.	25	25	-	-	-	-	-	-	-	-	-	-	-	-	-	-	-	-	-
Kansas	-	-	-	-	-	-	-	-	-	-	-	-	-	-	22	16	18	17	12
Kentucky	9	8	7	10	15	23	19	18	19	-	-	-	-	-	-	-	-	-	-
LSU	-	-	-	25	-	-	-	-	-	-	-	-	24	-	25	24	21	18	19
Louisville	7	7	6	7	5	4	11	10	9	10	17	22	-	-	-	-	-	-	-
Maryland	23	24	23	23	21	17	16	16	14	23	22	18	-	-	-	-	-	-	-
Memphis	12	12	11	9	7	5	4	4	4	5	4	3	3	3	3	4	3	5	4
Michigan	-	-	-	-	-	-	-	-	-	-	-	-	21	22	-	-	-	-	-
Michigan St.	4	4	12	13	14	12	10	9	7	14	11	11	12	12	16	18	25	-	-
Nevada	22	22	22	20	17	20	20	20	-	-	-	-	-	-	-	25	24	21	20
North Carolina	-	-	-	-	23	19	17	23	25	20	24	-	-	23	23	21	13	10	10
North Caro. St.	-	-	-	24	25	21	21	19	13	18	14	15	18	16	21	15	22	25	-
UNI	-	-	-	-	-	-	-	-	-	-	-	-	25	25	-	25	-	-	-
Ohio St.	-	-	-	-	-	-	24	21	18	19	19	16	20	19	12	13	9	7	6
Oklahoma	6	6	5	5	8	8	7	14	12	22	25	24	19	20	19	22	19	22	24
Pittsburgh	-	-	-	-	-	-	-	-	22	12	9	12	9	14	9	9	8	15	16
Stanford	13	13	-	-	-	-	-	-	-	-	-	-	-	-	-	-	-	-	-
Syracuse	16	16	17	-	-	-	-	-	-	-	20	25	-	-	-	-	-	-	21
Tennessee	-	-	-	-	-	-	23	-	-	-	-	19	13	11	8	10	11	14	18
Texas	2	2	2	2	2	6	15	15	15	8	5	4	7	6	6	7	6	8	9
UCLA	19	18	16	16	16	14	12	11	17	11	18	17	14	13	15	19	15	13	7
Villanova	5	5	4	4	4	3	3	3	3	3	8	6	4	4	4	2	4	2	3
Wake Forest	18	19	24	22	20	16	22	22	23	-	-	-	-	-	-	-	-	-	-
Washington	-	-	25	18	13	11	9	7	10	13	10	10	16	21	20	17	14	12	17
West Virginia	14	14	13	-	-	-	-	25	24	16	12	9	11	9	11	14	16	19	22
Wisconsin	-	-	-	-	-	-	-	24	-	21	15	23	-	-	-	-	-	-	-

2006-07

	November				December				January					February				Mar.	
	PS	14	21	28	5	12	19	26	2	9	16	23	30	6	13	20	27	6	13
Air Force	-	-	-	-	-	24	24	23	20	18	13	16	17	15	17	14	25	-	-
Alabama	11	10	8	6	4	9	10	8	8	14	10	12	19	18	25	25	-	-	-
Arizona	10	15	15	16	14	10	9	7	7	10	11	17	20	24	19	-	-	-	-
Boston College	15	14	23	-	-	-	-	-	-	-	-	-	-	-	21	-	-	-	-
BYU	-	-	-	-	-	-	-	-	-	-	-	-	-	-	-	21	-	23	24
Butler	-	-	-	19	15	18	16	15	13	12	18	14	13	10	13	15	18	19	21
Clemson	-	-	-	-	-	-	-	25	23	17	19	19	25	-	-	-	-	-	-
Connecticut	18	21	18	20	19	14	14	12	18	24	-	-	-	-	-	-	-	-	-
Creighton	19	20	-	-	-	-	-	-	-	-	-	-	-	-	-	-	-	-	-
Duke	12	11	9	11	7	6	6	5	5	11	14	10	8	16	-	18	14	21	-

	November PS	14	21	28	December 5	12	19	26	January 2	9	16	23	30	February 6	13	20	27	Mar. 6	13
Florida	1	1	1	4	7	5	5	3	3	2	1	1	1	1	1	3	5	6	3
Georgetown	8	8	14	18	-	-	-	-	-	-	-	-	-	22	14	12	9	9	8
Georgia Tech	23	23	19	21	25	-	-	-	-	-	-	-	-	-	-	-	-	-	-
Gonzaga	-	-	-	22	18	16	22	-	-	-	-	-	-	-	-	-	-	-	-
Indiana	-	-	-	-	-	-	-	-	23	-	24	-	-	-	-	-	-	-	-
Kansas	3	3	10	5	12	11	11	9	9	6	5	8	6	9	9	6	3	2	2
Kentucky	22	22	20	-	-	-	-	-	-	-	25	-	-	20	20	-	-	-	-
LSU	5	7	6	10	9	12	12	17	14	13	16	21	-	-	-	-	-	-	-
Louisville	-	-	-	-	-	-	-	-	-	-	-	-	-	-	-	20	16	12	16
Marquette	16	16	13	8	17	20	19	18	15	-	24	15	14	11	12	16	20	18	20
Maryland	-	-	25	23	23	-	-	-	-	-	-	-	-	-	-	-	24	17	18
Memphis	14	13	12	14	16	19	18	22	22	20	17	11	11	8	8	7	6	5	5
Nevada	24	24	21	24	20	25	25	24	21	19	15	18	15	12	11	11	10	10	15
UNLV	-	-	-	-	-	-	-	-	-	-	-	-	-	-	-	-	-	25	19
North Carolina	2	2	2	7	3	3	2	2	2	1	4	4	3	5	4	5	8	8	4
Notre Dame	-	-	-	-	21	20	19	17	22	20	22	21	-	-	-	-	22	20	17
Ohio St.	7	5	4	3	5	4	3	6	6	5	7	5	4	3	2	2	1	1	1
Oklahoma St.	-	-	22	15	15	13	12	9	12	13	12	17	18	-	-	-	-	-	-
Oregon	-	-	-	-	22	21	20	16	15	9	7	9	13	15	23	17	16	10	-
Pittsburgh	4	4	3	2	2	2	7	10	10	7	6	9	7	7	7	10	12	13	12
Southern Cal	-	-	-	-	-	-	-	-	-	-	-	25	-	19	22	-	23	-	23
Southern Ill.	-	-	-	-	-	-	-	-	-	-	-	-	-	21	16	13	11	14	14
Syracuse	20	18	17	15	21	23	23	-	-	-	-	-	-	-	-	-	-	-	-
Stanford	-	-	-	-	-	-	-	-	-	-	23	25	-	-	-	-	-	22	25
Tennessee	25	25	22	-	-	-	-	21	19	16	22	-	-	-	-	-	-	22	25
Texas	21	19	-	-	-	-	-	-	-	25	21	-	22	-	19	15	15	15	11
Texas A&M	13	12	11	9	6	13	13	11	11	8	8	6	10	6	6	8	7	7	9
UCLA	6	6	5	1	1	1	1	1	1	4	3	3	5	2	5	4	2	4	7
Vanderbilt	-	-	-	-	-	-	-	-	-	-	-	24	23	-	17	19	-	-	-
Virginia	-	-	-	25	-	-	-	-	-	-	-	-	-	-	24	-	-	-	-
Virginia Tech	-	-	-	-	-	-	-	-	-	-	23	24	16	-	-	21	-	-	-
Washington	17	17	16	13	13	17	17	14	24	-	-	-	-	-	-	-	-	-	-
Washington St.	-	-	-	-	-	-	-	-	-	23	-	20	18	14	10	9	13	11	13
West Virginia	-	-	-	-	-	-	-	-	25	21	-	-	-	23	22	-	-	-	-
Wichita St.	-	-	24	17	10	8	18	16	-	-	-	-	-	-	-	-	-	-	-
Winthrop	-	-	-	-	-	-	-	-	-	-	-	-	-	-	-	-	-	24	22
Wisconsin	9	9	7	12	11	7	4	4	4	3	2	2	2	4	3	1	4	3	6
Xavier	-	-	-	-	24	-	-	-	-	-	-	-	-	-	-	-	-	-	-

(Note: AP does not do a post-tournament poll.)

2007-08

	November PS	13	20	27	December 4	11	18	25	January 1	8	15	22	29	February 5	12	19	26	March 4	11	18
Arizona	17	17	-	-	22	21	19	17	21	-	-	-	-	-	-	-	-	-	-	-
Arizona St.	-	-	-	-	-	-	-	-	-	-	22	24	-	-	-	-	-	-	-	-
Arkansas	19	18	-	-	-	-	-	-	-	-	-	-	-	-	-	-	-	-	-	-
Baylor	-	-	-	-	-	-	-	-	-	-	25	25	-	-	-	-	-	-	-	-
BYU	-	-	-	21	20	25	21	20	-	-	-	-	-	-	-	-	-	-	24	-
Butler	-	25	22	16	13	18	16	16	16	14	12	15	12	10	9	8	14	14	12	11
Clemson	-	-	24	18	18	15	15	21	19	18	24	-	-	-	-	-	-	24	-	22
Connecticut	-	-	-	-	-	-	-	-	-	-	-	-	-	19	17	13	15	13	15	16
Davidson	-	-	-	-	-	-	-	-	-	-	-	-	-	-	-	-	-	25	23	23
Dayton	-	-	-	-	-	-	-	20	17	14	16	-	-	-	-	-	-	-	-	-
Drake	-	-	-	-	-	-	-	-	-	-	-	22	16	15	14	16	20	20	16	14
Duke	13	13	13	7	6	6	6	10	9	9	7	4	3	2	2	5	7	6	7	9
Florida	-	-	25	-	-	-	-	-	20	-	-	-	-	-	-	-	-	-	-	-
Georgetown	5	5	5	5	5	5	5	8	7	7	5	9	6	6	8	12	11	11	9	8
Gonzaga	14	14	14	19	17	19	18	-	-	-	-	-	-	-	-	-	24	22	20	24
Indiana	9	8	8	15	15	13	13	13	11	10	9	7	11	14	13	15	12	18	22	-
Kansas	4	4	4	3	3	3	3	3	3	2	2	4	3	4	6	5	5	4	4	3
Kansas St.	25	22	18	25	-	-	-	-	-	22	20	18	24	-	-	23	-	-	-	-
Kent St.	-	-	-	-	-	-	-	-	-	-	-	-	-	-	-	23	-	-	-	-
Kentucky	20	-	-	-	-	-	-	-	-	-	-	-	-	-	-	-	-	-	-	-
Louisville	6	6	6	12	14	22	-	-	-	-	-	-	-	-	23	18	13	12	13	13
Marquette	11	10	11	13	11	10	10	12	10	15	13	21	17	16	-	25	21	21	25	25
Memphis	3	3	3	3	2	2	2	2	2	2	1	1	1	1	1	2	2	2	2	2
Miami (Fla.)	-	-	-	-	-	-	22	19	-	25	21	-	-	-	-	-	-	-	-	-
Michigan St.	8	12	10	10	9	9	9	7	6	6	11	10	8	11	10	19	19	17	19	18
Mississippi	-	-	-	-	-	-	-	-	-	-	-	22	18	16	18	17	24	-	-	-
North Carolina	1	1	1	1	1	1	1	1	1	1	5	4	3	5	3	3	3	1	1	1
North Caro. St.	21	21	-	24	-	-	-	-	-	-	-	-	-	-	-	-	-	-	-	-
Notre Dame	-	-	-	-	-	-	-	-	-	-	-	-	-	22	20	21	17	19	14	15
Oregon	12	11	12	17	19	16	23	-	-	-	-	-	-	-	-	-	-	-	-	-
Pittsburgh	22	19	17	14	12	11	11	6	13	20	15	13	18	21	22	-	-	-	-	17
Purdue	-	-	-	-	-	-	-	-	-	-	-	-	-	24	19	14	16	15	17	20
St. Mary's (Cal.)	-	-	-	-	-	-	-	-	24	-	-	-	-	-	-	21	25	25	23	25
Southern Cal	18	-	22	24	-	25	24	22	-	-	-	-	-	-	-	-	-	-	-	-
Southern Ill.	24	23	19	-	-	-	-	-	-	-	-	-	-	-	-	-	-	-	-	-
Stanford	23	20	-	-	-	-	-	-	24	23	-	20	14	9	7	9	8	7	11	10
Syracuse	-	21	-	-	-	-	-	-	-	-	-	-	-	-	-	-	-	-	-	-
Tennessee	7	7	7	11	10	12	12	11	8	8	6	3	7	7	4	2	1	4	4	5
Texas	15	16	15	8	4	4	4	9	14	12	19	12	10	12	11	7	5	9	6	7
Texas A&M	16	15	16	9	16	14	14	14	12	11	10	18	23	18	16	22	-	-	-	-
UCLA	2	2	2	7	8	8	5	5	5	4	8	5	5	6	6	4	3	3	3	3
Vanderbilt	-	-	-	-	-	23	20	17	15	15	16	14	19	23	24	20	18	16	18	19
Villanova	-	24	20	-	25	23	20	18	17	19	25	18	-	-	-	-	-	-	-	-
Virginia	-	23	-	-	-	-	-	-	-	-	-	-	-	-	-	-	-	-	-	-
Washington St.	10	9	9	6	8	7	7	4	4	4	8	6	9	17	21	17	22	23	21	21
West Virginia	-	-	-	-	-	-	-	-	-	-	-	24	23	-	-	-	-	-	-	-
Wisconsin	-	-	20	-	-	-	-	-	25	21	17	11	13	8	15	11	10	10	8	6
Xavier	-	-	-	-	23	21	17	-	-	24	20	23	15	13	12	10	9	8	10	12

DIVISION I

Final Season Polls

Final Regular-Season Polls

The Helms Foundation of Los Angeles selected the national college men's basketball champions from 1942-82 and researched retroactive picks from 1901-41. The Helms winners are listed in this section to the time The Associated Press (AP) poll started in 1949. The AP is the writers' poll, while the UPI and USA Today/CNN and USA Today/NABC polls are the coaches' polls.

HELMS

1901 Yale	1913 Navy	1925 Princeton	1937 Stanford
1902 Minnesota	1914 Wisconsin	1926 Syracuse	1938 Temple
1903 Yale	1915 Illinois	1927 Notre Dame	1939 Long Island
1904 Columbia	1916 Wisconsin	1928 Pittsburgh	1940 Southern Cal.
1905 Columbia	1917 Washington St.	1929 Montana St.	1941 Wisconsin
1906 Dartmouth	1918 Syracuse	1930 Pittsburgh	1942 Stanford
1907 Chicago	1919 Minnesota	1931 Northwestern	1943 Wyoming
1908 Chicago	1920 Penn	1932 Purdue	1944 Army
1909 Chicago	1921 Penn	1933 Kentucky	1945 Oklahoma St.
1910 Columbia	1922 Kansas	1934 Wyoming	1946 Oklahoma St.
1911 St. John's (N.Y.)	1923 Kansas	1935 New York U.	1947 Holy Cross
1912 Wisconsin	1924 North Carolina	1936 Notre Dame	1948 Kentucky

1949

AP
1. Kentucky
2. Oklahoma St.
3. St. Louis
4. Illinois
5. Western Ky.
6. Minnesota
7. Bradley
8. San Francisco
9. Tulane
10. Bowling Green
11. Yale
12. Utah
13. North Carolina St.
14. Villanova
15. UCLA
16. Loyola (Ill.)
17. Wyoming
18. Butler
19. Hamline
20. Ohio St.

1950

AP
1. Bradley
2. Ohio St.
3. Kentucky
4. Holy Cross
5. North Carolina St.
6. Duquesne
7. UCLA
8. Western Ky.
9. St. John's (N.Y.)
10. La Salle
11. Villanova
12. San Francisco
13. Long Island
14. Kansas St.
15. Arizona
16. Wisconsin
17. San Jose St.
18. Washington St.
19. Kansas
20. Indiana

1951

AP
1. Kentucky
2. Oklahoma St.
3. Columbia
4. Kansas St.
5. Illinois
6. Bradley
7. Indiana
8. North Carolina St.
9. St. John's (N.Y.)
10. St. Louis
11. BYU
12. Arizona
13. Dayton
14. Toledo
15. Washington
16. Murray St.
17. Cincinnati
18. Siena
19. Southern California
20. Villanova

UPI
1. Kentucky
2. Oklahoma St.
3. Kansas St.
4. Illinois
5. Columbia
6. Bradley
7. North Carolina St.
8. Indiana
9. St. John's (N.Y.)
10. BYU
11. St. Louis
12. Arizona
13. Washington
14. Beloit
14. Villanova
16. UCLA
17. Cincinnati
18. Dayton
18. St. Bonaventure
18. Seton Hall
18. Texas A&M

1952

AP
1. Kentucky
2. Illinois
3. Kansas St.
4. Duquesne
5. St. Louis
6. Washington
7. Iowa
8. Kansas
9. West Virginia
10. St. John's (N.Y.)
11. Dayton
12. Duke
13. Holy Cross
14. Seton Hall
15. St. Bonaventure
16. Wyoming
17. Louisville
18. Seattle
19. UCLA
20. Texas St.

UPI
1. Kentucky
2. Illinois
3. Kansas
4. Duquesne
5. Washington
6. Kansas St.
7. St. Louis
8. Iowa
9. St. John's (N.Y.)
10. Wyoming
11. St. Bonaventure
12. Seton Hall
13. TCU
14. West Virginia
15. Holy Cross
16. Western Ky.
17. La Salle
18. Dayton
19. Louisville
20. UCLA
20. Indiana

1953

AP
1. Indiana
2. Seton Hall
3. Kansas
4. Washington
5. LSU
6. La Salle
7. St. John's (N.Y.)
8. Oklahoma St.
9. Duquesne
10. Notre Dame
11. Illinois
12. Kansas St.
13. Holy Cross
14. Seattle
15. Wake Forest
16. Santa Clara
17. Western Ky.
18. North Carolina St.
19. DePaul
20. Missouri St.

UPI
1. Indiana
2. Seton Hall
3. Washington
4. La Salle
5. Kansas
6. LSU
7. Oklahoma St.
8. North Carolina St.
9. Kansas St.
10. Illinois
11. Western Ky.
12. California
13. Notre Dame
14. DePaul
14. Wyoming
16. St. Louis
17. Holy Cross
18. Oklahoma City
19. BYU
20. Duquesne

1954

AP
1. Kentucky
2. La Salle
3. Holy Cross
4. Indiana
5. Duquesne
6. Notre Dame
7. Bradley
8. Western Ky.
9. Penn St.
10. Oklahoma St.
11. Southern California
12. George Washington
13. Iowa
14. LSU
15. Duke
16. Niagara
17. Seattle
18. Kansas
19. Illinois
20. Maryland

UPI
1. Indiana
2. Kentucky

1955

3. Duquesne
4. Oklahoma St.
5. Notre Dame
6. Western Ky.
7. Kansas
8. LSU
9. Holy Cross
10. Iowa
11. La Salle
12. Illinois
13. Colorado St.
14. North Carolina St.
14. Southern California
16. Oregon St.
17. Seattle
18. Dayton
19. Rice
20. Duke

AP
1. San Francisco
2. Kentucky
3. La Salle
4. North Carolina St.
5. Iowa
6. Duquesne
7. Utah
8. Marquette
9. Dayton
10. Oregon St.
11. Minnesota
12. Alabama
13. UCLA
14. George Washington
15. Colorado
16. Tulsa
17. Vanderbilt
18. Illinois
19. West Virginia
20. St. Louis

UPI
1. San Francisco
2. Kentucky
3. La Salle
4. Utah
5. Iowa
6. North Carolina St.
7. Duquesne
8. Oregon St.
9. Marquette
10. Dayton
11. Colorado
12. UCLA
13. Minnesota
14. Tulsa
15. George Washington
16. Illinois
17. Niagara
18. St. Louis
19. Holy Cross
20. Cincinnati

1956

AP
1. San Francisco
2. North Carolina St.
3. Dayton
4. Iowa
5. Alabama

6. Louisville
7. SMU
8. UCLA
9. Kentucky
10. Illinois
11. Oklahoma City
12. Vanderbilt
13. North Carolina
14. Holy Cross
15. Temple
16. Wake Forest
17. Duke
18. Utah
19. Oklahoma St.
20. West Virginia

UPI
1. San Francisco
2. North Carolina St.
3. Dayton
4. Iowa
5. Alabama
6. SMU
7. Louisville
8. Illinois
9. UCLA
10. Vanderbilt
11. North Carolina
12. Kentucky
13. Utah
14. Temple
15. Holy Cross
16. Oklahoma St.
16. St. Louis
18. Seattle
18. Duke
18. Canisius

1957

AP
1. North Carolina
2. Kansas
3. Kentucky
4. SMU
5. Seattle
6. Louisville
7. West Virginia
8. Vanderbilt
9. Oklahoma City
10. St. Louis
11. Michigan St.
12. Memphis
13. California
14. UCLA
15. Mississippi St.
16. Idaho St.
17. Notre Dame
18. Wake Forest
19. Canisius
19. Oklahoma St.

UPI
1. North Carolina
2. Kansas
3. Kentucky
4. SMU
5. Seattle
6. California
7. Michigan St.
8. Louisville
9. UCLA
9. St. Louis

11. West Virginia
12. Dayton
13. Bradley
14. BYU
15. Indiana
16. Vanderbilt
16. Xavier
16. Oklahoma City
19. Notre Dame
20. Kansas St.

1958

AP
1. West Virginia
2. Cincinnati
3. Kansas St.
4. San Francisco
5. Temple
6. Maryland
7. Kansas
8. Notre Dame
9. Kentucky
10. Duke
11. Dayton
12. Indiana
13. North Carolina
14. Bradley
15. Mississippi St.
16. Auburn
17. Michigan St.
18. Seattle
19. Oklahoma St.
20. North Carolina St.

UPI
1. West Virginia
2. Cincinnati
3. San Francisco
4. Kansas St.
5. Temple
6. Maryland
7. Notre Dame
8. Kansas
9. Dayton
10. Indiana
11. Bradley
12. North Carolina
13. Duke
14. Kentucky
15. Oklahoma St.
16. Oregon St.
16. North Carolina St.
18. St. Bonaventure
19. Michigan St.
19. Wyoming
19. Seattle

1959

AP
1. Kansas St.
2. Kentucky
3. Mississippi St.
4. Bradley
5. Cincinnati
6. North Carolina St.
7. Michigan St.
8. Auburn
9. North Carolina
10. West Virginia
11. California
12. St. Louis

13. Seattle
14. St. Joseph's
15. St. Mary's (Cal.)
16. TCU
17. Oklahoma City
18. Utah
19. St. Bonaventure
20. Marquette

UPI
1. Kansas St.
2. Kentucky
3. Michigan St.
4. Cincinnati
5. North Carolina St.
6. North Carolina
6. Mississippi St.
8. Bradley
9. California
10. Auburn
11. West Virginia
12. TCU
13. St. Louis
14. Utah
15. Marquette
16. Tennessee Tech
17. St. John's (N.Y.)
18. Navy
18. St. Mary's (Cal.)
20. St. Joseph's

1960

AP
1. Cincinnati
2. California
3. Ohio St.
4. Bradley
5. West Virginia
6. Utah
7. Indiana
8. Utah St.
9. St. Bonaventure
10. Miami (Fla.)
11. Auburn
12. New York U.
13. Georgia Tech
14. Providence
15. St. Louis
16. Holy Cross
17. Villanova
18. Duke
19. Wake Forest
20. St. John's (N.Y.)

UPI
1. California
2. Cincinnati
3. Ohio St.
4. Bradley
5. Utah
6. West Virginia
7. Utah St.
8. Georgia Tech
9. Villanova
10. Indiana
11. St. Bonaventure
12. New York U.
13. Texas
14. North Carolina
15. Duke
16. Kansas St.
17. Auburn
18. Providence
19. St. Louis
20. Dayton

1961

AP
1. Ohio St.
2. Cincinnati
3. St. Bonaventure
4. Kansas St.
5. North Carolina
6. Bradley
7. Southern California
8. Iowa
9. West Virginia
10. Duke
11. Utah
12. Texas Tech
13. Niagara

14. Memphis
15. Wake Forest
16. St. John's (N.Y.)
17. St. Joseph's
18. Drake
19. Holy Cross
20. Kentucky

UPI
1. Ohio St.
2. Cincinnati
3. St. Bonaventure
4. Kansas St.
5. Southern California
6. North Carolina
7. Bradley
8. St. John's (N.Y.)
9. Duke
10. Wake Forest
11. Iowa
12. West Virginia
13. Utah
14. St. Louis
15. Louisville
16. St. Joseph's
17. Dayton
18. Kentucky
19. Texas Tech
20. Memphis

1962

AP
1. Ohio St.
2. Cincinnati
3. Kentucky
4. Mississippi St.
5. Bradley
6. Kansas St.
7. Utah
8. Bowling Green
9. Colorado
10. Duke
11. Loyola (Ill.)
12. St. John's (N.Y.)
13. Wake Forest
14. Oregon St.
15. West Virginia
16. Arizona St.
17. Duquesne
18. Utah St.
19. UCLA
20. Villanova

UPI
1. Ohio St.
2. Cincinnati
3. Kentucky
4. Mississippi St.
5. Kansas St.
6. Bradley
7. Wake Forest
8. Colorado
9. Bowling Green
10. Utah
11. Oregon St.
12. St. John's (N.Y.)
13. Duke
13. Loyola (Ill.)
15. Arizona St.
16. West Virginia
17. UCLA
18. Duquesne
19. Utah St.
20. Villanova

1963

AP
1. Cincinnati
2. Duke
3. Loyola (Ill.)
4. Arizona St.
5. Wichita St.
6. Mississippi St.
7. Ohio St.
8. Illinois
9. New York U.
10. Colorado

UPI
1. Cincinnati
2. Duke

3. Arizona St.
4. Loyola (Ill.)
5. Illinois
6. Wichita St.
7. Mississippi St.
8. Ohio St.
9. Colorado
10. Stanford
11. New York U.
12. Texas
13. Providence
14. Oregon St.
15. UCLA
16. St. Joseph's
16. West Virginia
18. Bowling Green
19. Kansas St.
19. Seattle

1964

AP
1. UCLA
2. Michigan
3. Duke
4. Kentucky
5. Wichita St.
6. Oregon St.
7. Villanova
8. Loyola (Ill.)
9. DePaul
10. Davidson

UPI
1. UCLA
2. Michigan
3. Kentucky
4. Duke
5. Oregon St.
6. Wichita St.
7. Villanova
8. Loyola (Ill.)
9. UTEP
10. Davidson
11. DePaul
12. Kansas St.
13. Drake
13. San Francisco
15. Utah St.
16. Ohio St.
16. New Mexico
18. Texas A&M
19. Arizona St.
19. Providence

1965

AP
1. Michigan
2. UCLA
3. St. Joseph's
4. Providence
5. Vanderbilt
6. Davidson
7. Minnesota
8. Villanova
9. BYU
10. Duke

UPI
1. Michigan
2. UCLA
3. St. Joseph's
4. Providence
5. Vanderbilt
6. BYU
7. Davidson
8. Minnesota
9. Duke
10. San Francisco
11. Villanova
12. North Carolina St.
13. Oklahoma St.
14. Wichita St.
15. Connecticut
16. Illinois
17. Tennessee
18. Indiana
19. Miami (Fla.)
20. Dayton

1966

AP
1. Kentucky
2. Duke
3. UTEP
4. Kansas
5. St. Joseph's
6. Loyola (Ill.)
7. Cincinnati
8. Vanderbilt
9. Michigan
10. Western Ky.

UPI
1. Kentucky
2. Duke
3. UTEP
4. Kansas
5. Loyola (Ill.)
6. St. Joseph's
7. Michigan
8. Vanderbilt
9. Cincinnati
10. Providence
11. Nebraska
12. Utah
13. Oklahoma City
14. Houston
15. Oregon St.
16. Syracuse
17. Pacific
18. Davidson
19. BYU
19. Dayton

1967

AP
1. UCLA
2. Louisville
3. Kansas
4. North Carolina
5. Princeton
6. Western Ky.
7. Houston
8. Tennessee
9. Boston College
10. UTEP

UPI
1. UCLA
2. Louisville
3. North Carolina
4. Kansas
5. Princeton
6. Houston
7. Western Ky.
8. UTEP
9. Tennessee
10. Boston College
11. Toledo
12. St. John's (N.Y.)
13. Tulsa
14. Vanderbilt
14. Utah St.
16. Pacific
17. Providence
18. New Mexico
19. Duke
20. Florida

1968

AP
1. Houston
2. UCLA
3. St. Bonaventure
4. North Carolina
5. Kentucky
6. New Mexico
7. Columbia
8. Davidson
9. Louisville
10. Duke

UPI
1. Houston
2. UCLA
3. St. Bonaventure
4. North Carolina
5. Kentucky
6. Columbia

7. New Mexico
8. Louisville
9. Davidson
10. Marquette
11. Duke
12. New Mexico St.
13. Vanderbilt
14. Kansas St.
15. Princeton
16. Army
17. Santa Clara
18. Utah
19. Bradley
20. Iowa

1969

AP
1. UCLA
2. La Salle
3. Santa Clara
4. North Carolina
5. Davidson
6. Purdue
7. Kentucky
8. St. John's (N.Y.)
9. Duquesne
10. Villanova
11. Drake
12. New Mexico St.
13. South Carolina
14. Marquette
15. Louisville
16. Boston College
17. Notre Dame
18. Colorado
19. Kansas
20. Illinois

UPI
1. UCLA
2. North Carolina
3. Davidson
4. Santa Clara
5. Kentucky
6. La Salle
7. Purdue
8. St. John's (N.Y.)
9. New Mexico St.
10. Duquesne
11. Drake
12. Colorado
13. Louisville
14. Marquette
15. Villanova
16. Boston College
17. Weber St.
17. Wyoming
19. Colorado St.
20. South Carolina
20. Kansas

1970

AP
1. Kentucky
2. UCLA
3. St. Bonaventure
4. Jacksonville
5. New Mexico St.
6. South Carolina
7. Iowa
8. Marquette
9. Notre Dame
10. North Carolina St.
11. Florida St.
12. Houston
13. Penn
14. Drake
15. Davidson
16. Utah St.
17. Niagara
18. Western Ky.
19. Long Beach St.
20. Southern California

UPI
1. Kentucky
2. UCLA
3. St. Bonaventure
4. New Mexico St.
5. Jacksonville

6. South Carolina
7. Iowa
8. Notre Dame
9. Drake
10. Marquette
11. Houston
12. North Carolina St.
13. Penn
14. Florida St.
15. Villanova
15. Long Beach St.
17. Western Ky.
17. Utah St.
17. Niagara
20. Cincinnati
20. UTEP

1971

AP
1. UCLA
2. Marquette
3. Penn
4. Kansas
5. Southern California
6. South Carolina
7. Western Ky.
8. Kentucky
9. Fordham
10. Ohio St.
11. Jacksonville
12. Notre Dame
13. North Carolina
14. Houston
15. Duquesne
16. Long Beach St.
17. Tennessee
18. Villanova
19. Drake
20. BYU

UPI
1. UCLA
2. Marquette
3. Penn
4. Kansas
5. Southern California
6. South Carolina
7. Western Ky.
8. Kentucky
9. Fordham
10. Ohio St.
11. Jacksonville
11. BYU
13. North Carolina
14. Notre Dame
14. Long Beach St.
16. Drake
17. Villanova
18. Duquesne
18. Houston
20. Weber St.

1972

AP
1. UCLA
2. North Carolina
3. Penn
4. Louisville
5. Long Beach St.
6. South Carolina
7. Marquette
8. La.-Lafayette
9. BYU
10. Florida St.
11. Minnesota
12. Marshall
13. Memphis
14. Maryland
15. Villanova
16. Oral Roberts
17. Indiana
18. Kentucky
19. Ohio St.
20. Virginia

UPI
1. UCLA
2. North Carolina
3. Penn
4. Louisville
5. South Carolina

6. Long Beach St.
7. Marquette
8. La.-Lafayette
9. BYU
10. Florida St.
11. Maryland
12. Minnesota
13. Memphis
14. Kentucky
15. Villanova
16. Kansas St.
17. UTEP
18. Marshall
19. Missouri
19. Weber St.

1973

AP
1. UCLA
2. North Carolina St.
3. Long Beach St.
4. Providence
5. Marquette
6. Indiana
7. La.-Lafayette
8. Maryland
9. Kansas St.
10. Minnesota
11. North Carolina
12. Memphis
13. Houston
14. Syracuse
15. Missouri
16. Arizona St.
17. Kentucky
18. Penn
19. Austin Peay
20. San Francisco

UPI
1. UCLA
2. North Carolina St.
3. Long Beach St.
4. Marquette
5. Providence
6. Indiana
7. La.-Lafayette
7. Kansas St.
9. Minnesota
10. Maryland
11. Memphis
12. North Carolina
13. Arizona St.
14. Syracuse
15. Kentucky
16. South Carolina
17. Missouri
18. Weber St.
18. Houston
20. Penn

1974

AP
1. North Carolina St.
2. UCLA
3. Marquette
4. Maryland
5. Notre Dame
6. Michigan
7. Kansas
8. Providence
9. Indiana
10. Long Beach St.
11. Purdue
12. North Carolina
13. Vanderbilt
14. Alabama
15. Utah
16. Pittsburgh
17. Southern California
18. Oral Roberts
19. South Carolina
20. Dayton

UPI
1. North Carolina St.
2. UCLA
3. Notre Dame
4. Maryland
5. Marquette
6. Providence

---

7. Vanderbilt
8. North Carolina
9. Indiana
10. Kansas
11. Long Beach St.
12. Michigan
13. Southern California
14. Pittsburgh
15. Louisville
16. South Carolina
17. Creighton
18. New Mexico
19. Alabama
19. Dayton

1975

AP
1. UCLA
2. Kentucky
3. Indiana
4. Louisville
5. Maryland
6. Syracuse
7. North Carolina St.
8. Arizona St.
9. North Carolina
10. Alabama
11. Marquette
12. Princeton
13. Cincinnati
14. Notre Dame
15. Kansas St.
16. Drake
17. UNLV
18. Oregon St.
19. Michigan
20. Penn

UPI
1. Indiana
2. UCLA
3. Louisville
4. Kentucky
5. Maryland
6. Marquette
7. Arizona St.
8. Alabama
9. North Carolina St.
10. North Carolina
11. Penn
12. Southern California
13. Utah St.
14. UNLV
14. Notre Dame
16. Creighton
17. Arizona
18. New Mexico St.
19. Clemson
20. UTEP

1976

AP
1. Indiana
2. Marquette
3. UNLV
4. Rutgers
5. UCLA
6. Alabama
7. Notre Dame
8. North Carolina
9. Michigan
10. Western Mich.
11. Maryland
12. Cincinnati
13. Tennessee
14. Missouri
15. Arizona
16. Texas Tech
17. DePaul
18. Virginia
19. Centenary (La.)
20. Pepperdine

UPI
1. Indiana
2. Marquette
3. Rutgers
4. UNLV
5. UCLA
6. North Carolina
7. Alabama

---

8. Notre Dame
9. Michigan
10. Washington
11. Missouri
12. Arizona
13. Maryland
14. Tennessee
15. Virginia
16. Cincinnati
16. Florida St.
18. St. John's (N.Y.)
19. Western Mich.
19. Princeton

1977

AP
1. Michigan
2. UCLA
3. Kentucky
4. UNLV
5. North Carolina
6. Syracuse
7. Marquette
8. San Francisco
9. Wake Forest
10. Notre Dame
11. Alabama
12. Detroit
13. Minnesota
14. Utah
15. Tennessee
16. Kansas St.
17. Charlotte
18. Arkansas
19. Louisville
20. VMI

UPI
1. Michigan
2. San Francisco
3. North Carolina
4. UCLA
5. Kentucky
6. UNLV
7. Arkansas
8. Tennessee
9. Syracuse
10. Utah
11. Kansas St.
12. Cincinnati
13. Louisville
14. Marquette
15. Providence
16. Indiana St.
17. Minnesota
18. Alabama
19. Detroit
20. Purdue

1978

AP
1. Kentucky
2. UCLA
3. DePaul
4. Michigan St.
5. Arkansas
6. Notre Dame
7. Duke
8. Marquette
9. Louisville
10. Kansas
11. San Francisco
12. New Mexico
13. Indiana
14. Utah
15. Florida St.
16. North Carolina
17. Texas
18. Detroit
19. Miami (Ohio)
20. Penn

UPI
1. Kentucky
2. UCLA
3. Marquette
4. New Mexico
5. Michigan St.
6. Arkansas
7. DePaul
8. Kansas

---

9. Duke
10. North Carolina
11. Notre Dame
12. Florida St.
13. San Francisco
14. Louisville
15. Indiana
16. Houston
17. Utah St.
18. Utah
19. Texas
20. Georgetown

1979

AP
1. Indiana St.
2. UCLA
3. Michigan St.
4. Notre Dame
5. Arkansas
6. DePaul
7. LSU
8. Syracuse
9. North Carolina
10. Marquette
11. Duke
12. San Francisco
13. Louisville
14. Penn
15. Purdue
16. Oklahoma
17. St. John's (N.Y.)
18. Rutgers
19. Toledo
20. Iowa

UPI
1. Indiana St.
2. UCLA
3. North Carolina
4. Michigan St.
5. Notre Dame
6. Arkansas
7. Duke
8. DePaul
9. LSU
10. Syracuse
11. Iowa
12. Georgetown
13. Marquette
14. Purdue
15. Texas
16. Temple
17. San Francisco
17. Tennessee
19. Louisville
20. Detroit

1980

AP
1. DePaul
2. Louisville
3. LSU
4. Kentucky
5. Oregon St.
6. Syracuse
7. Indiana
8. Maryland
9. Notre Dame
10. Ohio St.
11. Georgetown
12. BYU
13. St. John's (N.Y.)
14. Duke
15. North Carolina
16. Missouri
17. Weber St.
18. Arizona St.
19. Iona
20. Purdue

UPI
1. DePaul
2. LSU
3. Kentucky
4. Louisville
5. Oregon St.
6. Syracuse
7. Indiana
8. Maryland
9. Ohio St.

---

10. Georgetown
11. Notre Dame
12. BYU
13. St. John's (N.Y.)
14. Missouri
15. North Carolina
16. Duke
17. Weber St.
18. Texas A&M
19. Arizona St.
20. Kansas St.

1981

AP
1. DePaul
2. Oregon St.
3. Arizona St.
4. LSU
5. Virginia
6. North Carolina
7. Notre Dame
8. Kentucky
9. Indiana
10. UCLA
11. Wake Forest
12. Louisville
13. Iowa
14. Utah
15. Tennessee
16. BYU
17. Wyoming
18. Maryland
19. Illinois
20. Arkansas

UPI
1. DePaul
2. Oregon St.
3. Virginia
4. LSU
5. Arizona St.
6. North Carolina
7. Indiana
8. Kentucky
9. Notre Dame
10. Utah
11. UCLA
12. Iowa
13. Louisville
14. Wake Forest
15. Tennessee
16. Wyoming
17. BYU
18. Illinois
19. Kansas
20. Maryland

1982

AP
1. North Carolina
2. DePaul
3. Virginia
4. Oregon St.
5. Missouri
6. Georgetown
7. Minnesota
8. Idaho
9. Memphis
10. Tulsa
11. Fresno St.
12. Arkansas
13. Alabama
14. West Virginia
15. Kentucky
16. Iowa
17. UAB
18. Wake Forest
19. UCLA
20. Louisville

UPI
1. North Carolina
2. DePaul
3. Virginia
4. Oregon St.
5. Missouri
6. Minnesota
7. Georgetown
8. Idaho
9. Memphis
10. Fresno St.

---

11. Tulsa
12. Alabama
13. Arkansas
14. Kentucky
15. Wyoming
16. Iowa
17. West Virginia
18. Kansas St.
19. Wake Forest
20. Louisville

1983

AP
1. Houston
2. Louisville
3. St. John's (N.Y.)
4. Virginia
5. Indiana
6. UNLV
7. UCLA
8. North Carolina
9. Arkansas
10. Missouri
11. Boston College
12. Kentucky
13. Villanova
14. Wichita St.
15. Chattanooga
16. North Carolina St.
17. Memphis
18. Georgia
19. Oklahoma St.
20. Georgetown

UPI
1. Houston
2. Louisville
3. St. John's (N.Y.)
4. Virginia
5. Indiana
6. UNLV
7. UCLA
8. North Carolina
9. Arkansas
10. Kentucky
11. Villanova
12. Missouri
13. Boston College
14. North Carolina St.
15. Georgia
16. Chattanooga
17. Memphis
18. Illinois St.
19. Oklahoma St.
20. Georgetown

1984

AP
1. North Carolina
2. Georgetown
3. Kentucky
4. DePaul
5. Houston
6. Illinois
7. Oklahoma
8. Arkansas
9. UTEP
10. Purdue
11. Maryland
12. Tulsa
13. UNLV
14. Duke
15. Washington
16. Memphis
17. Oregon St.
18. Syracuse
19. Wake Forest
20. Temple

UPI
1. North Carolina
2. Georgetown
3. Kentucky
4. DePaul
5. Houston
6. Illinois
7. Arkansas
8. Oklahoma
9. UTEP
10. Maryland
11. Purdue

12. Tulsa
13. UNLV
14. Duke
15. Washington
16. Memphis
16. Syracuse
18. Indiana
19. Auburn
20. Oregon St.

1985

AP
1. Georgetown
2. Michigan
3. St. John's (N.Y.)
4. Oklahoma
5. Memphis
6. Georgia Tech
7. North Carolina
8. Louisiana Tech
9. UNLV
10. Duke
11. VCU
12. Illinois
13. Kansas
14. Loyola (Ill.)
15. Syracuse
16. North Carolina St.
17. Texas Tech
18. Tulsa
19. Georgia
20. LSU

UPI
1. Georgetown
2. Michigan
3. St. John's (N.Y.)
4. Memphis
5. Oklahoma
6. Georgia Tech
7. North Carolina
8. Louisiana Tech
9. UNLV
10. Illinois
11. VCU
12. Duke
13. Kansas
14. Tulsa
15. Syracuse
16. Texas Tech
17. Loyola (Ill.)
18. North Carolina St.
19. LSU
20. Michigan St.

1986

AP
1. Duke
2. Kansas
3. Kentucky
4. St. John's (N.Y.)
5. Michigan
6. Georgia Tech
7. Louisville
8. North Carolina
9. Syracuse
10. Notre Dame
11. UNLV
12. Memphis
13. Georgetown
14. Bradley
15. Oklahoma
16. Indiana
17. Navy
18. Michigan St.
19. Illinois
20. UTEP

UPI
1. Duke
2. Kansas
3. St. John's (N.Y.)
4. Kentucky
5. Michigan
6. Georgia Tech
7. Louisville
8. North Carolina
9. Syracuse
10. UNLV
11. Notre Dame
12. Memphis
13. Bradley
14. Indiana
15. Georgetown
16. UTEP
17. Oklahoma
18. Michigan St.
19. Alabama
20. Illinois

1987

AP
1. UNLV
2. North Carolina
3. Indiana
4. Georgetown
5. DePaul
6. Iowa
7. Purdue
8. Temple
9. Alabama
10. Syracuse
11. Illinois
12. Pittsburgh
13. Clemson
14. Missouri
15. UCLA
16. New Orleans
17. Duke
18. Notre Dame
19. TCU
20. Kansas

UPI
1. UNLV
2. Indiana
3. North Carolina
4. Georgetown
5. DePaul
6. Purdue
7. Iowa
8. Temple
9. Alabama
10. Syracuse
11. Illinois
12. Pittsburgh
13. UCLA
14. Missouri
15. Clemson
16. TCU
17. Wyoming
18. Notre Dame
19. New Orleans
19. Oklahoma
19. UTEP

1988

AP
1. Temple
2. Arizona
3. Purdue
4. Oklahoma
5. Duke
6. Kentucky
7. North Carolina
8. Pittsburgh
9. Syracuse
10. Michigan
11. Bradley
12. UNLV
13. Wyoming
14. North Carolina St.
15. Loyola Marymount
16. Illinois
17. Iowa
18. Xavier
19. BYU
20. Kansas St.

UPI
1. Temple
2. Arizona
3. Purdue
4. Oklahoma
5. Duke
6. Kentucky
7. Pittsburgh
8. North Carolina
9. Syracuse
10. Michigan
11. UNLV
12. Bradley
13. North Carolina St.
14. Wyoming
15. Illinois
16. Loyola Marymount
17. BYU
18. Iowa
19. Indiana
20. Kansas St.

1989

AP
1. Arizona
2. Georgetown
3. Illinois
4. Oklahoma
5. North Carolina
6. Missouri
7. Syracuse
8. Indiana
9. Duke
10. Michigan
11. Seton Hall
12. Louisville
13. Stanford
14. Iowa
15. UNLV
16. Florida St.
17. West Virginia
18. Ball St.
19. North Carolina St.
20. Alabama

UPI
1. Arizona
2. Georgetown
3. Illinois
4. North Carolina
5. Oklahoma
6. Indiana
7. Duke
8. Missouri
9. Syracuse
10. Michigan
11. Seton Hall
12. Stanford
13. Louisville
14. UNLV
15. Iowa
16. Florida St.
17. Arkansas
18. North Carolina St.
19. West Virginia
20. Alabama

1990

AP
1. Oklahoma
2. UNLV
3. Connecticut
4. Michigan St.
5. Kansas
6. Syracuse
7. Arkansas
8. Georgetown
9. Georgia Tech
10. Purdue
11. Missouri
12. La Salle
13. Michigan
14. Arizona
15. Duke
16. Louisville
17. Clemson
18. Illinois
19. LSU
20. Minnesota
21. Loyola Marymount
22. Oregon St.
23. Alabama
24. New Mexico St.
25. Xavier

UPI
1. Oklahoma
2. UNLV
3. Connecticut
4. Michigan St.
5. Kansas
6. Syracuse
7. Georgia Tech
8. Arkansas
9. Georgetown
10. Purdue
11. Missouri
12. Arizona
13. La Salle
14. Duke
15. Michigan
16. Louisville
17. Clemson
18. Illinois
19. Alabama
20. New Mexico St.

1991

AP
1. UNLV
2. Arkansas
3. Indiana
4. North Carolina
5. Ohio St.
6. Duke
7. Syracuse
8. Arizona
9. Kentucky
10. Utah
11. Nebraska
12. Kansas
13. Seton Hall
14. Oklahoma St.
15. New Mexico St.
16. UCLA
17. East Tenn. St.
18. Princeton
19. Alabama
20. St. John's (N.Y.)
21. Mississippi St.
22. LSU
23. Texas
24. DePaul
25. Southern Miss.

UPI
1. UNLV
2. Arkansas
3. Indiana
4. North Carolina
5. Ohio St.
6. Duke
7. Arizona
8. Syracuse
9. Nebraska
10. Utah
11. Seton Hall
12. Kansas
13. Oklahoma St.
14. UCLA
15. East Tenn. St.
16. Alabama
17. New Mexico St.
18. Mississippi St.
19. St. John's (N.Y.)
20. Princeton
21. LSU
22. Michigan St.
23. Georgetown
24. North Carolina St.
25. Texas

1992

AP
1. Duke
2. Kansas
3. Ohio St.
4. UCLA
5. Indiana
6. Kentucky
7. UNLV
8. Southern California
9. Arkansas
10. Arizona
11. Oklahoma St.
12. Cincinnati
13. Alabama
14. Michigan St.
15. Michigan
16. Missouri
17. Massachusetts
18. North Carolina
19. Seton Hall
20. Florida St.
21. Syracuse
22. Georgetown
23. Oklahoma
24. DePaul
25. LSU

UPI
1. Duke
2. Kansas
3. UCLA
4. Ohio St.
5. Arizona
6. Indiana
7. Southern California
8. Arkansas
9. Kentucky
10. Oklahoma St.
11. Michigan St.
12. Missouri
13. Alabama
14. Cincinnati
15. North Carolina
16. Florida St.
17. Michigan
18. Seton Hall
19. Georgetown
20. Syracuse
21. Massachusetts
22. Oklahoma
23. DePaul
24. St. John's (N.Y.)
25. Tulane

1993

AP
1. Indiana
2. Kentucky
3. Michigan
4. North Carolina
5. Arizona
6. Seton Hall
7. Cincinnati
8. Vanderbilt
9. Kansas
10. Duke
11. Florida St.
12. Arkansas
13. Iowa
14. Massachusetts
15. Louisville
16. Wake Forest
17. New Orleans
18. Georgia Tech
19. Utah
20. Western Ky.
21. New Mexico
22. Purdue
23. Oklahoma St.
24. New Mexico St.
25. UNLV

USA TODAY/CNN
1. Indiana
2. North Carolina
3. Kentucky
4. Michigan
5. Arizona
6. Seton Hall
7. Cincinnati
8. Kansas
9. Vanderbilt
10. Duke
11. Florida St.
12. Arkansas
13. Iowa
14. Louisville
15. Wake Forest
16. Utah
17. Massachusetts
18. New Orleans
19. UNLV
20. Georgia Tech
21. Purdue
22. Virginia
23. Oklahoma St.
24. New Mexico St.
25. Western Ky.

1994

AP
1. North Carolina
2. Arkansas
3. Purdue
4. Connecticut
5. Missouri
6. Duke
7. Kentucky
8. Massachusetts
9. Arizona
10. Louisville
11. Michigan
12. Temple
13. Kansas
14. Florida
15. Syracuse
16. California
17. UCLA
18. Indiana
19. Oklahoma St.
20. Texas
21. Marquette
22. Nebraska
23. Minnesota
24. St. Louis
25. Cincinnati

USA TODAY/CNN
1. Arkansas
2. North Carolina
3. Connecticut
4. Purdue
5. Missouri
6. Duke
7. Massachusetts
8. Kentucky
9. Louisville
10. Arizona
11. Michigan
12. Temple
13. Kansas
14. Syracuse
15. Florida
16. UCLA
17. California
18. Indiana
19. Oklahoma St.
20. Minnesota
21. St. Louis
22. Marquette
23. UAB
24. Texas
25. Cincinnati

1995

AP
1. UCLA
2. Kentucky
3. Wake Forest
4. North Carolina
5. Kansas
6. Arkansas
7. Massachusetts
8. Connecticut
9. Villanova
10. Maryland
11. Michigan St.
12. Purdue
13. Virginia
14. Oklahoma St.
15. Arizona
16. Arizona St.
17. Oklahoma
18. Mississippi St.
19. Utah
20. Alabama
21. Western Ky.
22. Georgetown
23. Missouri
24. Iowa St.
25. Syracuse

USA TODAY/NABC
1. UCLA
2. Kentucky
3. Wake Forest
4. Kansas
5. North Carolina
6. Arkansas
7. Massachusetts
8. Connecticut
9. Michigan St.
10. Maryland
11. Purdue

DIVISION I

12. Villanova
13. Arizona
14. Oklahoma St.
15. Virginia
16. Arizona St.
17. Utah
18. Iowa St.
19. Mississippi St.
20. Oklahoma
21. Alabama
22. Syracuse
23. Missouri
24. Oregon
25. Stanford

1996

AP
1. Massachusetts
2. Kentucky
3. Connecticut
4. Georgetown
4. Kansas
4. Purdue
7. Cincinnati
8. Texas Tech
9. Wake Forest
10. Villanova
11. Arizona
12. Utah
13. Georgia Tech
14. UCLA
15. Syracuse
16. Memphis
17. Iowa St.
18. Penn St.
19. Mississippi St.
20. Marquette
21. Iowa
22. Virginia Tech
23. New Mexico
24. Louisville
25. North Carolina

USA TODAY/NABC
1. Massachusetts
2. Kentucky
3. Connecticut
4. Purdue
5. Georgetown
6. Cincinnati
7. Texas Tech
8. Kansas
9. Wake Forest
10. Utah
11. Arizona
12. Villanova
13. UCLA
14. Syracuse
15. Georgia Tech
16. Iowa St.
17. Memphis
18. Penn St.
19. Iowa
20. Mississippi St.
21. Virginia Tech
22. Marquette
23. Louisville
24. North Carolina
25. Stanford

1997

AP
1. Kansas
2. Utah
3. Minnesota
4. North Carolina
5. Kentucky
6. South Carolina
7. UCLA
8. Duke
9. Wake Forest
10. Cincinnati
11. New Mexico
12. St. Joseph's
13. Xavier
14. Clemson
15. Arizona
16. Col. of Charleston
17. Georgia
18. Iowa St.
19. Illinois
20. Villanova
21. Stanford
22. Maryland
23. Boston College
24. Colorado
25. Louisville

USA TODAY/NABC
1. Kansas
2. Utah
3. Minnesota
4. Kentucky
5. North Carolina
6. South Carolina
7. UCLA
8. Duke
9. Wake Forest
10. Cincinnati
11. New Mexico
12. Clemson
13. Arizona
14. Xavier
15. St. Joseph's
16. Villanova
17. Iowa St.
18. Col. of Charleston
19. Maryland
20. Boston College
21. Stanford
22. Georgia
23. Colorado
24. Illinois
25. Louisville

1998

AP
1. North Carolina
2. Kansas
3. Duke
4. Arizona
5. Kentucky
6. Connecticut
7. Utah
8. Princeton
9. Cincinnati
10. Stanford
11. Purdue
12. Michigan
13. Mississippi
14. South Carolina
15. TCU
16. Michigan St.
17. Arkansas
18. New Mexico
19. UCLA
20. Maryland
21. Syracuse
22. Illinois
23. Xavier
24. Temple
25. Murray St.

USA TODAY/NABC
1. North Carolina
2. Kansas
3. Duke
4. Arizona
5. Connecticut
6. Kentucky
7. Utah
8. Princeton
9. Purdue
10. Stanford
11. Cincinnati
12. Michigan
13. South Carolina
14. Mississippi
15. Michigan St.
16. TCU
17. Arkansas
18. New Mexico
19. Syracuse
20. UCLA
21. Xavier
22. Maryland
23. Illinois
24. Temple
25. Oklahoma

1999

AP
1. Duke
2. Michigan St.
3. Connecticut
4. Auburn
5. Maryland
6. Utah
7. Stanford
8. Kentucky
9. St. John's (N.Y.)
10. Miami (Fla.)
11. Cincinnati
12. Arizona
13. North Carolina
14. Ohio St.
15. UCLA
16. Col. of Charleston
17. Arkansas
18. Wisconson
19. Indiana
20. Texas
21. Iowa
22. Kansas
23. Florida
24. Charlotte
25. New Mexico

USA TODAY/NABC
1. Duke
2. Michigan St.
3. Connecticut
4. Auburn
5. Maryland
6. Utah
7. Stanford
8. St. John's (N.Y.)
9. Cincinnati
10. Arizona
11. Kentucky
12. Miami (Fla.)
13. North Carolina
14. Ohio St.
15. UCLA
16. Col. of Charleston
17. Wisconsin
18. Indiana
19. Arkansas
20. Iowa
21. Syracuse
22. Kansas
23. Texas
24. New Mexico
25. Florida

2000

AP
1. Duke
2. Michigan St.
3. Stanford
4. Arizona
5. Temple
6. Iowa St.
7. Cincinnati
8. Ohio St.
9. St. John's (N.Y.)
10. LSU
11. Tennessee
12. Oklahoma
13. Florida
14. Oklahoma St.
15. Texas
16. Syracuse
17. Maryland
18. Tulsa
19. Kentucky
20. Connecticut
21. Illinois
22. Indiana
23. Miami (Fla.)
24. Auburn
25. Purdue

USA TODAY/NABC
1. Duke
2. Michigan St.
3. Stanford
4. Arizona
5. Temple
6. Cincinnati
7. Iowa St.
8. Ohio St.
9. LSU
10. Tennessee
11. Florida
12. St. John's (N.Y.)
13. Oklahoma
14. Syracuse
15. Oklahoma St.
16. Maryland
17. Indiana
18. Texas
19. Tulsa
20. Kentucky
21. Connecticut
22. Auburn
23. Illinois
24. Purdue
25. Miami (Fla.)

2001

AP
1. Duke
2. Stanford
3. Michigan St.
4. Illinois
5. Arizona
6. North Carolina
7. Boston College
8. Florida
9. Kentucky
10. Iowa St.
11. Maryland
12. Kansas
13. Oklahoma
14. Mississippi
15. UCLA
16. Virginia
17. Syracuse
18. Texas
19. Notre Dame
20. Indiana
21. Georgetown
22. St. Joseph's
23. Wake Forest
24. Iowa
25. Wisconsin

USA TODAY/NABC
1. Duke
2. Stanford
3. Michigan St.
4. Arizona
5. North Carolina
6. Illinois
7. Boston College
8. Florida
9. Iowa St.
10. Kentucky
11. Maryland
12. Kansas
13. Mississippi
14. Oklahoma
15. Virginia
16. Syracuse
17. Texas
18. UCLA
19. Notre Dame
20. Georgetown
21. Indiana
22. Wake Forest
23. St. Joseph's
24. Wisconsin
25. Iowa

2002

AP
1. Duke
2. Kansas
3. Oklahoma
4. Maryland
5. Cincinnati
6. Gonzaga
7. Arizona
8. Alabama
9. Pittsburgh
10. Connecticut
11. Oregon
12. Marquette
13. Illinois
14. Ohio St.
15. Florida
16. Kentucky
17. Mississippi St.
18. Southern California
19. Western Ky.
20. Oklahoma St.
21. Miami (Fla.)
22. Xavier
23. Georgia
24. Stanford
25. Hawaii

USA TODAY/ESPN
1. Duke
2. Kansas
3. Oklahoma
4. Maryland
5. Cincinnati
6. Gonzaga
7. Pittsburgh
8. Alabama
9. Arizona
10. Marquette
11. Oregon
12. Ohio St.
13. Connecticut
14. Florida
15. Kentucky
16. Illinois
17. Southern California
18. Mississippi St.
19. Xavier
20. Western Ky.
21. Miami (Fla.)
22. Oklahoma St.
23. Stanford
24. Hawaii
25. North Carolina St.

2003

AP
1. Kentucky
2. Arizona
3. Oklahoma
4. Pittsburgh
5. Texas
6. Kansas
7. Duke
8. Wake Forest
9. Marquette
10. Florida
11. Illinois
12. Xavier
13. Syracuse
14. Louisville
15. Creighton
16. Dayton
17. Maryland
18. Stanford
19. Memphis
20. Mississippi St.
21. Wisconsin
22. Notre Dame
23. Connecticut
24. Missouri
25. Georgia

USA TODAY/ESPN
1. Kentucky
2. Arizona
3. Oklahoma
4. Pittsburgh
5. Texas
6. Kansas
7. Duke
8. Florida
9. Wake Forest
10. Illinois
11. Marquette
12. Syracuse
13. Louisville
14. Xavier
15. Creighton
16. Stanford
17. Maryland
18. Dayton
19. Wisconsin
20. Notre Dame
21. Mississippi St.
22. Memphis
23. Oklahoma St.
24. Connecticut
25. Missouri

2004

AP
1. Stanford
2. Kentucky
3. Gonzaga
4. Oklahoma St.
5. St. Joseph's
6. Duke
7. Connecticut
8. Mississippi St.
9. Pittsburgh
10. Wisconsin
11. Cincinnati
12. Texas
13. Illinois
14. Georgia Tech
15. North Carolina St.
16. Kansas
17. Wake Forest
18. North Carolina
19. Maryland
20. Syracuse
21. Providence
22. Arizona
23. South Carolina
24. Memphis
25. Boston College
    Utah St.

USA TODAY/ESPN
1. Stanford
2. Gonzaga
3. Oklahoma St.
4. Kentucky
5. St. Joseph's
6. Duke
7. Connecticut
8. Pittsburgh
9. Mississippi St.
10. Wisconsin
11. Texas
12. Cincinnati
13. Illinois
14. Kansas
15. Georgia Tech
16. Wake Forest
17. North Carolina St.
18. Arizona
19. Providence
20. North Carolina
21. Maryland
22. Utah St.
23. Southern Ill.
24. Syracuse
25. Michigan St.

2005

AP
1. Illinois
2. North Carolina
3. Duke
4. Louisville
5. Wake Forest
6. Oklahoma St.
7. Kentucky
8. Washington
9. Arizona
10. Gonzaga
11. Syracuse
12. Kansas
13. Connecticut
14. Boston College
15. Michigan St.
16. Florida
17. Oklahoma
18. Utah
19. Villanova
20. Wisconsin
21. Alabama
22. Pacific
23. Cincinnati
24. Texas Tech
25. Georgia Tech

USA TODAY/ESPN
1. Illinois
2. Duke
3. North Carolina
4. Louisville

5. Kentucky
6. Wake Forest
7. Washington
8. Oklahoma St.
9. Arizona
10. Kansas
11. Gonzaga
12. Boston College
13. Syracuse
14. Connecticut
15. Michigan St.
16. Oklahoma
17. Utah
18. Florida
19. Wisconsin
20. Pacific
21. Alabama
22. Villanova
23. Cincinnati
24. Texas Tech
25. Georgia Tech

2006
AP
1. Duke
2. Connecticut
3. Villanova
4. Memphis
5. Gonzaga
6. Ohio St.
7. Boston College
   UCLA
9. Texas
10. North Carolina
11. Florida
12. Kansas
13. Illinois
14. George Washington
15. Iowa
16. Pittsburgh
17. Washington
18. Tennessee
19. LSU
20. Nevada
21. Syracuse
22. West Virginia
23. Georgetown
24. Oklahoma
25. UAB

USA TODAY/ESPN
1. Duke
2. Connecticut
3. Memphis
4. Villanova
5. Gonzaga
6. Ohio St.
7. Boston College
8. UCLA
9. Texas
10. Florida
11. George Washington
12. North Carolina
13. Kansas
14. Illinois
15. Iowa
16. Pittsburgh
17. Washington
18. LSU
19. Tennessee
20. Oklahoma
21. Nevada
22. Syracuse
23. West Virginia
24. Georgetown
25. UAB

2007
AP
1. Ohio St.
2. Kansas
3. Florida
4. North Carolina
5. Memphis
6. Wisconsin
7. UCLA
8. Georgetown
9. Texas A&M
10. Oregon
11. Texas
12. Pittsburgh
13. Washington St.
14. Southern Ill.
15. Nevada
16. Louisville
17. Notre Dame
18. Maryland
19. UNLV
20. Marquette
21. Butler
22. Winthrop
23. Southern California
24. BYU
25. Tennessee

USA TODAY/ESPN
1. Ohio St.
2. Kansas
3. Florida
4. North Carolina
5. Memphis
6. UCLA
7. Wisconsin
8. Georgetown
9. Texas A&M
10. Pittsburgh
11. Texas
12. Oregon
13. Nevada
    Washington St.
15. Southern Ill.
16. Louisville
17. Notre Dame
18. UNLV
19. Butler
20. Marquette
21. Winthrop
22. Maryland
23. BYU
24. Creighton
25. Southern California

2008
AP
1. North Carolina
2. Memphis
3. UCLA
4. Kansas
5. Tennessee
6. Wisconsin
7. Texas
8. Georgetown
9. Duke
10. Stanford
11. Butler
12. Xavier
13. Louisville
14. Drake
15. Notre Dame
16. Connecticut
17. Pittsburgh
18. Michigan St.
19. Vanderbilt
20. Purdue
21. Washington St.
22. Clemson
23. Davidson
24. Gonzaga
25. Marquette

2008
USA TODAY/ESPN
1. North Carolina
2. UCLA
3. Memphis
4. Kansas
5. Wisconsin
6. Tennessee
7. Texas
8. Georgetown
9. Duke
10. Butler
11. Stanford
12. Xavier
13. Louisville
14. Drake
15. Notre Dame
16. Vanderbilt
17. Connecticut
18. Purdue
19. Pittsburgh
20. Michigan St.
21. Washington St.
22. Clemson
23. Davidson
24. Indiana
25. Marquette

Final Post-Tournament Polls

1994
USA TODAY/CNN
1. Arkansas
2. Duke
3. Arizona
4. Florida
5. Purdue
6. Missouri
7. Connecticut
8. Michigan
9. North Carolina
10. Louisville
11. Boston College
12. Kansas
13. Kentucky
14. Syracuse
15. Massachusetts
16. Indiana
17. Marquette
18. Temple
19. Tulsa
20. Maryland
21. Oklahoma St.
22. UCLA
23. Minnesota
24. Texas
25. Penn

1995
USA TODAY/NABC
1. UCLA
2. Arkansas
3. North Carolina
4. Oklahoma St.
5. Kentucky
6. Connecticut
7. Massachusetts
8. Virginia
9. Wake Forest
10. Kansas
11. Maryland
12. Mississippi St.
13. Arizona St.
14. Memphis
15. Tulsa
16. Georgetown
17. Syracuse
18. Missouri
19. Purdue
20. Michigan St.
21. Alabama
22. Utah
23. Villanova
24. Texas
25. Arizona

1996
USA TODAY/NABC
1. Kentucky
2. Massachusetts
3. Syracuse
4. Mississippi St.
5. Kansas
6. Cincinnati
7. Georgetown
8. Connecticut
9. Wake Forest
10. Texas Tech
11. Arizona
12. Utah
13. Georgia Tech
14. Louisville
15. Purdue
16. Georgia
17. Villanova
18. Arkansas
19. UCLA
20. Iowa St.
21. Virginia Tech
22. Iowa
23. Marquette
24. North Carolina
25. New Mexico

1997
USA TODAY/NABC
1. Arizona
2. Kentucky
3. Minnesota
4. North Carolina
5. Kansas
6. Utah
7. UCLA
8. Clemson
9. Wake Forest
10. Louisville
11. Duke
12. Stanford
13. Iowa St.
14. South Carolina
15. Providence
16. Cincinnati
17. St. Joseph's
18. California
19. New Mexico
20. Texas
21. Col. of Charleston
22. Xavier
23. Boston College
24. Michigan
25. Colorado

1998
USA TODAY/NABC
1. Kentucky
2. Utah
3. North Carolina
4. Stanford
5. Duke
6. Arizona
7. Connecticut
8. Kansas
9. Purdue
10. Michigan St.
11. Rhode Island
12. UCLA
13. Syracuse
14. Cincinnati
15. Maryland
16. Princeton
17. Michigan
18. West Virginia
19. South Carolina
20. Mississippi
21. New Mexico
22. Arkansas
23. Valparaiso
24. Washington
25. TCU

1999
USA TODAY/NABC
1. Connecticut
2. Duke
3. Michigan St.
4. Ohio St.
5. Kentucky
5. St. John's (N.Y.)
7. Auburn
8. Maryland
9. Stanford
10. Utah
11. Cincinnati
12. Gonzaga
12. Miami (Fla.)
14. Temple
15. Iowa
16. Arizona
17. Florida
18. North Carolina
19. Oklahoma
20. Miami (Ohio)

2000
USA TODAY/NABC
1. Michigan St.
2. Florida
3. Iowa St.
4. Duke
5. Stanford
6. Oklahoma St.
7. Cincinnati
8. Arizona
9. Tulsa
10. Temple
11. North Carolina
12. Syracuse
13. LSU
14. Tennessee
15. Purdue
16. Wisconsin
17. Ohio St.
18. St. John's (N.Y.)
19. Oklahoma
20. Miami (Fla.)
21. Texas
22. Kentucky
23. UCLA
24. Gonzaga
25. Maryland

21. UCLA
22. Purdue
23. Kansas
24. Missouri St.
25. Arkansas

2001
USA TODAY/NABC
1. Duke
2. Arizona
3. Michigan St.
4. Maryland
5. Stanford
6. Illinois
7. Kansas
8. Kentucky
9. Mississippi
10. North Carolina
11. Boston College
12. UCLA
13. Florida
14. Southern California
15. Iowa St.
16. Temple
17. Georgetown
18. Syracuse
19. Oklahoma
20. Gonzaga
21. Virginia
22. Cincinnati
23. Notre Dame
24. St. Joseph's
25. Penn St.

2002
USA/ESPN
1. Maryland
2. Kansas
3. Indiana
4. Oklahoma
5. Duke
6. Connecticut
7. Oregon
8. Cincinnati
9. Pittsburgh
10. Arizona
11. Illinois
12. Kent St.
13. Kentucky
14. Alabama
15. Missouri
16. Gonzaga
17. Ohio St.
18. Marquette
19. Texas
20. UCLA
21. Mississippi St.
22. Southern Ill.
23. Florida
24. Xavier
25. North Carolina St.

2003
USA/ESPN
1. Syracuse
2. Kansas
3. Texas
4. Kentucky
5. Arizona
6. Marquette
7. Oklahoma
8. Pittsburgh
9. Duke
10. Maryland
11. Connecticut
12. Wake Forest
13. Illinois
14. Wisconsin
15. Notre Dame
16. Florida
17. Xavier
18. Michigan St.
19. Louisville
20. Stanford
21. Butler
22. Missouri
23. Creighton
24. Oklahoma St.
25. Dayton

2004
USA/ESPN
1. Connecticut
2. Duke
3. Georgia Tech
4. Oklahoma St.
5. St. Joseph's
6. Stanford
7. Pittsburgh
8. Kentucky
9. Kansas
10. Texas
11. Illinois
12. Gonzaga
13. Mississippi St.
14. Xavier
15. Wake Forest
16. Wisconsin
17. Alabama
18. Cincinnati
19. Syracuse
20. North Carolina St.
21. Nevada
22. North Carolina
23. UAB
24. Maryland
25. Vanderbilt

2005
USA/ESPN
1. North Carolina
2. Illinois
3. Louisville
4. Michigan St.
5. Kentucky
6. Arizona
7. Duke
8. Oklahoma St.
9. Washington
10. Wisconsin
11. Wake Forest
12. West Virginia
13. Syracuse
14. Utah
15. Kansas
16. Texas Tech
17. Connecticut
18. Gonzaga
19. Boston College
20. Oklahoma
21. Syracuse
22. North Carolina St.
23. Milwaukee
24. Florida
25. Cincinnati

2006
USA/ESPN
1. Florida
2. UCLA
3. LSU

4. Connecticut
5. Villanova
6. Memphis
7. Duke
8. George Mason
9. Texas
10. Gonzaga
11. Boston College
12. Washington
13. Ohio St.
14. North Carolina
15. West Virginia
16. Georgetown
17. Illinois
18. Pittsburgh
19. George Washington
20. Tennessee
21. Wichita St.
22. Kansas
23. Iowa
24. Bradley
25. Bucknell

2007

USA/ESPN
1. Florida
2. Ohio St.
3. UCLA
4. Georgetown
5. Kansas
   North Carolina
7. Memphis
8. Oregon
9. Texas A&M
10. Pittsburgh

11. Southern Ill.
    Wisconsin
13. Butler
14. UNLV
15. Southern California
16. Texas
17. Washington St.
18. Tennessee
19. Vanderbilt
20. Louisville
21. Nevada
22. Winthrop
23. Maryland
24. Virginia
25. Virginia Tech

2008

USA/ESPN
1. Kansas
2. Memphis
3. North Carolina
4. UCLA
5. Texas
6. Louisville
7. Tennessee
8. Xavier
9. Davidson
10. Wisconsin
11. Stanford
12. Georgetown
13. Michigan St.
14. Butler
15. Washington St.
16. Duke
17. West Virginia

18. Pittsburgh
19. Notre Dame
20. Purdue
21. Marquette
22. Western Ky.
23. Drake
24. Villanova
25. Vanderbilt

American Sports Wire Poll

The following poll ranks the top historically black institutions of the NCAA as selected by American Sports Wire and compiled by Dick Simpson.

Year	Team	Coach	Won	Lost
1992	Howard	Butch Beard	17	14
1993	Jackson St.	Andy Stoglin	25	9
1994	Texas Southern	Robert Moreland	19	11
1995	Texas Southern	Robert Moreland	22	7
1996	South Carolina St.	Cy Alexander	22	8
1997	Coppin St.	Fang Mitchell	22	9
1998	South Carolina St.	Cy Alexander	22	8
1999	Alcorn St.	Davey L. Whitney	23	7
2000	South Carolina St.	Cy Alexander	20	14
2001	Hampton	Steve Merfeld	25	7
2002	Hampton	Steve Merfeld	25	7
2003	South Carolina St.	Cy Alexander	20	11
2004	Florida A&M	Michael Gillespie	15	17
2005	Delaware St.	Greg Jackson	19	14
2006	Delaware St.	Greg Jackson	21	14
2007	Delaware St.	Greg Jackson	21	13
2008	Alabama St.	Lewis Jackson	20	11

Division II Records

Individual Records

Basketball records are confined to the "modern era," which began with the 1937-38 season, the first without the center jump after each goal scored. Official weekly statistics rankings in scoring and shooting began with the 1947-48 season. Individual rebounds were added for the 1950-51 season, while team rebounds were added for the 1959-60 season. Assists were added for the 1988-89 season. Blocked shots and steals were added for the 1992-93 season. Scoring and rebounding are ranked on per-game average; shooting, on percentage. Beginning with the 1967-68 season, Division II rankings were limited only to NCAA members. The 1973-74 season was the first under a three-division reorganization plan adopted by the special NCAA Convention of August 1973. In statistical rankings, the rounding of percentages and/or averages may indicate ties where none exist. In these cases, the numerical order of the rankings is accurate.

Scoring

POINTS
Game
113—Clarence "Bevo" Francis, Rio Grande vs. Hillsdale, Feb. 2, 1954
Season
1,329—Earl Monroe, Winston-Salem, 1967 (32 games)
Career
4,045—Travis Grant, Kentucky St., 1969-72 (121 games)

AVERAGE PER GAME
Season
†46.5—Clarence "Bevo" Francis, Rio Grande, 1954 (1,255 in 27)
Career
(Min. 1,400) 33.4—Travis Grant, Kentucky St., 1969-72 (4,045 in 121)

†Season and career figures for Francis limited only to his 39 games (27 in 1954) against four-year colleges.

GAMES SCORING AT LEAST 50 POINTS
Season
†8—Clarence "Bevo" Francis, Rio Grande, 1954
Career
†14—Clarence "Bevo" Francis, Rio Grande, 1953-54

†Season and career figures for Francis limited only to his 39 games (27 in 1954) against four-year colleges.

MOST GAMES SCORING IN DOUBLE FIGURES
Career
130—Lambert Shell, Bridgeport, 1989-92

POINTS SCORED IN OVERTIME
18—John Green, Barton vs. St. Andrews, Feb. 5, 2004 (team scored 19)

Field Goals

FIELD GOALS
Game
38—Clarence "Bevo" Francis, Rio Grande vs. Alliance, Jan. 16, 1954 (71 attempts) and vs. Hillsdale, Feb. 2, 1954 (70 attempts)
Season
539—Travis Grant, Kentucky St., 1972 (869 attempts)
Career
1,760—Travis Grant, Kentucky St., 1969-72 (2,759 attempts)

CONSECUTIVE FIELD GOALS
Game
20—Lance Berwald, North Dakota St. vs. Augustana (S.D.), Feb. 17, 1984
Season
28—Don McAllister, Hartwick, 1980 (during six games, Jan. 26-Feb. 9); Lance Berwald, North Dakota St., 1984 (during three games, Feb. 13-18)

FIELD-GOAL ATTEMPTS
Game
71—Clarence "Bevo" Francis, Rio Grande vs. Alliance, Jan. 16, 1954 (38 made)
Season
925—Jim Toombs, Stillman, 1965 (388 made)
Career
3,309—Bob Hopkins, Grambling, 1953-56 (1,403 made)

FIELD-GOAL PERCENTAGE
Game
(Min. 20 made) 100%—Lance Berwald, North Dakota St. vs. Augustana (S.D.), Feb. 17, 1984 (20 of 20)
*Season
76.2%—Garrett Siler, Augusta St., 2008 (211 of 277)

*based on qualifiers for annual championship
Career
(Min. 400 made) 70.8%—Todd Linder, Tampa, 1984-87 (909 of 1,284)

Three-Point Field Goals

THREE-POINT FIELD GOALS
Game
16—Thomas Vincent, Emporia St. vs. Southwest Baptist, Feb. 28, 2004 (23 attempts); Markus Hallgrimson, Mont. St.-Billings vs. Western N.M., Feb. 12, 2000 (28 attempts)
Season
167—Alex Williams, Sacramento St., 1988 (369 attempts)
Career
451—Cameron Munoz, Mont. St.-Billings, 2003-06 (1,042 attempts)

THREE-POINT FIELD GOALS MADE PER GAME
Season
6.2—Markus Hallgrimson, Mont. St.-Billings, 2000 (160 in 26)
Career
4.7—Antonio Harris, LeMoyne-Owen, 1998-99 (245 in 52)

CONSECUTIVE THREE-POINT FIELD GOALS
Game
10—Duane Huddleston, Missouri S&T vs. Truman, Jan. 23, 1988
Season
18—Dan Drews, Le Moyne (during 11 games, Dec. 11, 1993 to Feb. 2, 1994)

CONSECUTIVE GAMES MAKING A THREE-POINT FIELD GOAL
Season
35—Tarvoris Uzoigwe, Henderson St., Nov. 15, 2002 to March 17, 2003 (one season)
Career
93—Daniel Parke, Rollins, Jan. 26, 1994, to Feb. 28, 1997

THREE-POINT FIELD-GOAL ATTEMPTS
Game
34—Markus Hallgrimson, Mont. St.-Billings vs. Western N.M., Feb. 26, 2000 (13 made)
Season
382—Markus Hallgrimson, Mont. St.-Billings, 2000 (160 made)
Career
1,100—Tavoris Uzoigwe, Henderson St., 2002-05 (404 made)

THREE-POINT FIELD-GOAL ATTEMPTS PER GAME
Season
14.7—Markus Hallgrimson, Mont. St.-Billings, 2000 (382 in 26)
Career
11.3—Markus Hallgrimson, Mont. St.-Billings, 1997-00 (927 in 82)

THREE-POINT FIELD-GOAL PERCENTAGE
Game
(Min. 10 made) 100%—Rodney Edgerson, Ky. Wesleyan vs. Wis.-Parkside, Jan. 25, 2007 (10 of 10)
*Season
(Min. 35 made) 65.0%—Ray Lee, Hampton, 1988 (39 of 60)

(Min. 50 made) 60.3%—Aaron Fehler, Oakland City, 1995 (73 of 121)
(Min. 100 made) 56.7%—Scott Martin, Rollins, 1991 (114 of 201)
(Min. 150 made) 45.3%—Alex Williams, Sacramento St., 1988 (167 of 369)

*based on qualifiers for annual championship
Career
(Min. 200 made) 51.3%—Scott Martin, Rollins, 1988-91 (236 of 460)

Free Throws

FREE THROWS
Game
37—Clarence "Bevo" Francis, Rio Grande vs. Hillsdale, Feb. 2, 1954 (45 attempts)
Season
401—Joe Miller, Alderson-Broaddus, 1957 (496 attempts)
Career
1,130—Joe Miller, Alderson-Broaddus, 1954-57 (1,460 attempts)

CONSECUTIVE FREE THROWS
Game
26—Jim Moore, St. Anselm vs. St. Rose, Feb. 18, 2006
Season
94—Paul Cluxton, Northern Ky., 1997 (during 34 games, Nov. 8-Mar. 20)

FREE-THROW ATTEMPTS
Game
45—Clarence "Bevo" Francis, Rio Grande vs. Hillsdale, Feb. 2, 1954 (37 made)
Season
†510—Clarence "Bevo" Francis, Rio Grande, 1954 (367 made)
Career
1,460—Joe Miller, Alderson-Broaddus, 1954-57 (1,130 made)

†Season figure for Francis limited to 27 games against four-year colleges.

FREE-THROW PERCENTAGE
Game
(Min. 20 made) 100%—Milosh Pujo, Lewis vs. Mt. St. Clare, Dec. 30, 1997 (20 of 20); Forrest "Butch" Meyeraan, Minn. St. Mankato vs. Wis.-River Falls, Feb. 21, 1961 (20 of 20)
*Season
100%—Paul Cluxton, Northern Ky., 1997 (94 of 94)

*based on qualifiers for annual championship
Career
(Min. 250 made) 93.5%—Paul Cluxton, Northern Ky., 1994-97 (272 of 291)
(Min. 500 made) 87.9%—Steve Nisenson, Hofstra, 1963-65 (602 of 685)

Rebounds

REBOUNDS
Game
46—Tom Hart, Middlebury vs. Trinity (Conn.), Feb. 5, 1955, and vs. Clarkson, Feb. 12, 1955
Season
799—Elmore Smith, Kentucky St., 1971 (33 games)
Career
2,334—Jim Smith, Steubenville, 1955-58 (112 games)

AVERAGE PER GAME
Season
29.5—Tom Hart, Middlebury, 1956 (620 in 21)
Career
(Min. 900) 27.6—Tom Hart, Middlebury, 1953, 55-56 (1,738 in 63)

Assists

ASSISTS
Game
25—Ali Baaqar, Morris Brown vs. Albany St. (Ga.), Jan. 26, 1991; Adrian Hutt, Metro St. vs. Sacramento St., Feb. 9, 1991
Season
400—Steve Ray, Bridgeport, 1989 (32 games)
Career
1,044—Demetri Beekman, Assumption, 1990-93 (119 games)

AVERAGE PER GAME
Season
12.5—Steve Ray, Bridgeport, 1989 (400 in 32)
Career
(Min. 550) 12.1—Steve Ray, Bridgeport, 1989-90 (785 in 65)

Blocked Shots

BLOCKED SHOTS
Game
15—Mark Hensel, Pitt.-Johnstown vs. Slippery Rock, Jan. 22, 1994

Season
170—Ryan McLemore, Edinboro, 2008 (31 games)
Career
455—Bryan Grier, Wingate, 2005-08 (122 games)

AVERAGE PER GAME
Season
5.48—Ryan McLemore, Edinboro, 2008, (170 in 31)
Career
4.00—Derek Moore, S.C.-Aiken, 1996-99 (408 in 102)

Steals

STEALS
Game
17—Antonio Walls, Alabama A&M vs. Albany St. (Ga.), Jan. 5, 1998
Season
139—J.R. Gamble, Queens (N.C.), 2001 (32 games)
Career
414—Jonte Flowers, Winona St., 2005-08, (141 games)

AVERAGE PER GAME
Season
4.96—Wayne Copeland, Lynn, 2000 (129 in 26)
Career
4.46—Wayne Copeland, Lynn, 1999-00 (254 in 57)

Games

GAMES PLAYED
Season
38—Terrence Hill, Rey Luque, Reggie McCoy, Kevin McDonald, Cardale Talley, Justin Thompson, Tommy Thompson, Kennesaw St., 2004
Career
146—John Smith, Winona St., 2005-08

Team Records

Note: Where records involve both teams, each team must be an NCAA Division II member institution.

SINGLE-GAME RECORDS

Scoring

POINTS
258—Troy vs. DeVry (Ga.) (141), Jan. 12, 1992
POINTS VS. DIVISION II TEAM
169—Stillman vs. Miles (123), Feb. 17, 1966
POINTS BY LOSING TEAM
146—Mississippi Col. vs. West Ala. (160), Dec. 2, 1969
POINTS, BOTH TEAMS
306—West Ala. (160) and Mississippi Col. (146), Dec. 2, 1969
POINTS IN A HALF
135—Troy vs. DeVry (Ga.), Jan. 12, 1992
FEWEST POINTS ALLOWED (SINCE 1938)
4—Albion (76) vs. Adrian, Dec. 12, 1938; Tennessee St. (7) vs. Oglethorpe, Feb. 16, 1971
FEWEST POINTS, BOTH TEAMS (SINCE 1938)
11—Tennessee St. (7) and Oglethorpe (4), Feb. 16, 1971
WIDEST MARGIN OF VICTORY
118—Mississippi Col. (168) vs. Dallas Bible (50), Dec. 9, 1971

Field Goals

FIELD GOALS
102—Troy vs. DeVry (Ga.), Jan. 12, 1992 (190 attempts)
FIELD-GOAL ATTEMPTS
190—Troy vs. DeVry (Ga.), Jan. 12, 1992 (102 made)
FEWEST FIELD GOALS (SINCE 1938)
0—Adrian vs. Albion, Dec. 12, 1938 (28 attempts)
FEWEST FIELD-GOAL ATTEMPTS
7—Mansfield vs. West Chester, Dec. 8, 1984 (4 made)
FIELD-GOAL PERCENTAGE
81.6%—Youngstown St. vs. UNI, Jan. 26, 1980 (31 of 38)
FIELD-GOAL PERCENTAGE, HALF
95.0%—Abilene Christian vs. Cameron, Jan. 21, 1989 (19 of 20)

Three-Point Field Goals

THREE-POINT FIELD GOALS
51—Troy vs. DeVry (Ga.), Jan. 12, 1992 (109 attempts)
THREE-POINT FIELD GOALS, BOTH TEAMS
39—Columbus St. (22) vs. Troy (17), Feb. 14, 1991
CONSECUTIVE THREE-POINT FIELD GOALS MADE WITHOUT A MISS
12—Southwest St. vs. Bemidji St., Jan. 22, 2000; Catawba vs. Wingate, Feb. 28, 1998; Pace vs. Medgar Evers, Nov. 27, 1991
NUMBER OF DIFFERENT PLAYERS TO SCORE A THREE-POINT FIELD GOAL, ONE TEAM
10—Troy vs. DeVry (Ga.), Jan. 12, 1992
THREE-POINT FIELD-GOAL ATTEMPTS
109—Troy vs. DeVry (Ga.), Jan. 12, 1992 (51 made)
THREE-POINT FIELD-GOAL ATTEMPTS, BOTH TEAMS
95—Columbus St. (52) vs. Troy (43), Feb. 14, 1991
THREE-POINT FIELD-GOAL PERCENTAGE
(Min. 10 made) 100%—LeMoyne-Owen vs. Delta St., Nov. 25, 2006 (10 of 10)
HIGHEST THREE-POINT FIELD-GOAL PERCENTAGE, BOTH TEAMS
(Min. 10 made) 83.3%—Tampa (9 of 10) vs. St. Leo (1 of 2), Jan. 21, 1987 (10 of 12)
(Min. 20 made) 77.8%—LeMoyne-Owen (10 of 10) vs. Delta St. (11 of 17), Nov. 25, 2006 (21 of 27)

Free Throws

FREE THROWS MADE
64—Wayne St. (Mich.) vs. Grand Valley St., Feb. 13, 1993 (79 attempts); Baltimore vs. Washington (Md.), Feb. 9, 1955 (84 attempts)
FREE THROWS MADE, BOTH TEAMS
89—Southern Ind. (50) vs. Northern St. (39), Nov. 15, 1997 (3ot); Baltimore (64) and Washington (Md.) (25), Feb. 9,1955
CONSECUTIVE FREE THROWS MADE
37—Southern Ind., January 23-30, 2003 (three games)
FREE-THROW ATTEMPTS
84—Baltimore vs. Washington (Md.), Feb. 9, 1955 (64 made)

FREE-THROW ATTEMPTS, BOTH TEAMS
142—Southern Ind. (80) vs. Northern St. (62), Nov. 15, 1997 (3 ot) (89 made)
FREE-THROW PERCENTAGE
(Min. 31 made) 100%—Dowling vs. Southampton, Feb. 6, 1985 (31 of 31)
FREE-THROW PERCENTAGE, BOTH TEAMS
(Min. 30 made) 97.0%—Hartford (17 of 17) vs. Bentley (15 of 16), Feb. 22, 1983 (32 of 33)

Rebounds

REBOUNDS
111—Central Mich. vs. Alma, Dec. 7, 1963
REBOUNDS, BOTH TEAMS
141—Loyola (Md.) (75) vs. McDaniel (66), Dec. 6, 1961; Concordia (Ill.) (72) vs. Concordia (Neb.) (69), Feb. 26, 1965
REBOUND MARGIN
65—Moravian (100) vs. Drew (35), Feb. 18, 1969

Assists

ASSISTS
65—Troy vs. DeVry (Ga.), Jan. 12, 1992
ASSISTS, BOTH TEAMS
65—Central Okla. (34) vs. Stonehill (31), Dec. 29, 1990

Personal Fouls

PERSONAL FOULS
51—Northern St. vs. Southern Ind., Nov. 15, 1997 (3 ot)
PERSONAL FOULS, BOTH TEAMS (Including Overtimes)
91—Northern St. (51) vs. Southern Ind. (40), Nov. 15, 1997 (3 ot)
PERSONAL FOULS, BOTH TEAMS (Regulation Time)
78—Cal St. Chico (41) vs. Cal St. San B'dino (37), Feb. 12, 2005 (85 total personal fouls including overtime)

DIVISION II

PLAYERS DISQUALIFIED
7—Northern St. vs. Southern Ind., Nov. 15, 1997 (3 ot); Illinois Col. vs. Illinois Tech, Dec. 13, 1952; Steubenville vs. West Liberty, 1952; Washington (Md.) vs. Baltimore, Feb. 9, 1955; Colorado St.-Pueblo vs. Air Force, Jan. 12, 1972; Edinboro vs. California (Pa.) (5 ot), Feb. 4, 1989

PLAYERS DISQUALIFIED, BOTH TEAMS
12—Alfred (6) and Rensselaer (6), Jan. 9, 1971

Overtimes

OVERTIME PERIODS
7—Yankton (79) vs. Black Hills (80), Feb. 18, 1956

POINTS IN ONE OVERTIME PERIOD
27—Southern Ind. vs. Central Mo., Jan. 5, 1985

POINTS IN ONE OVERTIME PERIOD, BOTH TEAMS
46—North Dakota St. (25) vs. St. Cloud St. (21), Jan. 16, 1999; North Dakota St. (25) vs. South Dakota (21), Jan. 9, 1999

POINTS IN OVERTIME PERIODS
60—California (Pa.) vs. Edinboro (5 ot), Feb. 4, 1989

POINTS IN OVERTIME PERIODS, BOTH TEAMS
114—California (Pa.) (60) vs. Edinboro (54) (5 ot), Feb. 4, 1989

WINNING MARGIN IN OVERTIME GAME
22—Pfeiffer (72) vs. Belmont Abbey (50), Dec. 8, 1960

SEASON RECORDS

Scoring

POINTS
3,566—Troy, 1993 (32 games); Central Okla., 1992 (32 games)

AVERAGE PER GAME
121.1—Troy, 1992 (3,513 in 29)

AVERAGE SCORING MARGIN
31.4—Bryan, 1961 (93.8 offense, 62.4 defense)

GAMES AT LEAST 100 POINTS
25—Troy, 1993 (32-game season)

CONSECUTIVE GAMES AT LEAST 100 POINTS
17—Norfolk St., 1970

Field Goals

FIELD GOALS
1,455—Kentucky St., 1971 (2,605 attempts)

FIELD GOALS PER GAME
46.9—Lincoln (Mo.), 1967 (1,267 in 27)

FIELD-GOAL ATTEMPTS
2,853—Ark.-Pine Bluff, 1967 (1,306 made)

FIELD-GOAL ATTEMPTS PER GAME
108.2—Stillman, 1968 (2,814 in 26)

FIELD-GOAL PERCENTAGE
62.4%—Kentucky St., 1976 (1,093 of 1,753)

Three-Point Field Goals

THREE-POINT FIELD GOALS
444—Troy, 1992 (1,303 attempts)

THREE-POINT FIELD GOALS PER GAME
15.3—Troy, 1992 (444 in 29)

THREE-POINT FIELD-GOAL ATTEMPTS
1,303—Troy, 1992 (444 made)

THREE-POINT FIELD-GOAL ATTEMPTS PER GAME
44.9—Troy, 1992 (1,303 in 29)

THREE-POINT FIELD-GOAL PERCENTAGE
(Min. 90 made) 53.8%—Winston-Salem, 1988 (98 of 182)
(Min. 200 made) 50.2%—Oakland City, 1992 (244 of 486)

CONSECUTIVE GAMES SCORING A THREE-POINT FIELD GOAL (Multiple Seasons)
567—Ky. Wesleyan, Nov. 22, 1986-Present

Free Throws

FREE THROWS MADE
896—Ouachita Baptist, 1965 (1,226 attempts)

FREE THROWS MADE PER GAME
36.1—Baltimore, 1955 (686 in 19)

FREE-THROW ATTEMPTS
1,226—Ouachita Baptist, 1965 (896 made)

FREE-THROW ATTEMPTS PER GAME
49.6—Baltimore, 1955 (943 in 19)

FREE-THROW PERCENTAGE
82.5%—Gannon, 1998 (473 of 573)

Rebounds

REBOUNDS
1,667—Norfolk St., 1973 (31 games)

AVERAGE PER GAME
65.8—Bentley, 1964 (1,513 in 23)

AVERAGE REBOUND MARGIN
24.4—Mississippi Val., 1976 (63.9 offense, 39.5 defense)

Assists

ASSISTS
736—Southern N.H., 1993 (33 games)

AVERAGE PER GAME
25.6—Quincy, 1994 (716 in 28)

Personal Fouls

PERSONAL FOULS
947—Seattle, 1952 (37 games)

PERSONAL FOULS PER GAME
29.9—Shaw, 1987 (748 in 25)

FEWEST PERSONAL FOULS
184—Sewanee, 1962 (17 games)

FEWEST PERSONAL FOULS PER GAME
10.0—Ashland, 1969 (301 in 30)

Defense

LOWEST POINTS PER GAME ALLOWED
20.2—Alcorn St., 1941 (323 in 16)

LOWEST POINTS PER GAME ALLOWED (Since 1948)
29.1—Miss. Industrial, 1948 (436 in 15)

LOWEST FIELD-GOAL PERCENTAGE ALLOWED (Since 1978)
35.8—Tarleton St., 2002 (657 of 1,837)

Overtimes

MOST OVERTIME GAMES
8—Barton, 2007 (won 8, lost 0); Belmont Abbey, 1983 (won 4, lost 4)

MOST CONSECUTIVE OVERTIME GAMES
3—10 times, most recent: Pace, 1996 (won 3, lost 0)

MOST OVERTIME WINS
8—Barton, 2007 (won 8, lost 0)

MOST MULTIPLE-OVERTIME GAMES
5—Cal St. Dom. Hills, 1987 (four 2 ot, one 3 ot; won 2, lost 3)

General Records

GAMES IN A SEASON
39—Winona St., 2008 (38-1); Kennesaw St., 2004 (35-4); Regis (Colo.), 1949 (36-3)

VICTORIES IN A SEASON
36—Regis (Colo.), 1949 (36-3)

VICTORIES IN A PERFECT SEASON
34—Fort Hays St., 1996

CONSECUTIVE VICTORIES
57—Winona St. (from Jan. 13, 2006-March 22, 2007)

CONSECUTIVE 30-WIN SEASONS
4—Ky. Wesleyan, 1998 (30); 1999 (35); 2000 (31); 2001 (31)

MOST-IMPROVED TEAM FROM ONE SEASON TO THE NEXT
17½ games—Lincoln (Mo.), 2001 (from 2-24 to 20-7)

CONSECUTIVE HOME-COURT VICTORIES
80—Philadelphia U. (from Jan. 8, 1991 to Nov. 21, 1995)

CONSECUTIVE REGULAR-SEASON VICTORIES (postseason tournaments not included)
54—Bentley (from Feb. 21, 2006-present)

CONSECUTIVE VICTORIES AGAINST AN OPPONENT
45—Fla. Southern vs. St. Leo, Feb. 11, 1985-current

DEFEATS IN A SEASON
28—UNC Pembroke, 2003 (0-28)

CONSECUTIVE DEFEATS IN A SEASON
28—UNC Pembroke, 2003 (0-28)

CONSECUTIVE DEFEATS
46—Olivet, Feb. 21, 1959, to Dec. 4, 1961; Southwest Minn. St., Dec. 11, 1971, to Dec. 1, 1973

CONSECUTIVE WINNING SEASONS
35—Norfolk St., 1963-97

CONSECUTIVE NON-LOSING SEASONS
35—Norfolk St., 1963-97

††UNBEATEN TEAMS (Since 1938; Number of Victories in Parentheses)
1938 Glenville St. (28)
1941 Milwaukee St. (16)
1942 Indianapolis (16)
1942 Rochester (16)
1944 Langston (23)
1945 Langston (24)
1948 West Virginia St. (23)
1949 Tennessee St. (24)
1956 Rochester Inst. (17)
1959 Grand Canyon (20)
1961 Calvin (20)
1964 Bethany (W.V.) (18)
1965 Central St. (Ohio) (30)
1965 Evansville (29)#
1993 Cal St. Bakersfield (33)#
1996 Fort Hays St. (34)#

††at least 15 victories; #NCAA Division II champion

All-Time Individual Leaders

Single-Game Records

SCORING HIGHS

Pts.	Player, Team vs. Opponent	Season
113	Clarence "Bevo" Francis, Rio Grande vs. Hillsdale	1954
84	Clarence "Bevo" Francis, Rio Grande vs. Alliance	1954
82	Clarence "Bevo" Francis, Rio Grande vs. Bluffton	1954
80	Paul Crissman, Southern California Col. vs. Pacific Christian	1966
77	William English, Winston-Salem vs. Fayetteville St.	1968
75	Travis Grant, Kentucky St. vs. Northwood (Mich.)	1970
72	Nate DeLong, Wis.-River Falls vs. Winona St.	1948
72	Lloyd Brown, Aquinas vs. Cleary	1953
72	Clarence "Bevo" Francis, Rio Grande vs. California (Pa.)	1953
72	John McElroy, Youngstown St. vs. Wayne St. (Mich.)	1969
71	Clayborn Jones, L.A. Pacific vs. L.A. Baptist	1965
70	Paul Wilcox, Davis & Elkins vs. Glenville St.	1959
70	Bo Clark, UCF vs. Fla. Memorial	1977

Season Records

SCORING AVERAGE

Player, Team	Season	G	FG	FT	Pts.	Avg.
Clarence "Bevo" Francis, Rio Grande	†1954	27	444	367	1,255	*46.5
Earl Glass, Miss. Industrial	†1963	19	322	171	815	42.9
Earl Monroe, Winston-Salem	†1967	32	509	311	*1,329	41.5
John Rinka, Kenyon	†1970	23	354	234	942	41.0
Willie Shaw, Lane	†1964	18	303	121	727	40.4
Travis Grant, Kentucky St.	†1972	33	*539	226	1,304	39.5
Thales McReynolds, Miles	†1965	18	294	118	706	39.2
Bob Johnson, Fitchburg St.	1963	18	213	277	703	39.1
Roger Kuss, Wis.-River Falls	†1953	21	291	235	817	38.9
Florindo Vieira, Quinnipiac	1954	14	191	138	520	37.1

†national champion; *record

FIELD-GOAL PERCENTAGE
(Based on qualifiers for annual championship)

Player, Team	Season	G	FG	FGA	Pct.
Garret Siler, Augusta St.	†2008	34	211	277	76.2
Todd Linder, Tampa	†1987	32	282	375	75.2
Maurice Stafford, North Ala.	†1984	34	198	264	75.0
Matthew Cornegay, Tuskegee	†1982	29	208	278	74.8
Callistus Eziukwu, Grand Valley St.	†2005	28	157	213	73.7
Brian Moten, West Ga.	†1992	26	141	192	73.4
Ed Phillips, Alabama A&M	†1968	22	154	210	73.3
Ray Strozier, Central Mo.	†1980	28	142	195	72.8
Harold Booker, Cheyney	†1965	24	144	198	72.7
Chad Scott, California (Pa.)	†1994	30	178	245	72.7
Tom Schurfranz, Bellarmine	†1991	30	245	339	72.3
Marv Lewis, Southampton	†1969	24	271	375	72.3
Louis Newsome, North Ala.	†1988	29	192	266	72.2
Ed Phillips, Alabama A&M	†1971	24	159	221	71.9
Gregg Northington, Alabama St.	1971	26	324	451	71.8

†national champion; *record

THREE-POINT FIELD GOALS

Player, Team	Season	G	3FG
Alex Williams, Sacramento St.	1988	30	167
Markus Hallgrimson, Mont. St.-Billings	2000	26	160
Yandel Brown, Columbus St.	2005	32	148
Eric Kline, Northern St.	1995	30	148
Eric Kline, Northern St.	1994	33	148
Cameron Munoz, Mont. St.-Billings	2006	28	147
Mike Taylor, West Virginia St.	2004	32	140
Shawn Pughsley, Central Okla.	1998	32	139
Jed Bedford, Columbus St.	2003	32	135
Reece Gliko, Mont. St.-Billings	1997	28	135
Ray Gutierrez, California (Pa.)	1993	27	135
Jason Garrow, Augustana (S.D.)	1992	27	135
Markus Hallgrimson, Mont. St.-Billings	1999	28	133
Stephen Dye, Alderson-Broaddus	2004	34	129
Shawn Williams, Central Okla.	1991	29	129
Tarvoris Uzoigwe, Henderson St.	2003	35	128
Robert Martin, Sacramento St.	1988	30	128
Steve Brown, West Ala.	2000	26	126
Antonio Harris, LeMoyne-Owen	1999	26	126
Tommie Spearman, Columbus	1995	29	126
Kwame Morton, Clarion	1994	26	126

THREE-POINT FIELD GOALS PER GAME

Player, Team	Season	G	3FG	Avg.
Markus Hallgrimson, Mont. St.-Billings	†2000	26	160	*6.2
Alex Williams, Sacramento St.	†1988	30	*167	5.6
Cameron Munoz, Mont. St.-Billings	†2006	28	147	5.3
Jason Garrow, Augustana (S.D.)	†1992	27	135	5.0
Eric Kline, Northern St.	†1995	30	148	4.9
Ray Gutierrez, California (Pa.)	†1993	29	142	4.9
Steve Brown, West Ala.	2000	26	126	4.8
Antonio Harris, LeMoyne-Owen	†1999	26	126	4.8
Kwame Morton, Clarion	†1994	26	126	4.8
Reece Gliko, Mont. St.-Billings	†1997	28	135	4.8
Markus Hallgrimson, Mont. St.-Billings	1999	28	133	4.8
John Boyd, LeMoyne-Owen	1992	26	123	4.7
Duane Huddleston, Missouri S&T	1988	25	118	4.7
Yandel Brown, Columbus St.	†2005	32	148	4.6
Antonio Harris, LeMoyne-Owen	†1998	26	119	4.6
Ricardo Watkins, Tuskegee	2000	24	110	4.6
Eric Kline, Northern St.	1994	33	148	4.5
Robbie Waldrop, Lees-McRae	2001	25	112	4.5
Damien Blair, West Chester	1994	28	125	4.5
Eric Carpenter, Cal St. San B'dino	1994	26	116	4.5

†national champion; *record

THREE-POINT FIELD-GOAL PERCENTAGE
(Based on qualifiers for annual championship)

Player, Team	Season	G	3FG	3FGA	Pct.
Ray Lee, Hampton	†1988	24	39	60	*65.0
Steve Hood, Winston-Salem	1988	28	42	67	62.7
Mark Willey, Fort Hays St.	†1990	29	49	81	60.5
Aaron Fehler, Oakland City	†1995	26	73	121	60.3
Aaron Baker, Mississippi Col.	†1989	27	69	117	59.0
Walter Hurd, Johnson C. Smith	1989	27	49	84	58.3
Matt Hopson, Oakland City	†1996	31	84	145	57.9
Jon Bryant, St. Cloud St.	1996	27	54	94	57.4
Adam Harness, Oakland City	†1997	26	39	68	57.4
Scott Martin, Rollins	†1991	28	114	201	56.7
Charles Byrd, West Tex. A&M	†1987	31	95	168	56.5
Aaron Buckoski, Michigan Tech	1997	26	39	69	56.5
Jay Nolan, Bowie St.	1987	27	70	124	56.5
Kris Kidwell, Oakland City	1996	28	44	78	56.4
Tony Harris, Dist. Columbia	1987	30	79	141	56.0
Rickey Barrett, Ala.-Huntsville	1987	26	63	113	55.8
Quinn Murphy, Drury	1995	27	45	81	55.6
Erik Fisher, San Fran. St.	1991	28	80	144	55.6
Mike Doyle, Philadelphia U.	1988	30	82	149	55.0

†national champion; *record

FREE-THROW PERCENTAGE
(Based on qualifiers for annual championship)

Player, Team	Season	G	FT	FTA	Pct.
Paul Cluxton, Northern Ky.	†1997	35	94	94	*100.0
Jake Linton, St. Martin's	†2008	27	162	168	96.4
Tomas Rimkus, Pace	1997	25	65	68	95.6
C. J. Cowgill, Chaminade	†2001	22	113	119	95.0
Rory Morgan, Colo. Christian	2008	31	85	90	94.4
Billy Newton, Morgan St.	†1976	28	85	90	94.4
Kent Andrews, McNeese St.	†1968	24	85	90	94.4
Darroll Phillips, Cal St. Chico	2008	27	83	88	94.3
Mike Sanders, Northern Colo.	†1987	28	82	87	94.3
Curtis Small, Southampton	†2002	29	109	116	94.0
Brent Mason, St. Joseph's (Ind.)	2001	31	125	133	94.0
Aaron Farley, Harding	†2003	30	137	146	93.8
Marcus Martinez, Cal St. Stanislaus	†2006	27	75	80	93.8
Travis Starns, Colorado Mines	†1999	26	87	93	93.5
Jay Harrie, Mont. St.-Billings	†1994	26	86	92	93.5
Joe Cullen, Hartwick	†1969	18	96	103	93.2
Dan Shanks, Coker	1997	27	119	128	93.0
Charles Byrd, West Tex. A&M	†1988	29	92	99	92.9
Jeremy Kudera, South Dakota	2001	28	78	84	92.9
Brian Koephick, Minn. St. Mankato	1988	28	104	112	92.9

†national champion; *record

DIVISION II

REBOUNDS (SINCE 1973)

Player, Team	Season	G	Reb.
Marvin Webster, Morgan St.	1974	33	740
Major Jones, Albany St. (Ga.)	1975	27	608
Earl Williams, Winston-Salem	1974	26	553
Antonio Garcia, Ky. Wesleyan	1999	37	540
Charles Oakley, Virginia Union	1985	31	535
Larry Johnson, Prairie View	1974	23	519
Andre Means, Sacred Heart	1977	32	516
Major Jones, Albany St. (Ga.)	1975	25	513
Harvey Jones, Alabama St.	1974	28	503
Andre Means, Sacred Heart	1978	30	493
Colin Duchacme, Longwood	2001	31	490
Rick Mahorn, Hampton	1980	31	490
Rob Roesch, Staten Island	1989	31	482
Leonard Robinson, Tennessee St.	1974	28	478
Major Jones, Albany St. (Ga.)	1976	24	475

REBOUND AVERAGE

Player, Team	Season	G	Reb.	Avg.
Tom Hart, Middlebury	†1956	21	620	*29.5
Tom Hart, Middlebury	†1955	22	649	29.5
Frank Stronczek, American Int'l	†1966	26	717	27.6
R.C. Owens, Albertson	†1954	25	677	27.1
Maurice Stokes, St. Francis (Pa.)	1954	26	689	26.5
Roman Turmon, Clark Atlanta	1954	23	602	26.2
Pat Callahan, Lewis	1955	20	523	26.2
Hank Brown, Mass.-Lowell	1966	19	496	26.1
Maurice Stokes, St. Francis (Pa.)	1955	28	726	25.9

†national champion; *record

(Since 1973)

Player, Team	Season	G	Reb.	Avg.
Larry Johnson, Prairie View	1974	23	519	22.6
Major Jones, Albany St. (Ga.)	1975	27	608	22.5
Marvin Webster, Morgan St.	1974	33	740	22.4
Earl Williams, Winston-Salem	1974	26	553	21.3
Major Jones, Albany St. (Ga.)	1974	25	513	20.5
Larry Gooding, St. Augustine's	1974	22	443	20.1
Major Jones, Albany St. (Ga.)	1976	24	475	19.8
Calvin Robinson, Mississippi Valley	1976	23	432	18.8
Scott Mountz, California (Pa.)	1978	24	431	18.0
Howard Shockley, Salisbury	1975	23	406	17.7
Charles Oakley, Virginia Union	1985	31	535	17.3
Marvin Webster, Morgan St.	1975	27	458	17.0
Larry Johnson, Ark.-Little Rock	1976	24	402	16.8
Keith Smith, Shaw	1979	20	329	16.5
Andre Means, Sacred Heart	1978	30	493	16.4
Donnie Roberts, St. Paul's	1975	25	406	16.2
Andre Means, Sacred Heart	1977	32	516	16.1
Dan Donahue, SIU Edwardsville	1975	26	419	16.1
Lorenzo Poole, Albany St. (Ga.)	1995	26	417	16.0
David Binion, N.C. Central	1983	25	400	16.0

ASSISTS

Player, Team	Season	G	Ast.
Steve Ray, Bridgeport	†1989	32	*400
Steve Ray, Bridgeport	†1990	33	385
Tony Smith, Pfeiffer	†1992	35	349
Luke Cooper, Alas. Anchorage	†2008	35	310
Rob Paternostro, Southern N.H.	1995	33	309
Jim Ferrer, Bentley	1989	31	309
Brian Gregory, Oakland	1989	28	300
Charles Jordan, Erskine	1992	34	298
Ernest Jenkins, N.M. Highlands	†1995	27	291
Pat Chambers, Philadelphia U.	1994	30	290
Zack Whiting, Chaminade	†2007	27	289
Craig Lottie, Alabama A&M	1995	32	287
Adrian Hutt, Metro St.	†1991	28	285
Javar Cheatham, Gannon	†2001	30	283
Patrick Boen, Stonehill	1989	32	278
Ernest Jenkins, N.M. Highlands	†1994	27	277
Clayton Smith, Metro St.	†2003	33	274
Adam Kaufman, Edinboro	1998	34	273
Darnell White, California (Pa.)	1994	30	273
Demetri Beekman, Assumption	1992	32	271

†national champion; *record

ASSIST AVERAGE

Player, Team	Season	G	Ast.	Avg.
Steve Ray, Bridgeport	†1989	32	*400	*12.5
Steve Ray, Bridgeport	†1990	33	385	11.7
Demetri Beekman, Assumption	†1993	23	264	11.5
Ernest Jenkins, N.M. Highlands	†1995	27	291	10.8
Brian Gregory, Oakland	1989	28	300	10.7

Player, Team	Season	G	Ast.	Avg.
Zack Whiting, Chaminade	†2007	27	289	10.7
Brent Schremp, Slippery Rock	1995	25	259	10.4
Ernest Jenkins, N.M. Highlands	†1994	27	277	10.3
Adrian Hutt, Metro St.	†1991	28	285	10.2
Tony Smith, Pfeiffer	†1992	35	349	10.0
Jim Ferrer, Bentley	1989	31	309	10.0
Ryan Nelson, Grand Canyon	†2006	27	263	9.7
Todd Chappell, Texas Wesleyan	†2000	27	263	9.7
Pat Chambers, Philadelphia U.	1994	30	290	9.7
Marcus Talbert, Colo. Christian	1994	27	261	9.7
Carlin Hughes, Mont. St.-Billings	2006	28	269	9.6
Paul Beaty, Miles	1992	26	248	9.5
Lawrence Jordan, IPFW	1990	28	266	9.5
Hal Chambers, Columbus St.	1993	24	227	9.5
Javar Cheatham, Gannon	†2001	30	283	9.4
Rob Paternostro, Southern N.H.	1995	33	309	9.4

†national champion; *record

BLOCKED SHOTS

Player, Team	Season	G	Blk.
Ryan McLemore, Edinboro	†2008	31	*170
James Doyle, Concord	†1998	30	157
Antonio Harvey, Pfeiffer	†1993	29	155
Bryan Grier, Wingate	†2006	31	151
Ramel Allen, Bridgeport	†2005	30	146
Kenyon Gamble, Tuskegee	†2004	28	142
John Burke, Southampton	†1996	28	142
Matthew Rogers, Southwest Baptist	2008	30	136
Vonzell McGrew, Mo. Western St.	†1995	31	132
Colin Ducharme, Longwood	2001	31	130
Corey Johnson, Pace	1995	30	130
Derek Moore, S.C.-Aiken	1998	30	129
John Smith, Winona St.	2006	36	127
Johnny Tyson, Central Okla.	†1994	27	126
Garth Joseph, St. Rose	†1997	34	124
Kino Outlaw, Mount Olive	1995	28	124
Martiniz Woody, Benedict	2008	33	121
Bryan Grier, Wingate	2008	29	120
Bryan Grier, Wingate	2007	34	119
Tyler Cain, South Dakota	2008	29	118
Kobby Acquah, Clark Atlanta	2005	28	118

†national champion; *record

BLOCKED-SHOT AVERAGE

Player, Team	Season	G	Blk.	Avg.
Ryan McLemore, Edinboro	†2008	31	*170	*5.48
Antonio Harvey, Pfeiffer	†1993	29	155	5.34
James Doyle, Concord	†1998	30	157	5.23
Kenyon Gamble, Tuskegee	†2004	28	142	5.07
John Burke, Southampton	†1996	28	142	5.07
Bryan Grier, Wingate	†2006	31	151	4.87
Ramel Allen, Bridgeport	†2005	30	146	4.86
Johnny Tyson, Central Okla.	†1994	27	126	4.66
Matthew Rogers, Southwest Baptist	2008	30	136	4.53
Kino Outlaw, Mount Olive	†1995	28	124	4.43
Kino Outlaw, Mount Olive	1996	27	117	4.33
Corey Johnson, Pace	1995	30	130	4.33
Derek Moore, S.C.-Aiken	1998	30	129	4.30
Vonzell McGrew, Mo. Western St.	1995	31	132	4.26
Jason Roseto, Edinboro	†2001	23	97	4.22
Kobby Acquah, Clark Atlanta	2005	28	118	4.21
Colin Ducharme, Longwood	2001	31	130	4.19
Mark Hensel, Pitt.-Johnstown	1994	27	113	4.19
Sean McKeon, Kutztown	†2007	28	117	4.18
Bryan Grier, Wingate	2008	29	120	4.14

†national champion; *record

STEALS

Player, Team	Season	G	Stl.
J.R. Gamble, Queens (N.C.)	†2001	32	*139
Wayne Copeland, Lynn	†2000	26	129
Japhet McNeil, Bridgeport	†2007	31	125
Wayne Copeland, Lynn	†1999	31	125
Terrance Gist, S.C. Upstate	†1998	29	122
Devlin Herring, Pitt.-Johnstown	†1997	27	122
Jonte Flowers, Winona St.	2008	36	121
Oronn Brown, Clarion	1997	29	120
Devlin Herring, Pitt.-Johnstown	1998	29	118
David Clark, Bluefield St.	1996	31	118
Tyrone McDaniel, Lenoir-Rhyne	1993	32	116
Ken Francis, Molloy	†1994	27	116
Darnell White, California (Pa.)	1994	30	115
Drew Williamson, Metro St.	†2006	31	114

Player, Team	Season	G	Stl.
Jayson Williams, Lane	2005	32	114
Luke Kendall, Metro St.	2004	34	114
Eddin Santiago, Mo. Southern St.	2001	30	114
Tracy Gross, High Point	1997	29	114
Robert Campbell, Armstrong Atlantic	2001	33	113
Shaun McKie, Salem Int'l	†2005	31	111

†national champion; *record

STEAL AVERAGE

Player, Team	Season	G	Stl.	Avg.
Wayne Copeland, Lynn	†2000	26	129	*4.96
John Morris, Bluefield St.	1994	23	104	4.52
Devlin Herring, Pitt.-Johnstown	†1997	27	122	4.52
J.R. Gamble, Queens (N.C.)	†2001	32	*139	4.34
Ken Francis, Molloy	†1994	27	116	4.29
Terrance Gist, S.C. Upstate	†1998	29	122	4.21
Oronn Brown, Clarion	1997	29	120	4.14
Devlin Herring, Pitt.-Johnstown	1998	29	118	4.07
Michael Dean, Cal St. East Bay	1998	26	105	4.04
Terryl Woolery, Cal Poly Pomona	1997	27	109	4.04
Japhet McNeil, Bridgeport	†2007	31	125	4.03
Wayne Copeland, Lynn	†1999	31	125	4.03
Kevin Nichols, Bemidji St.	1994	26	104	4.00
Tracy Gross, High Point	1997	29	114	3.93
Peron Austin, Colorado St.-Pueblo	1997	28	110	3.93
Marcus Stubblefield, Queens (N.C.)	1993	28	110	3.93
Demetri Beekman, Assumption	1993	23	89	3.87
Darnell White, California (Pa.)	1994	30	115	3.83
J.R. Gamble, Queens (N.C.)	2000	28	107	3.82
David Clark, Bluefield St.	†1996	31	118	3.81

†national champion; *record

Career Records

POINTS

Player, Team	Seasons	Pts.
Travis Grant, Kentucky St.	1969-72	*4,045
Bob Hopkins, Grambling	1953-56	3,759
Tony Smith, Pfeiffer	1989-92	3,350
Earnest Lee, Clark Atlanta	1984-87	3,298
Joe Miller, Alderson-Broaddus	1954-57	3,294
Henry Logan, Western Caro.	1965-68	3,290
John Rinka, Kenyon	1967-70	3,251
Dick Barnett, Tennessee St.	1956-59	3,209
Willie Scott, Alabama St.	1966-69	3,155
Johnnie Allen, Bethune-Cookman	1966-69	3,058
Bennie Swain, Texas Southern	1955-58	3,008
Lambert Shell, Bridgeport	1989-92	3,001
Carl Hartman, Alderson-Broaddus	1952-55	2,959
Earl Monroe, Winston-Salem	1964-67	2,935

*record

SCORING AVERAGE
(Minimum 1,400 points)

Player, Team	Seasons	G	FG	3FG	FT	Pts.	Avg.
Travis Grant, Kentucky St.	1969-72	121	*1,760	—	525	*4,045	*33.4
John Rinka, Kenyon	1967-70	99	1,261	—	729	3,251	32.8
Florindo Vieira, Quinnipiac	1954-57	69	761	—	741	2,263	32.8
Willie Shaw, Lane	1961-64	76	960	—	459	2,379	31.3
Mike Davis, Virginia Union	1966-69	89	1,014	—	730	2,758	31.0
Henry Logan, Western Caro.	1965-68	107	1,263	—	764	3,290	30.7
Willie Scott, Alabama St.	1966-69	103	1,277	—	601	3,155	30.6
Carlos Knox, IUPUI	1995-98	85	832	208	684	2,556	30.1
George Gilmore, Chaminade	1991-92	51	485	174	387	1,531	30.0
Brett Beeson, Minn. St. Moorhead	1995-96	54	551	92	421	1,615	29.9
Bob Hopkins, Grambling	1953-56	126	1,403	—	953	3,759	29.8
Rod Butler, Western New Eng.	1968-70	59	697	—	331	1,725	29.2
Gregg Northington, Alabama St.	1970-72	75	894	—	403	2,191	29.2
Isaiah Wilson, Baltimore	1969-71	67	731	—	471	1,933	28.9

*record

FIELD-GOAL PERCENTAGE
(Minimum 400 field goals made)

Player, Team	Seasons	G	FG	FGA	Pct.
Todd Linder, Tampa	1984-87	122	909	1,284	*70.8
Tom Schurfranz, Bellarmine	1987-88, 91-92	112	742	1,057	70.2
Chad Scott, California (Pa.)	1991-94	115	465	664	70.0
Ed Phillips, Alabama A&M	1968-71	95	610	885	68.9
Ulysses Hackett, S.C. Upstate	1990-92	90	824	1,213	67.9

Player, Team	Seasons	G	FG	FGA	Pct.
Larry Tucker, Lewis	1981-83	84	677	999	67.8
Otis Evans, Wayne St. (Mich.)	1989-92	106	472	697	67.7
Matthew Cornegay, Tuskegee	1979-82	105	524	783	66.9
Ray Strozier, Central Mo.	1978-81	110	563	843	66.8
Dennis Edwards, Fort Hays St.	1994-95	59	666	998	66.7
James Morris, Central Okla.	1990-93	76	532	798	66.7
Lance Berwald, North Dakota St.	1983-84	58	475	717	66.2
Harold Booker, Cheyney	1965-67, 69	108	662	1,002	66.1

*record

THREE-POINT FIELD GOALS MADE

Player, Team	Seasons	G	3FG
Cameron Munoz, Mont. St.-Billings	2003-06	99	*451
Stephen Dye, Alderson-Broaddus	2002-05	121	443
Steve Moyer, Gannon	1996-99	112	442
Tony Smith, Pfeiffer	1989-92	126	431
Kwame Morton, Clarion	1991-94	105	411
Tarvoris Uzoigwe, Henderson St.	2002-05	119	404
Gary Duda, Merrimack	1989-92	122	389
Mike Taylor, West Virginia St.	2001-04	116	378
Markus Hallgrimson, Mont. St.-Billings	1998-00	82	371
Craig Sanders, Northern Ky.	1999-02	122	356
Nate Newell, Ark.-Monticello	2004-07	112	355
Columbus Parker, Johnson C. Smith	1990-93	115	354
Gary Paul, Indianapolis	1987-90	111	354
Jared Hembree, West Ala.	2004-07	108	353
Matt Miller, Drury	1999-02	106	351
Travis Tuttle, North Dakota	1994-97	108	350
Mike Ziegler, Colorado Mines	1987-90	118	344
Chris Benson, Queens (N.C.)	2000-03	119	343
Ryan Williams, Pace	2005-08	107	340
James Sorrentine, St. Michael's	2005-08	107	340
Chris Brown, Tuskegee	1993-96	104	339
Stephen Hamrick, Eastern N.M.	1993-96	107	339
Jason Marcotte, Michigan Tech	2002-05	120	335
Mike Kuhens, Queens (N.Y.)	1995-98	104	334
Jesse Ogden, Edinboro	1995-98	110	334

*record

THREE-POINT FIELD GOALS MADE PER GAME
(Minimum 200 three-point field goals made)

Player, Team	Seasons	G	3FG	Avg.
Antonio Harris, LeMoyne-Owen	1998-99	52	245	*4.71
Cameron Munoz, Mont. St.-Billings	2003-06	99	*451	4.56
Markus Hallgrimson, Mont. St.-Billings	1998-00	82	371	4.52
Alex Williams, Sacramento St.	1987-88	58	247	4.26
Yandel Brown, Columbus St.	2004-05	63	264	4.19
Tommie Spearman, Columbus St.	1994-95	56	233	4.16
Reece Gliko, Mont. St.-Billings	1996-97	56	231	4.13
Danny Phillips, Mont. St.-Billings	2001-02	55	222	4.03
Steve Moyer, Gannon	1996-99	112	442	3.95
Kwame Morton, Clarion	1991-94	105	411	3.91
Quinn Beckwith, North Ala.	2007-08	55	205	3.73
Zoderick Green, Central Okla.	1993-95	57	212	3.72
Shawn Williams, Central Okla.	1989-91	57	212	3.72
Derrick Brown, Coker	1999-02	77	285	3.70
Stephen Dye, Alderson-Broaddus	2002-05	121	443	3.66
Mike Sinclair, Bowie St.	1987-89	82	299	3.65
Tai Crutchfield, Philadelphia U.	2000-01	58	210	3.62
Nate Allen, Western St.	1996-97	57	205	3.60
Ryan Stefanski, California (Pa.)	2001-03	88	305	3.47
Robert Martin, Sacramento St.	1987-89	85	294	3.46
Tony Smith, Pfeiffer	1989-92	126	431	3.42
Tarvoris Uzoigwe, Henderson St.	2002-05	119	404	3.39
Brett Rector, Davis & Elkins	2006-08	79	266	3.37
Michael Shue, Lock Haven	1994-97	92	308	3.35
Matt Miller, Drury	1999-02	106	351	3.31

*record

THREE-POINT FIELD-GOAL PERCENTAGE
(Minimum 200 three-point field goals made)

Player, Team	Seasons	G	3FG	3FGA	Pct.
Scott Martin, Rollins	1988-91	104	236	460	*51.3
Todd Woelfle, Oakland City	1995-98	103	210	412	51.0
Matt Markle, Shippensburg	1989-92	101	202	408	49.5
Paul Cluxton, Northern Ky.	1994-97	122	303	619	48.9
Lance Gelnett, Millersville	1989-92	109	266	547	48.6
Antonio Harris, LeMoyne-Owen	1998-99	52	245	510	48.0
Mark Willey, Fort Hays St.	1989-92	117	224	478	46.9
Todd Bowden, Randolph-Macon	1987-89	84	229	491	46.6
Gary Paul, Indianapolis	1987-90	111	354	768	46.1
Ben Nemmers, North Dakota St.	2001-04	110	257	558	46.1

Player, Team	Seasons	G	3FG	3FGA	Pct.
Brad Oleson, Alas. Fairbanks	2003-05	87	229	499	45.9
Matt Ripaldi, Southern N.H.	1993-96	123	277	604	45.9
Chad Miller, Oakland City	2004-07	113	315	688	45.8
Chris Conroy, St. Anselm	2002-05	114	234	511	45.8
Alex Williams, Sacramento St.	1987-88	58	247	541	45.7
Craig Nelson, Northern St.	2005-08	122	262	574	45.6
Jordan Nuness, Minn.-Duluth	2006-08	85	242	534	45.3
Steven Gum, Drury	2005-08	116	277	612	45.3
Benjamin Chasten, Johnson C. Smith	2002-05	92	202	448	45.1
Jason Bullock, Indiana (Pa.)	1993-96	119	287	637	45.1
Boyd Printy, Truman	1990-92	77	201	447	45.0

*record

FREE-THROW PERCENTAGE
(Minimum 250 free throws made)

Player, Team	Seasons	G	FT	FTA	Pct.
Paul Cluxton, Northern Ky.	1994-97	122	272	291	*93.5
Kent Andrews, McNeese St.	1967-69	67	252	275	91.6
Cris Brunson, Southern Ind.	2002-05	129	317	352	90.1
Jon Hagen, Minn. St. Mankato	1963-65	73	252	280	90.0
Drew Carlson, Minn. St. Mankato	2000-03	107	306	342	89.5
Lance Den Boer, Central Wash.	2005-07	80	386	432	89.4
Dave Reynolds, Davis & Elkins	1986-89	107	383	429	89.3
Cory Coe, Hillsdale	2003-06	110	258	290	89.0
Michael Shue, Lock Haven	1994-97	92	354	400	88.5
Craig Nelson, Northern St.	2005-08	122	253	286	88.5
Tony Budzik, Mansfield	1989-92	107	367	416	88.2
Terry Gill, New Orleans	1972-74	79	261	296	88.2
Matt Miller, Drury	1999-02	106	371	421	88.1
Bryan Vacca, Randolph-Macon	1980-83	94	262	298	87.9
Steve Nisenson, Hofstra	1963-65	83	602	685	87.9
Jeff Gore, St. Rose	1991-93	91	333	379	87.9
Jack Sparks, Bentley	1976-80	99	253	288	87.8
Todd Manuel, St. Anselm	2000-02	90	455	519	87.7
Dan Shanks, Coker	1994-97	102	467	533	87.6
Troy Nesmith, Gannon	1997-98	54	274	313	87.5
Wayne Profitt, Lynchburg	1965-67	57	482	551	87.5
Clyde Briley, McNeese St.	1962-65	101	561	642	87.4
Jason Sempsrott, South Dakota St.	1994-97	110	462	529	87.3
Foy Ballance, Armstrong Atlantic	1978-81	108	351	402	87.3
Jehu Brabham, Mississippi Col.	1969-71	72	452	518	87.3
Pete Chambers, West Chester	1966-68	67	267	306	87.3

*record

REBOUNDS
(For careers beginning in 1973 or after)

Player, Team	Seasons	G	Reb.
Major Jones, Albany St. (Ga.)	1973-76	105	2,052
Clemon Johnson, Florida A&M	1975-78	109	1,494
Wayne Robertson, Southern N.H.	1991-94	127	1,487
Carlos Terry, Winston-Salem	1975-78	117	1,467
James Hector, American Int'l	1991-94	115	1,446
Jeff Covington, Youngstown St.	1975-78	106	1,381
John Ebeling, Fla. Southern	1979-82	127	1,362
John Smith, Winona St.	2005-08	*146	1,334
Damon Reed, St. Rose	1997-00	128	1,280
Fred Hooks, Humboldt St.	2001-04	120	1,268
Kelvin Hicks, NYIT	1977-80	94	1,258
Jonathan Roberts, East Stroudsburg	1987-90	112	1,247
John Edwards, Fla. Southern	1973-76	94	1,214
John Fox, Millersville	1984-87	118	1,214
Dave Vonesh, North Dakota	1988-91	122	1,207
Marvin Webster, Morgan St.	1975-76	60	1,198
Billy McDaniel, Ark.-Monticello	2003-06	115	1,197
Tony Cornett, West Virginia St.	2004-07	126	1,190
Brian Atkins, Concord	2001-04	111	1,144
Ramzee Stanton, West Chester	2000-03	111	1,142
Mark Tetzlaff, South Dakota St.	1982-85	118	1,132
Chris Bowles, Southern Ind.	1991-94	114	1,129
Jakim Donaldson, Edinboro	2002-05	109	1,100
Steve O'Neill, American Int'l	1977-81	108	1,093
Garth Joseph, St. Rose	1995-97	89	1,072
Dusty Jura, Neb.-Kearney	2004-07	122	1,069
Bob Stanley, Missouri S&T	1974-77	95	1,049
Samario Clancy, Alderson-Broaddus	2005-08	125	1,046
Ernie DeWitt, Bryant	1978-81	107	1,036
Gerald Lavender, North Ala.	1977-80	118	1,033

*record

REBOUND AVERAGE
(Minimum 800 rebounds)

Player, Team	Seasons	G	Reb.	Avg.
Tom Hart, Middlebury	1953, 55-56	63	1,738	*27.6
Maurice Stokes, St. Francis (Pa.)	1953-55	72	1,812	25.2
Frank Stronczek, American Int'l	1965-67	62	1,549	25.0
Bill Thieben, Hofstra	1954-56	76	1,837	24.2
Hank Brown, Mass.-Lowell	1965-67	49	1,129	23.0
Elmore Smith, Kentucky St.	1969-71	85	1,917	22.6
Charles Wrinn, Trinity (Conn.)	1951-53	53	1,176	22.2
Roman Turmon, Clark Atlanta	1952-54	60	1,312	21.9
Tony Missere, Pratt	1966-68	62	1,348	21.7
Ron Horton, Delaware St.	1966-68	64	1,384	21.6

*record

(For careers beginning in 1973 or after; minimum 800 rebounds)

Player, Team	Seasons	G	Reb.	Avg.
Marvin Webster, Morgan St.	1975-76	60	1,198	20.0
Major Jones, Albany St. (Ga.)	1973-76	105	2,052	19.5
Howard Shockley, Salisbury	1975-76	49	817	16.7
Andre Means, Sacred Heart	1977-78	62	1,009	16.3
Antonio Garcia, Ky. Wesleyan	1998-99	70	997	14.2
Clemon Johnson, Florida A&M	1975-78	109	1,494	13.7
Larry Johnson, Ark.-Little Rock	1976-78	69	944	13.7
Kelvin Hicks, NYIT	1977-80	94	1,258	13.4
John Edwards, Fla. Southern	1973-76	94	1,214	12.9
James Hector, American Int'l	1991-94	115	1,446	12.6
Garth Joseph, St. Rose	1995-97	89	1,072	12.0
Wayne Robertson, Southern N.H.	1991-94	127	1,487	11.7
Wayne Armstrong, Armstrong Atlantic	1975-77	78	897	11.5
Jonathan Roberts, East Stroudsburg	1987-90	112	1,247	11.1
Bob Stanley, Missouri S&T	1974-77	95	1,049	11.0
Leo Parent, Mass.-Lowell	1987-89	92	1,011	11.0

ASSISTS

Player, Team	Seasons	G	Ast.
Demetri Beekman, Assumption	1990-93	119	*1,044
Adam Kaufman, Edinboro	1998-01	116	936
Rob Paternostro, Southern N.H.	1992-95	129	919
Luke Cooper, Alas. Anchorage	2005-08	121	880
Tony Smith, Pfeiffer	1989-92	126	828
Jamie Stevens, Mont. St.-Billings	1996-99	110	805
Josh Mueller, South Dakota	2002-05	120	801
Steve Ray, Bridgeport	1989-90	65	785
Dan Ward, St. Cloud St.	1992-95	100	774
Chris Dunn, West Virginia St.	2003-06	123	769
Jordan Canfield, Washburn	1994-97	126	756
Pat Delaney, St. Anselm	1999-02	118	731
Charles Jordan, Erskine	1989-92	119	727
Jamie Holden, St. Joseph's (Ind.)	2001-04	110	723
Donald Johnson, Franklin Pierce	1998-01	114	722
Dennis Springs, Ferris St.	2003-06	115	713
Patrick Chambers, Philadelphia U.	1991-94	123	709
Lamont Jones, Bridgeport	1992-95	119	708
Zack Whiting, Chaminade	2004-07	86	703
Ernest Jenkins, N.M. Highlands	1992-95	84	699
Antoine Campbell, Ashland	1995-98	113	697
Jonny Reibel, Rollins	2005-08	120	688
Pat Madden, Jacksonville St.	1989-91	88	688
Nate Tibbetts, South Dakota	1998-01	112	678
Candice Pickens, California (Pa.)	1993-96	121	675

*record

ASSIST AVERAGE
(Minimum 550 assists)

Player, Team	Seasons	G	Ast.	Avg.
Steve Ray, Bridgeport	1989-90	65	785	*12.1
Demetri Beekman, Assumption	1990-93	119	*1,044	8.8
Ernest Jenkins, N.M. Highlands	1992-95	84	699	8.3
Zack Whiting, Chaminade	2004-07	86	703	8.2
Adam Kaufman, Edinboro	1998-01	116	936	8.1
Mark Benson, Tex. A&M-Kingsville	1989-91	86	674	7.8
Pat Madden, Jacksonville St.	1989-91	88	688	7.8
Dan Ward, St. Cloud St.	1992-95	100	774	7.7
Mark Borders, Tampa	2004-06	86	649	7.5
Jamie Stevens, Mont. St.-Billings	1996-99	110	805	7.3
Luke Cooper, Alas. Anchorage	2005-08	121	880	7.3
Craig Lottie, Alabama A&M	1992-95	93	673	7.2
Rob Paternostro, Southern N.H.	1992-95	129	919	7.1
Eddin Santiago, Mo. Southern St.	1999-02	117	804	6.9
Josh Mueller, South Dakota	2002-05	120	801	6.7
Jamie Holden, St. Joseph's (Ind.)	2001-04	110	723	6.6
Tony Smith, Pfeiffer	1989-92	126	828	6.6

Player, Team	Seasons	G	Ast.	Avg.
Donald Johnson, Franklin Pierce	1998-01	114	722	6.3
Mike Buscetto, Quinnipiac	1990-93	99	624	6.3
Chris Dunn, West Virginia St.	2003-06	123	769	6.3
Patrick Herron, Winston-Salem	1992-95	97	604	6.2
Dennis Springs, Ferris St.	2003-06	115	713	6.2
Pat Delaney, St. Anselm	1999-02	118	731	6.2
Antoine Campbell, Ashland	1995-98	113	697	6.2
Charles Jordan, Erskine	1989-92	119	727	6.1
Mark White, Humboldt St.	2001-04	98	594	6.1
Nate Tibbetts, South Dakota	1998-01	112	678	6.1

record

BLOCKED SHOTS

Player, Team	Seasons	G	Blk.
Bryan Grier, Wingate	2005-08	122	455
John Smith, Winona St.	2005-08	*146	423
James Doyle, Concord	1995-98	120	416
Bilal Salaam, Kutztown	2002-05	109	408
Derek Moore, S.C.-Aiken	1996-99	102	408
Ryan McLemore, Edinboro	2005-08	117	354
Avis Wyatt, Virginia St.	2003-05, 07	113	350
Callistus Eziukwu, Grand Valley St.	2005-08	120	329
Rich Edwards, Adelphi	1999-02	123	305
Kino Outlaw, Mount Olive	1994-96	81	305
Mike Williams, Bryant	2001-05	129	301
Garth Joseph, St. Rose	1995-97	89	300
Kenyon Gamble, Florida Tech/Tuskegee	2001-02, 04-05	103	297
Sylvere Bryan, Tampa	1999-02	116	294
Kerwin Thompson, Eckerd	1993-96	116	284
Aaron Davis, Southern Conn. St.	2000-03	94	269
Jeff Weirsma, Erskine	2000-03	109	268
Eugene Haith, Philadelphia U.	1993-95	86	267
John Tomsich, Le Moyne	1996-99	114	264
Chandar Bingham, Virginia Union	1997-00	106	261
Coata Malone, Alabama A&M	1994-96	90	243
Alonzo Goldston, Fort Hays St.	1995-97	96	240
Damon Reed, St. Rose	1997-00	128	236
Brian Robinson, Assumption	2002-05	115	234
Robert Strickland, Charleston (W.V.)	2005-08	112	229

record.

BLOCKED-SHOT AVERAGE
(Minimum 175 blocked shots)

Player, Team	Seasons	G	Blk.	Avg.
Derek Moore, S.C.-Aiken	1996-99	102	408	4.00
John Burke, Southampton	1995-96	54	205	3.80
Kino Outlaw, Mount Olive	1994-96	81	305	3.77
Bilal Salaam, Kutztown	2002-05	109	408	3.74
Bryan Grier, Wingate	2005-08	122	*455	3.73
Vonzell McGrew, Mo. Western St.	1993-95	57	211	3.70
Tihomir Juric, Wis.-Parkside	1993-94	53	193	3.64
Ben Wallace, Virginia Union	1995-96	62	225	3.63
Corey Johnson, Pace	1993-95	58	210	3.62
Kobby Acquah, Clark Atlanta	2005-06	56	198	3.54
James Doyle, Concord	1995-98	120	416	3.47
Mark Hensel, Pitt.-Johnstown	1993-94	53	180	3.40
Garth Joseph, St. Rose	1995-97	89	300	3.37
Moustapha Diouf, Queens (N.C.)	2003-04	61	201	3.30
Eugene Haith, Philadelphia U.	1993-95	86	267	3.10
Avis Wyatt, Virginia St.	2003-05, 07	113	350	3.10
Ryan McLemore, Edinboro	2005-08	117	354	3.03
John Smith, Winona St.	2005-08	*146	423	2.90
Kenyon Gamble, Florida Tech/Tuskegee	2001-02, 04-05	103	297	2.88
Aaron Davis, Southern Conn. St.	2000-03	94	269	2.86
Callistus Eziukwu, Grand Valley St.	2005-08	120	329	2.74

Player, Team	Seasons	G	Blk.	Avg.
Coata Malone, Alabama A&M	1994-96	90	243	2.70
Sylvere Bryan, Tampa	1999-02	116	294	2.53
Alonzo Goldston, Fort Hays St.	1995-97	96	240	2.50
Rich Edwards, Adelphi	1999-02	123	305	2.48

record

STEALS

Player, Team	Seasons	G	Stl.
Jonte Flowers, Winona St.	2005-08	141	414
Eddin Santiago, Mo. Southern St.	1999-02	117	383
Oronn Brown, Clarion	1994-97	106	361
Robert Campbell, Armstrong Atlantic	1998-01	118	357
Jeremy Byrd, S.C. Upstate	2005-08	115	350
Marcus Best, Winston-Salem	1999-02	119	345
Shaun McKie, Salem Int'l	2004-07	113	340
Luke Kendall, Metro St.	2001-04	132	338
Devlin Herring, Pitt.-Johnstown	1995-98	106	333
Dustin Pfeifer, Findlay	2003-06	127	328
Luqman Jaaber, Virginia St./Virginia Union	2000, 03-05	114	316
Rolondo Hall, Davis & Elkins	1998-01	106	314
John Baiano, Southern N.H.	2003-06	122	304
Andre Dabney, Bloomfield	2004-07	120	294
Shahar Golan, Assumption	2001-04	115	293
Charlie Parker, Millersville	2005-08	121	288
Andre Dabney, Bloomfield	2004-07	120	283
Terrence Baxter, Pfeiffer	1998-01	108	281
David Clark, Bluefield St.	1994-96	83	278
Chris Dunn, West Virginia St.	2003-06	123	277
Eric Faber, Rollins	2002-05	119	276
Terrance Gist, S.C. Upstate	1994-97	112	276
Tony Cornett, West Virginia St.	2004-07	126	272
Omar Kasi, Molloy	1997-00	109	272
DeMarcos Anzures, Metro St.	1997-00	125	271
Mike Hancock, Neb.-Kearney	1995-98	121	271

record

STEAL AVERAGE
(Minimum 150 steals)

Player, Team	Seasons	G	Stl.	Avg.
Wayne Copeland, Lynn	1999-00	57	254	4.46
J.R. Gamble, Queens (N.C.)	2000-01	60	246	4.10
John Morris, Bluefield St.	1994-95	50	185	3.70
Oronn Brown, Clarion	1994-97	106	361	3.41
Patrick Herron, Winston-Salem	1993-95	78	263	3.37
David Clark, Bluefield St.	1994-96	83	278	3.35
Peron Austin, Colorado St.-Pueblo	1997-98	58	190	3.28
Eddin Santiago, Mo. Southern St.	1999-02	117	*383	3.27
Gallagher Driscoll, St. Rose	1991-92	59	192	3.25
Darnell White, California (Pa.)	1993-94	59	192	3.25
Rudy Berry, Cal St. Stanislaus	1993-94	51	164	3.21
Ken Francis, Molloy	1993-95	81	260	3.21
Bob Cunningham, NYIT	1995-96	55	175	3.18
Devlin Herring, Pitt.-Johnstown	1995-98	106	333	3.14
Craig Fergeson, Columbus St.	1995-96	61	191	3.13
Ron Harris, Caldwell	2004-05	59	181	3.07
Bryan Heaps, Abilene Christian	1993-94	56	171	3.05
Lamont Jones, Bridgeport	1993-95	84	256	3.05
Jeremy Byrd, S.C. Upstate	2005-08	115	350	3.04
Shaun McKie, Salem Int'l	2004-07	113	340	3.01
Kelly Mann, Concord	1997-98	62	185	2.98
Javar Cheatham, Gannon	2000-01	58	172	2.97
Rolondo Hall, Davis & Elkins	1998-01	106	314	2.96
Rickey Gibson, Stillman	2005-06	58	171	2.95
Brandon Hughes, Newberry	1997-00	88	259	2.94

record

DIVISION II

Annual Individual Champions

Scoring Average

Season	Player, Team	G	FG	FT	Pts.	Avg.
1948	Nate DeLong, Wis.-River Falls	22	206	206	618	28.1
1949	George King, Charleston (W.V.)	26	289	179	757	29.1
1950	George King, Charleston (W.V.)	31	354	259	967	31.2
1951	Scott Seagall, Millikin	31	314	260	888	28.6
1952	Harold Wolfe, Findlay	22	285	101	671	30.5
1953	Roger Kuss, Wis.-River Falls	21	291	235	817	38.9
1954	Clarence "Bevo" Francis, Rio Grande	27	444	367	1,255	*46.5
1955	Bill Warden, North Central (Ill.)	13	162	127	451	34.7
1956	Bill Reigel, McNeese St.	36	425	370	1,220	33.9
1957	Ken Hammond, West Va. Tech	27	334	274	942	34.9
1958	John Lee Butcher, Pikeville	27	330	210	870	32.2
1959	Paul Wilcox, Davis & Elkins	23	289	195	773	33.6
1960	Don Perrelli, Southern Conn. St.	22	263	168	694	31.5
1961	Lebron Bell, Bryant	14	174	114	462	33.0
1962	Willie Shaw, Lane	18	239	115	593	32.9
1963	Earl Glass, Miss. Industrial	19	322	171	815	42.9
1964	Willie Shaw, Lane	18	303	121	727	40.4
1965	Thales McReynolds, Miles	18	294	118	706	39.2
1966	Paul Crissman, Vanguard	23	373	90	836	36.3
1967	Earl Monroe, Winston-Salem	32	509	311	*1,329	41.5
1968	Mike Davis, Virginia Union	25	351	206	908	36.3
1969	John Rinka, Kenyon	26	340	202	882	33.9
1970	John Rinka, Kenyon	23	354	234	942	41.0
1971	Bo Lamar, La.-Lafayette	29	424	196	1,044	36.0
1972	Travis Grant, Kentucky St.	33	*539	226	1,304	39.5
1973	Claude White, Elmhurst	18	248	101	597	33.2
1974	Aaron James, Grambling	27	366	137	869	32.2
1975	Ron Barrow, Southern U.	23	296	115	707	30.7
1976	Ron Barrow, Southern U.	27	318	136	772	28.6
1977	Ed Murphy, Merrimack	28	369	158	896	32.0
1978	Harold Robertson, Lincoln (Mo.)	28	408	149	965	34.5
1979	Bo Clark, UCF	23	315	97	727	31.6
1980	Bill Fennelly, Central Mo.	28	337	189	863	30.8
1981	Gregory Jackson, St. Paul's	26	267	183	717	27.6
1982	John Ebeling, Fla. Southern	32	286	284	856	26.8
1983	Danny Dixon, Alabama A&M	27	379	152	910	33.7
1984	Earl Jones, Dist. Columbia	22	215	200	630	28.6
1985	Earnest Lee, Clark Atlanta	29	380	230	990	34.1
1986	Earnest Lee, Clark Atlanta	28	314	191	819	29.3

Season	Player, Team	G	FG	3FG	FT	Pts.	Avg.
1987	Earnest Lee, Clark Atlanta	29	326	35	174	861	29.7
1988	Daryl Cambrelen, Southampton	25	242	32	170	686	27.4
1989	Steve deLaveaga, Cal Lutheran	28	278	79	151	786	28.1
1990	A.J. English, Virginia Union	30	333	65	270	1,001	33.4
1991	Gary Mattison, St. Augustine's	26	277	53	159	766	29.5
1992	George Gilmore, Chaminade	28	280	82	238	880	31.4
1993	Darrin Robinson, Sacred Heart	26	313	75	130	831	32.0
1994	Kwame Mortin, Clarion	26	264	126	191	845	32.5
1995	Carlos Knox, IUPUI	29	284	39	218	825	28.4
1996	Brett Beeson, Minn. St. Moorhead	27	305	58	232	900	33.3
1997	Dan Sancomb, Wheeling Jesuit	27	295	11	125	726	26.9
1998	Carlos Knox, IUPUI	26	238	96	209	781	30.0
1999	Eddie Robinson, Central Okla.	26	305	24	95	729	28.0
2000	David Evans, BYU-Hawaii	28	300	48	134	782	27.9
2001	Marlon Dawson, Central Okla.	26	206	101	155	668	25.7
2002	Angel Figueroa, Dowling	25	216	79	143	654	26.2
2003	Ron Christy, Post	29	295	64	134	788	27.2
2004	Lewis Muse, Concord	26	308	0	125	741	28.5
2005	David Logan, Indianapolis	29	291	121	126	829	28.6
2006	Tayron Thomas, Philadelphia U.	31	298	42	260	898	29.0
2007	Ted Scott, West Virginia St.	33	315	125	137	892	27.0
2008	Michael Sturns, Holy Family	31	292	56	184	824	26.6

*record

Field-Goal Percentage

Season	Player, Team	G	FG	FGA	Pct.
1949	Vern Mikkelson, Hamline	30	203	377	53.8
1950	Nate DeLong, Wis.-River Falls	29	287	492	58.3
1951	Johnny O'Brien, Seattle	33	248	434	57.1
1952	Forrest Hamilton, Missouri St.	30	147	246	59.8
1953	Bob Buis, Carleton	21	149	246	60.6
1954	Paul Lauritzen, Augustana (Ill.)	19	158	251	62.9
1955	Jim O'Hara, UC Santa Barb.	24	140	214	65.4

Season	Player, Team	G	FG	FGA	Pct.
1956	Logan Gipe, Ky. Wesleyan	22	134	224	59.8
1957	John Wilfred, Winston-Salem	30	229	381	60.1
1958	Bennie Swain, Texas Southern	35	363	587	61.8
1959	Dick O'Meara, Babson	18	144	225	64.0
1960	Edwin Cox, Howard Payne	26	126	194	64.9
1961	Tony Solomon, St. Paul's	20	94	149	63.1
1962	Tom Morris, St. Paul's	17	108	168	64.3
1963	Howard Trice, Howard Payne	26	168	237	70.9
1964	Robert Springer, Howard Payne	24	119	174	68.4
1965	Harold Booker, Cheyney	24	144	198	72.7
1966	Harold Booker, Cheyney	27	170	240	70.8
1967	John Dickson, Arkansas St.	24	214	308	69.5
1968	Edward Phillips, Alabama A&M	22	154	210	73.3
1969	Marvin Lewis, Southampton	24	271	375	72.3
1970	Travis Grant, Kentucky St.	31	482	688	70.1
1971	Edward Phillips, Alabama A&M	24	159	221	71.9
1972	Don Manley, Otterbein	23	146	207	70.5
1973	Glynn Berry, Southampton	26	191	302	63.2
1974	Kirby Thurston, Western Caro.	25	242	367	65.9
1975	Gerald Cunningham, Kentucky St.	29	280	411	68.1
1976	Thomas Blue, Elizabeth City St.	24	270	388	69.6
1977	Kelvin Hicks, NYIT	24	161	232	69.4
1978	Ron Ripley, Green Bay	32	162	239	67.8
1979	Carl Bailey, Tuskegee	27	210	307	68.4
1980	Ray Strozier, Central Mo.	28	142	195	72.8
1981	Matthew Cornegay, Tuskegee	26	177	247	71.7
1982	Matthew Cornegay, Tuskegee	29	208	278	74.8
1983	Rudy Burton, Elizabeth City St.	24	142	201	70.6
1984	Maurice Stafford, North Ala.	34	198	264	75.0
1985	Todd Linder, Tampa	31	219	306	71.6
1986	Todd Linder, Tampa	28	204	291	70.1
1987	Todd Linder, Tampa	32	282	375	75.2
1988	Louis Newsome, North Ala.	29	192	266	72.2
1989	Tom Schurfranz, Bellarmine	28	164	240	68.2
1990	Ulysses Hackett, S.C. Upstate	32	301	426	70.7
1991	Tom Schurfranz, Bellarmine	30	245	339	72.3
1992	Brian Moten, West Ga.	26	141	192	73.4
1993	Chad Scott, California (Pa.)	28	173	245	70.6
1994	Chad Scott, California (Pa.)	30	178	245	72.7
1995	John Pruett, SIU Edwardsville	26	138	193	71.5
1996	Kyle Kirby, IPFW	26	133	195	68.2
1997	Andy Robertson, Fla. Southern	32	183	269	68.0
1998	Anthony Russell, West Fla.	28	191	284	67.3
1999	DaVonn Harp, Kutztown	27	140	205	68.3
2000	Shaun Bass, Drury	28	156	237	65.8
2001	Charles Ward, St. Augustine's	27	159	243	65.4
2002	Brett Barnard, Le Moyne	27	141	211	66.8
2003	Anthony Greenup, Shaw	30	172	242	71.1
2004	Anthony Greenup, Shaw	24	210	296	70.9
2005	Callistus Eziukwu, Grand Valley St.	28	157	213	73.7
2006	Chris Gilliam, Pitt.-Johnstown	27	199	290	68.6
2007	Garret Siler, Augusta St.	31	166	241	68.9
2008	Garret Siler, Augusta St.	34	211	277	*76.2

*record

Three-Point Field Goals Made Per Game

Season	Player, Team	G	3FG	Avg.
1987	Bill Harris, Northern Mich.	27	117	4.3
1988	Alex Williams, Sacramento St.	30	*167	5.6
1989	Robert Martin, Sacramento St.	28	118	4.2
1990	Gary Paul, Indianapolis	28	110	3.9
1991	Shawn Williams, Central Okla.	29	129	4.4
1992	Jason Garrow, Augustana (S.D.)	27	135	5.0
1993	Ray Gutierrez, California (Pa.)	29	142	4.9
1994	Kwame Morton, Clarion	26	126	4.8
1995	Eric Kline, Northern St.	30	148	4.9
1996	Daren Alix, Merrimack	28	114	4.1
1997	Reece Gliko, Mont. St-Billings	28	135	4.8
1998	Antonio Harris, LeMoyne-Owen	26	119	4.6
1999	Antonio Harris, LeMoyne-Owen	26	126	4.8
2000	Markus Hallgrimson, Mont. St.-Billings	26	160	*6.2
2001	Blake Johnson, Edinboro	28	111	4.0
2002	Danny Phillips, Mont. St.-Billings	28	120	4.3
2003	Jed Bedford, Columbus St.	32	135	4.2
2004	Mike Taylor, West Virginia St.	32	140	4.4
2005	Yandel Brown, Columbus St.	32	148	4.6
2006	Cameron Munoz, Mont. St.-Billings	28	147	5.3

Season	Player, Team	G	3FG	Avg.
2007	Brett Rector, Davis & Elkins	24	99	4.1
2008	Brandon Wright, Erskine	27	117	4.3

*record

Three-Point Field-Goal Percentage

Season	Player, Team	G	3FG	3FGA	Pct.
1987	Charles Byrd, West Tex. A&M	31	95	168	56.5
1988	Ray Lee, Hampton	24	39	60	*65.0
1989	Aaron Baker, Mississippi Col.	27	69	117	59.0
1990	Mark Willey, Fort Hays St.	29	49	81	60.5
1991	Scott Martin, Rollins	28	114	201	56.7
1992	Jeff Duvall, Oakland City	30	49	91	53.8
1993	Greg Wilkinson, Oakland City	32	82	152	53.9
1994	Todd Jones, Southern Ind.	29	56	105	53.3
1995	Aaron Fehler, Oakland City	26	73	121	†60.3
1996	Matt Hopson, Oakland City	31	84	145	57.9
1997	Adam Harness, Oakland City	26	39	68	57.4
1998	Todd Woelfe, Oakland City	27	87	162	53.7
1999	John Cabanilla, Oakland City	29	46	85	54.1
2000	Jasen Gast, Incarnate Word	26	39	72	54.2
2001	Bobby Hoegh, Southwest Baptist	23	72	147	49.0
2002	Jared Ramirez, Northern Colo.	27	60	115	52.2
2003	Ben Nemmers, North Dakota St.	30	83	159	52.2
2004	Derek Archer, Wayne St. (Neb.)	28	77	142	54.2
	Shawn Opunui, BYU-Hawaii	29	77	142	54.2
2005	Justin Belcastro, Fairmont St.	27	69	134	51.5
2006	Rich Davis, Grand Canyon	27	107	210	51.0
2007	Michael Bahl, Metro St.	32	105	202	52.0
2008	Andre Coleman	23	68	131	51.9

*record for minimum 35 made; †record for minimum 50 made

Free-Throw Percentage

Season	Player, Team	G	FT	FTA	Pct.
1948	Frank Cochran, Delta St.	22	36	43	83.7
1949	Jim Walsh, Spring Hill	25	62	75	82.7
1950	Dean Ehlers, Central Methodist	33	186	213	87.3
1951	Jim Hoverder, Central Mo.	23	75	85	88.2
1952	Jim Fenton, Akron	24	104	121	86.0
1953	Dick Parfitt, Central Mich.	22	93	105	88.6
1954	Bill Parrott, David Lipscomb	24	174	198	87.9
1955	Pete Kovacs, Monmouth (Ill.)	20	175	199	87.9
1956	Fred May, Loras	22	127	146	87.0
1957	Jim Sutton, South Dakota St.	22	127	138	92.0
1958	Arnold Smith, Allen	22	103	113	91.2
1959	Bill Reece, Lenoir-Rhyne	27	84	92	91.3
1960	Ron Slaymaker, Emporia St.	20	80	88	90.9
1961	Harvey Rosen, Wilkes	22	105	115	91.3
1962	Wayne Mahone, Stephen F. Austin	26	76	84	90.5
1963	Jon Hagen, Minn. St. Mankato	25	76	82	92.7
1964	Steve Nisenson, Hofstra	28	230	252	91.3
1965	Jon Hagen, Minn. St. Mankato	23	103	112	92.0
1966	Jack Cryan, Rider	25	182	198	91.9
1967	Kent Andrews, McNeese St.	22	101	110	91.8
1968	Kent Andrews, McNeese St.	24	85	90	94.4
1969	Joe Cullen, Hartwick	18	96	103	93.2
1970	John Rinka, Kenyon	23	234	263	89.0
1971	Ed Roeth, Defiance	26	138	152	90.8
1972	Jeff Kuntz, St. Norbert	25	142	155	91.6
1973	Bob Kronisch, Brooklyn	30	93	105	88.6
1974	Terry Gill, New Orleans	30	97	105	92.4
1975	Clarence Rand, Alabama St.	29	91	101	90.1
1976	Billy Newton, Morgan St.	28	85	90	94.4
1977	Emery Sammons, Philadelphia U.	28	145	157	92.4
1978	Dana Skinner, Merrimack	28	142	154	92.2
1979	Jack Sparks, Bentley	28	76	84	90.5
1980	Grey Giovanine, Central Mo.	28	75	83	90.4
1981	Ted Smith, SIU Edwardsville	26	67	73	91.8
1982	Carl Gonder, Augustana (S.D.)	27	86	93	92.5
1983	Joe Sclafani, New Haven	28	86	98	87.8
1984	Darrell Johnston, Southern N.H.	29	74	81	91.4
1985	Tom McDonald, South Dakota St.	33	88	97	90.7
1986	Todd Mezzulo, Alas. Fairbanks	27	114	125	91.2
1987	Mike Sanders, Northern Colo.	28	82	87	94.3
1988	Charles Byrd, West Tex. A&M	29	92	99	92.8
1989	Mike Boschee, North Dakota	28	71	77	92.2
1990	Mike Morris, Ala.-Huntsville	28	114	125	91.2
1991	Ryun Williams, South Dakota	30	114	125	91.2

Season	Player, Team	G	FT	FTA	Pct.
1992	Hal McManus, Lander	28	110	119	92.4
1993	Jason Williams, New Haven	27	115	125	92.0
1994	Jay Harrie, Mont. St.-Billings	26	86	92	93.5
1995	Jim Borodawka, Mass.-Lowell	27	74	80	92.5
1996	Paul Cluxton, Northern Ky.	32	100	108	92.6
1997	Paul Cluxton, Northern Ky.	35	94	94	*100.0
1998	Troy Nesmith, Gannon	27	146	158	92.4
1999	Travis Starns, Colorado Mines	26	87	93	93.5
2000	Jason Kreider, Michigan Tech.	31	84	91	92.3
2001	C.J. Cowgill, Chaminade	22	113	119	95.0
2002	Curtis Small, Southampton	29	109	116	94.0
2003	Aaron Farley, Harding	30	137	146	93.8
2004	Ralph Steele, Seattle Pacific	27	82	90	91.1
2005	Luqman Jaaber, Virginia Union	34	125	139	89.9
2006	Marcus Martinez, Cal St. Stanislaus	27	75	80	93.8
2007	Richard Stone, St. Andrews	28	101	110	91.8
2008	Jake Linton, St. Martin's	27	162	168	96.4

*record

Rebound Average

Season	Player, Team	G	Reb.	Avg.
1951	Walter Lenz, Frank. & Marsh.	17	338	19.9
1952	Charley Wrinn, Trinity (Conn.)	19	486	25.6
1953	Ellerbe Neal, Wofford	23	609	26.5
1954	R.C. Owens, Albertson	25	677	27.1
1955	Tom Hart, Middlebury	22	649	29.5
1956	Tom Hart, Middlebury	21	620	*29.5
1957	Jim Smith, Steubenville	26	651	25.0
1958	Marv Becker, Widener	18	450	25.0
1959	Jim Davis, King's (Pa.)	17	384	22.6
1960	Jackie Jackson, Virginia Union	19	424	†.241
1961	Jackie Jackson, Virginia Union	26	641	24.7
1962	Jim Ahrens, Buena Vista	28	682	24.4
1963	Gerry Govan, St. Mary's (Kan.)	18	445	24.7
1964	Ernie Brock, Virginia St.	24	597	24.9
1965	Dean Sandifer, Lakeland	23	592	25.7
1966	Frank Stronczek, American Int'l	26	717	27.6
1967	Frank Stronczek, American Int'l	25	602	24.1
1968	Ron Horton, Delaware St.	23	543	23.6
1969	Wilbert Jones, Albany St. (Ga.)	28	670	23.9
1970	Russell Jackson, Southern U.	22	544	24.7
1971	Tony Williams, St. Francis (Me.)	24	599	25.0
1972	No rankings			
1973	No rankings			
1974	Larry Johnson, Prairie View	23	519	22.6
1975	Major Jones, Albany St. (Ga.)	27	608	22.5
1976	Major Jones, Albany St. (Ga.)	24	475	19.8
1977	Andre Means, Sacred Heart	32	516	16.1
1978	Scott Mountz, California (Pa.)	24	431	18.0
1979	Keith Smith, Shaw	20	329	16.5
1980	Ricky Mahorn, Hampton	31	490	15.8
1981	Earl Jones, Dist. Columbia	25	333	13.3
1982	Donnie Carter, Tuskegee	29	372	12.8
1983	David Binion, N.C. Central	25	400	16.0
1984	Jerome Kersey, Longwood	27	383	14.2
1985	Charles Oakley, Virginia Union	31	535	17.3
1986	Raheem Muhammad, Wayne St. (Mich.)	31	428	13.8
1987	Andre Porter, Southampton	23	309	13.4
1988	Anthony Ikeobi, Clark Atlanta	27	380	14.1
1989	Toby Barber, Winston-Salem	24	327	13.6
1990	Leroy Gasque, Morris Brown	24	375	15.6
1991	Sheldon Owens, Shaw	27	325	12.0
1992	David Allen, Wayne St. (Neb.)	28	362	12.9
1993	James Hector, American Int'l	28	389	13.9
1994	Pat Armour, Jacksonville St.	25	363	14.5
1995	Lorenzo Poole, Albany St. (Ga.)	26	417	16.0
1996	J.J. Sims, West Ga.	28	374	13.4
1997	Kebu Stewart, Cal St. Bakersfield	33	442	13.4
1998	Antonio Garcia, Ky. Wesleyan	33	457	13.8
1999	Antonio Garcia, Ky. Wesleyan	37	540	14.6
2000	Howard Jackson, Lincoln Memorial	24	321	13.4
2001	Colin Duchacme, Longwood	31	490	15.8
2002	Danny Jones, Tarleton St.	33	416	13.0
2003	Billy McDaniel, Ark.-Monticello	27	345	12.8
2004	Jack Bain, UC-Colo. Spgs.	27	336	12.4
2005	Ramel Allen, Bridgeport	30	423	14.1
2006	Raheim Lowery, Dowling	27	342	12.7
2007	Eric Dawson, Midwestern St.	30	341	11.4
2008	Vincent Falzone, Molloy	27	334	12.4

*record; †Championship determined by highest individual recoveries out of total by both teams in all games.

DIVISION II

Assist Average

Season	Player, Team	G	Ast.	Avg.
1989	Steve Ray, Bridgeport	32	*400	*12.5
1990	Steve Ray, Bridgeport	33	385	11.7
1991	Adrian Hutt, Metro St.	28	285	10.2
1992	Tony Smith, Pfeiffer	35	349	10.0
1993	Demetri Beekman, Assumption	23	264	11.5
1994	Ernest Jenkins, N.M. Highlands	27	277	10.3
1995	Ernest Jenkins, N.M. Highlands	27	291	10.8
1996	Bobby Banks, Metro St.	27	244	9.0
1997	Emanuel Richardson, Pitt.-Johnstown	27	235	8.7
1998	Emanuel Richardson, Pitt.-Johnstown	29	260	9.0
1999	Shawn Brown, Merrimack	27	223	8.3
2000	Todd Chappell, Texas Wesleyan	27	263	9.7
2001	Javar Cheatham, Gannon	30	283	9.4
2002	Pat Delany, St. Anselm	30	234	7.8
2003	Clayton Smith, Metro St.	33	274	8.3
2004	Deshawn Bowman, Columbus St.	27	220	8.1
2005	Darnell Miller, West Ga.	28	219	7.8
2006	Ryan Nelson, Grand Canyon	27	263	9.7
2007	Zack Whiting, Chaminade	27	289	10.7
2008	Luke Cooper, Alas. Anchorage	35	310	8.9

*record

Blocked-Shot Average

Season	Player, Team	G	Blk.	Avg.
1993	Antonio Harvey, Pfeiffer	29	155	*5.3
1994	Johnny Tyson, Central Okla.	27	126	4.7
1995	Kino Outlaw, Mount Olive	28	124	4.4
1996	John Burke, Southampton	28	142	5.1
1997	Garth Joseph, St. Rose	34	124	3.6
1998	James Doyle, Concord	30	*157	5.2
1999	Chandar Bingham, Virginia Union	27	95	3.5
2000	Josh Stanhiser, Columbia Union	25	87	3.5
2001	Jason Roseto, Edinboro	23	97	4.2
2002	George Bailey, Lock Haven	20	79	4.0
2003	Aaron Davis, Southern Conn. St.	25	103	4.1
2004	Kenyon Gamble, Tuskegee	28	142	5.1
2005	Ramel Allen, Bridgeport	30	146	4.9
2006	Bryan Grier, Wingate	31	151	4.9
2007	Sean McKeon, Kutztown	28	117	4.2
2008	Ryan McLemore, Edinboro	31	170	5.5

*record

Steal Average

Season	Player, Team	G	Stl.	Avg.
1993	Marcus Stubblefield, Queens (N.C.)	28	110	3.9
1994	Ken Francis, Molloy	27	116	4.3
1995	Shannon Holmes, NYIT	30	110	3.7
1996	David Clark, Bluefield St.	31	118	3.8
1997	Devlin Herring, Pitt.-Johnstown	27	122	4.5
1998	Terrance Gist, S.C. Upstate	29	122	4.2
1999	Wayne Copeland, Lynn	31	125	4.0
2000	Wayne Copeland, Lynn	26	129	*5.0
2001	J.R. Gamble, Queens (N.C.)	32	*139	4.3
2002	Shahar Golan, Assumption	30	106	3.5
2003	Gerry McNair, C.W. Post	30	103	3.4
2004	Luqman Jaaber, Virginia Union	30	103	3.4
2005	Shaun McKie, Salem Int'l	31	111	3.6
2006	Drew Williamson, Metro St.	31	114	3.7
2007	Japhet McNeil, Bridgeport	31	125	4.0
2008	Garrett Lever, Neb.-Kearney	25	80	3.6

*record

Annual Team Champions

Won-Lost Percentage

Season	Team	Won	Lost	Pct.
1968	Monmouth	27	2	.931
1969	Alcorn St.	26	1	.963
1970	Central Wash.	31	2	.939
1971	Kentucky St.	31	2	.939
1972	Olivet	22	1	.957
1973	Coe	24	1	.960
1974	West Ga.	29	4	.879
1975	Bentley	23	2	.920
1976	Philadelphia U.	25	3	.893
1977	Clarion	27	3	.900
	Kentucky St.	27	3	.900
	Towson	27	3	.900
1978	Green Bay	30	2	.938
1979	Roanoke	25	3	.893
1980	Alabama St.	32	2	.941
1981	Mt. St. Mary's	28	3	.903
1982	Cheyney	28	3	.903
1983	Dist. Columbia	29	3	.906
1984	Norfolk St.	29	2	.935
1985	Jacksonville St.	31	1	.969
	Virginia Union	31	1	.969
1986	Wright St.	28	3	.903
1987	Norfolk St.	28	3	.903
1988	Fla. Southern	31	3	.912
1989	UC Riverside	30	4	.882
1990	Ky. Wesleyan	31	2	.939
1991	Southwest Baptist	29	3	.906
1992	California (Pa.)	31	2	.939
1993	Cal St. Bakersfield	33	0	1.000
1994	Philadelphia U.	29	2	.935
1995	Jacksonville St.	24	1	.960
1996	Fort Hays St.	34	0	1.000
1997	Fort Hays St.	29	2	.935
1998	UC Davis	31	2	.939
1999	Ky. Wesleyan	35	2	.946
2000	Fla. Southern	32	2	.941
2001	Adelphi	31	1	.969
2002	Cal St. San B'dino	28	2	.933
	Northeastern St.	28	2	.933
2003	Northeastern St.	32	3	.914
2004	Metro St.	32	3	.914
2005	Virginia Union	30	4	.882
	Findlay	30	4	.882
2006	Delta St.	30	2	.938
2007	Winona St.	35	1	.972
2008	Winona St.	38	1	.974

Scoring Offense

Season	Team	G	W-L	Pts.	Avg.
1948	St. Anselm	19	12-7	1,329	69.9
1949	Charleston (W.V.)	26	18-8	2,023	77.8
1950	Charleston (W.V.)	31	22-9	2,477	79.9
1951	Beloit	23	18-5	1,961	85.3
1952	Lambuth	22	17-5	1,985	90.2
1953	Arkansas Tech	21	20-1	1,976	94.1
1954	Montclair St.	22	18-4	2,128	96.7
1955	West Va. Tech	20	15-5	2,150	107.5
1956	West Va. Tech	22	16-6	2,210	100.5
1957	West Va. Tech	29	26-3	2,976	102.6
1958	West Va. Tech	29	24-5	2,941	101.4
1959	Grambling	29	28-1	2,764	95.3
1960	Mississippi Col.	19	15-4	2,169	114.2
1961	Lawrence Tech	25	19-6	2,409	96.4
1962	Troy	25	20-5	2,402	96.1
1963	Miles	21	17-4	2,011	95.8
1964	Benedict	27	19-8	2,730	101.1
1965	Ark.-Pine Bluff	26	22-4	2,655	102.1
1966	Southern Cal College	23	15-8	2,480	107.8
1967	Lincoln (Mo.)	27	24-3	2,925	108.3
1968	Stillman	26	17-9	2,898	111.5
1969	Norfolk St.	25	21-4	2,653	106.1
1970	Norfolk St.	26	19-7	2,796	107.5
1971	Savannah St.	29	18-11	3,051	105.2
1972	Florida A&M	28	18-10	2,869	102.5
1973	Md.-East. Shore	31	26-5	2,974	95.9
1974	Texas Southern	28	15-13	2,884	103.0

Season	Team	G	W-L	Pts.	Avg.
1975	Prairie View	26	16-10	2,774	106.7
1976	Southern U.	27	13-14	2,637	97.7
1977	Virginia Union	30	25-5	2,966	98.9
1978	Merrimack	28	22-6	2,606	93.1
1979	Armstrong Atlantic	27	21-6	2,626	97.3
1980	Ashland	27	11-16	2,514	93.1
1981	Virginia St.	31	20-11	2,761	89.1
1982	Alabama St.	28	22-6	2,429	86.8
1983	Virginia St.	29	19-10	2,802	96.6
1984	Southern N.H.	29	18-11	2,564	88.4
1985	Alabama A&M	31	21-10	2,881	92.9
1986	Alabama A&M	32	23-9	2,897	90.5
1987	Alabama A&M	30	23-7	2,826	94.2
1988	Oakland	28	19-9	2,685	95.9
1989	Stonehill	32	23-9	3,244	101.4
1990	Jacksonville St.	29	24-5	2,872	99.0
1991	Troy	30	22-8	3,259	108.6
1992	Troy	29	23-6	3,513	*121.1
1993	Central Okla.	29	23-6	3,293	113.6
1994	Central Okla.	27	17-10	2,782	103.0
1995	Central Okla.	30	23-7	3,219	107.3
1996	Central Okla.	29	19-10	2,933	101.1
1997	Mont. St.-Billings	28	22-6	2,904	103.7
1998	Mont. St.-Billings	28	21-7	2,945	105.2
1999	Central Okla.	27	16-11	2,657	98.4
2000	Mont. St.-Billings	26	17.9	2,460	94.6
2001	Mont. St.-Billings	27	18-9	2,648	98.1
2002	Mont. St.-Billings	28	21-7	2,559	91.4
2003	Pfeiffer	31	22-9	2,926	94.4
2004	Pfeiffer	34	31-3	3,278	96.4
2005	Pfeiffer	32	27-5	3,042	95.1
2006	West Liberty St.	29	21-8	2,841	98.0
2007	West Liberty St.	30	25-5	2,962	98.7
2008	West Liberty St.	29	23-6	2,827	97.5

*record

Season	Team	G	W-L	Pts.	Avg.
1990	Humboldt St.	31	20-11	1,831	59.1
1991	Minn. Duluth	32	27-5	1,899	59.3
1992	Pace	30	23-7	1,517	50.6
1993	Philadelphia U.	32	30-2	1,898	59.3
1994	Pace	29	19-10	1,715	59.1
1995	Armstrong Atlantic	31	20-11	1,929	62.2
1996	Coker	26	16-10	1,592	61.2
1997	Fort Hays St.	31	29-2	1,837	59.3
1998	Presbyterian	28	16-12	1,704	60.9
1999	Incarnate Word	30	28-2	1,727	57.6
2000	Wingate	30	26-4	1,775	59.2
2001	Henderson St.	32	22-10	1,919	60.0
2002	Tusculum	28	15-13	1,600	57.1
2003	Barry	28	18-10	1,490	53.2
2004	Valdosta St.	29	25-4	1,514	52.2
2005	Adelphi	29	22-7	1,609	55.5
2006	Adelphi	32	27-5	1,749	54.7
2007	Bentley	33	32-1	1,898	57.5
2008	Grand Valley St.	37	36-1	2,009	54.3

‡record since 1948

Scoring Defense

Season	Team	G	W-L	Pts.	Avg.
1948	Miss. Industrial	15	13-2	436	‡29.1
1949	Gordon	20	16-4	655	32.8
1950	A&M-Corpus Christi	26	25-1	1,030	39.6
1951	St. Martin's	24	11-13	1,137	47.4
1952	Truman	19	12-7	876	46.1
1953	Sacramento St.	26	18-8	1,381	53.1
1954	Sacramento St.	18	9-9	883	49.1
1955	Amherst	22	16-6	1,233	56.0
1956	Amherst	22	16-6	1,277	58.0
1957	Stephen F. Austin	26	23-3	1,337	51.4
1958	McNeese St.	23	19-4	1,068	46.4
1959	Humboldt St.	23	14-9	1,166	50.7
1960	Wittenberg	24	22-2	1,122	46.8
1961	Wittenberg	29	25-4	1,270	43.8
1962	Wittenberg	26	21-5	1,089	41.9
1963	Wittenberg	28	26-2	1,285	45.9
1964	Wittenberg	23	18-5	1,186	51.6
1965	Cheyney	25	24-1	1,393	55.7
1966	Chicago	16	12-4	894	55.9
1967	Ashland	24	21-3	1,025	42.7
1968	Ashland	30	23-7	1,164	38.8
1969	Ashland	30	26-4	1,017	33.9
1970	Ashland	27	23-4	1,118	41.4
1971	Ashland	28	25-3	1,523	54.4
1972	Chicago	20	16-4	1,132	56.6
1973	Steubenville	29	22-7	1,271	43.8
1974	Steubenville	26	14-12	1,336	51.4
1975	Cal Poly	26	15-11	1,590	61.2
1976	Green Bay	29	21-8	1,768	61.0
1977	Green Bay	29	26-3	1,682	58.0
1978	Green Bay	32	30-2	1,682	52.6
1979	Green Bay	32	24-8	1,612	50.4
1980	Green Bay	27	15-12	1,577	58.4
1981	San Fran. St.	26	17-9	1,463	56.3
1982	Cal Poly	29	23-6	1,537	53.0
1983	Cal Poly	28	18-10	1,553	55.5
1984	Cal Poly	28	20-8	1,458	52.1
1985	Cal Poly	27	16-11	1,430	53.0
1986	Lewis	30	24-6	1,702	56.7
1987	Denver	29	20-9	1,844	63.6
1988	N.C. Central	29	26-3	1,683	58.0
1989	N.C. Central	32	28-4	1,791	56.0

Scoring Margin

Season	Team	Off.	Def.	Mar.
1950	Montana	77.4	57.7	19.7
1951	Eastern Ill.	84.7	57.9	26.8
1952	Texas St.	77.4	48.9	28.5
1953	Arkansas Tech	94.7	74.3	20.4
1954	Texas Southern	89.2	63.3	25.9
1955	Mt. St. Mary's	95.2	73.3	21.9
1956	Western Ill.	92.5	72.1	20.4
1957	West Va. Tech	102.6	77.2	25.4
1958	Tennessee St.	88.7	64.1	24.6
1959	Grambling	95.3	73.3	22.0
1960	Mississippi Col.	114.2	92.9	21.3
1961	Bryan	93.8	62.4	*31.4
1962	Mansfield	87.6	64.7	22.9
1963	Gorham St.	94.7	69.7	25.0
1964	Central Conn. St.	94.5	67.7	26.8
1965	Cheyney	80.7	55.7	25.0
1966	Cheyney	90.0	64.4	25.6
1967	Lincoln (Mo.)	108.3	82.2	26.1
1968	Western New Eng.	104.7	76.8	27.9
1969	Indiana (Pa.)	88.6	64.5	24.1
1970	Husson	106.1	79.0	27.1
1971	Kentucky St.	103.5	78.2	25.3
1972	Brockport St.	93.8	70.3	23.5
1973	Green Bay	71.2	52.1	19.1
1974	Alcorn St.	96.9	79.8	17.1
1975	Bentley	95.2	78.7	16.5
1976	UCF	94.8	78.4	16.4
1977	Texas Southern	88.4	71.9	16.5
1978	Green Bay	68.8	52.5	16.2
1979	Roanoke	77.8	60.8	17.0
1980	UCF	91.7	72.1	19.6
1981	West Ga.	88.5	70.2	18.3
1982	Minn. Duluth	81.7	64.8	16.9
1983	Minn. Duluth	84.8	69.8	15.0
1984	Chicago St.	85.9	70.2	15.7
1985	Virginia Union	87.6	67.8	19.8
1986	Mt. St. Mary's	80.0	65.7	14.3
1987	Ky. Wesleyan	92.4	72.9	19.8
1988	Fla. Southern	89.6	70.5	19.1
1989	Virginia Union	88.2	69.6	18.6
1990	Ky. Wesleyan	97.3	76.8	20.5
1991	Ashland	99.8	78.2	21.6
1992	Oakland City	99.5	77.1	22.4
1993	Philadelphia U.	78.8	59.3	19.4
1994	Oakland City	87.8	65.5	22.3
1995	Jacksonville St.	101.2	77.6	23.6
1996	Fort Hays St.	92.1	70.2	21.9
1997	Fort Hays St.	84.1	59.3	24.8
1998	Oakland City	85.8	64.1	21.7
1999	Incarnate Word	78.5	57.6	21.0
2000	Metro St.	87.0	67.9	19.1
2001	Adelphi	85.3	65.7	19.7
2002	Ky. Wesleyan	91.3	72.7	18.6
2003	Ky. Wesleyan	88.9	72.7	16.3
2004	Metro St.	93.4	65.3	28.1
2005	Oakland City	83.5	63.2	20.3
2006	Pitt.-Johnstown	80.1	62.9	17.2

DIVISION II

Season	Team	Off.	Def.	Mar.
2007	Winona St.	85.6	66.5	19.1
2008	Winona St.	82.9	61.7	21.2

*record

Field-Goal Percentage

Season	Team	FG	FGA	Pct.
1948	Tex. A&M-Commerce	445	1,119	39.8
1949	Missouri St.	482	1,106	43.6
1950	A&M-Corpus Christi	555	1,290	43.0
1951	Beloit	773	1,734	44.6
1952	Missouri St.	890	1,903	46.8
1953	Lebanon Valley	637	1,349	47.2
1954	San Diego St.	675	1,502	44.9
1955	UC Santa Barb.	672	1,383	48.6
1956	UC Santa Barb.	552	1,142	48.3
1957	Alderson-Broaddus	1,006	2,094	48.0
1958	N.C. A&T	552	1,072	51.5
1959	Grambling	1,111	2,205	50.4
1960	William Carey	708	1,372	51.6
1961	Virginia Union	908	1,735	52.3
1962	West Va. Tech	871	1,575	55.3
1963	Lenoir-Rhyne	869	1,647	52.8
1964	LeMoyne-Owen	844	1,520	55.5
1965	Southern U.	1,036	1,915	54.1
1966	Howard Payne	932	1,710	54.5
1967	Alabama St.	874	1,555	56.2
1968	South Carolina St.	588	1,010	58.2
1969	Southampton	846	1,588	53.3
1970	Savannah St.	1,145	1,969	58.2
1971	Alabama St.	1,196	2,100	57.0
1972	Florida A&M	1,194	2,143	55.7
1973	Green Bay	929	1,700	54.6
1974	Kentucky St.	1,252	2,266	55.3
1975	Kentucky St.	1,121	1,979	56.6
1976	Kentucky St.	1,093	1,753	*62.4
1977	Merrimack	1,120	2,008	55.8
1978	Green Bay	840	1,509	55.7
1979	Morris Brown	980	1,763	55.6
1980	UNC Pembroke	849	1,544	55.0
1981	Bellarmine	851	1,561	54.5
1982	Fla. Southern	943	1,644	57.4
1983	Lewis	807	1,448	55.7
1984	Lewis	851	1,494	57.0
1985	Virginia Union	1,132	1,967	57.5
1986	Tampa	856	1,546	55.4
1987	Johnson Smith	995	1,817	54.8
1988	Fla. Southern	1,118	2,026	55.2
1989	Millersville	1,119	2,079	53.8
1990	S.C. Upstate	954	1,745	54.7
1991	S.C. Upstate	923	1,631	56.6
1992	S.C. Upstate	898	1,664	54.0
1993	Cal St. Bakersfield	1,002	1,849	54.2
1994	Southern Ind.	1,171	2,142	54.7
1995	High Point	862	1,603	53.8
1996	Fort Hays St.	1,158	2,145	54.0
1997	Oakland City	961	1,821	52.8
1998	West Tex. A&M	953	1,841	51.8
1999	South Dakota	835	1,631	51.2
2000	Mo. Western St.	845	1,621	52.1
2001	Southern Ind.	1,014	1,937	52.3
2002	Neb.-Kearney	899	1,762	51.0
2003	Michigan Tech	920	1,740	52.9
2004	BYU-Hawaii	824	1,573	52.4
2005	Colo. Christian	859	1,642	52.3
2006	Southern Ind.	1,042	1,974	52.8
2007	Winona St.	1,128	2,162	52.2
2008	Pitt.-Johnstown	931	1,761	52.9

*record

Field-Goal Percentage Defense

Season	Team	FG	FGA	Pct.
1978	Green Bay	681	1,830	37.2
1979	Green Bay	639	1,709	37.4
1980	Wis.-Parkside	688	1,666	41.3
1981	Central St. (Ohio)	675	1,724	39.2
1982	Minn. St. Mankato	699	1,735	40.3
1983	Central Mo.	746	1,838	40.6
1984	Norfolk St.	812	1,910	42.5

Season	Team	FG	FGA	Pct.
1985	Central Mo.	683	1,660	41.1
1986	Norfolk St.	782	1,925	40.6
1987	Denver	691	1,709	40.4
1988	Minn. Duluth	702	1,691	41.5
1989	N.C. Central	633	1,642	38.6
1990	Central Mo.	696	1,757	39.6
1991	Southwest Baptist	758	1,942	39.0
1992	Virginia Union	766	2,069	37.0
1993	Pfeiffer	767	2,028	37.8
1994	Virginia Union	705	1,966	35.9
1995	Virginia Union	723	1,973	36.6
1996	Virginia Union	718	1,944	36.9
1997	St. Rose	887	2,409	36.8
1998	Delta St.	705	1,930	36.5
1999	Delta St.	610	1,652	36.9
2000	Fla. Southern	702	1,887	37.2
2001	Tampa	631	1,723	36.6
2002	Tarleton St.	657	1,837	*35.8
2003	Tarleton St.	655	1,757	37.3
2004	Central Ark.	624	1,699	36.7
2005	Adelphi	539	1,432	37.6
2006	Adelphi	546	1,524	35.8
2007	Grand Valley St.	677	1,831	37.0
2008	Grand Valley St.	705	1,942	36.3

*record

Three-Point Field Goals Made Per Game

Season	Team	G	3FG	Avg.
1987	Northern Mich.	27	187	6.9
1988	Sacramento St.	30	303	10.1
1989	Central Okla.	27	280	10.4
1990	Stonehill	27	259	9.6
1991	Hillsdale	27	318	11.8
1992	Troy	29	*444	*15.3
1993	Hillsdale	28	366	13.1
1994	Hillsdale	25	315	12.6
1995	Hillsdale	29	330	11.4
1996	Mont. St.-Billings	28	304	10.9
1997	Mont. St.-Billings	28	394	14.1
1998	Mont. St.-Billings	28	375	13.4
1999	Mont. St.-Billings	28	355	12.7
2000	Mont. St.-Billings	26	294	11.3
2001	Mont. St.-Billings	27	284	10.5
2002	St. Anselm	30	301	10.0
2003	Bemidji St.	29	338	11.7
2004	Mont. St.-Billings	27	334	12.4
2005	Oakland City	31	394	12.7
2006	Mont. St.-Billings	28	360	12.9
2007	Fairmont St.	28	296	10.6
2008	Rollins	28	313	11.2

*record

Three-Point Field-Goal Percentage

Season	Team	G	3FG	3FGA	Pct.
1987	St. Anselm	30	97	189	51.3
1988	Winston-Salem	28	98	182	*53.8
1989	Mississippi Col.	27	144	276	52.2
1990	Shaw	27	74	143	51.7
1991	Rollins	28	278	585	47.5
1992	Oakland City	30	244	486	50.2
1993	Oakland City	32	215	465	46.2
1994	Oakland City	28	225	495	45.5
1995	Oakland City	30	256	561	45.6
1996	Oakland City	31	260	537	48.4
1997	Oakland City	30	311	651	47.8
1998	Michigan Tech	31	267	613	43.6
1999	South Dakota	29	258	577	44.7
2000	Eckerd	28	156	366	42.6
2001	Mesa St.	27	152	346	43.9
2002	Michigan Tech	30	216	499	43.3
2003	Michigan Tech	32	252	581	43.4
2004	Alas. Anchorage	30	280	612	45.8
2005	Colo. Christian	28	220	493	44.6
2006	Grand Canyon	27	286	640	44.7
2007	Metro St.	32	298	675	44.1
2008	Northern St.	33	257	577	44.5

*record

Free-Throw Percentage

Season	Team	FT	FTA	Pct.
1948	Charleston (W.V.)	446	659	67.7
1949	Linfield	276	402	68.7
1950	Jacksonville St.	452	613	73.7
1951	Millikin	603	846	71.3
1952	Eastern Ill.	521	688	75.7
1953	Upsala	513	69	74.0
1954	Central Mich.	376	509	73.9
1955	Mississippi Col.	559	733	76.3
1956	Wheaton (Ill.)	625	842	74.2
1957	Wheaton (Ill.)	689	936	73.6
1958	Wheaton (Ill.)	517	689	75.0
1959	Wabash	418	545	76.7
1960	Allen	225	297	75.8
1961	Missouri St.	453	605	74.9
1962	Lenoir-Rhyne	477	599	79.6
1963	Hampden-Sydney	442	559	79.1
1964	Western Caro.	492	621	79.2
1965	Mississippi Col.	529	663	79.8
1966	Athens St.	631	802	78.7
1967	Northwestern St.	528	678	77.9
1968	Kenyon	684	858	79.7
1969	Kenyon	583	727	80.2
1970	Wooster	571	714	80.0
1971	South Ala.	422	518	81.5
1972	Clark Atlanta	409	520	78.7
1973	Rockford (Ill.)	367	481	76.3
1974	New Orleans	537	701	76.6
1975	Alabama St.	456	565	80.7
1976	Alabama St.	451	576	78.3
1977	Puget Sound	495	637	77.7
1978	Merrimack	508	636	79.9
1979	Bentley	506	652	77.6
1980	Philadelphia U.	436	549	79.4
1981	Coppin St.	401	514	78.0
1982	Fla. Southern	726	936	77.6
1983	Transylvania	463	606	76.4
1984	Transylvania	491	639	76.8
1985	Minn. St. Mankato	349	445	78.4
1986	Southern N.H.	507	672	75.4
1987	Columbus St.	339	433	78.3
1988	Rollins	631	795	79.4
1989	Rollins	477	607	78.6
1990	Rollins	449	582	77.1
1991	Lenoir-Rhyne	441	564	78.2
1992	Adams St.	397	512	77.5
1993	Philadelphia U.	491	630	77.9
1994	West Liberty St.	473	602	78.6
1995	Western St.	469	603	77.8
1996	South Dakota	501	648	77.3
1997	Hawaii-Hilo	471	606	77.7

Season	Team	FT	FTA	Pct.
1998	Gannon	473	573	*82.5
1999	Minn.-Duluth	430	547	78.6
2000	Bemidji St.	386	492	78.5
2001	Morningside	383	485	79.0
2002	St. Cloud St.	461	587	78.5
2003	South Dakota	452	566	79.9
2004	Seattle Pacific	455	573	79.4
2005	St. Anselm	549	676	81.2
2006	Western Wash.	590	751	78.6
2007	Northwest Nazarene	384	473	81.2
2008	Neb.-Omaha	593	744	79.7

*record

Rebound Margin

Season	Team	Off.	Def.	Mar.
1976	Mississippi Val.	63.9	39.5	*24.4
1977	Philadelphia U.	38.7	24.1	14.6
1978	Mass.-Lowell	49.0	37.5	11.5
1979	Dowling	48.2	32.6	15.6
1980	Ark.-Pine Bluff	40.3	25.9	14.4
1981	Green Bay	40.6	26.5	14.1
1982	Central St. (Ohio)	48.0	37.2	10.8
1983	Hampton	50.2	38.5	11.8
1984	California (Pa.)	46.4	33.1	13.3
1985	Virginia Union	44.1	32.0	12.1
1986	Tampa	39.9	28.0	11.8
1987	Millersville	44.7	33.8	10.9
1988	Clark Atlanta	44.7	32.5	12.1
1989	Hampton	46.7	36.3	10.3
1990	Fla. Atlantic	41.0	29.4	11.6
1991	California (Pa.)	44.6	32.0	12.6
1992	Oakland City	43.4	31.8	11.6
1993	Metro St.	45.5	32.0	13.5
1994	Oakland City	44.0	33.7	10.3
1995	Jacksonville St.	47.7	35.2	12.5
1996	Virginia Union	48.0	36.1	11.9
1997	Southern Conn. St.	41.6	32.3	9.3
1998	South Dakota St.	46.5	35.9	10.6
1999	Ky. Wesleyan	44.8	32.6	12.2
2000	Salem Int'l	44.2	32.1	12.1
2001	Salem Int'l	42.6	31.3	11.4
2002	Tarleton St.	43.0	32.0	11.1
2003	South Dakota St.	44.1	32.5	11.6
2004	Washburn	42.5	30.7	11.8
2005	Fla. Gulf Coast	41.5	31.3	10.2
2006	Gannon	38.8	27.5	11.3
2007	Fla. Gulf Coast	44.5	33.7	10.8
2008	Ky. Wesleyan	36.8	25.4	11.4

*record

2008 Most-Improved Teams

School (Coach)	2008	2007	*Games Improved
1. S.C.-Aiken (Vince Alexander)	27-4	9-22	18
2. Gannon (John Reilly)	26-5	9-17	14½
3. Fla. Southern (Linc Darner)	24-9	8-20	13½
4. Clark Atlanta (Darryl Jacobs)	16-14	2-26	13
5. Florida Tech (Billy Mims)	20-8	10-21	11½
6. Arkansas Tech (Mark Downey)	18-11	6-21	11
Neb.-Omaha (Derrin Hansen)	25-7	12-16	11
8. San Fran. St. (Bill Treseler)	17-12	6-21	10
9. Assumption (Serge DeBari)	24-11	11-17	9½
Wilmington (Del.) (Kevin Welch)	10-16	1-26	9½
11. Carson-Newman (Dale Clayton)	18-9	10-19	9
Washburn (Bob Chipman)	18-11	8-19	9
13. Abilene Christian ((Jason Copeland)	20-9	10-16	8½
Ky. Wesleyan (Todd Lee)	24-8	13-14	8½

School (Coach)	2008	2007	*Games Improved
Merrimack (Bert Hammel)	17-12	8-20	8½
North Ala. (Bobby Champagne)	27-9	15-14	8½
17. Anderson (S.C.) (Jason Taylor)	12-16	4-24	8
Belmont Abbey (Stephen Miss)	16-12	8-20	8
Mansfield (Rich Miller)	17-10	9-18	8
20. Angelo St. (Fred Rike)	17-11	9-17	7
Mo. Southern St. (Robert Corn)	17-11	10-18	7
Northwest Nazarene (Tim Hills)	17-10	10-17	7
West Va. Wesleyan (Bill Lilly)	10-18	3-25	7

*To determine games improved, add the difference in victories between the two seasons to the difference in losses, then divide by two.

All-Time Winningest Teams

Includes records as a senior college only; minimum 10 seasons of competition. Postseason games are included.

By Percentage

	Team	Yrs.	Won	Lost	Pct.
1.	Metro St.	24	506	216	.701
2.	Philadelphia U.	73	1,229	539	.695
3.	Virginia Union	83	1,381	623	.689
4.	Lynn	15	296	139	.680
5.	Cheyney	45	829	413	.667
6.	Southern N.H.	45	844	429	.663
7.	Southern Ind.	39	734	379	.659
8.	St. Rose	34	644	335	.658
9.	Ky. Wesleyan	94	1,367	717	.656
10.	Central Wash.	101	1,566	832	.653
11.	Bentley	45	800	427	.652
12.	St. Mary's (Tex.)	54	985	532	.649
13.	Gannon	64	1,070	602	.640
14.	Northern St.	105	1,459	824	.639
15.	LeMoyne-Owen	50	855	496	.633
16.	Fairmont St.	83	1,371	804	.630
17.	Drury	100	1,390	822	.628
18.	Cal St. San B'dino	24	410	244	.627
19.	Mesa St.	33	578	344	.627
20.	Fort Hays St.	99	1,365	820	.625
21.	Carson-Newman	50	937	563	.625
22.	Central Mo.	103	1,469	883	.625
23.	Alas. Anchorage	31	564	342	.623
24.	California (Pa.)	46	747	456	.621
25.	Millersville	107	1,293	790	.621
26.	Incarnate Word	25	443	274	.618
27.	C.W. Post	52	838	519	.618
28.	St. Cloud St.	83	1,163	723	.617
29.	Fla. Southern	81	1,189	740	.616
30.	Grand Valley St.	42	727	453	.616

By Victories

	Team	Yrs.	Won	Lost	Pct.
1.	Central Wash.	101	1,566	832	.653
2.	Central Mo.	103	1,469	883	.625
3.	Northern St.	105	1,459	824	.639
4.	Drury	100	1,390	822	.628
5.	Virginia Union	83	1,381	623	.689
6.	Fairmont St.	83	1,371	804	.630
7.	Ky. Wesleyan	94	1,367	717	.656
8.	Fort Hays St.	99	1,365	820	.625
9.	Washburn	102	1,354	936	.591
10.	West Tex. A&M	87	1,350	870	.608
11.	Millersville	107	1,293	790	.621
12.	Pittsburg St.	99	1,291	1,031	.556
13.	Emporia St.	102	1,259	1,026	.551
14.	Neb.-Kearney	101	1,258	866	.592
15.	Western Wash.	106	1,249	942	.570
16.	Lenoir-Rhyne	87	1,230	952	.564
17.	Philadelphia U.	73	1,229	539	.695
18.	Northwest Mo. St.	92	1,228	882	.582
19.	West Chester	108	1,220	978	.555
20.	Rockhurst	87	1,217	952	.561
21.	Cal St. Chico	95	1,200	1,071	.528
22.	Bloomsburg	103	1,192	799	.599
23.	Fla. Southern	81	1,189	740	.616
24.	Tex. A&M-Commerce	91	1,187	967	.551
25.	East Central	81	1,170	817	.589
	Indianapolis	84	1,170	829	.585
27.	Catawba	82	1,165	966	.547
28.	St. Cloud St.	83	1,163	723	.617
29.	Northern Mich.	98	1,150	807	.588
30.	Glenville St.	89	1,149	970	.542

Winningest Teams of the 2000s

BY PERCENTAGE
(Minimum 6 seasons as NCAA member)

	Team	Yrs.	Won	Lost	Pct.
1.	Metro St.	9	242	55	.815
2.	Findlay	8	202	46	.815
3.	Cal St. San B'dino	9	206	55	.789
4.	Southern Ind.	9	224	62	.783
5.	Northwest Mo. St.	9	216	67	.763
5.	Neb.-Kearney	9	206	67	.755
7.	Virginia Union	9	200	66	.752
8.	Adelphi	9	206	68	.752
9.	Tarleton St.	9	207	71	.745
10.	Alderson-Broaddus	9	205	72	.740
11.	South Dakota	9	196	69	.740
12.	Bentley	9	207	74	.737
13.	Pfeiffer	9	198	71	.736
14.	Winona St.	9	211	77	.733
15.	Ky. Wesleyan	9	200	73	.733
16.	California (Pa.)	9	194	75	.721
17.	Seattle Pacific	9	187	73	.719
18.	Benedict	6	124	49	.717
19.	Eckerd	9	195	78	.714
20.	Northern St.	9	189	79	.705
21.	St. Cloud St.	9	184	79	.700
22.	Humboldt St.	9	181	78	.699
23.	Charleston (W.V.)	9	189	82	.697
	Rollins	9	189	82	.697
25.	Fla. Southern	9	189	83	.695
26.	Salem Int'l	9	189	84	.692
27.	Grand Valley St.	9	188	84	.691
28.	Bowie St.	9	184	83	.689
29.	Fort Hays St.	9	179	81	.689
30.	Northern Ky.	9	189	86	.687

BY VICTORIES

	Team	Yrs.	Won	Lost	Pct.
1.	Metro St.	9	242	55	.815
2.	Southern Ind.	9	224	62	.783
3.	Northwest Mo. St.	9	216	67	.763
4.	Winona St.	9	211	77	.733
5.	Tarleton St.	9	207	71	.745
	Bentley	9	207	74	.737
7.	Cal St. San B'dino	9	206	55	.789
	Neb.-Kearney	9	206	67	.755
	Adelphi	9	206	68	.752
10.	Alderson-Broaddus	9	205	72	.740
11.	Findlay	8	202	46	.815
12.	Virginia Union	9	200	66	.752
	Ky. Wesleyan	9	200	73	.733
14.	Pfeiffer	9	198	71	.736
15.	South Dakota	9	196	69	.740
16.	Eckerd	9	195	78	.714
17.	California (Pa.)	9	194	75	.721
18.	Northern St.	9	189	79	.705
	Charleston (W.V.)	9	189	82	.697
	Rollins	9	189	82	.697
	Fla. Southern	9	189	83	.695
	Salem Int'l	9	189	84	.692
	Northern Ky.	9	189	86	.687
24.	Grand Valley St.	9	188	84	.691
25.	Seattle Pacific	9	187	73	.719
26.	Washburn	9	185	85	.685
	Philadelphia U.	9	185	88	.678
28.	St. Cloud St.	9	184	79	.700
	Bowie St.	9	184	83	.689
30.	Queens (N.C.)	9	183	85	.683

All-Time Won-Lost Records

(Alphabetical Listing; No Minimum Seasons of Competition)

Team	First Year	Yrs.	Won	Lost	Pct.
Abilene Christian	1920	87	1,035	962	.518
Adams St.	1947	44	552	608	.476
Adelphi	1947	62	950	685	.581
Ala.-Huntsville	1974	35	493	505	.494
Alas. Anchorage	1978	31	564	342	.623
Alas. Fairbanks	1953	52	562	654	.462
Albany St. (Ga.)	1961	48	757	601	.557
Alderson-Broaddus	1935	71	1,112	874	.560
American Int'l	1934	74	874	908	.490
Angelo St.	1966	43	583	585	.499
Ark.-Monticello	1946	63	729	898	.448
Arkansas Tech	1915	85	1,102	916	.546
Armstrong Atlantic	1967	42	651	527	.553
Ashland	1921	88	1,041	890	.539
Assumption	1924	81	1,015	826	.551
Augusta St.	1966	43	663	542	.550
Augustana (S.D.)	1922	82	852	933	.477
Barry	1985	24	330	340	.493
Bellarmine	1951	58	761	739	.507
Belmont Abbey	1954	55	840	675	.555
Bemidji St.	1922	86	872	1,000	.466
Bentley	1964	45	800	427	.652
Bloomsburg	1902	103	1,192	799	.599
Bridgeport	1948	61	875	748	.539
BYU-Hawaii	1978	31	538	357	.601
C.W. Post	1957	52	838	519	.618
UC San Diego	1966	43	553	560	.497
Cal Poly Pomona	1948	61	849	781	.521
Cal St. Chico	1914	95	1,200	1,071	.528
Cal St. Dom. Hills	1978	31	401	430	.483
Cal St. L.A.	1949	60	738	813	.476
Cal St. San B'dino	1985	24	410	244	.627
Cal St. Stanislaus	1967	42	510	608	.456
California (Pa.)	1963	46	747	456	.621
Carson-Newman	1959	50	937	563	.625
Catawba	1927	82	1,165	966	.547
Central Mo.	1906	103	1,469	883	.625
Central Okla.	1922	82	1,123	880	.561
Central Wash.	1902	101	1,566	832	.653
Chadron St.	1922	84	978	978	.500
Chaminade	1978	31	485	379	.561
Cheyney	1964	45	829	413	.667
Christian Bros.	1955	54	795	734	.520
Clark Atlanta	1950	59	831	732	.532
Clayton St.	1991	18	282	241	.539
UC-Colo. Spgs.	1988	21	140	422	.249
Colo. Christian	1991	18	210	284	.425
Colorado Mines	1912	96	719	1,245	.366
Colorado St.-Pueblo	1964	45	739	501	.596
Columbus St.	1968	40	666	444	.600
Concordia-St. Paul	1968	41	423	633	.401
Delta St.	1928	77	1,122	737	.604
Dowling	1967	42	629	541	.538
Drury	1909	100	1,390	822	.628
East Central	1928	81	1,170	817	.589
East Stroudsburg	1927	81	879	920	.489
Eastern N.M.	1935	72	897	977	.479
Eckerd	1964	45	662	478	.581
Edinboro	1929	78	999	702	.587
Elizabeth City St.	1950	59	846	699	.548
Emporia St.	1902	102	1,259	1,026	.551
Erskine	1914	83	1,000	932	.518
Fairmont St.	1917	83	1,371	804	.630
Fayetteville St.	1937	65	821	838	.495
Felician	1997	12	137	208	.397
Ferris St.	1926	80	953	894	.516
Findlay	1911	86	1,124	714	.612
Fla. Southern	1924	81	1,189	740	.616
Florida Tech	1965	44	469	686	.406
Fort Hays St.	1908	99	1,365	820	.625
Fort Lewis	1964	45	584	605	.491
Francis Marion	1971	38	504	554	.476
Franklin Pierce	1964	45	690	487	.586
Gannon	1945	64	1,070	602	.640
Georgia College	1971	38	548	519	.514
Glenville St.	1909	89	1,149	970	.542
Grand Canyon	1950	59	974	612	.614
Grand Valley St.	1967	42	727	453	.616

Team	First Year	Yrs.	Won	Lost	Pct.
Harding	1958	51	676	735	.479
Hawaii Pacific	1979	30	513	381	.574
Hawaii-Hilo	1977	32	537	392	.578
Henderson St.	1913	93	1,142	885	.563
Hillsdale	1900	105	996	1,160	.462
Humboldt St.	1924	85	852	937	.476
Incarnate Word	1981	25	443	274	.618
Indiana (Pa.)	1928	79	1,096	692	.613
Indianapolis	1923	84	1,170	829	.585
Johnson Smith	1929	80	1,022	699	.594
Ky. Wesleyan	1908	94	1,367	717	.656
Lake Superior St.	1947	62	786	710	.525
Lander	1969	40	647	540	.545
Le Moyne	1949	60	837	654	.561
LeMoyne-Owen	1959	50	855	496	.633
Lenoir-Rhyne	1920	87	1,230	952	.564
Lewis	1949	60	957	642	.598
Lincoln Memorial	1923	86	1,124	948	.542
Lock Haven	1919	84	631	1,011	.384
Lynn	1994	15	296	139	.680
Mansfield	1918	85	909	795	.533
Mars Hill	1964	45	524	731	.418
Mass.-Lowell	1967	42	562	562	.500
Mercyhurst	1972	37	510	478	.516
Merrimack	1950	59	749	755	.498
Mesa St.	1976	33	578	344	.627
Metro St.	1985	24	506	216	.701
Michigan Tech	1918	88	794	931	.460
Midwestern St.	1947	62	1,129	749	.601
Miles	1971	38	487	537	.476
Millersville	1900	107	1,293	790	.621
Minn. St. Mankato	1921	84	1,101	803	.578
Minn.-Duluth	1931	75	1,076	704	.604
Minn. St.-Moorhead	1925	84	980	969	.503
Mo. Southern St.	1969	40	618	539	.534
Mo. Western St.	1970	39	669	469	.588
Missouri S&T	1910	96	764	1,183	.392
Mo.-St. Louis	1967	42	517	585	.469
Molloy	1993	16	152	285	.348
Mont. St.-Billings	1928	78	983	870	.530
Montevallo	1965	44	668	586	.533
Morehouse	1911	97	1,070	963	.526
Neb.-Kearney	1907	101	1,258	866	.592
Neb.-Omaha	1913	91	1,004	1,000	.501
N.M. Highlands	1924	82	830	1,008	.452
NYIT	1971	37	521	456	.533
Newberry	1913	93	938	1,198	.439
North Ala.	1932	74	968	774	.556
UNC-Pembroke	1940	69	839	867	.492
North Georgia	1942	39	626	555	.530
Northeastern St.	1925	72	962	866	.526
Northern Ky.	1972	37	625	426	.595
Northern Mich.	1907	98	1,150	807	.588
Northern St.	1903	105	1,459	824	.639
Northwest Mo. St.	1917	92	1,228	882	.582
Northwood (Mich.)	1961	48	554	683	.448
Nova Southeastern	1983	26	293	441	.399
Oakland City	1923	67	842	739	.533
Ouachita Baptist	1921	82	1,045	870	.546
Pace	1948	61	768	744	.508
Philadelphia U.	1921	73	1,229	539	.695
Philadelphia Sciences	1902	100	1,133	836	.575
Pitt.-Johnstown	1970	39	492	507	.492
Pittsburg St.	1909	99	1,291	1,031	.556
Quincy	1941	64	1,022	772	.570
Regis (Colo.)	1946	61	854	752	.532
Rockhurst	1922	87	1,217	952	.561
Rollins	1951	58	831	688	.547
Saginaw Valley	1970	39	543	531	.506
St. Andrews	1975	34	428	484	.469
St. Anselm	1935	71	966	717	.574
St. Cloud St.	1923	83	1,163	723	.617
St. Joseph's (Ind.)	1906	92	1,040	947	.523
St. Leo	1966	43	446	672	.399
St. Mary's (Tex.)	1955	54	985	532	.649
St. Michael's	1920	88	1,004	944	.515
St. Rose	1974	34	644	335	.658
San Fran. St.	1930	77	979	989	.497
Seattle Pacific	1944	65	1,039	758	.578
Shepherd	1907	101	1,126	1,067	.513
Slippery Rock	1910	97	1,041	986	.514
Sonoma St.	1964	41	466	586	.443
S.C.-Aiken	1970	39	531	605	.467

Team	First Year	Yrs.	Won	Lost	Pct.	Team	First Year	Yrs.	Won	Lost	Pct.
Southern Conn. St.	1960	49	565	721	.439	Wayne St. (Mich.)	1918	90	1,084	907	.544
Southern Ind.	1970	39	734	379	.659	Wayne St. (Neb.)	1913	94	1,128	.974	.537
Southern N.H.	1964	45	844	429	.663	West Ala.	1957	52	599	727	.452
Southwest Baptist	1966	43	632	538	.540	West Chester	1898	108	1,220	978	.555
Southwest Minn. St.	1968	41	466	643	.420	West Fla.	1968	24	349	287	.549
Stonehill	1950	59	839	679	.553	West Ga.	1958	51	781	561	.582
Tampa	1951	46	734	529	.581	West Liberty St.	1924	85	833	883	.485
Tarleton St.	1962	47	597	684	.466	West Tex. A&M	1921	87	1,350	870	.608
Tex. A&M-Commerce	1917	91	1,187	967	.551	West Va. St.	1945	64	923	767	.546
Tex. A&M-Kingsville	1926	74	816	926	.468	Western Ore.	1921	84	1,033	998	.509
Truman	1920	88	1,051	956	.524	Western St.	1924	82	736	1,152	.390
Tuskegee	1909	79	1,039	988	.513	Western Wash.	1903	106	1,249	942	.570
Upper Iowa	1916	93	826	978	.458	Wheeling Jesuit	1958	51	674	676	.499
Valdosta St.	1955	54	837	552	.603	Winona St.	1916	92	991	1,024	.492
Virginia Union	1926	83	1,381	623	.689	Wis.-Parkside	1970	39	534	554	.491
Washburn	1906	102	1,354	936	.591						

Division III Records

Individual Records

Division III men's basketball records are based on the performances of Division III teams since the three-division reorganization plan was adopted by the special NCAA Convention in August 1973. Assists were added for the 1988-89 season; blocked shots and steals were added for the 1992-93 season. In statistical rankings, the rounding of percentages and/or averages may indicate ties where none exist. In these cases, the numerical order of the rankings is accurate.

Scoring

POINTS
Game
77—Jeff Clement, Grinnell vs. Illinois Col., Feb. 18, 1998
Season
1,044—Greg Grant, TCNJ, 1989 (32 games)
Career
2,940—Andre Foreman, Salisbury, 1988-89, 91-92 (109 games)

AVERAGE PER GAME
Season
37.3—Steve Diekmann, Grinnell, 1995 (745 in 20)
Career
(Min. 1,400) 32.8—Dwain Govan, Bishop, 1974-75 (1,805 in 55)

POINTS SCORED WITH NO TIME ELAPSING
Game
24—Rob Rittgers, UC San Diego vs. Menlo, Jan. 16, 1988 (made 24 consecutive free throws due to 12 bench technical fouls)

CONSECUTIVE POINTS SCORED
Game
25—Andy Panko, Lebanon Valley vs. Frank. & Marsh., Jan. 19, 1998

GAMES SCORING AT LEAST 50 POINTS
Season
4—Mike Hoyt, Mt. St. Mary (N.Y.), 2007
Career
4—Mike Hoyt, Mt. St. Mary (N.Y.), 2004-07; Jeff Clement, Grinnell, 1996-99; Steve Diekmann, Grinnell, 1993-95

GAMES SCORING IN DOUBLE FIGURES
Career
116—Lamont Strothers, Chris. Newport, 1988-91

CONSECUTIVE GAMES SCORING IN DOUBLE FIGURES
Career
116—Lamont Strothers, Chris. Newport, from Nov. 20, 1987, to March 8, 1991

Field Goals

FIELD GOALS
Game
29—Ryan Hodges, Cal Lutheran vs. Redlands, Jan. 15, 2005 (31 attempts); Shannon Lilly, Bishop vs. Southwest Assembly of God, Jan. 31, 1983 (36 attempts)
Season
394—Dave Russell, Shepherd, 1975 (687 attempts)
Career
1,140—Andre Foreman, Salisbury, 1988-89, 91-92 (2,125 attempts)

CONSECUTIVE FIELD GOALS
Game
18—Franklyn Beckford, Lake Forest vs. Grinnell, Feb. 14, 2004; Jason Light, Emory & Henry vs. King (Tenn.), Dec. 2, 1995
Season
24—Todd Richards, Mount Union, 2000 (during five games)

FIELD-GOAL ATTEMPTS
Game
68—Jeff Clement, Grinnell vs. Illinois Col., Feb. 18, 1998 (26 made)
Season
742—Greg Grant, TCNJ, 1989 (387 made)
Career
2,149—Lamont Strothers, Chris. Newport, 1988-91 (1,016 made)

FIELD-GOAL PERCENTAGE
Game
(Min. 18 made) 100%— Franklyn Beckford, Lake Forest vs. Grinnell, Feb. 14, 2004 (18 of 18); Jason Light, Emory & Henry vs. King (Tenn.), Dec. 2, 1995 (18 of 18)
*Season
76.6—Travis Weiss, St. John's (Minn.), 1994 (160 of 209)
Based on qualifiers for annual championship.
Career
(Min. 400 made) 73.6%—Tony Rychlec, Mass. Maritime, 1981-83 (509 of 692)

Three-Point Field Goals

THREE-POINT FIELD GOALS
Game
21—Sami Wylie, Lincoln (Pa.) vs. Ohio St.-Marion, Dec. 2, 2006
Season
186—Jeff Clement, Grinnell, 1998 (511 attempts)
Career
516—Jeff Clement, Grinnell, 1996-99 (1,532 attempts)

THREE-POINT FIELD GOALS MADE PER GAME
Season
8.5—Jeff Clement, Grinnell, 1998 (186 in 22)
Career
5.7—Jeff Clement, Grinnell, 1996-99 (516 in 91)

CONSECUTIVE THREE-POINT FIELD GOALS
Game
11—Joe Goldin, Randolph-Macon vs. Emory & Henry, Feb. 16, 1997
Season
16—John Richards, Sewanee (during five games, Feb. 10 to Feb. 25, 1990)

CONSECUTIVE GAMES MAKING A THREE-POINT FIELD GOAL
Season
31—Troy Greenlee, DePauw, Nov. 17, 1989, to March 17, 1990
Career
75—Chris Carideo, Widener, 1992-95

THREE-POINT FIELD-GOAL ATTEMPTS
Game
52—Jeff Clement, Grinnell vs. Illinois Col., Feb. 18, 1998 (19 made)
Season
511—Jeff Clement, Grinnell, 1998 (186 made)
Career
1,532—Jeff Clement, Grinnell, 1996-99 (516 made)

THREE-POINT FIELD-GOAL ATTEMPTS PER GAME
Season
23.2—Jeff Clement, Grinnell, 1998 (511 in 22)
Career
16.8—Jeff Clement, Grinnell, 1996-99 (1,532 in 91)

THREE-POINT FIELD-GOAL PERCENTAGE
Game
(Min. 11 made) 100%—Joe Goldin, Randolph-Macon vs. Emory & Henry, Feb. 16, 1997 (11 of 11)
Season
(Min. 40 made) 67.0%—Reggie James, NJIT, 1989 (59 of 88)
(Min. 90 made) 56.9%—Eric Harris, Bishop, 1987 (91 of 160)
Career
(Min. 200 made) 51.3%—Jeff Seifriz, Wis.-Whitewater, 1987-89 (217 of 423)

Free Throws

FREE THROWS
Game
30—Rob Rittgers, UC San Diego vs. Menlo, Jan. 16, 1988 (30 attempts)
Season
249—Dave Russell, Shepherd, 1975 (293 attempts)
Career
792—Matt Hancock, Colby, 1987-90 (928 attempts)

CONSECUTIVE FREE THROWS MADE
Game
30—Rob Rittgers, UC San Diego vs. Menlo, Jan. 16, 1988
Season
59—Mike Michelson, Coast Guard (during 13 games, Jan. 16 to Feb. 27, 1990)
Career
84—Dirk Rhinehart, Kalamazoo (16 games, Jan. 3, 2001 to Dec. 17, 2001)

FREE THROWS ATTEMPTED
Game
30—Rob Rittgers, UC San Diego vs. Menlo, Jan. 16, 1988 (30 made)
Season
326—Moses Jean-Pierre, Plymouth St., 1994 (243 made)
Career
928—Matt Hancock, Colby, 1987-90 (792 made)

FREE-THROW PERCENTAGE
Game
(Min. 30 made) 100%—Rob Rittgers, UC San Diego vs. Menlo, Jan. 16, 1988 (30 of 30)
*Season
96.3%—Korey Coon, Ill. Wesleyan, 2000 (157 of 163)
based on qualifiers for annual championship
Career
(Min. 250 made) 92.5%—Andy Enfield, Johns Hopkins, 1988-91 (431 of 466)
(Min. 500 made) 86.2%—Brad Clark, Wis.-Oshkosh, 1997-00 (535 of 621)

Rebounds

REBOUNDS
Game
36—Mark Veenstra, Calvin vs. Colorado St.-Pueblo, Feb. 3, 1976; Clinton Montford, Methodist vs. Warren Wilson, Jan. 21, 1989
Season
579—Joe Manley, Bowie St., 1976 (29 games)
Career
1,628—Michael Smith, Hamilton, 1989-92 (107 games)

AVERAGE PER GAME
Season
19.97—Joe Manley, Bowie St., 1976 (579 in 29)
Career
(Min. 900) 17.4—Larry Parker, Plattsburgh St., 1975-78 (1,482 in 85)

Assists

ASSISTS
Game
26—Robert James, Kean vs. NJIT, March 11, 1989
Season
391—Robert James, Kean, 1989 (29 games)
Career
917—Tennyson Whitted, Ramapo, 2000-03 (108 games)

AVERAGE PER GAME
Season
13.5—Robert James, Kean, 1989 (391 in 29)
Career
(Min. 550) 8.6—Phil Dixon, Shenandoah, 1993-96 (889 in 103)

Blocked Shots

BLOCKED SHOTS
Game
18—John Bunch, Lincoln (Pa.) vs. New Jersey City, Jan. 19, 2004; John Bunch, Lincoln (Pa.) vs. Valley Forge, Dec. 13, 2003
Season
198—Tory Black, NJIT, 1997 (26 games)
Career
576—Ira Nicholson, Mt. St. Vincent, 1994-97 (100 games)

AVERAGE PER GAME
Season
7.6—Tory Black, NJIT, 1997 (198 in 26)
Career
6.1—Neil Edwards, York (N.Y.), 1998-00 (337 in 55)

Steals

STEALS
Game
17—Matt Newton, Principia vs. Harris-Stowe, Jan. 4, 1994
Season
189—Moses Jean-Pierre, Plymouth St., 1994 (30 games)
Career
448—Tennyson Whitted, Ramapo, 2000-03 (108 games)

AVERAGE PER GAME
Season
6.3—Moses Jean-Pierre, Plymouth St., 1994 (189 in 30)
Career
5.5—Moses Jean-Pierre, Plymouth St., 1993-94 (303 in 55 games)

Games

GAMES PLAYED
Season
34—Nick Bennett, Kyle Gruszcynski, Jason Kaslow, Neal Krajnik, Eric Maus and Tamaris Releford, Wis.-Stevens Point, 2004; Thane Anderson, Matt Benedict, Tim Blair, Lanse Carter, Mike Johnson, Todd Oehrlein, Mike Prasher and Derrick Shelton, Wis.-Eau Claire, 1990
Career
124—Tonton Balenga, Va. Wesleyan, 2005-08

Team Records

Note: Where records involve both teams, each team must be an NCAA Division III member institution.

SINGLE-GAME RECORDS

Scoring

POINTS
201—Lincoln (Pa.) vs. Ohio St.-Marion (78), Dec. 2, 2006
POINTS BY LOSING TEAM
153—Redlands vs. Cal Baptist, Dec. 10, 2004; Chapman vs. Redlands, December 4, 2003 (3ot)
POINTS, BOTH TEAMS
315—Simpson (167) vs. Grinnell (148), Nov. 19, 1994
POINTS IN A HALF
104—Lincoln (Pa.) vs. Ohio St.-Marion (78), Dec. 2, 2006 (second half)
POINTS SCORED WITH NO TIME ELAPSING OFF OF THE CLOCK
24—UC San Diego vs. Menlo, Jan. 16, 1988 (made 24 consecutive free throws due to 12 bench technical fouls)
FEWEST POINTS ALLOWED
6—Dickinson (15) vs. Muhlenberg, Feb. 3, 1982
FEWEST POINTS ALLOWED IN A HALF
0—Dickinson (2) vs. Muhlenberg (first), Feb. 3, 1982
FEWEST POINTS, BOTH TEAMS
21—Dickinson (15) vs. Muhlenberg (6), Feb. 3, 1982
FEWEST POINTS, HALF, BOTH TEAMS
2—Dickinson (2) vs. Muhlenberg (0) (first), Feb. 3, 1982
MARGIN OF VICTORY
123—Lincoln (Pa.) (201) vs. Ohio St.-Marion (78), Dec. 2, 2006

Field Goals

FIELD GOALS
79—Lincoln (Pa.) vs. Ohio St.-Marion, Dec. 2, 2006 (141 attempts)
FIELD-GOAL ATTEMPTS
141—Lincoln (Pa.) vs. Ohio St.-Marion, Dec. 2, 2006 (made 79)
FEWEST FIELD GOALS
3—Muhlenberg vs. Dickinson, Feb. 3, 1982 (11 attempts)
FEWEST FIELD-GOAL ATTEMPTS
11—Muhlenberg vs. Dickinson, Feb. 3, 1982 (3 made)

FIELD-GOAL PERCENTAGE
89.8%—St. Norbert vs. Grinnell, Jan. 28, 2000
FIELD-GOAL PERCENTAGE, HALF
95.7—Beloit vs. Grinnell, Jan. 27, 2001 (22 of 23)

Three-Point Field Goals

THREE-POINT FIELD GOALS
37—Redlands vs. La Sierra, Dec. 13, 2003 (97 attempts)
THREE-POINT FIELD GOALS, BOTH TEAMS
47—Redlands (35) vs. Whittier (12), Feb. 21, 2004
CONSECUTIVE THREE-POINT FIELD GOALS MADE WITHOUT A MISS
11—Willamette vs. Western Baptist, Jan. 8, 1987
NUMBER OF DIFFERENT PLAYERS TO SCORE A THREE-POINT FIELD GOAL, ONE TEAM
14—Redlands vs. Caltech, Jan. 29, 2005
THREE-POINT FIELD-GOAL ATTEMPTS
106—Redlands vs. La Sierra, Jan. 6, 2005 (35 made)
THREE-POINT FIELD-GOAL ATTEMPTS, BOTH TEAMS
119—Redlands (82) vs. Chapman (37), Dec. 5, 2003
THREE-POINT FIELD-GOAL PERCENTAGE
(Min. 10 made) 100%—Willamette vs. Western Baptist, Jan. 8, 1987 (11 of 11); Kean vs. Ramapo, Feb. 11, 1987 (10 of 10)
(Min. 15 made) 89.5%—Simpson vs. Dubuque, Feb. 22, 2003 (17 of 19)
THREE-POINT FIELD-GOAL PERCENTAGE, BOTH TEAMS
(Min. 10 made) 92.9%—Luther (8 of 8) vs. Wartburg (5 of 6), Feb. 14, 1987 (13 of 14)
(Min. 15 made) 75.0%—Anna Maria (4 of 6) vs. Nichols (11 of 14), Feb. 10, 1987 (15 of 20)
(Min. 20 made) 62.9%—Simpson (17 of 19) vs. Dubuque (5 of 16), Feb. 22, 2003 (22 of 35)

Free Throws

FREE THROWS MADE
53—UC San Diego vs. Menlo, Jan. 16, 1988 (59 attempts)
FREE THROWS MADE, BOTH TEAMS
93—Grinnell (50) vs. Beloit (43), Jan. 10, 1998
FREE THROWS ATTEMPTED
71—Earlham vs. Oberlin, Dec. 5, 1992 (46 made)
FREE THROWS ATTEMPTED, BOTH TEAMS
105—Earlham (71) vs. Oberlin (34), Dec. 5, 1992

FEWEST FREE THROWS MADE
0—Many teams
FEWEST FREE-THROW ATTEMPTS
0—Many teams
FREE-THROW PERCENTAGE
(Min. 28 made) 10.0%—Albany (N.Y.) vs. Potsdam St., Feb. 19, 1994 (28 of 28)
(Min. 30 made) 97.2%—Ill. Wesleyan vs. North Park, Feb. 19, 2003 (35 of 36)
(Min. 45 made) 92.6%—Grinnell vs. Beloit, Jan. 10, 1998 (50 of 54)
FREE-THROW PERCENTAGE, BOTH TEAMS
(Min. 20 made) 100%—Bethel (Minn.) (15 of 15) vs. Carleton (5 of 5), Feb. 24, 2004
(Min. 30 made) 94.9%—Muskingum (30 of 31) vs. Ohio Wesleyan (7 of 8), Jan. 10, 1981 (37 of 39)

Rebounds

REBOUNDS
98—Alma vs. Marion, Dec. 28, 1973
REBOUNDS, BOTH TEAMS
124—Chapman (65) vs. Redlands (59), Dec. 5, 2003; Ill. Wesleyan (62) vs. North Central (Ill.) (62), Feb. 8, 1977; Rochester Inst. (72) vs. Thiel (52), Nov. 18, 1988
REBOUND MARGIN
56—MIT (74) vs. Emerson-MCA (18), Feb. 21, 1990

Assists

ASSISTS
53—Simpson vs. Grinnell, Nov. 25, 1995
ASSISTS, BOTH TEAMS
79—Simpson (53) vs. Grinnell (26), Nov. 25, 1995

Personal Fouls

PERSONAL FOULS
47—Concordia Chicago vs. Trinity Christian, Feb. 26, 1988
PERSONAL FOULS, BOTH TEAMS
80—Grinnell (46) vs. St. Norbert (34), Jan. 28, 2000
PLAYERS DISQUALIFIED
6—Thomas More vs. Franklin, Feb. 2, 2002; Wheaton (Mass.) vs. Babson, Feb. 18, 1999; Union (N.Y.) vs. Rochester, Feb. 15, 1985; Haverford vs. Drew, Jan. 10, 1990; Manhattanville vs. Drew, Jan. 11, 1992; Roger Williams vs. Curry, Jan. 14, 1995

DIVISION III

PLAYERS DISQUALIFIED, BOTH TEAMS
11—Union (N.Y.) (6) vs. Rochester (5), Feb. 15, 1985

Overtimes

OVERTIME PERIODS
5—Babson (115) vs. Wheaton (Mass.) (107), Feb. 18, 1999; Capital (86) vs. Muskingum (89), Jan. 5, 1980; Carnegie Mellon (81) vs. Allegheny (76), Feb. 12, 1983; Rochester (99) vs. Union (N.Y.) (98), Feb. 15, 1985

POINTS IN ONE OVERTIME PERIOD
31—Marymount (Va.) vs. Catholic, Jan. 30, 1999

POINTS IN ONE OVERTIME PERIOD, BOTH TEAMS
51—Wash. & Lee (28) vs. Mary Washington (23), Jan. 9, 1995

POINTS IN OVERTIME PERIODS
50—Babson (50) vs. Wheaton (Mass.) (5 ot), Feb. 18, 1999

POINTS IN OVERTIME PERIODS, BOTH TEAMS
92—Babson (50) vs. Wheaton (Mass.) (42) (5 ot), Feb. 18, 1999

SEASON RECORDS

Scoring

POINTS
3,310—Redlands, 2005 (25 games)

AVERAGE PER GAME
132.4—Redlands, 2005 (3,310 in 25)

AVERAGE SCORING MARGIN
31.1—Husson, 1976 (98.7 offense, 67.6 defense)

GAMES AT LEAST 100 POINTS
23—Redlands, 2005 (25-game season); Grinnell, 2002 (24-game season)

CONSECUTIVE GAMES AT LEAST 100 POINTS
19—Grinnell, from Nov. 23, 2002, to Feb. 8, 2003

CONSECUTIVE GAMES AT LEAST 100 POINTS (Multiple Seasons)
28—Grinnell, from Jan. 25, 2002, to Feb. 8, 2003

Field Goals

FIELD GOALS
1,323—Shepherd, 1975 (2,644 attempts)

FIELD GOALS PER GAME
44.6—Redlands, 2005 (1,116 in 25)

FIELD-GOAL ATTEMPTS
2,757—Redlands, 2005 (1,116 made)

FIELD-GOAL ATTEMPTS PER GAME
110.3—Redlands, 2005 (2,757 in 25)

FIELD-GOAL PERCENTAGE
60.0—Stony Brook, 1978 (1,033 of 1,721)

Three-Point Field Goals

THREE-POINT FIELD GOALS
595—Redlands, 2005 (1,813 attempts)

THREE-POINT FIELD GOALS PER GAME
23.8—Redlands, 2005 (595 in 25)

THREE-POINT FIELD-GOAL ATTEMPTS
1,813—Redlands, 2005 (595 made)

THREE-POINT FIELD-GOAL ATTEMPTS PER GAME
72.5—Redlands, 2005 (1,813 in 25)

THREE-POINT FIELD-GOAL PERCENTAGE
(Min. 100 made) 62.0%—NJIT, 1989 (124 of 200)
(Min. 150 made) 49.1%—Eureka, 1994 (317 of 646)

CONSECUTIVE GAMES SCORING A THREE-POINT FIELD GOAL
474—Salisbury, Nov. 25, 1986-Present

Free Throws

FREE THROWS MADE
698—Ohio Wesleyan, 1988 (888 attempts)

FREE THROWS MADE PER GAME
23.7—Grinnell, 1995 (498 in 21)

FREE-THROW ATTEMPTS
930—Queens (N.Y.), 1981 (636 made)

FREE-THROW ATTEMPTS PER GAME
33.2—Grinnell, 1995 (698 in 21)

FREE-THROW PERCENTAGE
81.8%—Wis.-Oshkosh, 1998 (516 of 631)

Rebounds

REBOUNDS
1,616—Keene St., 1976 (29 games)

AVERAGE PER GAME
56.3—Mercy, 1977 (1,408 in 25)

AVERAGE REBOUND MARGIN
17.0—Hamilton, 1991 (49.6 offense, 32.5 defense)

Assists

ASSISTS
861—Salisbury, 1991 (29 games)

AVERAGE PER GAME
31.2—Me.-Farmington, 1991 (748 in 24)

Fouls

FOULS
801—McMurry, 2001 (28 games)

FOULS PER GAME
3.9—Grinnell, 1998 (679 in 22)

FEWEST FOULS
177—Caltech, 1997 (20 games)

FEWEST FOULS PER GAME
8.9—Caltech, 1997 (177 in 20)

Defense

FEWEST POINTS PER GAME ALLOWED
47.5—Wis.-Platteville, 1997 (1,283 in 27)

LOWEST FIELD-GOAL PERCENTAGE ALLOWED (Since 1978)
35.4—New York U., 2007 (552 of 1,560)

Overtimes

OVERTIME GAMES
7—Lakeland, 2008 (won 3, lost 4); McMurry, 2003 (won 7, lost 0); Albany (N.Y.), 1981 (won 5, lost 2); TCNJ, 1982 (won 6, lost 1); St. John's (Minn.), 1983 (won 4, lost 3); New Jersey City, 1994 (won 4, lost 3)

CONSECUTIVE OVERTIME GAMES
4—Goucher, Nov. 20-Nov. 30, 2007 (won 0, lost 4); Dominican (Ill.)), Feb. 1-Feb. 10, 2007 (won 2, lost 2)

OVERTIME WINS
7—McMurry, 2003 (7-0)

OVERTIME HOME WINS
5—McMurry, 2003 (5-0)

General Records

GAMES PLAYED IN A SEASON
34—Wis.-Stevens Point, 2004 (29-5); Wis.-Eau Claire, 1990 (30-4); LeMoyne-Owen, 1980 (26-8)

VICTORIES IN A SEASON
32—Potsdam St., 1986 (32-0)

CONSECUTIVE VICTORIES
60—Potsdam St. (from first game of 1985-86 season to March 14, 1987)

MOST-IMPROVED TEAM FROM ONE SEASON TO THE NEXT
17games—Hunter, 1998 (from 9-17 to 28-2)

CONSECUTIVE HOME-COURT VICTORIES
62—North Park (from Feb. 8, 1984, to Feb. 3, 1988)

CONSECUTIVE REGULAR-SEASON VICTORIES
59—Potsdam St. (from Nov. 22, 1985, to Dec. 12, 1987)

DEFEATS IN A SEASON
26—Otterbein, 1988 (1-26); Maryville (Mo.), 1991 (0-26)

CONSECUTIVE DEFEATS IN A SEASON
26—Maryville (Mo.), 1991 (0-26)

CONSECUTIVE DEFEATS
117—Rutgers-Camden (from Jan. 22, 1992, to Jan. 3, 1997; ended with 77-72 win vs. Bloomfield on Jan. 7, 1997)

CONSECUTIVE WINNING SEASONS
40—Wittenberg, 1969-08 (current)

CONSECUTIVE NON-LOSING SEASONS
52—Wittenberg, 1957-08 (current)

UNBEATEN TEAMS (Number of victories in parentheses)
Potsdam St., 1986 (32); Wis.-Platteville, 1995 (31); Wis.-Platteville, 1998 (30)

All-Time Individual Leaders

Single-Game Records

SCORING HIGHS

Pts.	Player, Team vs. Opponent	Season
77	Jeff Clement, Grinnell vs. Illinois Col.	1998
69	Sami Wylie, Lincoln (Pa.) vs. Ohio St.-Marion	2007
69	Steve Diekmann, Grinnell vs. Simpson	1995
64	Tim Russell, Albertus Magnus vs. Mitchell	2005
63	Ryan Hodges, Cal Lutheran vs. Redlands	2005
63	Joe DeRoche, Thomas vs. St. Joseph's (Me.)	1988
62	Kyle Myrick, Lincoln (Pa.) vs. Penn St.-Abington	2006
62	Nick Pelotte, Plymouth St. vs. Western Conn. St.	2005
62	Shannon Lilly, Bishop vs. Southwest Assembly of God	1983
61	Josh Metzger, Wis.-Lutheran vs. Grinnell	2001
61	Steve Honderd, Calvin vs. Kalamazoo	1993
61	Dana Wilson, Husson vs. Ricker	1974
60	Ed Brands, Grinnell vs. Ripon	1996
60	Steve Diekmann, Grinnell vs. Coe	1994
59	Ben Strong, Guilford vs. Lincoln (Pa.)	2007
59	Mike Hoyt, Mt. St. Mary (N.Y.) vs. Farmingdale	2007
59	Ed Brands, Grinnell vs. Chicago	1996
59	Steve Diekmann, Grinnell vs. Monmouth (Ill.)	1995
58	Andy Panko, Lebanon Valley vs. Juniata	1999
58	Jeff Clement, Grinnell vs. Clarke	1998

Season Records

SCORING AVERAGE

Player, Team	Season	G	FG	3FG	FT	Pts.	Avg.
Steve Diekmann, Grinnell	†1995	20	223	137	162	745	*37.3
Rickey Sutton, Lyndon St.	†1976	14	207	—	93	507	36.2
Shannon Lilly, Bishop	†1983	26	345	—	218	908	34.9
Dana Wilson, Husson	†1974	20	288	—	122	698	34.9
Rickey Sutton, Lyndon St.	†1977	16	223	—	112	558	34.9
Mike Hoyt, Mt. St. Mary (N.Y.)	†2007	26	274	121	229	898	34.5
Steve Diekmann, Grinnell	†1994	21	250	117	106	723	34.4
Ed Brands, Grinnell	†1996	24	260	158	136	814	33.9
Jeff Clement, Grinnell	†1998	22	238	*186	84	746	33.9
Kyle Myrick, Lincoln (Pa.)	†2006	30	387	59	177	1,010	33.7
Dwain Govan, Bishop	†1975	29	392	—	179	963	33.2
Clarence Caldwell, Greensboro	1976	22	306	—	111	723	32.8
Jeff Clement, Grinnell	†1999	22	217	166	121	721	32.8
Tim Russell, Albertus Magnus	†2005	25	292	74	161	819	32.8
Greg Grant, TCNJ	†1989	32	387	76	194	*1,044	32.6
Dennis Stanton, Ursinus	†2004	27	261	140	217	879	32.6
Dave Russell, Shepherd	1975	32	*394	—	*249	1,037	32.4
Dwain Govan, Bishop	1974	26	358	—	126	842	32.4
Ron Stewart, Otterbein	1983	24	297	—	166	760	31.7

†national champion; *record

FIELD-GOAL PERCENTAGE
(Based on qualifiers for annual championship)

Player, Team	Season	G	FG	FGA	Pct.
Travis Weiss, St. John's (Minn.)	†1994	26	160	209	*76.6
Brian Schmitting, Ripon	†2006	21	122	160	76.3
Pete Metzelaars, Wabash	†1982	28	271	360	75.3
Tony Rychlec, Mass. Maritime	†1981	25	233	311	74.9
Tony Rychlec, Mass. Maritime	1982	20	193	264	73.1
Russ Newnan, Menlo	1991	26	130	178	73.0
Ed Owens, Hampden-Sydney	†1979	24	140	192	72.9
Scott Baxter, Capital	†1991	26	164	226	72.6
Maurice Woods, Potsdam St.	1982	30	203	280	72.5
Earl Keith, Stony Brook	1979	24	164	227	72.2
Pete Metzelaars, Wabash	1981	25	204	283	72.1
Brandon King, Rowan	†2005	26	141	196	71.9
Jon Rosner, Yeshiva	1991	22	141	196	71.9
Pete Metzelaars, Wabash	1979	24	122	170	71.8
Anthony Farley, Miles	1982	26	168	235	71.5

†national champion; *record

THREE-POINT FIELD GOALS MADE

Player, Team	Season	G	3FG
Jeff Clement, Grinnell	1998	22	*186
Jeff Clement, Grinnell	1999	22	166
Ed Brands, Grinnell	1996	24	158
Billy Shivers, Redlands	2004	25	153
Chris Peterson, Eureka	1994	31	145
Amir Mazarei, Redlands	2007	23	143
John Grotberg, Grinnell	2008	24	140
Dennis Stanton, Ursinus	2004	27	140
Amir Mazarei, Redlands	2006	24	138
Steve Nordlund, Grinnell	2002	24	137
Steve Diekmann, Grinnell	1995	20	137
Chris Jans, Loras	1991	25	133
Eric Burdette, Wis.-Whitewater	1996	28	130
Ed Brands, Grinnell	1995	20	129
Sami Wylie, Lincoln (Pa.)	2006	30	128
Kyle Seyboth, Elms	2005	29	125
Tommy Doyle, Salem St.	1996	28	124
Everett Foxx, Ferrum	1992	29	124
Kirk Anderson, Augustana (Ill.)	1993	30	123
Jeff deLaveaga, Cal Lutheran	1992	28	122

*record

THREE-POINT FIELD GOALS MADE PER GAME

Player, Team	Season	G	3FG	Avg.
Jeff Clement, Grinnell	†1998	22	*186	*8.5
Jeff Clement, Grinnell	†1999	22	166	7.5
Steve Diekmann, Grinnell	†1995	20	137	6.9
Ed Brands, Grinnell	†1996	24	158	6.6
Ed Brands, Grinnell	1995	29	129	6.5
Amir Mazarei, Redlands	†2007	23	143	6.2
Billy Shivers, Redlands	†2004	25	153	6.1
John Grotberg, Grinnell	†2008	24	140	5.8
Amir Mazarei, Redlands	†2006	24	138	5.8
Steve Nordlund, Grinnell	†2002	24	137	5.7
Steve Diekmann, Grinnell	†1994	21	117	5.6
Chris Jans, Loras	†1991	25	133	5.3
Woody Piirto, Grinnell	1999	22	117	5.3
John Grotberg, Grinnell	2006	23	120	5.2
Dennis Stanton, Ursinus	2004	27	140	5.2
Jeff Clement, Grinnell	†1997	22	113	5.1
Mark Bedell, Fisk	1997	19	97	5.1
David Bailey, Concordia Chicago	1994	24	120	5.0
Jarett Kearse, Lincoln (Pa.)	†2005	22	105	4.8
Steve Nordlund, Grinnell	†2003	25	119	4.8
Steve Nordlund, Grinnell	2004	24	114	4.8

†national champion; *record

THREE-POINT FIELD-GOAL PERCENTAGE
(Based on qualifiers for annual championship)

Player, Team	Season	G	3FG	3FGA	Pct.
Reggie James, NJIT	†1989	29	59	88	*67.0
Chris Miles, NJIT	†1987	26	41	65	63.1
Chris Miles, NJIT	1989	29	46	75	61.3
Matt Miota, Lawrence	†1990	22	33	54	61.1
Mike Bachman, Alma	†1991	26	46	76	60.5
Ray Magee, Richard Stockton	†1988	26	41	71	57.7
Keith Orchard, Whitman	1988	26	42	73	57.5
Brian O'Donnell, Rutgers-Camden	1988	24	65	114	57.0
Erick Hunt, Methodist	1989	27	45	79	57.0
Eric Harris, Bishop	1987	26	91	160	56.9
Rick Brown, Muskingum	1988	30	71	125	56.8
Jamie Eichel, Fredonia St.	1989	24	51	90	56.7

†national champion; *record

FREE-THROW PERCENTAGE
(Based on qualifiers for annual championship)

Player, Team	Season	G	FT	FTA	Pct.
Korey Coon, Ill. Wesleyan	†2000	25	157	163	*96.3
Ryan Junghans, Hood	†2008	26	118	123	95.9
Nick Wilkins, Coe	†2003	26	66	69	95.7
Chanse Young, Manchester	†1998	25	65	68	95.6
Andy Enfield, Johns Hopkins	†1991	29	123	129	95.3
Chris Carideo, Widener	†1992	26	80	84	95.2
Yudi Teichman, Yeshiva	†1989	21	119	125	95.2
Joseph Chatman, Lesley	†2007	27	126	133	94.7
Brett Davis, Wis.-Oshkosh	1998	27	72	76	94.7
Joe Bueckers, Concordia-M'head	†2004	26	71	75	94.7
Mark Giovino, Babson	†1997	28	86	91	94.5
Ryan Miller, Moravian	2008	25	64	68	94.1
Aaron Faulkner, St. Norbert	2004	23	64	68	94.1

DIVISION III

Player, Team	Season	G	FT	FTA	Pct.
Mike Scheib, Susquehanna	†1977	22	80	85	94.1
Jason Prenevost, Middlebury	†1994	22	60	64	93.8
Kris Saiberlich, Lakeland	2008	28	89	95	93.7
Derrick Rogers, Averett	†2001	27	72	77	93.5
Hans Hoeg, Wis.-River Falls	†2005	25	113	121	93.4
Jerry Prestier, Baldwin-Wallace	†1978	25	125	134	93.3
Charlie Nanick, Scranton	†1996	25	96	103	93.2

†national champion; *record

REBOUND AVERAGE

Player, Team	Season	G	Reb.	Avg.
Joe Manley, Bowie St.	†1976	29	*579	*19.97
Fred Petty, Southern N.H.	†1974	22	436	19.8
Larry Williams, Pratt	†1977	24	457	19.0
Charles Greer, Thomas	1977	17	318	18.7
Larry Parker, Plattsburgh St.	†1975	23	430	18.7
John Jordan, Southern Me.	†1978	29	536	18.5
Keith Woolfolk, Upper Iowa	1978	26	479	18.4
Michael Stubbs, Trinity (Conn.)	†1990	22	398	18.1
Mike Taylor, Pratt	1978	23	414	18.0
Walt Edwards, Husson	1976	26	467	18.0
Dave Kufeld, Yeshiva	†1979	20	355	17.8

†national champion; *record

ASSISTS

Player, Team	Season	G	Ast.
Robert James, Kean	†1989	29	*391
Tennyson Whitted, Ramapo	†2002	29	319
Ricky Spicer, Wis.-Whitewater	1989	31	295
Joe Marcotte, NJIT	†1995	30	292
Andre Bolton, Chris. Newport	†1996	30	289
Ron Torgalski, Hamilton	1989	26	275
Albert Kirchner, Mt. St. Vincent	†1990	24	267
Steve Artis, Chris. Newport	1991	29	262
Phil Dixon, Shenandoah	1996	27	258
Tennyson Whitted, Ramapo	†2003	30	253
Phil Dixon, Shenandoah	†1994	26	253
Steve Artis, Chris. Newport	1990	28	251
Michael Crotty, Williams	†2004	32	249
David Genovese, Mt. St. Vincent	1994	27	248
Russell Springman, Salisbury	1990	27	246
John Ancrum, Elms	†2005	29	245
Michael Crotty, Williams	2003	32	245
Corey McAdam, Nazareth	2008	28	244
Tom Genco, Manhattanville	1990	26	244
Andrew Olson, Amherst	†2007	32	243
Andre Bolton, Chris. Newport	1995	28	243

†national champion; *record

ASSIST AVERAGE

Player, Team	Season	G	Ast.	Avg.
Robert James, Kean	†1989	29	*391	*13.5
Albert Kirchner, Mt. St. Vincent	†1990	24	267	11.1
Tennyson Whitted, Ramapo	†2002	29	319	11.0
Ron Torgalski, Hamilton	1989	26	275	10.6
David Arseneault, Grinnell	†2008	21	219	10.4
Louis Adams, Rust	1989	22	227	10.3
Eric Johnson, Coe	†1991	24	238	9.9
Joe Marcotte, NJIT	†1995	30	292	9.7
Phil Dixon, Shenandoah	†1994	26	253	9.7
Mark Cottom, Ferrum	1991	25	242	9.7
Andre Bolton, Chris. Newport	†1996	30	289	9.6
Phil Dixon, Shenandoah	1996	27	258	9.6
Ricky Spicer, Wis.-Whitewater	1989	31	295	9.5
David Rubin, Hobart	†1998	25	237	9.5
Pat Heldman, Maryville (Tenn.)	1989	25	236	9.4
Deshone Bond, Stillman	†1997	25	235	9.4
Tom Genco, Manhattanville	1990	26	244	9.4
Justin Culhane, Suffolk	1992	24	225	9.4

†national champion; *record

BLOCKED SHOTS

Player, Team	Season	G	Blk.
Tory Black, NJIT	†1997	26	*198
Neil Edwards, York (N.Y.)	†2000	26	193
Ira Nicholson, Mt. St. Vincent	†1995	28	188
John Bunch, Lincoln (Pa.)	†2004	25	173
Shacun Malave, City Tech	2004	28	167
Ira Nicholson, Mt. St. Vincent	†1996	27	163
Ira Nicholson, Mt. St. Vincent	1997	24	151
Antoine Hyman, Keuka	1997	26	148
Matt Cusano, Scranton	†1993	29	145
Neil Edwards, York (N.Y.)	†1999	26	144
Johnny Woods, Wesley	2000	24	132
Badou Gaye, Gwynedd-Mercy	2004	29	131
Antoine Hyman, Keuka	1996	25	131
Ifesinachi Anosike, Salem St.	†2005	29	129
Andrew South, NJIT	†1994	27	128
Mike Mientus, Allentown	1995	27	118
Roy Woods, Fontbonne	1995	25	117
Eric Lidecis, Maritime (N.Y.)	1994	26	116
Steve Juskin, Frank. & Marsh.	2004	30	114
Antonio Ramos, Clarke	2001	25	114

†national champion; *record

BLOCKED-SHOT AVERAGE

Player, Team	Season	G	Blk.	Avg.
Tory Black, NJIT	†1997	26	*198	*7.62
Neil Edwards, York (N.Y.)	†2000	26	193	7.42
John Bunch, Lincoln (Pa.)	†2004	25	173	6.92
Ira Nicholson, Mt. St. Vincent	†1995	28	188	6.71
Ira Nicholson, Mt. St. Vincent	1997	24	151	6.29
Ira Nicholson, Mt. St. Vincent	†1996	27	163	6.04
Shacun Malave, City Tech	2004	28	167	5.96
Antoine Hyman, Keuka	1997	26	148	5.69
Neil Edwards, York (N.Y.)	†1999	26	144	5.54
Johnny Woods, Wesley	2000	24	132	5.50
Antoine Hyman, Keuka	1996	25	131	5.24
Joe Henderson, Hunter	1999	22	112	5.09
Matt Cusano, Scranton	†1993	29	145	5.00
Drew Cohen, Colby	†2006	23	111	4.83
Andrew South, NJIT	†1994	27	128	4.74
Roy Woods, Fontbonne	1995	25	117	4.68
Johnny Woods, Wesley	†2001	22	101	4.59
Antonio Ramos, Clarke	2001	25	114	4.56
Douglas Hammond, Green Mountain	†2008	25	113	4.52
Badou Gaye, Gwynedd-Mercy	2004	29	131	4.52

†national champion; *record

STEALS

Player, Team	Season	G	Stl.
Moses Jean-Pierre, Plymouth St.	†1994	30	*189
Daniel Martinez, McMurry	†2000	29	178
Purvis Presha, Stillman	†1996	25	144
Tennyson Whitted, Ramapo	†2002	29	138
Matt Newton, Principia	1994	25	138
John Gallogly, Salve Regina	†1997	24	137
Elbie Murphy, St. Joseph's (Me.)	†2007	30	126
Greg Dean, Concordia-M'head	1997	23	126
Scott Clarke, Utica	†1995	24	126
Deron Black, Allegheny	1996	27	123
David Brown, Westfield St.	1994	25	122
Ricky Hollis, Brockport St.	2000	27	121
John Gallogly, Salve Regina	†1998	23	121
Barry Aranoff, Yeshiva	1995	22	121
Horace Jenkins, Wm. Paterson	2001	31	120
Brian Meehan, Salve Regina	1995	28	120
Tennyson Whitted, Ramapo	†2003	30	118
Scott Clarke, Utica	1996	26	118
Quameir Harding, Ramapo	†2006	29	116
Benny West, Howard Payne	†2004	25	116

†national champion; *record

STEAL AVERAGE

Player, Team	Season	G	Stl.	Avg.
Moses Jean-Pierre, Plymouth St.	†1994	30	*189	*6.30
Daniel Martinez, McMurry	†2000	29	178	6.14
Purvis Presha, Stillman	†1996	25	144	5.76
John Gallogly, Salve Regina	†1997	24	137	5.71
Matt Newton, Principia	1994	25	138	5.52
Barry Aranoff, Yeshiva	†1995	22	121	5.50
Greg Dean, Concordia-M'head	1997	23	126	5.48
John Gallogly, Salve Regina	†1998	23	121	5.26
Scott Clarke, Utica	1995	24	126	5.25
Joel Heckendorf, Martin Luther	1996	17	84	4.94
David Brown, Westfield St.	1994	25	122	4.88
Ivo Moyano, Polytechnic (N.Y.)	1994	19	91	4.78
Tennyson Whitted, Ramapo	†2002	29	138	4.76
Mario Thompson, Occidental	†1999	24	114	4.75
Benny West, Howard Payne	†2004	25	116	4.64
Keith Darden, Concordia (Tex.)	†2001	24	111	4.63
Moses Jean-Pierre, Plymouth St.	†1993	25	114	4.56
Deron Black, Allegheny	1996	27	123	4.55

Player, Team	Season	G	Stl.	Avg.
Scott Clarke, Utica	1996	26	118	4.54
Ricky Hollis, Brockport St.	2000	27	121	4.48

†national champion; *record

Career Records

POINTS

Player, Team	Seasons	Pts.
Andre Foreman, Salisbury	1988-89, 91-92	*2,940
Willie Chandler, Misericordia	2000-03	2,898
Lamont Strothers, Chris. Newport	1988-91	2,709
Matt Hancock, Colby	1987-90	2,678
Scott Fitch, Geneseo St.	1990-91, 93-94	2,634
Greg Grant, TCNJ	1987-89	2,611
Rick Hughes, Thomas More	1993-96	2,605
Mike Hoyt, Mt. St. Mary (N.Y.)	2004-07	2,586
Wil Peterson, St. Andrews	1980-83	2,553
Ron Stewart, Otterbein	1980-83	2,549
Andy Panko, Lebanon Valley	1996-99	2,515
Scott Tedder, Ohio Wesleyan	1985-88	2,501
Moses Jean-Pierre, Plymouth St.	1991-94	2,483
Steve Honderd, Calvin	1990-93	2,469
Herman Alston, Kean	1988-91	2,457
Dick Hempy, Otterbein	1984-87	2,439
John Patraitis, Anna Maria	1995-98	2,434
Kevin Moran, Curry	1983-86	2,415
Alex Butler, Rhode Island Col.	1994-97	2,398
Steve Wood, Grinnell	2001-04	2,381
Rickey Sutton, Lyndon St.	1976-79	2,379
Frank Wachlarowicz, St. John's (Minn.)	1975-79	2,357
Henry Shannon, Maryville (Mo.)	1996-99	2,352
Cedric Oliver, Hamilton	1976-79	2,349
Dana Janssen, Neb. Wesleyan	1983-86	2,333

*record

SCORING AVERAGE
(Minimum 1,400 points)

Player, Team	Seasons	G	FG	3FG	FT	Pts.	Avg.
Dwain Govan, Bishop	1974-75	55	750	—	305	1,805	*32.8
Dave Russell, Shepherd	1974-75	60	710	—	413	1,833	30.6
Kyle Myrick, Lincoln (Pa.)	2005-06	57	667	78	309	1,721	30.2
Rickey Sutton, Lyndon St.	1976-79	80	960	—	459	2,379	29.7
John Atkins, Knoxville	1976-78	70	845	—	322	2,012	28.7
Steve Peknik, Windham	1974-77	76	816	—	467	2,099	27.6
Clarence Caldwell, Greensboro	1975-77	70	802	—	299	1,903	27.2
Andre Foreman, Salisbury	1988-89, 91-92	109	*1,140	68	592	*2,940	27.0
Darrel Lewis, Lincoln (Pa.)	1996-99	86	796	265	409	2,267	26.4
Willie Chandler, Misericordia	2000-03	—	1,005	346	542	2,898	26.3
Matt Hancock, Colby	1987-90	102	844	198	*792	2,678	26.3
Terrence Dupree, Polytechnic (N.Y.)	1990-92	70	700	22	407	1,829	26.1
Steve Diekmann, Grinnell	1992-95	85	741	371	365	2,218	26.1
Rick Hughes, Thomas More	1993-96	101	1,039	13	514	2,605	25.8
Mark Veenstra, Calvin	1974-77	89	960	—	341	2,261	25.4
Ron Swartz, Hiram	1984-87	90	883	78	408	2,252	25.0
Clarence Caldwell, Greensboro	1974-77	93	971	—	363	2,309	24.8
James Rehnquist, Amherst	1975-77	61	614	—	284	1,512	24.8

*record

FIELD-GOAL PERCENTAGE
(Minimum 400 field goals made)

Player, Team	Seasons	G	FG	FGA	Pct.
Tony Rychlec, Mass. Maritime	1981-83	55	509	692	*73.6
Pete Metzelaars, Wabash	1979-82	103	784	1,083	72.4
Brian Schmitting, Ripon	2004-07	78	418	602	69.4
Maurice Woods, Potsdam St.	1980-82	93	559	829	67.4
Earl Keith, Stony Brook	1975-76, 78-79	94	777	1,161	66.9
Dan Rush, Bridgewater (Va.)	1992-95	102	712	1,069	66.6
Ryan Hodges, Cal Lutheran	2001, 03-05	94	518	787	65.8
Wade Gugino, Hope	1989-92	97	664	1,010	65.7
David Otte, Simpson	1992-95	76	549	840	65.4
Rick Batt, UC San Diego	1989-92	106	558	855	65.2
Phil Hawley, Randolph-Macon	2004-07	99	416	640	65.0
Kevin Ryan, TCNJ	1987-90	102	619	955	64.8
Greg Kemp, Aurora	1991-94	102	680	1,051	64.7
Scott Baxter, Capital	1988-91	104	505	782	64.6
Pat Fitzsimmons, Amherst	2000-03	101	452	700	64.6
Paul Rich, Geneseo St.	1978-81	88	452	700	64.6

Player, Team	Seasons	G	FG	FGA	Pct.
Nate Thomas, Neb. Wesleyan	1995-98	98	497	772	64.4
Tod Hart, Ithaca	1980-83	97	726	1,133	64.1
Tony Seay, Averett	1989-90	55	465	726	64.0
John Ellenwood, Wooster	1997-00	98	442	692	63.9
Jon Konzelman, Baptist Bible (Pa.)	2004-06	84	469	735	63.8
Jeff Gibbs, Otterbein	1999-02	109	758	1,188	63.8
Dick Hempy, Otterbein	1984-87	112	923	1,447	63.8
John Wassenbergh, St. Joseph's (Me.)	1993-96	108	815	1,281	63.6
Jason Boone, New York U.	2004-07	104	496	780	63.6

*record

THREE-POINT FIELD GOALS MADE

Player, Team	Seasons	G	3FG
Jeff Clement, Grinnell	1996-99	91	*516
Amir Mazarei, Redlands	2004-07	97	470
Steve Nordlund, Grinnell	2001-04	97	449
Chris Carideo, Widener	1992-95	103	402
Mike Hoyt, Mt. St. Mary (N.Y.)	2004-07	105	376
John Grotberg, Grinnell#	2006-08	71	372
Steve Diekmann, Grinnell	1992-95	85	371
Greg Cole, Western Conn. St.	2002, 04-06	110	367
Brendan Twomey, Mt. St. Mary (N.Y.)/Oneonta St.	2000, 02-04	109	362
Matt Garvey, Bates	1994-97	95	361
Craig Hannon, Westminster (Pa.)	2005-08	106	355
Ray Wilson, UC Santa Cruz	1989-92	100	354
Ed Brands, Grinnell	1993-96	78	347
Willie Chandler, Misericordia	2000-03	110	346
Robert Hennigan, Emerson	2001-04	105	342
Steve Matthews, Emerson/Wentworth Inst.	1998-00	81	334
Chris Hamilton, Blackburn	1988-91	101	334
Scott Fitch, Geneseo St.	1990-91, 93-94	109	332
Billy Collins, Nichols	1992-95	92	331
John Estelle, Wabash	1997-00	109	328
Tony Barros, Mass.-Boston	2004-07	101	326
Kris Saiberlich, Lakeland	2005-08	106	324
Mike Lee, Mary Washington	2004-07	106	323
Mark Bedell, Fisk	1994-97	94	321
James Mooney, Mt. St. Vincent	2003-06	102	318

#active player *record

THREE-POINT FIELD GOALS MADE PER GAME
(Minimum 200 three-point field goals made)

Player, Team	Season	G	3FG	Avg.
Jeff Clement, Grinnell	1996-99	91	*516	*5.67
Amir Mazarei, Redlands	2004-07	97	470	4.85
Steve Nordlund, Grinnell	2001-04	97	449	4.63
Ed Brands, Grinnell	1993-96	78	347	4.45
Steve Diekmann, Grinnell	1992-95	85	371	4.36
Steve Matthews, Emerson/Wentworth Inst.	1998-00	81	334	4.12
Chris Carideo, Widener	1992-95	103	402	3.90
Matt Garvey, Bates	1994-97	95	361	3.80
Sami Wylie, Lincoln (Pa.)	2006-07	58	220	3.79
Rohan Russell, Johnson & Wales (R.I.)	2003-04	54	202	3.74
Mark DeMonaco, Westminster (Pa.)	2004-06	81	295	3.64
Billy Collins, Nichols	1992-95	92	331	3.60
Mike Hoyt, Mt. St. Mary (N.Y.)	2004-07	105	376	3.58
Ray Wilson, UC Santa Cruz	1989-92	100	354	3.54
James Mooney, Mt. St. Vincent	2004-06	76	264	3.47
Chris Geruschat, Bethany (W.V.)	1989-92	89	307	3.45
Mark Bedell, Fisk	1994-97	94	321	3.41
Craig Hannon, Westminster (Pa.)	2005-08	106	355	3.35
Greg Cole, Western Conn. St.	2002, 04-06	110	367	3.34
Brendan Twomey, Mt. St. Mary (N.Y.)/Oneonta St.	2000, 02-04	109	362	3.32
Chris Hamilton, Blackburn	1988-91	101	334	3.31
Jeff Jones, Lycoming	1987-89	71	232	3.27
Robert Hennigan, Emerson	2001-04	105	342	3.26
Tony Barros, Mass.-Boston	2004-07	101	326	3.23
Casey Meador, Louisiana Col.	2003-06	99	315	3.18

*record

THREE-POINT FIELD-GOAL PERCENTAGE
(Minimum 200 three-point field goals made)

Player, Team	Season	G	3FG	3FGA	Pct.
Jeff Seifriz, Wis.-Whitewater	1987-89	85	217	423	*51.3
Chris Peterson, Eureka	1991-94	78	215	421	51.1
Everett Foxx, Ferrum	1989-92	104	315	630	50.0
Brad Alberts, Ripon	1989-92	95	277	563	49.2
Jeff Jones, Lycoming	1987-89	71	232	472	49.2
Troy Greenlee, DePauw	1988-91	106	232	473	49.0
David Todd, Pomona-Pitzer	1987-90	84	212	439	48.3
Al Callejas, Scranton	1998-01	90	225	466	48.3

*record

DIVISION III

FREE-THROW PERCENTAGE
(Minimum 250 free throws made)

Player, Team	Season	G	FT	FTA	Pct.
Andy Enfield, Johns Hopkins	1988-91	108	431	466	*92.5
Korey Coon, Ill. Wesleyan	1997-00	109	449	492	91.3
Joseph Chatman, Lesley	2007-08	55	271	298	90.9
Ryan Knuppel, Elmhurst	1998-01	102	288	317	90.9
Doug Brown, Elizabethtown	1976-80	96	252	279	90.3
Al Callejas, Scranton	1998-01	90	333	372	89.5
Tim McGraw, Hartwick	1985-88	107	330	371	88.9
Eric Jacobs, Wilkes/Scranton	1984-87	106	303	343	88.3
John Luisi, Suffolk	1999-02	105	265	300	88.3
Charles Nenick, Scranton	1994-97	98	259	294	88.1
Kevin Guyden, Mary Hardin-Baylor	2004-07	94	277	315	87.9
Todd Reinhardt, Wartburg	1988-91	105	283	322	87.9
Jeff Thomas, King's (Pa.)	1989-92	110	466	532	87.6
Ross Banaszak, Otterbein	2005-08	102	294	336	87.5
Brian Andrews, Alfred	1984-87	101	306	350	87.4
Matt Freesemann, Wartburg	1994-96	73	297	340	87.4
Dave Jannuzzi, Wilkes	1997-99, 2001	112	425	487	87.3
Nick Bennett, Wis.-Stevens Point	2002-05	117	322	369	87.3
Ryan Cain, WPI	2004-07	109	525	602	87.2
Sean O'Brien, St. John Fisher	2003-06	96	305	350	87.1
Ryan Wietor, Wis.-Eau Claire/Concordia (Wis.)	2002-05	92	298	342	87.1
Eric Elliott, Hope	1988-91	103	350	403	86.8
Chad Onofrio, Tufts	1993-96	100	329	379	86.8
Pat Pruitt, Albright	1989-92	87	261	301	86.7
Ryan Billet, Elizabethtown	1995-98	98	434	501	86.6
Mike Johnson, Wis.-Eau Claire	1989-91	89	421	486	86.6
Sean Fleming, Clark (Mass.)	2000-03	109	371	429	86.6

*record

REBOUND AVERAGE
(Minimum 900 rebounds)

Player, Team	Season	G	Reb.	Avg.
Larry Parker, Plattsburgh St.	1975-78	85	1,482	*17.4
Charles Greer, Thomas	1975-77	58	926	16.0
Willie Parr, LeMoyne-Owen	1974-76	76	1,182	15.6
Michael Smith, Hamilton	1989-92	107	*1,628	15.2
Dave Kufeld, Yeshiva	1977-80	81	1,222	15.1
Ed Owens, Hampden-Sydney	1977-80	77	1,160	15.1
Kevin Clark, Clark (Mass.)	1978-81	101	1,450	14.4
Mark Veenstra, Calvin	1974-77	89	1,260	14.2
Anthony Fitzgerald, Villa Julie	2003-06	107	1,496	14.0

*record

ASSISTS

Player, Team	Seasons	G	Ast.
Tennyson Whitted, Ramapo	2000-03	108	*917
Steve Artis, Chris. Newport	1990-93	112	909
Phil Dixon, Shenandoah	1993-96	103	889
Michael Crotty, Williams	2001-04	122	819
David Genovese, Mt. St. Vincent	1992-95	107	800
Andrew Olson, Amherst	2005-08	*123	758
Mike McGarvey, Ursinus	2003-06	111	754
Andre Bolton, Chris. Newport	1993-96	109	737
Tim Gaspar, Mass.-Dartmouth	2000-03	97	690
Eddie Ohlson, DeSales	2005-08	111	688
Matt Lucero, Austin	1998-01	99	677
Brian Nigro, Mt. St. Vincent	1997-00	99	674
Greg Dunne, Nazareth	1996-99	106	671
Moses Jean-Pierre, Plymouth St.	1991-94	109	669
Mike Rhoades, Lebanon Valley	1992-95	114	668
Lance Andrews, NJIT	1990-93	113	664
Dennis Jacobi, Bowdoin	1989-92	93	662
Tim Lawrence, Maryville (Tenn.)	1989-92	106	660
Pat Skerry, Tufts	1989-92	95	650
Donte Chisolm, Manhattanville	2005-08	112	646
Eric Prendeville, Salisbury	1996-99	107	641
Eric Johnson, Coe	1989-92	90	637
John Snyder, King's (Pa.)	1989-92	107	631
Jake Green, Piedmont	2005-08	103	624
Jason Saurbaugh, York (Pa.)	1997-00	101	624

*record

ASSIST AVERAGE
(Minimum 550 assists)

Player, Team	Season	G	Ast.	Avg.
Phil Dixon, Shenandoah	1993-96	103	889	*8.6
Tennyson Whitted, Ramapo	2000-03	108	*917	8.5
Steve Artis, Chris. Newport	1990-93	112	909	8.1
David Genovese, Mt. St. Vincent	1992-95	107	800	7.5

Player, Team	Season	G	Ast.	Avg.
Kevin Root, Eureka	1989-91	81	579	7.1
Dennis Jacobi, Bowdoin	1989-92	93	662	7.1
Tim Gaspar, Mass.-Dartmouth	2000-03	97	690	7.1
Eric Johnson, Coe	1989-92	90	637	7.1
Nathan Reeves, York (N.Y.)	1994-97	81	572	7.1
Pat Skerry, Tufts	1989-92	95	650	6.8
Matt Lucero, Austin	1998-01	99	677	6.8
Brian Nigro, Mt. St. Vincent	1997-00	99	674	6.8
Mike McGarvey, Ursinus	2003-06	111	754	6.8
Andre Bolton, Chris. Newport	1993-96	109	737	6.8
Michael Crotty, Williams	2001-04	*122	819	6.7
Tony Wyzzard, Emerson-MCA	1992-95	90	604	6.7
Greg Dunne, Nazareth	1996-99	106	671	6.3
Tim Lawrence, Maryville (Tenn.)	1989-92	106	660	6.2
Eddie Ohlson, DeSales	2005-08	111	688	6.2
Jason Saurbaugh, York (Pa.)	1997-00	101	624	6.2
Andrew Olson, Amherst	2005-08	*123	758	6.2
Kevin Clipperton, Upper Iowa	1994-97	99	610	6.2
Moses Jean-Pierre, Plymouth St.	1991-94	109	669	6.1
Paul Ferrell, Guilford	1991-94	99	607	6.1
Alex Morrison, Daniel Webster	1997-00	100	613	6.1

*record

BLOCKED SHOTS

Player, Team	Seasons	G	Blk.
Ira Nicholson, Mt. St. Vincent	1994-97	100	*576
Antoine Hyman, Keuka	1994-97	101	440
Kerry Gibson, Wis.-Oshkosh	2004-07	107	351
Shacun Malave, City Tech	2003-05	70	346
Andrew South, NJIT	1993-95	80	344
Badou Gaye, Gwynedd-Mercy	2002-05	104	340
Neil Edwards, York (N.Y.)	1998-00	55	337
Steve Juskin, Frank. & Marsh.	2001-04	114	330
Sean Devins, Trinity (Tex.)	2002-05	107	329
Mike Mientus, DeSales	1994-97	87	324
Arthur Hatch, Methodist	2001-04	97	321
Johnny Woods, Wesley	1999-02	78	319
Antonio Ramos, Clarke	2001-03	77	318
Terry Gray, Chris. Newport	2000-03	104	300
Mardochee Jean, Hardin-Simmons	2005-08	106	296
Jacob Nonemacher, Wis.-Stout	2004-07	100	292
Drew Cohen, Colby	2004-07	84	285
Jarriott Rook, Washington-St. Louis	2000-03	107	285
Jason Alexander, Catholic	1995-98	107	283
Jeremy Putman, Dubuque	1993-96	99	274
Matt Hilleary, Catholic	2000-03	118	273
Terry Thomas, Chris. Newport	1993-96	113	271
Ken LaFlamme, Emerson-MCA	1994-97	91	269
David Apple, Averett	1998-00	76	268
John Bunch, Lincoln (Pa.)	2003-04	48	265

*record

BLOCKED-SHOT AVERAGE
(Minimum 175 blocked shots)

Player, Team	Seasons	G	Blk.	Avg.
Neil Edwards, York (N.Y.)	1998-00	55	337	*6.13
Ira Nicholson, Mt. St. Vincent	1994-97	100	*576	5.76
John Bunch, Lincoln (Pa.)	2003-04	48	265	5.52
Shacun Malave, City Tech	2003-05	70	346	4.94
Tory Black, NJIT	1995-96	53	261	4.92
Antoine Hyman, Keuka	1994-97	101	440	4.36
Andrew South, NJIT	1993-95	80	344	4.30
Antonio Ramos, Clarke	2001-03	77	318	4.13
Johnny Woods, Wesley	1999-02	78	319	4.09
Ifesinachi Anosike, Salem St.	2004-05	56	221	3.95
Mike Mientus, DeSales	1994-97	87	324	3.72
Steve Butler, Chris. Newport	1997-98	55	196	3.56
David Apple, Averett	1998-00	76	268	3.53
Drew Cohen, Colby	2004-07	84	285	3.39
Arthur Hatch, Methodist	2001-04	97	321	3.31
Kerry Gibson, Wis.-Oshkosh	2004-07	107	351	3.28
Badou Gaye, Gwynedd-Mercy	2002-05	104	340	3.27
Sean Devins, Trinity (Tex.)	2002-05	107	329	3.07
Ken LaFlamme, Emerson-MCA	1994-97	91	269	2.96
Jacob Nonemacher, Wis.-Stout	2004-07	100	292	2.92
Steve Juskin, Frank. & Marsh.	2001-04	114	330	2.89
Terry Gray, Chris. Newport	2000-03	104	300	2.88
Mardochee Jean, Hardin-Simmons	2005-08	106	296	2.79
Jeremy Putman, Dubuque	1993-96	99	274	2.77
Mike Brown, Clark (Mass.)	1997-00	71	195	2.75

*record

STEALS

Player, Team	Seasons	G	Stl.
Tennyson Whitted, Ramapo	2000-03	108	*448
John Gallogly, Salve Regina	1995-98	98	413
Daniel Martinez, McMurry	1998-00	76	380
Ivo Moyano, Polytechnic (N.Y.)	1994-97	87	368
Benny West, Howard Payne	2001-04	98	363
Eric Bell, New Paltz St.	1993-96	94	355
Keith Darden, Concordia (Tex.)	2001-02, 04-05	90	348
Scott Clarke, Utica	1993-96	96	346
Jeff Mikos, Milwaukee Engr.	2003-06	105	340
Ricky Hollis, Brockport St.	1999-02	90	322
Adam Harper, Amherst	2001-04	111	321
Greg Dean, Concordia-M'head	1995-97	75	307
Tom Roeder, St. Joseph's (L.I.)	1999-02	98	303
Moses Jean-Pierre, Plymouth St.	1993-94	55	303
Joel Holstege, Hope	1995-98	118	301
Mike McGarvey, Ursinus	2003-06	111	300
Mario Thompson, Occidental	1999-01	71	300
Darrell Lewis, Lincoln (Pa.)	1996-99	86	298
Henry Shannon, Maryville (Mo.)	1996-99	106	292
Alex Morrison, Daniel Webster	1997-00	100	289
B.J. Reilly, Montclair St.	1997-00	101	287
Damien Hunter, Alvernia	1995-98	110	287
Keith Poppor, Amherst	1993-96	98	283
Carl Cochran, Richard Stockton	1994-97	113	281
Elbie Murphy, St. Joseph's (Me.)#	2006-08	83	280

#active player *record

STEAL AVERAGE
(Minimum 175 steals)

Player, Team	Seasons	G	Stl.	Avg.
Moses Jean-Pierre, Plymouth St.	1993-94	55	303	*5.51
Daniel Martinez, McMurry	1998-00	76	380	5.00
Ivo Moyano, Polytechnic (N.Y.)	1994-97	87	368	4.23
Mario Thompson, Occidental	1999-01	71	300	4.23
John Gallogly, Salve Regina	1995-98	98	413	4.21
Tennyson Whitted, Ramapo	2000-03	108	*448	4.15
Greg Dean, Concordia-M'head	1995-97	75	307	4.09
Keith Darden, Concordia (Tex.)	2001-02, 04-05	90	348	3.87
Rodney Lusain, UC San Diego	1993-94	50	193	3.86
Eric Bell, New Paltz St.	1993-96	94	355	3.78
Benny West, Howard Payne	2001-04	98	363	3.70
David Brown, Westfield St.	1993-95	53	193	3.64
Scott Clarke, Utica	1993-96	96	346	3.60
Ricky Hollis, Brockport St.	1999-02	90	322	3.58
Gerald Garlic, Goucher	1993-95	70	244	3.49
Darrel Lewis, Lincoln (Pa.)	1996-99	86	298	3.47
Shuron Woodyard, Villa Julie	1995-97	73	238	3.26
Jeff Mikos, Milwaukee Engr.	2003-06	105	340	3.24
Shawn McCarthy, Hunter	1993-95	81	261	3.22
Carl Small, Cornell College	1993-95	69	222	3.22
Horace Jenkins, Wm. Paterson	1998-01	82	263	3.21
Tom Roeder, St. Joseph's (L.I.)	1999-02	98	303	3.09
Deron Black, Allegheny	1993-96	78	240	3.08
Reuben Reyes, Salve Regina	1993-95	74	226	3.05
Ernie Peavy, Wis.-Platteville	1993-95	87	264	3.03

*record

Annual Individual Champions

Scoring Average

Season	Player, Team	G	FG	FT	Pts.	Avg.
1974	Dana Wilson, Husson	20	288	122	698	34.9
1975	Dwain Govan, Bishop	29	392	179	963	33.2
1976	Rickey Sutton, Lyndon St.	14	207	93	507	36.2
1977	Rickey Sutton, Lyndon St.	16	223	112	558	34.9
1978	John Atkins, Knoxville	25	340	103	783	31.3
1979	Scott Rogers, Kenyon	24	289	109	687	28.6
1980	Ray Buckland, Mass.-Boston	25	271	153	695	27.8
1981	Gerald Reece, William Penn	27	306	145	757	28.0
1982	Ashley Cooper, Ripon	22	256	89	601	27.3
1983	Shannon Lilly, Bishop	26	345	218	908	34.9
1984	Mark Van Valkenburg, Framingham St.	25	312	133	757	30.3
1985	Adam St. John, Maine Maritime	18	193	135	521	28.9
1986	John Saintignon, UC Santa Cruz	22	291	104	686	31.2

Season	Player, Team	G	FG	3FG	FT	Pts.	Avg.
1987	Rod Swartz, Hiram	23	232	78	133	675	29.3
1988	Matt Hancock, Colby	27	275	56	247	853	31.6
1989	Greg Grant, TCNJ	32	387	76	194	*1,044	32.6
1990	Grant Glover, Rust	23	235	1	164	635	27.6
1991	Andre Foreman, Salisbury	29	350	39	175	914	31.5
1992	Jeff deLaveaga, Cal Lutheran	28	258	122	187	825	29.5
1993	Dave Shaw, Drew	23	210	74	169	663	28.8
1994	Steve Diekmann, Grinnell	21	250	117	106	723	34.4
1995	Steve Diekmann, Grinnell	20	223	137	162	745	*37.3
1996	Ed Brands, Grinnell	24	260	158	136	814	33.9
1997	Mark Bedell, Fisk	19	177	97	88	539	28.4
1998	Jeff Clement, Grinnell	22	238	*186	84	746	33.9
1999	Jeff Clement, Grinnell	22	217	166	121	721	32.8
2000	Willie Chandler, Misericordia	27	249	92	114	704	26.1
2001	Willie Chandler, Misericordia	26	271	96	125	763	29.3
2002	Patrick Glover, Johnson St.	24	237	28	147	649	27.0
2003	Patrick Glover, Johnson St.	26	269	37	188	763	29.3
2004	Dennis Stanton, Ursinus	27	261	140	217	879	32.6
2005	Tim Russell, Albertus Magnus	25	292	74	161	819	32.8
2006	Kyle Myrick, Lincoln (Pa.)	30	387	59	177	1,010	33.7
2007	Mike Hoyt, Mt. St. Mary (N.Y.)	26	274	121	229	898	34.5
2008	John Grotberg, Grinnell	24	212	140	111	675	28.1

*record

Field-Goal Percentage

Season	Player, Team	G	FG	FGA	Pct.
1974	Fred Waldstein, Wartburg	28	163	248	65.7
1975	Dan Woodard, Elizabethtown	23	190	299	63.5
1976	Paul Merlis, Yeshiva	21	145	217	66.8
1977	Brent Cawelti, Trinity (Conn.)	20	107	164	65.2
1978	Earl Keith, Stony Brook	29	228	322	70.8
1979	Ed Owens, Hampden-Sydney	24	140	192	72.9
1980	E.D. Schechterley, Lynchburg	25	184	259	71.0
1981	Tony Rychlec, Mass. Maritime	25	233	311	74.9
1982	Pete Metzelaars, Wabash	28	271	360	75.3
1983	Mike Johnson, Drew	23	138	205	67.3
1984	Mark Van Valkenburg, Framingham St.	25	312	467	66.8
1985	Reinout Brugman, Muhlenberg	26	176	266	66.2
1986	Oliver Kyler, Frostburg St.	28	183	266	68.8
1987	Tim Ervin, Albion	21	127	194	65.5
1988	Matt Strong, Hope	27	163	232	70.3
1989	Kevin Ryan, TCNJ	32	246	345	71.3
1990	Bill Triplett, NJIT	28	169	237	71.3
1991	Scott Baxter, Capital	26	164	226	72.6
1992	Brett Grebing, Redlands	23	125	176	71.0
1993	Jim Leibel, St. Thomas (Minn.)	28	141	202	69.8
1994	Travis Weiss, St. John's (Minn.)	26	160	209	*76.6
1995	Justin Wilkins, Neb. Wesleyan	28	163	237	68.8
1996	Jason Light, Emory & Henry	25	207	294	70.4
1997	Jason Hayes, Marietta	25	184	271	67.9
1998	Lonnie Walker, Alvernia	27	165	237	69.6
1999	Jason Nickerson, Va. Wesleyan	26	242	363	66.7
2000	Jack Jirak, Hampden-Sydney	28	147	220	66.8
2001	John Thomas, Fontbonne	22	157	223	70.4
2002	Omar Warthen, Neumann	27	135	202	66.8
2003	Aaron Marshall, St. Lawrence	27	206	305	67.5
2004	Jon Konzelman, Baptist Bible (Pa.)	26	144	212	67.9
2005	Brandon King, Rowan	26	141	196	71.9
2006	Brian Schmitting, Ripon	21	122	160	76.3
2007	Brandon Adair, Va. Wesleyan	32	246	356	69.1
2008	Keith Pedersen, Central (Iowa)	24	124	178	69.7

*record

DIVISION III

Three-Point Field Goals Made Per Game

Season	Player, Team	G	3FG	Avg.
1987	Scott Fearrin, MacMurray	25	96	3.8
1988	Jeff Jones, Lycoming	23	97	4.2
1989	Brad Block, Aurora	26	112	4.3
1990	Chris Hamilton, Blackburn	24	109	4.5
1991	Chris Jans, Loras	25	133	5.3
1992	Jeff deLaveaga, Cal Lutheran	28	122	4.4
1993	Mike Connelly, Catholic	27	111	4.1
1994	Steve Diekmann, Grinnell	21	117	5.6
1995	Steve Diekmann, Grinnell	20	137	6.8
1996	Ed Brands, Grinnell	24	158	6.6
1997	Jeff Clement, Grinnell	22	113	5.1
1998	Jeff Clement, Grinnell	22	*186	*8.5
1999	Jeff Clement, Grinnell	22	166	7.5
2000	Woody Piirto, Grinnell	20	87	4.3
2001	Nevada Smith, Bethany (W.V.)	26	101	3.9
2002	Steve Nordlund, Grinnell	24	137	5.7
2003	Steve Nordlund, Grinnell	28	119	4.8
2004	Billy Shivers, Redlands	25	153	6.1
2005	Jarett Kearse, Lincoln (Pa.)	22	105	4.8
2006	Amir Mazarei, Redlands	24	138	5.8
2007	Amir Mazarei, Redlands	23	143	6.2
2008	John Grotberg, Grinnell	24	140	5.8

*record

Three-Point Field-Goal Percentage

Season	Player, Team	G	3FG	3FGA	Pct.
1987	Chris Miles, NJIT	26	41	65	63.1
1988	Ray Magee, Richard Stockton	26	41	71	57.7
1989	Reggie James, NJIT	29	59	88	*67.0
1990	Matt Miota, Lawrence	22	33	54	61.1
1991	Mike Bachman, Alma	26	46	76	60.5
1992	John Kmack, Plattsburgh St.	26	44	84	52.4
1993	Brad Apple, Greensboro	26	49	91	53.8
1994	Trever George, Coast Guard	23	38	72	52.8
1995	Tony Frieden, Manchester	32	58	107	54.2
1996	Joey Bigler, John Carroll	27	54	111	48.6
1997	Andy Strommen, Chicago	27	49	93	52.7
1998	Pat Maloney, Catholic	29	59	114	51.8
1999	Al Callejas, Scranton	26	66	122	54.1
2000	Brett Lively, Mary Washington	20	40	78	51.3
2001	Bryan Bertola, Lake Forest	23	58	110	52.7
2002	Doug Schneider, Pitt.-Bradford	28	78	143	54.5
2003	Jeremy Currier, Endicott	28	74	144	51.4
2004	Landon Lewis, Chapman	24	84	159	52.8
2005	John McAllen, Rivier	26	68	135	50.4
2006	Peter Lipka, Farmingdale	26	67	121	55.4
2007	Nate Stahl, Capital	28	74	146	50.7
2008	Nathan Edick, Marietta	25	63	115	54.8

*record

Free-Throw Percentage

Season	Player, Team	G	FT	FTA	Pct.
1974	Bruce Johnson, Plymouth St.	17	73	81	90.1
1975	Harold Howard, Austin	24	83	92	90.2
1976	Tim Mieure, Hamline	25	88	95	92.6
1977	Mike Scheib, Susquehanna	22	80	85	94.1
1978	Jerry Prestier, Baldwin-Wallace	25	125	134	93.3
1979	Joe Purcell, King's (Pa.)	26	66	71	93.0
1980	David Whiteside, UNC Greensboro	28	120	132	90.9
1981	Jim Cooney, Elmhurst	26	65	72	90.3
1982	Shannon Lilly, Bishop	22	142	153	92.8
1983	Mike Sain, Eureka	26	66	72	91.7
1984	Chris Genian, Redlands	24	71	78	91.0
1985	Bob Possehl, Coe	22	59	65	90.8
1986	Eric Jacobs, Scranton	29	81	87	93.1
1987	Chris Miles, NJIT	26	70	76	92.1
1988	Jeff Bowers, Southern Me.	29	95	102	93.1
1989	Yudi Teichman, Yeshiva	21	119	125	95.2
1990	Todd Reinhardt, Wartburg	26	91	98	92.9
1991	Andy Enfield, Johns Hopkins	29	123	129	95.3
1992	Chris Carideo, Widener	26	80	84	95.2
1993	Jim Durrell, Colby-Sawyer	25	67	72	93.1
1994	Jason Prenevost, Middlebury	22	60	64	93.8
1995	Matt Freesemann, Wartburg	24	128	138	92.8
1996	Charlie Nanick, Scranton	25	96	103	93.2

Season	Player, Team	G	FT	FTA	Pct.
1997	Mark Giovino, Babson	28	86	91	94.5
1998	Chanse Young, Manchester	25	65	68	95.6
1999	Ryan Eklund, Wis.-La Crosse	26	80	87	92.0
2000	Korey Coon, Ill. Wesleyan	25	157	163	*96.3
2001	Derrick Rogers, Averett	27	72	77	93.5
2002	Jason Luisi, Suffolk	28	87	94	92.6
2003	Nick Wilkins, Coe	26	66	69	95.7
2004	Joe Bueckers, Concordia-M'head	26	71	75	94.7
2005	Hans Hoeg, Wis.-River Falls	25	113	121	93.4
2006	Tony Bollier, Wheaton (Ill.)	25	104	112	92.9
	Matt Secrease, Hendrix	24	65	70	92.9
2007	Joseph Chatman, Lesley	27	126	133	94.7
2008	Ryan Junghans, Hood	26	118	123	95.9

*record

Rebound Average

Season	Player, Team	G	Reb.	Avg.
1974	Fred Petty, Southern N.H.	22	436	19.8
1975	Larry Parker, Plattsburgh St.	23	430	18.7
1976	Joe Manley, Bowie St.	29	*579	*19.97
1977	Larry Williams, Pratt	24	457	19.0
1978	John Jordan, Southern Me.	29	536	18.5
1979	Dave Kufeld, Yeshiva	20	355	17.8
1980	Dave Kufeld, Yeshiva	20	353	17.7
1981	Kevin Clark, Clark (Mass.)	27	465	17.2
1982	Len Washington, Mass.-Boston	23	361	15.7
1983	Luis Frias, Anna Maria	23	320	13.9
1984	Joe Weber, Aurora	27	370	13.7
1985	Albert Wells, Rust	22	326	14.8
1986	Russell Thompson, Westfield St.	22	338	15.4
1987	Randy Gorniak, Penn St.-Behrend	25	410	16.4
1988	Mike Nelson, Hamilton	26	349	13.4
1989	Clinton Montford, Methodist	27	459	17.0
1990	Michael Stubbs, Trinity (Conn.)	22	398	18.1
1991	Mike Smith, Hamilton	27	435	16.1
1992	Jeff Black, Fitchburg St.	22	363	16.5
1993	Steve Lemmer, Hamilton	27	404	15.0
1994	Chris Sullivan, St. John Fisher	23	319	13.9
1995	Scott Suhr, Milwaukee Engr.	25	349	14.0
1996	Craig Jones, Rochester Inst.	26	363	14.0
1997	Lonnie Walker, Alvernia	32	430	13.4
1998	Adam Doll, Simpson	25	366	14.6
1999	Anthony Peeples, Montclair St.	24	345	14.4
2000	Jeff Gibbs, Otterbein	23	307	13.3
2001	Jeff Gibbs, Otterbein	25	390	15.6
2002	Jeff Gibbs, Otterbein	32	523	16.3
2003	Jed Johnson, Maine Maritime	25	414	16.6
2004	Matt Clement, Maine Maritime	19	303	15.9
2005	Jeremy Coleman, Phila. Bible	28	391	14.0
2006	Anthony Fitzgerald, Villa Julie	29	416	14.3
2007	Nick Harrington, Southern Vt.	21	281	13.4
2008	Nick Harrington, Southern Vt.	24	369	15.4

*record

Assist Average

Season	Player, Team	G	Ast.	Avg.
1989	Robert James, Kean	27	*391	*13.5
1990	Albert Kirchner, Mt. St. Vincent	24	267	11.1
1991	Eric Johnson, Coe	24	238	9.9
1992	Edgar Loera, La Verne	23	202	8.8
1993	David Genovese, Mt. St. Vincent	27	237	8.8
1994	Phil Dixon, Shenandoah	26	253	9.7
1995	Joe Marcotte, N.J. Inst. of Tech	30	292	9.7
1996	Andre Bolton, Chris. Newport	30	289	9.6
1997	Deshone Bond, Stillman	25	235	9.4
1998	David Rubin, Hobart	25	237	9.5
1999	Tim Kelly, Pacific Lutheran	25	214	8.6
2000	Daniel Martinez, McMurry	29	229	7.9
2001	Jimmy Driggs, Hamilton	25	213	8.5
2002	Tennyson Whitted, Ramapo	29	319	11.0
2003	Tennyson Whitted, Ramapo	30	253	8.4
2004	Michael Crotty, Williams	32	249	7.8
2005	John Ancrum, Elms	29	245	8.4
2006	David Arseneault, Grinnell	23	198	8.6
2007	David Arseneault, Grinnell	24	203	8.5
2008	David Arseneault, Grinnell	21	219	10.4

*record

Blocked-Shot Average

Season	Player, Team	G	Blk.	Avg.
1993	Matt Cusano, Scranton	29	145	5.0
1994	Andrew South, NJIT	27	128	4.7
1995	Ira Nicholson, Mt. St. Vincent	28	188	6.7
1996	Ira Nicholson, Mt. St. Vincent	27	163	6.0
1997	Tory Black, NJIT	26	*198	*7.6
1998	Tony Seehase, Upper Iowa	23	89	3.9
1999	Neil Edwards, York (N.Y.)	26	144	5.5
2000	Neil Edwards, York (N.Y.)	26	193	7.4
2001	Johnny Woods, Wesley	22	101	4.6
2002	Kyle McNamar, Curry	25	107	4.3
2003	John Bunch, Lincoln (Pa.)	23	92	4.0
2004	John Bunch, Lincoln (Pa.)	25	173	6.9
2005	Ifesinachi Anosike, Salem St.	29	129	4.4
2006	Drew Cohen, Colby	23	111	4.8
2007	Kerry Gibson, Wis.-Oshkosh	27	103	3.8
2008	Douglas Hammond, Green Mountain	25	113	4.5

*record

Steal Average

Season	Player, Team	G	Stl.	Avg.
1993	Moses Jean-Pierre, Plymouth St.	25	114	4.6
1994	Moses Jean-Pierre, Plymouth St.	30	*189	*6.3
1995	Barry Aranoff, Yeshiva	22	121	5.5
1996	Purvis Presha, Stillman	25	144	5.8
1997	John Gallogly, Salve Regina	24	137	5.7
1998	John Gallogly, Salve Regina	23	121	5.3
1999	Mario Thompson, Occidental	24	114	4.8
2000	Daniel Martinez, McMurry	29	178	6.1
2001	Keith Darden, Concordia (Tex.)	24	111	4.6
2002	Tennyson Whitted, Ramapo	29	138	4.8
2003	Benny West, Howard Payne	24	99	4.1
2004	Benny West, Howard Payne	25	116	4.6
2005	Keith Darden, Concordia (Tex.)	25	96	3.8
2006	Quameir Harding, Ramapo	29	116	4.0
2007	Elbie Murphy, St. Joseph's (Me.)	30	126	4.2
2008	Tyler Gordon, Finlandia	25	99	4.0

*record

Annual Team Champions

Won-Lost Percentage

Season	Team	Won	Lost	Pct.
1974	Calvin	21	2	.913
1975	Calvin	22	1	.957
1976	Husson	25	1	.961
1977	Mass.-Boston	25	3	.893
1978	North Park	29	2	.935
1979	Stony Brook	24	3	.889
1980	Franklin Pierce	29	2	.935
1981	Potsdam St.	30	2	.938
1982	St. Andrews	27	3	.900
1983	Roanoke	31	2	.939
1984	Roanoke	27	2	.931
1985	Colby	22	3	.880
1986	Potsdam St.	32	0	1.000
1987	Potsdam St.	28	1	.966
1988	Scranton	29	3	.906
1989	TCNJ	30	2	.938
1990	Colby	26	1	.963
1991	Hamilton	26	1	.963
1992	Calvin	31	1	.969
1993	Rowan	29	2	.935
1994	Wittenberg	30	2	.938
1995	Wis.-Platteville	31	0	1.000
1996	Wilkes	28	2	.933
1997	Ill. Wesleyan	29	2	.935
1998	Wis.-Platteville	30	0	1.000
1999	Connecticut Col.	28	1	.966
2000	Calvin	30	2	.938
2001	Mass.-Dartmouth	25	3	.893
2002	Carthage	28	2	.933
2003	Williams	31	1	.969
2004	Williams	30	2	.938
2005	St. John Fisher	28	1	.966
2006	Lawrence	25	1	.962
2007	Amherst	30	2	.938
2008	Plattsburgh St.	27	3	.900

Scoring Offense

Season	Team	G	W-L	Pts.	Avg.
1974	Bishop	26	14-12	2,527	97.2
1975	Bishop	29	25-4	2,932	101.1
1976	Husson	26	25-1	2,567	98.7
1977	Mercy	25	16-9	2,587	103.5
1978	Mercy	26	16-10	2,602	10.1
1979	Ashland	25	14-11	2,375	95.0
1980	Franklin Pierce	31	29-2	3,073	99.1
1981	Husson	23	20-3	2,173	94.5
1982	Husson	26	19-7	2,279	87.7
1983	Bishop	26	18-8	2,529	97.3
1984	St. Joseph's (Me.)	29	24-5	2,666	91.9
1985	St. Joseph's (Me.)	30	22-8	2,752	91.7
1986	St. Joseph's (Me.)	30	26-4	2,837	94.6

Season	Team	G	W-L	Pts.	Avg.
1987	Bishop	26	13-13	2,534	97.5
1988	St. Joseph's (Me.)	29	20-9	2,785	96.0
1989	Redlands	25	15-10	2,507	10.3
1990	Salisbury	27	14-13	2,822	104.5
1991	Redlands	26	15-11	2,726	104.8
1992	Redlands	25	18-7	2,510	10.4
1993	Salisbury	26	18-8	2,551	98.1
1994	Grinnell	21	13-8	2,297	109.4
1995	Grinnell	21	14-7	2,422	115.3
1996	Grinnell	25	17-8	2,587	103.5
1997	Grinnell	22	10-12	2,254	102.5
1998	Grinnell	22	10-12	2,434	11.6
1999	Grinnell	22	11-11	2,509	114.0
2000	Grinnell	21	6-15	2,175	103.6
2001	Grinnell	24	16-8	2,837	118.2
2002	Grinnell	24	12-12	2,997	124.9
2003	Grinnell	25	19-6	3,119	124.8
2004	Grinnell	24	18-6	3,029	126.2
2005	Redlands	25	14-11	*3,310	*132.4
2006	Grinnell	23	14-9	2,699	117.3
2007	Redlands	24	17-7	2,810	117.1
2008	Grinnell	24	16-8	2,589	107.9

*record

Scoring Defense

Season	Team	G	W-L	Pts.	Avg.
1974	Fredonia St.	22	13-9	1,049	47.7
1975	Chicago	15	9-6	790	52.7
1976	Fredonia St.	23	10-13	1,223	53.2
1977	Hamline	30	22-8	1,560	52.0
1978	Widener	31	26-5	1,693	54.6
1979	Coast Guard	24	21-3	1,160	48.3
1980	John Jay	27	10-17	1,411	52.3
1981	Wis.-Stevens Point	26	19-7	1,394	53.6
1982	Wis.-Stevens Point	28	22-6	1,491	53.3
1983	Ohio Northern	26	18-8	1,379	53.0
1984	Wis.-Stevens Point	32	28-4	1,559	48.7
1985	Wis.-Stevens Point	30	25-3	1,438	47.9
1986	Widener	27	15-12	1,356	50.2
1987	Muskingum	27	16-11	1,454	53.9
1988	Ohio Northern	30	21-9	1,734	57.8
1989	Wooster	28	21-7	1,600	57.1
1990	Randolph-Macon	29	24-5	1,646	56.8
1991	Ohio Northern	27	14-13	1,508	55.9
1992	Wittenberg	29	23-6	1,651	56.9
1993	St. Thomas (Minn.)	28	19-9	1,599	57.1
1994	Yeshiva	22	12-10	1,308	59.5
1995	Johnson St.	26	15-11	1,559	60.0
1996	Upper Iowa	26	21-5	1,500	57.7
1997	Wis.-Platteville	27	24-3	1,283	*47.5
1998	Wis.-Platteville	30	30-0	1,552	51.7
1999	Rowan	27	25-2	1,549	57.4
2000	Baruch	28	19-9	1,639	58.5

Season	Team	G	W-L	Pts.	Avg.
2001	Cortland St.	28	21-7	1,678	59.9
2002	Babson	30	25-5	1,693	56.4
2003	Randolph-Macon	30	28-2	1,599	53.3
2004	Penn St.-Behrend	26	22-4	1,366	52.5
2005	Wittenberg	29	25-4	1,613	55.6
2006	Wittenberg	34	30-4	1,857	54.6
2007	Mississippi Col.	30	27-3	1,711	57.0
2008	Penn St.-Behrend	29	24-5	1,583	54.6

*record

Scoring Margin

Season	Team	Off.	Def.	Mar.
1974	Fisk	83.3	65.7	17.6
1975	Monmouth (Ill.)	83.9	66.0	17.9
1976	Husson	98.7	67.6	*31.1
1977	Husson	101.2	78.6	22.6
1978	Stony Brook	86.6	68.7	17.9
1979	North Park	84.4	67.3	17.1
1980	Franklin Pierce	99.1	76.5	22.6
1981	Husson	94.5	70.1	24.4
1982	Hope	83.9	70.0	13.8
1983	Trinity (Conn.)	79.8	61.4	18.4
1984	Wis.-Stevens Point	68.4	48.7	19.7
1985	Hope	85.4	66.0	19.4
1986	Potsdam St.	81.5	57.3	24.2
1987	NJIT	90.8	63.9	26.9
1988	Cal St. San B'dino	89.4	69.4	20.0
1989	TCNJ	92.3	68.5	23.8
1990	Colby	94.7	71.9	22.8
1991	Hamilton	89.8	66.2	23.6
1992	NJIT	95.0	73.4	21.6
1993	NJIT	90.4	65.7	24.7
1994	Rowan	89.6	64.4	25.3
1995	Colby-Sawyer	94.4	71.7	22.6
1996	Cabrini	89.4	67.6	21.8
1997	Williams	83.6	62.5	21.0
1998	Wis.-Platteville	73.9	51.7	22.2
1999	Hampden-Sydney	84.2	62.3	21.9
2000	Hampden-Sydney	88.2	66.4	21.8
2001	Chapman	81.2	63.4	17.9
2002	Brockport St.	84.5	64.9	19.6
2003	Williams	83.1	62.4	20.7
2004	Amherst	87.1	66.3	20.8
2005	Wittenberg	74.2	55.6	18.6
2006	Wooster	98.2	76.6	21.5
2007	Amherst	81.4	60.8	20.6
2008	Hope	80.6	63.5	17.1

*record

Field-Goal Percentage

Season	Team	FG	FGA	Pct.
1974	Muskingum	560	1,056	53.0
1975	Savannah St.	1,072	1,978	54.2
1976	Stony Brook	778	1,401	55.5
1977	Stony Brook	842	1,455	57.9
1978	Stony Brook	1,033	1,721	*60.0
1979	Stony Brook	980	1,651	59.4
1980	Framingham St.	924	1,613	57.3
1981	Averett	845	1,447	58.4
1982	Lebanon Valley	608	1,098	55.4
1983	Bishop	1,037	1,775	58.4
1984	Framingham St.	849	1,446	58.7
1985	Me.-Farmington	751	1,347	55.8
1986	Frostburg St.	971	1,747	55.6
1987	NJIT	969	1,799	53.9
1988	Rust	878	1,493	58.8
1989	Bridgewater (Va.)	650	1,181	55.0
1990	Wartburg	792	1,474	53.7
1991	Otterbein	1,104	2,050	53.9
1992	Bridgewater (Va.)	706	1,315	53.7
1993	St. John's (Minn.)	744	1,415	52.6
1994	Oglethorpe	774	1,491	51.9
1995	Simpson	892	1,627	54.8
1996	Simpson	946	1,749	54.1
1997	Neb. Wesleyan	968	1,834	52.8
1998	Ill. Wesleyan	843	1,546	54.5
1999	Lebanon Valley	751	1,445	52.0

Season	Team	FG	FGA	Pct.
2000	Franklin	814	1,577	51.6
2001	St. John's (Minn.)	772	1,471	52.5
2002	Wis.-Oshkosh	784	1,500	52.3
2003	Wis.-Oshkosh	849	1,600	53.1
2004	Chapman	648	1,266	51.2
2005	Cal Lutheran	659	1,251	52.7
2006	Baldwin-Wallace	933	1,743	53.5
2007	Mississippi Col.	789	1,504	52.5
2008	Emerson	838	1,591	52.7

*record

Field-Goal Percentage Defense

Season	Team	FG	FGA	Pct.
1978	Grove City	589	1,477	39.9
1979	Coast Guard	464	1,172	39.6
1980	Calvin	552	1,364	40.5
1981	Wittenberg	670	1,651	40.6
1982	Tufts	622	1,505	41.3
1983	Trinity (Conn.)	580	1,408	41.2
1984	Widener	617	1,557	39.6
1985	Colby	679	1,712	39.7
1986	Widener	531	1,344	39.5
1987	Widener	608	1,636	37.2
1988	Rust	603	1,499	40.2
1989	Wooster	595	1,563	38.1
1990	Rochester	760	1,990	38.2
1991	Hamilton	679	1,771	38.3
1992	Scranton	589	1,547	38.1
1993	Scranton	659	1,806	36.5
1994	Lebanon Valley	708	1,925	36.8
1995	New Jersey City	702	1,897	37.0
1996	Bowdoin	569	1,482	38.4
1997	NJIT	572	1,565	36.5
1998	Rhodes	552	1,488	37.1
1999	Grove City	533	1,469	36.3
2000	Baruch	608	1,689	36.0
2001	Endicott	575	1,569	36.6
2002	Rowan	503	1,377	36.5
2003	Trinity (Tex.)	589	1,587	37.1
2004	Kean	517	1,398	37.0
2005	Lebanon Valley	576	1,595	36.1
2006	Huntingdon	568	1,604	*35.4
2007	New York U.	552	1,560	*35.4
2008	Stevens Tech	637	1,698	37.5

*record

Three-Point Field Goals Made Per Game

Season	Team	G	3FG	Avg.
1987	Grinnell	22	166	7.5
1988	Southern Me.	29	233	8.0
1989	Redlands	25	261	10.4
1990	Augsburg	25	266	10.6
1991	Redlands	26	307	11.8
1992	Catholic	26	335	12.9
1993	Anna Maria	27	302	11.2
1994	Grinnell	21	297	14.1
1995	Grinnell	21	368	17.5
1996	Grinnell	25	415	16.6
1997	Grinnell	22	367	16.7
1998	Grinnell	22	406	18.5
1999	Grinnell	22	436	19.8
2000	Grinnell	21	353	16.8
2001	Grinnell	24	443	18.5
2002	Grinnell	24	490	20.4
2003	Grinnell	25	522	20.9
2004	Redlands	25	585	23.4
2005	Redlands	25	*595	*23.8
2006	Redlands	24	507	21.1
2007	Redlands	24	440	18.3
2008	Grinnell	24	462	19.3

*record

Three-Point Field-Goal Percentage

Season	Team	G	3FG	3FGA	Pct.
1987	Mass.-Dartmouth	28	102	198	51.5
1988	Richard Stockton	26	122	211	57.8
1989	NJIT	29	124	200	*62.0
1990	Western New Eng.	26	85	167	50.9
1991	Ripon	26	154	331	46.5
1992	Dickinson	27	126	267	47.2
1993	DePauw	26	191	419	45.6
1994	Eureka	31	317	646	49.1
1995	Manchester	32	222	487	45.6
1996	John Carroll	27	169	388	43.6
1997	Williams	30	235	507	46.4
1998	Franklin	29	168	390	43.1
1999	Union (N.Y.)	25	233	512	45.5
2000	Franklin	28	195	467	41.8
2001	Albion	25	192	417	46.0
2002	Gordon	27	262	590	44.4
2003	Wis.-Oshkosh	32	229	532	43.0
2004	Ill. Wesleyan	28	201	458	43.9
2005	Concordia-M'head	25	140	322	43.5
2006	Potsdam St.	28	210	485	43.3
2007	Augustana (Ill.)	28	159	361	44.0
2008	Wooster	28	248	559	44.4

*record

Free-Throw Percentage

Season	Team	FT	FTA	Pct.
1974	Lake Superior St.	369	461	80.0
1975	Muskingum	298	379	78.6
1976	Case Reserve	266	343	77.6
1977	Hamilton	491	640	76.7
1978	Case Reserve	278	351	79.2
1979	Marietta	364	460	79.1
1980	Denison	377	478	78.9
1981	Ripon	378	494	76.5
1982	Otterbein	458	589	77.8
1983	DePauw	368	475	77.5
1984	Redlands	426	534	79.8
1985	Wis.-Stevens Point	363	455	79.8
1986	Heidelberg	375	489	76.7
1987	Denison	442	560	78.9
1988	Capital	377	473	79.7
1989	Colby	464	585	79.3
1990	Colby	485	605	80.2
1991	Wartburg	565	711	79.5
1992	Thiel	393	491	80.0
1993	Colby	391	506	77.3
1994	Wheaton (Ill.)	455	572	79.5
1995	Baldwin-Wallace	454	582	78.0

Season	Team	FT	FTA	Pct.
1996	Anderson	454	592	76.7
1997	Ill. Wesleyan	616	790	78.0
1998	Wis.-Oshkosh	516	631	*81.8
1999	Carleton	423	540	78.3
2000	Ill. Wesleyan	426	543	78.5
2001	Franklin	570	713	79.9
2002	Moravian	407	512	79.5
2003	Wooster	543	685	79.3
2004	St. Norbert	307	377	81.4
2005	Louisiana Col.	358	455	78.7
2006	Wis.-Stevens Point	419	529	79.2
2007	Wis.-Stevens Point	339	412	82.3
2008	Elmhurst	415	509	81.5

*record

Rebound Margin

Season	Team	Off.	Def.	Mar.
1976	Bowie St.	54.0	37.5	16.5
1977	Husson	51.6	35.0	16.7
1978	Gallaudet	46.3	33.0	13.3
1979	St. Lawrence	43.2	28.7	14.5
1980	Elmira	41.4	28.7	12.7
1981	Clark (Mass.)	40.0	25.0	15.0
1982	Maryville (Mo.)	41.0	26.7	14.4
1983	Framingham St.	38.0	22.2	15.8
1984	New England Col.	43.3	29.3	14.0
1985	Bethel (Minn.)	45.0	32.2	12.8
1986	St. Joseph's (Me.)	43.7	29.5	14.2
1987	Elmira	40.6	29.3	11.3
1988	Cal St. San B'dino	46.6	29.7	16.9
1989	Yeshiva	49.8	34.6	15.2
1990	Bethel (Minn.)	42.2	30.3	12.0
1991	Hamilton	49.6	32.5	*17.0
1992	Bethel (Minn.)	42.3	31.0	11.3
1993	Eureka	33.9	22.2	11.7
1994	Maritime (N.Y.)	46.3	32.3	14.1
1995	Wittenberg	43.1	29.2	13.9
1996	Cabrini	47.9	34.7	13.1
1997	Rochester Inst.	42.8	31.9	10.8
1998	Chris. Newport	47.5	33.7	13.9
1999	Rensselaer	41.5	29.8	11.7
2000	Albright	41.3	29.6	11.7
2001	Wittenberg	44.7	30.7	14.0
2002	Wittenberg	42.5	30.1	12.4
2003	Williams	43.7	31.1	12.6
2004	Wooster	40.6	27.8	12.8
2005	Norwich	45.1	32.6	12.5
2006	Coast Guard	40.6	29.5	11.1
2007	New York U.	39.9	29.4	10.5
2008	Guilford	43.7	32.3	11.4

*record

2008 Most-Improved Teams

	School (Coach)	2008	2007	*Games Improved
1.	Mass.-Dartmouth (Brian Baptiste)	25-4	14-13	10
	New England (Jason Mulligan)	17-12	5-20	10
3.	Cortland St. (Tom Spanbauer)	21-8	10-16	9½
	Gettysburg (George Petrie)	24-5	13-13	9½
	Ursinus (Kevin Small)	29-4	16-10	9½
6.	Albion (Mike Turner)	19-6	10-15	9
	Becker (Brian Gorman)	13-14	3-22	9
	Brooklyn (Steve Podias)	21-7	10-14	9
9.	Coast Guard (Peter Barry)	24-7	14-14	8½
	Concordia-M'head (Duane Siverson)	13-13	4-21	8½
	Fitchburg St. (Derek Shell)	16-10	7-18	8½
	Heidelberg (Duane Sheldon)	23-6	13-13	8½
	Shenandoah (Robert Harris)	16-10	7-18	8½
14.	Concordia (Tex.) (Stan Bonewitz)	19-9	10-16	8
	Lawrence (Joel DePagter)	22-3	13-10	8

	School (Coach)	2008	2007	*Games Improved
	Maritime (N.Y.) (Jody King)	13-14	4-21	8
17.	Carleton (Guy Kalland)	19-8	11-15	7½
	Millsaps (Tim Wise)	28-4	18-9	7½
	Misericordia (Trevor Woodruff)	19-9	10-15	7½
	Nazareth (Mike Daley)	20-8	11-14	7½
	Pitt.-Greensburg (Marcus Kahn)	11-15	3-22	7½
	Southern Me. (Karl Henrikson)	14-13	6-20	7½
	Thomas More (John Ellenwood)	11-16	3-23	7½
24.	La Verne (Richard Reed)	12-13	5-20	7
	Widener (Chris Carideo)	22-6	15-13	7

*To determine games improved, add the difference in victories between the two seasons to the difference in losses, then divide by two.

DIVISION III

All-Time Winningest Teams

Includes records as a senior college only; minimum 10 seasons of competition. Postseason games are included.

By Percentage

	Team	Yrs.	Won	Lost	Pct.
1.	Husson	54	1,013	392	.721
2.	Wittenberg	97	1,575	628	.715
3.	Calvin	89	1,236	602	.672
4.	Colby-Sawyer	18	319	159	.667
5.	Hope	103	1,408	704	.667
6.	Wooster	108	1,472	750	.662
7.	Cabrini	28	509	264	.658
8.	Williams	107	1,301	687	.654
9.	St. Joseph's (Me.)	37	642	341	.653
10.	Richard Stockton	36	628	337	.651
11.	Chris. Newport	41	702	378	.650
12.	Westminster (Pa.)	105	1,439	789	.646
13.	Staten Island	30	538	297	.644
14.	Wis.-Eau Claire	92	1,293	718	.643
15.	Ill. Wesleyan	99	1,447	818	.639
16.	St. Thomas (Minn.)	99	1,420	808	.637
17.	St. John Fisher	46	719	411	.636
18.	New Jersey City	66	989	568	.635
19.	New York U.	90	1,173	677	.634
20.	Wis.-Stevens Point	110	1,276	752	.629
21.	Roanoke	95	1,260	751	.627
22.	Mass.-Dartmouth	44	709	435	.620
23.	Wartburg	73	1,064	659	.618
24.	Amherst	107	1,086	690	.611
25.	Defiance	99	1,266	814	.609
26.	Randolph-Macon	95	1,308	850	.606
27.	Augustana (Ill.)	103	1,299	848	.605
28.	Springfield	99	1,310	869	.601
29.	Scranton	91	1,286	855	.601
30.	Capital	102	1,207	805	.600

By Victories

	Team	Yrs.	Won	Lost	Pct.
1.	Wittenberg	97	1,575	628	.715
2.	Wooster	108	1,472	750	.662
3.	Ill. Wesleyan	99	1,447	818	.639
4.	Westminster (Pa.)	105	1,439	789	.646
5.	St. Thomas (Minn.)	99	1,420	808	.637
6.	Hope	103	1,408	704	.667
7.	Neb. Wesleyan	103	1,321	923	.589
8.	Springfield	99	1,310	869	.601
9.	Randolph-Macon	95	1,308	850	.606
10.	Gust. Adolphus	99	1,303	893	.593
11.	Williams	107	1,301	687	.654
12.	Augustana (Ill.)	103	1,299	848	.605
13.	Wis.-Eau Claire	92	1,293	718	.643
14.	Scranton	91	1,286	855	.601
15.	Wis.-Stevens Point	110	1,276	752	.629
16.	Defiance	99	1,266	814	.609
	Wheaton (Ill.)	107	1,266	969	.566
18.	Roanoke	95	1,260	751	.627
19.	Calvin	89	1,236	602	.672
20.	Loras	100	1,224	933	.567
21.	Willamette	84	1,216	915	.571
22.	Capital	102	1,207	805	.600
23.	Rochester (N.Y.)	106	1,206	842	.589
24.	Muskingum	106	1,201	907	.570
25.	DePauw	102	1,193	917	.565
26.	Hampden-Sydney	97	1,184	882	.573
27.	Hamline	98	1,182	935	.558
28.	Ohio Wesleyan	103	1,180	1,043	.531
29.	Frank. & Marsh.	105	1,178	834	.585
30.	Mount Union	111	1,175	1,013	.537

Winningest Teams of the 2000s

BY PERCENTAGE
(Minimum six seasons as NCAA member)

	Team	Yrs.	Won	Lost	Pct.
1.	Wooster	9	232	38	.859
2.	Amherst	9	225	41	.846
3.	Wis.-Stevens Point	9	212	50	.809
4.	Mississippi Col.	9	200	48	.806
5.	Wittenberg	9	205	50	.804
6.	Maryville (Tenn.)	9	205	51	.801
	Salem St.	9	205	51	.801
8.	Washington-St. Louis	9	191	50	.793
9.	Buena Vista	9	203	57	.781
10.	Williams	9	190	57	.769
11.	Catholic	9	200	62	.763
12.	Hampden-Sydney	9	195	63	.756
13.	Rochester (N.Y.)	9	183	60	.753
14.	St. Thomas (Minn.)	9	184	61	.751
15.	Hope	9	193	64	.751
16.	Hanover	9	181	62	.745
17.	St. John Fisher	9	186	65	.741
18.	Trinity (Conn.)	9	167	59	.739
19.	Chapman	9	168	60	.737
20.	Calvin	9	193	69	.737
21.	Aurora	9	180	65	.735
22.	Penn St.-Behrend	9	184	67	.733
23.	Va. Wesleyan	9	188	70	.729
24.	Gust. Adolphus	9	182	69	.725
25.	Trinity (Tex.)	9	179	68	.725
26.	Randolph-Macon	9	177	70	.717
27.	Brockport	9	189	76	.713
28.	McMurry	9	171	69	.713
29.	Chris. Newport	9	175	71	.711
30.	Wis.-Whitewater	9	174	71	.710

BY VICTORIES
(Minimum six seasons as NCAA member)

	Team	Yrs.	Won	Lost	Pct.
1.	Wooster	9	232	38	.859
2.	Amherst	9	225	41	.846
3.	Wis.-Stevens Point	9	212	50	.809
4.	Wittenberg	9	205	50	.804
	Maryville (Tenn.)	9	205	51	.801
	Salem St.	9	205	51	.801
7.	Buena Vista	9	203	57	.781
8.	Mississippi Col.	9	200	48	.806
	Catholic	9	200	62	.763
10.	Hampden-Sydney	9	195	63	.756
11.	Hope	9	193	64	.751
	Calvin	9	193	69	.737
13.	Washington-St. Louis	9	191	50	.793
14.	Williams	9	190	57	.769
15.	Brockport	9	189	76	.713
16.	Va. Wesleyan	9	188	70	.729
17.	St. John Fisher	9	186	65	.741
18.	St. Thomas (Minn.)	9	184	61	.751
	Penn St.-Behrend	9	184	67	.733
20.	Rochester (N.Y.)	9	183	60	.753
21.	Gust. Adolphus	9	182	69	.725
22.	Hanover	9	181	62	.745
23.	Aurora	9	180	65	.735
24.	Trinity (Tex.)	9	179	68	.725
25.	Alvernia	9	178	74	.706
	Keene St.	9	178	76	.701
27.	Randolph-Macon	9	177	70	.717
28.	Chris. Newport	9	175	71	.711
	Wm. Paterson	9	175	73	.706
	Ramapo	9	175	77	.694

All-Time Won-Lost Records

(Alphabetical Listing; No Minimum Seasons of Competition)

Team	First Year	Yrs.	Won	Lost	Pct.
Adrian	1903	97	760	1,219	.384
Albion	1898	97	1,039	872	.544
Albright	1901	101	1,172	1,020	.535
Alfred	1908	91	763	1,022	.427
Allegheny	1896	113	1,101	936	.541
Alma	1912	95	890	1,073	.453
Alvernia	1975	34	541	372	.593
Amherst	1902	107	1,086	690	.611
Anderson (Ind.)	1932	76	924	926	.499
Anna Maria	1983	26	300	366	.450
Augustana (Ill.)	1902	103	1,299	848	.605
Aurora	1913	92	911	901	.503
Austin	1912	78	559	1,041	.349
Babson	1931	68	744	700	.515
Baldwin-Wallace	1904	103	1,094	1,017	.518
Bates	1901	79	690	874	.441
Beloit	1906	98	1,103	778	.586
Benedictine (Ill.)	1966	43	591	504	.540
Bethany (W.Va.)	1906	100	899	1,057	.460
Bethel (Minn.)	1947	62	723	727	.499
Bluffton	1915	93	806	1,115	.420
Bowdoin	1942	67	627	745	.457
Bridgewater (Va.)	1903	87	821	976	.457
Bridgewater St.	1906	88	851	867	.495
Brockport	1929	76	890	717	.554
Buena Vista	1917	89	858	1,009	.460
Buffalo St.	1927	79	1,006	695	.591
Cabrini	1981	28	509	264	.658
Cal Lutheran	1962	47	589	673	.467
Cal St. East Bay	1962	47	530	717	.425
Caltech	1919	89	289	1,270	.185
Calvin	1920	89	1,236	602	.672
Capital	1907	102	1,207	805	.600
Carleton	1910	99	1,129	867	.566
Carnegie Mellon	1907	100	846	1,203	.413
Carroll (Wis.)	1949	60	591	796	.426
Carthage	1907	101	982	1,094	.473
Case Reserve	1902	107	1,090	953	.534
Castleton	1952	57	608	700	.465
Catholic	1912	96	1,120	986	.532
Central (Iowa)	1910	98	946	977	.492
Centre	1953	56	680	661	.507
Chapman	1923	83	1,125	848	.570
Chicago	1896	107	1,088	1,043	.511
Chris. Newport	1968	41	702	378	.650
CCNY	1906	103	1,011	995	.504
Claremont-M-S	1958	50	665	585	.532
Clark (Mass.)	1921	86	874	846	.508
Clarkson	1930	79	619	981	.387
Coast Guard	1926	82	698	907	.435
Coe	1901	108	983	986	.499
Colby	1938	68	946	642	.596
Colby-Sawyer	1991	18	319	159	.667
Colorado Col.	1915	94	822	1,082	.432
Concordia Chicago	1924	85	794	1,007	.441
Concordia (Tex.)	1959	41	352	666	.346
Concordia (Wis.)	1916	93	958	880	.521
Concordia-M'head	1923	86	870	1,096	.443
Connecticut Col.	1970	39	412	409	.502
Cornell College	1910	99	895	1,007	.471
Cortland St.	1924	83	897	776	.536
Curry	1942	67	809	819	.497
Dallas	1917	35	235	498	.321
Daniel Webster	1991	18	115	329	.259
Defiance	1905	99	1,266	814	.609
Delaware Valley	1927	79	555	965	.365
Denison	1900	106	971	1,102	.468
DePauw	1905	102	1,193	917	.565
DeSales	1969	40	488	498	.495
Dickinson	1901	98	834	1,007	.453
Drew	1930	77	552	945	.369
Dubuque	1916	91	870	982	.470
Earlham	1896	108	894	1,195	.428
Eastern	1959	42	461	537	.462
East. Mennonite	1967	42	361	650	.357
Eastern Conn. St.	1942	64	735	715	.507
Eastern Nazarene	1957	52	678	616	.524
Edgewood	1972	33	479	352	.576
Elizabethtown	1929	80	900	876	.507
Elmhurst	1922	84	793	1,007	.441
Elmira	1971	38	443	492	.474
Elms	1999	10	133	132	.502
Emory	1987	22	250	301	.454
Emory & Henry	1921	84	927	962	.491
Endicott	1995	14	213	160	.571
Eureka	1920	87	977	893	.522
Farmingdale St.	2000	9	154	91	.629
FDU-Florham	1961	48	549	602	.477
Ferrum	1986	23	254	335	.431
Fitchburg St.	1968	39	334	628	.347
Framingham St.	1968	41	449	542	.453
Franklin	1907	101	1,130	965	.539
Frank. & Marsh.	1900	105	1,178	834	.585
Fredonia St.	1935	70	659	794	.454
Frostburg St.	1937	66	728	788	.480
Gallaudet	1904	105	553	1,363	.289
Geneseo St.	1915	90	803	825	.493
Gettysburg	1901	105	1,136	1,001	.532
Gordon	1923	71	709	827	.462
Goucher	1991	18	234	231	.503
Greensboro	1967	42	494	572	.463
Grinnell	1901	106	853	1,127	.431
Grove City	1899	104	1,113	900	.553
Guilford	1906	94	881	999	.469
Gust. Adolphus	1904	99	1,303	893	.593
Gwynedd-Mercy	1994	15	235	168	.583
Hamilton	1901	96	1,003	734	.577
Hamline	1910	98	1,182	935	.558
Hampden-Sydney	1909	97	1,184	882	.573
Hanover	1901	103	1,125	899	.556
Hardin-Simmons	1908	99	1,068	1,079	.497
Hartwick	1929	78	971	725	.573
Haverford	1920	88	549	1,069	.339
Heidelberg	1903	102	894	1,075	.454
Hendrix	1908	85	974	830	.540
Hiram	1894	110	778	1,221	.389
Hobart	1902	98	691	1,035	.400
Hope	1902	103	1,408	704	.667
Howard Payne	1913	91	1,085	925	.540
Hunter	1953	54	639	648	.497
Husson	1954	54	1013	392	.721
Illinois Col.	1957	52	463	719	.392
Ill. Wesleyan	1910	99	1,447	818	.639
Immaculata	2006	3	33	46	.418
Ithaca	1930	78	970	722	.573
John Carroll	1920	87	921	898	.506
Johns Hopkins	1920	83	799	897	.471
Johnson & Wales (R.I.)	1998	11	134	158	.459
Juniata	1905	104	800	1,155	.409
Kalamazoo	1908	101	1,044	950	.524
Kean	1931	68	735	836	.468
Keene St.	1925	72	768	852	.474
Kenyon	1900	106	711	1,223	.368
Keuka	1986	23	260	307	.459
King's (Pa.)	1947	62	814	665	.550
Knox	1908	99	914	924	.497
LaGrange	1955	54	642	823	.438
Lake Erie	1988	21	175	362	.326
Lake Forest	1905	98	750	1,105	.404
Lakeland	1934	75	1,114	836	.571
Lawrence	1896	106	861	975	.469
Lebanon Valley	1904	101	1,038	983	.514
LeTourneau	1955	54	469	792	.372
Lewis & Clark	1946	63	924	756	.550
Loras	1909	100	1,224	933	.567
Louisiana Col.	1954	33	395	452	.466
Luther	1904	105	1,037	1,026	.503
Lycoming	1949	60	676	695	.493
Lynchburg	1957	52	516	779	.398
MacMurray	1958	51	555	728	.433
Me.-Farmington	1948	59	669	591	.531
Manchester	1915	93	951	1,014	.484
Manhattanville	1975	34	478	415	.535
Marian (Wis.)	1973	36	484	457	.514
Marietta	1902	104	936	1,112	.457
Mary Washington	1975	34	383	479	.444
Marymount (Va.)	1988	21	254	291	.466
Maryville (Mo.)	1977	32	353	483	.422
Maryville (Tenn.)	1903	105	1,148	886	.564
Marywood	1994	15	75	285	.208

DIVISION III

Team	First Year	Yrs.	Won	Lost	Pct.
Mass. Liberal Arts	1960	48	545	598	.477
Mass.-Boston	1981	28	282	437	.392
Mass.-Dartmouth	1965	44	709	435	.620
MIT	1953	56	539	730	.425
McDaniel	1922	86	702	1,139	.381
McMurry	1924	83	996	917	.521
Menlo	1987	22	304	268	.531
Merchant Marine	1946	63	673	792	.459
Messiah	1962	47	531	561	.486
Methodist	1964	45	497	612	.448
Middlebury	1918	91	698	1,050	.399
Millikin	1904	102	1,144	991	.536
Millsaps	1911	98	851	1,188	.417
Misericordia	1991	18	224	245	.478
Mississippi Col.	1909	96	1,130	884	.561
Monmouth (Ill.)	1900	108	1,118	894	.556
Montclair St.	1929	80	1,026	799	.562
Moravian	1936	67	791	777	.504
Mount Union	1896	111	1,175	1,013	.537
Mt. St. Joseph	1999	10	125	133	.484
Mt. St. Vincent	1982	27	381	310	.551
Muhlenberg	1901	101	1,142	1,013	.530
Muskingum	1903	106	1,201	907	.570
Nazareth	1978	31	457	339	.574
Neb. Wesleyan	1906	103	1,321	923	.589
New Jersey City	1932	66	989	568	.635
New York U.	1907	90	1,173	677	.634
Nichols	1959	50	461	706	.395
N.C. Wesleyan	1964	45	525	579	.476
North Central (Ill.)	1948	60	589	855	.408
North Park	1959	50	720	542	.571
Oberlin	1903	106	772	1,233	.385
Occidental	1955	53	719	593	.548
Ohio Northern	1911	97	1,167	864	.575
Ohio Wesleyan	1906	103	1,180	1,043	.531
Olivet	1899	96	688	1,181	.368
Otterbein	1903	106	1,112	903	.552
Ozarks (Ark.)	1948	61	676	890	.432
Pacific (Ore.)	1912	93	871	1,257	.409
Pacific Lutheran	1939	68	977	781	.556
Pitt.-Bradford	1980	29	385	383	.501
Plattsburgh St.	1926	79	702	671	.511
Plymouth St.	1948	61	782	613	.561
Randolph-Macon	1910	95	1,308	850	.606
Redlands	1918	91	977	887	.524
Rensselaer	1904	105	908	950	.489
Rhode Island Col.	1959	50	687	585	.540
Richard Stockton	1973	36	628	337	.651
Ripon	1901	104	1,097	838	.567
Roanoke	1912	95	1,260	751	.627
Rochester (N.Y.)	1902	106	1,206	842	.589
Rochester Inst.	1916	87	960	841	.533
Rockford	1956	53	500	773	.393
Roger Williams	1970	34	431	442	.494
Rose-Hulman	1898	101	960	970	.497
Rowan	1923	69	920	635	.592
St. John Fisher	1963	46	719	411	.636
St. John's (Minn.)	1903	106	1,062	1,042	.505
St. Joseph's (Me.)	1972	37	642	341	.653
St. Mary's (Md.)	1967	42	463	605	.434
St. Mary's (Minn.)	1920	87	751	1,116	.402
St. Norbert	1917	90	878	819	.517
St. Olaf	1907	102	973	1,039	.484
St. Scholastica	1981	27	285	433	.397
St. Thomas (Minn.)	1905	99	1,420	808	.637
Salisbury	1963	46	547	597	.478
Salve Regina	1975	33	325	428	.432
Scranton	1917	91	1,286	855	.601
Sewanee	1909	83	695	939	.425
Shenandoah	1975	34	385	482	.444
Simpson	1902	107	1,108	1,079	.507
Southern Me.	1923	81	807	730	.525
Springfield	1906	99	1,310	869	.601
Staten Island	1979	30	538	297	.644
Stevens Tech	1917	92	742	803	.480
Suffolk	1947	62	613	750	.450
Susquehanna	1902	105	905	1,085	.455
Swarthmore	1902	107	774	1,168	.399
Thiel	1917	88	544	1,163	.319
Thomas More	1948	58	606	864	.412
Transylvania	1903	87	1,093	807	.575
Trinity (Conn.)	1906	95	1,016	718	.586
Trinity (Tex.)	1949	59	706	727	.493
Tufts	1905	97	1,015	924	.523
Ursinus	1915	94	820	1,030	.443
Vassar	1970	37	298	481	.383
Va. Wesleyan	1969	40	543	485	.528
Wabash	1897	112	1,149	1,032	.527
Wartburg	1936	73	1,064	659	.618
Wash. & Jeff.	1913	93	896	868	.508
Wash. & Lee	1907	100	1,049	1,061	.497
Washington (Md.)	1913	96	1,002	949	.514
Washington-St. Louis	1905	93	1,074	876	.551
Waynesburg	1921	85	1,059	883	.545
Webster	1985	24	240	357	.402
Wentworth Inst.	1985	24	229	370	.382
Wesleyan (Conn.)	1902	107	990	924	.517
Western Conn. St.	1947	62	723	672	.518
Western New Eng.	1967	42	506	543	.482
Westfield St.	1951	58	671	677	.498
Westminster (Mo.)	1909	93	924	1,013	.477
Westminster (Pa.)	1898	105	1,439	789	.646
Wheaton (Ill.)	1902	107	1,266	969	.566
Wheaton (Mass.)	1990	19	256	242	.514
Widener	1906	100	1,128	808	.583
Wilkes	1947	62	751	704	.516
Willamette	1925	84	1,216	915	.571
Wm. Paterson	1939	67	869	763	.532
Williams	1901	107	1,301	687	.654
Wilmington (Ohio)	1917	91	820	1,108	.425
Wis.-Eau Claire	1917	92	1,293	718	.643
Wis.-La Crosse	1911	98	1,027	878	.539
Wis.-Oshkosh	1899	110	1,101	939	.540
Wis.-Platteville	1909	86	1,034	731	.586
Wis.-River Falls	1912	97	946	1,009	.484
Wis.-Stevens Point	1898	110	1,276	752	.629
Wis.-Stout	1907	99	914	984	.482
Wis.-Whitewater	1903	99	1,085	834	.565
Wittenberg	1912	97	1,575	628	.715
Wooster	1901	108	1,472	750	.662
Worcester St.	1951	58	652	699	.483
WPI	1903	98	871	945	.480
Yeshiva	1936	73	658	821	.445
York (Pa.)	1970	39	492	512	.490

Individual Collegiate Records

Individual Collegiate Records

Individual collegiate leaders are determined by comparing the best records in all three divisions in equivalent categories. Included are players whose careers were split between two divisions (e.g., Dwight Lamar of Louisiana-Lafayette or Howard Shockley of Salisbury).

Single-Game Records

POINTS

Pts.	Div.	Player, Team vs. Opponent	Date
113	II	Clarence "Bevo" Francis, Rio Grande vs. Hillsdale	Feb. 2, 1954
100	I	Frank Selvy, Furman vs. Newberry	Feb. 13, 1954
85	I	Paul Arizin, Villanova vs. Philadelphia NAMC	Feb. 12, 1949
84	II	Clarence "Bevo" Francis, Rio Grande vs. Alliance	1954
82	II	Clarence "Bevo" Francis, Rio Grande vs. Bluffton	1954
81	I	Freeman Williams, Portland St. vs. Rocky Mountain	Feb. 3, 1978
80	II	Paul Crissman, Southern Cal Col. vs. Pacific Christian	Feb. 18, 1966
77	II	William English, Winston-Salem vs. Fayetteville St.	Feb. 19, 1968
77	III	Jeff Clement, Grinnell vs. Illinois Col.	Feb. 18, 1998
75	II	Travis Grant, Kentucky St. vs. Northwood (Mich.)	1970
73	I	Bill Mlkvy, Temple vs. Wilkes	Mar. 3, 1951
72	II	Nate DeLong, Wis.-River Falls vs. Winona St.	Feb. 24, 1948
72	II	Lloyd Brown, Aquinas vs. Cleary	1953
72	II	Clarence "Bevo" Francis, Rio Grande vs. California (Pa.)	1953
72	II	John McElroy, Youngstown St. vs. Wayne St. (Mich.)	Feb. 26, 1969
72	I	Kevin Bradshaw, Alliant Int'l vs. Loyola Marymount	Jan. 5, 1991
71	II	Clayborn Jones, L.A. Pacific vs. L.A. Baptist	Jan. 30, 1965
71	I	Freeman Williams, Portland St. vs. Southern Ore.	Feb. 9, 1977
70	II	Paul Wilcox, Davis & Elkins vs. Glenville St.	1959
70	II	Bo Clark, UCF vs. Fla. Memorial	Jan. 31, 1977
69	II	Clarence "Bevo" Francis, Rio Grande vs. Wilberforce	1953
69	II	Clarence Burks, St. Augustine's vs. St. Paul's	1955
69	II	John Rinka, Kenyon vs. Wooster	Dec. 9, 1969
69	I	Pete Maravich, LSU vs. Alabama	Feb. 7, 1970
69	III	Steve Diekmann, Grinnell vs. Simpson	Nov. 19, 1994

FIELD-GOAL PERCENTAGE
(Minimum 13 field goals made)

Pct.	Div.	Player, Team vs. Opponent (FG-FGA)	Date
100	II	Lance Berwald, North Dakota St. vs. Augustana (S.D.) (20 of 20)	Feb. 17, 1984
100	III	Jason Light, Emory & Henry vs. King (Tenn.) (18 of 18)	Dec. 2, 1995
100	III	Franklyn Beckford, Lake Forest vs. Grinnell (18 of 18)	Feb. 14, 2004
100	I	Clifford Rozier, Louisville vs. Eastern Ky. (15 of 15)	Dec. 11, 1993
100	II	Patrick Hannaway, UC-Colo. Springs vs. Carroll (Wis.) (15 of 15)	Nov. 25, 2006
100	III	Dan Beyer, Wis.-Eau Claire vs. Grinnell (15 of 15)	Nov. 16, 2007
100	I	Dan Henderson, Arkansas St. vs. Ga. Southern (14 of 14)	Feb. 26, 1976
100	I	Cornelius Holden, Louisville vs. Southern Miss. (14 of 14)	Mar. 3, 1990
100	I	Dana Jones, Pepperdine vs. Boise St. (14 of 14)	Nov. 30, 1991
100	III	Waverly Yates, Clark (Mass.) vs. Suffolk (14 of 14)	Feb. 10, 1993
100	II	Derrick Scott, California (Pa.) vs. Columbia Union (14 of 14)	Dec. 6, 1995
100	II	Kyle Boast, Central Wash. vs. Alas. Anchorage (14 of 14)	Feb. 12, 2005
100	I	Ted Guzek, Butler vs. Michigan (13 of 13)	Dec. 15, 1956
100	I	Rick Dean, Syracuse vs. Colgate (13 of 13)	Feb. 14, 1966
100	I	Gary Lechman, Gonzaga vs. Portland St. (13 of 13)	Jan. 21, 1967
100	I	Kevin King, Charlotte vs. South Ala. (13 of 13)	Feb. 20, 1978
100	I	Vernon Smith, Texas A&M vs. Alas. Anchorage (13 of 13)	Nov. 26, 1978
100	I	Steve Johnson, Oregon St. vs. Hawaii Hilo (13 of 13)	Dec. 5, 1979
100	I	Antoine Carr, Wichita St. vs. Abilene Christian (13 of 13)	Nov. 28, 1980
100	III	Rich Lengieza, Nichols vs. Mass.-Dartmouth (13 of 13)	Feb. 22, 1981
100	I	Doug Hashley, Montana St. vs. Idaho St. (13 of 13)	Feb. 5, 1982
100	I	Brad Daugherty, North Carolina vs. UCLA (13 of 13)	Nov. 24, 1985
100	II	Bruce Merklinger, Susquehanna vs. Drew (13 of 13)	Jan. 22, 1986
100	III	Antonio Randolph, Averett vs. Methodist (13 of 13)	Jan. 26, 1991
100	III	Pat Holland, Randolph-Macon vs. East. Mennonite (13 of 13)	Feb. 9, 1991
100	I	Ricky Butler, UC Irvine vs. Cal St. Fullerton (13 of 13)	Feb. 21, 1991
100	I	Rafael Solis, Brooklyn vs. Wagner (13 of 13)	Dec. 11, 1991
100	III	Todd Seifferlein, DePauw vs. Franklin (13 of 13)	Jan. 18, 1992
100	II	Ralfs Jansons, St. Rose vs. Concordia (N.Y.) (13 of 13)	Jan. 13, 1996
100	I	Ben Handlogten, Western Mich. vs. Toledo (13 of 13)	Jan. 27, 1996
100	II	Derrick Freeman, Indiana (Pa.) vs. Clarion (13 of 13)	Feb. 17, 1996

Pct.	Div.	Player, Team vs. Opponent (FG-FGA)	Date
100	I	Mate Milisa, Long Beach St. vs. Cal St. Monterey Bay (13 of 13)	Dec. 22, 1999
100	I	Nathan Blessen, South Dakota vs. Neb.-Omaha (13 of 13)	Jan. 9, 2000
100	III	Dallin Wilson, Occidental vs. Redlands (13 of 13)	Feb. 18, 2004
100	III	Dee Dee Drake, Henderson St. vs. Rhema (13 of 13)	Dec. 4, 2006
100	III	Esmir Guzonjic, North Ala. vs. West Fla. (13 of 13)	Feb. 3, 2007
100	III	Kyle Huckins, Emory & Henry vs. LaGrange (13 of 13)	Nov. 16, 2007
100	III	Keith Pederson, Central (Iowa) vs. William Woods (13 of 13)	Dec. 29, 2007
100	II	Robbie Will, Seattle Pacific vs. Alas. Fairbanks (13 of 13)	Feb. 28, 2008

THREE-POINT FIELD GOALS MADE

3FG	Div.	Player, Team vs. Opponent	Date
19	III	Jeff Clement, Grinnell vs. Illinois Col.	Feb. 18, 1998
17	III	Jeff Clement, Grinnell vs. Clarke	Dec. 3, 1997
17	III	Billy Shivers, Redlands vs. Whittier	Feb. 21, 2004
16	III	Jeff Clement, Grinnell vs. Monmouth (Ill.)	Feb. 8, 1997
16	III	Jeff Clement, Grinnell vs. Lawrence	Feb. 21, 1998
16	II	Markus Hallgrimson, Mont. St.-Billings vs. Western N.M.	Feb. 9, 2000
16	II	Thomas Vincent, Emporia St. vs. Southwest Baptist	Feb. 28, 2004
15	I	Keith Veney, Marshall vs. Morehead St.	Dec. 14, 1996
14	II	Andy Schmidtmann, Wis.-Parkside vs. Lakeland	Feb. 14, 1989
14	I	Dave Jamerson, Ohio vs. Col. of Charleston	Dec. 21, 1989
14	III	Steve Diekmann, Grinnell vs. Illinois Col.	Feb. 18, 1994
14	I	Askia Jones, Kansas St. vs. Fresno St.	Mar. 24, 1994
14	III	Steve Diekmann, Grinnell vs. Simpson	Nov. 19, 1994
14	III	Ed Brands, Grinnell vs. Ripon	Feb. 24, 1996
14	II	Antonio Harris, LeMoyne-Owen vs. Savannah St.	Feb. 6, 1999
14	I	Ronald Blackshear, Marshall vs. Akron	Mar. 1, 2002
14	II	Taylor Patterson, Kennesaw St. vs. Carver Bible	Dec. 15, 2003
14	III	Scott Stone, Washington-St. Louis vs. Fontbonne	Dec. 17, 2005
14	III	John Grotberg, Grinnell vs. North Central (Minn.)	Dec. 8, 2007
13	II	Danny Lewis, Wayne St. (Mich.) vs. Michigan Tech	Feb. 20, 1993
13	III	Eric Ochel, Sewanee vs. Emory	Feb. 22, 1995
13	II	Rodney Thomas, IUPUI vs. Wilberforce	Feb. 24, 1997
13	II	Markus Hallgrimson, Mont. St.-Billings vs. Chaminade	Feb. 5, 2000
13	II	Markus Hallgrimson, Mont. St.-Billings vs. Western N.M.	Feb. 26, 2000
13	II	Bobby Ewing, Tusculum vs. Augusta St.	Dec. 30, 2004
13	III	Sami Wylie, Lincoln (Pa.) vs. Delaware Valley	Feb. 2, 2006
13	II	Kevin Hill, Mansfield vs. Seton Hill	Nov. 17, 2007
13	II	Patrick McCoy, Fontbonne vs. Principia	Jan. 12, 2008

REBOUNDS

Reb.	Div.	Player, Team vs. Opponent	Date
51	I	Bill Chambers, William & Mary vs. Virginia	Feb. 14, 1953
46	II	Tom Hart, Middlebury vs. Trinity (Conn.)	Feb. 5, 1955
46	II	Tom Hart, Middlebury vs. Clarkson	Feb. 12, 1955
45	II	William Henrikson, Windham vs. New England Col.	Feb. 4, 1970
44	II	Charles McCullough, Loyola (Md.) vs. McDaniel	Feb. 17, 1955
44	II	Norman Rokeach, Long Island vs. Brooklyn Poly	Dec. 28, 1963
43	I	Charlie Slack, Marshall vs. Morris Harvey	Jan. 12, 1954
43	II	Bob Bessoir, Scranton vs. King's (Pa.)	Mar. 5, 1955
42	I	Tom Heinsohn, Holy Cross vs. Boston College	Mar. 1, 1955
42	II	Larry Gooding, St. Augustine's vs. Shaw	Jan. 12, 1974
41	II	Richard Kross, American Int'l vs. Springfield	Feb. 19, 1958
40	II	Ellerbe Neal, Wofford vs. Presbyterian	Jan. 3, 1953
40	I	Art Quimby, Connecticut vs. Boston U.	Jan. 11, 1955
40	II	Donnie Fowler, Wofford vs. Mercer	Jan. 22, 1955
40	II	Charlie Harrison, N.C. A&T vs. Johnson C. Smith	Feb. 8, 1958
40	II	Anthony Romano, Willimantic St. vs. Fitchburg St.	Jan. 5, 1963
40	II	Ed Halicki, Monmouth vs. Southeastern	Dec. 4, 1970
39	II	Maurice Stokes, St. Francis (Pa.) vs. John Carroll	Jan. 28, 1955
39	II	Roger Lotchin, Millikin vs. Lake Forest	Feb. 11, 1956
39	II	Joe Cole, Texas St. vs. Texas Lutheran	Dec. 10, 1956
39	II	Dave DeBusschere, Detroit vs. Central Mich.	Jan. 30, 1960
39	I	Keith Swagerty, Pacific vs. UC Santa Barbara	Mar. 5, 1965
39	II	Curtis Pritchett, St. Augustine vs. St. Paul's	Jan. 24, 1970
38		14 tied	

(Since 1973)

Reb.	Div.	Player, Team vs. Opponent	Date
42	II	Larry Gooding, St. Augustine's vs. Shaw	Jan. 12, 1974
36	III	Mark Veenstra, Calvin vs. Colorado St.-Pueblo	Feb. 3, 1976
36	III	Clinton Montford, Methodist vs. Warren Wilson	Jan. 21, 1989
36	III	Josh Hinz, Beloit vs. Grinnell	Feb. 4, 2006
35	III	Ayal Hod, Yeshiva vs. Vassar	Feb. 22, 1989
35	I	Larry Abney, Fresno St. vs. SMU	Feb. 17, 2000
34	I	David Vaughn, Oral Roberts vs. Brandeis	Jan. 8, 1973

Reb.	Div.	Player, Team vs. Opponent	Date
34	II	Major Jones, Albany St. (Ga.) vs. Valdosta St.	Jan. 23, 1975
34	II	Herman Harris, Mississippi Val. vs. Texas Southern	Jan. 12, 1976
34	III	Walt Edwards, Husson vs. Me.-Farmington	Feb. 24, 1976
33	II	Lee Roy Williams, Cal Poly Pomona vs. Wheaton (Ill.)	Dec. 15, 1973
33	II	Joe Dombrowski, St. Anselm vs. New Hampshire	Dec. 8, 1974
33	III	Willie Parr, LeMoyne-Owen vs. Southern U.	Jan. 10, 1976
33	II	Larry Williams, Pratt vs. Mercy	Jan. 22, 1977
33	III	Nick Harrington, Southern Vt. vs. Mitchell	Jan. 6, 2008
32	II	Marvin Webster, Morgan St. vs. South Carolina St.	Dec. 8, 1973
32	II	Earl Williams, Winston-Salem vs. N.C. Central	Dec. 13, 1973
32	II	Fred Petty, Southern N.H. vs. Curry	Jan. 28, 1974
32	II	George Wilson, Union (Ky.) vs. Southwestern	1974
32	II	Tony DuCros, Regis vs. Neb. Wesleyan	Feb. 28, 1975
32	I	Durand Macklin, LSU vs. Tulane	Nov. 26, 1976
32	II	Robert Clements, Jacksonville vs. Shorter	Jan. 12, 1977
32	II	Jervaughn Scales, Southern U. vs. Grambling	Feb. 7, 1994
31	II	Pete Harris, Stephen F. Austin vs. Texas A&M	Jan. 22, 1973
31	I	Jim Bradley, Northern Ill. vs. Milwaukee	Feb. 19, 1973
31	III	John Humphrie, Swarthmore vs. Ursinus	Dec. 8, 1973
31	II	Roy Smith, Kentucky St. vs. Union (Ky.)	Feb. 10, 1975
31	III	Larry Parker, Plattsburgh St. vs. Clarkson	Jan. 19, 1976
31	I	Calvin Natt, La.-Monroe vs. Ga. Southern	Dec. 29, 1976
31	II	Charles Wode, Mississippi Val. vs. Miss. Industrial	Dec. 10, 1977
31	III	Jon Ford, Norwich vs. Johnson St.	Feb. 16, 1982

ASSISTS

Ast.	Div.	Player, Team vs. Opponent	Date
34	III	David Arseneault, Grinnell vs. North Central (Minn.)	Dec. 8, 2007
26	III	Robert James, Kean vs. NJIT	Mar. 11, 1989
25	II	Ali Baaqar, Morris Brown vs. Albany St. (Ga.)	Jan. 26, 1991
25	II	Adrian Hutt, Metro St. vs. Sacramento St.	Feb. 9, 1991
24	II	Steve Ray, Bridgeport vs. Sacred Heart	Jan. 25, 1989
24	II	Steve Ray, Bridgeport vs. New Haven	Feb. 8, 1989
24	III	Adam Dzierzynski, Chapman vs. Amer. Indian Bible	Feb. 5, 1995
23	II	Steve Ray, Bridgeport vs. St. Anselm	Nov. 26, 1989
23	II	Jeff Duvall, Oakland City vs. St. Meinrad	Dec. 3, 1991
23	II	Todd Chappell, Texas Wesleyan vs. Texas Lutheran	Feb. 12, 2000
22	I	Tony Fairley, Charleston So. vs. Armstrong Atlantic	Feb. 9, 1987
22	I	Avery Johnson, Southern U. vs. Texas Southern	Jan. 25, 1988
22	I	Sherman Douglas, Syracuse vs. Providence	Jan. 28, 1989
22	I	Antonio Whitley, St. Augustine's vs. Shaw	Feb. 1, 1992
22	II	Ernest Jenkins, N.M. Highlands vs. Panhandle St.	Jan. 29, 1994
22	II	Darnell Johnson, Slippery Rock vs. Glenville	Dec. 6, 2007
22	II	Perrick Robinson, West Virginia St. vs. Bluefield St.	Feb. 21, 2008
21	I	Mark Wade, UNLV vs. Navy	Dec. 29, 1986
21	I	Kelvin Scarborough, New Mexico vs. Hawaii	Feb. 13, 1987
21	I	Anthony Manuel, Bradley vs. UC Irvine	Dec. 19, 1987
21	I	Avery Johnson, Southern U. vs. Alabama St.	Jan. 16, 1988
21	III	Ron Torgalski, Hamilton vs. Vassar	Jan. 28, 1989
21	III	Mark Cottom, Ferrum vs. Concord	Dec. 15, 1990
21	II	Candice Pickens, California (Pa.) vs. Slippery Rock	Feb. 8, 1995

BLOCKED SHOTS

Blk.	Div.	Player, Team vs. Opponent	Date
18	III	John Bunch, Lincoln (Pa.) vs. Valley Forge Christian	Dec. 13, 2003
18	III	John Bunch, Lincoln (Pa.) vs. New Jersey City	Jan. 19, 2004
16	III	Tory Black, NJIT vs. Polytechnic (N.Y.)	Feb. 5, 1997
16	I	Mickell Gladness, Alabama A&M vs. Texas Southern	Feb. 24, 2007
15	III	Erick Lidecis, Maritime (N.Y.) vs. Stevens Institute	Nov. 30, 1993
15	II	Mark Hensel, Pitt.-Johnstown vs. Slippery Rock	Jan. 22, 1994
15	III	Ira Nicholson, Mt. St. Vincent vs. Stevens Institute	Nov. 27, 1994
15	III	Roy Woods, Fontbonne vs. MacMurray	Jan. 26, 1995
15	III	Antoine Hyman, Keuka vs. Hobart	Feb. 21, 1996
15	III	Johnny Woods, Wesley vs. Salisbury	Feb. 14, 2000
14	I	David Robinson, Navy vs. UNC Wilmington	Jan. 4, 1986
14	I	Shawn Bradley, BYU vs. Eastern Ky.	Dec. 7, 1990
14	II	Maurice Barnett, Elizabeth City St. vs. Bowie St.	Feb. 3, 1994
14	III	Andrew South, NJIT vs. Stevens Institute	Feb. 14, 1994
14	II	Victorlus Payne, Lane vs. Talladega	Jan. 26, 1996
14	I	Roy Rogers, Alabama vs. Georgia	Feb. 10, 1996
14	I	Loren Woods, Arizona vs. Oregon	Feb. 3, 2000
14	III	Neil Edwards, York (N.Y.) vs. Lehman	Feb. 12, 2000
14	III	Johnny Woods, Wesley vs. Eastern	Jan. 17, 2001
14	III	Lester Prosper, Old Westbury vs. Mt. St. Mary's (N.Y.)	Jan. 26, 2008
13	I	Kevin Roberson, Vermont vs. New Hampshire	Jan. 9, 1992
13	I	Jim McIlvaine, Marquette vs. Northeastern Ill.	Dec. 9, 1992
13	II	Mark Hensel, Pitt.-Johnstown vs. Wheeling Jesuit	Jan. 31, 1994
13	I	Keith Closs, Central Conn. St. vs. St. Francis (Pa.)	Dec. 21, 1994
13	III	Damon Avinger, CCNY vs. St. Joseph's (N.Y.)	Jan. 8, 1996
13	III	Antoine Hyman, Keuka vs. Hobart	Jan. 8, 1997
13	III	Neil Edwards, York (N.Y.) vs. Brooklyn	Feb. 22, 2000
13	I	D'or Fischer, Northwestern St. vs. Texas St.	Jan. 22, 2001
13	I	Kyle Davis, Auburn vs. Miami (Fla.)	Mar. 14, 2001

Blk.	Div.	Player, Team vs. Opponent	Date
13	I	Wojciech Myrda, La.-Monroe vs. UTSA	Jan. 17, 2002
13	I	Anthony King, Miami (Fla.) vs. Fla. Atlantic	Nov. 29, 2004
13	I	Deng Gai, Fairfield vs. Siena	Jan. 22, 2005
13	II	Callistus Eziukwu, Grand Valley St. vs. Ferris St.	Feb. 7, 2005
13	II	Mervyn Clarke, Oakland City vs. Ind.-East	Nov. 15, 2006
13	I	Sean Williams, Boston College vs. Duquesne	Dec. 28, 2006
13	I	Joel Anthony, UNLV vs. TCU	Feb. 7, 2007

STEALS

Stl.	Div.	Player, Team vs. Opponent	Date
17	III	Matt Newton, Principia vs. Harris-Stowe	Jan. 4, 1994
17	II	Antonio Walls, Alabama A&M vs. Albany St. (Ga.)	Jan. 5, 1998
15	II	David Clark, Delta St. vs. LeMoyne-Owen	Nov. 25, 2006
14	III	Moses Jean-Pierre, Plymouth St. vs. Rivier	Dec. 7, 1993
13	I	Mookie Blaylock, Oklahoma vs. Centenary (La.)	Dec. 12, 1987
13	I	Mookie Blaylock, Oklahoma vs. Loyola Marymount	Dec. 17, 1988
13	III	John Gallogly, Salve Regina vs. Roger Williams	Feb. 10, 1997
13	III	Todd Lange, Pomona-Pitzer vs. LaSierra	Jan. 7, 1999
13	III	Daniel Martinez, McMurry vs. Concordia (Tex.)	Feb. 3, 2000
12	I	Kenny Robertson, Cleveland St. vs. Wagner	Dec. 3, 1988
12	III	Moses Jean-Pierre, Plymouth St. vs. Rhode Island Col.	Jan. 23, 1993
12	I	Terry Evans, Oklahoma vs. Florida A&M	Jan. 27, 1993
12	III	David Brown, Westfield St. vs. Albertus Magnus	Jan. 8, 1994
12	III	Barry Aranoff, Yeshiva vs. Purchase	Feb. 13, 1995
12	III	Jamal Elliott, Haverford vs. Gwynedd-Mercy	Jan. 15, 1996
12	III	Deron Black, Allegheny vs. Case Reserve	Jan. 17, 1996
12	III	Mario Thompson, Occidental vs. LIFE Bible	Nov. 21, 1998
12	III	Freddy Conyers, Mass.-Boston vs. Westfield St.	Dec. 10, 1998
12	II	Marche' Bearad, Ark.-Monticello vs. Christian Bros.	Feb. 8, 1999
12	II	Derrick Brown, Davis & Elkins vs. Ohio Valley	Feb. 9, 1999
12	I	Richard Duncan, Middle Tenn. vs. Eastern Ky.	Feb. 20, 1999
12	III	Daniel Martinez, McMurry vs. Ozarks (Ark.)	Dec. 2, 1999
12	III	Greg Brown, Albertus Magnus vs. Rivier	Feb. 3, 2000
12	II	Terrence Baxter, Pfeiffer vs. Livingstone	Nov. 22, 2000
12	I	Greedy Daniels, TCU vs. Ark.-Pine Bluff	Dec. 30, 2000
12	I	Jehiel Lewis, Navy vs. Bucknell	Jan. 12, 2002
12	III	Benny West, Howard Payne vs. Sul Ross St.	Dec. 13, 2003
12	III	Curtis Miller, Albertus Magnus vs. Emmanuel (Mass.)	Jan. 22, 2004
12	I	Carldwell Johnson, UAB vs. South Carolina St.	Nov. 27, 2005

Season Records

(Based on qualifiers for annual statistical championship)

POINTS

Player, Team (Division)	Season	G	FG	3FG	FT	Pts.
Pete Maravich, LSU (I)	1970	31	522	—	337	1,381
Earl Monroe, Winston-Salem (II)	1967	32	509	—	311	1,329
Travis Grant, Kentucky St. (II)	1972	33	539	—	226	1,304
Clarence "Bevo" Francis, Rio Grande (II)	1954	27	444	—	367	1,255
Bill Reigel, McNeese St. (II)	1956	36	425	—	370	1,220
Elvin Hayes, Houston (I)	1968	33	519	—	176	1,214
Frank Selvy, Furman (I)	1954	29	427	—	355	1,209
Pete Maravich, LSU (I)	1969	26	433	—	282	1,148
Pete Maravich, LSU (I)	1968	26	432	—	274	1,138
Bo Kimble, Loyola Marymount (I)	1990	32	404	92	231	1,131
Hersey Hawkins, Bradley (I)	1988	31	377	87	284	1,125
Austin Carr, Notre Dame (I)	1970	29	444	—	218	1,106
Austin Carr, Notre Dame (I)	1971	29	430	—	241	1,101
Otis Birdsong, Houston (I)	1977	36	452	—	186	1,090
Dwight Lamar, La.-Lafayette (I)	1972	29	429	—	196	1,054
Kevin Bradshaw, Alliant Int'l (I)	1991	28	358	60	278	1,054
Dwight Lamar, La.-Lafayette (II)	1971	29	424	—	196	1,044
Greg Grant, TCNJ (III)	1989	32	387	76	194	1,044
Dave Russell, Shepherd (III)	1975	32	394	—	249	1,037
Glenn Robinson, Purdue (I)	1994	34	368	79	215	1,030
Kyle Myrick, Lincoln (Pa.) (III)	2006	30	387	59	177	1,010
Oscar Robertson, Cincinnati (I)	1958	28	352	—	280	984
Oscar Robertson, Cincinnati (I)	1959	30	331	—	316	978
Rick Barry, Miami (Fla.) (I)	1965	26	340	—	221	973
Larry Bird, Indiana St. (I)	1979	34	376	—	221	973

SCORING AVERAGE

Player, Team (Division)	Season	G	FG	3FG	FT	Pts.	Avg.
Clarence "Bevo" Francis, Rio Grande (II)	1954	27	444	—	367	1,255	46.5
Pete Maravich, LSU (I)	1970	31	522	—	337	1,381	44.5
Pete Maravich, LSU (I)	1969	26	433	—	282	1,148	44.2
Pete Maravich, LSU (I)	1968	26	432	—	274	1,138	43.8
Earl Glass, Miss. Industrial (II)	1963	19	322	—	171	815	42.9

Player, Team (Division)	Season	G	FG	3FG	FT	Pts.	Avg.
Frank Selvy, Furman (I)	1954	29	427	—	355	1,209	41.7
Earl Monroe, Winston-Salem (II)	1967	32	509	—	311	1,329	41.5
John Rinka, Kenyon (II)	1970	23	354	—	234	942	41.0
Willie Shaw, Lane (II)	1964	18	303	—	121	727	40.4
Johnny Neumann, Mississippi (I)	1971	23	366	—	191	923	40.1
Travis Grant, Kentucky St. (II)	1972	33	539	—	226	1,304	39.5
Thales McReynolds, Miles (II)	1965	18	294	—	118	706	39.2
Bob Johnson, Fitchburg St. (II)	1963	18	213	—	277	703	39.1
Roger Kuss, Wis.-River Falls (II)	1953	21	291	—	235	817	38.9
Freeman Williams, Portland St. (I)	1977	26	417	—	176	1,010	38.8
Billy McGill, Utah (I)	1962	26	394	—	221	1,009	38.8
Calvin Murphy, Niagara (I)	1968	24	337	—	242	916	38.2
Austin Carr, Notre Dame (I)	1970	29	444	—	218	1,106	38.1
Austin Carr, Notre Dame (I)	1971	29	430	—	241	1,101	38.0
Kevin Bradshaw, Alliant Int'l (I)	1991	28	358	60	278	1,054	37.6
Rick Barry, Miami (Fla.) (I)	1965	26	340	—	221	973	37.4
Steve Diekmann, Grinnell (III)	1995	20	223	137	162	745	37.3
Florindo Vieira, Quinnipiac (II)	1954	14	191	—	138	520	37.1
Elvin Hayes, Houston (I)	1968	33	519	—	176	1,214	36.8
Marshall Rogers, Tex.-Pan American (I)	1976	25	361	—	197	919	36.8

FIELD-GOAL PERCENTAGE

Player, Team (Division)	Season	G	FG	FGA	Pct.
Travis Weiss, St. John's (Minn.) (III)	1994	26	160	209	76.6
Brian Schmitting, Ripon (III)	2006	21	122	160	76.3
Garrett Siler, Augusta St. (II)	2008	34	211	277	76.2
Pete Metzelaars, Wabash (III)	1982	28	271	360	75.3
Todd Linder, Tampa (II)	1987	32	282	375	75.2
Maurice Stafford, North Ala. (II)	1984	34	198	264	75.0
Tony Rychlec, Mass. Maritime (II)	1981	25	233	311	74.9
Matthew Cornegay, Tuskegee (II)	1982	29	208	278	74.8
Steve Johnson, Oregon St. (I)	1981	28	235	315	74.6
Callistus Eziukwu, Grand Valley St. (II)	2005	28	157	213	73.7
Brian Moten, West Ga. (II)	1992	26	141	192	73.4
Ed Phillips, Alabama A&M (II)	1968	22	154	210	73.3
Tony Rychlec, Mass. Maritime (II)	1982	20	193	264	73.1
Russ Newman, Menlo (III)	1991	26	130	178	73.0
Ed Owens, Hampden-Sydney (III)	1979	24	140	192	72.9
Ray Strozier, Central Mo. (II)	1980	28	142	195	72.8
Harold Booker, Cheyney (II)	1965	24	144	198	72.7
Chad Scott, California (Pa.) (II)	1994	30	178	245	72.7
Scott Baxter, Capital (III)	1991	26	164	226	72.6
Maurice Woods, SUNY Potsdam (III)	1982	30	203	280	72.5
Tom Schurfranz, Bellarmine (II)	1991	30	245	339	72.3
Marv Lewis, Southampton (II)	1969	24	271	375	72.3
Earl Keith, Stony Brook (III)	1979	24	164	227	72.2
Louis Newsome, North Ala. (II)	1988	29	192	266	72.2
Pete Metzelaars, Wabash (III)	1981	25	204	283	72.1
Ed Phillips, Alabama A&M (II)	1971	24	159	221	71.9
Brandon King, Rowan (III)	2005	26	141	196	71.9
Jon Rosner, Yeshiva (III)	1991	22	141	196	71.9

THREE-POINT FIELD GOALS MADE

Player, Team (Division)	Season	G	3FG
Jeff Clement, Grinnell (III)	1998	22	186
Alex Williams, Sacramento St. (II)	1988	30	167
Jeff Clement, Grinnell (III)	1999	22	166
Stephen Curry, Davidson (I)	2008	36	162
Markus Hallgrimson, Mont. St.-Billings (II)	2000	26	160
Darrin Fitzgerald, Butler (I)	1987	28	158
Ed Brands, Grinnell (III)	1996	24	158
Billy Shivers, Redlands (III)	2004	25	153
Freddie Banks, UNLV (I)	1987	39	152
Eric Kline, Northern St. (II)	1994	33	148
Eric Kline, Northern St. (II)	1995	30	148
Yandel Brown, Columbus St. (II)	2005	32	148
Cameron Munoz, Mont. St.-Billings (II)	2006	28	147
Randy Rutherford, Oklahoma St. (I)	1995	37	146
Chris Peterson, Eureka (III)	1994	31	145
Robert McKiver, Houston (I)	2008	34	145
Amir Mazarei, Redlands (III)	2007	23	143
Robert Vaden, UAB (I)	2008	33	142
Dennis Stanton, Ursinus (III)	2004	27	140
Terrence Woods, Florida A&M (I)	2004	31	140
Mike Taylor, West Virginia St. (II)	2004	32	140
John Grotberg, Grinnell (III)	2008	24	140
Shawn Pughsley, Central Okla. (II)	1998	32	139
Terrence Woods, Florida A&M (I)	2003	28	139
J.J. Redick, Duke (I)	2006	36	139

THREE-POINT FIELD GOALS MADE PER GAME

Player, Team (Division)	Season	G	3FG	Avg.
Jeff Clement, Grinnell (III)	1998	22	186	8.45
Jeff Clement, Grinnell (III)	1999	22	166	7.55
Steve Diekmann, Grinnell (III)	1995	20	137	6.85
Ed Brands, Grinnell (III)	1996	24	158	6.58
Ed Brands, Grinnell (III)	1995	20	129	6.45
Amir Mazarei, Redlands (III)	2007	23	143	6.22
Markus Hallgrimson, Mont. St.-Billings (II)	2000	26	160	6.15
Billy Shivers, Redlands (III)	2004	25	153	6.12
John Grotberg, Grinnell (III)	2008	24	140	5.83
Amir Mazarei, Redlands (III)	2006	24	138	5.75
Steve Nordlund, Grinnell (III)	2002	24	137	5.71
Darrin Fitzgerald, Butler (I)	1987	28	158	5.64
Steve Diekmann, Grinnell (III)	1994	21	117	5.57
Alex Williams, Sacramento St. (II)	1988	30	167	5.57
Chris Jans, Loras (III)	1991	25	133	5.32
Woody Piirto, Grinnell (III)	1999	22	117	5.32
Cameron Munoz, Mont. St.-Billings (II)	2006	28	147	5.25
John Grotberg, Grinnell (III)	2006	23	120	5.22
Dennis Stanton, Ursinus (III)	2004	27	140	5.19
Jeff Clement, Grinnell (III)	1997	22	113	5.14
Mark Bedell, Fisk (III)	1997	19	97	5.11
Jason Garrow, Augustana (S.D.) (II)	1992	27	135	5.00
David Bailey, Concordia Chicago (III)	1994	24	120	5.00
Terrence Woods, Florida A&M (I)	2003	28	139	4.96
Eric Kline, Northern St. (II)	1995	30	148	4.93

THREE-POINT FIELD-GOAL PERCENTAGE

Player, Team (Division)	Season	G	3FG	3FGA	Pct.
Reggie James, NJIT (III)	1989	29	59	88	67.0
Ray Lee, Hampton (II)	1988	24	39	60	65.0
Glenn Tropf, Holy Cross (I)	1988	29	52	82	63.4
Sean Wightman, Western Mich. (I)	1992	30	48	76	63.2
Chris Miles, NJIT (III)	1987	26	41	65	63.1
Steve Hood, Winston-Salem (II)	1988	28	42	67	62.7
Chris Miles, NJIT (III)	1989	29	46	75	61.3
Matt Miota, Lawrence (III)	1990	22	33	54	61.1
Mike Bachman, Alma (III)	1991	26	46	76	60.5
Mark Wiley, Fort Hays St. (II)	1990	29	49	81	60.5
Aaron Fehler, Oakland City (II)	1995	26	73	121	60.3
Keith Jennings, East Tenn. St. (I)	1991	33	84	142	59.2
Aaron Baker, Mississippi Col. (II)	1989	27	69	117	59.0
Dave Calloway, Monmouth (I)	1989	28	48	82	58.5
Walter Hurd, Johnson C. Smith (II)	1989	27	49	84	58.3
Matt Hopson, Oakland City (II)	1996	31	84	145	57.9
Ray Magee, Richard Stockton (III)	1988	26	41	71	57.7
Keith Orchard, Whitman (III)	1988	26	42	73	57.5
Jon Bryant, St. Cloud St. (II)	1996	27	54	94	57.4
Adam Harness, Oakland City (II)	1997	26	39	68	57.4
Steve Kerr, Arizona (I)	1988	38	114	199	57.3
Reginald Jones, Prairie View (I)	1987	28	64	112	57.1
Brian O'Donnell, Rutgers-Camden (III)	1988	24	65	114	57.0
Erick Hunt, Methodist (III)	1989	27	45	79	57.0
Eric Harris, Bishop (III)	1987	26	91	160	56.9

FREE-THROW PERCENTAGE

Player, Team (Division)	Season	G	FT	FTA	Pct.
Paul Cluxton, Northern Ky. (II)	1997	35	94	94	100.0
Blake Ahearn, Missouri St. (I)	2004	33	117	120	97.5
Jack Linton, St. Martin's (II)	2008	27	162	168	96.4
Korey Coon, Ill. Wesleyan (III)	2000	25	157	163	96.3
Derek Raivio, Gonzaga (I)	2007	34	148	154	96.1
Ryan Junghans, Hood (III)	2008	26	118	123	95.9
Craig Collins, Penn St. (I)	1985	27	94	98	95.9
Nick Wilkins, Coe (III)	2003	26	66	69	95.7
Chanse Young, Manchester (III)	1998	25	65	68	95.6
Tomas Rimkus, Pace (II)	1997	25	65	68	95.6
Andy Enfield, Johns Hopkins (III)	1991	29	123	129	95.3
J.J. Redick, Duke (I)	2004	37	143	150	95.3
Chris Carideo, Eureka (III)	1992	26	80	84	95.2
Yudi Teichman, Yeshiva (III)	1989	21	119	125	95.2
Steve Drabyn, Belmont (I)	2003	29	78	82	95.1
Rod Foster, UCLA (I)	1982	27	95	100	95.0
C.J. Cowgill, Chaminade (II)	2001	22	113	119	95.0
Clay McKnight, Pacific (I)	2000	24	74	78	94.9
Matt Logie, Lehigh (I)	2003	28	91	96	94.8
A.J. Graves, Butler (I)	2007	35	145	153	94.8
Joseph Chatman, Lesley (III)	2007	27	126	133	94.7
Blake Ahearn, Missouri St. (I)	2005	32	90	95	94.7
Brett Davis, Wis.-Oshkosh (III)	1998	27	72	76	94.7
Joe Bueckers, Concordia-M'head (III)	2004	26	71	75	94.7
Mark Giovino, Babson (III)	1997	28	86	91	94.5

REBOUNDS

Player, Team (Division)	Season	G	Reb.
Elmore Smith, Kentucky St. (II)	1972	33	799
Marvin Webster, Morgan St. (II)	1974	33	740
Walt Dukes, Seton Hall (I)	1953	33	734
Maurice Stokes, St. Francis (Pa.) (II)	1955	28	726
Frank Stronczek, American Int'l (II)	1966	26	717
Maurice Stokes, St. Francis (Pa.) (II)	1954	26	689
Jim Ahrens, Buena Vista (II)	1962	28	682
Elmore Smith, Kentucky St. (II)	1970	30	682
R.C. Owens, Albertson (II)	1954	25	677
Wilbert Jones, Albany St. (Ga.) (II)	1969	28	670
Tom Gola, La Salle (I)	1954	30	652
Leroy Wright, Pacific (I)	1959	26	652
Jim Smith, Steubenville (II)	1957	26	651
Marvin Webster, Morgan St. (II)	1973	28	650
Tom Hart, Middlebury (II)	1955	22	649
Charlie Tyra, Louisville (I)	1956	29	645
Jackie Jackson, Virginia Union (II)	1961	26	641
Vincent White, Savannah St. (II)	1972	29	633
Paul Silas, Creighton (I)	1964	29	631
Bill Thieben, Hofstra (II)	1955	26	627
Lucious Jackson, Tex.-Pan American (II)	1963	32	626
Elvin Hayes, Houston (I)	1968	33	624
Vincent White, Savannah St. (II)	1970	27	624
Artis Gilmore, Jacksonville (I)	1970	28	621
Bill Thieben, Hofstra (II)	1954	24	620
Tom Hart, Middlebury (II)	1956	21	620

(Since 1973)

Player, Team (Division)	Season	G	Reb.
Marvin Webster, Morgan St. (II)	1974	33	740
Marvin Webster, Morgan St. (II)	1973	28	650
Major Jones, Albany St. (Ga.) (II)	1975	27	608
Marvin Barnes, Providence (I)	1974	32	597
Joe Manley, Bowie St. (III)	1976	29	579
Marvin Barnes, Providence (I)	1973	30	571
Earl Williams, Winston-Salem (II)	1974	26	553
John Jordan, Southern Me. (III)	1978	29	536
Charles Oakley, Virginia Union (III)	1985	31	535
Lawrence Johnson, Prairie View (II)	1974	23	519
Andre Means, Sacred Heart (II)	1977	32	516
Major Jones, Albany St. (Ga.) (II)	1975	25	513
Kermit Washington, American (I)	1973	25	511
Bill Walton, UCLA (I)	1973	30	506
Larry Bird, Indiana St. (I)	1979	34	505
Harvey Jones, Alabama St. (II)	1974	28	503
Larry Kenon, Memphis (I)	1973	30	501
Akeem Olajuwon, Houston (I)	1984	37	500
Andre Means, Sacred Heart (II)	1978	30	493
Ricky Mahorn, Hampton (II)	1980	31	490
Howard Shockley, Salisbury (III)	1974	27	482
Rob Roesch, Staten Island (II)	1989	31	482
Keith Woolfolk, Upper Iowa (III)	1978	26	479
Leonard Robinson, Tennessee St. (II)	1974	28	478
Major Jones, Albany St. (Ga.) (II)	1976	24	475

REBOUND AVERAGE

Player, Team (Division)	Season	G	Reb.	Avg.
Tom Hart, Middlebury (II)	1956	21	620	29.5
Tom Hart, Middlebury (II)	1955	22	649	29.5
Frank Stronczek, American Int'l (II)	1966	26	717	27.6
R.C. Owens, Albertson (II)	1954	25	677	27.1
Maurice Stokes, St. Francis (Pa.) (II)	1954	26	689	26.5
Ellerbe Neal, Wofford (II)	1953	23	609	26.5
Roman Turmon, Clark Atlanta (II)	1954	23	602	26.2
Pat Callahan, Lewis (II)	1955	20	523	26.2
Hank Brown, Mass.-Lowell (II)	1966	19	496	26.1
Maurice Stokes, St. Francis (Pa.) (II)	1955	28	726	25.9
Bill Thieben, Hofstra (II)	1954	24	620	25.8
Dean Sandifer, Lakeland (II)	1965	23	592	25.7
Charlie Slack, Marshall (I)	1955	21	538	25.6
Charles Wrinn, Trinity (Conn.) (II)	1952	19	486	25.6
Leroy Wright, Pacific (I)	1959	26	652	25.1
Jim Smith, Steubenville (II)	1957	26	651	25.0
Marv Becker, Widener (II)	1958	18	450	25.0
Tony Williams, St. Francis (Me.) (II)	1971	24	599	25.0
Ernie Brock, Virginia St. (II)	1964	24	597	24.9
Russell Jackson, Southern U. (II)	1970	22	544	24.7
Gerry Govan, St. Mary's (Kan.) (II)	1963	18	445	24.7
Merv Shorr, CCNY (II)	1954	18	444	24.7
Art Quimby, Connecticut (I)	1955	25	611	24.4
Charlie Slack, Marshall (I)	1956	22	520	23.6
Ed Conlin, Fordham (I)	1953	26	612	23.5

Player, Team (Division) (Since 1973)	Season	G	Reb.	Avg.
Marvin Webster, Morgan St. (II)	1973	28	650	23.2
Lawrence Johnson, Prairie View (II)	1974	23	519	22.6
Major Jones, Albany St. (Ga.) (II)	1975	27	608	22.5
Marvin Webster, Morgan St. (II)	1974	33	740	22.4
Earl Williams, Winston-Salem (II)	1974	26	553	21.3
Major Jones, Albany St. (Ga.) (II)	1975	25	513	20.5
Kermit Washington, American (I)	1973	25	511	20.4
Larry Gooding, St. Augustine's (II)	1974	22	443	20.1
Joe Manley, Bowie St. (III)	1976	29	579	20.0
Fred Petty, Southern N.H. (III)	1974	22	436	19.8
Major Jones, Albany St. (Ga.) (II)	1976	24	475	19.8
Larry Williams, Pratt (III)	1977	24	457	19.0
Marvin Barnes, Providence (I)	1973	30	571	19.0
Calvin Robinson, Mississippi Val. (II)	1976	23	432	18.8
Larry Williams, Pratt (III)	1977	17	318	18.7
Larry Parker, Plattsburgh St. (III)	1975	23	430	18.7
Marvin Barnes, Providence (I)	1974	32	597	18.7
Charles Greer, Thomas (III)	1977	17	318	18.7
John Jordan, Southern Me. (III)	1978	29	536	18.5
Keith Woolfolk, Upper Iowa (III)	1978	26	479	18.4
Michael Stubbs, Trinity (Conn.) (III)	1990	22	398	18.1
Mike Taylor, Pratt (III)	1978	23	414	18.0
Harvey Jones, Alabama St. (II)	1974	28	503	18.0
Walt Edwards, Husson (III)	1976	26	467	18.0
Scott Mountz, California (Pa.) (II)	1978	24	431	18.0

ASSISTS

Player, Team (Division)	Season	G	Ast.
Mark Wade, UNLV (I)	1987	38	406
Steve Ray, Bridgeport (II)	1989	32	400
Avery Johnson, Southern U. (I)	1988	30	399
Robert James, Kean (III)	1989	29	391
Steve Ray, Bridgeport (II)	1990	33	385
Anthony Manuel, Bradley (I)	1988	31	373
Tony Smith, Pfeiffer (II)	1992	35	349
Avery Johnson, Southern U. (I)	1987	31	333
Mark Jackson, St. John's (N.Y.) (I)	1986	32	328
Sherman Douglas, Syracuse (I)	1989	38	326
Tennyson Whitted, Ramapo (III)	2002	29	319
Greg Anthony, UNLV (I)	1991	35	310
Sam Crawford, New Mexico St. (I)	1993	34	310
Luke Cooper, Alas. Anchorage (II)	2008	35	310
Reid Gettys, Houston (I)	1984	37	309
Jim Ferrer, Bentley (II)	1989	31	309
Rob Paternostro, Southern N.H. (II)	1995	33	309
Carl Golson, Loyola (Ill.) (I)	1985	33	305
Craig Neal, Georgia Tech (I)	1988	32	303
Keith Jennings, East Tenn. St. (I)	1991	33	301
Brian Gregory, Oakland (II)	1989	28	300
Chris Corchiani, North Carolina St. (I)	1991	31	299
Doug Gottlieb, Oklahoma St. (I)	1999	34	299
Charles Jordan, Erskine (II)	1992	34	298
Keith Jennings, East Tenn. St. (I)	1990	34	297

ASSIST AVERAGE

Player, Team (Division)	Season	G	Ast.	Avg.
Robert James, Kean (III)	1989	29	391	13.48
Avery Johnson, Southern U. (I)	1988	30	399	13.30
Steve Ray, Bridgeport (II)	1989	32	400	12.50
Anthony Manuel, Bradley (I)	1988	31	373	12.03
Steve Ray, Bridgeport (II)	1990	33	385	11.66
Demetri Beekman, Assumption (II)	1993	23	264	11.47
Albert Kirchner, Mt. St. Vincent (III)	1990	24	267	11.12
Tennyson Whitted, Ramapo (III)	2002	29	319	11.00
Ernest Jenkins, N.M. Highlands (II)	1995	27	291	10.78
Avery Johnson, Southern U. (I)	1987	31	333	10.74
Brian Gregory, Oakland (II)	1989	28	300	10.71
Zack Whiting, Chaminade (II)	2007	27	289	10.70
Mark Wade, UNLV (I)	1987	38	406	10.68
Ron Torgalski, Hamilton (III)	1989	26	275	10.57
David Arseneault, Grinnell (III)	2008	21	219	10.43
Brent Schremp, Slippery Rock (II)	1995	25	259	10.36
Louis Adams, Rust (III)	1989	22	227	10.31
Ernest Jenkins, N.M. Highlands (II)	1994	27	277	10.31
Adrian Hutt, Metro St. (II)	1991	28	285	10.17
Nelson Haggerty, Baylor (I)	1995	28	284	10.14
Tony Smith, Pfeiffer (II)	1992	35	349	9.97
Jim Ferrer, Bentley (II)	1989	31	309	9.96
Glenn Williams, Holy Cross (I)	1989	28	278	9.92
Eric Johnson, Coe (III)	1991	24	238	9.91
Ryan Nelson, Grand Canyon (II)	2006	27	263	9.74
Todd Chappell, Texas Wesleyan (II)	2000	27	263	9.74

INDIVIDUAL COLLEGIATE

BLOCKED SHOTS

Player, Team (Division)	Season	G	Blk.
David Robinson, Navy (I)	1986	35	207
Tory Black, NJIT (III)	1997	26	198
Shawn James, Northeastern (I)	2006	30	196
Neil Edwards, York (N.Y.) (III)	2000	26	193
Ira Nicholson, Mt. St. Vincent (III)	1995	28	188
Mickell Gladness, Alabama A&M (I)	2007	30	188
Adonal Foyle, Colgate (I)	1997	28	180
Keith Closs, Central Conn. St. (I)	1996	28	178
Shawn Bradley, BYU (I)	1991	34	177
John Bunch, Lincoln (Pa.) (III)	2004	25	173
Wojciech Mydra, La.-Monroe (I)	2002	32	172
Ryan McLemore, Edinboro (II)	2008	31	170
Alonzo Mourning, Georgetown (I)	1989	34	169
Stephane Lasme, Massachusetts (I)	2007	33	168
Shacun Malave, City Tech (III)	2004	28	167
Adonal Foyle, Colgate (I)	1996	29	165
Deng Gai, Fairfield (I)	2005	30	165
Ira Nicholson, Mt. St. Vincent (III)	1996	27	163
Justin Williams, Wyoming (I)	2006	30	163
Ken Johnson, Ohio St. (I)	2000	30	161
Alonzo Mourning, Georgetown (I)	1992	32	160
Shaquille O'Neal, LSU (I)	1992	30	157
James Doyle, Concord (II)	1998	30	157
Jarvis Varnado, Mississippi St. (I)	2008	34	157
Roy Rogers, Alabama (I)	1996	32	156
Emeka Okafor, Connecticut (I)	2003	33	156

BLOCKED-SHOT AVERAGE

Player, Team (Division)	Season	G	Blk.	Avg.
Tory Black, NJIT (III)	1997	26	198	7.62
Neil Edwards, York (N.Y.) (III)	2000	26	193	7.42
John Bunch, Lincoln (Pa.) (III)	2004	25	173	6.92
Ira Nicholson, Mt. St. Vincent (III)	1995	28	188	6.71
Shawn James, Northeastern (I)	2006	30	196	6.53
Adonal Foyle, Colgate (I)	1997	28	180	6.43
Keith Closs, Central Conn. St. (I)	1996	28	178	6.36
Ira Nicholson, Mt. St. Vincent (III)	1997	24	151	6.29
Ira Nicholson, Mt. St. Vincent (III)	1996	27	163	6.04
Shacun Malave, City Tech (III)	2004	28	167	5.96
David Robinson, Navy (I)	1986	35	207	5.91
Antoine Hyman, Keuka (III)	1997	26	148	5.69
Adonal Foyle, Colgate (I)	1996	29	165	5.69
Neil Edwards, York (N.Y.) (III)	1999	26	144	5.54
Deng Gai, Fairfield (I)	2005	30	165	5.50
Johnny Woods, Wesley (II)	2000	24	132	5.50
Ryan McLemore, Edinboro (II)	2008	31	170	5.48
Shawn James, Northeastern (I)	2005	25	136	5.44
Justin Williams, Wyoming (I)	2006	30	163	5.43
Wojciech Mydra, La.-Monroe (I)	2002	32	172	5.38
Ken Johnson, Ohio St. (I)	2000	30	161	5.37
Keith Closs, Central Conn. St. (I)	1995	26	139	5.35
Antonio Harvey, Pfeiffer (II)	1993	29	155	5.34
Antoine Hyman, Keuka (III)	1996	25	131	5.24
James Doyle, Concord (II)	1998	30	157	5.23
Shaquille O'Neal, LSU (I)	1992	30	157	5.23

STEALS

Player, Team (Division)	Season	G	Stl.
Moses Jean-Pierre, Plymouth St. (III)	1994	30	189
Daniel Martinez, McMurry (III)	2000	29	178
Desmond Cambridge, Alabama A&M (I)	2002	29	160
Mookie Blaylock, Oklahoma (I)	1988	39	150
Purvis Presha, Stillman (III)	1996	25	144
Aldwin Ware, Florida A&M (I)	1988	29	142
Darron Brittman, Chicago St. (I)	1986	28	139
J.R. Gamble, Queens (N.C.) (II)	2001	32	139
John Linehan, Providence (I)	2002	31	139
Nadav Henefeld, Connecticut (I)	1990	37	138
Matt Newton, Principia (III)	1994	25	138
Tennyson Whitted, Ramapo (III)	2002	29	138
John Gallogly, Salve Regina (III)	1997	24	137
Mookie Blaylock, Oklahoma (I)	1989	35	131
Ronn McMahon, Eastern Wash. (I)	1990	29	130
Wayne Copeland, Lynn (II)	2000	26	129
Scott Clarke, Utica (III)	1995	24	126
Greg Dean, Concordia-M'head (III)	1997	23	126
Elbie Murphy, St. Joseph's (Me.) (III)	2007	30	126
Wayne Copeland, Lynn (II)	1999	31	125
Obie Trotter, Alabama A&M (I)	2005	32	125
Japhet McNeil, Bridgeport (II)	2007	31	125
Marty Johnson, Towson (I)	1988	30	124

Player, Team (Division)	Season	G	Stl.
Allen Iverson, Georgetown (I)	1996	37	124
Eric Coley, Tulsa (I)	2000	37	123
Deron Black, Allegheny (III)	1996	27	123

STEAL AVERAGE

Player, Team (Division)	Season	G	Stl.	Avg.
Moses Jean-Pierre, Plymouth St. (III)	1994	30	189	6.30
Daniel Martinez, McMurry (III)	2000	29	178	6.14
Purvis Presha, Stillman (III)	1996	25	144	5.76
John Gallogly, Salve Regina (III)	1997	24	137	5.71
Matt Newton, Principia (III)	1994	25	138	5.52
Desmond Cambridge, Alabama A&M (I)	2002	29	160	5.52
Barry Aranoff, Yeshiva (III)	1995	22	121	5.50
Greg Dean, Concordia-M'head (III)	1997	23	126	5.48
John Gallogly, Salve Regina (III)	1998	23	121	5.26
Scott Clarke, Utica (III)	1995	24	126	5.25
Darron Brittman, Chicago St. (I)	1986	28	139	4.96
Wayne Copeland, Lynn (II)	2000	26	129	4.96
Joel Heckendorf, Martin Luther (III)	1996	17	84	4.94
Aldwin Ware, Florida A&M (I)	1988	29	142	4.90
David Brown, Westfield St. (III)	1994	25	122	4.88
Ivo Moyano, Polytechnic (N.Y.) (III)	1994	19	91	4.78
Tennyson Whitted, Ramapo (III)	2002	29	138	4.76
Mario Thompson, Occidental (III)	1999	24	114	4.75
Benny West, Howard Payne (III)	2004	25	116	4.64
Keith Darden, Concordia (Tex.) (III)	2001	24	111	4.63
Moses Jean-Pierre, Plymouth St. (III)	1993	25	114	4.56
Deron Black, Allegheny (III)	1996	27	123	4.56
Scott Clark, Utica (III)	1996	26	118	4.54
John Morris, Bluefield St. (II)	1994	23	104	4.52
Devlin Herring, Pitt.-Johnstown (II)	1997	27	122	4.52

ASSIST TO TURNOVER RATIO

Player, Team (Division)	Season	G	Ast.	TO	Ratio
Ross Nakamura, Whitworth (III)	2008	27	128	30	4.27
Kyle Couvion, Christian Bros. (II)	2008	32	122	32	3.81
Cliff Clinkscales, DePaul (I)	2008	30	123	34	3.62
Luke Cooper, Alas. Anchorage (II)	2008	35	310	87	3.56
Jay Greene, UMBC (I)	2008	33	236	68	3.47
Jesse Clark, Minn. St. Mankato (II)	2008	29	125	36	3.47
Max Kaplan, Rochester (N.Y.) (III)	2008	28	122	36	3.39
Ben Fischer, Winona St. (II)	2008	37	116	35	3.31
Travis Whipple, Winona St. (II)	2008	39	121	37	3.27
D'Juan Tucker, Va. Wesleyan (III)	2008	30	111	35	3.17
Ronnie Means, Fairmont St. (II)	2008	29	238	76	3.13
Jermaine Beal, Vanderbilt (I)	2008	34	158	51	3.10
David Arseneault, Grinnell (III)	2008	21	219	71	3.08
Nick Perioli, Oswego St. (III)	2008	29	159	52	3.06
Dusty Wabiszewski, St. Cloud St. (II)	2008	28	189	63	3.00
DeAndre Bray, Jacksonville St. (I)	2008	29	185	62	2.98
Reece Freeman, Mass.-Dartmouth (III)	2008	29	222	75	2.96
Jared Laverdiere, Maryville (Tenn.) (III)	2008	27	91	31	2.94
Matt Bauscher, Boise St. (I)	2008	33	105	36	2.92
Timmy Crowell, Fort Lewis (II)	2008	30	206	71	2.90
Corey Fava, Roger Williams (III)	2008	28	87	30	2.90
Justin Kovac, Penn St.-Behrend (III)	2008	29	110	38	2.89
Jason Horton, Missouri (I)	2008	29	94	33	2.85
Drew Neitzel, Michigan St. (I)	2008	36	145	51	2.84
Khalifa El-Amin, Wis.-Stevens Point (III)	2008	29	91	32	2.84

Career Records

POINTS

Player, Team (Division)	Last Season	Yrs.	G	FG	3FG	FT	Pts.
Travis Grant, Kentucky St. (II)	1972	4	121	1,760	—	525	4,045
Bob Hopkins, Grambling (II)	1956	4	126	1,403	—	953	3,759
Pete Maravich, LSU (I)	1970	3	83	1,387	—	893	3,667
Dwight Lamar, La.-Lafayette (II & I)	1973	4	112	1,445	—	603	3,493
Tony Smith, Pfeiffer (II)	1992	4	126	1,150	431	619	3,350
Earnest Lee, Clark Atlanta (II)	1987	4	115	1,270	35	723	3,298
Joe Miller, Alderson-Broaddus (II)	1957	4	129	1,082	—	1,130	3,294
John Rinka, Kenyon (II)	1970	4	99	1,261	—	729	3,251
Freeman Williams, Portland St. (I)	1978	4	106	1,369	—	511	3,249
Lionel Simmons, La Salle (I)	1990	4	131	1,244	56	673	3,217
Dick Barnett, Tennessee St. (II)	1959	4	136	1,312	—	585	3,209
Alphonso Ford, Mississippi Val. (I)	1993	4	109	1,121	333	590	3,165
Willie Scott, Alabama St. (II)	1969	4	103	1,277	—	601	3,155
Harry Kelly, Texas Southern (I)	1983	4	110	1,234	—	598	3,066
Johnnie Allen, Bethune-Cookman (II)	1969	4	111	1,306	—	446	3,058

Player, Team (Division)	Last Season	Yrs.	G	FG	3FG	FT	Pts.
Keydren Clark, St. Peter's (I)	2006	4	118	967	435	689	3,058
Bennie Swain, Texas Southern (II)	1958	4	137	1,157	—	694	3,008
Hersey Hawkins, Bradley (I)	1988	4	125	1,100	118	690	3,008
Rich Fuqua, Oral Roberts (II & I)	1973	4	111	1,273	—	458	3,004
Lambert Shell, Bridgeport (II)	1992	4	132	1,102	22	775	3,001
Oscar Robertson, Cincinnati (I)	1960	3	88	1,052	—	869	2,973
Carl Hartman, Alderson-Broaddus (II)	1955	4	118	1,124	—	711	2,959
Danny Manning, Kansas (I)	1988	4	147	1,216	10	509	2,951
Andre Foreman, Salisbury (III)	1992	5	109	1,141	68	592	2,940
Earl Monroe, Winston-Salem (II)	1967	4	110	1,158	—	619	2,935

SCORING AVERAGE
(Minimum 1,500 points)

Player, Team (Division)	Last Season	Yrs.	G	FG	3FG	FT	Pts.	Avg.
Pete Maravich, LSU (I)	1970	3	83	1,387	—	893	3,667	44.2
Austin Carr, Notre Dame (I)	1971	3	74	1,017	—	526	2,560	34.6
Oscar Robertson, Cincinnati (I)	1960	3	88	1,052	—	869	2,973	33.8
Travis Grant, Kentucky St. (II)	1972	4	121	1,760	—	525	4,045	33.4
Calvin Murphy, Niagara (I)	1970	3	77	947	—	654	2,548	33.1
John Rinka, Kenyon (II)	1970	4	99	1,261	—	729	3,251	32.8
Dwain Govan, Bishop (III)	1975	2	55	750	—	305	1,805	32.8
Florindo Vieira, Quinnipiac (II)	1957	4	69	761	—	741	2,263	32.8
Dwight Lamar, La.-Lafayette (I)	1973	2	57	768	—	326	1,862	32.7
Frank Selvy, Furman (I)	1954	3	78	922	—	694	2,538	32.5
Rick Mount, Purdue (I)	1970	3	72	910	—	503	2,323	32.3
Darrell Floyd, Furman (I)	1956	3	71	868	—	545	2,281	32.1
Nick Werkman, Seton Hall (I)	1964	3	71	812	—	649	2,273	32.0
Willie Humes, Idaho St. (I)	1971	2	48	565	—	380	1,510	31.5
William Averitt, Pepperdine (I)	1973	2	48	615	—	311	1,541	31.4
Elgin Baylor, Albertson/Seattle (I)	1958	3	80	956	—	588	2,500	31.3
Willie Shaw, Lane (II)	1964	4	76	960	—	459	2,379	31.3
Mike Davis, Virginia Union (II)	1969	4	89	1,014	—	730	2,758	31.0
Elvin Hayes, Houston (I)	1968	3	93	1,215	—	454	2,884	31.0
Freeman Williams, Portland St. (I)	1978	4	106	1,369	—	511	3,249	30.7
Willie Scott, Alabama St. (I)	1969	4	103	1,277	—	601	3,155	30.6
Dave Russell, Shepherd (III)	1975	2	60	710	—	413	1,833	30.6
Larry Bird, Indiana St. (I)	1979	3	94	1,154	—	542	2,850	30.3
Kyle Myrick, Lincoln (Pa.) (III)	2006	2	57	667	78	309	1,721	30.2
Carlos Knox, IUPUI (II)	1998	4	85	832	208	684	2,556	30.1

FIELD-GOAL PERCENTAGE
(Minimum 400 field goals)

Player, Team (Division)	Last Season	Yrs.	G	FG	FGA	Pct.
Tony Rychlec, Mass. Maritime (III)	1983	3	55	509	692	73.6
Pete Metzelaars, Wabash (III)	1982	4	103	784	1,083	72.4
Todd Linder, Tampa (II)	1987	4	122	909	1,284	70.8
Tom Schurfranz, Bellarmine (II)	1992	4	112	742	1,057	70.2
Chad Scott, California (Pa.) (II)	1994	4	115	465	664	70.0
Brian Schmitting, Ripon (III)	2007	4	78	418	602	69.4
Ricky Nedd, Appalachian St. (I)	1994	4	113	412	597	69.0
Ed Phillips, Alabama A&M (II)	1971	4	95	610	885	68.9
Stephen Scheffler, Purdue (I)	1990	4	110	408	596	68.5
Ulysses Hackett, S.C. Upstate (II)	1992	3	90	824	1,213	67.9
Larry Tucker, Lewis (II)	1983	3	84	677	994	67.8
Steve Johnson, Oregon St. (I)	1981	4	116	828	1,222	67.8
Michael Bradley, Kentucky/Villanova (I)	2001	4	100	441	651	67.7
Otis Evans, Wayne St. (Mich.) (II)	1992	4	106	472	697	67.7
Maurice Woods, SUNY Potsdam (III)	1982	3	93	559	829	67.4
Matthew Cornegay, Tuskegee (II)	1982	4	105	524	783	66.9
Earl Keith, Stony Brook (III)	1979	4	94	777	1,161	66.9
Murray Brown, Florida St. (I)	1980	4	106	566	847	66.8
Ray Strozier, Central Mo. (II)	1981	4	110	563	843	66.8
Dennis Edwards, Fort Hays St. (II)	1995	2	59	666	998	66.7
James Morris, Central Okla. (II)	1993	4	76	532	798	66.7
Dan Rush, Bridgewater (Va.) (III)	1995	4	102	712	1,069	66.6
Lee Campbell, Middle Tenn./Missouri St. (I)	1990	3	88	411	618	66.5
Warren Kidd, Middle Tenn. (I)	1993	3	83	496	747	66.4
Todd MacCulloch, Washington (I)	1999	4	115	702	1,058	66.4

THREE-POINT FIELD GOALS

Player, Team (Division)	Last Season	Yrs.	G	3FG
Jeff Clement, Grinnell (III)	1999	4	91	516
Amir Mazarei, Redlands (III)	2007	4	97	470
J.J. Redick, Duke (I)	2006	4	139	457
Cameron Munoz, Mont. St.-Billings (II)	2006	4	99	451
Steve Nordlund, Grinnell (III)	2004	4	97	449
Stephen Dye, Alderson-Broaddus (II)	2005	4	121	443
Steve Moyer, Gannon (II)	1999	4	112	442
Keydren Clark, St. Peter's (I)	2006	4	118	435

Player, Team (Division)	Last Season	Yrs.	G	3FG
Tony Smith, Pfeiffer (II)	1992	4	126	431
Chris Lofton, Tennessee (I)	2008	4	128	431
Curtis Staples, Virginia (I)	1998	4	122	413
Kwame Morton, Clarion (II)	1994	4	105	411
Jack Leasure, Coastal Caro. (I)	2008	4	117	411
Keith Veney, Lamar/Marshall (I)	1997	4	111	409
Tarvoris Uzoigwe, Henderson St. (II)	2005	4	119	404
Chris Carideo, Widener (III)	1995	4	103	402
Doug Day, Radford (I)	1993	4	117	401
Gerry McNamara, Syracuse (I)	2006	4	135	400
Michael Watson, UMKC (I)	2004	4	117	391
Gary Duda, Merrimack (II)	1992	4	122	389
Ronnie Schmitz, UMKC (I)	1993	4	112	378
Mike Taylor, West Virginia St. (II)	2004	4	116	378
Mike Hoyt, Mt. St. Mary (N.Y.) (III)	2007	4	105	376
Mark Alberts, Akron (I)	1993	4	107	375
John Grotberg, Grinnell (III)+	2008	3	71	372

+active player

THREE-POINT FIELD GOALS PER GAME
(Minimum 200 three-point field goals)

Player, Team (Division)	Last Season	Yrs.	G	3FG	Avg.
Jeff Clement, Grinnell (III)	1999	4	91	516	5.67
Amir Mazarei, Redlands (III)	2007	4	97	470	4.85
Antonio Harris, LeMoyne-Owen (II)	1999	2	52	245	4.71
Steve Nordlund, Grinnell (III)	2004	4	97	449	4.63
Timothy Pollard, Mississippi Val. (I)	1989	2	56	256	4.57
Cameron Munoz, Mont. St.-Billings (II)	2006	4	99	451	4.56
Markus Hallgrimson, Mont. St.-Billings (II)	2000	3	82	371	4.52
Ed Brands, Grinnell (III)	1996	4	78	347	4.45
Steve Diekmann, Grinnell (III)	1995	4	85	371	4.36
Sydney Grider, La.-Lafayette (I)	1990	2	58	253	4.36
Alex Williams, Sacramento St. (II)	1988	2	58	247	4.26
Yandel Brown, Columbus St. (II)	2005	2	63	264	4.19
Tommie Spearman, Columbus St. (II)	1995	2	56	233	4.16
Reece Gliko, Mont. St.-Billings (II)	1997	2	56	231	4.13
Steve Matthews, Emerson/Wentworth Inst. (III)	2000	3	81	334	4.12
Danny Phillips, Mont. St.-Billings (II)	2002	2	55	222	4.03
Brian Merriweather, Tex.-Pan American (I)	2001	3	84	332	3.95
Steve Moyer, Gannon (II)	1999	4	112	442	3.95
Kwame Morton, Clarion (II)	1994	4	105	411	3.91
Chris Carideo, Widener (III)	1995	4	103	402	3.90
Robert McKiver, Providence/Houston (I)	2008	3	67	261	3.90
Josh Heard, Tennessee Tech (I)	2000	2	55	210	3.82
Matt Garvey, Bates (III)	1997	4	95	361	3.80
Sami Wylie, Lincoln (Pa.) (III)	2007	2	58	220	3.79
Quinn Beckwith, North Ala. (I)	2008	2	55	205	3.73

THREE-POINT FIELD-GOAL PERCENTAGE
(Minimum 200 three-point field goals)

Player, Team (Division)	Last Season	Yrs.	G	3FG	3FGA	Pct.
Scott Martin, Rollins (II)	1991	4	104	236	460	51.3
Jeff Seifriz, Wis.-Whitewater (III)	1989	3	85	217	423	51.3
Chris Peterson, Eureka (III)	1994	4	78	215	421	51.1
Todd Woelfle, Oakland City (II)	1998	4	103	210	412	51.0
Everett Foxx, Ferrum (III)	1992	4	104	315	630	50.0
Tony Bennett, Green Bay (I)	1992	4	118	290	584	49.7
Matt Markle, Shippensburg (II)	1992	4	101	202	408	49.5
Keith Jennings, East Tenn. St. (I)	1991	4	127	223	452	49.3
Brad Alberts, Ripon (III)	1992	4	95	277	563	49.2
Jeff Jones, Lycoming (III)	1989	3	71	232	472	49.2
Troy Greenlee, DePauw (III)	1991	4	106	232	473	49.0
Paul Cluxton, Northern Ky. (II)	1997	4	122	303	619	48.9
Devin Fulk, Wooster (III)	2008	4	122	204	419	48.7
Lance Gelnett, Millersville (II)	1992	4	109	266	547	48.6
David Todd, Pomona-Pitzer (III)	1990	4	84	212	439	48.3
Al Callejas, Scranton (III)	2001	4	90	225	466	48.3
Antonio Harris, LeMoyne-Owen (II)	1999	2	52	245	510	48.0
Jason Bullock, Indiana (Pa.) (II)	1995	4	88	235	491	47.9
Keelan Amelianovich, Ill.-Wesleyan (III)	2006	4	104	252	529	47.6
Matt Ripaldi, Southern N.H. (II)	1995	4	95	205	431	47.6
Kirk Manns, Michigan St. (I)	1990	4	120	212	446	47.5
Tim Locum, Wisconsin (I)	1991	4	118	227	481	47.2
Peter Lipka, Farmingdale (III)	2008	4	111	235	498	47.2
Stephen Sir, San Diego St./ Northern Ariz. (I)	2007	5	111	323	689	46.9
Mark Willey, Fort Hays St. (II)	1992	4	117	224	478	46.9

FREE-THROW PERCENTAGE
(Minimum 300 free throws made)

Player, Team (Division)	Last Season	Yrs.	G	FT	FTA	Pct.
Blake Ahearn, Missouri St. (I)	2007	4	129	435	460	94.6
Derek Raivio, Gonzaga (I)	2007	4	127	343	370	92.7
Andy Enfield, Johns Hopkins (III)	1991	4	108	431	466	92.5
Gary Buchanan, Villanova (I)	2003	4	122	324	355	91.3
Korey Coon, Ill. Wesleyan (III)	2000	4	109	449	492	91.3
J.J. Redick, Duke (I)	2006	4	139	662	726	91.2
Greg Starrick, Kentucky/Southern Ill. (I)	1972	4	72	341	375	90.9
Ryan Knuppel, Elmhurst (III)	2001	4	102	288	317	90.9
Jack Moore, Nebraska (I)	1982	4	105	446	495	90.1
Cris Brunson, Southern Ind. (II)	2005	4	129	317	352	90.1
A.J. Graves, Butler (I)	2008	4	130	362	402	90.0
Steve Henson, Kansas St. (I)	1990	4	127	361	401	90.0
Steve Alford, Indiana (I)	1987	4	125	535	596	89.8
Bob Lloyd, Rutgers (I)	1967	3	77	543	605	89.8
Jake Sullivan, Iowa St. (I)	2004	4	123	354	395	89.6
Jim Barton, Dartmouth (I)	1989	4	104	394	440	89.5
Al Callejas, Scranton (III)	2001	4	90	333	372	89.5
Dave Reynolds, Davis & Elkins (II)	1989	4	107	383	429	89.3
Tommy Boyer, Arkansas (I)	1963	3	70	315	353	89.2
Kyle Korver, Creighton (I)	2003	4	128	312	350	89.1
Lance Den Boer, Central Wash. (II)/ Washington St. (I)	2007	4	94	391	439	89.1
Tim McGraw, Hartwick (III)	1988	4	107	330	371	88.9
Rob Robbins, New Mexico (I)	1991	4	133	309	348	88.8
Gerry McNamara, Syracuse (I)	2006	4	135	435	490	88.8
Brent Jolly, Tennessee Tech (I)	2003	4	123	347	391	88.7
Marcus Wilson, Evansville (I)	1999	4	119	455	513	88.7

REBOUNDS

Player, Team (Division)	Last Season	Yrs.	G	Reb.
Jim Smith, Steubenville (II)	1958	4	112	2,334
Marvin Webster, Morgan St. (II)	1975	4	114	2,267
Tom Gola, La Salle (I)	1955	4	118	2,201
Major Jones, Albany St. (Ga.) (II)	1976	4	105	2,052
Joe Holup, George Washington (I)	1956	4	104	2,030
Charles Hardnett, Grambling (II)	1962	4	117	1,983
Jim Ahrens, Buena Vista (II)	1962	4	95	1,977
Elmore Smith, Kentucky St. (II)	1971	3	85	1,917
Charlie Slack, Marshall (I)	1956	4	88	1,916
Zelmo Beaty, Prairie View (II)	1962	4	97	1,916
Ed Conlin, Fordham (I)	1955	4	102	1,884
Hal Booker, Cheyney (II)	1969	4	103	1,882
Bill Thieben, Hofstra (II)	1956	3	76	1,837
Maurice Stokes, St. Francis (Pa.) (II)	1955	3	72	1,812
Dickie Hemric, Wake Forest (I)	1955	4	104	1,802
Paul Silas, Creighton (I)	1964	3	81	1,751
James Morgan, Md.-East. Shore (II)	1970	4	95	1,747
Tom Hart, Middlebury (II)	1956	3	63	1,738
Joe Casey, Boston St. (II)	1969	4	102	1,733
Art Quimby, Connecticut (I)	1955	4	80	1,716
Jerry Harper, Alabama (I)	1956	4	93	1,688
Jeff Cohen, William & Mary (I)	1961	4	103	1,679
Steve Hamilton, Morehead St. (I)	1958	4	102	1,675
Herb Lake, Youngstown St. (II)	1959	4	95	1,638
Jim Fay, St. Ambrose (I)	1953	4	95	1,633

(For careers beginning in 1973 or after)

Player, Team (Division)	Last Season	Yrs.	G	Reb.
Major Jones, Albany St. (Ga.) (II)	1976	4	105	2,052
Michael Smith, Hamilton (III)	1992	4	107	1,628
Tim Duncan, Wake Forest (I)	1997	4	128	1,570
Derrick Coleman, Syracuse (I)	1990	4	143	1,537
Malik Rose, Drexel (I)	1996	4	120	1,514
Ralph Sampson, Virginia (I)	1983	4	132	1,511
John Jordan, Southern Me. (III)	1981	4	105	1,504
Anthony Fitzgerald, Stevenson (III)	2006	4	107	1,496
Clemon Johnson, Florida A&M (II)	1978	4	109	1,494
Wayne Robertson, Southern N.H. (II)	1994	4	127	1,487
Larry Parker, Plattsburgh St. (III)	1978	4	85	1,482
Carlos Terry, Winston-Salem (II)	1978	4	117	1,467
Pete Padgett, Nevada (I)	1976	4	104	1,464
Kevin Clark, Clark (Mass.) (III)	1981	4	101	1,450
James Hector, American Int'l (II)	1994	4	115	1,446
Lionel Simmons, La Salle (I)	1990	4	131	1,429
Anthony Bonner, St. Louis (I)	1990	4	133	1,424
E.D. Schecterly, Lynchburg (III)	1980	4	104	1,404
Jeff Covington, Youngstown St. (II)	1978	4	106	1,381
Tyrone Hill, Xavier (I)	1990	4	126	1,380
Larry Sheets, East. Mennonite (III)	1983	4	105	1,378
Popeye Jones, Murray St. (I)	1992	4	123	1,374
Michael Brooks, La Salle (I)	1980	4	114	1,372

Player, Team (Division)	Last Season	Yrs.	G	Reb.
John Ebeling, Fla. Southern (II)	1982	4	127	1,362
Xavier McDaniel, Wichita St. (I)	1985	4	117	1,359

REBOUND AVERAGE
(Minimum 800 rebounds)

Player, Team (Division)	Last Season	Yrs.	G	Reb.	Avg.
Tom Hart, Middlebury (II)	1956	3	63	1,738	27.6
Maurice Stokes, St. Francis (Pa.) (II)	1955	3	72	1,812	25.2
Frank Stronczek, American Int'l (II)	1967	3	62	1,549	25.0
Bill Thieben, Hofstra (II)	1956	3	76	1,837	24.2
Hank Brown, Mass.-Lowell (II)	1967	3	49	1,129	23.0
Artis Gilmore, Jacksonville (I)	1970	2	54	1,224	22.7
Elmore Smith, Kentucky St. (II)	1971	3	85	1,917	22.6
Charles Wrinn, Trinity (Conn.) (II)	1953	3	53	1,176	22.2
Roman Turmon, Clark Atlanta (II)	1954	3	60	1,312	21.9
Charlie Slack, Marshall (I)	1956	4	88	1,916	21.8
Tony Missere, Pratt (II)	1968	3	62	1,348	21.7
Ron Horton, Delaware St. (II)	1968	3	64	1,384	21.6
Paul Silas, Creighton (I)	1964	3	81	1,751	21.6
Leroy Wright, Pacific (I)	1960	3	67	1,442	21.5
Art Quimby, Connecticut (I)	1955	4	80	1,716	21.5
Walt Dukes, Seton Hall (I)	1953	2	59	1,247	21.1
Jim Smith, Steubenville (II)	1958	4	112	2,334	20.8
Jim Ahrens, Buena Vista (II)	1962	4	95	1,977	20.8
Bob Brandes, Upsala (II)	1962	3	74	1,520	20.5
Jackie Jackson, Virginia Union (II)	1961	3	66	1,351	20.5
Bill Russell, San Francisco (I)	1956	3	79	1,606	20.3
Kermit Washington, American (I)	1973	3	73	1,478	20.2
Julius Erving, Massachusetts (I)	1971	2	52	1,049	20.2
Frank Hunter, Northland (II)	1962	4	79	1,581	20.0
Marvin Webster, Morgan St. (II)	1975	4	114	2,267	19.9

(For careers beginning in 1973 or after)

Player, Team (Division)	Last Season	Yrs.	G	Reb.	Avg.
Major Jones, Albany St. (Ga.) (II)	1976	4	105	2,052	19.5
Larry Parker, Plattsburgh St. (III)	1978	4	85	1,482	17.4
Howard Shockley, Salisbury (III & II)	1976	3	76	1,299	17.1
Andre Means, Sacred Heart (II)	1978	2	62	1,009	16.3
Charles Greer, Thomas (III)	1977	3	58	926	16.0
Willie Parr, LeMoyne-Owen (III)	1976	3	76	1,182	15.6
Glenn Mosley, Seton Hall (I)	1977	4	83	1,263	15.2
Michael Smith, Hamilton (III)	1992	4	107	1,628	15.2
Dave Kufeld, Yeshiva (III)	1980	4	81	1,222	15.1
Ed Owens, Hampden-Sydney (III)	1980	4	77	1,160	15.1
Tony Rychlec, Mass. Maritime (III)	1983	3	55	812	14.8
Bill Campion, Manhattan (I)	1975	3	74	1,070	14.5
John Jordan, Southern Me. (III)	1981	4	105	1,504	14.4
Kevin Clark, Clark (Mass.) (III)	1981	4	101	1,450	14.4
Antonio Garcia, Ky. Wesleyan (II)	1999	2	70	997	14.2
Mark Veenstra, Calvin (III)	1977	4	89	1,260	14.2
Pete Padgett, Nevada (I)	1976	4	104	1,464	14.1
Anthony Fitzgerald, Stevenson (III)	2006	4	107	1,496	14.0
Rob Roesch, Staten Island (III)	1989	2	61	850	13.9
Clemon Johnson, Florida A&M (II)	1978	4	109	1,494	13.7
Larry Johnson, UALR (II)	1978	3	69	944	13.7
Carlo DeTommaso, Rhode Island Col. (III)	1976	3	72	984	13.7
Bob Warner, Maine (I)	1976	4	96	1,304	13.5
Shaquille O'Neal, LSU (I)	1992	3	90	1,217	13.5
Cornelius Cash, Bowling Green (I)	1975	3	79	1,068	13.5
E.D. Schecterly, Lynchburg (III)	1980	4	104	1,404	13.5
Ira Terrell, SMU (I)	1976	3	80	1,077	13.5

ASSISTS

Player, Team (Division)	Last Season	Yrs.	G	Ast.
Bobby Hurley, Duke (I)	1993	4	140	1,076
Demetri Beekman, Assumption (II)	1993	4	119	1,044
Chris Corchiani, North Carolina St. (I)	1991	4	124	1,038
Ed Cota, North Carolina (I)	2000	4	138	1,030
Keith Jennings, East Tenn. St. (I)	1991	4	127	983
Steve Blake, Maryland (I)	2003	4	138	972
Sherman Douglas, Syracuse (I)	1989	4	138	960
Tony Miller, Marquette (I)	1995	4	123	956
Aaron Miles, Kansas (I)	2005	4	138	954
Greg Anthony, Portland/UNLV (I)	1991	4	138	950
Doug Gottlieb, Notre Dame/Oklahoma St. (I)	2000	4	124	947
Gary Payton, Oregon St. (I)	1990	4	120	938
Adam Kaufman, Edinboro (II)	2001	4	116	936
Rob Paternostro, Southern N.H. (II)	1995	4	129	919
Tennyson Whitted, Ramapo (III)	2003	4	108	917
Steve Artis, Chris. Newport (III)	1993	4	112	909
Orlando Smart, San Francisco (I)	1994	4	116	902
Andre LaFleur, Northeastern (I)	1987	4	128	894

Player, Team (Division)	Last Season	Yrs.	G	Ast.
Chico Fletcher, Arkansas St. (I)	2000	4	114	893
Phil Dixon, Shenandoah (III)	1996	4	103	889
Jim Les, Bradley (I)	1986	4	118	884
Frank Smith, Old Dominion (I)	1988	4	120	883
Luke Cooper, Alas. Anchorage (II)	2008	4	121	880
Taurence Chisholm, Delaware (I)	1988	4	110	877
Grayson Marshall, Clemson (I)	1988	4	122	857

ASSIST AVERAGE
(Minimum 550 assists)

Player, Team (Division)	Last Season	Yrs.	G	Ast.	Avg.
Steve Ray, Bridgeport (II)	1990	2	65	785	12.08
Avery Johnson, Southern U. (I)	1988	2	61	732	12.00
Sam Crawford, New Mexico St. (I)	1993	2	67	592	8.84
Mark Wade, Oklahoma/UNLV (I)	1987	3	79	693	8.77
Demetri Beekman, Assumption (II)	1993	4	119	1,044	8.77
Phil Dixon, Shenandoah (III)	1996	4	103	889	8.63
Tennyson Whitted, Ramapo (III)	2003	4	108	917	8.49
Chris Corchiani, North Carolina St. (I)	1991	4	124	1,038	8.37
Ernest Jenkins, N.M. Highlands (II)	1995	4	84	699	8.32
Zack Whiting, Chaminade (II)	2007	4	86	703	8.17
Steve Artis, Chris. Newport (III)	1993	4	112	909	8.12
Adam Kaufman, Edinboro (II)	2001	4	116	936	8.07
Taurence Chisholm, Delaware (I)	1988	4	110	877	7.97
Van Usher, Tennessee Tech (I)	1992	3	85	676	7.95
Anthony Manuel, Bradley (I)	1989	4	108	855	7.92
Mark Benson, Tex. A&M-Kingsville (II)	1991	3	86	674	7.84
Chico Fletcher, Arkansas St. (I)	2000	4	114	893	7.83
Pat Madden, Jacksonville St. (II)	1991	3	88	688	7.82
Gary Payton, Oregon St. (I)	1990	4	120	938	7.82
Orlando Smart, San Francisco (I)	1994	4	116	902	7.78
Tony Miller, Marquette (I)	1995	4	123	956	7.77
Keith Jennings, East Tenn. St. (I)	1991	4	127	983	7.74
Dan Ward, St. Cloud St. (II)	1995	4	100	774	7.74
Bobby Hurley, Duke (I)	1993	4	140	1,076	7.69
Doug Gottlieb, Notre Dame/Oklahoma St. (I)	2000	4	124	947	7.63

BLOCKED SHOTS

Player, Team (Division)	Last Season	Yrs.	G	Blk.
Ira Nicholson, Mt. St. Vincent (III)	1997	4	100	576
Wojciech Mydra, La.-Monroe (I)	2002	4	115	535
Adonal Foyle, Colgate (I)	1997	3	87	492
Tim Duncan, Wake Forest (I)	1997	4	128	481
Bryan Grier, Wingate (II)	2008	4	122	455
Alonzo Mourning, Georgetown (I)	1992	4	120	453
Tarvis Williams, Hampton (II)	2001	4	114	452
Ken Johnson, Ohio St. (I)	2001	4	127	444
Shawn James, Northeastern/Duquesne (I)	2008	3	83	443
Deng Gai, Fairfield (I)	2005	4	100	442
Emeka Okafor, Connecticut (I)	2004	3	103	441
Antoine Hyman, Keuka (III)	1997	4	101	440
Lorenzo Coleman, Tennessee Tech (I)	1997	4	113	437
Calvin Booth, Penn St. (I)	1999	4	114	428
Theo Ratliff, Wyoming (I)	1995	4	111	425
Troy Murphy, Notre Dame (I)	2001	3	94	425
Etan Thomas, Syracuse (I)	2000	4	122	424
John Smith, Winona St. (II)	2008	4	146	423
Shelden Williams, Duke (I)	2006	4	139	422
Rodney Blake, St. Joseph's (I)	1988	4	116	419
James Doyle, Concord (II)	1998	4	120	416
Shaquille O'Neal, LSU (I)	1992	3	90	412
Kevin Roberson, Vermont (I)	1992	4	112	409
Derek Moore, S.C. Aiken (II)	1999	4	102	408
Bilal Salaam, Kutztown (II)	2005	4	109	408

BLOCKED-SHOT AVERAGE
(Minimum 200 blocked shots)

Player, Team (Division)	Last Season	Yrs.	G	Blk.	Avg.
Neil Edwards, York (N.Y.) (III)	2000	3	55	337	6.13
Ira Nicholson, Mt. St. Vincent (III)	1997	4	100	576	5.76
Adonal Foyle, Colgate (I)	1997	3	87	492	5.66
John Bunch, Lincoln (Pa.) (III)	2004	2	48	265	5.52
Shawn James, Northeastern/Duquesne (I)	2008	3	83	443	5.34
David Robinson, Navy (I)	1987	2	67	351	5.24
Shacun Malave, City Tech (III)	2005	3	70	346	4.94
Mickell Gladness, Alabama A&M (I)	2008	3	85	396	4.66
Wojciech Mydra, La.-Monroe (I)	2002	4	115	535	4.65
Shaquille O'Neal, LSU (I)	1992	3	90	412	4.58
Troy Murphy, Notre Dame (I)	2001	3	94	425	4.52

Player, Team (Division)	Last Season	Yrs.	G	Blk.	Avg.
Jerome James, Florida A&M (I)	1998	3	81	363	4.48
Deng Gai, Fairfield (I)	2005	4	100	442	4.42
Antoine Hyman, Keuka (III)	1997	4	101	440	4.36
Andrew South, NJIT (III)	1995	3	80	344	4.30
Emeka Okafor, Connecticut (I)	2004	3	103	441	4.28
Justin Williams, Wyoming (I)	2006	2	58	244	4.21
Antonio Ramos, Clarke (III)	2003	3	77	318	4.13
Justin Rowe, Maine (I)	2003	2	55	226	4.11
Johnny Woods, Wesley (III)	2002	4	78	319	4.09
Derek Moore, S.C. Aiken (II)	1999	4	102	408	4.00
Tarvis Williams, Hampton (II)	2001	4	114	452	3.96
Ifesinachi Anosike, Salem St. (III)	2005	2	56	221	3.95
Lorenzo Coleman, Tennessee Tech (I)	1997	4	113	437	3.87
Theo Ratliff, Wyoming (I)	1995	4	111	425	3.83

STEALS

Player, Team (Division)	Last Season	Yrs.	G	Stl.
Tennyson Whitted, Ramapo (III)	2003	4	108	448
Jonte Flowers, Winona St. (II)	2008	4	141	414
John Gallogly, Salve Regina (III)	1998	4	98	413
John Linehan, Providence (I)	2002	5	122	385
Eddin Santiago, Mo. Southern St. (II)	2002	4	117	383
Daniel Martinez, McMurry (III)	2000	3	76	380
Eric Murdock, Providence (I)	1991	4	117	376
Ivo Moyano, Polytechnic (N.Y.) (III)	1997	4	87	368
Pepe Sanchez, Temple (I)	2000	4	116	365
Benny West, Howard Payne (III)	2004	4	98	363
Oronn Brown, Clarion (II)	1997	4	106	361
Robert Campbell, Armstrong Atlantic (II)	2001	4	118	357
Eric Bell, New Paltz St. (III)	1996	4	94	355
Cookie Belcher, Nebraska (I)	2001	5	131	353
Jeremy Byrd, S.C.-Upstate (II)	2008	4	115	350
Kevin Braswell, Georgetown (I)	2002	4	128	349
Keith Darden, Concordia (Tex.) (III)	2005	4	90	348
Bonzi Wells, Ball St. (I)	1998	4	116	347
Scott Clarke, Utica (III)	1996	4	96	346
Obie Trotter, Alabama A&M (I)	2006	4	114	346
Marcus Best, Winston-Salem (II)	2002	4	119	345
Gerald Walker, San Francisco (I)	1996	4	111	344
Johnny Rhodes, Maryland (I)	1996	4	122	344
Michael Anderson, Drexel (I)	1988	4	115	341
Kenny Robertson, Cleveland St. (I)	1990	4	119	341

STEAL AVERAGE
(Minimum 200 steals)

Player, Team (Division)	Last Season	Yrs.	G	Stl.	Avg.
Moses Jean-Pierre, Plymouth St. (III)	1994	2	55	303	5.51
Daniel Martinez, McMurry (III)	2000	3	76	380	5.00
Wayne Copeland, Lynn (II)	2000	2	57	254	4.46
Ivo Moyano, Polytechnic (N.Y.) (III)	1997	4	87	368	4.23
Mario Thompson, Occidental (III)	2001	3	71	300	4.23
John Gallogly, Salve Regina (III)	1998	4	98	413	4.21
Tennyson Whitted, Ramapo (III)	2003	4	108	448	4.15
Greg Dean, Concordia-M'head (III)	1997	3	75	307	4.09
Desmond Cambridge, Alabama A&M (I)	2002	3	84	330	3.93
Keith Darden, Concordia (Tex.) (III)	2005	4	90	348	3.87
Mookie Blaylock, Oklahoma (I)	1989	2	74	281	3.80
Eric Bell, New Paltz St. (III)	1996	4	94	355	3.78
Benny West, Howard Payne (III)	2004	4	98	363	3.70
Scott Clarke, Utica (III)	1996	4	96	346	3.60
Ricky Hollis, Brockport (III)	2002	4	90	322	3.58
Ronn McMahon, Eastern Wash. (I)	1990	3	64	225	3.52
Gerald Garlic, Goucher (III)	1995	3	70	244	3.49
Darrel Lewis, Lincoln (Pa.) (III)	1999	4	86	298	3.47
Oronn Brown, Clarion (II)	1997	4	106	361	3.41
Patrick Herron, Winston-Salem (II)	1995	3	78	263	3.37
David Clark, Bluefield St. (II)	1996	3	83	278	3.35
Eddin Santiago, Mo. Southern St. (II)	2002	4	117	383	3.27
Shuron Woodyard, Stevenson (III)	1997	3	73	238	3.26
Jeff Mikos, Milwaukee Engr. (III)	2006	4	105	340	3.24
Shawn McCartney, Hunter (III)	1995	3	81	261	3.22
Carl Small, Cornell College (III)	1995	3	69	222	3.22

INDIVIDUAL COLLEGIATE

Award Winners

Division I Consensus All-American Selections

By Season

1905
Oliver deGray Vanderbilt, Princeton; Harry Fisher, Yale; Marcus Hurley, Columbia; Willard Hyatt, Yale; Gilmore Kinney, Yale; C.D. McLees, Wisconsin; James Ozanne, Chicago; Walter Runge, Colgate; Chris Steinmetz, Wisconsin; George Tuck, Minnesota.

1906
Harold Amberg, Harvard; Garfield Brown, Minnesota; Eugene Cowell, Williams; George Flint, Penn; George Grebenstein, Dartmouth; Ralph Griffiths, Harvard; Marcus Hurley, Columbia; Charles Keinath, Penn; James McKeag, Chicago; John Schommer, Chicago.

1907
Frank Arthur, Wisconsin; George Flint, Penn; Albert Houghton, Chicago; Marcus Hurley, Columbia; Charles Keinath, Penn; Gilmore Kinney, Yale; John Ryan, Columbia; John Schommer, Chicago; Oswald Tower, Williams; L. Parson Warren, Williams.

1908
Hugh Harper, Wisconsin; Julian Hayward, Wesleyan; Charles Keinath, Penn; Haskell Noyes, Yale; Pat Page, Chicago; John Pryor, Brown; John Ryan, Columbia; John Schommer, Chicago; Ira Streusand, CCNY; Helmer Swenholt, Wisconsin.

1909
Biaggio Gerussi, Columbia; Julian Hayward, Wesleyan; Tommy Johnson, Kansas; Charles Keinath, Penn; Ted Kiendl, Columbia; Pat Page, Chicago; John Ryan, Columbia; Raymond Scanlon, Notre Dame; John Schommer, Chicago; Helmer Swenholt, Wisconsin.

1910
William Broadhead, New York U.; Leon Campbell, Colgate; Dave Charters, Purdue; William Copthorne, Army; Charles Eberle, Swarthmore; Samuel Harman, Rochester; Ted Kiendl, Columbia; Ernest Lambert, Oklahoma; W. Vaughn Lewis, Williams; Pat Page, Chicago.

1911
A.D. Alexander, Columbia; Dave Charters, Purdue; C.C. Clementson, Washington; Harry Hill, Navy; John Keenan, St. John's (N.Y.); Ted Kiendl, Columbia; Frank Lawler, Minnesota; W.M. Lee, Columbia; Walter Scoville, Wisconsin; Lewis Walton, Penn.

1912
Claus Benson, Columbia; Thomas Canfield, St. Lawrence; Lewis Castle, Syracuse; Fred Gieg, Swarthmore; Ernst Mensel, Dartmouth; Emil Schradieck, Colgate; Alphonse Schumacher, Dayton; Rufus Sisson, Dartmouth; Otto Stangel, Wisconsin; William Turner, Penn.

1913
Eddie Calder, St. Lawrence; Sam Carrier, Nebraska; George Halstead, Cornell; Edward Hayward, Wesleyan; Allen Johnson, Wisconsin; William Roberts, Army; Hamilton Salmon, Princeton; Alphonse Schumacher, Dayton; Larry Teeple, Purdue; Laurence Wild, Navy.

1914
Lewis Castle, Syracuse; Gil Halstead, Cornell; Carl Harper, Wisconsin; Ernest Houghton, Union (N.Y.); Walter Lunden, Cornell; Dan Meenan, Columbia; Nelson Norgren, Chicago; Elmer Oliphant, Purdue; Everett Southwick, CCNY; Eugene Van Gent, Wisconsin.

1915
W.P. Arnold, Yale; Leslie Brown, Cornell; Ernest Houghton, Union (N.Y.); Charlie Lee, Columbia; George Levis, Wisconsin; Elmer Oliphant, Purdue; Tony Savage, Washington; Ralph Sproull, Kansas; Wellington Strickley, Virginia; Ray Woods, Illinois.

1916
Roy Bohler, Washington St.; William Chandler, Wisconsin; Cyril Haas, Princeton; George Levis, Wisconsin; Clyde Littlefield, Texas; Edward McNichol, Penn; Dick Romney, Utah; Ade Sieberts, Oregon St.; Fred Williams, Missouri; Ray Woods, Illinois.

1917
Clyde Alwood, Illinois; Cyril Haas, Princeton; George Hjelte, California; Orson Kinney, Yale; Harold Olsen, Wisconsin; F.I. Reynolds, Kansas St.; Francis Stadsvold, Minnesota; Charles Taft, Yale; Ray Woods, Illinois; Harry Young, Wash. & Lee.

1918
Earl Anderson, Illinois; William Chandler, Wisconsin; Harold Gillen, Minnesota; Hubert Peck, Penn; Craig Ruby, Missouri; Joseph Schwarzer, Syracuse; Eber Simpson, Wisconsin; Alfred Sorenson, Washington St.; George Sweeney, Penn; Gene Vidal, Army.

1919
Lance Farwell, Navy; Tony Hinkle, Chicago; Dutch Lonborg, Kansas; Leon Marcus, Syracuse; Dan McNichol, Penn; Arnold Oss, Minnesota; George Parrish, Virginia Tech; Erling Platou, Minnesota; Craig Ruby, Missouri; Andrew Stannard, Penn.

1920
Howard Cann, New York U.; Charles Carney, Illinois; Erving Cook, Washington; Forrest DeBernardi, Westminster (Mo.); George Gardner, Southwestern (Kan.); Tony Hinkle, Chicago; Dan McNichol, Penn; Hubert Peck, Penn; George Sweeney, Penn; George Williams, Missouri.

1921
R.D. Birkhoff, Chicago; Herbert Bunker, Missouri; Everett Dean, Indiana; Forrest DeBernardi, Westminster (Mo.); Eddie Durno, Oregon; Basil Hayden, Kentucky; Dan McNichol, Penn; Arnold Oss, Minnesota; Donald White, Purdue; George Williams, Missouri.

1922
Arthur Browning, Missouri; Herbert Bunker, Missouri; Charles Carney, Illinois; Paul Endacott, Kansas; George Gardner, Southwestern (Kan.); William Graves, Penn; Marshall Hjelte, Oregon St.; Arthur Loeb, Princeton; Ira McKee, Navy; Ray Miller, Purdue.

1923
Charlie T. Black, Kansas; Arthur Browning, Missouri; Herbert Bunker, Missouri; Cartwright Carmichael, North Carolina; Paul Endacott, Kansas; Al Fox, Idaho; Ira McKee, Navy; Arthur Loeb, Princeton; Jimmy Lovley, Creighton; John Luther, Cornell.

1924
Arthur Ackerman, Kansas; Charlie T. Black, Kansas; Cartwright Carmichael, North Carolina; Jack Cobb, North Carolina; Abb Curtis, Texas; Slats Gill, Oregon St.; Harry Kipke, Michigan; Hugh Latham, Oregon; Jimmy Lovley, Creighton; Hugh Middlesworth, Butler.

1925
Arthur Ackerman, Kansas; Burgess Carey, Kentucky; Jack Cobb, North Carolina; Emanuel Goldblatt, Penn; Victor Hanson, Syracuse; Noble Kizer, Notre Dame; Johnny Miner, Ohio St.; Earl Mueller, Colorado Col.; Gerald Spohn, Washburn; Carlos Steele, Oregon St.

1926
Jack Cobb, North Carolina; George Dixon, California; Richard Doyle, Michigan; Emanuel Goldblatt, Penn; Gale Gordon, Kansas; Victor Hanson, Syracuse; Carl Loeb, Princeton; Albert Peterson, Kansas; George Spradling, Purdue; Algot Westergren, Oregon.

1927
Sidney Corenman, Creighton; George Dixon, California; Victor Hanson, Syracuse; John Lorch, Columbia; Ross McBurney, Wichita St.; John Nyikos, Notre Dame; Bennie Oosterbaan, Michigan; Gerald Spohn, Washburn; Cat Thompson, Montana St.; Harry Wilson, Army.

1928
Victor Holt, Oklahoma; Charley Hyatt, Pittsburgh; Alfred James, Washington; Charles Murphy, Purdue; Bennie Oosterbaan, Michigan; Wallace Reed, Pittsburgh; Glen Rose, Arkansas; Joe Schaaf, Penn; Ernest Simpson, Colorado Col.; Cat Thompson, Montana St.

1929
Vern Corbin, California; Thomas Churchill, Oklahoma; Charley Hyatt, Pittsburgh; Charles Murphy, Purdue; Joe Schaaf, Penn; John Thompson, Montana St.

1930
Charley Hyatt, Pittsburgh; Branch McCracken, Indiana; Charles Murphy, Purdue; John Thompson, Montana St.; Frank Ward, Montana St.; John Wooden, Purdue.

1931
Wes Fesler, Ohio St.; George Gregory, Columbia; Joe Reiff, Northwestern; Elwood Romney, BYU; John Wooden, Purdue.

1932
Louis Berger, Maryland; Ed Krause, Notre Dame; Forest Sale, Kentucky; Les Witte, Wyoming; John Wooden, Purdue.

1933
Ed Krause, Notre Dame; Elliott Loughlin, Navy; Jerry Nemer, Southern California; Joe Reiff, Northwestern; Forest Sale, Kentucky; Don Smith, Pittsburgh.

1934
Norman Cottom, Purdue; Claire Cribbs, Pittsburgh; Ed Krause, Notre Dame; Hal Lee, Washington; Les Witte, Wyoming.

1935
Bud Browning, Oklahoma; Claire Cribbs, Pittsburgh; Leroy Edwards, Kentucky; Jack Gray, Texas; Lee Guttero, Southern California.

1936
Vern Huffman, Indiana; Bob Kessler, Purdue; Bill Kinner, Utah; Hank Luisetti, Stanford; John Moir, Notre Dame; Paul Nowak, Notre Dame; Ike Poole, Arkansas.

1937
Jules Bender, Long Island; Hank Luisetti, Stanford; John Moir, Notre Dame; Paul Nowak, Notre Dame; Jewell Young, Purdue.

1938
Meyer Bloom, Temple; Hank Luisetti, Stanford; John Moir, Notre Dame; Paul Nowak, Notre Dame; Fred Pralle, Kansas; Jewell Young, Purdue.

1939
First Team—Ernie Andres, Indiana; Jimmy Hull, Ohio St.; Chet Jaworski, Rhode Island; Irving Torgoff, Long Island; Urgel Wintermute, Oregon.

Second Team—Robert Anet, Oregon; Bob Calihan, Detroit; Bob Hassmiller, Fordham; Michael Novak, Loyola (Ill.); Bernard Opper, Kentucky.

1940
First Team—Gus Broberg, Dartmouth; John Dick, Oregon; George Glamack, North Carolina; Bill Hapac, Illinois; Ralph Vaughn, Southern California.

Second Team—Jack Harvey, Colorado; Marvin Huffman, Indiana; James McNatt, Oklahoma; Jesse Renick, Oklahoma St.

1941
First Team—John Adams, Arkansas; Gus Broberg, Dartmouth; Howard Engleman, Kansas; Gene Englund, Wisconsin; George Glamack, North Carolina.

Second Team—Frank Baumholtz, Ohio; Robert Kinney, Rice; Paul Lindeman, Washington St.; Stan Modzelewski, Rhode Island; Oscar Schechtman, Long Island.

1942
First Team—Price Brookfield, West Tex. A&M; Robert Davies, Seton Hall; Bob Kinney, Rice; John Kotz, Wisconsin; Andrew Phillip, Illinois.

Second Team—Donald Burness, Stanford; Wilfred Doerner, Evansville; Robert Doll, Colorado; John Mandic, Oregon St.; Stan Modzelewski, Rhode Island; George Munroe, Dartmouth.

1943
First Team—Ed Beisser, Creighton; Charles Black, Kansas; Harry Boykoff, St. John's (N.Y.); William Closs, Rice; Andrew Phillip, Illinois; Ken Sailors, Wyoming; George Senesky, St. Joseph's.

Second Team—Gale Bishop, Washington St.; Otto Graham, Northwestern; John Kotz, Wisconsin; Bob Rensberger, Notre Dame; Gene Rock, Southern California; Gerald Tucker, Oklahoma.

1944
First Team—Robert Brannum, Kentucky; Audley Brindley, Dartmouth; Otto Graham, Northwestern; Leo Klier, Notre Dame; Robert Kurland, Oklahoma St.; George Mikan, DePaul; Alva Paine, Oklahoma.

Second Team—Howard Dallmar, Penn; Bob Dille, Valparaiso; Arnold Ferrin, Utah; Don Grate, Ohio St.; Dale Hall, Army; William Henry, Rice; Dick Triptow, DePaul.

1945
First Team—Arnold Ferrin, Utah; Wyndol Gray, Bowling Green; William Hassett, Notre Dame; William Henry, Rice; Walton Kirk, Illinois; Robert Kurland, Oklahoma St.; George Mikan, DePaul.

Second Team—Don Grate, Ohio St.; Dale Hall, Army; Vince Hanson, Washington St.; Richard Ives, Iowa; Max Norris, Northwestern; Herb Wilkinson, Iowa.

1946
First Team—Leo Klier, Notre Dame, 6-2, Washington, IN; Robert Kurland, Oklahoma St., 7-0, Jennings, MO; George Mikan, DePaul, 6-10, Joliet, IL; Max Norris, Northwestern, 6-2, West Frankfort, IL; Sid Tanenbaum, New York U., 6-0, New York.

Second Team—Charles Black, Kansas; John Dillon, North Carolina; William Hassett, Notre Dame; Tony Lavelli, Yale; Jack Parkinson, Kentucky; Ken Sailors, Wyoming.

1947
First Team—Ralph Beard, Kentucky, 5-10, Louisville, KY; Alex Groza, Kentucky, 6-7, Martin's Ferry, OH; Ralph Hamilton, Indiana, 6-1, Fort Wayne, IN; Sid Tanenbaum, New York U., 6-0, New York; Gerald Tucker, Oklahoma, 6-6, Winfield, KS.

Second Team—Don Barksdale, UCLA; Arnold Ferrin, Utah; Vern Gardner, Utah; John Hargis, Texas; George Kaftan, Holy Cross; Ed Koffenberger, Duke; Andrew Phillip, Illinois.

1948
First Team—Ralph Beard, Kentucky, 5-10, Jr., Louisville, KY; Ed Macauley, St. Louis, 6-8, Jr., St. Louis; Jim McIntyre, Minnesota, 6-10, Jr., Minneapolis; Kevin O'Shea, Notre Dame, 6-1, So., San Francisco; Murray Wier, Iowa, 5-9, Sr., Muscatine, IA.

Second Team—Dick Dickey, North Carolina St.; Arnold Ferrin, Utah; Alex Groza, Kentucky; Harold Haskins, Hamline; George Kaftan, Holy Cross; Duane Klueh, Indiana St.; Tony Lavelli, Yale; Jack Nichols, Washington; Andy Wolfe, California.

1949
First Team—Ralph Beard, Kentucky, 5-10, Sr., Louisville, KY; Vince Boryla, Denver, 6-5, Jr., East Chicago, IN; Alex Groza, Kentucky, 6-7, Sr., Martin's Ferry, OH; Tony Lavelli, Yale, 6-3, Sr., Somerville, MA; Ed Macauley, St. Louis, 6-8, Sr., St. Louis.

Second Team—Bill Erickson, Illinois, 6-1, Jr.; Vern Gardner, Utah, 6-5, Sr.; Wallace Jones, Kentucky, 6-4, Sr.; Jim McIntyre, Minnesota, 6-10, Sr.; Ernie Vandeweghe, Colgate, 6-3, Sr.

1950
First Team—Paul Arizin, Villanova, 6-3, Sr., Philadelphia; Bob Cousy, Holy Cross, 6-1, Sr., St. Albans, NY; Dick Schnittker, Ohio St., 6-5, Sr., Sandusky, OH; Bill Sharman, Southern California, 6-2, Sr., Porterville, CA; Paul Unruh, Bradley, 6-4, Sr., Toulon, IL.

Second Team—Charles Cooper, Duquesne, 6-5, Sr.; Don Lofgran, San Francisco, 6-6, Sr.; Kevin O'Shea, Notre Dame, 6-1, Sr.; Don Rehfeldt, Wisconsin, 6-6, Sr.; Sherman White, Long Island, 6-8, Jr.

1951
First Team—Clyde Lovellette, Kansas, 6-9, Jr., Terre Haute, IN; Gene Melchiorre, Bradley, 5-8, Sr., Highland Park, IL; Bill Mlkvy, Temple, 6-4, Jr., Palmerton, PA; Sam Ranzino, North Carolina St., 6-1, Sr., Gary, IN; Bill Spivey, Kentucky, 7-0, Jr., Macon, GA.

Second Team—Ernie Barrett, Kansas St., 6-3, Sr.; Bill Garrett, Indiana, 6-3, Sr.; Dick Groat, Duke, 6-0, Jr.; Mel Hutchins, BYU, 6-5, Jr.; Gale McArthur, Oklahoma St., 6-2, Sr.

1952
First Team—Chuck Darling, Iowa, 6-8, Sr., Denver; Rod Fletcher, Illinois, 6-4, Sr., Champaign, IL; Dick Groat, Duke, 6-0, Sr., Swissvale, PA; Cliff Hagan, Kentucky, 6-4, Jr., Owensboro, KY; Clyde Lovellette, Kansas, 6-9, Sr., Terre Haute, IN.

Second Team—Bob Houbregs, Washington, 6-7, Jr.; Don Meineke, Dayton, 6-7, Sr.; Johnny O'Brien, Seattle, 5-8, Jr.; Mark Workman, West Virginia, 6-9, Sr.; Bob Zawoluk, St. John's (N.Y.), 6-6, Sr.

1953
First Team—Ernie Beck, Penn, 6-4, Sr., Philadelphia; Walt Dukes, Seton Hall, 6-11, Sr., Rochester, NY; Tom Gola, La Salle, 6-6, So., Philadelphia; Bob Houbregs, Washington, 6-7, Sr., Seattle; Johnny O'Brien, Seattle, 5-8, Sr., South Amboy, NJ.

Second Team—Dick Knostman, Kansas St., 6-6, Sr.; Bob Pettit, LSU, 6-9, Jr.; Joe Richey, BYU, 6-1, Sr.; Don Schlundt, Indiana, 6-10, So.; Frank Selvy, Furman, 6-3, Jr.

1954
First Team—Tom Gola, La Salle, 6-6, Jr., Philadelphia; Cliff Hagan, Kentucky, 6-4, Sr., Owensboro, KY; Bob Pettit, LSU, 6-9, Sr., Baton Rouge, LA; Don Schlundt, Indiana, 6-10, Jr., South Bend, IN; Frank Selvy, Furman, 6-3, Sr., Corbin, KY.

Second Team—Bob Leonard, Indiana, 6-3, Sr.; Tom Marshall, Western Ky., 6-4, Sr.; Bob Mattick, Oklahoma St., 6-10, Sr.; Frank Ramsey, Kentucky, 6-3, Sr.; Dick Ricketts, Duquesne, 6-8, Jr.

1955
First Team—Dick Garmaker, Minnesota, 6-3, Sr., Hibbing, MN; Tom Gola, La Salle, 6-6, Sr., Philadelphia; Si Green, Duquesne, 6-3, Jr., Brooklyn, NY; Dick Ricketts, Duquesne, 6-8, Sr., Pottstown, PA; Bill Russell, San Francisco, 6-9, Jr., Oakland, CA.

Second Team—Darrell Floyd, Furman, 6-1, Jr.; Robin Freeman, Ohio St., 5-11, Jr.; Dickie Hemric, Wake Forest, 6-6, Sr.; Don Schlundt, Indiana, 6-10, Sr.; Ron Shavlik, North Carolina St., 6-9, Jr.

1956
First Team—Robin Freeman, Ohio St., 5-11, Sr., Cincinnati; Si Green, Duquesne, 6-3, Sr., Brooklyn, NY; Tom Heinsohn, Holy Cross, 6-7, Sr., Union City, NJ; Ron Shavlik, North Carolina St., 6-9, Sr., Denver; Bill Russell, San Francisco, 6-9, Sr., Oakland, CA.

Second Team—Bob Burrow, Kentucky, 6-7, Sr.; Darrell Floyd, Furman, 6-1, Sr.; Rod Hundley, West Virginia, 6-4, Jr.; K.C. Jones, San Francisco, 6-2, Sr.; Willie Naulls, UCLA, 6-5, Sr.; Bill Uhl, Dayton, 7-0, Sr.

1957
First Team—Wilt Chamberlain, Kansas, 7-0, So., Philadelphia; Chet Forte, Columbia, 5-9, Sr., Hackensack, NJ; Rod Hundley, West Virginia, 6-4, Sr., Charleston, WV; Jim Krebs, SMU, 6-8, Sr., Webster Groves, MO; Lenny Rosenbluth, North Carolina, 6-5, Sr., New York; Charlie Tyra, Louisville, 6-8, Sr., Louisville, KY.

Second Team—Elgin Baylor, Seattle, 6-6, So.; Frank Howard, Ohio St., 6-6, Jr.; Guy Rodgers, Temple, 6-0, Jr.; Gary Thompson, Iowa St., 5-10, Sr.; Grady Wallace, South Carolina, 6-4, Sr.

1958
First Team—Elgin Baylor, Seattle, 6-6, Jr., Washington, DC; Bob Boozer, Kansas St., 6-8, Jr., Omaha, NE; Wilt Chamberlain, Kansas, 7-0, Jr., Philadelphia; Don Hennon, Pittsburgh, 5-9, Jr., Wampum, PA; Oscar Robertson, Cincinnati, 6-5, So., Indianapolis; Guy Rodgers, Temple, 6-0, Sr., Philadelphia.

Second Team—Pete Brennan, North Carolina, 6-6, Jr.; Archie Dees, Indiana, 6-8, Sr.; Mike Farmer, San Francisco, 6-7, Sr.; Dave Gambee, Oregon St., 6-7, Sr.; Bailey Howell, Mississippi St., 6-7, Jr.

1959
First Team—Bob Boozer, Kansas St., 6-8, Sr., Omaha, NE; Johnny Cox, Kentucky, 6-4, Sr., Hazard, KY; Bailey Howell, Mississippi St., 6-7, Sr., Middleton, TN; Oscar Robertson, Cincinnati, 6-5, So., Indianapolis; Jerry West, West Virginia, 6-3, Jr., Cabin Creek, WV.

Second Team—Leo Byrd, Marshall, 6-2, Sr.; Johnny Green, Michigan St., 6-5, Sr.; Tom Hawkins, Notre Dame, 6-5, Sr.; Don Hennon, Pittsburgh, 5-9, Sr.; Alan Seiden, St. John's (N.Y.), 5-11, Sr.

1960
First Team—Darrall Imhoff, California, 6-10, Sr., Alhambra, CA; Jerry Lucas, Ohio St., 6-8, So., Middletown, OH; Oscar Robertson, Cincinnati, 6-5, Sr., Indianapolis; Tom Stith, St. Bonaventure, 6-5, Jr., Brooklyn, NY; Jerry West, West Virginia, 6-3, Sr., Cabin Creek, WV.

Second Team—Terry Dischinger, Purdue, 6-7, So.; Tony Jackson, St. John's (N.Y.), 6-4, Jr.; Roger Kaiser, Georgia Tech, 6-1, Jr.; Lee Shaffer, North Carolina, 6-7, Sr.; Len Wilkens, Providence, 6-1, Sr.

1961
First Team—Terry Dischinger, Purdue, 6-7, Jr., Terre Haute, IN; Roger Kaiser, Georgia Tech, 6-1, Sr., Dale, IN; Jerry Lucas, Ohio St., 6-8, Jr., Middletown, OH; Tom Stith, St. Bonaventure, 6-5, Sr., Brooklyn, NY; Chet Walker, Bradley, 6-6, Jr., Benton Harbor, MI.

Second Team—Walt Bellamy, Indiana, 6-10, Sr.; Frank Burgess, Gonzaga, 6-1, Sr.; Tony Jackson, St. John's (N.Y.), 6-1, Sr.; Billy McGill, Utah, 6-9, Jr.; Larry Siegfried, Ohio St., 6-4, Sr.

1962
First Team—Len Chappell, Wake Forest, 6-8, Sr., Portage Area, PA; Terry Dischinger, Purdue, 6-7, Sr., Terre Haute, IN; Jerry Lucas, Ohio St., 6-8, Sr., Middletown, OH; Billy McGill, Utah, 6-9, Sr., Los Angeles; Chet Walker, Bradley, 6-6, Sr., Benton Harbor, MI.

Second Team—Jack Foley, Holy Cross, 6-5, Sr.; John Havlicek, Ohio St., 6-5, Sr.; Art Heyman, Duke, 6-5, Jr.; Cotton Nash, Kentucky, 6-5, So.; John Rudometkin, Southern California, 6-6, Sr.; Rod Thorn, West Virginia, 6-4, Jr.

1963
First Team—Ron Bonham, Cincinnati, 6-5, Jr., Muncie, IN; Jerry Harkness, Loyola (Ill.), 6-3, Sr., New York; Art Heyman, Duke, 6-5, Sr., Rockville Center, NY; Barry Kramer, New York U., 6-4, Jr., Schenectady, NY; Tom Thacker, Cincinnati, 6-2, Sr., Covington, KY.

Second Team—Gary Bradds, Ohio St., 6-8, Jr.; Bill Green, Colorado St., 6-6, Sr.; Cotton Nash, Kentucky, 6-5, Jr.; Rod Thorn, West Virginia, 6-4, Sr.; Nate Thurmond, Bowling Green, 6-10, Sr.

1964
First Team—Gary Bradds, Ohio St., 6-8, Sr., Jamestown, OH; Bill Bradley, Princeton, 6-5, Jr., Crystal City, MO; Walt Hazzard, UCLA, 6-2, Sr., Philadelphia; Cotton Nash, Kentucky, 6-5, Sr., Leominster, MA; Dave Stallworth, Wichita St., 6-7, Jr., Dallas.

Second Team—Ron Bonham, Cincinnati, 6-5, Sr.; Mel Counts, Oregon St., 7-0, Sr.; Fred Hetzel, Davidson, 6-8, Jr.; Jeff Mullins, Duke, 6-4, Sr.; Cazzie Russell, Michigan, 6-5, So.

1965
First Team—Rick Barry, Miami (Fla.), 6-7, Sr., Roselle Park, NJ; Bill Bradley, Princeton, 6-5, Sr., Crystal City, MO; Gail Goodrich, UCLA, 6-1, Sr., North Hollywood, CA; Fred Hetzel, Davidson, 6-8, Sr., Washington, DC; Cazzie Russell, Michigan, 6-5, Jr., Chicago.

Second Team—Bill Buntin, Michigan, 6-7, Sr.; Wayne Estes, Utah St., 6-6, Sr.; Clyde Lee, Vanderbilt, 6-9, Jr.; Dave Schellhase, Purdue, 6-4, Jr.; Dave Stallworth, Wichita St., 6-7, Sr.

1966
First Team—Dave Bing, Syracuse, 6-3, Sr., Washington, DC; Clyde Lee, Vanderbilt, 6-9, Sr., Nashville, TN; Cazzie Russell, Michigan, 6-5, Sr., Chicago; Dave Schellhase, Purdue, 6-4, Sr., Evansville, IN; Jim Walker, Providence, 6-3, Jr., Boston.

Second Team—Lou Dampier, Kentucky, 6-0, Jr.; Matt Guokas, St. Joseph's, 6-5, Jr.; Jack Marin, Duke, 6-6, Sr.; Dick Snyder, Davidson, 6-5, Sr.; Bob Verga, Duke; Walt Wesley, Kansas, 6-11, Sr.

1967
First Team—Lew Alcindor, UCLA, 7-2, New York; Clem Haskins, Western Ky., 6-3, Campbellsville, KY; Elvin Hayes, Houston, 6-8, Rayville, LA; Bob Lloyd, Rutgers, 6-1, Upper Darby, PA; Wes Unseld, Louisville, 6-8, Louisville, KY; Bob Verga, Duke, 6-0, Sea Girt, NJ; Jim Walker, Providence, 6-3, Boston.

Second Team—Lou Dampier, Kentucky, 6-0, Sr.; Mel Daniels, New Mexico, 6-9, Sr.; Sonny Dove, St. John's (N.Y.), 6-8, Sr.; Don May, Dayton, 6-4, Jr.; Larry Miller, North Carolina, 6-4, Jr.

1968
First Team—Lew Alcindor, UCLA, 7-2, Jr., New York; Elvin Hayes, Houston, 6-8, Sr., Rayville, LA; Pete Maravich, LSU, 6-5, So., Raleigh, NC; Larry Miller, North Carolina, 6-4, Sr., Catasauga, PA; Wes Unseld, Louisville, 6-8, Sr., Louisville, KY.
Second Team—Lucius Allen, UCLA, 6-2, Jr.; Bob Lanier, St. Bonaventure, 6-11, So.; Don May, Dayton, 6-4, Sr.; Calvin Murphy, Niagara, 5-10, So.; Jo Jo White, Kansas, 6-3, Jr.

1969
First Team—Lew Alcindor, UCLA, 7-2, Sr., New York; Spencer Haywood, Detroit, 6-8, So., Detroit; Pete Maravich, LSU, 6-5, Jr., Raleigh, NC; Rick Mount, Purdue, 6-4, Jr., Lebanon, IN; Calvin Murphy, Niagara, 5-10, Jr., Norwalk, CT.
Second Team—Dan Issel, Kentucky, 6-9, Jr.; Mike Maloy, Davidson, 6-7, Jr.; Bud Ogden, Santa Clara, 6-6, Sr.; Charlie Scott, North Carolina, 6-5, Jr.; Jo Jo White, Kansas, 6-3, Sr.

1970
First Team—Dan Issel, Kentucky, 6-9, Sr., Batavia, IL; Bob Lanier, St. Bonaventure, 6-11, Sr., Buffalo, NY; Pete Maravich, LSU, 6-5, Sr., Raleigh, NC; Rick Mount, Purdue, 6-4, Sr., Lebanon, IN; Calvin Murphy, Niagara, 5-10, Sr., Norwalk, CT.
Second Team—Austin Carr, Notre Dame, 6-3, Jr.; Jim Collins, New Mexico St., 6-2, Sr.; John Roche, South Carolina, 6-3, Jr.; Charlie Scott, North Carolina, 6-6, Sr.; Sidney Wicks, UCLA, 6-8, Jr.

1971
First Team—Austin Carr, Notre Dame, 6-3, Sr., Washington, DC; Artis Gilmore, Jacksonville, 7-2, Sr., Dothan, AL; Jim McDaniels, Western Ky., 7-0, Sr., Scottsville, KY; Dean Meminger, Marquette, 6-1, Sr., New York; Sidney Wicks, UCLA, 6-8, Sr., Los Angeles.
Second Team—Ken Durrett, La Salle, 6-7, Sr.; Johnny Neumann, Mississippi, 6-7, So.; Howard Porter, Villanova, 6-8, Sr.; John Roche, South Carolina, 6-3, Sr.; Curtis Rowe, UCLA, 6-7, Sr.

1972
First Team—Henry Bibby, UCLA, 6-1, Sr., Franklinton, NC; Jim Chones, Marquette, 6-11, Jr., Racine, WI; Dwight Lamar, La.-Lafayette, 6-1, Jr., Columbus, OH; Bob McAdoo, North Carolina, 6-8, Jr., Greensboro, NC; Ed Ratleff, Long Beach St., 6-6, Jr., Columbus, OH; Tom Riker, South Carolina, 6-10, Sr., Oyster Bay, NY; Bill Walton, UCLA, 6-11, So., La Mesa, CA.
Second Team—Rich Fuqua, Oral Roberts, 6-3, Jr.; Barry Parkhill, Virginia 6-4, Jr.; Jim Price, Louisville 6-3, Sr.; Bud Stallworth, Kansas 6-5, Sr.; Henry Willmore, Michigan 6-3, Jr.

1973
First Team—Doug Collins, Illinois St., 6-6, Sr., Benton, IL; Ernie DiGregorio, Providence, 6-0, Sr., North Providence, RI; Dwight Lamar, La.-Lafayette, 6-1, Sr., Columbus, OH; Ed Ratleff, Long Beach St., 6-6, Sr., Columbus, OH; David Thompson, North Carolina St., 6-4, So., Shelby, NC; Bill Walton, UCLA, 6-11, Jr., La Mesa, CA; Keith Wilkes, UCLA, 6-6, Jr., Santa Barbara, CA.
Second Team—Jim Brewer, Minnesota, 6-9, Sr.; Tom Burleson, North Carolina St., 7-4, Jr.; Larry Finch, Memphis, 6-2, Sr.; Kevin Joyce, South Carolina, 6-3, Sr.; Tom McMillen, Maryland, 6-11, Jr.; Kermit Washington, American, 6-8, Sr.

1974
First Team—Marvin Barnes, Providence, 6-9, Sr., Providence, RI; John Shumate, Notre Dame, 6-9, Jr., Elizabeth, NJ; David Thompson, North Carolina St., 6-4, Jr., Shelby, NC; Bill Walton, UCLA, 6-11, Sr., La Mesa, CA; Keith Wilkes, UCLA, 6-6, Sr., Santa Barbara, CA.
Second Team—Len Elmore, Maryland, 6-9, Jr.; Larry Fogle, Canisius, 6-5, So.; Bobby Jones, North Carolina, 6-8, Sr.; Bill Knight, Pittsburgh, 6-7, Sr.; Campy Russell, Michigan, 6-8, Jr.

1975
First Team—Adrian Dantley, Notre Dame, 6-5, So., Washington, DC; John Lucas, Maryland, 6-4, Jr., Durham, NC; Scott May, Indiana, 6-7, Jr., Sandusky, OH; Dave Meyers, UCLA, 6-8, Sr., La Habra, CA; David Thompson, North Carolina St., 6-4, Sr., Shelby, NC.
Second Team—Luther Burden, Utah, 6-2, Jr.; Leon Douglas, Alabama, 6-10, Jr.; Kevin Grevey, Kentucky, 6-5, Sr.; Ron Lee, Oregon, 6-4, Jr.; Gus Williams, Southern California, 6-2, Sr.

1976
First Team—Kent Benson, Indiana, 6-11, Jr., New Castle, IN; Adrian Dantley, Notre Dame, 6-5, Jr., Washington, DC; John Lucas, Maryland, 6-4, Sr., Durham, NC; Scott May, Indiana, 6-7, Sr., Sandusky, OH; Richard Washington, UCLA, 6-10, Jr., Portland, OR.
Second Team—Phil Ford, North Carolina, 6-2, So.; Bernard King, Tennessee, 6-7, So.; Mitch Kupchak, North Carolina, 6-9, Sr.; Phil Sellers, Rutgers, 6-5, Sr.; Earl Tatum, Marquette, 6-6, Sr.

1977
First Team—Kent Benson, Indiana, 6-11, New Castle, IN; Otis Birdsong, Houston, 6-4, Winter Haven, FL; Phil Ford, North Carolina, 6-2, Rocky Mount, NC; Rickey Green, Michigan, 6-2, Chicago; Marques Johnson, UCLA, 6-7, Los Angeles; Bernard King, Tennessee, 6-7, Brooklyn, NY.
Second Team—Greg Ballard, Oregon, 6-7, Sr.; Bill Cartwright, San Francisco, 6-11, So.; Rod Griffin, Wake Forest, 6-6, Jr.; Ernie Grunfeld, Tennessee, 6-6, Sr.; Phil Hubbard, Michigan; Butch Lee, Marquette, 6-2, Jr.; Mychal Thompson, Minnesota, 6-10, Jr.

1978
First Team—Larry Bird, Indiana St., 6-9, Jr., French Lick, IN; Phil Ford, North Carolina, 6-2, Sr., Rocky Mount, NC; David Greenwood, UCLA, 6-9, Jr., Los Angeles; Butch Lee, Marquette, 6-2, Sr., Bronx, NY; Mychal Thompson, Minnesota, 6-10, Sr., Nassau, Bahamas.
Second Team—Ron Brewer, Arkansas, 6-4, Sr.; Jack Givens, Kentucky, 6-6, Sr.; Rod Griffin, Wake Forest, 6-4, Sr.; Rick Robey, Kentucky, 6-10, Sr.; Freeman Williams, Portland St., 6-4, Sr.

1979
First Team—Larry Bird, Indiana St., 6-9, Sr., French Lick, IN; Mike Gminski, Duke, 6-11, Jr., Monroe, CT; David Greenwood, UCLA, Sr., Los Angeles; Earvin Johnson, Michigan St., 6-8, So., Lansing, MI; Sidney Moncrief, Arkansas, 6-4, Sr., Little Rock, AR.
Second Team—Bill Cartwright, San Francisco, 7-1, Sr.; Calvin Natt, La.-Monroe, 6-5, Sr.; Mike O'Koren, North Carolina, 6-7, Jr.; Jim Paxson, Dayton, 6-6, Sr.; Jim Spanarkel, Duke, 6-5, Sr.; Kelly Tripucka, Notre Dame, 6-7, So.; Sly Williams, Rhode Island, 6-7, Jr.

1980
First Team—Mark Aguirre, DePaul, 6-7, So., Chicago; Michael Brooks, La Salle, 6-7, Sr., Philadelphia; Joe Barry Carroll, Purdue, 7-1, Sr., Denver; Darrell Griffith, Louisville, 6-4, Sr., Louisville, KY; Kyle Macy, Kentucky, 6-3, Sr., Peru, IN.
Second Team—Mike Gminski, Duke, 6-11, Sr.; Albert King, Maryland, 6-6, Jr.; Mike O'Koren, North Carolina, 6-8, Sr.; Kelvin Ransey, Ohio St., 6-1, Sr.; Sam Worthen, Marquette, 6-5, Sr.

1981
First Team—Mark Aguirre, DePaul, 6-7, Jr., Chicago; Danny Ainge, BYU, 6-5, Sr., Eugene, OR; Steve Johnson, Oregon St., 6-11, Sr., San Bernardino, CA; Ralph Sampson, Virginia, 7-4, So., Harrisonburg, VA; Isiah Thomas, Indiana, 6-1, So., Chicago.
Second Team—Sam Bowie, Kentucky, 7-1, So.; Jeff Lamp, Virginia, 6-6, Sr.; Durand Macklin, LSU, 6-7, Sr.; Kelly Tripucka, Notre Dame, 6-6, Sr.; Danny Vranes, Utah, 6-7, Sr.; Al Wood, North Carolina, 6-6, Sr.

1982
First Team—Terry Cummings, DePaul, 6-9, Jr., Chicago; Quintin Dailey, San Francisco, 6-4, Jr., Baltimore; Eric Floyd, Georgetown, 6-3, Sr., Gastonia, NC; Ralph Sampson, Virginia, 7-4, Jr., Harrisonburg, VA; James Worthy, North Carolina, 6-9, Jr., Gastonia, NC.
Second Team—Dale Ellis, Tennessee, 6-7, Jr.; Kevin Magee, UC Irvine, 6-8, Sr.; John Paxson, Notre Dame, 6-2, Jr.; Sam Perkins, North Carolina, 6-9, So.; Paul Pressey, Tulsa, 6-5, Sr.

1983
First Team—Dale Ellis, Tennessee, 6-7, Sr., Marietta, GA; Patrick Ewing, Georgetown, 7-0, So., Cambridge, MA; Michael Jordan, North Carolina, 6-6, So., Wilmington, NC; Keith Lee, Memphis, 6-9, So., West Memphis, AR; Sam Perkins, North Carolina, 6-9, Jr., Latham, NY; Ralph Sampson, Virginia, 7-4, Sr., Harrisonburg, VA; Wayman Tisdale, Oklahoma, 6-9, Fr., Tulsa, OK.
Second Team—Clyde Drexler, Houston, 6-7, Jr.; Sidney Green, UNLV, 6-9, Sr.; John Paxson, Notre Dame, 6-2, Sr.; Steve Stipanovich, Missouri, 6-11, Sr.; Jon Sundvold, Missouri, 6-2, Sr.; Darrell Walker, Arkansas, 6-4, Sr.; Randy Wittman, Indiana, 6-6, Sr.

1984
First Team—Patrick Ewing, Georgetown, 7-0, Jr., Cambridge, MA; Michael Jordan, North Carolina, 6-5, Jr., Wilmington, NC; Akeem Olajuwon, Houston, 7-0, Jr., Lagos, Nigeria; Sam Perkins, North Carolina, 6-10, Sr., Latham, NY; Wayman Tisdale, Oklahoma, 6-9, So., Tulsa, OK.
Second Team—Michael Cage, San Diego St., 6-9, Sr.; Devin Durrant, BYU, 6-7, Sr.; Keith Lee, Memphis, 6-10, Jr.; Chris Mullin, St. John's (N.Y.), 6-6, Jr.; Melvin Turpin, Kentucky, 6-11, Sr.; Leon Wood, Cal St. Fullerton, 6-3, Sr.

1985
First Team—Johnny Dawkins, Duke, 6-2, Jr., Washington, DC.; Patrick Ewing, Georgetown, 7-0, Sr., Cambridge, MA; Keith Lee, Memphis, 6-10, Sr., West Memphis, AR; Xavier McDaniel, Wichita St., 6-7, Sr., Columbia, SC; Chris Mullin, St. John's (N.Y.), 6-6, Sr., Brooklyn, NY; Wayman Tisdale, Oklahoma, 6-9, Jr., Tulsa, OK.
Second Team—Len Bias, Maryland, 6-8, Jr.; Jon Koncak, SMU, 7-0, Sr.; Mark Price, Georgia Tech, 6-0, Jr.; Kenny Walker, Kentucky, 6-8, Jr.; Dwayne Washington, Syracuse, 6-2, So.

1986
First Team—Steve Alford, Indiana, 6-2, Jr., New Castle, IN; Walter Berry, St. John's (N.Y.), 6-8, Jr., Bronx, NY; Len Bias, Maryland, 6-8, Sr., Landover, MD; Johnny Dawkins, Duke, 6-2, Sr., Washington, DC; Kenny Walker, Kentucky, 6-8, Sr., Roberta, GA.
Second Team—Dell Curry, Virginia Tech, 6-5, Sr.; Brad Daugherty, North Carolina, 6-11, Sr.; Ron Harper, Miami (Ohio), 6-6, Sr.; Danny Manning, Kansas, 6-11, So.; David Robinson, Navy, 6-11, Jr.; Scott Skiles, Michigan St., 6-1, Sr.

1987
First Team—Steve Alford, Indiana, 6-2 , Sr., New Castle, IN; Danny Manning, Kansas, 6-11 , Jr., Lawrence, KS; David Robinson, Navy, 7-1, Sr., Woodbridge, VA; Kenny Smith, North Carolina, 6-3 , Sr., Queens, NY; Reggie Williams, Georgetown, 6-7 , Sr., Baltimore.
Second Team—Armon Gilliam, UNLV, 6-9, Sr.; Horace Grant, Clemson, 6-10 , Sr.; Dennis Hopson, Ohio St., 6-5, Sr.; Mark Jackson, St. John's (N.Y.), 6-4, Sr.; Ken Norman, Illinois, 6-8, Sr.

1988
First Team—Sean Elliott, Arizona, 6-8, Jr., Tucson, AZ; Gary Grant, Michigan, 6-3, Sr., Canton, OH; Hersey Hawkins, Bradley, 6-3, Sr., Chicago; Danny Manning, Kansas, 6-11, Sr., Lawrence, KS; J.R. Reid, North Carolina, 6-9, So., Virginia Beach, VA.
Second Team—Danny Ferry, Duke, 6-10, Jr.; Jerome Lane, Pittsburgh, 6-6, Jr.; Mark Macon, Temple, 6-5, Fr.; Mitch Richmond, Kansas St., 6-5, Sr.; Rony Seikaly, Syracuse, 6-11, Sr.; Michael Smith, BYU, 6-10, Jr.

1989
First Team—Sean Elliott, Arizona, 6-8, Sr., Tucson, AZ; Pervis Ellison, Louisville, 6-9, Sr., Savannah, GA; Danny Ferry, Duke, 6-10, Sr., Bowie, MD; Chris Jackson, LSU, 6-1, Fr., Gulfport, MS; Stacey King, Oklahoma, 6-11, Sr., Lawton, OK.
Second Team—Mookie Blaylock, Oklahoma, 6-1, Sr.; Sherman Douglas, Syracuse, 6-0, Sr.; Jay Edwards, Indiana, 6-4, So.; Todd Lichti, Stanford, 6-4, Sr.; Glen Rice, Michigan, 6-7, Sr.; Lionel Simmons, La Salle, 6-6, Jr.

1990

First Team—Derrick Coleman, Syracuse, 6-10, Sr., Detroit; Chris Jackson, LSU, 6-1, So., Gulfport, MS; Larry Johnson, UNLV, 6-7, Jr., Dallas; Gary Payton, Oregon St., 6-3, Sr., Oakland, CA; Lionel Simmons, La Salle, 6-6, Sr., Philadelphia.

Second Team—Hank Gathers, Loyola Marymount, 6-7, Sr.; Kendall Gill, Illinois, 6-5, Sr.; Bo Kimble, Loyola Marymount, 6-5, Sr.; Alonzo Mourning, Georgetown, 6-10, So.; Rumeal Robinson, Michigan, 6-2, Sr.; Dennis Scott, Georgia Tech, 6-8, Jr.; Doug Smith, Missouri, 6-10, Jr.

1991

First Team—Kenny Anderson, Georgia Tech, 6-2, So., Rego Park, NY; Jim Jackson, Ohio St., 6-6, So., Toledo, OH; Larry Johnson, UNLV, 6-7, Sr., Dallas; Shaquille O'Neal, LSU, 7-1, So., San Antonio; Billy Owens, Syracuse, 6-9, Jr., Carlisle, PA.

Second Team—Stacey Augmon, UNLV, 6-8, Sr.; Keith Jennings, East Tenn. St., 5-7, Sr.; Christian Laettner, Duke, 6-11, Jr.; Eric Murdock, Providence, 6-2, Sr.; Steve Smith, Michigan St., 6-6, Sr.

1992

First Team—Jim Jackson, Ohio St., 6-6, Jr., Toledo, OH; Christian Laettner, Duke, 6-11, Sr., Angola, NY; Harold Miner, Southern California, 6-5, Jr., Inglewood, CA; Alonzo Mourning, Georgetown, 6-10, Sr., Chesapeake, VA; Shaquille O'Neal, LSU, 7-1, Jr., San Antonio.

Second Team—Byron Houston, Oklahoma St., 6-7, Sr.; Don MacLean, UCLA, 6-10, Sr.; Anthony Peeler, Missouri, 6-4, Sr.; Malik Sealy, St. John's (N.Y.), 6-7, Sr.; Walt Williams, Maryland, 6-8, Sr.

1993

First Team—Calbert Cheaney, Indiana, 6-7, Sr., Evansville, IN; Anfernee Hardaway, Memphis, 6-7, Jr., Memphis, TN; Bobby Hurley, Duke, 6-0, Sr., Jersey City, NJ; Jamal Mashburn, Kentucky, 6-8, Jr., New York; Chris Webber, Michigan, 6-9, So., Detroit.

Second Team—Terry Dehere, Seton Hall, 6-3, Sr.; Grant Hill, Duke, 6-7, Jr.; Billy McCaffrey, Vanderbilt, 6-3, Jr.; Eric Montross, North Carolina, 7-0, Jr.; J.R. Rider, UNLV, 6-7, Sr.; Glenn Robinson, Purdue, 6-9, So.; Rodney Rogers, Wake Forest, 6-8, Jr.

1994

First Team—Grant Hill, Duke, 6-8, Sr., Reston, VA; Jason Kidd, California, 6-4, So., Oakland, CA; Donyell Marshall, Connecticut, 6-9, Jr., Reading, PA; Glenn Robinson, Purdue, 6-8, Jr., Gary, IN; Clifford Rozier, Louisville, 6-9, Jr., Bradenton, FL.

Second Team—Melvin Booker, Missouri, 6-2, Sr.; Eric Montross, North Carolina, 7-0, Sr.; Lamond Murray, California, 6-7, Jr.; Khalid Reeves, Arizona, 6-2, Sr.; Jalen Rose, Michigan, 6-8, Jr.; Corliss Williamson, Arkansas, 6-7, So.

1995

First Team—Ed O'Bannon, UCLA, 6-8, Sr., Lakewood, CA; Shawn Respert, Michigan St., 6-3, Sr., Detroit; Joe Smith, Maryland, 6-10, So., Norfolk, VA; Jerry Stackhouse, North Carolina, 6-6, So., Kingston, NC; Damon Stoudamire, Arizona, 6-10, Sr., Portland, OR.

Second Team—Randolph Childress, Wake Forest, 6-2, Sr.; Kerry Kittles, Villanova, 6-5, Jr.; Lou Roe, Massachusetts, 6-7, Sr.; Rasheed Wallace, North Carolina, 6-10, So.; Corliss Williamson, Arkansas, 6-7, Jr.

1996

First Team—Ray Allen, Connecticut, 6-5, Jr., Dalzell, SC; Marcus Camby, Massachusetts, 6-11, Jr., Hartford, CT; Tony Delk, Kentucky, 6-1, Sr., Brownsville, TN; Tim Duncan, Wake Forest, 6-10, Jr., St. Croix, Virgin Islands; Allen Iverson, Georgetown, 6-1, So., Hampton, VA; Kerry Kittles, Villanova, 6-5, Sr., New Orleans.

Second Team—Danny Fortson, Cincinnati, 6-7, So.; Keith Van Horn, Utah, 6-9, Jr.; Jacque Vaughn, Kansas, 6-1, Jr.; John Wallace, Syracuse, 6-8, Sr.; Lorenzen Wright, Memphis, 6-11, So.

1997

First Team—Tim Duncan, Wake Forest, 6-10, Sr., St. Croix, Virgin Islands; Danny Fortson, Cincinnati, 6-7, Jr., Pittsburgh; Raef LaFrentz, Kansas, 6-11, Jr., Monona, IA; Ron Mercer, Kentucky, 6-7, So., Nashville, TN; Keith Van Horn, Utah, 6-9, Sr., Diamond Bar, CA.

Second Team—Chauncey Billups, Colorado, 6-3, So.; Bobby Jackson, Minnesota, 6-1, Sr.; Antawn Jamison, North Carolina, 6-9, So.; Brevin Knight, Stanford, 5-10, Sr.; Jacque Vaughn, Kansas, 6-1, Sr.

1998

First Team—Mike Bibby, Arizona, 6-2, So., Phoenix, AZ; Antawn Jamison, North Carolina, 6-9, Jr., Charlotte, NC; Raef LaFrentz, Kansas, 6-11, Sr., Monona, IA; Paul Pierce, Kansas, 6-7, Jr., Inglewood, CA; Miles Simon, Arizona, 6-5, Sr., Fullerton, CA.

Second Team—Vince Carter, North Carolina, 6-6, Jr.; Mateen Cleaves, Michigan St., 6-2, So.; Pat Garrity, Notre Dame, 6-9, Sr.; Richard Hamilton, Connecticut, 6-6, So.; Ansu Sesay, Mississippi, 6-9, Sr.

1999

First Team—Elton Brand, Duke, 6-8, So., Peekskill, NY; Mateen Cleaves, Michigan St., 6-2, Jr., Flint, MI; Richard Hamilton, Connecticut, 6-6, Jr., Coatesville, PA; Andre Miller, Utah, 6-2, Sr., Los Angeles; Jason Terry, Arizona, 6-2, Sr., Seattle.

Second Team—Evan Eschmeyer, Northwestern, 6-11, Sr.; Steve Francis, Maryland, 6-3, Jr.; Trajan Langdon, Duke, 6-3, Sr.; Chris Porter, Auburn, 6-7, Jr.; Wally Szczerbiak, Miami (Ohio), 6-8, Sr.

2000

First Team—Chris Carrawell, Duke, 6-6, Sr., St. Louis; Marcus Fizer, Iowa St., 6-8, Jr., Arcadia, LA; A.J. Guyton, Indiana, 6-1, Sr., Peoria, IL; Kenyon Martin, Cincinnati, 6-9, Sr., Dallas; Chris Mihm, Texas, 7-0, Jr., Austin, TX; Troy Murphy, Notre Dame, 6-10, So., Morristown, NJ.

Second Team—Courtney Alexander, Fresno St., 6-6, Sr.; Shane Battier, Duke, 6-8, Jr.; Mateen Cleaves, Michigan St., 6-2, Sr.; Scoonie Penn, Ohio St., 5-10, Sr.; Morrison Peterson, Michigan St., 6-6, Sr.; Stromile Swift, LSU, 6-9, So.

2001

First Team—Shane Battier, Duke, 6-8, Sr., Birmingham, MI; Joseph Forte, North Carolina, 6-4, So., Greenbelt, MD; Casey Jacobsen, Stanford, 6-6, So., Glendora, CA; Troy Murphy, Notre Dame, 6-10, Jr., Morristown, NJ; Jason Williams, Duke, 6-2, So., Plainfield, NJ.

Second Team—Troy Bell, Boston College, 6-1, So.; Michael Bradley, Villanova, 6-10, Jr.; Tayshaun Prince, Kentucky, 6-9, Jr.; Jason Richardson, Michigan St., 6-6, So.; Jamaal Tinsley, Iowa St., 6-3, Sr.

2002

First Team—Juan Dixon, Maryland, 6-3, Sr., Baltimore; Dan Dickau, Gonzaga, 6-1, Sr., Vancouver, WA; Drew Gooden, Kansas, 6-10, Jr., Richmond, CA; Steve Logan, Cincinnati, 6-1, Sr., Cleveland; Jason Williams, Duke, 6-2, Jr., Plainfield, NJ.

Second Team—Sam Clancy, Southern California, 6-7, Sr.; Mike Dunleavy, Duke, 6-9, Jr.; Casey Jacobsen, Stanford, 6-6, Jr.; Jared Jeffries, Indiana, 6-10, So.; David West, Xavier, 6-8, Jr.

2003

First Team—Nick Collison, Kansas, 6-9, Sr., Iowa Falls, IA; T.J. Ford, Texas, 5-10, So., Houston; Josh Howard, Wake Forest, 6-6, Sr., Winston-Salem, NC; Dwyane Wade, Marquette, 6-4, Jr., Robbins, IL; David West, Xavier, 6-9, Sr., Garner, NC.

Second Team—Carmelo Anthony, Syracuse, 6-8, Fr.; Troy Bell, Boston College, 6-1, Sr.; Jason Gardner, Arizona, 5-10, Sr.; Kyle Korver, Creighton, 6-7, Sr.; Hollis Price, Oklahoma, 6-1, Sr.

2004

First Team—Andre Emmett, Texas Tech, 6-5, Sr., Dallas; Ryan Gomes, Providence, 6-7, Jr., Waterbury, CT; Jameer Nelson, St. Joseph's, 6-0, Sr., Chester, PA; Emeka Okafor, Connecticut, 6-10, Jr., Houston; Lawrence Roberts, Mississippi St., 6-9, Jr., Houston.

Second Team—Josh Childress, Stanford, 6-8, Jr.; Devin Harris, Wisconsin, 6-3, Jr.; Julius Hodge, North Carolina St., 6-6, Jr.; Luke Jackson, Oregon, 6-7, Sr.; Blake Stepp, Gonzaga, 6-4, Sr.

2005

First Team—Andrew Bogut, Utah, 7-0, So., Melbourne, Australia; Dee Brown, Illinois, 6-0, Jr., Maywood, IL; Chris Paul, Wake Forest, 6-0, So., Lewisville, NC; J.J. Redick, Duke, 6-4, Jr., Roanoke, VA; Wayne Simien, Kansas, 6-9, Sr., Leavenworth, KS; Hakim Warrick, Syracuse, 6-9, Sr., Philadelphia.

Second Team—Ike Diogu, Arizona St., 6-8, Jr.; Luther Head, Illinois, 6-3, Sr.; Sean May, North Carolina, 6-9, Jr.; Salim Stoudamire, Arizona, 6-1, Sr.; Deron Williams, Illinois, 6-3, Jr.

2006

First Team—Randy Foye, Villanova, 6-4, Sr., Newark, NJ; Adam Morrison, Gonzaga, 6-8, Jr., Spokane, WA; J.J. Redick, Duke, 6-4, Sr., Roanoke, VA; Brandon Roy, Washington, 6-6, Sr., Seattle; Shelden Williams, Duke, 6-9, Sr., Forest Park, OK.

Second Team—Dee Brown, Illinois, 6-0, Sr.; Rodney Carney, Memphis, 6-7, Sr.; Rudy Gay, Connecticut, 6-9, So.; Tyler Hansbrough, North Carolina, 6-9, Fr.; Leon Powe, California, 6-8, So.; Allan Ray, Villanova, 6-2, Sr.; P.J. Tucker, Texas, 6-5, Jr.

2007

First Team—Arron Afflalo, UCLA, 6-5, Jr., Compton, CA; Kevin Durant, Texas, 6-9, Fr., Suitland, MD; Tyler Hansbrough, North Carolina, 6-9, So., Poplar Bluff, MO; Acie Law IV, Texas A&M, 6-3, Sr., Dallas; Alando Tucker, Wisconsin, 6-6, Sr., Lockport, IL.

Second Team—Jared Dudley, Boston College, 6-7, Sr.; Nick Fazekas, Nevada, 6-11, Sr.; Chris Lofton, Tennessee, 6-2, Jr.; Joakim Noah, Florida, 6-11, Jr.; Greg Oden, Ohio St., 7-0, Fr.

2008

First Team—D.J. Augustin, Texas, 6-0, So., New Orleans; Michael Beasley, Kansas St., 6-10, Fr., Washington, DC; Chris Douglas-Roberts, Memphis, 6-7, Jr., Detroit; Tyler Hansbrough, North Carolina, 6-9, Jr., Poplar Bluff, MO; Kevin Love, UCLA, 6-10, Fr., Lake Oswego, OR.

Second Team—Stephen Curry, Davidson, 6-2, So.; Shan Foster, Vanderbilt, 6-6, Sr.; Luke Harangody, Notre Dame, 6-8, So.; Roy Hibbert, Georgetown, 7-2, Sr.; Chris Lofton, Tennessee, 6-2, Sr; D.J. White, Indiana, 6-9, Sr.

Teams used for consensus selections:

Helms Foundation—1905-48
Converse Yearbook—1932-48
College Humor Magazine—1929-33, 1936
Christy Walsh Syndicate—1929-30
Literary Digest Magazine—1934
Madison Square Garden—1937-42
Omaha World Newspaper—1937
Newspaper Enterprises Assn.—1938, 1953-63
Colliers (Basketball Coaches)—1939, 1949-56
Pic Magazine—1942-44
Argosy Magazine—1945
True Magazine—1946-47
International News Service—1950-58
Look Magazine—1949-63
United Press International—1949-96
Sporting News—1943-46, 1997-2008
The Associated Press—1948-2008
National Assoc. of Basketball Coaches—1957-2008
U.S. Basketball Writers Association—1960-2008

Consensus First-Team All-Americans By Team

ARIZONA
1988—Sean Elliott
1989—Sean Elliott
1995—Damon Stoudamire
1998—Mike Bibby
    Miles Simon
1999—Jason Terry

ARKANSAS
1928—Glen Rose
1936—Ike Poole
1941—John Adams
1979—Sidney Moncrief

ARMY
1910—William Copthorne
1913—William Roberts
1918—Gene Vidal
1927—Harry Wilson

BOWLING GREEN
1945—Wyndol Gray

BRADLEY
1950—Paul Unruh
1951—Gene Melchiorre
1961—Chet Walker
1962—Chet Walker
1988—Hersey Hawkins

BYU
1931—Elwood Romney
1981—Danny Ainge

BROWN
1908—John Pryor

BUTLER
1924—Hugh Middlesworth

CALIFORNIA
1917—George Hjelte
1926—George Dixon
1927—George Dixon
1929—Vern Corbin
1960—Darrall Imhoff
1994—Jason Kidd

CHICAGO
1905—James Ozanne
1906—James McKeag
    John Schommer
1907—Albert Houghton
    John Schommer
1908—Pat Page
    John Schommer
1909—Pat Page
    John Schommer
1910—Pat Page
1914—Nelson Norgren
1919—Tony Hinkle
1920—Tony Hinkle
1921—R.D. Birkhoff

CINCINNATI
1958—Oscar Robertson
1959—Oscar Robertson
1960—Oscar Robertson
1963—Ron Bonham
    Tom Thacker
1997—Danny Fortson
2000—Kenyon Martin
2002—Steve Logan

CCNY
1908—Ira Streusand
1914—Everett Southwick

COLGATE
1905—Walter Runge
1910—Leon Campbell
1912—Emil Schradieck

COLORADO COL.
1925—Earl Mueller
1928—Ernest Simpson

COLUMBIA
1905—Marcus Hurley

1906—Marcus Hurley
1907—Marcus Hurley
    John Ryan
1908—John Ryan
1909—Biaggio Gerussi
    Ted Kiendl
    John Ryan
1910—Ted Kiendl
1911—A.D. Alexander
    Ted Kiendl
    W.M. Lee
1912—Claus Benson
1914—Dan Meenan
1915—Charlie Lee
1927—John Lorch
1931—George Gregory
1957—Chet Forte

CONNECTICUT
1994—Donyell Marshall
1996—Ray Allen
1999—Richard Hamilton
2004—Emeka Okafor

CORNELL
1913—George Halstead
1914—George Halstead
    Walter Lunden
1915—Leslie Brown
1923—John Luther

CREIGHTON
1923—Jimmy Lovley
1924—Jimmy Lovley
1927—Sidney Corenman
1943—Ed Beisser

DARTMOUTH
1906—George Grebenstein
1912—Ernst Mensel
    Rufus Sisson
1940—Gus Broberg
1941—Gus Broberg
1944—Audley Brindley

DAVIDSON
1965—Fred Hetzel

DAYTON
1912—Alphonse Schumacher
1913—Alphonse Schumacher

DENVER
1949—Vince Boryla

DePAUL
1944—George Mikan
1945—George Mikan
1946—George Mikan
1980—Mark Aguirre
1981—Mark Aguirre
1982—Terry Cummings

DETROIT
1969—Spencer Haywood

DUKE
1952—Dick Groat
1963—Art Heyman
1967—Bob Verga
1979—Mike Gminski
1985—Johnny Dawkins
1986—Johnny Dawkins
1989—Danny Ferry
1992—Christian Laettner
1993—Bobby Hurley
1994—Grant Hill
1999—Elton Brand
2000—Chris Carrawell
2001—Shane Battier
    Jason Williams
2002—Jason Williams
2005—J.J. Redick
2006—J.J. Redick
    Shelden Williams

DUQUESNE
1955—Dick Ricketts
    Si Green
1956—Si Green

FURMAN
1954—Frank Selvy

GEORGETOWN
1982—Eric Floyd
1983—Patrick Ewing

1984—Patrick Ewing
1985—Patrick Ewing
1987—Reggie Williams
1992—Alonzo Mourning
1996—Allen Iverson

GEORGIA TECH
1961—Roger Kaiser
1991—Kenny Anderson

GONZAGA
2002—Dan Dickau
2006—Adam Morrison

HARVARD
1906—Harold Amberg
    Ralph Griffiths

HOLY CROSS
1950—Bob Cousy
1956—Tom Heinsohn

HOUSTON
1967—Elvin Hayes
1968—Elvin Hayes
1977—Otis Birdsong
1984—Akeem Olajuwon

IDAHO
1923—Al Fox

ILLINOIS
1915—Ray Woods
1916—Ray Woods
1917—Clyde Alwood
    Ray Woods
1918—Earl Anderson
1920—Charles Carney
1922—Charles Carney
1940—Bill Hapac
1942—Andrew Phillip
1943—Andrew Phillip
1945—Walton Kirk
1952—Rod Fletcher
2005—Dee Brown

ILLINOIS ST.
1973—Doug Collins

INDIANA
1921—Everett Dean
1930—Branch McCracken
1936—Vern Huffman
1939—Ernie Andres
1947—Ralph Hamilton
1954—Don Schlundt
1975—Scott May
1976—Scott May
    Kent Benson
1977—Kent Benson
1981—Isiah Thomas
1986—Steve Alford
1987—Steve Alford
1993—Calbert Cheaney
2000—A.J. Guyton

INDIANA ST.
1978—Larry Bird
1979—Larry Bird

IOWA
1948—Murray Wier
1952—Chuck Darling

IOWA ST.
2000—Marcus Fizer

JACKSONVILLE
1971—Artis Gilmore

KANSAS
1909—Tommy Johnson
1915—Ralph Sproull
1919—Dutch Lonborg
1922—Paul Endacott
1923—Charlie T. Black
    Paul Endacott
1924—Arthur Ackerman
    Charlie T. Black
1925—Arthur Ackerman
1926—Gale Gordon
    Albert Peterson
1938—Fred Pralle
1941—Howard Engleman
1943—Charles Black
1951—Clyde Lovellette
1952—Clyde Lovellette
1957—Wilt Chamberlain

1958—Wilt Chamberlain
1987—Danny Manning
1988—Danny Manning
1997—Raef LaFrentz
1998—Raef LaFrentz
    Paul Pierce
2002—Drew Gooden
2003—Nick Collison
2005—Wayne Simien

KANSAS ST.
1917—F.I. Reynolds
1958—Bob Boozer
1959—Bob Boozer
2008—Michael Beasley

KENTUCKY
1921—Basil Hayden
1925—Burgess Carey
1932—Forest Sale
1933—Forest Sale
1935—Leroy Edwards
1944—Robert Brannum
1947—Ralph Beard
    Alex Groza
1948—Ralph Beard
1949—Ralph Beard
    Alex Groza
1951—Bill Spivey
1952—Cliff Hagan
1954—Cliff Hagan
1959—Johnny Cox
1964—Cotton Nash
1970—Dan Issel
1980—Kyle Macy
1986—Kenny Walker
1993—Jamal Mashburn
1996—Tony Delk
1997—Ron Mercer

LA SALLE
1953—Tom Gola
1954—Tom Gola
1955—Tom Gola
1980—Michael Brooks
1990—Lionel Simmons

LONG BEACH ST.
1972—Ed Ratleff
1973—Ed Ratleff

LONG ISLAND
1937—Jules Bender
1939—Irving Torgoff

LA.-LAFAYETTE
1972—Dwight Lamar
1973—Dwight Lamar

LSU
1954—Bob Pettit
1968—Pete Maravich
1969—Pete Maravich
1970—Pete Maravich
1989—Chris Jackson
1990—Chris Jackson
1991—Shaquille O'Neal
1992—Shaquille O'Neal

LOUISVILLE
1957—Charlie Tyra
1967—Wes Unseld
1968—Wes Unseld
1980—Darrell Griffith
1989—Pervis Ellison
1994—Clifford Rozier

LOYOLA (ILL.)
1963—Jerry Harkness

MARQUETTE
1971—Dean Meminger
1972—Jim Chones
1978—Butch Lee
2003—Dwyane Wade

MARYLAND
1932—Louis Berger
1975—John Lucas
1976—John Lucas
1986—Len Bias
1995—Joe Smith
2002—Juan Dixon

MASSACHUSETTS
1996—Marcus Camby

MEMPHIS
1983—Keith Lee
1985—Keith Lee
1993—Anfernee Hardaway
2008—Chris Douglas-Roberts

MIAMI (FLA.)
1965—Rick Barry

MICHIGAN
1924—Harry Kipke
1926—Richard Doyle
1927—Bennie Oosterbaan
1928—Bennie Oosterbaan
1965—Cazzie Russell
1966—Cazzie Russell
1977—Rickey Green
1988—Gary Grant
1993—Chris Webber

MICHIGAN ST.
1979—Earvin Johnson
1995—Shawn Respert
1999—Mateen Cleaves

MINNESOTA
1905—George Tuck
1906—Garfield Brown
1911—Frank Lawler
1917—Francis Stadsvold
1918—Harold Gillen
1919—Arnold Oss
    Erling Platou
1921—Arnold Oss
1948—Jim McIntyre
1955—Dick Garmaker
1978—Mychal Thompson

MISSISSIPPI ST.
1959—Bailey Howell
2004—Lawrence Roberts

MISSOURI
1916—Fred Williams
1918—Craig Ruby
1919—Craig Ruby
1920—George Williams
1921—Herbert Bunker
    George Williams
1922—Arthur Browning
    Herbert Bunker
1923—Arthur Browning
    Herbert Bunker

MONTANA ST.
1927—John Thompson
1928—John Thompson
1929—John Thompson
1930—John Thompson
    Frank Ward

NAVY
1911—Harry Hill
1913—Laurence Wild
1919—Lance Farwell
1922—Ira McKee
1923—Ira McKee
1933—Elliott Loughlin
1987—David Robinson

NEBRASKA
1913—Sam Carrier

UNLV
1990—Larry Johnson
1991—Larry Johnson

NEW YORK U.
1910—William Broadhead
1920—Howard Cann
1946—Sid Tanenbaum
1947—Sid Tanenbaum
1963—Barry Kramer

NIAGARA
1969—Calvin Murphy
1970—Calvin Murphy

NORTH CAROLINA
1923—Cartwright Carmichael
1924—Cartwright Carmichael
    Jack Cobb
1925—Jack Cobb
1926—Jack Cobb
1940—George Glamack
1941—George Glamack
1957—Lenny Rosenbluth

1968—Larry Miller
1972—Bob McAdoo
1977—Phil Ford
1978—Phil Ford
1982—James Worthy
1983—Michael Jordan
   Sam Perkins
1984—Michael Jordan
   Sam Perkins
1987—Kenny Smith
1988—J.R. Reid
1995—Jerry Stackhouse
1998—Antawn Jamison
2001—Joseph Forte
2007—Tyler Hansbrough
2008—Tyler Hansbrough

NORTH CAROLINA ST.
1951—Sam Ranzino
1956—Ron Shavlik
1973—David Thompson
1974—David Thompson
1975—David Thompson

NORTHWESTERN
1931—Joe Reiff
1933—Joe Reiff
1944—Otto Graham
1946—Max Norris

NOTRE DAME
1909—Raymond Scanlon
1925—Noble Kizer
1927—John Nyikos
1932—Ed Krause
1933—Ed Krause
1934—Ed Krause
1936—Paul Nowak
   John Moir
1937—Paul Nowak
   John Moir
1938—Paul Nowak
   John Moir
1944—Leo Klier
1945—William Hassett
1946—Leo Klier
1948—Kevin O'Shea
1971—Austin Carr
1974—John Shumate
1975—Adrian Dantley
1976—Adrian Dantley
2000—Troy Murphy
2001—Troy Murphy

OHIO ST.
1925—Johnny Miner
1931—Wes Fesler
1939—Jimmy Hull
1950—Dick Schnittker
1956—Robin Freeman
1960—Jerry Lucas
1961—Jerry Lucas
1962—Jerry Lucas
1964—Gary Bradds
1991—Jim Jackson
1992—Jim Jackson

OKLAHOMA
1910—Ernest Lambert
1928—Victor Holt
1929—Thomas Churchill
1935—Bud Browning
1944—Alva Paine
1947—Gerald Tucker
1983—Wayman Tisdale
1984—Wayman Tisdale
1985—Wayman Tisdale
1989—Stacey King

OKLAHOMA ST.
1944—Robert Kurland
1945—Robert Kurland
1946—Robert Kurland

OREGON
1921—Eddie Durno
1924—Hugh Latham
1926—Algot Westergren
1939—Urgel Wintermute
1940—John Dick

OREGON ST.
1916—Ade Sieberts
1922—Marshall Hjelte
1924—Slats Gill

1925—Carlos Steele
1981—Steve Johnson
1990—Gary Payton

PENN
1906—George Flint
   Charles Keinath
1907—George Flint
   Charles Keinath
1908—Charles Keinath
1909—Charles Keinath
1911—Lewis Walton
1912—William Turner
1916—Edward McNichol
1918—Hubert Peck
   George Sweeney
1919—Dan McNichol
   Andrew Stannard
1920—Dan McNichol
   Hubert Peck
   George Sweeney
1921—Dan McNichol
1920—William Graves
1925—Emanuel Goldblatt
1926—Emanuel Goldblatt
1928—Joe Schaaf
1929—Joe Schaaf
1945—Howard Dallmar
1953—Ernie Beck

PITTSBURGH
1928—Charley Hyatt
   Wallace Reed
1929—Charley Hyatt
1930—Charley Hyatt
1933—Don Smith
1934—Claire Cribbs
1935—Claire Cribbs
1958—Don Hennon

PRINCETON
1905—Oliver deGray Vanderbilt
1913—Hamilton Salmon
1916—Cyril Haas
1917—Cyril Haas
1922—Arthur Loeb
1923—Arthur Loeb
1926—Carl Loeb
1964—Bill Bradley
1965—Bill Bradley

PROVIDENCE
1966—Jim Walker
1967—Jim Walker
1973—Ernie DiGregorio
1974—Marvin Barnes
2004—Ryan Gomes

PURDUE
1910—Dave Charters
1911—Dave Charters
1913—Larry Teeple
1914—Elmer Oliphant
1915—Elmer Oliphant
1921—Donald White
1922—Ray Miller
1926—George Spradling
1928—Charles Murphy
1929—Charles Murphy
1930—Charles Murphy
   John Wooden
1931—John Wooden
1932—John Wooden
1934—Norman Cottom
1936—Bob Kessler
1937—Jewell Young
1938—Jewell Young
1961—Terry Dischinger
1962—Terry Dischinger
1966—Dave Schellhase
1969—Rick Mount
1970—Rick Mount
1980—Joe Barry Carroll
1994—Glenn Robinson

RHODE ISLAND
1939—Chet Jaworski

RICE
1942—Bob Kinney
1943—William Closs
1945—William Henry

ROCHESTER (N.Y.)
1910—Samuel Harman

RUTGERS
1967—Bob Lloyd

ST. BONAVENTURE
1960—Tom Stith
1961—Tom Stith
1970—Bob Lanier

ST. JOHN'S (N.Y.)
1911—John Keenan
1943—Harry Boykoff
1985—Chris Mullin
1986—Walter Berry

ST. JOSEPH'S
1943—George Senesky
2004—Jameer Nelson

ST. LAWRENCE
1912—Thomas Canfield
1913—Eddie Calder

ST. LOUIS
1948—Ed Macauley
1949—Ed Macauley

SAN FRANCISCO
1955—Bill Russell
1956—Bill Russell
1982—Quintin Dailey

SEATTLE
1953—Johnny O'Brien
1958—Elgin Baylor

SETON HALL
1942—Robert Davies
1953—Walt Dukes

SOUTH CAROLINA
1972—Tom Riker

SOUTHERN CALIFORNIA
1933—Jerry Nemer
1935—Lee Guttero
1940—Ralph Vaughn
1950—Bill Sharman
1992—Harold Miner

SMU
1957—Jim Krebs

SOUTHWESTERN (KAN.)
1920—George Gardner
1922—George Gardner

STANFORD
1936—Hank Luisetti
1937—Hank Luisetti
1938—Hank Luisetti
2001—Casey Jacobsen

SWARTHMORE
1910—Charles Eberle
1912—Fred Gieg

SYRACUSE
1912—Lewis Castle
1914—Lewis Castle
1918—Joseph Schwarzer
1919—Leon Marcus
1925—Victor Hanson
1926—Victor Hanson
1927—Victor Hanson
1966—Dave Bing
1990—Derrick Coleman
1991—Billy Owens
2005—Hakim Warrick

TEMPLE
1938—Meyer Bloom
1951—Bill Mlkvy
1958—Guy Rodgers

TENNESSEE
1977—Bernard King
1983—Dale Ellis

TEXAS
1916—Clyde Littlefield
1924—Abb Curtis
1935—Jack Gray
2000—Chris Mihm
2003—T.J. Ford
2007—Kevin Durant
2008—D.J. Augustin

TEXAS A&M
2007—Acie Law IV

TEXAS TECH
2004—Andre Emmett

UCLA
1964—Walt Hazzard
1965—Gail Goodrich
1967—Lew Alcindor
1968—Lew Alcindor
1969—Lew Alcindor
1971—Sidney Wicks
1972—Bill Walton
   Henry Bibby
1973—Bill Walton
   Keith Wilkes
1974—Bill Walton
   Keith Wilkes
1975—Dave Meyers
1976—Richard Washington
1977—Marques Johnson
1978—David Greenwood
1979—David Greenwood
1995—Ed O'Bannon
2007—Arron Afflalo
2008—Kevin Love

UNION (N.Y.)
1914—Ernest Houghton
1915—Ernest Houghton

UTAH
1916—Dick Romney
1936—Bill Kinner
1945—Arnold Ferrin
1962—Billy McGill
1997—Keith Van Horn
1999—Andre Miller
2005—Andre Bogut

VANDERBILT
1966—Clyde Lee

VILLANOVA
1950—Paul Arizin
1996—Kerry Kittles
2006—Randy Foye

VIRGINIA
1915—Wellington Strickley
1981—Ralph Sampson
1982—Ralph Sampson
1983—Ralph Sampson

VIRGINIA TECH
1919—George Parrish

WAKE FOREST
1962—Len Chappell
1996—Tim Duncan
1997—Tim Duncan
2003—Josh Howard
2005—Chris Paul

WASHBURN
1925—Gerald Spohn
1927—Gerald Spohn

WASHINGTON
1911—C.C. Clementson
1915—Tony Savage
1920—Erving Cook
1928—Alfred James
1934—Hal Lee
1953—Bob Houbregs
2006—Brandon Roy

WASH. & LEE
1917—Harry Young

WASHINGTON ST.
1916—Roy Bohler
1918—Alfred Sorenson

WESLEYAN
1908—Julian Hayward
1909—Julian Hayward
1913—Edward Hayward

WEST TEX. A&M
1942—Price Brookfield

WEST VIRGINIA
1957—Rod Hundley
1959—Jerry West
1960—Jerry West

WESTERN KY.
1967—Clem Haskins
1971—Jim McDaniels

WESTMINSTER (MO.)
1920—Forrest DeBernardi
1921—Forrest DeBernardi

WICHITA ST.
1927—Ross McBurney
1964—Dave Stallworth
1985—Xavier McDaniel

WILLIAMS
1906—Eugene Cowell
1907—Oswald Tower
   L. Parson Warren
1910—W. Vaughn Lewis

WISCONSIN
1905—C.D. McLees
   Chris Steinmetz
1907—Frank Arthur
1908—Hugh Harper
   Helmer Swenholt
1909—Helmer Swenholt
1911—Walter Scoville
1912—Otto Stangel
1913—Allen Johnson
1914—Carl Harper
   Eugene Van Gent
1915—George Levis
1916—William Chandler
   George Levis
1917—Harold Olsen
1918—William Chandler
   Eber Simpson
1941—Gene Englund
1942—John Kotz
2007—Alando Tucker

WYOMING
1932—Les Witte
1934—Les Witte
1943—Ken Sailors

XAVIER
2003—David West

YALE
1905—Harry Fisher
   Willard Hyatt
   Gilmore Kinney
1907—Gilmore Kinney
1908—Haskell Noyes
1915—W.P. Arnold
1917—Orson Kinney
   Charles Taft
1949—Tony Lavelli

Team Leaders in Consensus First-Team All-Americans

(Ranked on total number of selections)

Team	No.	Players	Team	No.	Players	Team	No.	Players
Kansas	26	19	Syracuse	11	8	Arizona	6	5
Purdue	25	16	Oklahoma	10	8	California	6	5
North Carolina	24	16	Missouri	10	5	Dartmouth	6	5
Penn	24	14	Yale	9	8	Louisville	6	5
Kentucky	22	17	Michigan	9	7	Maryland	6	5
Notre Dame	22	13	Princeton	9	6	DePaul	6	3
Wisconsin	20	17	Cincinnati	8	6	Oregon	5	5
UCLA	20	14	Pittsburgh	8	5	Southern California	5	5
Duke	18	14	LSU	8	4	Bradley	5	4
Columbia	18	12	Texas	7	7	Cornell	5	4
Indiana	15	12	Utah	7	7	New York U.	5	4
Chicago	14	8	Washington	7	7	Providence	5	4
Illinois	13	9	Navy	7	6	Wake Forest	5	4
Minnesota	11	10	Georgetown	7	5	La Salle	5	3
Ohio St.	11	8	Oregon St.	6	6	North Carolina St.	5	3
						Montana St.	5	2

Division I Academic All-Americans by Team

AIR FORCE
1968—Cliff Parsons
1970—Jim Cooper
1978—Tom Schneeberger

AMERICAN
1972—Kermit Washington
1973—Kermit Washington
1987—Patrick Witting

ARIZONA
1976—Bob Elliott
1977—Bob Elliott

ARIZONA ST.
1964—Art Becker
1999—Bobby Lazor

ARKANSAS
1978—Jim Counce

ARMY
1964—Mike Silliman

BALL ST.
2002—Patrick Jackson

BAYLOR
1996—Doug Brandt
1997—Doug Brandt

BELMONT
2002—Wes Burtner
2003—Adam Mark
2004—Adam Mark
2008—Justin Hare

BOSTON COLLEGE
1968—Terry Driscoll

BYU
1980—Danny Ainge
1981—Danny Ainge
1983—Devin Durrant
1984—Devin Durrant
1987—Michael Smith
1988—Michael Smith
1989—Michael Smith
1990—Andy Toolson

BROWN
1986—Jim Turner

BUCKNELL
1999—Valter Karavanic

BUTLER
2007—A.J. Graves

CALIFORNIA
1987—David Butler

CENTRAL MICH.
1993—Sander Scott

COL. OF CHARLESTON
2000—Jody Lumpkin
2001—Jody Lumpkin

CINCINNATI
1967—Mike Rolf

CLEVELAND ST.
1973—Pat Lyons

COASTAL CARO.
2008—Jack Leasure

COLGATE
1997—Adonal Foyle

CONNECTICUT
1967—Wes Bialosuknia
2003—Emeka Okafor
2004—Emeka Okafor

CORNELL
2007—Graham Dow

CREIGHTON
1964—Paul Silas
1978—Rick Apke

DARTMOUTH
1984—Paul Anderson
1996—Seamus Lonergan

DAVIDSON
1988—Derek Rucker

DAYTON
1979—Jim Paxson
1981—Mike Kanieski
1982—Mike Kanieski

DENVER
2003—Brett Starkey

DePAUL
1991—Stephen Howard
1992—Stephen Howard

DRAKE
2008—Adam Emmenecker

DUKE
1963—Jay Buckley
1964—Jay Buckley
1971—Dick DeVenzio
1972—Gary Melchionni

1975—Bob Fleischer
1978—Mike Gminski
        Jim Spanarkel
1979—Mike Gminski
        Jim Spanarkel
1980—Mike Gminski
2000—Shane Battier
2001—Shane Battier

DUQUESNE
1969—Bill Zopf
1970—Bill Zopf

EVANSVILLE
1989—Scott Haffner
2003—Clint Cuffle

FAIRLEIGH DICKINSON
1978—John Jorgensen

FLORIDA
2002—Matt Bonner
2003—Matt Bonner
2007—Lee Humphrey

FORDHAM
1975—Darryl Brown

GEORGE WASHINGTON
1976—Pat Tallent
1986—Steve Frick

GEORGIA
1988—Alec Kessler
1989—Alec Kessler
1990—Alec Kessler

GEORGIA TECH
1964—Jim Caldwell
1969—Rich Yunkus
1970—Rich Yunkus
1971—Rich Yunkus
1998—Matt Harpring

GONZAGA
1984—Bryce McPhee
        John Stockton
1985—Bryce McPhee
1992—Jarrod Davis
1993—Jeff Brown
1994—Jeff Brown
2002—Dan Dickau

GREEN BAY
1992—Tony Bennett

HARVARD
1985—Joe Carrabino
1987—Arne Duncan

HAWAII
2004—Michael Kuebler

HOLY CROSS
1969—Ed Siudut
1978—Ronnie Perry
1979—Ronnie Perry
1980—Ronnie Perry
1991—Jim Nairus

ILLINOIS
1968—Dave Scholz
1969—Dave Scholz
1971—Rich Howatt
1974—Rick Schmidt
1975—Rick Schmidt

ILLINOIS ST.
1973—Doug Collins

INDIANA
1964—Dick Van Arsdale
1965—Dick Van Arsdale
1965—Tom Van Arsdale
1973—John Ritter
1974—Steve Green
1975—Steve Green
1976—Kent Benson
1977—Kent Benson
1978—Wayne Radford
1982—Randy Wittman
1983—Randy Wittman
1985—Uwe Blab
1989—Joe Hillman

IOWA
2007—Adam Haluska

IOWA ST.
1995—Fred Hoiberg

JACKSONVILLE
1971—Vaughan Wedeking
1983—Maurice Roulhac

KANSAS
1971—Bud Stallworth
1974—Tom Kivisto
1977—Ken Koenigs
        Chris Barnthouse
1978—Ken Koenigs
1979—Darnell Valentine
1980—Darnell Valentine
1981—Darnell Valentine
1982—David Magley
1996—Jacque Vaughn
1997—Jerod Haase
        Jacque Vaughn

1999—Ryan Robertson

KANSAS ST.
1968—Earl Seyfert
1982—Tim Jankovich
        Ed Nealy

KENTUCKY
1966—Lou Dampier
1967—Lou Dampier
1969—Larry Conley
1970—Dan Issel
        Mike Pratt
1971—Mike Casey
1975—Bob Guyette
        Jimmy Dan Conner
1979—Kyle Macy

LA SALLE
1977—Tony DiLeo
1988—Tim Legler
1992—Jack Hurd

LAMAR
1999—Matt Sundblad

LEWIS
1989—Jamie Martin

LOUISVILLE
1976—Phil Bond

LOYOLA MARYMOUNT
1973—Steve Smith

MANHATTAN
1990—Peter Runge

MARQUETTE
1982—Marc Marotta
1983—Marc Marotta
1984—Marc Marotta

MARSHALL
1972—Mike D'Antoni
1973—Mike D'Antoni

MARYLAND
1972—Tom McMillen
1973—Tom McMillen
1974—Tom McMillen
1991—Matt Roe

MERCER
2005—Will Emerson
2006—Will Emerson

MIAMI (OHIO)
1993—Craig Michaelis

MICHIGAN
1976—Steve Grote
1981—Marty Bodnar

MICHIGAN ST.
1970—Ralph Simpson
1979—Greg Kelser
2004—Chris Hill
2005—Chris Hill

MISSISSIPPI
1975—Dave Shepherd

MISSOURI
1983—Steve Stipanovich

MONTANA
1981—Craig Zanon
1985—Larry Krystkowiak
1986—Larry Krystkowiak

MURRAY ST.
1985—Mike Lahm

NEBRASKA
1984—John Matzke

UNLV
1983—Danny Tarkanian
1984—Danny Tarkanian

NEW MEXICO
1969—Ron Becker
1970—Ron Becker

NEW MEXICO ST.
2001—Eric Channing
2002—Eric Channing

NORTH CAROLINA
1965—Billy Cunningham
1970—Charlie Scott
1972—Dennis Wuycik
        Steve Previs
1976—Tommy LaGarde
1986—Steve Hale
1994—Eric Montross

UNC GREENSBORO
2001—Nathan Jameson

NORTH CAROLINA ST.
1984—Terry Gannon
1985—Terry Gannon
1995—Todd Fuller
1996—Todd Fuller

NORTH DAKOTA ST.
2008—Brett Winkelman

NORTHEASTERN
1977—David Caligaris
1978—David Caligaris

NORTHERN ILL.
1984—Tim Dillion
1998—T.J. Lux
2000—T.J. Lux

UNI
1984—Randy Kraayenbrink

NORTHWESTERN
1967—Jim Burns
1980—Mike Campbell
1987—Shon Morris
1988—Shon Morris

NOTRE DAME
1967—Bob Arnzen
1968—Bob Arnzen
1969—Bob Arnzen
1974—Gary Novak
1979—Kelly Tripucka
1980—Rich Branning
1982—John Paxson
1983—John Paxson
1997—Pat Garrity
1998—Pat Garrity
2005—Chris Quinn

OHIO
1971—Craig Love
1977—Steve Skaggs
1990—Dave Jamerson

OHIO ST.
1968—Bill Hosket

OKLAHOMA
1974—Alvan Adams
1975—Alvan Adams
1980—Terry Stotts

OKLAHOMA ST.
1964—Gary Hassmann
1969—Joe Smith

PACIFIC
1967—Keith Swagerty

PENN
1972—Robert Morse

PENN ST.
1994—John Amaechi
1995—John Amaechi

PRINCETON
1965—Bill Bradley
1991—Kit Mueller

PURDUE
1965—Dave Schellhase
1966—Dave Schellhase
1972—Robert Ford
1981—Brian Walker
1982—Keith Edmonson
1983—Steve Reid
1985—Steve Reid

RADFORD
1998—Corey Reed

RICE
1994—Adam Peakes

SACRED HEART
2006—Kibwe Trim

ST. FRANCIS (PA.)
1990—Michael Iuzzolino
1991—Michael Iuzzolino

ST. LOUIS
1968—Rich Niemann
1994—Scott Highmark
1995—Scott Highmark

SAN DIEGO ST.
1976—Steve Copp

SANTA CLARA
1968—Dennis Awtrey
1969—Dennis Awtrey
1970—Dennis Awtrey

SIENA
1985—Doug Peotzch
1992—Bruce Schroeder

SOUTH CAROLINA
1970—John Roche
1971—John Roche

SOUTHEAST MO. ST.
2005—Derek Winans

SOUTHERN ILL.
1976—Mike Glenn
1977—Mike Glenn

SMU
1977—Pete Lodwick
2005—Eric Castro

STANFORD
2000—Mark Madsen
2006—Dan Grunfeld

SYRACUSE
1981—Dan Schayes

TENNESSEE
1968—Bill Justus
1993—Lang Wiseman

TEXAS
1979—Jim Krivacs
2008—D.J. Augustin

UTEP
2000—Brandon Wolfram
2001—Brandon Wolfram

TEXAS A&M
1964—Bill Robinette

TULSA
1999—Michael Ruffin

UCLA
1967—Mike Warren
1969—Kenny Heitz
1971—Sidney Wicks
1972—Bill Walton
        Keith Wilkes
        Greg Lee
1973—Bill Walton
        Keith Wilkes
        Greg Lee
1974—Bill Walton
        Keith Wilkes
        Greg Lee
1975—Ralph Drollinger
1977—Marques Johnson
1979—Kiki Vandeweghe
1980—Kiki Vandeweghe
1995—George Zidek

UTAH
1970—Mike Newlin
1971—Mike Newlin
1977—Jeff Jonas
1998—Michael Doleac

UTAH ST.
1964—Gary Watts
1980—Dean Hunger
1982—Larry Bergeson
1996—Eric Franson

VANDERBILT
1975—Jeff Fosnes
1976—Jeff Fosnes
1993—Bruce Elder

VILLANOVA
1973—Tom Inglesby
1982—John Pinone
1983—John Pinone
1986—Harold Jensen
1987—Harold Jensen

VIRGINIA
1976—Wally Walker
1981—Jeff Lamp
        Lee Raker

VMI
1980—Andy Kolesar
1981—Andy Kolesar

WASHINGTON
1982—Dave Henley

WASHINGTON ST.
1989—Brian Quinnett

WEBER ST.
1985—Randy Worster

WEST VIRGINIA
2005—Johannes Herber
2006—Johannes Herber

WESTERN MICH.
2007—Joe Reitz

WICHITA ST.
1967—Jamie Thompson
1969—Ron Mendell

WILLIAM & MARY
1985—Keith Cieplicki
2004—Adam Hess

WISCONSIN
1974—Dan Anderson

Division I Player of the Year

Season	United Press International	The Associated Press	Oscar Robertson Trophy (USBWA)	Wooden Award	Nat'l Assn. of Basketball Coaches	Naismith Award	Adolph Rupp Trophy
1955	Tom Gola La Salle						
1956	Bill Russell San Francisco						
1957	Chet Forte Columbia						
1958	Oscar Robertson Cincinnati						
1959	Oscar Robertson Cincinnati		Oscar Robertson Cincinnati				
1960	Oscar Robertson Cincinnati		Oscar Robertson Cincinnati				
1961	Jerry Lucas Ohio St.	Jerry Lucas Ohio St.	Jerry Lucas Ohio St.				
1962	Jerry Lucas Ohio St.	Jerry Lucas Ohio St.	Jerry Lucas Ohio St.				
1963	Art Heyman Duke	Art Heyman Duke	Art Heyman Duke				
1964	Gary Bradds Ohio St.	Gary Bradds Ohio St.	Walt Hazzard UCLA				
1965	Bill Bradley Princeton	Bill Bradley Princeton	Bill Bradley Princeton				
1966	Cazzie Russell Michigan	Cazzie Russell Michigan	Cazzie Russell Michigan				
1967	Lew Alcindor UCLA	Lew Alcindor UCLA	Lew Alcindor UCLA				
1968	Elvin Hayes Houston	Elvin Hayes Houston	Elvin Hayes Houston				
1969	Lew Alcindor UCLA	Lew Alcindor UCLA	Lew Alcindor UCLA			Lew Alcindor UCLA	
1970	Pete Maravich LSU	Pete Maravich LSU	Pete Maravich LSU			Pete Maravich LSU	
1971	Austin Carr Notre Dame	Austin Carr Notre Dame	Sidney Wicks UCLA			Austin Carr Notre Dame	
1972	Bill Walton UCLA	Bill Walton UCLA	Bill Walton UCLA			Bill Walton UCLA	Bill Walton UCLA
1973	Bill Walton UCLA	Bill Walton UCLA	Bill Walton UCLA			Bill Walton UCLA	Bill Walton UCLA
1974	Bill Walton UCLA	David Thompson North Carolina St.	Bill Walton UCLA			Bill Walton UCLA	Bill Walton UCLA
1975	David Thompson North Carolina St.	David Thompson North Carolina St.	David Thompson North Carolina St.		David Thompson North Carolina St.	David Thompson North Carolina St.	David Thompson North Carolina St.
1976	Scott May Indiana	Scott May Indiana	Adrian Dantley Notre Dame		Scott May Indiana	Scott May Indiana	Scott May Indiana
1977	Marques Johnson UCLA	Marques Johnson UCLA	Marques Johnson UCLA	Marques Johnson UCLA	Marques Johnson UCLA	Marques Johnson UCLA	Marques Johnson UCLA
1978	Butch Lee Marquette	Butch Lee Marquette	Phil Ford North Carolina	Phil Ford North Carolina	Phil Ford North Carolina	Butch Lee Marquette	Butch Lee Marquette
1979	Larry Bird Indiana St.	Larry Bird Indiana St.	Larry Bird Indiana St.	Larry Bird Indiana St.	Larry Bird Indiana St.	Larry Bird Indiana St.	Larry Bird Indiana St.
1980	Mark Aguirre DePaul	Mark Aguirre DePaul	Mark Aguirre DePaul	Darrell Griffith Louisville	Michael Brooks La Salle	Mark Aguirre DePaul	Mark Aguirre DePaul
1981	Ralph Sampson Virginia	Ralph Sampson Virginia	Ralph Sampson Virginia	Danny Ainge BYU	Danny Ainge BYU	Ralph Sampson Virginia	Ralph Sampson Virginia
1982	Ralph Sampson Virginia	Ralph Sampson Virginia	Ralph Sampson Virginia	Ralph Sampson Virginia	Ralph Sampson Virginia	Ralph Sampson Virginia	Ralph Sampson Virginia
1983	Ralph Sampson Virginia	Ralph Sampson Virginia	Ralph Sampson Virginia	Ralph Sampson Virginia	Ralph Sampson Virginia	Ralph Sampson Virginia	Ralph Sampson Virginia
1984	Michael Jordan North Carolina	Michael Jordan North Carolina	Michael Jordan North Carolina	Michael Jordan North Carolina	Michael Jordan North Carolina	Michael Jordan North Carolina	Michael Jordan North Carolina
1985	Chris Mullin St. John's (N.Y.)	Patrick Ewing Georgetown	Chris Mullin St. John's (N.Y.)	Chris Mullin St. John's (N.Y.)	Patrick Ewing Georgetown	Patrick Ewing Georgetown	Patrick Ewing Georgetown
1986	Walter Berry St. John's (N.Y.)	Walter Berry St. John's (N.Y.)	Walter Berry St. John's (N.Y.)	Walter Berry St. John's (N.Y.)	Walter Berry St. John's (N.Y.)	Johnny Dawkins Duke	Walter Berry St. John's (N.Y.)
1987	David Robinson Navy	David Robinson Navy	David Robinson Navy	David Robinson Navy	David Robinson Navy	David Robinson Navy	David Robinson Navy
1988	Hersey Hawkins Bradley	Hersey Hawkins Bradley	Hersey Hawkins Bradley	Danny Manning Kansas	Danny Manning Kansas	Danny Manning Kansas	Hersey Hawkins Bradley
1989	Danny Ferry Duke	Sean Elliott Arizona	Danny Ferry Duke	Sean Elliott Arizona	Sean Elliott Arizona	Danny Ferry Duke	Sean Elliott Airzona
1990	Lionel Simmons La Salle	Lionel Simmons La Salle	Lionel Simmons La Salle	Lionel Simmons La Salle	Lionel Simmons La Salle	Lionel Simmons La Salle	Lionel Simmons La Salle

AWARD WINNERS

Season	United Press International	The Associated Press	Oscar Robertson Trophy (USBWA)	Wooden Award	Nat'l Assn. of Basketball Coaches	Naismith Award	Adolph Rupp Trophy
1991	Shaquille O'Neal LSU	Shaquille O'Neal LSU	Larry Johnson UNLV	Larry Johnson UNLV	Larry Johnson UNLV	Larry Johnson UNLV	Shaquille O'Neal LSU
1992	Jim Jackson Ohio St.	Christian Laettner Duke	Christian Laettner Duke	Christian Laettner Duke	Christian Laettner Duke	Christian Laettner Duke	Christian Laettner Duke
1993	Calbert Cheaney Indiana	Calbert Cheaney Indiana	Calbert Cheaney Indiana	Calbert Cheaney Indiana	Calbert Cheaney Indiana	Calbert Cheaney Indiana	Calbert Cheaney Indiana
1994	Glenn Robinson Purdue	Glenn Robinson Purdue	Glenn Robinson Purdue	Glenn Robinson Purdue	Glenn Robinson Purdue	Glenn Robinson Purdue	Glenn Robinson Purdue
1995	Joe Smith Maryland	Joe Smith Maryland	Ed O'Bannon UCLA	Ed O'Bannon UCLA	Shawn Respert Michigan St.	Joe Smith Maryland	Joe Smith Maryland
1996	Marcus Camby Massachusetts	Marcus Camby Massachusetts	Marcus Camby Massachusetts	Marcus Camby Massachusetts	Marcus Camby Massachusetts	Marcus Camby Massachusetts	Marcus Camby Massachusetts
1997		Tim Duncan Wake Forest	Tim Duncan Wake Forest	Tim Duncan Wake Forest	Tim Duncan Wake Forest	Tim Duncan Wake Forest	Tim Duncan Wake Forest
1998		Antawn Jamison North Carolina	Antawn Jamison North Carolina	Antawn Jamison North Carolina	Antawn Jamison North Carolina	Antawn Jamison North Carolina	Antawn Jamison North Carolina
1999		Elton Brand Duke	Elton Brand Duke	Elton Brand Duke	Elton Brand Duke	Elton Brand Duke	Elton Brand Duke
2000		Kenyon Martin Cincinnati	Kenyon Martin Cincinnati	Kenyon Martin Cincinnati	Kenyon Martin Cincinnati	Kenyon Martin Cincinnati	Kenyon Martin Cincinnati
2001		Shane Battier Duke	Shane Battier Duke	Shane Battier Duke	Jason Williams Duke	Shane Battier Duke	Shane Battier Duke
2002		Jason Williams Duke	Jason Williams Duke	Jason Williams Duke	Jason Williams Duke Drew Gooden Kansas	Jason Williams Duke	Jason Williams Duke
2003		David West Xavier	David West Xavier	T.J. Ford Texas	Nick Collison Kansas	T.J. Ford Texas	David West Xavier
2004		Jameer Nelson St. Joseph's	Jameer Nelson St. Joseph's	Jameer Nelson St. Joseph's	Jameer Nelson St. Joseph's Emeka Okafor Connecticut	Jameer Nelson St. Joseph's	Jameer Nelson St. Joseph's
2005		Andrew Bogut Utah	Andrew Bogut Utah	Andrew Bogut Utah	Andrew Bogut Utah	Andrew Bogut Utah	J.J. Redick Duke
2006		J.J. Redick Duke	J.J. Redick Duke Adam Morrison Gonzaga	J.J. Redick Duke	J.J. Redick Duke	J.J. Redick Duke Adam Morrison Gonzaga	J.J. Redick Duke
2007		Kevin Durant Texas	Kevin Durant Texas	Kevin Durant Texas	Kevin Durant Texas	Kevin Durant Texas	Kevin Durant Texas
2008		Tyler Hansbrough North Carolina	Tyler Hansbrough North Carolina	Tyler Hansbrough North Carolina	Tyler Hansbrough North Carolina	Tyler Hansbrough North Carolina	Tyler Hansbrough North Carolina

Basketball Times Player of the Year: 1982-Ralph Sampson, Virginia; 1983-Ralph Sampson, Virginia; 1984-Akeem Olajuwon, Houston; 1985-Patrick Ewing, Georgetown; 1986-Scott Skiles, Michigan St.; 1987-Kenny Smith, North Carolina; 1988-Hersey Hawkins, Bradley; 1989-Sean Elliot, Arizona; 1990-Derrick Coleman, Syracuse; 1991-Larry Johnson, UNLV; 1992-Christian Laettner, Duke; 1993-Jamaal Mashburn, Kentucky; 1994-Glenn Robinson, Purdue; 1995-Ed O'Bannon, UCLA; 1996-Marcus Camby, Massachusetts; 1997-Tim Duncan, Wake Forest; 1998-Antawn Jamison, North Carolina; 1999-Jason Terry, Arizona; 2000-Kenyon Martin, Cincinnati; 2001-Shane Battier, Duke; 2002-Jason Williams, Duke; 2003-David West, Xavier; 2004-Jameer Nelson, St. Joseph's; 2005-Andrew Bogut, Utah; 2006-J.J. Redick, Duke, & Adam Morrison, Gonzaga; 2007-Kevin Durant, Texas; 2008-Tyler Hansbrough, North Carolina.

The Sporting News Player of the Year (no selection made in missing years): 1943-Andy Phillips, Illinois; 1944-Dale Hall, Army; 1945-George Mikan, DePaul; 1946-Bob Kurland, Oklahoma St.; 1950-Paul Arizin, Villanova; 1951-Sherman White, Long Island; 1958-Oscar Robertson, Cincinnati; 1959-Oscar Robertson, Cincinnati; 1960-Oscar Robertson, Cincinnati; 1961-Jerry Lucas, Ohio St.; 1962-Jerry Lucas, Ohio St.; 1963-Art Heyman, Duke; 1964-Bill Bradley, Princeton; 1965-Bill Bradley, Princeton; 1966-Cazzie Russell, Michigan; 1967-Lew Alcindor, UCLA; 1968-Elvin Hayes, Houston; 1969-Lew Alcindor, UCLA; 1970-Pete Maravich, LSU; 1971-Sidney Wicks, UCLA; 1972-Bill Walton, UCLA; 1973-Bill Walton, UCLA; 1974-Bill Walton, UCLA; 1975-David Thompson, North Carolina St.; 1976-Scott May, Indiana; 1977-Marques Johnson, UCLA; 1978-Phil Ford, North Carolina; 1979-Larry Bird, Indiana St.; 1980-Darrell Griffith, Louisville; 1981-Mark Aguirre, DePaul; 1982-Ralph Sampson, Virginia; 1983-Michael Jordan, North Carolina; 1984-Michael Jordan, North Carolina; 1985-Patrick Ewing, Georgetown; 1986-Walter Berry, St. John's (N.Y.); 1987-David Robinson, Navy; 1988-Hersey Hawkins, Bradley; 1989-Stacey King, Oklahoma; 1990-Dennis Scott, Georgia Tech; 1991-Larry Johnson, UNLV; 1992-Christian Laettner, Duke; 1993-Calbert Cheaney, Indiana; 1994-Glenn Robinson, Purdue; 1995-Shawn Respert, Michigan St.; 1996-Marcus Camby, Massachusetts; 1997-Tim Duncan, Wake Forest; 1998-Antawn Jamison, North Carolina; 1999-Elton Brand, Duke; 2000-Kenyon Martin, Cincinnati; 2001-Shane Battier, Duke; 2002-Jason Williams, Duke; 2003-T.J. Ford, Texas; 2004-Jameer Nelson, St. Joseph's; 2005-Dee Brown, Illinois; 2006-J.J. Redick, Duke; 2007-Kevin Durant, Texas ; 2008-Tyler Hansbrough, North Carolina.

Frances Pomeroy Naismith Award (Most Outstanding Player who stands 6-foot tall or under): 1969-Billy Keller, Purdue; 1970-John Rinka, Kenyon; 1971- Charlie Johnson, California; 1972-Scott Martin, Oklahoma; 1973-Bobby Sherwin, Army; 1974-Mike Robinson, Michigan St.; 1975-Monty Towe, North Carolina St.; 1976-Frank Algia, St. John's (N.Y.); 1977-Jeff Jonas, Utah; 1978-Mike Scheib, Susquehanna; 1979-Alton Byrd, Columbia; 1980-Jim Sweeney, Boston College; 1981-Terry Adolph, West Texas A&M; 1982-Jack Moore, Nebraska; 1983-Ray McCallum, Ball St.; 1984-Ricky Stokes, Virginia; 1985-Bubba Jennings, Texas Tech; 1986-Jim Les, Bradley; 1987-Muggsy Bogues, Wake Forest; 1988-Jerry Johnson, Fla. Southern; 1989-Tim Hardaway, UTEP; 1990-Boo Harvey, St. John's (N.Y.); 1991-Keith Jennings, East Tenn. St.; 1992-Tony Bennett, Green Bay; 1993-Sam Crawford, New Mexico St.; 1994-Greg Brown, Evansville; 1995-Tyus Edney, UCLA; 1996-Eddie Benton, Vermont; 1997-Kent McCausland, Iowa; 1998-Earl Boykins, Eastern Mich.; 1999-Shawnta Rogers, George Washington; 2000-Scoonie Penn, Ohio St.; 2001-Rashad Phillips, Detroit; 2002-Steve Logan, Cincinnati; 2003-Jason Gardner, Arizona; 2004-Jameer Nelson, St. Joseph's; 2005-Nate Robinson, Washington; 2006-Dee Brown, Illinois; 2007-Tre' Kelly, South Carolina; 2008-Mike Green, Butler.

Defensive Player of the Year: 1987-Tommy Amaker, Duke; 1988-Billy King, Duke; 1989-Stacey Augmon, UNLV; 1990-Stacey Augmon, UNLV; 1991-Stacey Augmon, UNLV; 1992-Alonzo Mourning, Georgetown; 1993-Grant Hill, Duke; 1994-Jim McIlvaine, Marquette; 1995-Tim Duncan, Wake Forest; 1996-Tim Duncan, Wake Forest; 1997-Tim Duncan, Wake Forest; 1998-Steve Wojciechowski, Duke; 1999-Shane Battier, Duke; 2000-Kenyon Martin, Cincinnatti & Shane Battier, Duke; 2001-Shane Battier, Duke; 2002-John Linehan, Providence; 2003-Emeka Okafor, Connecticut; 2004-Emeka Okafor, Connecticut; 2005-Shelden Williams, Duke; 2006-Shelden Williams, Duke; 2007-Greg Oden, Ohio St; 2008-Hasheem Thabeet, Connecticut.

Bob Cousy Award (top point guard): 2004-Jameer Nelson, St. Joseph's; 2005-Raymond Felton, North Carolina; 2006-Dee Brown, Illinois; 2007-Acie Law IV, Texas A&M; 2008-D.J. Augustin, Texas.

Pete Newell Big Man Award: 2000-Marcus Fizer, Iowa; 2001-Jason Collins, Stanford; 2002-Drew Gooden, Kansas; 2003-David West, Xavier; 2004-Emeka Okafor, Connecticut; 2005-Andrew Bogut, Utah; 2006-Glen Davis, LSU; 2007-Greg Oden, Ohio St.; 2008-Michael Beasley, Kansas St.

Chip Hilton Award (personal character): 1997-Tim Duncan, Wake Forest; 1998-Hassan Booker, Navy; 1999-Tim Hill, Harvard; 2000-Eduardo Najera, Oklahoma; 2001-Shane Battier, Duke; 2002-Juan Dixon, Maryland; 2003-Brandon Miller, Butler; 2004-Emeka Okafor, Connecticut; 2005-Ronald Ross, Texas Tech; 2006-Gerry McNamara, Syracuse; 2007-Acie Law IV, Texas A&M; 2008-Mike Green, Butler.

Divisions II & III Player Of The Year

The Divisions II and III Player of the Year are chosen by the National Association of Basketball Coaches (NABC).

	Division II		Division III
1983	Earl Jones, Dist. of Columbia	1983	Leroy Witherspoon, Potsdam St.
1984	Earl Jones, Dist. of Columbia	1984	Leroy Witherspoon, Potsdam St.
1985	Charles Oakley, Virginia Union	1985	Tim Casey, Wittenberg
1986	Todd Linder, Tampa	1986	Dick Hempy, Otterbein
1987	Ralph Talley, Norfolk St.	1987	Brendan Mitchell, Potsdam St.
1988	Jerry Johnson, Fla. Southern	1988	Scott Tedder, Ohio Wesleyan
1989	Kris Kearney, Fla. Southern	1989	Greg Grant, TCNJ
1990	A.J. English, Virginia Union	1990	Matt Hancock, Colby
1991	Corey Crowder, Ky. Wesleyan	1991	Brad Baldridge, Wittenberg
1992	Eric Manuel, Oklahoma City	1992	Andre Foreman, Salisbury
1993	Alex Wright, Central Okla.	1993	Steve Hondred, Calvin
1994	Derrick Johnson, Virginia Union	1994	Scott Fitch, Geneseo St.
1995	Stan Gourard, Southern Ind.	1995	D'Artis Jones, Ohio Northern
1996	Stan Gourard, Southern Ind.	1996	David Benter, Hanover
1997	Kebu Stewart, Cal St. Bakersfield	1997	Bryan Crabtree, Ill. Wesleyan
1998	Joe Newton, Central Okla.	1998	Mike Nogelo, Williams
1999	Antonio Garica, Ky. Wesleyan	1999	Merrill Berunson, Wis.-Platteville
2000	Ajumu Gaines, Charleston (W.V.)	2000	Aaron Winkle, Calvin
2001	Colin Ducharme, Longwood	2001	Horace Jenkins, Wm. Paterson
2002	Ronald Murray, Shaw	2002	Jeff Gibbs, Otterbein
2003	Marlon Parmer, Ky. Wesleyan	2003	Bryan Nelson, Williams
2004	Elad Inbar, Mass.-Lowell	2004	Richard Melzer, Wis.-River Falls
2005	Mark Worthington, Metro St.	2005	Jason Kalsow, Wis.-Stevens Point
2006	Daruis Hargrove, Virginia Union	2006	Brandon Adair, Va. Wesleyan
	Turner Trofholz, South Dakota	2007	Andrew Olson, Amherst
2007	John Smith, Winona St.		Ben Strong, Guilford
2008	John Smith, Winona St.	2008	Andrew Olson, Amherst

Divisions II and III First-Team All-Americans by Team

Current Division I member denoted by (*). Non-NCAA member denoted by (†).

ABILENE CHRISTIAN
1968—John Godfrey

ADELPHI
2001—Ryan McCormack

AKRON*
1967—Bill Turner
1972—Len Paul

ALA.-HUNTSVILLE
1978—Tony Vann
2006—Jason Smith

ALAS. ANCHORAGE
1987—Jesse Jackson
1987—Hansi Gnad
1989—Michael Johnson
1990—Todd Fisher
2005—Brad Oleson
2008—Carl Arts

ALBANY ST. (GA.)
1975—Major Jones

ALBION
2005—Travis Dupree
2006—Brandon Crawford

ALCORN ST.*
1976—John McGill

ALFRED
2001—Devon Downing

AMERICAN*
1960—Willie Jones

AMERICAN INT'L
1969—Greg Hill
1970—Greg Hill
2002—Malik Moore

AMHERST
1970—Dave Auten
1971—James Rehnquist
2003—Steve Zieja
2005—Andrew Schiel
2007—Andrew Olson
2008—Andrew Olson

ARK.-MONTICELLO
2004—Billy McDaniel

ARKANSAS ST.*
1965—Jerry Rook

ARMSTRONG ATLANTIC
1975—Ike Williams

ASSUMPTION
1970—Jake Jones
1971—Jake Jones
1973—Mike Boylan
1974—John Grochowalski
1975—John Grochowalski
1976—Bill Wurm

AUGUSTA ST.
2007—AJ Bowman
2008—AJ Bowman

AUGUSTANA (ILL.)
1973—John Laing

BABSON
1992—Jim Pierrakos

BARTON
2007—Anthony Atkinson

BEMIDJI ST.
2004—Charles Hanks

BENTLEY
1974—Brian Hammel
1975—Brian Hammel
2005—Tim Forbes
2008—Nate Fritsch

BISHOP
1983—Shannon Lilly

BOWIE ST.
2005—Letheal Cook
2007—Gail Goodrich

BRIDGEPORT
1969—Gary Baum
1976—Lee Hollerbach
1985—Manute Bol
1991—Lambert Shell
1992—Lambert Shell
1995—Lamont Jones

BRIDGEWATER (VA.)
1995—Dan Rush
2002—Kyle Williford

BYU-HAWAII
2000—David Evans

BROCKPORT
2002—Mike Medbury

BRYANT
1981—Ernie DeWitt
2004—Romuald Augustin

UC RIVERSIDE*
1989—Maurice Pullum

CAL POLY POMONA
2005—Jeff Bonds

CAL ST. BAKERSFIELD
1996—Kebu Stewart
1997—Kebu Stewart

CAL ST. SAN B'DINO
2004—Jonathan Levy

CALIFORNIA (PA.)
1993—Ray Gutierrez

CALVIN
1993—Steve Honderd
2000—Aaron Winkle

CAMERON
1974—Jerry Davenport

CARLETON
1993—Gerrick Monroe

CARTHAGE
2002—Antoine McDaniel

CENTENARY (LA.)*
1957—Milt Williams

CENTRAL CONN. ST.*
1969—Howie Dickenman

UCF*
1979—Bo Clark
1980—Bo Clark

CENTRAL MO. ST.
1981—Bill Fennelly
1985—Ron Nunnelly
1991—Armando Becker
2006—Michael Hicks

CENTRAL OKLA.
1993—Alex Wright
1997—Tyrone Hopkins
1998—Joe Newton
1999—Eddie Robinson
2008—Sam Belt

CENTRAL WASH.
1967—Mel Cox

CHARLESTON (W.V.)
2000—Ajamu Gaines

CHATTANOOGA*
1977—Wayne Golden

CHEYNEY
1979—Andrew Fields
1981—George Melton
1982—George Melton

CHICAGO
2003—Derek Reich

CHRIS. NEWPORT
1991—Lamont Strothers
2001—Antoine Sinclair

CLAREMONT-M-S
1992—Chris Greene

CLARION
1994—Kwame Morton

CLARK (MASS.)
1980—Kevin Clark
1981—Kevin Clark
1988—Kermit Sharp

COLBY
1977—Paul Harvey
1978—Paul Harvey
1989—Matt Hancock
1990—Matt Hancock

COLUMBUS ST.
2004—Yandel Brown
2005—Yandel Brown

CONCORD
2004—Lewis Muse

CORTLAND ST.
2000—Tom Williams

DAVIS & ELKINS
1959—Paul Wilcox

DELTA ST.
1969—Sammy Little
2006—Jasper Johnson

DePAUW
1987—David Galle

DIST. COLUMBIA
1982—Earl Jones
1983—Earl Jones
     Michael Britt
1984—Earl Jones

EASTERN MICH.*
1971—Ken McIntosh
1972—George Gervin

EDINBORO
1996—Tyrone Mason
2002—Kenny Tate
2005—Jakim Donaldson

ELMHURST
2001—Ryan Knuppel

EMORY
1990—Tim Garrett

EMORY & HENRY
2004—Justin Call

EVANSVILLE*
1959—Hugh Ahlering
1960—Ed Smallwood
1965—Jerry Sloan
     Larry Humes
1966—Larry Humes

FINDLAY
2006—Dustin Pfeiffer
2007—Frank Phillips
2008—Josh Bostic

FLA. SOUTHERN
1981—John Ebeling
1982—John Ebeling
1988—Jerry Johnson
     Kris Kearney
1989—Kris Kearney
1990—Donolly Tyrell

FORT HAYS ST.
1997—Alonzo Goldston

FRAMINGHAM ST.
1984—Mark Van Valkenburg

FRANKLIN
1999—Jason Sibley

FRANK. & MARSH.
1992—Will Lasky
1996—Jeremiah Henry
2000—Alex Kraft

GANNON
1985—Butch Warner
1998—Troy Nesmith

GENESEO ST.
1994—Scott Fitch

GEORGETOWN (KY.)†
1964—Cecil Tuttle

GRAMBLING*
1961—Charles Hardnett
1962—Charles Hardnett
1964—Willis Reed
1966—Johnny Comeaux
1976—Larry Wright

GRAND CANYON
1976—Bayard Forest

GRAND VALLEY ST.
1997—Joe Modderman
2008—Callistus Eziukwu

GREEN BAY*
1978—Tom Anderson
1979—Ron Ripley

GUILFORD
1968—Bob Kauffman
1975—Lloyd Free
2007—Ben Strong
2008—Ben Strong

HAMILTON
1977—Cedric Oliver
1978—Cedric Oliver
1979—Cedric Oliver
1987—John Cavanaugh
1998—Mike Schantz
1999—Michael Schantz
2003—Joe Finley

HAMPDEN-SYDNEY
1992—Russell Turner
2000—T.J. Grimes

HANOVER
1996—David Benter

HARTFORD*
1979—Mark Noon

HARTWICK
1977—Dana Gahres
1983—Tim O'Brien

HAVERFORD
1977—Dick Vioth

HENDERSON ST.
2002—Niki Arinze
2004—Tarvoris Uzoique

HOPE
1984—Chip Henry
1998—Joel Holstege
2008—Marcus Vanderheide

HUMBOLDT ST.
2004—Austin Nichols
2007—Kevin Johnson
2008—Devin Peal

ILLINOIS ST.*
1968—Jerry McGreal

ILL. WESLEYAN
1977—Jack Sikma
1989—Jeff Kuehl
1995—Chris Simich
1997—Bryan Crabtree
1998—Brent Niebrugge
2000—Korey Coon
2004—Keelan Amelianovich
2005—Adam Dauksas

INDIANA (PA.)
1995—Derrick Freeman

IUPUI*
1996—Carlos Knox

INDIANA ST.*
1968—Jerry Newsome

INDIANAPOLIS
2005—David Logan

ITHACA
2000—Pat Britton

JACKSON ST.*
1974—Eugene Short
1975—Eugene Short
1977—Purvis Short

JACKSONVILLE*
1962—Roger Strickland
1963—Roger Strickland

JOHNSON C. SMITH
2001—Wiyle Perry

KEAN
1993—Fred Drains

KEENE ST.
2001—Chris Coates

KENNESAW ST.
2004—Terrence Hill

KENTUCKY ST.
1971—Travis Grant
     Elmore Smith
1972—Travis Grant
1975—Gerald Cunningham
1977—Gerald Cunningham

KY. WESLEYAN
1957—Mason Cope
1967—Sam Smith
1968—Dallas Thornton
1969—George Tinsley
1984—Rod Drake
     Dwight Higgs
1988—J.B. Brown
1990—Corey Crowder
1991—Corey Crowder
1995—Willis Cheaney
1998—Antonio Garcia
1999—Antonio Garcia
     Dana Williams
2000—LeRoy John
2001—Lorico Duncan
2002—Ronald Evans

KENYON
1969—John Rinka
1970—John Rinka
1979—Scott Rogers
1980—Scott Rogers

LAWRENCE
2006—Chris Braier

LEBANON VALLEY
1995—Mike Rhodes
1997—Andy Panko
1998—Andy Panko
1999—Andy Panko
2005—J.D. Byers

LEWIS
2004—Monta McGhee

LEWIS & CLARK
1963—Jim Boutin
1964—Jim Boutin
1999—Andy Panko

LINCOLN (MO.)
1978—Harold Robertson

LIPSCOMB*
1988—Phillip Hutcheson
1989—Phillip Hutcheson
1990—Phillip Hutcheson
1992—John Pierce

LONG ISLAND*
1968—Luther Green
     Larry Newbold

LONGWOOD*
1984—Jerome Kersey
2001—Colin Ducharme

LA.-LAFAYETTE*
1965—Dean Church
1970—Marvin Winkler
1971—Dwight Lamar

LOUISIANA COL.
1979—Paul Poe

LOUISIANA TECH*
1973—Mike Green

MAINE*
1961—Tom Chappelle

MASS.-DARTMOUTH
1993—Steve Haynes

MASS.-LOWELL
1989—Leo Parent
2004—Elad Inbar
2005—Stacey Moragne
2006—Stacey Moragne

MERCHANT MARINE
1990—Kevin D'Arcy

MERRIMACK
1977—Ed Murphy
1978—Ed Murphy
        Dana Skinner
1983—Joe Dickson

METHODIST
1997—Jason Childers

METRO ST.
2005—Mark Worthington

MICHIGAN TECH
2003—Matt Cameron
2004—Josh Buettner
2005—Josh Buettner

MILLERSVILLE
2008—Charlie Parker

MINN. DULUTH
1977—Bob Bone

MINN. ST. MANKATO
2005—Jamel Staten
2006—Luke Anderson
2007—Luke Anderson
2008—Atila Santos

MISERICORDIA
2003—Willie Chandler

MO.-ST. LOUIS
1977—Bob Bone

MONTCLAIR ST.
1999—Anthony Peoples
2006—Gian Paul Gonzalez

MONTEVALLO
2005—James Hall
2007—Greg Brown
        Marcus Kennedy

MORGAN ST.*
1974—Marvin Webster
1975—Marvin Webster
1999—Tim West

MT. ST. MARY'S*
1957—Jack Sullivan

MOUNT UNION
1997—Aaron Shipp

MUHLENBERG
2002—Mark Lesko

MUSKINGUM
1992—Andy Moore

NEB.-OMAHA
1992—Phil Cartwright

NEB. WESLEYAN
1986—Dana Janssen

NEW HAVEN
1988—Herb Watkins

TCNJ
1988—Greg Grant
1989—Greg Grant

NEW JERSEY CITY
1979—Brett Wyatt
2004—Samar Battle

NJIT
1996—Clarence Pierce

NEW ORLEANS*
1971—Xavier Webster

NYIT
1980—Kelvin Hicks

NICHOLLS ST.*
1978—Larry Wilson

NORFOLK ST.*
1979—Ken Evans
1984—David Pope
1987—Ralph Talley
1995—Corey Williams

NORTH ALA.
1980—Otis Boddie

N.C. WESLEYAN
1999—Marquis McDougald

NORTH DAKOTA
1966—Phil Jackson
1967—Phil Jackson
1991—Dave Vonesh
1993—Scott Guldseth
2003—Jerome Beasley

NORTH DAKOTA ST.*
1960—Marvin Bachmeier

NORTH PARK
1979—Mike Harper
1980—Mike Harper
1981—Mike Thomas

NORTHEASTERN ST.
2003—Jon Shepherd
2004—Darnell Hinson

NORTHERN MICH.
1987—Bill Harris
2000—Cory Brathol
2007—Ricky Volcy

NORTHWOOD
1973—Fred Smile

OHIO NORTHERN
1982—Stan Mories
1995—D'Artis Jones
2001—Kris Oberdick
2004—Jim Conrad

OHIO WESLEYAN
1987—Scott Tedder
1988—Scott Tedder

OKLAHOMA CITY†
1992—Eric Manuel

OLD DOMINION*
1972—Dave Twardzik
1974—Joel Copeland
1976—Wilson Washington

OTTERBEIN
1966—Don Carlos
1982—Ron Stewart
1983—Ron Stewart
1985—Dick Hempy
1986—Dick Hempy
1987—Dick Hempy
1991—James Bradley
1994—Nick Gutman
1999—Kevin Weakley
2002—Jeff Gibbs

PACIFIC LUTHERAN
1959—Chuck Curtis

PFEIFFER
1992—Tony Smith
2005—Rico Grier
2006—DeMario Grier

PHILADELPHIA U.
1976—Emory Sammons
1977—Emory Sammons
2006—Tayron Thomas
2007—Christian Burns

PITTSBURG ST.
2005—Eddie Jackson

PITT.-JOHNSTOWN
2008—Chris Gilliam

PLATTSBURGH ST.
2008—Anthony Williams

PLYMOUTH ST.
1994—Moses Jean-Pierre
1999—Adam DeChristopher

POTSDAM ST.
1980—Derrick Rowland
1981—Derrick Rowland
1982—Maurice Woods
1983—Leroy Witherspoon

1984—Leroy Witherspoon
1986—Roosevelt Bullock
1986—Brendan Mitchell
1987—Brendan Mitchell
1988—Steve Babiarz
1989—Steve Babiarz

PRAIRIE VIEW*
1962—Zelmo Beaty

PUGET SOUND
1979—Joe Leonard

QUEENS (N.C.)
1998—Soce Faye

RAMAPO
2003—Charles Ransom
2005—Amin Wright

RANDOLPH-MACON
1983—Bryan Vacca
2003—Jared Mills
2005—Justin Wansley

RICHARD STOCKTON
1997—Carl Cochrane

ROANOKE
1972—Hal Johnston
1973—Jay Piccola
1974—Jay Piccola
1983—Gerald Holmes
1984—Reggie Thomas
1985—Reggie Thomas
1994—Hilliary Scott

ROCHESTER (N.Y.)
1991—Chris Fite
1992—Chris Fite
2004—Seth Hauben
2005—Seth Hauben

ROCHESTER INST.
1996—Craig Jones
1997—Craig Jones

ROLLINS
2008—Jonny Reibel

ROWAN
1998—Rob Scott
2007—Thomas Baker
2008—Matt Byrnes

RUTGERS-CAMDEN
2002—Brian Turner

SACRED HEART*
1972—Ed Czernota
1978—Hector Olivencia
        Andre Means
1982—Keith Bennett
1983—Keith Bennett
1986—Roger Younger
1993—Darrin Robinson

ST. CLOUD ST.
1957—Vern Baggenstoss
1986—Kevin Catron

ST. JOHN FISHER
2006—Sean O'Brien

ST. JOSEPH'S (IND.)
1960—Bobby Williams
2006—Sullivan Sykes

ST. MICHAEL'S
1965—Richie Tarrant

ST. NORBERT
1963—Mike Wisneski

ST. ROSE
2007—Steve Dagostino
2008—Steve Dagostino

ST. THOMAS
2006—Isaac Rosefelt
2007—Isaac Rosefelt

SALEM INT'L
1976—Archie Talley
2006—Shaun McKie

SALEM ST.
2000—Tishaun Jenkins

SALISBURY
1991—Andre Foreman
1992—Andre Foreman

SAM HOUSTON ST.*
1973—James Lister

SCRANTON
1963—Bill Witaconis
1977—Irvin Johnson
1978—Irvin Johnson
1984—Bill Bessoir
1985—Bill Bessoir
1993—Matt Cusano

SEATTLE PACIFIC
2006—Tony Binetti
2007—Dustin Bremerman

SEWANEE
1998—Ryan Harrigan

SHAW
2002—Ronald Murray

SHENANDOAH
1996—Phil Dixon

SLIPPERY ROCK
1991—Myron Brown

S.C. AIKEN
2008—Chris Commons

SOUTH DAKOTA
1958—Jim Daniels
2004—Tommie King
2006—Turner Trofholz

SOUTH DAKOTA ST.*
1961—Don Jacobsen
1964—Tom Black
2005—Turner Trofholz

SOUTHEASTERN OKLA.
1957—Jim Spivey
2007—Eric Babers

SOUTHERN ILL.*
1966—George McNeil
1967—Walt Frazier

SOUTHERN IND.
1995—Stan Gouard
1996—Stan Gouard

SOUTHERN N.H.
2003—Sotirios Karapostolou

SOUTHWEST BAPTIST
2006—Sheldon Pace

SPRINGFIELD
1970—Dennis Clark
1986—Ivan Olivares

STEPHEN F. AUSTIN*
1970—Surry Oliver

STETSON*
1970—Ernie Killum

STEUBENVILLE†
1958—Jim Smith

STONEHILL
1979—Bill Zolga
1980—Bill Zolga
1982—Bob Reitz

STONY BROOK*
1979—Earl Keith

SUSQUEHANNA
1986—Dan Harnum

TAMPA
1985—Todd Linder
1986—Todd Linder
1987—Todd Linder
1994—DeCarlo Deveaux
2008—Jeremy Black

TARLETON ST.
2004—Tim Burnette

TENNESSEE ST.*
1958—Dick Barnett
1959—Dick Barnett
1971—Ted McClain
1972—Lloyd Neal
1974—Leonard Robinson

TEX.-PAN AMERICAN*
1964—Lucious Jackson
1968—Otto Moore

TEXAS SOUTHERN*
1958—Bennie Swain
1977—Alonzo Bradley

TEXAS ST.*
1959—Charles Sharp
1960—Charles Sharp

THOMAS MORE
1996—Rick Hughes

TRINITY (CONN.)
2006—Tyler Rhoten

TRINITY (TEX.)
1968—Larry Jeffries
1969—Larry Jeffries
2002—Colin Tabb

TROY*
1993—Terry McCord

TUFTS
1995—Chris McMahon

UPSALA
1981—Steve Keenan
1982—Steve Keenan

URSINUS
2004—Dennis Stanton
2008—Nick Shattuck

UTICA
2007—Ray Bryant

VIRGINIA UNION
1985—Charles Oakley
1990—A.J. English
1994—Derrick Johnson
        Warren Peebles
1996—Ben Wallace
1998—Marquise Newbie
2006—Duane Crockett
        Darius Hargrove

VA. WESLEYAN
2006—Brandon Adair

WABASH
1982—Pete Metzelaars

WASHBURN
1994—Clarence Tyson
1997—Dan Buie
2001—Ewan Auguste
2005—Travis Robbins

WASH. & LEE
1978—Pat Dennis

WAYNE ST. (NEB.)
1999—Tyler Johnson

WEST CHESTER
2003—Ramzee Stanton

WEST GA.
1974—Clarence Walker

WEST TEXAS A&M
2007—Damien Lolar
2008—Robert Lee

WEST VIRGINIA ST.
2004—Mike Taylor
2007—Ted Scott

WESTERN CARO.*
1968—Henry Logan

WESTERN WASH.
2006—Grant Dykstra

WESTMINSTER (PA.)
1962—Ron Galbreath

WESTMINSTER (UTAH)†
1969—Ken Hall

WHEATON (ILL.)
1958—Mel Peterson
2007—Kent Raymond
2008—Kent Raymond

WIDENER
1978—Dennis James
1988—Lou Stevens
2006—Kristian Clarkson

WILKES
2001—Dave Jannuzzi

WM. PATERSON
2000—Horace Jenkins
2001—Horace Jenkins

WILLIAMS
1961—Bob Mahland
1962—Bob Mahland
1996—Mike Nogelo
1997—Mike Nogelo
1998—Mike Nogelo
2004—Ben Coffin

WINONA ST.
2007—John Smith
2008—John Smith

WINSTON-SALEM*
1967—Earl Monroe
1980—Reginald Gaines

WIS.-EAU CLAIRE
1972—Mike Ratliff

WIS.-OSHKOSH
1996—Dennis Ruedinger
2002—Tim Dworak

WIS.-PARKSIDE
1976—Gary Cole

WIS.-PLATTEVILLE
1992—T.J. Van Wie
1998—Ben Hoffmann
1999—Merrill Brunson

WIS.-RIVER FALLS
2003—Richard Melzer
2004—Richard Melzer

WIS.-STEVENS POINT
1985—Terry Porter
2000—Brant Bailey
2005—Jason Kalsow

WIS.-SUPERIOR
2001—Vince Thomas

WIS.-WHITEWATER
1990—Ricky Spicer
1994—Ty Evans
1997—James Stewart
2008—Matt Goodwin

WITTENBERG
1961—George Fisher
1963—Al Thrasher
1980—Brian Agler
1981—Tyrone Curtis
1985—Tim Casey
1989—Steve Allison
1990—Brad Baldridge
1991—Brad Baldridge

WOOSTER
2003—Bryan Nelson
2007—Tom Port

WRIGHT ST.*
1981—Rodney Benson
1986—Mark Vest

XAVIER (LA.)†
1973—Bruce Seals

YORK (PA.)
2007—Chad McGowan

YOUNGSTOWN ST.*
1977—Jeff Covington
1978—Jeff Covington

Teams used for selections:
AP Little All-America—
 1957-79
NABC College Division—
 1967-76
NABC Divisions II, III—
 1977-2008

Divisions II and III Academic All-Americans by Team

ABILENE CHRISTIAN
1999—Jared Mosley

AKRON
1972—Wil Schwarzinger

ALBANY (N.Y.)
1988—John Carmello

ALBION
1979—John Nibert

ALDERSON-BROADDUS
2002—Kevyn McBride

ARKANSAS TECH
1990—Gray Townsend
1994—David Bevis
1995—David Bevis

ASHLAND
1967—Jim Basista
1970—Jay Franson

ASSUMPTION
1967—George Ridick

AUGUSTANA (ILL.)
1973—Bruce Hamming
1974—Bruce Hamming
1975—Bruce Hamming
1979—Glen Heiden

AUGUSTANA (S.D.)
1974—John Ritterbusch
1975—John Ritterbusch

BALDWIN-WALLACE
1985—Bob Scelza

BARRINGTON
1982—Shawn Smith

BATES
1983—Herb Taylor
1984—Herb Taylor

BEMIDJI ST.
1976—Steve Vogel
1977—Steve Vogel
1978—Steve Vogel
2003—Royce Bryan

BENTLEY
1980—Joe Betley

BETHANY (W.V.)
2006—Matt Drahos

BETHEL (MINN.)
1994—Jason Mekelburg

BLOOMSBURG
1978—Steve Bright

BRANDEIS
1978—John Martin

BRIAR CLIFF
1989—Chad Neubrand

BRIDGEWATER (VA.)
1985—Sean O'Connell

BRYAN
1981—Dean Ropp

C.W. POST
1973—Ed Fields

CALIFORNIA (PA.)
1993—Raymond Guttierez

UC DAVIS
1970—Tom Cupps
1983—Preston Neumayr

UC RIVERSIDE
1971—Kirby Gordon

CAL LUTHERAN
1983—Bill Burgess

CALVIN
1992—Steve Honderd
1993—Steve Honderd
1994—Chris Knoester

CAPITAL
1973—Charles Gashill

CARNEGIE MELLON
1973—Mike Wegener
1979—Larry Hufnagel
1980—Larry Hufnagel

CASE RESERVE
1996—Jim Fox
1997—Jim Fox

CASTLETON ST.
1985—Bryan DeLoatch

CATHOLIC
1997—Jeremy Borys

UCF
1982—Jimmie Farrell

CENTRAL MICH.
1967—John Berends
1971—Mike Hackett

CENTRAL ST. (OHIO)
1971—Sterling Quant

CHADRON ST.
1992—Josh Robinson

CHAPMAN
2006—Zach Wheatley

CLAREMONT-M-S
2002—Bob Donlan

COAST GUARD
1971—Ken Bicknell

COLBY-SAWYER
2006—Andrew St. Clair

COLORADO MINES
1991—Daniel McKeon
1991—Hank Prey

UC-COLO. SPRINGS
2007—Patrick Hannaway

COLORADO ST.-PUEBLO
1972—Jim Von Loh

CORNELL COLLEGE
1974—Randy Kuhlman
1977—Dick Grant
1978—Robert Wisco
1979—Robert Wisco
1987—Jeff Fleming

DAVID LIPSCOMB
1989—Phil Hutcheson
1990—Phil Hutcheson
1992—Jerry Meyer

DELTA ST.
1972—Larry MaGee

DENISON
1967—Bill Druckemiller
1970—Charles Claggett
1987—Kevin Locke
1988—Kevin Locke
1997—Casey Chroust

DENVER
1987—Joe Fisher

DePAUW
1970—Richard Tharp
1973—Gordon Pittenger
1987—David Galle

DICKINSON
1971—Lloyd Bonner
1981—David Freysinger
1982—David Freysinger

DREXEL
1967—Joe Hertrich

ELMHURST
2001—Ryan Knuppel

ELON
1988—Brian Branson
1988—Steve Page
1998—Christopher Kiger

EMBRY-RIDDLE
2001—Kyle Mas

EMORY
2000—Neil Bhutta
2005—Chase Fawsett

EMORY & HENRY
2004—Justin Call

FLA. GULF COAST
2007—Beau Bauer

FORT HAYS ST.
1978—Mike Pauls

FORT LEWIS
1998—Ryan Ostrom

FRANK. & MARSH.
2000—Jerome Maiatico

GANNON
2007—Aurimas Truskauskas

GETTYSBURG
1975—Jeffrey Clark

GREEN BAY
1974—Tom Jones

GRINNELL
1976—John Haigh
1994—Steve Diekmann
1995—Steve Diekmann
1996—Ed Brands

GROVE CITY
1979—Mike Donahoe
1984—Curt Silverling
1985—Curt Silverling

GUST. ADOLPHUS
1983—Mark Hanson

HAMILTON
1978—John Klauberg

HAMLINE
1986—Paul Westling
1989—John Banovetz

HAMPDEN-SYDNEY
1992—Russell Turner

HARDING
1985—Kenneth Collins
1986—Kenneth Collins

HOWARD PAYNE
1973—Garland Bullock
1974—Garland Bullock

ILL. WESLEYAN
1972—Dean Gravlin
1973—Dean Gravlin
1975—Jack Sikma
 Bob Spear
1976—Jack Sikma
 Bob Spear
1977—Jack Sikma
 Bob Spear
1979—Al Black
1981—Greg Yess
1982—Greg Yess
1987—Brian Coderre
1999—Korey Coon
2000—Korey Coon
2006—Keelan Amelianovich

INCARNATE WORD
1993—Randy Henderson

JAMES MADISON
1976—Sherman Dillard

JAMESTOWN
1980—Pete Anderson
1981—Pete Anderson

JOHN CARROLL
1999—Mark Heidorf

JOHNS HOPKINS
1991—Andy Enfield

KENYON
1970—John Rinka

1977—Tim Appleton
1985—Chris Coe Russell

LaGRANGE
1980—Todd Whitsitt

LEBANON VALLEY
2005—J.D. Byers

LIBERTY
1980—Karl Hess

LUTHER
1981—Doug Kintzinger
1982—Doug Kintzinger

MacMURRAY
1970—Tom Peters

MARIAN (WIS.)
2002—Scott Jaeger

MARIETTA
1982—Rick Clark
1983—Rick Clark

MARYVILLE (MO.)
2003—Kevin Bartow

MASS.-LOWELL
1970—Alfred Spinell
1984—John Paganetti

MIT
1980—Ray Nagem
1991—David Tomlinson
2008—Jimmy Bartolotta

McDANIEL
1983—Douglas Pinto
1985—David Malin

McGILL
1983—Willie Hinz

McNEESE ST.
1972—David Wallace

MERRIMACK
1983—Joseph Dickson
1984—Joseph Dickson

MICHIGAN TECH
1981—Russ VanDuine
1985—Wayne Helmila
2003—J.T. Luginski

MILLIKIN
1977—Roy Mosser
 Dale Wills
1978—Gregg Finigan
1979—Rich Rames
 Gary Jackson
1980—Gary Jackson
1981—Gary Jackson
1989—Brian Horst

MILWAUKEE ENGR.
1983—Jeffrey Brezovar

MINN. ST. MANKATO
1997—David Kruse

MINN. ST. MOORHEAD
1996—Brett Beeson
MISSOURI S&T
1984—Todd Wentz
2004—Brian Westre
MO.-ST. LOUIS
1975—Bobby Bone
1976—Bobby Bone
1977—Bobby Bone
MONMOUTH (ILL.)
1990—S. Juan Mitchell
MONT. ST.-BILLINGS
2004—Jerett Skrifvars
MOUNT UNION
1971—Jim Howell
MUHLENBERG
1979—Greg Campisi
1981—Dan Barletta
NEB.-KEARNEY
1974—Tom Kropp
1975—Tom Kropp
2004—Nick Branting
2006—Dusty Jura
NEB.-OMAHA
1981—Jim Gregory
NEB. WESLEYAN
1984—Kevin Cook
1986—Kevin Cook
1995—Justin Wilkins
1997—Kipp Kissinger
1998—Kipp Kissinger
UNC ASHEVILLE
1974—Randy Pallas
NORTHERN COLO.
1967—Dennis Colson
NORTHWESTERN (MINN.)
2005—Jeff VerSteeg

OBERLIN
1971—Vic Guerrieri
1972—Vic Guerrieri
OHIO NORTHERN
2001—Kris Oberdick
OHIO WESLEYAN
1990—Mark Slayman
1998—John Camillus
OLD DOMINION
1974—Gray Eubank
1975—Gray Eubank
OTTERBEIN
1980—Mike Cochran
PACIFIC LUTHERAN
1967—Doug Leeland
POINT PARK
1986—Richard Condo
RIPON
1999—Bret Van Dyken
ROCHESTER
1984—Joe Augustine
ROCKFORD
1976—John Morrissey
1977—John Morrissey
ROSE-HULMAN
2002—Christopher Unton
ST. JOHN'S (MINN.)
1995—Joe Deignan
ST. JOSEPH'S (IND.)
1975—James Thordsen
ST. LEO
1977—Ralph Nelson
ST. NORBERT
2008—Eric Bieniasz

ST. ROSE
2007—Steve Dagostino
2008—Steve Dagostino
ST. THOMAS (FLA.)
1976—Arthur Collins
1977—Mike LaPrete
ST. THOMAS (MINN.)
1967—Dan Hansard
1978—Terry Fleming
SCRANTON
1983—Michael Banas
1984—Michael Banas
1985—Dan Polacheck
1993—Matt Cusano
SHIPPENSBURG
1979—John Whitmer
1981—Brian Cozzens
1982—Brian Cozzens
SIMPSON
2002—Jesse Harris
2003—Jesse Harris
SLIPPERY ROCK
1971—Robert Wiegand
1979—Mike Hardy
1983—John Samsa
1995—Mark Metzka
SOUTH DAKOTA
1970—Bill Hamer
1975—Rick Nissen
1976—Rick Nissen
1978—Jeff Nannen
1980—Jeff Nannen
1985—Rob Swanhorst
SOUTH DAKOTA ST.
1971—Jim Higgins
1972—Jim Higgins
SOUTHERN N.H.
2003—Brian Larrabee

SOUTHERN VA.
2008—Chris Pendleton
SUSQUEHANNA
1986—Donald Harnum
1994—Tres Wolf
TENNESSEE TEMPLE
1977—Dan Smith
1978—Dan Smith
TEXAS LUTHERAN
2005—Tommy Stolhandske
TRINITY (CONN.)
1996—Keith Wolff
TRUMAN
1984—Mark Campbell
1999—Jason Reinberg
2000—Jason Reinberg
UNION (N.Y.)
1970—Jim Tedisco
URSINUS
2004—Dennis Stanton
VIRGINIA TECH
1968—Ted Ware
WABASH
1973—Joe Haklin
WARTBURG
1971—Dave Platte
1972—Dave Platte
1974—Fred Waldstein
1990—Dan Nettleton
1991—Dan Nettleton
WASHBURN
2001—Ewan Auguste
WASHINGTON-ST. LOUIS
1988—Paul Jackson
2007—Troy Ruths
2008—Troy Ruths

WASH. & JEFF.
1980—David Damico
WENTWORTH INST.
2000—Kevin Hanlon
WESLEYAN (CONN.)
1972—James Akin
1974—Rich Fairbrother
1982—Steven Maizes
WESTERN ST.
1970—Michael Adams
1973—Rod Smith
WESTMINSTER (PA.)
1967—John Fontanella
WILKES
2001—Dave Jannuzzi
WM. PATERSON
2001—Horace Jenkins
WIS.-EAU CLAIRE
1972—Steven Johnson
1975—Ken Kaiser
1976—Ken Kaiser
WIS.-OSHKOSH
1998—Joe Imhoff
WIS.-PLATTEVILLE
1992—T.J. Van Wie
1993—T.J. Van Wie
WIS.-SUPERIOR
2001—Vince Thomas
WITTENBERG
1967—Jim Appleby
WOOSTER
2005—Matt Schlingman
WPI
1996—James Naughton

NCAA Postgraduate Scholarship Winners by Team

ABILENE CHRISTIAN
1999—Jared Mosley
AIR FORCE
1970—James Cooper
1973—Thomas Blase
1974—Richard Nickelson
1978—Thomas Schneeberger
1992—Brent Roberts
1993—Brad Boyer
UAB
1999—Damon Cobb
ALBANY (N.Y.)
1988—John Carmello
ALLEGHENY
1976—Robert Del Greco
ALMA
1976—Stuart TenHoor
AMERICAN
1973—Kermit Washington
1998—Nathan Smith
ARIZONA
1988—Steve Kerr
1991—Matt Muehlebach
ARIZONA ST.
1965—Dennis Dairman
ARKANSAS ST.
1975—J.H. Williams
ARMY
1965—John Ritch III
1972—Edward Mueller
1973—Robert Sherwin Jr.
1985—Randall Cozzens
1994—David Ardayfio

ASSUMPTION
1975—Paul Brennan
1977—William Wurm
2004—Shahar Golan
AUBURN
1976—Gary Redding
AUGUSTANA (ILL.)
1975—Bruce Hamming
AUGUSTANA (S.D.)
1975—Neil Klutman
1992—Jason Garrow
BALL ST.
1989—Richard Hall
BATES
1984—Herbert Taylor
BAYLOR
1997—Doug Brandt
BELLARMINE
1992—Tom Schurfranz
2001—Ronald Brooks
BELMONT
2004—Adam Mark
2008—Justin Hare
BENTLEY
1980—Joseph Betley
BOSTON COLLEGE
1967—William Wolters
1970—Thomas Veronneau
1972—James Phelan
1980—James Sweeney
1995—Marc Molinsky

BOWDOIN
1966—Howard Pease
BOWLING GREEN
1965—Robert Dwors
BRANDEIS
1972—Donald Fishman
1978—John Martin
BRIDGEWATER (VA.)
1970—Frederick Wampler
BYU
1966—Richard Nemelka
1983—Gregory Kite
1984—Devin Durrant
1987—Brent Stephenson
1989—Michael Smith
1990—Andy Toolson
1991—Steve Schreiner
BYU-HAWAII
2000—David Evans
BROWN
1972—Arnold Berman
1997—Jade Newburn
BUENA VISTA
2000—Landon Roth
BUTLER
1977—Wayne Burris
1991—John Karaffa
2008—Drew Streicher
CALIFORNIA
1987—David Butler
UC DAVIS
1970—Thomas Cupps
1977—Mark Ford

1983—Preston Neumayr
1991—Matt Cordova
UC IRVINE
1975—Carl Baker
UC RIVERSIDE
1975—Randy Burnett
UC SAN DIEGO
1997—Matt Aune
UC SANTA BARBARA
1973—Robert Schachter
1993—Michael Meyer
CAL POLY POMONA
1978—Thomas Ispas
CAL ST. DOM. HILLS
1987—John Nojima
CAL ST. STANISLAUS
1983—Richard Thompson
CALIFORNIA (PA.)
1984—William Belko
CALTECH
1966—Alden Holford
1967—James Pearson
1968—James Stanley
1971—Thomas Heinz
CALVIN
1977—Mark Veenstra
1993—Steve Honderd
CARLETON
1969—Thomas Weaver
1982—James Tolf
1999—Joshua Wilhelm

CARNEGIE MELLON
1980—Lawrence Hufnagel
CASE RESERVE
1971—Mark Estes
CATHOLIC
1972—Joseph Good
1997—Jeremy Borys
CENTRAL (IOWA)
1973—Dana Snoap
1980—Jeffrey Verhoef
CENTRAL MICH.
1993—Sander Scott
CENTRE
1985—Thomas Cowens
CHAPMAN
1970—Anthony Mason
CHICAGO
1969—Dennis Waldon
1974—Gerald Clark
1985—Keith Libert
CINCINNATI
1977—Gary Yoder
CLAREMONT-M-S
1972—Jeffrey Naslund
CLARION
1973—Joseph Sebestyen
CLEMSON
1967—James Sutherland
1980—Robert Conrad Jr.
1999—Tom Wideman
COASTAL CARO.
2008—Jack Leasure

COE
1965—Gary Schlarbaum

COLBY
1972—Matthew Zweig

COLGATE
1999—Ben Wandtke

COLORADO
1966—Charles Gardner
1985—Alex Stivrins

COLORADO MINES
1991—Hank Prey
1994—Todd Kenyon

UC-COLO. SPRINGS
2007—Patrick Hannaway

COLORADO ST.
1986—Richard Strong Jr.

COLUMBIA
1968—William Ames

CORNELL COLLEGE
1967—David Crow
1979—Robert Wisco
1981—Eric Reitan
1987—Jefferson Fleming
1994—Abram Tubbs
　　　Chad Reed

CREIGHTON
1971—Dennis Bresnahan Jr.
1978—Richard Apke

DARTMOUTH
1968—Joseph Colgan
1976—William Healey
1984—Paul Anderson
1997—Sea Lonergan

DAVIDSON
1969—Wayne Huckel
1983—Clifford Tribus

DAYTON
1979—Jim Paxson
1985—Larry Schellenberg

DELAWARE
1978—Brian Downie

DENISON
1968—William Druckemiller Jr.
1988—Kevin Locke
1993—Kevin Frye
1997—Casey Chroust
1999—John Rusnak

DENVER
1968—Richard Callahan
2000—Tyler Church
2004—Brett Starkey

DePAUL
1992—Stephen Howard

DePAUW
1969—Thomas McCormick
1970—Richard Tharp
1973—Gordon Pittenger
1986—Phillip Wendel

DeSALES
1985—George Bilicic Jr.

DICKINSON
1982—David Freysinger
1987—Michael Erdos

DREW
1989—Joe Novak

DUKE
1975—Robert Fleischer

EASTERN WASH.
2000—Ryan Hansen

ELON
1998—Christopher Kiger

EMORY
1993—Kevin Felner
1999—Lewis Satterwhite
2000—Neil Bhutta

EVANSVILLE
1989—Scott Haffner

FAIRLEIGH DICKINSON
1978—John Jorgensen
1993—Kevin Conway

FLORIDA
1970—Andrew Owens Jr.
1973—Anthony Miller
2003—Matthew Bonner
2007—Lee Humphrey

FLA. SOUTHERN
1969—Richard Lewis
1979—Larry Tucker
1989—Kris Kearney

FORT LEWIS
1998—Ryan Ostrom

FRANKLIN
1994—David Dunkle

FRANK. & MARSH.
2000—Jerome Maiatico

GEORGE WASHINGTON
1976—Pat Tallent
1987—Steve Frick

GEORGETOWN
1968—Bruce Stinebrickner

GEORGIA
1965—McCarthy Crenshaw Jr.
1987—Chad Kessler
1990—Alec Kessler

GEORGIA TECH
1998—Matt Harping

GONZAGA
1992—Jarrod Davis
1994—Jeff Brown
1996—Jon Kinloch

GRAMBLING
1983—William Hobdy

GRINNELL
1968—James Schwartz
1976—John Haigh

GUST. ADOLPHUS
2008—Trevor Wittwer

HAMILTON
1969—Brooks McCuen
1978—John Klauberg

HAMLINE
1989—John Banovetz

HAMPDEN-SYDNEY
1983—Christopher Kelly
1999—David Hobbs

HARVARD
1979—Glenn Fine

HAVERFORD
1966—Hunter Rawlings III
1967—Michael Bratman
1977—Richard Voith

HIRAM
1977—Edwin Niehaus

HOLY CROSS
1969—Edward Siudut
1977—William Doran Jr.
1979—John O'Connor
1980—Ronnie Perry

HOUSTON BAPTIST
1985—Albert Almanza

IDAHO
1967—Michael Wicks

IDAHO ST.
1993—Corey Bruce

ILLINOIS
1971—Rich Howat

ILLINOIS ST.
1988—Jeffrey Harris
1998—Dan Muller

ILLINOIS TECH
1969—Eric Wilson

ILL. WESLEYAN
1988—Brian Coderre
2000—Korey Coon

2006—Adam Dauksas

INDIANA
1975—Steven Green
1982—Randy Wittman
1985—Uwe Blab

INDIANA ST.
1972—Danny Bush
1981—Steven Reed

IOWA
1966—Dennis Pauling
1976—G. Scott Thompson
1981—Steven Waite
1998—Jess Settles

IOWA ST.
1989—Marc Urquhart

ITHACA
1973—David Hollowell

JACKSONVILLE
1971—Vaughn Wedeking
1983—Maurice Roulhac
1986—Thomas Terrell

JAMES MADISON
1978—Sherman Dillard

JAMESTOWN
1981—Peter Anderson

JOHNS HOPKINS
1965—Robert Smith
1975—Andrew Schreiber
1991—Andy Enfield
1992—Jay Gangemi
1997—Matt Gorman
1998—Greg Roehrig

KALAMAZOO
1965—Thomas Nicolai
1973—James Van Sweden
1979—David Dame
1982—John Schelske
1996—Jeremy Cole

KANSAS
1974—Thomas Kivisto
1978—Kenneth Koenigs
1997—Jerod Haase
1999—Ryan Robertson
　　　T.J. Pugh

KANSAS ST.
1968—Earl Seyfert

KENT ST.
1994—Rodney Koch
2002—Demetric Shaw

KENTUCKY
1975—Robert Guyette
1996—Mark Pope

KENYON
1995—Jamie Harless

KING'S (PA.)
1981—James Shea

KNOX
1965—James Jepson

LA SALLE
1992—John Hurd

LA VERNE
2001—Kevin Gustafson

LAFAYETTE
1972—Joseph Mottola
1980—Robert Falconiero
1991—Bruce Stankavage
1994—Keith Brazzo

LAKE FOREST
1968—Frederick Broda

LAMAR
1970—James Nicholson
1999—Matt Sundblad

LEWIS
1989—James Martin

LONG BEACH ST.
1990—Tyrone Mitchell

LORAS
1971—Patrick Lillis

1972—John Buri

LOUISVILLE
1977—Phillip Bond

LOYOLA (MD.)
1979—John Vogt

LOYOLA MARYMOUNT
1973—Stephen Smith

LUTHER
1968—David Mueller
1974—Timothy O'Neill
1982—Douglas Kintzinger
1986—Scott Sawyer

MAINE
1990—Dean Smith

MARQUETTE
1984—Marc Marotta

MARSHALL
1973—Michael D'Antoni
1997—John Brannen

MARYLAND
1974—Tom McMillen
1981—Gregory Manning
1991—Matt Roe

MARYVILLE (MO.)
2003—Kevin Bartow

MASS.-LOWELL
1970—Alfred Spinell Jr.

MIT
1966—John Mazola
1967—Robert Hardt
1968—David Jansson
1971—Bruce Wheeler
1991—David Tomlinson

McDANIEL
1983—Douglas Pinto

McNEESE ST.
1978—John Rudd

MERCER
2006—Will Emerson

MIAMI (OHIO)
1982—George Sweigert

MICHIGAN
1981—Martin Bodnar
1993—Rob Pelinka

MICHIGAN ST.
2005—Chris Hill

MICHIGAN TECH
1978—Michael Trewhella
1981—Russell Van Duine

MIDDLEBURY
1975—David Pentkowski
1982—Paul Righi

MINNESOTA
1970—Michael Regenfuss

MINN. MORRIS
1997—Todd Hanson

MINN. ST. MANKATO
1997—David Kruse

MINN. ST. MOORHEAD
1980—Kevin Mulder
1996—Brett Beeson

MISSISSIPPI COL.
2008—Tyler Winford

MISSISSIPPI ST.
1976—Richard Knarr

MISSOURI
1972—Gregory Flaker

MISSOURI S&T
1977—Ross Klie

MO.-ST. LOUIS
1977—Robert Bone

MISSOURI ST.
1971—Tillman Williams

MONMOUTH (ILL.)
1992—Steve Swanson

MONTANA
1968—Gregory Hanson
1981—Craig Zanon
1986—Larry Krystkowiak
1992—Daren Engellant
1995—Jeremy Lake

MONTANA ST.
1988—Ray Willis Jr.
1996—Nico Harrison
2004—Jason Erikson

MONT. ST.-BILLINGS
2007—Jonathan Wiley

MORNINGSIDE
1986—John Kelzenberg

MT. ST. MARY'S
1976—Richard Kidwell

MUHLENBERG
1976—Glenn Salo

MUSKINGUM
1974—Gary Ferber
1983—Myron Dulkoski Jr.

NAVY
1979—Kevin Sinnett
1984—Clifford Maurer
1995—Wesley Cooper

NEBRASKA
1972—Alan Nissen
1986—John Matzke
1987—William Jackman
1991—Beau Reid
2006—Bronsen Schliep

NEB.-KEARNEY
2004—Nicholas Branting

NEB.-OMAHA
1981—James Gregory

NEB. WESLEYAN
1995—Justin Wilkins
1998—Kipp Kissinger

UNLV
1984—Danny Tarkanian

NEW MEXICO
1973—Breck Roberts

NEW YORK U.
1996—Greg Belinfanti

NORTH CAROLINA
1966—Robert Bennett Jr.
1974—John O'Donnell
1977—Bruce Buckley
1986—Steve Hale
1995—Pearce Landry

UNC GREENSBORO
2001—Nathan Jameson

UNC WILMINGTON
1997—Bill Mayew

NORTH CAROLINA ST.
1966—Peter Coker
1985—Terrence Gannon
1996—Todd Fuller

NORTH DAKOTA ST.
1981—Brady Lipp
1989—Joe Regnier
2000—Jason Retzlaff

NORTHEASTERN
1978—David Caligaris

NORTHERN ARIZ.
1979—Troy Hudson
2006—Kelly Golob

NORTHERN COLO.
1968—Dennis Colson
1990—Toby Moser

NORTHERN ILL.
1984—Timothy Dillion
2000—A.J. Lux

UNI
1979—Michael Kemp

NORTHERN KY.
2000—Kevin Listerman

NORTHWEST MO. ST.
1989—Robert Sundell

NORTHWESTERN
1973—Richard Sund
1980—Michael Campbell
1990—Walker Lambiotte
1994—Kevin Rankin

NORTHWOOD
1999—Jeremy Piggott

NOTRE DAME
1969—Robert Arnzen
1974—Gary Novak
1983—John Paxson
1998—Pat Garrity

OAKLAND
1990—Brian Gregory

OBERLIN
1972—Victor Guerrieri

OCCIDENTAL
1973—Douglas McAdam
1981—Miles Glidden
1996—John Pike

OGLETHORPE
1992—David Fischer

OHIO
1967—John Hamilton
1968—Wayne Young
1979—Steven Skaggs

OHIO ST.
1968—Wilmer Hosket

OHIO WESLEYAN
2007—Benjamin Chojnacki

OKLAHOMA
1972—Scott Martin
1975—Robert Pritchard
1980—Terry Stotts
1988—Dave Sieger

OKLAHOMA CITY
1967—Gary Gray

OKLAHOMA ST.
1965—Gary Hassmann
1969—Joseph Smith

OLD DOMINION
1975—Gray Eubank

OLIVET
1999—Jeff Bell

OREGON
1971—William Drozdiak
1988—Keith Balderston
2000—Adrian Smith

OREGON ST.
1967—Edward Fredenburg

PACIFIC
1967—Bruce Parsons Jr.
1979—Terence Carney
1986—Richard Anema
1992—Delano Demps

PENN
1972—Robert Morse

PENN ST.
1982—Michael Edelman
1995—John Amaechi

PITTSBURGH
1976—Thomas Richards
1986—Joseph David
1992—Darren Morningstar

POMONA-PITZER
1966—Gordon Schloming
1970—Douglas Covey
1986—David Di Cesaris

PORTLAND ST.
1966—John Nelson

POTSDAM ST.
2005—Christian Turner

POLYTECHNIC (N.Y.)
1968—Charles Privalsky

PRINCETON
1969—Christopher Thomforde
1997—Sydney Johnson

PRINCIPIA
1979—William Kelsey

PUGET SOUND
1974—Richard Brown

PURDUE
1971—George Faerber
1981—Brian Walker

RADFORD
1998—Corey Reed

REDLANDS
1990—Robert Stone

REGIS (COLO.)
1988—John Nilles
1994—Pat Holloway

RENSSELAER
1967—Kurt Hollasch

RHODES
1994—Greg Gonda
1996—Scott Brown

RICE
1995—Adam Peakes
2001—Michael Wilks

RICHMOND
1986—John Davis Jr.

RIPON
1978—Ludwig Wurtz
1999—Bret Van Dyken

ROANOKE
2000—Paris Butler

ROLLINS
1993—David Wolf

RUTGERS
1985—Stephen Perry

ST. ANSELM
1980—Sean Canning

ST. FRANCIS (PA.)
1997—Eric Shaner

ST. JOHN FISHER
1997—Eric Shaner

ST. JOHN'S (N.Y.)
1981—Frank Gilroy

ST. JOSEPH'S (IND.)
1975—James Thordsen

ST. JOSEPH'S
1966—Charles McKenna

ST. LAWRENCE
1969—Philip McWhorter

ST. LEO
1981—Kevin McDonald

ST. LOUIS
1967—John Kilo
1995—Scott Highmark

ST. MARY'S (CAL.)
1980—Calvin Wood
1999—Eric Schraeder

ST. NORBERT
1987—Andris Arians

ST. OLAF
1966—Eric Grimsrud
1971—David Finholt

ST. THOMAS (MINN.)
1967—Daniel Hansard
1995—John Tauer

SAN DIEGO
1978—Michael Strode

SAN DIEGO ST.
1976—Steven Copp

SAN FRANCISCO
1990—Joel DeBortoli

SANTA CLARA
1994—Peter Eisenrich

SCRANTON
1974—Joseph Cantafio
1984—Michael Banas
1985—Daniel Polacheck
1988—John Andrejko
1993—Matt Cusano

SEATTLE PACIFIC
1997—Geoffrey Ping
2006—Michael Binetti

SETON HALL
1969—John Suminski

SEWANEE
1967—Thomas Ward Jr.
1976—Henry Hoffman Jr.
1982—James Sherman
1998—Ryan Harrigan

SIENA
1992—Bruce Schroeder

SIMPSON
1980—John Hines
1995—David Otte
2003—Jesse Harris

SLIPPERY ROCK
1975—Clyde Long

SOUTH ALA.
1998—Toby Madison

SOUTH DAKOTA
1976—Rick Nissen
2001—Jeremy Kudera

SOUTH DAKOTA ST.
1973—David Thomas
1997—Jason Sempsrott
2000—Casey Estling

SOUTH FLA.
1992—Radenko Dobras

SOUTHERN CALIFORNIA
1974—Daniel Anderson
1975—John Lambert

SOUTHERN ILL.
1977—Michael Glenn

SMU
1977—Peter Lodwick

SOUTHERN UTAH
1991—Peter Johnson
1993—Richard Barton

STANFORD
1976—Edward Schweitzer
1980—Kimberly Belton
2000—Mark Madsen

SUSQUEHANNA
1986—Donald Harnum
1994—Lloyd Wolf

SWARTHMORE
1965—Cavin Wright
1987—Michael Dell

SYRACUSE
1981—Dan Schayes
1998—Marius Janulis

TENNESSEE
1993—Lang Wiseman

TENN.-MARTIN
1976—Michael Baker

TEXAS
1974—Harry Larrabee
1979—Jim Krivacs

TEXAS-ARLINGTON
1980—Paul Renfor

TEX.-PAN AMERICAN
1976—Jesus Guerra Jr.

TEXAS A&M
1970—James Heitmann

TCU
1970—Jeffrey Harp
1981—Larry Frevert

TEXAS TECH
1985—Brooks Jennings Jr.
1986—Tobin Doda

TOLEDO
1967—William Backensto
1980—Timothy Selgo

TRANSYLVANIA
1972—Robert Jobe Jr.
1980—Lawrence Kopczyk

TRINITY (CONN.)
1971—Howard Greenblatt
1996—Keith Wolff

TRINITY (TEX.)
1975—Phillip Miller

TRUMAN
2000—Jason Reinberg

TUFTS
1981—Scott Brown

TULSA
1999—Michael Ruffin

UCLA
1969—Kenneth Heitz
1971—George Schofield
1980—Kiki Vandeweghe
1995—George Zidek

UTAH
1968—Lyndon MacKay
1971—Michael Newlin
1977—Jeffrey Jonas
1998—Drew Hansen

UTAH ST.
1996—Eric Franson

VANDERBILT
1976—Jeffrey Fosnes

VILLANOVA
1983—John Pinone

VIRGINIA
1973—James Hobgood

VMI
1969—John Mitchell
1971—Jan Essenburg
1977—William Bynum III
1981—Andrew Kolesar
1987—Gay Elmore Jr.
1996—Bobby Prince

VIRGINIA TECH
1972—Robert McNeer

WABASH
1976—Len Fulkerson

WAKE FOREST
1969—Jerry Montgomery
1994—Marcus Blucas
1996—Rusty LaRue

WARTBURG
1972—David Platte
1974—Fred Waldstein
1991—Dan Nettleton

WASHINGTON
1970—Vincent Stone
1974—Raymond Price
1987—Rodney Ripley

WASHINGTON (MD.)
1979—Joseph Wilson
1990—Tim Keehan

1998—Bradd Burkhart

WASHINGTON-ST. LOUIS
1991—Jed Bargen
2008—Troy Ruths

WASH. & JEFF.
1970—Terry Evans
1981—David Damico

WASH. & LEE
1983—Brian Hanson
1984—John Graves

WEBER ST.
1980—Mark Mattos
1985—Kent Hagan

WESLEYAN (CONN.)
1973—Brad Rogers
1974—Richard Fairbrother
1977—Steve Malinowski
1982—Steven Maizes
1985—Gregory Porydzy

WEST TEX. A&M
2008—Tyler Cooper

WEST VIRGINIA
2006—Johannes Herber

WESTERN CARO.
1982—Gregory Dennis
1987—Richard Rogers

WESTERN ILL.
1984—Todd Hutcheson

WESTMINSTER (PA.)
1967—John Fontanella

WHEATON (ILL.)
1995—Nathan Frank

WHITTIER
1977—Rodney Snook

WICHITA ST.
1969—Ronald Mendell
1991—Paul Guffrovich

WIDENER
1983—Louis DeRogatis

WILLIAM & MARY
1985—Keith Cieplicki
2004—Adam Hess

WILLIAMS
1965—Edgar Coolidge III
1986—Timothy Walsh

WISCONSIN
1987—Rodney Ripley

WIS.-OSHKOSH
1998—Joe Imhoff

WIS.-PLATTEVILLE
1993—T.J. Van Wie

WIS.-STEVENS POINT
1983—John Mack

WITTENBERG
1984—Jay Ferguson
1996—Scott Schwartz

WOOSTER
1995—Scott Meech
2005—Matt Schlingman
2006—Kyle Witucky

WRIGHT ST.
1978—Alan McGee

XAVIER
1975—Peter Accetta
1981—Gary Massa

YALE
1967—Richard Johnson
1968—Robert McCallum Jr.

YORK (PA.)
2006—Brandon Bushey

Coaching Records

All-Divisions Coaching Records

Some of the won-lost records included in this coaches section have been adjusted because of action by the NCAA Committee on Infractions to forfeit particular regular-season games or vacate particular NCAA tournament games.

Coaches with at Least 600 Career Wins

(This list includes all coaches who have won at least 600 games regardless of classification with a minimum 10 head coaching seasons at NCAA schools.)

	Coach (Alma Mater), Teams Coached, Tenure	Yrs.	Won	Lost	Pct.
1.	Bob Knight (Ohio St. 1962) Army 1966-71, Indiana 72-2000, Texas Tech 02-08	42	902	371	.709
2.	Don Meyer (Northern Colo. 1967) Hamline 1973-75, Lipscomb 76-99, Northern St. 2000-08*	36	891	299	.749
3.	Dean Smith (Kansas 1953) North Carolina 1962-97	36	879	254	.776
4.	Adolph Rupp (Kansas 1923) Kentucky 1931-52, 54-72	41	876	190	.822
5.	Herb Magee (Philadelphia U. 1963) Philadelphia U. 1968-2008*	41	855	339	.716
6.	Jim Phelan (La Salle 1951) Mt. St. Mary's 1955-2003	49	830	524	.613
7.	Clarence "Big House" Gaines (Morgan St. 1945) Winston-Salem 1947-93	47	828	447	.649
8.	Jerry Johnson (Fayetteville St. 1951) LeMoyne-Owen 1959-2005	47	821	447	.647
9.	Eddie Sutton (Oklahoma St. 1958) Creighton 1970-74, Arkansas 75-85, Kentucky 86-89, Oklahoma St. 91-2006, San Francisco 08	37	804	328	.710
10.	Mike Krzyzewski (Army 1969) Army 1976-80, Duke 81-2008*	33	803	267	.750
11.	Lefty Driesell (Duke 1954) Davidson 1961-69, Maryland 70-86, James Madison 89-97, Georgia St. 98-2003	41	786	394	.666
12.	Lute Olson (Augsburg 1956) Long Beach St. 1974, Iowa 75-83, Arizona 84-2007*	34	780	280	.736
13.	Lou Henson (New Mexico St. 1955) Hardin-Simmons 1963-66, Illinois 76-96, New Mexico St. 67-75, 98-2005	41	779	412	.654
14.	Jim Calhoun (American Int'l 1968) Northeastern 1973-86, Connecticut 87-2008*	36	774	337	.697
15.	Jim Boeheim (Syracuse 1966) Syracuse 1977-2008*	32	771	278	.735
16.	Henry Iba [Westminster (Mo.) 1928] Northwest Mo. St. 1930-33, Colorado 34, Oklahoma St. 35-70	41	764	339	.693
17.	Ed Diddle (Centre 1921) Western Ky. 1923-64	42	759	302	.715
18.	Phog Allen (Kansas 1906) Baker 1906-08, Haskell 09, Central Mo. 13-19, Kansas 08-20, 20-56	48	746	264	.739
19.	John Chaney (Bethune-Cookman 1955) Cheyney 1973-82, Temple 83-2006	34	741	312	.704
20.	Glenn Robinson (West Chester 1967) Frank. & Marsh. 1972-2008*	37	730	284	.720
21.	Jerry Tarkanian (Fresno St. 1955) Long Beach St. 1969-73, UNLV 74-92, Fresno St. 96-2002	31	729	201	.784
22.	Norm Stewart (Missouri 1956) UNI 1962-67, Missouri 68-99	38	728	374	.661
23.	Ray Meyer (Notre Dame 1938) DePaul 1943-84	42	724	354	.672
24.	Don Haskins (Oklahoma St. 1952) UTEP 1962-99	38	719	353	.671
25.	Dave Robbins (Catawba 1966) Virginia Union 1979-2008*	30	713	194	.786
26.	Dick Sauers (Slippery Rock 1951) Albany (N.Y.) 1956-87, 89-97	41	702	330	.680

	Coach (Alma Mater), Teams Coached, Tenure	Yrs.	Won	Lost	Pct.
27.	Jim Smith (Marquette 1956) St. John's (Minn.) 1965-2008*	44	685	475	.591
28.	Denny Crum (UCLA 1958) Louisville 1972-2001	30	675	295	.696
29.	Dennis Bridges (Ill. Wesleyan 1961) Ill. Wesleyan 1966-2001	36	666	320	.675
30.	John Wooden (Purdue 1932) Indiana St. 1947-48, UCLA 49-75	29	664	162	.804
31.	Ralph Miller (Kansas 1942) Wichita St. 1952-64, Iowa 65-70, Oregon St. 71-89	38	657	382	.632
32.	Gene Bartow (Truman 1953) Central Mo. 1962-64, Valparaiso 65-70, Memphis 71-74, Illinois 75, UCLA 76-77, UAB 79-96	34	647	353	.647
33.	Bob Chipman (Kansas St. 1973) Washburn 1980-2008*	29	646	251	.720
34.	Billy Tubbs (Lamar 1958) Southwestern (Tex.) 1972-73, Oklahoma 81-94, TCU 95-2002, Lamar 1977-80, 2004-06	31	641	340	.653
35.	Marv Harshman (Pacific Lutheran 1942) Pacific Lutheran 1946-58, Washington St. 59-71, Washington 72-85	40	637	443	.590
36.	Hugh Durham (Florida St. 1959) Florida St. 1967-78, Georgia 79-95, Jacksonville 98-2005	37	633	429	.596
37.	John Lance (Pittsburg St. 1918) Southwestern Okla. 1919-22, Pittsburg St. 23-34, 36-63	44	632	340	.650
38.	Ken Anderson (Wis.-Eau Claire 1955) Wis.-Eau Claire 1969-95	27	631	152	.806
39.	Cam Henderson (Salem 1917) Muskingum 1920-23, Davis & Elkins 24-35, Marshall 36-55	36	630	243	.722
39.	Ed Messbarger (Northwest Mo. St. 1956) Benedictine Hts. 1958-60, Dallas 61-63, St. Mary's (Tex.) 64-78, Angelo St. 79-98	41	630	518	.549
41.	Norm Sloan (North Carolina St. 1951) Presbyterian 1952-55, Citadel 57-60, Florida 61-66, North Carolina St. 67-80, Florida 81-89	37	624	393	.614
42.	Dean Nicholson (Central Wash. 1950) Central Wash. 1965-90	26	620	199	.757
43.	Glenn Van Wieren (Hope 1964) Hope 1978-2008*	31	618	203	.753
43.	Tom Murphy (Springfield 1960) Hamilton 1971-2004, SUNYIT 06	35	618	274	.693
43.	Dick Reynolds (Otterbein 1965) Otterbein 1973-2008*	36	618	359	.633
46.	Bob Huggins (West Virginia 1977) Walsh 1981-83, Akron 85-89, Cincinnati 90-2005, Kansas St. 07, West Virginia 08*	26	616	222	.735
47.	Ed Adams (Tuskegee 1934) N.C. Central 1935-36, Tuskegee 37-49, Texas Southern 50-58	24	612	150	.803
48.	Jerry Slocum [King's (N.Y.) 1975] Nyack 1976-87, Geneva 1988-96, Gannon 97-2005, Youngstown St. 06-08*	33	610	384	.614
49.	Jerry Steele (Wake Forest 1961) Guilford 1963-70, High Point 73-2003	39	609	486	.556
50.	Tom Penders (Connecticut 1967) Tufts 1972-74, Columbia 75-78, Fordham 79-86, Rhode Island 87-88, Texas 89-98, George Washington 99-2001, Houston 05-08*	34	608	410	.597
51.	Gary Williams (Maryland 1968) American 1979-82, Boston College 83-86, Ohio St. 87-89, Maryland 90-2008*	30	604	343	.638

*active

Division I Coaching Records

Winningest Active Coaches

(Minimum five years as a Division I head coach; includes record at four-year U.S. colleges only.)

BY PERCENTAGE

No.	Coach	Team	Yrs.	Won	Lost	Pct.
1.	Roy Williams	North Carolina	20	560	134	.807
2.	Mark Few	Gonzaga	9	236	60	.797
3.	Bruce Pearl	Tennessee	16	394	108	.785
4.	Bo Ryan	Wisconsin	24	556	163	.773
5.	Jamie Dixon	Pittsburgh	5	132	40	.767
6.	Thad Matta	Ohio St.	8	207	66	.758
7.	John Calipari	Memphis	16	408	135	.751
8.	Mike Krzyzewski	Duke	33	803	267	.750
9.	Lute Olson	Arizona	34	780	280	.736
10.	Bob Huggins	West Virginia	26	616	222	.735
11.	Jim Boeheim	Syracuse	32	771	278	.735
12.	Rick Pitino	Louisville	22	521	191	.732
13.	Rick Majerus	St. Louis	21	438	162	.730
14.	Tubby Smith	Minnesota	17	407	159	.719
15.	Bill Self	Kansas	15	349	137	.718
16.	Danny Kaspar	Stephen F. Austin	17	353	148	.705
17.	Billy Donovan	Florida	14	320	135	.703
18.	Tom Izzo	Michigan St.	13	305	130	.701
19.	Jim Christian	TCU	6	137	59	.699
20.	Darrin Horn	South Carolina	5	111	48	.698
21.	Jim Calhoun	Connecticut	36	774	337	.697
22.	Bruce Weber	Illinois	10	231	101	.696

No.	Coach	Team	Yrs.	Won	Lost	Pct.
23.	Mike Montgomery	California	26	547	244	.692
24.	John Thompson III	Georgetown	8	168	78	.683
25.	Brad Brownell	Wright St.	6	127	60	.679
26.	Ben Howland	UCLA	14	294	144	.671
27.	Stew Morrill	Utah St.	22	455	224	.670
28.	Pat Douglass	UC Irvine	27	547	273	.667
29.	Gregg Marshall	Wichita St.	10	205	103	.666
30.	Bob Hoffman	Mercer	14	310	156	.665
31.	Tom Crean	Indiana	9	190	96	.664
32.	Rick Barnes	Texas	21	449	227	.664
33.	Tony Shaver	William & Mary	22	413	214	.659
34.	Mike Brey	Notre Dame	13	266	138	.658
35.	Larry Hunter	Western Caro.	28	543	282	.658
36.	Bart Lundy	High Point	10	202	106	.656
37.	Jeff Price	Ga. Southern	15	291	155	.652
38.	Keith Dambrot	Akron	10	200	108	.649
39.	Blaine Taylor	Old Dominion	14	277	150	.649
40.	L. Vann Pettaway	Alabama A&M	22	421	229	.648
41.	Tim Floyd	Southern California	15	306	167	.647
42.	Mark Gottfried	Alabama	13	267	147	.645
43.	Rick Stansbury	Mississippi St.	10	208	115	.644
44.	Roger Reid	Southern Utah	8	162	90	.643
44.	Todd Lickliter	Iowa	7	144	80	.643
46.	Rick Byrd	Belmont	27	541	303	.641
47.	Mike Anderson	Missouri	6	123	69	.641
48.	Fran Dunphy	Temple	19	343	194	.639
49.	Gary Williams	Maryland	30	604	343	.638
50.	Jeff Capel III	Oklahoma	6	118	68	.634
51.	Steve Alford	New Mexico	17	332	192	.634
52.	Phil Martelli	St. Joseph's	13	261	152	.632
53.	Bobby Lutz	Charlotte	19	368	215	.631
54.	Dana Altman	Creighton	19	365	219	.625
55.	Billy Gillispie	Kentucky	6	118	71	.624

No.	Coach	Team	Yrs.	Won	Lost	Pct.
56.	Bob Marlin	Sam Houston St.	10	182	111	.621
57.	Kevin Stallings	Vanderbilt	15	293	179	.621
58.	John Beilein	Michigan	26	486	297	.621
59.	Brian Gregory	Dayton	5	98	60	.620
60.	Mack McCarthy	East Carolina	17	320	196	.620
61.	John Giannini	La Salle	19	346	215	.617
62.	Jay Wright	Villanova	14	270	168	.616
63.	Mike Jarvis	Fla. Atlantic	19	321	201	.615
64.	Homer Drew	Valparaiso	31	593	376	.612
65.	Greg Jackson	Delaware St.	17	295	189	.610
66.	Cliff Ellis	Coastal Caro.	30	547	352	.608
67.	Greg McDermott	Iowa St.	14	250	161	.608
68.	Larry Eustachy	Southern Miss.	17	320	208	.606
69.	Bob Burton	Cal St. Fullerton	5	92	60	.605
70.	Scott Sutton	Oral Roberts	9	168	111	.602
71.	Bob McKillop	Davidson	19	340	225	.602
72.	Bob Williams	UC Santa Barb.	20	348	232	.600
72.	Karl Hobbs	George Washington	7	123	82	.600
72.	Mick Cronin	Cincinnati	5	93	62	.600

(Coaches with five or more years coached but less than five years as a Division I head coach; includes record at four-year U.S. colleges only.)

No.	Coach	Team	Yrs.	Won	Lost	Pct.
1.	Mike Lonergan	Vermont	15	305	128	.704
2.	David Paulsen	Bucknell	14	262	120	.686
3.	Kevin McKenna	Indiana St.	5	104	49	.680
4.	Jeff Reynolds	Air Force	5	98	48	.671
5.	Ken Bone	Portland St.	16	311	157	.665
6.	Ricky Duckett	Grambling	8	148	81	.646
7.	Jim Yarbrough	Southeastern La.	8	146	81	.643
8.	Scott Nagy	South Dakota St.	13	243	142	.631
9.	Don Friday	St. Francis (Pa.)	5	83	49	.629
10.	Jerry Slocum	Youngstown St.	33	610	384	.614

BY VICTORIES

No.	Coach, Team	Won
1.	Mike Krzyzewski, Duke	803
2.	Lute Olson, Arizona	780
3.	Jim Calhoun, Connecticut	774
4.	Jim Boeheim, Syracuse	771
5.	Bob Huggins, West Virginia	616
6.	Tom Penders, Houston	608
7.	Gary Williams, Maryland	604
8.	Homer Drew, Valparaiso	593
9.	Roy Williams, North Carolina	560
10.	Bo Ryan, Wisconsin	556
10.	Ben Braun, Rice	556
12.	Mike Montgomery, California	547
12.	Pat Douglass, UC Irvine	547
12.	Cliff Ellis, Coastal Caro.	547
15.	Larry Hunter, Western Caro.	543
16.	Rick Byrd, Belmont	541
17.	Rick Pitino, Louisville	521
18.	Bobby Cremins, Col. of Charleston	492
19.	John Beilein, Michigan	486
20.	Dave Bike, Sacred Heart	463
21.	Pat Kennedy, Towson	461
22.	Stew Morrill, Utah St.	455
23.	Rick Barnes, Texas	449
24.	Rick Majerus, St. Louis	438
25.	Don Maestri, Troy	433
26.	L. Vann Pettaway, Alabama A&M	421
27.	Mike Deane, Wagner	415
28.	Tony Shaver, William & Mary	413
29.	Lon Kruger, UNLV	409
30.	John Calipari, Memphis	408

No.	Coach, Team	Won
31.	Tubby Smith, Minnesota	407
32.	Jim Larranaga, George Mason	404
33.	Tom Green, Fairleigh Dickinson	400
34.	Bob Thomason, Pacific	396
35.	Bruce Pearl, Tennessee	394
35.	Greg Kampe, Oakland	394
37.	Rick Scruggs, Gardner-Webb	378
38.	Dave Loos, Austin Peay	377
39.	Bobby Lutz, Charlotte	368
40.	Dana Altman, Creighton	365
41.	Fang Mitchell, Coppin St.	358
42.	Danny Kaspar, Stephen F. Austin	353
43.	Oliver Purnell, Clemson	350
44.	Bill Self, Kansas	349
45.	Bob Williams, UC Santa Barb.	348
45.	Al Skinner, Boston College	348
47.	John Giannini, La Salle	346
48.	Rob Spivery, Southern U.	344
49.	Fran Dunphy, Temple	343
50.	Jim Crews, Army	342
51.	Bob McKillop, Davidson	340
52.	Cy Alexander, Tennessee St.	337
53.	Steve Alford, New Mexico	332
54.	Mike Jarvis, Fla. Atlantic	321
55.	Billy Donovan, Florida	320
55.	Mack McCarthy, East Carolina	320
55.	Larry Eustachy, Southern Miss.	320
55.	Jim Wooldridge, UC Riverside	320
59.	Ralph Willard, Holy Cross	318
60.	Jim Baron, Rhode Island	313

No.	Coach, Team	Won
61.	Bob Hoffman, Mercer	310
62.	Mike Dement, UNC Greensboro	309
63.	Tim Floyd, Southern California	306
63.	Leonard Hamilton, Florida St.	306
65.	Tom Izzo, Michigan St.	305
66.	Charlie Coles, Miami (Ohio)	302
67.	Ernie Kent, Oregon	301
67.	Seth Greenberg, Virginia Tech	301
69.	Greg Jackson, Delaware St.	295
70.	Ben Howland, UCLA	294
71.	Kevin Stallings, Vanderbilt	293
72.	Jeff Price, Ga. Southern	291
73.	Herb Sendek, Arizona St.	283
74.	John Brady, Arkansas St.	281
75.	Blaine Taylor, Old Dominion	277
76.	Ronnie Arrow, South Ala.	274
77.	Jay Wright, Villanova	270
77.	Jeff Jones, American	270
79.	Bill Herrion, New Hampshire	268
80.	Mark Gottfried, Alabama	267
81.	Mike Brey, Notre Dame	266
82.	Phil Martelli, St. Joseph's	261
83.	Dennis Wolff, Boston U.	260
84.	Perry Clark, A&M-Corpus Chris.	259
85.	Steve Fisher, San Diego St.	256
86.	Greg McDermott, Iowa St.	250
87.	Kirk Speraw, UCF	247
88.	Mark Few, Gonzaga	236
89.	Steve Hawkins, Western Mich.	233
90.	Ron Hunter, IUPUI	232

No.	Coach, Team	Won
91.	Bruce Weber, Illinois	231
92.	Jerry Wainwright, DePaul	228
93.	Glen Miller, Penn	223
93.	Jim Molinari, Western Ill.	223
93.	Frankie Allen, Md.-East. Shore	223
96.	Lorenzo Romar, Washington	212
97.	Tom Asbury, Pepperdine	210
98.	Rick Stansbury, Mississippi St.	208
98.	Paul Hewitt, Georgia Tech	208
100.	Thad Matta, Ohio St.	207
101.	Gregg Marshall, Wichita St.	205
102.	Bruiser Flint, Drexel	204
103.	Bart Lundy, High Point	202
103.	Gary Waters, Cleveland St.	202
105.	Ron Everhart, Duquesne	201
106.	Keith Dambrot, Akron	200

(Coaches with five or more years coached but less than five years as a Division I head coach; includes record at four-year U.S. colleges only.)

No.	Coach, Team	Won
1.	Jerry Slocum, Youngstown St.	610
2.	Jim Whitesell, Loyola (Ill.)	343
3.	Ken Bone, Portland St.	311
4.	Mike Lonergan, Vermont	305
5.	David Paulsen, Bucknell	262
6.	Scott Nagy, South Dakota St.	243
7.	Tim Miles, Colorado St.	219

Winningest Coaches All-Time

BY PERCENTAGE
(Minimum 10 head coaching seasons in Division I)

	Coach, team coached & tenure	Yrs.	Won	Lost	Pct.
1.	Clair Bee, Rider 1929-31, Long Island 1932-43, 46-51	21	412	87	.826
2.	Adolph Rupp, Kentucky 1931-52, 54-72	41	876	190	.822
3.	Roy Williams, Kansas 1989-2003, North Carolina 04-08*	20	560	134	.807
4.	John Wooden, Indiana St. 1947-48, UCLA 49-75	29	664	162	.804
5.	John Kresse, Col. of Charleston 1980-02	23	560	143	.797
6.	Jerry Tarkanian, Long Beach St. 1969-73, UNLV 74-92, Fresno St. 96-2002	31	729	201	.784
7.	Francis Schmidt, Tulsa 1916-17, 19-22, Arkansas 24-29, TCU 30-34	17	258	72	.782
8.	Dean Smith, North Carolina 1962-97	36	879	254	.776
9.	Jack Ramsay, St. Joseph's 1956-66	11	231	71	.765
10.	Frank Keaney, Rhode Island 1921-48	28	401	124	.764
11.	George Keogan, Wis.-Superior 1913-14, St. Louis 16, St. Thomas (Minn.) 18, Allegheny 19, Valparaiso 20-21, Notre Dame 24-43 #	27	414	127	.764
12.	Vic Bubas, Duke 1960-69	10	213	67	.761
13.	Harry Fisher, Fordham 1905, Columbia 1907-16, St. John's (N.Y.) 1910, Army 07, 22-23, 25	16	189	60	.759
14.	John Calipari, Massachusetts 1989-96, Memphis 2001-08*	16	408	135	.751
15.	Mike Krzyzewski, Army 1976-80, Duke 81-2008*	33	803	267	.750
16.	Fred Bennion, BYU 1909-10, Utah 11-14, Montana St. 15-19	11	95	32	.748
17.	Chick Davies, Duquesne 1925-43, 47-48	21	314	106	.748
18.	Ray Mears, Wittenberg 1957-62, Tennessee 63-77	21	399	135	.747
19.	Edward McNichol, Pennsylvania 1921-30	10	186	63	.747
20.	Al McGuire, Belmont Abbey 1958-64, Marquette 65-77	20	406	142	.741
21.	Phog Allen, Baker 1906-08, Haskell 09, Central Mo. 13-19, Kansas 08-09, 20-56	50	746	264	.739
22.	Everett Case, North Carolina St. 1947-65	19	377	134	.738
23.	Lute Olson, Long Beach St. 1974, Iowa 75-83, Arizona 84-2007*	34	780	280	.736
24.	Arthur Schabinger, Ottawa 1917-20, Emporia St. 21-22, Creighton 23-35	19	245	88	.736
25.	Bob Huggins, Walsh 1981-83, Akron 85-89, Cincinnati 90-2005, Kansas St. 07, West Virginia 08*	26	616	222	.735
26.	G. Ott Romney, Montana St. 1923-28, BYU 29-35	13	283	102	.735
27.	Jim Boeheim, Syracuse 1977-2008*	32	771	278	.735
28.	Doc Meanwell, Wisconsin 1912-17, Missouri 18, Wisconsin 21-34	22	280	101	.735
29.	Rick Pitino, Boston U. 1979-83, Providence 86-87, Kentucky 90-97, Louisville 2002-08*	22	521	191	.732
30.	Rick Majerus, Marquette 1984-86, Ball St. 88-89, Utah 1990-2004, St. Louis 08*	21	438	162	.730
31.	Henry Lannigan, Virginia 1906-29 #	24	254	95	.727
32.	Lew Andreas, Syracuse 1925-50	25	358	135	.726
33.	Lou Carnesecca, St. John's (N.Y.) 1966-70, 74-92	24	526	200	.725
34.	Fred Schaus, West Virginia 1955-60, Purdue 1973-78	12	251	96	.723
35.	James Usilton, Temple 1927-39	13	205	79	.722
36.	Cam Henderson, Muskingum 1920-23, Davis & Elkins 24-35, Marshall 36-55	36	630	243	.722
37.	Joe Lapchick, St. John's (N.Y.) 1937-47, 57-65	20	334	130	.720
38.	Tubby Smith, Tulsa 1992-95, Georgia 96-97, Kentucky 98-2007, Minnesota 08*	17	407	159	.719
39.	Edmund Dollard, Syracuse 1912-24	13	151	59	.719
40.	Hugh Greer, Connecticut 1947-63	17	286	112	.719
41.	Bill Self, Oral Roberts 1994-97, Tulsa 98-2000, Illinois 01-03, Kansas 04-08*	15	349	137	.718
42.	Dudey Moore, Duquesne 1949-58, La Salle 59-63	15	270	107	.716
43.	Ed Diddle, Western Ky. 1923-64	42	759	302	.715
44.	Tom Blackburn, Dayton 1948-64	17	352	141	.714
45.	John Lawther, Westminster (Pa.) 1927-36, Penn St. 37-49	23	317	127	.714
46.	John Thompson, Georgetown 1973-99	27	596	239	.714
47.	Hec Edmundson, Idaho 1917-18, Washington 21-47	29	508	204	.713
48.	Nolan Richardson, Tulsa 1981-85, Arkansas 86-2002	22	509	207	.711
49.	Edward Kelleher, St. John's (N.Y.) 1922, Fordham 23-34, 39-43, Army 44-45	19	258	105	.711
50.	Eddie Sutton, Creighton 1970-74, Arkansas 75-85, Kentucky 86-89, Oklahoma St. 91-2006, San Francisco 08	37	804	328	.710
51.	Piggy Lambert, Purdue 1917-17, 19-46	29	371	152	.709
52.	Bob Knight, Army 1966-71, Indiana 72-2000, Texas Tech 02-08	42	902	371	.709
53.	Pat Page, Chicago 1912-20, Butler 21-26	15	257	106	.708
54.	Peck Hickman, Louisville 1945-67	23	443	183	.708
55.	Lee Rose, Transylvania 1965-65, 69-75, Charlotte 76-78, Purdue 79-80, South Fla. 81-86	19	388	162	.705
56.	Joe B. Hall, Regis (Colo.) 1960-64, Central Mo. 65, Kentucky 73-85	19	373	156	.705
57.	John Chaney, Cheyney 1973-82, Temple 83-2006	34	741	312	.704
58.	Billy Donovan, Marshall 1995-96, Florida 97-2008*	14	320	135	.703
59.	Tom Izzo, Michigan St. 1996-2008*	13	305	130	.701
60.	Harlan Dykes, Santa Clara 1927-35, St. Mary's (Cal.) 38-39	11	147	63	.700
61.	Frank McGuire, St. John's (N.Y.) 1948-52, North Carolina 53-61, South Carolina 65-80	30	549	236	.699
62.	Bennie Owen, Oklahoma 1909-21	13	113	49	.698
63.	Jim Calhoun, Northeastern 1973-86, Connecticut 87-2008*	36	774	337	.697
64.	E.C. Hayes, Mississippi St. 1912-24	12	124	54	.697
65.	Boyd Grant, Fresno St. 1978-86, Colorado St. 88-91	13	275	120	.696
66.	Denny Crum, Louisville 1972-01	30	675	295	.696
67.	Douglas R. Mills, Illinois 1937-47	11	151	66	.696
68.	Bruce Weber, Southern Ill. 1999-2003, Illinois 04-08*	10	231	101	.696
69.	Honey Russell, Seton Hall 1937-43, Manhattan 46, Seton Hall 50-60	19	310	137	.694
70.	Henry Iba, Northwest Mo. St. 1930-33, Colorado 34, Oklahoma St. 35-70	41	764	339	.693
71.	Eddie M. Cameron, Wash. & Lee 1925, Duke 29-42	15	234	104	.692
72.	Larry Weise, St. Bonaventure 1962-73	12	202	90	.692
73.	Mike Montgomery, Montana 1979-86, Stanford 87-04, California*	26	547	244	.692
74.	Gene Smithson, Illinois St. 1976-78, Wichita St. 79-86	11	221	99	.691
75.	Harold Anderson, Toledo 1935-42, Bowling Green 43-63	29	504	226	.690
76.	Nat Holman, CCNY 1920-52, 55-56, 59-60	37	423	190	.690
77.	Ralph R. Jones, Butler 1904, Wabash 05-09, Purdue 10-12, Illinois 13-20, Lake Forest 34-39, 46	24	232	106	.686
78.	John R. Wilson, Navy 1927-39	20	204	94	.685
79.	Dana Kirk, Tampa 1967-71, Va. Commonwealth 77-79, Memphis 80-86	15	281	131	.682
80.	Guy Lewis, Houston 1957-86	30	592	279	.680
81.	John Oldham, Tennessee Tech 1956-64, Western Ky. 65-71	16	260	123	.679
82.	Harry Combes, Illinois 1948-67	20	316	150	.678
83.	Zora Clevenger, Indiana 1905-06, Neb. Wesleyan 08-11, Tennessee 12-16, Kansas St. 17-20	15	151	72	.677
84.	Digger Phelps, Fordham 1971, Notre Dame 72-91	21	419	200	.677
85.	Bob King, New Mexico 1963-72, Indiana St. 76-78	13	236	113	.676
86.	Buck Read, Western Mich. 1922-49	28	358	173	.674
87.	Jack Gardner, Kansas St. 1940-42, 47-53, Utah 54-71	28	486	235	.674
88.	Leo Novak, Army 1927-39	13	126	61	.674
89.	J.R. Crozier, Wake Forest 1906-17	12	95	46	.674
90.	Roy Skinner, Vanderbilt 1959-59, 62-76	16	278	135	.673
91.	Thomas Haggerty, DePaul 1937-40, Loyola (Ill.) 46-50, Loyola (La.) 51-53	12	224	109	.673
92.	Alex Severence, Villanova 1937-61	25	413	201	.673
93.	Ray Meyer, DePaul 1943-84	42	724	354	.672
94.	Ben Howland, Northern Ariz. 1995-99, Pittsburgh 2000-03, UCLA 04-08*	14	294	144	.671
95.	Don Haskins, UTEP 1962-99	38	719	353	.671
96.	Stew Morrill, Montana 1987-91, Colorado St. 92-98, Utah St. 99-2008*	22	455	224	.670
97.	Dutch Hermann, Penn St. 1916-17, 20-32	15	148	73	.670
98.	Don Corbett, Lincoln (Mo.) 1972-79, N.C. A&T 80-93	22	413	204	.669
99.	Ozzie Cowles, Carleton 1925-30, Wis.-River Falls 33-36, Dartmouth 37-43, 45-46, Michigan 47-48, Minnesota 49-59	32	421	208	.669
100.	Jim Harrick, Pepperdine 1980-88, UCLA 89-96, Rhode Island 98-99, Georgia 2000-03	23	470	233	.669
101.	Neil Cohalan, Manhattan 1930-42	13	165	82	.668
102.	Pat Douglass, Mont. St.-Billings 1982-87, Cal St. Bakersfield 88-97, UC Irvine 98-2008*	27	547	273	.667
103.	Charles Moir, Roanoke 1968-73, Tulane 74-76, Virginia Tech 77-87	20	392	196	.667
103.	Jack Gray, Texas 1937-42, 46-51	12	194	97	.667
103.	Herman Stegeman, Monmouth (Ill.) 1917, Georgia 20-31	13	178	89	.667
106.	Neil McCarthy, Weber St. 1975-85, New Mexico St. 86-97	22	431	216	.666
107.	Lefty Driesell, Davidson 1961-69, Maryland 70-86, James Madison 89-97, Georgia St. 98-2003	41	786	394	.666
108.	Harold Bradley, Hartwick 1948-50, Duke 51-59, Texas 60-67	20	337	169	.666
109.	Skip Prosser, Loyola (Md.) 1994, Xavier 95-2001, Wake Forest 02-07	14	291	146	.666
110.	Gregg Marshall, Winthrop 1999-2007, Wichita St. 08*	10	205	103	.666
111.	Wimp Sanderson, Alabama 1981-92, UALR 95-99	17	350	176	.665
112.	Hank Crisp, Alabama 1924-42, 46	20	264	133	.665
113.	Rick Barnes, George Mason 1988, Providence 89-94, Clemson 95-98, Texas 99-2008*	21	449	227	.664
114.	Edward J. Stewart, Mount Union 1908, Purdue 09, Oregon St. 12-16, Nebraska 17-19, Texas 24-27, UTEP 28	15	193	98	.663
115.	Branch McCracken, Ball St. 1931-38, Indiana 39-43, 47-65	32	450	231	.661
116.	Norm Stewart, UNI 1962-67, Missouri 68-99	38	728	374	.661

Coach, team coached & tenure	Yrs.	Won	Lost	Pct.
117. W.O. Hamilton, William Jewell 1899-1900, 07-08, Kansas 10-19	14	144	74	.661
118. Dave Gavitt, Dartmouth 1968-69, Providence 70-79	12	227	117	.660
119. Terry Holland, Davidson 1970-74, Virginia 75-90	21	418	216	.659
120. Harry Litwack, Temple 1953-73	21	373	193	.659
121. Mike Brey, Delaware 1996-2000, Notre Dame 01-08*..	13	266	138	.658
122. Larry Hunter, Wittenberg 1977-89, Ohio 90-2001, Western Caro. 06-08*	28	543	282	.658
123. Pete Carril, Lehigh 1967, Princeton 68-96	30	525	273	.658
124. Pete Newell, San Francisco 1947-50, Michigan St. 51-54, California 55-60	14	234	123	.655
125. Louis Cooke, Minnesota 1898-1924 #	27	242	127	.655
126. Dick Tarrant, Richmond 1982-93	12	239	126	.655
127. Lou Henson, Hardin-Simmons 1963-66, Illinois 76-96, New Mexico St. 67-75, 1998-2005	41	779	412	.654
128. Billy Tubbs, Southwestern (Tex.) 1972-73, Lamar 77-80, Oklahoma 81-94, TCU 95-2002, Lamar 04-06..	31	641	340	.653
129. Fred Taylor, Ohio St. 1959-76	18	297	158	.653
130. Jack Hartman, Southern Ill. 1963-70, Kansas St. 71-86.	24	437	233	.652
131. Paul Evans, St. Lawrence 1974-80, Navy 81-86, Pittsburgh 87-94	21	390	208	.652
132. Eddie Hickey, Creighton 1936-43, 47, St. Louis 48-58, Marquette 59-64	26	433	231	.652
133. George King, Charleston (W.Va.) 1957, West Virginia 61-65, Purdue 66-72	13	223	119	.652
134. Leonard Palmer, CCNY 1907-16	10	71	38	.651
135. J. Craig Ruby, Missouri 1921-22, Illinois 23-36	16	181	97	.651
136. John Kraft, Villanova 1962-73, Rhode Island 74-81	20	341	183	.651

*active; # ties included in calculating the winning percentages for: George Keogan 3 ties, Henry Lannigan 1 and Louis Cooke 1.

BY VICTORIES

(Minimum 10 head coaching seasons in Division I)

Coach	Wins
1. Bob Knight	902
2. Dean Smith	879
3. Adolph Rupp	876
4. Jim Phelan, Mt. St. Mary's 1955-2003	830
5. Eddie Sutton	804
6. Mike Krzyzewski*	803
7. Lefty Driesell	786
8. Lute Olson*	780
9. Lou Henson	779
10. Jim Calhoun*	774
11. Jim Boeheim*	771
12. Henry Iba	764
13. Ed Diddle	759
14. Phog Allen	746
15. John Chaney	741
16. Jerry Tarkanian	729
17. Norm Stewart	728
18. Ray Meyer	724
19. Don Haskins	719
20. Denny Crum	675
21. John Wooden	664
22. Ralph Miller, Wichita St. 1952-64, Iowa 65-70, Oregon St. 71-89	657
23. Gene Bartow, Central Mo. 1962-64, Valparaiso 65-70, Memphis 71-74, Illinois 75, UCLA 76-77, UAB 79-96	647
24. Billy Tubbs	641
25. Marv Harshman, Pacific Lutheran 1946-58, Washington St. 59-71, Washington 72-85	637
26. Hugh Durham, Florida St. 1967-78, Georgia 79-95, Jacksonville 98-2005	633
27. Cam Henderson	630
28. Norm Sloan, Presbyterian 1952-55, Citadel 57-60, Florida 61-66, North Carolina St. 67-80, Florida 81-89	624
29. Bob Huggins*	616
30. Tom Penders, Tufts 1972-74, Columbia 75-78, Fordham 79-86, Rhode Island 87-88, Texas 89-98, George Washington 99-2001, Houston 05-08*	608
31. Gary Williams, American 1979-82, Boston College 83-86, Ohio St. 87-89, Maryland 90-2008*	604
32. Slats Gill, Oregon St. 1929-64	599
33. Tom Davis, Lafayette 1972-77, Boston College 78-82, Stanford 83-86, Iowa 87-99, Drake 2004-07	598
34. Abe Lemons, Tex.-Pan American 1974-76, Texas 77-82, Oklahoma City 56-73, 84-90	597
35. John Thompson	596
36. Homer Drew, Bethel (Ind.) 1977-87, Ind.-South Bend 88, Valparaiso 89-2002, 04-08*	593
37. Guy Lewis	592
38. Eldon Miller, Wittenberg 1963-70, Western Mich. 71-76, Ohio St. 77-86, UNI 87-98	568
39. Davey L. Whitney, Texas Southern 1965-69, Alcorn St. 70-89, 97-2003	566
40. Gale Catlett, Cincinnati 1973-78, West Virginia 79-2002	565

Coach	Wins
41. Gary Colson, Valdosta St. 1959-68, Pepperdine 69-79, New Mexico 81-88, Fresno St. 91-95	563
42. John Kresse	560
43. Roy Williams*	560
44. Tony Hinkle, Butler 1927-42, 46-70	558
45. Ben Braun, Siena Heights 1978-85, Eastern Mich. 86-96, California 97-2008, Rice*	556
46. Glenn Wilkes, Stetson 1958-93	551
47. Frank McGuire	549
48. Pat Douglass*	547
48. Cliff Ellis, South Ala. 1976-84, Clemson 85-94, Auburn 95-2004, Coastal Caro. 08*	547
48. Mike Montgomery*	547
51. Larry Hunter*	543
52. Harry Miller, Western St. 1953-58, Fresno St. 61-65, Eastern N.M. 66-70, North Texas 71, Wichita St. 72-78, Stephen F. Austin 79-88	536
53. Bill C. Foster, Shorter 1963-67, Charlotte 71-75, Clemson 76-84, Miami (Fla.) 86-90, Virginia Tech 92-97	532
54. Gene Keady, Western Ky. 1979-80, Purdue 81-2005	531
55. Dave Bliss, Oklahoma 1976-80, Southern Methodist 81-88, New Mexico 89-99, Baylor 2000-03	526
55. Lou Carnesecca	526
57. Pete Carril	525
58. Ben Jobe, Talladega 1965-67, Alabama St. 68, South Carolina St. 69-73, Denver 79-80, Alabama A&M 83-86, Southern U. 87-96, Tuskegee 97-2000, Southern U. 02-03	524
58. Tom Young, Catholic 1959-67, American 70-73, Rutgers 74-85, Old Dominion 86-91	524
60. Fred Enke, Louisville 1924-25, Arizona 26-61	523
61. Rick Pitino*	521
62. Rollie Massimino, Stony Brook 1970-71, Villanova 74-92, UNLV 93-94, Cleveland St. 97-2003	515
63. Don DeVoe, Virginia Tech 1972-76, Wyoming 77-78, Tennessee 79-89, Florida 90, Navy 93-2004	512
64. C.M. Newton, Transylvania 1956-64, 66-68, Alabama 69-80, Vanderbilt 82-89	509
64. Nolan Richardson	509
66. Hec Edmundson	508
67. Harold Anderson	504
68. Cal Luther, DePauw 1955-58, Murray St. 59-74, Longwood 82-90, Tenn.-Martin 91-99, Bethel (Tenn.) 2000	500
69. Bill Reinhart, Oregon 1924-35, George Washington 36-42, 50-66	499
69. Kelvin Sampson, Montana Tech 1982-85, Washington St. 88-94, Oklahoma 95-2006, Indiana 07-08	499
71. Jack Friel, Washington St. 1929-58	495
71. Everett Shelton, Phillips (Okla.) 1924-26, Wyoming 40-43, 45-59, Sacramento St. 60-68	495
71. Ned Wulk, Xavier 1952-57, Arizona St. 58-82	495
74. Bobby Cremins, Appalachian St. 1976-81, Georgia Tech 82-2000, Col. of Charleston 07-08*	492
75. Dick Bennett, Wis.-Stevens Point 1977-85, Green Bay 86-95, Wisconsin 96-2001, Washington St. 04-06	490
76. John Beilein, Nazareth 1983, Le Moyne 84-92, Canisius 93-97, Richmond 98-2002, West Virginia 03-07, Michigan 08*	486
76. Jack Gardner	486
78. Bob Hallberg, St. Xavier 1972-77, Chicago St. 78-87, Ill.-Chicago 88-96	485
79. Butch van Breda Kolff, Princeton 1963-67, New Orleans 78-79, Lafayette 52-55, 85-88, Hofstra 56-62, 89-94	482
80. Jim Harrick	470
81. Gene Iba, Houston Baptist 1978-85, Baylor 86-92, Pittsburg St. 96-2008*	468
82. Bill E. Foster, Bloomsburg 1961-63, Rutgers 64-71, Utah 72-74, Duke 75-80, South Carolina 81-86, Northwestern 87-93	467
83. Johnny Orr, Massachusetts 1964-66, Michigan 69-80, Iowa St. 81-94	466
84. Taps Gallagher, Niagara 1932-43, 47-65	465
85. Pat Kennedy, Iona 1981-86, Florida St. 87-97, DePaul 98-2002, Montana 03-04, Towson 05-08*	461
86. George Blaney, Stonehill 1968-69, Dartmouth 70-72, Holy Cross 73-94, Seton Hall 95-97	460
86. Ken Hayes, Tulsa 1969-75, New Mexico St. 76-79, Oral Roberts 80-83, Northeastern St. 84-97	460
88. Stew Morrill*	455
89. Tex Winter, Marquette 1952-53, Kansas St. 54-68, Washington 69-71, Northwestern 74-78, Long Beach St. 79-83	453
90. Branch McCracken	450
91. Rick Barnes*	449
91. Nibs Price, California 1925-54	449
93. Dale Brown, LSU 1973-97	448
94. Peck Hickman	443
94. Shelby Metcalf, Texas A&M 1964-90	443
96. Rick Majerus*	438
97. Don Donoher, Dayton 1965-89	437
97. Jack Hartman	437
99. Eddie S. Hickey	433
99. Don Maestri, Troy 1983-2008*	433

*active

Division I Active Coaches Listed by School

Coach	School	Yrs.	Won	Lost	Pct.
Perry Clark	A&M-Corpus Chris.	16	259	219	.542
Jeff Reynolds	Air Force	5	98	48	.671
Keith Dambrot	Akron	10	200	108	.649
Mark Gottfried	Alabama	13	267	147	.645
L. Vann Pettaway	Alabama A&M	22	421	229	.648
Lewis Jackson	Alabama St.	3	42	49	.462
Will Brown	Albany (N.Y.)	7	91	108	.457
Larry Smith	Alcorn St.	0	0	0	.000
Jeff Jones	American	16	270	218	.553
Houston Fancher	Appalachian St.	8	124	118	.512
Lute Olson	Arizona	34	780	280	.736
Herb Sendek	Arizona St.	15	283	193	.595
George Ivory	Ark.-Pine Bluff	0	0	0	.000
John Pelphrey	Arkansas	6	103	79	.566
John Brady	Arkansas St.	17	281	216	.565
Jim Crews	Army	23	342	330	.509
Jeff Lebo	Auburn	10	172	127	.575
Dave Loos	Austin Peay	22	377	300	.557
Billy Taylor	Ball St.	6	87	93	.483
Scott Drew	Baylor	6	77	91	.458
Rick Byrd	Belmont	27	541	303	.641
Clifford Reed Jr.	Bethune-Cookman	7	70	121	.366
Kevin Broadus	Binghamton	1	14	16	.467
Greg Graham	Boise St.	7	126	87	.592
Al Skinner	Boston College	20	348	263	.570
Dennis Wolff	Boston U.	16	260	202	.563
Louis Orr	Bowling Green	7	113	97	.538
Jim Les	Bradley	6	105	90	.538
Jesse Agel	Brown	0	0	0	.000
David Paulsen	Bucknell	14	262	120	.686
Reggie Witherspoon	Buffalo	9	105	159	.398
Brad Stevens	Butler	1	30	4	.882
Dave Rose	BYU	3	72	26	.735
Kevin Bromley	Cal Poly	8	92	124	.426
Bob Burton	Cal St. Fullerton	5	92	60	.605
Bobby Braswell	Cal St. Northridge	12	188	167	.530
Mike Montgomery	California	26	547	244	.692
Robbie Laing	Campbell	5	39	104	.273
Tom Parrotta	Canisius	2	18	44	.290
Greg Gary	Centenary (La.)	0	0	0	.000
Howie Dickenman	Central Conn. St.	12	192	161	.544
Ernie Zeigler	Central Mich.	2	27	35	.435
Barclay Radebaugh	Charleston So.	4	52	66	.441
Bobby Lutz	Charlotte	19	368	215	.631
John Shulman	Chattanooga	4	72	55	.567
Benjy Taylor	Chicago St.	4	39	63	.382
Mick Cronin	Cincinnati	5	93	62	.600
Ed Conroy	Citadel	5	54	87	.383
Oliver Purnell	Clemson	20	350	259	.575
Gary Waters	Cleveland St.	12	202	169	.544
Cliff Ellis	Coastal Caro.	30	547	352	.608
Bobby Cremins	Col. of Charleston	27	492	335	.595
Emmett Davis	Colgate	10	136	152	.472
Jeff Bzdelik	Colorado	5	87	67	.565
Tim Miles	Colorado St.	13	219	157	.582
Joe Jones	Columbia	5	63	75	.457
Jim Calhoun	Connecticut	36	774	337	.697
Fang Mitchell	Coppin St.	22	358	302	.542
Steve Donahue	Cornell	8	96	123	.438
Dana Altman	Creighton	19	365	219	.625
Terry Dunn	Dartmouth	4	35	74	.321
Bob McKillop	Davidson	19	340	225	.602
Brian Gregory	Dayton	5	98	60	.620
Monte Ross	Delaware	2	19	43	.306
Greg Jackson	Delaware St.	17	295	189	.610
Joe Scott	Denver	8	100	127	.441
Jerry Wainwright	DePaul	14	228	193	.542
Ray McCallum	Detroit	11	170	149	.533
Mark Phelps	Drake	0	0	0	.000
Bruiser Flint	Drexel	12	204	166	.551
Mike Krzyzewski	Duke	33	803	267	.750
Ron Everhart	Duquesne	14	201	204	.496
Mack McCarthy	East Carolina	17	320	196	.620
Murry Bartow	East Tenn. St.	11	198	144	.579
Mike Miller	Eastern Ill.	9	110	142	.437
Jeff Neubauer	Eastern Ky.	3	49	44	.527
Charles Ramsey	Eastern Mich.	3	34	57	.374
Kirk Earlywine	Eastern Wash.	2	32	27	.542
Ernie Nestor	Elon	10	124	178	.411

Coach	School	Yrs.	Won	Lost	Pct.
Marty Simmons	Evansville	7	108	93	.537
Ed Cooley	Fairfield	2	27	35	.435
Tom Green	Fairleigh Dickinson	25	400	328	.549
Mike Jarvis	Fla. Atlantic	19	321	201	.615
Billy Donovan	Florida	14	320	135	.703
Eugene Harris	Florida A&M	1	15	17	.469
Sergio Rouco	Florida Int'l	4	22	74	.229
Leonard Hamilton	Florida St.	20	306	296	.508
Dereck Whittenburg	Fordham	9	132	133	.498
Steve Cleveland	Fresno St.	11	188	150	.556
Jeff Jackson	Furman	5	43	99	.303
Jeff Price	Ga. Southern	15	291	155	.652
Rick Scruggs	Gardner-Webb	22	378	293	.563
Jim Larranaga	George Mason	24	404	301	.573
Karl Hobbs	George Washington	7	123	82	.600
John Thompson III	Georgetown	8	168	78	.683
Dennis Felton	Georgia	10	175	134	.566
Rod Barnes	Georgia St.	9	150	130	.536
Paul Hewitt	Georgia Tech	11	208	139	.599
Mark Few	Gonzaga	9	236	60	.797
Ricky Duckett	Grambling	8	148	81	.646
Tod Kowalczyk	Green Bay	6	92	88	.511
Kevin Nickelberry	Hampton	2	33	28	.541
Dan Leibovitz	Hartford	2	31	34	.477
Tommy Amaker	Harvard	11	184	161	.533
Bob Nash	Hawaii	1	11	19	.367
Bart Lundy	High Point	10	202	106	.656
Tom Pecora	Hofstra	7	115	100	.535
Ralph Willard	Holy Cross	18	318	227	.583
Tom Penders	Houston	34	608	410	.597
Gil Jackson	Howard	3	22	70	.239
Don Verlin	Idaho	0	0	0	.000
Joe O'Brien	Idaho St.	2	25	36	.410
Jimmy Collins	Ill.-Chicago	12	194	171	.532
Bruce Weber	Illinois	10	231	101	.696
Tim Jankovich	Illinois St.	5	78	67	.538
Tom Crean	Indiana	9	190	96	.664
Kevin McKenna	Indiana St.	5	104	49	.680
Kevin Willard	Iona	1	12	20	.375
Todd Lickliter	Iowa	7	144	80	.643
Greg McDermott	Iowa St.	14	250	161	.608
Dane Fife	IPFW	3	35	53	.398
Ron Hunter	IUPUI	14	232	180	.563
Tevester Anderson	Jackson St.	10	180	137	.568
Cliff Warren	Jacksonville	3	34	53	.391
James Green	Jacksonville St.	11	167	162	.508
Matt Brady	James Madison	4	73	50	.593
Bill Self	Kansas	15	349	137	.718
Frank Martin	Kansas St.	1	21	12	.636
Geno Ford	Kent St.	3	51	32	.614
Billy Gillispie	Kentucky	6	118	71	.624
John Giannini	La Salle	19	346	215	.617
Robert Lee	La.-Lafayette	4	40	62	.392
Orlando Early	La.-Monroe	3	38	53	.418
Fran O'Hanlon	Lafayette	13	185	189	.495
Steve Roccaforte	Lamar	2	34	28	.548
Brett Reed	Lehigh	1	14	15	.483
Ritchie McKay	Liberty	12	181	174	.510
Scott Sanderson	Lipscomb	8	112	121	.481
Dan Monson	Long Beach St.	11	176	148	.543
Jim Ferry	Long Island	10	172	122	.585
Mike Gillian	Longwood	5	34	116	.227
Kerry Rupp	Louisiana Tech	2	15	28	.349
Rick Pitino	Louisville	22	521	191	.732
Jim Whitesell	Loyola (Ill.)	21	343	252	.576
Jimmy Patsos	Loyola (Md.)	4	58	62	.483
Bill Bayno	Loyola Marymount	6	94	64	.595
Trent Johnson	LSU	9	159	122	.566
Ted Woodward	Maine	4	45	72	.385
Barry Rohrssen	Manhattan	2	25	36	.410
Chuck Martin	Marist	0	0	0	.000
Buzz Williams	Marquette	1	14	17	.452
Donnie Jones	Marshall	1	16	14	.533
Gary Williams	Maryland	30	604	343	.638
Derek Kellogg	Massachusetts	0	0	0	.000
Dave Simmons	McNeese St.	2	28	33	.459
Frankie Allen	Md.-East. Shore	18	223	294	.431
John Calipari	Memphis	16	408	135	.751
Bob Hoffman	Mercer	14	310	156	.665
Frank Haith	Miami (Fla.)	4	69	60	.535
Charlie Coles	Miami (Ohio)	18	302	241	.556
John Beilein	Michigan	26	486	297	.621
Tom Izzo	Michigan St.	13	305	130	.701

Coach	School	Yrs.	Won	Lost	Pct.
Kermit Davis Jr.	Middle Tenn.	10	171	132	.564
Rob Jeter	Milwaukee	3	45	47	.489
Tubby Smith	Minnesota	17	407	159	.719
Andy Kennedy	Mississippi	3	66	37	.641
Rick Stansbury	Mississippi St.	10	208	115	.644
Sean Woods	Mississippi Val.	0	0	0	.000
Mike Anderson	Missouri	6	123	69	.641
Cuonzo Martin	Missouri St.	0	0	0	.000
Dave Calloway	Monmouth	10	146	154	.487
Wayne Tinkle	Montana	2	31	31	.500
Brad Huse	Montana St.	2	26	34	.433
Donnie Tyndall	Morehead St.	2	27	33	.450
Todd Bozeman	Morgan St.	6	70	91	.435
Milan Brown	Mt. St. Mary's	5	60	91	.397
Billy Kennedy	Murray St.	10	138	153	.474
Jerry Eaves	N.C. A&T	5	45	105	.300
Billy Lange	Navy	6	88	86	.506
Doc Sadler	Nebraska	4	85	45	.654
Mark Fox	Nevada	4	102	30	.773
Bill Herrion	New Hampshire	17	268	226	.543
Steve Alford	New Mexico	17	332	192	.634
Marvin Menzies	New Mexico St.	1	21	14	.600
Joe Pasternack	New Orleans	1	19	13	.594
Joe Mihalich	Niagara	10	179	123	.593
J.P. Piper	Nicholls St.	4	33	82	.287
Anthony Evans	Norfolk St.	1	16	15	.516
Roy Williams	North Carolina	20	560	134	.807
Sidney Lowe	North Carolina St.	2	35	32	.522
Saul Phillips	North Dakota St.	1	16	13	.552
Johnny Jones	North Texas	8	121	116	.511
Bill Coen	Northeastern	2	27	36	.429
Mike Adras	Northern Ariz.	9	150	117	.562
Tad Boyle	Northern Colo.	2	17	40	.298
Ricardo Patton	Northern Ill.	13	190	182	.511
Bill Carmody	Northwestern	12	195	160	.549
Mike McConathy	Northwestern St.	9	145	135	.518
Mike Brey	Notre Dame	13	266	138	.658
Greg Kampe	Oakland	24	394	304	.564
John Groce	Ohio	0	0	0	.000
Thad Matta	Ohio St.	8	207	66	.758
Jeff Capel III	Oklahoma	6	118	68	.634
Travis Ford	Oklahoma St.	11	181	155	.539
Blaine Taylor	Old Dominion	14	277	150	.649
Scott Sutton	Oral Roberts	9	168	111	.602
Ernie Kent	Oregon	17	301	214	.584
Craig Robinson	Oregon St.	2	30	28	.517
Bob Thomason	Pacific	23	396	276	.589
Glen Miller	Penn	15	223	184	.548
Ed DeChellis	Penn St.	12	162	185	.467
Tom Asbury	Pepperdine	12	210	147	.588
Jamie Dixon	Pittsburgh	5	132	40	.767
Eric Reveno	Portland	2	18	45	.286
Ken Bone	Portland St.	16	311	157	.665
Byron Rimm II	Prairie View	5	63	83	.432
Sydney Johnson	Princeton	1	6	23	.207
Keno Davis	Providence	1	28	5	.848
Matt Painter	Purdue	4	81	45	.643
Tom Moore	Quinnipiac	6	91	74	.552
Brad Greenberg	Radford	1	10	20	.333
Jim Baron	Rhode Island	21	313	310	.502
Ben Braun	Rice	31	556	397	.583
Chris Mooney	Richmond	6	79	93	.459
Tommy Dempsey	Rider	3	47	46	.505
Mike Rice	Robert Morris	1	26	8	.765
Fred Hill Jr.	Rutgers	2	21	39	.350
Brian Katz	Sacramento St.	0	0	0	.000
Dave Bike	Sacred Heart	30	463	415	.527
Bob Marlin	Sam Houston St.	10	182	111	.621
Jimmy Tillette	Samford	11	179	145	.552
Bill Grier	San Diego	1	22	14	.611
Steve Fisher	San Diego St.	18	256	210	.549
Rex Walters	San Francisco	2	31	33	.484
George Nessman	San Jose St.	3	24	69	.258
Kerry Keating	Santa Clara	1	15	16	.484
Horace Broadnax	Savannah St.	8	69	153	.311
Bobby Gonzalez	Seton Hall	9	159	108	.596
Fran McCaffery	Siena	12	197	162	.549
Matt Doherty	SMU	7	114	108	.514
Ronnie Arrow	South Ala.	17	274	191	.589
Darrin Horn	South Carolina	5	111	48	.698
Tim Carter	South Carolina St.	13	184	188	.495
Scott Nagy	South Dakota St.	13	243	142	.631
Stan Heath	South Fla.	7	124	96	.564
Scott Edgar	Southeast Mo. St.	9	131	134	.494
Jim Yarbrough	Southeastern La.	8	146	81	.643
Tim Floyd	Southern California	15	306	167	.647
Chris Lowery	Southern Ill.	4	96	41	.701
Larry Eustachy	Southern Miss.	17	320	208	.606
Rob Spivery	Southern U.	23	344	333	.508
Roger Reid	Southern Utah	8	162	90	.643
Mark Schmidt	St. Bonaventure	7	90	112	.446
Brian Nash	St. Francis (N.Y.)	3	26	61	.299
Don Friday	St. Francis (Pa.)	5	83	49	.629
Norm Roberts	St. John's (N.Y.)	8	72	151	.323
Phil Martelli	St. Joseph's	13	261	152	.632
Rick Majerus	St. Louis	21	438	162	.730
Randy Bennett	St. Mary's (Cal.)	7	127	90	.585
John Dunne	St. Peter's	2	11	49	.183
Johnny Dawkins	Stanford	0	0	0	.000
Danny Kaspar	Stephen F. Austin	17	353	148	.705
Derek Waugh	Stetson	8	93	130	.417
Steve Pikiell	Stony Brook	4	25	85	.227
Jim Boeheim	Syracuse	32	771	278	.735
Jim Christian	TCU	6	137	59	.699
Fran Dunphy	Temple	19	343	194	.639
Bret Campbell	Tenn.-Martin	9	103	158	.395
Bruce Pearl	Tennessee	16	394	108	.785
Cy Alexander	Tennessee St.	21	337	290	.537
Mike Sutton	Tennessee Tech.	6	102	82	.554
Tom Schuberth	Tex.-Pan American	2	32	28	.533
Rick Barnes	Texas	21	449	227	.664
Mark Turgeon	Texas A&M	10	178	130	.578
Tony Harvey	Texas Southern	0	0	0	.000
Doug Davalos	Texas St.	6	94	71	.570
Pat Knight	Texas Tech	1	4	7	.364
Scott Cross	Texas-Arlington	2	34	29	.540
Gene Cross	Toledo	0	0	0	.000
Pat Kennedy	Towson	28	461	386	.544
Don Maestri	Troy	26	433	316	.578
Dave Dickerson	Tulane	3	46	45	.505
Doug Wojcik	Tulsa	3	56	42	.571
Mike Davis	UAB	8	153	106	.591
Steve Shields	UALR	5	82	65	.558
Gary Stewart	UC Davis	15	193	210	.479
Pat Douglass	UC Irvine	27	547	273	.667
Jim Wooldridge	UC Riverside	20	320	259	.553
Bob Williams	UC Santa Barb.	20	348	232	.600
Kirk Speraw	UCF	15	247	202	.550
Ben Howland	UCLA	14	294	144	.671
Randy Monroe	UMBC	4	57	65	.467
Matt Brown	UMKC	1	11	21	.344
Eddie Biedenbach	UNC Asheville	15	195	237	.451
Mike Dement	UNC Greensboro	21	309	291	.515
Benny Moss	UNC Wilmington	2	27	35	.435
Ben Jacobson	UNI	2	36	27	.571
Lon Kruger	UNLV	22	409	275	.598
Jim Boylen	Utah	1	18	15	.545
Stew Morrill	Utah St.	22	455	224	.670
Tony Barbee	UTEP	2	33	31	.516
Brooks Thompson	UTSA	2	20	39	.339
Homer Drew	Valparaiso	31	593	376	.612
Kevin Stallings	Vanderbilt	15	293	179	.621
Anthony Grant	VCU	2	52	15	.776
Mike Lonergan	Vermont	15	305	128	.704
Jay Wright	Villanova	14	270	168	.616
Dave Leitao	Virginia	8	133	111	.545
Seth Greenberg	Virginia Tech	18	301	240	.556
Duggar Baucom	VMI	5	72	73	.497
Mike Deane	Wagner	24	415	294	.585
Dino Gaudio	Wake Forest	8	85	137	.383
Lorenzo Romar	Washington	12	212	160	.570
Tony Bennett	Washington St.	2	52	17	.754
Randy Rahe	Weber St.	2	36	26	.581
Bob Huggins	West Virginia	26	616	222	.735
Larry Hunter	Western Caro.	28	543	282	.658
Jim Molinari	Western Ill.	14	223	186	.545
Ken McDonald	Western Ky.	0	0	0	.000
Steve Hawkins	Western Mich.	14	233	174	.572
Gregg Marshall	Wichita St.	10	205	103	.666
Tony Shaver	William & Mary	22	413	214	.659
Randy Peele	Winthrop	5	68	81	.456
Bo Ryan	Wisconsin	24	556	163	.773
Mike Young	Wofford	6	74	103	.418
Brad Brownell	Wright St.	6	127	60	.679
Heath Schroyer	Wyoming	4	47	65	.420
Sean Miller	Xavier	4	93	39	.705
James Jones	Yale	9	117	134	.466
Jerry Slocum	Youngstown St.	33	610	384	.614

Fastest To Milestone Wins

(Head coaches with at least half their seasons at Division I.)

FASTEST TO 100 WINS

Rk. Name, School	G	W	L	Pct.	Yr.	Season
1. Doc Meanwell, Wisconsin & Missouri	109	100	9	.917	7th	1918
2. Buck Freeman, St. John's (N.Y.)	110	100	10	.909	5th	1932
3. Adolph Rupp, Kentucky	116	100	16	.862	6th	1936
4. Jim Boeheim, Syracuse	117	100	17	.855	4th	1980
4. Jerry Tarkanian, Long Beach St.	117	100	17	.855	5th	1973
6. Everett Case, North Carolina St.	120	100	20	.833	4th	1950
6. Fred Taylor, Ohio St.	120	100	20	.833	5th	1963
7. Lew Andreas, Syracuse	122	100	22	.820	7th	1931
7. Denny Crum, Louisville	122	100	22	.820	5th	1976
7. Everett Dean, Carleton & Indiana	122	100	22	.820	7th	1929
11. Clair Bee, Rider & Long Island	123	100	23	.813	5th	1934
12. Don Haskins, UTEP	125	100	25	.800	5th	1966
12. Nat Holman, CCNY	125	100	25	.800	10th	1929
12. Buster Sheary, Holy Cross	125	100	25	.800	5th	1953
15. Jamie Dixon, Pittsburgh	126	100	26	.794	4th	2007
15. Mark Few, Gonzaga	126	100	26	.794	4th	2003
15. Tony Hinkle, Butler	126	100	26	.794	7th	1933
15. Ray Meyer, DePaul	126	100	26	.794	6th	1948
19. Harry Combes, Illinois	127	100	27	.787	6th	1953
19. Peck Hickman, Louisville	127	100	27	.787	5th	1949
21. Vic Bubas, Duke	128	100	28	.781	5th	1964
21. Mark Fox, Nevada	128	100	28	.781	4th	2008
23. Hugh Greer, Connecticut	129	100	29	.775	6th	1952
23. Roy Williams, Kansas	129	100	29	.775	4th	1992
25. Speedy Morris, La Salle	130	100	30	.769	4th	1990
25. Fred Schaus, West Virginia	130	100	30	.769	5th	1959
25. Clifford Wells, Tulane	130	100	30	.769	6th	1951
25. Thad Matta, Butler & Xavier	130	100	30	.769	4th	2004

FASTEST TO 200 WINS

Rk. Name, School	G	W	L	Pct.	Yr.	Season
1. Clair Bee, Rider & Long Island	231	200	31	.866	12th	1938
2. Jerry Tarkanian, Long Beach St. & UNLV	234	200	34	.855	9th	1977
3. Mark Few, Gonzaga	247	200	47	.810	8th	2007
4. Everett Case, North Carolina St.	250	200	50	.800	9th	1954
5. Harold Anderson, Toledo & Bowling Green	251	200	51	.797	10th	1945
5. Lew Andreas, Syracuse	251	200	51	.797	14th	1939
5. Nat Holman, CCNY	251	200	51	.797	18th	1937
5. Adolph Rupp, Kentucky	251	200	51	.797	13th	1943
9. Roy Williams, Kansas	252	200	52	.794	8th	1996
10. Vic Bubas, Duke	254	200	54	.787	10th	1969
10. Denny Crum, Louisville	254	200	54	.787	9th	1980
10. Henry Iba, Northwest Mo. St., Colorado & Oklahoma St.	254	200	54	.787	11th	1940
10. Doc Meanwell, Missouri & Wisconsin	254	200	54	.787	15th	1927
14. Hec Edmundson, Washington	261	200	61	.766	13th	1931
14. Hugh Greer, Connecticut	261	200	61	.766	11th	1957
14. Thad Matta, Butler, Xavier & Ohio St.	261	200	61	.766	8th	2008
17. George Keogan, Wis.-Superior, St. Louis, St. Thomas (Minn.), Allegheny, Valparaiso & Notre Dame	263	200	63	.760	14th	1930
17. Joseph Lapchick, St. John's (N.Y.)	263	200	63	.760	13th	1958
19. Jack Ramsay, St. Joseph's	264	200	64	.758	10th	1965
20. Peck Hickman, Louisville	265	200	65	.755	10th	1954
21. Jim Boeheim, Syracuse	266	200	66	.752	9th	1985
21. Fred Schaus, West Virginia & Purdue	266	200	66	.752	10th	1976
23. Don Haskins, UTEP	269	200	69	.743	11th	1972
24. Bob Knight, Army & Indiana	270	200	70	.741	11th	1976
25. Lou Carnesecca, St. John's (N.Y.)	271	200	71	.738	10th	1978
25. Harry Combes, Illinois	271	200	71	.738	12th	1959
25. Arthur Schabinger, Ottawa, Emporia St. & Creighton	271	200	71	.738	16th	1932

FASTEST TO 300 WINS

Rk. Name, School	G	W	L	Pct.	Yr.	Season
1. Clair Bee, Rider & Long Island	344	300	44	.872	15th	1943
2. Adolph Rupp, Kentucky	366	300	66	.820	17th	1947
3. Jerry Tarkanian, Long Beach St. & UNLV	370	300	70	.811	13th	1982
3. Roy Williams, Kansas	370	300	70	.811	11th	1999
5. Everett Case, North Carolina St.	377	300	77	.796	13th	1959
6. Harold Anderson, Toledo & Bowling Green	378	300	78	.794	14th	1949
7. Denny Crum, Louisville	382	300	82	.785	13th	1984
7. Henry Iba, Northwest Mo. St., Colorado & Oklahoma St.	382	300	82	.785	15th	1944
9. Hec Edmundson, Washington	392	300	92	.765	18th	1936
10. Jim Boeheim, Syracuse	393	300	93	.763	13th	1989
10. Frank Keaney, Rhode Island	393	300	93	.763	24th	1944
12. George Keogan, Wis.-Superior, St. Louis, St. Thomas (Minn.), Allegheny, Valparaiso & Notre Dame	394	300	94	.761	20th	1936
13. Ray Mears, Wittenberg & Tennessee	395	300	95	.759	16th	1972
14. Piggy Lambert, Purdue	397	300	97	.756	23rd	1940
15. Lew Andreas, Syracuse	400	300	100	.750	23rd	1947
15. Chick Davies, Duquesne	400	300	100	.750	21st	1948
17. John Lawther, Westminster (Pa.) & Penn St.	402	300	102	.746	21st	1947
18. Nolan Richardson, Tulsa & Arkansas	404	300	104	.743	13th	1993
19. Peck Hickman, Louisville	405	300	105	.741	15th	1959
20. Dean Smith, North Carolina	406	300	106	.739	15th	1976
20. Eddie Sutton, Creighton & Arkansas	406	300	106	.739	15th	1984
22. Bob Knight, Army & Indiana	407	300	107	.737	15th	1980
22. John Thompson, Georgetown	407	300	107	.737	14th	1986
24. Nat Holman, CCNY	408	300	108	.735	27th	1946
25. Rick Majerus, Marquette, Ball St. & Utah	409	300	109	.733	14th	1998

FASTEST TO 400 WINS

Rk. Name, School	G	W	L	Pct.	Yr.	Season
1. Adolph Rupp, Kentucky	477	400	77	.839	20th	1950
2. Clair Bee, Rider & Long Island	483	400	83	.828	21st	1951
3. Jerry Tarkanian, Long Beach St. & UNLV	492	400	92	.813	17th	1985
4. Roy Williams, Kansas	496	400	96	.806	15th	2003
5. Henry Iba, Northwest Mo. St., Colorado & Oklahoma St.	500	400	100	.800	19th	1948
6. Frank Keaney, Rhode Island	521	400	121	.768	28th	1948
7. Phog Allen, Baker, Haskell, Central Mo. & Kansas	522	400	122	.766	29th	1935
8. George Keogan, Wis.-Superior, St. Louis, St. Thomas (Minn.), Allegheny, Valparaiso & Notre Dame	522	400	122	.766	26th	1942
9. Jim Boeheim, Syracuse	527	400	127	.759	17th	1993
10. Dean Smith, North Carolina	531	400	131	.753	19th	1980
11. John Calipari, Massachusetts & Memphis	534	400	134	.749	16th	2008
12. Lou Carnesecca, St. John's (N.Y.)	535	400	135	.748	18th	1986
12. John Thompson, Georgetown	535	400	135	.748	18th	1990
14. Denny Crum, Louisville	536	400	136	.746	17th	1988
14. Ed Diddle, Western Ky.	536	400	136	.746	24th	1946
14. Nolan Richardson, Tulsa & Arkansas	536	400	136	.746	17th	1997
17. Rick Majerus, Marquette, Ball St. & Utah	538	400	138	.743	19th	2003
18. Nat Holman, CCNY	539	400	139	.742	32nd	1952
19. Eddie Sutton, Creighton, Arkansas & Kentucky	541	400	141	.739	19th	1988
20. Al McGuire, Belmont Abbey & Marquette	542	400	142	.738	20th	1977
21. Bob Knight, Army & Indiana	545	400	145	.734	20th	1985
21. Rick Pitino, Boston U., Providence, Kentucky & Louisville	545	400	145	.734	18th	2004
23. Bob Huggins, Walsh, Akron & Cincinnati	548	400	148	.730	19th	1999
23. John Wooden, Indiana St. & UCLA	548	400	148	.730	20th	1966
25. Harold Anderson, Toledo & Bowling Green	561	400	161	.713	23rd	1957

FASTEST TO 500 WINS

Rk. Name, School	G	W	L	Pct.	Yr.	Season
1. Adolph Rupp, Kentucky	583	500	83	.858	23rd	1955
2. Jerry Tarkanian, Long Beach St. & UNLV	604	500	104	.828	20th	1988
3. Roy Williams, Kansas & North Carolina	627	500	127	.797	19th	2007
4. Henry Iba, Northwest Mo. St., Colorado & Oklahoma St.	631	500	131	.792	23rd	1952

Rk. Name, School	G	W	L	Pct.	Yr.	Season
5. Phog Allen, Baker, Haskell, Central Mo. & Kansas	646	500	146	.774	34th	1940
6. John Wooden, Indiana St. & UCLA	652	500	152	.767	24th	1970
7. Dean Smith, North Carolina	653	500	153	.766	23rd	1984
8. John Chaney, Cheyney & Temple	662	500	162	.755	22nd	1994
9. Ed Diddle, Western Ky.	667	500	167	.750	28th	1950
10. Jim Boeheim, Syracuse	669	500	169	.747	21st	1997
11. Bob Huggins, Walsh, Akron & Cincinnati	671	500	171	.745	21st	2002
12. Lou Carnesecca, St. John's (N.Y.)	683	500	183	.732	23rd	1991
12. Bob Knight, Army & Indiana	683	500	183	.732	24th	1989
14. Eddie Sutton, Creighton, Arkansas, Kentucky & Oklahoma St.	685	500	185	.730	23rd	1993
14. John Thompson, Georgetown	685	500	185	.730	22nd	1994
14. Rick Pitino, Boston U., Providence, Kentucky & Louisville	685	500	185	.730	22nd	2008
17. Denny Crum, Louisville	687	500	187	.728	22nd	1993
18. Lute Olson, Long Beach St., Iowa & Arizona	690	500	190	.725	23rd	1996
19. Nolan Richardson, Tulsa & Arkansas	695	500	195	.719	22nd	2002
20. Frank McGuire, St. John's (N.Y.)	699	500	199	.715	27th	1977
21. Mike Krzyzewski, Army & Duke	710	500	210	.704	23rd	1998
22. Harold Anderson, Toledo & Bowling Green	724	500	224	.691	29th	1963
23. Fred Enke, Louisville & Arizona	811	500	311	.617	34th	1959
24. Tony Hinkle, Butler	830	500	330	.602	37th	1966

FASTEST TO 600 WINS

Rk. Name, School	G	W	L	Pct.	Yr.	Season
1. Adolph Rupp, Kentucky	704	600	104	.852	27th	1959
2. Jerry Tarkanian, Long Beach St. & UNLV	720	600	120	.833	24th	1992
3. John Wooden, Indiana St. & UCLA	755	600	155	.795	27th	1973
4. Dean Smith, North Carolina	773	600	173	.776	26th	1987
5. Henry Iba, Northwest Mo. St., Colorado & Oklahoma St.	775	600	175	.774	29th	1958
6. Phog Allen, Baker, Haskell, Central Mo. & Kansas	780	600	180	.769	41st	1947
7. Ed Diddle, Western Ky.	790	600	190	.759	32nd	1954
8. Jim Boeheim, Syracuse	807	600	207	.743	25th	2001
9. Bob Knight, Army & Indiana	812	600	212	.739	27th	1993
9. Bob Huggins, Walsh, Akron, Cincinnati, Kansas St. & West Virginia	812	600	212	.739	26th	2008
11. Lute Olson, Long Beach St., Iowa & Arizona	815	600	215	.736	27th	2000
12. John Chaney, Cheyney & Temple	816	600	216	.735	27th	1999
13. Mike Krzyzewski, Army & Duke	823	600	223	.729	26th	2001
14. Denny Crum, Louisville	825	600	225	.727	26th	1997
15. Cam Henderson, Muskingum, Davis & Elkins, & Marshall	830	600	230	.723	34th	1953
16. Eddie Sutton, Creighton, Arkansas, Kentucky & Oklahoma St.	837	600	237	.717	28th	1998
17. Don Haskins, UTEP	861	600	261	.697	31st	1992
18. Lefty Driesell, Davidson, Maryland & James Madison	868	600	268	.691	30th	1992
19. Jim Calhoun, Northeastern & Connecticut	879	600	279	.683	30th	2001
20. Guy Lewis, Houston	882	600	282	.680	31st	1987
21. Lou Henson, Hardin-Simmons, New Mexico St. & Illinois	887	600	287	.676	32nd	1993
22. Norm Stewart, UNI & Missouri	894	600	294	.671	32nd	1993
23. Gene Bartow, Central Mo., Valparaiso, Memphis, Illinois, UCLA & UAB	916	600	316	.655	32nd	1994
24. Ray Meyer, DePaul	933	600	333	.643	37th	1980
25. Ralph Miller, Wichita St., Iowa & Oregon St.	952	600	352	.630	36th	1987

FASTEST TO 700 WINS

Rk. Name, School	G	W	L	Pct.	Yr.	Season
1. Adolph Rupp, Kentucky	836	700	136	.837	32nd	1964
2. Jerry Tarkanian, Long Beach St., UNLV & Fresno St.	876	700	176	.799	29th	2000
3. Dean Smith, North Carolina	904	700	204	.774	30th	1991
4. Phog Allen, Baker, Haskell, Central Mo. & Kansas	938	700	238	.746	47th	1953
5. Jim Boeheim, Syracuse	939	700	239	.745	29th	2005
6. Mike Krzyzewski, Army & Duke	940	700	240	.745	30th	2005
6. Lute Olson, Long Beach St., Iowa & Arizona	940	700	240	.745	31st	2004
8. Ed Diddle, Western Ky.	946	700	246	.740	28th	1960

Rk. Name, School	G	W	L	Pct.	Yr.	Season
9. Henry Iba, Northwest Mo. St., Colorado & Oklahoma St.	953	700	253	.735	36th	1965
10. Bob Knight, Army & Indiana	956	700	256	.732	32nd	1997
11. Eddie Sutton, Creighton, Arkansas, Kentucky & Oklahoma St.	975	700	275	.718	32nd	2002
12. John Chaney, Cheyney & Temple	978	700	278	.716	32nd	2004
13. Jim Calhoun, Northeastern & Connecticut	1,008	700	308	.694	33rd	2005
14. Don Haskins, UTEP	1,029	700	329	.680	37th	1998
15. Lou Henson, Hardin-Simmons, Illinois & New Mexico St.	1,046	700	346	.669	36th	2000
16. Lefty Driesell, Davidson, Maryland, James Madison & Georgia St.	1,048	700	348	.668	37th	1999
17. Ray Meyer, DePaul	1,051	700	351	.666	52nd	1984
18. Norm Stewart, UNI & Missouri	1,055	700	355	.664	36th	1998

FASTEST TO 800 WINS

Rk. Name, School	G	W	L	Pct.	Yr.	Season
1. Adolph Rupp, Kentucky	972	800	172	.823	37th	1969
2. Dean Smith, North Carolina	1,029	800	229	.777	33rd	1994
3. Mike Krzyzewski, Army & Duke	1,064	800	264	.752	33rd	2008
4. Bob Knight, Army, Indiana & Texas Tech	1,102	800	302	.726	37th	2003
5. Eddie Sutton, Creighton, Arkansas, Kentucky, Oklahoma St. & San Francisco	1,122	800	322	.713	37th	2008

FASTEST TO 900 WINS

Rk. Name, School	G	W	L	Pct.	Yr.	Season
1. Bob Knight, Army, Indiana & Texas Tech	1,269	900	369	.709	42nd	2008

Top 10 Best Career Starts By Percentage

(Head coaches with at least half of their seasons at Division I)

1 SEASON

Coach, Team	Season	W	L	Pct.
Norman Shepard, North Carolina	1924	23	0	1.000
Bill Hodges, Indiana St.	1979	33	1	.970
Tom Gola, La Salle	1969	23	1	.958
Lou Rossini, Columbia	1951	21	1	.955
Earl Brown, Dartmouth	1944	19	2	.905
Phil Johnson, Weber St.	1969	27	3	.900
Bill Guthridge, North Carolina	1998	34	4	.895
Gary Cunningham, UCLA	1978	25	3	.893
Bob Davies, Seton Hall	1947	24	3	.889
Jerry Tarkanian, Long Beach St.	1969	23	3	.885

2 SEASONS

Coach, Team	Seasons	W	L	Pct.
Lew Andreas, Syracuse	1925-26	33	3	.917
Bill Carmody, Princeton	1997-98	51	6	.895
Everett Case, North Carolina St.	1947-48	55	8	.873
Buck Freeman, St. John's (N.Y.)	1928-29	41	6	.872
Gary Cunningham, UCLA	1978-79	50	8	.862
Nibs Price, California	1925-26	25	4	.862
Denny Crum, Louisville	1972-73	49	8	.860
Adolph Rupp, Kentucky	1931-32	30	5	.857
Jerry Tarkanian, Long Beach St.	1969-70	47	8	.855
John Castellani, Seattle	1957-58	45	9	.833

3 SEASONS

Coach, Team	Seasons	W	L	Pct.
Nibs Price, California	1925-27	38	4	.905
Buck Freeman, St. John's (N.Y.)	1928-30	64	7	.901
Lew Andreas, Syracuse	1925-27	48	7	.873
Adolph Rupp, Kentucky	1931-33	51	8	.864
Jerry Tarkanian, Long Beach St.	1969-71	69	12	.852
Jim Boeheim, Syracuse	1977-79	74	14	.841
Bill Carmody, Princeton	1997-99	73	14	.841
Everett Case, North Carolina St.	1947-49	80	16	.833
Ben Carnevale, North Carolina & Navy	1945-47	68	14	.829
Mark Fox, Nevada	2005-07	81	18	.818

4 SEASONS

Coach, Team	Seasons	W	L	Pct.
Buck Freeman, St. John's (N.Y.)	1928-31	85	8	.914
Adolph Rupp, Kentucky	1931-34	67	9	.882
Jerry Tarkanian, Long Beach St.	1969-72	92	15	.860
Jim Boeheim, Syracuse	1977-80	100	18	.847

Coach, Team	Seasons	W	L	Pct.
Fred Taylor, Ohio St.	1959-62	89	17	.840
Everett Case, North Carolina St.	1947-50	107	22	.829
Nibs Price, California	1925-28	47	10	.825
Nat Holman, CCNY	1920-23	46	10	.821
Denny Crum, Louisville	1972-75	98	22	.817
Lew Andreas, Syracuse	1925-28	58	13	.817

5 SEASONS

Coach, Team	Seasons	W	L	Pct.
Buck Freeman, St. John's (N.Y.)	1928-32	107	12	.899
Adolph Rupp, Kentucky	1931-35	86	11	.887
Jerry Tarkanian, Long Beach St. & UNLV	1969-73	116	17	.872
Nat Holman, CCNY	1920-24	58	11	.841
Fred Taylor, Ohio St.	1959-63	109	21	.838
Nibs Price, California	1925-29	64	13	.831
Everett Case, North Carolina St.	1947-51	137	29	.825
Charles Orsborn, Bradley	1957-61	115	25	.821
Mark Few, Gonzaga	2000-04	133	32	.806
Buster Sheary, Holy Cross	1949-53	110	27	.803
Jim Boeheim, Syracuse	1977-81	122	30	.803

6 SEASONS

Coach, Team	Seasons	W	L	Pct.
Buck Freeman, St. John's (N.Y.)	1928-33	130	16	.890
Adolph Rupp, Kentucky	1931-36	101	17	.856
Jerry Tarkanian, Long Beach St. & UNLV	1969-74	136	23	.855
Nat Holman, CCNY	1920-25	70	13	.843
Buster Sheary, Holy Cross	1949-54	136	29	.824
Lew Andreas, Syracuse	1925-30	87	19	.821
Everett Dean, Carleton & Indiana	1922-27	82	18	.820
Clair Bee, Rider & Long Island	1929-34	101	23	.815
Fred Taylor, Ohio St.	1959-64	125	29	.812
Mark Few, Gonzaga	2000-05	159	37	.811

7 SEASONS

Coach, Team	Seasons	W	L	Pct.
Buck Freeman, St. John's (N.Y.)	1928-34	146	19	.885
Jerry Tarkanian, Long Beach St. & UNLV	1969-75	160	28	.851
Adolph Rupp, Kentucky	1931-37	118	22	.843
Clair Bee, Rider & Long Island	1929-35	125	25	.833
Everett Dean, Carleton & Indiana	1922-28	97	20	.829
Mark Few, Gonzaga	2000-06	188	41	.821
Lew Andreas, Syracuse	1925-31	103	23	.817
Nat Holman, CCNY	1920-26	79	18	.814
Buster Sheary, Holy Cross	1949-55	155	36	.812
Everett Case, North Carolina St.	1947-53	187	45	.806

8 SEASONS

Coach, Team	Seasons	W	L	Pct.
Jerry Tarkanian, Long Beach St. & UNLV	1969-76	189	30	.863
Clair Bee, Rider & Long Island	1929-36	150	25	.857
Buck Freeman, St. John's (N.Y.)	1928-35	159	27	.855
Adolph Rupp, Kentucky	1931-38	131	27	.829
Nat Holman, CCNY	1920-27	88	21	.807
Everett Case, North Carolina St.	1947-54	213	52	.804
Mark Few, Gonzaga	2000-07	211	52	.802
Hugh Greer, Connecticut	1947-54	131	38	.799
Lew Andreas, Syracuse	1925-32	116	30	.795
Roy Williams, Kansas	1989-96	213	56	.792

9 SEASONS

Coach, Team	Seasons	W	L	Pct.
Jerry Tarkanian, Long Beach St. & UNLV	1969-77	218	33	.869
Clair Bee, Rider & Long Island	1929-37	177	28	.863
Buck Freeman, St. John's (N.Y.)	1928-36	177	31	.851
Adolph Rupp, Kentucky	1931-39	147	31	.826
Everett Case, North Carolina St.	1947-55	241	56	.811
Roy Williams, Kansas	1989-97	247	58	.810
Lew Andreas, Syracuse	1925-33	130	32	.802
Henry Iba, Northwest Mo. St., Colorado & Oklahoma St.	1930-38	180	45	.800
Denny Crum, Louisville	1972-80	219	55	.799
Hugh Greer, Connecticut	1947-55	171	43	.799

10 SEASONS

Coach, Team	Seasons	W	L	Pct.
Clair Bee, Rider & Long Island	1929-38	200	32	.862
Jerry Tarkanian, Long Beach St. & UNLV	1969-78	238	41	.853
Roy Williams, Kansas	1989-98	282	62	.820
Everett Case, North Carolina St.	1947-56	265	60	.815
Adolph Rupp, Kentucky	1931-40	162	37	.814
Lew Andreas, Syracuse	1925-34	145	34	.810

Coach, Team	Seasons	W	L	Pct.
Henry Iba, Northwest Mo. St., Colorado & Oklahoma St.	1930-39	199	53	.790
Denny Crum, Louisville	1972-81	240	64	.789
Harold Anderson, Toledo & Bowling Green	1935-44	182	50	.784
Nat Holman, CCNY	1920-29	108	30	.783

11 SEASONS

Coach, Team	Seasons	W	L	Pct.
Clair Bee, Rider & Long Island	1929-39	223	32	.875
Jerry Tarkanian, Long Beach St. & UNLV	1969-79	259	49	.841
Lew Andreas, Syracuse	1925-35	160	36	.816
Roy Williams, Kansas	1989-99	305	72	.809
Henry Iba, Northwest Mo. St., Colorado & Oklahoma St.	1930-40	225	56	.801
Adolph Rupp, Kentucky	1931-41	179	45	.799
Everett Case, North Carolina St.	1947-57	280	71	.798
Harold Anderson, Toledo & Bowling Green	1935-45	206	54	.792
Nat Holman, CCNY	1920-30	119	33	.783
Denny Crum, Louisville	1972-82	263	74	.780

12 SEASONS

Coach, Team	Seasons	W	L	Pct.
Clair Bee, Rider & Long Island	1929-40	242	36	.871
Jerry Tarkanian, Long Beach St. & UNLV	1969-80	282	58	.829
Lew Andreas, Syracuse	1925-36	172	41	.806
Roy Williams, Kansas	1989-2000	329	82	.800
Harold Anderson, Toledo & Bowling Green	1935-46	233	59	.798
Adolph Rupp, Kentucky	1931-42	198	51	.795
Everett Case, North Carolina St.	1947-58	298	77	.795
Henry Iba, Northwest Mo. St., Colorado & Oklahoma St.	1930-41	243	63	.794
Denny Crum, Louisville	1972-83	295	78	.791
Joe Mullaney, Norwich & Providence	1955-66	243	68	.781

13 SEASONS

Coach, Team	Seasons	W	L	Pct.
Clair Bee, Rider & Long Island	1929-41	267	38	.875
Jerry Tarkanian, Long Beach St. & UNLV	1969-81	298	70	.810
Lew Andreas, Syracuse	1925-37	185	45	.804
Roy Williams, Kansas	1989-2001	355	89	.800
Harold Anderson, Toledo & Bowling Green	1935-47	261	66	.798
Everett Case, North Carolina St.	1947-59	320	81	.798
Nat Holman, CCNY	1920-32	147	38	.795
Henry Iba, Northwest Mo. St., Colorado & Oklahoma St.	1930-42	263	69	.792
Adolph Rupp, Kentucky	1931-43	215	57	.790
Denny Crum, Louisville	1972-84	319	89	.782

14 SEASONS

Coach, Team	Seasons	W	L	Pct.
Clair Bee, Rider & Long Island	1929-42	291	41	.877
Roy Williams, Kansas	1989-2002	388	93	.807
Nat Holman, CCNY	1920-33	160	39	.804
Harold Anderson, Toledo & Bowling Green	1935-48	288	72	.800
Jerry Tarkanian, Long Beach St. & UNLV	1969-82	318	80	.799
Adolph Rupp, Kentucky	1931-44	234	59	.799
Lew Andreas, Syracuse	1925-38	198	50	.798
Henry Iba, Northwest Mo. St., Colorado & Oklahoma St.	1930-43	277	79	.778
Everett Case, North Carolina St.	1947-60	331	96	.775
Jim Boeheim, Syracuse	1977-90	343	108	.761

15 SEASONS

Coach, Team	Seasons	W	L	Pct.
Clair Bee, Rider & Long Island	1929-43	304	47	.866
Nat Holman, CCNY	1920-34	174	40	.813
Jerry Tarkanian, Long Beach St. & UNLV	1969-83	346	83	.807
Roy Williams, Kansas	1989-2003	418	101	.805
Adolph Rupp, Kentucky	1931-45	256	63	.803
Harold Anderson, Toledo & Bowling Green	1935-49	312	79	.798
Lew Andreas, Syracuse	1925-39	212	54	.797
Henry Iba, Northwest Mo. St., Colorado & Oklahoma St.	1930-44	304	85	.781
Everett Case, North Carolina St.	1947-61	347	105	.768
Denny Crum, Louisville	1972-86	370	114	.764
Jim Boeheim, Syracuse	1977-91	369	114	.764

16 SEASONS

Coach, Team	Seasons	W	L	Pct.
Clair Bee, Rider & Long Island	1929-43, 46	318	56	.850
Adolph Rupp, Kentucky	1931-46	284	65	.814
Jerry Tarkanian, Long Beach St. & UNLV	1969-84	375	89	.808

Coach, Team	Seasons	W	L	Pct.
Nat Holman, CCNY	1920-35	184	46	.800
Roy Williams, Kansas & North Carolina	1989-2004	437	112	.796
Henry Iba, Northwest Mo. St., Colorado & Oklahoma St.	1930-45	331	89	.788
Harold Anderson, Toledo & Bowling Green	1935-50	331	90	.786
Lew Andreas, Syracuse	1925-40	222	62	.782
Everett Case, North Carolina St.	1947-62	358	111	.763
Ray Mears, Wittenberg & Tennessee	1957-72	306	97	.759
Jim Boeheim, Syracuse	1977-92	391	124	.759

17 SEASONS

Coach, Team	Seasons	W	L	Pct.
Clair Bee, Rider & Long Island	1929-43, 46-47	335	61	.850
Adolph Rupp, Kentucky	1931-47	318	68	.824
Jerry Tarkanian, Long Beach St. & UNLV	1969-85	403	93	.813
Roy Williams, Kansas & North Carolina	1989-2005	470	116	.802
Henry Iba, Northwest Mo. St., Colorado & Oklahoma St.	1930-46	362	91	.799
Nat Holman, CCNY	1920-36	194	50	.795
Harold Anderson, Toledo & Bowling Green	1935-51	341	94	.784
Lew Andreas, Syracuse	1925-41	236	67	.779
Jim Boeheim, Syracuse	1977-93	411	133	.756
Joseph Lapchick, St. John's (N.Y.)	1937-47, 57-62	291	95	.754

18 SEASONS

Coach, Team	Seasons	W	L	Pct.
Clair Bee, Rider & Long Island	1929-43, 46-48	352	65	.844
Adolph Rupp, Kentucky	1931-48	354	71	.833
Jerry Tarkanian, Long Beach St. & UNLV	1969-86	436	98	.816
Roy Williams, Kansas & North Carolina	1989-2006	493	124	.799
Henry Iba, Northwest Mo. St., Colorado & Oklahoma St.	1930-47	386	99	.796
Nat Holman, CCNY	1920-37	204	56	.785
Harold Anderson, Toledo & Bowling Green	1935-52	358	104	.775
Lew Andreas, Syracuse	1925-42	251	73	.775
Jim Boeheim, Syracuse	1977-94	434	140	.756
Dean Smith, North Carolina	1962-79	386	127	.752

19 SEASONS

Coach, Team	Seasons	W	L	Pct.
Adolph Rupp, Kentucky	1931-49	386	73	.841
Clair Bee, Rider & Long Island	1929-43, 46-49	370	77	.828
Jerry Tarkanian, Long Beach St. & UNLV	1969-87	473	100	.825
Henry Iba, Northwest Mo. St., Colorado & Oklahoma St.	1930-48	413	103	.800
Roy Williams, Kansas & North Carolina	1989-2007	524	131	.800
Nat Holman, CCNY	1920-38	217	59	.786
Lew Andreas, Syracuse	1925-43	259	83	.757
Harold Anderson, Toledo & Bowling Green	1935-53	370	119	.757
Jim Boeheim, Syracuse	1977-95	454	150	.752
Dean Smith, North Carolina	1962-80	407	135	.751

20 SEASONS

Coach, Team	Seasons	W	L	Pct.
Adolph Rupp, Kentucky	1931-50	411	78	.840
Clair Bee, Rider & Long Island	1929-43, 46-50	390	82	.826
Jerry Tarkanian, Long Beach St. & UNLV	1969-88	501	106	.825
Roy Williams, Kansas & North Carolina	1989-2008	560	134	.807
Henry Iba, Northwest Mo. St., Colorado & Oklahoma St.	1930-49	436	108	.801
Phog Allen, Baker, Kansas, Haskell, Central Mo. & Kansas	1906-09, 13-28	325	89	.785
Nat Holman, CCNY	1920-39	228	65	.778
John Chaney, Cheyney & Temple	1973-92	458	143	.762
Frank Keaney, Rhode Island	1922-41	265	86	.755
Harold Anderson, Toledo & Bowling Green	1935-54	387	126	.754

21 SEASONS

Coach, Team	Seasons	W	L	Pct.
Adolph Rupp, Kentucky	1931-51	443	80	.847
Clair Bee, Rider & Long Island	1929-43, 46-51	410	86	.827
Jerry Tarkanian, Long Beach St. & UNLV	1969-89	530	114	.823
Henry Iba, Northwest Mo. St., Colorado & Oklahoma St.	1930-50	454	117	.795
Nat Holman, CCNY	1920-40	236	73	.764
Dean Smith, North Carolina	1962-82	468	145	.763
Phog Allen, Baker, Kansas, Haskell, Central Mo. & Kansas	1906-09, 13-29	328	104	.759
Frank Keaney, Rhode Island	1922-42	283	90	.759
John Chaney, Cheyney & Temple	1973-93	478	156	.754
Chick Davies, Duquesne	1925-40, 47-48	314	106	.748

22 SEASONS

Coach, Team	Seasons	W	L	Pct.
Adolph Rupp, Kentucky	1931-52	472	83	.850
Jerry Tarkanian, Long Beach St. & UNLV	1969-90	565	119	.826
Henry Iba, Northwest Mo. St., Colorado & Oklahoma St.	1930-51	483	123	.797
Nat Holman, CCNY	1920-41	253	78	.764
Dean Smith, North Carolina	1962-83	496	153	.764
Frank Keaney, Rhode Island	1922-43	299	93	.763
Phog Allen, Baker, Kansas, Haskell, Central Mo. & Kansas	1906-09, 13-30	342	108	.760
John Wooden, Indiana St. & UCLA	1947-68	464	151	.754
John Chaney, Cheyney & Temple	1973-94	501	164	.753
Lew Andreas, Syracuse	1925-47	308	105	.746

23 SEASONS

Coach, Team	Seasons	W	L	Pct.
Adolph Rupp, Kentucky	1931-52, 54	497	83	.857
Jerry Tarkanian, Long Beach St. & UNLV	1969-91	599	120	.833
Henry Iba, Northwest Mo. St., Colorado & Oklahoma St.	1930-52	502	131	.793
Dean Smith, North Carolina	1962-84	524	156	.771
Nat Holman, CCNY	1920-42	269	81	.769
John Wooden, Indiana St. & UCLA	1947-69	493	152	.764
Phog Allen, Baker, Kansas, Haskell, Central Mo. & Kansas	1906-09, 13-31	357	111	.763
Frank Keaney, Rhode Island	1922-44	313	99	.760
John Chaney, Cheyney & Temple	1973-95	520	175	.748
Ed Diddle, Western Ky.	1923-45	395	134	.747

24 SEASONS

Coach, Team	Seasons	W	L	Pct.
Adolph Rupp, Kentucky	1931-52, 54-55	520	86	.858
Jerry Tarkanian, Long Beach St. & UNLV	1969-92	625	122	.837
Henry Iba, Northwest Mo. St., Colorado & Oklahoma St.	1930-53	525	138	.792
John Wooden, Indiana St. & UCLA	1947-70	521	154	.772
Dean Smith, North Carolina	1962-85	551	165	.770
Frank Keaney, Rhode Island	1922-45	333	104	.762
Phog Allen, Baker, Kansas, Haskell, Central Mo. & Kansas	1906-09, 13-32	370	116	.761
Nat Holman, CCNY	1920-43	277	91	.753
Jim Boeheim, Syracuse	1977-2000	575	199	.743
Bob Huggins, Walsh, Akron & Cincinnati	1981-2005	567	199	.740

25 SEASONS

Coach, Team	Seasons	W	L	Pct.
Adolph Rupp, Kentucky	1931-52, 54-56	540	92	.854
Jerry Tarkanian, Long Beach St., UNLV & Fresno St.	1969-92, 96	647	133	.829
Henry Iba, Northwest Mo. St., Colorado & Oklahoma St.	1930-54	549	143	.793
John Wooden, Indiana St. & UCLA	1947-71	550	155	.780
Dean Smith, North Carolina	1962-86	579	171	.772
Frank Keaney, Rhode Island	1922-46	354	107	.768
Phog Allen, Baker, Kansas, Haskell, Central Mo. & Kansas	1906-09, 13-33	383	120	.761
Jim Boeheim, Syracuse	1977-2001	600	208	.743
John Chaney, Cheyney & Temple	1973-97	560	199	.738
Bob Huggins, Walsh, Akron, Cincinnati & Kansas St.	1981-2005, 07	590	211	.737

26 SEASONS

Coach, Team	Seasons	W	L	Pct.
Adolph Rupp, Kentucky	1931-52, 54-57	563	97	.853
Jerry Tarkanian, Long Beach St., UNLV & Fresno St.	1969-92, 96-97	667	145	.821
John Wooden, Indiana St. & UCLA	1947-72	580	155	.789
Henry Iba, Northwest Mo. St., Colorado & Oklahoma St.	1930-55	561	156	.782
Dean Smith, North Carolina	1962-87	611	175	.777
Frank Keaney, Rhode Island	1922-47	371	110	.771
Phog Allen, Baker, Kansas, Haskell, Central Mo. & Kansas	1906-09, 13-34	399	121	.767
Ed Diddle, Western Ky.	1923-48	463	159	.744
Jim Boeheim, Syracuse	1977-2002	623	221	.738
John Chaney, Cheyney & Temple	1973-98	581	208	.736
Nat Holman, CCNY	1920-45	295	106	.736

27 SEASONS

Coach, Team	Seasons	W	L	Pct.
Adolph Rupp, Kentucky	1931-52, 54-58	586	103	.851
Jerry Tarkanian, Long Beach St., UNLV & Fresno St.	1969-92, 96-98	688	158	.813

Coach, Team	Seasons	W	L	Pct.
John Wooden, Indiana St. & UCLA	1947-73	610	155	.797
Henry Iba, Northwest Mo. St., Colorado & Oklahoma St.	1930-56	579	165	.778
Dean Smith, North Carolina	1962-88	638	182	.778
Frank Keaney, Rhode Island	1922-48	387	117	.768
Phog Allen, Baker, Kansas, Haskell, Central Mo. & Kansas	1906-09, 13-35	414	126	.767
Ed Diddle, Western Ky.	1923-49	488	163	.750
Jim Boeheim, Syracuse	1977-2003	653	226	.743
Nat Holman, CCNY	1920-46	309	110	.737
Bob Knight, Army & Indiana	1966-92	588	210	.737

28 SEASONS

Coach, Team	Seasons	W	L	Pct.
Adolph Rupp, Kentucky	1931-52, 54-59	610	106	.852
Jerry Tarkanian, Long Beach St., UNLV & Fresno St.	1969-92, 96-99	689	170	.802
John Wooden, Indiana St. & UCLA	1947-74	636	159	.800
Dean Smith, North Carolina	1962-89	667	190	.778
Henry Iba, Northwest Mo. St., Colorado & Oklahoma St.	1930-57	596	174	.774
Phog Allen, Baker, Kansas, Haskell, Central Mo. & Kansas	1906-09, 13-36	435	128	.773
Ed Diddle, Western Ky.	1923-50	513	169	.752
Bob Knight, Army & Indiana	1966-93	619	214	.743
Jim Boeheim, Syracuse	1977-2004	676	234	.743
Mike Krzyzewski, Army & Duke	1976-2003	663	234	.739

29 SEASONS

Coach, Team	Seasons	W	L	Pct.
Adolph Rupp, Kentucky	1931-52, 54-60	628	113	.848
John Wooden, Indiana St. & UCLA	1947-75	664	162	.804
Jerry Tarkanian, Long Beach St., UNLV & Fresno St.	1969-92, 96-2000	701	179	.797
Phog Allen, Baker, Kansas, Haskell, Central Mo. & Kansas	1906-09, 13-37	450	132	.773
Henry Iba, Northwest Mo. St., Colorado & Oklahoma St.	1930-58	617	182	.772
Dean Smith, North Carolina	1962-90	688	203	.772
Ed Diddle, Western Ky.	1923-51	532	179	.748
Jim Boeheim, Syracuse	1977-2005	703	241	.745
Mike Krzyzewski, Army & Duke	1976-2004	694	240	.743
Nat Holman, CCNY	1920-48	344	119	.743

30 SEASONS

Coach, Team	Seasons	W	L	Pct.
Adolph Rupp, Kentucky	1931-52, 54-61	647	122	.841
Jerry Tarkanian, Long Beach St., UNLV & Fresno St.	1969-92, 96-2001	710	186	.792
Phog Allen, Baker, Kansas, Haskell, Central Mo. & Kansas	1906-09, 13-38	468	134	.777
Dean Smith, North Carolina	1962-91	717	209	.774
Henry Iba, Northwest Mo. St., Colorado & Oklahoma St.	1930-59	628	196	.762
Ed Diddle, Western Ky.	1923-52	558	184	.752
Mike Krzyzewski, Army & Duke	1976-2005	721	246	.746
Lute Olson, Long Beach St., Iowa & Arizona	1974-2003	690	240	.742
Jim Boeheim, Syracuse	1977-2006	726	253	.742
Nat Holman, CCNY	1920-49	361	127	.740

31 SEASONS

Coach, Team	Seasons	W	L	Pct.
Adolph Rupp, Kentucky	1931-52, 54-62	670	125	.843
Jerry Tarkanian, Long Beach St., UNLV & Fresno St.	1969-92, 96-2000	729	201	.784
Phog Allen, Baker, Kansas, Haskell, Central Mo. & Kansas	1906-09, 13-39	481	141	.773
Dean Smith, North Carolina	1962-92	740	219	.772
Ed Diddle, Western Ky.	1923-53	583	190	.754
Henry Iba, Northwest Mo. St., Colorado & Oklahoma St.	1930-60	638	211	.751
Mike Krzyzewski, Army & Duke	1976-2006	753	250	.751
Nat Holman, CCNY	1920-50	385	132	.745
Lute Olson, Long Beach St., Iowa & Arizona	1974-2004	710	249	.740
Jim Boeheim, Syracuse	1977-2007	750	264	.740

32 SEASONS

Coach, Team	Seasons	W	L	Pct.
Adolph Rupp, Kentucky	1931-52, 54-63	686	134	.837
Dean Smith, North Carolina	1962-93	774	223	.776
Phog Allen, Baker, Kansas, Haskell, Central Mo. & Kansas	1906-09, 13-40	500	147	.773
Ed Diddle, Western Ky.	1923-54	612	193	.760

Coach, Team	Seasons	W	L	Pct.
Mike Krzyzewski, Army & Duke	1976-2007	775	261	.748
Henry Iba, Northwest Mo. St., Colorado & Oklahoma St.	1930-61	652	222	.746
Lute Olson, Long Beach St., Iowa & Arizona	1974-2005	740	256	.743
Nat Holman, CCNY	1920-51	397	139	.741
Jim Boeheim, Syracuse	1977-2008	771	278	.735
Bob Knight, Army & Indiana	1966-97	700	258	.731

33 SEASONS

Coach, Team	Seasons	W	L	Pct.
Adolph Rupp, Kentucky	1931-52, 54-64	707	140	.835
Dean Smith, North Carolina	1962-94	802	230	.777
Phog Allen, Baker, Kansas, Haskell, Central Mo. & Kansas	1906-09, 13-41	512	153	.770
Ed Diddle, Western Ky.	1923-55	630	203	.756
Mike Krzyzewski, Army & Duke	1976-2008	803	267	.750
Henry Iba, Northwest Mo. St., Colorado & Oklahoma St.	1930-62	666	233	.741
Lute Olson, Long Beach St., Iowa & Arizona	1974-2006	760	269	.739
Nat Holman, CCNY	1920-52	405	150	.730
Bob Knight, Army & Indiana	1966-98	720	270	.727
Eddie Sutton, Creighton, Arkansas, Kentucky & Oklahoma St.	1970-89, 91-2003	724	288	.715

34 SEASONS

Coach, Team	Seasons	W	L	Pct.
Adolph Rupp, Kentucky	1931-52, 54-65	722	150	.828
Dean Smith, North Carolina	1962-95	830	236	.779
Phog Allen, Baker, Kansas, Haskell, Central Mo. & Kansas	1906-09, 13-42	529	158	.770
Ed Diddle, Western Ky.	1923-56	646	215	.750
Henry Iba, Northwest Mo. St., Colorado & Oklahoma St.	1930-63	682	242	.738
Lute Olson, Long Beach St., Iowa & Arizona	1974-2007	780	280	.736
Bob Knight, Army & Indiana	1966-99	743	281	.726
Eddie Sutton, Creighton, Arkansas, Kentucky & Oklahoma St.	1970-89, 91-2004	755	292	.721
Nat Holman, CCNY	1920-52, 55	413	160	.721
John Chaney, Cheyney & Temple	1973-2006	741	312	.704

35 SEASONS

Coach, Team	Seasons	W	L	Pct.
Adolph Rupp, Kentucky	1931-52, 54-66	749	152	.831
Dean Smith, North Carolina	1962-96	851	247	.775
Phog Allen, Baker, Kansas, Haskell, Central Mo. & Kansas	1906-09, 13-43	551	164	.771
Ed Diddle, Western Ky.	1923-57	663	224	.747
Henry Iba, Northwest Mo. St., Colorado & Oklahoma St.	1930-64	697	252	.734
Bob Knight, Army & Indiana	1966-2000	764	289	.726
Eddie Sutton, Creighton, Arkansas, Kentucky & Oklahoma St.	1970-89, 91-2005	781	299	.723
Nat Holman, CCNY	1920-52, 55-56	417	174	.706
Jim Calhoun, Northeastern & Connecticut	1973-2007	750	328	.696
Don Haskins, UTEP	1962-96	678	313	.684

36 SEASONS

Coach, Team	Seasons	W	L	Pct.
Adolph Rupp, Kentucky	1931-52, 54-67	762	165	.822
Dean Smith, North Carolina	1962-97	879	254	.776
Phog Allen, Baker, Kansas, Haskell, Central Mo. & Kansas	1906-09, 13-44	568	173	.767
Ed Diddle, Western Ky.	1923-58	677	235	.742
Henry Iba, Northwest Mo. St., Colorado & Oklahoma St.	1930-65	717	259	.735
Bob Knight, Army, Indiana & Texas Tech	1966-2000, 02	787	298	.725
Eddie Sutton, Creighton, Arkansas, Kentucky & Oklahoma St.	1970-89, 91-2006	798	315	.717
Jim Calhoun, Northeastern & Connecticut	1973-2008	774	337	.697
Nat Holman, CCNY	1920-52, 55-56, 59	423	186	.695
Don Haskins, UTEP	1962-97	691	351	.679

37 SEASONS

Coach, Team	Seasons	W	L	Pct.
Adolph Rupp, Kentucky	1931-52, 54-68	784	170	.822
Phog Allen, Baker, Kansas, Haskell, Central Mo. & Kansas	1906-09, 13-45	580	178	.765
Ed Diddle, Western Ky.	1923-59	693	245	.739
Bob Knight, Army, Indiana & Texas Tech	1966-2000, 02-03	809	311	.722
Henry Iba, Northwest Mo. St., Colorado & Oklahoma St.	1930-66	721	280	.720
Eddie Sutton, Creighton, Arkansas, Kentucky Oklahoma St. & San Francisco	1970-89, 91-2006, 08	804	328	.710
Nat Holman, CCNY	1920-52, 55-56, 59-60	423	190	.690

Coach, Team	Seasons	W	L	Pct.
Don Haskins, UTEP	1962-98	703	341	.673
Lefty Driesell, Davidson, Maryland, James Madison & Georgia St.	1961-86, 89-99	716	360	.665
Lou Henson, Hardin-Simmons, New Mexico St., Illinois & New Mexico St.	1963-96, 99-2001	722	365	.664

38 SEASONS

Coach, Team	Seasons	W	L	Pct.
Adolph Rupp, Kentucky	1931-52, 54-69	807	175	.822
Phog Allen, Baker, Kansas, Haskell, Central Mo. & Kansas	1906-09, 13-46	599	180	.769
Ed Diddle, Western Ky.	1923-60	714	252	.739
Bob Knight, Army, Indiana & Texas Tech	1966-2000, 02-04	832	322	.721
Henry Iba, Northwest Mo. St., Colorado & Oklahoma St.	1930-67	728	298	.710
Don Haskins, UTEP	1962-99	719	353	.671
Lefty Driesell, Davidson, Maryland, James Madison & Georgia St.	1961-86, 89-2000	733	372	.663
Lou Henson, Hardin-Simmons, New Mexico St., Illinois & New Mexico St.	1963-96, 99-2002	742	377	.663
Norm Stewart, UNI & Missouri	1962-99	731	375	.661
Ray Meyer, DePaul	1943-80	623	335	.650

39 SEASONS

Coach, Team	Seasons	W	L	Pct.
Adolph Rupp, Kentucky	1931-52, 54-70	833	177	.825
Phog Allen, Baker, Kansas, Haskell, Central Mo. & Kansas	1906-09, 13-47	607	185	.766
Ed Diddle, Western Ky.	1923-61	732	260	.740
Bob Knight, Army, Indiana & Texas Tech	1966-2000, 02-05	854	333	.719
Henry Iba, Northwest Mo. St., Colorado & Oklahoma St.	1930-68	738	314	.702
Lefty Driesell, Davidson, Maryland, James Madison & Georgia St.	1961-86, 89-2001	762	377	.669
Ray Meyer, DePaul	1943-81	650	337	.659
Lou Henson, Hardin-Simmons, New Mexico St., Illinois & New Mexico St.	1963-96, 99-2003	762	386	.664
Tony Hinkle, Butler	1927-42, 46-68	531	367	.591
Marv Harshman, Pacific Lutheran, Washington St. & Washington	1946-84	632	439	.590

40 SEASONS

Coach, Team	Seasons	W	L	Pct.
Adolph Rupp, Kentucky	1931-52, 54-71	855	183	.824
Phog Allen, Baker, Kansas, Haskell, Central Mo. & Kansas	1906-09, 13-48	616	200	.755
Ed Diddle, Western Ky.	1923-62	749	270	.735
Bob Knight, Army, Indiana & Texas Tech	1966-2000, 02-06	869	350	.713
Henry Iba, Northwest Mo. St., Colorado & Oklahoma St.	1930-69	750	327	.696
Lefty Driesell, Davidson, Maryland, James Madison & Georgia St.	1961-86, 89-2002	782	388	.668
Ray Meyer, DePaul	1943-82	676	339	.666
Lou Henson, Hardin-Simmons, New Mexico St., Illinois & New Mexico St.	1963-96, 99-2004	775	400	.660
Marv Harshman, Pacific Lutheran, Washington St. & Washington	1946-85	654	449	.593
Tony Hinkle, Butler	1927-42, 46-69	542	382	.587

41 SEASONS

Coach, Team	Seasons	W	L	Pct.
Adolph Rupp, Kentucky	1931-52, 54-72	876	190	.822
Phog Allen, Baker, Kansas, Haskell, Central Mo. & Kansas	1906-09, 13-49	628	212	.748
Ed Diddle, Western Ky.	1923-63	754	286	.725
Bob Knight, Army, Indiana & Texas Tech	1966-2000, 02-07	890	363	.710
Henry Iba, Northwest Mo. St., Colorado & Oklahoma St.	1930-70	764	339	.693
Ray Meyer, DePaul	1943-83	697	351	.665
Lefty Driesell, Davidson, Maryland, James Madison & Georgia St.	1961-86, 89-2003	800	409	.662
Lou Henson, Hardin-Simmons, New Mexico St., Illinois & New Mexico St.	1963-96, 99-2005	779	412	.654
Tony Hinkle, Butler	1927-42, 46-70	557	393	.586

42 SEASONS

Coach, Team	Seasons	W	L	Pct.
Phog Allen, Baker, Kansas, Haskell, Central Mo. & Kansas	1906-09, 13-50	642	223	.742
Ed Diddle, Western Ky.	1923-64	759	302	.715
Bob Knight, Army, Indiana & Texas Tech	1966-2000, 02-08	902	371	.709
Ray Meyer, DePaul	1943-84	724	354	.672

Top 10 Best Career Starts By Wins

(Head coaches with at least half their seasons at Division I)

1 SEASON

Coach, Team	Season	W	L	Pct.
Bill Guthridge, North Carolina	1998	34	4	.895
Bill Hodges, Indiana St.	1979	33	1	.970
Jamie Dixon, Pittsburgh	2004	31	5	.861
Brad Stevens, Butler	2008	30	4	.882
Stan Heath, Kent St.	2002	30	6	.833
John Warren, Oregon	1945	30	13	.698
Keno Davis, Drake	2008	28	5	.848
Mick Cronin, Murray St.	2004	28	6	.824
Anthony Grant, VCU	2007	28	7	.800
Phil Johnson, Weber St.	1969	27	3	.900
Blaine Taylor, Montana	1992	27	4	.871
Tevester Anderson, Murray St.	1999	27	6	.818
John Phillips, Tulsa	2002	27	7	.794
Chris Lowery, Southern Ill.	2005	27	8	.771
Doc Sadler, UTEP	2005	27	8	.771

2 SEASONS

Coach, Team	Seasons	W	L	Pct.
Bill Guthridge, North Carolina	1998-99	58	14	.806
Everett Case, North Carolina St.	1947-48	55	8	.873
Todd Lickliter, Butler	2002-03	53	12	.815
Ben Carnevale, North Carolina	1945-46	52	11	.825
Mark Fox, Nevada	2005-06	52	13	.800
Anthony Grant, VCU	2007-08	52	15	.776
Mark Few, Gonzaga	2000-01	52	16	.765
Don Monson, Gonzaga	1998-99	52	17	.754
Tony Bennett, Washington St.	2007-08	52	17	.754
Bill Carmody, Princeton	1997-98	51	6	.895
Jamie Dixon, Pittsburgh	2004-05	51	14	.785

3 SEASONS

Coach, Team	Seasons	W	L	Pct.
Mark Fox, Nevada	2005-07	81	18	.818
Mark Few, Gonzaga	2000-02	81	20	.802
Everett Case, North Carolina St.	1947-49	80	16	.833
Bill Guthridge, North Carolina	1998-2000	80	28	.741
Chris Lowery, Southern Ill.	2005-07	78	26	.750
Thad Matta, Butler & Xavier	2001-03	76	20	.792
Jamie Dixon, Pittsburgh	2004-06	76	22	.776
Roy Williams, Kansas	1989-91	76	25	.752
Jim Boeheim, Syracuse	1977-79	74	14	.841
Bill Carmody, Princeton	1997-99	73	14	.839

4 SEASONS

Coach, Team	Seasons	W	L	Pct.
Everett Case, North Carolina St.	1947-50	107	22	.829
Mark Few, Gonzaga	2000-03	105	29	.784
Jamie Dixon, Pittsburgh	2004-07	105	30	.778
Bruce Stewart, West Va. Wesleyan & Middle Tenn.	1983-86	104	34	.754
Roy Williams, Kansas	1989-92	103	30	.774
Mark Fox, Nevada	2005-08	102	30	.773
Thad Matta, Butler & Xavier	2001-04	102	31	.767
Jim Boeheim, Syracuse	1977-80	100	18	.847
Speedy Morris, La Salle	1987-90	100	31	.763
Paul Westphal, Grand Canyon & Pepperdine	1987-88, 2002-03	100	40	.714

5 SEASONS

Coach, Team	Seasons	W	L	Pct.
Everett Case, North Carolina St.	1947-51	137	29	.825
Mark Few, Gonzaga	2000-04	133	32	.806
Roy Williams, Kansas	1989-93	132	37	.781
Jamie Dixon, Pittsburgh	2004-08	132	40	.767
Bruce Stewart, West Va. Wesleyan & Middle Tenn.	1983-87	126	41	.754
Forddy Anderson, Drake & Bradley	1947-51	123	42	.745
Jerry Tarkanian, Long Beach St. & UNLV	1969-73	122	20	.859
Jim Boeheim, Syracuse	1977-81	122	30	.803
Thad Matta, Butler, Xavier & Ohio St.	2001-05	122	43	.739
Fred Schaus, West Virginia	1955-59	120	32	.789
Larry Brown, UCLA & Kansas	1980-81, 84-86	120	38	.759
Tom Izzo, Michigan St.	1996-2000	120	48	.714

6 SEASONS

Coach, Team	Seasons	W	L	Pct.
Everett Case, North Carolina St.	1947-52	161	39	.805
Roy Williams, Kansas	1989-94	159	45	.779

COACHING RECORDS

Coach, Team	Seasons	W	L	Pct.
Mark Few, Gonzaga	2000-05	159	37	.811
Bruce Stewart, West Va. Wesleyan & Middle Tenn.	1983-88	149	52	.741
Thad Matta, Butler, Xavier & Ohio St.	2001-06	148	49	.751
Tom Izzo, Michigan St.	1996-2001	148	53	.736
Fred Schaus, West Virginia	1955-60	146	37	.798
Larry Brown, UCLA & Kansas	1980-81, 84-87	145	49	.747
Pete Gillen, Xavier	1986-91	141	49	.742
Forddy Anderson, Drake & Bradley	1947-52	140	54	.722

7 SEASONS

Coach, Team	Seasons	W	L	Pct.
Mark Few, Gonzaga	2000-06	188	41	.821
Everett Case, North Carolina St.	1947-53	187	45	.806
Roy Williams, Kansas	1989-95	184	51	.783
Thad Matta, Butler, Xavier & Ohio St.	2001-07	183	53	.775
Larry Brown, UCLA & Kansas	1980-81, 84-88	172	60	.741
Bruce Stewart, West Va. Wesleyan & Middle Tenn.	1983-89	172	60	.741
Tom Izzo, Michigan St.	1996-2002	167	65	.720
Bruce Weber, Southern Ill. & Illinois	1999-2005	166	63	.725
Jerry Tarkanian, Long Beach St. & UNLV	1969-75	160	28	.851
Denny Crum, Louisville	1972-78	162	44	.786
Howard Hobson, Southern Ore. & Oregon	1933-39	162	48	.771

8 SEASONS

Coach, Team	Seasons	W	L	Pct.
Everett Case, North Carolina St.	1947-54	213	52	.804
Roy Williams, Kansas	1989-96	213	56	.792
Mark Few, Gonzaga	2000-07	211	52	.802
Thad Matta, Butler, Xavier & Ohio St.	2001-08	207	66	.758
Bruce Weber, Southern Ill. & Illinois	1999-2006	192	70	.733
Jerry Tarkanian, Long Beach St. & UNLV	1969-76	189	30	.863
John Calipari, Massachusetts	1989-96	189	70	.730
Tom Izzo, Michigan St.	1996-2003	189	78	.708
Tubby Smith, Tulsa, Georgia & Kentucky	1992-99	187	75	.714
Denny Crum, Louisville	1972-79	186	52	.782

9 SEASONS

Coach, Team	Seasons	W	L	Pct.
Roy Williams, Kansas	1989-97	247	58	.810
Everett Case, North Carolina St.	1947-55	241	56	.811
Mark Few, Gonzaga	2000-08	236	60	.797
Denny Crum, Louisville	1972-80	219	55	.799
Jerry Tarkanian, Long Beach St. & UNLV	1969-77	218	33	.869
Bruce Weber, Southern Ill. & Illinois	1999-2007	215	82	.724
John Calipari, Massachusetts & Memphis	1989-96, 2001	210	85	.712
Tubby Smith, Tulsa, Georgia & Kentucky	1992-2000	210	85	.712
Tom Izzo, Michigan St.	1996-2004	207	90	.697
Jim Boeheim, Syracuse	1977-85	204	71	.742

10 SEASONS

Coach, Team	Seasons	W	L	Pct.
Roy Williams, Kansas	1989-98	282	62	.820
Everett Case, North Carolina St.	1947-56	265	60	.815
Denny Crum, Louisville	1972-81	240	64	.789
Jerry Tarkanian, Long Beach St. & UNLV	1969-78	238	41	.853
John Calipari, Massachusetts & Memphis	1989-96, 2001-02	237	94	.716
Tubby Smith, Tulsa, Georgia & Kentucky	1992-2001	234	95	.711
Tom Izzo, Michigan St.	1996-2005	233	97	.706
Bruce Weber, Southern Ill. & Illinois	1999-2008	231	101	.696
Jim Boeheim, Syracuse	1977-86	230	77	.749
Nolan Richardson, Tulsa & Arkansas	1981-90	226	88	.720

11 SEASONS

Coach, Team	Seasons	W	L	Pct.
Roy Williams, Kansas	1989-99	305	72	.809
Everett Case, North Carolina St.	1947-57	280	71	.798
Denny Crum, Louisville	1972-82	263	74	.780
Jim Boeheim, Syracuse	1977-87	261	84	.757
Nolan Richardson, Tulsa & Arkansas	1981-91	260	92	.739
John Calipari, Massachusetts & Memphis	1989-96, 2001-03	260	101	.720
Jerry Tarkanian, Long Beach St. & UNLV	1969-79	259	49	.841
Tubby Smith, Tulsa, Georgia & Kentucky	1992-2002	256	105	.709
Tom Izzo, Michigan St.	1996-2006	255	109	.701
Tom Blackburn, Dayton	1948-58	242	87	.736

12 SEASONS

Coach, Team	Seasons	W	L	Pct.
Roy Williams, Kansas	1989-2000	329	82	.800
Everett Case, North Carolina St.	1947-58	298	77	.795
Denny Crum, Louisville	1972-83	295	78	.791
Tubby Smith, Tulsa, Georgia & Kentucky	1992-2003	288	109	.725
Jim Boeheim, Syracuse	1977-88	287	93	.755
Nolan Richardson, Tulsa & Arkansas	1981-92	286	100	.741
Jerry Tarkanian, Long Beach St. & UNLV	1969-80	282	58	.829
John Calipari, Massachusetts & Memphis	1989-96, 2001-04	282	109	.721
Tom Izzo, Michigan St.	1996-2007	278	121	.697
Wimp Sanderson, Alabama	1981-92	265	118	.692

13 SEASONS

Coach, Team	Seasons	W	L	Pct.
Roy Williams, Kansas	1989-2001	355	89	.800
Everett Case, North Carolina St.	1947-59	320	81	.798
Denny Crum, Louisville	1972-84	319	89	.782
Jim Boeheim, Syracuse	1977-89	317	101	.758
Tubby Smith, Tulsa, Georgia & Kentucky	1992-2004	315	114	.734
Nolan Richardson, Tulsa & Arkansas	1981-93	308	109	.739
Tom Izzo, Michigan St.	1996-2008	305	130	.701
John Calipari, Massachusetts & Memphis	1989-96, 2001-05	304	125	.709
Jerry Tarkanian, Long Beach St. & UNLV	1969-81	298	70	.810
John Thompson, Georgetown	1973-85	297	107	.735

14 SEASONS

Coach, Team	Seasons	W	L	Pct.
Roy Williams, Kansas	1989-2002	388	93	.807
Jim Boeheim, Syracuse	1977-90	343	108	.761
Tubby Smith, Tulsa, Georgia & Kentucky	1992-2005	343	120	.741
Nolan Richardson, Tulsa & Arkansas	1981-94	339	112	.752
Denny Crum, Louisville	1972-85	338	107	.760
John Calipari, Massachusetts & Memphis	1989-96, 2001-06	337	129	.723
Everett Case, North Carolina St.	1947-60	331	96	.775
John Thompson, Georgetown	1973-86	321	115	.736
Billy Donovan, Marshall & Florida	1995-2008	320	135	.703
Jerry Tarkanian, Long Beach St. & UNLV	1969-82	318	80	.799

15 SEASONS

Coach, Team	Seasons	W	L	Pct.
Roy Williams, Kansas	1989-2003	418	101	.805
Nolan Richardson, Tulsa & Arkansas	1981-95	371	119	.757
Denny Crum, Louisville	1972-86	370	114	.764
John Calipari, Massachusetts & Memphis	1989-96, 2001-07	370	133	.736
Jim Boeheim, Syracuse	1977-91	369	114	.764
Tubby Smith, Tulsa, Georgia & Kentucky	1992-2006	365	133	.733
Rick Pitino, Boston U., Providence & Kentucky	1979-83, 86-87, 90--97	352	124	.739
John Thompson, Georgetown	1973-87	350	120	.745
Bill Self, Oral Roberts, Tulsa, Illinois & Kansas	1994-2008	349	137	.718
Everett Case, North Carolina St.	1947-61	347	105	.768

16 SEASONS

Coach, Team	Seasons	W	L	Pct.
Roy Williams, Kansas & North Carolina	1989-2004	437	112	.796
John Calipari, Massachusetts & Memphis	1989-96, 2001-08	408	135	.751
Jim Boeheim, Syracuse	1977-92	391	124	.759
Nolan Richardson, Tulsa & Arkansas	1981-96	391	132	.748
Denny Crum, Louisville	1972-87	388	128	.752
Tubby Smith, Tulsa, Georgia & Kentucky	1992-2007	387	145	.727
Jerry Tarkanian, Long Beach St. & UNLV	1969-84	375	89	.808
Rick Pitino, Boston U., Providence, Kentucky & Louisville	1979-83, 86-87, 90-97, 2002	371	137	.730
John Thompson, Georgetown	1973-88	370	130	.740
Billy Tubbs, Texas St., Lamar & Oklahoma	1972-73, 77-90	363	153	.703

17 SEASONS

Coach, Team	Seasons	W	L	Pct.
Roy Williams, Kansas & North Carolina	1989-2005	470	116	.802
Denny Crum, Louisville	1972-88	412	139	.748
Jim Boeheim, Syracuse	1977-93	411	133	.756
Nolan Richardson, Tulsa & Arkansas	1981-97	409	146	.737
Tubby Smith, Tulsa, Georgia, Kentucky & Minnesota	1992-2008	407	159	.719
Jerry Tarkanian, Long Beach St. & UNLV	1969-85	403	93	.813
John Thompson, Georgetown	1973-89	399	135	.747
Rick Pitino, Boston U., Providence, Kentucky & Louisville	1979-83, 86-87, 90-97, 2002-03	396	144	.733
Bob Huggins, Walsh, Akron & Cincinnati	1981-98	388	148	.724
Billy Tubbs, Texas St., Lamar & Oklahoma	1972-73, 77-91	383	168	.695

18 SEASONS

Coach, Team	Seasons	W	L	Pct.
Roy Williams, Kansas & North Carolina	1989-2006	493	124	.799
Jerry Tarkanian, Long Beach St. & UNLV	1969-86	436	98	.816
Denny Crum, Louisville	1972-89	436	148	.747
Jim Boeheim, Syracuse	1977-94	434	140	.756

Coach, Team	Seasons	W	L	Pct.
Nolan Richardson, Tulsa & Arkansas	1981-98	433	155	.736
John Thompson, Georgetown	1973-90	423	142	.749
Rick Pitino, Boston U., Providence, Kentucky & Louisville	1979-83, 86-87, 90-97, 2002-04	416	154	.730
Bob Huggins, Walsh, Akron & Cincinnati	1981-99	415	154	.729
Billy Tubbs, Texas St., Lamar & Oklahoma	1972-73, 77-92	404	177	.695
Lou Carnesecca, St. John's (N.Y.)	1966-70, 74-86	402	136	.747

19 SEASONS

Coach, Team	Seasons	W	L	Pct.
Roy Williams, Kansas & North Carolina	1989-2007	524	131	.800
Jerry Tarkanian, Long Beach St. & UNLV	1969-87	473	100	.825
Denny Crum, Louisville	1972-90	463	156	.748
Nolan Richardson, Tulsa & Arkansas	1981-99	456	166	.733
Jim Boeheim, Syracuse	1977-95	454	150	.752
Rick Pitino, Boston U., Providence, Kentucky & Louisville	1979-83, 86-87, 90-97, 2002-05	449	159	.738
Bob Huggins, Walsh, Akron & Cincinnati	1981-2000	444	158	.738
John Thompson, Georgetown	1973-91	442	155	.740
Billy Tubbs, Texas St., Lamar & Oklahoma	1972-73, 77-93	424	189	.692
Lou Carnesecca, St. John's (N.Y.)	1966-70, 74-87	423	145	.745

20 SEASONS

Coach, Team	Seasons	W	L	Pct.
Roy Williams, Kansas & North Carolina	1989-2008	560	134	.807
Jerry Tarkanian, Long Beach St. & UNLV	1969-88	501	106	.825
Jim Boeheim, Syracuse	1977-96	483	159	.752
Denny Crum, Louisville	1972-91	477	172	.735
Nolan Richardson, Tulsa & Arkansas	1981-2000	475	181	.724
Rick Pitino, Boston U., Providence, Kentucky & Louisville	1979-83, 86-87, 90-97, 2002-06	470	172	.732
Bob Huggins, Walsh, Akron & Cincinnati	1981-2001	469	168	.736
John Thompson, Georgetown	1973-92	464	165	.738
John Chaney, Cheyney & Temple	1973-92	458	143	.762
Lou Carnesecca, St. John's (N.Y.)	1966-70, 74-88	440	157	.737

21 SEASONS

Coach, Team	Seasons	W	L	Pct.
Jerry Tarkanian, Long Beach St. & UNLV	1969-89	530	114	.823
Jim Boeheim, Syracuse	1977-97	502	172	.745
Bob Huggins, Walsh, Akron & Cincinnati	1981-2002	500	172	.744
Denny Crum, Louisville	1972-92	496	183	.730
Nolan Richardson, Tulsa & Arkansas	1981-2001	495	192	.721
Rick Pitino, Boston U., Providence, Kentucky & Louisville	1979-83, 86-87, 90-97, 2002-07	494	182	.731
John Thompson, Georgetown	1973-93	484	178	.731
John Chaney, Cheyney & Temple	1973-93	478	156	.754
Dean Smith, North Carolina	1962-82	468	145	.763
Lou Carnesecca, St. John's (N.Y.)	1966-70, 74-89	460	170	.730

22 SEASONS

Coach, Team	Seasons	W	L	Pct.
Jerry Tarkanian, Long Beach St. & UNLV	1969-90	565	119	.826
Jim Boeheim, Syracuse	1977-98	528	181	.745
Rick Pitino, Boston U., Providence, Kentucky & Louisville	1979-83, 86-87, 90-97, 2002-08	521	191	.732
Denny Crum, Louisville	1972-93	518	192	.730
Bob Huggins, Walsh, Akron & Cincinnati	1981-2003	517	184	.738
John Thompson, Georgetown	1973-94	503	190	.726
John Chaney, Cheyney & Temple	1973-94	501	164	.753
Dean Smith, North Carolina	1962-83	496	153	.764
Lou Carnesecca, St. John's (N.Y.)	1966-70, 74-90	484	180	.729
Henry Iba, Northwest Mo. St., Colorado & Oklahoma St.	1930-51	483	123	.797

23 SEASONS

Coach, Team	Seasons	W	L	Pct.
Jerry Tarkanian, Long Beach St. & UNLV	1969-91	599	120	.833
Jim Boeheim, Syracuse	1977-99	549	193	.740
Denny Crum, Louisville	1972-94	546	198	.734
Bob Huggins, Walsh, Akron & Cincinnati	1981-2004	542	191	.739
Dean Smith, North Carolina	1962-84	524	156	.771
John Thompson, Georgetown	1973-95	524	200	.724
John Chaney, Cheyney & Temple	1973-95	520	175	.748
Lute Olson, Long Beach St., Iowa & Arizona	1974-96	509	192	.726
Lou Carnesecca, St. John's (N.Y.)	1966-70, 74-91	507	189	.728
Mike Krzyzewski, Army & Duke	1976-98	505	212	.704

24 SEASONS

Coach, Team	Seasons	W	L	Pct.
Jerry Tarkanian, Long Beach St. & UNLV	1969-92	625	122	.837
Jim Boeheim, Syracuse	1977-2000	575	199	.743
Bob Huggins, Walsh, Akron & Cincinnati	1981-2005	567	199	.740

Coach, Team	Seasons	W	L	Pct.
Denny Crum, Louisville	1972-95	565	212	.727
John Thompson, Georgetown	1973-96	553	208	.727
Dean Smith, North Carolina	1962-85	551	165	.770
Mike Krzyzewski, Army & Duke	1976-99	542	214	.717
John Chaney, Cheyney & Temple	1973-96	540	188	.742
Lute Olson, Long Beach St., Iowa & Arizona	1974-97	534	201	.718
Eddie Sutton, Creighton, Arkansas, Kentucky & Oklahoma St.	1970-89, 91-94	526	199	.726
Lou Carnesecca, St. John's (N.Y.)	1966-70, 74-92	526	200	.725

25 SEASONS

Coach, Team	Seasons	W	L	Pct.
Jerry Tarkanian, Long Beach St., UNLV & Fresno St.	1969-92, 96	647	133	.829
Jim Boeheim, Syracuse	1977-2001	600	208	.743
Bob Huggins, Walsh, Akron, Cincinnati & Kansas St.	1981-2005, 07	590	211	.737
Denny Crum, Louisville	1972-96	587	224	.724
Dean Smith, North Carolina	1962-86	579	171	.772
John Thompson, Georgetown	1973-97	573	218	.724
Mike Krzyzewski, Army & Duke	1976-2000	571	219	.723
Lute Olson, Long Beach St., Iowa & Arizona	1974-98	564	206	.732
John Chaney, Cheyney & Temple	1973-97	560	199	.738
Eddie Sutton, Creighton, Arkansas, Kentucky & Oklahoma St.	1970-89, 91-95	553	209	.726

26 SEASONS

Coach, Team	Seasons	W	L	Pct.
Jerry Tarkanian, Long Beach St., UNLV & Fresno St.	1969-92, 96-97	667	145	.821
Jim Boeheim, Syracuse	1977-2002	623	221	.738
Bob Huggins, Walsh, Akron, Cincinnati, Kansas St. & West Virginia	1981-2005, 07-08	616	222	.735
Denny Crum, Louisville	1972-97	613	233	.725
Dean Smith, North Carolina	1962-87	611	175	.777
Mike Krzyzewski, Army & Duke	1976-2001	606	223	.731
John Thompson, Georgetown	1973-98	589	233	.717
Lute Olson, Long Beach St., Iowa & Arizona	1974-99	586	213	.733
John Chaney, Cheyney & Temple	1973-98	581	208	.736
John Wooden, Indiana St. & UCLA	1947-72	580	155	.789

27 SEASONS

Coach, Team	Seasons	W	L	Pct.
Jerry Tarkanian, Long Beach St., UNLV & Fresno St.	1969-92, 96-98	688	158	.813
Jim Boeheim, Syracuse	1977-2003	653	226	.743
Dean Smith, North Carolina	1962-88	638	182	.778
Mike Krzyzewski, Army & Duke	1976-2002	637	227	.737
Denny Crum, Louisville	1972-98	625	253	.712
Lute Olson, Long Beach St., Iowa & Arizona	1974-2000	613	220	.736
John Wooden, Indiana St. & UCLA	1947-73	610	155	.797
John Chaney, Cheyney & Temple	1973-99	605	219	.734
John Thompson, Georgetown	1973-99	596	239	.714
Bob Knight, Army & Indiana	1966-92	588	210	.737

28 SEASONS

Coach, Team	Seasons	W	L	Pct.
Jerry Tarkanian, Long Beach St., UNLV & Fresno St.	1969-92, 96-99	689	170	.802
Jim Boeheim, Syracuse	1977-2004	676	234	.743
Dean Smith, North Carolina	1962-89	667	190	.778
Mike Krzyzewski, Army & Duke	1976-2003	663	234	.739
Denny Crum, Louisville	1972-99	644	264	.709
Lute Olson, Long Beach St., Iowa & Arizona	1974-2001	638	226	.738
John Wooden, Indiana St. & UCLA	1947-74	636	159	.800
John Chaney, Cheyney & Temple	1973-2000	632	225	.737
Bob Knight, Army & Indiana	1966-93	619	214	.743
Adolph Rupp, Kentucky	1931-52, 54-59	610	106	.852

29 SEASONS

Coach, Team	Seasons	W	L	Pct.
Jim Boeheim, Syracuse	1977-2005	703	241	.745
Jerry Tarkanian, Long Beach St., UNLV & Fresno St.	1969-92, 96-2000	701	179	.797
Mike Krzyzewski, Army & Duke	1976-2004	694	240	.743
Dean Smith, North Carolina	1962-90	688	203	.772
John Wooden, Indiana St. & UCLA	1947-75	664	162	.804
Denny Crum, Louisville	1972-2000	663	276	.706
Lute Olson, Long Beach St., Iowa & Arizona	1974-2002	662	236	.737
John Chaney, Cheyney & Temple	1973-2001	656	238	.734
Bob Knight, Army & Indiana	1966-94	640	223	.742
Eddie Sutton, Creighton, Arkansas, Kentucky & Oklahoma St.	1970-89, 91-99	632	252	.715

30 SEASONS

Coach, Team	Seasons	W	L	Pct.
Jim Boeheim, Syracuse	1977-2006	726	253	.742
Mike Krzyzewski, Army & Duke	1976-2005	721	246	.746
Dean Smith, North Carolina	1962-91	717	209	.774
Jerry Tarkanian, Long Beach St., UNLV & Fresno St.	1969-92, 96-2001	710	186	.792
Lute Olson, Long Beach St., Iowa & Arizona	1974-2003	690	240	.742
John Chaney, Cheyney & Temple	1973-2002	675	253	.727
Denny Crum, Louisville	1972-2001	675	295	.696
Bob Knight, Army & Indiana	1966-95	659	235	.737
Eddie Sutton, Creighton, Arkansas, Kentucky & Oklahoma St.	1970-89, 91-2000	659	259	.718
Adolph Rupp, Kentucky	1931-52, 54-61	647	122	.841

31 SEASONS

Coach, Team	Seasons	W	L	Pct.
Mike Krzyzewski, Army & Duke	1976-2006	753	250	.751
Jim Boeheim, Syracuse	1977-2007	750	264	.740
Dean Smith, North Carolina	1962-92	740	219	.772
Jerry Tarkanian, Long Beach St., UNLV & Fresno St.	1969-92, 96-2002	729	201	.784
Lute Olson, Long Beach St., Iowa & Arizona	1974-2004	710	249	.740
John Chaney, Cheyney & Temple	1973-2003	693	269	.720
Bob Knight, Army & Indiana	1966-96	679	246	.734
Eddie Sutton, Creighton, Arkansas, Kentucky & Oklahoma St.	1970-89, 91-2001	679	269	.716
Adolph Rupp, Kentucky	1931-52, 54-62	670	125	.843
Jim Calhoun, Northeastern & Connecticut	1973-2003	647	296	.686

32 SEASONS

Coach, Team	Seasons	W	L	Pct.
Mike Krzyzewski, Army & Duke	1976-2007	775	261	.748
Dean Smith, North Carolina	1962-93	774	223	.776
Jim Boeheim, Syracuse	1977-2008	771	278	.735
Lute Olson, Long Beach St., Iowa & Arizona	1974-2005	740	256	.743
John Chaney, Cheyney & Temple	1973-2004	708	283	.714
Eddie Sutton, Creighton, Arkansas, Kentucky & Oklahoma St.	1970-89, 91-2002	702	278	.716
Bob Knight, Army & Indiana	1966-97	701	257	.732
Adolph Rupp, Kentucky	1931-52, 54-63	686	134	.837
Jim Calhoun, Northeastern & Connecticut	1973-2004	680	302	.692
Henry Iba, Northwest Mo. St., Colorado & Oklahoma St.	1930-61	652	221	.746

33 SEASONS

Coach, Team	Seasons	W	L	Pct.
Mike Krzyzewski, Army & Duke	1976-2008	803	267	.750
Dean Smith, North Carolina	1962-94	802	230	.777
Lute Olson, Long Beach St., Iowa & Arizona	1974-2006	760	269	.739
Eddie Sutton, Creighton, Arkansas, Kentucky & Oklahoma St.	1970-89, 91-2003	724	288	.715
John Chaney, Cheyney & Temple	1973-2005	724	297	.709
Bob Knight, Army & Indiana	1966-98	721	269	.728
Adolph Rupp, Kentucky	1931-52, 54-64	707	140	.835
Jim Calhoun, Northeastern & Connecticut	1973-2005	703	310	.694
Henry Iba, Northwest Mo. St., Colorado & Oklahoma St.	1930-62	666	233	.741
Lefty Driesell, Davidson, Maryland & James Madison	1961-86, 89-95	657	302	.685

34 SEASONS

Coach, Team	Seasons	W	L	Pct.
Dean Smith, North Carolina	1962-95	830	236	.779
Lute Olson, Long Beach St., Iowa & Arizona	1974-2007	780	280	.736
Eddie Sutton, Creighton, Arkansas, Kentucky & Oklahoma St.	1970-89, 91-2004	755	292	.721
Bob Knight, Army & Indiana	1966-99	744	280	.727
John Chaney, Cheyney & Temple	1973-2006	741	312	.704
Jim Calhoun, Northeastern & Connecticut	1973-2006	733	314	.700
Adolph Rupp, Kentucky	1931-52, 54-65	722	150	.828
Henry Iba, Northwest Mo. St., Colorado & Oklahoma St.	1930-63	682	242	.738
Lefty Driesell, Davidson, Maryland & James Madison	1961-86, 89-96	667	322	.674
Don Haskins, UTEP	1962-95	665	298	.691

35 SEASONS

Coach, Team	Seasons	W	L	Pct.
Dean Smith, North Carolina	1962-96	851	247	.775
Eddie Sutton, Creighton, Arkansas, Kentucky & Oklahoma St.	1970-89, 91-2005	781	299	.723
Bob Knight, Army & Indiana	1966-2000	764	289	.726
Jim Calhoun, Northeastern & Connecticut	1973-2007	750	328	.696
Adolph Rupp, Kentucky	1931-52, 54-66	749	152	.831

Coach, Team	Seasons	W	L	Pct.
Henry Iba, Northwest Mo. St., Colorado & Oklahoma St.	1930-64	697	252	.734
Lou Henson, Hardin-Simmons, New Mexico St., Illinois & New Mexico St.	1963-96, 99	686	341	.668
Lefty Driesell, Davidson, Maryland & James Madison	1961-86, 89-97	683	335	.671
Don Haskins, UTEP	1962-96	678	313	.684
Norm Stewart, UNI & Missouri	1962-96	678	334	.670

36 SEASONS

Coach, Team	Seasons	W	L	Pct.
Dean Smith, North Carolina	1962-97	879	254	.776
Eddie Sutton, Creighton, Arkansas, Kentucky & Oklahoma St.	1970-89, 91-2006	798	315	.717
Bob Knight, Army, Indiana & Texas Tech	1966-2000, 02	787	298	.725
Jim Calhoun, Northeastern & Connecticut	1973-2008	774	337	.697
Adolph Rupp, Kentucky	1931-52, 54-67	762	165	.822
Henry Iba, Northwest Mo. St., Colorado & Oklahoma St.	1930-65	717	259	.735
Lou Henson, Hardin-Simmons, New Mexico St., Illinois & New Mexico St.	1963-96, 99-2000	708	351	.669
Lefty Driesell, Davidson, Maryland, James Madison & Georgia St.	1961-86, 89-98	699	347	.668
Norm Stewart, UNI & Missouri	1962-97	694	351	.664
Don Haskins, UTEP	1962-97	691	327	.679

37 SEASONS

Coach, Team	Seasons	W	L	Pct.
Bob Knight, Army, Indiana & Texas Tech	1966-2000, 02-03	809	311	.722
Eddie Sutton, Creighton, Arkansas, Kentucky Oklahoma St. & San Francisco	1970-89, 91-2006, 08	804	328	.710
Adolph Rupp, Kentucky	1931-52, 54-68	784	170	.822
Lou Henson, Hardin-Simmons, New Mexico St., Illinois & New Mexico St.	1963-96, 99-2001	722	365	.664
Henry Iba, Northwest Mo. St., Colorado & Oklahoma St.	1930-66	721	280	.720
Lefty Driesell, Davidson, Maryland, James Madison & Georgia St.	1961-86, 89-99	716	360	.665
Norm Stewart, UNI & Missouri	1962-98	711	366	.660
Don Haskins, UTEP	1962-98	703	341	.673
Ed Diddle, Western Ky.	1923-59	693	245	.739
Ralph Miller, Wichita St., Iowa & Oregon St.	1952-88	635	374	.629

38 SEASONS

Coach, Team	Seasons	W	L	Pct.
Bob Knight, Army, Indiana & Texas Tech	1966-2000, 02-04	832	322	.721
Adolph Rupp, Kentucky	1931-52, 54-69	807	175	.822
Lou Henson, Hardin-Simmons, New Mexico St., Illinois & New Mexico St.	1963-96, 99-2002	742	377	.663
Lefty Driesell, Davidson, Maryland, James Madison & Georgia St.	1961-86, 89-2000	733	372	.663
Norm Stewart, UNI & Missouri	1962-99	731	375	.661
Henry Iba, Northwest Mo. St., Colorado & Oklahoma St.	1930-67	728	298	.710
Don Haskins, UTEP	1962-99	719	353	.671
Ed Diddle, Western Ky.	1923-60	714	252	.739
Ralph Miller, Wichita St., Iowa & Oregon St.	1952-89	657	382	.632
Ray Meyer, DePaul	1943-80	623	335	.650

39 SEASONS

Coach, Team	Seasons	W	L	Pct.
Bob Knight, Army, Indiana & Texas Tech	1966-2000, 02-05	854	333	.719
Adolph Rupp, Kentucky	1931-52, 54-70	833	177	.825
Lefty Driesell, Davidson, Maryland, James Madison & Georgia St.	1961-86, 89-2001	762	377	.669
Lou Henson, Hardin-Simmons, New Mexico St., Illinois & New Mexico St.	1963-96, 99-2003	762	386	.664
Henry Iba, Northwest Mo. St., Colorado & Oklahoma St.	1930-68	738	314	.702
Ed Diddle, Western Ky.	1923-61	732	260	.740
Ray Meyer, DePaul	1943-81	650	337	.659
Marv Harshman, Pacific Lutheran, Washington St. & Washington	1946-84	632	439	.590
Phog Allen, Baker, Kansas, Haskell, Central Mo. & Kansas	1906-09, 13-47	607	185	.766
Tony Hinkle, Butler	1927-42, 46-68	531	367	.591

40 SEASONS

Coach, Team	Seasons	W	L	Pct.
Bob Knight, Army, Indiana & Texas Tech	1966-2000, 02-06	869	350	.713
Adolph Rupp, Kentucky	1931-52, 54-71	855	183	.824
Lefty Driesell, Davidson, Maryland, James Madison & Georgia St.	1961-86, 89-2002	782	388	.668

Coach, Team	Seasons	W	L	Pct.
Lou Henson, Hardin-Simmons, New Mexico St., Illinois & New Mexico St.	1963-96, 99-2004	775	400	.660
Henry Iba, Northwest Mo. St., Colorado & Oklahoma St.	1930-69	750	327	.696
Ed Diddle, Western Ky.	1923-62	749	270	.735
Ray Meyer, DePaul	1943-82	676	339	.666
Marv Harshman, Pacific Lutheran, Washington St. & Washington	1946-85	654	449	.593
Phog Allen, Baker, Kansas, Haskell, Central Mo. & Kansas	1906-09, 13-40	616	200	.755
Tony Hinkle, Butler	1927-42, 46-69	542	382	.587

41 SEASONS

Coach, Team	Seasons	W	L	Pct.
Bob Knight, Army, Indiana & Texas Tech	1966-2000, 02-07	890	363	.710
Adolph Rupp, Kentucky	1931-52, 54-72	876	190	.822
Lefty Driesell, Davidson, Maryland, James Madison & Georgia St.	1961-86, 89-2003	800	409	.662
Lou Henson, Hardin-Simmons, New Mexico St., Illinois & New Mexico St.	1963-96, 99-2005	779	412	.654
Henry Iba, Northwest Mo. St., Colorado & Oklahoma St.	1930-70	764	339	.693
Ed Diddle, Western Ky.	1923-63	754	286	.725
Ray Meyer, DePaul	1943-83	697	351	.665
Phog Allen, Baker, Kansas, Haskell, Central Mo. & Kansas	1906-09, 13-49	628	212	.748
Tony Hinkle, Butler	1927-42, 46-70	557	393	.586

42 SEASONS

Coach, Team	Seasons	W	L	Pct.
Bob Knight, Army, Indiana & Texas Tech	1966-2000, 02-08	902	371	.709
Ed Diddle, Western Ky.	1923-64	759	302	.715
Ray Meyer, DePaul	1943-84	724	354	.672
Phog Allen, Baker, Kansas, Haskell, Central Mo. & Kansas	1906-09, 13-50	642	223	.742

Active Coaching Longevity Records

(Minimum five years as a Division I head coach)

MOST GAMES

No.	Coach, Team and Seasons
1,111	Jim Calhoun, Northeastern 1973-86, Connecticut 87-2008
1,060	Lute Olson, Long Beach St. 1974, Iowa 75-83, Arizona 84-2007
1,070	Mike Krzyzewski, Army 1976-80, Duke 81-2008
1,049	Jim Boeheim, Syracuse 1977-2008
1,018	Tom Penders, Tufts 1972-74, Columbia 75-78, Fordham 79-86, Rhode Island 87-88, Texas 89-98, George Washington 99-2001, Houston 05-08
969	Homer Drew, Bethel (Ind.) 1977-87, Ind.-South Bend 88, Valparaiso 89-2002, 04-08
953	Ben Braun, Siena Heights 1978-85, Eastern Mich. 86-96, California 97-2008, Rice
947	Gary Williams, American 1979-82, Boston College 83-86, Ohio St. 87-89, Maryland 90-2008
899	Cliff Ellis, South Ala. 1976-84, Clemson 85-94, Auburn 95-2004, Coastal Caro. 08
878	Dave Bike, Sacred Heart 1979-2008
847	Pat Kennedy, Iona 1981-86, Florida St. 87-97, DePaul 98-2002, Montana 03-04, Towson 05-08
844	Rick Byrd, Maryville (Tenn.) 1979-80, Lincoln Memorial 84-86, Belmont 87-2008
838	Bob Huggins, Walsh 1981-83, Akron 1985-89, Cincinnati 90-2005, Kansas St. 07, West Virginia 08
827	Bobby Cremins, Appalachian St. 1976-81, Georgia Tech 82-2000, Col. of Charleston 07-08
825	Larry Hunter, Wittenberg 1977-89, Ohio 1990-2001, Western Caro. 06-08
820	Pat Douglass, Mont. St.-Billings 1982-87, Cal St. Bakersfield 88-97, UC Irvine 98-2008
791	Mike Montgomery, Montana 1979-86, Stanford 87-2004, California
783	John Beilein, Nazareth 1983, Le Moyne 84-92, Canisius 93-97, Richmond 98-2002, West Virginia 03-07, Michigan 08
749	Don Maestri, Troy 1983-2008
728	Tom Green, Fairleigh Dickinson 1984-2008

MOST SEASONS

No.	Coach, Team and Seasons
36	Jim Calhoun, Northeastern 1973-86, Connecticut 87-2008
34	Lute Olson, Long Beach St. 1974, Iowa 75-83, Arizona 84-2007
34	Tom Penders, Tufts 1972-74, Columbia 75-78, Fordham 79-86, Rhode Island 87-88, Texas 89-98, George Washington 99-2001, Houston 05-08
33	Mike Krzyzewski, Army 1976-80, Duke 81-2008
32	Jim Boeheim, Syracuse 1977-2008
31	Ben Braun, Siena Heights 1978-85, Eastern Mich. 86-96, California 97-2008, Rice
31	Homer Drew, Bethel (Ind.) 1977-87, Ind.-South Bend 88, Valparaiso 89-2002, 04-08
30	Dave Bike, Sacred Heart 1979-2008
30	Cliff Ellis, South Ala. 1976-84, Clemson 85-94, Auburn 95-2004, Coastal Caro. 08
30	Gary Williams, American 1979-82, Boston College 83-86, Ohio St. 87-89, Maryland 90-2008
28	Larry Hunter, Wittenberg 1977-89, Ohio 1990-2001, Western Caro. 06-08
28	Pat Kennedy, Iona 1981-86, Florida St. 87-97, DePaul 98-2002, Montana 03-04, Towson 05-08
27	Bobby Cremins, Appalachian St. 1976-81, Georgia Tech 82-2000, Col. of Charleston 07-08
27	Pat Douglass, Mont. St.-Billings 1982-87, Cal St. Bakersfield 88-97, UC Irvine 98-2008
27	Rick Byrd, Maryville (Tenn.) 1979-80, Lincoln Memorial 84-86, Belmont 87-2008
26	John Beilein, Nazareth 1983, Le Moyne 84-92, Canisius 93-97, Richmond 98-2002, West Virginia 03-07, Michigan 08
26	Bob Huggins, Walsh 1981-83, Akron 1985-89, Cincinnati 90-2005, Kansas St. 07, West Virginia 08
26	Don Maestri, Troy 1983-2008
26	Mike Montgomery, Montana 1979-86, Stanford 87-2004, California
25	Tom Green, Fairleigh Dickinson 1984-2008

MOST SEASONS WITH CURRENT SCHOOL

No.	Coach, Team and Seasons
32	Jim Boeheim, #Syracuse 1977-2008
30	Dave Bike, #Sacred Heart 1979-2008
28	Mike Krzyzewski, Duke 1981-2008
26	Don Maestri, #Troy 1983-2008
25	Tom Green, #Fairleigh Dickinson 1984-2008
24	Lute Olson, Arizona 1984-2007
24	Greg Kampe, #Oakland 1985-2008
22	Rick Byrd, Belmont 1987-2008
22	Jim Calhoun, Connecticut 1987-2008
22	Fang Mitchell, #Coppin St. 1987-2008
22	L. Vann Pettaway, #Alabama A&M 1987-2008
20	Bob Thomason, Pacific 1989-2008
19	Homer Drew, Valparaiso 89-2002, 04-08
19	Bob McKillop, #Davidson 1990-2008
19	Gary Williams, Maryland 1990-2007
18	Dave Loos, Austin Peay 1991-2008
15	Kirk Speraw, #UCF 1994-2008
15	Dana Altman, Creighton 1995-2008
14	Ron Hunter, #IUPUI 1995-2008
14	Dennis Wolff, Boston U., 1995-2008
13	Tom Izzo, #Michigan St. , 1996-2008
13	Phil Martelli, #St. Joseph's, 1996-2008
13	Fran O'Hanlon, Lafayette, 1996-2008
13	Rick Scruggs, Gardner-Webb, 1996-2008
12	Eddie Biedenback, UNC Asheville, 1997-2008
12	Bobby Braswell, Cal St. Northridge, 1997-2008
12	Charlie Coles, Miami (Ohio), 1997-2008
12	Jimmy Collins, Ill.-Chicago, 1997-2008
12	Howie Dickenman, Central Conn. St. , 1997-2008
12	Billy Donovan, Florida, 1997-2008

#has coached only at this school

MOST DIVISION I 20-WIN SEASONS

No.	Coach, Team and Seasons
30	Jim Boeheim, Syracuse 1977-2008
29	Lute Olson, Long Beach St. 1974, Iowa 75-83, Arizona 84-2007
24	Mike Krzyzewski, Army 1976-80, Duke 81-2008
22	Jim Calhoun, Northeastern 1973-86, Connecticut 87-2008
20	Bob Huggins, Walsh 1981-83, Akron 1985-89, Cincinnati 90-2005, Kansas St. 07, West Virginia 08
18	Roy Williams, Kansas 1989-2003, North Carolina 04-08
16	Rick Pitino, Boston U. 1979-83, Providence 86-87, Kentucky 90-97, Louisville 2002-08
16	Gary Williams, American 1979-82, Boston College 83-86, Ohio St. 87-89, Maryland 90-2008
15	Tubby Smith, Tulsa 1992-95, Georgia 96-97, Kentucky 98-2007, Minnesota 08
14	John Calipari, Massachusetts 1989-96, Memphis 2001-08
13	Rick Barnes, George Mason 1988, Providence 89-94, Clemson 95-98, Texas 99-2000
13	Rick Byrd, Maryville (Tenn.) 1979-80, Lincoln Memorial 84-86, Belmont 87-2008
13	Stew Morrill, Montana 1987-91, Colorado St. 92-98, Utah St. 99-2008
12	Tom Penders, Tufts 1972-74, Columbia 1975-78, Fordham 79-86, Rhode Island 87-88, Texas 89-98, George Washington 99-2001, Houston 05-08
11	Dana Altman, Marshall 1990, Kansas St. 91-94, Creighton 95-2008

COACHING RECORDS

No.	Coach, Team and Seasons
10	Ben Braun, Eastern Mich. 1986-96, California 97-2008, Rice
10	Billy Donovan, Marshall 1995-96, Florida 97-2008
10	Pat Kennedy, Iona 1981-86, Florida St. 87-97, DePaul 98-2002, Montana 03-04, Towson 05-08
10	Dave Odom, East Carolina 1980-82, Wake Forest 90-2001, South Carolina 02-08
9	Cliff Ellis, South Ala. 1976-84, Clemson 85-94, Auburn 95-2004, Coastal Caro. 08

MOST CONSECUTIVE DIVISION I 20-WIN SEASONS

No.	Coach, Team and Seasons
20	Lute Olson, Arizona 1988-2007
15	Tubby Smith, Tulsa 1994-95, Georgia 96-97, Kentucky 98-2007, Minnesota 08
14	Jim Boeheim, Syracuse 1983-96
14	Roy Williams, Kansas 1990-2003
12	Mike Krzyzewski, Duke 1997-2008
11	Jim Boeheim, Syracuse 1998-2008
11	Bob Huggins, Cincinnati 1992-2002
11	Mike Krzyzewski, Duke 1984-94
10	Dana Altman, Creighton 1999-2008
10	Bill Self, Tulsa 1999-2000, Illinois 01-04, Kansas 04-08
9	Rick Barnes, Texas 2000-08
9	Jim Calhoun, Connecticut 1998-2006
9	Billy Donovan, Florida 1999-2007
9	Mark Few, Gonzaga 2000-08
9	Stew Morrill, Utah St. 2000-08
8	John Calipari, Memphis 2001-08
8	Thad Matta, Butler 2001, Xavier 02-04, Ohio St. 05-08
8	Gary Williams, Maryland 1997-2004
7	Rick Pitino, Kentucky 1991-97
6	Mike Brey, Delaware 1998-2000, Notre Dame 01-03
6	John Calipari, Massachusetts 1991-96
6	Jim Christian, Kent St. 2003-08
6	Homer Drew, Valparaiso 1994-99
6	Bruce Pearl, Milwaukee 2003-05, Tennessee 06-08
6	Tom Penders, Rhode Island 1987-88, Texas 89-92
6	Rick Pitino, Louisville 2003-08
6	Bruce Weber, Southern Ill. 2002-03, Illinois 04-07

CURRENT MOST CONSECUTIVE DIVISION I 20-WIN SEASONS

No.	Coach, Team and Seasons
20	Lute Olson, Arizona 1988-2007
15	Tubby Smith, Tulsa 1994-95, Georgia 96-97, Kentucky 98-2007, Minnesota 08
12	Mike Krzyzewski, Duke 1997-2008
11	Jim Boeheim, Syracuse 1998-2008
10	Dana Altman, Creighton 1999-2008
10	Billy Donovan, Florida 1999-2008
10	Bill Self, Tulsa 1999-2000, Illinois 01-04, Kansas 04-08
9	Rick Barnes, Texas 2000-08
9	Mark Few, Gonzaga 2000-08
9	Stew Morrill, Utah St. 2000-08
8	John Calipari, Memphis 2001-08
8	Thad Matta, Butler 2001, Xavier 02-04, Ohio St. 05-08
6	Jim Christian, Kent St. 2003-08
6	Bruce Pearl, Milwaukee 2004-05, Tennessee 06-08
6	Rick Pitino, Louisville 2003-08
4	Ronnie Arrow, A&M-Corpus Christi 2005-07, South Ala. 08
4	Bob Huggins, Cincinnati 2004-05, Kansas St. 07, West Virginia 08
4	Tom Izzo, Michigan St. 2005-08
4	Bob McKillop, Davidson 2005-08
4	Scott Sutton, Oral Roberts 2005-08
4	Roy Williams, North Carolina 2005-08
4	Jay Wright, Villanova 2005-08

MOST DIVISION I 30-WIN SEASONS

No.	Coach, Team and Seasons
9	Mike Krzyzewski, Army 1976-80, Duke 81-2008
8	Roy Williams, Kansas 1989-2003, North Carolina 04-08
6	Jim Calhoun, Northeastern 1973-86, Connecticut 87-2008
5	John Calipari, Massachusetts 1989-96, Memphis 2001-08
4	Rick Pitino, Boston U. 1979-83, Providence 86-87, Kentucky 90-97, Louisville 2002-08
3	Jim Boeheim, Syracuse 1977-2008
3	Ben Howland, Northern Ariz. 1995-99, Pittsburgh 2000-03, UCLA 04-08
3	Lute Olson, Long Beach St. 1974, Iowa 75-83, Arizona 84-2007
3	Bill Self, Oral Roberts 1994-97, Tulsa 98-2000, Illinois 01-03, Kansas 04-08
2	Rick Barnes, George Mason 1988, Providence 89-94, Clemson 95-98, Texas 99-2008
2	Billy Donovan, Marshall 1995-96, Florida 97-2008
2	Tom Izzo, Michigan St. 1996-2008

No.	Coach, Team and Seasons
2	Bo Ryan, Milwauee 2000-01, Wisconsin 02-08
2	Tubby Smith, Tulsa 1992-95, Georgia 96-97, Kentucky 98-2007, Minnesota 08

MOST TEAMS

No.	Coach, Team and Seasons
7	Tom Penders, Tufts 1972-74, Columbia 75-78, Fordham 79-86, Rhode Island 87-88, Texas 89-98, George Washington 99-2001, Houston 05-08
6	John Beilein, Nazareth 1983, Le Moyne 84-92, Canisius 93-97, Richmond 98-2002, West Virginia 03-07, Michigan 08
5	Mike Deane, Oswego St. 1981-82, Siena 87-94, Marquette 95-99, Lamar 2000-2003, Wagner 04-08
5	Bob Huggins, Walsh 1981-83, Akron 1985-89, Cincinnati 90-2005, Kansas St. 07, West Virginia 08
5	Pat Kennedy, Iona 1981-86, Florida St. 87-97, DePaul 98-2002, Montana 03-04, Towson 05-08
5	Lon Kruger, Tex.-Pan American 1983-86, Kansas St. 87-90, Florida 91-92, 94-96, Illinois 97-2000, UNLV 05-08
5	Ritchie McKay, Portland St. 1997-98, Colorado St. 99-2000, Oregon St. 01-02, New Mexico 03-07, Liberty 08
5	Rick Scruggs, North Greenville 1987-89, Belmont Abbey 90-91, Pikeville 92-94, Milligan 95, Gardner-Webb 96-2008
5	Jim Wooldridge, Central Mo. 1986-91, Texas St. 92-94, Louisiana Tech 95-98, Kansas St. 2001-06, UC Riverside 08
4	Steve Alford, Manchester 92-95, Missouri St. 96-99, Iowa 2000-07, New Mexico 08
4	Frankie Allen, Virginia Tech 1988-91, Tennessee St. 92-2000, Howard 01-05, Md.-East. Shore
4	Rick Barnes, George Mason 1988, Providence 89-94, Clemson 95-98, Texas 99-2008
4	Ben Braun, Siena Heights 1978-85, Eastern Mich. 86-96, California 97-2008, Rice
4	Keith Dambrot, Tiffin 1985-86, Ashland 90-91, Central Mich. 92-93, Akron 2005-08
4	Matt Doherty, Notre Dame 2000, North Carolina 01-03, Fla. Atlantic 06, SMU 07-08
4	Cliff Ellis, South Ala. 1976-84, Clemson 85-94, Auburn 95-2004, Coastal Caro. 08
4	Larry Eustachy, Idaho 1991-93, Utah St. 94-98, Iowa St. 99-2003, Southern Miss. 05-08
4	Tim Floyd, Idaho 1987-88, New Orleans 89-94, Iowa St. 95-98, Southern California 06-08
4	Travis Ford, Campbellsville 1998-2000, Eastern Ky. 01-05, Massachusetts 06-08, Oklahoma St.
4	Mike Jarvis, Boston U. 1986-90, George Washington 91-98, St. John's (N.Y.) 99-2004, Fla. Atlantic
4	Rick Majerus, Marquette 1984-86, Ball St. 88-89, Utah 90-2004, St. Louis 08
4	Greg McDermott, Wayne St. (Neb.) 1995-2000, North Dakota St. 01, UNI 02-06, Iowa St. 07-08
4	Jim Molinari, Northern Ill. 1990-91, Bradley 92-2002, Minnesota 07, Western Ill.
4	Rick Pitino, Boston U. 1979-83, Providence 86-87, Kentucky 90-97, Louisville 2002-08
4	Oliver Purnell, Radford 1989-91, Old Dominion 92-94, Dayton 95-2003, Clemson 04-08
4	Bill Self, Oral Roberts 1994-97, Tulsa 98-2000, Illinois 01-03, Kansas 04-08
4	Tubby Smith, Tulsa 1992-95, Georgia 96-97, Kentucky 98-2007, Minnesota 08
4	Rob Spivery, Montevallo 1986-95, Ashland 96, Alabama St. 97-2005, Southern U. 06-08
4	Al Walker, Colorado Col. 1989-93, Cornell 94-96, Chaminade 97-2000, Binghamton 01-08
4	Gary Williams, American 1979-82, Boston College 83-86, Ohio St. 87-89, Maryland 90-2008

All-Time Coaching Longevity Records

(Minimum 10 years as a Division I head coach)

MOST GAMES

No.	Coach, Team and Seasons
1,354	Jim Phelan, Mt. St. Mary's 1955-03
1,273	Bob Knight, Army 1966-71, Indiana 72-2000, Texas Tech 02-08
1,191	Lou Henson, Hardin-Simmons 1963-66, Illinois 76-96, New Mexico St. 67-75, 98-2005
1,180	Lefty Driesell, Davidson 1961-69, Maryland 70-86, James Madison 89-97, Georgia St. 1998-2003
1,133	Dean Smith, North Carolina 1962-97
1,132	Eddie Sutton, Creighton 1970-74, Arkansas 75-85, Kentucky 86-89, Oklahoma St. 91-2006, San Francisco 08
1,111	Jim Calhoun, Northeastern 1973-86, Connecticut 87-2008*
1,103	Henry Iba, Northwest Mo. St. 1930-33, Colorado 34, Oklahoma St. 35-70
1,102	Norm Stewart, UNI 1962-67, Missouri 68-99

No.	Coach, Team and Seasons
1,080	Marv Harshman, Pacific Lutheran 1946-58, Washington St. 59-71, Washington 72-85
1,078	Ray Meyer, DePaul 1943-84
1,072	Don Haskins, UTEP 1962-99
1,070	Mike Krzyzewski, Army 1976-80, Duke 81-2008*
1,066	Adolph Rupp, Kentucky 1931-52, 54-72
1,062	Hugh Durham, Florida St. 1967-78, Georgia 79-95, Jacksonville 98-2005
1,061	Ed Diddle, Western Ky. 1923-64
1,060	Lute Olson, Long Beach St. 1974, Iowa 75-83, Arizona 84-2007*
1,053	John Chaney, Cheyney 1973-82, Temple 83-2006
1,039	Ralph Miller, Wichita St. 1952-64, Iowa 65-70, Oregon St. 71-89
1,049	Jim Boeheim, Syracuse 1977-2008

active

MOST SEASONS

No.	Coach, Team and Seasons
50	Phog Allen, Baker 1906-08, Haskell 09, Central Mo. 13-19, Kansas 08-09, 20-56
49	Jim Phelan, Mt. St. Mary's 1955-03
46	Frank J. Hill, Seton Hall 1912-18, 20-30, Rutgers 16-43
42	Ed Diddle, Western Ky. 1923-64
42	Bob Knight, Army 1966-71, Indiana 72-2000, Texas Tech 02-08
42	Ray Meyer, DePaul 1943-84
41	Lefty Driesell, Davidson 1961-69, Maryland 70-86, James Madison 89-97, Georgia St. 98-2003
41	Lou Henson, Hardin-Simmons 1963-66, Illinois 76-96, New Mexico St. 67-75, 98-2005
41	Tony Hinkle, Butler 1927-42, 46-70
41	Henry Iba, Northwest Mo. St. 1930-33, Colorado 34, Oklahoma St. 35-70
41	Adolph Rupp, Kentucky 1931-52, 54-72
40	Marv Harshman, Pacific Lutheran 1946-58, Washington St. 59-71, Washington 72-85
39	Cal Luther, DePauw 1955-58, Murray St. 59-74, Longwood 82-90, Tenn.-Martin 91-99, Bethel (Tenn.) 2000
38	Fred Enke, Louisville 1924-25, Arizona 26-61
38	Don Haskins, UTEP 1962-99
38	Ralph Miller, Wichita St. 1952-64, Iowa 65-70, Oregon St. 71-89
38	Norm Stewart, UNI 1962-67, Missouri 68-99
37	Hugh Durham, Florida St. 1967-78, Georgia 79-95, Jacksonville 98-2005
37	Nat Holman, CCNY 1920-52, 55-56, 59-60
37	Norm Sloan, Presbyterian 1952-55, Citadel 57-60, North Carolina St. 67-80, Florida 61-66, 81-89
37	Eddie Sutton, Creighton 1970-74, Arkansas 75-85, Kentucky 86-89, Oklahoma St. 91-2006, San Francisco 08

active

MOST SEASONS AT ONE SCHOOL

No.	Coach, Team and Seasons
49	James Phelan, #Mt. St. Mary's 1955-2003
42	Ed Diddle, #Western Ky. 1923-64
42	Ray Meyer, #DePaul 1943-84
41	Tony Hinkle, #Butler 1927-42, 46-70
41	Adolph Rupp, #Kentucky 1931-52, 54-72
39	Phog Allen, Kansas 1908-09, 20-56
38	Don Haskins, #UTEP 1962-99
37	Nat Holman, #CCNY 1920-52, 55-56, 59-60
36	Fred Enke, Arizona 1926-61
36	Slats Gill, #Oregon St. 1929-64
36	Henry Iba, Oklahoma St. 1935-70
36	Dean Smith, #North Carolina 1962-97
36	Glenn Wilkes, #Stetson 1958-93
35	Howard Cann, #New York U. 1924-58
34	Nelson Norgren, #Chicago 1922-42, 45-57
32	Jim Boeheim, #Syracuse 1977-2008*
32	Norm Stewart, Missouri 1968-99
31	Doc Carlson, #Pittsburgh 1923-53
31	Taps Gallagher, #Niagara 1932-43, 47-65
31	Cy McClairen, #Bethune-Cookman 1962-66, 68-93

active; #has coached only at this school

COACHES WITH 100 OR MORE WINS AT FOUR DIVISION I SCHOOLS

Coach, Total Wins (Schools, Wins)

Lefty Driesell, 786 wins, 1961-86, 89-2003 (Davidson 176, Maryland 348, James Madison 159, Georgia St. 103)

COACHES WITH 100 OR MORE WINS AT THREE DIVISION I SCHOOLS

Coach, Total Wins (Schools, Wins)

Tom Davis, 581 wins, 1972-99, 2004-06 (Lafayette 116, Boston College 100, Iowa 270)
Hugh Durham, 633 wins, 1967-95, 98-2005 (Florida St. 230, Georgia 297, Jacksonville 106)
Cliff Ellis, 534 wins, 1976-2004 (South Ala. 171, Clemson 177, Auburn 186)
Mike Jarvis, 369 wins, 1986-2004 [Boston U. 101, George Washington 152, St. John's (N.Y.) 116]
Bob Knight, 902 wins, 1966-2000, 02-09 (Army 102, Indiana 662, Texas Tech 138)
Frank McGuire, 549 wins [St. John's (N.Y.) 102, North Carolina 164, South Carolina 283]
Jerry Tarkanian, 729 wins (Long Beach St. 116, UNLV 509, Fresno St. 104)
Billy Tubbs, 641 wins (Oklahoma 333, TCU 156, Lamar 121)
Butch van Breda Kolff, 482 wins (Lafayette 132, Hofstra 215, Princeton 103)

active.

COACHES WITH 200 OR MORE WINS AT TWO DIVISION I SCHOOLS

Coach, Total Wins (Schools, Wins)

Jim Calhoun, 774 wins, 1973-2008 (Northeastern 248, Connecticut 526)*
Hugh Durham, 633 wins, 1967-95 (Florida St. 230, Georgia 297)
Lou Henson, 779 wins, 1963-96, 98-2005 (Illinois 423, New Mexico St. 289)
Neil McCarthy, 431 wins, 1975-96 (Weber St. 205, New Mexico St. 226)
Ralph Miller, 657 wins, 1952-89 (Wichita St. 220, Oregon St. 342)
Johnny Orr, 466 wins, 1964-66, 69-94 (Michigan 209, Iowa St. 218)
Norm Sloan, 624 wins, 1952-55, 57-89 (Florida 232, North Carolina St. 266)
Eddie Sutton, 804 wins, 1972-89, 91-2006, 08 (Arkansas 260, Oklahoma 368)

* active.

MOST DIVISION I 20-WIN SEASONS

No.	Coach, Team and Seasons
30	Jim Boeheim, Syracuse 1977-2008*
30	Dean Smith, North Carolina 1962-97
29	Bob Knight, Army 1966-71, Indiana 72-2000, Texas Tech 02-08
29	Lute Olson, Long Beach St. 1974, Iowa 75-83, Arizona 84-2007*
25	Eddie Sutton, Creighton 1970-74, Arkansas 75-85, Kentucky 86-89, Oklahoma St. 91-2006, San Francisco 08
25	Jerry Tarkanian, Long Beach St. 1969-73, UNLV 74-92, Fresno St. 96-2002
24	Mike Krzyzewski, Army 1976-80, Duke 81-2008*
23	Adolph Rupp, Kentucky 1931-52, 54-72
22	Jim Calhoun, Northeastern 1973-86, Connecticut 87-2008*
22	Lefty Driesell, Davidson 1961-69, Maryland 70-86, James Madison 89-97, Georgia St. 1998-2003
21	Denny Crum, Louisville 1972-2001
20	Lou Henson, Hardin-Simmons 1963-66, Illinois 76-96, New Mexico St. 67-75, 99-2005
20	Bob Huggins, Walsh 1981-83, Akron 1985-89, Cincinnati 90-2005, Kansas St. 07, West Virginia 08*
19	John Thompson, Georgetown 1973-99
18	Lou Carnesecca, St. John's (N.Y.) 1966-92
18	Ed Diddle, Western Ky. 1923-64
18	Billy Tubbs, Southwestern (Tex.) 1972-73, Oklahoma 81-94, TCU 95-2002, Lamar 1977-80, 2004-06
18	Roy Williams, Kansas 1989-2003, North Carolina 04-2008*
18	John Wooden, Indiana St. 1947-48, UCLA 49-75
17	Don Haskins, UTEP 1962-99
17	Mike Montgomery, Montana 1979-86, Stanford 87-2004
17	Norm Stewart, UNI 1962-67, Missouri 1968-99

active

MOST CONSECUTIVE DIVISION I 20-WIN SEASONS

No.	Coach, Team and Seasons
27	Dean Smith, North Carolina 1971-97
20	Lute Olson, Arizona 1988-2007*
14	Jim Boeheim, Syracuse 1983-96*
15	Tubby Smith, Tulsa 1994-95, Georgia 96-97, Kentucky 98-2007, Minnesota 08*
14	Roy Williams, Kansas 1990-2003*
13	Denny Crum, Louisville 1972-84
13	John Thompson, Georgetown 1978-90
12	Mike Krzyzewski, Duke 1997-2008*
12	Billy Tubbs, Oklahoma 1982-93
11	Jim Boeheim, Syracuse 1998-2008*
11	Bob Huggins, Cincinnati 1992-2002
11	Mike Krzyzewski, Duke 1984-94*
11	Al McGuire, Marquette 1967-77
11	Jerry Tarkanian, Long Beach St. 1970-73, UNLV 74-80
11	Jerry Tarkanian, UNLV 1982-92
10	Dana Altman, Creighton 1999-2008*

No.	Coach, Team and Seasons
10	Everett Case, North Carolina St. 1947-56
10	Mike Montgomery, Stanford 1995-2004
10	G. Ott Romney, Montana St. 1924-28, BYU 29-33
10	Kelvin Sampson, Oklahoma 1998-2006, Indiana 07-08
10	Bill Self, Tulsa 1999-2000, Illinois 01-04, Kansas 04-08*
10	Eddie Sutton, Arkansas 1977-85, Kentucky 86

active

MOST DIVISION I 30-WIN SEASONS

No.	Coach, Team and Seasons
9	Mike Krzyzewski, Army 1976-80, Duke 1981-2008*
8	Roy Williams, Kansas 1989-2003, North Carolina 2004-08*
6	Jim Calhoun, Northeastern 1973-86, Connecticut 87-2008*
5	John Calipari, Massachusetts 1989-96, Memphis 2001-08*
4	Bob Knight, Army 1966-71, Indiana 1972-2000, Texas Tech 02-08
4	Rick Pitino, Boston U. 1979-83, Providence 86-87, Kentucky 1990-97, Louisville 2002-08*
4	Nolan Richardson, Tulsa 1981-85, Arkansas 1986-2002
4	Adolph Rupp, Kentucky 1931-52, 54-72
4	Jerry Tarkanian, Long Beach St. 1969-73, UNLV 1974-92, Fresno St. 96-2002
4	John Wooden, Indiana St. 1947-48, UCLA 1949-1975
3	Jim Boeheim, Syracuse 1977-2008*
3	Denny Crum, Louisville 1972-2001
3	Ben Howland, Northern Ariz. 1995-99, Pittsburgh 2000-03, UCLA 04-08*
3	Guy Lewis, Houston 1957-86
3	Mike Montgomery, Montana 1979-86, Stanford 1987-2004
3	Lute Olson, Long Beach St. 1974, Iowa 75-83, Arizona 1984-2007*
3	Bill Self, Oral Roberts 1994-97, Tulsa 98-2000, Illinois 01-03, Kansas 04-08*
3	Dean Smith, North Carolina 1962-97
3	Eddie Sutton, Creighton 1970-74, Arkansas 1975-85, Kentucky 86-89, Oklahoma St. 91-2006
3	John Thompson, Georgetown 1973-99
3	Billy Tubbs, Southwestern (Tex.) 1972-73, Oklahoma 1981-94, TCU 95-2002, Lamar 1977-80, 2004-06
2	Forddy Anderson, Drake 1947-48, Bradley 1949-54, Michigan St, 55-65, Hiram Scott 66-70
2	Rick Barnes, George Mason 1988, Providence 89-94, Clemson 95-98, Texas 99-2008*
2	Lou Carnesecca, St. John's (N.Y.) 1966-92
2	John Chaney, Cheyney 1973-82, Temple 1983-2006
2	Billy Donovan, Marshall 1995-96, Florida 97-2008*
2	Tom Izzo, Michigan St. 1996-2008*
2	Rick Majerus, Marquette 1984-86, Ball St. 88-89, Utah 1990-2004
2	G. Ott Romney, Montana St. 1923-28, BYU 29-35
2	Tubby Smith, Tulsa 1992-95, Georgia 96-97, Kentucky 1998-2007, Minnostota*

active

MOST TEAMS

No.	Coach, Team and Seasons
7	Ben Jobe, Talladega 1965-67, Alabama St. 68, South Carolina St. 69-73, Denver 79-80, Alabama A&M 83-86, Tuskegee 97-2000, Southern U. 1987-96, 2002-03
7	Tom Penders, Tufts 1972-74, Columbia 75-78, Fordham 79-86, Rhode Island 87-88, Texas 89-98, George Washington 99-2001, Houston 05-08*.
7	Elmer Ripley, Wagner 1923-25, Georgetown 28-29, 39-43, 47-49, Yale 30-35, Columbia 44-45, Notre Dame 46, John Carroll 50-51, Army 52-53

No.	Coach, Team and Seasons
7	Bob Vanatta, Central Methodist 1943, 48-50, Missouri St. 51-53, Army 54, Bradley 55-56, Memphis 57-62, Missouri 63-67, Delta St. 73
6	J.D. Barnett, Lenoir Rhyne 1970, High Point 71, Louisiana Tech 78-79, Va. Commonwealth 80-85, Tulsa 86-91, Northwestern St. 95-99
6	Gene Bartow, Central Mo. 1962-64, Valparaiso 65-70, Memphis 71-74, Illinois 75, UCLA 76-77, UAB 79-96
6	John Beilein, Nazareth 1983, Le Moyne 84-92, Canisius 93-97, Richmond 99-2002, West Virginia 03-07, Michigan 08*
6	Bill E. Foster, Bloomsburg 1961-63, Rutgers 64-71, Utah 72-74, Duke 75-80, South Carolina 81-86, Northwestern 87-93
6	George Keogan, Wis.-Superior 1913-14, St. Louis 16, St. Thomas (Minn.)18, Allegheny 19, Valparaiso 20-21, Notre Dame 24-43
6	Press Maravich, West Va. Wesleyan 1950, Davis & Elkins 51-52, Clemson 57-62, North Carolina St. 65-66, LSU 67-72, Appalachian St. 73-75
6	Harry Miller, Western St. 1953-58, Fresno St. 61-65, Eastern N.M. 66-70, North Texas 71, Wichita St. 72-78, Stephen F. Austin 79-88
6	Hal Wissel, TCNJ 1965-67, Lafayette 68-71, Fordham 72-76, Fla. Southern 78-82, Charlotte 83-85, Springfield 87-90
5	Ozzie Cowles, Carleton 1925-30, Wis.-River Falls 34-36, Dartmouth 37-43, 45-46, Michigan 47-48, Minnesota 49-59
5	Tom Davis, Lafayette 1972-77, Boston College 78-82, Stanford 83-86, Iowa 87-99, Drake 2004-07
5	Mike Deane, Oswego St. 1981-82, Siena 87-94, Marquette 95-99, Lamar 2000-03, Wagner 04-08*
5	Don DeVoe, Virginia Tech 1972-76, Wyoming 77-78, Tennessee 79-89, Florida 90, Navy 93-2004
5	Bill C. Foster, Shorter 1963-67, Charlotte 71-75, Clemson 76-84, Miami (Fla.) 86-90, Virginia Tech 92-97
5	Ron Greene, Loyola (La.) 1968-69, New Orleans 70-77, Mississippi St. 78, Murray St. 79-85, Indiana St. 86-89
5	Blair Gullion, Earlham 1928-35, Tennessee 36-38, Cornell 39-42, Connecticut 46-47, Washington-St. Louis 48-52, 54-59
5	Bob Huggins, Walsh 1981-83, Akron 85-89, Cincinnati 90-2005, Kansas St. 07, West Virginia 08*
5	Pat Kennedy, Iona 1981-86, Florida St. 87-97, DePaul 98-2002, Montana 03-04, Towson 05-08*
5	Lon Kruger, Tex.-Pan American 1983-86, Kansas St. 87-90, Florida 91-92, Illinois 97-2000, UNLV 05-08*
5	Tates Locke, Army 1964-65, Miami (Ohio) 67-70, Clemson 71-75, Jacksonville 79-81, Indiana St. 90-94
5	Ken Loeffler, Geneva 1929-35, Yale 36-42, Denver 46, La Salle 50-55, Texas A&M 56-57
5	Cal Luther, DePauw 1955-58, Murray St. 59-74, Longwood 82-90, Tenn.-Martin 91-99, Bethel (Tenn.) 2000
5	John Mauer, Kentucky 1928-30, Miami (Ohio) 31-38, Tennessee 39-43, 45-47, Army 48-51, Florida 52-60
5	Lynn Nance, Iowa St. 1977-80, Central Mo. 81-85, St. Mary's (Cal.) 87-89, Washington 90-93, Southwest Baptist 97-99
5	Norm Shepard, North Carolina 1924, Guilford 29, Randolph-Macon 30-36, Davidson 38-49, Harvard 50-54
5	Gordon Stauffer, Washburn 1967, Indiana St. 68-75, IPFW 76-79, Geneva 80-81, Nicholls 82-90
5	E.J. Stewart, Purdue 1909, Oregon St. 12-16, Nebraska 17-19, Texas 24-27, UTEP 28
5	Eddie Sutton, Creighton 1970-74, Arkansas 75-85, Kentucky 86-89, Oklahoma St. 91-2006, San Francisco 08
5	Tex Winter, Marquette 1952-53, Kansas St. 54-68, Washington 69-71, Northwestern 74-78, Long Beach St. 79-83
5	Jim Wooldrige, Central Mo. 1986-91, Texas St. 92-94, Louisana Tech 95-98, Kansas St. 2001-06, UC Riverside 08*

active

Division I Head Coaching Changes

Year	Teams	Chngs.	Pct.	1st Yr.	Year	Teams	Chngs.	Pct.	1st Yr.
1950	145	22	15.2	11	1963	178	24	13.5	15
1951	153	28	18.3	15	1964	179	23	12.8	17
1952	156	23	14.7	18	1965	182	15	8.2	8
1953	158	20	12.7	13	1966	182	24	13.2	20
1954	160	12	7.5	7	1967	185	33	17.8	18
1955	162	21	13.0	9	1968	189	26	13.8	16
1956	166	18	10.8	12	1969	193	29	15.0	19
1957	167	18	10.8	9	1970	196	29	14.8	17
1958	173	14	8.1	8	1971	203	30	14.8	17
1959	174	20	11.5	10	1972	210	37	17.6	21
1960	175	23	13.1	15	1973	216	38	17.6	24
1961	173	15	8.7	11	1974	233	41	17.6	23
1962	178	15	8.4	14					

Year	Teams	Chngs.	Pct.	1st Yr.	Year	Teams	Chngs.	Pct.	1st Yr.
1975	235	44	18.7	30	1992	298	39	13.1	15
1976	235	34	14.5	20	1993	298	34	11.4	15
1977	245	39	15.9	21	1994	301	33	11.0	17
1978	254	39	15.4	24	1995	302	58	19.2	28
1979	257	53	20.6	28	1996	305	42	13.8	31
1980	261	43	16.5	23	1997	305	52	17.0	29
1981	264	42	15.9	21	1998	306	63	20.6	31
1982	273	37	13.6	20	1999	310	45	14.5	30
1983	274	37	13.5	18	2000	318	55	17.3	27
1984	276	38	13.8	21	2001	318	53	16.7	31
1985	282	26	9.2	15	2002	321	47	14.6	22
1986	283	56	19.8	21	2003	325	44	13.5	29
1987	290	66	22.8	35	2004	326	46	14.1	20
1988	290	39	13.4	16	2005	326	40	12.3	25
1989	293	42	14.3	24	2006	326	47	14.4	25
1990	292	54	18.5	29	2007	325	61	18.8	35
1991	295	41	13.9	16	2008	328	63	19.2	28

Division I Coach of the Year

Season	United Press International	The Associated Press	U.S. Basketball Writers Assn.	National Assn. of Basketball Coaches	Naismith	The Sporting News	CBS/Chevrolet
1955	Phil Woolpert San Francisco						
1956	Phil Woolpert San Francisco						
1957	Frank McGuire North Carolina						
1958	Tex Winter Kansas St.						
1959	Adolph Rupp Kentucky		Eddie Hickey Marquette				
1960	Pete Newell California		Pete Newell California				
1961	Fred Taylor Ohio St.		Fred Taylor Ohio St.				
1962	Fred Taylor Ohio St.		Fred Taylor Ohio St.				
1963	Ed Jucker Cincinnati		Ed Jucker Cincinnati				
1964	John Wooden UCLA		John Wooden UCLA			John Wooden UCLA	
1965	Dave Strack Michigan		Bill van Breda Kolff Princeton				
1966	Adolph Rupp Kentucky		Adolph Rupp Kentucky			Adolph Rupp Kentucky	
1967	John Wooden UCLA	John Wooden UCLA	John Wooden UCLA			Jack Hartman Southern Ill.	
1968	Guy Lewis Houston	Guy Lewis Houston	Guy Lewis Houston			Guy Lewis Houston	
1969	John Wooden UCLA	John Wooden UCLA	Maury John Drake	John Wooden UCLA		John Wooden UCLA	
1970	John Wooden UCLA	John Wooden UCLA	John Wooden UCLA	John Wooden UCLA		Adolph Rupp Kentucky	
1971	Al McGuire Marquette	Al McGuire Marquette	Al McGuire Marquette	Jack Kraft Villanova		Al McGuire Marquette	
1972	John Wooden UCLA	John Wooden UCLA	John Wooden UCLA	John Wooden UCLA		John Wooden UCLA	
1973	John Wooden UCLA	John Wooden UCLA	John Wooden UCLA	Gene Bartow Memphis		John Wooden UCLA	
1974	Digger Phelps Notre Dame	Norm Sloan North Carolina St.	Norm Sloan North Carolina St.	Al McGuire Marquette		Digger Phelps Notre Dame	
1975	Bob Knight Indiana	Bob Knight Indiana	Bob Knight Indiana	Bob Knight Indiana		Bob Knight Indiana	
1976	Tom Young Rutgers	Bob Knight Indiana	Bob Knight Indiana	Johnny Orr Michigan		Tom Young Rutgers	
1977	Bob Gaillard San Francisco	Bob Gaillard San Francisco	Eddie Sutton Arkansas	Dean Smith North Carolina		Lee Rose Charlotte	
1978	Eddie Sutton Arkansas	Eddie Sutton Arkansas	Ray Meyer DePaul	Bill Foster Duke Abe Lemons Texas		Bill Foster Duke	
1979	Bill Hodges Indiana St.	Bill Hodges Indiana St.	Dean Smith North Carolina	Ray Meyer DePaul		Bill Hodges Indiana St.	
1980	Ray Meyer DePaul	Ray Meyer DePaul	Ray Meyer DePaul	Lute Olson Iowa		Lute Olson Iowa	
1981	Ralph Miller Oregon St.	Ralph Miller Oregon St.	Ralph Miller Oregon St.	Ralph Miller Oregon St. Jack Hartman Kansas St.		Dale Brown LSU	Dale Brown LSU
1982	Norm Stewart Missouri	Ralph Miller Oregon St.	John Thompson Georgetown	Don Monson Idaho		Ralph Miller Oregon St.	Gene Keady Purdue
1983	Jerry Tarkanian UNLV	Guy Lewis Houston	Lou Carnesecca St. John's (N.Y.)	Lou Carnesecca St. John's (N.Y.)		Denny Crum Louisville	Lou Carnesecca St. John's (N.Y)
1984	Ray Meyer DePaul	Ray Meyer DePaul	Gene Keady Purdue	Marv Harshman Washington		John Thompson Georgetown	Gene Keady Purdue
1985	Lou Carnesecca St. John's (N.Y.)	Bill Frieder Michigan	Lou Carnesecca St. John's (N.Y.)	John Thompson Georgetown		Lou Carnesecca St. John's (N.Y.)	Dale Brown LSU
1986	Mike Krzyzewski Duke	Eddie Sutton Kentucky	Dick Versace Bradley	Eddie Sutton Kentucky		Denny Crum Louisville	Mike Krzyzewski Duke
1987	John Thompson Georgetown	Tom Davis Iowa	John Chaney Temple	Rick Pitino Providence	Bob Knight Indiana	Rick Pitino Providence	Joey Meyer DePaul
1988	John Chaney Temple	John Chaney Temple	John Chaney Temple	John Chaney Temple	Larry Brown Kansas	John Chaney Temple	John Chaney Temple
1989	Bob Knight Indiana	Bob Knight Indiana	Bob Knight Indiana	P.J. Carlesimo Seton Hall	Mike Krzyzewski Duke	P.J. Carlisemo Seton Hall	Lute Olson Arizona
1990	Jim Calhoun Connecticut	Jim Calhoun Connecticut	Roy Williams Kansas	Jud Heathcote Michigan St.	Bobby Cremins Georgia Tech	Jim Calhoun Connecticut	Jim Calhoun Connecticut
1991	Rick Majerus Utah	Randy Ayers Ohio St.	Randy Ayers Ohio St.	Mike Krzyzewski Duke	Randy Ayers Ohio St.	Rick Pitino Kentucky	Randy Ayers Ohio St.
1992	Perry Clark Tulane	Roy Williams Kansas	Perry Clark Tulane	George Raveling Southern California	Mike Krzyzewski Duke	Mike Krzyzewski Duke	George Raveling Southern California
1993	Eddie Fogler Vanderbilt	Eddie Fogler Vanderbilt	Eddie Fogler Vanderbilt	Eddie Fogler Vanderbilt	Dean Smith North Carolina	Eddie Fogler Vanderbilt	Eddie Fogler Vanderbilt

COACHING RECORDS

Season	United Press International	The Associated Press	U.S. Basketball Writers Assn.	National Assn. of Basketball Coaches	Naismith	The Sporting News	CBS/Chevrolet
1994	Norm Stewart Missouri	Norm Stewart Missouri	Charlie Spoonhour St. Louis	Nolan Richardson Arkansas / Gene Keady Purdue	Nolan Richardson Arkansas	Norm Stewart Missouri	Nolan Richardson Arkansas
1995	Leonard Hamilton Miami (Fla.)	Kelvin Sampson Oklahoma	Kelvin Sampson Oklahoma	Jim Harrick UCLA	Jim Harrick UCLA	Jud Heathcote Michigan St.	Gene Keady Purdue
1996	Gene Keady Purdue	Gene Keady Purdue	Gene Keady Purdue	John Calipari Massachusetts	John Calipari Massachusetts	John Calipari Massachusetts	Gene Keady Purdue
1997		Clem Haskins Minnesota	Clem Haskins Minnesota	Clem Haskins Minnesota	Roy Williams Kansas	Roy Williams Kansas	Clem Haskins Minnesota
1998		Tom Izzo Michigan St.	Tom Izzo Michigan St.	Bill Guthridge North Carolina	Bill Guthridge North Carolina	Bill Guthridge North Carolina	Bill Guthridge North Carolina
1999		Cliff Ellis Auburn	Cliff Ellis Auburn	Mike Krzyzewski Duke	Mike Krzyzewski Duke	Cliff Ellis Auburn	Cliff Ellis Auburn
2000		Larry Eustachy Iowa St.	Larry Eustachy Iowa St.	Gene Keady Purdue	Mike Montgomery Stanford	Bob Huggins Cincinnati / Bill Self Tulsa	Mike Krzyzewski Duke
2001		Matt Doherty North Carolina	Al Skinner Boston College	Tom Izzo Michigan St.	Rod Barnes Mississippi	Al Skinner Boston College	Al Skinner Boston College
2002		Ben Howland Pittsburgh	Ben Howland Pittsburgh	Kelvin Sampson Oklahoma	Ben Howland Pittsburgh	Ben Howland Pittsburgh	Kelvin Sampson Oklahoma
2003		Tubby Smith Kentucky	Tubby Smith Kentucky	Tubby Smith Kentucky	Tubby Smith Kentucky	Tubby Smith Kentucky	Tubby Smith Kentucky
2004		Phil Martelli St. Joseph's	Phil Martelli St. Joseph's	Phil Martelli St. Joseph's / Mike Montgomery Stanford	Phil Martelli St. Joseph's	Mike Montgomery Stanford	Phil Martelli St. Joseph's
2005		Bruce Weber Illinois	Bruce Weber Illinois	Bruce Weber Illinois	Bruce Weber Illinois	Bruce Weber Illinois	Bruce Weber Illinois
2006		Roy Williams North Carolina	Roy Williams North Carolina	Jay Wright Villanova	Jay Wright Villanova	Bruce Pearl Tennessee	Jay Wright Villanova
2007		Tony Bennett Washington St.	Tony Bennett Washington St.	Todd Lickliter Butler	Tony Bennett Washington St.	Tony Bennett Washington St.	Tony Bennett Washington St.
2008		Keno Davis Drake	Keno Davis Drake	Bob McKillop Davidson	John Calipari Memphis	Keno Davis Drake	Keno Davis Drake

Adolph Rupp Cup: 2004-Phil Martelli, St. Joseph's; 2005-Bruce Weber, Illinois; 2006-Roy Williams, North Carolina; 2007-Bo Ryan, Wisconsin; 2008-Bruce Pearl, Tennessee.

Basketball Times **Coach of the Year:** 1982-Gale Catlett, West Virginia; 1983-Lou Carnesecca, St. John's (N.Y.); 1984-Jerry Tarkanian, UNLV; 1985-Bobby Cremins, Georgia Tech; 1986-Mike Krzyzewski, Duke; 1987-Wimp Sanderson, Alabama; 1988-Lute Olson, Arizona; 1989-Bob Knight, Indiana; 1990-Rick Pitino, Kentucky; 1991-Rick Majerus, Utah; 1992-Steve Fisher, Michigan; 1993-Dean Smith, North Carolina; 1994-Norm Stewart, Missouri; 1995-Eddie Sutton, Oklahoma St.; 1996-John Calipari, Massachusetts; 1997-Mike Krzyzewski, Duke; 1998-Bob Huggins, Cincinnati; 1999-Tom Izzo, Michigan St.; 2000-Mike Montgomery, Stanford; 2001-Al Skinner, Boston College; 2002-Bob Knight, Texas Tech; 2003-Tubby Smith, Kentucky; 2004-Mike Montgomery, Stanford; 2005-Bruce Weber, Illinois; 2006-Bruce Pearl, Tennessee; 2007-Tony Bennett, Washington St.; 2008-Keno Davis, Drake.

Jim Phelan Award: 2003-Mark Slonaker, Mercer; 2004-Phil Martelli, St. Joseph's; 2005-Tubby Smith, Kentucky; 2006-Ben Howland, UCLA; 2007- Tony Bennett, Washington St.; 2008-Bo Ryan, Wisconsin.

Legends of Coaching Award: 1999-Dean Smith, North Carolina; 2000-Mike Krzyzewski, Duke; 2001-Lute Olson, Arizona; 2002-Denny Crum, Louisville; 2003-Roy Williams, Kansas; 2004-Mike Montgomery, Stanford; 2005-Jim Calhoun, Connecticut; 2006-Jim Boeheim, Syracuse; 2007- Gene Keady, Purdue; 2008-Pat Summit, Tennessee (women's coach).

Divisions II and III Coach of the Year

NABC Division II Coach of the Year Award: 1962-James Phelan, Mt. St. Mary's; 1963-James Iverson, South Dakota St.; 1964-Arad McCutchan, Evansville; 1965-Arad McCutchan, Evansville; 1966-Guy Strong, Ky. Wesleyan; 1967-Clarence Gaines, Winston-Salem; 1968-Bob Polk, Trinity (Tex.); 1969-William Callahan, American Int'l; 1970-Lucias Mitchell, Kentucky St.; 1971-Bob Daniels, Ky. Wesleyan; 1972-Charles Moir, Roanoke; 1973-Bob Jones, Ky. Wesleyan; 1974-Bill Thomas, Missouri St.; 1975-Sonny Allen, Old Dominion; 1976-Herb McGee, Philadelphia U./Don Zech, Puget Sound; 1977-Ron Shumate, Chattanooga; 1978-John Chaney, Cheyney St.; 1979-Dave Buss, Green Bay; 1980-Hal Wissel, Fla. Southern; 1981-James Phelan, Mt. St. Mary's ; 1982-Mac Petty, Wabash ; 1983-Ralph Underhill, Wright St.; 1984-Lynn Nance, Central Mo.; 1985-Bill Jones, Jacksonville St.; 1986-Dave Bike, Sacred Heart; 1987-Wayne Chapman, Ky. Wesleyan; 1988-Don Doucette, Lowell; 1989-Michael Bernard, N.C. Central; 1990-Wayne Chapman, Ky. Wesleyan; 1991-Gary Elliott, North Ala.; 1992-Bruce Webster, Bridgeport; 1993-Pat Douglass, Cal St. Bakersfield; 1994-Pat Douglass, Cal St. Bakersfield; 1995-Bruce Pearl, Southern Ind.; 1996-Gary Garner, Fort Hays St.; 1997-Pat Douglass, Cal St. Bakersfield; 1998-Bob Williams, UC Davis; 1999-Ray Harper, Ky. Wesleyan; 2000-Mike Dunlap, Metro St.; 2001-Ray Harper, Ky. Wesleyan; 2002-Mike Dunlap, Metro St.; 2003-Larry Gipson, Northeastern St.; 2004-Tony Ingle, Kennesaw St.; 2005-Dave Robbins, Virginia Union; 2006-Mike Leaf, Winona St.; 2007-Ron Lievense, Barton; 2008-Mike Leaf, Winona St.

NABC Division III Coach of the Year Award: 1976-Bob Hamilton, Wittenberg; 1977-Larry Hunter, Wittenberg; 1978-Dan McCarrell, North Park; 1979-Dan McCarrell, North Park; 1980-Dan McCarrell, North Park; 1981-Jerry Welsh, SUNY Potsdam; 1982-Bobby Dye, Cal St. Bakersfield; 1983-Robert Bessoir, Scranton; 1984-Dave Vander Meulen, Wis.-Whitewater; 1985-Richard Sauers, Albany (N.Y.); 1986-Jerry Welsh, SUNY Potsdam; 1987-Bosco Djurickovic, North Park; 1988-Gene Mehaffey, Ohio Wesleyan; 1989-Dave Vander Meulen, Wis.-Whitewater; 1990-Michael Neer, Rochester (N.Y.); 1991-Bo Ryan, Wis.-Platteville; 1992-Ed Douma, Calvin; 1993-Joe Campoli, Ohio Northern; 1994-Pat Flannery, Lebanon Valley; 1995-Bo Ryan, Wis.-Platteville; 1996-John Giannini, Rowan; 1997-Dennie Bridges, Ill. Wesleyan; 1998-Bo Ryan, Wis.-Platteville; 1999-Bo Ryan, Wis.-Platteville; 2000-Kevin Vande Streek, Calvin; 2001-Mike Lonergan, Catholic; 2002-Dick Reynolds, Otterbein; 2003-David Paulsen, Williams; 2004-David Paulsen, Williams; 2005-Jeff Gamber, York (Pa.); 2006-Dave Macedo, Va. Wesleyan; 2007-David Hixon, Amherst; 2008-Mark Edwards, Washington-St. Louis.

Division II Coaching Records

Winningest Active Coaches

(Minimum five years as a head coach; includes record at four-year colleges only.)

BY PERCENTAGE

Coach, Team	Years	Won	Lost	Pct.
1. Greg Zimmerman, Alderson-Broaddus	7	172	49	.778
2. Rick Herdes, Southern Ind.	7	173	52	.769
3. Freddrell Watson, Benedict	5	113	36	.758
4. Danny Young, Montevallo	7	169	55	.754
5. Jeff Oliver, Cal St. San B'dino	6	131	43	.753
6. Don Meyer, Northern St.	36	891	299	.749
7. Ron Niekamp, Findlay	23	505	174	.744
8. Tom Kropp, Neb.-Kearney	18	389	148	.724
9. Brian Beaury, St. Rose	22	490	189	.722
10. Gordon Gibbons, Clayton St.	18	388	150	.721
11. Bob Chipman, Washburn	29	646	251	.720
12. Mike Leaf, Winona St.	10	226	89	.717
13. Herb Magee, Philadelphia U.	41	855	339	.716
14. Rick Cooper, West Tex. A&M	21	447	188	.704
15. Kim Anderson, Central Mo.	6	127	55	.698
16. Lonn Reisman, Tarleton St.	20	417	186	.692
17. Richard Schmidt, Tampa	27	548	245	.691
18. Luke D'Alessio, Bowie St.	9	184	83	.689
19. Mark Johnson, Fort Hays St.	7	138	66	.676
20. Stan Spirou, Southern N.H.	23	466	223	.676
21. Matt Margenthaler, Minn. St. Mankato	7	140	67	.676
22. Greg Kamansky, Cal Poly Pomona	8	153	74	.674
23. Jay Lawson, Bentley	17	338	164	.673
24. Steve Tappmeyer, Northwest Mo. St.	20	395	193	.672
25. Jeff Hironaka, Seattle Pacific	6	115	57	.669
26. Ken Wagner, BYU-Hawaii	18	343	171	.667
27. Greg Walcavich, Edinboro	27	509	260	.662
28. Kevin Schlagel, St. Cloud St.	12	216	113	.657
29. Tom Ryan, Eckerd	12	232	122	.655
30. Jeff Guiot, Southwest Baptist	7	135	71	.655
31. Terry Evans, Central Okla.	6	117	62	.654
32. Keith Dickson, St. Anselm	22	420	231	.645
33. Scott McMillin, Lynn	5	96	53	.644
34. Jim Baker, Catawba	14	262	145	.644
35. Jeff Ray, Midwestern St.	11	205	114	.643
36. Kevin Luke, Michigan Tech	14	260	145	.642
37. Fred Thompson, Millersville	10	183	104	.638
38. Dave Davis, Pfeiffer	17	309	178	.634
39. Bill Brown, California (Pa.)	22	383	224	.631
40. Tom Klusman, Rollins	28	502	296	.629
41. Jim Heaps, Mesa St.	12	208	123	.628
42. Brad Jackson, Western Wash.	23	424	251	.628
43. James Cosgrove, Adelphi	11	197	117	.627
44. Jeff Burkhamer, Armstrong Atlantic	6	111	66	.627
45. Darren Metress, Augusta St.	12	219	131	.626
46. Steve Joyner, Johnson C. Smith	21	379	227	.625
47. David McLaughlin, Stonehill	5	86	53	.619
48. Grady Brewer, Morehouse	8	140	87	.617
49. Bryan Poore, West Virginia St.	10	181	115	.611
50. Mike Ruane, Bridgeport	8	145	93	.609
51. Mike Sandifar, Oakland City	26	452	292	.608
52. Mark Corino, Caldwell	25	441	291	.602
53. Jeff Morgan, Harding	16	271	180	.601
54. Terry Sellers, Georgia College	15	254	171	.598
55. Greg Sparling, Central Wash.	14	220	149	.596
56. Ron Righter, Clarion	22	350	238	.595
57. Tom Smith, Mo. Western St.	33	555	385	.590
58. Bob Hofman, Fort Lewis	20	335	233	.590
59. Linc Darner, Fla. Southern	6	106	74	.589
60. Marty Bell, Quincy	5	87	61	.588
61. Larry Gipson, Northeastern St.	16	268	189	.586
62. Gene Iba, Pittsburg St.	28	468	339	.580
63. Ron Spry, Paine	28	453	332	.577
64. Gary Edwards, Francis Marion	24	404	297	.576
65. Dennis O'Donnell, St. Thomas Aquinas	17	291	215	.575
66. Stu Engen, Minn. St. Moorhead	16	243	180	.574
67. Bobby Champagne, North Ala.	5	86	64	.573
68. John Lentz, Lenior-Rhyne	25	402	301	.572
69. Lonnie Porter, Regis (Colo.)	31	490	367	.572
70. Roger Lyons, Ashland	15	235	177	.570

BY VICTORIES

(Minimum five years as a head coach; includes record at four-year colleges only.)

Coach, Team	Years	Won	Lost	Pct.
1. Don Meyer, Northern St.	36	891	299	.749
2. Herb Magee, Philadelphia U.	41	855	339	.716
3. Bob Chipman, Washburn	29	646	251	.720
4. Tom Smith, Mo. Western St.	33	555	385	.590
5. Richard Schmidt, Tampa	27	548	245	.691
6. Greg Walcavich, Edinboro	27	509	260	.662
7. Ron Niekamp, Findlay	23	505	174	.744
8. Tom Klusman, Rollins	28	502	296	.629
9. Brian Beaury, St. Rose	22	490	189	.722
Lonnie Porter, Regis (Colo.)	31	490	367	.572
11. Tim Hills, Northwest Nazarene	29	478	436	.523
12. Gene Iba, Pittsburg St.	28	468	339	.580
13. Stan Spirou, Southern N.H.	23	466	223	.676
14. Ron Spry, Paine	28	453	332	.577
15. Mike Sandifar, Oakland City	26	452	292	.608
16. Rick Cooper, West Tex. A&M	21	447	188	.704
17. Mark Corino, Caldwell	25	441	291	.602
18. Brad Jackson, Western Wash.	23	424	251	.628
19. Tom Wood, Humboldt St.	27	421	331	.560
20. Keith Dickson, St. Anselm	22	420	231	.645
21. Lonn Reisman, Tarleton St.	20	417	186	.692
22. Gary Edwards, Francis Marion	24	404	297	.576
Bert Hammel, Merrimack	28	404	391	.508
24. John Lentz, Lenoir-Rhyne	25	402	301	.572
25. Steve Tappmeyer, Northwest Mo. St.	20	395	193	.672
26. Tom Kropp, Neb.-Kearney	18	389	148	.724
27. Gordon Gibbons, Clayton St.	18	388	150	.721
28. Mike Nienaber, Christian Bros.	25	385	392	.495
29. Bill Brown, California (Pa.)	22	383	224	.631
30. Steve Joyner, Johnson C. Smith	21	379	227	.625
31. Jim Boone, Tusculum	22	360	278	.564
32. Gary Tuell, Nova Southeastern	21	356	270	.569
33. Ron Righter, Clarion	22	350	238	.595
34. Dean Ellis, Northern Mich.	22	346	273	.559
35. Ken Wagner, BYU-Hawaii	18	343	171	.667
36. Jay Lawson, Bentley	17	338	164	.673
37. Bob Hofman, Fort Lewis	20	335	233	.590
38. Greg White, Charleston (W.V.)	22	326	291	.528
39. Serge DeBari, Assumption	22	324	255	.560
40. Art Luptowski, American Int'l	19	311	235	.570
41. Dave Davis, Pfeiffer	17	309	178	.634
42. Steve Cox, Concord	19	306	244	.556
43. Bob Rukavina, Pitt.-Johnstown	19	302	212	.588
44. Lennie Acuff, Ala.-Huntsville	18	299	237	.558
45. Dale Clayton, Carson-Newman	20	295	268	.524
46. Dennis O'Donnell, St. Thomas Aquinas	17	291	215	.575
47. Robert Corn, Mo. Southern St.	19	290	248	.539
48. Ron Lievense, Barton	20	288	262	.524
49. Jeff Morgan, Harding	16	271	180	.601
Dan Schmotzer, Coker	21	271	296	.478
51. Larry Gipson, Northeastern St.	16	268	189	.586
52. Mike Newell, Ark.-Monticello	16	267	207	.563
53. Jim Baker, Catawba	14	262	145	.644
54. Kevin Luke, Michigan Tech	14	260	145	.642
55. Terry Sellers, Georgia College	15	254	171	.598
56. Joe Clinton, Dominican (N.Y.)	17	249	256	.493
57. Stu Engen, Minn. St. Moorhead	16	243	180	.574
58. Tony Robinson, Southeastern Okla.	17	242	232	.511
59. Roger Lyons, Ashland	15	235	177	.570
60. Dale Martin, Missouri S&T	21	234	327	.417
61. Tom Ryan, Eckerd	12	232	122	.655
62. Pat Fuscaldo, Sonoma St.	17	230	222	.509
63. Cesar Odio, Barry	14	227	173	.568
64. Mike Leaf, Winona St.	10	226	89	.717
65. Don Hogan, West Fla.	15	225	186	.547
66. Greg Sparling, Central Wash.	14	220	149	.596
67. Darren Metress, Augusta St.	12	219	131	.626
68. Kevin Schlagel, St. Cloud St.	12	216	113	.657
69. Jim Heaps, Mesa St.	12	208	123	.628
70. Gary Manchel, Mercyhurst	14	206	190	.520

COACHING RECORDS

Winningest Coaches All-Time

(Minimum 10 head coaching seasons in Division II)

BY PERCENTAGE

	Coach (Team coached, tenure)	Years	Won	Lost	Pct.
1.	Walter Harris (Philadelphia U. 1954-65, 67)	13	240	56	.811
2.	Dolph Stanley (Beloit 1946-57)	12	238	56	.810
3.	Ed Adams (N.C. Central 1936-37, Tuskegee 37-49, Texas Southern 50-58)	24	612	150	.803
4.	Dave Robbins (Virginia Union 1979-08)	30	713	194	.786
5.	Charles Christian (Norfolk St. 1974-78, 82-90)	14	318	95	.770
6.	Lucias Mitchell (Alabama St. 1964-67, Kentucky St. 68-75, Norfolk St. 79-81)	15	325	103	.759
7.	Mike Dunlap (Cal Lutheran 1990-94, Metro St. 98-06)	14	328	105	.758
8.	Dean Nicholson (Central Wash. 1965-90)	26	620	199	.757
9.	Don Meyer (Hamline 1973-75, Lipscomb 76-99, Northern St. 00-08)*	36	891	299	.749
10.	John Kochan (Millersville 1984-96)	13	285	96	.748
11.	Joe Hutton (Hamline 1932-65)	34	591	207	.741
12.	Ed Oglesby (Florida A&M 1951-70, 72)	21	386	138	.737
13.	John McLendon (N.C. Central 1941-52, Hampton 53-54, Tennessee St. 55-59, Kentucky St. 64-66, Cleveland St. 67-69)	25	496	179	.735
14.	Moco Mercer (Dubuque 1941-50)	10	119	43	.735
15.	Calvin Irvin (Johnson C. Smith 1948-51, N.C. A&T 55-72)	22	397	144	.734
16.	Garland Pinholster (Oglethorpe 1957-66)	10	180	68	.726
17.	Tom Kropp (Neb.-Kearney 1991-08)*	18	389	148	.724
18.	Brian Beaury (St. Rose 1987-08)*	22	490	189	.722
19.	Gordon Gibbons (South Fla. 1980; Fla. Southern 91-00, Clayton St. 2002-08)*	18	388	150	.721
20.	Bob Chipman (Washburn 1980-08)*	29	646	251	.720
21.	Albert Muyskens (Calvin 1936-45)	10	118	46	.720
22.	Bob Leaf (Winona St. 1999-08)*	10	226	89	.717
23.	Herb Magee (Philadelphia U. 1968-08)*	41	855	339	.716
24.	Fred Sefton (Akron 1916-24, 26-27)	11	103	42	.710
25.	Butch Haswell (Fairmont St. 1994-04)	11	226	93	.708
26.	Andrew Laska (Assumption 1952-67)	16	224	93	.707
27.	Al Shields (Bentley 1964-78)	15	257	107	.706
28.	Dave Boots (Augsburg 1983-88, South Dakota 89-08)*.	26	523	219	.705
29.	Rick Cooper (Wayland Baptist 1988-93; West Tex. A&M 94-08)*	21	447	188	.704
30.	Lou D'Allesandro (Southern N.H. 1964-70, 73-75)	10	183	77	.704
31.	Bill Boylan (Monmouth 1957-77)	21	368	155	.704
32.	Beryl Shipley (La.-Lafayette 1958-73)	16	293	126	.699
33.	Edwin Nihiser (Brockport 1929-34, 36-39, 41-42)	12	104	45	.698
34.	Ernest Hole (Wooster 1927-58)	32	412	181	.695
35.	Sam Cozen (Drexel 1953-68)	16	213	94	.694
36.	Barney Steen (Calvin 1954-66)	13	189	84	.692
37.	Lonn Reisman (Tarleton St. 1989-08)*	20	417	186	.692
38.	Richard Schmidt (Vanderbilt 1980-81, Tampa 84-08)*.	27	548	245	.691
39.	Ed Jucker (Merchant Marine 1946-47, Rensselaer 49-53, Cincinnati 61-65, Rollins 73-77) ..	17	266	109	.709
40.	Robert Rainey (Albany St. [Ga.] 1961-72)	12	243	112	.685
41.	Dick Sauers (Albany [N.Y.] 1956-87, 89-97)	41	702	330	.680
42.	Clem Leitch (North Dakota 1926-43)	18	224	106	.679
43.	Bill E. Jones (Florence St. 1973, North Ala. 74, Jacksonville St. 75-98)	26	477	226	.679
44.	Rutherford Baker (Albany [N.Y.] 1925-35)	11	63	30	.677
45.	Danny Rose (Central Mich. 1938-43, 47-54)	14	176	84	.677
46.	Stan Spirou (Southern N.H. 1986-08)*	23	466	223	.676
47.	Jay Lawson (Bentley 1992-08)*	17	338	164	.673
48.	Albin Schneidler (St. Joseph's [Ind.] 1912-25)	14	111	54	.673
49.	Dale Race (Milton 1976-79, Minn. Duluth 85-98)	18	363	177	.672
50.	Steve Tappmeyer (Northwest Mo. St. 1989-08)*	20	395	193	.672
51.	Russell Beichly (Akron 1941-59)	19	288	141	.671
52.	Steve Rives (Louisiana Col. 1986, Delta St. 87-06)	21	402	200	.668
53.	William Lucas (Central St. 1961-74)	14	241	120	.668
54.	Ken Wagner (BYU Hawaii 1991-08)	18	343	171	.667
55.	Fred Hobdy (Grambling 1957-86)	30	571	287	.666
56.	Paul Webb (Randolph-Macon 1957-75, Old Dominion 76-85)	29	511	257	.665
57.	Ken Bone (Cal St. Stanislaus 1985, Seattle Pacific 91-02, Portland St. 07-08)*	16	311	157	.665
58.	Ed Martin (South Carolina St. 1956-68, Tennessee St. 69-85)	30	501	253	.664
59.	Marlowe Severson (St. Cloud St. 1959-69, Minn. St. Mankato 70-73)	15	250	127	.663
60.	Don Zech (Puget Sound 1969-89)	21	386	197	.662
61.	Greg Walcavich (Birmingham-So. 1979-83, Rice 87, West Va. Wesleyan 88-89, Edinboro 90-08)*	27	509	260	.662
62.	Dave Buss (Green Bay 1970-82, Long Beach St. 84, St. Olaf 88-94)	21	381	195	.661
63.	Charles Chronister (Bloomsburg 1972-02)	31	559	288	.660
64.	Wayne Boultinghouse (Southern Ind. 1975-81; Ky. Wesleyan 91-96)	13	240	124	.659
65.	Donald Feeley (Sacred Heart 1966-78, Fairleigh Dickinson 81-83)	16	285	148	.658
66.	Kevin Schlagel (St. Cloud St. 1984, 98-08)*	12	216	113	.657
67.	Tom Ryan (Eckerd 1997-07)*	12	232	122	.655
68.	Roger Kaiser (West Ga. 1970-90)	21	387	204	.655
69.	Boyd King (Truman 1947-71)	25	377	199	.655
70.	Ernie Wheeler (Cal Poly 1973-86; Mont. St.-Billings 89-91)	17	314	166	.654

*Active coaches

BY VICTORIES

(Minimum 10 head coaching seasons in Division II)

	Coach (Team coached, tenure)	Years	Won	Lost	Pct.
1.	Don Meyer (Hamline 1973-75, Lipscomb 76-99, Northern St. 00-08)*	36	891	299	.749
2.	Herb Magee (Philadelphia U. 1968-08)*	41	855	339	.716
3.	Clarence Gaines (Winston-Salem 1947-93)	47	828	447	.649
4.	Jerry Johnson (LeMoyne-Owen 1959-05)	47	821	447	.647
5.	Dave Robbins (Virginia Union 1979-08)	30	713	194	.786
6.	Dick Sauers (Albany [N.Y.] 1956-87, 89-97)	41	702	330	.680
7.	Bob Chipman (Washburn 1980-08)*	29	646	251	.720
8.	John Lance (Southwestern Okla. 1919-22, Pittsburg St. 23-34, 36-63)	44	632	340	.650
9.	Ed Messbarger (Benedictine Hts. 1958-60, Dallas 61-63, St. Mary's [Tex.] 64-78, Angelo St. 79-98)	41	630	518	.549
10.	Dean Nicholson (Central Wash. 1965-90)	26	620	199	.757
11.	Ed Adams (N.C. Central 1936-37, Tuskegee 37-49, Texas Southern 50-58)	24	612	150	.803
12.	Joe Hutton (Hamline 1932-65)	34	591	207	.741
13.	Dom Rosselli (Youngstown St. 1941-42, 47-82)	38	590	387	.604
14.	Dan McCarrell, (North Park 1968-84, Minn. St. Mankato 85-01)	34	579	347	.625
15.	Fred Hobdy (Grambling 1957-86)	30	571	287	.666
16.	Charles Chronister (Bloomsburg 1972-02)	31	559	288	.660
17.	Ed Douma (Alma 1974, Lake Superior St. 75-78, Kent St. 79-82, UNC Greensboro 83-84, Calvin 85-96, Hillsdale 99-07)	32	555	302	.648
	Bill Knapton (Beloit 1958-97)	40	555	344	.617
	Tom Smith (Central Mo. 1976-80, Valparaiso 81-88, Mo. Western St. 89-08)*	33	555	385	.590
20.	Bruce Webster (Bridgeport 1966-99)	34	549	405	.575
21.	Richard Schmidt (Vanderbilt 1980-81, Tampa 84-08)*.	27	548	245	.691
22.	Dave Boots (Augsburg 1983-88, South Dakota 89-08)*	26	523	219	.705
23.	Arthur McAfee (Lane 1961, Mississippi Val. 62, Lincoln [Mo.] 63, Bishop 64-65, Morehouse 66-2000)	40	516	510	.503
24.	Arad McCutchan (Evansville 1947-77)	31	514	314	.621
	Jim Gudger (Western Caro. 1951-69, Tex. A&M-Commerce 70-83)	33	514	415	.553
25.	Paul Webb (Randolph-Macon 1957-75, Old Dominion 76-85)	29	511	257	.665
26.	Herbert Greene (Aub.-Montgomery 1976-77, Columbus St. 82-06)	27	510	270	.654
	Aubrey Bonham (Whittier 1938-43, 46-68)	29	510	285	.642
28.	Greg Walcavich (Birmingham-So. 1979-83, Rice 87, West Va. Wesleyan 88-89, Edinboro 90-08)*	27	509	260	.662
29.	Leo Nicholson (Central Wash. 1930-64)	33	505	281	.642
30.	Tom Klusman (Rollins 1981-08)*	28	502	296	.629
31.	Ed Martin (South Carolina St. 1956-68, Tennessee St. 69-85)	30	501	253	.664
	Bobby Vaughan (Elizabeth City St. 1952-66, 68-86)	34	501	363	.580
33.	Will Renken (Bloomfield 1948-52, Albright 56-88)	38	497	466	.516
34.	John McLendon (N.C. Central 1941-52, Hampton 53-54, Tennessee St. 55-59, Kentucky St. 64-66, Cleveland St. 67-69)	25	496	179	.735
35.	Ed Murphy (West Ala. 1979-83, Delta St. 84-86, Mississippi 87-92, West Ga. 94-07)	28	493	309	.615
36.	Brian Beaury (St. Rose 1987-08)*	22	490	189	.722
	Rich Glas (Minn.-Morris 1975-79, Willamette 80-84, North Dakota 89-06)	28	490	302	.619
	Lonnie Porter (Regis [Colo.] 1978-08)*	31	490	367	.572
39.	Angus Nicoson (Indianapolis 1948-76)	29	482	274	.638
40.	Hamlet Peterson (Luther 1923-65)	43	481	356	.575
41.	Bill Detrick (Central Conn. St. 1960-87, Coast Guard 90)	30	479	278	.633
42.	Bill E. Jones (Florence St. 1973, North Ala. 74, Jacksonville St. 75-98)	26	477	226	.679

Coach (Team coached, tenure)	Years	Won	Lost	Pct.
43. Dave Gunther (Wayne St. [Neb.] 1968-70, North Dakota 71-88, Buena Vista 94-95, Bemidji St. 96-01)	29	476	328	.592
44. Gene Iba (Houston Baptist 1978-85, Baylor 86-92, Pittsburg St. 96-08)*	28	468	339	.580
45. Tom Galeazzi (C.W. Post 1982-06)	25	467	259	.643
46. Stan Spirou (Southern N.H. 1986-08)*	23	466	223	.676
47. John Masi (UC Riverside 1980-05)	26	462	269	.632
48. Burt Kahn (Quinnipiac 1962-91)	30	459	355	.564
Richard Meckfessel (Charleston [W.V.] 1966-79, Mo.-St. Louis 83-99)	31	459	420	.522
Oliver Jones (Albany St. [Ga.] 1973-00, Tuskegee 01-04)	32	459	424	.520
51. Jim Seward (Wayne St. [Neb.] 1975-78, Ashland 79-83, Kansas Newman 84-87, Central Okla. 88-02)	28	454	339	.573
52. Ron Spry (Paine 1981-08)*	28	453	332	.577
53. Mike Sandifar (Averett 1979-81, Southwestern [Kan.] 82-87, Oakland City 88-99, 04-08)*	26	452	292	.608
54. Rick Cooper (Wayland Baptist 1988-93, West Tex. A&M 94-08)*	21	447	188	.704

Coach (Team coached, tenure)	Years	Won	Lost	Pct.
55. J.B. Scearce (North Ga. 1942-43, Cumberland 47, Ga. Southern 48-79)	26	447	244	.647
Butch Raymond (Augsburg 1971-73, Minn. St. Mankato 74-84, St. Cloud St. 85-97)	27	447	302	.597
57. Ron Shumate (Chattanooga 1973-79, Southeast Mo. St. 82-97)	23	445	232	.657
58. Tom Villemure (Detroit Business 1967, Grand Valley St. 73-96)	25	437	268	.620
59. James Dominey (Valdosta St. 1972-00)	29	436	343	.560
60. Hal Nunnally (Randolph-Macon 1976-99)	24	431	232	.650
Leonidas Epps (Clark Atlanta 1950-78)	29	431	291	.597
62. Ollie Gelston (New Jersey City 1960-67, Montclair St. 68-91)	32	429	347	.553
63. Brad Jackson (Western Wash. 1986-08)*	23	424	251	.628
64. L. Vann Pettaway (Alabama A&M 1987-08)*	22	421	229	.648
Tom Wood (Humboldt St. 1982-08)*	27	421	331	.560
66. Keith Dickson (St. Anselm 1987-08)*	22	420	231	.645
Jim Harley (Eckerd 1964-96)	32	420	349	.546
68. Irvin Peterson (Neb. Wesleyan 1949-51, 54-80)	30	419	314	.572
69. Lonn Reisman (Tarleton St. 1989-08)*	20	417	186	.692
Tom Feely (St. Thomas [Minn.] 1955-80)	26	417	269	.608

*active

Division III Coaching Records

Winningest Active Coaches

(Minimum five years as a head coach; includes record at four-year colleges only.)

BY PERCENTAGE

Coach, Team	Years	Won	Lost	Pct.
1. Steve Moore, Wooster	27	577	178	.764
2. Rob Kornaker, St. John Fisher	7	151	48	.759
3. Brian VanHaaften, Buena Vista	12	255	82	.757
4. David Macedo, Va. Wesleyan	8	175	57	.754
5. Glenn Van Wieren, Hope	31	618	203	.753
6. Pat Miller, Wis.-Whitewater	7	146	49	.749
7. Chris Harvey, Salem St.	6	125	43	.744
8. Brian Meehan, Brandeis	12	238	92	.721
9. Joe Cassidy, Rowan	12	230	89	.721
10. Mark Hanson, Gust. Adolphus	18	358	139	.720
11. Glenn Robinson, Frank. & Marsh.	37	730	284	.720
12. David Hixon, Amherst	31	577	226	.719
13. Jerry Rickrode, Wilkes	16	303	119	.718
14. Mike Rhoades, Randolph-Macon	9	177	70	.717
15. Stan Ogrodnik, Trinity (Conn.)	27	469	186	.716
16. J.P. Andrejko, King's (Pa.)	7	138	56	.711
17. Jim Hayford, Whitworth	9	177	73	.708
18. Bob Campbell, Western Conn. St.	24	463	193	.706
19. Greg Mason, Centre	9	169	71	.704
20. James Lancaster, Aurora	14	261	110	.704
21. C.J. Woollum, Chris. Newport	24	469	199	.702
22. Bill Foti, Colby-Sawyer	16	300	128	.701
23. Rob Colbert, Keene St.	9	178	76	.701
24. Randy Lambert, Maryville (Tenn.)	28	525	225	.700
25. Gerry Matthews, Richard Stockton	22	427	186	.697
26. Brian Baptiste, Mass.-Dartmouth	25	476	210	.694
27. Dave Niland, Penn St.-Behrend	14	264	118	.691
28. Bill Brown, Wittenberg	21	403	184	.687
29. Warren Caruso, Husson	14	278	127	.686
30. Bob Gillespie, Ripon	28	456	209	.686
31. Joe Nesci, New York U.	20	353	165	.681
32. Bosko Djurickovic, Carthage	22	398	187	.680
33. Steve Fritz, St. Thomas (Minn.)	28	509	240	.680
34. Chuck McBreen, Ramapo	10	186	90	.674
35. Jose Rebimas, Wm. Paterson	14	253	123	.673
36. Bill Harris, Wheaton (Ill.)	23	421	205	.673
37. Ryan Smith, Sewanee	5	94	46	.671
38. Mark Edwards, Washington-St. Louis	27	476	234	.670
39. Todd Raridon, North Central (Ill.)	19	332	166	.667
40. Mike Bokosky, Chapman	16	266	134	.665
41. Bob Gaillard, Lewis & Clark	27	485	247	.663
42. Kevin Small, Ursinus	8	145	74	.662
43. Kevin Van de Streek, Calvin	18	338	175	.659
44. Ted Van Dellen, Wis.-Oshkosh	18	316	165	.657
45. Rick Van Pelt, Messiah	5	86	45	.656
46. Mike McGrath, Chicago	9	152	80	.655
47. Dick Whitmore, Colby	37	590	314	.653

Coach, Team	Years	Won	Lost	Pct.
48. Chris Bartley, WPI	7	122	65	.652
49. Ron Holmes, McMurry	18	311	167	.651
50. Eric Bridgeland, Whitman	7	108	58	.651
51. John Baron, Gwynedd-Mercy	6	109	59	.649
52. Ken DeWeese, Mary Hardin-Baylor	10	171	93	.648
53. Page Moir, Roanoke	19	332	181	.647
54. Dick Peth, Wartburg	23	411	225	.646
55. Bill Nelson, Johns Hopkins	28	472	259	.646
56. Nelson Whitmore, Hamline	10	184	101	.646
57. Mike Moran, John Carroll	16	283	158	.642
58. Scott Coval, DeSales	15	256	144	.640
59. Carl Danzig, Scranton	7	120	69	.635
60. Mike Neer, Rochester	32	532	307	.634
61. Bill Fenlon, DePauw	23	376	217	.634
62. Chris Carideo, Widener	7	123	71	.634
63. Tom Palombo, Guilford	11	190	110	.633
64. Dick Reynolds, Otterbein	36	618	359	.633
65. Mark Scherer, Elmhurst	12	193	113	.631
66. Ken Scalmanini, Claremont-M-S.	10	157	93	.628
67. David Schultz, Carroll (Wis.)	6	93	56	.624
68. Mike Turner, Albion	34	527	319	.623
69. Rich Rider, Cal Lutheran	23	365	225	.619
70. Paul Phillips, Clark (Mass.)	20	329	203	.618

BY VICTORIES

(Minimum five years as a head coach; includes record at four-year colleges only.)

Coach, Team	Years	Won	Lost	Pct.
1. Glenn Robinson, Frank. & Marsh.	37	730	284	.720
2. Jim Smith, St. John's (Minn.)	44	685	475	.591
3. Glenn Van Wieren, Hope	31	618	203	.753
4. Dick Reynolds, Otterbein	36	618	359	.633
5. Dick Whitmore, Colby	37	590	314	.653
6. Steve Moore, Wooster	27	577	178	.764
7. David Hixon, Amherst	31	577	226	.719
8. Mike Neer, Rochester	32	532	307	.634
9. Mike Turner, Albion	34	527	319	.623
10. Randy Lambert, Maryville (Tenn.)	28	525	225	.700
11. Steve Fritz, St. Thomas (Minn.)	28	509	240	.680
12. Mac Petty, Wabash	35	492	390	.558
13. Lee McKinney, Fontbonne	30	486	354	.579
14. Bob Gaillard, Lewis & Clark	27	485	247	.663
15. Brian Baptiste, Mass.-Dartmouth	25	476	210	.694
Mark Edwards, Washington-St. Louis	27	476	234	.670
17. Bill Nelson, Johns Hopkins	28	472	259	.646
18. Stan Ogrodnik, Trinity (Conn.)	27	469	186	.716
C.J. Woollum, Chris. Newport	24	469	199	.702
20. Bob Campbell, Western Conn. St.	24	463	193	.706
21. Bob Gillespie, Ripon	28	456	209	.686
22. Herb Hilgeman, Rhodes	32	455	328	.581
23. Bob McVean, Rochester Inst.	30	438	326	.573
24. Jeff Gamber, York (Pa.)	31	429	379	.531
25. Gerry Matthews, Richard Stockton	22	427	186	.697
26. Bill Harris, Wheaton (Ill.)	23	421	205	.673

Coach, Team	Years	Won	Lost	Pct.
27. Dick Peth, Wartburg	23	411	225	.646
28. Kerry Prather, Franklin	25	408	268	.604
29. Bill Brown, Wittenberg	21	403	184	.687
30. Peter Barry, Coast Guard	26	401	302	.570
31. Bosko Djurickovic, Carthage	22	398	187	.680
32. Jim Walker, Moravian	29	386	345	.528
33. Charlie Brock, Springfield	28	380	349	.521
34. Bill Fenlon, DePauw	23	376	217	.634
35. Jonathon Halpert, Yeshiva	36	367	446	.451
36. Rich Rider, Cal Lutheran	23	365	225	.619
37. Mike Griffin, Rensselaer	31	360	419	.462
38. Mark Hanson, Gust. Adolphus	18	358	139	.720
Ed Andrist, Wis.-Stout	19	358	288	.554
39. Joe Nesci, New York U.	20	353	165	.681
40. Dick Meader, Me.-Farmington	32	350	415	.458
41. Gordie James, Willamette	21	345	219	.612
42. Ray Rankis, Baruch	25	344	322	.517
43. Kevin Van de Streek, Calvin	18	338	175	.659
44. Todd Raridon, North Central (Ill.)	19	332	166	.667
Page Moir, Roanoke	19	332	181	.647
46. Pat Cunningham, Trinity (Tex.)	20	313	225	.582
47. Paul Phillips, Clark (Mass.)	20	329	203	.618
48. Guy Kalland, Carleton	24	329	282	.538
49. Charles Katsiaficas, Pomona-Pitzer	21	328	212	.607
50. Bruce Wilson, Simpson	23	328	268	.550
51. Tim Gilbride, Bowdoin	23	320	242	.569
52. Ted Van Dellen, Wis.-Oshkosh	18	316	165	.657
53. Ron Holmes, McMurry	18	311	167	.651
54. Ted Fiore, Montclair St.	19	305	213	.589
55. Mike Daley, Nazareth	22	304	269	.531
56. Jerry Rickrode, Wilkes	16	303	119	.718
57. Brian Newhall, Occidental	20	302	202	.599
58. Bill Foti, Colby-Sawyer	16	300	128	.701
59. Robert Sheldon, Tufts	20	299	203	.596
60. Dave Madeira, Muhlenburg	21	295	236	.556
61. Anthony Petosa, Staten Island	18	289	202	.589
62. Larry Doty, Staten Island	21	288	263	.523
63. Mike Moran, John Carroll	16	283	158	.642
64. Ronald St. John, York (N.Y.)	20	282	253	.527
65. Warren Caruso, Husson	14	278	127	.686
66. Robert Schlosser, Elizabethtown	18	278	187	.598
67. Mark Boyle, Marian (Wis.)	20	275	278	.497
68. Gene Rushing, Louisiana Col.	22	267	324	.452
69. Buck Riley, Adrian	26	267	383	.411
70. Mike Bokosky, Chapman	16	266	134	.665

Winningest Coaches All-Time

(Minimum 10 head coaching seasons in Division III)

BY PERCENTAGE

Coach (Team coached, tenure)	Years	Won	Lost	Pct.
1. Bo Ryan (Wis.-Platteville 1985-99, Milwaukee 00-01, Wisconsin 02-08)*	24	556	163	.773
2. Steve Moore (Muhlenberg 1982-87, Wooster 88-08)*	27	577	178	.764
3. Jim Borcherding (Augustana [Ill.] 1970-84)	15	313	100	.758
4. Harry Sheehy (Williams 1984-00)	17	324	104	.757
5. Brian VanHaaften (Buena Vista 1997-08)*	12	255	82	.757
6. Glenn Van Wieren (Hope 1978-08)*	31	618	203	.753
7. Rick Simonds (St. Joseph's [Me.] 1980-03)	23	463	176	.725
8. Brian Meehan (Salem St. 1997-03, Brandeis 04-08)*	12	238	92	.721
9. Joe Cassidy (Rowan 1997-08)*	12	230	89	.721
10. Mark Hanson (Gust. Adolphus 1991-08)*	18	358	139	.720
11. Glenn Robinson (Frank. & Marsh. 1972-08)*	37	730	284	.720
12. Dave Darnall (Eureka 1975-94)	20	383	150	.719
13. David Hixon (Amherst 1978-08)*	31	577	226	.719
14. Jerry Rickrode (Wilkes 1993-08)*	16	303	119	.718
15. Stan Ogrodnik (Trinity [Conn.] 1982-08)*	27	469	186	.716
16. Joe Campoli (Ohio Northern 1993-05)	13	254	101	.715
17. Bob Ward (St. John Fisher 1988-01)	14	261	106	.711
18. James Catalano (NJIT 1980-01)	22	431	176	.710
19. Jerry Welsh (SUNY Potsdam 1969, 71-91, Iona 92-95)	26	502	205	.710
20. Dave Vander Meulen (Wis.-Whitewater 1979-01)	23	440	182	.707
21. Bob Campbell (Western Conn. St. 1985-08)*	24	463	193	.706
22. Mike Lonergan (Catholic 1993-04, Vermont 06-08)*	15	305	128	.704
23. James Lancaster (Aurora 1995-08)*	14	261	110	.704
24. C.J. Woollum (Chris. Newport 85-08)*	24	469	199	.702
25. Bill Foti (Colby-Sawyer 1993-08)*	16	300	128	.701
26. Randy Lambert (Maryville [Tenn.] 1981-08)*	28	525	225	.700
27. John Reynders (Allegheny 1980-89)	10	180	78	.698

Coach (Team coached, tenure)	Years	Won	Lost	Pct.
28. Gerry Mathews (Richard Stockton 1986-94, 96-08)*	22	427	186	.697
29. Lewis Levick (Wartburg 1966-93)	28	510	225	.694
30. Brian Baptiste (Mass.-Dartmouth 1984-08)*	25	476	210	.694
31. Tom Murphy (Hamilton 1971-04, SUNYIT 06)	35	618	274	.693
32. Dave Niland (Penn St.-Behrend 1995-08)*	14	264	118	.691
33. John Dzik (Cabrini 1981-05)	25	481	216	.690
34. Jim Todd (Fitchburg St. 1978-79, Salem St. 88-96)	11	207	93	.690
35. Charles Brown (New Jersey City 1983-07)	25	483	218	.689
36. Bill Brown (Wooster 1983, Kenyon 84-88, Wittenberg 94-08)*	21	403	184	.687
37. David Paulsen (St. Lawrence 1995-97, Le Moyne 98-00, Williams 01-08)*	14	262	120	.686
38. Bob Gillespie (Ripon 1981-08)*	28	456	209	.686
39. Joe Nesci (New York U. 1989-08)*	20	353	165	.681
40. Bosko Djurickovic (North Park 1985-94, Carthage 97-08)*	22	398	187	.680
41. Richard Bihr (Buffalo St. 1980-99, 01-05)	25	449	211	.680
42. Steve Fritz (St. Thomas [Minn.] 1981-08)*	28	509	240	.680
43. Bob Bessoir (Scranton 1973-01)	29	554	263	.678
44. Dennie Bridges (Ill. Wesleyan 1966-01)	36	666	320	.675
45. Chuck McBreen (Ramapo 1999-08)*	10	186	90	.674
46. Jose Rebimbas (Montclair St. 1995, Wm. Paterson 96-08)*	14	253	123	.673
47. Bill Harris (King's [N.Y.] 1986-91, Wheaton [Ill.] 92-08)*	23	421	205	.673
48. John McCloskey (Alvernia 1992-97, 99-04)	12	227	111	.672
49. Mark Edwards (Washington-St. Louis 1982-08)*	27	476	234	.670
50. Todd Raridon (Neb. Wesleyan 1990-04, North Central [Ill.] 05-08)*	19	332	166	.667
51. Naylond Hayes (Rust 1970-88)	18	338	169	.667
52. Mike Bokosky (Chapman 1993-08)*	16	266	134	.665
53. Bob Gaillard (San Francisco 1971-78, Lewis & Clark 90-08)*	27	485	247	.663
54. Kevin Van de Streek (Sioux Falls 1991-96, Calvin 97-08)*	18	338	175	.659
55. Tony Shaver (Hampden-Sydney 1987-03, William & Mary 04-08)*	22	413	214	.659
56. Ted Van Dellen (Wis.-Oshkosh 1991-08)*	18	316	165	.657
57. Dick Whitmore (Colby 1971-01, 03-08)*	37	590	314	.653
58. Rudy Marisa (Waynesburg 1970-03)	34	563	300	.652
59. Ron Holmes (McMurry 1991-08)*	18	311	167	.651
60. Nick Lambros (Hartwick 1978-98)	21	352	191	.648
61. Page Moir (Roanoke 1990-08)*	19	332	181	.647
62. Bill Nelson (Rochester Inst. 1981-83, Nazareth 84-86, Johns Hopkins 87-08)*	28	472	259	.646
63. Nelson Whitmore (Brockport 1999-07, Hamline 08)*	10	184	101	.646
64. Mike Beitzel (Northern Ky. 1981-88, Hanover 89-08)*	28	494	275	.642
65. Mike Moran (John Carroll 1993-08)*	16	283	158	.642
66. John Tharp (Lawrence 1995-07, Hillsdale 08)*	14	217	122	.640
67. Scott Coval (DeSales 1994-08)*	15	256	144	.640
68. Doug Riley (St. Andrews 1978-86, Plattsburgh St. 87, Armstrong Atlantic 88-92)	15	245	139	.638
69. Mike Neer (Rochester 1977-08)*	32	532	307	.634
70. Bill Fenlon (Sewanee 1986-88, Rose-Hulman 89-91, Southwestern [Tex.] 92, DePauw 93-08)*	23	376	217	.634

*active

BY VICTORIES
(Minimum 10 head coaching seasons in Division III)

Coach (Team coached, tenure)	Years	Won	Lost	Pct.
1. Glenn Robinson (Frank. & Marsh. 1972-08)*	37	730	284	.720
2. Jim Smith (St. John's [Minn.] 1965-08)*	44	685	475	.591
3. Dennie Bridges (Ill. Wesleyan 1966-01)	36	666	320	.675
4. Glenn Van Wieren (Hope 1978-08)*	31	618	203	.753
Tom Murphy (Hamilton 1971-04, SUNYIT 06)	35	618	274	.693
Dick Reynolds (Otterbein 73-08)*	36	618	359	.633
7. Dick Whitmore (Colby 1971-01, 03-08)*	37	590	314	.653
8. Steve Moore (Muhlenberg 1982-87, Wooster 88-08)*	27	577	178	.764
David Hixon (Amherst 1978-08)*	31	577	226	.719
10. Rudy Marisa (Waynesburg 1970-03)	34	563	300	.652
11. Bo Ryan (Wis.-Platteville 1985-99, Milwaukee 00-01, Wisconsin 02-08)*	24	556	163	.773
12. Bob Bessoir (Scranton 1973-01)	29	554	263	.678
13. Jim Burson (Muskingum 1968-05)	38	543	425	.561
14. C. Alan Rowe (Widener 1966-98)	33	536	324	.623
15. Mike Neer (Rochester 1977-08)*	32	532	307	.634
16. Mike Turner (Albion 1975-08)*	34	527	319	.623
17. Randy Lambert (Maryville [Tenn.] 1981-08)*	28	525	225	.700
Gene Mehaffey (Carson-Newman 1968-78, Ohio Wesleyan 80-99)	31	525	384	.578
19. Lewis Levick (Wartburg 1966-93)	28	510	225	.694
20. Steve Fritz (St. Thomas [Minn.] 1981-08)*	28	509	240	.680

Coach (Team coached, tenure)	Years	Won	Lost	Pct.
21. Jerry Welsh (SUNY Potsdam 1969, 71-91, Iona 92-95)	26	502	205	.710
22. Jon Davison (Dubuque 1967-93, Clarke 97-07)*	38	499	478	.511
23. Mike Beitzel (Northern Ky. 1981-88, Hanover 89-08)	28	494	275	.642
24. Mac Petty (Sewanee 1974-76, Wabash 77-08)*	35	492	390	.558
25. Lee McKinney (Mo. Baptist 1979-88, Fontbonne 89-08)*	30	486	354	.579
26. Bob Gaillard (San Francisco 1971-78 Lewis & Clark 90-08)*	27	485	247	.663
27. Charles Brown (New Jersey City 1983-07)	25	483	218	.689
28. John Dzik (Cabrini 1981-05)	25	481	216	.690
29. Brian Baptiste (Mass.-Dartmouth 1984-08)*	25	476	210	.694
Mark Edwards (Washington-St. Louis 1982-08)*	27	476	234	.670
31. Bill Nelson (Rochester Inst. 1981-83, Nazareth 84-86, Johns Hopkins 87-08)*	28	472	259	.646
32. Stan Ogrodnik (Trinity [Conn.] 1982-08)*	27	469	186	.716
C.J. Woollum (Chris. Newport 1985-08)*	24	469	199	.702
Terry Glasgow (Monmouth [Ill.] 1973-07)	35	469	313	.600
35. Rick Simonds (St. Joseph's [Me.] 1980-03)	23	463	176	.725
Bob Campbell (Western Conn. St. 1985-08)*	24	463	193	.706
Cliff Garrison (Hendrix 1973-03)	31	463	376	.552
38. Verne Canfield (Wash. & Lee 1965-95)	31	460	337	.577
39. Bob Gillespie (Ripon 1981-08)*	28	456	209	.686

Coach (Team coached, tenure)	Years	Won	Lost	Pct.
40. Herb Hilgeman (Rhodes 1977-08)*	32	455	328	.581
41. Gary Smith (Redlands 1972-07)	36	450	467	.491
42. Richard Bihr (Buffalo St. 1980-99, 01-05)	25	449	211	.680
43. Dave Vander Meulen (Wis.-Whitewater 1979-01)	23	440	182	.707
44. Bob McVean (Eisenhower 1979-83, Rochester Inst. 84-08)*	30	438	326	.573
45. James Catalano (NJIT 1980-01)	22	431	176	.710
46. Ollie Gelston (New Jersey City 1960-67, Montclair St. 68-91)	32	429	347	.553
Jeff Gamber (York [Pa.] 1978-08)*	31	429	379	.531
48. Gerry Mathews (Richard Stockton 1986-94, 96-08)*	22	427	186	.697
49. Leon Richardson (Ozarks [Ark.] 1956, Dubuque 58-59, Drury 60-65, William Penn 75-02)	37	422	459	.479
50. Bill Harris (King's [N.Y.] 1986-91, Wheaton (Ill.) 92-08)*.	23	421	205	.673
51. Steve Bankston (Baldwin-Wallace 1981-08)	28	419	329	.560
52. Tony Shaver (Hampden-Sydney 1987-03, William & Mary 04-08)*	22	413	214	.659
Don Smith (Elizabethtown 1955-64, Bucknell 65-72, Elizabethtown 73-88)	34	413	381	.520
54. Kerry Prather (Franklin 1984-08)*	25	408	268	.604
55. Bill Brown (Wooster 1983, Kenyon 84-88, Wittenberg 94-08)*	21	403	184	.687

active

Attendance Records

Attendance

2008 Attendance Summary

(For All NCAA Varsity Teams)

	Total Teams	Games or Sessions	2008 Attendance	Avg.	Change in Total	Change in Avg.
Home Attendance, NCAA Division I	*328	*4,844	*25,793,112	5,325	568,991	-2
NCAA Championship Tournament		35	*763,607	*21,817	66,615	1,903
Other Division I Neutral-Site Attendance		214	1,579,182	7,379	-205,617	-589
NCAA DIVISION I TOTALS	***328**	***5,093**	***28,135,901**	**5,524**	**429,989**	**-24**
Home Attendance, NCAA Division II	^258	3,538	2,700,151	763	-192,669	-52
Home Attendance, NCAA Division III	388	*4,637	1,973,368	426	25,638	-4
Reclassifying Teams	*43	*491	*386,928	788	--	--
Neutral-Site Attendance for Divisions II & III		179	*170,149	951	--	--
NCAA Division II Tournament Neutral Sites		14	23,207	1,658	--	--
NCAA Division III Tournament Neutral Sites		6	6,612	1,102	--	--
NATIONAL TOTALS FOR 2008	***1,017**	***13,958**	***33,396,316**	**2,393**	**560,453**	**-56**

*Record high. NOTES: The Neutral-Site Attendance for Divisions II and III does not include the NCAA tournaments. The total attendance for the Division II Tournament was 75,225 for a 2,090 average over 36 sessions and the Division III Tournament was 54,231 for a 1,291 average over 42 sessions.

^ Division II attendance figures do not include five NCAA Puerto Rican schools.

Division I Championship Tournament

Round	Site	Att.	Site	Att.	Site	Att.	Site	Att.
Opening Round	Dayton	8,464						
First Round	Anaheim	17,600	Denver	19,282	Omaha	17,162	Tampa	15,328
	Anaheim	17,600	Denver	19,010	Omaha	17,839	Tampa	15,920
	Birmingham	14,420	Little Rock	16,060	Raleigh	19,477	Washington	18,400
	Birmingham	14,315	Little Rock	16,060	Raleigh	19,477	Washington	18,400
Second Round	Anaheim	17,600	Denver	19,299	Omaha	17,162	Tampa	14,504
	Birmingham	14,606	Little Rock	16,060	Raleigh	19,477	Washington	18,400
Regional Semifinals	Charlotte	19,092	Detroit	57,028	Houston	32,931	Phoenix	18,103
Regional Finals	Charlotte	19,092	Detroit	57,563	Houston	32,798	Phoenix	18,103

Final Four

National Semifinal	San Antonio	43,718
National Final	San Antonio	43,257
Final Four Total		86,975
Total Tournament Attendance		**763,607**
Average Per Session		**21,817**

All Division I Conferences

	Total Teams	Games or Sessions	Entire Season 2008 Attendance	Average	Change In Avg.	Conference Tournament Total Sessions	Total Attendance	Average
1. Big Ten	11	194	2,517,685	12,978	218	5	80,012	16,002
2. Southeastern	12	211	2,561,545	12,140	168	7	73,942	10,563
3. Atlantic Coast	12	209	2,355,822	11,272	154	6	120,210	20,035
4. Big East	16	274	3,054,190	11,147	-17	6	117,372	19,562
5. Big 12	12	216	*2,374,927	*10,995	276	6	113,254	18,876
6. Pacific-10	10	176	*1,573,505	8,940	416	5	81,809	16,362
7. Mountain West	9	146	1,218,466	8,346	48	5	51,899	10,380
8. Missouri Valley	10	168	1,323,352	7,877	-143	5	64,551	12,910
9. Atlantic 10	14	212	*1,252,485	5,908	484	6	34,636	5,773
10. Conference USA	12	207	1,194,432	5,770	717	6	70,073	11,679
11. Western Athletic	9	146	833,675	5,710	-920	5	36,950	7,390
12. Colonial	12	174	*668,418	3,841	140	6	42,160	7,027
13. Horizon#	10	152	544,112	3,580	-110	7	20,021	2,860
14. Mid-American	12	165	498,736	3,023	-122	5	38,036	7,607
15. Sun Belt	13	201	606,814	3,019	620	9	35,014	3,890
16. West Coast	8	111	309,587	2,789	99	4	20,400	5,100
17. Southern	11	156	388,029	2,487	117	5	23,857	4,771
18. Metro Atlantic	10	136	335,150	2,464	70	5	30,944	6,189
19. Ohio Valley	11	156	365,830	2,345	-87	6	16,123	2,687
20. Big Sky#	9	121	279,213	2,308	-233	4	12,009	3,002
21. Ivy	8	106	230,460	2,174	244	-	-	-
22. Summit#	8	115	238,301	2,072	-458	4	11,898	2,975
23. America East	9	124	248,533	2,004	-9	5	16,883	3,377
24. Atlantic Sun	8	104	201,590	1,938	-75	4	8,176	2,044
25. Mid-Eastern	11	133	257,207	1,934	160	6	32,796	5,466
26. Patriot	8	112	*209,691	1,872	26	7	11,851	1,693
27. Big South	8	119	*213,932	1,798	67	6	8,194	1,366
28. Big West#	9	126	222,496	1,766	-85	4	11,055	2,764
29. Southland	11	161	269,617	1,675	58	4	4,942	1,236
30. Southwestern	10	119	181,393	1,524	62	4	2,537	634
31. Northeast	11	157	180,261	1,148	-58	7	12,698	1,814
Independent#	4	43	39,750	924	-255	-	-	-

*Record high for that conference. # Different alignment from the previous year.

NOTE: Entire season total attendance includes the conference tournaments.

Leading Division II Conferences

Rank	Conference	Total Teams	Games or Sessions	2008 Attendance	Average	Change In Avg.
1.	North Central	7	105	204,328	1,946	-2
2.	Mid-America	10	139	231,767	1,667	-227
3.	Northern Sun	9	134	184,699	1,378	-129
4.	CIAA	10	122	167,034	1,369	-22
5.	SIAC	12	156	167,626	1,075	40
6.	Great Lakes Valley	14	211	200,547	950	-81
7.	Lone Star	14	186	167,552	901	-56
8.	Great Northwest	10	142	125,914	887	-44
9.	Peach Belt	9	131	106,808	815	35
10.	GLIAC	13	187	150,721	806	31

Leading Division III Conferences

Rank	Conference	Total Teams	Games or Sessions	2008 Attendance	Average	Change In Avg.
1.	Michigan	8	92	95,181	1,035	-65
2.	Illinois & Wisconsin	7	84	68,705	818	14
3.	Wisconsin	9	114	82,791	726	-63
4.	Iowa	9	108	78,040	723	159
5.	Ohio	10	113	80,162	709	-65
6.	Northwest	9	93	63,936	687	54
7.	UAA	8	112	76,339	682	114
8.	MAC Commonwealth	6	73	48,686	667	138
9.	Little East	8	104	62,286	599	113
10.	North Coast	10	120	71,599	597	-86

Leading Teams

DIVISION I

Rank	School	G	Attendance	Average
1.	Kentucky	18	405,964	22,554
2.	North Carolina	16	327,953	20,497
3.	Syracuse	22	447,587	20,345
4.	Tennessee	16	324,274	20,267
5.	Louisville	17	331,184	19,481
6.	Maryland	19	341,050	17,950
7.	Wisconsin	18	309,420	17,190
8.	Arkansas	16	274,360	17,148
9.	Indiana	19	320,641	16,876
10.	Memphis	21	351,718	16,748
11.	Illinois	15	249,270	16,618
12.	Ohio St.	20	331,731	16,587
13.	Kansas	20	328,182	16,409
14.	Marquette	17	276,064	16,239
15.	Creighton	18	276,000	15,333
16.	North Carolina St.	16	240,682	15,043
17.	Michigan St.	17	250,903	14,759
18.	New Mexico	18	258,493	14,361
19.	Arizona	17	241,703	14,218
20.	Texas	18	248,673	13,815
21.	BYU	16	216,295	13,518
22.	Vanderbilt	19	254,945	13,418
23.	Iowa St.	18	239,697	13,317
24.	Georgetown	16	207,286	12,955
25.	Kansas St.	17	212,987	12,529
26.	Oklahoma St.	16	200,056	12,504
27.	Dayton	18	224,623	12,479
28.	Minnesota	17	211,685	12,452
29.	South Carolina	17	209,880	12,346
30.	Purdue	17	209,870	12,345

2008 DIVISION I TEAM-BY-TEAM ATTENDANCE

School	G	Attendance	Average
A&M-Corpus Christi	14	28,539	2,039
Air Force	16	61,888	3,868
Akron	16	55,265	3,454
Alabama	18	186,640	10,369
Alabama A&M	12	23,741	1,978
Alabama St.	12	40,268	3,356
Albany (N.Y.)	13	39,409	3,031
Alcorn St.	11	8,425	766
American	15	27,867	1,858
Appalachian St.	13	31,790	2,445
Arizona	17	241,703	14,218
Arizona St.	20	160,152	8,008
UALR	16	59,783	3,736
Ark.-Pine Bluff	11	10,490	954
Arkansas	16	274,360	17,148
Arkansas St.	15	48,106	3,207
Army	14	12,408	886
Auburn	15	80,882	5,392
Austin Peay	14	44,911	3,208
Ball St.	15	50,971	3,398
Baylor	16	116,015	7,251
Belmont	12	19,877	1,656
Bethune-Cookman	15	31,907	2,127
Binghamton	15	54,670	3,645
Boise St.	16	89,249	5,578
Boston College	19	109,789	5,778
Boston U.	13	15,346	1,180
Bowling Green	13	17,574	1,352
Bradley	19	182,392	9,600

School	G	Attendance	Average
Brown	12	18,407	1,534
Bucknell	13	44,189	3,399
Buffalo	13	24,200	1,862
Butler	15	89,169	5,945
BYU	16	216,295	13,518
Cal Poly	12	23,362	1,947
Cal St. Fullerton	14	12,850	918
Cal St. Northridge	13	16,065	1,236
California	19	150,383	7,915
Campbell	15	12,414	828
Canisius	14	18,602	1,329
Centenary (La.)	12	10,440	870
Central Conn. St.	14	23,210	1,658
Central Mich.	11	17,716	1,611
Charleston So.	15	16,749	1,117
Charlotte	16	116,944	7,309
Chattanooga	16	67,725	4,233
Chicago St.	9	5,420	602
Cincinnati	17	145,081	8,534
Citadel	16	20,684	1,293
Clemson	16	137,739	8,609
Cleveland St.	15	49,603	3,307
Coastal Caro.	14	13,861	990
Col. of Charleston	13	40,979	3,152
Colgate	14	7,871	562
Colorado	15	77,417	5,161
Colorado St.	13	43,588	3,353
Columbia	13	14,883	1,145
Connecticut	17	202,082	11,887
Coppin St.	10	4,534	453
Cornell	13	38,440	2,957
Creighton	18	276,000	15,333
Dartmouth	12	9,236	770
Davidson	14	86,993	6,214
Dayton	18	224,623	12,479
Delaware	12	38,605	3,217
Delaware St.	10	9,078	908
Denver	12	29,454	2,455
DePaul	15	138,927	9,262
Detroit	16	31,157	1,947
Drake	15	90,571	6,038
Drexel	16	32,264	2,017
Duke	16	149,024	9,314
Duquesne	15	46,370	3,091
East Carolina	19	89,406	4,706
East Tenn. St.	13	50,716	3,901
Eastern Ill.	13	13,116	1,009
Eastern Ky.	16	42,350	2,647
Eastern Mich.	14	12,805	915
Eastern Wash.	13	19,863	1,528
Elon	14	13,210	944
Evansville	15	82,292	5,486
Fairfield	13	36,371	2,798
Fairleigh Dickinson	12	5,719	477
Fla. Atlantic	15	11,522	768
Florida	21	226,815	10,801
Florida A&M	12	15,155	1,263
Florida Int'l	17	14,888	876
Florida St.	18	137,508	7,639
Fordham	14	32,285	2,306
Fresno St.	17	173,065	10,180
Furman	11	15,217	1,383
Ga. Southern	13	32,152	2,473
Gardner-Webb	12	24,511	2,043
George Mason	14	90,920	6,494
George Washington	12	36,226	3,019

School	G	Attendance	Average	School	G	Attendance	Average
Georgetown	16	207,286	12,955	Navy	14	31,329	2,238
Georgia	16	125,172	7,823	Nebraska	20	205,722	10,286
Georgia St.	14	18,746	1,339	Nevada	16	119,488	7,468
Georgia Tech	13	119,483	9,191	New Hampshire	15	12,344	823
Gonzaga	14	84,000	6,000	New Mexico	18	258,493	14,361
Grambling	11	13,067	1,188	New Mexico St.	20	123,055	6,153
Green Bay	14	54,145	3,868	New Orleans	15	10,165	678
Hampton	13	27,213	2,093	Niagara	12	25,345	2,112
Hartford	13	18,993	1,461	Nicholls St.	11	4,554	414
Harvard	13	15,855	1,220	Norfolk St.	10	19,699	1,970
Hawaii	18	111,072	6,171	North Carolina	16	327,953	20,497
High Point	14	18,809	1,344	North Carolina St.	16	240,682	15,043
Hofstra	13	35,623	2,740	North Texas	17	54,028	3,178
Holy Cross	14	37,486	2,678	Northeastern	10	14,449	1,445
Houston	19	84,240	4,434	Northern Ariz.	16	20,793	1,300
Howard	10	14,792	1,479	Northern Colo.	13	16,794	1,292
Idaho	13	14,781	1,137	Northern Ill.	12	20,404	1,700
Idaho St.	13	30,807	2,370	Northwestern	16	73,256	4,579
Ill.-Chicago	14	55,272	3,948	Northwestern St.	14	21,168	1,512
Illinois	15	249,270	16,618	Notre Dame	17	165,337	9,726
Illinois St.	18	117,293	6,516	Oakland	14	29,150	2,082
Indiana	19	320,641	16,876	Ohio	14	71,886	5,135
Indiana St.	14	60,039	4,289	Ohio St.	20	331,731	16,587
Iona	12	22,119	1,843	Oklahoma	17	174,422	10,260
Iowa	18	193,700	10,761	Oklahoma St.	16	200,056	12,504
Iowa St.	18	239,697	13,317	Old Dominion	17	114,857	6,756
IPFW	13	23,999	1,846	Oral Roberts	13	75,795	5,830
IUPUI	15	14,358	957	Oregon	15	130,521	8,701
Jackson St.	12	11,987	999	Oregon St.	15	68,688	4,579
Jacksonville	11	28,915	2,629	Pacific	14	47,047	3,361
Jacksonville St.	15	21,686	1,446	Penn	17	82,614	4,860
James Madison	14	50,846	3,632	Penn St.	17	136,693	8,041
Kansas	20	328,182	16,409	Pepperdine	10	14,211	1,421
Kansas St.	17	212,987	12,529	Pittsburgh	18	197,447	10,969
Kent St.	16	59,361	3,710	Portland	13	28,502	2,192
Kentucky	18	405,964	22,554	Portland St.	12	11,561	963
La Salle	12	27,352	2,279	Prairie View	12	23,124	1,927
La.-Lafayette	14	57,692	4,121	Princeton	13	31,080	2,391
La.-Monroe	12	16,056	1,338	Providence	15	127,907	8,527
Lafayette	13	29,736	2,287	Purdue	17	209,870	12,345
Lamar	16	59,268	3,704	Quinnipiac	14	23,581	1,684
Lehigh	15	18,805	1,254	Radford	13	25,796	1,984
Liberty	15	37,580	2,505	Rhode Island	15	81,886	5,459
Lipscomb	12	22,033	1,836	Rice	13	15,065	1,159
Long Beach St.	13	25,241	1,942	Richmond	15	59,868	3,991
Long Island	14	10,964	783	Rider	13	20,985	1,614
Longwood	12	10,487	874	Robert Morris	15	20,594	1,373
Louisiana Tech	14	18,417	1,316	Rutgers	18	93,175	5,176
Louisville	17	331,184	19,481	Sacramento St.	13	7,583	583
Loyola (Ill.)	14	24,857	1,776	Sacred Heart	15	16,372	1,091
Loyola (Md.)	13	19,225	1,479	Sam Houston St.	16	29,504	1,844
Loyola Marymount	13	25,700	1,977	Samford	14	15,998	1,143
LSU	15	128,469	8,565	San Diego	18	52,194	2,900
Maine	13	17,613	1,355	San Diego St.	14	94,638	6,760
Manhattan	14	30,485	2,178	San Francisco	13	22,758	1,751
Marist	12	28,571	2,381	San Jose St.	13	21,233	1,633
Marquette	17	276,064	16,239	Santa Clara	13	29,844	2,296
Marshall	17	85,710	5,042	Savannah St.	12	8,101	675
Maryland	19	341,050	17,950	Seton Hall	17	122,834	7,226
Massachusetts	16	78,392	4,900	Siena	17	110,012	6,471
McNeese St.	12	10,043	837	SMU	18	52,990	2,944
Md.-East. Shore	11	17,212	1,565	South Ala.	18	90,382	5,021
Memphis	21	351,718	16,748	South Carolina	17	209,880	12,346
Mercer	13	14,734	1,133	South Carolina St.	13	18,365	1,413
Miami (Fla.)	16	69,152	4,322	South Fla.	15	76,839	5,123
Miami (Ohio)	12	32,807	2,734	Southeast Mo. St.	13	44,685	3,437
Michigan	15	150,504	10,034	Southeastern La.	15	14,740	983
Michigan St.	17	250,903	14,759	Southern California	15	127,014	8,468
Middle Tenn.	17	71,828	4,225	Southern Ill.	16	106,555	6,660
Milwaukee	17	61,746	3,632	Southern Miss.	14	50,644	3,617
Minnesota	17	211,685	12,452	Southern U.	11	11,224	1,020
Mississippi	18	131,413	7,301	Southern Utah	14	34,150	2,439
Mississippi St.	15	138,789	9,253	St. Bonaventure	13	54,984	4,230
Mississippi Val.	12	25,914	2,160	St. Francis (N.Y.)	14	5,215	373
Missouri	17	137,027	8,060	St. Francis (Pa.)	15	16,788	1,119
Missouri St.	16	99,859	6,241	St. John's (N.Y.)	16	94,183	5,886
Monmouth	13	19,917	1,532	St. Joseph's	13	61,762	4,751
Montana	13	54,986	4,230	St. Louis	16	141,387	8,837
Montana St.	14	66,751	4,768	St. Mary's (Cal.)	16	47,278	2,955
Morehead St.	14	33,499	2,393	St. Peter's	14	16,241	1,160
Morgan St.	12	27,514	2,293	Stanford	17	124,621	7,331
Mt. St. Mary's	15	17,837	1,189	Stephen F. Austin	14	36,386	2,599
Murray St.	16	50,962	3,185	Stetson	13	22,395	1,723
N.C. A&T	11	38,942	3,540				

School	G	Attendance	Average
Stony Brook	13	12,214	940
Syracuse	22	447,587	20,345
TCU	17	60,000	3,529
Temple	14	85,637	6,117
Tenn.-Martin	14	38,031	2,717
Tennessee	16	324,274	20,267
Tennessee St.	12	30,270	2,523
Tennessee Tech	13	24,331	1,872
Tex.-Pan American	10	15,742	1,574
Texas	18	248,673	13,815
Texas A&M	20	206,860	10,343
Texas Southern	11	10,616	965
Texas St.	13	27,287	2,099
Texas Tech	16	114,615	7,163
Texas-Arlington	17	12,389	729
Toledo	12	55,256	4,605
Towson	15	30,263	2,018
Troy	15	30,584	2,039
Tulane	16	32,964	2,060
Tulsa	20	115,027	5,751
UAB	15	75,162	5,011
UC Davis	15	27,481	1,832
UC Irvine	14	24,790	1,771
UC Riverside	13	6,040	465
UC Santa Barbara	14	28,565	2,040
UCF	16	78,253	4,891
UCLA	18	190,438	10,580
UMBC	14	37,884	2,706
UMKC	16	29,705	1,857
UNC Asheville	19	20,076	1,057
UNC Greensboro	13	16,730	1,287
UNC Wilmington	15	79,626	5,308
UNI	17	86,630	5,096
UNLV	21	249,171	11,865
Utah	15	149,687	9,979
Utah St.	17	154,302	9,077
UTEP	16	130,321	8,145
UTSA	15	20,797	1,386
Valparaiso	17	62,316	3,666
Vanderbilt	19	254,945	13,418
VCU	14	86,369	6,169
Vermont	12	32,003	2,667
Villanova	15	147,570	9,838
Virginia	20	234,092	11,705
Virginia Tech	17	166,858	9,815
VMI	14	27,735	1,981
Wagner	16	20,064	1,254
Wake Forest	17	202,282	11,899
Washington	19	166,475	8,762
Washington St.	16	131,701	8,231
Weber St.	14	50,075	3,577
West Virginia	16	163,315	10,207
Western Caro.	14	21,166	1,512
Western Ill.	14	8,806	629
Western Ky.	15	95,961	6,397
Western Mich.	12	42,455	3,538
Wichita St.	15	157,170	10,478
William & Mary	14	33,690	2,406
Winthrop	15	53,326	3,555
Wisconsin	18	309,420	17,190
Wofford	14	17,526	1,252
Wright St.	16	78,450	4,903
Wyoming	14	73,673	5,262
Xavier	17	170,133	10,008
Yale	13	19,945	1,534
Youngstown St.	13	36,051	2,773

RECLASSIFYING TEAMS TO DIVISION I

School	G	Attendance	Average
Cal St. Bakersfield	14	30,158	2,154
Central Ark.	15	18,031	1,202
Fla. Gulf Coast	11	25,561	2,324
Kennesaw St.	13	12,673	975
N.C. Central	7	8,952	1,279
NJIT	12	7,150	596
North Dakota St.	13	39,441	3,034
North Fla.	12	12,389	1,032
Presbyterian	5	7,811	1,562
S.C. Upstate	10	9,081	908
South Dakota St.	15	32,790	2,186
Winston-Salem	14	17,071	1,219

LARGEST DIVISION I AVERAGE ATTENDANCE INCREASE FROM PREVIOUS YEAR

Rank	School	G	2008 Avg.	2007 Avg.	Change in Avg.
1.	Southern California	15	8,468	5,798	2,670
2.	Georgetown	16	12,955	10,441	2,514
3.	Davidson	14	6,214	3,721	2,493
4.	Memphis	21	16,748	14,527	2,221
5.	UCF	16	4,891	2,706	2,185
6.	Mississippi	18	7,301	5,406	1,895
7.	Colorado	15	5,161	3,324	1,837
8.	Temple	14	6,117	4,312	1,805
9.	Montana St.	14	4,768	3,024	1,744
10.	Cornell	13	2,957	1,340	1,617
11.	Wake Forest	17	11,899	10,294	1,605
12.	South Ala.	18	5,021	3,422	1,599
13.	New Mexico	18	14,361	12,853	1,508
14.	Marshall	17	5,042	3,544	1,498
15.	Minnesota	17	12,452	10,974	1,478
16.	La.-Lafayette	14	4,121	2,654	1,467
17.	BYU	16	13,518	12,073	1,445
18.	Illinois St.	18	6,516	5,092	1,424
19.	Vanderbilt	19	13,418	12,030	1,388
20.	Charlotte	16	7,309	6,026	1,283
21.	Clemson	16	8,609	7,329	1,280
22.	South Fla.	15	5,123	3,852	1,271
23.	Baylor	16	7,251	6,065	1,186
24.	Boise St.	16	5,578	4,393	1,185
25.	Western Ky.	15	6,397	5,229	1,168
26.	Maryland	19	17,950	16,822	1,128
27.	North Texas	17	3,178	2,067	1,111
28.	SMU	18	2,944	1,838	1,106
29.	North Carolina St.	16	15,043	13,952	1,091
30.	Arizona St.	20	8,008	6,931	1,077

DIVISION I ALL GAMES ATTENDANCE (HOME, ROAD, NEUTRAL)

Rank	School	Attendance
1.	Kansas	756,830
2.	North Carolina	688,940
3.	Memphis	644,435
4.	Syracuse	615,934
5.	Wisconsin	603,644
6.	Louisville	590,898
7.	Tennessee	581,146
8.	Michigan St.	569,808
9.	Kentucky	562,086
10.	Texas	551,310
11.	Ohio St.	544,353
12.	Maryland	526,152
13.	Illinois	519,586
14.	UCLA	516,931
15.	Marquette	513,656
16.	Indiana	494,847
17.	Georgetown	484,930
18.	Pittsburgh	477,315
19.	Arkansas	474,050
20.	Arizona	449,677
21.	Florida	439,227
22.	Minnesota	438,069
23.	Villanova	433,286
24.	Vanderbilt	430,536

DIVISION II

Rank	School	Games	Attendance	Average
1.	Northern St.	18	58,869	3,270
2.	Morehouse	14	42,816	3,058
3.	Elizabeth City St.	12	35,520	2,960
4.	South Dakota	16	46,165	2,885
5.	Augustana (S.D.)	15	40,882	2,725
6.	Central Mo.	15	39,766	2,651
7.	St. Cloud St.	16	41,576	2,598
8.	Winona St.	23	57,490	2,499
9.	Virginia St.	12	29,664	2,472
10.	Washburn	13	31,107	2,392
11.	Emporia St.	14	30,187	2,156
12.	Alas. Anchorage	21	41,894	1,994
13.	Harding	13	25,104	1,931
14.	Southern Ind.	18	33,875	1,881
15.	Minn. St. Mankato	16	29,936	1,871
16.	North Dakota	14	26,122	1,865
17.	Mo. Western St.	14	25,668	1,833
18.	Southwest Minn. St.	14	25,617	1,829
19.	Ky. Wesleyan	17	29,300	1,723

Rank	School	Games	Attendance	Average
20.	Tarleton St.	19	32,355	1,702
21.	Pittsburg St.	13	20,844	1,603
22.	Gannon	17	26,773	1,574
23.	Grand Valley St.	21	33,020	1,572
24.	Fort Hays St.	16	25,080	1,567
25.	Virginia Union	15	23,519	1,567
26.	Fayetteville St.	11	16,719	1,519
27.	Adams St.	11	16,457	1,496
28.	S.C. Aiken	16	23,667	1,479
29.	California (Pa.)	17	23,633	1,390
30.	Mo. Southern St.	14	19,298	1,378

DIVISION III

Rank	School	Games	Attendance	Average
1.	Hope	17	51,278	3,016
2.	Wooster	15	24,318	1,621
3.	Ill. Wesleyan	11	16,350	1,486
4.	Buena Vista	13	18,525	1,425
5.	Calvin	13	17,856	1,373
6.	Wis.-Stevens Point	14	18,901	1,350
7.	Keene St.	13	17,132	1,317
8.	Mass.-Dartmouth	17	22,375	1,316
9.	Lincoln (Pa.)	8	10,411	1,301
10.	Puget Sound	12	14,580	1,215
11.	Capital	15	18,221	1,214
12.	Messiah	11	13,213	1,201
13.	Augustana (Ill.)	16	16,999	1,062
14.	Rochester (N.Y.)	16	16,508	1,031
15.	York (Pa.)	14	14,296	1,021
16.	Chris. Newport	15	15,162	1,010
17.	Maryville (Tenn.)	13	12,981	998
18.	Wheaton (Ill.)	10	9,955	995
19.	New York U.	16	15,539	971
20.	Whitworth	11	10,495	954
21.	Mississippi Col.	12	11,411	950
22.	St. John's (Minn.)	11	10,309	937
23.	Pomona-Pitzer	11	10,246	931
24.	Washington-St. Louis	14	13,013	929
25.	Wartburg	13	11,959	919
26.	Brandeis	14	12,850	917
27.	Howard Payne	12	10,612	884
28.	Muskingum	12	10,586	882
29.	Otterbein	11	9,593	872
30.	Mary Hardin-Baylor	16	13,675	854

All-Time Attendance Leaders

DIVISION I

CONFERENCE LEADERS BY TOTAL ATTENDANCE

Conference	Season	Teams	Attendance	P/G Avg.
Big East	†2007	16	3,259,992	11,164
Big East	†2008	16	3,054,190	11,147
Big East	†2006	16	2,964,418	11,061
Big Ten	2007	11	2,564,662	12,760
Southeastern	2007	12	2,562,073	11,972
Southeastern	2008	12	2,561,545	12,140
Big Ten	2008	11	2,517,685	12,978
Atlantic Coast	2007	12	2,434,902	11,118
Atlantic Coast	2008	12	2,355,822	11,272
Big Ten	†2001	11	2,342,022	13,383
Big Ten	2006	11	2,277,085	12,581
Atlantic Coast	2006	12	2,277,076	11,273
Big 12	2007	12	2,261,697	10,719
Big Ten	†2002	11	2,258,255	13,362
Big Ten	†2000	11	2,255,913	13,428
Big Ten	†2005	11	2,255,332	12,530
Big Ten	†2003	11	2,254,658	12,526
Southeastern	†2004	12	2,230,546	11,439
Southeastern	2006	12	2,205,320	11,082
Big Ten	†1999	11	2,204,556	13,361

DIVISION I

CONFERENCE LEADERS BY AVERAGE ATTENDANCE

Conference	Season	Teams	Attendance	P/G Avg.
Big Ten	†1990	10	2,017,407	13,449
Big Ten	†2000	11	2,255,913	13,428
Big Ten	†2001	11	2,342,022	13,383
Big Ten	†2002	11	2,258,255	13,362
Big Ten	†1999	11	2,204,556	13,361
Big Ten	†1991	10	2,042,836	13,095

Conference	Season	Teams	Attendance	P/G Avg.
Big Ten	†2008	11	2,517,685	12,978
Big Ten	†1992	10	1,994,144	12,865
Big Ten	†2004	11	2,122,586	12,787
Big Ten	†1996	11	2,106,810	12,769
Big Ten	†2007	11	2,564,662	12,760
Big Ten	†1993	11	2,163,693	12,728
Big Ten	†1995	11	2,058,763	12,708
Big Ten	†1994	11	2,107,600	12,696
Big Ten	†1989	10	1,971,110	12,635
Big Ten	†2006	11	2,277,085	12,581
Big East	1991	9	1,771,386	12,563
Big Ten	†2005	11	2,255,332	12,530
Big Ten	†2003	11	2,254,658	12,526
Big Ten	†1998	11	2,166,264	12,450

DIVISION II

CONFERENCE LEADERS BY TOTAL ATTENDANCE

Conference	Season	Teams	Attendance	P/G Avg.
North Central Intercollegiate	†1992	10	482,213	3,014
North Central Intercollegiate	†1991	10	438,746	2,868
North Central Intercollegiate	†1989	10	438,403	2,923
North Central Intercollegiate	†1990	10	436,292	2,889
North Central Intercollegiate	†1988	10	413,956	2,797
North Central Intercollegiate	†1993	10	408,624	2,919
Central Intercollegiate	1990	14	395,884	2,262
North Central Intercollegiate	†1987	10	393,940	2,626
North Central Intercollegiate	†1984	10	392,154	2,801
Central Intercollegiate	1991	14	384,978	2,139
North Central Intercollegiate	†1995	10	382,042	2,497
Central Intercollegiate	†1980	13	380,798	2,457
North Central Intercollegiate	†1985	10	380,087	2,639
North Central Intercollegiate	†1986	10	379,701	2,601
Central Intercollegiate	1989	14	378,046	2,211
Central Intercollegiate	†1981	14	377,322	2,233
Central Intercollegiate	†1979	12	375,370	2,760
Central Intercollegiate	1988	14	374,803	2,142
Central Intercollegiate	†1982	14	373,236	2,290
Central Intercollegiate	1987	14	370,957	2,169

DIVISION II

CONFERENCE LEADERS BY AVERAGE ATTENDANCE

Conference	Season	Teams	Attendance	P/G Avg.
North Central Intercollegiate	†1992	10	482,213	3,014
North Central Intercollegiate	†1989	10	438,403	2,923
North Central Intercollegiate	†1993	10	408,624	2,919
North Central Intercollegiate	†1990	10	436,292	2,889
North Central Intercollegiate	†1991	10	438,746	2,868
North Central Intercollegiate	†1981	8	312,410	2,840
North Central Intercollegiate	†1984	10	392,154	2,801
North Central Intercollegiate	†1988	10	413,956	2,797
Mid-Continent	†1980	5	189,193	2,782
North Central Intercollegiate	1980	8	302,752	2,778
Central Intercollegiate	†1979	12	375,370	2,760
North Central Intercollegiate	1979	7	257,030	2,677
North Central Intercollegiate	†1985	10	380,087	2,639
North Central Intercollegiate	†1994	10	362,572	2,627
North Central Intercollegiate	†1987	10	393,940	2,626
North Central Intercollegiate	†1982	8	290,995	2,622
North Central Intercollegiate	†1986	10	379,701	2,601
North Central Intercollegiate	†2004	8	301,111	2,574
North Central Intercollegiate	†1983	8	356,777	2,567
North Central Intercollegiate	†2002	10	369,858	2,551

DIVISION III

CONFERENCE LEADERS BY TOTAL ATTENDANCE

Conference	Season	Teams	Attendance	P/G Avg.
Wisconsin State University	†1979	9	183,122	1,621
Wisconsin State University	†1990	9	170,276	1,362
Wisconsin State University	†1986	9	164,207	1,368
Wisconsin State University	†1982	9	160,860	1,411
Wisconsin State University	†1980	9	154,665	1,333
Wisconsin State University	†1985	9	153,102	1,255
Minnesota Intercollegiate	†1987	11	153,090	1,169
Wisconsin State University	†1991	9	152,289	1,238
Minnesota Intercollegiate	†1984	11	148,041	1,130
Wisconsin State University	1984	9	142,859	1,181
Illinois & Wisconsin	1980	9	138,820	1,251
Wisconsin State University	†1992	9	135,735	1,122
Wisconsin State University	†1993	9	130,870	1,091
Minnesota Intercollegiate	1990	9	120,849	1,079
Minnesota Intercollegiate	1992	11	118,504	898
Middle Atlantic	†1998	16	115,253	597

Conference	Season	Teams	Attendance	P/G Avg.
Middle Atlantic	†2003	16	111,519	575
Michigan Intercollegiate	†2000	8	111,310	1,091
Illinois & Wisconsin	†2001	8	110,868	1,131
Middle Atlantic	2000	16	110,833	568

DIVISION III
CONFERENCE LEADERS BY AVERAGE ATTENDANCE

Conference	Season	Teams	Attendance	P/G Avg.
Wisconsin State University	†1979	9	183,122	1,621
Wisconsin State University	†1982	9	160,860	1,411
Wisconsin State University	†1986	9	164,207	1,368
Wisconsin State University	†1990	9	170,276	1,362
Wisconsin State University	†1980	9	154,665	1,333
Wisconsin State University	†1985	9	153,102	1,255
Illinois & Wisconsin	1980	9	138,820	1,251
Michigan Intercollegiate	†2002	7	98,263	1,244
Wisconsin State University	†1991	9	152,289	1,238
Michigan Intercollegiate	†1993	7	97,624	1,236
Michigan Intercollegiate	†2006	7	107,400	1,234
Michigan Intercollegiate	†1994	7	97,418	1,203
Michigan Intercollegiate	†1990	7	84,548	1,191
Michigan Intercollegiate	†1995	7	86,353	1,183
Wisconsin State University	†1984	9	142,859	1,181
Minnesota Intercollegiate	†1987	11	153,090	1,169
Michigan Intercollegiate	†1992	7	89,549	1,163
Michigan Intercollegiate	†2001	7	95,378	1,163
Illinois & Wisconsin	2001	8	110,868	1,131
Minnesota Intercollegiate	1984	11	148,041	1,130

DIVISION I
TEAM LEADERS BY TOTAL ATTENDANCE

Conference	Season	Games	Attendance	P/G Avg.
Syracuse	†1989	19	537,949	28,313
Syracuse	†1986	19	498,850	26,255
Syracuse	†1991	17	497,179	29,246
Syracuse	†1990	16	478,686	29,918
Syracuse	†1987	19	474,214	24,959
Syracuse	†2007	22	473,353	21,516
Syracuse	†1988	16	461,223	28,826
Syracuse	†1992	17	460,752	27,103
Syracuse	†2008	22	447,587	20,345
Kentucky	1986	19	426,740	22,460
Syracuse	†1994	17	419,039	24,649
Syracuse	†2005	18	413,605	22,978
Syracuse	†2006	19	410,153	21,587
Kentucky	2008	18	405,964	22,554
Syracuse	†1993	16	405,620	25,351
Louisville	2006	22	402,963	18,316
Kentucky	1992	17	396,688	23,335
Kentucky	1988	17	393,725	23,160
Syracuse	†1985	15	388,049	25,870
Syracuse	†1995	16	387,925	24,245

DIVISION I
TEAM LEADERS BY AVERAGE ATTENDANCE

Conference	Season	Games	Attendance	P/G Avg.
Syracuse	†1990	16	478,686	29,918
Syracuse	†1991	17	497,179	29,246
Syracuse	†1988	16	461,223	28,826
Syracuse	†1989	19	537,949	28,313
Syracuse	†1992	17	460,752	27,103
Syracuse	†1986	19	498,850	26,255
Syracuse	†1985	15	388,049	25,870
Syracuse	†1993	16	405,620	25,351
Syracuse	†1987	19	474,214	24,959
Syracuse	†1994	17	419,039	24,649
Syracuse	†1995	16	387,925	24,245
Kentucky	†1998	12	287,354	23,946
Kentucky	1993	16	382,869	23,929
Kentucky	1996	13	310,633	23,895
Kentucky	1995	13	309,477	23,806
Kentucky	†1997	13	309,457	23,804
Kentucky	†1983	15	356,776	23,785
Kentucky	1984	16	380,453	23,778
Kentucky	1991	14	331,404	23,672
Kentucky	†1981	15	354,996	23,666

DIVISION II
TEAM LEADERS BY TOTAL ATTENDANCE

Conference	Season	Games	Attendance	P/G Avg.
Norfolk St.	†1984	18	119,925	6,663
Southeast Mo. St.	†1989	21	106,102	5,052

Conference	Season	G/S	Attendance	P/G Avg.
Southeast Mo. St.	†1988	20	104,538	5,227
Norfolk St.	†1983	17	101,854	5,991
Southeast Mo. St.	†1990	19	100,448	5,287
Norfolk St.	†1985	16	97,854	6,116
Norfolk St.	†1979	19	97,700	4,984
Ky. Wesleyan	1984	19	96,344	5,071
North Dakota St.	1983	15	90,850	6,057
Ky. Wesleyan	1985	19	88,612	4,664
Ky. Wesleyan	1990	20	87,371	4,369
Southeast Mo. St.	†1991	16	85,927	5,370
South Dakota St.	†1998	16	85,599	5,350
Ky. Wesleyan	1988	19	84,009	4,422
Ky. Wesleyan	†1982	20	84,008	4,200
Ky. Wesleyan	†1987	19	82,459	4,340
Alabama A&M	†1995	16	82,249	5,141
Alabama A&M	†1994	17	80,877	4,757
North Dakota St.	1984	15	79,000	5,267
Ky. Wesleyan	1983	17	78,895	4,461

DIVISION II
TEAM LEADERS BY AVERAGE ATTENDANCE

Conference	Season	Games	Attendance	P/G Avg.
Norfolk St.	†1984	18	119,925	6,663
Norfolk St.	†1985	16	97,854	6,116
North Dakota St.	†1983	15	90,850	6,057
Norfolk St.	1983	17	101,854	5,991
Southeast Mo. St.	†1991	16	85,927	5,370
South Dakota St.	†1998	16	85,599	5,350
North Dakota St.	†1981	13	69,000	5,308
Southeast Mo. St.	†1990	19	100,448	5,287
North Dakota St.	1984	15	79,000	5,267
Southeast Mo. St.	†1988	20	104,538	5,227
Alabama A&M	†1995	16	82,249	5,141
Ky. Wesleyan	1984	19	96,344	5,071
Southeast Mo. St.	†1989	21	106,102	5,052
Norfolk St.	†1979	19	94,700	4,984
Norfolk St.	1990	14	69,536	4,967
South Dakota St.	1996	14	69,229	4,945
North Dakota	†1992	13	64,261	4,943
Norfolk St.	†1980	15	73,750	4,917
Alabama A&M	1992	15	73,633	4,909
North Dakota St.	1985	15	73,100	4,873

DIVISION III
TEAM LEADERS BY TOTAL ATTENDANCE

Conference	Season	Games	Attendance	P/G Avg.
Hope	†2006	18	52,719	2,928
Hope	†2008	17	51,278	3,016
Calvin	†2000	14	48,941	3,496
Calvin	†1993	12	48,215	4,018
St. John's (Minn.)	†1978	15	45,000	3,000
Hope	†2007	15	43,848	2,923
Calvin	†2001	13	43,796	3,369
Wis.-Stevens Point	†1982	14	41,000	2,929
Wis.-Eau Claire	†1989	17	40,900	2,406
Otterbein	†1983	17	40,900	2,406
Otterbein	†1991	18	40,101	2,228
Wis.-Whitewater	†1986	16	40,000	2,500
Wis.-Eau Claire	†1987	17	39,800	2,341
Concordia (Minn.)	1982	14	39,700	2,836
Augustana (Ill.)	1982	14	38,700	2,764
Calvin	†1992	14	38,600	2,757
Calvin	†1994	14	38,271	2,734
Scranton	†1977	14	37,900	2,707
Wis.-Eau Claire	1991	18	37,750	2,097
Ill. Wesleyan	†1995	15	37,700	2,513

DIVISION III
TEAM LEADERS BY AVERAGE ATTENDANCE

Conference	Season	Games	Attendance	P/G Avg.
Calvin	†1993	12	48,215	4,018
Calvin	†1978	10	36,300	3,630
Calvin	†2000	14	48,941	3,496
Calvin	†2001	13	43,796	3,369
Augustana (Ill.)	†1983	12	36,400	3,033
Hope	†2008	17	51,278	3,016
St. John's (Minn.)	1978	15	45,000	3,000
Wis.-Stevens Point	†1982	14	41,000	2,929
Hope	†2006	18	52,719	2,928
Hope	†2007	15	43,848	2,923
Savannah St.	†1980	6	17,502	2,917
Calvin	†2002	13	37,613	2,893

Conference	Season	G/S	Attendance	P/G Avg.
SUNY Potsdam	†1981	11	31,600	2,873
Savannah St.	†1979	10	28,700	2,870
Concordia-M'head	†1987	13	37,300	2,869
Concordia (Minn.)	1982	14	39,700	2,836
Calvin	†1997	10	28,206	2,821
Calvin	†1995	11	30,717	2,792
Augustana (Ill.)	1982	14	38,700	2,764
Calvin	†1992	14	38,600	2,757

†national leader

Annual NCAA Attendance

ALL DIVISIONS

Season	Teams	Attendance	Per Game Average	Change in Avg.	
1977	717	23,324,040	2,710	—	—
1978	726	23,590,952	2,678	Down	32
1979	718	24,482,516	2,757	Up	79
1980	715	24,861,722	2,765	Up	8
1981	730	25,159,358	2,737	Down	28
1982	741	25,416,017	2,727	Down	10
1983	755	26,122,785	2,706	Down	21
1984	750	26,271,613	2,728	Up	22
1985	753	26,584,426	2,712	Down	16
1986	760	26,368,815	2,654	Down	58
1987	760	26,797,644	2,698	Up	44
1988	761	27,452,948	2,777	Up	79
1989	772	28,270,260	2,814	Up	37
1990	767	28,740,819	*2,860	Up	46
1991	796	29,249,583	2,796	Down	64
1992	813	29,378,161	2,747	Down	49
1993	831	28,527,348	2,703	Down	44
1994	858	28,390,491	2,604	Down	99
1995	868	28,548,158	2,581	Down	23
1996	866	28,225,352	2,563	Down	18
1997	865	27,738,284	2,508	Down	55
1998	895	28,031,879	2,445	Down	63
1999	926	28,505,428	2,401	Down	44
2000	932	29,024,876	2,410	Up	9
2001	937	28,949,093	2,392	Down	18
2002	936	29,395,240	2,373	Down	19
2003	967	30,124,304	2,339	Down	34
2004	981	30,760,510	2,355	Up	16
2005	983	30,568,645	2,327	Down	28
2006	984	30,939,715	2,351	Up	24
2007	982	32,835,863	2,449	Up	98
2008	*1,017	*33,396,316	2,393	Down	56

DIVISION I

Season	Teams	Attendance	Per Game Average	Change in Avg.	
1976	235	15,059,892	4,759	—	—
1977	245	16,469,250	5,021	Up	262
1978	254	17,669,080	5,124	Up	103
1979	257	18,649,383	5,271	Up	147
1980	261	19,052,743	5,217	Down	54
1981	264	19,355,690	5,131	Down	86
1982	273	19,789,706	5,191	Up	60
1983	274	20,488,437	5,212	Up	21
1984	276	20,715,426	5,243	Up	31
1985	282	21,394,261	5,258	Up	15
1986	283	21,244,519	5,175	Down	83
1987	290	21,756,709	5,205	Up	30
1988	290	22,463,476	5,443	Up	238
1989	293	23,059,429	5,565	Up	122
1990	292	23,581,823	5,721	Up	156
1991	295	23,777,437	*5,735	Up	14
1992	298	23,893,993	5,643	Down	92
1993	298	23,321,655	5,635	Down	8
1994	301	23,275,158	5,571	Down	64
1995	302	23,560,495	5,641	Up	70
1996	305	23,542,652	5,588	Down	53
1997	305	23,190,856	5,485	Down	103
1998	306	23,282,774	5,459	Down	26
1999	310	23,587,824	5,451	Down	8
2000	318	24,281,774	5,386	Down	65
2001	318	24,100,555	5,311	Down	75
2002	321	24,499,611	5,287	Down	24
2003	325	25,001,678	5,372	Up	85
2004	326	25,548,468	5,443	Up	71
2005	326	25,366,317	5,334	Down	109
2006	326	25,808,346	5,426	Up	92
2007	325	27,705,912	5,548	Up	122
2008	*328	*28,135,901	5,524	Down	24

DIVISION II

Season	Teams	Attendance	Per Game Average	Change in Avg.	
1977	177	*3,846,907	*1,811	—	—
1978	173	3,168,419	1,515	Down	296
1979	172	3,295,149	1,535	Up	20
1980	177	3,324,670	1,479	Down	56
1981	190	3,543,766	1,486	Up	7
1982	190	3,329,518	1,391	Down	95
1983	195	3,364,184	1,324	Down	67
1984	189	3,199,307	1,306	Down	18
1985	181	2,988,083	1,255	Down	51
1986	184	2,946,020	1,204	Down	51
1987	179	2,893,392	1,220	Up	16
1988	175	2,902,400	1,242	Up	22
1989	189	3,157,464	1,273	Up	31
1990	189	3,104,462	1,223	Down	50
1991	204	3,388,278	1,221	Down	2
1992	214	3,395,684	1,188	Down	33
1993	220	3,201,765	1,145	Down	43
1994	243	3,219,979	1,036	Down	109
1995	244	3,125,974	992	Down	44
1996	242	2,918,802	938	Down	54
1997	242	2,873,311	915	Down	23
1998	252	2,976,420	904	Down	8
1999	266	3,063,436	892	Down	15
2000	258	2,942,477	882	Down	10
2001	261	2,951,969	877	Down	5
2002	258	2,990,641	888	Up	11
2003	269	3,076,804	855	Down	33
2004	*271	3,107,628	864	Up	9
2005	268	3,054,549	854	Down	10
2006	264	2,913,513	825	Down	29
2007	262	2,892,820	815	Down	10
2008	258	2,700,151	763	Down	52

DIVISION III

Season	Teams	Attendance	Per Game Average	Change in Avg.	
1977	295	*2,881,400	*912	—	—
1978	299	2,632,678	816	Down	96
1979	289	2,427,688	770	Down	46
1980	277	2,387,142	783	Up	13
1981	276	2,132,000	693	Down	90
1982	278	2,183,895	711	Up	18
1983	286	2,148,736	685	Down	26
1984	286	2,233,340	701	Up	16
1985	290	2,081,452	629	Down	72
1986	293	2,053,693	615	Down	14
1987	291	2,021,459	606	Down	9
1988	296	1,970,823	583	Down	23
1989	290	1,935,058	573	Down	10
1990	286	1,939,795	581	Up	8
1991	297	1,967,087	564	Down	1
1992	301	1,962,598	553	Down	11
1993	313	1,883,283	531	Down	22
1994	314	1,741,867	493	Down	38
1995	322	1,802,301	487	Down	6
1996	319	1,730,357	472	Down	15
1997	318	1,626,240	444	Down	28
1998	337	1,736,409	447	Up	3
1999	350	1,824,391	446	Down	1
2000	356	1,750,621	426	Down	20
2001	358	1,846,043	444	Up	18
2002	357	1,804,209	424	Down	20
2003	373	1,869,592	426	Up	2
2004	384	1,944,957	427	Up	1
2005	383	1,960,141	431	Up	4
2006	382	1,955,720	430	Down	1
2007	380	1,947,730	430	None	0
2008	*388	1,973,368	426	Down	4

*record

Annual Conference Attendance Champions

DIVISION I

Season	Conference	Teams	Attendance	P/G Avg.
1976	Atlantic Coast	7	863,082	9,590
1977	Big Ten	10	1,346,889	9,977
1978	Big Ten	10	1,539,589	11,238
1979	Big Ten	10	1,713,380	12,238
1980	Big Ten	10	1,877,048	12,189
1981	Big Ten	10	1,779,892	12,026
1982	Big Ten	10	1,688,834	11,810
1983	Big Ten	10	1,747,910	11,499
1984	Big Ten	10	1,774,140	12,069
1985	Big Ten	10	1,911,325	12,097
1986	Big Ten	10	1,908,629	11,929
1987	Big Ten	10	1,805,263	11,877
1988	Big Ten	10	1,925,617	12,423
1989	Big Ten	10	1,971,110	12,635
1990	Big Ten	10	2,017,407	*13,449
1991	Big Ten	10	2,042,836	13,095
1992	Big Ten	10	1,994,144	12,865
1993	Big Ten	11	2,163,693	12,728
1994	Big Ten	11	2,107,600	12,696
1995	Big Ten	11	2,058,763	12,708
1996	Big Ten	11	2,106,810	12,769
1997	Big Ten	11	2,004,893	12,376
1998	Big Ten	11	2,166,264	12,450
1999	Big Ten	11	2,204,556	13,361
2000	Big Ten	11	2,255,913	13,428
2001	Big Ten	11	2,342,022	13,383
2002	Big Ten	11	2,258,255	13,362
2003	Big Ten	11	2,254,658	12,526
2004	Big Ten	11	2,122,586	12,787
2005	Big Ten	11	2,255,332	12,530
2006	Big Ten	11	2,277,085	12,581
2007	Big Ten	11	2,564,662	12,760
2008	Big Ten	11	2,517,685	12,978

DIVISION II

Season	Conference	Teams	Attendance	P/G Avg.
1979	Central Intercollegiate	12	375,370	2,760
1980	Mid-Continent	5	189,193	2,782
1981	North Central Intercollegiate	8	312,410	2,840
1982	North Central Intercollegiate	8	290,995	2,622
1983	North Central Intercollegiate	8	356,777	2,567
1984	North Central Intercollegiate	10	392,154	2,801
1985	North Central Intercollegiate	10	380,087	2,639
1986	North Central Intercollegiate	10	379,701	2,601
1987	North Central Intercollegiate	10	393,940	2,626
1988	North Central Intercollegiate	10	413,956	2,797
1989	North Central Intercollegiate	10	438,403	2,923
1990	North Central Intercollegiate	10	436,292	2,889
1991	North Central Intercollegiate	10	438,746	2,868
1992	North Central Intercollegiate	10	*482,213	*3,014
1993	North Central Intercollegiate	10	408,624	2,919
1994	North Central Intercollegiate	10	362,572	2,627
1995	North Central Intercollegiate	10	382,042	2,497
1996	North Central Intercollegiate	10	341,119	2,336
1997	North Central Intercollegiate	10	319,703	2,160
1998	North Central Intercollegiate	10	315,918	2,225
1999	North Central Intercollegiate	10	299,228	2,050
2000	North Central Intercollegiate	10	300,257	2,114
2001	North Central Intercollegiate	10	300,822	2,118
2002	North Central Intercollegiate	10	369,858	2,551
2003	North Central Intercollegiate	9	328,903	2,473
2004	North Central Intercollegiate	8	301,111	2,574
2005	North Central Intercollegiate	7	229,745	2,252
2006	North Central Intercollegiate	7	197,739	1,920
2007	North Central Intercollegiate	7	198,653	1,948
2008	North Central Intercollegiate	7	204,328	1,946

DIVISION III

Season	Conference	Teams	Attendance	P/G Avg.
1990	Wisconsin State University	9	*170,276	*1,362
1991	Wisconsin State University	9	152,289	1,238
1992	Michigan Intercollegiate	7	89,549	1,163
1993	Michigan Intercollegiate	7	97,624	1,236
1994	Michigan Intercollegiate	7	97,418	1,203
1995	Michigan Intercollegiate	7	86,353	1,183
1996	Michigan Intercollegiate	7	80,376	1,058
1997	Michigan Intercollegiate	7	81,370	1,085
1998	Michigan Intercollegiate	8	91,267	941
1999	Michigan Intercollegiate	8	87,055	957
2000	Michigan Intercollegiate	8	111,310	1,091
2001	Michigan Intercollegiate	7	95,378	1,163
2002	Michigan Intercollegiate	7	98,263	1,244
2003	Michigan Intercollegiate	8	79,798	1,050
2004	Michigan Intercollegiate	8	88,153	1,049
2005	Michigan Intercollegiate	7	89,165	1,115
2006	Michigan Intercollegiate	7	107,400	1,234
2007	Michigan Intercollegiate	7	88,039	1,100
2008	Michigan Intercollegiate	8	95,181	1,035

*record

Annual Team Attendance Champions

DIVISION I

Season	Champion	Games	Attendance	Avg.
1970	Illinois	11	157,206	14,291
1971	Illinois	11	177,408	16,128
1972	BYU	12	261,815	21,818
1973	BYU	14	260,102	18,579
1974	BYU	10	162,510	16,251
1975	Minnesota	13	219,047	16,850
1976	Indiana	12	202,700	16,892
1977	Kentucky	14	312,527	22,323
1978	Kentucky	16	373,367	23,335
1979	Kentucky	15	351,042	23,403
1980	Kentucky	15	352,511	23,501
1981	Kentucky	15	354,996	23,666
1982	Kentucky	16	371,093	23,193
1983	Kentucky	15	356,776	23,785
1984	Kentucky	16	380,453	23,778
1985	Syracuse	15	388,049	25,870
1986	Syracuse	19	498,850	26,255
1987	Syracuse	19	474,214	24,959
1988	Syracuse	16	461,223	28,826
1989	Syracuse	19	*537,949	28,313
1990	Syracuse	16	478,686	*29,918
1991	Syracuse	17	497,179	29,246
1992	Syracuse	17	460,752	27,103
1993	Syracuse	16	405,620	25,351
1994	Syracuse	17	419,039	24,649
1995	Syracuse	16	387,925	24,245
1996	Kentucky	13	310,633	23,895
1997	Kentucky	13	309,457	23,804
1998	Kentucky	12	287,354	23,946
1999	Kentucky	13	303,771	23,367
2000	Kentucky	14	314,267	22,448
2001	Kentucky	12	261,435	21,786
2002	Kentucky	15	315,203	21,014
2003	Kentucky	13	289,526	22,271
2004	Kentucky	13	295,227	22,710
2005	Syracuse	18	413,605	22,978
2006	Kentucky	15	341,445	22,763
2007	Kentucky	16	374,737	23,421
2008	Kentucky	18	405,964	22,554

DIVISION I LARGEST INCREASE FROM PREVIOUS YEAR

Season	Champion	Games	Att. Avg.	Previous Yr. Avg.	Increase
1977	Kentucky	14	22,323	11,511	10,812
1978	Texas	15	12,583	5,846	6,737
1979	Illinois	13	14,209	8,719	5,490
1980	Missouri	16	9,460	6,624	2,836
1981	DePaul	14	15,410	5,308	10,102
1982	Georgetown	17	8,591	4,197	4,394
1983	Chattanooga	16	7,547	3,931	3,616
1984	UNLV	16	15,779	6,380	9,399
1985	Villanova	9	10,218	5,744	4,474
1986	North Carolina	15	15,838	9,954	5,884
1987	North Carolina	13	20,149	15,838	4,311
1988	Tennessee	16	20,823	12,191	8,632
1989	Texas	14	10,011	4,028	5,983
1990	Cincinnati	15	9,273	3,572	5,701
1991	Wright St.	15	8,503	2,716	5,787
1992	Memphis	16	16,142	10,935	5,207
1993	Boise St.	15	12,113	7,536	4,577
1994	Arkansas	16	20,134	8,975	*11,159
1995	St. Louis	16	17,714	13,008	4,706
1996	Memphis	17	14,235	9,765	4,470
1997	Wichita St.	15	9,449	5,528	3,921
1998	Temple	13	7,964	3,891	4,073

Season	Champion	Games	Att. Avg.	Previous Yr. Avg.	Increase
1999	Ohio St.	15	17,223	9,970	7,253
2000	North Carolina St.	20	16,535	10,800	5,735
2001	Oklahoma St.	12	12,044	5,907	6,137
2002	Texas Tech	17	13,743	9,557	4,186
2003	BYU	16	14,468	8,630	5,838
2004	UTEP	17	10,282	6,038	4,244
2005	Virginia Tech	16	9,405	6,342	3,063
2006	Tennessee	15	17,954	12,225	5,729
2007	Virginia	17	13,521	7,796	5,725
2008	Southern California	15	8,468	5,798	2,670

DIVISION I ALL GAMES (HOME, ROAD & NEUTRAL)

Season	Champion	Games	Attendance	Avg.
1978	Kentucky	30	586,250	19,542
1979	Kentucky	31	546,288	17,622
1980	Kentucky	35	563,160	16,090
1981	Kentucky	28	499,461	17,838
1982	Kentucky	30	541,786	18,060
1983	Kentucky	31	562,947	18,160
1984	Kentucky	34	633,618	18,636
1985	Syracuse	31	581,347	18,753
1986	Syracuse	32	641,146	20,036
1987	Syracuse	38	826,182	21,742
1988	Syracuse	35	719,910	20,569
1989	Syracuse	38	*855,053	*22,501
1990	Syracuse	33	716,945	21,726
1991	Syracuse	32	680,261	21,258
1992	Kentucky	36	709,078	19,697
1993	North Carolina	38	721,760	18,994
1994	Kentucky	34	647,722	19,051
1995	Arkansas	39	695,026	17,821
1996	Kentucky	36	725,884	20,163
1997	Kentucky	40	822,863	20,572
1998	Kentucky	39	784,614	20,118
1999	Kentucky	37	737,738	19,939
2000	Michigan St.	39	621,108	15,926
2001	Duke	39	650,550	16,681
2002	Indiana	37	644,641	17,423
2003	Syracuse	35	686,997	19,628
2004	Kentucky	32	663,298	20,728
2005	Illinois	39	711,798	18,251
2006	Syracuse	35	640,949	18,313
2007	Ohio St.	39	747,457	19,166
2008	Kansas	40	756,830	18,920

DIVISION II

Season	Champion	Avg.
1977	Evansville	4,576
1978	Norfolk St.	4,226
1979	Norfolk St.	4,984
1980	Norfolk St.	4,917
1981	North Dakota St.	5,300
1982	North Dakota St.	4,385
1983	North Dakota St.	6,057
1984	Norfolk St.	*6,663
1985	Norfolk St.	6,116
1986	St. Cloud St.	4,539
1987	North Dakota St.	4,820
1988	Southeast Mo. St.	5,227
1989	Southeast Mo. St.	5,052
1990	Southeast Mo. St.	5,287
1991	Southeast Mo. St.	5,370
1992	North Dakota	4,943
1993	Alabama A&M	4,748
1994	South Dakota St.	4,852
1995	Alabama A&M	5,141
1996	South Dakota St.	4,945
1997	South Dakota St.	4,423
1998	South Dakota St.	5,350
1999	Ky. Wesleyan	4,247
2000	South Dakota St.	4,077
2001	Morehouse	4,404
2002	South Dakota St.	4,449
2003	Neb.-Kearney	3,839
2004	South Dakota St.	3,375
2005	Virginia St.	3,471
2006	Northern St.	3,916
2007	Central Mo. St.	3,640
2008	Northern St.	3,270

*record

DIVISION III

Season	Champion	Avg.
1977	Scranton	2,707
1978	Calvin	3,630
1979	Savannah St.	2,870
1980	Savannah St.	2,917
1981	SUNY Potsdam	2,873
1982	Wis.-Stevens Point	2,929
1983	Augustana (Ill.)	3,033
1984	Hope	2,144
1985	Wis.-Stevens Point	2,313
1986	Calvin	2,570
1987	Concordia-M'head	2,869
1988	Calvin	2,627
1989	Calvin	2,544
1990	Calvin	2,622
1991	Hope	2,480
1992	Calvin	2,757
1993	Calvin	*4,018
1994	Calvin	2,734
1995	Calvin	2,792
1996	Hope	2,409
1997	Calvin	2,821
1998	Ill. Wesleyan	2,615
1999	Hope	2,440
2000	Calvin	3,496
2001	Calvin	3,369
2002	Calvin	2,893
2003	Hope	2,383
2004	Hope	2,491
2005	Hope	2,462
2006	Hope	2,928
2007	Hope	2,923
2008	Hope	3,016

*record

Annual NCAA Tournament Attendance

DIVISION I

Season	Sess.	Attend.	P/G Avg.
1939	5	15,025	3,005
1940	5	36,880	7,376
1941	5	48,055	9,611
1942	5	24,372	4,874
1943	5	56,876	11,375
1944	5	59,369	11,874
1945	5	67,780	13,556
1946	5	73,116	14,623
1947	5	72,959	14,592
1948	5	72,523	14,505
1949	5	66,077	13,215
1950	5	75,464	15,093
1951	9	110,645	12,294
1952	10	115,712	11,571
1953	14	127,149	9,082
1954	15	115,391	7,693
1955	15	116,983	7,799
1956	15	132,513	8,834
1957	14	108,891	7,778
1958	14	176,878	12,634
1959	14	161,809	11,558
1960	16	155,491	9,718
1961	14	169,520	12,109
1962	14	177,469	12,676
1963	14	153,065	10,933
1964	14	140,790	10,056
1965	13	140,673	10,821
1966	13	140,925	10,840
1967	14	159,570	11,398
1968	14	160,888	11,492
1969	15	165,712	11,047
1970	16	146,794	9,175
1971	16	207,200	12,950
1972	16	147,304	9,207
1973	16	163,160	10,198
1974	16	154,112	9,632
1975	18	183,857	10,214
1976	18	202,502	11,250
1977	18	241,610	13,423
1978	18	227,149	12,619
1979	22	262,101	11,914
1980	26	321,260	12,356
1981	26	347,414	13,362
1982	26	427,251	16,433
1983	28	364,356	13,013
1984	28	397,481	14,196
1985	34	422,519	12,427
1986	34	499,704	14,697
1987	34	654,744	19,257
1988	34	558,990	16,441
1989	34	613,242	18,037
1990	34	537,138	15,798
1991	34	665,707	19,580
1992	34	580,462	17,072
1993	34	707,719	20,815
1994	34	578,007	17,000

Season	Sess.	Attend.	P/G Avg.
1995	34	539,440	15,866
1996	34	643,290	18,920
1997	34	634,584	18,664
1998	34	682,530	20,074
1999	34	720,685	21,197
2000	34	638,577	18,782
2001	35	596,075	17,031
2002	35	720,433	20,584
2003	35	715,080	20,431
2004	35	716,899	20,483
2005	35	689,317	19,695
2006	35	670,254	19,150
2007	35	696,992	19,914
2008	35	*763,607	*21,817

*record

DIVISION II

Season	Sess.	Attend.	P/G Avg.
1977	22	*87,602	*3,982
1978	22	83,058	3,775
1979	22	66,446	3,020
1980	22	50,649	2,302
1981	22	69,470	3,158
1982	22	67,925	3,088
1983	22	70,335	3,197
1984	22	81,388	3,699
1985	22	81,476	3,703
1986	22	71,083	3,231
1987	22	77,934	3,542
1988	22	72,462	3,294
1989	20	69,008	3,450
1990	20	64,212	3,211
1991	20	59,839	2,992
1992	20	60,629	3,031
1993	20	56,125	2,806
1994	20	60,511	3,026
1995	36	86,767	2,410
1996	28	65,882	2,353
1997	28	66,626	2,380
1998	28	59,946	2,141
1999	28	49,144	1,755
2000	28	50,130	1,790
2001	28	60,418	2,158
2002	28	60,258	2,152

Season	Sess.	Attend.	P/G Avg.
2003	36	51,054	1,418
2004	36	41,126	1,142
2005	36	51,896	1,442
2006	36	60,640	1,684
2007	36	76,073	2,113
2008	36	75,225	2,090

*record

DIVISION III

Season	Sess.	Attend.	P/G Avg.
1977	21	38,881	1,851
1978	21	37,717	1,796
1979	22	43,850	1,993
1980	22	46,518	2,114
1981	22	58,432	*2,656
1982	22	44,973	2,044
1983	22	51,093	2,322
1984	22	42,152	1,916
1985	22	39,154	1,780
1986	22	53,500	2,432
1987	22	48,150	2,189
1988	22	43,787	1,990
1989	28	49,301	1,761
1990	26	50,527	1,943
1991	34	56,942	1,675
1992	34	65,257	1,919
1993	34	49,675	1,461
1994	34	54,848	1,613
1995	59	*88,684	1,503
1996	58	87,437	1,508
1997	58	70,647	1,218
1998	42	63,330	1,508
1999	42	53,928	1,284
2000	42	62,527	1,489
2001	42	77,110	1,836
2002	46	74,437	1,618
2003	42	66,379	1,580
2004	42	66,693	1,588
2005	42	64,289	1,531
2006	42	99,394	2,367
2007	42	60,619	1,443
2008	42	54,231	1,291

*record

Division I Attendance Records

SINGLE GAME (PAID)
78,129—Kentucky (79) vs. Michigan St. (74), Dec. 13, 2003, at Ford Field, Detroit (regular-season game)

SINGLE GAME (TURNSTILE)
58,903—North Carolina (78) vs. Kansas (68) and Michigan (81) vs. Kentucky (78) (ot), Apr. 3, 1993 (NCAA semifinals), at Louisiana Superdome, New Orleans

HOME COURT, SINGLE GAME
33,633—Villanova (92) at Syracuse (82), Mar. 5, 2006, Carrier Dome, Syracuse, NY

HOME-COURT AVERAGE, SEASON
29,918—Syracuse, 1990 (478,686 in 16 games at Carrier Dome)

HOME-COURT TOTAL, SEASON
537,949—Syracuse, 1989 (19 games)

FULL-SEASON AVERAGE, ALL GAMES
(home, road, neutral, tournaments)
22,501—Syracuse, 1989 (855,053 in 38 games)

FULL-SEASON TOTAL, ALL GAMES
(home, road, neutral, tournaments)
855,053—Syracuse, 1989 (38 games)

TOP 10 ATTENDANCE GAMES (PAID)*
78,129—Kentucky (79) vs. Michigan St. (74), Dec. 13, 2003, at Ford Field, Detroit

68,112—LSU (87) vs. Notre Dame (64), Jan. 20, 1990, at Louisiana Superdome, New Orleans

66,144—LSU (82) vs. Georgetown (80), Jan. 28, 1989, at Louisiana Superdome, New Orleans

64,959—Indiana (74) vs. Syracuse (73), Mar. 30, 1987 (NCAA final); Indiana (97) vs. UNLV (93) and Syracuse (77) vs. Providence (63), Mar. 28, 1987 (NCAA semifinals), at Louisiana Superdome, New Orleans

64,151—North Carolina (77) vs. Michigan (71), Apr. 5, 1993 (NCAA final); North Carolina (78) vs. Kansas (68) and Michigan (81) vs. Kentucky (78) (ot), Apr. 3, 1993 (NCAA semifinals), at Louisiana Superdome, New Orleans

61,612—North Carolina (63) vs. Georgetown (62), Mar. 29, 1982 (NCAA final); North Carolina (68) vs. Houston (63) and Georgetown (50) vs. Louisville (46), Mar. 27, 1982 (NCAA semifinals), at Louisiana Superdome, New Orleans

61,304—LSU (84) vs. Texas (83), Jan. 3, 1992, at Louisiana Superdome, New Orleans

57,563—Kansas (59) vs. Davidson (57), Mar. 30, 2008 (Midwest Regional final), at Ford Field, Detroit (attendance for the semifinals was 57,028)

54,524—Syracuse (81) vs. Kansas (78), Apr. 7, 2003 (NCAA final), at Louisiana Superdome, New Orleans (attendance for the semifinals was 54,432)

53,510—Florida (76) vs. UCLA (66) and Ohio St. (67) vs. Georgetown (60), Mar. 31, 2007 (NCAA semifinals), at Georgia Dome, Atlanta (attendance for the final was 51,458)

* Figures for games at the Final Four include the media.

TOP FIVE ATTENDANCE GAMES (TURNSTILE)
58,903—North Carolina (78) vs. Kansas (68) and Michigan (81) vs. Kentucky (78) (ot), Apr. 3, 1993 (NCAA semifinals), at Louisiana Superdome, New Orleans

56,707—Indiana (74) vs. Syracuse (73), Mar. 30, 1987 (NCAA final), at Louisiana Superdome, New Orleans

56,264—North Carolina (77) vs. Michigan (71), Apr. 5, 1993 (NCAA final), at Louisiana Superdome, New Orleans

55,841—Indiana (97) vs. UNLV (93) and Syracuse (77) vs. Providence (63), Mar. 28, 1987 (NCAA semifinals), at Louisiana Superdome, New Orleans

54,321—LSU (82) vs. Georgetown (80), Jan. 28, 1989, at Louisiana Superdome, New Orleans

TOP 10 REGULAR-SEASON GAMES (PAID)
78,129—Kentucky (79) vs. Michigan St. (74), Dec. 13, 2003, at Ford Field, Detroit

68,112—LSU (87) vs. Notre Dame (64), Jan. 20, 1990, at Louisiana Superdome, New Orleans

66,144—LSU (82) vs. Georgetown (80), Jan. 28, 1989, at Louisiana Superdome, New Orleans

61,304—LSU (84) vs. Texas (83), Jan. 3, 1992, at Louisiana Superdome, New Orleans

52,693—Houston (71) vs. UCLA (69), Jan. 20, 1968, at Astrodome, Houston

45,214—Louisville (101) vs. Indiana (79) and Notre Dame (81) vs. Kentucky (65), Dec. 3, 1988, at RCA Dome, Indianapolis

43,601—Notre Dame (69) vs. Louisville (54) and Kentucky (82) vs. Indiana (76), Dec. 5, 1987, at RCA Dome, Indianapolis

41,071—Kentucky (89) vs. Indiana (82), Dec. 2, 1995, at RCA Dome, Indianapolis

40,128—Louisville (84) vs. Notre Dame (73) and Indiana (71) vs. Kentucky (69), Dec. 2, 1989, at RCA Dome, Indianapolis

38,504—Kentucky (75) vs. Indiana (72), Dec. 6, 1997, at RCA Dome, Indianapolis

ON-CAMPUS REGULAR-SEASON, SINGLE GAME

33,633—Villanova (92) at Syracuse (82), Mar. 5, 2006, Carrier Dome, Syracuse, NY

33,199—Notre Dame (57) at Syracuse (60), Feb. 5, 2005, Carrier Dome, Syracuse, NY

33,071—Rutgers (74) at Syracuse (82), Mar. 9, 2003, Carrier Dome, Syracuse, NY

33,048—Georgetown (58) at Syracuse (62), Mar. 3, 1991, Carrier Dome, Syracuse, NY

33,015—Georgetown (87) at Syracuse (89), Mar. 4, 1990 (ot), Carrier Dome, Syracuse, NY

32,996—Georgetown (72) at Syracuse (68), Feb. 23, 1992, Carrier Dome, Syracuse, NY

32,944—Connecticut (56) at Syracuse (67), Mar. 7, 2004, Carrier Dome, Syracuse, NY

32,820—Connecticut (86) at Syracuse (90), Feb. 10, 1990, Carrier Dome, Syracuse, NY

32,804—Providence (66) at Syracuse (91), Feb. 26, 2005, Carrier Dome, Syracuse, NY

32,763—Pittsburgh (68) at Syracuse (89), Feb. 24, 1991, Carrier Dome, Syracuse, NY

2008 Division I Attendance Single-Game Highs

REGULAR-SEASON

31,327—Georgetown (70) at Syracuse (77), Feb. 16, 2008, at Carrier Dome, Syracuse, NY

26,632—Pittsburgh (82) at Syracuse (77), Mar. 1, 2008, at Carrier Dome in Syracuse, NY

26,494—Villanova (81) vs. Syracuse (71), Jan. 19, 2008, at Carrier Dome in Syracuse, NY

24,386—Louisville (89) at Kentucky (75), Jan. 5, 2008, at Rupp Arena in Lexington, KY

24,371—Arkansas (58) at Kentucky (63), Feb. 23, 2008, at Rupp Arena in Lexington, KY

POSTSEASON

57,563—Kansas (59) vs. Davidson (57), Mar. 30, 2008 (NCAA Midwest Regional final), at Ford Field in Detroit

57,028—Kansas (72) vs. Villanova (57) and Davidson (73) vs. Wisconsin (56), Mar. 28, 2008 (NCAA Midwest Regional semifinals) at Ford Field in Detroit

43,718—Memphis (78) vs. UCLA (63) and Kansas (84) vs. North Carolina (66), Apr. 5, 2008 (NCAA semifinals), at Alamodome in San Antonio

43,257—Kansas (75) vs. Memphis (68) in overtime, Apr. 7, 2008 (NCAA final), at Alamodome in San Antonio

32,931—Texas (82) vs. Stanford (62) and Memphis (92) vs. Michigan St. (74), Mar. 28, 2008 (NCAA South Regional semifinals), at Reliant Stadium in Houston

Division II Attendance Records

PAID ATTENDANCE, SINGLE GAME

21,786—Bowie St. (72) vs. Virginia Union (71), Mar. 1, 2003, at RBC Center, Raleigh, NC (Central Intercollegiate Athletic Association final; early rounds had crowds of 16,536, 15,786 and 11,761)

20,432—Shaw (82) vs. Johnson Smith (68), Mar. 2, 2002, at RBC Center, Raleigh, NC (Central Intercollegiate Athletic Association final; early rounds had crowds of 18,054, 17,827 and 14,386)

15,731—Virginia Union (80) vs. N.C. Central (72), Feb. 28, 2004, at RBC Center, Raleigh, NC (CIAA final; early rounds had crowds of 9,718, 8,493 & 7,115)

13,913—Evansville (93) vs. Ky. Wesleyan (87), Feb. 13, 1960, at Roberts Stadium, Evansville, IN

13,240—La.-Lafayette (105) vs. Ky. Wesleyan (83), Mar. 19, 1971, at Roberts Stadium, Evansville, IN (NCAA third place)

2008 ATTENDANCE SINGLE-GAME HIGHS

7,981—Virginia Union (68) at Virginia St. (61), Jan. 20, 2008

5,980—Augustana (S.D.) (78) at South Dakota (69), Feb. 28, 2008

5,920—Minn. St. Mankato (61) at South Dakota (80), Feb. 2, 2008

5,645—Clark Atlanta (60) at Morehouse (58), Jan. 31, 2008

5,562—South Dakota (90) at Augustana (S.D.) (95), Jan. 12, 2008

Division III Attendance Records

PAID ATTENDANCE, SINGLE GAME

11,442—Hope (70) vs. Calvin (56), Jan. 29, 1997, at Van Andel Arena, Grand Rapids, Michigan

2008 ATTENDANCE SINGLE-GAME HIGHS

4,700—Claremont-M-S (53) at Pomona-Pitzer (55), Mar. 1, 2008

4,700—Claremont-M-S (42) at Pomona-Pitzer (52), Feb. 13, 2008

3,653—Calvin (72) at Hope (88), Mar. 1, 2008

3,611—Wheaton (Ill.) (70) at Hope (83), Mar. 15, 2008

3,603—Calvin (59) at Hope (76), Feb. 20, 2008

3,603—Ohio Wesleyan (63) at Hope (71), Mar. 14, 2008

Playing-Rules History

Dr. James Naismith's 13 Original Rules of Basketball

Photo from NCAA archives

1. The ball could be thrown in any direction with one or both hands.
2. The ball could be batted in any direction with one or both hands (never with the fist).
3. A player cannot run with the ball. The player must throw it from the spot on which he catches it, allowance to be made for a man who catches the ball when running at a good speed if he tries to stop.
4. The ball had to be held in or between the hands; the arms or body must not be used for holding it.
5. No shouldering, holding, pushing, tripping, or striking in any way the person of an opponent should be allowed; the first infringement of this rule by any player should count as a foul, the second should disqualify him until the next goal was made, or, if there was evident intent to injure the person, for the whole of the game, no substitute allowed.
6. A foul was striking at the ball with the fist, violation of Rules 3, 4, and such as described in Rule 5.
7. If either side makes three consecutive fouls, it should count a goal for the opponents (consecutive means without the opponents in the meantime making a foul).
8. A goal should be made when the ball was thrown or batted from the grounds into the basket and stays there, providing those defending the goal do not touch or disturb the goal. If the ball rests on the edges, and the opponent moves the basket, it should count as a goal.
9. When the ball goes out of bounds, it should be thrown into the field of play by the person first touching it. In case of a dispute, the umpire should throw it straight into the field. The thrower-in was allowed five seconds; if he holds it longer, it should go to the opponent. If any side persists in delaying the game, the umpire should call a foul on that side.
10. The umpire should be judge of the men and should note the fouls and notify the referee when three consecutive fouls have been made. He should have power to disqualify men according to Rule 5.
11. The referee should be judge of the ball and should decide when the ball was in play, in bounds, to which side it belongs, and should keep the time. He should decide when a goal had been made, and keep account of the goals with any other duties that were usually performed by a referee.
12. The time should be two 15-minute halves, with five minutes' rest between.
13. The side making the most goals in that time should be declared the winner. In case of a draw, the game may, by agreement of the captains, be continued until another goal was made.

Note: These original rules were published in January 1892 in the Springfield College school newspaper, The Triangle.

Important Rules Changes by Year

The earliest rules book available for this research was from the 1905-06 season. Some of the rules listed in 1905-06 could have actually been instituted before that season.

1891-92
- The 13 original rules of basketball were written by Dr. James Naismith in December 1891 in Springfield, Massachusetts.

1894-95
- The free-throw line was set at 20 feet.

1895-96
- Points awarded for field goal change from three to two, and points awarded for each successful free throw from three points to one point.

1896-97
- Backboards were installed.

1900-01
- A dribbler could not shoot for a field goal and could dribble only once, and then with two hands.

1905-06
- Personal fouls were separated into two classes: "A" for general fouls and "B" for more flagrant fouls. Class A fouls were called for delay of game, tackling the ball (touching the ball when a teammate was already touching it), kicking the ball, striking the ball, advancing the ball, hugging the ball, shooting after dribbling, tackling the opponent, holding the opponent, pushing the opponent, or addressing the game officials. Class B fouls could lead to possible game disqualification and were called for striking the opponent, kicking the opponent, shouldering the opponent, tripping the opponent, hacking the opponent, unnecessary roughness, or using profane or abusive language. If two class B fouls were committed by one player, he was disqualified for the rest of the game.
- If a player was fouled during the act of shooting, his team was automatically awarded one point and one free-throw attempt. If the original shot from the field for goal was good, it counted along with the awarded extra point and free-throw attempt.
- Each game had one referee, one umpire and two inspectors. The referee was the superior officer of the game and had supreme authority once the game began until it concluded. The referee's main duties were calling fouls and stopping play. The umpire could call fouls and reported to the referee. Inspectors were the referee's assistants and were stationed one at each end of the court. Inspectors had no power to make decisions but noted whether goals were made in accordance with the rules and reported such to the referee. The official scorer kept a book containing the scoring and fouls made for each player and each team. The duties of the official scorer have basically remained the same through all the years.
- One timekeeper was appointed by the home team. The visiting team could appoint an assistant timekeeper if it chose to.
- A timeout called while the ball was in play resulted in a jump ball when play was resumed. If the ball was out-of-bounds when a timeout was called, the team in possession of the ball kept possession.
- Time stopped only when ordered by the referee. It did not stop for dead-ball situations such as free throws or when the ball was out-of-bounds.
- Halftime increased to 10 minutes.
- Although not yet known as defensive goaltending, if a player touched the ball or basket when the ball was on the edge of the rim, the referee awarded one point to the shooting team.

1906-07
- The free-throw line was moved from 20 to 15 feet.

1907-08
- Inspector was no longer a game official position.

1908-09
- A dribbler became permitted to shoot. The dribble was defined as the "continuous passage of the ball," making the double dribble illegal.

- A second official was added for games in an effort to curb the rough play.

1910-11
- Within Class B fouls, personal fouls were distinguished from the other.
- Players were disqualified upon committing their fourth personal foul.
- No coaching was allowed during the progress of the game by anybody connected with either team. A warning was given for the first violation and a free throw was awarded after that.

1913-14
- The bottom of the net was left open.

1914-15
- College, YMCA and AAU rules were made the same.

1915-16
- Class A fouls were changed to violations, and Class B fouls became technical and personal fouls.
- If a player was fouled in the act of shooting, his team was awarded two free throws regardless of whether the original field goal was made or missed. If it was made, those two points counted.
- Defensive interference with the ball or basket while the ball was on the basket's rim resulted in one free throw attempt for the shooting team.

1920-21
- A player could re-enter the game once. Before this rule, if a player left the game, he could not re-enter for the rest of the game.
- The backboards were moved two feet from the wall of the court. Before this rule, players would "climb" the padded wall to sink baskets.

1921-22
- Running with the ball changed from a foul to a violation.

1922-23
- Defensive interference with the ball or basket while the ball was on the basket's rim was declared a goal for the shooting team.

1923-24
- The player fouled must shoot his own free throws. Before this rule, one person usually shot all his team's free throws.

1924-25
- Time stopped when ordered by the referee for injuries, substitutions, two-shot fouls and timeouts requested by the team captain. The clock kept running at all other times including dead-ball situations, such as out-of-bounds.
- Two timekeepers were used, one from each team, and shared a watch placed on a table so both could see it. The timekeepers kept track of all the incidents that time was out and added that to the game time. The timekeepers indicated when time expired by using a gong, pistol or whistle.
- Only team captains could call for a timeout. Each team had three timeouts per game.

1928-29
- The charging foul by the dribbler was introduced.

1930-31
- A held ball could be called when a closely guarded player was withholding the ball from play for five seconds. The result was a jump ball.
- The maximum circumference of the ball was reduced from 32 to 31 inches, and the maximum weight from 23 to 22 ounces.
- If a player was fouled in the act of shooting, his team was awarded two free throws if the original field goal was missed. If it was made, those two points counted and only one free throw was attempted.

1932-33
- The 10-second center (division) line was introduced to reduce stalling.
- No player could stand in the free-throw lane with the ball for more than three seconds.

1933-34
- A player could re-enter the game twice.

1934-35
- The circumference of the ball again was reduced to between 29½ and 30¼ inches.

1935-36
- No offensive player could remain in the free-throw lane, with or without the ball, for more than three seconds.
- After a made free throw, the team scored upon put the ball in play at the end of the court where the goal had been scored.

1937-38
- The center jump after every goal scored was eliminated.

1938-39
- The ball was thrown in from out of bounds at mid-court by the team shooting a free throw after a technical foul. Before this rule, the ball was put into play with a center jump after a technical-foul free throw.
- The circumference of the ball was established as 30 inches.

1939-40
- Teams had the choice of whether to take a free throw or take the ball out of bounds at mid-court. If two or more free throws were awarded, this option applied to the last throw.
- The backboards were moved from 2 to 4 feet from the end line to permit freer movement under the basket.

1940-41
- Fan-shaped backboards were made legal.

1942-43
- Any player who was eligible to start an overtime period was allowed an extra personal foul, increasing the total so disqualification was on the fifth foul.

1944-45
- Along with the ball on the rim, defensive interference by touching the ball after it had started its downward flight during an opponent's field goal attempt was declared a goal for the shooting team.
- Five personal fouls disqualify a player. An extra foul was not permitted in overtime games.
- Unlimited substitution was introduced.
- It became a violation for an offensive player to remain in the free-throw lane for more than three seconds.

1946-47
- Transparent backboards were authorized.

1947-48
- The clock was stopped on every dead ball the last three minutes of the second half and of every overtime period. This included every time a goal was scored because the ball was considered dead until put into play again. (This rule was abolished in 1951.)

1948-49
- Coaches were allowed to speak to players during a timeout.

1951-52
- Games were played in four 10-minute quarters.

1952-53
- Teams could no longer waive free throws in favor of taking the ball out of bounds.
- The one-and-one free-throw rule was introduced, although the bonus was used only if the first shot was missed. The rule was in effect the entire game except the last three minutes, when every foul resulted in two free throws.

1954-55
- The one-and-one free throw was changed so that the bonus shot was given only if the first shot was made.
- Games were changed back to being played in two 20-minute halves.

1955-56
- The free-throw lane was increased from 6 feet to 12 feet.
- The two-shot penalty in the last three minutes of the game was eliminated. The one-and-one became in effect the entire game.

1956-57
- On the lineup for a free throw, the two spaces adjacent to the end line were occupied by opponents of the free-thrower. In the past, one space was marked "H" for a home team player to occupy, and across the lane the first space was marked "V" for a visiting team player to stand in.
- Grasping the basket became classified as a technical foul under unsportsmanlike tactics.

1957-58
- Offensive goaltending was banned so that no player from either team could touch the ball or basket when the ball was on the basket's rim or above the cylinder. The only exception was the shooter in the original act of shooting.
- One free throw for each common foul was taken for the first six personal fouls by one team in each half, and the one-and-one was used thereafter.
- On uniforms, the use of the single digit numbers one and two and any digit greater than five was prohibited.
- A ball that passed over the backboard—either front to back or back to front—was considered out of bounds.

1964-65

- Coaches had to remain seated on the bench except while the clock was stopped or to direct or encourage players on the court. This rule was to help keep coaches from inciting undesirable crowd reactions toward the officials.

1967-68

- The dunk was made illegal during the game and pregame warm-up.

1970-71

- During a jump ball, a nonjumper could not change his position from the time the official was ready to make the toss until after the ball had been touched.

1972-73

- The free throw on the first six common fouls each half by a team was eliminated.
- Players could not attempt to create the false impression that they had been fouled in charging/guarding situations or while screening when the contact was only incidental. An official could charge the "actor" with a technical foul for unsportsmanlike conduct if, in the official's opinion, the actor was making a travesty of the game.
- Freshmen became eligible to play varsity basketball. This was the result of a change in the NCAA bylaws, not the basketball playing rules.

1973-74

- Officials could now penalize players for fouls occurring away from the ball, such as grabbing, holding and setting illegal screens.

1974-75

- During a jump ball, a non-jumper on the restraining circle could move around the circle after the ball had left the official's hands.
- A player charged with a foul was no longer required to raise his hand. (In 1978, however, it was strongly recommended that a player start raising his hand again.)

1976-77

- The dunk was made legal again.

1980-81

- Conferences began experimenting with the three-point field-goal at different distances.

1981-82

- The jump ball was used only at the beginning of the game and the start of each overtime. An alternating arrow was used to indicate possession in jump-ball situations during the game.
- All fouls charged to bench personnel were assessed to the head coach.

1982-83

- When the closely guarded five-second count was reached, it was no longer a jump-ball situation. It was a violation, and the ball was awarded to the defensive team out of bounds.

1983-84

- Two free throws were taken for each common foul committed within the last two minutes of the second half and the entire overtime period, if the bonus rule was in effect. (This rule was rescinded one month into the season.)

1984-85

- The coaching box was introduced, whereby a coach and all bench personnel had to remain in the 28-foot-long coaching box unless seeking information from the scorers' table.

1985-86

- The 45-second clock was introduced. The team in control of the ball had to shoot for a goal within 45 seconds after it attained team control.
- If a shooter was fouled intentionally and the shot was missed, the penalty was two shots and possession of the ball out of bounds to the team that was fouled.
- The head coach could stand throughout the game, while all other bench personnel had to remain seated.

1986-87

- The three-point field goal was introduced and set at 19 feet 9 inches from the center of the basket.
- A coach could leave the confines of the bench at any time without penalty to correct a scorer's or timer's mistake. A technical foul was assessed if there was no mistake. (This was changed the next year to a timeout.) Also, a television replay could be used to prevent or rectify a scorer's or timer's mistake or a malfunction of the clock.

1987-88

- Each intentional personal foul carried a two-shot penalty plus possession of the ball.

1988-89

- Any squad member who participated in a fight was ejected from the game and was placed on probation. If that player participated in a second fight during the season, he was suspended for one game. A third fight involving the same person resulted in suspension for the rest of the season including championship competition.

1990-91

- Beginning with the team's 10th personal foul in a half, two free throws were awarded for each common foul, except player-control fouls.
- Three free throws were awarded when a shooter was fouled during an unsuccessful three-point try.
- The fighting rule was amended. The first time any squad member or bench personnel participated in a fight, he was suspended for the team's next game. If that same person participated in a second fight, he was suspended for the rest of the season, including championship competition.

1991-92

- Contact technical fouls counted toward the five fouls for player disqualification and toward the team fouls in reaching bonus free-throw situations.
- The shot clock was reset when the ball struck the basket ring, not when a shot left the shooter's hands as it had been since the rule was introduced in 1986.

1992-93

- Unsporting technical fouls, in addition to contact technical fouls, counted toward the five fouls for player disqualification and toward the team fouls in reaching bonus free-throw situations.

1993-94

- The shot clock was reduced from 45 seconds to 35. The team in control of the ball must shoot for a goal within 35 seconds after it attained team control.
- A foul was ruled intentional if, while playing the ball, a player caused excessive contact with an opponent.
- The game clock was stopped after successful field goals in the last minute of the game and the last minute of any overtime period with no substitution allowed.
- The five-second dribbling violation when closely guarded was eliminated.
- The rule concerning the use of profanity was expanded to include abusive and obscene language in an effort to curtail verbal misconduct by players and coaches.

1994-95

- The inner circle at mid-court was eliminated.
- Scoring was restricted to a tap-in when (³⁄₁₀) (.3) of a second or less remained on the game clock or shot clock.
- The fighting and suspension rules were expanded to include coaches and team personnel.

1995-96

- All unsporting technical fouls charged to anyone on the bench counted toward the team foul total.
- Teams were allowed one 20-second timeout per half. This was an experimental rule in the 1994-95 season.

1996-97

- Teams had to warm up and shoot at the end of the court farthest from their own bench for the first half. Previously, teams had the choice of baskets in the first half.
- In games not involving commercial electronic media, teams were entitled to four full-length timeouts and two 20-second timeouts per game. In games involving commercial electronic media, teams were entitled to two full-length timeouts and three 20-second timeouts per game.

1997-98

- The five-second dribbling violation when closely guarded was reinstated.
- Timeout requests could be made by a player on the court or by the head coach.

1998-99

- In a held-ball situation initiated by the defense, the ball would be awarded to the defensive team. Previously, possession was awarded by the direction of the possession arrow.

1999-00

- Held-ball change from previous season rescinded.
- Twenty-second timeouts increased to 30 seconds in length. New electronic- media timeout format adopted.
- Uniform numbers one and two were permitted.
- Officials must consult courtside television monitors, when available, to judge whether a game-deciding last-second shot in the second half or any extra period counts. (This was passed during the season.)

2000-01

- Technical fouls divided into direct (two-shot penalty) and indirect (one-shot penalty) with ball returned to point of interruption.

2001-02

- Both direct and indirect technical fouls penalized by two shots and returned to point of interruption.
- Officials could check an official courtside monitor to determine if a try was a three- or two-point attempt, regardless of whether the try was successful.

2002-03

- Composite ball could be used without mutual consent of coaches.
- Two free-throw lane spaces closest to the free-thrower would remain unoccupied.
- No free throws were awarded to the offended team in bonus for personal fouls committed by a team while in team control or in possession of the ball during a throw-in (team-control foul).

2003-04

- Officials could consult courtside monitor at the end of either half or any extra period to determine: (1) if a field-goal try beat the horn; (2) whether a shot-clock violation at the end of the first half beat the horn; or, (3) whether a shot-clock violation that would determine the outcome of a game beat the horn. The officials also could use a courtside monitor to correct a timer's mistake or to determine if the game clock or shot clock expired at or near the end of a period.
- A team would have control when a player of that team had disposal of the ball for a throw-in.

2005-06

- Expanding on the rule from two seasons before, officials who consult a courtside monitor at the end of either half or any extra period could correct the official game time if needed and/or determine whether a foul was committed before time expired. Officials could also consult a courtside monitor any time during the game to correct a timer's mistake.
- The time allowed to replace a disqualified player was reduced from 30 to 20 seconds and the warning signal was sounded five seconds before the expiration of the time limit.
- Violations when the ball had been intentionally kicked no longer resulted in the reset of the shot clock to 35 seconds. When the violation occured with 15 or fewer seconds remaining, the shot clock was reset to 15 seconds. Otherwise, when the violation occured with more than 15 seconds remaining, there was no reset of the shot clock.

2006-07

- A timeout would not be recognized when an airborne player's momentum carried him either out-of-bounds or into the backcourt.

2007-08

- During free throws, eliminated the first lane space nearest the basket on each side of the lane and used the second, third and fourth lane space on each side as an alignment for free throws.
- Use of courtside monitor allowed for determining whether a flagrant foul occurred or to assess the situation during a fight.

2008-09

- The three-point was line extended to 20 feet, 9 inches.
- When the entire ball is above the level of the ring during a field-goal try and contacts the backboard, it is considered to be on its downward flight. In such a case, it is goaltending when that ball is touched by a player.

2009-10

- Division II and III institutions will be required to have a game clock with a 10th-of-a-second display, a red light or LED lights, and shot clocks mounted on the backboard.

Important Rules Changes by Subject

Ball: 1930-31, The maximum circumference of the ball was reduced from 32 to 31 inches, and the maximum weight from 23 to 22 ounces. 1934-35, The circumference of the ball again was reduced to between 29½ and 30¼ inches. 1938-39, The circumference of the ball was established as 30 inches. 2002-03, Mutual consent no longer needed for composite ball to be legal.

Basket Equipment: 1896-97, Backboards were installed. 1913-14, The bottom of the net was left open. 1920-21, The backboards were moved two feet from the wall of the court. Before this rule, players would "climb" the padded wall to sink baskets. 1939-40, The backboards were moved from 2 to 4 feet from the end line to permit freer movement under the basket. 1940-41, Fan-shaped backboards were made legal. 1946-47, Transparent backboards were authorized. 1957-58, A ball that passed over the backboard—either front to back or back to front—was considered out of bounds. 1996-97, Teams had to warm up and shoot at the end of the court farthest from their own bench for the first half. Previously, teams had the choice of baskets in the first half. 2002-03, For Division I, shot clocks had to be mounted and recessed on backboard, red warning light had to be added and game clock had to show 10th-of-a-second display. 2003-04, for Division II, shot clocks were recessed and mounted. 2009-10, Division II and III institutions were required to have a game clock with a 10th-of-a-second display, a red light or LED lights, and shot clocks mounted on the backboard. 2009-10, Division II and III institutions will be required to have a game clock with a 10th-of-a-second display, a red light or LED lights, and shot clocks mounted on the backboard.

Block/Charge: 1928-29, The charging foul by the dribbler was introduced. 1972-73, Players could not attempt to create the false impression that they had been fouled in charging/guarding situations or while screening when the contact was only incidental. An official could charge the "actor" with a technical foul for unsportsmanlike conduct if, in the official's opinion, the actor was making a travesty of the game. 2002, Prior rule was deleted because of lack of use.

Clock Stoppage: 1947-48, The clock was stopped on every dead ball the last three minutes of the second half and of every extra period. This includes every time a goal was scored because the ball was considered dead until put into play again. (This rule was abolished in 1951.)

Closely Guarded: 1982-83, When the closely guarded five-second count was reached, it was no longer a jump-ball situation. It was a violation, and the ball was awarded to the defensive team out of bounds. 1993-94, The five-second dribbling violation when closely guarded was eliminated. 1997-98, The five-second dribbling violation when closely guarded was reinstated.

Coaching: 1910-11, No coaching was allowed during the progress of the game by anybody connected with either team. A warning was given for the first violation and a free throw was awarded after that. 1948-49, Coaches were allowed to speak to players during a timeout. 1964-65, Coaches had to remain seated on the bench except while the clock was stopped or to direct or encourage players on the court. This rule was to help keep coaches from inciting undesirable crowd reactions toward the officials. 1984-85, The coaching box was introduced, whereby a coach and all bench personnel had to remain in the 28-foot-long coaching box unless seeking information from the scorers' table. 1985-86, The head coach could stand throughout the game, while all other bench personnel had to remain seated. 1986-87, A coach could leave the confines of the bench at any time without penalty to correct a scorer's or timer's mistake. A technical foul was assessed if there was no mistake. (This penalty was changed the next year to a timeout.) Also, a television replay could be used to prevent or rectify a scorer's or timer's mistake or a malfunction of the clock. 1994-95, The fighting and suspension rules were expanded to include coaches and team personnel. 1995-96, All unsporting technical fouls charged to anyone on the bench counted toward the team foul total.

Dribbling: 1900-01, A dribbler could not shoot for a field goal and could dribble only once, and then with two hands. 1905-06, Personal fouls were separated into two classes: "A" for general fouls and "B" for more flagrant fouls. Shooting after dribbling became a Class A foul, which later became known as a violation. 1908-09, A dribbler became permitted to shoot. The dribble was defined as the "continuous passage of the ball," making the double dribble illegal. 1928-29, The charging foul by the dribbler was introduced. 1993-94, The five-second dribbling violation when closely guarded was eliminated. 1997-98, The five-second dribbling violation when closely guarded was reinstated.

Field Goals: 1895-96, A field goal changes from three to two points, and free throws from three points to one point. 1905-06, If a player was fouled during the act of shooting, his team was automatically awarded one point and one free-throw attempt. If the original shot from the field for goal was good, it counted along with the awarded extra point and free-throw attempt. 1915-16, If a player was fouled in the act of shooting, his team was awarded two free throws regardless of whether the original field goal was made or missed. If it was made, those two points counted. 1930-31, If a player was fouled in the act of shooting, his team was awarded two free throws if the original field goal was missed. If it was made, those two points counted and only one free throw was attempted.

Fighting: 1988-89, Any squad member who participated in a fight was ejected from the game and placed on probation. If that individual participated in a second fight during the season, he was suspended for one game. A third fight involving the same person resulted in suspension for the rest of the season including championship competition. 1990-91, The fighting rule was amended. The first time any squad member or bench personnel participated in a fight, he was suspended for the team's next game. If that same person participated in a second fight, he was suspended for the rest of the season, including championship competition. 1994-95, The fighting and suspension rules were expanded to include coaches and team personnel.

Fouls: 1905-06, Personal fouls were separated into two classes: "A" for general fouls and "B" for more flagrant fouls. Class A fouls were called for delay of game, tackling the ball (touching the ball when a teammate was already touching it), kicking the ball, striking the ball, advancing the ball, hugging the ball, shooting after dribbling, tackling the opponent, holding the opponent, pushing the opponent, or addressing the game officials. Class B fouls could lead to possible game disqualification and were called for striking the opponent, kicking the opponent, shouldering the opponent, tripping the opponent, hacking the opponent unnecessary roughness, or using profane or abusive language. If two Class B fouls were committed by one player, he was disqualified for the rest of the game. 1910-11, Within Class B fouls, personal fouls were distinguished from the other. 1915-16, Class A fouls were changed to violations, and Class B fouls became technical and personal fouls.

Fouling Out: 1905-06, Players were disqualified upon committing their second Class "B" foul (as described in the preceding "Fouls" section). 1910-11, Players were disqualified upon committing their fourth personal foul. 1942-43, Any player who was eligible to start an extra period was allowed an extra personal foul, increasing the total so disqualification was on the fifth foul. 1944-45, Five personal fouls disqualify a player. An extra foul was not permitted in overtime games. 1991-92, Contact technical fouls counted toward the five fouls for player disqualification and toward the team fouls in reaching bonus free-throw situations.

Free Throws: 1894-95, The free-throw line was set at 20 feet. 1906-07, The free-throw line was moved from 20 to 15 feet. 1923-24, The player fouled must shoot his own free throws. Before this rule, one person usually shot all his team's free throws. 1935-36, After a made free throw, the team scored upon would put the ball in play at the end of the court where the goal had been scored. 1939-40, Teams had the choice of whether to take a free throw or take the ball out of bounds at mid-court. If two or more free throws were awarded, this option applied to the last throw. 1952-53, Teams could no longer waive free throws in favor of taking the ball out of bounds. 1952-53, The one-and-one free-throw rule was introduced, although the bonus was used only if the first shot was missed. The rule was in effect the entire game except the last three minutes, when every foul was two shots. 1954-55, The one-and-one free throw was changed so that the bonus shot was given only if the first shot was made. 1955-56, The two-shot penalty in the last three minutes of the game was eliminated. The one-and-one became in effect the entire game. 1956-57, The free-throw lane was increased from 6 feet to 12 feet. On the lineup for a free throw, the two spaces adjacent to the end line were occupied by opponents of the free thrower. In the past, one space was marked "H" for a home team player to occupy, and across the lane the first space was marked "V" for a visiting team player to stand in. 1957-58, One free throw for each common foul was taken for the first six personal fouls by one team in each half, and the one-and-one was used thereafter. 1972-73, The free throw on the first six common fouls each half by a team was eliminated. 1974-75, A player charged with a foul was no longer required to raise his hand. (In 1978, however, it was strongly recommended that a player start raising his hand again.) 1983-84, Two free throws were taken for each common foul committed within the last two minutes of the second half and the entire overtime period, if the bonus rule was in effect. (This rule was rescinded one month into the season.) 1985-86, If a shooter was fouled intentionally and the shot was missed, the penalty was two shots and possession of the ball out of bounds to the team that was fouled. 1987-88, Each intentional personal foul carried a two-shot penalty plus possession of the ball. 1990-91, Beginning with the team's 10th personal foul in a half, two free throws were awarded for each common foul, except player-control fouls. 1990-91, Three free throws were awarded when a shooter was fouled during an unsuccessful three-point try. 1991-92, Contact technical fouls counted toward the five fouls for player disqualification and toward the team fouls in reaching bonus free-throw situations. 1992-93, Unsporting technical fouls, in addition to contact technical fouls, counted toward the five fouls for player disqualification and toward the team fouls in reaching bonus free-throw situations. 1995-96, All unsporting technical fouls charged to anyone on the bench counted toward the team foul total. 2000-01, Number of players permitted on free-throw lane reduced from eight to six. 2002-03, Lane spaces closest to the free-thrower would remain unoccupied. 2007-08, During free throws, eliminated the first lane space nearest the basket on each side of the lane and used the second, third and fourth lane space on each side as an alignment for free throws.

Freshmen: 1972-73, Freshmen became eligible to play varsity basketball. This was the result of a change in the NCAA bylaws, not the basketball playing rules.

Game Officials: 1905-06, Each game had one referee, one umpire and two inspectors. The referee was the superior officer of the game and had supreme authority once the game began until it concluded. The referee's main duties were calling fouls and stopping play. The umpire could call fouls and reported to the referee. Inspectors were the referee's assistants and were stationed one at each end of the court. Inspectors had no power to make decisions but noted whether goals were made in accordance with the rules and reported such to the referee. The official scorer kept a book containing the scoring and fouls made for each player and each team. The duties of the official scorer have basically remained the same through all the years. For timekeepers, see the section on timekeepers. 1907-08, Inspector was no longer a game official position.

Goaltending/Basket Interference: 1905-06, Although not yet known as defensive goaltending, if a player touched the ball or basket when the ball was on the edge of the rim, the referee awarded one point to the shooting team. 1915-16, Defensive interference with the ball or basket while the ball was on the basket's rim resulted in one free throw attempt for the shooting team. 1922-23, Defensive interference with the ball or basket while the ball was on the basket's rim was declared a goal for the shooting team. 1944-45, Along with the ball on the rim, defensive interference by touching the ball after it had started its downward flight during an opponent's field goal attempt was declared a goal for the shooting team. 1957-58, Offensive goaltending was banned so that no player from either team could touch the ball or basket when the ball was on the basket's rim or above the cylinder. The only exception was the shooter in the original act of shooting. 2008-09, When the entire ball is above the level of the ring during a field-goal try and contacts the backboard, it is considered to be on its downward flight. In such a case, it is goaltending when that ball is touched by a player.

Held Ball: 1930-31, A held ball could be called when a closely guarded player was withholding the ball from play for five seconds. The result was a jump ball. 1998-99, In a held-ball situation initiated by the defense, the ball would be awarded to the defensive team. Previously, possession was awarded by the direction of the possession arrow. This was rescinded the next season.

Intentional Foul: 1985-86, If a shooter was fouled intentionally and the shot was missed, the penalty was two shots and possession of the ball out of bounds to the team that was fouled. 1987-88, Each intentional personal foul carried a two-shot penalty plus possession of the ball. 1993-94, A foul would be ruled intentional if, while playing the ball, a player caused excessive contact with an opponent.

Jump Ball/Alternate Possession: 1905-06, A timeout called while the ball was in play resulted in a jump ball when play was resumed. If the ball was out-of-bounds when a timeout was called, the team in possession of the ball kept possession. 1930-31, A held ball could be called when a closely guarded player was withholding the ball from play for five seconds. The result was a jump ball. 1937-38, The center jump after every goal scored was eliminated. 1970-71, During a jump ball, a non-jumper could not change his position from the time the official was ready to make the toss until after the ball had been touched. 1974-75, During a jump ball, a non-jumper on the restraining circle could move around it after the ball had left the official's hands. 1981-82, The jump ball was used only at the beginning of the game and the start of each extra period. An alternating arrow would indicate possession in held-ball situations during the game. 1994-95, The inner circle at mid-court was eliminated.

Lines: 1894-95, The free-throw line was moved from 20 to 15 feet. 1932-33, The 10-second center (division) line was introduced to reduce stalling. 1956-57, The free-throw lane was increased from 6 feet to 12 feet. On the lineup for a free throw, the two spaces adjacent to the end line were occupied by opponents of the free-thrower. In the past, one space was marked "H" for a home team player to occupy, and across the lane the first space was marked "V" for a visiting team player to stand in. 1984-85, The coaching box was introduced, whereby a coach and all bench personnel had to remain in the 28-foot-long coaching box unless seeking information from the scorers' table. 1986-87, The three-point field goal was introduced and set at 19 feet 9 inches from the center of the basket. 1994-95, The inner circle at mid-court was eliminated.

Officials: 1908-09, A second official was added for games in an effort to curb the rough play. 1977-78, The option of a third official was allowed.

Out of Bounds: 1957-58, A ball that passed over the backboard—either front to back or back to front—was considered out of bounds.

Overtime: 1942-43, Any player who was eligible to start an extra period was allowed an extra personal foul, increasing the total so disqualification was on the fifth foul. 1944-45, An extra foul was not permitted in overtime games. 1993-94, The game clock was stopped after successful field goals in the last minute of the game and the last minute of any extra period with no substitution allowed.

Periods: 1905-06, Games were played in two 20-minute halves with a 10-minute rest time between the halves. 1951-52, Games were played in four 10-minute quarters. 1954-55, Games were changed back to being played in two 20-minute halves. 1996-97, Teams had to warm up and shoot at the end of the court farthest from their own bench for the first half. Previously, teams had the choice of baskets in the first half.

Rough Play: 1908-09, A second official was added for games in an effort to curb the rough play. 1939-40, Teams had the choice of whether to take a free throw or take the ball out of bounds at mid-court. If two or more free throws were awarded, this option applied to the last throw. 1952-53, Teams could no longer waive free throws in favor of taking the ball out of bounds. 1957-58, One free throw for each common foul was taken for the first six personal fouls by one team in each half, and the one-and-one was used thereafter. 1972-73, The free throw on the first six common fouls each half by a team was eliminated. 1973-74, Officials could now penalize players for fouls occurring away from the ball, such as grabbing, holding and setting illegal screens. 1974-75, A player charged with a foul was no longer required to raise his hand. (In 1978, however, it was strongly recommended that a player start raising his hand again.) 1983-84, Two free throws were taken for each common foul committed within the last two minutes of the second half and the entire overtime period, if the bonus rule was in effect. (This rule was rescinded one month into the season.) 1987-88, Each intentional personal foul carried a two-shot penalty plus possession of the ball. 1990-91, Beginning with the team's 10th personal foul in a half, two free throws were awarded for each common foul, except player-control fouls. 1991-92, Contact technical fouls counted toward the five fouls for player disqualification and toward the team fouls in reaching bonus free-throw situations. 1992-93, Unsporting technical fouls, in addition to contact technical fouls, counted toward the five fouls for player disqualification and toward the team fouls in reaching bonus free-throw situations. 1993-94, A foul would be ruled intentional if, while playing the ball, a player caused excessive contact with an opponent. 2000-01, Number of players permitted on free-throw lane reduced from eight to six. 2007-08, Use of courtside monitor allowed for determining whether a flagrant foul occurred or to assess the situation during a fight.

Shot Clock/Stalling: 1932-33, The 10-second center (division) line was introduced to reduce stalling. 1985-86, The 45-second clock was introduced. The team in control of the ball must now shoot for a goal within 45 seconds after it attains team control. 1991-92, The shot clock was reset when the ball struck the basket ring, not when a shot left the shooter's hands as it had been since the rule was introduced in 1986. 1993-94, The shot clock was reduced to 35 seconds from 45. The team in control of the ball must shoot for a goal within 35 seconds after it attained team control. 1993-94, The game clock was stopped after successful field goals in the last minute of the game and the last minute of any overtime period with no substitution allowed. Officials could consult courtside monitor at the end of either half or any extra period to determine: (1) if a field-goal try beat the horn; (2) whether a shot-clock violation at the end of the first half beat the horn; or, (3) whether a shot-clock violation that would determine the outcome of a game beat the horn. The officials also could use a courtside monitor to correct a timer's mistake or to determine if the game clock or shot clock expired at or near the end of a period. 2005-06, Violations when the ball had been intentionally kicked would no longer result in the reset of the shot clock to 35 seconds. When the violation occured with 15 or fewer seconds remaining, the shot clock was reset to 15 seconds. Otherwise, when the violation occured with more than 15 seconds remaining, there was no reset of the shot clock.

Shot in Closing Seconds: 1994-95, Scoring was restricted to a tap-in when 3/10 (.3) of a second or less remained on the game clock or shot clock. 1999-2000, During the season, the rules committee made a rule that required the official to look at the courtside monitor to determine if a potential game-winning shot in the last second of the game or overtime would count. 2003-04, Officials could consult courtside monitor at the end of either half or any extra period to determine: (1) if a field-goal try beat the horn; (2) whether a shot-clock violation at the end of the first half beat the horn; or, (3) whether a shot-clock violation that would determine the outcome of a game beat the horn. The officials also could use a courtside monitor to correct a timer's mistake or to determine if the game clock or shot clock expired at or near the end of a period.

Substitution: 1920-21, A player could re-enter the game once. Before this rule, if a player left the game, he could not re-enter for the rest of the game. 1933-34, A player could re-enter the game twice. 1944-45, Unlimited substitution was introduced. 1993-94, The game clock was stopped after successful field goals in the last minute of the game and the last minute of any extra period with no substitution allowed. 2005-06, The time allowed to replace a disqualified player was reduced from 30 to 20 seconds and the warning signal was sounded five seconds before the expiration of the time limit.

Technical Fouls: 1938-39, The ball was thrown in from out of bounds at mid-court by the team shooting a free throw after a technical foul. Before, the ball was put into play with a center jump after a technical-foul free throw. 1956-57, Grasping the basket became classified as a technical foul under unsportsmanlike tactics. 1981-82, All fouls charged to bench personnel were assessed to the head coach. 1988-89, Any squad member who participated in a fight was ejected from the game and was placed on probation. If that player participated in a second fight during the season, he was suspended for one game. A third fight involving the same person resulted in suspension for the rest of the season including championship competition. 1990-91, The fighting rule was amended. The first time any squad member or bench personnel participated in a fight, he was suspended for the team's next game. If that same person participated in a second fight, he was suspended for the rest of the season, including championship competition. 1991-92, Contact technical fouls counted toward the five fouls for player disqualification and toward the team fouls in reaching bonus free-throw situations. 1992-93, Unsporting technical fouls, in addition to contact technical fouls, counted toward the five fouls for player disqualification and toward the team fouls in reaching bonus free-throw situations. 1993-94, The rule concerning the use of profanity was expanded to include abusive and obscene language in an effort to curtail verbal misconduct by players and coaches. 1994-95, The fighting and suspension rules were expanded to include coaches and team personnel. 2000-01, technical fouls divided into direct (two-shot penalty) and indirect (one-shot penalty) with ball returned to point of interruption. 2001-02, Both direct and indirect technical fouls penalized by two shots and return to point of interruption.

Television Replay: 1986-87, A coach could leave the confines of the bench at any time without penalty to correct a scorer's or timer's mistake. A technical foul was assessed if there was no mistake. (This was changed the next year to a timeout.) Also, a television replay could be used to prevent or rectify a scorer's or timer's mistake or a malfunction of the clock. 1999-00, Officials must consult courtside television monitors, when available, to

judge whether a game-deciding last-second shot in the second half or any extra period counts. (This was passed during season.) 2001-02, Officials could check an official courtside monitor to determine if a try was a three- or two-point attempt, regardless of whether the try was successful. 2003-04, Officials could consult courtside monitor at the end of either half or any extra period to determine: (1) if a field-goal try beat the horn; (2) whether a shot-clock violation at the end of the first half beat the horn; or, (3) whether a shot-clock violation that would determine the outcome of a game beat the horn. The officials also could use a courtside monitor to correct a timer's mistake or to determine if the game clock or shot clock expired at or near the end of a period. 2005-06, Expanding on the rule from two seasons before, officials who consult a courtside monitor at the end of either half or any extra period could correct the official game time if needed and/or determine whether a foul was committed before time expired. Officials could also consult a courtside monitor any time during the game to correct a timer's mistake. 2007-08, Use of courtside monitor allowed for determining whether a flagrant foul occurred or to assess the situation during a fight.

Three Seconds: 1932-33, No player could stand in the free-throw lane with the ball more than three seconds. 1935-36, No offensive player could remain in the free-throw lane, with or without the ball, for more than three seconds. 1944-45, It became a violation for an offensive player to remain in the free-throw lane more than three seconds.

Three-Point Shot: 1980-81, Conferences began experimenting with the three-point field-goal at different distances. 1986-87, The three-point field goal was introduced nationally and set at 19 feet 9 inches from the center of the basket. 1990-91, Three free throws were awarded when a shooter was fouled during an unsuccessful three-point try. 2008-09, The three-point line was extended to 20 feet, 9 inches.

Time Stoppage: 1905-06, Time stopped only when ordered by the referee. It did not stop for dead-ball situations such as free throws or when the ball was out-of-bounds. 1924-25, Time stopped when ordered by the referee for injuries, substitutions, two-shot fouls and timeouts requested by the team captain. The clock kept running at all other times including dead-ball situations, such as out-of-bounds.

Timekeepers: 1905-06, One timekeeper was appointed by the home team. The visiting team could appoint an assistant timekeeper if it chose to. 1924-25, Two timekeepers were used, one from each team, and shared a watch placed on a table so both could see it. The timekeepers kept track of all the incidents that time was out and added that to the game time. The timekeepers indicated when time expired by using a gong, pistol or whistle.

Timeouts: 1924-25, Only team captains could call for a timeout. Each team had three timeouts per game. 1948-49, Coaches were allowed to speak to players during a timeout. 1995-96, Teams were allowed one 20-second timeout per half. This was an experimental rule in the 1994-95 season. 1996-97, In games not involving commercial electronic media, teams were entitled to four full-length timeouts and two 20-second timeouts per game. In games involving commercial electronic media, teams were entitled to two full-length timeouts and three 20-second timeouts per game. 1997-98, Timeout requests could be made by a player on the court or by the head coach. 1999-00, Twenty-second timeouts increased to 30 seconds in length. New electronic-media timeout format adopted. 2006-07, A timeout would not be recognized when an airborne player's momentum carried him either out-of-bounds or into the backcourt.

Traveling: 1900-01, A dribbler could not shoot for a field goal and could dribble only once, and then only with two hands. 1908-09, A dribbler was permitted to shoot. The dribble was defined as the "continuous passage of the ball," making the double dribble illegal. 1921-22, Running with the ball changes from a foul to a violation.

Uniforms: 1957-58, On uniforms, the use of the single digit numbers one and two and any digit greater than five was prohibited. 1999-00, Uniform numbers one and two were permitted.

Basketball Rules Committee Secretary-Rules Editor Roster

Name	Affiliation	Years
Oswald Tower	non-NCAA	1939-59
John Bunn	Colorado St.	1960-67
Ed Steitz	Springfield	1967-91
Henry Nichols	Villanova	1992-96
Ed Bilik	Springfield	1997-present

Division I Basketball Rules Committee Chair Roster

Name	Affiliation	Years
H.H. Salmon Jr.	Princeton	1939-40
Floyd Rowe	non-NCAA	1941
James W. St. Clair	SMU	1942-44
E.J. Hickox	non-NCAA	1945, 1947
H.G. Olsen	Ohio St.	1946
George Edwards	Missouri	1948-51
Bruce Drake	Oklahoma	1952-55
Paul Hinkle	Butler	1956-59

Name	Affiliation	Years
H.E. Foster	Wisconsin	1960-65
Polk Robison	Texas Tech	1966
Norvall Neve	Atlantic Coast, Missouri Valley Conferences	1967-75
Richard Wilson	Amherst	1976
John Carpenter	Rider	1977-78
Jack Thurnblad	Carleton	1979-80
C.M. Newton	Alabama, Southeastern Conference	1981-85
James Dutcher	Minnesota	1986
Jerry Krause	Eastern Wash.	1987
Richard Sauers	Albany (N.Y.)	1988
Gene Bartow	UAB	1989-93
George Raveling	Southern California	1994-96
Larry Keating Jr.	Seton Hall	1997
Herb Kenny	Wesleyan (Conn.)	1998
Reggie Minton	Air Force	1999-2000
Roy Williams	Kansas	2001
Art Hyland	Big East Conference	2002-03
Willis Wilson	Rice	2004
Perry Watson	Detroit	2005
Larry Keating Jr.	Kansas	2006-07
Brad Jackson	Western Wash.	2008
Dick Hack	Pitt.-Greensburg	2009

Basketball Rules Committee Roster

Name	Affiliation	Years
Phog Allen	Kansas	1939-41
William Anderson	Lafayette	1951-54
Lewis Andreas	Syracuse	1946-49
Tom Apke	Creighton, Colorado	1979-84
Tim Autry	South Carolina St.	1998-2002
Joe Baker	Wis.-La Crosse	2003-05
Ralph Barkey	Sonoma St.	1996
Sam Barry	Southern California	1946-48
Justin Barry	Southern California	1949-51
Gene Bartow	Memphis, Illinois, UCLA, UAB	1974-78, 88-93
Mike Brey	Notre Dame	2008-present
Steve Belko	Oregon	1966-69
John Bennington	St. Louis, Michigan St.	1960-65
Bill Berry	San Jose St.	1988-90
Ed Bilik	Springfield	1968-69, 72-78, 96-2002
Hoyt Brawner	Denver	1960-66
Adam Brick	George Mason	2009-present
Charlie Brock	Springfield	2003-07
Clint Bryant	Augusta St.	1996-99
Tom Bryant	Centre	1996-98
John Bunn	Stanford, Springfield, Colorado St.	1939-40, 54-67
Clarence Burch	Lycoming	1979-82
Jim Burson	Muskingum	1987-92
L.C. Butler	Colorado St.	1951-53
E.M. Cameron	Duke	1956-61
John Carpenter	Rider	1973-78
Don Casey	Temple	1979-82
Dale Clayton	Carson-Newman	2003-07
Gary Colson	New Mexico, California	1986-92
Robert Corn	Mo. Southern St.	2008-present
Forrest Cox	Colorado	1940-44
Joe Dean Jr.	Birmingham So.	2003-07
Sumner A. Dole	Connecticut	1939-41
Ed Douma	Hillsdale	2001-04
Bruce Drake	Oklahoma	1947-55
Fran Dunphy	Penn	2004-06
James Dutcher	Minnesota	1983-86
W.H.H. Dye	Washington	1955-59
Scott Eaton	Northern Ky.	2009-present
C.S. Edmundson	Washington	1941-45
George Edwards	Missouri	1942-51
Fred Enke	Arizona	1957-61
Wesley E. Fesler	Wesleyan (Conn.)	1944
Dan Fitzgerald	Gonzaga	1996-97
H.E. Foster	Wisconsin	1958-66
Clarence Gaines	Winston-Salem	1992-93
Jayson Gee	Charleston (W.V.)	2001-03
Pete Gillen	Xavier	1993-97
Jack Gray	Texas	1951-52
Hugh Greer	Connecticut	1963
Jim Gudger	Tex. A&M-Commerce	1976, 78
Dick Hack	Medaille, Pitt.-Greensburg	2006-present
Richard Harter	Penn	1972
Rick Hartzell	UNI	2008
Clem Haskins	Minnesota	1992-96
E.O. "Doc" Hayes	SMU	1967-69
R.E. Henderson	Baylor	1953-56
Paul Hinkle	Butler	1954-59
Howard Hobson	Yale	1952-55
Ron Holmes	McMurry	1999-2002
Art Hyland	Big East Conference	1998-2003
Henry Iba	Oklahoma St.	1952-54, 67-69
Clarence Iba	Tulsa	1956-59
George Ireland	Loyola (Ill.)	1963-66
Calvin Irvin	N.C. A&T	1979
Brad Jackson	Western Wash.	2004-08
Bill Jones	North Ala.	1985-91
Larry Keating, Jr.	Seton Hall, Kansas	1994-97; 2003-07
Herb Kenny	Wesleyan (Conn.)	1993-98
William Knapton	Beloit	1981-86
Jack Kraft	Villanova	1968-69
Jerry Krause	Eastern Wash. St.	1976-78, 83-87
Mike Kryzyewski	Duke	1991
John Kundla	Minnesota	1968-69, 72-74
Eugene Lambert	Arkansas	1945-49
Dale Lash	Springfield	1942-43
Debora Lazorik	Marietta	1999-2002
Harry Litwack	Temple	1960-65
Bobby Lutz	Charlotte	2007-present
Edward P. Markey	St. Michael's	1992-95
Jack Martin	Lamar	1974-79
Rollie Massimino	UNLV	1993-95
Arthur McAfee	Morehouse	1975-80
Walter "Doc" Meanwell	Wisconsin	1939
Gene Mehaffey	Ohio Wesleyan	1993-98
Bill Menefee	Baylor	1972-73
Ray Meyer	DePaul	1979-82
Joey Meyer	DePaul	1993-95
Douglas Mills	Illinois	1947-53
Reggie Minton	Air Force	1997-2000
Mike Montgomery	Stanford	1997-2000
Steve Moore	Wooster	2007-present
Gerald Myers	Texas Tech	1986-92, 2009-present
Norvall Neve	Atlantic Coast, Missouri Valley Conferences	1967-75
C.M. Newton	Alabama, Southeastern Conference	1981-85
Henry Nichols	Villanova	1992-96
Thomas Niland Jr.	Le Moyne	1985-91
Kenneth Norton	Manhattan	1955-59
Tom O'Connor	George Mason	1998-2003
Dave Odom	Wake Forest	2001-04
H.G. Olsen	Ohio St.	1940-46
Ray Oosting	Trinity (Conn.)	1946-49, 51, 58-62
James Padgett	California, Nevada	1972-74
Curtis Parker	Centenary (La.)	1939-41
Ted Paulauskas	St. Anselm	1997-99
Richard H. Perry	UC Riverside	1992
Vadal Peterson	Utah	1945-48
Mac Petty	Wabash	1987-92
Digger Phelps	Notre Dame	1988-91
Jerry Pimm	Utah	1979-84
Lonnie Porter	Regis (Colo.)	2004-08
Clarence Price	California	1952-54
Skip Prosser	Wake Forest	2004-07
Jack Ramsay	St. Joseph's	1966-67
George Raveling	Southern California	1993-96
Lonn Reisman	Tarleton St.	2000-03
Polk Robison	Texas Tech	1962-66
Paul Rundell	San Fran. St.	1980-81
Adolph Rupp	Kentucky	1962-66
Andy Russo	Florida Tech, Lynn	1997-2000
H.H. Salmon Jr.	Princeton	1939-40
Richard Sauers	Albany (N.Y.)	1983-87
William Scanlon	Union (N.Y.)	1989-94
Jim Schaus	Ohio	2009-present
Norman Shepard	Davidson	1942-47
J. Dallas Shirley	Southern Conference	1984-87
Dean Smith	North Carolina	1967-69, 72-73
James W. St. Clair	SMU	1939-44
Floyd Stahl	Ohio St.	1956-57, 60-61
Ed Steitz	Springfield	1959-91
Norm Stewart	Missouri	1985-91
Kenneth Stibler	Biscayne	1978-84
Eddie Sutton	Arkansas	1980-85
H. Jamison Swarts	Penn	1941-45
A.K. Tebell	Virginia	1948-52
Bob Thomason	Pacific	2004-08
John M. Thompson	N.C. Wesleyan	2008-present
John Thompson III	Princeton	2003-04
Jack Thurnblad	Carleton	1975-80
Alvin J. Van Wie	Wooster	1981-86
Bob Vanatta	Sunshine State Conference	1994-95
Kevin Vande Streek	Calvin	2003-06
A. Kenyon Wagner	BYU-Hawaii	2009-present
M. Edward Wagner	California Collegiate Athletic Association	1976-79
Russell Walseth	Colorado	1972-75, 77-78
Perry Watson	Detroit	2002-05
Stanley Watts	BYU	1954-57
Clifford Wells	Tulane	1953-56
Don White	Connecticut	1945
Reggie Witherspoon	Buffalo	2006-present
Vining William	Ouachita Baptist	1977
James Williams	Colorado St.	1972-78
Roy Williams	Kansas	1997-2000
Floyd Wilson	Harvard	1964-69
Richard Wilson	Amherst	1972-75
Willis Wilson	Rice	2001-04
Willard A. Witte	Wyoming	1939
John Wooden	UCLA	1961-64
Ned Wulk	Arizona St.	1968-69
Jim Zalacca	New Paltz St., Potsdam St.	1999-2002

Division I Basketball Firsts

The First Time...

Playing rules were published:
January 1892 in the Springfield College school newspaper, The Triangle.

A game was played:
January 20, 1892, at the Training School of the International YMCA College, now known as Springfield College in Massachusetts.

A game was played in public:
March 11, 1892, at Springfield College. A crowd of 200 saw the students defeat the teachers, 5-1.

A full schedule of games was played by a college:
1894, when the University of Chicago compiled a 6-1 season record.

A game between two colleges was played:
February 9, 1895, when the Minnesota School of Agriculture defeated Hamline, 9-3. Nine players were allowed on the court at the same time for both teams.

A game between two colleges was played with five players on each team:
January 16, 1896, when Chicago defeated Iowa, 15-12, in Iowa City. Iowa's starting lineup was composed of a YMCA team that just happened to be university students.

A game between two true college teams with five players on a team was played:
1897, when Yale defeated Penn, 32-10.

A conference season was played:
1901-02 by the East League, known today as the Ivy Group.

A conference tournament was played:
1921 by the Southern Conference. Kentucky was the winner.

A consensus all-America team was selected:
1929. Members were Charley Hyatt, Pittsburgh; Joe Schaaf, Penn; Charles Murphy, Purdue; Vern Corbin, California; Thomas Churchill, Oklahoma; and John Thompson, Montana State.

A game was filmed for a newsreel:
February 20, 1931, St. John's (N.Y.) against Carnegie Mellon.

The National Invitation Tournament was played:
1938, when Temple was the winner.

A college game was televised:
February 28, 1940, when Pittsburgh defeated Fordham, 50-37, at Madison Square Garden in New York City. In the second game, New York University defeated Georgetown, 50-27. The games were broadcast on New York station W2XBS.

The three-point shot was used experimentally in a game:
February 7, 1945, Columbia defeated Fordham, 73-58. The three-point line was set at 21 feet from the basket and Columbia scored 11 "long goals" to Fordham's nine. Also, free-throwers had an option to take their shots from the regular 15-foot distance for one point or from 21 feet for two points. Eight "long fouls" were made during the game.

The 12-foot free-throw lane was used experimentally in a game:
February 7, 1945, Columbia defeated Fordham, 73-58 in the same game as mentioned above. The free-throw lane was widened from 6 feet to 12 for this game and the rule was adopted 11 years later.

An Associated Press poll was published:
1949, when St. Louis was ranked No. 1. By the end of the season, Kentucky had taken over the top spot.

Five African-Americans were on the court for a Major College (Division I) team:
December 29,1962, Loyola (Ill.) against Wyoming in the All-City Tournament in Oklahoma City. In the second half of the game, starter John Egan was replaced by Pablo Robertson to make all five players in the game for Loyola African-American. Three months later Loyola won the NCAA title.

All the games of a conference tournament were televised:
1979, the Sun Belt on ESPN.

The RPI was released to the public:
Febuary 1, 2006, when the Rating Percentage Index (RPI) appeared on the NCAA Web site.

NCAA Tournament Firsts

The first game:
March 17, 1939, when Villanova defeated Brown, 42-30, in Philadelphia.

The first championship game:
March 27, 1939, when Oregon defeated Ohio State, 46-33, in Evanston, Illinois.

The first NCAA tournament MOP:
1939, Jimmy Hull of Ohio State was named the tournament's Most Outstanding Player.

The first player to score 30 points or more in a tournament game:
1941, George Glamack of North Carolina scored 31 points against Dartmouth in a regional third-place game.

The first time two teams from the same conference played in the NCAA tournament:
1944, when Iowa State and Missouri, both of the Big Six, played in the Western regional.

The first freshman named NCAA tournament MOP:
1944, Arnie Ferrin of Utah.

The first two-time NCAA tournament MOP:
1946, Bob Kurland of Oklahoma State was MOP in 1945 and 1946.

The first time four teams advanced to the final site:
1946 (North Carolina, Ohio State, Oklahoma State and California).

The first championship game televised:
1946, locally in New York City by WCBS-TV. Oklahoma State defeated North Carolina, 43-40. An estimated 500,000 watched the game on television.

The first player to dunk:
March 26 1946, when Bob Kurland, the 7-foot center for Oklahoma State, threw down two dunks late in the game to help preserve a 43-40 victory over North Carolina in the championship game.

The first repeat champion:
1946, Oklahoma State followed its 1945 championship with a title in 1946.

The first player to score 30 points or more in a Final Four game:
1947, George Kaftan of Holy Cross scored 30 points against CCNY in the national semifinal game.

The first school to win the NCAA championship in its home town:
1950, CCNY won the title in New York.

The first NCAA championship team to have an integrated roster of white and black players:
1950, CCNY's squad was the first integrated championship team, starting three black players

The first time conference champions qualified automatically:
1951.

The first time a team entered the tournament undefeated:
1951, Columbia at 21-0. The Lions lost to Illinois in the first round, 79-71.

The first time a conference tournament champion qualified automatically for the NCAA tournament instead of the regular-season champion:
1952, North Carolina State finished second in the Southern Conference but won the conference postseason tournament.

The first time there were four regional sites:
1952.

The first time games were televised regionally:
1952.

The first NCAA tournament MOP not to play on the national championship team:
1953, B.H. Born of Kansas.

The first player to score 40 points or more in a tournament game:
1952, Clyde Lovellette of Kansas scored 44 points against St. Louis in the regional final game.

The first player to score 40 points or more in a Final Four game:
1953, Bob Houbregs of Washington scored 42 points against LSU in the national third-place game.

The first time a Final Four was played on Friday and Saturday:
1954.

The first tournament championship game televised nationally:
1954, for a broadcast rights fee of $7,500.

The first time an undefeated team won the NCAA championship:
1956, when San Francisco went 29-0.

The first player to score 50 points or more in a tournament game:
1958, Oscar Robertson of Cincinnati scored 56 points against Arkansas in the regional third-place game.

The first time two teams from the same state played in the NCAA title game:
1961, when Cincinnati defeated Ohio State, 70-65, in overtime.

The first football Heisman Trophy winner to play in the Final Four:
1963, Terry Baker of Oregon State.

The first player to score 50 points or more in a Final Four game:
1965, Bill Bradley of Princeton scored 58 points against Wichita State in the national third-place game.

The first championship team to start five African-Americans:
1966, UTEP with Harry Flournoy, David Lattin, Bobby Joe Hill, Orsten Artis and Willie Worsley.

The first three-time NCAA tournament MOP:
1969, Lew Alcindor of UCLA was MOP in 1967, 1968 and 1969.

The first time the Final Four was played on Thursday and Saturday:
1969.

The first time the Final Four was played on Saturday and Monday:
1973.

The first NCAA title game televised during prime time:
1973, UCLA's win over Memphis was televised by NBC.

The first time television rights totaled more than $1 million:
1973.

The first public draw for Final Four tickets:
1973 for the 1974 championship.

The first time teams other than the conference champion could be chosen at large from the same conference:
1975.

The first reference to the term "Final Four":
1975 Official Collegiate Basketball Guide, page 5 in national preview-review section written by Ed Chay of the Cleveland Plain Dealer. Chay wrote, "Outspoken Al McGuire of Marquette, whose team was one of the

final four in Greensboro, was among several coaches who said it was good for college basketball that UCLA was finally beaten."

The first time two African-American coaches played each other in a tournament game:
March 13, 1976, when Fred Snowden's Arizona Wildcats defeated John Thompson's Georgetown Hoyas, 83-76, in a first round game.

The first time two teams from the same conference played in the Final Four title game:
March 29, 1976, when Indiana defeated Michigan, 86-68. Both teams were Big Ten members.

The first player to play for two teams in the Final Four championship game:
1978, Bob Bender with Indiana in 1976 and Duke in 1978.

The first time the seeding process was used to align teams in the bracket:
1978.

The first reference to term "Final Four" was capitalized:
1978 Official Collegiate Basketball Guide (page 7, first line).

The first time all teams were seeded in the bracket:
1979.

The first public lottery for Final Four tickets:
1979.

The first time more than two teams from the same conference were allowed in the NCAA tournament:
1980.

The first time none of the No. 1 seeds in the NCAA tournament advanced to the Final Four:
1980.

The first time the Rating Percentage Index (RPI), a computer ranking system, was used as an aid in evaluating teams for at-large selections and seeding:
1981.

The first time two No. 1 seeds in the NCAA tournament advanced to the Final Four:
1981.

The first time a Final Four logo was produced that was specific to the site of the championship game:
1981, when the final game was played in Philadelphia and the logo included the Liberty Bell.

The first live television broadcast of the selection show announcing the NCAA tournament bracket:
1982.

The first time CBS was awarded the television rights for the NCAA tournament:
1982.

The first TV announcer to use "March Madness" in referring the tournament:
1982, Brent Musburger of CBS Sports.

The first African-American to coach a team into the Final Four:
1982, John Thompson of Georgetown.

The first time a men's and women's team from the same school advanced to the Final Four in the same year:
1983, when both Georgia teams lost in the national semifinals.

The first time awards were presented to all participating teams in the NCAA championship tournament:
1984.

The first African-American to coach a team to the NCAA basketball championship:
1984, John Thompson of Georgetown.

The first time 64 teams participated in the NCAA tournament:
1985.

The first unranked team to win the championship:
1985, Villanova.

The first double-digit seed to reach the Final Four:
1986, LSU as an 11-seed.

The first coach to win the NCAA title in his first year as a head coach:
Steve Fisher of Michigan in 1989.

The first time 65 teams participated in the NCAA tournament:
2001.

The first time two persons of color faced each other as coaches in a Final Four game:
March 30, 2002, when Mike Davis' Indiana Hoosiers defeated Kelvin Sampson's Oklahoma Sooners, 73-64, in a national semifinal game.

The first time three teams from the same conference advanced to the Final Four:
1985, when Georgetown, St. John's (New York) and Villanova represented the Big East.

The first time all 64 NCAA tournament teams were subject to drug testing:
1987.

The first time neutral courts were used in all rounds of the NCAA tournament:
1989.

The first time all the Nos. 1 and 2 seeds in the NCAA tournament advanced to the Sweet Sixteen:
1989.

The first time a bearded coach advanced to the Final Four:
1989, P.J. Carlesimo of Seton Hall.

The first No. 15-seed to defeat a No. 2-seed:
1991, Richmond over Syracuse, 73-69.

The first time a minimum facility seating capacity of 12,000 for first and second rounds and regionals was established:
1993.

The first time three No. 1 seeds in the NCAA tournament advanced to the Final Four:
1993.

The first time two former Final Four most outstanding players returned to the Final Four:
1995, when North Carolina's Donald Williams (1993) and Arkansas' Corliss Williamson (1994) returned to the Final Four.

The First School...

To play in both the NIT and the NCAA tournaments in the same year:
Duquesne in 1940

To win 30 games in a season:
Wyoming went 31-2 in 1943.

To win a football bowl game and the NCAA tournament title in the same academic year:
Oklahoma State won the Cotton Bowl and the NCAA championship in 1944-45.

To be ranked No. 1 in the final regular-season poll and go on to win the NCAA championship:
Kentucky ended the 1949 regular season ranked No. 1 and proceeded to win its second NCAA title.

To win the NCAA tournament and the NIT in the same year:
CCNY won both tournaments in 1950.

To play for the national championship in both football and basketball in the same academic year:
Oklahoma lost in both the Orange Bowl and the Final Four title game in 1987-88.

To be ranked No. 1 in the men's and women's polls:
Connecticut's men's and women's basketball programs were ranked No. 1 in their respective top-25 polls February 13, 1995.

To be voted the national champion in football and win the NCAA basketball tournament in the same academic year:
Florida in 2006-07

The First Coach...

Who also happened to be the inventor of the game:
Dr. James Naismith invented the game in December 1891 at Springfield College in Massachusetts.

To have won the NCAA tournament at his alma mater:
Howard Hobson of Oregon in 1939.

To lead his team to a finish among the final four teams in the nation in his first season as a head coach:
Bruce Drake of Oklahoma in 1939.

To take two different teams to the NCAA tournament:
Ben Carnevale—North Carolina in 1946 and Navy in 1947.

To lead his alma mater into the NCAA tournament after having played in the tournament:
Elmer Gross played for Penn State in the 1942 NCAA tournament and later coached them in the 1952 tournament.

To lead a school other than his alma mater into the NCAA tournament after having played in the tournament:
Doyle Parrack played for Oklahoma State in the 1945 NCAA tournament and later coached Oklahoma City in the 1952 tournament.

To be recognized as national coach of the year:
Phil Woolpert of San Francisco was named the 1955 coach of the year by United Press International.

To take two different teams to the Final Four:
Forddy Anderson and Frank McGuire. Anderson—Bradley in 1950 and Michigan State in 1957; McGuire—St. John's (New York) in 1952 and North Carolina in 1957.

To take two different schools to the NCAA championship game:
Frank McGuire in 1957 with North Carolina after St. John's (New York) in 1952.

To take three different teams to the NCAA tournament:
Eddie Hickey—Creighton in 1941 (first year), Saint Louis in 1952 and Marquette in 1959.

To have won the NCAA championship his first year at a school:
Ed Jucker at Cincinnati in 1961.

Who was African-American to coach at a Division I school:
Will Robinson at Illinois State in the 1971-72 season.

To win the NCAA championship after playing for an NCAA championship team:
Bob Knight coached Indiana to the championship in 1976 after playing for the 1960 Ohio State champions.

To take four different teams to the NCAA tournament:
Eddie Sutton—Creighton in 1974 (first year), Arkansas in 1977, Kentucky in 1986 and Oklahoma State in 1991.

To take a school to the Final Four in four different decades:
Dean Smith took North Carolina to the Final Four 11 times from 1967 to 1997.

To take three different teams to the Final Four:
Rick Pitino—Providence in 1987, Kentucky in 1993 and Louisville in 2005.

The First Player...

To score 1,000 points in his career:
Christian Steinmetz of Wisconsin from 1903-05.

To be named consensus all-American three times:
John Wooden of Purdue from 1930-32.

To popularize the jump shot:
John Cooper of Missouri in 1932-34, Hank Luisetti of Stanford in 1936-38 and Kenny Sailors of Wyoming in 1941-43 and 1946.

To score 50 points in one game:
Hank Luisetti of Stanford, who scored 50 in a win over Duquesne, January 1, 1938.

To dribble behind his back:
Hank Luisetti of Stanford and Bob Davies of Seton Hall, are believed to be two of the first innovators of the behind-the-back dribble in the 1930s and early 1940s. Davies was photographed doing so.

To dunk in a game:
Bob Kurland, the 7-foot center for Oklahoma State, in 1946. His first dunk was disallowed, although his subsequent dunks were allowed.

Who was African-American to be named to the consensus all-America team:
Don Barksdale of UCLA in 1947.

Who was African-American to play on the U.S. Olympic team:
Don Barksdale of UCLA in 1948.

To score 2,000 points in his career:
Jim Lacy of Loyola (Md.) scored 2,154 points from 1946-49.

To lead the nation in scoring during the regular season and play for the NCAA championship team in the same year:
Clyde Lovellette of Kansas in 1952.

To grab 50 rebounds in one game:
Bill Chambers of William and Mary brought down 51 boards against Virginia on February 14, 1953.

To grab 700 rebounds in a season:
Walt Dukes of Seton Hall brought down 734 boards during the 1953 season.

To score 100 points in a game:
Frank Selvy of Furman scored 100 points in a 149-95 victory over Newberry on February 13, 1954, in Greenville, South Carolina.

To score 1,000 points in a single season:
Frank Selvy of Furman scored 1,209 during the 1954 season.

To average 40 points a game for a season:
Frank Selvy of Furman averaged 41.7 points a game during the 1954 season.

To average 30 points a game for a career:
Frank Selvy of Furman averaged 32.5 points a game from 1952-54.

To achieve 2,000 points and 2,000 rebounds in his career:
Tom Gola of La Salle scored 2,462 points and pulled down 2,201 rebounds from 1952-55.

Recognized as the national player of the year:
Tom Gola of La Salle was named the 1955 player of the year by United Press International.

To average more than 20 points and 20 rebounds per game during his career:
Bill Russell of San Francisco from 1954-56. He averaged 20.7 points and 20.3 rebounds.

To score 3,000 points in his career:
Pete Maravich of LSU scored 3,667 points from 1968-70.

To average 40 points a game for a career:
Pete Maravich of LSU averaged 44.2 points a game from 1968-70.

To score a three-point field goal (not counting the Columbia-Fordham game in 1945):
Ronnie Carr of Western Carolina drilled a 23-footer against Middle Tennessee State at 7:06 p.m. on November 29, 1980. The three-pointer was used as an experiment by several conferences until the rule was adopted nationally for the 1986-87 season.

To be named consensus all-American his freshman season:
Wayman Tisdale of Oklahoma in 1983.

To lead the nation in scoring and rebounding in the same season:
Xavier McDaniel of Wichita State in 1985.

To make 400 three-point field goals in his career:
Doug Day of Radford hit 401 three-pointers from 1990-93.

To be named national player-of-the-year his freshman season:
Kevin Durant of Texas in 2007.

Conferences

2008 Division I Conference Standings

AMERICA EAST CONFERENCE

	Conference			Full Season		
	W	L	Pct.	W	L	Pct.
UMBC #	13	3	.813	24	9	.727
Hartford	10	6	.625	18	16	.529
Albany (N.Y.)	10	6	.625	15	15	.500
Vermont	9	7	.563	16	15	.516
Binghamton	9	7	.563	14	16	.467
Boston U.	9	7	.563	14	17	.452
New Hampshire	6	10	.375	9	20	.310
Maine	3	13	.188	7	23	.233
Stony Brook	3	13	.188	7	23	.233

ATLANTIC COAST CONFERENCE

	Conference			Full Season		
	W	L	Pct.	W	L	Pct.
North Carolina #	14	2	.875	36	3	.923
Duke	13	3	.813	28	6	.824
Clemson	10	6	.625	24	10	.706
Virginia Tech	9	7	.563	21	14	.600
Miami (Fla.)	8	8	.500	23	11	.676
Maryland	8	8	.500	19	15	.559
Wake Forest	7	9	.438	17	13	.567
Florida St.	7	9	.438	19	15	.559
Georgia Tech	7	9	.438	15	17	.469
Virginia	5	11	.313	17	16	.515
North Carolina St.	4	12	.250	15	16	.484
Boston College	4	12	.250	14	17	.452

ATLANTIC SUN CONFERENCE

	Conference			Full Season		
	W	L	Pct.	W	L	Pct.
Belmont #	14	2	.875	25	9	.735
Jacksonville	12	4	.750	18	13	.581
Stetson	11	5	.688	16	16	.500
East Tenn. St.	11	5	.688	19	13	.594
Lipscomb	9	7	.563	15	16	.484
Gardner-Webb	9	7	.563	16	16	.500
Kennesaw St.*	7	9	.438	10	20	.333
Mercer	6	10	.375	11	19	.367
Fla. Gulf Coast*	6	10	.375	10	21	.323
Campbell	5	11	.313	10	20	.333
S.C. Upstate*	5	11	.313	7	23	.233
North Fla.*	1	15	.063	3	26	.103

ATLANTIC 10 CONFERENCE

	Conference			Full Season		
	W	L	Pct.	W	L	Pct.
Xavier	14	2	.875	30	7	.811
Temple #	11	5	.688	21	13	.618
Massachusetts	10	6	.625	25	11	.694
Richmond	9	7	.563	16	15	.516
St. Joseph's	9	7	.563	21	13	.618
Charlotte	9	7	.563	20	14	.588
La Salle	8	8	.500	15	17	.469
Dayton	9	8	.529	23	11	.676
St. Louis	7	9	.438	16	15	.516
Duquesne	7	9	.438	17	13	.567
Rhode Island	7	9	.438	21	12	.636
Fordham	6	10	.375	12	17	.414
George Washington	5	11	.313	9	17	.346
St. Bonaventure	2	14	.125	8	22	.267

BIG EAST CONFERENCE

	Conference			Full Season		
	W	L	Pct.	W	L	Pct.
Georgetown	15	3	.833	28	6	.824
Louisville	14	4	.778	27	9	.750
Notre Dame	14	4	.778	25	8	.758
Connecticut	13	5	.722	24	9	.727
West Virginia	11	7	.611	26	11	.703
Marquette	11	7	.611	25	10	.714
Pittsburgh #	10	8	.556	27	10	.730
Villanova	9	9	.500	22	13	.629
Syracuse	9	9	.500	21	14	.600
Cincinnati	8	10	.444	13	19	.406
Seton Hall	7	11	.389	17	15	.531
Providence	6	12	.333	15	16	.484
DePaul	6	12	.333	11	19	.367
St. John's (N.Y.)	5	13	.278	11	19	.367
South Fla.	3	15	.167	12	19	.387
Rutgers	3	15	.167	11	20	.355

BIG SKY CONFERENCE

	Conference			Full Season		
	W	L	Pct.	W	L	Pct.
Portland St. #	14	2	.875	23	10	.697
Northern Ariz.	11	5	.688	21	11	.656
Weber St.	10	6	.625	16	14	.533
Idaho St.	8	8	.500	12	19	.387
Montana	8	8	.500	14	16	.467
Montana St.	9	9	.438	15	15	.500
Northern Colo.	6	10	.375	13	16	.448
Eastern Wash.	6	10	.375	11	19	.367
Sacramento St.	2	14	.125	4	24	.143

BIG SOUTH CONFERENCE

	Conference			Full Season		
	W	L	Pct.	W	L	Pct.
UNC Asheville	10	4	.714	23	10	.697
Winthrop #	10	4	.714	22	12	.647
High Point	8	6	.571	17	14	.548
Liberty	7	7	.500	16	16	.500
VMI	6	8	.429	14	15	.483
Coastal Caro.	6	8	.429	13	15	.464
Radford	5	9	.357	10	20	.333
Charleston So.	4	10	.286	10	20	.333

BIG TEN CONFERENCE

	Conference			Full Season		
	W	L	Pct.	W	L	Pct.
Wisconsin #	16	2	.889	31	5	.861
Purdue	15	3	.833	25	9	.735
Indiana	14	4	.778	25	8	.758
Michigan St.	12	6	.667	27	9	.750
Ohio St.	10	8	.556	24	13	.649
Minnesota	8	10	.444	20	14	.588
Penn St.	7	11	.389	15	16	.484
Iowa	6	12	.333	13	19	.406
Illinois	5	13	.278	16	19	.457
Michigan	5	13	.278	10	22	.313
Northwestern	1	17	.056	8	22	.267

BIG 12 CONFERENCE

	Conference			Full Season		
	W	L	Pct.	W	L	Pct.
Texas	13	3	.813	31	7	.816
Kansas #	13	3	.813	37	3	.925
Kansas St.	10	6	.625	21	12	.636
Oklahoma	9	7	.563	23	12	.657
Baylor	9	7	.563	21	11	.656
Texas A&M	8	8	.500	25	11	.694
Nebraska	7	9	.438	20	13	.606
Texas Tech	7	9	.438	16	15	.516
Oklahoma St.	7	9	.438	17	16	.515
Missouri	6	10	.375	16	16	.500
Iowa St.	4	12	.250	14	18	.438
Colorado	3	13	.188	12	20	.375

BIG WEST CONFERENCE

	Conference			Full Season		
	W	L	Pct.	W	L	Pct.
UC Santa Barbara	12	4	.750	23	9	.719
Cal St. Northridge	12	4	.750	20	10	.667
Cal St. Fullerton #	12	4	.750	24	9	.727
Pacific	11	5	.688	21	10	.677
UC Irvine	9	7	.563	18	16	.529
Cal Poly	7	9	.438	12	18	.400
UC Riverside	4	12	.250	9	21	.300
Long Beach St.	3	13	.188	6	25	.194
UC Davis	2	14	.125	9	22	.290

COLONIAL ATHLETIC ASSOCIATION

	Conference			Full Season		
	W	L	Pct.	W	L	Pct.
VCU	15	3	.833	24	8	.750
George Mason #	12	6	.667	23	11	.676
UNC Wilmington	12	6	.667	20	13	.606
Old Dominion	11	7	.611	18	16	.529
William & Mary	10	8	.556	17	16	.515
Northeastern	9	9	.500	14	17	.452
Delaware	9	9	.500	14	17	.452
Hofstra	8	10	.444	12	18	.400
Towson	7	11	.389	13	18	.419
James Madison	5	13	.278	13	17	.433
Drexel	5	13	.278	12	20	.375
Georgia St.	5	13	.278	9	21	.300

CONFERENCE USA

	Conference			Full Season		
	W	L	Pct.	W	L	Pct.
Memphis #	16	0	1.000	38	2	.950
UAB	12	4	.750	23	11	.676
Houston	11	5	.688	24	10	.706
UCF	9	7	.563	16	15	.516
Southern Miss.	9	7	.563	19	14	.576
UTEP	8	8	.500	19	14	.576
Tulsa	8	8	.500	25	14	.641
Marshall	8	8	.500	16	14	.533
Tulane	6	10	.375	17	15	.531
East Carolina	5	11	.313	11	19	.367
SMU	4	12	.250	10	20	.333
Rice	0	16	.000	3	27	.100

HORIZON LEAGUE

	Conference			Full Season		
	W	L	Pct.	W	L	Pct.
Butler #	16	2	.889	30	4	.882
Cleveland St.	12	6	.667	21	13	.618
Wright St.	12	6	.667	21	10	.677
Ill.-Chicago	9	9	.500	18	15	.545
Milwaukee	9	9	.500	14	16	.467
Valparaiso	9	9	.500	22	14	.611
Green Bay	9	9	.500	15	15	.500
Loyola (Ill.)	6	12	.333	12	19	.387
Youngtown St.	5	13	.278	9	21	.300
Detroit	3	15	.167	7	23	.233

IVY GROUP

	Conference			Full Season		
	W	L	Pct.	W	L	Pct.
Cornell	14	0	1.000	22	6	.786
Brown	11	3	.786	19	10	.655
Penn	8	6	.571	13	18	.419
Columbia	7	7	.500	14	15	.483
Yale	7	7	.500	13	15	.464
Dartmouth	3	11	.214	10	18	.357
Harvard	3	11	.214	8	22	.267
Princeton	3	11	.214	6	23	.207

METRO ATLANTIC ATHLETIC CONFERENCE

	Conference			Full Season		
	W	L	Pct.	W	L	Pct.
Siena #	13	5	.722	23	11	.676
Rider	13	5	.722	23	11	.676
Niagara	12	6	.667	19	10	.655
Loyola (Md.)	12	6	.667	19	14	.576
Fairfield	11	7	.611	14	16	.467
Marist	11	7	.611	18	14	.563
Iona	8	10	.444	12	20	.375
Manhattan	5	13	.278	12	19	.387
St. Peter's	3	15	.167	6	24	.200
Canisius	2	16	.111	6	25	.194

MID-AMERICAN CONFERENCE

East Division	Conference			Full Season		
	W	L	Pct.	W	L	Pct.
Kent St. #	13	3	.813	28	7	.800
Akron	11	5	.688	24	11	.686
Ohio	9	7	.563	20	13	.606
Miami (Ohio)	9	7	.563	17	16	.515
Bowling Green	7	9	.438	13	17	.433
Buffalo	3	13	.188	10	20	.333
West Division						
Western Mich.	12	4	.750	20	12	.625
Central Mich.	8	8	.500	14	17	.452
Eastern Mich.	8	8	.500	14	17	.452
Toledo	7	8	.467	11	19	.367
Ball St.	5	11	.313	6	24	.200
Northern Ill.	3	12	.200	6	22	.214

MID-EASTERN ATHLETIC CONFERENCE

	Conference			Full Season		
	W	L	Pct.	W	L	Pct.
Morgan St.	14	2	.875	22	11	.667
Hampton	11	5	.688	18	12	.600
Norfolk St.	11	5	.688	16	15	.516
Delaware St.	10	6	.625	14	16	.467
N.C. A&T	9	7	.563	15	16	.484
Florida A&M	9	7	.563	15	17	.469
Coppin St. #	7	9	.438	16	21	.432
South Carolina St.	7	9	.438	13	20	.394
Bethune-Cookman	5	11	.313	11	21	.344
Howard	3	13	.188	6	26	.188
Md.-East. Shore	2	14	.125	4	28	.125

MISSOURI VALLEY CONFERENCE

	Conference			Full Season		
	W	L	Pct.	W	L	Pct.
Drake #	15	3	.833	28	5	.848
Illinois St.	13	5	.722	25	10	.714
Southern Ill.	11	7	.611	18	15	.545
Creighton	10	8	.556	22	11	.667
UNI	9	9	.500	18	14	.563
Bradley	9	9	.500	21	17	.553
Missouri St.	8	10	.444	17	16	.515
Indiana St.	8	10	.444	15	16	.484
Wichita St.	4	14	.222	11	20	.355
Evansville	3	15	.167	9	21	.300

MOUNTAIN WEST CONFERENCE

	Conference			Full Season		
	W	L	Pct.	W	L	Pct.
BYU	14	2	.875	27	8	.771
UNLV #	12	4	.750	27	8	.771
New Mexico	11	5	.688	24	9	.727
San Diego St.	9	7	.563	20	13	.606
Air Force	8	8	.500	16	14	.533
Utah	7	9	.438	18	15	.545
TCU	6	10	.375	14	16	.467
Wyoming	5	11	.313	12	18	.400
Colorado St.	0	16	.000	7	25	.219

NORTHEAST CONFERENCE

	Conference			Full Season		
	W	L	Pct.	W	L	Pct.
Robert Morris	16	2	.889	26	8	.765
Wagner	15	3	.833	23	8	.742
Sacred Heart	13	5	.722	18	14	.563
Mt. St. Mary's #	11	7	.611	19	15	.559
Quinnipiac	11	7	.611	15	15	.500
Central Conn. St.	10	8	.556	14	16	.467
Long Island	7	11	.389	15	15	.500
Fairleigh Dickinson	4	14	.222	8	20	.286
St. Francis (N.Y.)	4	14	.222	7	22	.241
Monmouth	4	14	.222	7	24	.226
St. Francis (Pa.)	4	14	.222	6	23	.207

OHIO VALLEY CONFERENCE

	Conference			Full Season		
	W	L	Pct.	W	L	Pct.
Austin Peay #	16	4	.800	24	11	.686
Murray St.	13	7	.650	18	13	.581
Morehead St.	12	8	.600	15	15	.500
Tenn.-Martin	11	9	.550	17	16	.515
Samford	10	10	.500	14	16	.467
Tennessee St.	10	10	.500	15	17	.469
Tennessee Tech	10	10	.500	13	19	.406
Eastern Ky.	10	10	.500	14	16	.467
Southeast Mo. St.	7	13	.350	12	19	.387
Eastern Ill.	6	14	.300	7	22	.241
Jacksonville St.	5	15	.250	7	22	.241

PACIFIC-10 CONFERENCE

	Conference			Full Season		
	W	L	Pct.	W	L	Pct.
UCLA #	16	2	.889	35	4	.897
Stanford	13	5	.722	28	8	.778
Washington St.	11	7	.611	26	9	.743
Southern California	11	7	.611	21	12	.636
Arizona St.	9	9	.500	21	13	.618
Oregon	9	9	.500	18	14	.563
Arizona	8	10	.444	19	15	.559
Washington	7	11	.389	16	17	.485
California	6	12	.333	17	16	.515
Oregon St.	0	18	.000	6	25	.194

PATRIOT LEAGUE

	Conference			Full Season		
	W	L	Pct.	W	L	Pct.
American #	10	4	.714	21	12	.636
Navy	9	5	.643	16	14	.533
Colgate	7	7	.500	18	14	.563
Lehigh	7	7	.500	14	15	.483
Army	6	8	.429	14	16	.467
Lafayette	6	8	.429	15	15	.500
Bucknell	6	8	.429	12	19	.387
Holy Cross	5	9	.357	15	14	.517

SOUTHEASTERN CONFERENCE

	Conference			Full Season		
Eastern Division	W	L	Pct.	W	L	Pct.
Tennessee	14	2	.875	31	5	.861
Kentucky	12	4	.750	18	13	.581
Vanderbilt	10	6	.625	26	8	.765
Florida	8	8	.500	24	12	.667
South Carolina	5	11	.313	14	18	.438
Georgia #	4	12	.250	17	17	.500
Western Division						
Mississippi St.	12	4	.750	23	11	.676
Arkansas	9	7	.563	23	12	.657
Mississippi	7	9	.438	24	11	.686
LSU	6	10	.375	13	18	.419
Alabama	5	11	.313	17	16	.515
Auburn	4	12	.250	14	16	.467

SOUTHERN CONFERENCE

	Conference			Full Season		
North Division	W	L	Pct.	W	L	Pct.
Appalachian St.	13	7	.650	18	13	.581
Chattanooga	13	7	.650	18	13	.581
UNC Greensboro	12	8	.600	19	12	.613
Elon	9	11	.450	14	19	.424
Western Caro.	6	14	.300	10	21	.323
South Division						
Davidson #	20	0	1.000	29	7	.806
Ga. Southern	13	7	.650	20	12	.625
Col. of Charleston	9	11	.450	16	17	.485
Wofford	8	12	.400	16	16	.500
Furman	6	14	.300	7	23	.233
Citadel	1	19	.050	6	24	.200

SOUTHLAND CONFERENCE

	Conference			Full Season		
East Division	W	L	Pct.	W	L	Pct.
Lamar	13	3	.813	19	11	.633
Southeastern La.	9	7	.563	17	13	.567
Northwestern St.	9	7	.563	15	18	.455
McNeese St.	7	9	.438	13	16	.448
Nicholls St.	5	11	.313	10	21	.323
Central Ark.*	4	12	.250	14	16	.467
West Division						
Stephen F. Austin	13	3	.813	26	6	.813
Sam Houston St.	10	6	.625	23	8	.742
Texas-Arlington #	7	9	.438	21	12	.636
UTSA	7	9	.438	13	17	.433
Texas St.	6	10	.375	13	16	.448
A&M Corpus Christi	6	10	.375	9	20	.310

SOUTHWESTERN ATHLETIC CONFERENCE

	Conference			Full Season		
	W	L	Pct.	W	L	Pct.
Alabama St.	15	3	.833	20	11	.645
Mississippi Val. #	12	6	.667	17	16	.515
Alabama A&M	11	7	.611	14	15	.483
Jackson St.	10	8	.556	14	20	.412
Southern U.	9	9	.500	11	19	.367
Ark.-Pine Bluff	8	10	.444	13	18	.419
Grambling	7	11	.389	7	19	.269
Prairie View	6	12	.333	8	22	.267
Alcorn St.	6	12	.333	7	24	.226
Texas Southern	6	12	.333	7	25	.219

SUMMIT LEAGUE

	Conference			Full Season		
	W	L	Pct.	W	L	Pct.
Oral Roberts #	16	2	.889	24	9	.727
IUPUI	15	3	.833	26	7	.788
Oakland	11	7	.611	17	14	.548
North Dakota St.*	10	8	.556	16	13	.552
IPFW	9	9	.500	13	18	.419
Southern Utah	9	9	.500	11	19	.367
Western Ill.	7	11	.389	12	18	.400
UMKC	6	12	.333	11	21	.344
Centenary (La.)	4	14	.222	10	21	.323
South Dakota St.*	3	15	.167	8	21	.276

SUN BELT CONFERENCE

	Conference			Full Season		
Eastern Division	W	L	Pct.	W	L	Pct.
South Ala.	16	2	.889	26	7	.788
Western Ky. #	16	2	.889	29	7	.806
Middle Tenn.	11	7	.611	17	15	.531
Fla. Atlantic	8	10	.444	15	18	.455
Florida Int'l	6	12	.333	9	20	.310
Troy	4	14	.222	12	19	.387
Western Division						
UALR	11	7	.611	20	11	.645
La.-Lafayette	11	7	.611	15	15	.500
North Texas	10	8	.556	20	11	.645
New Orleans	8	10	.444	19	13	.594
Denver	7	11	.389	11	19	.367
Arkansas St.	5	13	.278	10	20	.333
La.-Monroe	4	14	.222	10	21	.323

WEST COAST CONFERENCE

	Conference			Full Season		
	W	L	Pct.	W	L	Pct.
Gonzaga	13	1	.929	25	8	.758
St. Mary's (Cal.)	12	2	.857	25	7	.781
San Diego #	11	3	.786	22	14	.611
Santa Clara	6	8	.429	15	16	.484
San Francisco	5	9	.357	10	21	.323
Pepperdine	4	10	.286	11	21	.344
Portland	3	11	.214	9	22	.290
Loyola Marymount	2	12	.143	5	26	.161

WESTERN ATHLETIC CONFERENCE

	Conference			Full Season		
	W	L	Pct.	W	L	Pct.
Utah St.	12	4	.750	24	11	.686
Nevada	12	4	.750	21	12	.636
New Mexico St.	12	4	.750	21	14	.600
Boise St. #	12	4	.750	25	9	.735
Hawaii	7	9	.438	11	19	.367
Idaho	5	11	.313	8	21	.276
Fresno St.	5	11	.313	13	19	.406
San Jose St.	4	12	.250	13	19	.406
Louisiana Tech	3	13	.188	6	24	.200

INDEPENDENTS

	W	L	Pct.
Tex.-Pan American	18	13	.581
Savannah St.	13	18	.419
Chicago St.	11	17	.393
Longwood	9	22	.290

RECLASSIFYING AND PROVISIONAL TEAMS

	W	L	Pct.
North Dakota St.	16	13	.552
Utah Valley St.	15	14	.517
Central Ark.	14	16	.467
Winston-Salem	12	18	.400
Kennesaw St.	10	20	.333
Fla. Gulf Coast	10	21	.323
Cal St. Bakersfield	8	21	.276
South Dakota St.	8	21	.276
S.C. Upstate	7	23	.233
Presbyterian	5	25	.167
North Fla.	3	26	.103
N.C. Central	4	26	.133
NJIT	0	29	.000

#won conference tournament
*ineligible for NCAA tournament

CONFERENCES

Division I Conference Champions Season-by-Season

Regular-season and conference tournament champions; No. refers to the number of teams in the conference or tournament.

AMERICA EAST CONFERENCE

Season	No.	Regular Season
1980	10	Boston U./Northeastern
1981	9	Northeastern
1982	9	Northeastern
1983	9	Boston U./New Hampshire
1984	8	Northeastern
1985	9	Northeastern/Canisius
1986	10	Northeastern
1987	10	Northeastern
1988	10	Siena
1989	10	Siena
1990	7	Northeastern
1991	6	Northeastern
1992	8	Delaware
1993	8	Drexel/Northeastern
1994	8	Drexel
1995	9	Drexel
1996	10	Drexel
1997	10	Boston U.
1998	10	Delaware/Boston U.
1999	10	Delaware/Drexel
2000	10	Hofstra
2001	10	Hofstra
2002	9	Boston U./Vermont
2003	9	Boston U.
2004	10	Boston U.
2005	10	Vermont
2006	9	Albany (N.Y.)
2007	9	Vermont
2008	9	UMBC

Season	No.	Conference Tournament
1980	8	Holy Cross
1981	6	Northeastern
1982	6	Northeastern
1983	8	Boston U.
1984	8	Northeastern
1985	9	Northeastern
1986	10	Northeastern
1987	10	Northeastern
1988	10	Boston U.
1989	10	Siena
1990	7	Boston U.
1991	6	Northeastern
1992	8	Delaware
1993	8	Delaware
1994	8	Drexel
1995	9	Drexel
1996	10	Drexel
1997	10	Boston U.
1998	10	Delaware
1999	10	Delaware
2000	10	Hofstra
2001	10	Hofstra
2002	8	Boston U.
2003	8	Vermont
2004	10	Vermont
2005	10	Vermont
2006	9	Albany (N.Y.)
2007	9	Albany (N.Y.)
2008	9	UMBC

AMERICAN SOUTH CONFERENCE

Season	No.	Regular Season
1988	6	Louisiana Tech/New Orleans
1989	6	New Orleans
1990	6	Louisiana Tech/New Orleans
1991	7	New Orleans/Arkansas St.

Season	No.	Conference Tournament
1988	6	Louisiana Tech
1989	6	Louisiana Tech
1990	6	New Orleans
1991	7	Louisiana Tech

AMERICAN WEST CONFERENCE

Season	No.	Regular Season
1995	4	Southern Utah
1996	4	Cal Poly

Season	No.	Conference Tournament
1995	4	Southern Utah
1996	4	Southern Utah

ATLANTIC COAST CONFERENCE

Season	No.	Regular Season
1954	8	Duke
1955	8	North Carolina St.
1956	8	North Carolina St./North Carolina
1957	8	North Carolina
1958	8	Duke
1959	8	North Carolina St./North Carolina
1960	8	North Carolina
1961	8	North Carolina
1962	8	Wake Forest
1963	8	Duke
1964	8	Duke
1965	8	Duke
1966	8	Duke
1967	8	North Carolina
1968	8	North Carolina
1969	8	North Carolina
1970	8	South Carolina
1971	8	North Carolina
1972	7	North Carolina
1973	7	North Carolina St.
1974	7	North Carolina St.
1975	7	Maryland
1976	7	North Carolina
1977	7	North Carolina
1978	7	North Carolina
1979	7	Duke/North Carolina
1980	8	Maryland
1981	8	Virginia
1982	8	North Carolina/Virginia
1983	8	North Carolina/Virginia
1984	8	North Carolina
1985	8	Georgia Tech/North Carolina/North Carolina St.
1986	8	Duke
1987	8	North Carolina
1988	8	North Carolina
1989	8	North Carolina St.
1990	8	Clemson
1991	8	Duke
1992	9	Duke
1993	9	North Carolina
1994	9	Duke
1995	9	Maryland/North Carolina/Virginia/Wake Forest
1996	9	Georgia Tech
1997	9	Duke
1998	9	Duke
1999	9	Duke
2000	9	Duke
2001	9	Duke/North Carolina
2002	9	Maryland
2003	9	Wake Forest
2004	9	Duke
2005	11	North Carolina
2006	12	Duke
2007	12	North Carolina/Virginia
2008	12	North Carolina

Season	No.	Conference Tournament
1954	8	North Carolina St.
1955	8	North Carolina St.
1956	8	North Carolina St.
1957	8	North Carolina
1958	8	Maryland
1959	8	North Carolina St.
1960	8	Duke
1961	7	Wake Forest
1962	8	Wake Forest
1963	8	Duke
1964	8	Duke
1965	8	North Carolina St.
1966	8	Duke
1967	8	North Carolina
1968	8	North Carolina
1969	8	North Carolina
1970	8	North Carolina St.
1971	8	South Carolina
1972	7	North Carolina
1973	7	North Carolina St.
1974	7	North Carolina St.
1975	7	North Carolina
1976	7	Virginia
1977	7	North Carolina
1978	7	Duke
1979	7	North Carolina
1980	8	Duke
1981	8	North Carolina
1982	8	North Carolina
1983	8	North Carolina St.
1984	8	Maryland
1985	8	Georgia Tech
1986	8	Duke
1987	8	North Carolina St.
1988	8	Duke
1989	8	North Carolina
1990	8	Georgia Tech
1991	7	North Carolina
1992	8	Duke
1993	9	Georgia Tech
1994	9	North Carolina
1995	9	Wake Forest
1996	9	Wake Forest
1997	9	North Carolina
1998	9	North Carolina
1999	9	Duke
2000	9	Duke
2001	9	Duke
2002	9	Duke
2003	9	Duke
2004	9	Maryland
2005	11	Duke
2006	12	Duke
2007	12	North Carolina
2008	12	North Carolina

ATLANTIC SUN CONFERENCE

Season	No.	Regular Season
1979	8	La.-Monroe
1980	7	La.-Monroe
1981	9	Houston Baptist
1982	9	UALR
1983	8	UALR
1984	8	Houston Baptist
1985	8	Ga. Southern
1986	8	UALR
1987	10	UALR
1988	10	UALR/Ga. Southern
1989	10	Ga. Southern
1990	9	Centenary (La.)
1991	8	UTSA
1992	8	Ga. Southern
1993	7	Florida Int'l
1994	10	Col. of Charleston
1995	11	Col. of Charleston
1996	12	Col. of Charleston (East)/Samford (West)/Southeastern La. (West)
1997	12	Col. of Charleston (East)/Samford (West)
1998	12	Col. of Charleston (East)/Georgia St. (West)
1999	11	Samford
2000	10	Georgia St./Troy
2001	10	Georgia
2002	11	Georgia St./Troy
2003	12	Belmont (North)/Mercer (South)/Troy (South)
2004	11	Troy
2005	11	UCF/Gardner-Webb
2006	11	Lipscomb/Belmont
2007	8	East Tenn. St.
2008	8	Belmont

Season	No.	Conference Tournament
1979	6	La.-Monroe
1980	7	Centenary (La.)
1981	9	Mercer
1982	7	La.-Monroe
1983	8	Ga. Southern
1984	8	Houston Baptist
1985	8	Mercer
1986	8	UALR
1987	8	Ga. Southern
1988	8	UTSA
1989	8	UALR
1990	8	UALR
1991	8	Georgia St.
1992	8	Ga. Southern
1993		DNP
1994	8	UCF
1995	8	Florida Int'l
1996	8	UCF
1997	8	Col. of Charleston
1998	8	Col. of Charleston

Season	No.	Conference Tournament
1999	8	Samford
2000	10	Samford
2001	10	Georgia St.
2002	8	Fla. Atlantic
2003	8	Troy
2004	8	UCF
2005	8	UCF
2006	8	Belmont
2007	8	Belmont
2008	8	Belmont

ATLANTIC 10 CONFERENCE

Season	No.	Regular Season
1977	8	Rutgers (Eastern)/West Virginia (Western)/Penn St. (Western)
1978	8	Rutgers/Villanova
1979	8	Villanova
1980	8	Villanova/Duquesne/Rutgers
1981	8	Rhode Island/Duquesne
1982	8	West Virginia
1983	10	Rutgers (Eastern)/St. Bonaventure (Western)/West Virginia (Western)
1984	10	Temple
1985	10	West Virginia
1986	10	St. Joseph's
1987	10	Temple
1988	10	Temple
1989	10	West Virginia
1990	10	Temple
1991	10	Rutgers
1992	9	Massachusetts
1993	8	Massachusetts
1994	9	Massachusetts
1995	9	Massachusetts
1996	12	Massachusetts (East)/George Washington (West)/Virginia Tech (West)
1997	12	St. Joseph's (East)/Xavier (West)
1998	12	Temple (East)/Xavier (West)/George Washington (West)/Dayton (West)
1999	12	Temple (East)/George Washington (West)
2000	12	Temple (East)/Dayton (West)
2001	11	St. Joseph's
2002	12	Temple (East)/St. Joseph's (East)/Xavier (West)
2003	12	St. Joseph's (East)/Xavier (West)
2004	12	St. Joseph's (East)/Dayton (West)
2005	12	St. Joseph's (East)/George Washington (West)
2006	14	George Washington
2007	14	Massachusetts/Xavier
2008	14	Xavier

Season	No.	Conference Tournament
1977	8	Duquesne
1978	8	Villanova
1979	8	Rutgers
1980	8	Villanova
1981	8	Pittsburgh
1982	8	Pittsburgh
1983	10	West Virginia
1984	10	West Virginia
1985	10	Temple
1986	10	St. Joseph's
1987	10	Temple
1988	10	Temple
1989	10	Rutgers
1990	10	Temple
1991	10	Penn St.
1992	9	Massachusetts
1993	8	Massachusetts
1994	9	Massachusetts
1995	9	Massachusetts
1996	12	Massachusetts
1997	12	St. Joseph's
1998	12	Xavier
1999	12	Rhode Island
2000	12	Temple
2001	11	Temple
2002	12	Xavier
2003	11	Dayton
2004	12	Xavier
2005	12	George Washington
2006	12	Xavier
2007	12	George Washington
2008	12	Temple

BIG EAST CONFERENCE

Season	No.	Regular Season
1980	7	Syracuse/Georgetown/St. John's (N.Y.)
1981	8	Boston College
1982	8	Villanova
1983	9	Boston College/Villanova/St. John's (N.Y.)
1984	9	Georgetown
1985	9	St. John's (N.Y.)
1986	9	St. John's (N.Y.)/Syracuse
1987	9	Syracuse/Georgetown/Pittsburgh
1988	9	Pittsburgh
1989	9	Georgetown
1990	9	Connecticut/Syracuse
1991	9	Syracuse
1992	10	Seton Hall/Georgetown/St. John's (N.Y.)
1993	10	Seton Hall
1994	10	Connecticut
1995	10	Connecticut
1996	13	Georgetown (Big East 7)/Connecticut (Big East 6)
1997	13	Georgetown (Big East 7)/Villanova (Big East 6)/Boston College (Big East 6)
1998	13	Syracuse (Big East 7)/Connecticut (Big East 6)
1999	13	Connecticut
2000	13	Syracuse/Miami (Fla.)
2001	14	Boston College (East)/Notre Dame (West)
2002	14	Connecticut (East)/Pittsburgh (West)
2003	14	Boston College (East)/Connecticut (East)/Pittsburgh (West)/Syracuse (West)
2004	14	Pittsburgh
2005	12	Boston College/Connecticut
2006	16	Connecticut/Villanova
2007	16	Georgetown
2008	16	Georgetown

Season	No.	Conference Tournament
1980	7	Georgetown
1981	8	Syracuse
1982	8	Georgetown
1983	9	St. John's (N.Y.)
1984	9	Georgetown
1985	9	Georgetown
1986	9	St. John's (N.Y.)
1987	9	Georgetown
1988	9	Syracuse
1989	9	Georgetown
1990	9	Connecticut
1991	9	Seton Hall
1992	10	Syracuse
1993	10	Seton Hall
1994	10	Providence
1995	10	Villanova
1996	13	Connecticut
1997	13	Boston College
1998	13	Connecticut
1999	13	Connecticut
2000	13	St. John's (N.Y.)
2001	12	Boston College
2002	12	Connecticut
2003	12	Pittsburgh
2004	12	Connecticut
2005	11	Syracuse
2006	12	Syracuse
2007	12	Georgetown
2008	12	Pittsburgh

BIG EIGHT CONFERENCE

(Note: The Big Eight and Missouri Valley conferences share the same history from 1908-28.)

Season	No.	Regular Season
1908	6	Kansas
1909	6	Kansas
1910	6	Kansas
1911	5	Kansas
1912	6	Nebraska/Kansas
1913	6	Nebraska
1914	7	Kansas/Nebraska
1915	7	Kansas
1916	7	Nebraska
1917	7	Kansas St.
1918	7	Missouri

Season	No.	Regular Season
1919	8	Kansas St.
1920	8	Missouri
1921	9	Missouri
1922	9	Missouri/Kansas
1923	9	Kansas
1924	9	Kansas
1925	9	Kansas
1926	10	Kansas
1927	10	Kansas
1928	10	Oklahoma
1929	6	Oklahoma
1930	6	Missouri
1931	6	Kansas
1932	6	Kansas
1933	6	Kansas
1934	6	Kansas
1935	6	Iowa St.
1936	6	Kansas
1937	6	Kansas/Nebraska
1938	6	Kansas
1939	6	Missouri/Oklahoma
1940	6	Kansas/Missouri/Oklahoma
1941	6	Iowa St./Kansas
1942	6	Kansas/Oklahoma
1943	6	Kansas
1944	6	Iowa St./Oklahoma
1945	6	Iowa St.
1946	6	Kansas
1947	6	Oklahoma
1948	7	Kansas St.
1949	7	Nebraska/Oklahoma
1950	7	Kansas/Kansas St./Nebraska
1951	7	Kansas St.
1952	7	Kansas
1953	7	Kansas
1954	7	Kansas/Colorado
1955	7	Colorado
1956	7	Kansas St.
1957	7	Kansas
1958	7	Kansas St.
1959	8	Kansas St.
1960	8	Kansas/Kansas St.
1961	8	Kansas St.
1962	8	Colorado
1963	8	Colorado/Kansas St.
1964	8	Kansas St.
1965	8	Oklahoma St.
1966	8	Kansas
1967	8	Kansas
1968	8	Kansas St.
1969	8	Colorado
1970	8	Kansas St.
1971	8	Kansas
1972	8	Kansas St.
1973	8	Kansas St.
1974	8	Kansas
1975	8	Kansas
1976	8	Missouri
1977	8	Kansas St.
1978	8	Kansas
1979	8	Oklahoma
1980	8	Missouri
1981	8	Missouri
1982	8	Missouri
1983	8	Missouri
1984	8	Oklahoma
1985	8	Oklahoma
1986	8	Kansas
1987	8	Missouri
1988	8	Oklahoma
1989	8	Oklahoma
1990	8	Missouri
1991	8	Oklahoma St./Kansas
1992	8	Kansas
1993	8	Kansas
1994	8	Missouri
1995	8	Kansas
1996	8	Kansas

Season	No.	Conference Tournament
1977	8	Kansas St.
1978	8	Missouri
1979	8	Oklahoma
1980	8	Kansas St.
1981	8	Kansas
1982	8	Missouri
1983	8	Oklahoma St.
1984	8	Kansas
1985	8	Oklahoma
1986	8	Kansas

CONFERENCES

Season	No.	Conference Tournament
1987	8	Missouri
1988	8	Oklahoma
1989	8	Missouri
1990	8	Oklahoma
1991	8	Missouri
1992	8	Kansas
1993	8	Missouri
1994	8	Nebraska
1995	8	Oklahoma St.
1996	8	Iowa St.

BIG SKY CONFERENCE

Season	No.	Regular Season
1964	6	Montana St.
1965	6	Weber St.
1966	6	Weber St./Gonzaga
1967	6	Gonzaga/Montana St.
1968	6	Weber St.
1969	6	Weber St.
1970	6	Weber St.
1971	6	Weber St.
1972	8	Weber St.
1973	8	Weber St.
1974	8	Idaho St./Montana
1975	8	Montana
1976	8	Boise St./Weber St./Idaho St.
1977	8	Idaho St.
1978	8	Montana
1979	8	Weber St.
1980	8	Weber St.
1981	8	Idaho
1982	8	Idaho
1983	8	Weber St./Nevada
1984	8	Weber St.
1985	8	Nevada
1986	8	Northern Ariz./Montana
1987	8	Montana St.
1988	9	Boise St.
1989	9	Boise St./Idaho
1990	9	Idaho
1991	9	Montana
1992	9	Montana
1993	8	Idaho
1994	8	Weber St./Idaho St.
1995	8	Montana/Weber St.
1996	8	Montana St.
1997	9	Northern Ariz.
1998	9	Northern Ariz.
1999	9	Weber St.
2000	9	Montana/Eastern Wash.
2001	9	Cal St. Northridge
2002	8	Montana St.
2003	8	Weber St.
2004	8	Eastern Wash.
2005	8	Portland St.
2006	8	Northern Ariz.
2007	8	Northern Ariz./Weber St.
2008	9	Portland St.

Season	No.	Conference Tournament
1976	8	Boise St.
1977	8	Idaho St.
1978	8	Weber St.
1979	8	Weber St.
1980	8	Weber St.
1981	8	Idaho
1982	8	Idaho
1983	8	Weber St.
1984	8	Nevada
1985	8	Nevada
1986	7	Montana St.
1987	8	Idaho St.
1988	9	Boise St.
1989	9	Idaho
1990	9	Idaho
1991	9	Montana
1992	9	Montana
1993	6	Boise St.
1994	6	Boise St.
1995	6	Weber St.
1996	6	Montana St.
1997	6	Montana
1998	6	Northern Ariz.
1999	6	Weber St.
2000	6	Northern Ariz.
2001	6	Cal St. Northridge
2002	6	Montana
2003	6	Weber St.
2004	6	Eastern Wash.

Season	No.	Conference Tournament
2005	6	Montana
2006	6	Montana
2007	6	Weber St.
2008	6	Portland St.

BIG SOUTH CONFERENCE

Season	No.	Regular Season
1986	8	Charleston So.
1987	8	Charleston So.
1988	7	Coastal Caro.
1989	7	Coastal Caro.
1990	7	Coastal Caro.
1991	8	Coastal Caro.
1992	8	Radford
1993	9	Towson
1994	10	Towson
1995	9	UNC Greensboro
1996	9	UNC Greensboro
1997	8	Liberty/UNC Asheville
1998	7	UNC Asheville
1999	6	Winthrop
2000	8	Radford
2001	8	Radford
2002	8	Winthrop/UNC Asheville
2003	8	Winthrop
2004	9	Birmingham So./Liberty
2005	9	Winthrop
2006	9	Winthrop
2007	8	Winthrop
2008	8	UNC Asheville/Winthrop

Season	No.	Conference Tournament
1986	8	Charleston So.
1987	8	Charleston So.
1988	7	Winthrop
1989	7	UNC Asheville
1990	7	Coastal Caro.
1991	8	Coastal Caro.
1992	8	Campbell
1993	9	Coastal Caro.
1994	8	Liberty
1995	8	Charleston So.
1996	8	UNC Greensboro
1997	8	Charleston So.
1998	7	Radford
1999	6	Winthrop
2000	6	Winthrop
2001	6	Winthrop
2002	8	Winthrop
2003	8	UNC Asheville
2004	8	Liberty
2005	8	Winthrop
2006	8	Winthrop
2007	8	Winthrop
2008	8	Winthrop

BIG TEN CONFERENCE

Season	No.	Regular Season
1906	6	Minnesota
1907	5	Chicago/Minnesota/Wisconsin
1908	5	Chicago/Wisconsin
1909	8	Chicago
1910	8	Chicago
1911	8	Purdue/Minnesota
1912	8	Purdue/Wisconsin
1913	9	Wisconsin
1914	9	Wisconsin
1915	9	Illinois
1916	9	Wisconsin
1917	9	Minnesota/Illinois
1918	10	Wisconsin
1919	10	Minnesota
1920	10	Chicago
1921	10	Michigan/Wisconsin/Purdue
1922	10	Purdue
1923	10	Iowa/Wisconsin
1924	10	Wisconsin/Illinois/Chicago
1925	10	Ohio St.
1926	10	Purdue/Indiana/Michigan/Iowa
1927	10	Michigan
1928	10	Indiana/Purdue
1929	10	Wisconsin/Michigan
1930	10	Purdue
1931	10	Northwestern
1932	10	Purdue
1933	10	Northwestern/Ohio St.
1934	10	Purdue
1935	10	Purdue/Illinois/Wisconsin
1936	10	Indiana/Purdue

Season	No.	Regular Season
1937	10	Minnesota/Illinois
1938	10	Purdue
1939	10	Ohio St.
1940	10	Purdue
1941	10	Wisconsin
1942	10	Illinois
1943	10	Illinois
1944	10	Ohio St.
1945	10	Iowa
1946	10	Ohio St.
1947	9	Wisconsin
1948	9	Michigan
1949	9	Illinois
1950	9	Ohio St.
1951	10	Illinois
1952	10	Illinois
1953	10	Indiana
1954	10	Indiana
1955	10	Iowa
1956	10	Iowa
1957	10	Indiana/Michigan St.
1958	10	Indiana
1959	10	Michigan St.
1960	10	Ohio St.
1961	10	Ohio St.
1962	10	Ohio St.
1963	10	Ohio St./Illinois
1964	10	Michigan/Ohio St.
1965	10	Michigan
1966	10	Michigan
1967	10	Indiana/Michigan St.
1968	10	Ohio St./Iowa
1969	10	Purdue
1970	10	Iowa
1971	10	Ohio St.
1972	10	Minnesota
1973	10	Indiana
1974	10	Indiana/Michigan
1975	10	Indiana
1976	10	Indiana
1977	10	Michigan
1978	10	Michigan St.
1979	10	Michigan St./Purdue/Iowa
1980	10	Indiana
1981	10	Indiana
1982	10	Minnesota
1983	10	Indiana
1984	10	Illinois/Purdue
1985	10	Michigan
1986	10	Michigan
1987	10	Indiana/Purdue
1988	10	Purdue
1989	10	Indiana
1990	10	Michigan St.
1991	10	Ohio St./Indiana
1992	10	Ohio St.
1993	11	Indiana
1994	11	Purdue
1995	11	Purdue
1996	11	Purdue
1997	11	Minnesota
1998	11	Michigan St./Illinois
1999	11	Michigan St.
2000	11	Michigan St./Ohio St.
2001	11	Michigan St./Illinois
2002	11	Illinois/Ohio St./Indiana/Wisconsin
2003	11	Wisconsin
2004	11	Illinois
2005	11	Illinois
2006	11	Ohio St.
2007	11	Ohio St.
2008	11	Wisconsin

Season	No.	Conference Tournament
1998	11	Michigan
1999	11	Michigan St.
2000	11	Michigan St.
2001	11	Iowa
2002	11	Ohio St.
2003	11	Illinois
2004	11	Wisconsin
2005	11	Illinois
2006	11	Iowa
2007	11	Ohio St.
2008	11	Wisconsin

BIG 12 CONFERENCE

Season	No.	Regular Season
1997	12	Kansas
1998	12	Kansas
1999	12	Texas
2000	12	Iowa St.
2001	12	Iowa St.
2002	12	Kansas
2003	12	Kansas
2004	12	Oklahoma St.
2005	12	Oklahoma/Kansas
2006	12	Texas/Kansas
2007	12	Kansas
2008	12	Kansas/Texas

Season	No.	Conference Tournament
1997	12	Kansas
1998	12	Kansas
1999	12	Kansas
2000	12	Iowa St.
2001	12	Oklahoma
2002	12	Oklahoma
2003	12	Oklahoma
2004	11	Oklahoma St.
2005	12	Oklahoma St.
2006	12	Kansas
2007	12	Kansas
2008	12	Kansas

BIG WEST CONFERENCE

Season	No.	Regular Season
1970	6	Long Beach St.
1971	6	Long Beach St.
1972	7	Long Beach St.
1973	7	Long Beach St.
1974	7	Long Beach St.
1975	6	Long Beach St.
1976	6	Long Beach St./Cal St. Fullerton
1977	7	Long Beach St./San Diego St.
1978	8	Fresno St./San Diego St.
1979	8	Pacific
1980	8	Utah St.
1981	8	Fresno St.
1982	8	Fresno St.
1983	9	UNLV
1984	10	UNLV
1985	10	UNLV
1986	10	UNLV
1987	10	UNLV
1988	10	UNLV
1989	10	UNLV
1990	10	UNLV
1991	10	UNLV
1992	10	UNLV
1993	10	New Mexico St.
1994	10	New Mexico St.
1995	10	Utah St.
1996	10	Long Beach St.
1997	12	Nevada (Eastern)/New Mexico St. (Eastern)/Utah St. (Eastern)/ Pacific (Western)
1998	12	Utah St. (Eastern)/ Pacific (Western)
1999	12	Boise St. (Eastern)/New Mexico St. (Eastern)/UC Santa Barbara (Western)
2000	12	Utah St. (Eastern)/Long Beach St. (Western)
2001	9	UC Irvine
2002	10	Utah St./UC Irvine
2003	10	UC Santa Barbara
2004	10	Utah St./Pacific
2005	10	Pacific
2006	8	Pacific
2007	8	Long Beach St.
2008	9	UC Santa Barbara/ Cal St. Northridge/Cal St. Fullerton

Season	No.	Conference Tournament
1976	4	San Diego St.
1977	7	Long Beach St.
1978	7	Cal St. Fullerton
1979	8	Pacific
1980	7	San Jose St.
1981	7	Fresno St.
1982	7	Fresno St.
1983	8	UNLV
1984	8	Fresno St.
1985	8	UNLV
1986	8	UNLV
1987	8	UNLV
1988	10	Utah St.

Season	No.	Conference Tournament
1989	10	UNLV
1990	10	UNLV
1991	8	UNLV
1992	8	New Mexico St.
1993	8	Long Beach St.
1994	10	New Mexico St.
1995	10	Long Beach St.
1996	6	San Jose St.
1997	8	Pacific
1998	8	Utah St.
1999	8	New Mexico St.
2000	8	Utah St.
2001	8	Utah St.
2002	8	UC Santa Barbara
2003	8	Utah St.
2004	8	Pacific
2005	8	Utah St.
2006	8	Pacific
2007	8	Long Beach St.
2008	8	Cal St. Fullerton

BORDER CONFERENCE

Season	No.	Regular Season
1932	5	Arizona
1933	6	Texas Tech
1934	6	Texas Tech
1935	6	Texas Tech
1936	7	Arizona
1937	7	New Mexico St.
1938	7	New Mexico St.
1939	7	New Mexico St.
1940	7	New Mexico St.
1941		DNP
1942	9	West Tex. A&M
1943	8	West Tex. A&M
1944	4	Northern Ariz.
1945	9	New Mexico
1946	9	Arizona
1947	9	Arizona
1948	9	Arizona
1949	9	Arizona
1950	9	Arizona
1951	9	Arizona
1952	8	New Mexico St./West Tex. A&M
1953	8	Arizona/Hardin-Simmons
1954	7	Texas Tech
1955	7	Texas Tech/West Tex. A&M
1956	7	Texas Tech
1957	6	UTEP
1958	6	Arizona St.
1959	6	Arizona St./New Mexico St./UTEP
1960	6	New Mexico St.
1961	6	Arizona St./New Mexico St.
1962	5	Arizona St.

COLONIAL ATHLETIC ASSOCIATION

Season	No.	Regular Season
1983	6	William & Mary
1984	6	Richmond
1985	8	Navy/Richmond
1986	8	Navy
1987	8	Navy
1988	8	Richmond
1989	8	Richmond
1990	8	James Madison
1991	8	James Madison
1992	8	Richmond/James Madison
1993	8	James Madison/Old Dominion
1994	8	James Madison/Old Dominion
1995	8	Old Dominion
1996	9	VCU
1997	9	Old Dominion/UNC Wilmington
1998	9	William & Mary/UNC Wilmington
1999	9	George Mason
2000	9	James Madison/George Mason
2001	9	Richmond
2002	10	UNC Wilmington
2003	10	UNC Wilmington
2004	10	VCU
2005	10	Old Dominion
2006	12	George Mason/UNC Wilmington
2007	12	VCU
2008	12	VCU

Season	No.	Conference Tournament
1983	6	James Madison
1984	6	Richmond
1985	8	Navy

Season	No.	Conference Tournament
1986	8	Navy
1987	8	Navy
1988	8	Richmond
1989	8	George Mason
1990	8	Richmond
1991	8	Richmond
1992	8	Old Dominion
1993	8	East Carolina
1994	8	James Madison
1995	8	Old Dominion
1996	9	VCU
1997	9	Old Dominion
1998	9	Richmond
1999	9	George Mason
2000	9	UNC Wilmington
2001	6	George Mason
2002	10	UNC Wilmington
2003	10	UNC Wilmington
2004	10	VCU
2005	10	Old Dominion
2006	12	UNC Wilmington
2007	12	VCU
2008	12	George Mason

CONFERENCE USA

Season	No.	Regular Season
1996	11	Tulane (Red)/Memphis (White)/ Cincinnati (Blue)
1997	12	Tulane (Red)/Memphis (White)/ Charlotte (White)/ Cincinnati (Blue)
1998	12	Cincinnati (American)/ Memphis (National)
1999	12	Cincinnati (American)/ UAB (National)
2000	12	Cincinnati (American)/ Tulane (National)/ South Fla. (National)
2001	12	Cincinnati (American)/ Southern Miss. (National)
2002	14	Cincinnati (American)/Memphis (National)
2003	14	Marquette (American)/Memphis (National)
2004	14	DePaul/Memphis/Cincinnati/ UAB/Charlotte
2005	14	Louisville
2006	12	Memphis
2007	12	Memphis
2008	12	Memphis

Season	No.	Conference Tournament
1996	11	Cincinnati
1997	12	Marquette
1998	12	Cincinnati
1999	12	Charlotte
2000	12	St. Louis
2001	12	Charlotte
2002	12	Cincinnati
2003	12	Louisville
2004	12	Cincinnati
2005	12	Louisville
2006	12	Memphis
2007	12	Memphis
2008	12	Memphis

EAST COAST CONFERENCE

Season	No.	Regular Season
1959	10	St. Joseph's
1960	10	St. Joseph's
1961	10	St. Joseph's
1962	10	St. Joseph's
1963	9	St. Joseph's
1964	8	Temple
1965	8	St. Joseph's
1966	10	St. Joseph's
1967	12	Temple
1968	11	La Salle
1969	12	Temple
1970	12	St. Joseph's (East)/ Rider (West)/Lehigh (West)/Lafayette (West)
1971	13	St. Joseph's (East)/ Lafayette (West)
1972	13	Temple (East)/Rider (West)
1973	13	St. Joseph's (East)/ Lafayette (West)
1974	13	St. Joseph's (East)/ La Salle (East)/Rider (West)

Season	No.	Conference Tournament
1975	12	American (East)/La Salle (East)/Lafayette (West)
1976	12	St. Joseph's (East)/Lafayette (West)
1977	12	Temple (East)/Hofstra (East)/Lafayette (West)
1978	12	La Salle (East)/Lafayette (West)
1979	12	Temple (East)/Bucknell (West)
1980	12	St. Joseph's (East)/Lafayette (West)
1981	12	American (East)/Lafayette (West)/Rider (West)
1982	12	Temple (East)/West Chester (West)
1983	10	American (East)/La Salle (East)/Hofstra (East)/Rider (West)
1984	9	Bucknell
1985	8	Bucknell
1986	8	Drexel
1987	8	Bucknell
1988	8	Lafayette
1989	8	Bucknell
1990	8	Towson/Hofstra/Lehigh
1991	7	Towson
1992	7	Hofstra
1993		DNP
1994	6	Troy

Season	No.	Conference Tournament
1975	12	La Salle
1976	12	Hofstra
1977	12	Hofstra
1978	12	La Salle
1979	12	Temple
1980	12	La Salle
1981	12	St. Joseph's
1982	12	St. Joseph's
1983	10	La Salle
1984	9	Rider
1985	8	Lehigh
1986	8	Drexel
1987	8	Bucknell
1988	8	Lehigh
1989	8	Bucknell
1990	8	Towson
1991	7	Towson
1992	7	Towson
1993		DNP
1994	6	Hofstra

EASTERN INTERCOLLEGIATE CONFERENCE

Season	No.	Regular Season
1933	5	Pittsburgh
1934	6	Pittsburgh
1935	5	Pittsburgh/West Virginia
1936	6	Carnegie Mellon/Pittsburgh
1937	6	Pittsburgh/Temple
1938	6	Temple
1939	6	Carnegie Mellon/Georgetown

GREAT MIDWEST CONFERENCE

Season	No.	Regular Season
1992	6	DePaul/Cincinnati
1993	6	Cincinnati
1994	7	Marquette
1995	7	Memphis

Season	No.	Conference Tournament
1992	6	Cincinnati
1993	6	Cincinnati
1994	7	Cincinnati
1995	7	Cincinnati

GULF STAR CONFERENCE

Season	No.	Regular Season
1985	6	Southeastern La.
1986	6	Sam Houston St.
1987	6	Stephen F. Austin

HORIZON LEAGUE

Season	No.	Regular Season
1980	6	Loyola (Ill.)
1981	7	Xavier
1982	7	Evansville
1983	8	Loyola (Ill.)
1984	8	Oral Roberts

Season	No.	Conference Tournament
1985	8	Loyola (Ill.)
1986	7	Xavier
1987	7	Evansville/Loyola (Ill.)
1988	6	Xavier
1989	7	Evansville
1990	8	Xavier
1991	8	Xavier
1992	6	Evansville
1993	8	Evansville/Xavier
1994	6	Xavier
1995	11	Xavier
1996	9	Green Bay
1997	9	Butler
1998	8	Detroit/Ill.-Chicago
1999	8	Detroit
2000	8	Butler
2001	8	Butler
2002	9	Butler
2003	9	Butler
2004	9	Milwaukee
2005	9	Milwaukee
2006	9	Milwaukee
2007	9	Butler/Wright St.
2008	10	Butler

Season	No.	Conference Tournament
1980	6	Oral Roberts
1981	7	Oklahoma City
1982	7	Evansville
1983	8	Xavier
1984	8	Oral Roberts
1985	8	Loyola (Ill.)
1986	7	Xavier
1987	7	Xavier
1988	6	Xavier
1989	7	Evansville
1990	8	Dayton
1991	8	Xavier
1992	6	Evansville
1993	8	Evansville
1994	6	Detroit
1995	10	Green Bay
1996	8	Northern Ill.
1997	9	Butler
1998	8	Butler
1999	8	Detroit
2000	8	Butler
2001	8	Butler
2002	9	Ill.-Chicago
2003	9	Milwaukee
2004	9	Ill.-Chicago
2005	9	Milwaukee
2006	9	Milwaukee
2007	9	Wright St.
2008	10	Butler

IVY GROUP

Season	No.	Regular Season
1902	5	Yale
1903	5	Yale
1904	6	Columbia
1905	5	Columbia
1906	6	Penn
1907	6	Yale
1908	5	Penn
1909-10		DNP
1911	5	Columbia
1912	6	Columbia
1913	5	Cornell
1914	6	Cornell/Columbia
1915	6	Yale
1916	6	Penn
1917	6	Yale
1918	6	Penn
1919	5	Penn
1920	6	Penn
1921	6	Penn
1922	6	Princeton
1923	6	Yale
1924	6	Cornell
1925	6	Princeton
1926	6	Columbia
1927	6	Dartmouth
1928	6	Penn
1929	6	Penn
1930	6	Columbia
1931	6	Columbia
1932	6	Princeton
1933	6	Yale

Season	No.	Regular Season
1934	7	Penn
1935	7	Penn
1936	7	Columbia
1937	7	Penn
1938	7	Dartmouth
1939	7	Dartmouth
1940	7	Dartmouth
1941	7	Dartmouth
1942	7	Dartmouth
1943	7	Dartmouth
1944	5	Dartmouth
1945	4	Penn
1946	5	Dartmouth
1947	7	Columbia
1948	7	Columbia
1949	7	Yale
1950	7	Princeton
1951	7	Columbia
1952	7	Princeton
1953	7	Penn
1954	8	Cornell
1955	8	Princeton
1956	8	Dartmouth
1957	8	Yale
1958	8	Dartmouth
1959	8	Dartmouth
1960	8	Princeton
1961	8	Princeton
1962	8	Yale
1963	8	Princeton
1964	8	Princeton
1965	8	Princeton
1966	8	Penn
1967	8	Princeton
1968	8	Columbia
1969	8	Princeton
1970	8	Penn
1971	8	Penn
1972	8	Penn
1973	8	Penn
1974	8	Penn
1975	8	Penn
1976	8	Princeton
1977	8	Princeton
1978	8	Penn
1979	8	Penn
1980	8	Penn
1981	8	Princeton
1982	8	Penn
1983	8	Princeton
1984	8	Princeton
1985	8	Penn
1986	8	Brown
1987	8	Penn
1988	8	Cornell
1989	8	Princeton
1990	8	Princeton
1991	8	Princeton
1992	8	Princeton
1993	8	Penn
1994	8	Penn
1995	8	Penn
1996	8	Princeton
1997	8	Princeton
1998	8	Princeton
1999	8	Penn
2000	8	Penn
2001	8	Princeton
2002	8	Penn/Yale/Princeton
2003	8	Penn
2004	8	Princeton
2005	8	Penn
2006	8	Penn
2007	8	Penn
2008	8	Cornell

METRO ATLANTIC ATHLETIC CONFERENCE

Season	No.	Regular Season
1982	6	St. Peter's
1983	6	Iona
1984	8	La Salle/St. Peter's/Iona
1985	8	Iona
1986	8	Fairfield
1987	8	St. Peter's
1988	8	La Salle
1989	8	La Salle
1990	12	Holy Cross (North)/La Salle (South)

Season	No.	Conference Tournament
1991	9	Siena
1992	9	Manhattan
1993	8	Manhattan
1994	8	Canisius
1995	8	Manhattan
1996	8	Fairfield/Iona
1997	8	Iona
1998	10	Iona
1999	10	Niagara/Siena
2000	10	Siena
2001	10	Iona/Siena/Niagara
2002	10	Marist/Rider
2003	10	Manhattan
2004	10	Manhattan
2005	10	Niagara/Rider
2006	10	Manhattan
2007	10	Marist
2008	10	Rider/Siena

Season	No.	Conference Tournament
1982	6	Fordham
1983	6	Fordham
1984	8	Iona
1985	8	Iona
1986	8	Fairfield
1987	8	Fairfield
1988	8	La Salle
1989	8	La Salle
1990	12	La Salle
1991	9	St. Peter's
1992	9	La Salle
1993	8	Manhattan
1994	8	Loyola (Md.)
1995	8	St. Peter's
1996	8	Canisius
1997	8	Fairfield
1998	10	Iona
1999	10	Siena
2000	10	Iona
2001	10	Iona
2002	10	Siena
2003	10	Manhattan
2004	10	Manhattan
2005	10	Niagara
2006	10	Iona
2007	10	Niagara
2008	10	Siena

METROPOLITAN COLLEGIATE ATHLETIC CONFERENCE

Season	No.	Regular Season
1976	6	Tulane
1977	7	Louisville
1978	7	Florida St.
1979	7	Louisville
1980	7	Louisville
1981	7	Louisville
1982	7	Memphis
1983	7	Louisville
1984	8	Memphis/Louisville
1985	8	Memphis
1986	7	Louisville
1987	7	Louisville
1988	7	Louisville
1989	7	Florida St.
1990	8	Louisville
1991	8	Southern Miss.
1992	7	Tulane
1993	7	Louisville
1994	7	Louisville
1995	7	Charlotte

Season	No.	Conference Tournament
1976	6	Cincinnati
1977	7	Cincinnati
1978	7	Louisville
1979	7	Virginia Tech
1980	7	Louisville
1981	7	Louisville
1982	7	Memphis
1983	7	Louisville
1984	8	Memphis
1985	8	Memphis
1986	7	Louisville
1987	7	Memphis
1988	7	Louisville
1989	5	Louisville
1990	8	Louisville
1991	8	Florida St.

Season	No.	Conference Tournament
1992	7	Charlotte
1993	7	Louisville
1994	7	Louisville
1995	7	Louisville

METROPOLITAN NEW YORK CONFERENCE

Season	No.	Regular Season
1943	8	St. John's (N.Y.)
1944-45		DNP
1946	7	New York U./St. John's (N.Y.)
1947	7	St. John's (N.Y.)
1948	7	New York U.
1949	7	Manhattan/St. John's (N.Y.)
1950	7	CCNY
1951	7	St. John's (N.Y.)
1952	7	St. John's (N.Y.)
1953	7	Manhattan
1954	7	St. Francis (N.Y.)
1955	7	Manhattan
1956	7	St. Francis (N.Y.)
1957	7	New York U.
1958	7	St. John's (N.Y.)
1959	7	Manhattan
1960	7	New York U.
1961	7	St. John's (N.Y.)
1962	7	St. John's (N.Y.)
1963	7	Fordham

MID-AMERICAN CONFERENCE

Season	No.	Regular Season
1947	5	Butler/Cincinnati
1948	6	Cincinnati
1949	6	Cincinnati
1950	6	Cincinnati
1951	5	Cincinnati
1952	7	Miami (Ohio)/Western Mich.
1953	7	Miami (Ohio)
1954	8	Toledo
1955	8	Miami (Ohio)
1956	7	Marshall
1957	7	Miami (Ohio)
1958	7	Miami (Ohio)
1959	7	Bowling Green
1960	7	Ohio
1961	7	Ohio
1962	7	Bowling Green
1963	7	Bowling Green
1964	7	Ohio
1965	7	Ohio
1966	7	Miami (Ohio)
1967	7	Toledo
1968	7	Bowling Green
1969	7	Miami (Ohio)
1970	6	Ohio
1971	6	Miami (Ohio)
1972	6	Ohio
1973	7	Miami (Ohio)
1974	7	Ohio
1975	8	Central Mich.
1976	10	Western Mich.
1977	10	Central Mich.
1978	10	Miami (Ohio)
1979	10	Toledo
1980	10	Toledo
1981	10	Ball St./Northern Ill./Toledo/Western Mich./Bowling Green
1982	10	Ball St.
1983	10	Bowling Green
1984	10	Miami (Ohio)
1985	10	Ohio
1986	10	Miami (Ohio)
1987	9	Central Mich.
1988	9	Eastern Mich.
1989	9	Ball St.
1990	9	Ball St.
1991	9	Eastern Mich.
1992	8	Miami (Ohio)
1993	10	Ball St./Miami (Ohio)
1994	10	Ohio
1995	10	Miami (Ohio)
1996	10	Eastern Mich.
1997	10	Bowling Green/Miami (Ohio)
1998	12	Akron (East)/Ball St. (West)/
1999	13	Miami (Ohio)(East)/Toledo (West)
2000	13	Bowling Green (East)/Ball St. (West)/Toledo (West)

Season	No.	Conference Tournament
2001	13	Kent St. (East)/Central Mich. (West)
2002	13	Kent St. (East)/Ball St. (West)
2003	13	Kent St. (East)/Central Mich. (West)
2004	13	Kent St. (East)/Western Mich. (West)
2005	13	Miami (Ohio) (East)/Toledo (West)/Western Mich. (West)
2006	12	Kent St. (East)/Northern Ill. (West)
2007	12	Akron (East)/Toledo (West)
2008	12	Kent St. (East)/Western Mich. (West)

Season	No.	Conference Tournament
1980	7	Toledo
1981	7	Ball St.
1982	7	Northern Ill.
1983	7	Ohio
1984	7	Miami (Ohio)
1985	7	Ohio
1986	7	Ball St.
1987	7	Central Mich.
1988	7	Eastern Mich.
1989	8	Ball St.
1990	8	Ball St.
1991	8	Eastern Mich.
1992	8	Miami (Ohio)
1993	10	Ball St.
1994	8	Ohio
1995	8	Ball St.
1996	8	Eastern Mich.
1997	8	Miami (Ohio)
1998	8	Eastern Mich.
1999	8	Kent St.
2000	13	Ball St.
2001	13	Kent St.
2002	13	Kent St.
2003	13	Central Mich.
2004	13	Western Mich.
2005	13	Ohio
2006	12	Kent St.
2007	12	Miami (Ohio)
2008	12	Kent St.

MID-EASTERN ATHLETIC CONFERENCE

Season	No.	Regular Season
1972	7	N.C. A&T
1973	7	Md.-East. Shore
1974	7	Md.-East. Shore/Morgan St.
1975	7	N.C. A&T
1976	7	N.C. A&T/Morgan St.
1977	7	South Carolina St.
1978	7	N.C. A&T
1979	7	N.C. A&T
1980	7	Howard
1981	6	N.C. A&T
1982	7	N.C. A&T
1983	7	Howard
1984	6	N.C. A&T
1985	7	N.C. A&T
1986	8	N.C. A&T
1987	8	Howard
1988	7	N.C. A&T
1989	9	South Carolina St.
1990	9	Coppin St.
1991	9	Coppin St.
1992	9	N.C. A&T/Howard
1993	9	Coppin St.
1994	9	Coppin St.
1995	9	Coppin St.
1996	10	Coppin St./South Carolina St.
1997	10	Coppin St.
1998	11	Coppin St.
1999	11	Coppin St./South Carolina St.
2000	11	South Carolina St.
2001	11	Hampton/South Carolina St.
2002	11	Hampton
2003	11	South Carolina St.
2004	11	South Carolina St./Coppin St.
2005	11	Delaware St.
2006	11	Delaware St.
2007	11	Delaware St.
2008	11	Morgan St.

CONFERENCES

Season	No.	Conference Tournament
1972	7	N.C. A&T
1973	7	N.C. A&T
1974	7	Md.-East. Shore
1975	7	N.C. A&T
1976	7	N.C. A&T
1977	7	Morgan St.
1978	7	N.C. A&T
1979	7	N.C. A&T
1980	7	Howard
1981	6	Howard
1982	7	N.C. A&T
1983	7	N.C. A&T
1984	6	N.C. A&T
1985	6	N.C. A&T
1986	6	N.C. A&T
1987	7	N.C. A&T
1988	7	N.C. A&T
1989	8	South Carolina St.
1990	8	Coppin St.
1991	9	Florida A&M
1992	9	Howard
1993	9	Coppin St.
1994	9	N.C. A&T
1995	9	N.C. A&T
1996	8	South Carolina St.
1997	9	Coppin St.
1998	9	South Carolina St.
1999	10	Florida A&M
2000	11	South Carolina St.
2001	11	Hampton
2002	11	Hampton
2003	11	South Carolina St.
2004	11	Florida A&M
2005	11	Delaware St.
2006	11	Hampton
2007	11	Florida A&M
2008	11	Coppin St.

MISSOURI VALLEY CONFERENCE

(Note: The Big Eight and Missouri Valley conferences share the same history from 1908-28.)

Season	No.	Regular Season
1908	6	Kansas
1909	6	Kansas
1910	6	Kansas
1911	5	Kansas
1912	6	Nebraska/Kansas
1913	6	Nebraska
1914	7	Kansas/Nebraska
1915	7	Kansas
1916	7	Nebraska
1917	7	Kansas St.
1918	7	Missouri
1919	8	Kansas St.
1920	8	Missouri
1921	9	Missouri
1922	9	Missouri/Kansas
1923	9	Kansas
1924	9	Kansas
1925	9	Kansas
1926	10	Kansas
1927	10	Kansas
1928	10	Oklahoma
1929	5	Washington-St. Louis
1930	5	Creighton/Washington-St. Louis
1931	5	Creighton/Oklahoma St.
1932	5	Creighton
1933	6	Butler
1934	6	Butler
1935	7	Creighton/Drake
1936	7	Creighton/Oklahoma St./Drake
1937	7	Oklahoma St.
1938	7	Oklahoma St.
1939	8	Oklahoma St./Drake
1940	7	Oklahoma St.
1941	7	Creighton
1942	6	Oklahoma St./Creighton
1943	6	Creighton
1944	4	Oklahoma St.
1945	5	Oklahoma St.
1946	7	Oklahoma St.
1947	7	St. Louis
1948	6	Oklahoma St.
1949	6	Oklahoma St.
1950	7	Bradley
1951	8	Oklahoma St.
1952	6	St. Louis
1953	6	Oklahoma St.
1954	6	Oklahoma St.

Season	No.	Regular Season
1955	6	Tulsa/St. Louis
1956	7	Houston
1957	8	St. Louis
1958	8	Cincinnati
1959	8	Cincinnati
1960	8	Cincinnati
1961	7	Cincinnati
1962	7	Bradley/Cincinnati
1963	7	Cincinnati
1964	7	Drake/Wichita St.
1965	8	Wichita St.
1966	8	Cincinnati
1967	8	Louisville
1968	9	Louisville
1969	9	Drake/Louisville
1970	9	Drake
1971	8	Drake/Louisville/St. Louis
1972	8	Memphis/Louisville
1973	10	Memphis
1974	9	Louisville
1975	8	Louisville
1976	7	Wichita St.
1977	7	Southern Ill./New Mexico St.
1978	9	Creighton
1979	9	Indiana St.
1980	9	Bradley
1981	9	Wichita St.
1982	10	Bradley
1983	10	Wichita St.
1984	9	Tulsa/Illinois St.
1985	9	Tulsa
1986	9	Bradley
1987	8	Tulsa
1988	8	Bradley
1989	8	Creighton
1990	8	Southern Ill.
1991	9	Creighton
1992	10	Southern Ill./Illinois St.
1993	10	Illinois St.
1994	10	Southern Ill./Tulsa
1995	11	Tulsa
1996	11	Bradley
1997	10	Illinois St.
1998	10	Illinois St.
1999	10	Evansville
2000	10	Indiana St.
2001	10	Creighton
2002	10	Southern Ill./Creighton
2003	10	Southern Ill.
2004	10	Southern Ill.
2005	10	Southern Ill.
2006	10	Wichita St.
2007	10	Southern Ill.
2008	10	Drake

Season	No.	Conference Tournament
1977	8	Southern Ill.
1978	9	Creighton
1979	8	Indiana St.
1980	8	Bradley
1981	8	Creighton
1982	8	Tulsa
1983	8	Illinois St.
1984	8	Tulsa
1985	8	Wichita St.
1986	8	Tulsa
1987	7	Wichita St.
1988	8	Bradley
1989	8	Creighton
1990	8	Illinois St.
1991	9	Creighton
1992	8	Missouri St.
1993	8	Southern Ill.
1994	8	Southern Ill.
1995	8	Southern Ill.
1996	8	Tulsa
1997	10	Illinois St.
1998	10	Illinois St.
1999	10	Creighton
2000	10	Creighton
2001	10	Indiana St.
2002	10	Creighton
2003	10	Creighton
2004	10	UNI
2005	10	Creighton
2006	10	Southern Ill.
2007	10	Creighton
2008	10	Drake

MOUNTAIN STATES CONFERENCE

Season	No.	Regular Season
1938	7	Colorado/Utah
1939	7	Colorado
1940	7	Colorado
1941	7	Wyoming
1942	7	Colorado
1943	5	Wyoming
1944	7	Utah
1945	7	Utah
1946	7	Wyoming
1947	7	Wyoming
1948	6	BYU
1949	6	Wyoming
1950	6	BYU
1951	6	BYU
1952	8	Wyoming
1953	8	Wyoming
1954	8	Colorado
1955	8	Utah
1956	8	Utah
1957	8	BYU
1958	8	Wyoming
1959	8	Utah
1960	8	Utah
1961	8	Colorado St./Utah
1962	8	Utah

MOUNTAIN WEST CONFERENCE

Season	No.	Regular Season
2000	8	UNLV/Utah
2001	8	BYU/Wyoming/Utah
2002	8	Wyoming
2003	8	BYU/Utah
2004	8	Air Force
2005	8	Utah
2006	9	San Diego St.
2007	9	BYU
2008	9	BYU

Season	No.	Conference Tournament
2000	8	UNLV
2001	8	BYU
2002	8	San Diego St.
2003	8	Colorado St.
2004	8	Utah
2005	8	New Mexico
2006	9	San Diego St.
2007	9	UNLV
2008	9	UNLV

NEW ENGLAND CONFERENCE

Season	No.	Regular Season
1938	5	Rhode Island
1939	5	Rhode Island
1940	5	Rhode Island
1941	5	Rhode Island
1942	5	Rhode Island
1943	5	Rhode Island
1944	4	Rhode Island
1945		DNP
1946	5	Rhode Island

NEW JERSEY-NEW YORK 7 CONFERENCE

Season	No.	Regular Season
1977	7	Columbia/Seton Hall
1978	7	Rutgers/St. John's (N.Y.)
1979	7	Rutgers

NORTHEAST CONFERENCE

Season	No.	Regular Season
1982	11	Fairleigh Dickinson (North)/Robert Morris (South)
1983	10	Long Island (North)/Robert Morris (South)
1984	9	Long Island/Robert Morris
1985	8	Marist
1986	9	Fairleigh Dickinson
1987	9	Marist
1988	9	Fairleigh Dickinson/Marist
1989	9	Robert Morris
1990	9	Robert Morris
1991	9	St. Francis (Pa.)/Fairleigh Dickinson
1992	9	Robert Morris

Season	No.	Conference Tournament
1993	10	Rider
1994	10	Rider
1995	10	Rider
1996	10	Mt. St. Mary's
1997	10	Long Island
1998	9	Long Island
1999	11	UMBC
2000	12	Central Conn. St.
2001	12	St. Francis (N.Y.)
2002	12	Central Conn. St.
2003	12	Wagner
2004	11	Monmouth/St. Francis (N.Y.)
2005	11	Monmouth
2006	11	Fairleigh Dickinson
2007	11	Central Conn. St.
2008	11	Robert Morris

Season	No.	Conference Tournament
1982	8	Robert Morris
1983	8	Robert Morris
1984	8	Long Island
1985	8	Fairleigh Dickinson
1986	8	Marist
1987	6	Marist
1988	6	Fairleigh Dickinson
1989	6	Robert Morris
1990	6	Robert Morris
1991	7	St. Francis (Pa.)
1992	9	Robert Morris
1993	10	Rider
1994	10	Rider
1995	10	Mt. St. Mary's
1996	10	Monmouth
1997	8	Long Island
1998	8	Fairleigh Dickinson
1999	8	Mt. St. Mary's
2000	8	Central Conn. St.
2001	7	Monmouth
2002	8	Central Conn. St.
2003	8	Wagner
2004	8	Monmouth
2005	8	Fairleigh Dickinson
2006	8	Monmouth
2007	8	Central Conn. St.
2008	8	Mt. St. Mary's

OHIO VALLEY CONFERENCE

Season	No.	Regular Season
1949	8	Western Ky.
1950	7	Western Ky.
1951	7	Murray St.
1952	7	Western Ky.
1953	6	Eastern Ky.
1954	6	Western Ky.
1955	6	Western Ky.
1956	6	Morehead St./Tennessee Tech/Western Ky.
1957	6	Morehead St./Western Ky.
1958	7	Tennessee Tech
1959	7	Eastern Ky.
1960	7	Western Ky.
1961	7	Morehead St./Western Ky./Eastern Ky.
1962	6	Western Ky.
1963	7	Tennessee Tech/Morehead St.
1964	8	Murray St.
1965	8	Eastern Ky.
1966	8	Western Ky.
1967	8	Western Ky.
1968	8	East Tenn. St./Murray St.
1969	8	Murray St./Morehead St.
1970	8	Western Ky.
1971	8	Western Ky.
1972	8	Eastern Ky./Morehead St./Western Ky.
1973	8	Austin Peay
1974	8	Austin Peay/Morehead St.
1975	8	Middle Tenn.
1976	8	Western Ky.
1977	8	Austin Peay
1978	8	Middle Tenn./Eastern Ky.
1979	7	Eastern Ky.
1980	7	Western Ky./Murray St.
1981	8	Western Ky.
1982	8	Murray St./Western Ky.
1983	8	Murray St.
1984	8	Morehead St.
1985	8	Tennessee Tech
1986	8	Akron/Middle Tenn.

Season	No.	Conference Tournament
1987	8	Middle Tenn.
1988	8	Murray St.
1989	7	Middle Tenn./Murray St.
1990	7	Murray St.
1991	7	Murray St.
1992	8	Murray St.
1993	9	Tennessee St.
1994	9	Murray St.
1995	9	Murray St./Tennessee St.
1996	9	Murray St.
1997	10	Austin Peay/Murray St.
1998	10	Murray St.
1999	10	Murray St.
2000	10	Southeast Mo. St./Murray St.
2001	9	Tennessee Tech
2002	9	Tennessee Tech
2003	9	Austin Peay/Morehead St.
2004	11	Austin Peay
2005	11	Tennessee Tech
2006	11	Murray St.
2007	11	Austin Peay
2008	11	Austin Peay

Season	No.	Conference Tournament
1949	8	Western Ky.
1950	7	Eastern Ky.
1951	7	Murray St.
1952	7	Western Ky.
1953	6	Western Ky.
1954	6	Western Ky.
1955	6	Eastern Ky.
1956-63		DNP
1964	8	Murray St.
1965	8	Western Ky.
1966	8	Western Ky.
1967	8	Tennessee Tech
1968-74		DNP
1975	4	Middle Tenn.
1976	8	Western Ky.
1977	4	Middle Tenn.
1978	4	Western Ky.
1979	4	Eastern Ky.
1980	4	Western Ky.
1981	4	Western Ky.
1982	4	Middle Tenn.
1983	4	Morehead St.
1984	4	Morehead St.
1985	7	Middle Tenn.
1986	7	Akron
1987	7	Austin Peay
1988	7	Murray St.
1989	7	Middle Tenn.
1990	7	Murray St.
1991	7	Murray St.
1992	7	Murray St.
1993	6	Tennessee St.
1994	7	Tennessee St.
1995	7	Murray St.
1996	7	Austin Peay
1997	8	Murray St.
1998	8	Murray St.
1999	8	Murray St.
2000	8	Southeast Mo. St.
2001	8	Eastern Ill.
2002	8	Murray St.
2003	8	Austin Peay
2004	8	Murray St.
2005	8	Eastern Ky.
2006	8	Murray St.
2007	8	Eastern Ky.
2008	8	Austin Peay

PACIFIC-10 CONFERENCE

Season	No.	Regular Season
1916	3	California/Oregon St.
1917	6	Washington St.
1918		DNP
1919	6	Oregon
1920	6	Stanford
1921	6	Stanford
1922	8	Idaho
1923	8	Idaho
1924	9	California
1925	8	California
1926	9	California
1927	9	California
1928	10	Southern California
1929	10	California
1930	9	Southern California

Season	No.	Regular Season
1931	9	Washington
1932	9	California
1933	9	Oregon St.
1934	9	Washington
1935	9	Southern California
1936	9	Stanford
1937	9	Stanford
1938	10	Stanford
1939	9	Oregon
1940	9	Southern California
1941	9	Washington St.
1942	9	Stanford
1943	9	Washington
1944	8	Washington (North)/California (South)
1945	8	Oregon (North)/UCLA (South)
1946	9	California
1947	9	Oregon St.
1948	9	Washington
1949	9	Oregon St.
1950	9	UCLA
1951	9	Washington
1952	9	UCLA
1953	9	Washington
1954	9	Southern California
1955	9	Oregon St.
1956	9	UCLA
1957	9	California
1958	9	Oregon St./California
1959	9	California
1960	5	California
1961	5	Southern California
1962	5	UCLA
1963	5	UCLA/Stanford
1964	6	UCLA
1965	8	UCLA
1966	8	Oregon St.
1967	8	UCLA
1968	8	UCLA
1969	8	UCLA
1970	8	UCLA
1971	8	UCLA
1972	8	UCLA
1973	8	UCLA
1974	8	UCLA
1975	8	UCLA
1976	8	UCLA
1977	8	UCLA
1978	8	UCLA
1979	10	UCLA
1980	10	Oregon St.
1981	10	Oregon St.
1982	10	Oregon St.
1983	10	UCLA
1984	10	Washington/Oregon St.
1985	10	Washington/Southern California
1986	10	Arizona
1987	10	UCLA
1988	10	Arizona
1989	10	Arizona
1990	10	Oregon St./Arizona
1991	10	Arizona
1992	10	UCLA
1993	10	Arizona
1994	10	Arizona
1995	10	UCLA
1996	10	UCLA
1997	10	UCLA
1998	10	Arizona
1999	10	Stanford
2000	10	Arizona/Stanford
2001	10	Stanford
2002	10	Oregon
2003	10	Arizona
2004	10	Stanford
2005	10	Arizona
2006	10	UCLA
2007	10	UCLA
2008	10	UCLA

Season	No.	Conference Tournament
1987	10	UCLA
1988	10	Arizona
1989	10	Arizona
1990	10	Arizona
1991-2001		DNP
2002	8	Arizona
2003	8	Oregon
2004	8	Stanford
2005	8	Washington

CONFERENCES

Season	No.	Regular Season
2006	10	UCLA
2007	10	Oregon
2008	10	UCLA

PATRIOT LEAGUE

Season	No.	Regular Season
1991	7	Fordham
1992	8	Bucknell/Fordham
1993	8	Bucknell
1994	8	Navy/Fordham/Colgate/Holy Cross
1995	8	Bucknell/Colgate
1996	7	Colgate/Navy
1997	7	Navy
1998	7	Lafayette/Navy
1999	7	Lafayette
2000	7	Lafayette/Navy
2001	7	Holy Cross
2002	8	American
2003	8	Holy Cross
2004	8	Lehigh/American
2005	8	Holy Cross
2006	8	Bucknell
2007	8	Holy Cross
2008	8	American

Season	No.	Conference Tournament
1991	7	Fordham
1992	8	Fordham
1993	8	Holy Cross
1994	8	Navy
1995	8	Colgate
1996	7	Colgate
1997	7	Navy
1998	7	Navy
1999	7	Lafayette
2000	7	Lafayette
2001	7	Holy Cross
2002	8	Holy Cross
2003	8	Holy Cross
2004	8	Lehigh
2005	8	Bucknell
2006	8	Bucknell
2007	8	Holy Cross
2008	8	American

ROCKY MOUNTAIN CONFERENCE

Season	No.	Regular Season
1922	6	Colorado Col.
1923	5	Colorado Col.
1924	6	Colorado Col.
1925	12	Colorado Col. (East)/BYU (West)
1926	12	Colorado St. (East)/Utah (West)
1927	12	Colorado Col. (East)/Montana St. (West)
1928	12	Wyoming (East)/Montana St. (West)
1929	12	Colorado (East)/Montana St. (West)
1929	12	Colorado (East)/Montana St. (West)
1930	12	Colorado (East)/Montana St. (West)/Utah St. (West)
1931	12	Wyoming (East)/Utah (West)
1932	12	Wyoming (East)/BYU (West)/Utah (West)
1933	12	Wyoming (East)/Colorado St. (East)/BYU (West)/Utah (West)
1934	12	Wyoming (East)/ BYU (West)
1935	12	Northern Colo. (East)/Utah St. (West)
1936	12	Wyoming (East)/Utah (West)
1937	12	Denver (East)/Colorado (East)/Montana St. (West)/Utah (West)
1938	5	Montana St.
1939	5	Northern Colo.
1940	5	Northern Colo.
1941	5	Northern Colo.
1942	5	Northern Colo.
1943	3	Northern Colo.
1944	3	Colorado Col.
1945	3	Colorado Col.
1946	5	Colorado St.
1947	5	Montana St.
1948	4	Colorado St.
1949	5	Colorado St.
1950	6	Montana St.
1951	6	Montana St.
1952	6	Colorado St./Montana St.

Season	No.	Regular Season
1953	6	Idaho St.
1954	6	Idaho St.
1955	6	Idaho St.
1956	6	Idaho St.
1957	6	Idaho St.
1958	6	Idaho St.
1959	6	Idaho St.
1960	6	Idaho St.

SOUTHEASTERN CONFERENCE

Season	No.	Regular Season
1933	13	Kentucky
1934	13	Alabama
1935	13	LSU/Kentucky
1936	13	Tennessee
1937	13	Kentucky
1938	13	Georgia Tech
1939	13	Kentucky
1940	13	Kentucky
1941	12	Tennessee
1942	12	Kentucky
1943	12	Tennessee
1944	6	Kentucky
1945	12	Kentucky
1946	12	Kentucky
1947	12	Kentucky
1948	12	Kentucky
1949	12	Kentucky
1950	12	Kentucky
1951	12	Kentucky
1952	12	Kentucky
1953	11	LSU
1954	12	Kentucky/LSU
1955	12	Kentucky
1956	12	Alabama
1957	12	Kentucky
1958	12	Kentucky
1959	12	Mississippi St.
1960	12	Auburn
1961	12	Mississippi St.
1962	12	Mississippi St./Kentucky
1963	12	Mississippi St.
1964	12	Kentucky
1965	11	Vanderbilt
1966	11	Kentucky
1967	10	Tennessee
1968	10	Kentucky
1969	10	Kentucky
1970	10	Kentucky
1971	10	Kentucky
1972	10	Tennessee/Kentucky
1973	10	Kentucky
1974	10	Vanderbilt/Alabama
1975	10	Kentucky/Alabama
1976	10	Alabama
1977	10	Kentucky/Tennessee
1978	10	Kentucky
1979	10	LSU
1980	10	Kentucky
1981	10	LSU
1982	10	Kentucky/Tennessee
1983	10	Kentucky
1984	10	Kentucky
1985	10	LSU
1986	10	Kentucky
1987	10	Alabama
1988	10	Kentucky*
1989	10	Florida
1990	10	Georgia
1991	10	Mississippi St./LSU
1992	12	Kentucky (Eastern)/Arkansas (Western)
1993	12	Vanderbilt (Eastern)/Arkansas (Western)
1994	12	Florida (Eastern)/Kentucky (Eastern)/Arkansas (Western)
1995	12	Kentucky (Eastern)/Arkansas (Western)/Mississippi St. (Western)
1996	12	Kentucky (Eastern)/Mississippi St. (Western)
1997	12	South Carolina (Eastern)/Mississippi (Western)
1998	12	Kentucky (Eastern)/Mississippi (Western)
1999	12	Tennessee (Eastern)/Auburn (Western)

Season	No.	Conference Tournament
2000	12	Tennessee (Eastern)/ Florida (Eastern)/Kentucky (Eastern)/LSU (Western)
2001	12	Florida (Eastern)/Kentucky (Eastern)/Mississippi (Western)
2002	12	Georgia (Eastern)/Kentucky (Eastern)/Florida (Eastern)/Alabama (Western)
2003	12	Kentucky (Eastern)/Mississippi St. (Western)
2004	12	Kentucky (Eastern)/Mississippi St. (Western)
2005	12	Kentucky (Eastern)/Alabama (Western)/LSU (Western)
2006	12	Tennessee (Eastern)/LSU (Western)
2007	12	Florida (Eastern)/Mississippi (Western)/Mississippi St. (Western)
2008	12	Tennessee (Eastern)/Mississippi St. (Western)

Season	No.	Conference Tournament
1933	13	Kentucky
1934	10	Alabama
1935		DNP
1936	9	Tennessee
1937	8	Kentucky
1938	11	Georgia Tech
1939	12	Kentucky
1940	12	Kentucky
1941	12	Tennessee
1942	12	Kentucky
1943	11	Tennessee
1944	6	Kentucky
1945	11	Kentucky
1946	12	Kentucky
1947	12	Kentucky
1948	12	Kentucky
1949	12	Kentucky
1950	12	Kentucky
1951	12	Vanderbilt
1952	12	Kentucky
1953-78		DNP
1979	10	Tennessee
1980	10	LSU
1981	10	Mississippi
1982	10	Alabama
1983	10	Georgia
1984	10	Kentucky
1985	10	Auburn
1986	10	Kentucky
1987	10	Alabama
1988	10	Kentucky*
1989	10	Alabama
1990	9	Alabama
1991	9	Alabama
1992	11	Kentucky
1993	12	Kentucky
1994	12	Kentucky
1995	12	Kentucky
1996	12	Mississippi St.
1997	12	Kentucky
1998	12	Kentucky
1999	12	Kentucky
2000	12	Arkansas
2001	12	Kentucky
2002	12	Mississippi St.
2003	11	Kentucky
2004	12	Kentucky
2005	12	Florida
2006	12	Florida
2007	12	Florida
2008	12	Georgia

*later vacated

SOUTHERN CONFERENCE

Season	No.	Regular Season
1922	13	Virginia
1923	19	North Carolina
1924	21	Tulane
1925	21	North Carolina
1926	22	Kentucky
1927	22	South Carolina
1928	22	Auburn
1929	23	Wash. & Lee
1930	23	Alabama
1931	22	Georgia
1932	23	Kentucky/Maryland
1933	10	South Carolina

Season	No.	Regular Season
1934	10	South Carolina
1935	10	North Carolina
1936	10	Wash. & Lee
1937	16	Wash. & Lee
1938	15	North Carolina
1939	15	Wake Forest
1940	15	Duke
1941	15	North Carolina
1942	15	Duke
1943	15	Duke
1944	12	North Carolina
1945	14	South Carolina
1946	16	North Carolina
1947	16	North Carolina St.
1948	16	North Carolina St.
1949	16	North Carolina St.
1950	16	North Carolina St.
1951	17	North Carolina St.
1952	17	West Virginia
1953	17	North Carolina St.
1954	10	George Washington
1955	10	West Virginia
1956	10	George Washington/West Virginia
1957	10	West Virginia
1958	10	West Virginia
1959	9	West Virginia
1960	9	Virginia Tech
1961	9	West Virginia
1962	9	West Virginia
1963	9	West Virginia
1964	9	Davidson
1965	10	Davidson
1966	9	Davidson
1967	9	West Virginia
1968	8	Davidson
1969	8	Davidson
1970	8	Davidson
1971	7	Davidson
1972	8	Davidson
1973	8	Davidson
1974	8	Furman
1975	8	Furman
1976	8	VMI
1977	10	Furman/VMI
1978	8	Appalachian St.
1979	9	Appalachian St.
1980	9	Furman
1981	9	Appalachian St./Davidson/Chattanooga
1982	9	Chattanooga
1983	9	Chattanooga
1984	9	Marshall
1985	9	Chattanooga
1986	9	Chattanooga
1987	9	Marshall
1988	9	Marshall
1989	8	Chattanooga
1990	8	East Tenn. St.
1991	8	East Tenn. St./Furman/Chattanooga
1992	8	East Tenn. St./Chattanooga
1993	10	Chattanooga
1994	10	Chattanooga
1995	10	Marshall (Northern)/Chattanooga (Southern)
1996	10	Davidson (Northern)/Western Caro. (Southern)
1997	10	Davidson (Northern)/Marshall (Northern)/Chattanooga (Southern)
1998	11	Appalachian St. (North)/Davidson (North)/Chattanooga (South)
1999	12	Appalachian St.(North)/Col. of Charleston (South)
2000	12	Appalachian St. (North)/Col. of Charleston (South)
2001	12	East Tenn. St. (North)/Col. of Charleston (South)
2002	12	Davidson (North)/UNC Greensboro (North)/East Tenn. St. (North)/Col. of Charleston (South)/Ga. Southern (South)/Chattanooga (South)
2003	12	Appalachian St. (North)/Davidson (North)/East Tenn. St. (North)/Col. of Charleston (South)
2004	12	East Tenn. St. (North)/Ga. Southern (South)/Davidson (South)/Col. of Charleston (South)

Season	No.	Conference Tournament
2005	12	Chattanooga (North)/Davidson (South)
2006	11	Elon (North)/Ga. Southern (South)
2007	11	Appalachian St. (North)/Davidson (South)
2008	11	Appalachian St. (North)/Chattanooga (North)/Davidson (South)

Season	No.	Conference Tournament
1921		Kentucky
1922	23	North Carolina
1923	22	Mississippi St.
1924	16	North Carolina
1925	17	North Carolina
1926	16	North Carolina
1927	14	Vanderbilt
1928	16	Mississippi
1929	16	North Carolina St.
1930	16	Alabama
1931	16	Maryland
1932	16	Georgia
1933	8	South Carolina
1934	8	Wash. & Lee
1935	8	North Carolina
1936	8	North Carolina
1937	8	Wash. & Lee
1938	8	Duke
1939	11	Clemson
1940	8	North Carolina
1941	8	Duke
1942	8	Duke
1943	8	George Washington
1944	8	Duke
1945	8	North Carolina
1946	8	Duke
1947	8	North Carolina St.
1948	10	North Carolina St.
1949	8	North Carolina St.
1950	8	North Carolina St.
1951	8	North Carolina St.
1952	8	North Carolina St.
1953	8	Wake Forest
1954	8	George Washington
1955	8	West Virginia
1956	8	West Virginia
1957	8	West Virginia
1958	8	West Virginia
1959	8	West Virginia
1960	8	West Virginia
1961	8	George Washington
1962	8	West Virginia
1963	8	West Virginia
1964	8	VMI
1965	8	West Virginia
1966	8	Davidson
1967	8	West Virginia
1968	8	Davidson
1969	8	Davidson
1970	8	Davidson
1971	7	Furman
1972	8	East Carolina
1973	8	Furman
1974	8	Furman
1975	8	Furman
1976	8	VMI
1977	7	VMI
1978	8	Furman
1979	8	Appalachian St.
1980	8	Furman
1981	8	Chattanooga
1982	8	Chattanooga
1983	8	Chattanooga
1984	8	Marshall
1985	8	Marshall
1986	8	Davidson
1987	8	Marshall
1988	8	Chattanooga
1989	8	East Tenn. St.
1990	8	East Tenn. St.
1991	8	East Tenn. St.
1992	8	East Tenn. St.
1993	10	Chattanooga
1994	10	Chattanooga
1995	10	Chattanooga
1996	9	Western Caro.
1997	10	Chattanooga
1998	10	Davidson
1999	12	Col. of Charleston
2000	12	Appalachian St.
2001	12	UNC Greensboro

Season	No.	Conference Tournament
2002	12	Davidson
2003	12	East Tenn. St.
2004	12	East Tenn. St.
2005	12	UNC Greensboro
2006	11	Davidson
2007	11	Davidson
2008	11	Davidson

SOUTHLAND CONFERENCE

Season	No.	Regular Season
1964	5	Lamar
1965	5	Abilene Christian/Arkansas St.
1966	5	Abilene Christian
1967	5	Arkansas St.
1968	5	Abilene Christian
1969	5	Trinity (Tex.)
1970	5	Lamar
1971	5	Arkansas St.
1972	7	Louisiana Tech
1973	7	Louisiana Tech
1974	3	Arkansas St.
1975	5	McNeese St.
1976	6	Louisiana Tech
1977	6	La.-Lafayette
1978	6	McNeese St./Lamar
1979	6	Lamar
1980	6	Lamar
1981	6	Lamar
1982	6	La.-Lafayette
1983	7	Lamar
1984	7	Lamar
1985	7	Louisiana Tech
1986	7	La.-Monroe
1987	6	Louisiana Tech
1988	8	North Texas
1989	8	North Texas
1990	8	La.-Monroe
1991	8	La.-Monroe
1992	10	UTSA
1993	10	La.-Monroe
1994	10	La.-Monroe
1995	10	Nicholls St.
1996	10	La.-Monroe
1997	10	McNeese St./La.-Monroe/Texas St.
1998	10	Nicholls St.
1999	10	Texas St.
2000	11	Sam Houston St.
2001	11	McNeese St.
2002	11	McNeese St.
2003	11	Sam Houston St.
2004	11	Southeastern La./Texas-Arlington/UTSA
2005	11	Northwestern St./Southeastern La.
2006	11	Northwestern St.
2007	11	Northwestern St. (East)/A&M Corpus Christi (West)
2008	11	Lamar (East)/Stephen F. Austin (West)

Season	No.	Conference Tournament
1981	6	Lamar
1982	5	La.-Lafayette
1983	7	Lamar
1984	7	Louisiana Tech
1985	7	Louisiana Tech
1986	7	La.-Monroe
1987	6	Louisiana Tech
1988	6	North Texas
1989	6	McNeese St.
1990	7	La.-Monroe
1991	4	La.-Monroe
1992	6	La.-Monroe
1993	6	La.-Monroe
1994	8	Texas St.
1995	8	Nicholls St.
1996	6	La.-Monroe
1997	6	Texas St.
1998	6	Nicholls St.
1999	6	UTSA
2000	8	Lamar
2001	8	Northwestern St.
2002	6	McNeese St.
2003	6	Sam Houston St.
2004	8	UTSA
2005	8	Southeastern La.
2006	8	Northwestern St.
2007	8	A&M Corpus Christi
2008	8	Texas-Arlington

CONFERENCES

SOUTHWEST CONFERENCE

Season	No.	Regular Season
1915	5	Texas
1916	5	Texas
1917	3	Texas
1918	5	Rice
1919	5	Texas
1920	6	Texas A&M
1921	5	Texas A&M
1922	6	Texas A&M
1923	6	Texas A&M
1924	8	Texas
1925	8	Oklahoma St.
1926	7	Arkansas
1927	7	Arkansas
1928	7	Arkansas
1929	7	Arkansas
1930	7	Arkansas
1931	7	TCU
1932	7	Baylor
1933	7	Texas
1934	7	TCU
1935	7	Arkansas/Rice/SMU
1936	7	Arkansas
1937	7	SMU
1938	7	Arkansas
1939	7	Texas
1940	7	Rice
1941	7	Arkansas
1942	7	Rice/Arkansas
1943	7	Texas/Rice
1944	7	Arkansas/Rice
1945	7	Rice
1946	7	Baylor
1947	7	Texas
1948	7	Baylor
1949	7	Arkansas/Baylor/Rice
1950	7	Baylor/Arkansas
1951	7	Texas A&M/TCU/Texas
1952	7	TCU
1953	7	TCU
1954	7	Rice/Texas
1955	7	SMU
1956	7	SMU
1957	7	SMU
1958	8	Arkansas/SMU
1959	8	TCU
1960	8	Texas
1961	8	Texas Tech
1962	8	SMU/Texas Tech
1963	8	Texas
1964	8	Texas A&M
1965	8	SMU/Texas
1966	8	SMU
1967	8	SMU
1968	8	TCU
1969	8	Texas A&M
1970	8	Rice
1971	8	TCU
1972	8	Texas/SMU
1973	8	Texas Tech
1974	8	Texas
1975	8	Texas A&M
1976	9	Texas A&M
1977	9	Arkansas
1978	9	Texas/Arkansas
1979	9	Texas/Arkansas
1980	9	Texas A&M
1981	9	Arkansas
1982	9	Arkansas
1983	9	Houston
1984	9	Houston
1985	9	Texas Tech
1986	9	TCU/Texas/Texas A&M
1987	9	TCU
1988	9	SMU
1989	9	Arkansas
1990	9	Arkansas
1991	9	Arkansas
1992	8	Houston/Texas
1993	8	SMU
1994	8	Texas
1995	8	Texas/Texas Tech
1996	8	Texas Tech

Season	No.	Conference Tournament
1976	9	Texas Tech
1977	9	Arkansas
1978	9	Houston
1979	9	Arkansas
1980	9	Texas A&M
1981	9	Houston
1982	9	Arkansas
1983	9	Houston
1984	9	Houston
1985	8	Texas Tech
1986	8	Texas Tech
1987	8	Texas A&M
1988	8	SMU
1989	8	Arkansas
1990	8	Arkansas
1991	9	Arkansas
1992	8	Houston
1993	8	Texas Tech
1994	8	Texas
1995	7	Texas
1996	8	Texas Tech

SOUTHWESTERN ATHLETIC CONFERENCE

Season	No.	Regular Season
1957	6	Texas Southern
1958	6	Texas Southern
1959	8	Grambling
1960	8	Grambling
1961	8	Prairie View
1962	7	Prairie View
1963	8	Grambling
1964	8	Grambling/Jackson St.
1965	8	Southern U.
1966	8	Alcorn St./Grambling
1967	8	Alcorn St./Ark.-Pine Bluff/Grambling
1968	8	Alcorn St./Jackson St.
1969	8	Alcorn St.
1970	8	Jackson St.
1971	7	Grambling
1972	7	Grambling
1973	7	Alcorn St.
1974	7	Jackson St.
1975	7	Jackson St.
1976	7	Alcorn St.
1977	7	Texas Southern
1978	7	Jackson St./Southern U.
1979	7	Alcorn St.
1980	7	Alcorn St.
1981	7	Alcorn St./Southern U.
1982	7	Alcorn St./Jackson St.
1983	8	Texas Southern
1984	8	Alcorn St.
1985	8	Alcorn St.
1986	8	Alcorn St./Southern U.
1987	8	Grambling
1988	8	Southern U.
1989	8	Grambling/Southern U./Texas Southern
1990	8	Southern U.
1991	8	Jackson St.
1992	8	Mississippi Val./Texas Southern
1993	8	Jackson St.
1994	8	Texas Southern
1995	8	Texas Southern
1996	8	Jackson St./Mississippi Val.
1997	8	Mississippi Val.
1998	9	Texas Southern
1999	9	Alcorn St.
2000	10	Alcorn St.
2001	10	Alabama St.
2002	10	Alcorn St.
2003	10	Prairie View
2004	10	Mississippi Val.
2005	10	Alabama A&M
2006	10	Southern U.
2007	10	Mississippi Val.
2008	10	Alabama St.

Season	No.	Conference Tournament
1980	7	Alcorn St.
1981	7	Southern U.
1982	7	Alcorn St.
1983	7	Alcorn St.
1984	8	Alcorn St.
1985	4	Southern U.
1986	8	Mississippi Val.
1987	8	Southern U.
1988	8	Southern U.
1989	8	Southern U.
1990	8	Texas Southern
1991	8	Jackson St.
1992	8	Mississippi Val.
1993	8	Southern U.
1994	8	Texas Southern
1995	6	Texas Southern
1996	6	Mississippi Val.
1997	8	Jackson St.
1998	8	Prairie View
1999	8	Alcorn St.
2000	8	Jackson St.
2001	8	Alabama St.
2002	8	Alcorn St.
2003	8	Texas Southern
2004	8	Alabama St.
2005	8	Alabama A&M
2006	8	Southern U.
2007	8	Jackson St.
2008	8	Mississippi Val.

SUMMIT LEAGUE

Season	No.	Regular Season
1983	8	Western Ill.
1984	8	Ill.-Chicago
1985	8	Cleveland St.
1986	8	Cleveland St.
1987	8	Missouri St.
1988	8	Missouri St.
1989	8	Missouri St.
1990	7	Missouri St.
1991	9	Northern Ill.
1992	9	Green Bay
1993	9	Cleveland St.
1994	10	Green Bay
1995	10	Valparaiso
1996	10	Valparaiso
1997	9	Valparaiso
1998	9	Valparaiso
1999	8	Valparaiso
2000	9	Oakland
2001	9	Southern Utah/Valparaiso
2002	9	Valparaiso
2003	8	Valparaiso
2004	9	Valparaiso
2005	9	Oral Roberts
2006	9	IUPUI/Oral Roberts
2007	8	Oral Roberts
2008	8	Oral Roberts

Season	No.	Conference Tournament
1984	8	Western Ill.
1985	8	Eastern Ill.
1986	8	Cleveland St.
1987	8	Missouri St.
1988		DNP
1989	7	Missouri St.
1990	7	UNI
1991	8	Green Bay
1992	8	Eastern Ill.
1993	8	Wright St.
1994	8	Green Bay
1995	6	Valparaiso
1996	8	Valparaiso
1997	8	Valparaiso
1998	7	Valpairaso
1999	7	Valparaiso
2000	7	Valparaiso
2001	8	Southern Utah
2002	8	Valparaiso
2003	8	IUPUI
2004	8	Valparaiso
2005	8	Oakland
2006	8	Oral Roberts
2007	8	Oral Roberts
2008	8	Oral Roberts

SUN BELT CONFERENCE

Season	No.	Regular Season
1977	6	Charlotte
1978	6	Charlotte
1979	6	South Ala.
1980	8	South Ala.
1981	7	VCU/South Ala./UAB
1982	8	UAB
1983	8	VCU/Old Dominion
1984	8	VCU
1985	8	VCU
1986	8	Old Dominion
1987	8	Western Ky.
1988	8	Charlotte
1989	8	South Ala.

Season	No.	Regular Season
1990	8	UAB
1991	8	South Ala.
1992	11	Louisiana Tech/La.-Lafayette
1993	10	New Orleans
1994	10	Western Ky.
1995	10	Western Ky.
1996	10	UALR/New Orleans
1997	10	New Orleans/South Ala.
1998	10	South Ala./Arkansas St.
1999	8	Louisiana Tech
2000	9	La.-Lafayette/South Ala.
2001	12	Western Ky. (East)/South Ala. (West)
2002	11	Western Ky. (East)/La.-Lafayette (West)/New Mexico St. (West)
2003	12	Western Ky. (East)/La.-Lafayette (West)
2004	11	UALR (East)/La.-Lafayette (West)
2005	11	UALR (East)/Denver (West)
2006	11	Western Ky. (East)/South Ala. (West)
2007	13	South Ala. (Eastern)/Arkansas St. (Western)/La.-Monroe (Western)
2008	13	South Ala. (Eastern)/Western Ky. (Eastern)/UALR (Western)/La.-Lafayette (Western)

Season	No.	Conference Tournament
1977	6	Charlotte
1978	6	New Orleans
1979	6	Jacksonville
1980	8	VCU
1981	7	VCU
1982	6	UAB
1983	8	UAB
1984	8	UAB
1985	8	VCU
1986	8	Jacksonville
1987	8	UAB
1988	8	Charlotte
1989	8	South Ala.
1990	8	South Fla.
1991	8	South Ala.
1992	11	La.-Lafayette
1993	9	Western Ky.
1994	10	La.-Lafayette
1995	10	Western Ky.
1996	10	New Orleans
1997	10	South Ala.
1998	10	South Ala.
1999	8	Arkansas St.
2000	9	La.-Lafayette
2001	11	Western Ky.
2002	11	Western Ky.
2003	11	Western Ky.
2004	8	La.-Lafayette
2005	11	La.-Lafayette
2006	11	South Ala.
2007	13	North Texas
2008	13	Western Ky.

WEST COAST CONFERENCE

Season	No.	Regular Season
1953	5	Santa Clara
1954	5	Santa Clara
1955	5	San Francisco
1956	8	San Francisco
1957	8	San Francisco
1958	7	San Francisco
1959	7	St. Mary's (Cal.)
1960	7	Santa Clara
1961	7	Loyola Marymount
1962	7	Pepperdine
1963	7	San Francisco
1964	7	San Francisco
1965	8	San Francisco
1966	8	Pacific
1967	8	Pacific
1968	8	Santa Clara
1969	8	Santa Clara
1970	8	Santa Clara
1971	8	Pacific
1972	8	San Francisco
1973	8	San Francisco
1974	8	San Francisco
1975	8	UNLV
1976	7	Pepperdine
1977	8	San Francisco
1978	8	San Francisco
1979	8	San Francisco
1980	9	San Francisco/St. Mary's (Cal.)
1981	8	San Francisco/Pepperdine
1982	8	Pepperdine
1983	7	Pepperdine
1984	7	San Diego
1985	7	Pepperdine
1986	8	Pepperdine
1987	8	San Diego
1988	8	Loyola Marymount
1989	8	St. Mary's (Cal.)
1990	8	Loyola Marymount
1991	8	Pepperdine
1992	8	Pepperdine
1993	8	Pepperdine
1994	8	Gonzaga
1995	8	Santa Clara
1996	8	Gonzaga/Santa Clara
1997	8	St. Mary's (Cal.)/Santa Clara
1998	8	Gonzaga
1999	8	Gonzaga
2000	8	Pepperdine
2001	8	Gonzaga
2002	8	Gonzaga/Pepperdine
2003	8	Gonzaga
2004	8	Gonzaga
2005	8	Gonzaga
2006	8	Gonzaga
2007	8	Gonzaga
2008	8	Gonzaga

Season	No.	Conference Tournament
1987	8	Santa Clara
1988	8	Loyola Marymount
1989	8	Loyola Marymount
1990		DNP
1991	8	Pepperdine
1992	8	Pepperdine
1993	8	Santa Clara
1994	8	Pepperdine
1995	8	Gonzaga
1996	8	Portland
1997	8	St. Mary's (Cal.)
1998	8	San Francisco
1999	8	Gonzaga
2000	8	Gonzaga
2001	8	Gonzaga
2002	8	Gonzaga
2003	6	San Diego
2004	8	Gonzaga
2005	8	Gonzaga
2006	8	Gonzaga
2007	8	Gonzaga
2008	8	San Diego

WESTERN ATHLETIC CONFERENCE

Season	No.	Regular Season
1963	6	Arizona St.
1964	6	New Mexico/Arizona St.
1965	6	BYU
1966	6	Utah
1967	6	Wyoming/BYU
1968	6	New Mexico
1969	6	BYU/Wyoming
1970	8	UTEP
1971	8	BYU
1972	8	BYU
1973	8	Arizona St.
1974	8	New Mexico
1975	8	Arizona St.
1976	8	Arizona
1977	8	Utah
1978	8	New Mexico
1979	7	BYU
1980	8	BYU
1981	9	Utah/Wyoming
1982	9	Wyoming
1983	9	UTEP/Utah
1984	9	UTEP
1985	9	UTEP
1986	9	Wyoming/UTEP/Utah
1987	9	UTEP
1988	9	BYU
1989	9	Colorado St.
1990	9	Colorado St./BYU
1991	9	Utah
1992	9	UTEP/BYU
1993	10	BYU/Utah
1994	10	New Mexico
1995	10	Utah
1996	10	Utah
1997	16	Fresno St. (Pacific)/Hawaii (Pacific)/Utah (Mountain)
1998	16	TCU (Pacific)/Utah (Mountain)
1999	16	UNLV (Mountain)/Tulsa (Mountain)/Utah (Pacific)
2000	8	Tulsa
2001	9	Fresno St.
2002	10	Hawaii/Tulsa
2003	10	Fresno St.
2004	10	UTEP/Nevada
2005	10	Nevada
2006	9	Nevada
2007	9	Nevada
2008	9	Boise St./Nevada/New Mexico St./Utah St.

Season	No.	Conference Tournament
1984	9	UTEP
1985	9	San Diego St.
1986	9	UTEP
1987	9	Wyoming
1988	9	Wyoming
1989	9	UTEP
1990	9	UTEP
1991	9	BYU
1992	8	BYU
1993	10	New Mexico
1994	10	Hawaii
1995	10	Utah
1996	10	New Mexico
1997	12	Utah
1998	12	UNLV
1999	12	Utah
2000	8	Fresno St.
2001	9	Hawaii
2002	10	Hawaii
2003	9	Tulsa
2004	10	Nevada
2005	10	UTEP
2006	8	Nevada
2007	9	New Mexico St.
2008	9	Boise St.

WESTERN NEW YORK LITTLE THREE CONFERENCE

Season	No.	Regular Season
1947	3	Canisius
1948	3	Niagara
1949	3	Niagara
1950	3	Canisius/Niagara/St. Bonaventure
1951	3	St. Bonaventure
1952		DNP
1953	3	Niagara
1954	3	Niagara
1955	3	Niagara
1956	3	Canisius
1957	3	Canisius/St. Bonaventure
1958	3	St. Bonaventure

YANKEE CONFERENCE

Season	No.	Regular Season
1947	6	Vermont
1948	6	Connecticut
1949	6	Connecticut
1950	6	Rhode Island
1951	6	Connecticut
1952	6	Connecticut
1953	6	Connecticut
1954	6	Connecticut
1955	6	Connecticut
1956	6	Connecticut
1957	6	Connecticut
1958	6	Connecticut
1959	6	Connecticut
1960	6	Connecticut
1961	6	Rhode Island
1962	6	Massachusetts
1963	6	Connecticut
1964	6	Connecticut/Rhode Island
1965	6	Connecticut
1966	6	Connecticut/Rhode Island
1967	6	Connecticut
1968	6	Massachusetts/Rhode Island
1969	6	Massachusetts
1970	6	Connecticut/Massachusetts

CONFERENCES

Season	No.	Regular Season
1971	6	Massachusetts
1972	6	Rhode Island
1973	7	Massachusetts
1974	7	Massachusetts
1975	7	Massachusetts

INDEPENDENTS
(Best Record)

Season	No.	Regular Season
1946	30	Yale
1947	32	Duquesne
1948	40	Bradley
1949	34	Villanova
1950	36	Toledo
1951	37	Dayton
1952	42	Seton Hall
1953	42	Seattle
1954	39	Holy Cross/Seattle
1955	41	Marquette
1956	35	Temple
1957	32	Seattle
1958	29	Temple
1959	32	St. Bonaventure
1960	34	Providence
1961	35	Memphis
1962	34	Loyola (Ill.)
1963	47	Loyola (Ill.)
1964	51	UTEP
1965	45	Providence
1966	44	UTEP
1967	47	Boston College
1968	47	Houston
1969	47	Boston College
1970	52	Jacksonville
1971	55	Marquette
1972	59	Oral Roberts
1973	68	Providence
1974	73	Notre Dame
1975	79	Tex.-Pan American
1976	79	Rutgers
1977	73	UNLV
1978	70	DePaul
1979	68	Syracuse
1980	55	DePaul
1981	54	DePaul
1982	52	DePaul
1983	19	New Orleans
1984	19	DePaul
1985	22	Notre Dame
1986	17	Notre Dame
1987	18	DePaul
1988	18	Akron
1989	22	Akron
1990	19	Wright St.
1991	17	DePaul
1992	12	Penn St.
1993	14	Milwaukee
1994	6	Southern Utah
1995	2	Notre Dame
1996	2	Oral Roberts
1997	3	Oral Roberts
1998	0	
1999	2	Denver
2000	5	Tex.-Pan American
2001	5	Stony Brook
2002	3	Tex.-Pan American
2003	4	Centenary (La.)
2004	4	A&M-Corpus Christi
2005	4	A&M-Corpus Christi
2006	4	A&M-Corpus Christi
2007	4	Tex.-Pan American
2008	4	Tex.-Pan American

CONSECUTIVE REGULAR-SEASON WINNER

No.	Team	Conference	Seasons
13	UCLA	Pacific-10	1967-79
10	Connecticut	Yankee	1951-60
10	UNLV	Big West	1983-92
9	Kentucky	Southeastern	1944-52
8	Gonzaga	West Coast	2001-08
8	Idaho St.	Rocky Mountain	1953-60
8	Long Beach St.	Big West	1970-77
7	Cincinnati	Conference USA	1996-2002
7	Coppin St.	Mid-Eastern	1993-99
7	Dartmouth	Ivy	1938-44
7	Murray St.	Ohio Valley	1994-2000

No.	Team	Conference	Seasons
7	Rhode Island	New England	1938-44
6	Arizona	Border	1946-51
6	Col. of Charleston	Southern	1999-2004
6	Cincinnati	Missouri Valley	1958-63
6	Davidson	Southern	1968-73
6	Kansas	Missouri Valley	1922-27
6	Kentucky	Southeastern	1968-73
6	Kentucky	Southeastern	2000-05
6	Penn	Ivy	1970-75
6	Weber St.	Big Sky	1968-73

CONSECUTIVE CONFERENCE TOURNAMENT WINNER

No.	Team	Conference	Seasons
7	Kentucky	Southeastern	1944-50
7	N.C. A&T	Mid-Eastern	1982-88
6	North Carolina St.	Southern	1947-52
6	Valparaiso	Mid-Continent	1995-2000
6	West Virginia	Southern	1955-60
5	Duke	Atlantic Coast	1999-2003
5	Massachusetts	Atlantic 10	1992-96
4	Arizona	Pacific-10	1988-90, 2002
4	Cincinnati	Great Midwest	1992-95
4	East Tenn. St.	Southern	1989-92
4	Gonzaga	West Coast	1999-2002
4	Gonzaga	West Coast	2004-07
4	Kentucky	Southeastern	1992-95
4	La.-Monroe	Southland	1990-93
4	Northeastern	America East	1984-87
4	Winthrop	Big South	1999-2002
4	Winthrop	Big South	2005-08
3	32 tied		

REGULAR SEASON CONFERENCE TITLES WON OR SHARED
(Includes divisional crowns)

No.	School	Conferences
51	Kansas	MVC, Big 8, Big 12
49	Kentucky	Southern, SEC
37	Penn	Ivy
33	North Carolina	Southern, ACC
31	Utah	Rocky Mountain, Mountain States, WAC, MWC
30	UCLA	Pac-10
28	Connecticut	Yankee, Big East
28	Princeton	Ivy
27	Western Ky.	OVC, Sun Belt
26	Arkansas	Southwest, SEC
25	Texas	Southwest, Big 12
23	BYU	Rocky Mountain Mountain States WAC, MWC
22	Cincinnati	MAC, MVC, Great Midwest, C-USA
21	Arizona	Border, WAC, Pac-10
21	Duke	Southern
21	Purdue	Big Ten
21	Wyoming	Rocky Mountain Mountain States WAC, MWC
20	Indiana	Big Ten
20	Louisville	MVC, Metropolitan, C-USA
20	Murray St.	OVC
20	St. Joseph's	East Coast, A-10

DIVISION I UNDEFEATED IN CONFERENCE PLAY
Minimum 6 conference games.

Year	Conference	Team	Conference W-L	Overall W-L
1904	Ivy	Columbia	10-0	14-0
1905	Ivy	Columbia	8-0	13-0
1908	Ivy	Penn	8-0	23-4
1908	Missouri Valley	Kansas	6-0	18-6
1909	Big Ten	Chicago	12-0	12-0
1912	Big Ten	Purdue	12-0	12-0
1912	Big Ten	Wisconsin	12-0	15-0
1912	Missouri Valley	Nebraska	8-0	14-1
1913	Big Ten	Wisconsin	12-0	14-1
1913	Missouri Valley	Nebraska	10-0	17-2

Year	Conference	Team	Conference W-L	Overall W-L
1914	Big Ten	Wisconsin	12-0	15-0
1914	Missouri Valley	Nebraska	7-0	15-3
1915	Big Ten	Illinois	12-0	16-0
1916	Big Ten	Wisconsin	12-0	20-1
1916	Missouri Valley	Nebraska	12-0	13-1
1916	Southwest	Texas	6-0	12-0
1920	Ivy	Penn	10-0	22-1
1920	Southwest	Texas A&M	16-0	19-0
1922	Pacific Coast	Idaho	7-0	19-1
1923	Missouri Valley	Kansas	16-0	17-1
1924	Southwest	Texas	20-0	23-0
1926	Pacific Coast	California	7-0	14-0
1927	Pacific Coast	California	7-0	13-0
1928	Missouri Valley	Oklahoma	18-0	18-0
1928	Southwest	Arkansas	12-0	19-1
1929	Big Six	Oklahoma	10-0	13-2
1929	Missouri Valley	Washington-St. Louis	7-0	11-7
1929	Pacific Coast	California	11-0	17-3
1930	Big Ten	Purdue	10-0	13-2
1931	Ivy	Columbia	10-0	20-2
1932	Missouri Valley	Creighton	8-0	17-4
1934	Eastern Intercollegiate	Pittsburgh	8-0	18-4
1936	Big Six	Kansas	10-0	21-2
1936	Ivy	Columbia	12-0	19-3
1937	Ivy	Penn	12-0	17-3
1938	Border	New Mex. St.	18-0	22-3
1940	Missouri Valley	Oklahoma St.	12-0	26-3
1941	Southwest	Arkansas	12-0	20-3
1942	Border	West Tex. A&M	16-0	28-3
1943	Big Six	Kansas	10-0	22-6
1943	Big Ten	Illinois	12-0	17-1
1943	Border	West Tex. A&M	16-0	15-7
1943	Missouri Valley	Creighton	10-0	16-1
1944	Ivy	Dartmouth	8-0	19-2
1945	Border	New Mexico	12-0	14-2
1945	Southwest	Rice	12-0	20-1
1946	Big Six	Kansas	10-0	19-2
1946	Missouri Valley	Oklahoma St.	12-0	31-2
1947	Southwest	Texas	12-0	26-2
1948	Missouri Valley	Oklahoma St.	10-0	27-4
1948	Southeastern	Kentucky	9-0	36-3
1949	Southeastern	Kentucky	13-0	32-2
1951	Ivy	Columbia	12-0	22-1
1951	Southeastern	Kentucky	14-0	32-2
1952	Southeastern	Kentucky	14-0	29-3
1953	Rocky Mountain	Idaho St.	10-0	18-7
1953	Southeastern	LSU	13-0	22-3
1954	Southeastern	Kentucky	14-0	25-0
1954	Southeastern	LSU	14-0	20-5
1954	Southern	George Washington	10-0	23-3
1954	Yankee	Connecticut	7-0	23-3
1955	West Coast	San Francisco	12-0	28-1
1955	Yankee	Connecticut	7-0	20-5
1956	Pacific Coast	UCLA	16-0	22-6
1956	Southeastern	Alabama	14-0	21-3
1956	Southwest	Southern Methodist	12-0	25-4
1956	West Coast	San Francisco	14-0	29-0
1957	Atlantic Coast	North Carolina	14-0	32-0
1957	Rocky Mountain	Idaho St.	12-0	25-4
1957	Southern	West Virginia	12-0	25-5
1957	Yankee	Connecticut	8-0	17-8
1958	Mid-American	Miami (Ohio)	12-0	18-9
1958	Rocky Mountain	Idaho St.	10-0	22-6
1958	Southern	West Virginia	12-0	26-2
1958	West Coast	San Francisco	12-0	25-2
1958	Yankee	Connecticut	10-0	17-10
1959	Big Eight	Kansas St.	14-0	25-2
1959	Middle Atlantic	St. Joseph's	7-0	22-5
1959	Southern	West Virginia	11-0	29-5
1960	Rocky Mountain	Idaho St.	8-0	21-5
1961	Big Ten	Ohio St.	14-0	27-1
1961	Middle Atlantic	St. Joseph's	8-0	25-5
1962	Border	Arizona St.	8-0	23-4
1963	Atlantic Coast	Duke	14-0	27-3
1963	Middle Atlantic	St. Joseph's	8-0	23-5
1964	AAWU	UCLA	15-0	30-0
1964	West Coast	San Francisco	12-0	23-5
1965	AAWU	UCLA	14-0	28-2
1965	Southern	Davidson	12-0	24-2

Year	Conference	Team	Conf W-L	Overall W-L
1965	Yankee	Connecticut	10-0	23-3
1966	Ohio Valley	Western Ky.	14-0	25-3
1967	AAWU	UCLA	14-0	30-0
1967	West Coast	Pacific	14-0	24-4
1968	AAWU	UCLA	14-0	29-1
1969	Big Sky	Weber St.	15-0	27-3
1969	Ivy	Princeton	14-0	19-7
1969	Southern	Davidson	9-0	27-3
1970	Atlantic Coast	South Carolina	14-0	25-3
1970	Big Ten	Iowa	14-0	20-5
1970	Ivy	Penn	14-0	25-2
1970	Ohio Valley	Western Ky.	14-0	22-3
1970	Pacific Coast	Long Beach St.	10-0	24-5
1970	Southern	Davidson	10-0	22-5
1971	Big Eight	Kansas	14-0	27-3
1971	Ivy	Penn	14-0	28-1
1971	Middle Atlantic (E)	St. Joseph's	6-0	19-9
1971	Pacific Coast	Long Beach St.	10-0	24-5
1971	Pacific-8	UCLA	14-0	29-1
1971	Yankee	Massachusetts	10-0	23-4
1972	Middle Atlantic (E)	Temple	6-0	23-8
1972	Pacific-8	UCLA	14-0	30-0
1972	Southland	La.-Lafayette	8-0	25-4
1973	Atlantic Coast	North Caro. St.	12-0	27-0
1973	Middle Atlantic (E)	St. Joseph's	6-0	22-6
1973	Pacific-8	UCLA	14-0	30-0
1973	Southland	La.-Lafayette	12-0	24-5
1974	Atlantic Coast	North Caro. St.	12-0	30-1
1974	Pacific Coast	Long Beach St.	12-0	24-2
1975	Big Ten	Indiana	18-0	31-1
1975	Southern	Furman	13-0	22-7
1976	Big Ten	Indiana	18-0	32-0
1976	Ivy	Princeton	14-0	22-5
1977	Southwest	Arkansas	16-0	26-2
1977	West Coast	San Francisco	14-0	29-2
1978	East Coast (W)	Lafayette	10-0	23-8
1978	Pacific-8	UCLA	14-0	25-3
1979	East Coast	Temple	13-0	25-4
1979	Missouri Valley	Indiana St.	16-0	33-1
1979	New Jersey-New York 7	Rutgers	6-0	22-9
1979	Southwestern	Alcorn St.	12-0	28-1
1979	Sun Belt	South Ala.	10-0	20-7
1980	Metro	Louisville	12-0	33-3
1980	Southwestern	Alcorn St.	12-0	28-2
1980	Trans America	La.-Monroe	6-0	17-11
1981	East Coast (E)	American	11-0	24-6
1982	East Coast	Temple	11-0	19-8
1982	West Coast	Pepperdine	14-0	22-7
1983	ECAC South	William & Mary	9-0	20-9
1983	Metro	Louisville	12-0	32-4
1983	Southwest	Houston	16-0	31-3
1984	Atlantic 10	Temple	18-0	26-5
1984	Atlantic Coast	North Carolina	14-0	28-3
1984	ECAC North Atlantic	Northeastern	14-0	27-5
1986	Missouri Valley	Bradley	16-0	32-3
1987	Atlantic Coast	North Carolina	14-0	32-4
1987	Gulf Star	Stephen F. Austin	10-0	22-6
1987	Pacific Coast	UNLV	18-0	37-2
1988	Atlantic 10	Temple	18-0	32-2
1988	Metro Atlantic	La Salle	14-0	24-10
1988	Mid-Eastern	N.C. A&T	16-0	26-3
1988	West Coast	Loyola Marymount	14-0	28-4
1990	Metro Atlantic	La Salle	16-0	30-2
1991	Big West	UNLV	18-0	34-1
1991	Ivy	Princeton	14-0	24-3
1992	Big West	UNLV	18-0	26-2
1992	North Atlantic	Delaware	14-0	27-4
1992	West Coast	Pepperdine	14-0	24-7
1993	Ivy	Penn	14-0	22-5
1993	Mid-Eastern	Coppin St.	16-0	22-8
1993	Sun Belt	New Orleans	18-0	26-4
1994	Big Eight	Missouri	14-0	28-4
1994	Ivy	Penn	14-0	25-3
1994	Mid-Eastern	Coppin St.	16-0	22-8
1995	American West	Southern Utah	6-0	17-11
1995	Ivy	Penn	14-0	22-6
1995	Midwestern	Xavier	14-0	23-5
1996	Midwestern	Wis.-G.B.	16-0	25-4
1996	Southeastern (E)	Kentucky	16-0	34-2
1996	Southern	Davidson	14-0	25-5
1996	Southwest	Texas Tech	14-0	30-2
1997	Ivy	Princeton	14-0	24-4
1997	Trans America (E)	Col. of Charleston	16-0	29-3
1998	Ivy	Princeton	14-0	27-2
1998	Western Athletic (P)	TCU	14-0	27-6
1999	Atlantic Coast	Duke	16-0	37-2
1999	Southern (S)	Col. of Charleston	16-0	28-3
1999	Western Athletic (P)	Utah	14-0	28-5
2000	Big West (E)	Utah St.	16-0	28-6
2000	Conference USA (A)	Cincinnati	16-0	29-4
2000	Ivy	Penn	14-0	21-8
2002	Big 12	Kansas	16-0	33-4
2003	Big Sky	Weber St.	14-0	26-6
2003	Ivy	Penn	14-0	22-6
2003	Southeastern	Kentucky	16-0	32-4
2004	Atlantic 10 (E)	St. Joseph's	16-0	30-2
2004	Ohio Valley	Austin Peay	16-0	22-10
2004	West Coast	Gonzaga	14-0	28-3
2005	Big West	Pacific	18-0	27-4
2005	Southern (S)	Davidson	16-0	23-9
2006	Atlantic 10	George Washington	16-0	27-3
2006	Patriot	Bucknell	14-0	27-5
2006	West Coast	Gonzaga	14-0	29-4
2007	Big South	Winthrop	14-0	29-5
2007	Conference USA	Memphis	16-0	32-5
2008	Conference USA	Memphis	16-0	38-2
2008	Ivy	Cornell	14-0	22-6
2008	Southern (S)	Davidson	20-0	29-7

Division I Conference Alignment History

CHANGES FOR 2008-09

Team	Old Conference	New Conference
Gardner-Webb	Atlantic Sun	Big South
North Dakota St.	Division II	Summit
Samford	Ohio Valley	Southern
South Dakota St.	Division II	Summit

CHANGES FOR TEAMS NOT YET FULL-FLEDGE DIVISION I

Team	Status	New Conference
Central Ark.	Reclassifying	Southland
Fla. Gulf Coast	Reclassifying	Atlantic Sun
Kennesaw St.	Reclassifying	Atlantic Sun
North Dakota St.	Reclassifying	Summit
North Fla.	Reclassifying	Atlantic Sun
Presbyterian	Reclassifying	Big South
S.C. Upstate	Reclassifying	Atlantic Sun
South Dakota St.	Reclassifying	Summit
Utah Valley St.	Provisional	Western Athletic

AMERICA EAST CONFERENCE
(1980-present)
ECAC North (1980-82)
ECAC North Atlantic (1983-89)
North Atlantic (1990-96)
America East (1997-present)

Albany (N.Y.)	2002-present
Binghamton	2002-present
Boston U.	1980-present
Canisius	1980-89
Colgate	1980-90
Delaware	1992-2001
Drexel	1992-2001
Hartford	1986-present
Hofstra	1995-2001
Holy Cross	1980-83
Maine	1980-present
UMBC	2004-present
New Hampshire	1980-present
Niagara	1980-89
Northeastern	1980-2005
Rhode Island	1980
Siena	1985-89
Stony Brook	2002-present
Towson	1996-2001
Vermont	1980-present

AMERICAN SOUTH CONFERENCE
(1988-91)

Arkansas St.	1988-91
UCF	1991
Lamar	1988-91
Louisiana Tech	1988-91
New Orleans	1988-91
La.-Lafayette	1988-91
Tex.-Pan American	1988-91

AMERICAN WEST CONFERENCE
(1995-96)

Cal Poly	1995-96
Cal St. Northridge	1995-96
Sacramento St.	1995-96
Southern Utah	1995-96

ATLANTIC COAST CONFERENCE
(1954-present)

Boston College	2006-present
Clemson	1954-present
Duke	1954-present
Florida St.	1992-present
Georgia Tech	1980-present
Maryland	1954-present
Miami (Fla.)	2005-present
North Carolina	1954-present
North Carolina St.	1954-present
South Carolina	1954-71
Virginia	1954-present
Virginia Tech	2005-present
Wake Forest	1954-present

ATLANTIC SUN CONFERENCE
(1979-present)
Trans America Athletic (1979-2001)

UALR	1981-91
Belmont	2002-present
Campbell	1995-present
Centenary (La.)	1979-99
UCF	1993-2005
Col. of Charleston	1993-98
East Tenn. St.	2006-present
Fla. Atlantic	1994-present
Florida Int'l	1992-98
Gardner-Webb	2003-08
Ga. Southern	1981-92
Georgia St.	1985-2005
Hardin-Simmons	1979-89
Houston Baptist	1979-89
Jacksonville	1999-present

Jacksonville St.	1996-2003
Lipscomb	2004-present
Mercer	1979-present
Nicholls St.	1983-84
La.-Monroe	1979-82
Northwestern St.	1981-84
Oklahoma City	1979
Samford	1979-2003
Southeastern La.	1992-97
Stetson	1987-present
Tex.-Pan American	1979-80
Troy	1998-2005

ATLANTIC 10 CONFERENCE
(1977-present)
Eastern Collegiate Basketball League (1977-78)
Eastern AA (1979-82)
Eastern 8
Atlantic 10 (1983-present)

Charlotte	2006-present
Dayton	1996-present
Duquesne	1977-92, 94-present
Fordham	1996-present
George Washington	1977-present
La Salle	1996-present
Massachusetts	1977-present
Penn St.	1977-79, 83-91
Pittsburgh	1977-82
Rhode Island	1981-present
Richmond	2002-present
Rutgers	1977-95
St. Bonaventure	1980-present
St. Joseph's	1983-present
St. Louis	2006-present
Temple	1983-present
Villanova	1977-80
Virginia Tech	1996-2000
West Virginia	1977-95
Xavier	1996-present

BIG EAST CONFERENCE
(1980-present)

Boston College	1980-2005
Cincinnati	2006-present
Connecticut	1980-present
DePaul	2006-present
Georgetown	1980-present
Louisville	2006-present
Marquette	2006-present
Miami (Fla.)	1992-2004
Notre Dame	1996-present
Pittsburgh	1983-present
Providence	1980-present
Rutgers	1996-present
St. John's (N.Y.)	1980-present
Seton Hall	1980-present
South Fla.	2006-present
Syracuse	1980-present
Villanova	1981-present
Virginia Tech	2001-2004
West Virginia	1996-present

BIG EIGHT CONFERENCE
(1908-96)
Missouri Valley (1908-28)
Big Six (1929-47)
Big Seven (1948-58)
Big Eight (1959-96)

Colorado	1948-96
Drake	1908-28
Grinnell	1919-28
Iowa St.	1908-96
Kansas	1908-96
Kansas St.	1914-96
Missouri	1908-96
Nebraska	1908-19, 21-96
Oklahoma	1920-96
Oklahoma St.	1926-28, 59-96
Washington-St. Louis	1908-10, 12-28

BIG SKY CONFERENCE
(1964-present)

Boise St.	1971-96
Cal St. Northridge	1997-2001
Eastern Wash.	1988-present
Gonzaga	1964-79

Idaho	1964-96
Idaho St.	1964-present
Montana	1964-present
Montana St.	1964-present
Nevada	1980-92
Northern Ariz.	1971-present
Northern Colo.	2008-present
Portland St.	1999-present
Sacramento St.	1997-present
Weber St.	1964-present

BIG SOUTH CONFERENCE
(1986-present)

Armstrong Atlantic	1986-87
Augusta St.	1986-91
Birmingham-So.	2004-06
Campbell	1986-94
Charleston So.	1986-present
Coastal Caro.	1986-present
Davidson	1991-92
Elon	2000-2003
Gardner-Webb	2009-present
High Point	2000-present
Liberty	1992-present
UMBC	1993-98
UNC Asheville	1986-present
UNC Greensboro	1993-97
Radford	1986-present
Towson	1993-95
VMI	2004-present
Winthrop	1986-present

BIG TEN CONFERENCE
(1895-present)
Intercollegiate Conference of Faculty Representatives
Western Intercollegiate
Big Nine (1947-48)
Big Ten (1912-46, 49-present)

Chicago	1895-46
Illinois	1895-present
Indiana	1899-present
Iowa	1899-present
Michigan	1895-present
Michigan St.	1949-present
Minnesota	1895-present
Northwestern	1895-present
Ohio St.	1912-present
Penn St.	1993-present
Purdue	1895-present
Wisconsin	1895-present

BIG 12 CONFERENCE
(1997-present)

Baylor	1997-present
Colorado	1997-present
Iowa St.	1997-present
Kansas	1997-present
Kansas St.	1997-present
Missouri	1997-present
Nebraska	1997-present
Oklahoma	1997-present
Oklahoma St.	1997-present
Texas	1997-present
Texas A&M	1997-present
Texas Tech	1997-present

BIG WEST CONFERENCE
(1970-present)
Pacific Coast (1970-88)
Big West (1989-present)

Boise St.	1997-2001
UC Davis	2008-present
UC Irvine	1978-present
UC Riverside	2002-present
UC Santa Barbara	1970-74, 77-present
Cal Poly	1997-present
Cal St. Fullerton	1975-present
Cal St. L.A.	1970-74
Cal St. Northridge	2002-present
Fresno St.	1970-92
Idaho	1997-2005
Long Beach St.	1970-present
Nevada	1993-2000
UNLV	1983-96
New Mexico St.	1984-2000
North Texas	1997-2000
Pacific	1972-present

San Diego St.	1970-78
San Jose St.	1970-96
Utah St.	1979-2005

BORDER CONFERENCE
(1932-40, 42-62)

Arizona	1932-40, 42-61
Arizona St.	1932-40, 42-43, 44-62
Hardin-Simmons	1942-43, 45-62
New Mexico	1932-40, 42, 45-51
New Mexico St.	1932-40, 42-62
Northern Ariz.	1932-40, 42-53
UTEP	1936-40, 42-43, 44-62
Texas Tech	1933-40, 42-56
West Tex. A&M	1942-43, 45-62

COLONIAL ATHLETIC ASSOCIATION
(1983-present)

American	1985-2001
Delaware	2002-present
Drexel	2002-present
East Carolina	1983-2001
George Mason	1983-present
Georgia St.	2006-present
Hofstra	2002-present
James Madison	1983-present
Navy	1983-91
UNC Wilmington	1985-present
Northeastern	2006-present
Old Dominion	1992-present
Richmond	1983-2001
Towson	2002-present
VCU	1996-present
William & Mary	1983-present

CONFERENCE USA
(1996-present)

UAB	1996-present
UCF	2006-present
Charlotte	1996-2005
Cincinnati	1996-2005
DePaul	1996-2005
East Carolina	2002-present
Houston	1997-present
Louisville	1996-2005
Marquette	1996-2005
Marshall	2006-present
Memphis	1996-present
Rice	2006-present
St. Louis	1996-2005
South Fla.	1996-2005
SMU	2006-present
Southern Miss.	1996-present
UTEP	2006-present
TCU	2002-05
Tulane	1996-present
Tulsa	2006-present

EAST COAST CONFERENCE
(1959-92, 94)
Middle Atlantic (1959-74)
East Coast (1975-92, 94)

American	1967-84
Brooklyn	1992
Bucknell	1959-90
Buffalo	1992, 94
Central Conn. St.	1991-92, 94
Chicago St.	1994
Delaware	1959-91
Drexel	1959-91
Gettysburg	1959-74
Hofstra	1966-92, 94
Lafayette	1959-90
La Salle	1959-83
Lehigh	1959-90
UMBC	1991-92
Muhlenberg	1959-64
Northeastern Ill.	1994
Rider	1967-92
Rutgers	1959-62
St. Joseph's	1959-82
Temple	1959-82
Towson	1983-92
Troy	1994
West Chester	1966-67, 69-74

EASTERN INTERCOLLEGIATE CONFERENCE
(1933-39)

Bucknell	1934
Carnegie Mellon	1933-39
Georgetown	1933-39
Penn St.	1936-39
Pittsburgh	1933-39
Temple	1933-39
West Virginia	1933-39

GREAT MIDWEST CONFERENCE
(1992-95)

UAB	1992-95
Cincinnati	1992-95
Dayton	1994-95
DePaul	1992-95
Marquette	1992-95
Memphis	1992-95
St. Louis	1992-95

GULF STAR CONFERENCE
(1985-87)

Nicholls St.	1985-87
Northwestern St.	1985-87
Sam Houston St.	1985-87
Southeastern La.	1985-87
Stephen F. Austin	1985-87
Texas St.	1985-87

HORIZON LEAGUE
(1980-present)
Midwestern Collegiate (1980-2001)

Butler	1980-present
Cleveland St.	1995-present
Dayton	1989-93
Detroit	1981-present
Duquesne	1993
Evansville	1980-94
Green Bay	1995-present
Ill.-Chicago	1995-present
La Salle	1993-95
Loyola (Ill.)	1980-present
Marquette	1990-91
Milwaukee	1995-present
Northern Ill.	1995-97
Oklahoma City	1980-85
Oral Roberts	1980-87
St. Louis	1983-91
Valparaiso	2008-present
Wright St.	1995-present
Xavier	1980-95
Youngstown St.	2002-present

IVY GROUP
(1902-08, 11-18, 20-present)
Eastern Intercollegiate League

Brown	1954-present
Columbia	1902-08, 11-18, 20-present
Cornell	1902-08, 11-18, 20-present
Dartmouth	1912-18, 20-present
Harvard	1902-04, 06-07, 34-43, 47-present
Penn	1904-08, 11-18, 20-present
Princeton	1902-08, 11-18, 20-44, 46-present
Yale	1902-08, 11-18, 20-43, 47-present

METRO ATLANTIC ATHLETIC CONFERENCE
(1982-present)

Army	1982-90
Canisius	1990-present
Fairfield	1982-present
Fordham	1982-90
Holy Cross	1984-90
Iona	1982-present
La Salle	1984-92
Loyola (Md.)	1990-present
Manhattan	1982-present
Marist	1998-present
Niagara	1990-present
Rider	1998-present
St. Peter's	1982-present
Siena	1990-present

METROPOLITAN COLLEGIATE ATHLETIC CONFERENCE
(1976-95)

Charlotte	1992-95
Cincinnati	1976-91
Florida St.	1977-91
Georgia Tech	1976-78
Louisville	1976-95
Memphis	1976-91
St. Louis	1976-82
South Carolina	1984-91
South Fla.	1992-95
Southern Miss.	1983-95
Tulane	1976-85, 90-95
VCU	1992-95
Virginia Tech	1979-95

METROPOLITAN COLLEGIATE CONFERENCE (1966-69)

Fairleigh Dickinson	1966-69
Hofstra	1966-69
Iona	1966-69
Long Island	1966-69
Manhattan	1966-69
New York U.	1966-67
St. Francis (N.Y.)	1966-68
St. Peter's	1966-69
Seton Hall	1966-69
Wagner	1966-69

METROPOLITAN NEW YORK CONFERENCE (1943, 46-63)

Brooklyn	1943, 46-63
CCNY	1943, 46-63
Fordham	1943, 46-63
Hofstra	1943
Manhattan	1943, 46-63
New York U.	1943, 46-63
St. Francis (N.Y.)	1943, 46-63
St. John's (N.Y.)	1943, 46-63

MID-AMERICAN CONFERENCE
(1947-present)

Akron	1993-present
Ball St.	1976-present
Bowling Green	1954-present
Buffalo	1999-present
Butler	1947-50
Case Reserve	1947-55
Central Mich.	1973-present
Cincinnati	1947-53
Eastern Mich.	1975-present
Kent St.	1952-present
Marshall	1954-69, 98-2005
Miami (Ohio)	1948-present
Northern Ill.	1976-86, 98-present
Ohio	1947-present
Toledo	1952-present
Wayne St. (Mich.)	1947
Western Mich.	1948-present

MID-EASTERN ATHLETIC CONFERENCE
(1972-present)

Bethune-Cookman	1981-present
Coppin St.	1986-present
Delaware St.	1972-87, 89-present
Florida A&M	1981-83, 88-present
Hampton	1996-present
Howard	1972-present
Md.-East. Shore	1972-79, 83-present
Morgan St.	1972-80, 85-present
Norfolk St.	1998-present
N.C. A&T	1972-present
N.C. Central	1972-80
South Carolina St.	1972-present

MISSOURI VALLEY CONFERENCE
(1908-present)

Bradley	1949-51, 56-present
Butler	1933-34
Cincinnati	1958-70
Creighton	1928-43, 46-48, 78-present
Detroit	1950-57
Drake	1908-51, 57-present
Evansville	1995-present
Grinnell	1919-39
Houston	1951-60
Illinois St.	1982-present
Indiana St.	1978-present
Iowa St.	1908-28
Kansas	1908-28
Kansas St.	1914-28
Louisville	1965-75
Memphis	1968-73
Missouri	1908-28
Missouri St.	1991-present
Nebraska	1908-19, 21-28
New Mexico St.	1973-83
North Texas	1958-75
UNI	1992-present
Oklahoma	1920-28
Oklahoma St.	1926-57
St. Louis	1938-43, 45-74
Southern Ill.	1976-present
Tulsa	1935-96
Washburn	1935-41
Washington-St. Louis	1908-10, 12-47
West Tex. A&M	1973-86
Wichita St.	1946-present

MOUNTAIN STATES CONFERENCE
(1911-43, 46-62)
Also known as:
Rocky Mountain (1911-37)
Big Seven (1938-43, 46-47)
Skyline Six (1948-51)
Skyline Eight (1952-62)
Mountain States (1938-43, 46-62)

BYU	1924-42, 46-62
Colorado	1911-42, 46-47
Colorado Col.	1911-37
Colorado Mines	1911-37
Colorado St.	1911-22, 24-42, 46-62
Denver	1911-42, 46-62
Montana	1952-62
Montana St.	1925-37
New Mexico	1952-62
Northern Colo.	1925-37
Utah	1924-42, 46-62
Utah St.	1924-42, 46-62
Western St.	1925-37
Wyoming	1923-43, 46-62

MOUNTAIN WEST CONFERENCE
(2000-present)

Air Force	2000-present
BYU	2000-present
Colorado St.	2000-present
UNLV	2000-present
New Mexico	2000-present
San Diego St.	2000-present
TCU	2006-present
Utah	2000-present
Wyoming	2000-present

NEW JERSEY-NEW YORK 7 CONFERENCE (1977-79)

Columbia	1977-79
Fordham	1977-79
Manhattan	1977-79
Princeton	1977-79
Rutgers	1977-79
St. John's (N.Y.)	1977-79
Seton Hall	1977-79

NORTHEAST CONFERENCE
(1982-present)
ECAC Metro (1982-88)
Northeast (1989-present)

Baltimore	1982-83
Central Conn. St.	1998-present
Fairleigh Dickinson	1982-present
Long Island	1982-present
Loyola (Md.)	1982-89
Marist	1982-97
UMBC	1999-2003
Monmouth	1986-present
Mt. St. Mary's	1990-present
Quinnipiac	1999-present
Rider	1993-97
Robert Morris	1982-present
Sacred Heart	2000-present
St. Francis (N.Y.)	1982-present
St. Francis (Pa.)	1982-present

CONFERENCES

Siena 1982-84
Towson 1982
Wagner 1982-present

OHIO VALLEY CONFERENCE
(1949-present)

Akron 1981-87
Austin Peay 1964-present
East Tenn. St. 1958-78
Eastern Ill. 1997-present
Eastern Ky. 1949-present
Evansville 1949-52
Jacksonville St. 2004-present
Louisville 1949
Marshall 1949-52
Middle Tenn. 1953-2000
Morehead St. 1949-present
Murray St. 1949-present
Samford 2004-08
Southeast Mo. St. 1992-present
Tenn.-Martin 1993-present
Tennessee St. 1988-present
Tennessee Tech 1949-present
Western Ky. 1949-82
Youngstown St. 1982-88

PACIFIC-10 CONFERENCE
(1916-17, 19-present)
Pacific Coast (1916-59)
Big Five (1960-62)
Big Six (1963)
Athletic Association of Western Universities—
AAWU (1963-68)
Pacific 8 (1969-78)
Pacific-10 (1979-present)

Arizona 1979-present
Arizona St. 1979-present
California 1916-17, 19-present
Idaho 1922-59
Montana 1924-29
Oregon 1917, 19-59, 65-present
Oregon St. 1916-17, 19-59, 65-present
Southern California 1922-24, 26-present
Stanford 1917, 19-43, 46-present
UCLA 1928-present
Washington 1916-17, 19-present
Washington St. 1917, 19-59, 64-present

PATRIOT LEAGUE
(1991-present)

American 2002-present
Army 1991-present
Bucknell 1991-present
Colgate 1991-present
Fordham 1991-95
Holy Cross 1991-present
Lafayette 1991-present
Lehigh 1991-present
Navy 1992-present

SOUTHEASTERN CONFERENCE
(1933-present)

Alabama 1933-43, 45-present
Arkansas 1992-present
Auburn 1933-43, 45-present
Florida 1933-43, 45-present
Georgia 1933-present
Georgia Tech 1933-64
Kentucky 1933-52, 54-present
LSU 1933-present
Mississippi 1933-43, 45-present
Mississippi St. 1933-43, 45-present
Sewanee 1933-40
South Carolina 1992-present
Tennessee 1933-43, 45-present
Tulane 1933-66
Vanderbilt 1933-present

SOUTHERN CONFERENCE
(1922-present)
Southern Intercollegiate Athletic Association—
SIAA (1895-1921)

Alabama 1922-32
Appalachian St. 1973-present
Auburn 1922-32
Col. of Charleston 1999-present
Chattanooga 1977-present

Citadel 1937-present
Clemson 1922-53
Davidson 1937-88, 93-present
Duke 1929-53
East Carolina 1966-77
East Tenn. St. 1979-2005
Elon 2004-present
Florida 1923-32
Furman 1937-42, 45-present
George Washington 1942-43, 46-70
Georgia 1922-32
Ga. Southern 1993-present
Georgia Tech 1922-32
Kentucky 1922-32
LSU 1923-32
Marshall 1977-97
Maryland 1924-53
Mississippi 1923-32
Mississippi St. 1922-30, 32
North Carolina 1922-53
UNC Greensboro 1998-present
North Carolina St. 1922-53
Richmond 1937-76
Samford 2009-present
Sewanee 1924-32
South Carolina 1923-53
Tennessee 1922-32
Tulane 1923-32
Vanderbilt 1923-32
Virginia 1922-37
VMI 1926-2003
Virginia Tech 1922-65
Wake Forest 1937-43, 45-53
Wash. & Lee 1922-43, 46-58
West Virginia 1951-68
Western Caro. 1977-present
William & Mary 1937-77
Wofford 1998-present

SOUTHLAND CONFERENCE
(1964-present)

Abilene Christian 1964-73
Arkansas St. 1964-87
Lamar 1964-87, 99-present
La.-Lafayette 1972-82
La.-Monroe 1983-2006
Louisiana Tech 1972-87
McNeese St. 1973-present
Nicholls St. 1992-present
North Texas 1983-96
Northwestern St. 1988-present
Sam Houston St. 1988-present
Southeastern La. 1998-present
Stephen F. Austin 1988-present
Texas-Arlington 1964-86, 88-present
UTSA 1992-present
A&M-Corpus Christi 2007-present
Texas St. 1988-present
Trinity (Tex.) 1964-72

SOUTHWEST CONFERENCE
(1915-96)

Arkansas 1924-91
Baylor 1915-96
Houston 1976-96
Oklahoma St. 1918, 22-25
Phillips 1920
Rice 1915-16, 18-96
SMU 1919-96
Southwestern (Tex.) 1915-16
Texas 1915-96
Texas A&M 1915-96
TCU 1924-96
Texas Tech 1958-96

SOUTHWESTERN ATHLETIC CONFERENCE
(1978-present)

Alabama A&M 2000-present
Alabama St. 1983-present
Alcorn St. 1978-present
Ark.-Pine Bluff 1999-present
Grambling 1978-present
Jackson St. 1978-present
Mississippi Val. 1978-present
Prairie View 1978-present
Southern U. 1978-present
Texas Southern 1978-present

SUMMIT LEAGUE
(1983-present)
Mid-Continent (1983-2007)

Akron 1991-92
Buffalo 1995-98
Centenary (La.) 2004-present
Central Conn. St. 1995-97
Chicago St. 1995-2006
Cleveland St. 1983-94
Eastern Ill. 1983-96
Green Bay 1983-94
Ill.-Chicago 1983-94
IPFW 2008-present
IUPUI 1999-present
Milwaukee 1994
UMKC 1995-present
Missouri St. 1983-90
North Dakota St. 2009-present
Northeastern Ill. 1995-98
Northern Ill. 1991-94
UNI 1983-91
Oakland 2000-present
Oral Roberts 1998-present
South Dakota St. 2009-present
Southern Utah 1998-present
Troy 1995-97
Valparaiso 1983-2007
Western Ill. 1983-present
Wright St. 1992-94
Youngstown St. 1993-2001

SUN BELT CONFERENCE
(1977-present)

UAB 1980-91
UALR 1992-present
Arkansas St. 1992-present
UCF 1992
Charlotte 1977-91
Denver 2000-present
Florida Int'l 1999-present
Georgia St. 1977-81
Jacksonville 1977-98
Lamar 1992-98
La.-Lafayette 1992-present
La.-Monroe 2007-present
Louisiana Tech 1992-2001
Middle Tenn. 2001-present
New Mexico St. 2001-05
New Orleans 1977-80, 92-present
North Texas 2001-present
Old Dominion 1983-91
South Ala. 1977-present
South Fla. 1977-91
Tex.-Pan American 1992-98
Troy 2006-present
VCU 1980-91
Western Ky. 1983-present

WEST COAST CONFERENCE
(1953-present)

UC Santa Barbara 1965-69
Fresno St. 1956-57
Gonzaga 1980-present
Loyola Marymount 1956-present
Nevada 1970-79
UNLV 1970-75
Pacific 1953-71
Pepperdine 1956-present
Portland 1977-present
St. Mary's (Cal.) 1953-present
San Diego 1980-present
San Francisco 1953-82, 86-present
San Jose St. 1953-69
Santa Clara 1953-present
Seattle 1972-80

WESTERN ATHLETIC CONFERENCE
(1963-present)

Air Force 1981-99
Arizona 1963-78
Arizona St. 1963-78
Boise St. 2002-present
BYU 1963-99
Colorado St. 1970-99
Fresno St. 1993-present
Hawaii 1980-present
Idaho 2006-present
Louisiana Tech 2002-present

Nevada	2001-present
UNLV	1997-99
New Mexico	1963-99
New Mexico St.	2006-present
Rice	1997-99
San Diego St.	1979-present
San Jose St.	1997-present
SMU	1997-2005
UTEP	1970-2005
TCU	1997-2001
Tulsa	1997-2005

Utah	1963-99
Utah St.	2006-present
Wyoming	1963-99

**WESTERN NEW YORK
LITTLE THREE CONFERENCE
(1947-51, 53-58)**

Canisius	1947-51, 53-58
Niagara	1947-51, 53-58
St. Bonaventure	1947-51, 53-58

**YANKEE CONFERENCE
(1938-43, 46-76)**

Boston U.	1973-76
Connecticut	1938-43, 46-76
Maine	1938-43, 46-76
Massachusetts	1947-76
New Hampshire	1938-43, 46-76
Northeastern	1938-43, 46
Rhode Island	1938-43, 46-76
Vermont	1947-76

Division I Alignment History

Abilene Christian	1971-73
Air Force	1958-present
Akron	1948-50, 1981-present
Alabama	1948-present
UAB	1980-present
Alabama A&M	2000-present
Alabama St.	1983-present
Albany (N.Y.)	2000-present
Alcorn St.	1978-present
Alliant Int'l	1982-91
American	1967-present
Appalachian St.	1974-present
Arizona	1948, 1951-present
Arizona St.	1951-present
Arkansas	1948-present
UALR	1979-present
Ark.-Pine Bluff	1999-present
Arkansas St.	1971-present
Armstrong Atlantic	1987
Army	1948-present
Auburn	1948-present
Augusta	1985-91
Austin Peay	1964-present
Baldwin-Wallace	1948-53
Ball St.	1972-present
Baltimore	1979-83
Baylor	1948-present
Belmont	2000-present
Bethune-Cookman	1981-present
Binghamton	2002-present
Birmingham-So.	2004-06
Boise St.	1972-present
Boston College	1948-present
Boston U.	1948-49, 1958-present
Bowling Green	1948-present
Bradley	1948-present
BYU	1948-present
Brooklyn	1948-49, 1983-92
Brown	1948-present
Bucknell	1948-present
Buffalo	1974-77, 1992-present
Butler	1948-present
California	1948-present
UC Davis	2008-present
UC Irvine	1978-present
UC Riverside	2002-present
UC Santa Barbara	1964-present
Cal Poly	1995-present
Cal St. Fullerton	1975-present
Cal St. L.A.	1971-75
Cal St. Northridge	1991-present
Campbell	1978-present
Canisius	1948-present
Case Reserve	1948-55
Catholic	1977-81
Centenary (La.)	1960-present
Central Conn. St.	1987-present
UCF	1985-present
Central Mich.	1974-present
Col. of Charleston	1992-present
Charleston So.	1975-present
Charlotte	1973-present
Chattanooga	1978-present
Chicago St.	1985-present
Cincinnati	1948-present
Citadel	1948-present
CCNY	1948-53
Clemson	1948-present

Cleveland St.	1973-present
Coastal Caro.	1987-present
Colgate	1948-present
Colorado	1948-present
Colorado St.	1948-present
Columbia	1948-present
Connecticut	1948, 1952-present
Coppin St.	1986-present
Cornell	1948-present
Creighton	1948-56, 1960-present
Dartmouth	1948-present
Davidson	1948-present
Dayton	1948-present
Delaware	1958-present
Delaware St.	1974-present
Denver	1948-80, 1999-present
DePaul	1948-present
Detroit	1948-present
Drake	1948-present
Drexel	1974-present
Duke	1948-present
Duquesne	1948-present
East Carolina	1965-present
East Tenn. St.	1959-present
Eastern Ill.	1982-present
Eastern Ky.	1948, 1952-present
Eastern Mich.	1974-present
Eastern Wash.	1984-present
Elon	2000-present
Evansville	1978-present
Fairfield	1965-present
Fairleigh Dickinson	1968-present
Florida	1948-present
Florida A&M	1979-present
Fla. Atlantic	1994-present
Florida Int'l	1988-present
Florida St.	1957-present
Fordham	1948-present
Fresno St.	1956-58, 1971-present
Furman	1948-present
Gardner-Webb	2003-present
George Mason	1979-present
George Washington	1948-present
Georgetown	1948-present
Georgia	1948-present
Ga. Southern	1974-present
Georgia St.	1974-present
Georgia Tech	1948-present
Gettysburg	1948-51, 1959-73
Gonzaga	1953-present
Grambling	1978-present
Green Bay	1982-present
Hamline	1948
Hampton	1996-present
Hardin-Simmons	1951-63, 1965-90
Hartford	1985-present
Harvard	1948-present
Hawaii	1971-present
High Point	2000-present
Hofstra	1967-present
Holy Cross	1948-present
Houston	1951-present
Houston Baptist	1974-89
Howard	1974-present
Idaho	1948-present
Idaho St.	1959-present
Illinois	1948-present

Ill.-Chicago	1982-present
Illinois St.	1972-present
Indiana	1948-present
IPFW	2003-present
IUPUI	1999-present
Indiana St.	1948, 1972-present
Iona	1954-present
Iowa	1948-present
Iowa St.	1948-present
Jackson St.	1978-present
Jacksonville	1967-present
Jacksonville St.	1996-present
James Madison	1977-present
John Carroll	1948-55
Kansas	1948-present
Kansas St.	1948-present
Kent St.	1948, 1952-present
Kentucky	1948-52, 1954-present
Ky. Wesleyan	1957-58
La Salle	1948-present
Lafayette	1948-present
Lamar	1970-present
Lawrence Tech	1948
Lehigh	1948-present
Liberty	1989-present
Lipscomb	2004-present
Long Beach St.	1970-present
Long Island	1948-51, 1969-present
Longwood	2008-present
La.-Lafayette	1972-73, 1976-present
La.-Monroe	1974-present
LSU	1948-present
Louisiana Tech	1974-present
Louisville	1948-present
Loyola Marymount	1950-present
Loyola (Ill.)	1948-present
Loyola (La.)	1952-53, 1955-72
Loyola (Md.)	1948-50, 1982-present
Maine	1962-present
Manhattan	1948-present
Marist	1982-present
Marquette	1948-present
Marshall	1948, 1954-present
Maryland	1948-present
UMBC	1987-present
Md.-East. Shore	1974-75, 1982-present
Massachusetts	1962-present
McNeese St.	1974-present
Memphis	1956-present
Mercer	1974-present
Miami (Fla.)	1949-53, 1955-71, 1986-present
Miami (Ohio)	1948-present
Michigan	1948-present
Michigan St.	1948-present
Middle Tenn.	1959-present
Milwaukee	1974-80, 1991-present
Minnesota	1948-present
Mississippi	1948-present
Mississippi St.	1948-present
Mississippi Val.	1980-present
Missouri	1948-present
UMKC	1990-present
Missouri St.	1983-present
Monmouth	1984-present
Montana	1948, 1952-present
Montana St.	1948, 1958-present
Morehead St.	1956-present

Morgan St.	1985-present
Morris Brown	2002-03
Mt. St. Mary's	1989-present
Muhlenberg	1948-63
Murray St.	1954-present
Navy	1948-present
Nebraska	1948-present
UNLV	1970-present
Nevada	1948, 1970-present
New Hampshire	1962-present
New Mexico	1951-present
New Mexico St.	1951-present
New Orleans	1976-present
New York U.	1948-71; 84
Niagara	1948-present
Nicholls St.	1981-present
Norfolk St.	1998-present
North Carolina	1948-present
UNC Asheville	1987-present
UNC Greensboro	1992-present
UNC Wilmington	1977-present
N.C. A&T	1974-present
North Carolina St.	1948-present
North Dakota St.	2009-present
North Texas	1958-present
Northeastern	1973-present
Northeastern Ill.	1991-98
Northern Ariz.	1951-53, 1972-present
Northern Colo.	1974-78, 2008-present
Northern Ill.	1968-present
UNI	1981-present
Northwestern	1948-present
Northwestern St.	1977-present
Notre Dame	1948-present
Oakland	2000-present
Ohio	1948-present
Ohio St.	1948-present
Oklahoma	1948-present
Oklahoma City	1951-85
Oklahoma St.	1948-present
Old Dominion	1977-present
Oral Roberts	1972-89, 1994-present
Oregon	1948-present
Oregon St.	1948-present
Pacific	1954-present
Penn	1948-present
Penn St.	1948-present
Pepperdine	1956-present
Pittsburgh	1948-present
Portland	1954-present
Portland St.	1973-81, 1999-present
Prairie View	1981-present
Princeton	1948-present
Providence	1949, 1958-present
Purdue	1948-present
Quinnipiac	1999-present
Radford	1985-present
Regis (Colo.)	1962-64
Rhode Island	1948-present
Rice	1948-present
Richmond	1948-present
Rider	1968-present
Robert Morris	1977-present
Rutgers	1948-present
Sacramento St.	1992-present
Sacred Heart	2000-present
St. Bonaventure	1948-present
St. Francis (N.Y.)	1948-present
St. Francis (Pa.)	1956-present
St. John's (N.Y.)	1948-present
St. Joseph's	1948-present
St. Louis	1948-present
St. Mary's (Cal.)	1948-present
St. Peter's	1965-present
Sam Houston St.	1987-present
Samford	1973-present
San Diego	1980-present
San Diego St.	1971-present
San Francisco	1948-82, 1986-present
San Jose St.	1953-present
Santa Clara	1948-present
Savannah St.	2003-present
Scranton	1948
Seattle	1953-80
Seton Hall	1948-present
Siena	1948-49, 1951-60, 1977-present
South Ala.	1972-present
South Carolina	1948-present
South Carolina St.	1974-present
South Dakota St.	2009-present
South Fla.	1974-present
Southeast Mo. St.	1992-present
Southeastern La.	1981-89, 1991-present
Southern U.	1978-present
Southern California	1948-present
Southern Ill.	1968-present
SMU	1948-present
Southern Miss.	1969, 1973-present
Southern Utah	1989-present
Stanford	1948-present
Stephen F. Austin	1987-present
Stetson	1972-present
Stony Brook	2000-present
Syracuse	1948-present
Temple	1948-present
Tennessee	1948-present
Tenn.-Martin	1993-present
Tennessee St.	1978-present
Tennessee Tech	1956-present
Texas	1948-present
Texas-Arlington	1969-present
UTEP	1951-present
Tex.-Pan American	1969-present
UTSA	1982-present
Texas A&M	1948-present
A&M-Corpus Christi	1973, 2003-present
TCU	1948-present
Texas Southern	1978-present
Texas St.	1985-present
Texas Tech	1951-present
Texas Wesleyan	1948
Toledo	1948-present
Towson	1980-present
Trinity (Tex.)	1971-73
Troy	1994-present
Tulane	1948-85, 1990-present
Tulsa	1948-present
UCLA	1948-present
Utah	1948-present
Utah St.	1948-present
Utica	1982-87
Valparaiso	1948-58, 1977-present
Vanderbilt	1948-present
Vermont	1962-present
Villanova	1948-present
Virginia	1948-present
VCU	1974-present
VMI	1948-present
Virginia Tech	1948-present
Wagner	1977-present
Wake Forest	1948-present
Washington	1948-present
Washington-St. Louis	1948-50, 1954-60
Wash. & Lee	1948-59
Washington St.	1948-present
Wayne St. (Neb.)	1948-50
Weber St.	1964-present
West Chester	1974-82
West Texas	1951-86
West Virginia	1948-present
Western Caro.	1977-present
Western Ill.	1982-present
Western Ky.	1948-present
Western Mich.	1948-present
Wichita St.	1948-present
William & Mary	1948-present
Winthrop	1987-present
Wisconsin	1948-present
Wofford	1996-present
Wright St.	1988-present
Wyoming	1948-present
Xavier	1948-present
Yale	1948-present
Youngstown St.	1948, 1982-present

2008 Division II Conference Standings

CALIFORNIA COLLEGIATE ATHLETIC ASSOCIATION

	Conference			Full Season		
	W	L	Pct.	W	L	Pct.
Cal St. San B'dino	15	5	.750	22	8	.733
Humboldt St.	15	5	.750	20	9	.690
Cal St. Dom. Hills	11	9	.550	17	11	.607
Cal St. L.A.	11	9	.550	17	11	.607
UC San Diego #	11	9	.550	18	11	.621
San Fran. St.	11	9	.550	17	12	.586
Cal St. Monterey Bay	11	9	.550	12	15	.444
Cal Poly Pomona	10	10	.500	13	15	.464
Sonoma St.	7	13	.350	11	15	.423
Cal St. Stanislaus	5	15	.250	6	21	.222
Cal St. Chico	3	17	.150	7	20	.259

CENTRAL ATLANTIC COLLEGIATE CONFERENCE

	Conference			Full Season		
North Division	W	L	Pct.	W	L	Pct.
Post	10	6	.625	14	15	.483
Caldwell	9	7	.563	12	17	.414
Dominican (N.Y.)	8	8	.500	13	15	.464
Bloomfield	6	10	.375	16	16	.500
Nyack	6	10	.375	11	16	.407
Felician	4	12	.250	10	17	.370
South Division.						
Philadelphia U. #	16	0	1.000	22	12	.647
Holy Family	12	4	.750	21	10	.677
Goldey-Beacom	8	8	.500	16	12	.571
Phila. Sciences	7	9	.438	13	15	.464
Wilmington (Del.)	6	10	.375	10	16	.385
Chestnut Hill	4	12	.250	6	21	.222

CENTRAL INTERCOLLEGIATE ATHLETIC ASSOCIATION

	Conference			Full Season		
East Division	W	L	Pct.	W	L	Pct.
Virginia Union	14	4	.778	22	8	.733
Elizabeth City St.	13	5	.722	20	7	.741
Bowie St.	13	5	.722	21	8	.724
Virginia St.	8	10	.444	11	18	.379
St. Paul's	3	15	.167	8	17	.320
West Division						
Johnson C. Smith #	11	7	.611	21	10	.677
St. Augustine's	11	7	.611	16	10	.615
Fayetteville St.	8	10	.444	14	15	.483
Livingstone	8	10	.444	14	14	.500
Shaw	1	17	.056	5	23	.179

CONFERENCE CAROLINAS

	Conference			Full Season		
	W	L	Pct.	W	L	Pct.
Mount Olive #	16	4	.800	24	7	.774
Pfeiffer	15	5	.750	21	8	.724
Queens (N.C.)	14	6	.700	21	10	.677
Barton	14	6	.700	19	10	.655
Belmont Abbey	14	6	.700	16	12	.571
Anderson (S.C.)	10	10	.500	12	16	.429
Limestone	7	13	.350	10	17	.370
Coker	7	13	.350	9	19	.321
St. Andrews	6	14	.300	7	20	.259
Lees-McRae	5	15	.250	6	21	.222
Erskine	2	18	.100	6	21	.222

EAST COAST CONFERENCE

	Conference			Full Season		
	W	L	Pct.	W	L	Pct.
C.W. Post #	18	2	.900	26	5	.839
Adelphi	14	6	.700	20	10	.667
NYIT	13	7	.650	16	12	.571
St. Thomas Aquinas	12	8	.600	17	12	.586
Bridgeport	11	9	.550	13	15	.464
Concordia (N.Y.)	10	10	.500	12	17	.414
Molloy	8	12	.400	10	18	.357
Dowling	8	12	.400	9	19	.321
New Haven	7	13	.350	11	16	.407
Mercy	7	13	.350	8	19	.296
Queens (N.Y.)	2	18	.100	4	23	.148

GREAT LAKES INTERCOLLEGIATE ATHLETIC CONFERENCE

	Conference			Full Season		
North Division	W	L	Pct.	W	L	Pct.
Grand Valley St. #	18	0	1.000	36	1	.973
Michigan Tech	8	10	.444	13	14	.481
Lake Superior St.	8	10	.444	12	16	.429
Saginaw Valley	7	11	.389	12	14	.462
Northwood (Mich.)	6	12	.333	11	16	.407
Northern Mich.	6	12	.333	7	20	.259
Ferris St.	5	13	.278	10	19	.345
South Division						
Gannon	15	2	.882	26	5	.839
Findlay	14	3	.824	28	5	.848
Mercyhurst	9	8	.529	15	13	.536
Ashland	7	10	.412	13	15	.464
Hillsdale	7	10	.412	14	14	.500
Wayne St. (Mich.)	4	13	.235	10	16	.385

GREAT LAKES VALLEY CONFERENCE

	Conference			Full Season		
East Division	W	L	Pct.	W	L	Pct.
Northern Ky.	14	5	.737	21	8	.724
Ky. Weslyean	14	5	.737	24	8	.750
St. Joseph's (Ind.)	13	6	.684	18	12	.600
Lewis	11	8	.579	20	11	.645
Bellarmine	11	8	.579	17	11	.607
Wis.-Parkside	9	10	.474	16	11	.593
Indianapolis	8	11	.421	14	13	.519
West Division						
Drury #	15	4	.789	25	6	.806
SIU Edwardsville	10	9	.526	17	11	.607
Quincy	9	10	.474	16	13	.552
Southern Ind.	9	10	.474	15	12	.556
Mo.-St. Louis	5	14	.263	10	17	.370
Rockhurst	5	14	.263	9	18	.333
Missouri S&T	0	19	.000	3	24	.111

GREAT NORTHWEST ATHLETIC CONFERENCE

	Conference			Full Season		
	W	L	Pct.	W	L	Pct.
Alas. Anchorage	16	2	.889	29	6	.829
Central Wash.	15	3	.833	21	7	.750
Seattle Pacific	12	6	.667	21	8	.724
Northwest Nazarene	9	9	.500	17	10	.630
Western Oregon	8	10	.444	15	12	.556
Western Wash.	8	10	.444	15	12	.556
St. Martin's	8	10	.444	13	14	.481
Seattle	11	7	.611	18	9	.667
Alas. Fairbanks	2	16	.111	5	22	.185
Mont. St.-Billings	1	17	.056	1	28	.034

GULF SOUTH CONFERENCE

	Conference			Full Season		
East Division	W	L	Pct.	W	L	Pct.
North Ala.	10	2	.833	27	9	.750
Valdosta St.	8	4	.667	18	11	.621
West Ga.	7	5	.583	16	12	.571
Ala.-Huntsville	6	6	.500	13	15	.464
Montevallo	5	7	.417	12	16	.429
West Fla.	3	9	.250	13	14	.481
West Ala.	3	9	.250	10	17	.370
West Division						
Christian Bros. #	10	4	.714	22	10	.688
Ouachita Baptist	10	4	.714	20	10	.667
Harding	10	4	.714	18	13	.581
Arkansas Tech	8	6	.571	18	11	.621
Ark.-Monticello	8	6	.571	17	12	.586
Delta St.	8	6	.571	14	12	.538
Southern Ark.	2	12	.143	11	16	.407
Henderson St.	0	14	.000	3	24	.111

HEARTLAND CONFERENCE

	Conference			Full Season		
	W	L	Pct.	W	L	Pct.
St. Edward's	9	1	.900	23	7	.767
Incarnate Word	6	4	.600	17	11	.607
St. Mary's (Tex.) #	6	4	.600	17	13	.567
Dallas Baptist	5	5	.500	16	16	.500
Okla. Panhandle	2	8	.200	10	17	.370
Lincoln (Mo.)	2	8	.200	7	20	.259
Newman*	0	0	.000	14	12	.538
Tex. Permian Basin*	0	0	.000	11	16	.407
Tex. A&M Int'l*	0	0	.000	10	16	.385

LONE STAR CONFERENCE

	Conference			Full Season		
North Division	W	L	Pct.	W	L	Pct.
Central Okla. #	11	1	.917	28	6	.824
Southwestern Okla.	9	3	.750	21	7	.750
Northeastern St.	7	5	.583	14	14	.500
Tex. A&M-Commerce	7	5	.583	14	16	.467
East Central	4	8	.333	14	13	.519
Cameron	4	8	.333	6	21	.222
Southeastern Okla.	0	12	.000	3	24	.111
South Division						
West Tex. A&M	11	1	.917	21	8	.724
Tarleton St.	9	3	.750	25	7	.781
Abilene Christian	6	6	.500	20	9	.690
Angelo St.	6	6	.500	17	11	.607
Tex. A&M-Kingsville	5	7	.417	16	11	.593
Midwestern St.	5	7	.417	13	13	.500
Eastern N.M.	0	12	.000	6	21	.222

MID-AMERICA INTERCOLLEGIATE ATHLETICS ASSOCIATION

	Conference			Full Season		
	W	L	Pct.	W	L	Pct.
Southwest Baptist	14	4	.778	22	8	.733
Northwest Mo. St. #	12	6	.667	24	8	.750
Central Mo.	11	7	.611	18	10	.643
Mo. Southern St.	11	7	.611	17	11	.607
Fort Hays St.	10	8	.556	19	11	.633
Pittsburg St.	9	9	.500	18	10	.643
Washburn	9	9	.500	18	11	.621
Emporia St.	7	11	.389	14	16	.467
Truman	4	14	.222	5	22	.185
Mo. Western St.	3	15	.167	9	18	.333

NORTH CENTRAL CONFERENCE

	Conference			Full Season		
	W	L	Pct.	W	L	Pct.
Minn. St. Mankato	11	1	.917	22	7	.759
Augustana (S.D.)	8	4	.667	22	9	.710
Neb.-Omaha #	7	5	.583	25	7	.781
South Dakota	7	5	.583	22	7	.759
St. Cloud St.	5	7	.417	17	11	.607
North Dakota	2	10	.167	15	15	.500
Minn. Duluth	2	10	.167	9	19	.321

NORTHEAST-10 CONFERENCE

	Conference			Full Season		
	W	L	Pct.	W	L	Pct.
Bentley #	22	0	1.000	34	1	.971
St. Rose	18	4	.818	23	8	.742
Assumption	14	8	.636	24	11	.686
Pace	13	9	.591	14	14	.500
Stonehill	12	10	.545	18	14	.563
Merrimack	12	10	.545	17	12	.586
Bryant	12	10	.545	18	13	.581
Le Moyne	12	10	.545	15	14	.517
St. Anselm	11	11	.500	13	14	.481
Southern N.H.	9	13	.409	12	16	.429
Mass.-Lowell	8	14	.364	12	17	.414
American Int'l	7	15	.318	10	18	.357
Franklin Pierce	6	16	.273	10	17	.370
St. Michael's	6	16	.273	8	18	.308
Southern Conn. St.	3	19	.136	7	20	.259

NORTHERN SUN INTERCOLLEGIATE CONFERENCE

	Conference			Full Season		
	W	L	Pct.	W	L	Pct.
Winona St. #	18	0	1.000	38	1	.974
Northern St.	16	2	.889	29	4	.879
Southwest Minn. St.	11	7	.611	17	12	.586
Concordia-St. Paul	10	8	.556	16	12	.571
Wayne St. (Neb.)	10	8	.556	16	13	.552
Upper Iowa	8	10	.444	9	19	.321
Minn. St. Moorhead	7	11	.389	14	14	.500
Mary	5	13	.278	8	20	.286
Bemidji St.	3	15	.167	6	21	.222
Minn.-Crookston	2	16	.111	5	22	.185

PACIFIC WEST CONFERENCE

	Conference			Full Season		
	W	L	Pct.	W	L	Pct.
Chaminade	15	3	.833	21	8	.724
BYU-Hawaii	13	5	.722	20	8	.714
Dixie St.*	10	8	.556	13	14	.481
Hawaii Hilo	8	10	.444	13	13	.500
Grand Canyon	6	12	.333	12	15	.444
Notre Dame de Namur*	6	12	.333	10	16	.385
Hawaii Pacific	5	13	.278	8	19	.296

PEACH BELT CONFERENCE

	Conference			Full Season		
	W	L	Pct.	W	L	Pct.
S.C. Aiken	19	1	.950	27	4	.871
Augusta St.	17	3	.850	27	7	.794
Georgia College	13	7	.650	20	9	.690
North Ga.	12	8	.600	18	11	.621
Armstrong Atlantic	11	9	.550	17	11	.607
Clayton St. #	9	11	.450	19	15	.559
Columbus St.	9	11	.450	13	18	.419
Francis Marion	6	14	.300	12	16	.429
Lander	6	14	.300	10	19	.345
Ga. Southwestern*	5	15	.250	8	19	.296
UNC Pembroke	3	17	.150	8	20	.286

PENNSYLVANIA STATE ATHLETIC CONFERENCE

	Conference			Full Season		
East Division	W	L	Pct.	W	L	Pct.
Cheyney	10	2	.833	19	10	.655
Kutztown	10	2	.833	19	9	.679
Millersville	8	4	.667	22	10	.688
East Stroudsburg	6	6	.500	18	10	.643
Mansfield	5	7	.417	17	10	.630
West Chester	3	9	.250	12	15	.444
Bloomsburg	0	12	.000	8	19	.296
West Division						
California (Pa.) #	11	1	.917	28	6	.824
Edinboro	11	1	.917	24	7	.774
Clarion	7	5	.583	16	12	.571
Indiana (Pa.)	5	7	.417	13	15	.464
Slippery Rock	4	8	.333	7	20	.259
Shippensburg	2	10	.167	8	19	.296
Lock Haven	2	10	.167	2	24	.077

ROCKY MOUNTAIN ATHLETIC CONFERENCE

East Division

	Conference			Full Season		
	W	L	Pct.	W	L	Pct.
Colo. Christian	13	6	.684	18	13	.581
Neb.-Kearney	13	6	.684	16	13	.552
Metro St.	12	7	.632	19	12	.613
Regis (Colo.)	9	10	.474	14	14	.500
Colorado Mines	8	11	.421	15	14	.517
UC-Colo. Springs	6	13	.316	10	17	.370
Chadron St.	6	13	.316	7	20	.259

West Division

	W	L	Pct.	W	L	Pct.
Fort Lewis #	16	3	.842	24	6	.800
Adams St.	12	7	.632	18	10	.643
Western N.M.	12	7	.632	17	12	.586
Mesa St.	10	9	.526	13	14	.481
Western St.	8	11	.421	10	17	.370
Colorado St.-Pueblo	7	12	.368	10	17	.370
N.M. Highlands	1	18	.053	1	26	.037

SOUTH ATLANTIC CONFERENCE

	Conference			Full Season		
	W	L	Pct.	W	L	Pct.
Wingate	12	2	.857	24	7	.774
Lenoir-Rhyne	12	2	.857	23	7	.767
Carson-Newman	8	6	.571	18	9	.667
Catawba #	7	7	.500	19	12	.613
Tusculum	6	8	.429	13	15	.464
Mars Hill	5	9	.357	14	16	.467
Newberry	5	9	.357	12	16	.429
Lincoln Memorial	1	13	.071	8	20	.286
Brevard*	0	0	.000	4	24	.143

SOUTHERN INTERCOLLEGIATE ATHLETIC CONFERENCE

	Conference			Full Season		
	W	L	Pct.	W	L	Pct.
Benedict #	20	2	.909	28	5	.848
LeMoyne-Owen	14	8	.636	14	13	.519
Miles	13	9	.591	15	13	.536
Clark Atlanta	13	9	.591	16	14	.533
Fort Valley St.	13	9	.591	15	14	.517
Paine	12	10	.545	13	15	.464
Tuskegee	11	11	.500	14	17	.452
Albany St. (Ga.)	11	12	.478	13	16	.448
Kentucky St.	11	12	.478	12	16	.429
Morehouse	9	13	.409	12	15	.444
Lane	5	17	.227	5	23	.179
Stillman	1	21	.045	1	27	.036
Claflin*	0	0	.000	24	2	.923

SUNSHINE STATE CONFERENCE

	Conference			Full Season		
	W	L	Pct.	W	L	Pct.
Fla. Southern #	12	4	.750	24	9	.727
Tampa	11	5	.688	21	9	.700
Eckerd	11	5	.688	19	10	.655
Florida Tech	9	7	.563	20	8	.714
Rollins	8	8	.500	19	9	.679
Lynn	8	8	.500	16	13	.552
St. Leo	6	10	.375	14	15	.483
Nova Southeastern	5	11	.313	10	18	.357
Barry	2	14	.125	10	20	.333

WEST VIRGINIA INTERCOLLEGIATE ATHLETIC CONFERENCE

	Conference			Full Season		
	W	L	Pct.	W	L	Pct.
Pitt.-Johnstown	17	3	.850	23	8	.742
Alderson-Broaddus #	17	3	.850	26	7	.788
West Virginia St.	16	4	.800	20	10	.667
West Liberty St.	15	5	.750	23	6	.793
Charleston (W.V.)	12	8	.600	19	10	.655
Fairmont St.	12	8	.600	19	10	.655
Seton Hill	11	9	.550	12	15	.444
Shepherd	9	11	.450	16	13	.552
Davis & Elkins	9	11	.450	12	16	.429
Concord	9	11	.450	15	14	.517
West Va. Wesleyan	8	12	.400	10	18	.357
Wheeling Jesuit	8	12	.400	13	15	.464
Glenville St.	7	13	.350	9	19	.321
Ohio Valley	6	14	.300	7	21	.250
Salem Int'l	2	18	.100	5	23	.179
Bluefield St.	2	18	.100	2	26	.071

DIVISION II INDEPENDENTS

	W	L	Pct.
Central St.	21	4	.840
King (Tenn.)	26	8	.765
Flagler	20	7	.741
Dist. Columbia	14	8	.636
Oakland City	17	13	.567
Minn.-Morris	14	12	.538
Chowan	13	17	.433
St. Thomas (Fla.)	10	18	.357
North Greenville	7	20	.259
Urbana	5	23	.179
Palm Beach Atl.	4	22	.154
Tiffin	3	24	.111
Columbia Union	2	24	.077
NJIT	0	29	.000

#won conference tournament
*not eligible for conference championship

2008 Division III Conference Standings

ALLEGHENY MOUNTAIN COLLEGIATE CONFERENCE

	Conference			Full Season		
	W	L	Pct.	W	L	Pct.
Penn St.-Behrend #	15	3	.833	24	5	.828
Lake Erie	13	5	.722	18	9	.667
Penn St.-Altoona	10	8	.556	14	13	.519
La Roche	10	8	.556	13	13	.500
Pitt.-Greensburg	10	8	.556	11	15	.423
Medaille	9	9	.500	15	13	.536
Hilbert	8	10	.444	12	13	.480
Frostburg St.	8	10	.444	9	16	.360
Pitt.-Bradford	6	12	.333	10	15	.400
Mount Aloysius*	1	17	.056	5	20	.200

AMERICAN SOUTHWEST CONFERENCE

East Division

	Conference			Full Season		
	W	L	Pct.	W	L	Pct.
Mississippi Col.	16	4	.800	19	6	.760
Texas-Dallas	13	7	.650	17	9	.654
Texas-Tyler	13	7	.650	14	12	.538
LeTourneau	9	11	.450	12	13	.480
East Tex. Baptist	9	11	.450	9	17	.346
Louisiana Col.	8	12	.400	9	16	.360
Ozarks (Ark.)	5	15	.250	8	17	.320

West Division

	W	L	Pct.	W	L	Pct.
Mary Hardin-Baylor #	19	2	.905	26	4	.867
Concordia (Tex.)	14	7	.667	19	9	.679
Hardin-Simmons	13	8	.619	15	12	.556
Howard Payne	11	10	.524	14	13	.519
McMurry	9	12	.429	12	13	.480
Sul Ross St.	7	14	.333	8	17	.320
Schreiner	5	16	.238	5	20	.200
Texas Lutheran	3	18	.143	3	22	.120

CAPITAL ATHLETIC CONFERENCE

	Conference			Full Season		
	W	L	Pct.	W	L	Pct.
York (Pa.)	13	3	.813	18	8	.692
Mary Washington	11	5	.688	18	9	.667
St. Mary's (Md.) #	9	7	.563	19	12	.613
Hood	9	7	.563	15	11	.577
Wesley	9	7	.563	14	12	.538
Marymount (Va.)	8	8	.500	15	12	.556
Stevenson	5	11	.313	7	19	.269
Salisbury	4	12	.250	7	20	.259
Gallaudet	4	12	.250	6	19	.240

CENTENNIAL CONFERENCE

	Conference			Full Season		
	W	L	Pct.	W	L	Pct.
Ursinus #	18	0	1.000	29	4	.879
Gettysburg	16	2	.889	24	5	.828
Johns Hopkins	12	6	.667	16	10	.615
McDaniel	10	8	.556	15	11	.577
Dickinson	9	9	.500	14	13	.519
Muhlenberg	8	10	.444	10	15	.400
Frank. & Marsh.	7	11	.389	12	13	.480
Haverford	6	12	.333	8	16	.333
Swarthmore	2	16	.111	6	19	.240
Washington (Md.)	2	16	.111	5	20	.200

CITY UNIVERSITY OF NEW YORK ATHLETIC CONFERENCE

	Conference			Full Season		
	W	L	Pct.	W	L	Pct.
Brooklyn	10	3	.769	21	7	.750
York (N.Y.)	10	3	.769	22	9	.710
Staten Island	9	4	.692	14	12	.538
Baruch	9	4	.692	13	13	.500
Hunter	8	5	.615	13	14	.481
John Jay #	6	7	.462	14	16	.467
City Tech	6	7	.462	8	19	.296
Lehman	5	8	.385	11	15	.423
CCNY	2	11	.154	4	21	.160
Medgar Evers	0	13	.000	1	24	.040

COMMONWEALTH CONFERENCE

	Conference			Full Season		
	W	L	Pct.	W	L	Pct.
Lycoming	7	3	.700	17	10	.630
Widener #	6	4	.600	22	6	.786
Albright	6	4	.600	17	9	.654
Lebanon Valley	5	5	.500	11	15	.423
Messiah	4	6	.400	15	10	.600
Elizabethtown	2	8	.200	15	9	.625

COMMONWEALTH COAST CONFERENCE

	Conference			Full Season		
	W	L	Pct.	W	L	Pct.
Curry #	11	2	.846	18	11	.621
Roger Williams	11	2	.846	17	11	.607
Gordon	9	4	.692	18	9	.667
Western New Eng.	9	4	.692	16	11	.593
New England	9	4	.692	17	12	.586
Wentworth Inst.	8	5	.615	14	11	.560
Colby-Sawyer	8	5	.615	13	11	.542
Endicott	7	6	.538	11	15	.423
Nichols	6	7	.462	10	15	.400
Salve Regina	4	9	.308	6	19	.240
Regis (Mass.)	3	10	.231	9	16	.360
Anna Maria	2	11	.154	8	17	.320
New England Col.	2	11	.154	7	18	.280
Eastern Nazarene	2	11	.154	5	20	.200

EMPIRE 8

	Conference			Full Season		
	W	L	Pct.	W	L	Pct.
Stevens Institute	12	4	.750	23	6	.793
Ithaca	12	4	.750	17	9	.654
Nazareth #	11	5	.688	20	8	.714
St. John Fisher	11	5	.688	17	12	.586
Utica	10	6	.625	16	9	.640
Rochester Inst.	8	8	.500	14	11	.560
Hartwick	5	11	.313	10	15	.400
Elmira	2	14	.125	6	19	.240
Alfred	1	15	.063	2	23	.080

FREEDOM CONFERENCE

	Conference			Full Season		
	W	L	Pct.	W	L	Pct.
DeSales	9	3	.750	21	6	.778
King's (Pa.) #	9	3	.750	20	9	.690
Manhattanville	9	3	.750	17	9	.654
Wilkes	7	5	.583	13	12	.520
Arcadia	6	6	.500	12	13	.480
FDU-Florham	2	10	.167	3	22	.120
Delaware Valley	0	12	.000	3	21	.125

GREAT NORTHEAST ATHLETIC CONFERENCE

	Conference			Full Season		
	W	L	Pct.	W	L	Pct.
Emerson	15	3	.833	24	5	.828
Lasell #	14	4	.778	20	9	.690
Emmanuel (Mass.)	14	4	.778	17	11	.607
Johnson & Wales (R.I.)	12	6	.667	15	12	.556
St. Joseph's (Me.)	11	7	.611	14	13	.519
Rivier	10	8	.556	13	13	.500
Norwich	8	10	.444	12	13	.480
Daniel Webster	5	13	.278	7	19	.269
Mount Ida	4	14	.222	7	18	.280
Albertus Magnus	3	15	.167	4	21	.160
Suffolk	3	15	.167	4	21	.160

GREAT SOUTH ATHLETIC CONFERENCE

	Conference			Full Season		
	W	L	Pct.	W	L	Pct.
Maryville (Tenn.) #	6	0	1.000	24	3	.889
Piedmont	2	4	.333	14	13	.519
Huntingdon	2	4	.333	9	17	.346
LaGrange	2	4	.333	6	19	.240

HEARTLAND COLLEGIATE ATHLETIC CONFERENCE

	Conference			Full Season		
	W	L	Pct.	W	L	Pct.
Defiance	13	3	.813	19	8	.704
Franklin #	10	6	.625	18	10	.643
Transylvania	10	6	.625	16	11	.593
Anderson (Ind.)	10	6	.625	15	12	.556
Hanover	9	7	.563	13	13	.500
Rose-Hulman	8	8	.500	12	14	.462
Bluffton	7	9	.438	13	12	.520
Mt. St. Joseph	3	13	.188	9	16	.360
Manchester	2	14	.125	4	21	.160

COLLEGE CONFERNCE OF ILLINOIS & WISCONSIN

	Conference			Full Season		
	W	L	Pct.	W	L	Pct.
Augustana (Ill.) #	11	3	.786	23	6	.793
Wheaton (Ill.)	9	5	.643	22	8	.733
Ill. Wesleyan	9	5	.643	16	11	.593
Elmhurst	8	6	.571	18	8	.692
Carthage	7	7	.500	13	12	.520
North Park	6	8	.429	14	11	.560
North Central (Ill.)	4	10	.286	10	15	.400
Millikin	2	12	.143	9	16	.360

IOWA INTERCOLLEGIATE ATHLETIC CONFERENCE

	Conference			Full Season		
	W	L	Pct.	W	L	Pct.
Buena Vista	14	2	.875	23	7	.767
Loras #	13	3	.813	22	7	.759
Coe	10	6	.625	16	11	.593
Central (Iowa)	8	8	.500	14	10	.583
Dubuque	7	9	.438	14	12	.538
Cornell Col.	7	9	.438	9	17	.346
Wartburg	6	10	.375	9	16	.360
Simpson	4	12	.250	7	18	.280
Luther	3	13	.188	7	18	.280

LANDMARK CONFERENCE

	Conference			Full Season		
	W	L	Pct.	W	L	Pct.
Susquehanna	10	4	.714	13	12	.520
Scranton #	9	5	.643	19	6	.679
Moravian	9	5	.643	18	9	.667
Juniata	9	5	.643	17	11	.607
Merchant Marine	7	7	.500	12	13	.480
Catholic	4	10	.286	10	15	.400
Drew	4	10	.286	7	18	.280
Goucher	4	10	.286	6	19	.240

LIBERTY LEAGUE

	Conference			Full Season		
	W	L	Pct.	W	L	Pct.
St. Lawrence	12	2	.857	17	9	.654
Vassar	9	5	.643	18	8	.692
Hamilton	9	5	.643	17	9	.654
Hobart	7	7	.500	12	13	.480
Clarkson #	7	7	.500	11	17	.393
Rensselear	6	8	.429	11	14	.440
Union (N.Y.)	5	9	.357	9	15	.375
Skidmore	1	13	.071	6	19	.240

LITTLE EAST CONFERENCE

	Conference			Full Season		
	W	L	Pct.	W	L	Pct.
Mass.-Dartmouth	12	2	.857	25	4	.862
Rhode Island Col. #	11	3	.786	23	7	.767
Keene St.	8	6	.571	16	11	.593
Southern Me.	8	6	.571	14	13	.519
Western Conn. St.	6	8	.429	15	12	.556
Eastern Conn. St.	6	8	.429	13	13	.500
Plymouth St.	4	10	.286	8	18	.308
Mass.-Boston	1	13	.071	2	24	.077

MASSACHUSETTS STATE COLLEGE ATHLETIC CONFERENCE

	Conference			Full Season		
	W	L	Pct.	W	L	Pct.
Salem St. #	9	3	.750	21	7	.750
Fitchburg St.	8	4	.667	16	10	.615
Westfield St.	7	5	.583	19	9	.679
Framingham St.	7	5	.583	12	14	.462
Bridgewater St.	6	6	.500	13	13	.500
Worcester St.	3	9	.250	10	16	.385
Mass. Liberal Arts	2	10	.167	7	18	.280

MICHIGAN INTERCOLLEGIATE ATHLETIC ASSOCIATION

	Conference			Full Season		
	W	L	Pct.	W	L	Pct.
Hope #	13	1	.929	28	4	.875
Albion	12	2	.857	19	6	.760
Calvin	9	5	.643	16	11	.593
Trine	6	8	.429	9	16	.360
Adrian	5	9	.357	11	15	.423
Olivet	5	9	.357	9	16	.360
Kalamazoo	3	11	.214	6	19	.240
Alma	3	11	.214	3	21	.125

MIDWEST CONFERENCE

	Conference			Full Season		
	W	L	Pct.	W	L	Pct.
Lawrence #	15	1	.938	22	3	.880
Grinnell	11	5	.688	16	8	.667
Carroll (Wis.)	10	6	.625	15	9	.625
St. Norbert	10	6	.625	14	10	.583
Lake Forest	7	9	.438	11	12	.478
Knox	7	9	.438	8	15	.348
Monmouth (Ill.)	7	9	.438	7	15	.318
Ripon	6	10	.375	11	12	.478
Illinois Col.	5	11	.313	9	14	.391
Beloit	2	14	.125	4	19	.174

MINNESOTA INTERCOLLEGIATE ATHLETIC CONFERENCE

	Conference			Full Season		
	W	L	Pct.	W	L	Pct.
St. Thomas (Minn.) #	17	3	.850	23	5	.821
Gust. Adolphus	14	6	.700	19	8	.704
Carleton	13	7	.650	19	8	.704
Concordia-M'head	12	8	.600	13	13	.500
Bethel (Minn.)	11	9	.550	16	11	.593
St. John's (Minn.)	11	9	.550	14	12	.538
Augsburg	10	10	.500	12	13	.480
St. Olaf	10	10	.500	12	13	.480
Hamline	6	14	.300	8	17	.320
Macalester	4	16	.200	6	19	.240
St. Mary's (Minn.)	2	18	.100	2	23	.080

NEW ENGLAND SMALL COLLEGE ATHLETIC CONFERENCE

	Conference			Full Season		
	W	L	Pct.	W	L	Pct.
Amherst	9	0	1.000	27	4	.871
Bowdoin	6	3	.667	22	7	.759
Trinity (Conn.) #	6	3	.667	21	7	.750
Middlebury	6	3	.667	19	8	.704
Bates	5	4	.556	17	8	.680
Connecticut Col.	4	5	.444	17	8	.680
Williams	4	5	.444	17	8	.680
Colby	3	6	.333	13	12	.520
Tufts	1	8	.111	11	13	.458
Wesleyan (Conn.)	1	8	.111	8	16	.333

NEW ENGLAND WOMEN'S AND MEN'S ATHLETICS CONFERENCE

	Conference			Full Season		
	W	L	Pct.	W	L	Pct.
WPI	11	1	.917	21	7	.750
Coast Guard #	7	5	.583	24	7	.774
Clark (Mass.)	7	5	.583	12	13	.480
Babson	6	6	.500	10	16	.385
Springfield	5	7	.417	10	15	.400
Wheaton (Mass.)	3	9	.250	13	12	.520
MIT	3	9	.250	12	14	.462

NEW JERSEY ATHLETIC CONFERENCE

North Division	Conference			Full Season		
	W	L	Pct.	W	L	Pct.
Wm. Paterson	10	3	.769	19	7	.731
Ramapo	9	4	.692	16	11	.593
Montclair St.	8	5	.615	16	11	.593
New Jersey City	6	7	.462	14	12	.538
Rutgers-Newark	6	7	.462	13	13	.500
South Division						
Richard Stockton #	10	3	.769	22	7	.759
Rowan	7	6	.538	18	8	.692
Kean	4	9	.308	9	17	.346
Rutgers-Camden	3	10	.231	6	19	.240
TCNJ	2	11	.154	6	19	.240

NORTH ATLANTIC CONFERENCE

East Division	Conference			Full Season		
	W	L	Pct.	W	L	Pct.
Husson	10	3	.769	18	11	.621
Lesley	8	5	.615	12	16	.429
Me.-Farmington	7	6	.538	11	15	.423
Maine Maritime	7	6	.538	10	14	.417
Thomas (Me.)	2	11	.154	9	16	.360
West Division						
Elms #	11	2	.846	23	7	.767
Castleton	8	5	.615	15	11	.577
Becker	8	5	.615	13	14	.481
Johnson St.	4	9	.308	9	17	.346
Wheelock	0	13	.000	1	24	.040

NORTH COAST ATHLETIC CONFERENCE

	Conference			Full Season		
	W	L	Pct.	W	L	Pct.
Wooster	15	1	.938	23	5	.821
Ohio Wesleyan #	12	4	.750	22	8	.733
Wittenberg	12	4	.750	16	10	.615
Kenyon	11	5	.688	13	13	.500
Wabash	10	6	.625	18	10	.643
Allegheny	6	10	.375	12	15	.444
Hiram	5	11	.313	8	18	.308
Oberlin	4	12	.250	5	21	.192
Denison	3	13	.188	3	22	.120
Earlham	2	14	.125	4	21	.160

NORTH EASTERN ATHLETIC CONFERENCE

	Conference			Full Season		
	W	L	Pct.	W	L	Pct.
Baptist Bible (Pa.) #	10	4	.714	18	10	.643
Cazenovia	10	4	.714	14	14	.500
Keystone	9	5	.643	14	12	.538
Penn St.-Berks*	7	7	.500	7	19	.269
Penn St.-Harrisburg*	6	8	.429	8	17	.320
Keuka	6	8	.429	7	16	.304
D'Youville	5	9	.357	8	17	.320
Phila. Biblical	3	11	.214	3	21	.125

NORTHERN ATHLETICS CONFERENCE

	Conference			Full Season		
	W	L	Pct.	W	L	Pct.
Aurora	16	2	.889	22	7	.759
Wis. Lutheran	12	6	.667	18	8	.692
Marian (Wis.)	12	6	.667	16	11	.593
Milwaukee Engr.	11	7	.611	17	10	.630
Dominican (Ill.)	11	7	.611	14	12	.538
Lakeland #	10	8	.556	17	11	.607
Edgewood	10	8	.556	13	13	.500
Benedictine (Ill.)	10	8	.556	11	15	.423
Concordia (Wis.)	9	9	.500	14	11	.560
Concordia Chicago	4	14	.222	5	20	.200
Maranatha Baptist	2	16	.111	8	20	.286
Rockford	1	17	.056	1	24	.040

NORTHWEST CONFERENCE

	Conference			Full Season		
	W	L	Pct.	W	L	Pct.
Whitworth #	12	4	.750	21	7	.750
Puget Sound	11	5	.688	19	7	.731
Lewis & Clark	9	7	.563	15	9	.625
Linfield	9	7	.563	14	11	.560
Pacific (Ore.)	9	7	.563	11	14	.440
Willamette	9	7	.563	11	15	.423
Pacific Lutheran	7	9	.438	11	13	.458
George Fox	5	11	.313	9	16	.360
Whitman	1	15	.063	5	19	.208

OHIO ATHLETIC CONFERENCE

	Conference			Full Season		
	W	L	Pct.	W	L	Pct.
Capital	16	2	.889	24	6	.800
Heidelberg #	14	4	.778	23	6	.793
Wilmington (Ohio)	11	7	.611	16	10	.615
Ohio Northern	10	8	.556	15	12	.556
Muskingum	9	9	.500	15	11	.577
Baldwin-Wallace	8	10	.444	12	15	.444
John Carroll	8	10	.444	11	14	.440
Mount Union	6	12	.333	9	17	.346
Otterbein	6	12	.333	7	18	.280
Marietta	2	16	.111	6	19	.240

OLD DOMINION ATHLETIC CONFERENCE

	Conference			Full Season		
	W	L	Pct.	W	L	Pct.
Guilford #	16	2	.889	24	5	.828
Randolph-Macon	14	4	.778	20	6	.769
Va. Wesleyan	14	4	.778	23	7	.767
Roanoke	11	7	.611	18	9	.667
Wash. & Lee	11	7	.611	15	11	.577
Hampden-Sydney	8	10	.444	15	12	.556
Bridgewater (Va.)	7	11	.389	13	13	.500
East. Mennonite	5	13	.278	9	17	.346
Emory & Henry	3	15	.167	7	18	.280
Lynchburg	1	17	.056	3	22	.120

PENNSYLVANIA ATHLETIC CONFERENCE

	Conference			Full Season		
	W	L	Pct.	W	L	Pct.
Alvernia	13	3	.813	15	11	.577
Misericordia	11	5	.688	19	10	.655
Immaculata #	11	5	.688	18	10	.643
Gwynedd-Mercy	10	6	.625	21	10	.677
Cabrini	9	7	.563	12	14	.462
Eastern	8	8	.500	11	14	.440
Neumann	8	8	.500	10	15	.400
Centenary (N.J.)	2	14	.125	4	20	.167
Marywood	0	16	.000	7	18	.280

PRESIDENTS' ATHLETIC CONFERENCE

	Conference			Full Season		
	W	L	Pct.	W	L	Pct.
Bethany (W.V.)	9	3	.750	17	11	.607
Grove City	9	3	.750	17	11	.607
Wash. & Jeff.	8	4	.667	14	14	.500
Thomas More	5	7	.417	11	16	.407
Westminster (Pa.)	5	7	.417	7	19	.269
Thiel	4	8	.333	10	15	.400
Waynesburg	2	10	.167	8	17	.320
St. Vincent*	0	0	.000	22	4	.846
Geneva*	0	0	.000	14	14	.500

ST. LOUIS INTERCOLLEGIATE ATHLETIC CONFERENCE

	Conference			Full Season		
	W	L	Pct.	W	L	Pct.
Webster	16	0	1.000	20	6	.769
Fontbonne #	12	4	.750	21	7	.750
Westminster (Mo.)	12	4	.750	17	8	.680
Maryville (Mo.)	9	7	.563	13	14	.481
Greenville	8	8	.500	13	13	.500
Eureka	8	8	.500	9	16	.360
Principia	3	13	.188	5	18	.217
Blackburn	3	13	.188	5	19	.208
MacMurray	1	15	.063	3	22	.120

SKYLINE CONFERENCE

	Conference			Full Season		
	W	L	Pct.	W	L	Pct.
Farmingdale St. #	16	2	.889	22	6	.786
St. Joseph's (L.I.)	16	2	.889	21	7	.750
Old Westbury	15	3	.833	16	10	.615
Maritime (N.Y.)	9	9	.500	13	14	.481
Mt. St. Mary (N.Y.)	8	10	.444	11	15	.423
Yeshiva	7	11	.389	11	16	.407
Mt. St. Vincent	6	12	.333	9	16	.360
Polytechnic (N.Y.)	6	12	.333	8	17	.320
Bard	5	13	.278	8	17	.320
Purchase*	2	16	.111	3	22	.120

SOUTHERN CALIFORNIA INTERCOLLEGIATE ATHLETIC CONFERENCE

	Conference			Full Season		
	W	L	Pct.	W	L	Pct.
Cal Lutheran	11	3	.786	21	5	.808
Occidental	11	3	.786	22	6	.786
Claremont-M-S	8	6	.571	15	12	.556
Pomona-Pitzer #	8	6	.571	15	13	.536
Whittier	7	7	.500	14	11	.560
La Verne	6	8	.429	12	13	.480
Redlands	5	9	.357	10	15	.400
Caltech	0	14	.000	1	24	.040

SOUTHERN COLLEGIATE ATHLETIC CONFERENCE

	Conference			Full Season		
	W	L	Pct.	W	L	Pct.
Centre	14	0	1.000	26	3	.897
Millsaps #	13	2	.867	28	4	.875
DePauw	10	4	.714	19	7	.731
Oglethorpe	10	4	.714	16	10	.615
Trinity (Tex.)	9	6	.600	18	9	.667
Hendrix	6	9	.400	14	12	.538
Southwestern (Tex.)	6	9	.400	11	14	.440
Austin	6	9	.400	9	17	.346
Rhodes	5	9	.357	11	15	.423
Sewanee	1	13	.071	7	18	.280
Colorado Col.	0	15	.000	0	24	.000
Birmingham-So.*	0	0	.000	13	12	.520

STATE UNIVERSITY OF NEW YORK ATHLETIC CONFERENCE

	Conference			Full Season		
	W	L	Pct.	W	L	Pct.
Plattsburgh St. #	16	0	1.000	27	3	.900
Brockport St.	14	2	.875	21	8	.724
Cortland St.	12	4	.750	21	8	.724
Oswego St.	12	4	.750	21	8	.724
Geneseo St.	11	5	.688	19	8	.704
Oneonta St.	7	9	.438	12	14	.462
SUNY Potsdam	7	9	.438	11	15	.423
Fredonia St.	6	10	.375	9	17	.346
Buffalo St.	5	11	.313	8	15	.348
SUNYIT	2	14	.125	7	18	.280
New Paltz St.	2	14	.125	6	19	.240
Morrisville St.*	2	14	.125	5	19	.208

USA SOUTH ATHLETIC CONFERENCE

	Conference			Full Season		
	W	L	Pct.	W	L	Pct.
Methodist	8	4	.667	16	10	.615
Ferrum	8	4	.667	14	12	.538
Shenandoah	6	6	.500	16	10	.615
Chris. Newport	6	6	.500	10	16	.385
Averett #	5	7	.417	14	15	.483
Greensboro	5	7	.417	13	15	.464
N.C. Wesleyan	4	8	.333	12	15	.444

UNIVERSITY ATHLETIC ASSOCIATION

	Conference			Full Season		
	W	L	Pct.	W	L	Pct.
Chicago	11	3	.786	18	8	.692
Washington-St. Louis	10	4	.714	25	6	.806
Brandeis	10	4	.714	23	6	.793
Rochester (N.Y.)	9	5	.643	22	6	.786
Carnegie Mellon	6	8	.429	19	9	.679
New York U.	6	8	.429	16	11	.593
Emory	3	11	.214	10	15	.400
Case Reserve	1	13	.071	8	17	.320

UPPER MIDWEST ATHLETIC CONFERENCE

	Conference			Full Season		
	W	L	Pct.	W	L	Pct.
Northwestern (Minn.)* #	12	2	.857	20	9	.690
Minn.-Morris*	9	5	.643	14	12	.538
Martin Luther	9	5	.643	13	13	.500
St. Scholastica	9	5	.643	11	15	.423
Bethany Lutheran*	9	5	.643	11	17	.393
Presentation*	5	9	.357	7	18	.280
Crown (Minn.)*	2	12	.143	5	20	.200
Northland	1	13	.071	3	22	.120

WISCONSIN INTERCOLLEGIATE ATHLETIC CONFERENCE

	Conference			Full Season		
	W	L	Pct.	W	L	Pct.
Wis.-Whitewater #	13	3	.813	24	5	.828
Wis.-Stevens Point	12	4	.750	23	7	.767
Wis.-Platteville	12	4	.750	19	7	.731
Wis.-Oshkosh	11	5	.688	17	9	.654
Wis.-Superior	6	10	.375	12	15	.444
Wis.-La Crosse	6	10	.375	11	15	.423
Wis.-Eau Claire	5	11	.313	12	15	.444
Wis.-Stout	4	12	.250	7	19	.269
Wis.-River Falls	3	13	.188	9	16	.360

DIVISION III INDEPENDENTS

	W	L	Pct.
Green Mountain	21	5	.808
Chapman	19	7	.731
Newbury	21	9	.700
Menlo	18	10	.643
Cal St. East Bay	13	12	.520
Finlandia	13	12	.520
Neb. Wesleyan	14	13	.519
Rust	11	12	.478
Dallas	11	15	.423
Randolph	8	13	.381
North Central (Minn.)	8	16	.333
Lyndon St.	5	15	.250
La Sierra	5	17	.227
Southern Vt.	5	19	.208
Me.-Presque Isle	3	15	.167
Lancaster Bible	4	20	.167
Lincoln (Pa.)	4	22	.154
Mitchell	3	22	.120
UC Santa Cruz	3	23	.115

#won conference tournament
*not eligible for conference championship